Raising Scores & Hands

- Develop concepts with solid time on task
- Practice with plentiful, meaningful activities
- Meet the needs of every child
- Teach real-life solutions with real-life problems
- Integrate technology for practical application

WITHDRAWN

Math in my World

McGraw-Hill
School Division

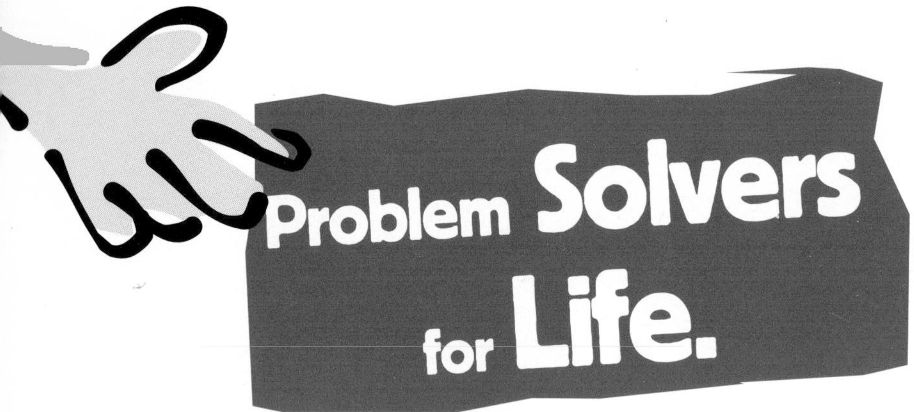

Motivate with Content

Students apply math skills developed through real-life themes that match their interests, problems that challenge and engage, situations they can share and investigations they can carry out.

Explore with Focus

Hands-on activities in Explore Lessons provide time on task — to assure understanding of key concepts and skills.

Practice with Purpose

Abundant practice in all different standardized and state test formats helps raise scores through skill mastery and critical thinking.

Assess with Assurance

Mixed Reviews, Mixed Applications, Midchapter Reviews, Chapter Reviews, and Cumulative Reviews maintain mastery and ensure achievement over time. Chapters are designed with built-in-the-Pupil's Edition assessment that starts with "What Do You Know?" for pre-assessment, includes Chapter Tests, and finishes with "What Did You Learn?" and "What Do You Think?" features.

Prepare for the Future with Technology

Math in my World is the first math program to come with technology that was developed side-by-side with the print program. Math Van delights students while teaching the same content, chapter by chapter, as the print program. Integrated software for teachers simplifies lesson planning and assessment. And Resource Village, our website for teachers, provides rich alternative instruction for every pupil edition chapter, too.

Solve Problems with Strategies

Problem solving through mixed applications and other strategies in "Problem Solvers at Work," "Problem-Solving Strategies," and "Real-life Investigations" builds the foundation for continued success in math.

Meet Diverse Needs with Teaching Choices

Teachers can meet the needs of every child with Alternative Teaching Strategies in every lesson, extensive ESL support, comprehensive Spanish language instruction, Reteaching and Remediation tools for all objectives, lesson resources and components for every special requirement.

Discover Simplicity – with Point-of-Use Features

Teaching support and features for meeting individual needs, are found chapter by chapter and lesson by lesson at point of use — right where teachers need them. Important topics that appear throughout the program — like algebra preparation — are clearly indicated with bold icons.

Program Components

	K	1	2	3	4	5	6
Teacher's Edition Volume 1	●	●	●	●	●	●	●
Teacher's Edition Volume 2		●	●	●	●	●	●
Pupil Edition, Consumable	●	●	●				
Pupil Edition, Non-Consumable				●	●	●	●
Testing Program Blackline Masters	●	●	●	●	●	●	●
Teacher's Assessment Resources	●	●	●	●	●	●	●
Practice Workbook	●	●	●	●	●	●	●
Reteach Workbook		●	●	●	●	●	●
Extend Workbook	●	●	●	●	●	●	●
Quick Review Blackline Masters		●	●	●	●	●	●
Daily Review Transparencies		●	●	●	●	●	●
Home/School Connection				●	●	●	●
Read-Aloud Anthology	●	●	●	●	●	●	●
Math Vocabulary Cards	●	●	●	●	●	●	●
Math Center Activity Pad	●	●	●	●	●	●	●
Problem of the Day Flip Chart	●	●	●	●	●	●	●
Teacher's Lesson Planner	●	●	●	●	●	●	●
Interactive Lesson Planner	●	●	●	●	●	●	●
Teacher Aids Blackline Masters	●	●	●	●	●	●	●
Calculator Blackline Masters		●	●	●	●	●	●
Puppet (Panda, Rhino, Toucan)	●	●	●				
Rubber Self-inking Stamps (Panda, Rhino, Toucan)	●	●	●				
Manipulative Counters (Panda, Rhino)	●	●					
Professional Handbook (one for K–6)	●	●	●	●	●	●	●
Jumbo Activity Book and Stickers	●	●	●				
Literature Big Books (six titles per grade)	●	●	●				
Floor Mats	●	●	●				
Student Workmats	●	●	●				
Problem Solving Audio Cassettes		●	●	●	●	●	●
Math Songs Audio Cassette (one for K–2)	●	●	●				
Customized Grade Level Manipulative Kits (K–2, 3–6)	●	●	●	●	●	●	●
Overhead Manipulative Kit (K–2, 3–6)	●	●	●	●	●	●	●
Essential Manipulative Kit	●	●	●	●	●	●	●
Supplementary Manipulative Kit	●	●	●	●	●	●	●
Teaching Aids Transparencies		●	●	●	●	●	●
Testing: Preparation and Strategies Video	●	●	●	●	●	●	●
Math Van Software	●	●	●	●	●	●	●
Computer Test Generator Software				●	●	●	●
Internet Project Handbook				●	●	●	●
Math for You and Me! Comprehensive Kit		●	●				

Program Authors

M*ath in My World* was developed by an experienced team of authors and consulting experts. The authors who collaborated to create the program represent McGraw-Hill's commitment to the most current thinking in mathematics education, and our deep sensitivity to the real-life challenges of today's classrooms.

DR. DOUGLAS H. CLEMENTS

Professor of Mathematics Education
State University of New York at Buffalo

Douglas H. Clements conducts research on computer applications in education, early development of mathematical ideas, and the learning and teaching of geometry. Dr. Clements taught kindergarten for five years and contributed to NCTM's Addenda series.

LOIS GORDON MOSELEY

Independent Mathematics Consultant
Houston, Texas

While she fulfilled her pivotal responsibilities as Coordinator of the Region IV Education Service Center in Houston, Lois Gordon Moseley served as the chairperson for the statewide Mathematics Texas Essential Knowledge and Skills writing team for grades PK - 12. She also served on the board of directors for the Association of African-American Mathematics Educators. Now she consults with Texas school districts and dedicates herself to the improvement of math education.

KENNETH W. JONES

Director OVEC - University of Louisville, Kentucky
Partnership for Professional Development

Ken Jones works closely with school districts in the Louisville region to develop ongoing professional development opportunities for teachers and administrators and to facilitate school improvement. He has been a middle school teacher and the director of several nationally-funded grant programs in mathematics. His special interest is performance assessment and portfolios.

DR. LINDA SCHULMAN

Professor of Mathematics and Mathematics Education
Lesley College
Cambridge, Massachusetts

Linda Schulman began her career as an elementary school teacher and is a leading author of innovative supplementary materials for the teaching of mathematics. Currently, her work focuses on the use of investigations and alternative assessment strategies in the elementary classroom.

Contributing Authors

DR. KATHY KELLY-BENJAMIN
Former Associate Professor - Mathematics Education
Florida Institute of Technology, Melbourne, Florida

Dr. Kelly-Benjamin is an instructional design manager and educational consultant with expertise in instructional technology and assessment. Dr. Kelly-Benjamin has also been a middle school mathematics teacher, consultant and writer.

CHRISTINE A. FERNSLER
First Grade Teacher
Sidwell Friends School
Washington, D.C.

Christine Fernsler is a recognized authority on classroom practice in elementary math education. She has served as a school mathematics coordinator, presented workshops for NCTM, Virginia Council for Teachers of Mathematics (VCTM) and V-Quest. Ms. Fernsler has also taught courses at George Mason University and Catholic University.

DR. LIANA FOREST
Executive Director
National Association for the Study of Cooperation in Education
Felton, California

Dr. Forest has taught at levels from preschool to graduate school. For twenty years she has conducted research and written on learning and teaching in cooperative settings. She also facilitates professional development for teachers, professors and administrators with a focus on cooperative student groups, collaborative school teams and creating cooperative communities. Dr. Forest writes for and is Executive Editor of Cooperative Learning Publications for the International Association for the Study of Cooperatives in Education (IASCE), where she also serves on the Executive Board.

MARIA R. MAROLDA
Mathematics Specialist
Behavioral Neurology/Learning Disabilities Program
Children's Hospital
Boston, Massachusetts

Maria R. Marolda has extensive expertise and practical experience in mathematics learning profiles, alternative assessment techniques, and differentiated teaching approaches designed to address learning differences in mathematics.

DR. RICHARD H. MOYER
Professor of Science Education
University of Michigan - Dearborn
Dearborn, Michigan

Dr. Richard H. Moyer is a senior author of Macmillan/ McGraw-Hill Science as well as numerous other books and publications. Dr. Moyer, who has taught at all levels, is the recipient of many teaching awards and consults on the use of inquiry teaching methods both nationally and abroad.

DR. WALTER G. SECADA
Professor of Curriculum and Instruction
University of Wisconsin - Madison
Madison, Wisconsin

Dr. Walter Secada has written extensively about equity, the education of bilingual learners of mathematics, and the reform of school mathematics. In addition, he has conducted workshops involving authentic assessment, how children reason when they do mathematics, and multiculturalism in the mathematics curriculum. Dr. Secada is editor of an NCTM series of professional books, *Changing the Faces of Mathematics*, which helps teachers address the diversity of today's classrooms.

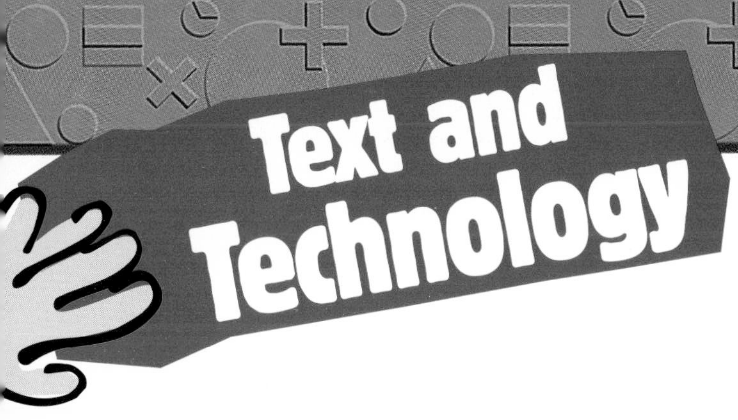

Integrated Technology for Management and Instruction

Math in my World management technology helps teachers develop and manage lesson plans, assess student performance, and interact with other teachers using the program. Instructional technology aids students in mastering key math concepts with multimedia and Internet-based lessons that are fully integrated with every chapter in their textbook.

PLANNERPLUS INTERACTIVE LESSON PLANNER

A good instructional plan is the heart of effective instruction. Teachers need easy access to the range of options available to them in each lesson. PlannerPlus shows every element of the program electronically, including:

- objectives
- resources and materials
- lesson content
- all blackline masters

It's easy for teachers to tailor their plans to meet individual needs.

Because teachers have little time to master complex software programs, PlannerPlus is designed to be intuitive and easy to use.

Based on the structure of the Teacher's Edition, teachers can create lesson plans on a daily, weekly, or chapter basis, using suggested outlines or creating custom lessons with their own materials.

In addition to identifying the components and references used in the lesson plan, PlannerPlus can display and print any *Math in my World* blackline master. Every curricular resource is available when needed, for group or individual lessons.

MATH IN MY WORLD TEST GENERATOR

The integrated Test Generator for Grades 3–6 comes with a computer databank of test items for each chapter correlated to:

- state standards
- national standardized testing objectives
- chapter content

Teachers can create tests customized to evaluate student progress from any perspective they need.

The Test Generator gives teachers the choice to:

- use existing questions or create their own
- print tests or give tests online
- customize based on any criteria the teacher selects

Each test item references the math program textbooks and/or technology.

MATHTALK FORUM

Always seeking ways to assist teachers in staff development, McGraw-Hill has established the MathTalk Forum, an online community of classroom teachers.

Hosted by math experts, MathTalk Forum is available for teachers to pose questions about teaching math, share classroom ideas, and gain new insights about their profession. MathTalk expands the professional community and provides the opportunity to participate in "teacher talk" about math with teachers from classrooms everywhere.

MATH VAN MULTIMEDIA SOFTWARE

Math Van is a feature-rich multimedia package developed to go hand-in-hand with the pupil editions of *Math in my World*.

Both the primary K-2 and the intermediate 3-6 programs include:

- grade-appropriate software
- teacher's guide
- user's guide

Special activity cards at intermediate grades support independent exploration and practice of key mathematical concepts.

Every chapter in every grade level of the Teacher's Edition includes a fully integrated, alternative lesson using Math Van, for flexible integration of multimedia technology into instruction. These alternative Teaching with Technology lessons explore the same objective identified in the introduction of each text chapter.

Math Van primary and intermediate activities challenge students to apply the knowledge they've gained in the classroom, and incorporate:

- colorful graphics
- engaging mathematical problems
- flexible tools

Math Van meets individual needs with:

- review and reinforcement of concepts and skills
- exploration and extension of content
- instructional support at every proficiency level

Other Math Van options provide:

- on-screen manipulatives for problem solving, skills practice and decision-making
- Tech Links that highlight opportunities for students to use manipulatives, tables and graphs
- online notes for more practice, reteaching, and extension
- an on-screen calculator
- a built-in notebook that allows students to save and print work, and to keep track of progress for assessment and sharing

INTERNET LESSONS AND CYBERSCOUT

Teachers with Internet access often struggle to find appropriate web sites for instruction. *Math in my World's* Internet resources offer easy access to web-based lesson plans that support guided explorations. Teachers simply select the chapter to teach, review the lesson plan, print the project sheet and answer keys, and they're ready.

For help in designing their own web-linked lessons, teachers can turn to Cyberscout, a classroom-specific search utility. Key-in basic information about the lesson being planned, and a reply e-mail will come back with a list of appropriate websites — so it's simple to develop unique online lessons without spending hours net-searching alone.

MATH IN MY WORLD INTEGRATES TECHNOLOGY

Students today deserve the preparation that both text and technology give them. But technology integration must be natural, closely connected to the expectations for achievement.

Math in my World is the most technologically rich program available. Full integration with the text, flexible application of the tools, and a focus on the needs of students and teachers together bring the power of technology to the service of instruction.

TEACHER'S EDITION

McGRAW-HILL MATHEMATICS

Math in my World

DOUGLAS H. CLEMENTS

KENNETH W. JONES

LOIS GORDON MOSELEY

LINDA SCHULMAN

McGraw-Hill School Division

New York Farmington

Contributors

Lodge Textbook QA 107 .M26 1999 Gr.4 TE-Pt.2

Author Team

Program Authors

Dr. Douglas H. Clements

Kenneth W. Jones

Lois Gordon Moseley

Dr. Linda Schulman

Contributing Authors

Christine A. Fernsler

Dr. Liana Forest

Dr. Kathleen Kelly-Benjamin

Maria R. Marolda

Dr. Richard H. Moyer

Dr. Walter G. Secada

Multicultural and Educational Consultants

Rim An
Teacher
UN International School
New York, New York

Sue Cantrell
Superintendent of Schools
Madison County Schools
Marshall, North Carolina

Mordessa Corbin
Instructional Specialist
Mathematics Pre K - 12
Gilbert, Louisiana

Dr. Carlos Diaz
Project Director
Cultural Foundations in Education
Florida Atlantic University
Boca Raton, Florida

Carl Downing
Director of Native American
Language Development Institute
Oklahoma City, Oklahoma

Linda Ferreira
Teacher
Pinellas Park, Florida

Judythe M. Hazel
Elementary School Principal
Tempe, Arizona

Roger Larson
Mathematics Coordinator
Ramsey, Minnesota

Josie Robles
Mathematics Coordinator
Silver Springs, Maryland

Veronica Rogers
Director, Secondary Education
Mobile, Alabama

Telkia Rutherford
Mathematics Facilitator
Chicago, Illinois

Sharon Searcy
Teacher
Mandarin, Florida

Elizabeth Sinor
Teacher/Trainer
Mathematics and Assessment
Waddy, Kentucky

Michael Wallpe
Curriculum Development
Indianapolis, Indiana

Claudia Zaslavsky
Author, Africa Counts
New York, New York

Career Professionals

Jim Anderson
Stained Glass Artist

Robert Beard
Leather Carver

Bill Becoat
Inventor

Jack Bertagnolli
Rancher

Alex Bhattacharji
Reporter, Sports Illustrated

Dr. Sherrilyn Brannon
Veterinarian

Yvonne Campos
Marketing Executive

Theresa Cebuhar
Highway Maintenance Worker

Dave Chin
School Adjustment Counselor

Steve Crockett
Engineer

Susannah Druck
Program Coordinator,
Ecosphere Magazine

Larry Felix
Communications Officer

La Tondra Finley
Veterinarian's Receptionist

Charlotte Garcia
School Superintendent

Rich Garcia
American League Umpire

Alyssa Goodman
Astrophysicist

Marla Grossberg
Market Researcher

Clair Hain, Jr.
President of Great Coasters
International

Ruth Handler
Designer of Barbie and Ken Dolls

Kevin Hanson
Track Official

Kim Harrison
Marine Biologist

Beverly Harvard
Chief of Police

Maria Hayashida
Musher, Winner of 1996
Alaskan Iditarod Race

Colleen Heminger-Cordell
Business Owner

Patrick Hong
Automobile Road-Tester

David Juarez
Olympic Mountain Biker

Pat Kambesis
Speleologist

Frank Mazzotti
Wildlife Biologist

Mishelle Michaels
Meteorologist

Sterling Monroe
Statistician

Rusty Moore
Cordwainer

Sharon O'Connell
Founder of the Sadako/Paper
Crane Project

Sandy Pandiscio
Treasury Analyst

Martha Puente &
Beatrice Gonzalez
Interior Decorators

Tom Rittenberry
Sales Representative,
Sun Microsystems

Raymond Rye
Museum Director

Susan Solomon
Ozone Researcher

Monty & Ann Stambler
Game Inventors

Donald Stull
Architect

Priscilla Warren
Rug Weaver

Tina Yao
Graphic Designer

Suzanne Yin
Marine Biologist

McGraw-Hill School Division
A Division of The ***McGraw-Hill*** *Companies*

Copyright © 1999 McGraw-Hill School Division, a Division of the Educational and Professional Publishing Group of The McGraw-Hill Companies, Inc.

All rights reserved. No part of this book may be reproduced or transmitted in any form or by any means, electronic or mechanical, including photocopying, recording, or by any information storage and retrieval system without permission in writing from the publisher.

McGraw-Hill School Division
1221 Avenue of the Americas
New York, New York 10020

Printed in the United States of America
ISBN 0-02-110333-X / 4, Pt. 2
2 3 4 5 6 7 8 9 073 04 03 02 01 00 99 98

Contributors

Thanks to all of the teachers, students, and schools who contributed to this project.

Educators and Schools

Phyllis Adcock
West Lake Elementary School
Apex, North Carolina

Leigh Anne Akey
Pauline O'Rourke Elementary School
Mobile, Alabama

Linda Allen
Goshen Elementary School
Goshen, Kentucky

Harriet Anagnostopoulos
John J. Shaughnessy
Humanities School
Lowell, Massachusetts

Susan Ardissono
Shoreline, Washington

Catherine Battle
Snowden Elementary School
Memphis, Tennessee

Sylvia Bednarski
Centerfield Elementary School
Crestwood, Kentucky

Lorraine Bege
Luis Munoz Marin School
Bridgeport, Connecticut

Tricia Bender
Pauline O'Rourke Elementary School
Mobile, Alabama

G. Renee Black
Pauline O'Rourke Elementary School
Mobile, Alabama

Sandy Blagborne
McPherson Middle School
Howell, Michigan

Denise Blume
Slidell, Louisiana

Kaye Bybee
Southland Elementary School
Riverton, Utah

Betty Byrne
Snowden Elementary School
Memphis, Tennessee

Brent Caldwell
Madison Middle School
Marshall, North Carolina

Ellen Carlson
Northwest Elementary School
Howell, Michigan

Walter Carr
Mandarin Middle School
Jacksonville, Florida

Hope Carter
Pauline O'Rourke Elementary School
Mobile, Alabama

Cynthia Carter
Mandarin Oaks Elementary School
Jacksonville, Florida

Denise Clark
Crestwood Elementary School
Crestwood, Kentucky

Patsy Cohen
Louisville Collegiate School
Louisville, Kentucky

Linda Colburn
E.N. Rogers School
Lowell, Massachusetts

Tammy Cooper
Latson Road Elementary School
Howell, Michigan

Lynne Copeland
John Yeates Middle School
Suffolk, Virginia

Naomi Damron
Southland Elementary School
Riverton, Utah

Peg Darcy
Kammerer Middle School
Louisville, Kentucky

Talmdage Darden
John Yeates Middle School
Suffolk, Virginia

Mary Davis
Snowden Elementary School
Memphis, Tennessee

Winifred Deavens
St. Louis Public Schools
St. Louis, Missouri

Terri Dickson
Snowden Elementary School
Memphis, Tennessee

Kris Dillon
Elephant's Fork Elementary School
Suffolk, Virginia

Karen Doidge
West Lake Elementary School
Apex, North Carolina

Hope Donato
Piney Grove Elementary School
Charlotte, North Carolina

Jo Doty
Mandarin Oaks Elementary School
Jacksonville, Florida

Marna Draper
Hawthorne Elementary School
Indianapolis, Indiana

Renee Duckenfield
West Lake Elementary School
Apex, North Carolina

Susan Farrar
Hawthorne Elementary School
Indianapolis, Indiana

Mary Jo Farrell
John J. Shaughnessy
Humanities School
Lowell, Massachusetts

Katrina Fives
Pauline O'Rourke Elementary School
Mobile, Alabama

Katie Flaherty
East Cobb Middle School
Marietta, Georgia

Ellen Flamer
Piney Grove Elementary School
Charlotte, North Carolina

Winston Fouche
Webster Middle School
St. Louis, Missouri

Gil French
Baltimore, Maryland

Melissa Garrone
Snowden Elementary School
Memphis, Tennessee

Dana Geils
P.S. 144/District 28 Queens
Forest Hills, New York

Vera Greer
Snowden Elementary School
Memphis, Tennessee

Paul Groth
Highlander Way Middle School
Howell, Michigan

Marguerite Guthrie
Anchorage Public School
Anchorage, Kentucky

Terri Haarala
Pauline O'Rourke Elementary School
Mobile, Alabama

Carol Harris
Elephant's Fork Elementary School
Suffolk, Virginia

Beverly Hartz
Elephant's Fork Elementary School
Suffolk, Virginia

Lori Harvey
Snowden Elementary School
Memphis, Tennessee

Judy Haskell
Northwest Elementary School
Howell, Michigan

Mary Lynne Havey
McPherson Middle School
Howell, Michigan

Diane Hayes
Pauline O'Rourke Elementary School
Mobile, Alabama

Gayle Hendershot
Garland, Texas

Hector Hirigoyen
Miami, Florida

Janice Holland
Elephant's Fork Elementary School
Suffolk, Virginia

Daisy Irvin
Luis Munoz Marin School
Bridgeport, Connecticut

Barbara Jacobs
H.B. Slaughter School
Louisville, Kentucky

Lisa James
Carroll Middle School
Carrollton, Kentucky

Roberta Johnson
Anchorage Public School
Anchorage, Kentucky

Barbara Jones
Mandarin Oaks Elementary School
Jacksonville, Florida

Faye Jones
West Lake Elementary School
Apex, North Carolina

Lori Jones
Mandarin Middle School
Jacksonville, Florida

Steve June
West Lake Elementary School
Apex, North Carolina

Sydell Kane
P.S. 144/District 28 Queens
Forest Hills, New York

Alisha Kelly
Southwest Elementary School
Howell, Michigan

Kathy Kelly
Hawthorne Elementary School
Indianapolis, Indiana

Mona Kennedy
Southland Elementary School
Riverton, Utah

Larry Kiernan
Raymond Park Middle School
Indianapolis, Indiana

Dina Kruckenberg
Ira Ogden Elementary School
San Antonio, Texas

Cathy Kuhns
Coral Springs, Florida

Judy Lane
Hawthorne Elementary School
Indianapolis, Indiana

Carol Lehrman
P.S. 144/District 28 Queens
Forest Hills, New York

Eleanor Levinson
West Lake Elementary School
Apex, North Carolina

Contributors

Clarice Loggins
Snowden Elementary School
Memphis, Tennessee

Jim Long
Snowden Elementary School
Memphis, Tennessee

Melanee Lucado
Snowden Elementary School
Memphis, Tennessee

Diane Lucas
Pauline O'Rourke Elementary School
Mobile, Alabama

Debra Luke
Pauline O'Rourke Elementary School
Mobile, Alabama

Debbie Lytle
Piney Grove Elementary School
Charlotte, North Carolina

Jim Madsen
Southland Elementary School
Riverton, Utah

Maria Marquez
Ira Ogden Elementary School
San Antonio, Texas

Ofelia Martinez
Ira Ogden Elementary School
San Antonio, Texas

Lisa Martire
Luis Munoz Marin School
Bridgeport, Connecticut

Rae Ann Maurer
P.S. 144/District 28 Queens
Forest Hills, New York

Ellen McClain
Hawthorne Elementary School
Indianapolis, Indiana

Kelley McDaniel
South Oldham County Middle School
Crestwood, Kentucky

Debra McElreath
Mandarin Oaks Elementary School
Jacksonville, Florida

Nancy McLaughlin
DeSoto, Texas

Jim McMann
Lowell Public Schools
Lowell, Massachusetts

Debbie Miller
Hawthorne Elementary School
Indianapolis, Indiana

Milvern Miller
South Bend, Indiana

Melinda Monserrate
Gateway Middle School
St. Louis, Missouri

Phyllis Moore
Madison Middle School
Marshall, North Carolina

Joan Murphy
E.N. Rogers School
Lowell, Massachusetts

Vickey Myrick
West Lake Elementary School
Apex, North Carolina

Dennis Nelson
Tempe, Arizona

Martha O'Donnell
St. Francis School
Goshen, Kentucky

Tom O'Hare
E.N. Rogers School
Lowell, Massachusetts

Wanda Peele
Emma Elementary School
Asheville, North Carolina

Linda Perry-Clarke
Elephant's Fork Elementary School
Suffolk, Virginia

Taylor Phelps
John Yeates Middle School
Suffolk, Virginia

Alda Pill
Mandarin Oaks Elementary School
Jacksonville, Florida

Kay Pitts
Snowden Elementary School
Memphis, Tennessee

Barbara Rea
North Oldham County Middle School
Goshen, Kentucky

Susan Rhyne
Piney Grove Elementary School
Charlotte, North Carolina

Mary Riley
Madison, Wisconsin

Carolyn Rooks
Snowden Elementary School
Memphis, Tennessee

Nancy Rose
Luis Munoz Marin School
Bridgeport, Connecticut

Jeffrey Rosen
East Cobb Middle School
Marietta, Georgia

Charlene Ruble
Centerfield Elementary School
Crestwood, Kentucky

Patricia Sanford
Mandarin Oaks Elementary School
Jacksonville, Florida

Jim Santo
Luis Munoz Marin School
Bridgeport, Connecticut

Lee Sawyer
West Lake Elementary School
Apex, North Carolina

Virginia Schurke
Mandarin Oaks Elementary School
Jacksonville, Florida

Shadonica Scruggs
Snowden Elementary School
Memphis, Tennessee

Ellen Sears
Anchorage Public School
Anchorage, Kentucky

Tim Sears
Anchorage Public School
Anchorage, Kentucky

Mary Sevigney
John J. Shaughnessy
Humanities School
Lowell, Massachusetts

Ann Sievert
Highlander Way Middle School
Howell, Michigan

Laura Silverman
P.S. 144/District 28 Queens
Forest Hills, New York

Ada Simmons
East Cobb Middle School
Marietta, Georgia

Dot Singleton
Winston Salem, North Carolina

Jo Ann Sipkin
West Lake Elementary School
Apex, North Carolina

Hilda Skiles
South Oldham County Middle School
Crestwood, Kentucky

Sue Slesnick
Louisville Collegiate School
Louisville, Kentucky

Venus Smith
Snowden Elementary School
Memphis, Tennessee

Judy Smizik
Pittsburgh, Pennsylvania

Doug Soards
Mt. Washington Middle School
Mt. Washington, Kentucky

Kristen Sousa
Pauline O'Rourke Elementary School
Mobile, Alabama

Nancy Souza
North Oldham County Middle School
Goshen, Kentucky

Laura Stander
John J. Shaughnessy Humanities School
Lowell, Massachusetts

Trish Strain
Mandarin Oaks Elementary School
Jacksonville, Florida

Mary Sullivan
Pauline O'Rourke Elementary School
Mobile, Alabama

Jeff Swensson
Raymond Park Middle School
Indianapolis, Indiana

Rebecca True
Raymond Park Middle School
Indianapolis, Indiana

Charlie Waller
Pauline O'Rourke Elementary School
Mobile, Alabama

Judy Wayne
E.N. Rogers School
Lowell, Massachusetts

Vickie Wheatley
LaGrange Elementary School
LaGrange, Kentucky

Carol Wietholter
Hawthorne Elementary School
Indianapolis, Indiana

Christine Wilcox
Centerfield Elementary School
Crestwood, Kentucky

Kathryn Williams
Pauline O'Rourke Elementary School
Mobile, Alabama

Ronna Young
Hawthorne Elementary School
Indianapolis, Indiana

Karen Zinman
Rye Brook, New York

Field Test Schools

Alexander Middle School
Huntersville, North Carolina

Benjamin Franklin Elementary School
Yorktown Heights, New York

Bow Elementary School
Detroit, Michigan

Burrville Elementary School
Washington, DC

Candler Elementary School
Candler, North Carolina

Cattell Elementary School
Des Moines, Iowa

Crestwood Elementary School
Crestwood, Kentucky

David Cox Elementary School
Henderson, Nevada

Emma Elementary School
Asheville, North Carolina

JHS 263K
Brooklyn, New York

Longfellow Elementary School
Des Moines, Iowa

Onalaska Middle School
Onalaska, Wisconsin

Studebaker Elementary School
Des Moines, Iowa

W.C. Pryor Middle School
Fort Walton Beach, Florida

Contents

 These lessons develop, practice or apply algebraic thinking through the study of patterns, relationships and functions, properties, equations, formulas, and inequalities.

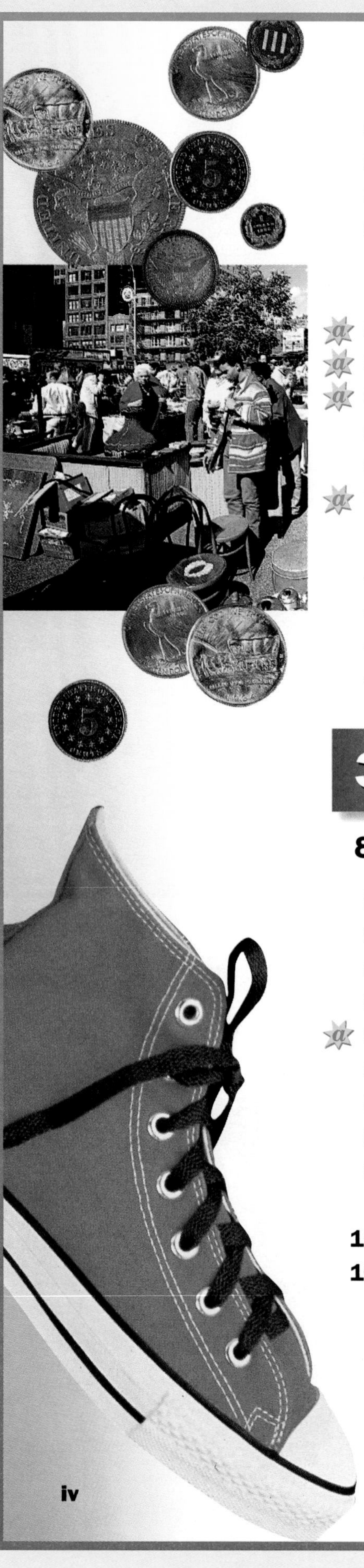

3 Time, Data, and Graphs

4 Multiplication and Division Facts

 These lessons develop, practice or apply algebraic thinking through the study of patterns, relationships and functions, properties, equations, formulas, and inequalities.

5 Multiply by 1-Digit Numbers

6 Multiply by 2-Digit Numbers

7 Measurement

 These lessons develop, practice or apply algebraic thinking through the study of patterns, relationships and functions, properties, equations, formulas, and inequalities.

8 Divide by 1- and 2-Digit Numbers

9 Geometry

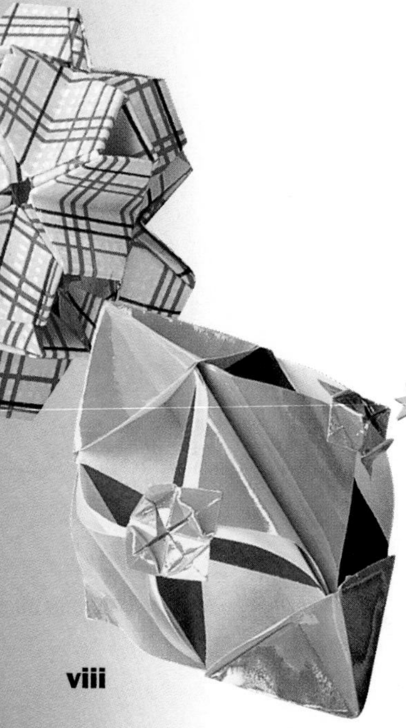

10 Fractions and Probability

 These lessons develop, practice or apply algebraic thinking through the study of patterns, relationships and functions, properties, equations, formulas, and inequalities.

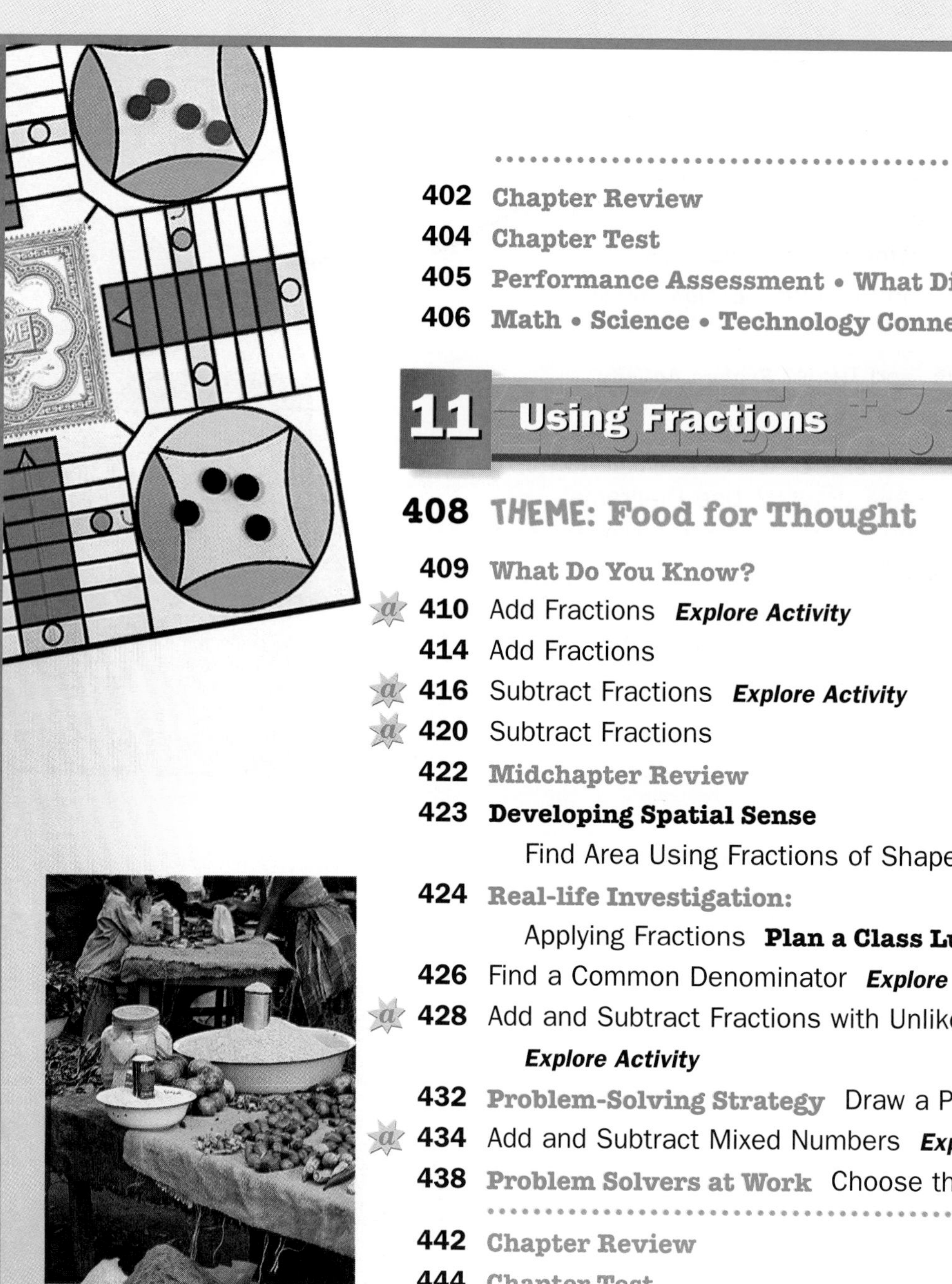

11 Using Fractions

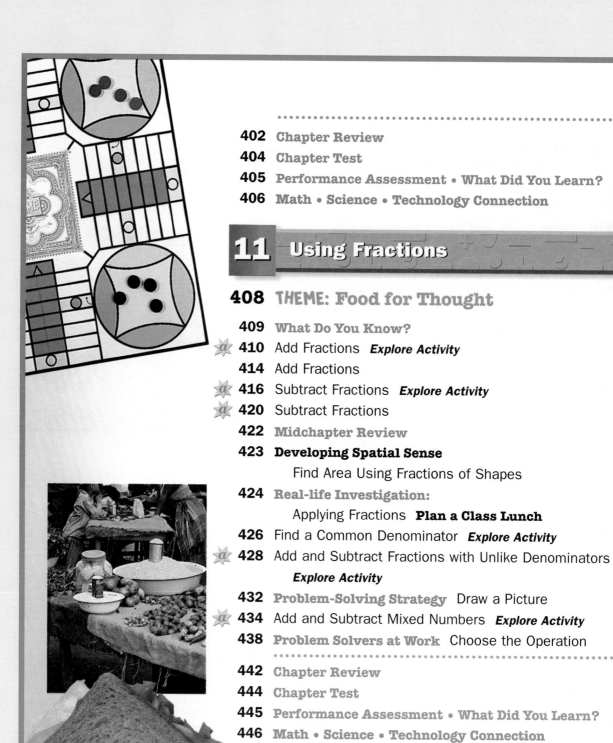

12 Decimals

These lessons develop, practice or apply algebraic thinking through the study of patterns, relationships and functions, properties, equations, formulas, and inequalities.

CHAPTER 7 AT A GLANCE: Measurement

Theme: Under the Sea   Suggested Pacing: 10–13 days

CHAPTER 7 ORGANIZER

	DAY 1	DAY 2	DAY 3
WEEK ONE	**PREASSESSMENT** Introduction **pp. 240** What Do You Know? **p. 241** **CHAPTER OBJECTIVES:** 7A, 7B, 7C, 7D, 7E **RESOURCES** Read-Aloud Anthology pp. 34–35 Pretest: Test Master Form A, B, or C Diagnostic Inventory Portfolio Journal **NCTM STANDARDS:** 1, 2, 3, 4, 10	**LESSON 7.1** EXPLORE ACTIVITY Length in Customary Units **pp. 242–243** **CHAPTER OBJECTIVES:** 7A **MATERIALS** inch rulers (TA 18) or measuring tapes (TA 19), calculators (opt.) **RESOURCES** Reteach/Practice/Extend: 58 Math Center Cards: 58 Extra Practice: 508 Daily Review TE p. 241B Technology Link **NCTM STANDARDS:** 4, 10	**LESSON 7.2** Rename Customary Units of Length **pp. 244–245** **CHAPTER OBJECTIVES:** 7C **MATERIALS** customary measuring tapes (TA 19), calculators (opt.) **RESOURCES** Reteach/Practice/Extend: 59 Math Center Cards: 59 Extra Practice: 508 Daily Review TE p. 243B Algebraic Thinking Technology Link **NCTM STANDARDS:** 8, 10
WEEK TWO	**MIDCHAPTER ASSESSMENT** Midchapter Review **p. 252** **CHAPTER OBJECTIVES:** 7A, 7C, 7D **MATERIALS** rulers (TA 18), calculators (opt.) Developing Number Sense **p. 253** **REAL-LIFE INVESTIGATION:** Applying Measurement **pp. 254–255** Portfolio Journal **NCTM STANDARDS:** 1, 2, 3, 4, 5, 10	**LESSON 7.5** Capacity and Weight in Customary Units **pp. 256–259** **CHAPTER OBJECTIVES:** 7B **MATERIALS** cup, pt, qt, gal containers; calculators (opt.) **RESOURCES** Reteach/Practice/Extend: 62 Math Center Cards: 62 Extra Practice: 510 Daily Review TE p. 255B Algebraic Thinking Journal Technology Link **NCTM STANDARDS:** 10	**LESSON 7.6** PROBLEM-SOLVING STRATEGY Use Logical Reasoning **pp. 260–261** **CHAPTER OBJECTIVES:** 7E **RESOURCES** Reteach/Practice/Extend: 63 Math Center Cards: 63 Extra Practice: 510 Daily Review TE p. 259B Technology Link **NCTM STANDARDS:** 1, 2, 3, 4, 10
WEEK THREE	**CHAPTER ASSESSMENT** Chapter Review **pp. 270–271** **MATERIALS** calculators (opt.) Chapter Test **p. 272** **RESOURCES** Posttest: Test Master Form A, B, or C Performance Assessment **p. 273** **RESOURCES** Performance Task: Test Master Math • Science • Technology Connection **pp. 274–275** Portfolio **NCTM STANDARDS:** 1, 4, 10		

DAY 4

LESSON 7.3

EXPLORE ACTIVITY

Length in Metric Units pp. 246–249

CHAPTER OBJECTIVES: 7A

MATERIALS centimeter rulers (TA 18) or metric measuring tapes (TA 20), calculators (opt.)

RESOURCES Reteach/Practice/Extend: 60
Math Center Cards: 60
Extra Practice: 509

Daily Review TE p. 245B

Algebraic Thinking

Technology Link

NCTM STANDARDS: 4, 10

LESSON 7.7

Capacity and Mass in Metric Units pp. 262–265

CHAPTER OBJECTIVES: 7B

MATERIALS plastic liter containers, plastic cups, eyedroppers

RESOURCES Reteach/Practice/Extend: 64
Math Center Cards: 64
Extra Practice: 511

Daily Review TE p. 261B

Algebraic Thinking

Technology Link

NCTM STANDARDS: 10

DAY 5

LESSON 7.4

Perimeter pp. 250–251

CHAPTER OBJECTIVES: 7D

MATERIALS measuring tapes (TA 19–20) and rulers (TA 18)

RESOURCES Reteach/Practice/Extend: 61
Math Center Cards: 61
Extra Practice: 509

TEACHING WITH TECHNOLOGY
Alternate Lesson TE pp. 251A–251B

Daily Review TE p. 249B

Algebraic Thinking

Technology Link

NCTM STANDARDS: 4, 9, 10

LESSON 7.8

PROBLEM SOLVERS AT WORK

Check for Reasonableness pp. 266–269

CHAPTER OBJECTIVES: 7E

MATERIALS C and F thermometers, calculators (opt.), computer drawing program (opt.)

RESOURCES Reteach/Practice/Extend: 65
Math Center Cards: 65
Extra Practice: 511

Daily Review TE p. 265B

Technology Link

NCTM STANDARDS: 1, 2, 3, 4, 10

Assessment Options

FORMAL

Chapter Tests

STUDENT BOOK

- Midchapter Review, p. 252
- Chapter Review, pp. 270–271
- Chapter Test, p. 272

BLACKLINE MASTERS

- Test Master Form A, B, or C
- Diagnostic Inventory

COMPUTER TEST GENERATOR

- Available on disk

Performance Assessment

- What Do You Know? p. 241
- Performance Assessment, p. 273
- Holistic Scoring Guide, Teacher's Assessment Resources, pp. 27–32
- Follow-Up Interviews, p. 273
- Performance Task, Test Masters

Teacher's Assessment Resources

- Portfolio Guidelines and Forms, pp. 6–9, 33–35
- Holistic Scoring Guide, pp. 27–32
- Samples of Student Work, pp. 37–72

INFORMAL

Ongoing Assessment

- Observation Checklist, pp. 244, 260
- Interview, pp. 242, 246, 262
- Anecdotal Report, pp. 250, 256, 266

Portfolio Opportunities

- Chapter Project, p. 239F
- What Do You Know? p. 241
- Investigation, pp. 254–255
- Journal Writing, pp. 241, 252, 257
- Performance Assessment, p. 273
- Self-Assessment: What Do You Think? p. 273

Chapter Objectives		Standardized Test Correlations
7A	Estimate and measure length in customary or metric units	MAT, CAT, SAT, CTBS, TN*
7B	Estimate and measure weight, mass, or capacity in customary or metric units	CAT, SAT, CTBS, TN*
7C	Convert between customary or metric units of length, weight, mass, or capacity	
7D	Find perimeter	MAT, CAT, CTBS, TN*
7E	Solve problems, including those that involve measurement and logical reasoning	MAT, CAT, SAT, ITBS, CTBS, TN*

*Terra Nova

NCTM Standards Grades K–4

1 Problem Solving
2 Communication
3 Reasoning
4 Connections
5 Estimation
6 Number Sense and Numeration
7 Concepts of Whole Number Operations
8 Whole Number Computation
9 Geometry and Spatial Sense
10 Measurement
11 Statistics and Probability
12 Fractions and Decimals
13 Patterns and Relationships

Meeting Individual Needs

LEARNING STYLES

- AUDITORY/LINGUISTIC
- LOGICAL/ANALYTICAL
- VISUAL/SPATIAL
- MUSICAL
- KINESTHETIC
- SOCIAL
- INDIVIDUAL

Students who are talented in art, language, and physical activity may better understand mathematical concepts when these concepts are connected to their areas of interest. Use the following activities to stimulate the different learning styles of some of your students.

Social Learners

Students can work together at a measuring center using different kinds of tools. Place lines made with masking tape in one area and label with letters of the alphabet. Have students work together to estimate and record the lengths of the lines.

Visual/Spatial Learners

Students will be making comparisons in this chapter. Display a poster comparing measurements so they can convert larger units within the metric and customary systems of measuring.

See Lesson Resources, pp. 241A, 243A, 245A, 249A, 255A, 259A, 261A, 265A.

GIFTED AND TALENTED

Have students select classroom objects and find the perimeters of each. They will choose an appropriate measuring tool and measure objects in the metric and customary systems. Students could measure their desk tops, the teacher's desk top, the chalkboard, the door, or other objects around the classroom. Ask students to record their results.

You may wish to have students explore distance in miles using an atlas or road map. Give students a map and have them find distances between places. Have them plan a trip and record daily distances traveled. Encourage them to use a key and convert the information from the key to actual measurements.

See also Meeting Individual Needs, pp. 248, 258, 264, 268.

ESL APPROPRIATE

EXTRA SUPPORT

Have available customary and metric measuring tapes and rulers and other measuring tools throughout the chapter. Specific suggestions for ways to provide extra support to students appear in every lesson in this chapter.

See Meeting Individual Needs, pp. 242, 244, 246, 250, 256, 260, 262, 266.

EARLY FINISHERS

Students who finish their class work early may write letters to other classes inviting them to view the mural, Sea It Now. (See *Chapter Project*, p. 239F.)

See also Meeting Individual Needs, pp. 242, 244, 248, 250, 258, 260, 264, 268.

LANGUAGE SUPPORT

This chapter will have many new measurement terms. Display a poster of new words with a description and a diagram so students can refer to it if needed. Post comparative measures as well, for example, 12 inches = 1 foot. When measuring, use terms to describe the tools being used and explain the process. As students repeat the process encourage them to talk about what they are doing.

See also Meeting Individual Needs, pp. 256, 262, 268.

ESL APPROPRIATE

INCLUSION

- **For inclusion ideas, information, and suggestions, see pp. 246, 258, 264, 266, T15.**
- **For gender fairness tips, see pp. 257, T15.**

USING MANIPULATIVES

Building Understanding Provide centimeter and inch rulers, meter sticks and yardsticks to give students a frame of reference. Keep measuring tools in an accessible area and allow students to select the appropriate tools when needed.

Easy-to-Make Manipulatives Use cardboard milk containers to measure ounces, cups, pints, quarts, and gallons. To make one pound weights, use film containers filled with pennies and glue. A kilogram weight can be made with rocks in a coffee can. A paper clip can be used for a gram weight.

ESL APPROPRIATE

USING COOPERATIVE LEARNING

Pairs Experiment This strategy develops teamwork by having pairs work together to do an experiment.

- **In a group of four, partners help each other with an experiment.**
- **Then the two sets of partners share results.**
- **The group discusses all results, then comes to an agreement and prepares a joint report.**

USING LITERATURE

Use the selection *Window on the Deep: The Adventures of Underwater Explorer Sylvia Earle* to introduce the chapter theme, Under the Sea. This selection is reprinted on pages 34–35 of the Read-Aloud Anthology.

Also available in the Read-Aloud Anthology is the story *Lightening the Load*, page 36.

Linking Technology

This integrated package of programs and services allows students to explore, develop, and practice concepts; solve problems; build portfolios; and assess their own progress. Teachers can enhance instruction, provide remediation, and share ideas with other educational professionals.

CD-ROM ACTIVITY

In *Treasure Hunt,* students use the geometry and measurement tools to discover the location of buried treasure. Students can use the online notebook to write about how they measure perimeter. To extend the activity, students use the Math Van tools to create their own maps. **Available on CD-ROM.**

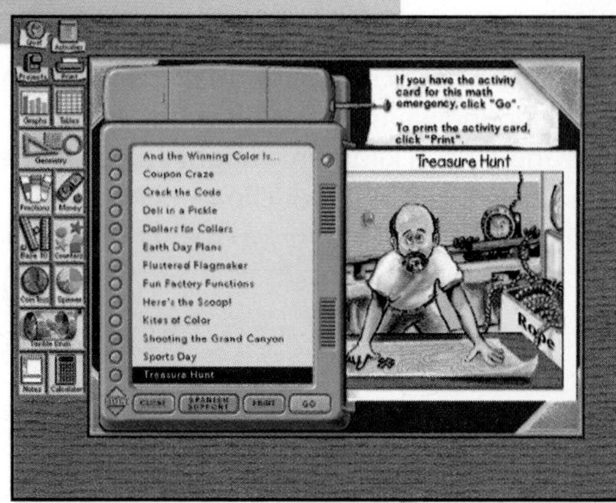

CD-ROM TOOLS

Students can use Math Van's geometry and measurement tools to explore the concept of measurement. The Tech Links on the Lesson Resources pages highlight opportunities for students to use these and other tools such as graphs, tables, online notes, and calculator to provide additional practice, reteaching, or extension. **Available on CD-ROM.**

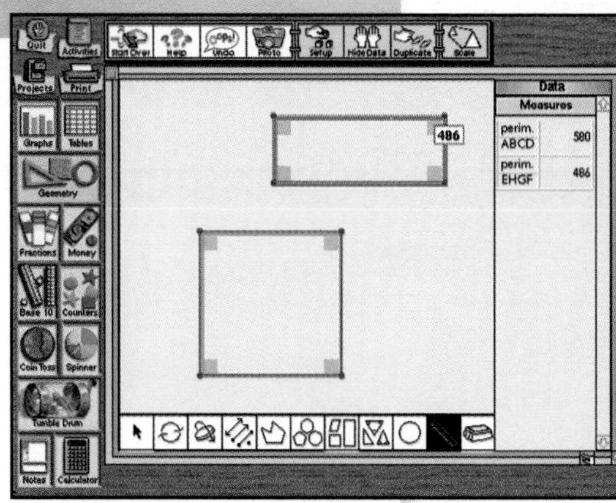

WEB SITE http://www.mhschool.com

Teachers can access the McGraw-Hill School Division World Wide Web site for additional curriculum support at http://www.mhschool.com. Click on our Resource Village for specially designed activities linking Web sites to measurement. Motivate children by inviting them to explore Web sites that develop the chapter theme of "Under the Sea." Exchange ideas on classroom management, cultural diversity, and other areas in the Math Forum.

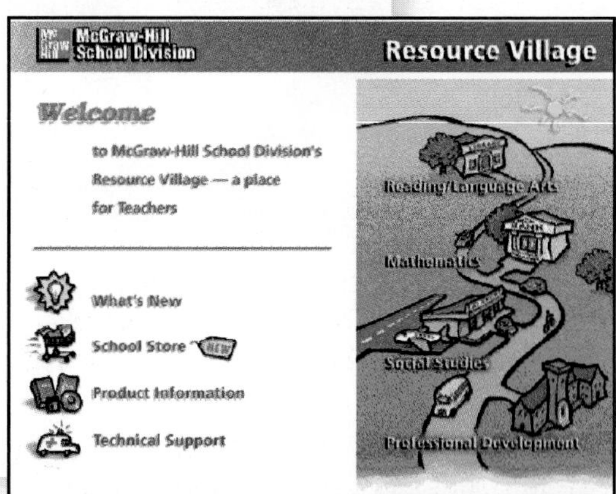

Chapter Project SEA IT NOW

Highlighting the Math

- construct physical models
- apply customary and metric measurement

1 Starting the Project

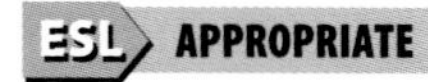

Introduce the idea of creating an underwater environment, Sea It Now. Have students discuss things that live in or may be found in the sea. List their responses on the chalkboard. Invite students to share any information they might know about the size or weight of specific creatures, or even how deep in the ocean they may be found.

Tell students that they will create a large mural incorporating the things they've been discussing. They will also research the creatures, plants, and objects for information about actual measurement, weight, and length. Assign students to groups.

Cut a large sheet of craft paper into as many sections as there are groups. Each group will create its own portion of the mural. Consider how family or community members may participate.

2 Continuing the Project

- Each group decides upon what to include in its portion of the mural. Members of the group research the creatures or objects in their environment and take notes on the measurements.
- Each group makes a chart displaying the measurement information they researched.
- The groups create drawings of the things they researched; taking turns drawing, painting, and/or coloring their section of mural; and attaching their researched creations to the appropriate part of the mural. If possible, take photographs of the mural.

3 Finishing the Project

Each group presents its portion of the mural, providing measurement information about things in the scene and making a math statement or two about the scene.

Community Involvement

Invite a speaker from your local aquarium or museum of natural history. Be sure the class is ready with thoughtful questions to pose to the speaker. Follow up the visit with a thank-you letter to the speaker.

BUILDING A PORTFOLIO

Each student's portfolio contains the drawings and measurement of the creatures or objects they researched. The portfolio may also include a photograph of the mural.

To assess students' work, refer to the Holistic Scoring Guide on page 27 in the Teacher's Assessment Resources.

PURPOSE Introduce theme of the chapter.

Resources Read-Aloud Anthology, pages 34–35

Using Literature

Read "Window on the Deep" from the Read-Aloud Anthology to introduce the chapter theme, "Under the Sea."

Developing the Theme

Encourage students to describe what they know about the sea. Create an idea web with the class about life under the sea. You may want to start with categories such as "animal life," "plant life," "the water," or "the ocean floor." Ask students to come up with other headings and brainstorm items appropriate to each heading.

Have students use the items from the idea web to discuss the importance of the sea to humans. Then ask students to think of math skills a person might need in a sea-related job or when enjoying the sea—for instance, a fisherman would need measuring and bookkeeping skills as well as map skills.

These under-the-sea subjects are discussed in this chapter:

Giant American Lobster p. 244
Carp p. 244
Siamese Fighting Fish p. 246
Sea Turtle p. 247
Giant Spider Crab p. 247
Scuba diving p. 250
Box Turtle p. 263
Leatherback Turtle p. 263
Bluefin Tuna p. 263
Kelp p. 265

On pages 254–255 students will investigate how salt affects ocean temperature.

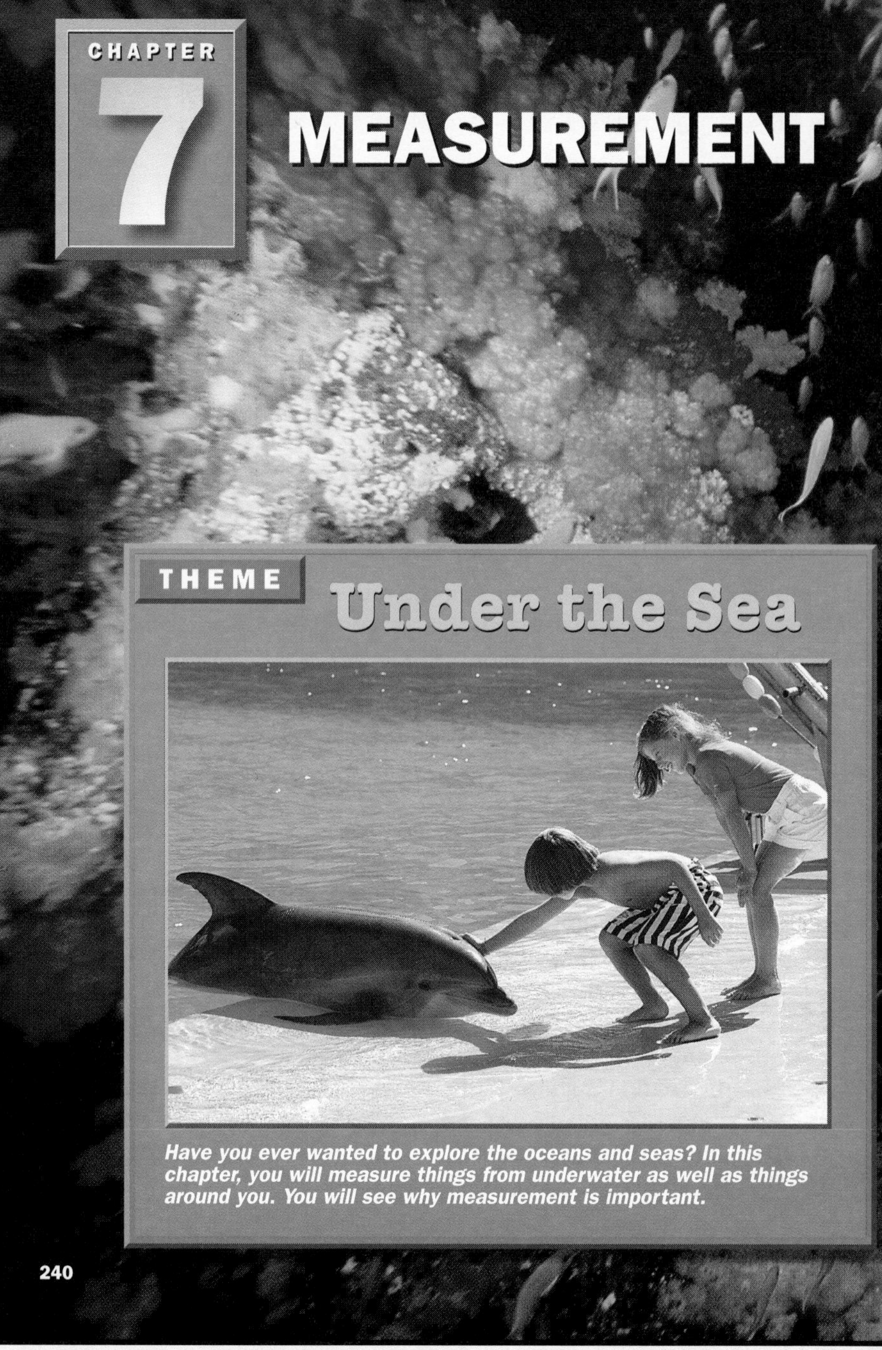

Have you ever wanted to explore the oceans and seas? In this chapter, you will measure things from underwater as well as things around you. You will see why measurement is important.

240

Chapter Bibliography

Dividing into Darkness: A Submersible Explores the Sea by Rebecca Johnson. Minneapolis, MN: Lerner Publications Co., 1989. ISBN 0–8225–1587–3.

The Magic School Bus On the Ocean Floor by Joanna Cole. New York: Scholastic, Inc., 1992. ISBN 0–590–41430–5.

Community Involvement

Help students organize a scuba demonstration at a local pool. To find a diver, students can write or call a local police department, rescue squad, or sports shops. Invite a certified scuba diver to demonstrate the equipment, show photographs taken underwater, and talk about fish, underwater wrecks, and water pollution. Students can publicize the event by making posters and displaying them at community centers and sports shops.

What Do You Know?

Scientists measure dolphins to learn more about how they grow. **2. Possible answer: scales, tape measures, thermometers, rulers, yardsticks, metersticks**

1 What different types of measurements could scientists take on a dolphin? **Possible answer: length, distance around, weight, temperature**

2 What measurement tools could scientists use to collect dolphin measurements? **See above.**

3 A 15-foot-long bottle-nosed dolphin gave birth to a 5-foot-long calf. Name at least three things that are about the same length as each of the dolphins. Explain how you made your choices. **Possible answer: dolphin—basketball pole, bulletin board, cafeteria table; calf—student's height, length of teacher's desk, kitchen shelf**

Use Diagrams **A dolphin is 14 feet long and a fourth-grade student is 4 feet tall. Draw a diagram to compare the length of the dolphin to the height of the student.**

A diagram is a drawing that shows what something looks like or how it works. A diagram often has labels to help you understand it better.

1 What does the diagram show you about the length of the dolphin and height of the student? **Possible answer: It shows that the dolphin is 10 feet longer than the student.**

Vocabulary*

*partial list

length, p.242	**meter (m),** p.246	**quart (qt),** p.256	**mass,** p.263
customary, p.242	**kilometer (km),** p.246	**gallon (gal),** p.256	**gram (g),** p.263
inch (in.), p.242	**perimeter,** p.250	**weight,** p.257	**kilogram (kg),** p.263
foot (ft), p.243	**capacity,** p.256	**ounce (oz),** p.257	**degrees Fahrenheit (°F),** p.266
yard (yd), p.243	**cup (c),** p.256	**pound (lb),** p.257	**degrees Celsius (°C),** p.266
mile (mi), p.243	**pint (pt),** p.256	**milliliter (mL),** p.262	
metric, p.246		**liter (L),** p.262	

Reading, Writing, Arithmetic

Use Diagrams Have students find several diagrams in Chapter 7, such as the diagrams on pages 242–243. Have them compare and contrast the diagrams, looking at labels and how the diagrams are used. Ask:

- **How could a diagram help you solve a problem?** *[Possible answers: It helps you to see the problem; it gives information needed to solve the problem.]*

Vocabulary

Students may record new words in their journals. Encourage them to show examples and draw diagrams to help them tell what the words mean.

PURPOSE Assess students' ability to apply prior knowledge of measurement.

Materials have available: measuring tools

Assessing Prior Knowledge

Ask students for examples of the types of measurements that people make. List the types they suggest on the board.

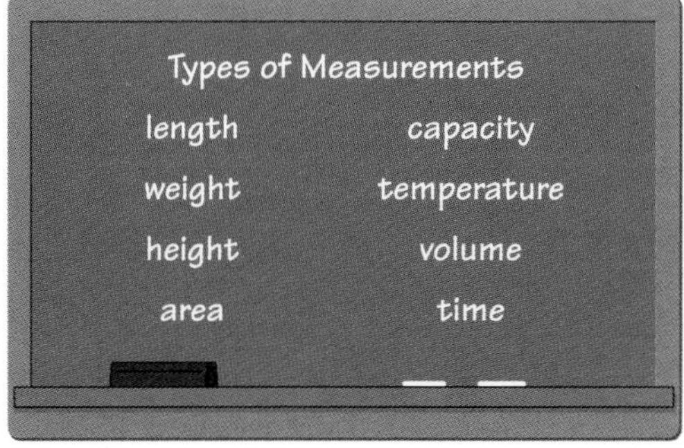

Types of Measurements
length
capacity
weight
temperature
height
volume
area
time

Encourage students to use whatever methods they wish to answer items 1–3. Observe students as they work. Look at the answers they give for item 3.

Building a Portfolio

Item 3 can be used as a benchmark to show where students are in their understanding of measurement.

A Portfolio Checklist for Students and a Checklist for Teachers are provided in Teacher's Assessment Resources, pp. 33–34.

Prerequisite Skills

- *Can students measure the length of an object to the nearest inch?*
- *Can students measure the length of an object to the nearest centimeter?*
- *Can students compare measurement units?*

Assessment Resources

Diagnostic Inventory

Use this blackline master to assess prerequisite skills that students will need in order to be successful in this chapter.

Test Masters

Use the multiple choice format (form A or B) or the free response format (form C) as a pretest of the skills in this chapter.

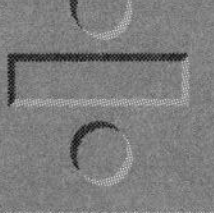

LESSON 7.1 RESOURCES

EXPLORE ACTIVITY

Length in Customary Units

OBJECTIVE Explore estimating, measuring, comparing, and ordering length in customary units.

RESOURCE REMINDER
Math Center Cards 58
Practice 58, Reteach 58, Extend 58

SKILLS TRACE

GRADE 3	• Explore estimating, measuring, comparing, and ordering length in customary units. *(Chapter 9)*
GRADE 4	• Explore estimating, measuring, comparing, and ordering length in customary units.
GRADE 5	• Explore estimating, measuring, comparing, and ordering length in customary units. *(Chapter 7)*

MANIPULATIVE WARM-UP

Cooperative Pairs — Visual/Spatial

OBJECTIVE Explore estimating and measuring length to the nearest inch.

Materials per pair: inch graph paper (TA 8)

▶ Distribute a piece of inch graph paper to each pair of students. Explain that each square on the sheet is 1 in. long.

▶ Have each pair choose several objects, such as a textbook, a calculator, and a pencil. Pairs estimate the length of each object and record their estimates.

▶ Partners use the inch graph paper to check their estimates.

ESL APPROPRIATE

STATISTICS CONNECTION

Whole Class — Logical/Analytical

OBJECTIVE Measure heights of students.

Materials customary measuring stick or tape measure

▶ Ask students to estimate their heights to the nearest inch.

▶ Have students take turns standing against a measuring stick or tape placed against a wall to get an exact measurement of their height in inches. Record each height to the nearest inch.

▶ Record the heights on the chalkboard. Have students compare these measurements with their estimates.

▶ Ask students to find the median, mode, and the range for the height of students.

ESL APPROPRIATE

Daily Review

PREVIOUS DAY QUICK REVIEW

Multiply.

1. 251 × 30 *[7,530]*
2. 1,012 × 12 *[12,144]*
3. 6,384 × 27 *[172,368]*
4. 28,506 × 17 *[484,602]*

FAST FACTS

1. 4 × 4 *[16]*
2. 5 × 8 *[40]*
3. 7 × 7 *[49]*
4. 6 × 0 *[0]*

Problem of the Day • 58

If sixteen players enter a ping-pong tournament, how many rounds of ping-pong would have to be played to determine the winner? *[4 rounds]*

TECH LINK

ONLINE EXPLORATION

Use our Web-linked activities and lesson plans to connect your students to the real world of life under the sea.

MATH FORUM

Idea I provide measurements in inches, feet, and yards for a scavenger hunt. Students hunt for classroom objects to fit each measurement and list the items they find.

Visit our Resource Village at http://www.mhschool.com to access the Online Exploration and the Math Forum.

MATH CENTER

Practice

OBJECTIVE Estimate and measure in inches.

Materials per pair: ruler, yardstick, string; per student: Math Center Recording Sheet (TA 31 optional)

Students use measuring tapes and rulers to find some personal measurements, such as the distance around their wrist.

MATH CENTER
Partners

PRACTICE ACTIVITY 58

Spatial Sense • Choose a Tool

YOU NEED
- ruler
- yardstick and string or tape measure

Take a personal inventory. Copy and complete the table. Estimate first, then measure in inches. Help each other with measurements you cannot do on your own.

If you don't have a tape measure, use a string and then measure the string with the yardstick or ruler.

Item	Estimate	Measurement
1. length of hand		
2. distance around head		
3. distance around wrist		
4. distance from elbow to wrist		
5. distance from floor to waist		

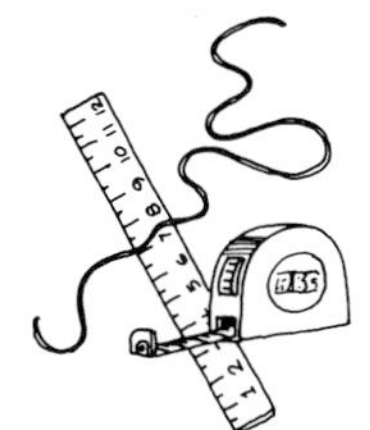

Grade Level 4 McGraw-Hill School Division

Chapter 7, Lesson 1, pages 242–243 Measurement

ESL APPROPRIATE

NCTM Standards
- ✓ Problem Solving
- Communication
- Reasoning
- ✓ Connections

Problem Solving

OBJECTIVE Estimate using nonstandard measures.

Materials inch ruler, Math Center Recording Sheet (TA 31 optional)

Students use descriptions of cubit, span, and fathom to estimate the lengths of classroom objects using their personal units. *[Answers may vary. Check students' work.]*

MATH CENTER
Partners

PROBLEM-SOLVING ACTIVITY 58

Spatial Reasoning • Ancient Body Measures

YOU NEED
- inch ruler

Before there were rulers, people used parts of the body to measure lengths.

Help each other measure the actual length of your cubit, span, and fathom to the nearest half inch. Be sure to record your results. Use these units of measure to find the length of the chalkboard, the height of the door, and the width of your desk.

Why do you think that this way of measuring is not used today?

Cubit length from the elbow to the end of the longest finger

Span length from little finger to thumb when the hand is stretched out

Fathom length from fingertip to fingertip when you stretch both arms

Grade Level 4 McGraw-Hill School Division

Chapter 7, Lesson 1, pages 242–243 Measurement

NCTM Standards
- ✓ Problem Solving
- Communication
- Reasoning
- ✓ Connections

EXPLORE ACTIVITY
Length in Customary Units

OBJECTIVE Estimate, measure, and compare units of length.

Materials per pair: inch ruler (TA 18) or customary measuring tape (TA 19)

Vocabulary customary, foot, inch, length, mile, yard

1 Introduce

Resources Read-Aloud Anthology, p. 36

Read "Lightening the Load" aloud. After finishing the story, have students discuss why the man's attempt at lightening the load was in fact no help at all. *[Possible answer: he only moved the sack of meal from the ass's back to his own shoulder.]*

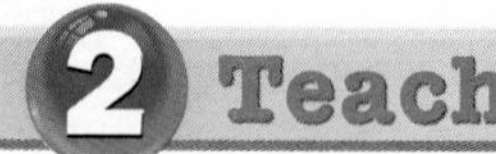

2 Teach *Cooperative Pairs*

LEARN Have volunteers explain how to find the three measurements for the length of the mussei on page 242.

Work Together Begin by having pairs of students identify the inch, $\frac{1}{2}$-inch, and $\frac{1}{4}$-inch marks on their rulers or tape. Ask:

- **Describe where $1\frac{1}{2}$ in. is on your tape.** *[It is halfway between the 1- and 2- inch marks.]*
- **When you measure to the nearest inch, how do you know whether to round up or down?** *[Round down when a length is between an inch mark and the next half inch. Round up lengths that are at the half-inch mark or between the half-inch mark and the next inch.]*

Point out that when measuring, students should start at the first line on the ruler, rather than at 1-inch mark.

MAKE CONNECTIONS
Have students discuss which units they would use to measure each of the items on their list, and why.

3 Close

Check for Understanding using items 1–4, page 243.

CRITICAL THINKING
Encourage students to give specific examples.

PRACTICE
Materials have available: inch ruler (TA 18) or customary measuring tape, calculators
Have students complete ex. 1–10 as independent work.

- Point out that more than one unit may be appropriate for exact measurements in ex. 1 and 2.
- For ex. 3 and 4, point out that a length used to estimate a measurement is called a *benchmark*.

EXPLORE ACTIVITY • MEASUREMENT

Length in Customary Units

LEARN

IN THE WORKPLACE
Dr. Kim Harrison, marine biologist, Northeast Regional Aquaculture Center, MA

Marine biologists estimate the lengths of sea animals to see if they are healthy.

An **inch (in.)** is a **customary** unit used to measure short lengths.

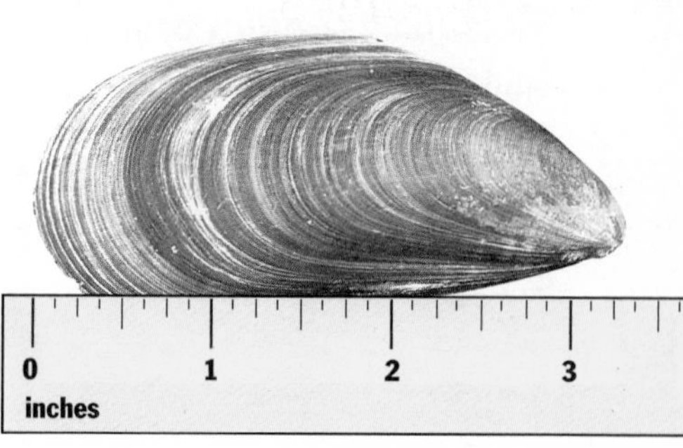

Check Out the Glossary
For vocabulary words
See page 544.

The length of the mussel is:
3 in. to the nearest inch.
$3\frac{1}{2}$ in. to the nearest half inch.
$3\frac{1}{4}$ in. to the nearest quarter inch.

Work Together
Practice estimating. Work with a partner to estimate and then measure some lengths in your classroom to the nearest inch.

You will need
- *inch ruler or measuring tape*

Record your work in a table.

Object	Estimate	Actual Measurement

- What methods did you use to estimate? Compare your methods with those of other pairs.
Possible answer: Used things of known length for comparisons.
- How did your estimates compare to your actual measurements?
Possible answer: My estimates were usually less than the actual measurements.

Meeting Individual Needs

Early Finishers

Have students slide a coin on the desk from a masking tape line and estimate how far the coin moved. Then have them measure the distance the coin moved to the nearest inch and compare it with their estimates.

ESL APPROPRIATE

Extra Support

For students having difficulty measuring, suggest they put an object on paper, mark its beginning and end points on the paper, and draw a line segment between the two marks that they can then measure.

Ongoing Assessment

Interview Determine if students associate distances with appropriate units of measure by asking:

- **What would you measure in miles? yards? feet? inches?** *[Possible answers: distance between towns; swimming pool length; couch width; postcard]*

Follow Up For students who need additional help and practice, assign **Reteach 58.**

Assign **Extend 58** for students who would like a challenge.

ake Connections: Possible answer: inch—length of a picture/shoe/eraser; foot—ight of student/ceiling/animal; yard—length of fabric/yarn/football field; mile—stance between homes/cities/states

ake Connections

u can also use the units **foot (ft)**, **rd (yd)**, and **mile (mi)** to measure nger lengths.

Item	Unit Used for Measurement
Carpet	foot
Football field	yard
Distance between cities	mile

Name three things you would measure with each unit—inch, foot, yard, mile. See above.

heck for Understanding

stimate and then measure. Explain your methods. Check students' work.

your stride
2 your height
3 your arm span

ritical Thinking: Generalize **Explain your reasoning.**

When would you choose to measure to the nearest half or quarter inch? Possible answers: when measuring things close in size, when a very exact measurement is needed

ractice

stimate and then measure. Check students' work for ex. 1–2.

length of your foot
2 distance you can reach

How could you use this part of your thumb to estimate length? See below.

4 How could you use this part of your arm to estimate length? See below.

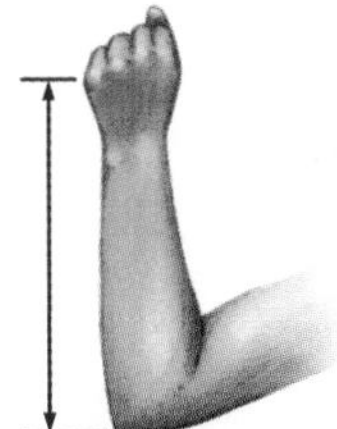

rite the letter of the best estimate.

height of a classmate b
a. 50 ft **b.** 50 in. **c.** 50 yd

6 length of a school bus a
a. 27 ft **b.** 27 in. **c.** 27 yd

distance around a running track c
a. 440 mi **b.** 440 ft **c.** 440 yd

8 depth out in the middle of the ocean
a. 6 ft **b.** 6 mi **c.** 6 in. b

Marta measured the length of her book to the nearest quarter inch as $13\frac{3}{4}$ in. What does it measure to the nearest inch? 14 in.

10 Don can walk a mile in about 15 minutes. About how long would it take him to walk 5 miles? about 1 h 15 min

Possible answer : The distance from the knuckle to the tip of the thumb is about 1 in.
Possible answer: The distance from the elbow to the middle of the hand is about 1 ft.

tra Practice, page 508

Alternate Teaching Strategy

Materials index cards; per group: inch ruler (TA 18)

Prepare index cards with line segments ranging from $2\frac{3}{4}$ in. to $4\frac{1}{4}$ in. Lengths should include whole numbers, lengths close to whole numbers, lengths to the $\frac{1}{2}$-inch mark, close to the $\frac{1}{2}$-inch mark, to the $\frac{1}{4}$-inch mark, and close to the $\frac{1}{4}$-inch mark. There should be one segment per index card.

Distribute the cards randomly to groups. Have students measure the lines to the nearest inch, half inch, and quarter inch.

Write the lengths 3 in. and 4 in. on the chalkboard. Have students tape their cards next to the closest measurement. Ask:

- **How did you decide where to tape your card?** *[For lengths thqt are not whole numbers, students should mention using $\frac{1}{2}$-inch marks to find the closest inch marks.]*

Now write $3\frac{1}{4}$ in., $3\frac{1}{2}$ in., and $4\frac{1}{4}$ in. on the chalkboard. Have volunteers decide which cards should be moved to a closer measurement. Have them explain their work.

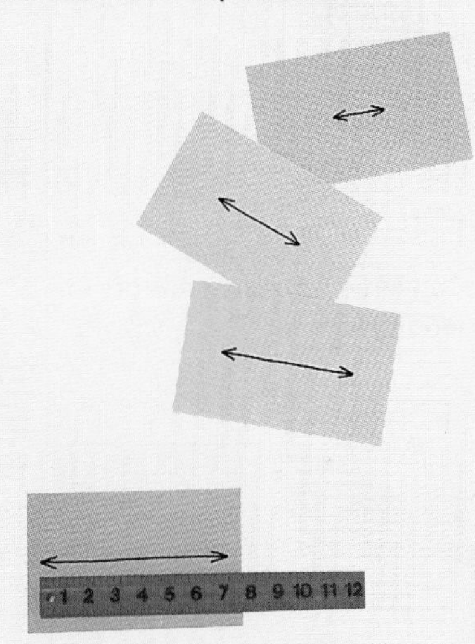

PRACTICE • 58

Practice 58

Name:

Length in Customary Units

Estimate and then measure. Check students' work.

1. length of your thumb ______
2. length of your longest strand of hair ______
3. width of your math book ______
4. height of your desk ______
5. length of your desk ______

Ring the letter of the best estimate.

	a.	b.	c.
6. height of a drinking glass	(a.) 6 in.	b. 6 ft	c. 6 yd
7. height of a sixth grader	a. 5 in.	(b.) 5 ft	c. 5 yd
8. length of a rug in your living room	a. 5 in.	(b.) 5 ft	c. 5 mi
9. distance you can ride your bike	a. 2 in.	b. 2 yd	(c.) 2 mi
10. length of someone's foot	(a.) 8 in.	b. 8 yd	c. 8 mi
11. height of a finger puppet	(a.) 4 in.	b. 4 ft	c. 4 yd
12. length of your pencil	(a.) 5 in.	b. 5 ft	c. 5 yd
13. distance from your house to school	a. 2 in.	b. 20 ft	(c.) 2 mi
14. length of your calculator	(a.) 4 in.	b. 4 ft	c. 4 yd
15. height of a tree	(a.) 40 ft	b. 4 yd	c. 40 mi

McGraw-Hill School Division

RETEACH • 58

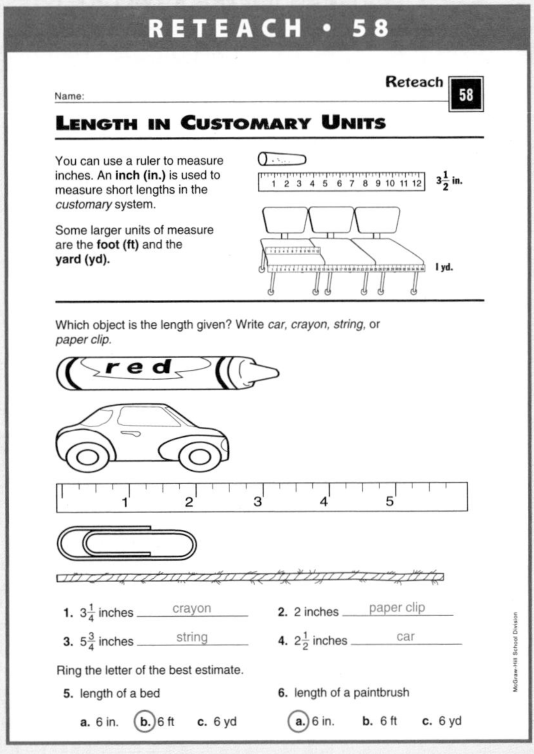
Reteach 58

Name:

Length in Customary Units

You can use a ruler to measure inches. An **inch (in.)** is used to measure short lengths in the *customary* system.

Some larger units of measure are the **foot (ft)** and the **yard (yd).**

Which object is the length given? Write *car, crayon, string,* or *paper clip.*

1. $3\frac{1}{4}$ inches crayon
2. 2 inches paper clip
3. $5\frac{3}{4}$ inches string
4. $2\frac{1}{2}$ inches car

Ring the letter of the best estimate.

5. length of a bed
a. 6 in. (b.) 6 ft c. 6 yd

6. length of a paintbrush
(a.) 6 in. b. 6 ft c. 6 yd

McGraw-Hill School Division

EXTEND • 58

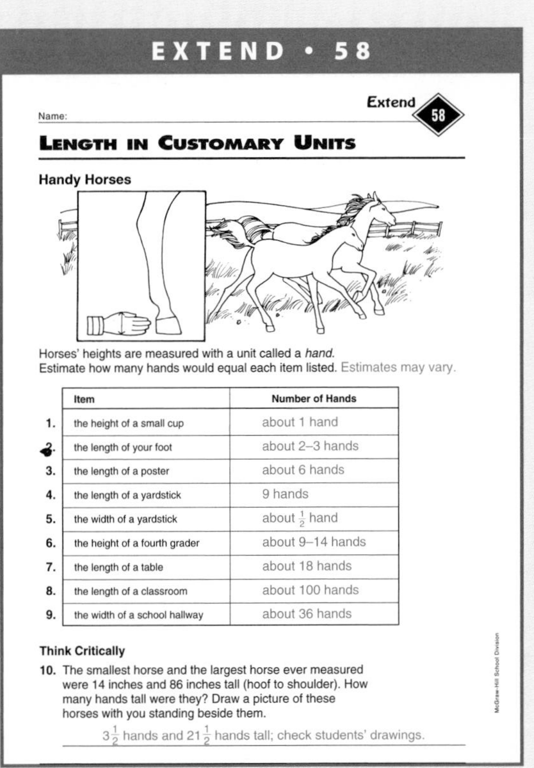
Extend 58

Name:

Length in Customary Units

Handy Horses

Horses' heights are measured with a unit called a *hand.* Estimate how many hands would equal each item listed. Estimates may vary.

	Item	Number of Hands
1.	the height of a small cup	about 1 hand
2.	the length of your foot	about 2–3 hands
3.	the length of a poster	about 6 hands
4.	the length of a yardstick	9 hands
5.	the width of a yardstick	about $\frac{1}{2}$ hand
6.	the height of a fourth grader	about 9–14 hands
7.	the length of a table	about 18 hands
8.	the length of a classroom	about 100 hands
9.	the width of a school hallway	about 36 hands

Think Critically

10. The smallest horse and the largest horse ever measured were 14 inches and 86 inches tall (hoof to shoulder). How many hands tall were they? Draw a picture of these horses with you standing beside them.
$3\frac{1}{2}$ hands and $21\frac{1}{2}$ hands tall; check students' drawings.

McGraw-Hill School Division

LESSON 7.2

Rename Customary Units of Length

OBJECTIVE Convert customary units of length.

RESOURCE REMINDER
Math Center Cards 59
Practice 59, Reteach 59, Extend 59

SKILLS TRACE	
GRADE 3	• Explore estimating, measuring, comparing, and ordering length in customary units. *(Chapter 9)*
GRADE 4	• Convert customary units of length.
GRADE 5	• Convert customary units of length. *(Chapter 7)*

MANIPULATIVE WARM-UP

Cooperative Pairs — **Kinesthetic**

OBJECTIVE Explore using different customary units of length to measure a given length.

Materials per pair: customary measuring tape (TA 19)

▶ One partner measures the length of a tabletop or desktop. The other partner measures the width of the tabletop or desktop. Partners record their measurements and discuss the customary unit of measure they used.

▶ Partners choose another customary unit of length to measure the length of a tabletop or desktop. They record these measurements.

▶ Partners discuss the best unit of measure to use for the height of the table or desk. They make the measurement and record it.

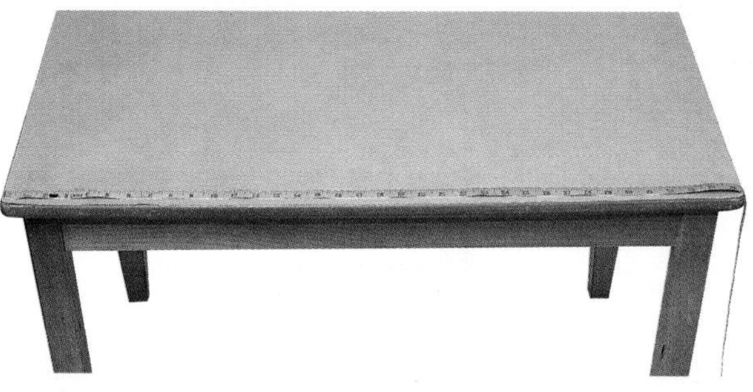

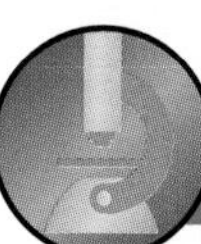

SCIENCE CONNECTION

Cooperative Groups — **Logical/Analytical**

OBJECTIVE Connect customary units of length to science.

Materials have available: large world map; per group: drawing paper, markers, computer graphing program (optional)

▶ Show this chart on the chalkboard:

DEPTHS OF OCEANS

Ocean	Greatest Depth
Arctic Ocean	17,880 ft
Atlantic Ocean	28,374 ft
Indian Ocean	23,376 ft
Pacific Ocean	36,198 ft

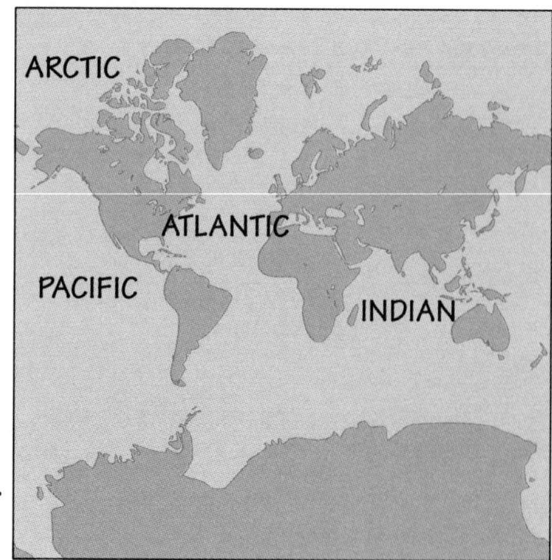

▶ As a class, locate the oceans on the world map. Have groups identify the oceans that are more than 5 miles deep. *[Atlantic Ocean and Pacific Ocean]*

▶ Have group members draw or use a graphing program to show the depth of the oceans using a bar graph. *[Check students' work.]*

Daily Review

PREVIOUS DAY QUICK REVIEW

Write the correct unit of measure.

1. A goldfish is 2 ___ long. *[in.]*
2. A table is 5 ___ long. *[ft]*
3. A long road is 34 ___ long. *[mi]*

FAST FACTS

1. 0 ÷ 10 *[0]*
2. 36 ÷ 6 *[6]*
3. 5 ÷ 5 *[1]*
4. 63 ÷ 9 *[7]*

Problem of the Day • 59

A photograph is 5 inches wide and 7 inches long. It has a 2-inch-wide frame around it. How wide and long is the picture with the frame? *[9 in. wide and 11 in. long]*

TECH LINK

Math Van

MATH VAN

Tool You may wish to use the Calculator with this lesson.

MATH FORUM

Multi-Age Classes You may wish to pair younger students who have less experience renaming measurements with older students who can help them understand the methods used.

Visit our Resource Village at http://www.mhschool.com to see more of the Math Forum.

MATH CENTER

Practice

OBJECTIVE Rename customary units of length.

Materials per pair: game board, 2 counters, 2 number cubes; per student: Math Center Recording Sheet (TA 31 optional)

Prepare Have students make the game board as shown.

Students move along a game board as they rename inches as feet or yards. *[Answers may vary. Check students' work.]*

MATH CENTER
Partners

PRACTICE ACTIVITY 59

Calculator • Length Game

YOU NEED
- 2 counters
- 2 number cubes

- Both partners put their counters on *Start* on the game board after they copy it.
- Roll both number cubes. Use the numbers to tell your partner a number of inches. For instance, if you rolled 2 and 4 you could say 24 in. or 42 in.
- Your partner must rename the length as feet and inches (if less than 36 in.) or yards, feet, and inches (if over 36 in.). If the answer is correct, your partner moves his or her counter to the next *foot* or *yard* space on the board. If the answer is incorrect, your partner moves to the next *inch* space.
- Switch roles. Keep playing until one player reaches the end.

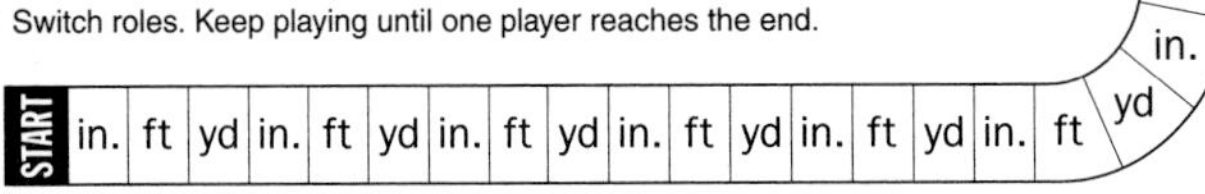

Grade Level 4 McGraw-Hill School Division

Chapter 7, Lesson 2, pages 244–245 Measurement

NCTM Standards
- ✓ Problem Solving
- Communication
- ✓ Reasoning
- Connections

Problem Solving

OBJECTIVE Explore measurement systems.

Materials per student: calculator, Math Center Recording Sheet (TA 31 optional)

Students make equivalency conversions in an obsolete surveyors' measurement system. *[1. 50 links = 2 rods; 2. 500 links = 5 chains; 3. 5 miles = 40,000 links; 4. 250 chains = 25,000 links; 5. 1 chain = 66 ft, 1 rod = $16\frac{1}{2}$ ft, or 16 feet 6 inches, 1 link = 0.66 ft, or about 8 inches]*

MATH CENTER
On Your Own

PROBLEM-SOLVING ACTIVITY 59

Using Data • Surveyors

YOU NEED
- calculator

Fifty years ago, surveyors measured distances in units called *rods, links,* and *chains.*

Copy and complete.

1. 50 links =	? rods
2. 500 links =	? chains
3. 5 miles =	? links
4. 250 chains =	? links

25 links = 1 rod
4 rods = 1 chain
100 links = 1 chain
80 chains = 1 mile

5. A mile is 5,280 feet long. About how long in feet and inches is a chain? a rod? a link?

Grade Level 4 McGraw-Hill School Division

Chapter 7, Lesson 2, pages 244–245 Measurement

NCTM Standards
- ✓ Problem Solving
- Communication
- ✓ Reasoning
- ✓ Connections

Rename Customary Units of Length

OBJECTIVE Convert customary units of length.

Materials per group: customary measuring tape (TA 19)

1 Introduce

Have students use a customary measuring tape that is at least a yard long to complete the following:

1 ft = ___ in. *[12]* 48 in. = ___ ft *[4]*
3 ft = ___ in. *[36]* 60 in. = ___ ft *[5]*
1 yd = ___ ft *[3]* 72 in. = ___ ft *[6]*
1 yd = ___ in. *[36]* 72 in. = ___ yd *[2]*

2 Teach *Whole Class*

LEARN Discuss the introductory problem on page 244.

- **Why does renaming the lobster's measurement in inches make it easier to solve the problem?** *[It is easier to compare measurements when they are in the same units.]*
- **When you rename feet using inches, why do you multiply the number of feet by 12?** *[Because each foot has 12 inches in it.]*
- **How do you rename any larger unit using a smaller unit?** *[Multiply the number of larger units by the number of smaller units in each larger unit.]*

More Examples Have students explain why multiplication by 1,760 is used in Example B.

3 Close

Check for Understanding using items 1–5, page 244.

CRITICAL THINKING
For item 5, ask:

- **How do you rename any smaller unit using a larger unit?** *[by counting on the smaller unit until you reach the larger unit or multiply the smaller unit to get a product that is equal to the larger unit]*

PRACTICE
Materials have available: calculators

Options for assigning exercises:
A—Ex. 1–2; odd ex. 3–19, **Mixed Review**
B—Ex. 1–2; even ex. 4–18, **Mixed Review**

- For ex. 1–10, students may multiply to rename to smaller units and count to rename to larger units.

Algebra: Patterns In ex. 1–2, students apply their knowledge of patterns and renaming units to complete the table.

Mixed Review/Test Preparation In ex. 1–2, students review addition and subtraction of money amounts, learned in Chapter 2. In ex. 3–5, students multiply money amounts, learned in Chapters 5 and 6.

Rename Customary Units of Length

LEARN

A carp is about 29 in. long. The giant American lobster is about 3 ft long. Which is longer?

You can rename units to make comparisons.

Compare 3 ft and 29 in.

Think: 1 ft = 12 in.

3 ft = 3 × 12 in. = 36 in.

36 in. > 29 in.

The lobster is longer.

Cultural Note
In Japan, families fly carp-shaped wind socks as a wish for healthy children.

12 **inches (in.)**	= 1 **foot (ft)**
3 **feet (ft)**	= 1 **yard (yd)**
1,760 **yards (yd)**	= 1 **mile (mi)**

More Examples

A Complete.
The marlin is about 8 ■ long.
a. inches
b. feet
c. yards

Think: The marlin is a little larger than the man.

The marlin is about 8 ft long.

B Suppose you take 1-yd-long strides as you walk. How many strides will you take to walk 3 mi

Complete.

3 mi = ■ yd **Think:** 1 mi = 1,760 y

3 mi = 3 × 1,760 yd
= 5,280 yd

You will take 5,280 strides to walk 3 mi.

CHECK

Check for Understanding

Complete.

1 4 ft = ■ in. 48 **2** 12 ft = ■ yd 4 **3** 4 mi = ■ yd 7,040 **4** 7 yd = ■ ft 21

Critical Thinking: Analyze
Explain your reasoning.

5 A Nassau grouper is 48 in. long. Tell how you would find this length in feet. See below.

Meeting Individual Needs

Early Finishers

Have pairs measure the longest step each of them can take, measuring one in feet and inches and the other in inches. Then have them change the measurements to the same units to compare the lengths of the giant steps.

Extra Support

Suggest students copy the conversion table on p. 244 and write sentences that describe how they use it. For example, "I multiply feet by 12 to find the number of inches; I count by 12s to find the number of feet."

Ongoing Assessment

Observation Checklist Determine if students understand how to rename units by observing whether they choose the correct operation—multiplication to rename to a smaller unit and counting to rename to a larger unit.

Follow Up If students have difficulty understanding how to rename to larger or smaller units, use a yard stick or measuring tape to give them additional practice. Then assign **Reteach 59.**

Assign **Extend 59** for students who would like a challenge.

'ractice

GEBRA: PATTERNS Copy and complete the table.

Feet	1	2	3	4	■ 5
Inches	12	■ 24	■ 36	■ 48	60

2

Yards	1	2	3	■ 4	5
Feet	3	■ 6	■ 9	12	■ 15

omplete.

12 yd = ■ ft 36 **4** 5 mi = ■ yd 8,800 **5** 9 ft = ■ in. 108 **6** 96 in. = ■ ft 8

15 ft = ■ yd 5 **8** 120 in. = ■ ft 10 **9** 300 ft = ■ yd 100 **10** 3,520 yd = ■ mi 2

ompare lengths. Write >, <, or =.

6 ft ● 60 in. > **12** 4 yd ● 12 ft = **13** 5,000 yd ● 5 mi < **14** 20 ft ● 6 yd >

Write the names in order from shortest to tallest height. **Marcus, Kay, Jo Beth, Tom.**

Jo Beth—70 in.	Kay—5 ft
Marcus—59 in.	Tom—6 ft

19. Possible answer: Use foot (9 ft by 12 ft) or yard (3 yd by 4 yd); use foot since this is the way many rugs are sold.

IXED APPLICATIONS

Problem Solving

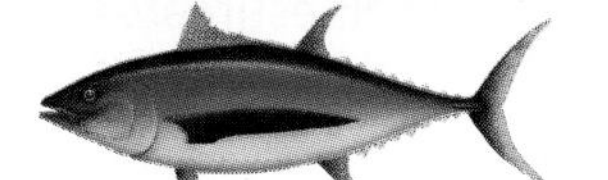

se the pictures of the sea animals for problems 16–17.

Porkfish 13 in. **Atlantic Albacore Tuna** 45 in. **Deep Sea Shrimp** 6 in.

Which animals are longer than 1 foot? **porkfish and tuna**

17 Which animal is longer than 1 yard? How much longer? **tuna; 9 in. longer**

Patti buys 2 *Great Underseas* videos. Each one costs $19.95 including tax. She gives the clerk 2 twenty-dollar bills. What is the cost? How much change will Patti get? **$39.90; $0.10**

19 **Make a decision** You want to buy a rug. Your floor space is 108 in. wide and 144 in. long. What other units could you use? Which unit will you use when you go to buy the rug? **See above.**

mixed review • test preparation

$925 + 637 = **$1,562**

2 $6.51 − 0.67 = **$5.84**

3 $60.71 × 9 = **$546.39**

4 $45 × 30 = **$1,350**

5 $9.99 × 12 = **$119.88**

xtra Practice, page 508

Alternate Teaching Strategy

Materials per student: five 12-inch strips of construction paper, 3 of the same color, 2 each a different color; tape, markers, inch ruler (TA 18)

Give each student three 12-inch strips of one color and one 12-inch strip of each of two other colors.

Have students tape 3 strips of one color edge to edge so they have a 36-inch strip. Have them label this long strip *yard,* and one of the other two strips *foot.* Then have them use an inch ruler to mark off 12 equal parts on the other piece of paper. Have them label one of the 12 parts *inch.*

Have students use the strips to answer questions such as the following:

- **How many inches are in 1 foot? 2 feet? 3 feet? 10 feet?** *[12; 24; 36; 120]*
- **How many feet are in 1 yard? 2 yards? 3 yards? 12 yards?** *[3; 6; 9; 36]*
- **Which is longer, 38 inches or 4 feet?** *[4 feet]*
- **Which is shorter, 1 yard or 4 feet?** *[1 yard]*

YARD

FOOT

INCH

PRACTICE • 59

HOMEWORK

Practice 59

Name:

Rename Customary Units of Length

Complete.

1.

Miles	1	2	3	4	5	6	7
Yards	1,760	3,520	5,280	7,040	8,800	10,560	12,320

2. 60 in. = 5 ft 3. 9 ft = 3 yd 4. 4 ft = 48 in.
5. 4 yd = 12 ft 6. 8 ft = 96 in. 7. 24 in. = 2 ft
8. 1 mi = 1,760 yd 9. 21 ft = 7 yd 10. 5,280 yd = 3 mi
11. 3 ft = 36 in. 12. 6 yd = 18 ft 13. 36 in. = 1 yd
14. 2 yd = 72 in. 15. 3 yd = 108 in. 16. 5 yd = 15 ft
17. 10 yd = 30 ft 18. 7,040 yd = 4 mi 19. 6 ft = 72 in.

Write >, <, or =.

20. 1 ft (>) 10 in. 21. 14 in. (<) 3 yd 22. 36 in. (<) 2 yd
23. 3 ft (>) 35 in. 24. 10 ft (>) 3 yd 25. 5 yd (=) 15 ft
26. 3 ft (>) 24 in. 27. 2 yd (>) 3 ft 28. 1 ft (=) 12 in.
29. 1 yd (=) 3 ft 30. 4 ft (<) 50 in. 31. 9 yd (>) 26 ft
32. 1 yd (>) 1 ft 33. 2 yd (=) 6 ft 34. 4 ft (=) 48 in.
35. 3 ft (>) 13 in. 36. 1 mi (>) 100 yd 37. 2 yd (<) 73 in.

Solve.

38. Greg planted an orange seed 3 years ago when he was in first grade. The plant grew about 4 inches every year. About how tall in feet is the orange plant now? about 1 ft

39. Greg planted an evergreen tree 1 yard tall. He thinks that in 8 years the tree will be twice as tall. How many feet will that be? How many inches? 6 ft; 72 in.

McGraw-Hill School Division

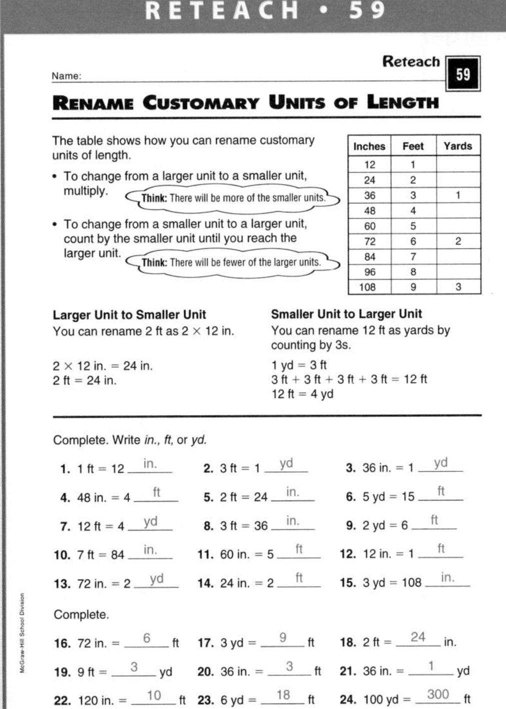

RETEACH • 59

Reteach 59

Name:

Rename Customary Units of Length

The table shows how you can rename customary units of length.

- To change from a larger unit to a smaller unit, multiply. **Think:** There will be more of the smaller units.
- To change from a smaller unit to a larger unit, count by the smaller unit until you reach the larger unit. **Think:** There will be fewer of the larger units.

Inches	Feet	Yards
12	1	
24	2	
36	3	1
48	4	
60	5	
72	6	2
84	7	
96	8	
108	9	3

Larger Unit to Smaller Unit
You can rename 2 ft as 2 × 12 in.

2 × 12 in. = 24 in.
2 ft = 24 in.

Smaller Unit to Larger Unit
You can rename 12 ft as yards by counting by 3s.

1 yd = 3 ft
3 ft + 3 ft + 3 ft + 3 ft = 12 ft
12 ft = 4 yd

Complete. Write *in., ft,* or *yd.*

1. 1 ft = 12 in. 2. 3 ft = 1 yd 3. 36 in. = 1 yd
4. 48 in. = 4 ft 5. 2 ft = 24 in. 6. 5 yd = 15 ft
7. 12 ft = 4 yd 8. 3 ft = 36 in. 9. 2 yd = 6 ft
10. 7 ft = 84 in. 11. 60 in. = 5 ft 12. 12 in. = 1 ft
13. 72 in. = 2 yd 14. 24 in. = 2 ft 15. 3 yd = 108 in.

Complete.

16. 72 in. = 6 ft 17. 3 yd = 9 ft 18. 2 ft = 24 in.
19. 9 ft = 3 yd 20. 36 in. = 3 ft 21. 36 in. = 1 yd
22. 120 in. = 10 ft 23. 6 yd = 18 ft 24. 100 yd = 300 ft

McGraw-Hill School Division

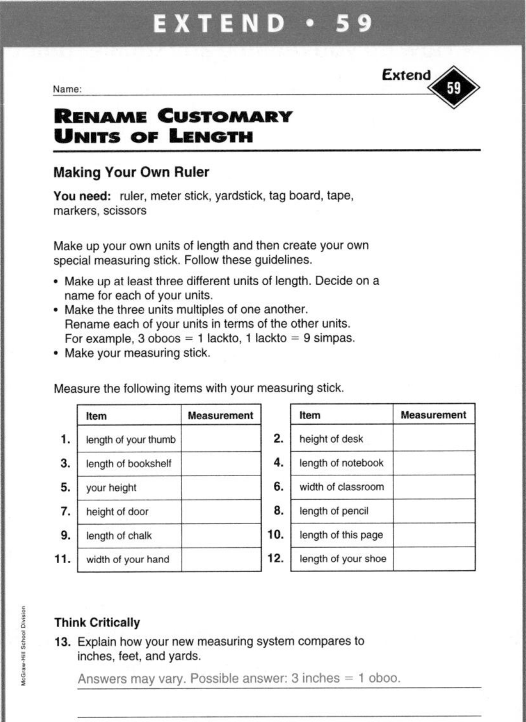

EXTEND • 59

Extend 59

Name:

Rename Customary Units of Length

Making Your Own Ruler

You need: ruler, meter stick, yardstick, tag board, tape, markers, scissors

Make up your own units of length and then create your own special measuring stick. Follow these guidelines.

- Make up at least three different units of length. Decide on a name for each of your units.
- Make the three units multiples of one another. Rename each of your units in terms of the other units. For example, 3 oboos = 1 lackto, 1 lackto = 9 simpas.
- Make your measuring stick.

Measure the following items with your measuring stick.

	Item	Measurement		Item	Measurement
1.	length of your thumb		2.	height of desk	
3.	length of bookshelf		4.	length of notebook	
5.	your height		6.	width of classroom	
7.	height of door		8.	length of pencil	
9.	length of chalk		10.	length of this page	
11.	width of your hand		12.	length of your shoe	

Think Critically

13. Explain how your new measuring system compares to inches, feet, and yards.
Answers may vary. Possible answer: 3 inches = 1 oboo.

McGraw-Hill School Division

LESSON 7.3

EXPLORE ACTIVITY

Length in Metric Units

OBJECTIVE Explore estimating, measuring, comparing, and ordering length in metric units.

RESOURCE REMINDER
Math Center Cards 60
Practice 60, Reteach 60, Extend 60

SKILLS TRACE

GRADE 3	• Explore estimating, measuring, comparing, and ordering length in metric units. *(Chapter 9)*
GRADE 4	• Explore estimating, measuring, comparing, and ordering length in metric units.
GRADE 5	• Explore estimating, measuring, comparing, and ordering length in metric units. *(Chapter 7)*

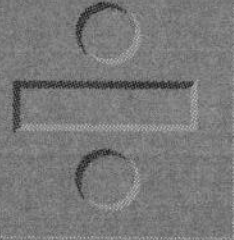

LESSON 7.3 RESOURCES

MANIPULATIVE WARM-UP

Cooperative Pairs — Kinesthetic

OBJECTIVE Explore estimating and measuring length to the nearest centimeter.

Materials per pair: centimeter graph paper (TA 7)

▶ Distribute a piece of centimeter graph paper to each pair of students. Explain that each square on the sheet is 1 cm long.

▶ Have each pair choose several small classroom objects, such as a paper clip, a pen, and an eraser. Pairs estimate the length of each object and record their estimates.

▶ Partners use the centimeter graph paper to check their estimates.

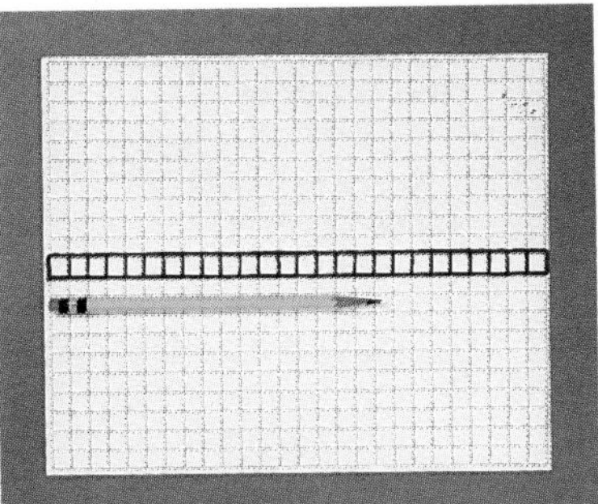

ESL APPROPRIATE

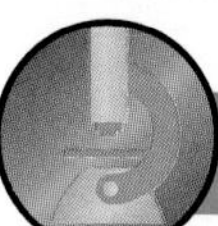

SCIENCE CONNECTION

Cooperative Pairs — Visual/Spatial

OBJECTIVE Relate metric units of length to marine life.

Materials metric measuring tape (TA 20), construction paper

▶ List on the chalkboard:

Fish	*Length*
Atlantic Herring	30 centimeters
Blue Marlin	3 meters
Bull Shark	24 meters
Clown Anemone	5 centimeters

▶ Have each group cut strips to show and compare the lengths of the fish above.

▶ Students may wish to research and compare other lengths of fish.

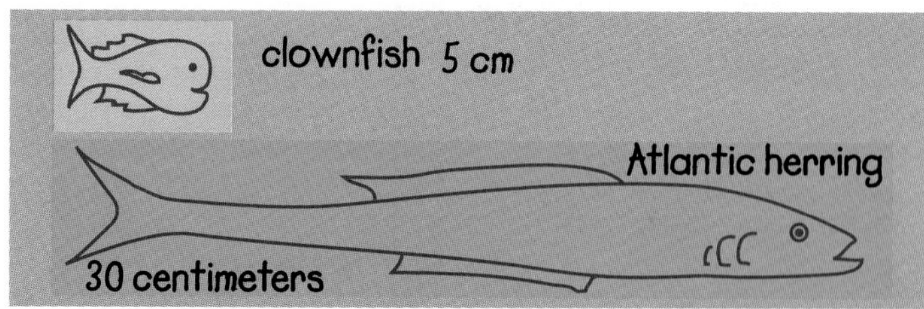

ESL APPROPRIATE

Daily Review

PREVIOUS DAY QUICK REVIEW

Complete.

1. 24 in. = __ ft *[2]*
2. 6 yd = __ ft *[18]*
3. 5__ = 60 in. *[feet]*
4. __ mi = 3,520 yds *[2]*

FAST FACTS

1. (5 + 4) + 1 *[10]*
2. (3 + 7) + 9 *[19]*
3. 8 + (6 + 5) *[19]*
4. 12 + (7 + 6) *[25]*

Problem of the Day • 60

Sue has a red pair of shorts and a blue pair of shorts. She has a white shirt, a yellow shirt, and a purple shirt. How many outfits can she make? *[6—red-white, red-yellow, red-purple, blue-white, blue-yellow, blue-purple]*

TECH LINK

MATH FORUM

Management Tip Have students work in groups to measure objects that are longer than their ruler. One student marks the end of the ruler. Another moves the ruler. The third counts the number of units.

Visit our Resource Village at http://www.mhschool.com to see more of the Math Forum.

MATH CENTER

Practice

OBJECTIVE Compare metric units of length.

Materials per pair: 20 index cards, meterstick

Students play a concentration game, matching equivalent metric lengths.

PRACTICE ACTIVITY 60

MATH CENTER
Partners

Game • Metric Match

- Use the index cards to make the cards shown.
- Mix them up and put them all facedown. Players take turns flipping over two cards.
- If both players agree the cards are equivalent, the player gets to keep the pair. If the cards are not equivalent they are turned facedown again and the other player turns over two cards. You can use the meter stick as a tool to help you compare the lengths listed on some of the cards.
- Play until no cards are left.
- The player who has more pairs wins.

YOU NEED
- 20 index cards
- meter stick

McGraw-Hill School Division Grade Level 4

Chapter 7, Lesson 3, pages 246–249 Measurement

ESL APPROPRIATE

NCTM Standards
- ✓ Problem Solving
- ✓ Communication
- ✓ Reasoning
- Connections

Problem Solving

OBJECTIVE Determine reasonable estimates of metric length.

Materials per student: 12 index cards, metric ruler or measuring tape, Math Center Recording Sheet (TA 31 optional)

Students mix and match numbers, units, and items until they have 4 sets of reasonable estimates.

PROBLEM-SOLVING ACTIVITY 60

MATH CENTER
On Your Own

Spatial Reasoning • What's My Measure?

Write one of the following on each of 12 index cards:

- numbers: *2, 22, 19, 12*
- metric units: *centimeter, decimeter, centimeter, meter*
- measures: *width of a piece of paper, length of a table, length of a new pencil, height of a fourth grader*

Arrange the cards into 4 sets of 3 cards each. Each set should include a number, a metric unit, and a matching distance. When you are finished, use the tape measure to measure a piece of paper, a table, a pencil, and a classmate to see if you were right.

YOU NEED
- 12 index cards
- metric tape measure

McGraw-Hill School Division Grade Level 4

Chapter 7, Lesson 3, pages 246–249 Measurement

NCTM Standards
- ✓ Problem Solving
- Communication
- ✓ Reasoning
- ✓ Connections

EXPLORE ACTIVITY

Length in Metric Units

OBJECTIVE Estimate, measure, compare, and order metric length.

Materials per pair: centimeter ruler (TA 18), meterstick, or metric measuring tape (TA 20)

Vocabulary centimeter, decimeter, kilometer, meter, metric, millimeter

Give students a centimeter ruler, meterstick, or measuring tape. To help students discover benchmarks for measuring with metric units, ask:

- **What part of your hand is about 1 centimeter wide?** *[a finger]*
- **What part of your finger is about 1 millimeter thick?** *[thickness of fingernail]*
- **What length is about 1 meter?** *[Possible answer: nose to fingertip]*
- **About how many centimeters wide is your math book?** *[about 20 cm]*

Cooperative Pairs

LEARN Have volunteers explain how to find the measurements for the Siamese fighting fish at the top of the page.

Work Together Begin by having students find the markings for millimeters, centimeters, decimeters, and a meter on a measuring tape. Make sure they understand that there are increments of 10 between each successive unit. Ask:

- **When you measure to the nearest centimeter, how do you know whether to round up or down?** *[When a length is less than 5 millimeters from the last centimeter mark, round down; when a length is 5 or more millimeters from the last centimeter mark, round up to the next centimeter.]*

Be sure students begin their measurements from zero, which is often not labeled on rulers.

Talk It Over Have students review their work to see if they consistently underestimate or overestimate when using a particular unit. If they do, they may find it useful to find benchmarks that they can think of when estimating with this unit.

Length in Metric Units

LEARN

Centimeter (cm) and millimeter (mm) are metric units of length.

The length of this Siamese fighting fish is:
6 cm to the nearest centimeter.
64 mm to the nearest millimeter.

You can also use the units **decimeter (dm), meter (m),** and **kilometer (km)** to measure longer lengths.

10 **millimeters (mm)**	=	1 **centimeter (cm)**
10 **centimeters (cm)**	=	1 **decimeter (dm)**
10 **decimeters (dm)**	=	1 **meter (m)**
1,000 **meters (m)**	=	1 **kilometer (km)**

Work Together

Choose one object in your classroom that you would use each unit to measure—millimeter, centimeter, decimeter, and meter. Work with a partner to estimate and then measure those lengths and heights.

You will need
- *centimeter ruler*
- *meterstick or measuring tape*

Record your work in a table.

Object	Estimate	Actual Measurement

Talk It Over

▶ Explain your choices. See below.

▶ How did your estimates compare to your actual measurements?
Possible answer: My estimates were usually less than the actual measurements.

Check Out the Glossary For vocabulary words See page 544.

Question 1. Check students' work. The most efficient choice would be to select a unit that would give the least number of units.

246 Lesson 7.3

Meeting Individual Needs

Extra Support

Since a decimeter is usually not indicated on a metric ruler, you may need to remind students that it is 10 centimeters when they are measuring or comparing units.

Inclusion

Have students write the names of the metric units of length on cards. Then have them work together to match the names of units with corresponding markings on a meterstick or metric measuring tape.

Ongoing Assessment

Interview Determine students' understanding of metric units of measure for length. Ask:

- **What unit of measure would you use to describe the distance between Houston and Chicago? the width of a sheet of paper?** *[kilometers; centimeters]*

Follow Up Have students who need additional help with metric units of measure for length complete **Reteach 60.**

Have students who understand metric units of measure for length complete **Extend 60.**

ake Connections
u can rename units to make comparisons.

m found that the width of the classroom orway is 95 cm. Could a sea turtle that 9 dm wide fit through the doorway?

mpare 9 dm and 95 cm.

ink: 1 dm = 10 cm

dm = 9 × 10 cm = 90 cm
cm < 95 cm
e sea turtle will fit through the doorway.

ore Examples

Complete.
The neon goby is about 5 ■ long.
a. mm **b.** cm **c.** dm

Think: The neon goby is about the length of your little finger.

A neon goby is about 5 cm long.

B How many kilometers do you walk if you walk 3,000 m?

Complete.
3,000 m = ■ km

Think: 1,000 m = 1 km
2,000 m = 2 km
3,000 m = 3 km

You walk 3 km.

heck for Understanding

stimate and then measure. Explain your methods. Check students' work.

your hand **2** your height **3** length of your stride

omplete.

7 m = ■ cm 700 **5** 4 m = ■ dm 40 **6** 60 mm = ■ cm 6 **7** 8,000 m = ■ km 8

ritical Thinking: Analyze

xplain your reasoning.

Could a 4-dm-wide giant spider crab fit on a table or desk in your classroom? If so, where? Answers may vary. Possible answer: Yes; it would fit on the 50-cm-square book table.

CHECK

MAKE CONNECTIONS

Help students understand the process for renaming a larger metric unit using a smaller metric unit. Ask:

- **How can you rename centimeters using millimeters?** *[Multiply the number of centimeters by 10.]*
- **How can you rename meters using centimeters?** *[Multiply the number of meters by 100.]*

More Examples For Example B, make sure students understand they are renaming a smaller unit using a larger unit. So, they must find out how many larger units can be made from a given number of smaller units.

3 Close

Check for Understanding using items 1–8, page 247.

Critical Thinking
Remind students that they will find it helpful to use the same units when comparing the sizes of tables and desks, and the width of the spider crab.

Practice See pages 248–249.

PRACTICE

Materials have available: calculators

Options for assigning exercises:
A—Odd ex. 1–39, **Mixed Review**
B—Even ex. 2–38, **Mixed Review**

- In ex. 3–6, students may want to look at a metric measuring tape to help them visualize lengths.
- For **Make It Right** (ex. 29), see Common Error below.
- In ex. 36, students may use the problem-solving strategy, working backward, to find the answer.

Algebra: Patterns In ex. 7, students apply their knowledge of patterns and renaming metric units to complete the table.

Mixed Review/Test Preparation Students add, subtract, and multiply money amounts, a skill they learned in Chapters 2, 5, and 6. They also will rename places in ex. 2 and 3 in order to successfully subtract.

PRACTICE

Practice

Estimate and then measure. Check students' work.

1. your arm span
2. distance you can reach

Write the letter of the best estimate.

		a.	**b.**	**c.**
3	length of your stride a	7 dm	7 cm	7 m
4	distance a plane travels c	7 dm	70 cm	700 km
5	length of a baseball bat a	100 cm	80 km	3 m
6	distance around a running track c	4 km	400 km	400 m

ALGEBRA: PATTERNS **Copy and complete the table.**

7.

Meters	1	2	■ 3	4	5	■ 6
Decimeters	10	■ 20	■ 30	40	■ 50	60
Centimeters	100	■ 200	300	■ 400	■ 500	■ 600

Complete.

8. 7 cm = ■ mm 70
9. 8 m = ■ cm 800
10. 4 km = ■ m 4,000
11. 10 m = ■ dm 100
12. 50 dm = ■ m 5
13. 9,000 m = ■ km 9
14. 100 cm = ■ dm 10
15. 100 mm = ■ cm 10
16. 12 dm = ■ cm 120
17. 200 mm = ■ cm 20
18. 15 m = ■ dm 150
19. 1,000 cm = ■ m 10

Write >, <, or =.

20. 60 cm ● 6 m <
21. 90 cm ● 9 dm =
22. 732 cm ● 7 m >
23. 15 cm ● 150 mm =
24. 32 cm ● 300 mm >
25. 4,000 m ● 40 km <
26. 50 dm ● 500 cm =
27. 250 mm ● 20 cm >
28. 40 cm ● 5 dm <

Make It Right

29. Cory wrote these names in order from shortest to tallest. Tell what the error is and correct it.

Mark	*2 m*
Roy	*14 dm*
Sandra	*165 cm*

Cory ordered the numbers without paying attention to the units—the order should be Roy, Sandra, Mark.

Meeting Individual Needs

Early Finishers

Have students write four problems like ex. 3–6 on page 248 to exchange with another student. Students should use objects they can actually measure or ones with available measurements.

Gifted And Talented

Have students play "Name that Length." One student points to an object, the other guesses its length using a metric unit of measure. The object is then measured and its length compared with the estimate.

Common Error

As in **Make It Right,** students may order the numbers in measurements without paying attention to the units of measure. Have students look at a metric measuring tape and write three measurements using different units of measure, rename the units so they all have the same unit of measure, and then order the measurements.

IXED APPLICATIONS

roblem Solving

se the bar graph for problems 30–35.

Which sharks are less than 500 cm long? **mako, hammerhead**

Which sharks are longer than 1,000 cm? **basking, whale**

Which shark is between 4 m and 6 m in length? **hammerhead**

Which shark is about as tall as your classroom? **mako**

Which shark is about as long as your classroom? **Possible answers: basking, whale**

How many meters longer is a whale shark than a basking shark? How many centimeters is that? **6 m longer; 600 cm longer**

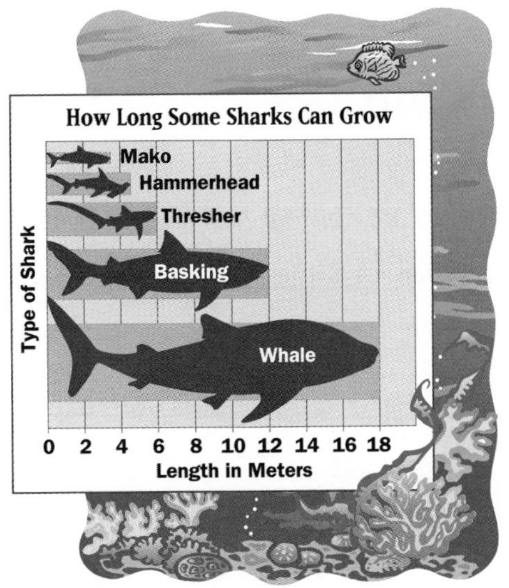

Alicia took a half hour to walk to the aquarium. She watched a dolphin show for 45 minutes. The show ended at 6:15 P.M. When did she leave to go to the aquarium? **5:00 P.M.**

Dom can walk 1 km in about 20 minutes. About how long would it take him to walk 5 km? Explain your reasoning. **See below.**

37 A ticket to the Shark Show costs $1.50. Orlando buys 15 tickets. He pays with a twenty-dollar bill and a ten-dollar bill. How much change does he get? **$7.50**

39 **Write a problem** about buying a shark poster for your classroom. Pick a place for it. Ask a classmate to pick a size for the poster. **Students should compare problems and solutions.**

mixed review • test preparation

1 $14.25 + $8.30 **$22.55**	2 $180 − $120.95 **$59.05**	3 $17.45 − $9.80 **$7.65**
4 4 × $12.50 **$50**	5 32 × $75 **$2,400**	6 20 × $9.95 **$199**
7 56 ÷ 7 **8**	8 36 ÷ 4 **9**	9 72 ÷ 8 **9**

8. Possible answer: about 110 min, or 1 h 50 min; 5 × 20 min = 100 min plus an extra 10 min to allow for him getting tired

xtra Practice, page 509

Alternate Teaching Strategy

Materials per group: centimeter ruler and meterstick, 10 index cards

Write the following statements on a chalkboard.

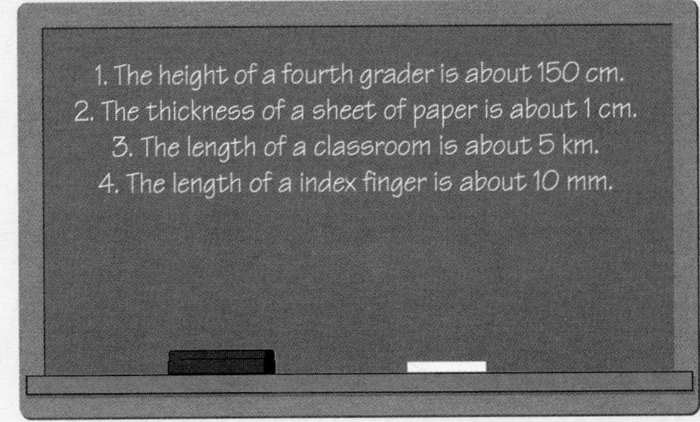

1. The height of a fourth grader is about 150 cm.
2. The thickness of a sheet of paper is about 1 cm.
3. The length of a classroom is about 5 km.
4. The length of a index finger is about 10 mm.

Ask students if each of the statements is true or false. *[**1.** True; **2.** False; **3.** False; **4.** False]*

Have students work in a small group to check each of the statements using metric rulers. Students compare their results.

Distribute 10 index cards to each group. On the cards, have students write five true statements and five false statements about lengths in metric units. Collect the cards. Read each statement to the class. Students discuss whether each statement is true or false.

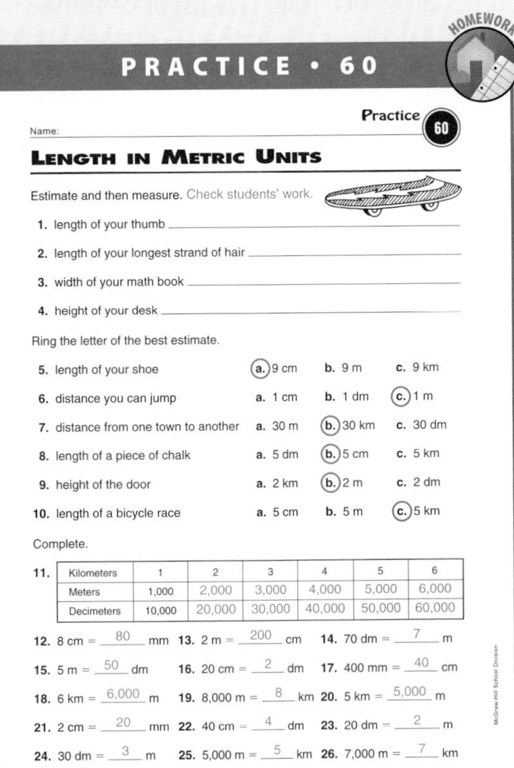

PRACTICE • 60

HOMEWORK

Practice 60

Name:

LENGTH IN METRIC UNITS

Estimate and then measure. Check students' work.

1. length of your thumb ____
2. length of your longest strand of hair ____
3. width of your math book ____
4. height of your desk ____

Ring the letter of the best estimate.

5. length of your shoe (a.) 9 cm b. 9 m c. 9 km
6. distance you can jump a. 1 cm b. 1 dm (c.) 1 m
7. distance from one town to another a. 30 m (b.) 30 km c. 30 dm
8. length of a piece of chalk a. 5 dm (b.) 5 cm c. 5 km
9. height of the door a. 2 km (b.) 2 m c. 2 dm
10. length of a bicycle race a. 5 cm b. 5 m (c.) 5 km

Complete.

11.

Kilometers	1	2	3	4	5	6
Meters	1,000	2,000	3,000	4,000	5,000	6,000
Decimeters	10,000	20,000	30,000	40,000	50,000	60,000

12. 8 cm = 80 mm 13. 2 m = 200 cm 14. 70 dm = 7 m
15. 5 m = 50 dm 16. 20 cm = 2 dm 17. 400 mm = 40 cm
18. 6 km = 6,000 m 19. 8,000 m = 8 km 20. 5 km = 5,000 m
21. 2 cm = 20 mm 22. 40 cm = 4 dm 23. 20 dm = 2 m
24. 30 dm = 3 m 25. 5,000 m = 5 km 26. 7,000 m = 7 km

McGraw-Hill School Division

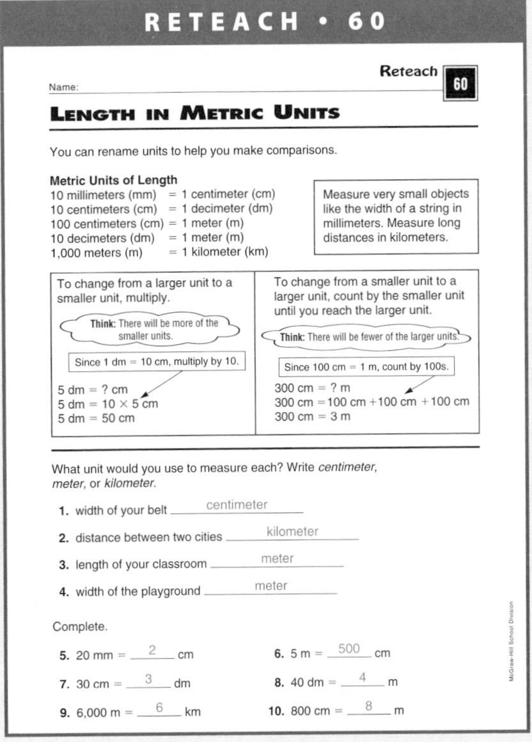

RETEACH • 60

Reteach 60

Name:

LENGTH IN METRIC UNITS

You can rename units to help you make comparisons.

Metric Units of Length
10 millimeters (mm) = 1 centimeter (cm)
10 centimeters (cm) = 1 decimeter (dm)
100 centimeters (cm) = 1 meter (m)
10 decimeters (dm) = 1 meter (m)
1,000 meters (m) = 1 kilometer (km)

Measure very small objects like the width of a string in millimeters. Measure long distances in kilometers.

To change from a larger unit to a smaller unit, multiply.	To change from a smaller unit to a larger unit, count by the smaller unit until you reach the larger unit.
Think: There will be more of the smaller units.	**Think:** There will be fewer of the larger units.
Since 1 dm = 10 cm, multiply by 10.	Since 100 cm = 1 m, count by 100s.
5 dm = ? cm 5 dm = 10 × 5 cm 5 dm = 50 cm	300 cm = ? m 300 cm = 100 cm + 100 cm + 100 cm 300 cm = 3 m

What unit would you use to measure each? Write *centimeter, meter,* or *kilometer.*

1. width of your belt centimeter
2. distance between two cities kilometer
3. length of your classroom meter
4. width of the playground meter

Complete.

5. 20 mm = 2 cm 6. 5 m = 500 cm
7. 30 cm = 3 dm 8. 40 dm = 4 m
9. 6,000 m = 6 km 10. 800 cm = 8 m

McGraw-Hill School Division

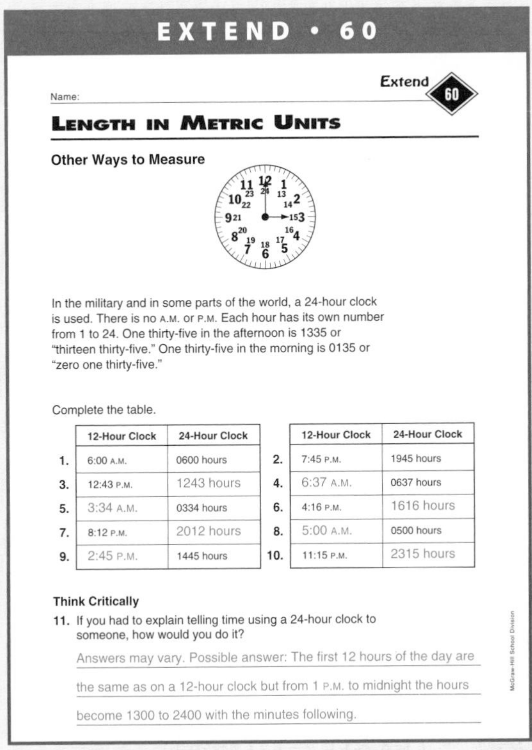

EXTEND • 60

Extend 60

Name:

LENGTH IN METRIC UNITS

Other Ways to Measure

In the military and in some parts of the world, a 24-hour clock is used. There is no A.M. or P.M. Each hour has its own number from 1 to 24. One thirty-five in the afternoon is 1335 or "thirteen thirty-five." One thirty-five in the morning is 0135 or "zero one thirty-five."

Complete the table.

	12-Hour Clock	24-Hour Clock		12-Hour Clock	24-Hour Clock
1.	6:00 A.M.	0600 hours	2.	7:45 P.M.	1945 hours
3.	12:43 P.M.	1243 hours	4.	6:37 A.M.	0637 hours
5.	3:34 A.M.	0334 hours	6.	4:16 P.M.	1616 hours
7.	8:12 P.M.	2012 hours	8.	5:00 A.M.	0500 hours
9.	2:45 P.M.	1445 hours	10.	11:15 P.M.	2315 hours

Think Critically

11. If you had to explain telling time using a 24-hour clock to someone, how would you do it?
Answers may vary. Possible answer: The first 12 hours of the day are the same as on a 12-hour clock but from 1 P.M. to midnight the hours become 1300 to 2400 with the minutes following.

McGraw-Hill School Division

Perimeter

OBJECTIVE Find the perimeter of regular and irregular shapes.

Teaching with Technology
See Alternate computer lesson, pp. 251A–251B.

RESOURCE REMINDER
Math Center Cards 61
Practice 61, Reteach 61, Extend 61

SKILLS TRACE

GRADE 3	• Explore finding the perimeter of regular and irregular shapes. *(Chapter 9)*
GRADE 4	• Find the perimeter of regular and irregular shapes.
GRADE 5	• Explore finding the perimeter and area of squares, rectangles, and polygons made up of squares. *(Chapter 12)*

MANIPULATIVE WARM-UP

Cooperative Pairs — **Visual/Spatial**

OBJECTIVE Find the perimeter of shapes by counting or using multiplication.

Materials per pair: centimeter graph paper (TA 7) or inch graph paper (TA 8); straightedge

▶ On graph paper, one partner draws a figure with sides that run along lines in the grid. Make sure students understand that they should not draw diagonal lines.

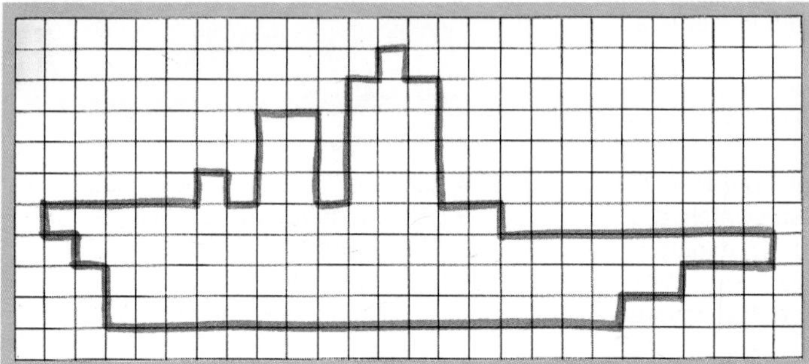

▶ The other partner finds the distance in units around the edge of the whole figure. The partner then explains how she or he found the answer. *[Possible answers: Counted the units for each side; counted the units for one or two sides and multiplied by the number of sides.]*

▶ Partners switch roles and repeat the activity.

SOCIAL STUDIES CONNECTION

Cooperative Groups — **Logical/Analytical**

OBJECTIVE Find the approximate perimeters of states.

Materials per group: map of the United States; inch ruler (TA 18) or centimeter ruler (TA 18)

▶ Have the class examine a map of the United States and look for states that have relatively straight sides as borders, such as Wyoming and Colorado. List the states on the chalkboard.

▶ Explain briefly how to use a map scale to calculate distances. You may have to provide students with the approximate length in miles of each side of the states that are listed on the chalkboard.

▶ Have group members work together to find the perimeter of the shapes listed on the chalkboard. Then have groups share their results.

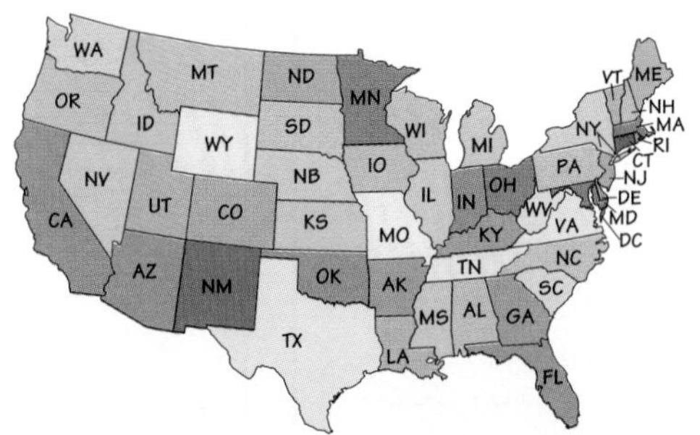

Daily Review

PREVIOUS DAY QUICK REVIEW

Complete.

1. 3 dm = □ cm *[30]*
2. 2 m = □ cm *[200]*
3. 80 cm = □ dm *[8]*
4. 500 cm = □ m *[5]*

FAST FACTS

1. 29 − 17 *[12]*
2. 53 − 28 *[25]*
3. 107 − 35 *[72]*
4. 99 − 24 *[75]*

Problem of the Day • 61

You have four coins. They are worth 36¢. What coins do you have? *[1 quarter, 2 nickels, 1 penny]*

TECH LINK

Math Van

MATH VAN

Activity You may wish to use *Treasure Hunt* to teach this lesson.

MATH FORUM

Multi-Age Classes Students may have different levels of experience in finding perimeter and working with regular and irregular shapes. Pair inexperienced students with experienced students.

Visit our Resource Village at http://www.mhschool.com to see more of the Math Forum.

MATH CENTER

Practice

OBJECTIVE Solve problems involving the greatest perimeter of squares and rectangles.

Materials per pair: number cube, metric ruler; per student: Math Center Recording Sheet (TA 31 optional)

Students randomly select digits to form dimensions that will result in squares or rectangles with the greatest possible perimeter. *[Answers may vary. Check students' drawings.]*

PRACTICE ACTIVITY 61 — MATH CENTER — Partners

Spatial Sense • The Increasing Perimeter

YOU NEED
- number cube
- metric ruler

- One player rolls the number cube 4 times. Each player uses the 4 numbers to make two 2-digit numbers. Let these be the length and width of a rectangle or square (use centimeters as the units).
- Race to draw a rectangle or square with these measurements. The player who finishes first earns 1 point. The player whose figure has the greater perimeter earns 1 point.
- Play until one person has earned 5 points.

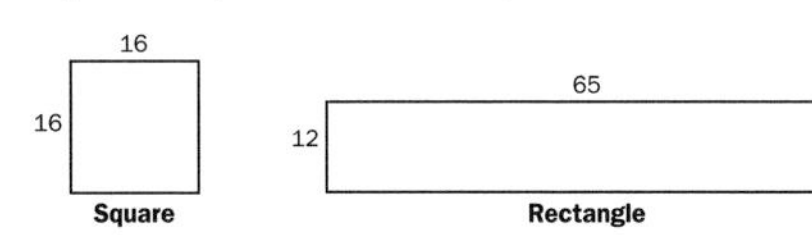

Grade Level 4 — McGraw-Hill School Division

Chapter 7, Lesson 4, pages 250–251 — Measurement

NCTM Standards
- ✓ Problem Solving
- Communication
- ✓ Reasoning
- ✓ Connections

Problem Solving

OBJECTIVE Solve multistep problems using measurement.

Materials Math Center Recording Sheet (TA 31 optional)

Students first determine the perimeter of a figure by finding missing measures. The lengths can be found using the lengths of the sides given. They then estimate perimeters based on drawings. *[**1.** The perimeter is 112 ft. Subtract 6 ft for the gates: you need 106 ft of fencing; **2.** Answers may vary. **a.** about 19 cm, **b.** about 17 ft]*

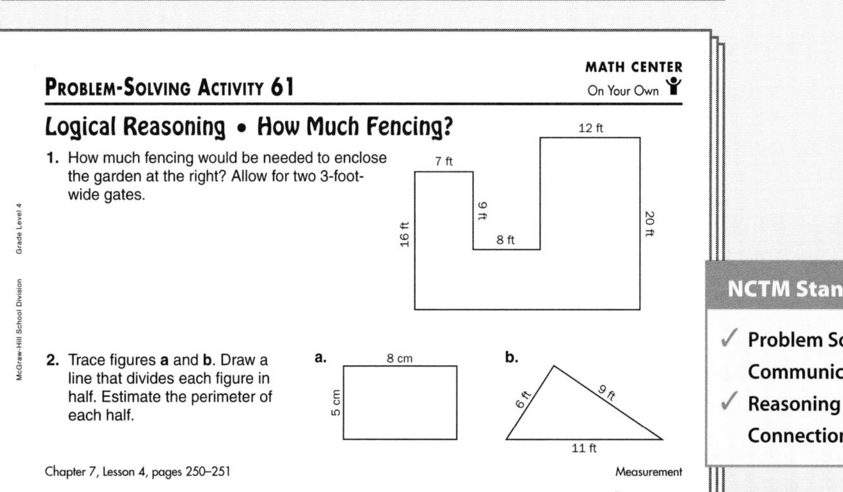

PROBLEM-SOLVING ACTIVITY 61 — MATH CENTER — On Your Own

Logical Reasoning • How Much Fencing?

1. How much fencing would be needed to enclose the garden at the right? Allow for two 3-foot-wide gates.

2. Trace figures **a** and **b**. Draw a line that divides each figure in half. Estimate the perimeter of each half.

Grade Level 4 — McGraw-Hill School Division

Chapter 7, Lesson 4, pages 250–251 — Measurement

NCTM Standards
- ✓ Problem Solving
- Communication
- ✓ Reasoning
- Connections

Perimeter

OBJECTIVE Find the perimeter of regular and irregular shapes.

Vocabulary perimeter

1 Introduce

To help students relate perimeter to real-life experience, ask:

- **The distance around an object is called its perimeter. What are some real-life things for which you might want to know the perimeter?** *[Possible answer: You might want to know the perimeter of a garden so that you would know how much fencing you needed for it.]*

2 Teach *Whole Class*

LEARN As students discuss the introductory problem, ask:

- **What is the length of the rope opposite the side labeled 140 ft? How do you know?** *[140 ft; Opposite sides of a rectangle are equal.]*
- **What is the length of the rope opposite the side labeled 50 ft? How do you know?** *[50 ft; Opposite sides of a rectangle are equal.]*

More Examples Ask students to explain another way they might find the perimeter of a square. *[Since all the sides of a square are equal, multiply the length of one of the sides by 4— 8 cm × 4 = 32 cm.]*

3 Close

Check for Understanding using items 1–5, page 250.

CRITICAL THINKING
For item 5, have students work in groups to find the perimeter of the classroom and record their work in a journal.

PRACTICE
Materials have available: calculators

Students complete ex. 1–8 as independent work.

Algebra Students apply algebraic thinking to find the missing length.

Use Diagrams Check students' diagrams. Discuss how students determined the answer. *[Possible answers: found the sum of the four sides; multiplied 2 × 12 and 2 × 8, then added the products]*

More to Explore Summarize students' findings by writing the following on the chalkboard:

Square: side + side + side + side = perimeter
side × 4 = perimeter
Rectangle: (2 × length) + (2 × width) = perimeter

Perimeter

LEARN

Imagine diving for lost treasure! Salvage companies place rope around the section they want to search. The diver needs to know how much rope to bring underwater.

Search Section	
Length	140 ft
Length	140 ft
Width	50 ft
Width	+ 50 ft
Perimeter	380 ft

Perimeter is the distance around an object or a shape. To find the perimeter of any shape, add the lengths of its sides.

The diver needs 380 ft of rope.

More Examples

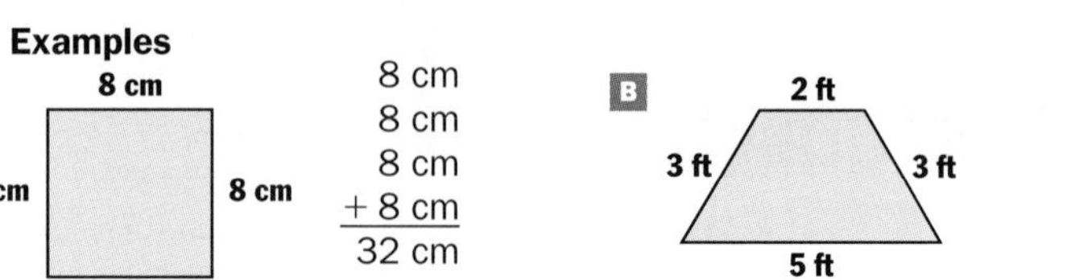

Perimeter = 32 cm

Perimeter = 13 ft

CHECK

Check for Understanding

Find the perimeter.

1 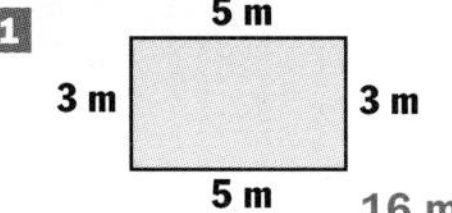

16 m

2 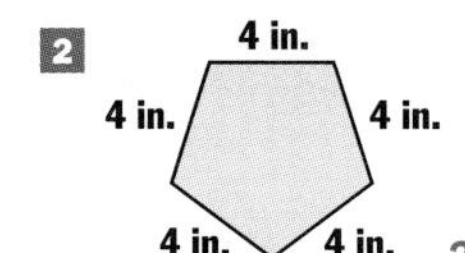

20 in.

3 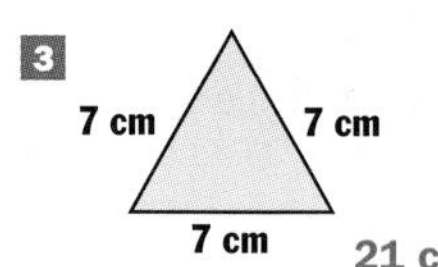

21 cm

Critical Thinking: Analyze **Explain your reasoning.**

4 How many addends will you have if you find the perimeter of:
a. a figure with 6 sides? **6 addends**
b. a figure with 18 sides? **18 addends**

Check Out the Glossary
For vocabulary words
See page 544.

5 Journal Tell how you would find the perimeter of your classroom. **See below.**

5. Students may suggest using a measuring tape or other measuring instruments to find the lengths of each side, then add all the lengths to find the perimeter.

Meeting Individual Needs

Early Finishers

Have students write a problem about buying a fence for a rectangular horse corral. Then have them exchange problems to solve, and check.

Extra Support

Suggest students count sides of an irregular shape, then check to see if the number of addends they use in finding perimeter equals the number of sides they counted on the shape.

Ongoing Assessment

Anecdotal Report Make notes on students' methods for finding perimeter. Do they take into account the length of all sides of regular and irregular shapes? Do they write addition or multiplication number sentences to express perimeter?

Follow Up Have students who need help with finding perimeter complete **Reteach 61.**

Assign **Extend 61** for students who are proficient at finding perimeter.

Students should draw a rectangle with sides labeled 12m by 8m; The perimeter is 40 m.

ractice

ind the perimeter.

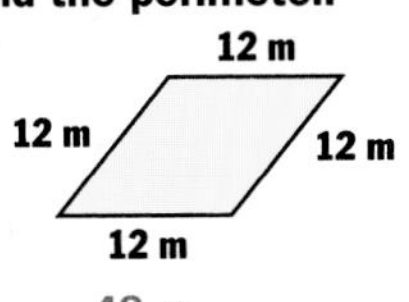

48 m

2 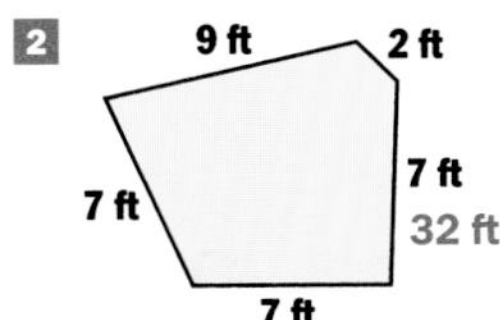

32 ft

3 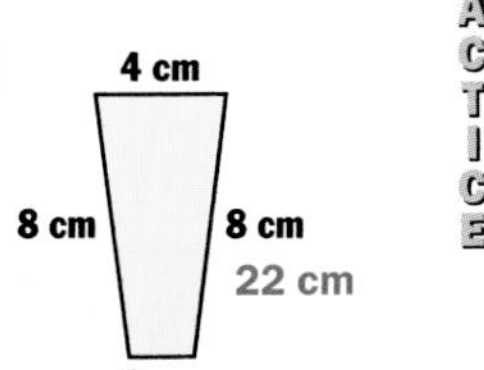

22 cm

LGEBRA Find the length of the missing side.

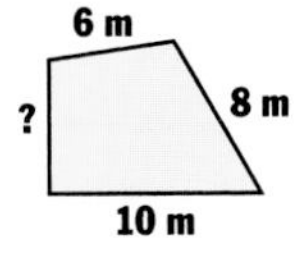

Perimeter = 30 m
6 m

5 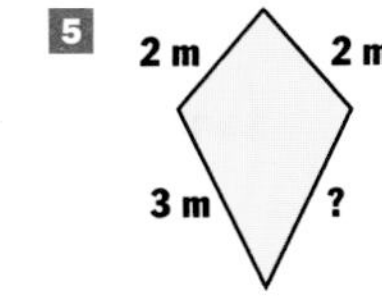

Perimeter = 10 m
3m

6 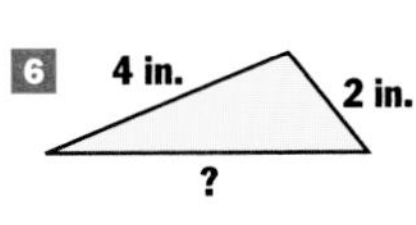

Perimeter = 11 in.
5 in.

MIXED APPLICATIONS

Problem Solving

Pencil & Paper · Calculator · Mental Math

7 **Use Diagrams** Draw a diagram to show the distance a diver swims around a rectangular pool measuring 12 m by 8 m. See above.

8 Divers use a waterproof notepad that costs $12.50. How much would it cost to supply a diving crew with 4 notepads? $50

more to explore

quares and Rectangles

ou can find the perimeter of a quare if you know the length of ne side.

3 yd **Think:** A square has four equal sides.

erimeter = (3 + 3 + 3 + 3) yd
= 12 yd

You can also find the perimeter of a rectangle if you know the length of two sides that touch.

2 m, 7 m **Think:** The opposite sides of a rectangle are equal.

Perimeter = (7 + 2 + 7 + 2) m
= 18 m

- How can you use multiplication to find the perimeters of the square and rectangle shown? Square—multiply the length of one side by 4, rectangle—multiply each of the two sides by 2 and then add the products.

xtra Practice, page 509

PRACTICE

Alternate Teaching Strategy

Materials per student: yarn, metric measuring tape (TA 20)

Have students measure the perimeter of a book or other rectangular object, with yarn. Students cut the yarn to fit exactly around the outside edge of the object being measured. They then use the centimeter measuring tape to measure the length of yarn.

Students then confirm that the perimeter equals the sum of the length of the sides. Students do this by measuring the length of each side of the object. They then write a number sentence with the lengths of the sides as addends. The sum equals the full length of the string, which is the perimeter.

ESL APPROPRIATE

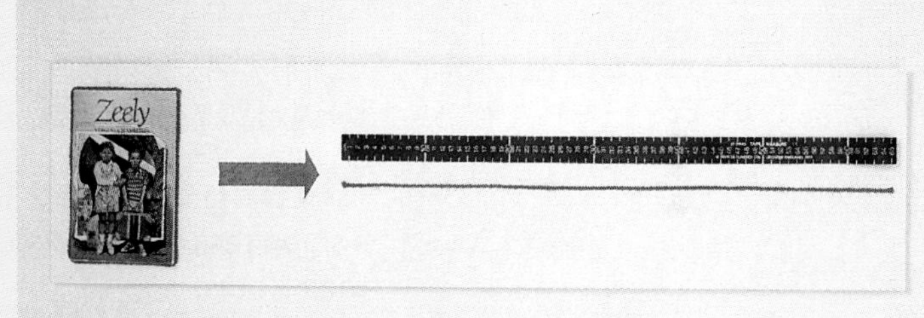

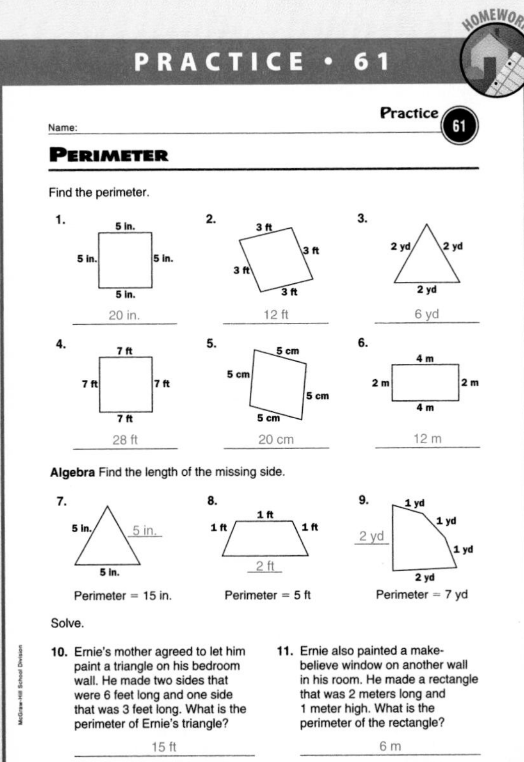

PRACTICE • 61

HOMEWORK

Name: Practice 61

PERIMETER

Find the perimeter.

1. 5 in., 5 in., 5 in., 5 in. — 20 in.
2. 3 ft, 3 ft, 3 ft, 3 ft — 12 ft
3. 2 yd, 2 yd, 2 yd — 6 yd
4. 7 ft, 7 ft, 7 ft, 7 ft — 28 ft
5. 5 cm, 5 cm, 5 cm, 5 cm — 20 cm
6. 4 m, 2 m, 2 m, 4 m — 12 m

Algebra Find the length of the missing side.

7. 5 in., 5 in., 5 in. Perimeter = 15 in.
8. 1 ft, 1 ft, 1 ft, 2 ft Perimeter = 5 ft
9. 1 yd, 1 yd, 1 yd, 2 yd, 2 yd Perimeter = 7 yd

Solve.

10. Ernie's mother agreed to let him paint a triangle on his bedroom wall. He made two sides that were 6 feet long and one side that was 3 feet long. What is the perimeter of Ernie's triangle? 15 ft

11. Ernie also painted a make-believe window on another wall in his room. He made a rectangle that was 2 meters long and 1 meter high. What is the perimeter of the rectangle? 6 m

McGraw-Hill School Division

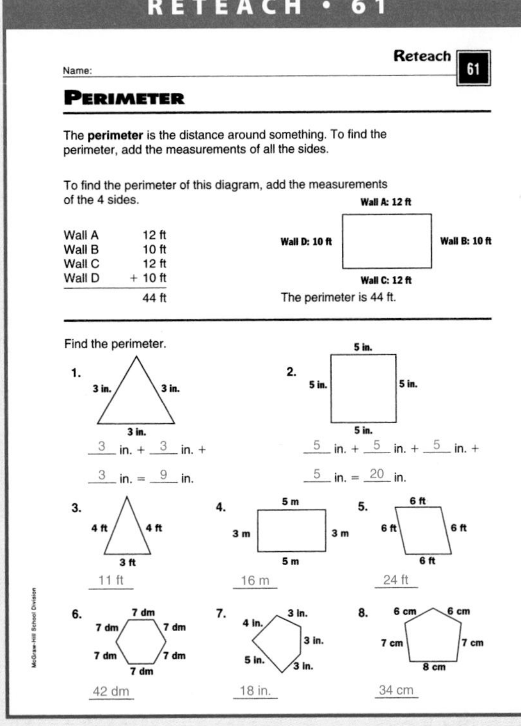

RETEACH • 61

Name: Reteach 61

PERIMETER

The **perimeter** is the distance around something. To find the perimeter, add the measurements of all the sides.

To find the perimeter of this diagram, add the measurements of the 4 sides.

Wall A	12 ft
Wall B	10 ft
Wall C	12 ft
Wall D	+ 10 ft
	44 ft

Wall A: 12 ft, Wall B: 10 ft, Wall C: 12 ft, Wall D: 10 ft

The perimeter is 44 ft.

Find the perimeter.

1. 3 in., 3 in., 3 in.
3 in. + 3 in. + 3 in. = 9 in.
2. 5 in., 5 in., 5 in., 5 in.
5 in. + 5 in. + 5 in. + 5 in. = 20 in.
3. 4 ft, 4 ft, 3 ft — 11 ft
4. 5 m, 3 m, 3 m, 5 m — 16 m
5. 6 ft, 6 ft, 6 ft, 6 ft — 24 ft
6. 7 dm, 7 dm, 7 dm, 7 dm, 7 dm, 7 dm — 42 dm
7. 3 in., 4 in., 3 in., 5 in., 3 in. — 18 in.
8. 6 cm, 6 cm, 7 cm, 7 cm, 8 cm — 34 cm

McGraw-Hill School Division

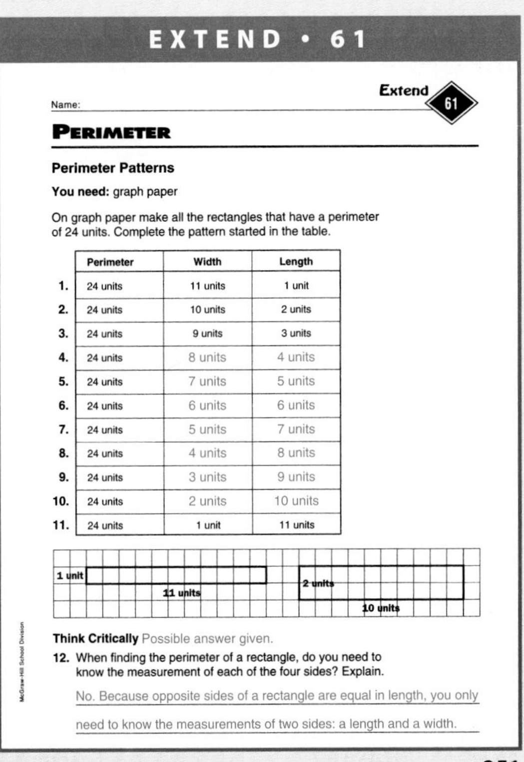

EXTEND • 61

Name: Extend 61

PERIMETER

Perimeter Patterns

You need: graph paper

On graph paper make all the rectangles that have a perimeter of 24 units. Complete the pattern started in the table.

	Perimeter	Width	Length
1.	24 units	11 units	1 unit
2.	24 units	10 units	2 units
3.	24 units	9 units	3 units
4.	24 units	8 units	4 units
5.	24 units	7 units	5 units
6.	24 units	6 units	6 units
7.	24 units	5 units	7 units
8.	24 units	4 units	8 units
9.	24 units	3 units	9 units
10.	24 units	2 units	10 units
11.	24 units	1 unit	11 units

1 unit, 11 units, 2 units, 10 units

Think Critically Possible answer given.

12. When finding the perimeter of a rectangle, do you need to know the measurement of each of the four sides? Explain.
No. Because opposite sides of a rectangle are equal in length, you only need to know the measurements of two sides: a length and a width.

McGraw-Hill School Division

Teaching With Technology

Perimeter

OBJECTIVE Students learn about perimeter by measuring the sides of a shape on an underwater treasure map.

Resource Math Van Activity: *Treasure Hunt*

SET UP

Provide students with the activity card for *Treasure Hunt*. Start ***Math Van*** and click the *Activities* button. Click the *Treasure Hunt* activity on the Fax Machine.

USING THE MATH VAN ACTIVITY

1 Getting Started Students use the Geometry tools to measure a shipwreck site's perimeter. Then they answer related questions in their Notes.

2 Practice and Apply Students make a scaled map of a shipwreck site. Then they use the Geometry tools to measure the lines in the map and to calculate the perimeter of the site.

3 Close You may want students to share how they found the perimeter of a site and discuss other methods that can be used to find the perimeter.

Extend Students use the Geometry tools to draw a map of another, more scattered shipwreck. They measure how much rope they will need to surround the site.

TIPS FOR TOOLS

If students have difficulty remembering which points they measured on their maps, advise them to click the Show Labels box in the Geometry Setup window to display the labels for each point.

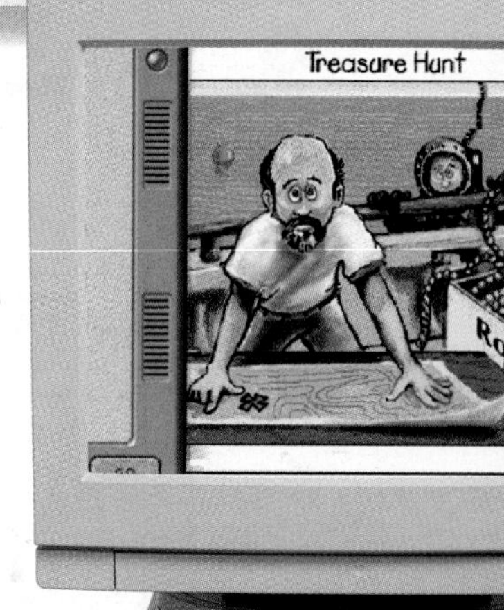

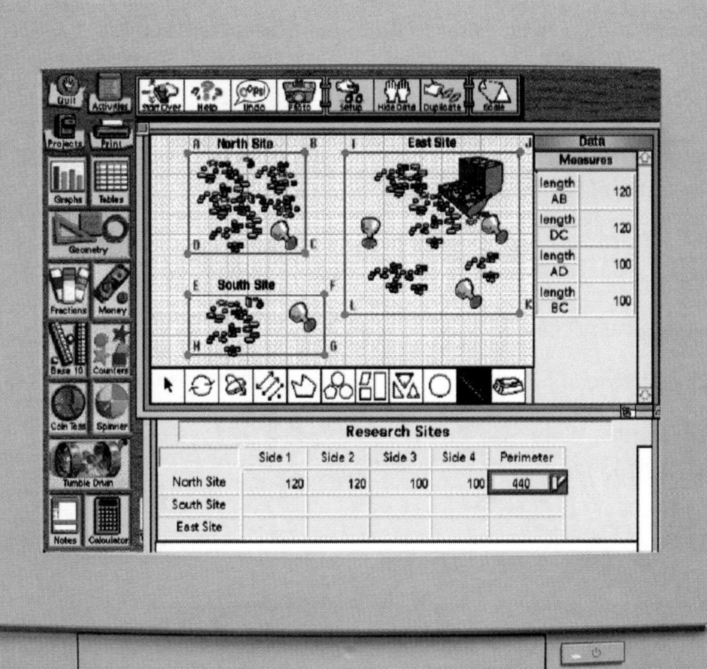

SCREEN 1

Students measure lengths of lines on the treasure map and type the measurements in the Table.

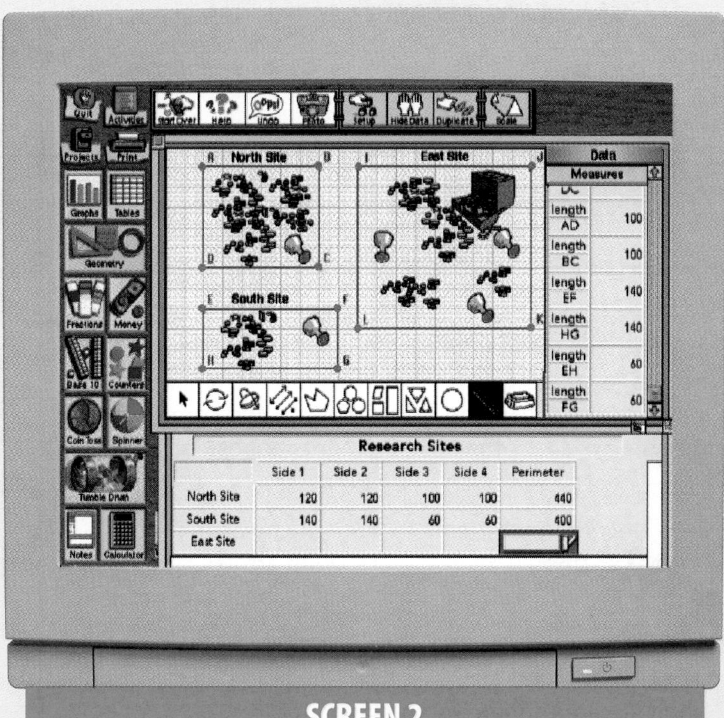

SCREEN 2

Students find the perimeter of quadrilaterals and type the perimeter in the Table.

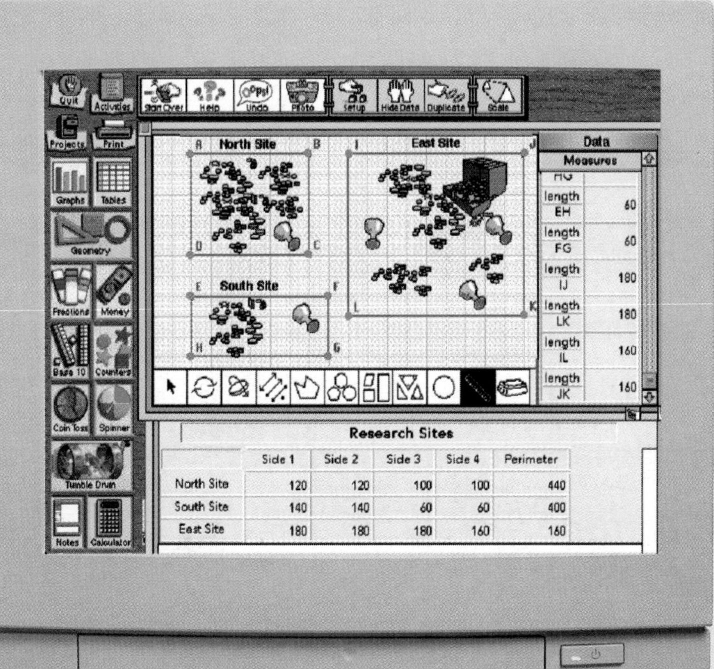

SCREEN 3

Students measure remaining lines, find the perimeters, and type them in the Table.

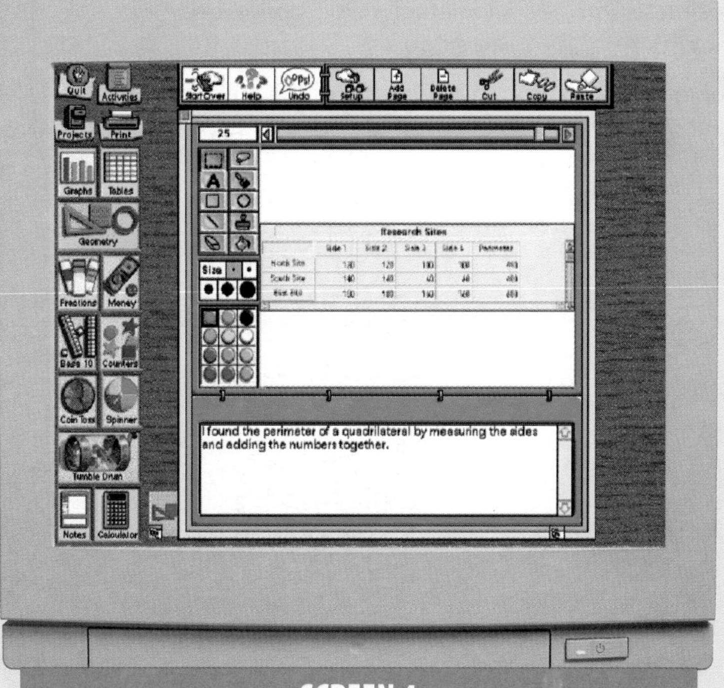

SCREEN 4

Students take a photo of their work and answer questions about how they found the site's perimeter.

MIDCHAPTER REVIEW

PURPOSE Maintain and review concepts, skills, and strategies that students have learned thus far in the chapter.

Materials per student: customary ruler, centimeter ruler, calculator (optional)

Using the Midchapter Review

Have students complete the **Midchapter Review** independently or use it with the whole class.

In ex. 9–14, to avoid errors with the greater than and less than signs, encourage students to write down both the renamed unit of measure and the unit of measure it is being compared with in the same order as the measurements appear in the text.

In ex. 15–16, encourage students to write the measurements given and the renamed units connected with arrows. After the renamed units are ordered, they can easily go back and order the equivalent given units.

Students should explain why their choices of tool and unit are appropriate for the task.

Vocabulary Review

Write the following words and abbreviations on the chalkboard:

centimeter (cm)	**inch (in.)**	**mile (mi)**
customary	**length**	**millimeter (mm)**
decimeter (dm)	**kilometer (km)**	**perimeter**
foot (ft)	**meter (m)**	**yard (yd)**

Ask volunteers to explain, show, or act out the meanings of these words.

Estimate and then measure the length to the nearest inch. Estimates may vary.

1
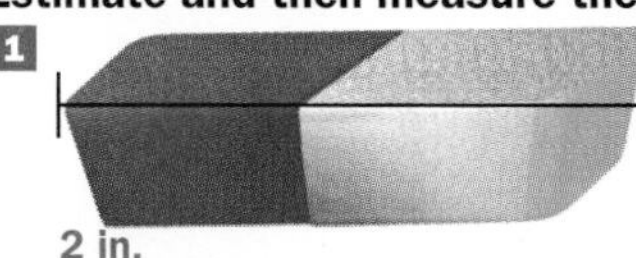
2 in.

2
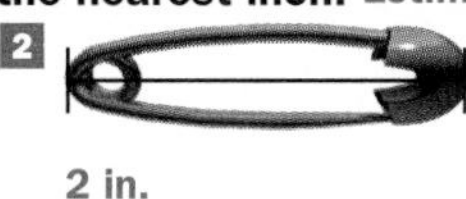
2 in.

Estimate and then measure the length to the nearest centimeter. Estimates may vary.

3
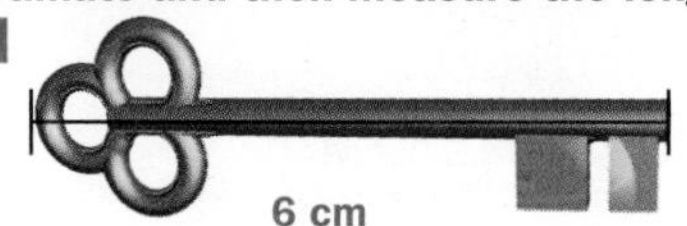
6 cm

4

5 cm

Write the letter of the best estimate.

	a.	b.	c.
5 length of tennis racket a	**a.** 3 ft	**b.** 3 in.	**c.** 3 mi
6 height of fire hydrant c	**a.** 80 mm	**b.** 80 m	**c.** 80 cm
7 width of baseball card b	**a.** 3 ft	**b.** 3 in.	**c.** 3 yd
8 distance between two cities c	**a.** 250 cm	**b.** 250 dm	**c.** 250 km

Compare lengths. Write >, <, or =.

9 480 cm ● 4 m > **10** 4 ft ● 72 in. < **11** 18 ft ● 6 yd =

Complete.

12 6 ft = ■ in. 72 **13** 18 ft = ■ yd 6 **14** 50 cm = ■ dm 5

Write the measurements in order from shortest to longest.

15 13 in., 5 ft, 1 yd, 2 ft, 72 in.
13 in., 2 ft, 1 yd, 5 ft, 72 in.

16 2 km, 19 cm, 25 mm, 3 dm, 1 m
25 mm, 19 cm, 3 dm, 1 m, 2 km

Find the perimeter.

17
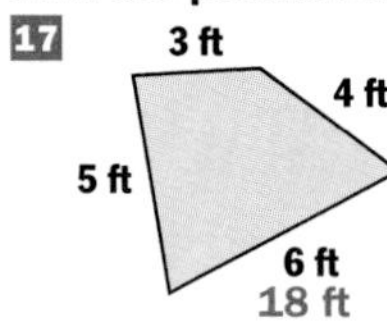

18 ft

18
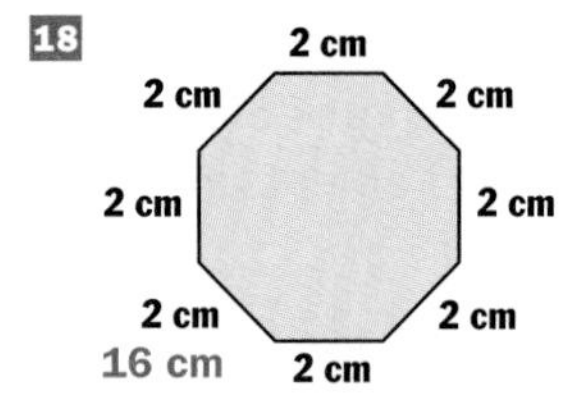

16 cm

19
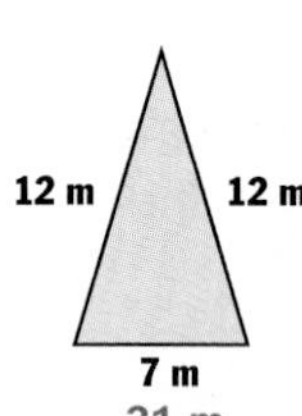

31 m

20 Suppose you want to hang four posters evenly on your wall. What measuring tools would you use? What units of measurement would you use? Tell why. Possible answer: If the poster is measured in feet, then a customary measuring tape should be used to find an appropriate distance from the ceiling and floor to hang the posters.

Reinforcement and Remediation

CHAPTER OBJECTIVES	MIDCHAPTER REVIEW ITEMS	STUDENT BOOK PAGES	TEACHER'S EDITION PAGES		TEACHER RESOURCES
			Activities	Alternate Teaching Strategy	Reteach
*7A	1–8	242–243, 246–249	241A, 245A	243, 245	58, 60
*7C	9–16	244–245	243A	245	59
*7D	17–20	250–251	249A	251	61

*7A Estimate and measure length in customary or metric units
*7C Convert between customary or metric units of length, weight, mass or capacity
*7D Find perimeter

developing number sense

MATH CONNECTION

Use Benchmarks

u can use common objects or parts of your body *benchmarks* to help you estimate the lengths of ıer things.

Some Metric Benchmarks	
Length, Width, or Height	**About . . .**
Width of little finger	1 cm
Width of hand	1 dm
Width of cassette tape	1 dm
Length of stride	1 m
Height from toes to waist	1 m
Width of door	1 m
Height of door from floor to doorknob	1 m

Which of the body benchmarks in the table work for your body? Which do not? **Students may find that some of the given body benchmarks are less than or greater than their measurements.**

Choose three objects whose lengths you would estimate by using the width of your little finger. Why did you choose them? **Answers may vary. The lengths should be small enough to justify the use of centimeters.**

Choose three objects whose lengths you would estimate by using the width of your hand and three by using the length of your stride. Are these the same or different from the lengths you chose in problem 2? Why? **See page T17.**

ll how you would estimate the length, width, or height by ıng one or more of the benchmarks in the table. Answers may vary. Possible answers are given.

height of a chair
use height from toes to waist.

5 length of a dining room table
use length of stride

length and width of a telephone book
use width of hand

7 width of a room
use length of stride

length of a hallway
use length of stride

9 height of a piano
use height from toes to waist

OBJECTIVE Use number sense to determine lengths.

Using Number Sense

Math Connection In Lessons 1 and 3, students estimated length with customary and metric units of measure. Here students use common objects and parts of their bodies as benchmarks to help them estimate lengths of other things.

After students read the table and answer questions 1–3, reinforce this method for estimating length by asking:

- **What benchmark would you use to measure the length of your classroom? Why?** *[Stride; a meter is the best unit to use for estimating a room length; since you can walk through the room, this benchmark is easier to use than other benchmarks for 1 meter.]*

Students may work in small groups or on their own to complete ex. 4–9.

Applying Measurement

OBJECTIVE Measure temperature in degrees Fahrenheit and Celsius.

Materials per group: 4 one-quart containers, salt, measuring spoon, thermometer, tape, markers

1 Engage

Tell students that salinity means saltiness, or the amount of salt dissolved in a liquid. Then ask the students to describe experiences they may have had in the ocean or other bodies of salt water.

2 Investigate *Cooperative Groups*

Note that the experiment requires about a half hour of direct sunlight. Students will also need access to a refrigerator.

Have students read the Steps 1–5. Encourage students to form a hypothesis about the results of the experiment before they begin.

Dissolving Salt Using the Pairs Experiment Strategy, in a group of four, partners help each other with an experiment. Then the two sets of partners share the results. The group discusses all results, then comes to an agreement and prepares a joint report. Demonstrate how to fill the containers so that each container holds 1 quart of water. While groups wait for the containers to warm or cool, group members can practice measuring a level teaspoon of salt and discuss their hypotheses.

In Step 3, have students measure the temperature twice, once to the nearest degree Fahrenheit and once to the nearest degree Celsius.

In Step 5, point out that if salt granules fall to the bottom of the container after the water has been stirred, then the salt did not dissolve completely.

3 Reflect and Share

Report Your Findings As groups compare posters, help point out similarities among their findings. Have students comment on the trends they observe. For example, some students may observe that although the original temperature of the water varied from group to group, the amount of salt that dissolved in the warm water was always greater than the amount of salt that dissolved in the cold water.

Ask each group to share their original hypothesis and compare it to their conclusions.

TEMPERATURE AND SALINITY OF Ocean Water

Did you know that the temperatures of oceans in different parts of the world vary? How do you think the temperature affects how well salt dissolves in the water?

Make your own samples to test how well salt dissolves in water of different temperatures.

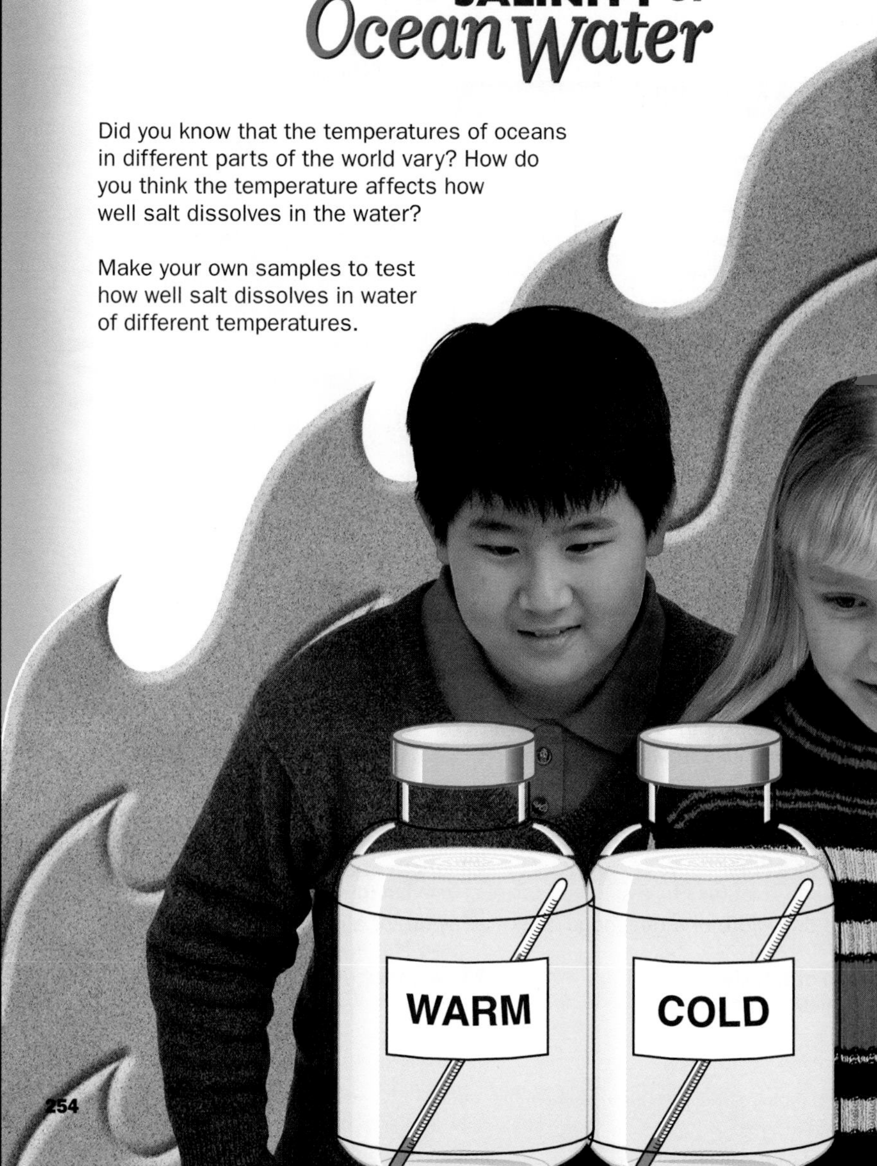

254

More To Investigate

Predict Sample answer: More salt will dissolve in the boiling water than in either container of water in our experiment.

Explore Sample answer: Salt lowers the temperature at which water freezes.

Find Ocean water helps keep fish warmer. The surface of the water may freeze but the water below the ice does not. The ice acts as a layer of insulation keeping the fish warmer than they would be near the surface.

Bibliography Students who wish to learn more about salt and oceans can read:

Be a Kid Physicist, by William R. Wellnitz. New York: McGraw-Hill Book Publishers, Inc., 1993. ISBN 0-07-073397-X.

Incredible Facts About the Ocean: The Land Below, The Life Within, Volume 2, by W. Wright Robinson. Morristown, NJ: Silver Burdett Press, 1987. ISBN 0-87518-358-1.

Salts and Solids, by Robert C. Mebane and Thomas R. Rybolt. New York: TFC Books, 1995. ISBN 0-8050-2841-2.

swers may vary.
eck students' work.

See Teacher's Edition
for sample of student work.

DECISION MAKING

Dissolving Salt

1 Work with a small group. Decide what each member of your group will do during the activity and how you will measure the temperature and amount of salt that is dissolved.

2 Fill two containers with 1 quart of water. Let one container sit in the classroom in sunlight. Place the other container in the refrigerator.

3 After 20 minutes, record the temperature of each container of water.

4 Add 1 level teaspoon of salt to each container at the same time. After each teaspoon is added, stir the containers until the salt is completely dissolved.

5 Continue to add 1 teaspoon of salt to each container until the salt will not dissolve completely. Record your findings in a table.

Reporting Your Findings

6 Portfolio Prepare a poster of the data and conclusions from your experiment. Include:

- a description of the experiment and an explanation of how to tell when salt is completely dissolved.
- a bar graph that shows the amount of salt that was dissolved in each container of water.
- a sentence that describes how water temperature affects how well salt dissolves in water.

7 Compare your results with those of other groups. Did they draw the same conclusion?

Revise your work.

- Does your display include all three parts?
- Is your graph clearly labeled and easy to read?
- Did you proofread your work?

MORE TO INVESTIGATE

See Teacher's Edition.

PREDICT whether more or less salt will dissolve in a container of boiling water than in the containers in your experiment.

EXPLORE how salt affects the freezing temperature of water.

FIND how salt in ocean water helps fish on sunny but very cold winter days.

Students' Work

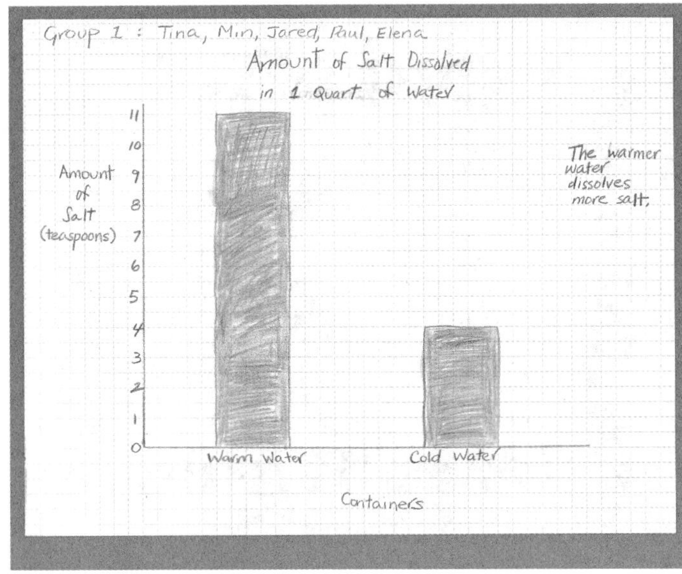

Building A Portfolio

This investigation will allow you to evaluate students' ability to organize data, present data, and draw conclusions from an experiment.

Allow students to revise their work for the portfolio. Each student's portfolio piece should consist of a copy of his or her poster summarizing the team's findings. The poster also includes a description of the experiment, a bar graph, and a conclusion about how temperature affects the salinity of water.

You may use the Holistic Scoring Guide to assess this task. See page 27 in Teacher's Assessment Resources.

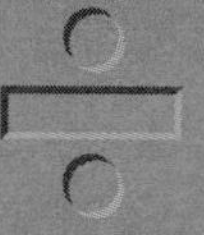

Capacity and Weight in Customary Units

OBJECTIVE Estimate, compare, and order capacity and weight in customary units.

RESOURCE REMINDER
Math Center Cards 62
Practice 62, Reteach 62, Extend 62

SKILLS TRACE

GRADE 3	• Estimate, compare, and order capacity and weight in customary units. *(Chapter 9)*
GRADE 4	• Estimate, compare, order, and convert capacity and weight in customary units.
GRADE 5	• Estimate, compare, order, and convert capacity and weight in customary units. *(Chapter 7)*

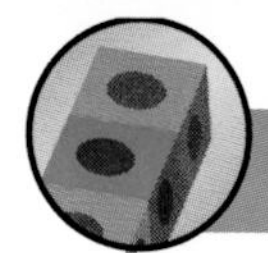

MANIPULATIVE WARM-UP

Cooperative Groups — Kinesthetic

OBJECTIVE Compare relative capacities of various size containers.

Materials per group: several containers of various sizes, dried beans

▶ Give each group several containers and a bag of dried beans.

▶ Ask the group to decide which of their containers is the smallest. Have the students estimate how many of the small containers full of dried beans would be needed to fill each of the larger containers.

▶ Have students check their estimates by using small containers full of dried beans to fill each of the larger containers.

▶ Ask them if their results would change if they filled the containers with water instead of dried beans. *[No]* You may wish to demonstrate this for students or let them discover it on their own.

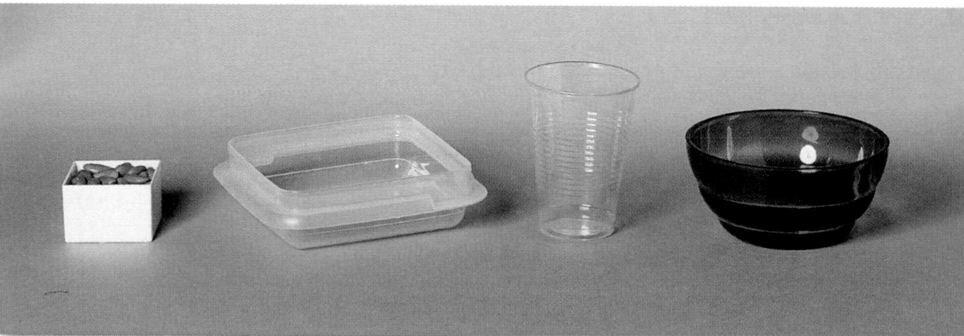

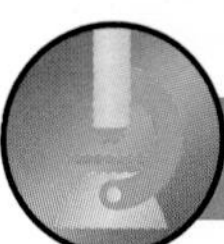

SCIENCE CONNECTION

Whole Class — Logical/Analytical

OBJECTIVE Use a balance to solve a problem.

Materials balance, 5 plastic film canisters, paper clips

▶ Label five canisters with the letters A to E. Put the same number of paper clips in four of the canisters. Put about half as many in the remaining canister. Display the canisters and a balance.

▶ Explain to the class that all but one of the containers have the same number of paper clips inside. The other container has fewer paper clips than the others. Students must think of a way to use the balance to discover which container is lighter than the others.

▶ Have students explain how they discover the lighter container.

ESL APPROPRIATE

Daily Review

PREVIOUS DAY QUICK REVIEW

Find the perimeter.

1. Square with 5 ft sides *[20 ft]*
2. Rectangle with sides 4 ft and 2 ft *[12 ft]*
3. Triangle with each side 3 ft *[9 ft]*

FAST FACTS

1. 10 × 10 *[100]*
2. 8 × 90 *[720]*
3. 50 × 1,000 *[50,000]*
4. 7 × 2,000 *[14,000]*

Problem of the Day • 62

You have 4 one-cup, 3 pint, and 1 quart containers. How can you store a half-gallon of lemonade you make in these containers? *[Possible answers: 1 quart and 2 pints, 1 quart and 4 cups]*

TECH LINK

Math Van

MATH VAN

Tools You may wish to use the Calculator with this lesson.

MATH FORUM

Idea Have students hold two objects of similar size but different weights, such as a rock and a ping-pong ball, so that they recognize that size and shape do not always give an indication of weight.

Visit our Resource Village at http://www.mhschool.com to see more of the Math Forum.

MATH CENTER

Practice

OBJECTIVE Discuss use of various units to describe everyday objects.

Materials per student: 16 counters, Math Center Recording Sheet (TA 31 optional)

Students use a bingo-type game board to select units that can be used to measure an item. Students have the opportunity to defend their answers.

PRACTICE ACTIVITY 62

MATH CENTER
Small Group

Number Sense • Measurement Bingo

YOU NEED
16 counters per player

- Each player draws a 4-by-4 grid. In each square, write a customary unit of weight (ounce, pound) or capacity (fluid ounce, cup, pint, quart, gallon). To fill all the squares, you will have to repeat some units.
- On each turn, a player names something packaged in any of these units. Each player covers one square that contains that unit. For instance, if someone says "milk," you could cover fluid ounce, cup, pint, quart, or gallon. You can cover only one square each time. The first player to fill a row or column wins.

pt	lb	gal	oz
cup	cup	lb	pt
fl oz	lb	qt	oz
gal	cup	oz	fl oz

Grade Level 4

McGraw-Hill School Division

Chapter 7, Lesson 5, pages 256–259

Measurement

NCTM Standards

✓ Problem Solving
✓ Communication
✓ Reasoning
✓ Connections

Problem Solving

OBJECTIVE Solve problems relating to customary units of capacity.

Materials per pair: number cube, drawing paper; per student: crayons, Math Center Recording Sheet (TA 31 optional)

Students randomly select numbers to represent a number of cups. They rename it into greater units and draw containers representing those units. The object is to use the fewest possible containers. *[Answers may vary.]*

PROBLEM-SOLVING ACTIVITY 62

MATH CENTER
Partners

Spatial Reasoning • The Fewer the Better Game

YOU NEED
number cube
drawing paper
crayon or marker

- Roll the cube twice. Use the two numbers to make a 2-digit number. It is the number of cups of water.
- Each player renames that number of cups into different units. Draw your answer by drawing sketches of the containers, labeled by unit, that you would use.
- The player who draws the fewest containers and is correct wins the round.
- Change roles and play again.

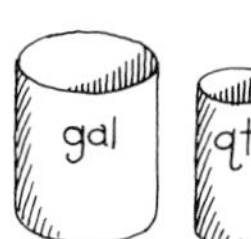

Grade Level 4

McGraw-Hill School Division

Chapter 7, Lesson 5, pages 256–259

Measurement

NCTM Standards

✓ Problem Solving
Communication
✓ Reasoning
Connections

Capacity and Weight in Customary Units

OBJECTIVE Estimate, compare, and order capacity and weight in customary units.

Vocabulary capacity, cup, fluid ounce, gallon, ounce, pint, pound, quart, weight

1 Introduce

Materials cup, pint, quart, and gallon containers

Show students the 1-cup container. Tell students the capacity, or amount of liquid that the container can hold is one cup. Then show the pint container. Ask:

- **How can you find the capacity of this container?** *[Fill it using the 1-cup container and count how many cups.]*

Fill the pint container using the 1-cup container. Ask students to give the capacity of the container. Tell students a container that holds 2 cups is a pint. Begin a chart on the chalkboard like the one on page 256.

Do the same for the other containers using the next smaller container to fill each.

2 Teach *Whole Class*

LEARN Point out the definition of *capacity,* and have students look at the benchmarks for the units on page 256. Then discuss the questions below the equivalencies chart. Ask:

- **When you rename gallons using quarts, why do you multiply the number of gallons by 4?** *[Because each gallon has 4 quarts in it.]*
- **How do you rename any larger unit using a smaller unit?** *[Multiply the number of larger units by the number of smaller units in each larger unit.]*
- **When you rename fluid ounces using cups, why do you divide by 8?** *[because there are 8 fluid ounces in a cup]*

Help students to estimate the capacity of a drinking glass and sink by first identifying the unit that is most appropriate for measuring the capacity of each.

MEASUREMENT

Capacity and Weight in Customary Units

LEARN

If you fill a 5-gallon aquarium with only 1 gallon of water, it is still a 5-gallon aquarium. The size of the aquarium has not changed. It can still hold 5 gallons.

Capacity is the amount of liquid a container can hold.

1 fluid ounce (fl oz)

1 cup (c)

1 pint (pt) 1 quart (qt) 1 gallon (gal)

8 **fluid ounces (fl oz)**	= 1 **cup (c)**
2 **cups (c)**	= 1 **pint (pt)**
2 **pints (pt)**	= 1 **quart (qt)**
4 **quarts (qt)**	= 1 **gallon (gal**

Check Out the Glossary
For vocabulary words
See page 544.

How many quart containers of water does it take to fill a 5-gal aquarium?

Think:
1 gal = 4 qt

5 gal = 5 × 4 qt
= 20 qt

It would take 20 quart containers.

A juice container holds 64 fl oz. How many cups is that?

Think: 1 c = 8 fl oz

64 fl oz = 64 fl oz ÷ 8
= 8 c

That is 8 cups of juice.

▶ What do you think is the capacity of a drinking glass? a kitchen sink? Why? **Possible answer: 6–16 fl oz; 4–8 gal; accept all reasonab explanations.**

256 Lesson 7.5

Meeting Individual Needs

Extra Support

Some students may need to review multiplication and division facts used when converting measures from smaller to larger units and vice versa.

Language Support

Use a measuring cup to familiarize students acquiring English with *fluid ounce, cup,* and *pint* markings. Help them realize that a container that says "half pint" is 1 cup and a "half gallon" is 2 quarts.

ESL APPROPRIATE

Ongoing Assessment

Anecdotal Report Make notes on students' ability to estimate capacity and weight. Note which units they have difficulty with so that you can provide additional practice.

Follow Up Have students create a table with models of containers or weights drawn under the equivalent units. Students who need additional help may complete **Reteach 62.**

Assign **Extend 62** for students who would like a challenge.

allon of water weighs 8 pounds.

16 **ounces (oz)** = 1 **pound (lb)**

ight is the amount of heaviness an object.

unce (oz) **1 ounce (oz)** **1 pound (lb)** **40 pounds (lb)**

Hold a dime in your hand. What items can you find in your classroom that weigh about the same as the dime?
Possible answer: large paper clip

▶ Hold your math book in one hand. What items can you find in your classroom that weigh about the same as your book?
Possible answer: dictionary

w many ounces does -lb bag weigh?

nk: 1 lb = 16 oz

b = 5 × 16 oz
= 80 oz

e bag weighs 80 oz.

How many pounds does a 48-oz lobster weigh?

Think: 1 lb = 16 oz
2 lb = 32 oz
3 lb = 48 oz

48 oz = 3 lb

The lobster weighs 3 lb.

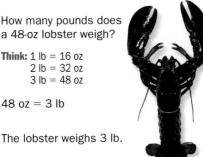

heck for Understanding

ite the letter of the best estimate.

amount of water in a bathtub c
a. 50 fl oz **b.** 50 c **c.** 50 gal

2 weight of a school bus a
a. 6,000 lb **b.** 6,000 oz **c.** 95 lb

mplete.

3 qt = ■ pt 6 **4** 4 pt = ■ qt 2 **5** 4 lb = ■ oz 64 **6** 80 oz = ■ lb 5

itical Thinking: Analyze **Explain your reasoning.**

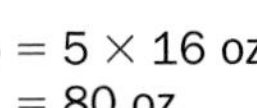
Marcy says that an aquarium filled with 10 gallons of water weighs 90 pounds. Is her statement reasonable? Why or why not? **Possible answer: Yes; the water would weigh 8 × 10 lb, or 80 lb, and the weight of the aquarium itself could be 10 lb.**

CHECK

Turn the page for Practice.

To help create a context for units of weight, discuss methods by which weight can be determined, such as using a scale to find an exact measurement or holding two objects to compare the weight of each.

Point out to students that the abbreviation for pound (lb) comes from the Latin word for pound, which is *libra.*

After students review the examples on the page, ask:

- **What unit do you use to describe your weight?** *[pounds]*
- **What are some items you buy in a store that are sold by weight?** *[Possible answers: foods, some hardware and construction materials like nails]*

Help students understand that not all weights found on grocery store items are an even number of pounds. Explain that weights between 1 and 2 pounds, for example, are expressed as 1 pound and a number of ounces.

3 Close

Check for Understanding using items 1–7, page 257.

CRITICAL THINKING
Remind students that multiplication shows how many groups there are. So, 8 gallons that weigh about 10 pounds each can be expressed as 8 × 10 = 80, which is close enough to the estimate of 90 to be reasonable.

Practice See pages 258–259.

Gender Fairness

Try alternating between girls and boys when calling on students. Be sure to provide adequate wait time for a student to answer.

PRACTICE

Materials Have available: calculators

Options for assigning exercises:
A—Odd ex. 1–17; choose six of ex. 19–27; **Mixed Review**
B—Even ex. 2–18; choose six of ex. 19–27; **Mixed Review**

- For ex. 1–6, students may want to rename amounts in the same unit, show those amounts in order, then choose a reasonable estimate.
- Ex. 20 is a multistep problem in which students first rename units, then add and compare.

Algebra: Patterns In ex. 15–16, students apply their knowledge of patterns and renaming units of capacity and weight to complete the table.

Mixed Review/Test Preparation In ex. 1–5, students review adding and subtracting money amounts, learned in Chapter 2. In ex. 6–10, students review multiplying whole numbers and money, learned in Chapters 5 and 6.

PRACTICE

Practice

Choose the most reasonable estimate.
Explain your reasoning. Explanations may vary.

1 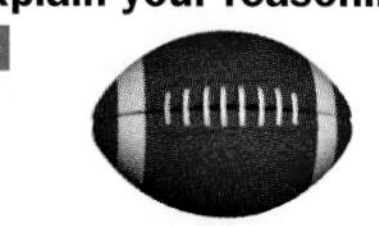
1 oz or 1 lb **1 lb**

2 
4 qt or 4 c or 4 fl oz **4 c**

3 

30 fl oz or 30 qt or 30 ... **30 f...**

4 
2 gal or 2 pt or 2 c **2 gal**

5 
30 oz or 30 lb **30 lb**

6 
14 oz or 14 lb **14 ...**

Choose the best unit. Write *cup, pint, quart,* or *gallon*. Accept all reasonable answers. Possible answers are g...

7 bucket **quart or gallon**
8 bud vase **cup**
9 milk pitcher **pint or quart**
10 garbage ca... **gallon**

Choose the better unit. Write *ounce* or *pound*.

11 eraser **ounce**
12 hiking boots **pound**
13 computer **pound**
14 compact d... **ounce**

ALGEBRA: PATTERNS Copy and complete the table.

15

Gallons	Quarts	Pints	Cups
1	4	■ 8	16
2	■ 8	16	32
3	12	24	48■
■ 4	16	■ 32	64
5	■ 20	40	80■

16

Pounds	Ounces
1	■ 16
■ 2	32
■ 3	48
4	■ 64
5	■ 80

Solve.

18. Possible answers: six 1-pt containers or twelve 1-c containers or four 1-pt containers plus eight 1-c contain...

17 **What if** your full name is spelled out with wood blocks. Each block is 1 letter and weighs 1 lb. Name an object that weighs about the same as your name. **Students' answers will depend on the number of letters in their names.**

18 How would you balance the second scale? (Hint: You can mix containers.) **See above.**

258 Lesson 7.5

Meeting Individual Needs

Early Finishers

Have students list five items in the classroom whose capacity can be measured and three whose weight can be measured. For each, have students identify the best unit of measure.

Gifted And Talented

Students create riddles to describe objects by capacity or weight, such as: "I am half the height of students. I help them when they're tired. You measure my weight in pounds. What am I?" *[a chair]*

Inclusion

It may be helpful for visually impaired students to write out measurement units, to help them avoid confusing "pt," "qt," and other abbreviations.

COMMON ERROR

Some students may divide to change from a larger unit to a smaller unit, or multiply to change from a smaller unit to a larger unit. Use models and drawings to review the relationships between units.

. Possible answer: No; a yardstick would make more sense because the distance is so long.
. No; 3 gal = 12 qt and 7 qt + 8 pt (4 qt) is only 11 qt, not 12.

IXED APPLICATIONS
roblem Solving

Pencil & Paper | Calculator | Mental Math

Brad decides to measure the school driveway with an inch ruler. Is this the best tool for him to use? Explain. **See above.**

20 Manuel needs 3 gal of juice for a party. He has 7 quart bottles and 8 pint containers of juice. Does he have enough? Why or why not? **See above.**

Jill's stride measures 26 in. She figures she can walk from her classroom door to the school library by taking no more than 15 steps. Her friend Aura measured the distance to be 32 ft. Is Jill's figuring correct? Explain your thinking. **Yes; 5 × 26 = 390 in., which is about 32 ft.**

22 **Logical reasoning** The largest whale ever recorded is a blue whale measuring just over 110 ft long. This whale was about as long as: **a**
a. a cafeteria.
b. a classroom.
c. a school bus.

Yoko brings enough juice so that each person at a party gets 4 c. There are 24 people at the party. How much juice does Yoko bring? **96 c, or 6 gal**

Josie caught three fish that weighed 25 oz, 14 oz, and 34 oz. Which one weighed under 1 lb? over 2 lb? **14-oz fish; 34-oz fish**

Estimate and then measure the length of your hand span. What unit of measure did you use? Why? How could you use your hand span to estimate other lengths? **See page T17.**

Dave starts a fishing trip at 6:30 A.M. If the trip lasts 4 hours 55 minutes, when does it end? **11:25 A.M.**

27 **Write a problem** about the perimeter of something in your classroom. Ask others to solve it. **Students should compare problems and solutions.**

mixed review • test preparation

$5.08 − 0.61 = **$4.47**	**2** $9.27 + 5.37 = **$14.64**	**3** $34.92 + 72.64 = **$107.56**	**4** $78.00 − 62.83 = **$15.17**	**5** $35.16 − 26.99 = **$8.17**
$2.83 × 7 = **$19.81**	**7** $17.52 × 3 = **$52.56**	**8** $9.41 × 23 = **$216.43**	**9** $4.99 × 15 = **$74.85**	**10** $37.65 × 50 = **$1,882.50**

Alternate Teaching Strategy

Materials balance, 1 pound and 16 1-ounce weights; per group: cup, pint, quart, and gallon containers labeled with the appropriate unit; water or rice

Have students work in small groups. Students fill larger containers with water or rice from the smaller containers, and use their findings to complete the following. *[2 cups = 1 pint, 2 pints = 1 quart, 4 quarts = 1 gallon]*

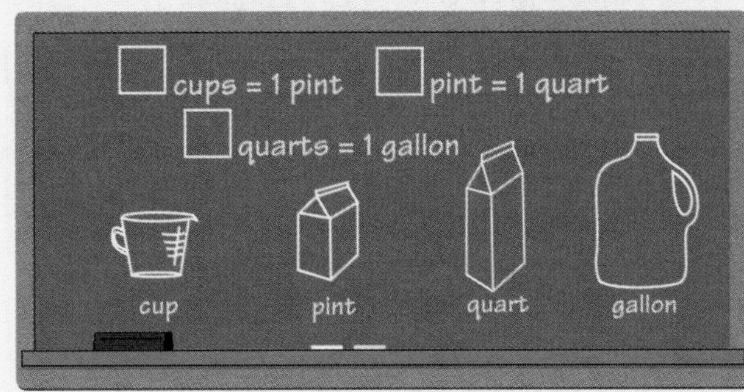

Complete a similar activity for customary units of weight. Have volunteers come to the front of the room and use a balance, ounce, and pound weights to find how many ounces equal 1 pound. *[16]*

ESL APPROPRIATE

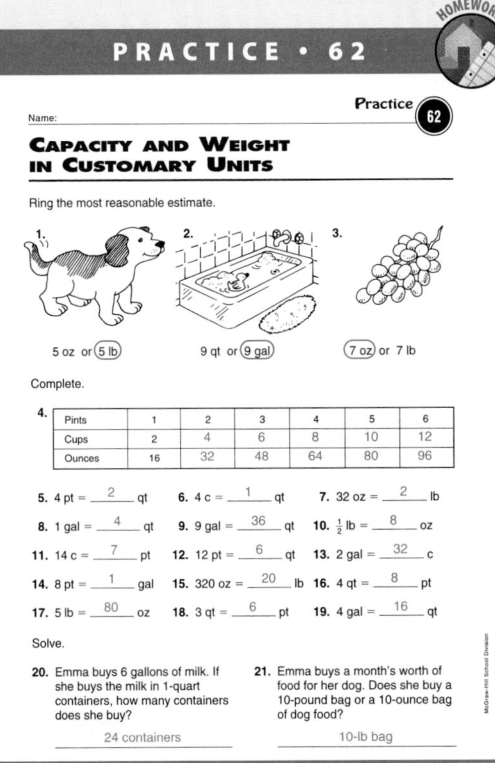
PRACTICE • 62 (HOMEWORK)

Name: Practice 62

Capacity and Weight in Customary Units

Ring the most reasonable estimate.

1. 5 oz or (5 lb)
2. 9 qt or (9 gal)
3. (7 oz) or 7 lb

Complete.

4.

Pints	1	2	3	4	5	6
Cups	2	4	6	8	10	12
Ounces	16	32	48	64	80	96

5. 4 pt = 2 qt
6. 4 c = 1 qt
7. 32 oz = 2 lb
8. 1 gal = 4 qt
9. 9 gal = 36 qt
10. $\frac{1}{2}$ lb = 8 oz
11. 14 c = 7 pt
12. 12 pt = 6 qt
13. 2 gal = 32 c
14. 8 pt = 1 gal
15. 320 oz = 20 lb
16. 4 qt = 8 pt
17. 5 lb = 80 oz
18. 3 qt = 6 pt
19. 4 gal = 16 qt

Solve.

20. Emma buys 6 gallons of milk. If she buys the milk in 1-quart containers, how many containers does she buy? 24 containers

21. Emma buys a month's worth of food for her dog. Does she buy a 10-pound bag or a 10-ounce bag of dog food? 10-lb bag

McGraw-Hill School Division

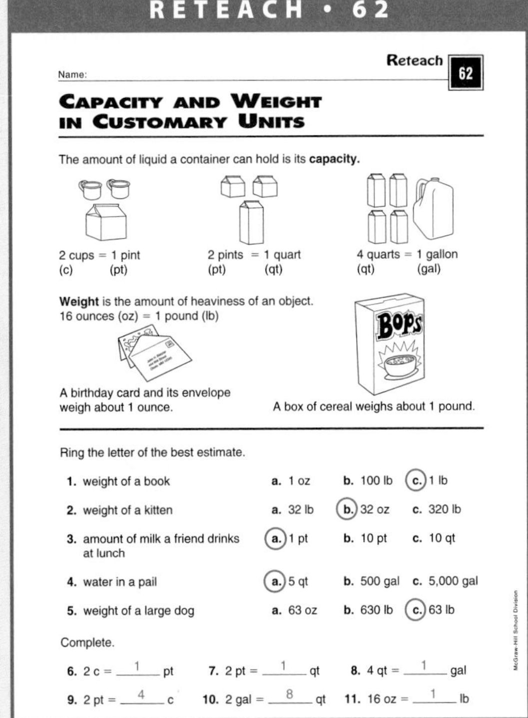
RETEACH • 62

Name: Reteach 62

Capacity and Weight in Customary Units

The amount of liquid a container can hold is its **capacity**.

2 cups = 1 pint (c) (pt)
2 pints = 1 quart (pt) (qt)
4 quarts = 1 gallon (qt) (gal)

Weight is the amount of heaviness of an object.
16 ounces (oz) = 1 pound (lb)

A birthday card and its envelope weigh about 1 ounce.
A box of cereal weighs about 1 pound.

Ring the letter of the best estimate.

1. weight of a book — a. 1 oz b. 100 lb (c.) 1 lb
2. weight of a kitten — a. 32 lb (b.) 32 oz c. 320 lb
3. amount of milk a friend drinks at lunch — (a.) 1 pt b. 10 pt c. 10 qt
4. water in a pail — (a.) 5 qt b. 500 gal c. 5,000 gal
5. weight of a large dog — a. 63 oz b. 630 lb (c.) 63 lb

Complete.

6. 2 c = 1 pt
7. 2 pt = 1 qt
8. 4 qt = 1 gal
9. 2 pt = 4 c
10. 2 gal = 8 qt
11. 16 oz = 1 lb

McGraw-Hill School Division

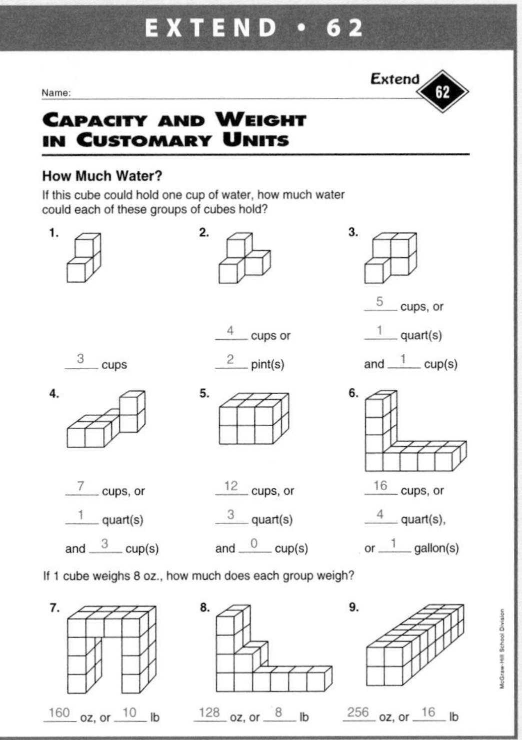
EXTEND • 62

Name: Extend 62

Capacity and Weight in Customary Units

How Much Water?

If this cube could hold one cup of water, how much water could each of these groups of cubes hold?

1. 3 cups
2. 4 cups or 2 pint(s)
3. 5 cups, or 1 quart(s) and 1 cup(s)
4. 7 cups, or 1 quart(s) and 3 cup(s)
5. 12 cups, or 3 quart(s) and 0 cup(s)
6. 16 cups, or 4 quart(s), or 1 gallon(s)

If 1 cube weighs 8 oz., how much does each group weigh?

7. 160 oz, or 10 lb
8. 128 oz, or 8 lb
9. 256 oz, or 16 lb

McGraw-Hill School Division

Problem-Solving Strategy: Use Logical Reasoning

OBJECTIVE Solve problems by using logical reasoning.

RESOURCE REMINDER
Math Center Cards 63
Practice 63, Reteach 63, Extend 63

SKILLS TRACE

GRADE 3	• Solve problems using logical reasoning. *(Chapter 9)*
GRADE 4	• Solve problems using logical reasoning.
GRADE 5	• Solve problems using logical reasoning. *(Chapter 8)*

LESSON 7.6 RESOURCES

MANIPULATIVE WARM-UP

Cooperative Groups | Visual/Spatial

OBJECTIVE Use logical reasoning to solve problems.

Materials two-color counters

▶ Display two-color counters. Explain that all the counters are the same weight. Then show counters in the following two arrangements:

▶ Have students look at the grouping which shows a stack of 5 counters and 2 counters. Have them add or subtract counters to make the stacks equal.

▶ Have students look at the second grouping which shows two stacks of 4 and 6 counters. Have them decide how to create one or more stacks of another color counters to equal these in weight. *[Possible answer: Any group or combinations of groups that has a total of 10 counters.]*

ESL APPROPRIATE

DISCRETE MATH CONNECTION

Cooperative Group | Kinesthetic

OBJECTIVE Use logical reasoning to solve a problem.

Materials per group: construction paper, scissors

▶ Have students draw and cut out 2 large, 2 medium, and 2 small fish. One large sheet of construction paper can represent the aquarium.

▶ Tell students that they have to put 4 fish at a time in the aquarium, and that the 4 fish must be of at least two different kinds. Have students find as many combinations as they can that fit these requirements. *[6 combinations: 2 large, 2 medium; 2 large, 2 small; 1 large, 2 medium, 1 small; 1 large, 1 medium, 2 small; 2 medium, 2 small; 1 medium, 2 large, 1 small]*

▶ Students record their findings in a list.

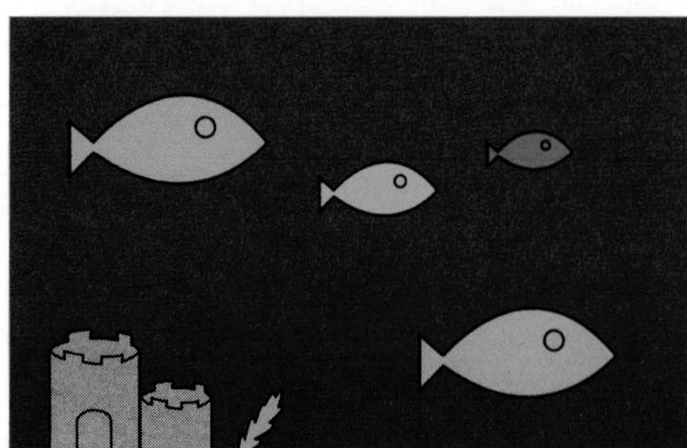

ESL APPROPRIATE

Daily Review

PREVIOUS DAY QUICK REVIEW

Complete.

1. 2 lb = □ oz *[32]*
2. 3 pt = □ c *[6]*
3. □ qt = 6 pt *[3]*
4. □ gal = 8 qt *[2]*

FAST FACTS

1. 36 ÷ 6 *[6]*
2. 40 ÷ 5 *[8]*
3. 63 ÷ 7 *[9]*
4. 56 ÷ 8 *[7]*

Problem of the Day • 63

Starting on Monday, you deliver newspapers to 20 customers per day during your first week. You gain 2 more customers each day starting Monday of the second week. How many newspapers have you delivered by the end of the second Thursday? *[228]*

TECH LINK

MATH FORUM

Idea I have students use pails without water to act out the solution to the introductory problem. After each step, they tell the amount of water in each pail.

Visit our Resource Village at http://www.mhschool.com to see more of the Math Forum.

MATH CENTER

Practice

OBJECTIVE Solve problems using logical reasoning.

Students solve problems about mass and money. *[**1.** 1 dog = 3 cats. Answers may vary. Possible answer: In the second picture, take 5 hamsters from each side. Since 20 hamsters = 2 cats, 3 cats = 1 dog; **2.** Todd: 14 quarters, Mia: 19 quarters. Possible answer: work backward from Sue's amount]*

MATH CENTER
On Your Own

PRACTICE ACTIVITY 63

Logical Reasoning • Cats, Dogs, and Quarters

1. How many cats does it take to balance one dog? Explain your reasoning.
2. Todd, Sue, and Mia together had $10.00 in quarters. Todd had 2 times as many quarters as Sue. Mia had 5 more quarters than Todd. If Sue had $1.75 in quarters, how many quarters did Todd and Mia have?

- Explain your reasoning.

?cats

Grade Level 4
McGraw-Hill School Division

Chapter 7, Lesson 6, pages 260–261 Measurement

NCTM Standards
✓ Problem Solving
Communication
✓ Reasoning
✓ Connections

Problem Solving

OBJECTIVE Explore and explain fairness of a game.

Material per group: number cube; per student: Math Center Recording Sheet (TA 31 optional)

Students play a circle game and discuss whether the game is fair or unfair. *[**1.** Answers may vary. Possible answer: Whoever starts at position 4 is the winner. It is fair since a toss of the number cube determines where you start; **2.** Changing the number to 8 shifts the position of the winning player.]*

MATH CENTER
Small Group

PROBLEM-SOLVING ACTIVITY 63

Decision Making • Fair or Unfair?

YOU NEED
- number cube
- 5 players

- Sit in a circle as shown. Each player tosses the number cube. The person who gets the greatest number goes first. If 2 or more players get the greatest number, they should toss again.
- The first player says "one." Students continue counting around the circle to "five."
- Whoever says "five" is out. Repeat this process until only one person is left. The last person wins 10 points. Remember to keep counting to 5 even when there are fewer than 5 players.

1. Do you think this game is fair or unfair? Explain.
2. How would saying numbers 1–8 change the game? Try it.

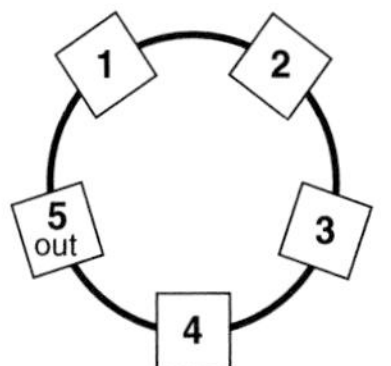

Grade Level 4
McGraw-Hill School Division

Chapter 7, Lesson 6, pages 260–261 Problem Solving

NCTM Standards
✓ Problem Solving
✓ Communication
✓ Reasoning
Connections

Problem-Solving Strategy: Use Logical Reasoning

OBJECTIVE Solve problems by using logical reasoning.

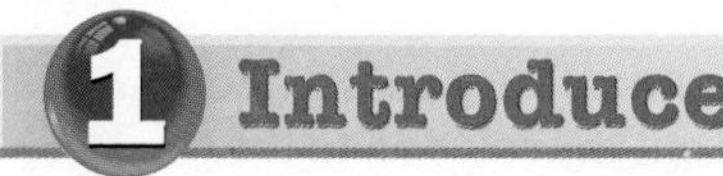

1 Introduce

To introduce students to the reasoning used in this lesson, ask:

- **What can you do if you have to measure a liquid but you do not have the exact size measuring cup?** *[Possible answers: Use part of a larger one or measure several times using a smaller one; estimate; calculate an equivalent amount using an alternate measure.]*

2 Teach *Whole Class*

LEARN Work through the introductory problem with the class. Have volunteers explain what happens in each step, and what the table shows.

The solution to the problem can be expressed using the number sentence shown below:

$(5 \text{ gal} - 3 \text{ gal}) + (5 \text{ gal} - 3 \text{ gal}) = 2 \text{ gal} + 2 \text{ gal} = 4 \text{ gal}$

You may wish to write this number sentence on the board, and have a volunteer explain how it describes the solution. *[The subtraction in the parentheses shows how you get 2 gallons in the large pail. You do this twice to get 4 gallons in the aquarium.]*

3 Close

Check for Understanding with items 1 and 2, page 260.

CRITICAL THINKING
For item 2, students should create tables to solve the problems and identify the number of steps it takes to solve each.

PRACTICE

Materials have available: calculators

Students complete ex. 1–10 as independent work.

- For ex. 4, students might want to draw a picture or use a table.
- For ex. 5, encourage students to create a table to help them solve the problem.
- Ex. 8 requires renaming feet as inches.

Problem-Solving Strategy

Read | Plan | Solve | Look Back

Use Logical Reasoning

LEARN

Read **Suppose you need to fill an aquarium with 4 gallons of water for an ocean project. You have only these two containers.**

How can you get exactly 4 gallons of water into the aquarium?

Plan Think about the difference in capacities of the two pails. How can you use this difference to help you fill the aquarium?

Solve The table below shows one way to measure 4 gallons using these two pails.

Steps	Water in 3-gal Pail	Water in 5-gal Pail	Water in Aquarium
1. Fill the 5-gallon pail.	0	5	0
2. Pour water from the 5-gallon pail into the 3-gallon pail to fill it.	3	2	0
3. Pour what remains in the 5-gallon pail into the aquarium.	3	0	2

You now have 2 gallons in the aquarium. Empty the 3-gallon pail and repeat steps 1–3 to get 4 gallons in the aquarium.

Look Back Why is making a table helpful for solving this problem?
It helps to keep track of the steps.

CHECK

Check for Understanding

1 How would you use the 3-gallon and the 5-gallon pails to fill the aquarium with each amount of water? **Possible answer: a. subtract 3 gal from 5 gal for 2 gal an then add 5 gal; b. use 3-gal pail onc and the 5-gal pail once; c. the 3-gal pail times.**

a. 7 gal **b.** 8 gal **c.** 9 gal

Critical Thinking: Analyze **Explain your reasoning.**

2 Which amount (7, 8, or 9 gallons) requires the least number of steps? Which requires the greatest number of steps?
8 gal only takes two steps; 7 and 9 each take three steps.

260 Lesson 7.6

Meeting Individual Needs

Early Finishers

Have students use the information in the Infobit and table of length of Coastal Waters Fish to write two word problems. They can exchange these problems with partners and solve.

Extra Support

Encourage students to write a numbered list of steps to solve the problem on the table they develop for item 1 on p. 260, then draw pictures that correspond to each step listed in the sequence.

Ongoing Assessment

Observation Checklist Determine if students understand how to use the logical reasoning strategy presented in this lesson by observing the steps they follow as they complete items 1 and 2 in **Check for Understanding.**

Follow Up For students who need additional help and practice, assign **Reteach 63.**

For students who can use logical reasoning to solve problems, assign **Extend 63.**

Possible answer: Fill 2-fl-oz glass three times; fill 8-fl-oz glass, fill 5-fl-oz and 2-fl-oz glasses from it, leaving 1 fl oz.

IXED APPLICATIONS

roblem Solving

Suppose you have 3 glasses—2 fl oz, 5 fl oz, and 8 fl oz. What is the easiest way to fill a pitcher with 6 fl oz? 1 fl oz? **See above.**

Dante collects seashells. At last count, he had 156 shells. His goal is to collect 500 shells. If he collects 8 shells each week, how long will it be before he reaches his goal? **43 wk**

The tanks at the Monterey Bay Aquarium in California hold 750,000 gal of water. Is this about 2 times, 4 times, or 6 times the capacity of the ocean tank at the New England Aquarium? SEE INFOBIT. **about 4 times**

INFOBIT
The giant ocean tank at the New England Aquarium is 23 feet deep and holds almost 190,000 gal of water.

Calvin has 3 times as many fish in his aquarium as Sheila. Sheila has 2 more than Cameron, who has twice as many as Carlos. If Carlos has 4 fish in his aquarium, how many do the others have in theirs? **See below.**

5 Amber presented her project 2 days after Brian. Marlene presented hers 4 days before Amber. The presentations were given on Monday, Wednesday, and Friday. When did each person present? **Marlene on Monday, Brian on Wednesday, Amber on Friday**

e the table for problems 6–10.

About how many swordfish would you need to equal the length of 3 smalltooth sawfish? **about 7 swordfish**

How long are the three shortest fish? the three longest? What is the difference between the shortest and the longest? **2 ft, 7 ft, and 10 ft; 11 ft, 16 ft, and 22 ft; 20 ft**

Which fish measures 132 in.? **ocean sunfish**

What object is about as long as an Atlantic manta ray? a bluefish? a swordfish? Explain your answers. **See above.**

Lengths of Coastal Waters Fish	
Atlantic manta ray	22 ft
Bluefish	2 ft
Blue marlin	10 ft
Ocean sunfish	11 ft
Smalltooth sawfish	16 ft
Swordfish	7 ft

9. Possible answers: length of a classroom; length of a puppy; a very tall basketball player. Explanations may vary.

10 **Write a problem** using any of the information from the table. Solve it. Then have a friend solve it. **Students should compare problems and solutions.**

Calvin—30 fish, Cameron—8 fish, Sheila—10 fish

ra Practice, page 510

PRACTICE

Alternate Teaching Strategy

Materials per pair: 3 pieces of strings—6 cm, 7 cm, and 9 cm

Distribute 3 pieces of strings to each group. Have students brainstorm how they would draw line segments of 1 cm, 2 cm, 3 cm, 4 cm, 5 cm, 8 cm, and 10 cm using the 3 pieces of strings.

Have groups report how they found the lengths using the 3 pieces of strings. Extend the activity by having students draw line segments of 23 cm, 26 cm, and 34 cm using the strings.

PRACTICE • 63

HOMEWORK

Practice 63

Name:

PROBLEM-SOLVING: USE LOGICAL REASONING

Read / Plan / Solve / Look Back

Solve using the logical-reasoning strategy.

1. Terry has been asked to make plaster of Paris for the class. She needs 6 quarts of water. She has a 5-quart jar and a 7-quart jar. How can she use them to measure 6 quarts?
   She could fill a 7-quart jar and use that to fill the 5-quart jar. What remains is 2 quarts. She could do this two more times.
2. The class used all the plaster of Paris, and now Terry needs to make a larger amount. She has one 7-quart jar and one 5-quart jar. How can she use them to measure 9 quarts of water?
   She could fill a 7-quart jar and use that to fill the 5-quart jar. What remains is 2 quarts. She adds one full 7-quart jar of water.
3. Carlos makes 2 more plaster frogs than Tina. Tina makes 2 more than Maria, who makes twice as many as Jeff. If Jeff makes 6, how many do the others make?
   Maria—12, Tina—14, Carlos—16
4. Keisha finishes her crafts project 15 minutes before David, who finishes 5 minutes after Mindy. Mindy finishes 20 minutes before Ben. Ben finishes at 10:30. When do the others finish?
   Keisha—10:00, David—10:15, Mindy—10:10

Solve using any method.

5. The class has been making papier-mâché fish all week. They use 5 pounds of papier-mâché. How many ounces of papier-mâché is that?
   80 oz
6. Some of the students display their papier-mâché fish on a window ledge in the classroom. Each fish is 4 inches long, and the window ledge is 1 yard long. How many fish can fit on the ledge?
   9 fish

McGraw-Hill School Division

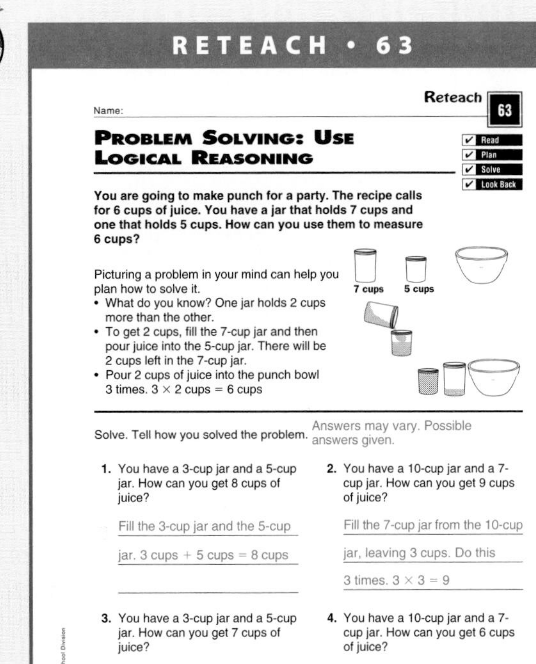

RETEACH • 63

Reteach 63

Name:

PROBLEM SOLVING: USE LOGICAL REASONING

Read / Plan / Solve / Look Back

You are going to make punch for a party. The recipe calls for 6 cups of juice. You have a jar that holds 7 cups and one that holds 5 cups. How can you use them to measure 6 cups?

Picturing a problem in your mind can help you plan how to solve it.

- What do you know? One jar holds 2 cups more than the other.
- To get 2 cups, fill the 7-cup jar and then pour juice into the 5-cup jar. There will be 2 cups left in the 7-cup jar.
- Pour 2 cups of juice into the punch bowl 3 times. 3×2 cups = 6 cups

Solve. Tell how you solved the problem. Answers may vary. Possible answers given.

1. You have a 3-cup jar and a 5-cup jar. How can you get 8 cups of juice?
   Fill the 3-cup jar and the 5-cup jar. 3 cups + 5 cups = 8 cups
2. You have a 10-cup jar and a 7-cup jar. How can you get 9 cups of juice?
   Fill the 7-cup jar from the 10-cup jar, leaving 3 cups. Do this 3 times. $3 \times 3 = 9$
3. You have a 3-cup jar and a 5-cup jar. How can you get 7 cups of juice?
   Fill the 3-cup jar from the 5-cup jar, leaving 2 cups. Add another filled 5-cup jar.
4. You have a 10-cup jar and a 7-cup jar. How can you get 6 cups of juice?
   Fill the 7-cup jar from the 10-cup jar, leaving 3 cups. Do this twice. $2 \times 3 = 6$

McGraw-Hill School Division

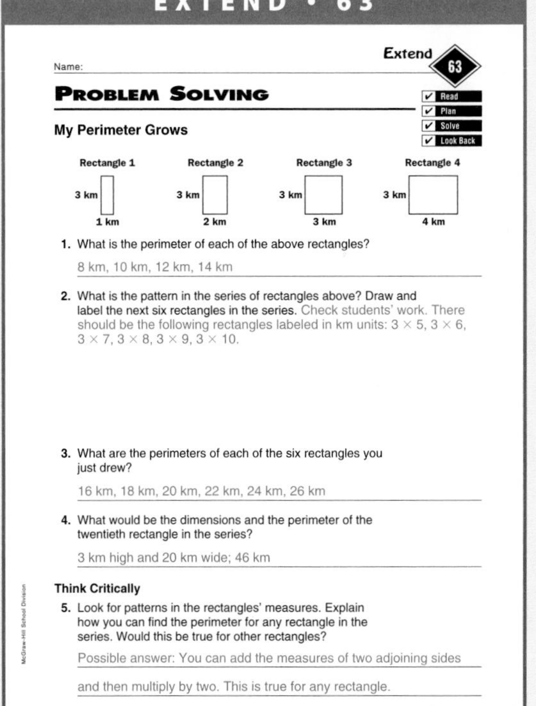

EXTEND • 63

Extend 63

Name:

PROBLEM SOLVING

Read / Plan / Solve / Look Back

My Perimeter Grows

1. What is the perimeter of each of the above rectangles?
   8 km, 10 km, 12 km, 14 km
2. What is the pattern in the series of rectangles above? Draw and label the next six rectangles in the series. Check students' work. There should be the following rectangles labeled in km units: 3×5, 3×6, 3×7, 3×8, 3×9, 3×10.
3. What are the perimeters of each of the six rectangles you just drew?
   16 km, 18 km, 20 km, 22 km, 24 km, 26 km
4. What would be the dimensions and the perimeter of the twentieth rectangle in the series?
   3 km high and 20 km wide; 46 km

Think Critically

5. Look for patterns in the rectangles' measures. Explain how you can find the perimeter for any rectangle in the series. Would this be true for other rectangles?
   Possible answer: You can add the measures of two adjoining sides and then multiply by two. This is true for any rectangle.

McGraw-Hill School Division

LESSON 7.7

Capacity and Mass in Metric Units

OBJECTIVE Estimate, compare, and order capacity and mass in metric units.

RESOURCE REMINDER
Math Center Cards 64
Practice 64, Reteach 64, Extend 64

SKILLS TRACE

GRADE 3	• Estimate, compare, and order capacity and mass in metric units. *(Chapter 9)*
GRADE 4	• Estimate, compare, and order capacity and mass in metric units.
GRADE 5	• Estimate, compare, order, and convert capacity and mass in metric units. *(Chapter 7)*

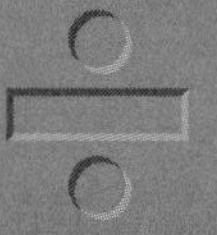

LESSON 7.7 RESOURCES

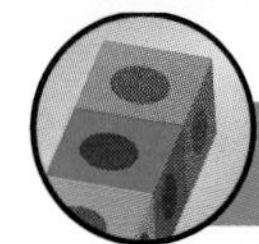

MANIPULATIVE WARM-UP

Whole Class — Visual/Spatial

OBJECTIVE Explore mass in grams and kilograms

Materials balance, box of 1,000 paper clips; 1 gram mass, 1 kg mass

► Use the balance to demonstrate to students that a 1 gram mass has about the same mass as a paper clip.

► Demonstrate to students that a kilogram mass has about the same mass as 1,000 paper clips.

► Ask students to bring up several items to determine if they have more or less mass than either the gram or kilogram. Students should tell you their guesses—greater than a unit or less than a unit—before the items are placed on the pan balance.

ESL APPROPRIATE

HEALTH CONNECTION

Whole Class — Logical/Analytical

OBJECTIVE Relate units of measure for capacity and mass to nutrition labels.

Materials nutrition labels from a variety of foods and beverages

► Write this nutrition information below on the board. Explain that it describes a pack of muffins, and that as written on this label, the amounts of nutrients in foods are often expressed in grams.

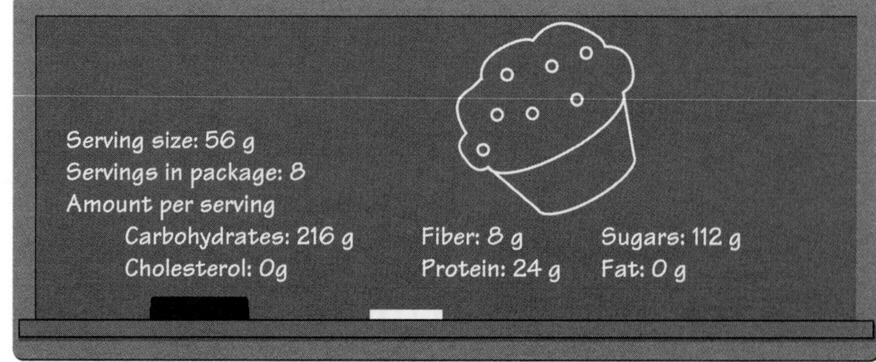

Serving size: 56 g
Servings in package: 8
Amount per serving
Carbohydrates: 216 g
Cholesterol: 0g
Fiber: 8 g
Protein: 24 g
Sugars: 112 g
Fat: 0 g

► Ask questions such as whether or not these muffins can be recommended to someone on a low-fat diet, and why. *[Yes, there are 0 g of fat.]*

► Invite students to compare this nutrition information to those from other foods and beverage labels you make available for the class.

Daily Review

PREVIOUS DAY QUICK REVIEW

Complete.

1. 5 lb = □ oz *[80]*
2. 8 pt = □ c *[16]*
3. □ qt = 20 pt *[10]*
4. □ gal = 64 pt *[8]*

FAST FACTS

1. 38 + 19 *[57]*
2. 17 + 25 *[42]*
3. 69 + 31 *[100]*
4. 116 + 58 *[174]*

Problem of the Day • 64

Ryan bought 1 gallon of spring water. He drank 6 cups. How many pints of spring water did he have left? *[5 pints or 10 cups]*

TECH LINK

Math Van

MATH VAN

Tools You may wish to use the Table and Graph tool for Data Point with this lesson.

MATH FORUM

Management Tip I find that students need practice with measuring tools before they develop the necessary experience to estimate capacity or mass. It also helps if students can work in pairs and discuss their observations with a partner.

Visit our Resource Village at http://www.mhschool.com to see more of the Math Forum.

MATH CENTER

Practice

OBJECTIVE Compare metric units of capacity.

Materials per group: 20 index cards

Students play a game involving matching metric units of mass and capacity.

PRACTICE ACTIVITY 64 — MATH CENTER, Small Group

Game • Are They the Same?

YOU NEED: 2 sets of 10 index cards

- Use the index cards to make the cards shown.
- Stack both sets of cards. Keep them separate.
- Mix up each set well. Put both decks facedown. The first player turns over the top card in each deck.
- If the two amounts are equivalent, that player gets 1 point and takes another turn. If the two amounts are not equivalent, the next player turns over 2 cards. Be sure to return the cards to the decks and mix up the decks after each turn.
- The student with the most points after three rounds wins.

1,000 mL	1 L
1,000 g	1 kg
5,000 mL	2 L
1 g	3,000 g
10 kg	25,000 mL

1 mL	1 L
1,000 mL	1 kg
1,000 g	5 L
2,000 mL	1,000 kg
3 kg	25 L

Grade Level 4 · McGraw-Hill School Division

Chapter 7, Lesson 7, pages 262–265 · Measurement

ESL APPROPRIATE

NCTM Standards
- ✓ Problem Solving
- Communication
- ✓ Reasoning
- ✓ Connections

Problem Solving

OBJECTIVE Solve word problems involving metric measures of mass.

Materials per student: Math Center Recording Sheet (TA 31 optional)

Students use what they know about metric mass equivalencies to solve a distribution problem. *[Answers may vary. Possible answer: The masses can be distributed so that each tray holds 14 kg: tray 1 will hold one 10 kg, one 2 kg, and two 1,000 g masses; tray 2 will hold one 10 kg, one 2,000 g, and two 1,000 g masses; tray 3 will hold one 10,000 g and one 4 kg; tray 4 will hold one 5 kg, one 5,000 g; and one 4 kg mass.]*

PROBLEM-SOLVING ACTIVITY 64 — MATH CENTER, On Your Own

Logical Reasoning • Fair Share

Can these four masses be arranged so that each tray holds the same amount? Explain.

10 kg · 10 kg · 10,000 g

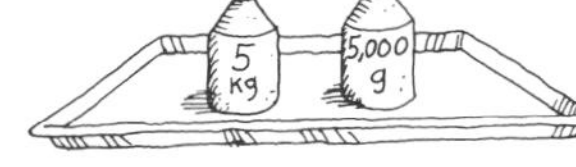

Grade Level 4 · McGraw-Hill School Division

Chapter 7, Lesson 7, pages 262–265 · Measurement

NCTM Standards
- ✓ Problem Solving
- Communication
- ✓ Reasoning
- ✓ Connections

Capacity and Mass in Metric Units

OBJECTIVE Estimate, compare, and order metric capacity and mass.

Materials plastic liter containers, plastic drinking glasses, and eyedroppers

Vocabulary capacity, gram, kilogram, liter, mass, milliliter

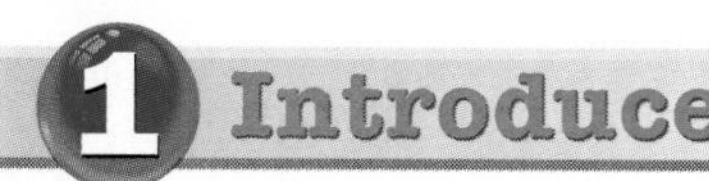

1 Introduce

Materials food and beverage containers with labels

To help students find a daily context for metric measures for capacity and mass, present containers for food and beverages that indicate capacity or mass in both customary and metric units or metric units only. Have students hold the containers to feel the mass and look at the size of the containers and note their capacities.

2 Teach *Whole Class*

LEARN Discuss the relationship between milliliters and liters and the examples of metric capacity on page 262. Then display the various containers you have collected. Have students make estimates such as the following:

- How much each container holds.
- How many glasses of water will fill the liter container.
- What part of a glass will 10 drops from an eyedropper fill.

Continue by having students use a metric measuring cup to find the capacities of some of the containers that are on display.

Discuss the two examples of renaming units. Have volunteers explain the procedure for renaming in each example.

Capacity and Mass in Metric Units

LEARN

Most scientists measure capacity with metric units.

Capacity is the amount a container can hold.

1 milliliter (mL)

1 liter (L)

5 liters (L)

1,000 **milliliters (mL)** = 1 **liter (L)**

How many 1-mL eyedroppers would it take to fill a 2-L bottle with water?

Think: 1 L = 1,000 mL

2 L = 2 × 1,000 mL
= 2,000 mL

It would take 2,000 eyedroppers.

There are 50,000 mL of water in an aquarium. How many liters is that?

Think: 1,000 mL = 1 L
50,000 mL = 50 L

The aquarium has 50 L of water.

▶ What do you think is the capacity of a drinking glass? a sink? Why?
Possible answer: 200–400 mL; 15–22 L; accept all reasonable explanations.

Check Out the Glossary
For vocabulary words
See page 544.

Meeting Individual Needs

Extra Support

Review using patterns to multiply numbers such as 2 × 1,000 and 15 × 1,000. Remind students to use the basic fact and count the number of zeros in the factor to determine the number of zeros in the product.

Language Support

Have students name as many liquids as they can to be sure they understand what a "liquid" is.

ESL APPROPRIATE

Ongoing Assessment

Interview Determine students' understanding of metric units of capacity and mass by asking:

- **What unit of measure would you use to show the amount of water a thimble can hold? the water you use to fill a bathtub?** *[milliliter, liter]*

Follow Up You may also wish to assign **Reteach 64** for students who need additional help.

Have students who understand metric units for capacity and mass try **Extend 64.**

logists measured the largest
therback turtle at 500 kilograms!

1,000 **grams (g)** = 1 **kilogram (kg)**

ss is the amount of matter that
kes up an object.

gram (g) each | 1 kilogram (kg) | Box Turtle 500 grams (g) | Leatherback Turtle 500 kilograms (kg)

e mass of a bicycle is 15 kg. How
any grams is that?

ink: 1 kg = 1,000 g

kg = 15 × 1,000 g
= 15,000 g

e bicycle's mass is 15,000 g.

A bluefin tuna's mass is 454,000 g.
Is it lighter or heavier than the
leatherback turtle?

Think: 1,000 g = 1 kg
454,000 g = 454 kg

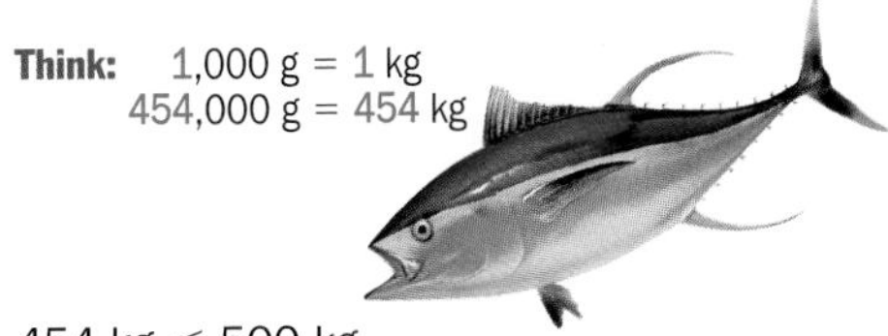

454 kg < 500 kg

The bluefin tuna is lighter than
the leatherback turtle.

heck for Understanding

rite the letter of the best estimate.

capacity of a soup can a
a. 350 mL **b.** 35 L **c.** 35 mL

2 mass of a television set c
a. 25 g **b.** 250 kg **c.** 25 kg

mplete.

3 L = ■ mL 3,000 **4** 7 kg = ■ g 7,000 **5** 2,000 g = ■ kg 2 **6** 10,000 mL = ■ L 10

ritical Thinking: Generalize **Explain your reasoning.**

Look at some 1-L containers. Are they all the same shape?
No; 1 L of liquid can fill many different sizes and shapes of containers.

What would you measure using grams? using kilograms?
Possible answer: light things; heavy things; it is more efficient to measure in the least number of units possible.

CHECK

Turn the page for Practice.

Discuss the examples of metric mass and the relationship between grams and kilograms presented on page 263. Make sure students understand that *matter* is "what a thing is made of" and *mass* expresses how much of something there is.

Discuss the two examples involving renaming units. Remind students that to find how many smaller units there are in a larger unit—such as how many grams in a 15 kilogram bicycle—you multiply:

15 kg = 15 × 1,000 = 15,000 g

To find out how many of a larger unit there are in a smaller unit—such as how many kilograms a 454,000 gram bluefin tuna weighs—you count by thousands or multiply:

454 kg × 1,000 = 454,000 g

There are 454 thousands in 454,000 or 454 kilograms

If you have a metric scale available, you may wish to weigh and compare the mass of a variety of classroom objects in grams and kilograms.

3 Close

Check for Understanding using items 1–8, page 263.

CRITICAL THINKING
For item 7, encourage students to use dimensional terms in their comparisons, such as *height, width,* and *depth.*

For item 8, encourage students to make a generalization based on examples given in the lesson and their own experiences.

Practice See pages 264–265.

PRACTICE

Materials have available: calculators

Options for assigning exercises:
A—Odd ex. 1–23; all ex. 25–30; **Cultural Connection**
B—Even ex. 2–24; all ex. 25–30; **Cultural Connection**

- For ex. 1–6, students may want to rename in the same unit, then order amounts from least to greatest to help them make the correct estimate.
- For ex. 11–24, students should multiply by 1,000 to rename to smaller units and count or multiply to rename to larger units.
- In ex. 26, students solve a problem using logical reasoning.
- For **Make It Right** (ex. 25), see Common Error below.

Algebra: Patterns In ex. 11–12, students apply their knowledge of patterns and renaming units of capacity and mass to complete the table.

Cultural Connection After discussing the origin and meaning of the word *carat,* have a volunteer explain how to complete ex. 2. Then let students complete the rest of the activity independently or in pairs.

You may wish to have students make up their own problems involving renaming carats using milligrams. You may also wish to let students look up the size of the world's largest diamond and describe the diamond's size using various units.

PRACTICE

Practice

Choose the more reasonable estimate. Explain your reasoning. Explanations may vary.

1. 300 kg or 300 g
300 g
2. 6 mL or 6 L
6 L
3. 2,000 kg or 20 kg
2,000 kg

4. 50 L or 500 mL
500 mL
5. 130 g or 13 g
130 g
6. 1 L or 10 mL
1 L

Choose the best unit. Write *milliliter, liter, gram,* or *kilogram.*

7. capacity of a milk jug liter
8. mass of a rowboat kilogram
9. mass of a clamshell gram
10. capacity of a straw milliliter

ALGEBRA: PATTERNS Copy and complete the table.

11.

Liter	1	2	■ 3	4	■ 5
Milliliter	1,000	■ 2,000	3,000	■ 4,000	■ 5,000

12.

Kilogram	■ 1	2	3	4	5
Gram	1,000	■ 2,000	■ 3,000	■ 4,000	5,000

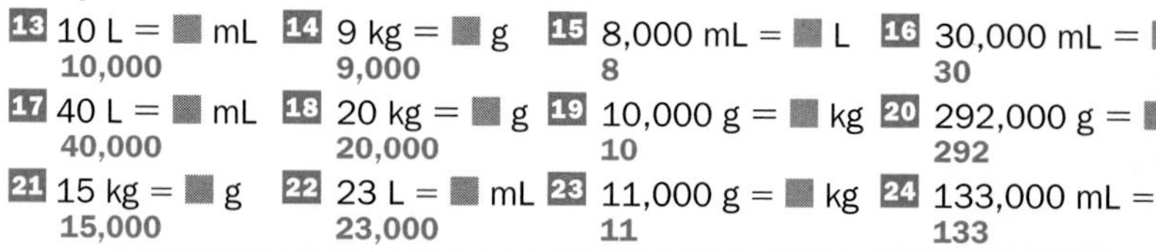

Complete.

13. 10 L = ■ mL 10,000
14. 9 kg = ■ g 9,000
15. 8,000 mL = ■ L 8
16. 30,000 mL = ■ 30
17. 40 L = ■ mL 40,000
18. 20 kg = ■ g 20,000
19. 10,000 g = ■ kg 10
20. 292,000 g = ■ 292
21. 15 kg = ■ g 15,000
22. 23 L = ■ mL 23,000
23. 11,000 g = ■ kg 11
24. 133,000 mL = ■ 133

Make It Right

25. Manny says that he drinks a 250-L glass of orange juice every morning. Write to him and explain why this is impossible.

Possible answer: 250 mL is a common capacity for a glass (about $8\frac{1}{2}$ fl oz), not 250

Meeting Individual Needs

Early Finishers

Have students brainstorm a list of items and appropriate units of measure for capacity or mass in their everyday experiences.

Inclusion

Students may remember the smaller and larger capacity units by their abbreviations. The uppercase "L" stands for liter, the larger unit. The smaller unit of milliliters—"mL"—has a smaller letter before the uppercase.

Common Error

As in **Make It Right,** students may confuse the sizes of different units of measure. Have students review the benchmark examples for each unit and the equivalency charts for metric units of capacity and mass.

Gifted And Talented

Have students solve the following problem:
On a balance, 3 spools balance 9 buttons. How many buttons will balance 5 spools? *[15 buttons]*

3. Agree, because there has to be less than 4 L in a gallon since a liter is a bit more than a quart.

MIXED APPLICATIONS

Problem Solving

Pencil & Paper | Calculator | Mental Math

INFOBIT
Kelp is a large type of seaweed. It can grow up to 60 cm a day. It can reach 60 m in length.

Rico knows that there are 4 qt in a gallon. He also knows that a liter is a little bit more than a quart. He says there are a little less than 4 L in a gallon. Explain why you agree or disagree with Rico. See above.

How many centimeters long can kelp grow? SEE INFOBIT. 6,000 cm

Could kelp grow to full length in 50 days? in 100 days? Show your work. SEE INFOBIT. No; yes; 100 × 60 cm = 6,000 cm = 60 m.

Data Point Choose ten objects in your classroom. Survey your classmates to see how they estimate the mass of each object. Show your results in a graph. Students may choose textbooks, erasers, notebooks, and so on.

30 Margaret has 800 cm of tape. She gives Alex 4 m for his project, she gives Carey 2 m for her project, and she keeps the rest for her project. How much does she keep? 2 m, or 200 cm

Cultural Connection

Measurement from the Middle East

In the Middle East, the first units of measure came from the plant world. The Arabic word *qirat* (KEE-raht) means the seed of the coral tree. Qirats were used for thousands of years to measure the weight of precious gems. Today, we say *carat*.

A carat is still the unit of measure by weight for jewels. In 1913, jewelers around the world agreed that a carat would be equivalent to 200 milligrams.

Find the weight in milligrams.

1 1 carat 200 mg
2 3 carats 600 mg
3 5 carats 1,000 mg
4 10 carats 2,000 mg
5 23 carats 4,600 mg

Extra Practice, page 511

Alternate Teaching Strategy

Materials balance, variety of classroom items, gram and kilogram weights

Have volunteers come to the front of the room and compare the masses of pairs of objects by placing the objects on a balance. Have students discuss and record the results. For example, the mass of a chalk eraser is greater than that of a piece of chalk.

Next, have volunteers place gram and kilogram weights on the scale and explore the relationship between them.

Finally, have students choose classroom items, estimate the mass of each, then use the balance to check the estimates.

ESL APPROPRIATE

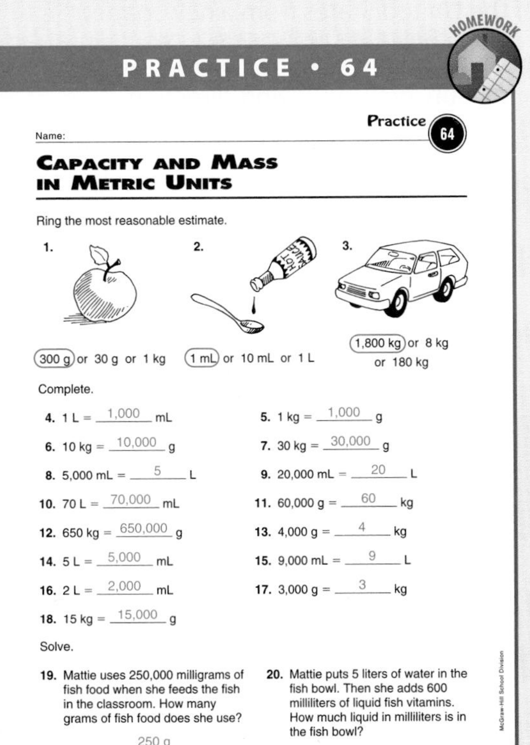

PRACTICE • 64

HOMEWORK

Practice 64

Name:

Capacity and Mass in Metric Units

Ring the most reasonable estimate.

1. (300 g) or 30 g or 1 kg
2. (1 mL) or 10 mL or 1 L
3. (1,800 kg) or 8 kg or 180 kg

Complete.

4. 1 L = 1,000 mL
5. 1 kg = 1,000 g
6. 10 kg = 10,000 g
7. 30 kg = 30,000 g
8. 5,000 mL = 5 L
9. 20,000 mL = 20 L
10. 70 L = 70,000 mL
11. 60,000 g = 60 kg
12. 650 kg = 650,000 g
13. 4,000 g = 4 kg
14. 5 L = 5,000 mL
15. 9,000 mL = 9 L
16. 2 L = 2,000 mL
17. 3,000 g = 3 kg
18. 15 kg = 15,000 g

Solve.

19. Mattie uses 250,000 milligrams of fish food when she feeds the fish in the classroom. How many grams of fish food does she use? 250 g

20. Mattie puts 5 liters of water in the fish bowl. Then she adds 600 milliliters of liquid fish vitamins. How much liquid in milliliters is in the fish bowl? 5,600 mL

McGraw-Hill School Division

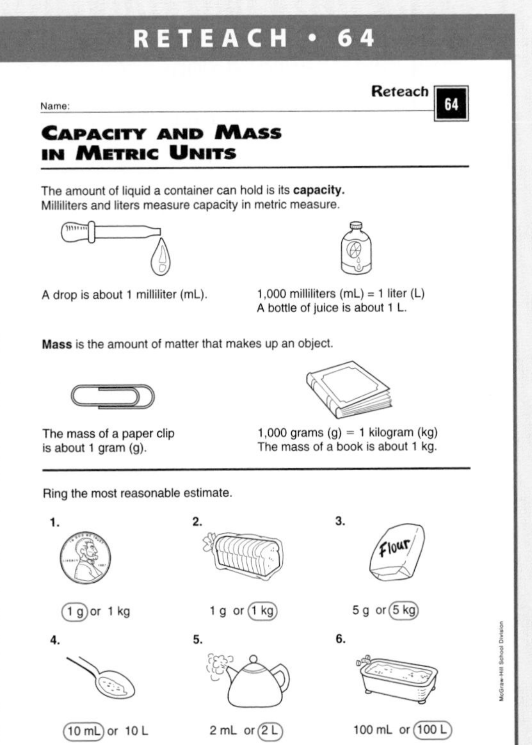

RETEACH • 64

Reteach 64

Name:

Capacity and Mass in Metric Units

The amount of liquid a container can hold is its **capacity**. Milliliters and liters measure capacity in metric measure.

A drop is about 1 milliliter (mL).

1,000 milliliters (mL) = 1 liter (L)
A bottle of juice is about 1 L.

Mass is the amount of matter that makes up an object.

The mass of a paper clip is about 1 gram (g).

1,000 grams (g) = 1 kilogram (kg)
The mass of a book is about 1 kg.

Ring the most reasonable estimate.

1. (1 g) or 1 kg
2. 1 g or (1 kg)
3. 5 g or (5 kg)
4. (10 mL) or 10 L
5. 2 mL or (2 L)
6. 100 mL or (100 L)

McGraw-Hill School Division

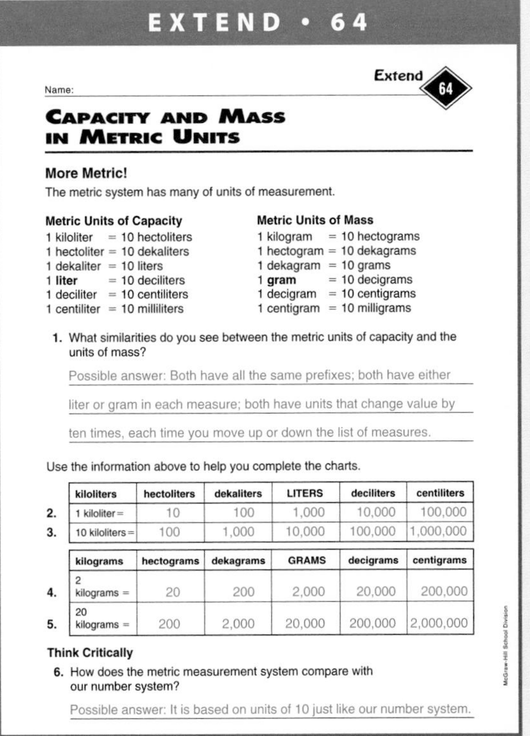

EXTEND • 64

Extend 64

Name:

Capacity and Mass in Metric Units

More Metric!

The metric system has many of units of measurement.

Metric Units of Capacity
1 kiloliter = 10 hectoliters
1 hectoliter = 10 dekaliters
1 dekaliter = 10 liters
1 **liter** = 10 deciliters
1 deciliter = 10 centiliters
1 centiliter = 10 milliliters

Metric Units of Mass
1 kilogram = 10 hectograms
1 hectogram = 10 dekagrams
1 dekagram = 10 grams
1 **gram** = 10 decigrams
1 decigram = 10 centigrams
1 centigram = 10 milligrams

1. What similarities do you see between the metric units of capacity and the units of mass?
Possible answer: Both have all the same prefixes; both have either liter or gram in each measure; both have units that change value by ten times, each time you move up or down the list of measures.

Use the information above to help you complete the charts.

	kiloliters	hectoliters	dekaliters	LITERS	deciliters	centiliters
2.	1 kiloliter =	10	100	1,000	10,000	100,000
3.	10 kiloliters =	100	1,000	10,000	100,000	1,000,000

	kilograms	hectograms	dekagrams	GRAMS	decigrams	centigrams
4.	2 kilograms =	20	200	2,000	20,000	200,000
5.	20 kilograms =	200	2,000	20,000	200,000	2,000,000

Think Critically

6. How does the metric measurement system compare with our number system?
Possible answer: It is based on units of 10 just like our number system.

McGraw-Hill School Division

Problem Solvers at Work

OBJECTIVE To solve problems and check for reasonableness.

RESOURCE REMINDER
Math Center Cards 65
Practice 65, Reteach 65, Extend 65

SKILLS TRACE	
GRADE 3	• Formulate and solve problems involving checking the reasonableness of answers for given situations involving Fahrenheit and Celsius thermometers. *(Chapter 9)*
GRADE 4	• Formulate and solve problems involving checking the reasonableness of answers for given situations involving Fahrenheit and Celsius thermometers.
GRADE 5	• Formulate and solve problems involving checking the reasonableness of answers for given situations. *(Chapter 7)*

LESSON 7.8 RESOURCES

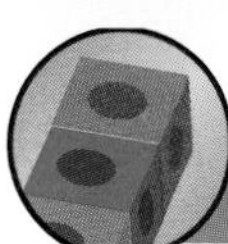

MANIPULATIVE WARM-UP

Cooperative Groups — **Social**

OBJECTIVE Check schedules for reasonableness.

Materials per group: analog clock (TA 12)

▶ Each student works independently to create a schedule of activities for a 3-hour period after school. Students may use the analog clock to help them.

▶ Students take turns sharing their schedules with the group, then asking questions about combinations of activities. For example:

- **Can I watch a movie for $2\frac{1}{2}$ hours, then play a basketball game to 100 points?** *[No, because 30 minutes is not a reasonable amount of time for a basketball game to 100 points.]*

▶ The group discusses whether each combination of activities is reasonable or unreasonable, using the clock to demonstrate their thinking.

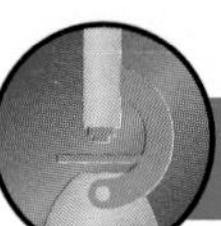

SCIENCE CONNECTION

Cooperative Groups — **Visual/Spatial**

OBJECTIVE Solve problems about temperature.

Materials copy of a weather map of the United States from a newspaper

▶ Have students examine a weather map and discuss how the map shows weather conditions such as rain, clouds, sunshine, and wind direction.

▶ Each group member creates a question that involves an activity that could be reasonable or unreasonable, depending on the temperature readings on the map. For example:

- **Could you build a snow sculpture in Boise, Idaho, today? How do you know?**

▶ Students take turns asking questions.

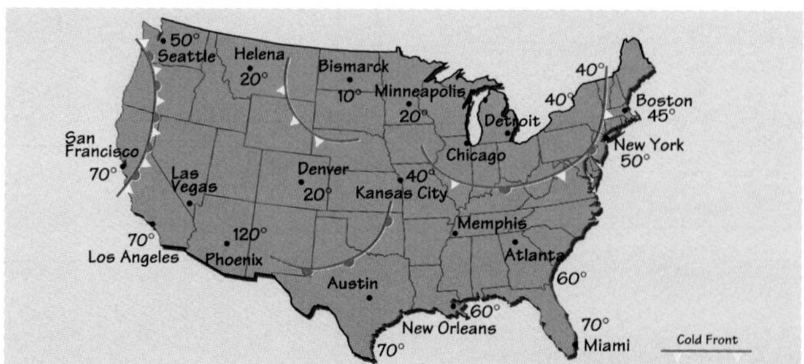

Daily Review

PREVIOUS DAY QUICK REVIEW

Complete.

1. 2 ☐ = 2,000 g *[kg]*
2. 4,000 mL = ☐ L *[4]*
3. 10 kg = ☐ g *[10,000]*
4. 6 L = ☐ mL *[6,000]*

FAST FACTS

1. (16 + 5) + 4 *[25]*
2. 27 + (52 + 13) *[92]*
3. 57 + (0 + 4 + 86) *[147]*
4. 38 + (28 + 62) *[128]*

Problem of the Day • 65

Tania's ruler is 10 cm long. She uses it to measure a 3 m long piece of string. How many times must she place the ruler along the string? *[30]*

TECH LINK

Math Van

MATH VAN

Aid You may wish to use the Electronic Teacher Aid with this lesson.

MATH FORUM

Cultural Diversity Have students from other regions compare the climates in those regions to the local one. Have students talk about how seasonal activities are different in those regions.

Visit our Resource Village at http://www.mhschool.com to see more of the Math Forum.

MATH CENTER

Practice

OBJECTIVE Determine reasonableness of measurement statements.

Materials per student: Math Center Recording Sheet (TA 31 optional)

Students use their knowledge of the metric system to decide what is reasonable. *[Possible answers: **1.** 4,500 gm is around 10 lb. It is reasonable; **2.** 5 km in 5 sec is unreasonable; **3.** 2,000 mL a day is about eight 8-ounce glasses. It is reasonable; **4.** 220 cm is about 7 ft 2 in. It is a reasonable height.]*

MATH CENTER
On Your Own

PRACTICE ACTIVITY 65

Logical Reasoning • How Much?

Decide if each possibility is reasonable. Support your answer with an explanation and examples. Draw pictures when it helps.

1. A teenager has declared to the world that she can lift 4,500 g with just one hand.
2. Another person has announced that he is the first one to run 5 km in 5 seconds.
3. A doctor has asked his patients to drink 2,000 mL of liquids daily.
4. A professional basketball player is around 220 cm tall.

- Make up some reasonable/unreasonable claims of your own. Invite your classmates to evaluate them.

Zorba, one of the world's largest dogs, weighs 157 kg.
—*The Guinness Book of Records*

McGraw-Hill School Division Grade Level 4

Chapter 7, Lesson 8, pages 266–269 Problem Solving

NCTM Standards

✓ Problem Solving
✓ Communication
✓ Reasoning
✓ Connections

Problem Solving

OBJECTIVE Make decisions about a class trip.

Materials per student: Math Center Recording Sheet (TA 31 optional)

Students work in pairs to make suggestions about taking a class trip. They consider cost and safety, as well as basic needs. *[Answers may vary. Check students' work.]*

MATH CENTER
On Your Own

PROBLEM-SOLVING ACTIVITY 65

Making Decisions • A Reasonable Trip

Your class is planning a weekend camping trip. You must do all the planning and make all the arrangements. Many questions need to be answered if this trip is going to happen! Some of the questions are:

- How will you get there?
- How much will transportation cost?
- What kind of equipment do you need?
- What food will you take?
- How many adults should come?

Make a list of all the things that need to be worked out before you can take this trip. Some questions need to have exact answers, while others can be estimates. Be sure your suggestions are reasonable.

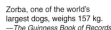

McGraw-Hill School Division Grade Level 4

Chapter 7, Lesson 8, pages 266–269 Problem Solving

NCTM Standards

✓ Problem Solving
Communication
Reasoning
✓ Connections

Problem Solvers at Work

OBJECTIVE To solve problems and check for reasonableness.

Materials have available: Celsius and Fahrenheit thermometers, computer drawing program

Resources drawing program, or Math Van Tools

Vocabulary degrees Celsius, degrees Fahrenheit, temperature

Let students examine Celsius and Fahrenheit thermometers. Have them locate various temperatures. Then ask:

- **What range of temperatures is your favorite? Why?**
- **How does the temperature where you live affect what activities you enjoy?**
- **How would the activities you participate in change if you moved to a different place with very different temperatures?**

Cooperative Groups

PART 1 CHECK FOR REASONABLENESS

LEARN Encourage students to use the picture of the thermometers on page 266 to help them estimate the temperatures outside and in the classroom in both degrees Fahrenheit and Celsius.

Students may be interested to learn that the Celsius thermometer was invented by A. Celsius (1701–1744), a Swedish astronomer and inventor. The Fahrenheit thermometer was invented by D. G. Fahrenheit (1686–1736), a German physicist.

Work Together For items 1–3, partners may first discuss whether or not the statement makes sense. Suggest they look at the thermometers on page 266 to check the statements for reasonableness.

For items 4 and 5, suggest pairs of students take turns guessing answers. The student who is not answering may use the thermometers on page 266 to check the answer for reasonableness.

Problem-Solvers at Work

Read · Plan · Solve · Look Back

Part 1 Checking for Reasonableness

LEARN

Did you ever check a thermometer before deciding what to wear? Suppose you are going to the ocean for the day. The air temperature is 70°F. The water temperature is 55°F.

°C: 110, 100, 90, 80, 70, 60, 50, 40, 30, 20, 10, 0, -10, -20, -30
°F: 230, 210, 190, 170, 150, 130, 110, 90, 70, 50, 30, 10, -10
water boils
human body temperature
room temperature
water freezes

Temperature can be measured in **degrees Fahrenheit (°F)** or in **degrees Celsius (°C).**

Work Together

For problems 1–3, decide if the statement is reasonable or unreasonable. Explain your answer.

1. You wear shorts and a sweatshirt while collecting seashells. **Reasonable; the air temperature is warm but not hot.**
2. You go into the ocean for a swim. **Unreasonable; the water temperature is too cold.**
3. You say that the water temperature is 13°C. If it rises about 8 degrees, you will go swimming. **Reasonable; 13°C + 8°C = 21°C, which is warm enough for swimming.**
4. **What if** the air temperature is 18°C. What should you wear? **Possible answers: jacket, sweater, sweatshirt**
5. **Make a decision** A thermometer reads ⁻6°C. What outdoor activities would it be reasonable for you to do? **Possible answer: ice skating, playing in the snow**

266 Lesson 7.8

Meeting Individual Needs

Extra Support

Some students may need to be alerted that the scales of the thermometers are different. The Celsius thermometer is marked in 1 degree intervals, while the Fahrenheit thermometer is marked in 2 degree intervals.

Inclusion

Some students may need help in reading the shorter lines of the scales of the thermometers on page 266.

Ongoing Assessment

Anecdotal Report Make notes on whether students make reasonable or unreasonable statements about temperatures both Fahrenheit and Celsius. In addition, note whether or not students use sources like the thermometers on page 266 to check their statements and answers for reasonableness.

Follow Up Assign **Reteach 65** for students who need additional practice.

For students who understand the difference between reasonable and unreasonable temperatures, assign **Extend 65.**

Part 2 Write and Share Problems

Lisa wrote a problem about a book.

A book is 8 in. wide and 12 in. long. It weighs 48 lb. Which of these measurements is not reasonable? What should it be?

CHECK

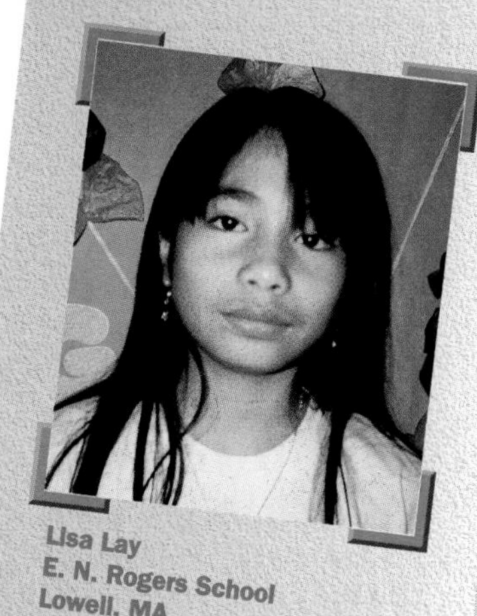

Lisa Lay
E. N. Rogers School
Lowell, MA

6 Solve Lisa's problem.
48 lb; possible answer: 48 oz

7 **Write a problem** of your own about one of the items on the table. Or choose any other item you wish. Include as many measurements as you can. Make one of the measurements unreasonable.
For problems 7–10, see Teacher's Edition

8 Trade problems. Solve at least three problems written by your classmates.

9  **Use Diagrams** Describe one of the items on the table. Challenge another student to draw a diagram from your description.

10 What was the most interesting problem you solved? Why?

Check Out the Glossary
For vocabulary words
See page 544.

Turn the page for Practice Strategies.

Part 2 Write and Share Problems

Check Invite students to explain how they solved the problem. Accept all reasonable responses.

Item 7 provides an opportunity for students to write a problem based on the items pictured on page 267. Students should be able to draw on prior knowledge and experience to estimate the approximate measurement of the items.

For items 8 and 10, encourage students to discuss the problems they solved and their reasons why a problem was most interesting.

 **Use Diagrams** For item 9, have students review the diagrams they drew from their partners' descriptions. Then have them revise their descriptions to more accurately reflect the object.

Encourage students' creativity by suggesting a variety of contexts and subjects that can be used in problems.

3 Close

Have students discuss how they wrote their own problems. Have them compare the methods they used to determine reasonableness or unreasonableness in other students' problems.

Practice See pages 268–269.

Part 3 Practice

Materials have available: calculators; computer drawing program (optional)

Students have the option of choosing any five problems from ex. 1–8 and any two problems from ex. 9–12. They may choose to do more problems if they wish. Have students describe how they made their choices.

- For ex. 4 and 10, drawing a picture and using a model are good strategies to use.
- For ex. 7, students may want to use an analog clock as a model to figure out elapsed time.
- For ex. 2, working backward is a good strategy to use.

At the Computer If computers are not available, students may use paper and pencil and calculators to do ex. 12.

Math Van Have students use the Drawing tool to make the squares and find any patterns. A project electronic teacher aid has been provided.

1. Possible answer: afternoon—light jackets; night—heavy jackets, gloves
4. If he wraps the ribbon around both the length and width, he will need at least 48 in. plus several inches for the bow.

Part 3 Practice Strategies

PRACTICE

Menu Explanations may vary.
Choose five problems and solve them. Explain your methods.

1 Robert and his family visited New York. The high temperature for their afternoon tour was 14°C. At night, the temperature dropped 20 degrees. How do you think they dressed in the afternoon? at night? **See above.**

2 Karla has scored the most goals on her team. She has scored 4 times as many as Barb, who has scored 2 more than Tanya. Tanya has scored 2 goals for her team. How many goals has Karla scored? **16 goals**

3 Helga claims to have a pet snake 3 m long. She says the snake is not as long as she is tall. Is this reasonable? Why or why not? What length might her snake be? **No; 3 m is about 3 yd, or 9 ft; it might be about 3 ft long.**

4 Glenn needs ribbon to wrap around the book he bought for a birthday present. The book measures 12 in. by 10 in. and is 1 in. thick. How much ribbon will he need? **See above.**

5 May recorded Tuesday's high and low temperatures as 100°F and 67°F. Estimate what these temperatures are in degrees Celsius. **Possible answer: 40°C and 20°C**

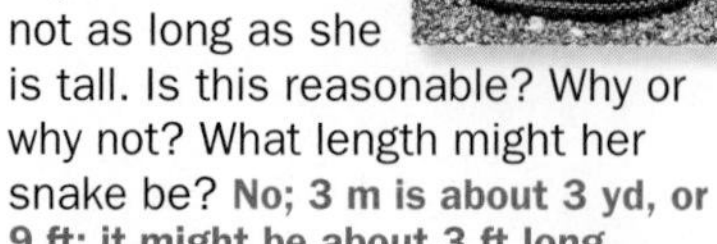

6 A bullfrog is 20 cm long. It makes a leap that is 15 times its body length. Is the leap greater than or less than 2 m? **greater than 2 m ($15 \times 20 =$ 300 cm, 300 cm > 2 m)**

7 Brenda ate breakfast and got dressed in 30 minutes. She then watched television for 1 hour 15 minutes, read a book for 35 minutes, and worked on the computer for 40 minutes. She then played outside with her friends. If she started at 7:30 A.M., what time did she go outside? **10:30 A.M.**

8 Brandy begins by doing 5 push-ups a day. She plans to increase the number of push-ups she does by 3 each day. How many days will it take her to reach her goal—50 push-ups a day? **What if** she starts out doing only 3 the first day. How many more days would it take? **16 days; 1 more day**

Meeting Individual Needs

Early Finishers

Invite students to do more than the required number of problems on pages 268–269.

Common Error

In item 4, students may forget to include all the measures. Instead of calculating the amount of ribbon needed to go entirely around the book, students may omit the thickness and use only length and width.

Language Support

Before assigning Menu items, pair students acquiring English with English-speaking students to ensure that students understand what the word problems are about.

ESL APPROPRIATE

Gifted And Talented

Students take turns stating a temperature in Fahrenheit or Celsius and naming an activity appropriate for that temperature. Each player has 30 seconds to give a correct response and receives 1 point.

Students may find differences between average depths, between average and deepest depths, between different ocean depths, and so on.

oose two problems and solve them. Explanations may vary.
plain your methods.

Use the table. Identify and find at least three differences between depths. See above.

World's Three Largest Oceans			
)cean	Rank	Average Depth	Deepest Point
'acific	1	4,028 m	11,500 m
‹tlantic	2	3,688 m	9,200 m
ndian	3	4,284 m	7,450 m

Spatial reasoning Jack built a large cube out of centimeter cubes. Each side is 4 cubes long. How many cubes did Jack use in all? What is the perimeter of each side of the large cube? 64 cubes; 16 cm

Write a problem that requires changing units of measure to find the answer. Solve your problem. Then give it to a classmate to solve. Compare your answers and the methods you used. How are they similar? How are they different? Students should compare problems and solutions.

At the Computer You can make squares out of smaller squares as shown on the right. Use a drawing program to construct squares that are 4 by 4, 5 by 5, 6 by 6, and 7 by 7. Make a table like the one below. Write about any patterns you see. See below.

Number of Squares	1	4	9
Dimensions	1 by 1	2 by 2	3 by 3
Perimeter	4	8	12

:. Possible answer: As the dimensions of the squares increase by 1, the perimeter increases by 4.

tra Practice, page 511

Alternate Teaching Strategy

Display a copy of the thermometers from page 266. Have students examine the thermometers, noting the temperature of boiling water, normal body temperature, room temperature, and the point at which water freezes.

Have students draw scenes of seasonal activities, such as raking leaves, swimming, or sledding. Students label each scene with a temperature in degrees Fahrenheit or degrees Celsius.

Have students display their pictures. Then have the class as a whole decide whether the temperature on each picture is reasonable. If it is not, students discuss and suggest a reasonable temperature.

PRACTICE • 65

HOMEWORK

Practice 65

Name:

PROBLEM SOLVING: CHECK FOR REASONABLENESS

✔ Read ✔ Plan ✔ Solve ✔ Look Back

Solve.

1. There is ice in your yard and snow is falling. The wind shakes the trees. Which temperature is reasonable, 75°F or 20°F? 20°F
2. You wear shorts and a T-shirt and sit in your yard in the shade of a tree. You want a cool breeze. Which temperature is reasonable, 5°C or 22°C? 22°C
3. You are boiling water to make hot chocolate. What is the temperature of the boiling water, 100°F or 212°F? 212°F
4. You are raking leaves in the fall wearing jeans and a sweatshirt. Which temperature is reasonable, 13°C or 25°C? 13°C
5. You want to buy a garden hose. You estimate that you will need a 2-foot-long hose. Is that reasonable? Why or why not? No; too short a length
6. You look at your flower garden. You think it must be 2 kilometers long. Is that reasonable? Why or why not? What might be more reasonable? No; 2 m or 2 yd

Solve using any method.

7. During hot weather, you water your flower garden with 10 gallons of water a day. How many gallons would you use in 3 weeks? Which operation did you use to solve this problem? 210 gal; multiplication
8. Your flower garden is 20 feet long and 15 feet wide. It also has a fence with a gate on each side. What is the perimeter of your flower garden? What information is not needed to find the perimeter? 70 ft; fences with gates

McGraw-Hill School Division

RETEACH • 65

Reteach 65

Name:

PROBLEM SOLVING: CHECK FOR REASONABLENESS

✔ Read ✔ Plan ✔ Solve ✔ Look Back

To measure air temperature, you can use either a **Celsius** or **Fahrenheit** thermometer.

At 30°C, it makes sense to wear shorts and go swimming.

At 0°C, it makes sense to wear a heavy jacket.

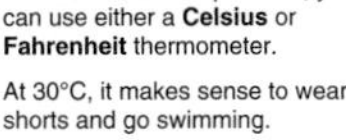
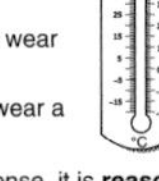
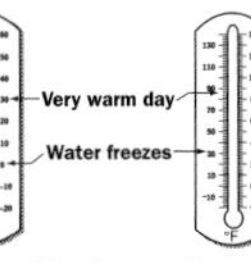

When something makes sense, it is **reasonable.** As you solve problems and answer questions, check to see if your answer makes sense, or is reasonable.

Solve. Use the thermometer above. Possible answers given.

1. Hyung reads the thermometer that shows 32°F. He puts on a jacket, scarf, cap, and gloves. Is that reasonable? Why or why not? Yes, the air is cold.
2. Marina reads the thermometer that shows 30°C. She decides to go to the beach. Is that reasonable? Why or why not? Yes, it's a warm day.
3. Kelly reads 42°C on the thermometer. She looks out the window at the snowstorm. Is the temperature reasonable? If not, what would be reasonable? No; 0°C.
4. Martin and Dorn jog for a half mile. Then they decide that 34°F is too hot to be running. Next time, they will wait for a cooler day. Is this reasonable? No, 34°F is a cold day.
5. Amy is going to make 2 sandwiches each for the 28 people in her scout troop. She estimates that she will need to make 90 sandwiches. Is this reasonable? Why or why not? No, 30 × 2 = 60 sandwiches.
6. Tanisha decides to save for a new bike. If she saves about 15¢ each day for 35 weeks, she will have between \$30 and \$40. Is this reasonable? Why or why not? Yes, 15¢ each day is about \$1 per week.

McGraw-Hill School Division

EXTEND • 65

Extend 65

Name:

PROBLEM SOLVING

✔ Read ✔ Plan ✔ Solve ✔ Look Back

They're Full of Beans!

You need: calculator

Alan has an enormous jelly bean collection. He keeps it in an old bathtub he found in a junkyard. The tub holds 100,555 jelly beans.

Alan also keeps jelly beans in these containers:

2,111 jelly beans 1,000 jelly beans 167 jelly beans

2,500 jelly beans 39 jelly beans 14,800 jelly beans

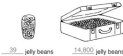

Work with a partner. Using the clues below, find out how many jelly beans each container holds.

- If Alan used jelly beans from the bathtub to fill the bucket, there would be 98,444 jelly beans left in the tub.
- He fills the jug with jelly beans from the bucket, and there are (370 × 3) + 1 jelly beans left in the bucket.
- The coffee can holds 1,944 fewer jelly beans than the bucket.
- Alan uses 6 suitcases, 4 shoeboxes, and 45 glasses to fill the bathtub completely.
- The shoebox holds 389 more jelly beans than the bucket.
- Alan fills the glass with jelly beans from the coffee can and there are 32 × 4 jelly beans left in the can.

McGraw-Hill School Division

CHAPTER REVIEW

PURPOSE Review and assess the concepts, skills, and strategies that students have learned in the chapter.

Materials per student: calculator (optional)

Chapter Objectives

7A Estimate and measure length in customary or metric units

7B Estimate and measure weight, mass, or capacity in customary or metric units

7C Convert between customary or metric units of length, weight, mass, or capacity

7D Find perimeter

7E Solve problems, including those that involve measurement and logical reasoning

Using the Chapter Review

The **Chapter Review** can be used as a review, practice test, or chapter test.

Think Critically Students' explanations for ex. 28 will indicate whether or not they understand how to find the perimeter of regular shapes, including rectangles. By knowing the length and width, students can multiply each by 2 and add the products to find out the perimeter of the entire figure.

Language and Mathematics

Complete the sentence. Use a word in the chart. (pages 242–265)

1 The ■ of an aquarium is usually found in gallons. **capacity**

2 By knowing the length and width of a rectangle, you can find its ■. **perimeter**

3 A kilometer is a ■ unit of measure. **metric**

4 The ■ of a car would be measured in kilograms. **mass**

Vocabulary
metric
customary
perimeter
length
capacity
weight
mass

Concepts and Skills

Write the letter of the best estimate. (pages 242, 244, 246, 256, 262)

	a.	b.	c.
5 width of a street **b**	18 in.	18 ft	18 mi
6 length of a mouse **a**	4 in.	4 ft	4 yd
7 height of a flagpole **b**	8 dm	8 m	8 cm
8 length of an envelope **a**	25 cm	25 km	25 m
9 capacity of a teacup **c**	10 pt	10 qt	1 c
10 capacity of a glue bottle **c**	120 L	12 L	120 m
11 weight of a kitten **c**	30 lb	3 oz	3 lb
12 mass of a city telephone book **c**	10 g	100 g	1 kg

Complete. (pages 242, 244, 246, 256, 262)

13 4 qt = ■ c **16**
14 3 gal = ■ pt **24**
15 4 lb = ■ oz **64**
16 6 ft = ■ in. **72**
17 2 yd = ■ in. **72**
18 108 in. = ■ yd **3**
19 5 L = ■ mL **5,000**
20 4 cm = ■ m **40**
21 7 km = ■ m **7,000**
22 25 dm = ■ cm **250**
23 6,000 g = ■ kg **6**
24 10 kg = ■ g **10,000**

Reinforcement and Remediation

CHAPTER OBJECTIVES	CHAPTER REVIEW ITEMS	STUDENT BOOK PAGES	TEACHER'S EDITION PAGES			TEACHER RESOURCES
		Lessons	Midchapter Review	Activities	Alternate Teaching Strategy	Reteach
7A	3, 5–8, 26	242–243, 246–249	252	241A, 243A	243, 249	58, 60
7B	9–12	256–259, 262–265		255A, 261A	259, 265	62
7C	13–24	244–245	252	243A	245	59
7D	2, 28	250–251	252	249A	251	61
7E	25–27, 29–33	260–261 266–269		259A, 265A	261, 269	63, 65

rite *reasonable* or *unreasonable* for the statement. If nreasonable, write the unit of measure that would make reasonable. (page 266)

Eli wore his bathing suit when it was 32°F. **unreasonable; degrees Celsius**

Lynda ran 2 mi after school. **reasonable**

Danica's little brother weighs 25 oz. **unreasonable; pounds**

hink critically. (page 250)

Generalize. Is this statement *true* or *false*? Explain why.
The perimeter of a rectangle can always be found if you know the length and the width. **True; perimeter is equal to twice the length plus twice the width.**

MIXED APPLICATIONS
Problem Solving

Pencil & Paper | Calculator | Mental Math

(pages 260, 266)

se the table for problems 29–31.

Which sea monster is about half as long as a man is tall? **American lobster**

How many sea monsters (and which ones) could you line up to equal the length of your classroom? **Possible answer: 15 starfish**

What in your school would compare to the length of the loggerhead sponge? the giant earthworm? the giant squid? **See below.**

Sea Monsters	
Jellyfish	120 ft
Giant squid	60 ft
Giant earthworm	22 ft
Starfish	5 ft
Loggerhead sponge	4 ft
American lobster	3 ft

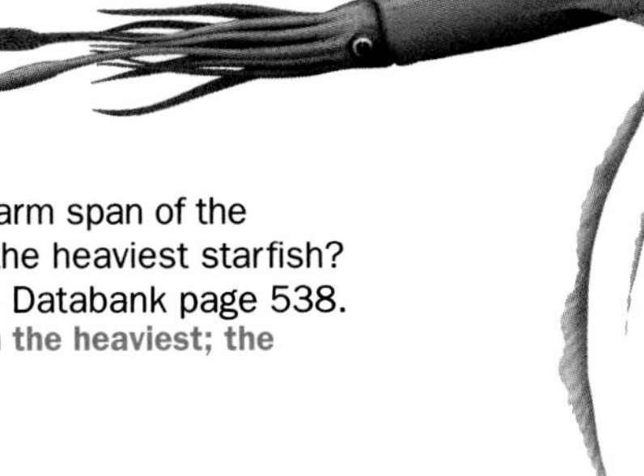

What is the easiest way to fill a 1-gal pitcher using only a 3-gal container and a 4-gal container? **See below.**

Data Point How much longer is the arm span of the largest starfish than the arm span of the heaviest starfish? What is their difference in weight? See Databank page 538. **The largest starfish is 29 in. longer than the heaviest; the difference in weight is 12 lb 13 oz.**

1. **Possible answers: length of a bookshelf; length of the classroom; length of hallway**
2. **Fill the 4-gal container and pour into the 3-gal container, then pour what is left in the 4-gal container into the pitcher.**

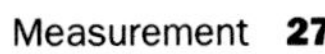

CHAPTER TEST

PURPOSE Assess the concepts, skills, and strategies students have learned in this chapter.

Chapter Objectives

- **7A** Estimate and measure length in customary or metric units
- **7B** Estimate and measure weight, mass, or capacity in customary or metric units
- **7C** Convert between customary or metric units of length, weight, mass or capacity
- **7D** Find perimeter
- **7E** Solve problems, including those that involve measurement and logical reasoning

Using the Chapter Test

The **Chapter Test** can be used as a practice test, a chapter test, or as an additional review. The **Performance Assessment** on Student Book page 273 provides an alternate means of assessing students' understanding of measurement in customary and metric units.

Assessment Resources

Test Masters

The Testing Program Blackline Masters provide three forms of the Chapter Test to assess students' understanding of the chapter concepts, skills, and strategies. Form C uses a free-response format. Forms A and B use a multiple-choice format.

Computer Test Generator

The Computer Test Generator supplies abundant multiple-choice and free-response test items, which you may use to generate tests and practice worksheets tailored to the needs of your class.

Teacher's Assessment Resources

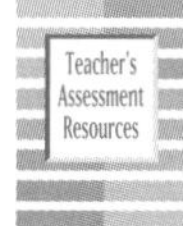

Teacher's Assessment Resources provides resources for alternate assessment. It includes guidelines for Building a Portfolio, page 6, and the Holistic Scoring Guide, page 27.

chapter test

Measure the line to the nearest inch.

1. ——— 1 in.
2. ——— 2 in.
3. ——— 3 in.
4. ——— 1 in.

Write the letter of the best estimate.

5. width of a window b
   a. 24 ft **b.** 24 in. **c.** 24 yd
6. length of a pen c
   a. 12 m **b.** 12 km **c.** 12 cm
7. mass of a paper clip a
   a. 1 g **b.** 10 g **c.** 1 kg
8. capacity of a soup bowl a
   a. 1 pt **b.** 1 gal **c.** 1 fl oz
9. capacity of a juice bottle b
   a. 2 mL **b.** 2 L **c.** 20 mL
10. weight of a textbook c
    a. 2 oz **b.** 20 lb **c.** 2 lb

Complete.

11. 6 qt = ■ c 24
12. 15 dm = ■ cm 150
13. 4 kg = ■ g 4,000
14. 6 yd = ■ 18
15. 5,000 m = ■ km 5
16. 4 yd = ■ in. 144
17. 44 qt = ■ gal 11
18. 2 L = ■ r 2,000

Find the perimeter.

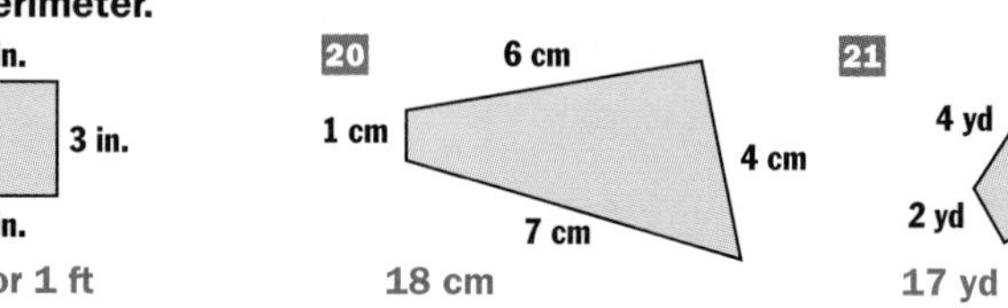

19. 12 in., or 1 ft
20. 18 cm
21. 17 yd

Solve.

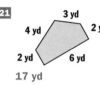

22. A bicycle is 5 ft 4 in. long and 3 ft 9 in. high. Will it fit in a shipping box that is 66 in. long and $44\frac{1}{2}$ in. high? Why or why not? **No; the box is too short—it needs to be at least 45 in. high.**
23. Mel walks 75 ft in 1 min. His brother walks 21 yd in 2 min. If they start together, how far from Mel will his brother be in 6 min? **87 yd**
24. The art teacher wants to put a border around a rectangular bulletin board that is 7 ft long and 5 ft wide. How many yards of border will he need? **8 yd**
25. José is twice as old as Alberto. In 2 years, Alberto will be half Corey's age at that time. Corey is now 14. How old are José and Alberto? **José—12, Alberto—**

Test Correlation		
CHAPTER OBJECTIVES	TEST ITEMS	TEXT PAGES
7A	1–4	242–243, 246–249
7B	5–10	256–259, 262–265
7C	11–18	244–245
7D	19–21	250–251
7E	22–25	260–261, 266–269

Teacher's Assessment Resources for samples of student k. Check students' work.

hat Did You Learn?

three objects that can be found in your school. Choose ects whose length, mass, weight, or capacity you can asure.

Describe the different ways that each object can be measured.

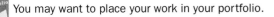

For each object:
a. describe the most important measurement and explain why you chose it.
b. estimate the measurement.
c. explain how you arrived at your estimate and decided which unit to use.
d. find the actual measurement.

A Good Answer
- explains the reasoning involved in choosing how an object should be measured
- gives reasonable estimates and accurate measurements

You may want to place your work in your portfolio.

What Do You Think?

See Teacher's Edition.

1 Do you understand which tools and units to use when you measure? If not, what do you find most difficult?

2 What do you think is the most important step when measuring an object? Why?
- Finding an estimate first.
- Deciding what measurement to take.
- Choosing an appropriate unit and tool.
- Other. Explain.

Reviewing A Portfolio

Have students review their portfolios. Consider including these items:
- Finished work on the Chapter Project (p. 239F) or **Investigation** (pp. 254–255).
- Selected math journal entries, pp. 241, 252.
- Finished work on the nonroutine problem in **What Do You Know?** (p. 241) and problems from the Menu (pp. 268–269).
- Each student's self-selected "best piece" from work completed during the chapter. Have each student attach a note explaining why he or she chose that piece.
- Any work you or an individual student wishes to keep for future reference.

You may take this opportunity to conduct conferences with students. The Portfolio Analysis Form can help you report students' progress. See Teacher's Assessment Resources, p. 33.

PURPOSE Review and assess the concepts, skills, and strategies learned in this chapter.

Materials have available: rulers, balance scales, kitchen scales, measuring cups, quart containers, beads of popcorn

Using the Performance Assessment

Have students read the problems and restate them in their own words. Make sure they understand they are to work with 3 objects and that they are to estimate before they measure each one.

Point out the section on the student page headed "A Good Answer." Make sure students understand that you will use these points to evaluate their answers.

Evaluating Student Work

As you read students' papers, look for the following:
- *Does the student describe the different ways that the objects could be measured and explain why he or she chose one of those measurements?*
- *Does the student make reasonable estimates?*
- *Can the student use measurement tools?*
- *Does the student make accurate measurements?*

The Holistic Scoring Guide and annotated samples of students' work can be used to assess this task. See pages 27–32 and 37–72 in Teacher's Assessment Resources.

Using the Self-Assessment

What Do You Think? Assure students that there are no right or wrong answers. Tell them the emphasis is on what they think and how they justify their answers.

Follow-Up Interviews

These questions can be used to gain insight into students' thinking:
- **How else could the first object be measured? the second? the third?**
- **How did you choose which measurement to use for your first object? your second? your third?**
- **How did you make your estimates?**
- **How did you choose a unit to use for each measurement?**
- **How did you make the actual measurement?**

OBJECTIVE Use information about the speed of sound to calculate ocean depths.

Science

Cultural Connection Read the **Cultural Note.** Tell students that the ability of bats to navigate by sound is called *echolocation.*

Read the remainder of page 274 with the class. Discuss the advantages and disadvantages echolocation can have for animals. You may wish to mention that Spallanzani found that bats who were blind could still navigate and feed on insects. Deaf bats could neither navigate nor feed.

After students answer the question on page 274, explain that dolphins make clicking sounds that bounce off underwater objects back to the dolphin. By listening to these echoes the dolphin can navigate under the ocean and find food.

Math

Have students work in pairs to complete items 1–3. Suggest students draw a diagram to help them answer items 1 and 2.

When finished have partners share and compare their answers and methods.

Tables for item 3 should look similar to the following:

Echoes Reach Ship	Ocean Depth (ft)
2 seconds	5,000
4 seconds	10,000
6 seconds	15,000
8 seconds	20,000

math science technology
CONNECTION

SONAR

Cultural Note
In 1793, the Italian biologist Lazzaro Spallanzani found that bats make very high squeaks that cannot be heard by people. These sounds bounce off objects and back to the bat like an echo.

By listening to echoes, a bat can tell the difference between an insect and the twig it is sitting on! People also are able to use sound to measure ocean depth.

In about 1920, scientists discovered how to bounce sounds off the ocean floor and record the echo. This is called *sonar*, which stands for **so**und **na**vigation and **r**anging.

Scientists measure the time it takes for the sound to travel from the ship to the floor of the ocean and back to the ship. Since we know how fast sound can travel in water, we can calculate the depth of the ocean by timing how long it takes for the echo to return to the ship.

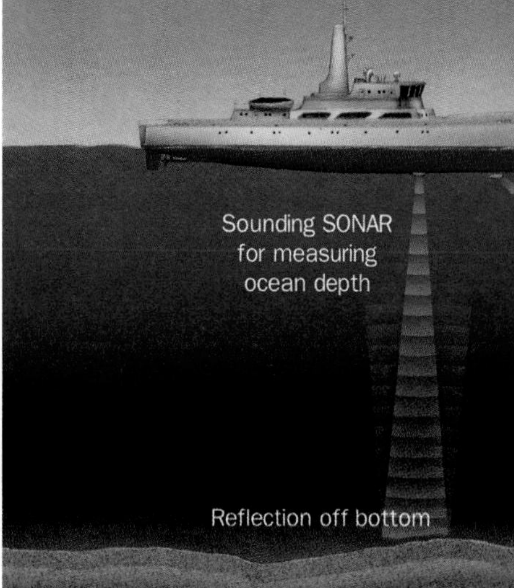

- What other animals do you know of that use sonar to tell distances? **Possible answer: dolphins**
- Harder surfaces reflect sound better. On the ocean floor, which would reflect sound better, rocks or mud? **rocks**

274 Math • Science • Technology Connection

Extending The Activity

1. Have students research other animals that use echolocation to navigate, such as beluga whales and guacharos, a cave-dwelling bird that lives in Venezuela. Students can work in pairs to research and prepare their reports. Have them present their findings using audio-visual aids such as posters, tape recorders, video recorders, and computers.
2. Plan a trip to a local zoo that has dolphins or bats to observe.

leasuring Ocean Depth

ound travels about 5,000 ft every econd in water. Suppose it takes seconds for an echo to travel from ship to the ocean floor and back. at means that the sound travels r 1 second before hitting the ocean or and another second to return to e boat. That means the ocean is 000 ft deep.

How deep is the ocean if it takes 4 seconds for the sound to return to the ship? **10,000 ft**

How long will it take the sound to return to a ship if the ocean is 20,000 ft deep? **8 s**

Make a table of times for an echo to return to a ship, and then calculate the ocean depth in feet. **Students' tables should show times in seconds and depth in feet.**

At the Computer

4 Use a graphing program to make a line graph for the distance traveled by sound and the time taken to return to the ship. What do you notice? **Check students' work.**

5 Use the line graph to estimate how many seconds it will take for sound to return to a ship if the ocean is 7,500 ft deep. **3 s**

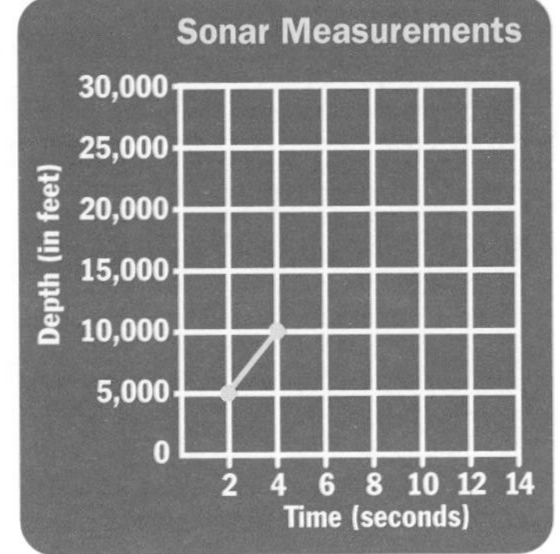

Technology

Students can use the data from the table they created for item 3 on page 275 to make their graph. They should notice that the graphs show that the distance and the time increase at the same rate.

For item 5, students can extend the lines on their graphs to help them predict the number of seconds.

Math Van Students may use the Graph tool to create a line graph for item 4. A project electronic teacher aid has been provided.

Interesting Facts

- **Sound travels faster through glass** than through iron, brick, wood, water, gold, or air. Sound moves through glass at up to 19,000 feet per second, through iron at almost 16,000 feet per second, through brick at about 12,000 feet per second, through gold at about 6,000 feet per second, and through water at about 5,000 feet per second.
- **Sound travels through sea-level air** at only 1,088 feet per second (about 741 miles per hour) and even slower at temperatures above 32° Fahrenheit.
- **A sound like thunder** occurs when a plane flies faster than the speed of sound, but the pilot does not hear it.

Bibliography

Bats: Mysterious Flyers of the Night, by Dee Stuart. Minneapolis, MN: Carolrhoda Books, Inc., 1994. ISBN 0-87614-814-3.

Bees Dance and Whales Sing: The Mysteries of Animal Communications, by Margery Facklam. San Francisco, CA: Sierra Club Books, 1992. ISBN 0-871-56573-0.

Theme: Our States   Suggested Pacing: 13–16 days

Divide by 1- and 2-Digit Numbers

	DAY 1	DAY 2	DAY 3
WEEK ONE	**PREASSESSMENT** Introduction pp. 276 What Do You Know? p.277 **CHAPTER OBJECTIVES:** 8A, 8B, 8C, 8D, 8E **RESOURCES** Read-Aloud Anthology pp. 37–39 Pretest: Test Master Form A, B, or C Diagnostic Inventory Portfolio Journal **NCTM STANDARDS:** 1, 2, 3, 4, 7, 8	**LESSON 8.1** MENTAL MATH Division Patterns pp. 278–279 **CHAPTER OBJECTIVES:** 8C **MATERIALS** calculators (opt.) **RESOURCES** Reteach/Practice/Extend: 66 Math Center Cards: 66 Extra Practice: 512 Daily Review TE p. 277B Algebraic Thinking Technology Link **NCTM STANDARDS:** 6, 8, 13	**LESSON 8.2** MENTAL MATH Estimate Quotients pp. 280–281 **CHAPTER OBJECTIVES:** 8A **MATERIALS** calculators (opt.) **RESOURCES** Reteach/Practice/Extend: 67 Math Center Cards: 67 Extra Practice: 512 Daily Review TE p. 279B Technology Link **NCTM STANDARDS:** 5, 8
WEEK TWO	**LESSON 8.5** Zeros in the Quotient pp. 290–291 **CHAPTER OBJECTIVES:** 8B **MATERIALS** place-value models (TA 22), calculators (opt.) **RESOURCES** Reteach/Practice/Extend: 70 Math Center Cards: 70 Extra Practice: 513 Daily Review TE p. 289B Technology Link **NCTM STANDARDS:** 8	**LESSON 8.6** Divide Greater Numbers pp. 292–293 **CHAPTER OBJECTIVES:** 8B **MATERIALS** calculators (opt.) **RESOURCES** Reteach/Practice/Extend: 71 Math Center Cards: 71 Extra Practice: 513 Daily Review TE p. 291B Technology Link **NCTM STANDARDS:** 8	**LESSON 8.7** PROBLEM-SOLVING STRATEGY Guess, Test, and Revise pp. 294–295 **CHAPTER OBJECTIVES:** 8E **MATERIALS** calculators (opt.) **RESOURCES** Reteach/Practice/Extend: 72 Math Center Cards: 72 Extra Practice: 514 Daily Review TE p. 293B Technology Link **NCTM STANDARDS:** 1, 2, 3, 4, 8
WEEK THREE	**LESSON 8.9** MENTAL MATH Divide by Multiples of Ten pp. 302–303 **CHAPTER OBJECTIVES:** 8C **MATERIALS** cm graph paper (TA 7), crayons, calculators (opt.) **RESOURCES** Reteach/Practice/Extend: 74 Math Center Cards: 74 Extra Practice: 515 Daily Review TE p. 301B Algebraic Thinking Journal Technology Link **NCTM STANDARDS:** 8, 13	**LESSON 8.10** EXPLORE ACTIVITY Divide by Tens pp. 304–307 **CHAPTER OBJECTIVES:** 8C **MATERIALS** spinner blanks (TA 2–3), place-value models (TA 22) **RESOURCES** Reteach/Practice/Extend: 75 Math Center Cards: 75 Extra Practice: 515 Daily Review TE p. 303B Algebraic Thinking Technology Link **NCTM STANDARDS:** 4, 8	**LESSON 8.11** PROBLEM SOLVERS AT WORK Interpret Quotient and Remainder pp. 308–311 **CHAPTER OBJECTIVES:** 8E **MATERIALS** place-value models (TA 22), calculators (opt.) **RESOURCES** Reteach/Practice/Extend: 76 Math Center Cards: 76 Extra Practice: 515 Daily Review TE p. 307B Technology Link **NCTM STANDARDS:** 1, 2, 3, 4, 8

DAY 4

LESSON 8.3

EXPLORE ACTIVITY

Divide by 1-Digit Numbers pp. 282–285

CHAPTER OBJECTIVES: 8B

MATERIALS 10-part spinners (TA 2), place-value models (TA 22), calculators (opt.)

RESOURCES Reteach/Practice/Extend: 68
Math Center Cards: 68
Extra Practice: 512

TEACHING WITH TECHNOLOGY
Alternate Lesson
TE pp. 285A–285B

Daily Review TE p. 281B

 Algebraic Thinking

 Technology Link

NCTM STANDARDS: 4, 7, 8

DAY 5

LESSON 8.4

Divide by 1-Digit Numbers pp. 286–289

CHAPTER OBJECTIVES: 8B

MATERIALS place-value models (TA 22), calculators (opt.)

RESOURCES Reteach/Practice/Extend: 69
Math Center Cards: 69
Extra Practice: 513

Daily Review TE p. 285D

 Algebraic Thinking

 Journal

 Technology Link

NCTM STANDARDS: 8

MIDCHAPTER ASSESSMENT

Midchapter Review p. 296

CHAPTER OBJECTIVES: 8A, 8B, 8C, 8E

MATERIALS calculators (opt.)

Developing Algebra Sense p. 297

REAL-LIFE INVESTIGATION:

Applying Division pp. 298–299

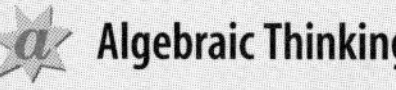 Algebraic Thinking

 Portfolio  Journal

NCTM STANDARDS: 1, 2, 3, 4, 8, 13

LESSON 8.8

EXPLORE ACTIVITY

Average pp. 300–301

CHAPTER OBJECTIVES: 8D

MATERIALS connecting cubes, calculators (opt.)

RESOURCES Reteach/Practice/Extend: 73
Math Center Cards: 73
Extra Practice: 514

Daily Review TE p. 299B

Technology Link

NCTM STANDARDS: 4, 8, 11

CHAPTER ASSESSMENT

Chapter Review pp. 312–313

MATERIALS calculators (opt.)

Chapter Test p. 314

RESOURCES Posttest: Test Master Form A, B, or C

Performance Assessment p. 315

RESOURCES Performance Task: Test Master

Math • Science • Technology Connection pp. 316–317

 Algebraic Thinking

 Portfolio

NCTM STANDARDS: 1, 4, 8

Assessment Options

FORMAL

Chapter Tests

STUDENT BOOK
- Midchapter Review, p. 296
- Chapter Review, pp. 312–313
- Chapter Test, p. 314

BLACKLINE MASTERS
- Test Master Form A, B, or C
- Diagnostic Inventory

COMPUTER TEST GENERATOR
- Available on disk

Performance Assessment
- What Do You Know? p. 277
- Performance Assessment, p. 315
- Holistic Scoring Guide, Teacher's Assessment Resources, pp. 27–32
- Follow-Up Interviews, p. 315
- Performance Task, Test Masters

Teacher's Assessment Resources
- Portfolio Guidelines and Forms, pp. 6–9, 33–35
- Holistic Scoring Guide, pp. 27–32
- Samples of Student Work, pp. 37–72

INFORMAL

Ongoing Assessment
- Observation Checklist, pp. 278, 280, 286, 292, 300, 304
- Interview, p. 302
- Anecdotal Report, pp. 282, 290, 294, 308

Portfolio Opportunities
- Chapter Project, p. 275F
- What Do You Know? p. 277
- Investigation, pp. 298–299
- Journal Writing, pp. 277, 287, 296, 302
- Performance Assessment, p. 315
- Self-Assessment: What Do You Think? p. 315

Chapter Objectives		Standardized Test Correlations
8A	Estimate quotients of whole numbers and money amounts	MAT, CAT, SAT, ITBS, CTBS, TN*
8B	Divide by 1-digit divisors	MAT, CAT, SAT, ITBS, CTBS, TN*
8C	Divide by multiples of 10	MAT, CAT, SAT, ITBS, CTBS, TN*
8D	Find the average of a group of numbers	ITBS, TN*
8E	Solve problems, including those that involve division and guessing, testing, and revising	MAT, CAT, SAT, ITBS, CTBS, TN*

*Terra Nova

NCTM Standards Grades K–4	
1 Problem Solving	8 Whole Number Computation
2 Communication	9 Geometry and Spatial Sense
3 Reasoning	10 Measurement
4 Connections	11 Statistics and Probability
5 Estimation	12 Fractions and Decimals
6 Number Sense and Numeration	13 Patterns and Relationships
7 Concepts of Whole Number Operations	

Meeting Individual Needs

LEARNING STYLES

- AUDITORY/LINGUISTIC
- LOGICAL/ANALYTICAL
- VISUAL/SPATIAL
- MUSICAL
- KINESTHETIC
- SOCIAL
- INDIVIDUAL

Students who are talented in art, language, and physical activity may better understand mathematical concepts when these concepts are connected to their areas of interest. Use the following activity to stimulate the different learning styles of some of your students.

Social Learners

Partners can practice division with a 0 to 9 spinner and a recording sheet.

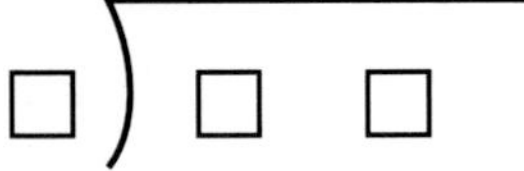

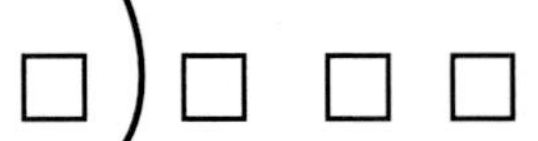

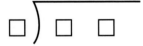

Students will spin and write the digits in the squares. When all the squares are filled, they solve the problems.

See Lesson Resources, pp. 277A, 279A, 281A, 285C, 289A, 291A, 293A, 299A, 301A, 303A, 307A.

GIFTED AND TALENTED

Some students may enjoy challenging each other with multiplication and division problems they have written. Have each student keep original multiplication and division problems in a booklet. Set aside one day a week when students can trade booklets and solve each other's problems. Encourage students to trade with as many students as possible during the course of the year.

See also Meeting Individual Needs, pp. 284, 288, 304, 310.

ESL APPROPRIATE

EXTRA SUPPORT

Some students may benefit from using counters or place-value models to help them divide. Specific suggestions for ways to provide extra support to students appear in every lesson in this chapter.

See Meeting Individual Needs, pp. 278, 280, 282, 286, 290, 292, 294, 300, 302, 304, 308.

EARLY FINISHERS

Students who finish their class work early may make posters for the classroom door as a welcome for any speakers who visit the class. (See *Chapter Project*, p. 275F.)

See also Meeting Individual Needs, pp. 278, 280, 284, 286, 290, 292, 294, 300, 302, 306, 310.

LANGUAGE SUPPORT

Display new words such as *prime, composite, quotient,* and *remainder* on a poster with examples. As new concepts are explained, add them to the poster and have students refer to the list as necessary. You may also wish to post the steps for division for students to refer to as needed.

See also Meeting Individual Needs, pp. 282, 310.

ESL APPROPRIATE

INCLUSION

- **For inclusion ideas, information, and suggestions, see pp. 288, 306, 310, T15.**
- **For gender fairness tips, see p. T15.**

USING MANIPULATIVES

Building Understanding Students can use place-value models to understand the concept of multiplication and division. To show 3 × 180, students can make three sets of 180. Have them sort the ones, tens, and hundreds together and count. To model division, have students divide 381 by 3. Students will need to regroup the hundreds, tens, and ones. Have them record as they work.

Easy-to-Make Manipulatives Place-value models can be made with centimeter graph paper glued on to cardboard. Cut into blocks of hundreds (10 by 10), tens (1 by 10) and ones (1 by 1).

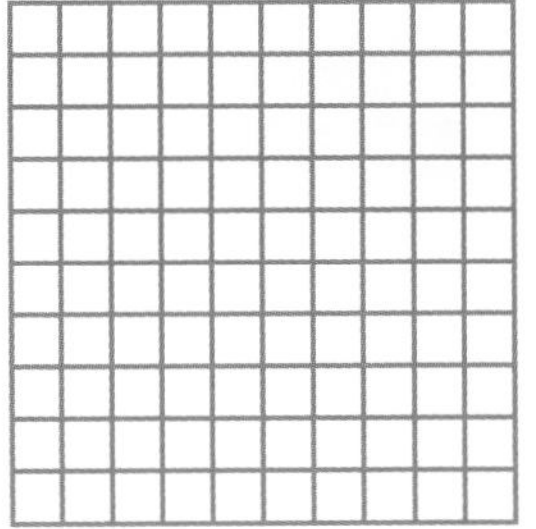

ESL APPROPRIATE

USING COOPERATIVE LEARNING

Group Discussion (with Round Robin) This strategy ensures equal participation by having each student respond verbally to a topic.

- **In a small group, students take turns contributing an idea, an answer, or a comment, orally.**
- **Students may say "pass" when they do not wish to contribute.**
- **The activity continues until the task is done, even though this may take several turns for each student.**

USING LITERATURE

Use the story *Your Best Friend, Kate* to introduce the chapter theme, Our States. This story is reprinted on pages 37–39 of the Read-Aloud Anthology.

Also available in the Read-Aloud Anthology is the story *One Hundred Hungry Ants*, page 40.

Linking Technology

This integrated package of programs and services allows students to explore, develop, and practice concepts; solve problems; build portfolios; and assess their own progress. Teachers can enhance instruction, provide remediation, and share ideas with other educational professionals.

CD-ROM ACTIVITY

In *Shooting the Grand Canyon,* students use place-value models to plan a photographic rafting trip. Students can use the online notebook to write about the ways they use division. To extend the activity, students use Math Van tools to complete an open-ended problem related to the concept. **Available on CD-ROM.**

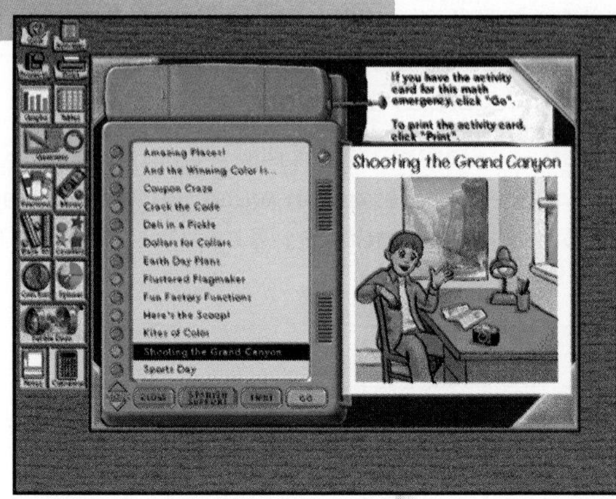

CD-ROM TOOLS

Students can use Math Van's place-value models to explore the concept of dividing by 1- and 2-digit numbers. The Tech Links on the Lesson Resources pages highlight opportunities for students to use this and other tools such as tables, graphs, online notes, and calculator to provide additional practice, reteaching, or extension.
Available on CD-ROM.

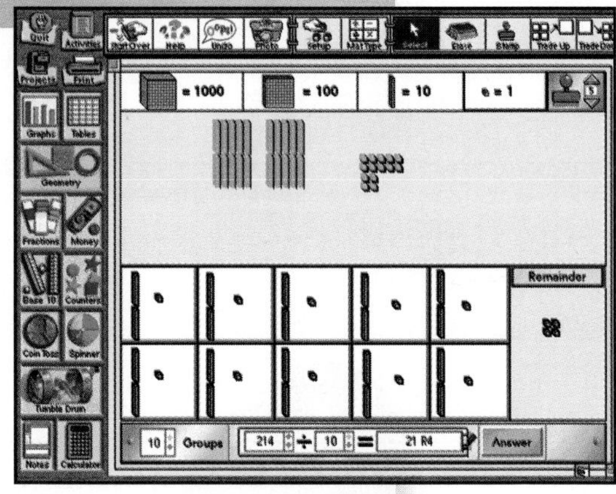

WEB SITE

http://www.mhschool.com

Teachers can access the McGraw-Hill School Division World Wide Web site for additional curriculum support at http://www.mhschool.com. Click on our Resource Village for specially designed activities linking Web sites to division. Motivate children by inviting them to explore Web sites that develop the chapter theme of "Our States." Exchange ideas on classroom management, cultural diversity, and other areas in the Math Forum.

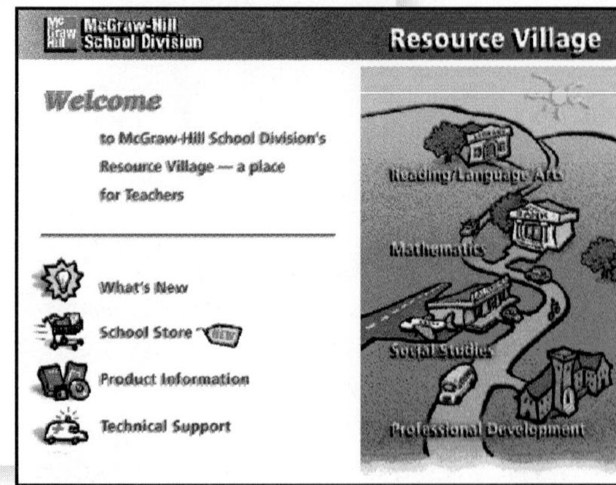

Chapter Project STATE ALMANACS

Highlighting the Math

- collect and organize data
- divide whole numbers

1 Starting the Project

Introduce the idea of a State Almanac. Review that an almanac is a yearly reference book containing general and statistical information. Assign students to groups to make their own State Almanacs. Write on paper slips as many state names (your state and others in your geographical region) as there are student groups. Fold paper slips and put them in a paper bag, and have one student from each group choose the state on which to base their almanac. Consider how family or community members can participate.

2 Continuing the Project

- Each group researches features for its selected state: state bird, flower, population of capital or other large cities, products, major bodies of water, number of counties, and per capita income.
- Each group designs and writes a mini-almanac for its assigned state, including three division story problems. Each story problem should be based on one of the features that have been researched. Examples: time to cross the state by car driving at a given speed, average per capita income over a period of years, average amount of a product harvested over a five-year period.

3 Finishing the Project

Have students present their almanacs to the class, describing the features and posing one or two of the story problems to the class. Take snapshots of the completed almanacs.

Community Involvement

Lend the State Almanacs to the school library for display or to be borrowed by other students. Also invite parents or community members who have lived in "almanac states" to speak to the class about those states.

BUILDING A PORTFOLIO

Have each student write a short paragraph about the experience of creating the almanac, focusing on the importance of math in creating it. The portfolio may also include a snapshot of the group almanac.

To assess students' work, refer to the Holistic Scoring Guide on page 27 in the Teacher's Assessment Resources.

PURPOSE Introduce the theme of the chapter.

Resources Read-Aloud Anthology, pages 37–39, newspapers

Using Literature

Read "Your Best Friend, Kate" from the Read-Aloud Anthology to introduce the theme of the chapter, "Our States."

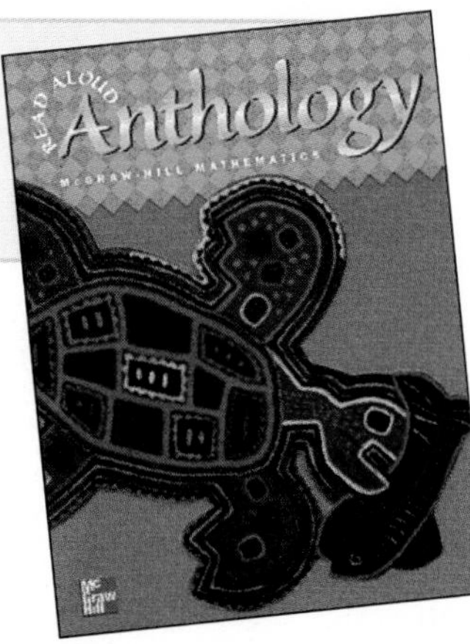

Developing the Theme

Encourage students to describe things that make their state important to them. Allow students who have lived in other states to describe what they like most about those states. Ask students to tell about states they would most like to visit and why.

Discuss states in the news. Articles of interest may reflect the economy, the environment, sports, or entertainment.

Discuss different geographical regions such as New England, the Pacific Northwest, the Southwest, and the Rocky Mountains. Have students list some of the states in each region and describe other geographical regions.

Suggest that students research several different states. They may enjoy making lists of state birds, state flowers, or state mottoes.

The following are discussed in this chapter:

Minnesota	pp. 278	Michigan	pp. 294
Pennsylvania	pp. 280	Texas	pp. 300
Florida	pp. 286	Washington, D.C.	pp. 302
New York	pp. 290	Missouri	pp. 308
Georgia	pp. 292		

On pages 298–299, students will apply division to plan a state tour.

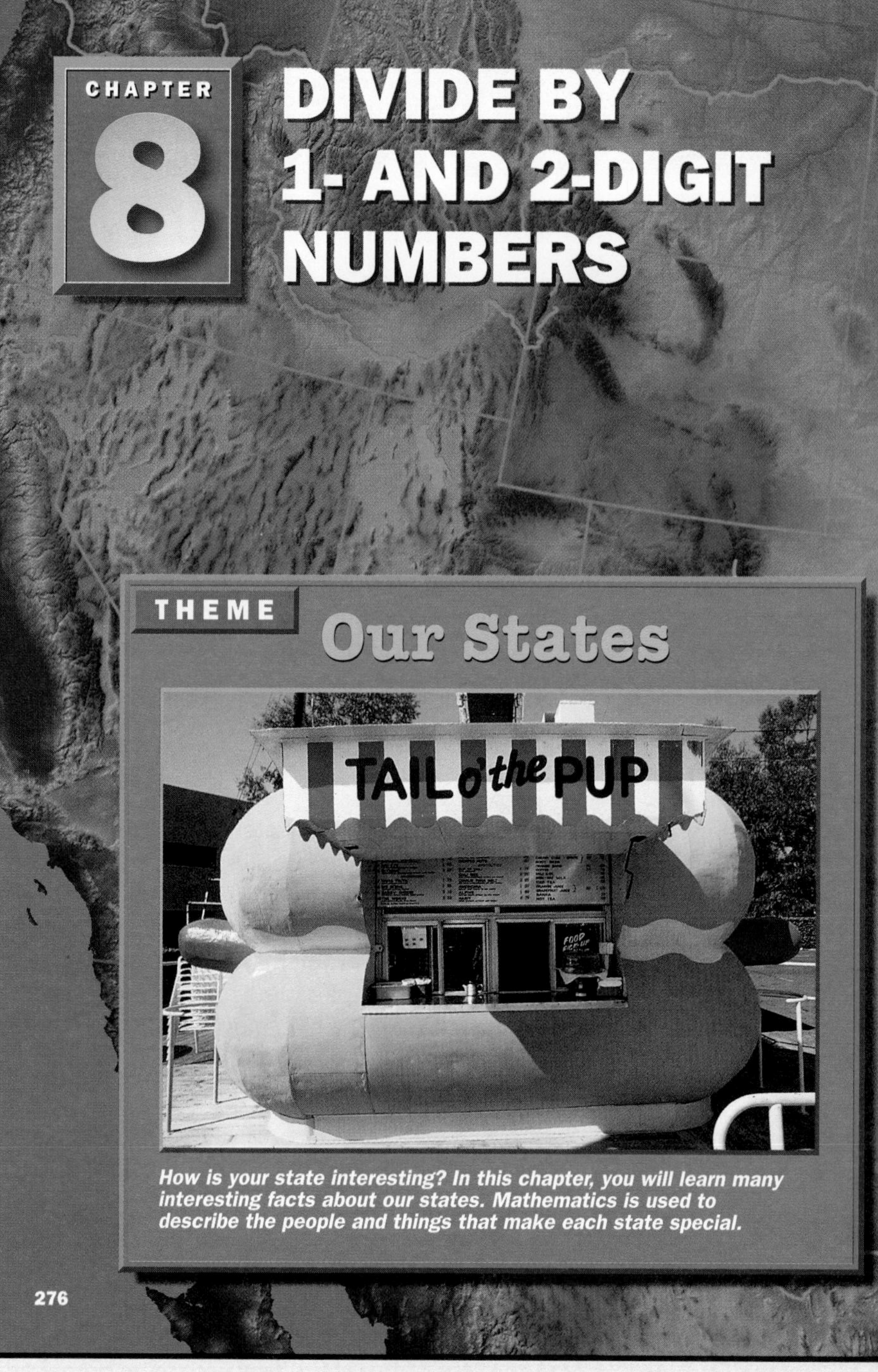

How is your state interesting? In this chapter, you will learn many interesting facts about our states. Mathematics is used to describe the people and things that make each state special.

276

Chapter Bibliography

The Doorbell Rang by Pat Hutchins. New York: Mulberry Books, 1989. ISBN 0–688–09234–9.

It Happened in America: True Stories From The Fifty States by Lila Perl. New York: Henry Holt & Company, 1993. ISBN 0–8050–1719–4.

Kids Learn America! Bringing Geography to Life With People, Places, and History by Patricia Gordon and Reed C. Snow. Charlotte, VT: Williamson Publishing Co., 1991. ISBN 0–913589–58–6.

Community Involvement

Have students conduct a survey of seniors and other adults who have lived in other states. Questions might include questions such as "What states have you lived in?" and "What do you like about our state?" Have students work in small groups to compile survey results. Students can present the results for a local newspaper.

What Do You Know?

The Travel Industry Association of America helps people arrange tours within the United States and abroad.

1. You want to visit all 50 states. If you visit 8 states a year, how many years will it take? Explain. **See above.**
2.  Choose the states you want to visit and how many you would like to visit each year. Find how many years it would take to visit these states. Explain your reasoning. **Students' answers should reflect how many states they wish to visit each year.**

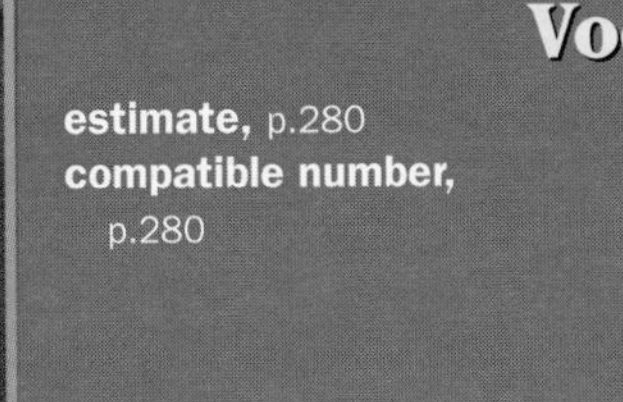

Problem/Solution **A class wants to plan a trip to a new park in their city. The only map of their city they have is dated 1980.**

In stories, if you identify a problem, it helps you understand the situation and the solution.

1. What problem might the students have? **The map may have been made before the park was built, so it won't show the park.**
2. How could students solve the problem? **Possible answers: get a new map; call the park for directions**

Vocabulary

estimate, p.280
compatible number, p.280
regroup, p.282
dividend, p.283
divisor, p.283
quotient, p.283
remainder, p.283
average, p.300

Divide by 1- and 2-Digit Numbers 277

Reading, Writing, Arithmetic

Problem/Solution List students' answers to item 2 on the chalkboard. Encourage creative thinking by accepting any reasonable solutions. Then invite students to tell about other problems they have identified and solved.

Vocabulary

Students may record new words in their journals. Encourage them to show examples and draw diagrams to help them tell what the words mean.

- **Draw a picture to show the quotient and remainder for 27 ÷ 6.**

[Possible answer:]

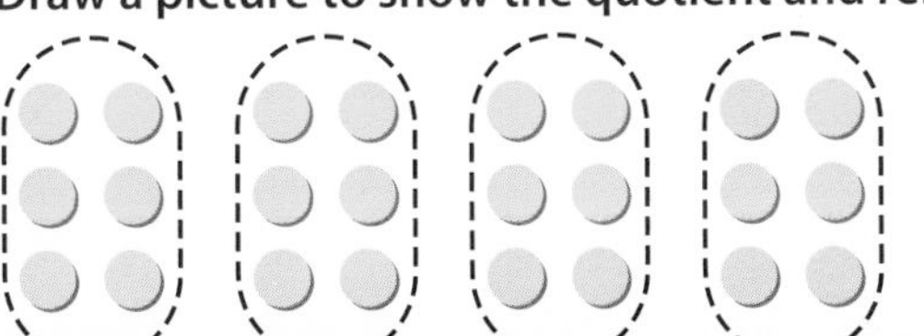

$$6\overline{)27}\quad 4\text{ R}3$$

PURPOSE Assess students' ability to apply prior knowledge of division.

Materials have available: counters, calculators (optional)

Assessing Prior Knowledge

Ask volunteers to give examples of strategies for dividing. List the students' examples on the board.

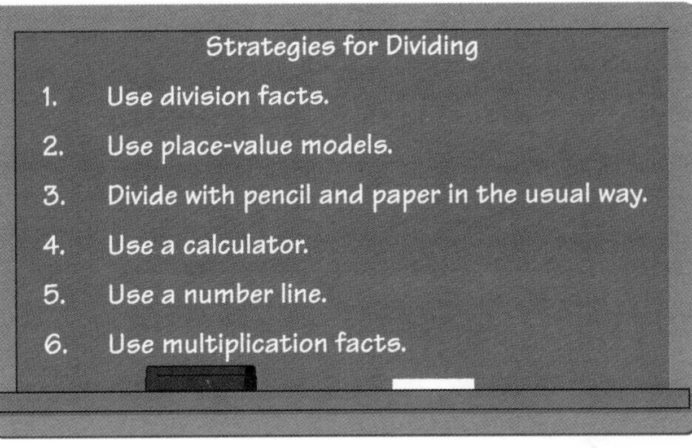

Strategies for Dividing
1. Use division facts.
2. Use place-value models.
3. Divide with pencil and paper in the usual way.
4. Use a calculator.
5. Use a number line.
6. Use multiplication facts.

Discuss the different methods students used to answer items 1–2. Some students may solve item 2 by choosing a number of states and how many they want to visit each year, and then divide the first number by the second. Other students may solve it by deciding how many states they would like to visit each year and how many years they want to do that, and then multiplying those two numbers to get the number of states they want to visit altogether.

Building a Portfolio

Item 2 can be used as a benchmark to show where students are in their understanding of division.

A Portfolio Checklist for Students and a Checklist for Teachers are provided in Teacher's Assessment Resources, pp. 33–34.

Prerequisite Skills

- *Can students relate multiplication and division facts?*
- *Can students multiply by 1-digit numbers?*
- *Can students multiply by multiples of 10?*

Assessment Resources

Diagnostic Inventory

Use this blackline master to assess prerequisite skills that students will need in order to be successful in this chapter.

Test Masters

Use the multiple choice format (form A or B) or the free response format (form C) as a pretest of the skills in this chapter.

MENTAL MATH

Division Patterns

OBJECTIVE Use mental math strategies to divide multiples of 10, 100, and 1,000 by 1-digit numbers.

RESOURCE REMINDER
Math Center Cards 66
Practice 66, Reteach 66, Extend 66

SKILLS TRACE

GRADE 3	• Use mental math strategies to divide multiples of 10 and 100 by 1-digit numbers. *(Chapter 12)*
GRADE 4	• Use mental math strategies to divide multiples of 10, 100, and 1,000.
GRADE 5	• Use mental math strategies to divide multiples of 10, 100, 1,000, and 10,000. *(Chapter 5)*

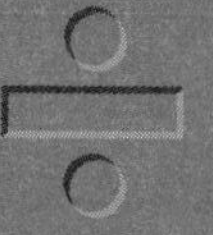

WARM-UP

Cooperative Pairs — Logical/Analytical

OBJECTIVE Review multiplication patterns.

Materials calculator (optional)

▶ Write this multiplication pattern on the board:

$4 \times 2 = 8$
$40 \times 2 = 80$
$400 \times 2 = 800$
$\square \times 2 = 8000$

▶ Have a volunteer find the missing number *[4,000]* and explain how they found it.

▶ Have pairs work together to find the missing numbers:

$6 \times 5 = 30$	$7 \times 3 = 21$	■ × 8 = 40 *[5]*
60 × 5 = ■ *[300]*	$70 \times 3 = 210$	■ × 8 = 400 *[50]*
$600 \times 5 = 3{,}000$	■ × 3 = 2,100 *[700]*	■ × 8 = 4,000 *[500]*
■ × 5 = 30,000 *[6,000]*	7,000 × 3 = ■ *[21,000]*	■ × 8 = 40,000 *[5,000]*

▶ Allow time for pairs to present their findings and methods to the class.

ALGEBRA CONNECTION

Cooperative Pairs — Logical/Analytical

OBJECTIVE Connect division facts with algebra.

Materials per pair: 0–9 spinner (TA 2)

▶ Each student spins the spinner twice and records the two numbers.

▶ Then each student makes a division sentence for the other student to solve, with the dividend missing. For example, if a student spins a 7 and a 3, the division sentence will be ■ ÷ 3 = 7 or ■ ÷ 7 = 3. *[21]*

▶ Have students continue spinning until each has ten division sentences to solve.

▶ Ask students to explain how they found the missing numbers in their division sentences. *[Possible answers: Used mental math, multiplied the divisor by the quotient.]*

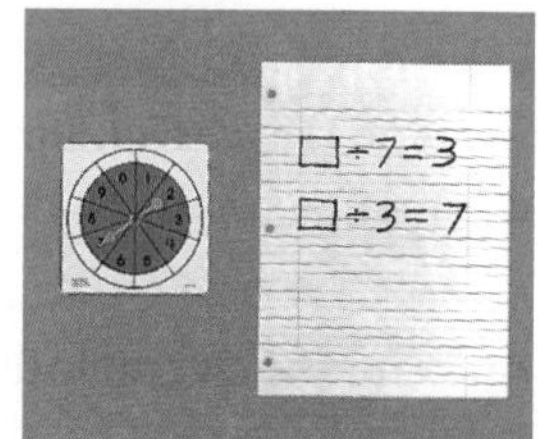

Daily Review

PREVIOUS DAY QUICK REVIEW

Which is greater?

1. 1 kg or 10 g *[1 kg]*
2. 30 mL or 1 L *[1 L]*
3. 50 g or 5 kg *[5 kg]*
4. 2 L or 1,000 ml *[2 L]*

FAST FACTS

1. 3 × 9 *[27]*
2. 4 × 4 *[16]*
3. 5 × 7 *[35]*
4. 6 × 8 *[48]*

Problem of the Day • 66

Mr. Kim has 640 pencils and 720 pens. Eight boxes of pencils contain the same number of pencils and nine boxes of pens contain the same number of pens. How does the number of pencils in each box compare to the number of pens? *[same]*

TECH LINK

ONLINE EXPLORATION

Use our Web-linked activities and lesson plans to connect your students to the real world of our states.

MATH FORUM

Idea My students benefit from using calculators to explore division patterns. Working through more examples helps some students better understand the pattern.

Visit our Resource Village at http://www.mhschool.com to access the Online Exploration and the Math Forum.

MATH CENTER

Practice

OBJECTIVE Use patterns to write division sentences.

Materials per group: 9 index cards, clock with second hand; per student: Math Center Recording Sheet (TA 31 optional)

Prepare Have students label the cards 1 through 9.

Students start with a multiple of 10 to use as a quotient and write as many division sentences for that quotient as they can in 1 minute. *[Check students' work.]*

MATH CENTER
Small Group

PRACTICE ACTIVITY 66

Game • Basic Fact Brainstorm

- Mix up the cards and place them facedown. Each player draws one card from the top. Each player writes the number that was picked. One player rolls the number cube to get a number from 1 to 3. (If you roll 4–6, roll again.) The number rolled is the number of zeros to write after the digit you have written.
- You have 1 minute to write as many division sentences as you can that have that number as the quotient. For example, if you chose 5 and rolled 2, you could write 1,000 ÷ 2 = 500. Give 1 point for each correct sentence. Keep playing until someone has 25 points.

YOU NEED
number cards (1–9)
number cube
clock or watch with second hand

6
6,000

Grade Level 4 · McGraw-Hill School Division

Chapter 8, Lesson 1, pages 278–279 · Division

ESL APPROPRIATE

NCTM Standards
Problem Solving
✓ Communication
✓ Reasoning
Connections

Problem Solving

OBJECTIVE Use division patterns to order quotients.

Materials per student: 4 blank slips of paper, Math Center Recording Sheet (TA 31 optional)

Students write 4 basic division facts and mix them up so that the quotients are not arranged in increasing order. Students must then add zeros to the quotients and dividends so that the quotients are in increasing order. They do not move the pieces of paper. *[Check students' work.]*

MATH CENTER
On Your Own

PROBLEM-SOLVING ACTIVITY 66

Logical Reasoning • Division Pattern Challenge

- On each slip of paper, write a basic division fact. Space out the numbers and signs.
- Line up the pieces of paper so that the quotients are *not* in order.
- Your goal is to fix the division so that they are in increasing order. You do that by adding zeros to any or all of the quotients and one of the other numbers, either the dividend or the divisor. Here is an example:

YOU NEED
sheet of paper folded in half twice and torn to make 4 slips of paper

12 ÷ 3 = 4	18 ÷ 6 = 3	25 ÷ 5 = 5	12 ÷ 6 = 2
12 ÷ 3 = 4	180 ÷ 6 = 30	250 ÷ 5 = 50	1,200 ÷ 6 = 200

Grade Level 4 · McGraw-Hill School Division

Chapter 8, Lesson 1, pages 278–279 · Division

ESL APPROPRIATE

NCTM Standards
✓ Problem Solving
Communication
✓ Reasoning
Connections

MENTAL MATH
Division Patterns

OBJECTIVE Use mental math to divide multiples of 10, 100, and 1,000.

Have students describe how they use the first product to find the second.

- 6 × 8; 60 × 8 *[Possible answers: Multiply 48 × 10, write a zero after 48 to find 480.]*
- 4 × 7; 400 × 7 *[Possible answers: Multiply 28 × 100, add two zeros after 28 to find 2,800.]*

2 Teach

▶ **LEARN** As students describe the patterns in the division sentences on page 278, list them on the board. Students should see that when there is an additional zero in the dividend, there is an additional zero in the quotient.

More Examples For Example C, students should see that since the basic fact has a zero in the dividend, the dividends in this pattern will have one more zero than the quotients.

▶ **Check for Understanding** using items 1–12, page 278.

CRITICAL THINKING
For item 12, students analyze how basic facts and place value can be used to find quotients mentally. Extend this analysis by asking:

- **How can you find 4,000 ÷ 8?** *[4,000 ÷ 8 = 40 hundreds ÷ 8 = 5 hundreds = 500]*

▶ **PRACTICE**
Materials have available: calculators

Options for assigning exercises:
A—Ex. 1–8, 17–26; **Mixed Review**
B—Ex. 9–26; **Mixed Review**

- For ex. 25, students can use mental math with other operations to make a decision about spending money.

Algebra In ex. 17–22, squares replace variables as the unknown in algebraic sentences. Students can use mental math to solve for the squares.

Mixed Review/Test Preparation In ex. 1–4, students review addition, subtraction, and multiplication, learned in Chapters 2 and 6. Students find perimeter in ex. 5–7, a skill they learned in Chapter 7.

Division Patterns

LEARN

Maria loves her dogs—all 120 of them! She takes people on dogsledding tours. She also races. A 3-day race can cover 180 mi. If the same distance is covered each day, how many miles are traveled a day?

IN THE WORKPLACE
Maria Hayashida, musher from Jackson Hole, WY, competed in the 1996 Alaskan Iditarod Race

ALGEBRA: PATTERNS You can use patterns to help you divide mentally. What patterns do you see below?

18 ÷ 3 = 6
180 ÷ 3 = 60
1,800 ÷ 3 = 600

Possible answer: Make new division sentences by multiplying the product and quotient of a division fact by 10 and by 100.

60 miles are traveled each day.

More Examples

A 7 ÷ 1 = 7
70 ÷ 1 = 70
700 ÷ 1 = 700
7,000 ÷ 1 = 7,000

B 12 ÷ 3 = 4
120 ÷ 3 = 40
1,200 ÷ 3 = 400

C 20 ÷ 5 = 4
200 ÷ 5 = 40
2,000 ÷ 5 = 400

CHECK

Check for Understanding

ALGEBRA: PATTERNS Complete. Describe the pattern. **Check students' descriptions.**

1 9 ÷ 3 = 3
90 ÷ 3 = ■ **30**
900 ÷ 3 = ■ **300**
9,000 ÷ 3 = ■ **3,000**

2 30 ÷ 6 = ■ **5**
300 ÷ 6 = ■ **50**
3,000 ÷ 6 = 500

3 72 ÷ 9 = ■ **8**
720 ÷ 9 = 80
7,200 ÷ 9 = ■ **800**

Divide mentally.

4 140 ÷ 2 **70** **5** 240 ÷ 6 **40** **6** 450 ÷ 9 **50** **7** 480 ÷ 8 **60**

8 1,500 ÷ 3 **500** **9** 1,800 ÷ 6 **300** **10** 6,400 ÷ 8 **800** **11** 8,100 ÷ 9 **900**

Critical Thinking: Analyze **Explain your reasoning.**

12 If you think of 180 as 18 tens, how can you find 180 ÷ 6 mentally? How can you find 1,800 ÷ 6? **Possible answer: 180 ÷ 6 = 18 tens ÷ 6 = 3 tens = 30; 1,800 ÷ 6 = 18 hundreds ÷ 6 = 3 hundreds = 300**

Meeting Individual Needs

Early Finishers

Tell students to write two basic-fact division sentences. Then have them append six zeros to each dividend. Let them use calculators to find the quotients of the new dividends and the original divisors.

ESL APPROPRIATE

Extra Support

As students complete exercises 1–16, have them begin by writing a basic fact that they can use to help them find the answer.

Ongoing Assessment

Observation Checklist
Observe if students understand how to divide multiples of 10, 100, and 1,000 by one-digit numbers by having them identify the basic facts that they use to find the answer.

Follow Up Have students who need help use calculators to make division patterns. They start with a basic fact, then multiply the dividend by 10, 100, and 1,000 to find other quotients in the pattern. You may also wish to assign **Reteach 66.**

Have students who are adept at mental math try **Extend 66.**

Answers may vary. Possible answers: 2 lb of apples and 1 lb of pears—$0.99 + $0.99 + $0.69 is less than $3, 1 lb of oranges and 1 lb of pineapples—$1.29 + $1.69 is just under $3.

actice 23. 2 lb of grapes; the pears cost $2.76 while the grapes cost $3.58; the grapes cost 82¢ more than the pears.

de mentally.

80 ÷ 2 **40**	**2** 60 ÷ 3 **20**	**3** 50 ÷ 5 **10**	**4** 60 ÷ 6 **10**
320 ÷ 4 **80**	**6** 160 ÷ 8 **20**	**7** 400 ÷ 5 **80**	**8** 490 ÷ 7 **70**
540 ÷ 9 **60**	**10** 630 ÷ 9 **70**	**11** 2,100 ÷ 3 **700**	**12** 3,000 ÷ 6 **500**
2,700 ÷ 3 **900**	**14** 3,600 ÷ 9 **400**	**15** 4,800 ÷ 6 **800**	**16** 7,200 ÷ 8 **900**

EBRA Find the missing number.

■ ÷ 2 = 300 **600**	**18** 540 ÷ ■ = 60 **9**	**19** 720 ÷ ■ = 90 **8**
3,500 ÷ ■ = 700 **5**	**21** ■ ÷ 4 = 300 **1,200**	**22** ■ ÷ 7 = 700 **4,900**

XED APPLICATIONS

roblem Solving Pencil & Paper · Calculator · Mental Math

the sign for problems 23–25.

Price for each Pound of Fruit

Oranges	$1.29
Pineapples	$1.69
Grapes	$1.79
Apples	$0.99
Pears	$0.69

Which costs more, 4 pounds of pears or 2 pounds of grapes? How much more? Explain. **See above.**

Gina buys a pound of apples and a pound of pineapples. She pays with a $5 bill. How much change will she get? **$2.32**

25 **Make a decision** You want to spend no more than $3 on fruit and get at least two different kinds of fruit. What would you buy? Why? **See above.**

A musher switches her 120 dogs around for her trips. She has 4 dogs on each sled. How many sleds are pulled before the same dogs are used again? **30 sleds**

mixed review • test preparation

861 + 246 **1,107**	**2** 947 − 540 **407**	**3** 40 × 51 **2,040**	**4** 9,000 × 40 **360,000**

d the perimeter.

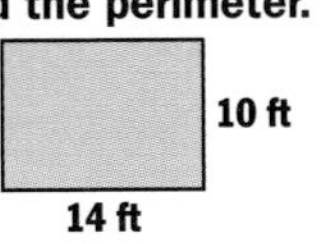

48 ft

6
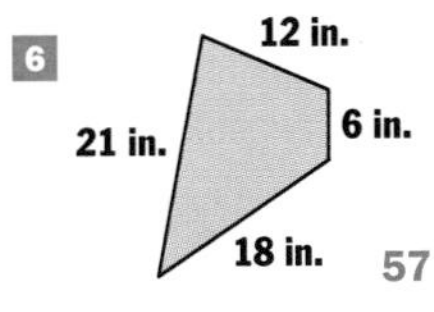

57 in.

7
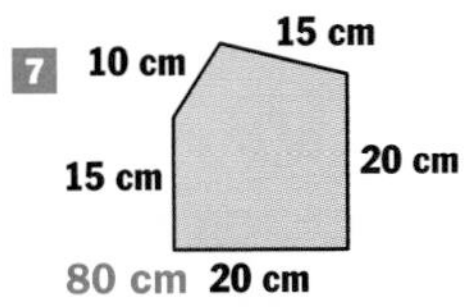

80 cm

ra Practice, page 512

PRACTICE

Alternate Teaching Strategy

Materials per group: place-value models—50 ones, 50 tens, 50 hundreds, 4 thousands (if available)

Have groups use models to show the following:

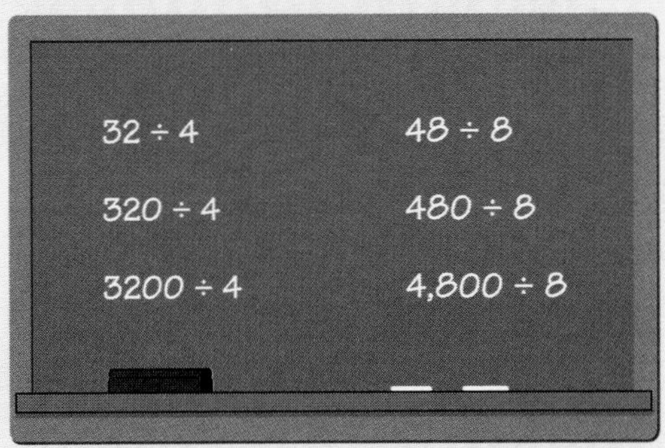

Before students begin, remind them that to divide they may need to use one type of place-value model for others. For example, to divide 32 into 4 equal groups, they must use 30 ones for 3 tens.

After students finish finding the patterns, ask:

- **How does the basic fact help you find how many of each model will be in the equal groups?** *[Possible answer: The number of ones in the quotient of the basic fact is the same as the number of hundreds and thousands in the next two quotients in the pattern.]*

Let students continue the activity by modeling some of the Practice exercises on page 279.

PRACTICE • 66

HOMEWORK

Practice 66

Name:

MENTAL MATH: DIVISION PATTERNS

Divide mentally.

1. 20 ÷ 2 = 10	**2.** 60 ÷ 2 = 30	**3.** 80 ÷ 4 = 20
4. 90 ÷ 3 = 30	**5.** 150 ÷ 3 = 50	**6.** 210 ÷ 7 = 30
7. 250 ÷ 5 = 50	**8.** 180 ÷ 6 = 30	**9.** 2,400 ÷ 6 = 400
10. 630 ÷ 7 = 90	**11.** 1,600 ÷ 4 = 400	**12.** 640 ÷ 8 = 80
13. 4,500 ÷ 9 = 500	**14.** 320 ÷ 8 = 40	**15.** 3,200 ÷ 8 = 400
16. 1,800 ÷ 3 = 600	**17.** 2,000 ÷ 4 = 500	**18.** 4,200 ÷ 7 = 600
19. 5,400 ÷ 9 = 600	**20.** 720 ÷ 8 = 90	**21.** 8,100 ÷ 9 = 900
22. 4,900 ÷ 7 = 700	**23.** 4,800 ÷ 8 = 600	**24.** 3,600 ÷ 6 = 600
25. 4,000 ÷ 5 = 800	**26.** 1,800 ÷ 9 = 200	**27.** 5,600 ÷ 8 = 700
28. 6,300 ÷ 9 = 700	**29.** 1,400 ÷ 7 = 200	**30.** 2,800 ÷ 7 = 400

Algebra Find the missing number.

31. 45 ÷ 5 = 9	**32.** 450 ÷ 5 = 90	**33.** 800 ÷ 2 = 400
34. 2,700 ÷ 3 = 900	**35.** 320 ÷ 8 = 40	**36.** 4,800 ÷ 6 = 800
37. 1,200 ÷ 3 = 400	**38.** 3,500 ÷ 7 = 500	**39.** 2,700 ÷ 9 = 300

Solve mentally.

40. There will be 200 tap dancers in 4 groups performing in the Park School Hollywood Talent Show. All the groups will have an equal number of dancers. How many dancers will be in each group?

50 tap dancers

41. Sixty actors will put on 6 funny skits at the Talent Show. All the skits will have an equal number of actors. How many actors will there be in each skit?

10 actors

McGraw-Hill School Division

RETEACH • 66

Reteach 66

Name:

MENTAL MATH: DIVISION PATTERNS

To divide mentally, you can use basic division facts and look for patterns. Count the zeros.

Divide. **Think:** The basic fact is 15 ÷ 5 = 3. **Think:** The basic fact is 40 ÷ 8 = 5.

15 ÷ 5 = 3	0 zeros	40 ÷ 8 = 5	0 extra zeros
15**0** ÷ 5 = 3**0**	1 zero	40**0** ÷ 8 = 5**0**	1 extra zero
1,5**00** ÷ 5 = 3**00**	2 zeros	4,0**00** ÷ 8 = 5**00**	2 extra zeros

Complete.

1. 8 ÷ 4 = 2
80 ÷ 4 = 2 0
800 ÷ 4 = 2 00

2. 16 ÷ 4 = 4
160 ÷ 4 = 4 0
1,600 ÷ 4 = 4 00

3. 20 ÷ 4 = 5
200 ÷ 4 = 5 0
2,000 ÷ 4 = 5 00

4. 32 ÷ 8 = 4
320 ÷ 8 = 4 0
3,200 ÷ 8 = 4 00

5. 30 ÷ 5 = 6
300 ÷ 5 = 60
3,000 ÷ 5 = 600

6. 45 ÷ 9 = 5
450 ÷ 9 = 50
4,500 ÷ 9 = 500

7. 48 ÷ 8 = 6
480 ÷ 8 = 60
4,800 ÷ 8 = 600

8. 64 ÷ 8 = 8
640 ÷ 8 = 80
6,400 ÷ 8 = 800

9. 140 ÷ 2 = 70	**10.** 360 ÷ 4 = 90	**11.** 800 ÷ 8 = 100
12. 1,400 ÷ 2 = 700	**13.** 360 ÷ 6 = 60	**14.** 540 ÷ 9 = 60
15. 4,200 ÷ 6 = 700	**16.** 4,900 ÷ 7 = 700	**17.** 2,700 ÷ 9 = 300

McGraw-Hill School Division

EXTEND • 66

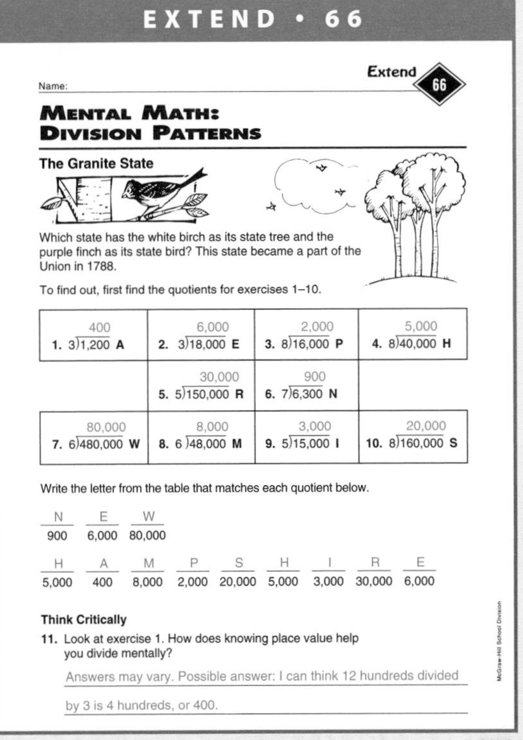

Extend 66

Name:

MENTAL MATH: DIVISION PATTERNS

The Granite State

Which state has the white birch as its state tree and the purple finch as its state bird? This state became a part of the Union in 1788.

To find out, first find the quotients for exercises 1–10.

1. 3)1,200 **A** — 400	**2.** 3)18,000 **E** — 6,000	**3.** 8)16,000 **P** — 2,000	**4.** 8)40,000 **H** — 5,000
	5. 5)150,000 **R** — 30,000	**6.** 7)6,300 **N** — 900	
7. 6)480,000 **W** — 80,000	**8.** 6)48,000 **M** — 8,000	**9.** 5)15,000 **I** — 3,000	**10.** 8)160,000 **S** — 20,000

Write the letter from the table that matches each quotient below.

N	E	W
900	6,000	80,000

H	A	M	P	S	H	I	R	E
5,000	400	8,000	2,000	20,000	5,000	3,000	30,000	6,000

Think Critically

11. Look at exercise 1. How does knowing place value help you divide mentally?

Answers may vary. Possible answer: I can think 12 hundreds divided by 3 is 4 hundreds, or 400.

McGraw-Hill School Division

LESSON 8.2

MENTAL MATH

Estimate Quotients

OBJECTIVE Estimate quotients using compatible numbers.

RESOURCE REMINDER
Math Center Cards 67
Practice 67, Reteach 67, Extend 67

SKILLS TRACE

GRADE 3	• Use mental math strategies to divide multiples of 10 and 100. *(Chapter 12)*
GRADE 4	• Estimate quotients mentally using compatible numbers.
GRADE 5	• Estimate quotients mentally using compatible numbers. *(Chapter 5)*

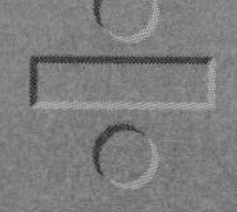

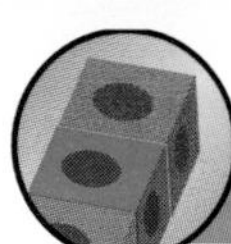

MANIPULATIVE WARM-UP

Cooperative Groups — Logical/Analytical

OBJECTIVE Explore estimating quotients.

Materials per group: place-value models—25 tens

► Write this division sentence on the chalkboard: 140 ÷ 7. Have students use mental math to find the answer. *[20]* Then use models to check.

► Write this division sentence on the chalkboard: 143 ÷ 7. Ask students to estimate the answer, and then to explain how they estimated. *[Possible answer: about 20, since 140 ÷ 7 = 20, and 143 is close to 140.]*

► Continue with other sentences, such as 120 ÷ 6, 121 ÷ 6; 210 ÷ 7, 213 ÷ 7; 240 ÷ 8, 242 ÷ 8. Have students use mental math to find the first quotient in each pair, use models to check the quotient, and then use the first quotient to estimate the second.

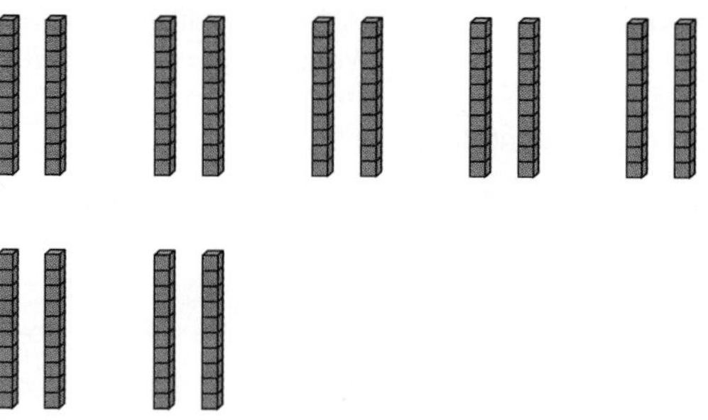

SOCIAL STUDIES CONNECTION

Cooperative Pairs — Visual/Spatial

OBJECTIVE Connect mental math and division to using maps.

Materials per pair: road atlas

► One student chooses two towns that are between 200 and 400 miles apart. If a road atlas or map is not available, use the map shown below.

► Students work together to estimate the number of miles per hour that they would have to travel to complete the trip between the two cities in seven hours. They then make the estimates for eight hours and nine hours.

► Students repeat the activity, with the second partner choosing two new cities.

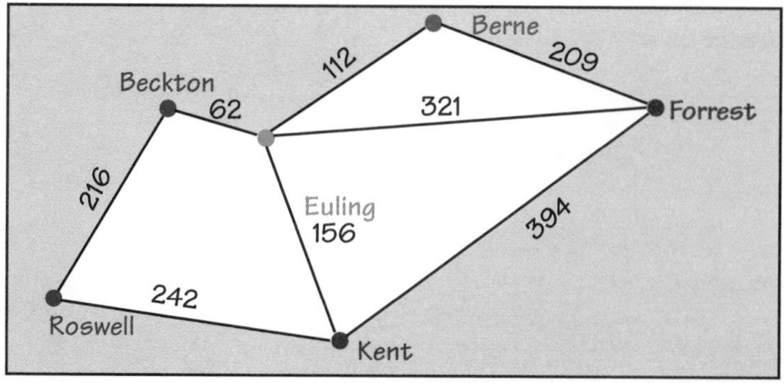

Daily Review

PREVIOUS DAY QUICK REVIEW

Divide mentally.

1. 300 ÷ 5 *[60]*
2. 480 ÷ 6 *[80]*
3. 1,200 ÷ 4 *[300]*
4. 6,400 ÷ 8 *[800]*

FAST FACTS

1. 7 × 4 *[28]*
2. 8 × 6 *[48]*
3. 2 × 3 *[6]*
4. 9 × 9 *[81]*

Problem of the Day • 67

Kyle has $2,592 to pay for 4 truckloads of vegetables. Each truckload costs the same amount. What two sets of compatible numbers can you use to estimate the quotient? How does the exact answer compare to these estimates? *[$2,400 ÷ 4 = $600; $2,800 ÷ 4 = $700; between $600 and $700]*

TECH LINK

Math Van

MATH VAN

Tool You may wish to use the Table and Graph tool for the Data Point in this lesson.

MATH FORUM

Multi-Age Classes I pair younger students who have difficulty finding compatible numbers with students who have mastered the skill. The younger students can do the division.

Visit our Resource Village at http://www.mhschool.com to see more of the Math Forum.

MATH CENTER

Practice

OBJECTIVE Use compatible numbers to estimate quotients.

Materials per student: counters, Math Center Recording Sheet (TA 31 optional)

Students work their way across a game board by using the numbers in the boxes as dividends and estimating quotients based on compatible numbers. *[Check students' work.]*

PRACTICE ACTIVITY 67 — MATH CENTER — Partners

Game • Compatibility Partner

YOU NEED
- 2 counters

- Copy the game board at right. Each player places a counter on *Start* and moves one space in any direction. The number in the space is the dividend. Use any number from 5 to 9 as the divisor. Estimate the quotient by using compatible numbers.
- The first player to do so gets to move his or her counter one space in any direction. The other player stays in the same place.

Players must always try new estimates if they are on a space twice. The winner is the first to get to a *Finish*.

START	155	3,421	787	312
167	152	652	4,198	532 FINISH
379	96	1,578	8,976	198
410	181	152	720	192 FINISH
40	2,010 FINISH	521	2,390 FINISH	3,781

McGraw-Hill School Division Grade Level 4

Chapter 8, Lesson 2, pages 280–281 — Division

ESL APPROPRIATE

NCTM Standards
- ✓ Problem Solving
- ✓ Communication
- ✓ Reasoning
- Connections

Problem Solving

OBJECTIVE Play a game using estimation of quotients.

Materials per group: number cube, 0–9 spinner (TA 2); per student: Math Center Recording Sheet (TA 31 optional)

Students form a dividend from a random selection of 4 digits and a divisor from a roll of a number cube. They are challenged to arrange the digits of the dividend to give the greatest quotient and to do it first. *[Check students' work.]*

PROBLEM-SOLVING ACTIVITY 67 — MATH CENTER — Small Group

Logical Reasoning • Estimate the Greatest Quotients

YOU NEED
- spinner (0–9)
- number cube

- One player spins four times. Record the numbers. You will use the numbers to form a dividend. Another player rolls the number cube to get the divisor. (If 1 is rolled, roll again.)
- Players use the four digits to write a dividend that will give a quotient anywhere from 101 to 600. The first player to finish gets the number of points listed in the table. All the other players who write a dividend earn 1 point.
- The first player to reach 20 points is the winner.

Score	1 point	2 points	3 points	4 points	5 points	6 points
Quotient	101–200	201–300	301–400	401–500	501–600	over 600

McGraw-Hill School Division Grade Level 4

Chapter 8, Lesson 2, pages 280–281 — Division

ESL APPROPRIATE

NCTM Standards
- ✓ Problem Solving
- Communication
- ✓ Reasoning
- Connections

MENTAL MATH

Estimate Quotients

OBJECTIVE Use mental math to estimate quotients.

Vocabulary compatible numbers, estimate

1 Introduce

Read the following problem to the class.

Gina runs 301 miles in 6 months. She runs about the same number of miles each month. About how many miles does Gina run each month?

Ask whether an exact answer or an estimate is needed to solve the problem. *[estimate]* Then have volunteers suggest ways to estimate the quotient. *[300 ÷ 6 = 50 mi]*

2 Teach *Whole Class*

LEARN Lead students to understand that for the problem on page 280, compatible numbers are easier to use than rounding. For example, rounding the dividend to the nearest ten gives 750 ÷ 8, which is not easy to solve; using the compatible numbers 720 ÷ 8 is easier, because the fact 72 ÷ 8 can be used.

More Examples As students discuss Examples A and B, have them suggest other compatible numbers that can be used to estimate the quotient. *[A: 360 ÷ 6 = 60; B: 150 ÷ 5 = 30]*

3 Close

Check for Understanding using items 1–9, page 280.

CRITICAL THINKING

For item 9, students use compatible numbers to estimate quotients.

PRACTICE

Materials have available: calculators

Options for assigning exercises:

A—Odd ex. 1–15, all ex. 17–22; **Mixed Review**

B—Even ex. 2–16; all ex. 17–22; **Mixed Review**

- For ex. 19, students must identify the information in the Infobit that pertains to each problem to solve.
- For ex. 20, students can make a bar graph or a pictograph to display their data.

Mixed Review/Test Preparation Students add and subtract money or multiply, learned in Chapters 2 and 5.

Estimate Quotients

LEARN

Each year, the Little League World Series is held in South Williamsport, PA.

A Little League team needs $752 f[...] buses and tickets. The team decide[...] to earn money by running a snack stand for 8 weeks. About how muc[...] do they need to earn each week?

You can **estimate** to solve this probl[...]

To estimate a quotient, you can use **compatible numbers** that help you divide mentally.

Estimate: 752 ÷ 8

Find a number close to 752 that you can divide by 8 mentally. You can us[...] the fact 72 ÷ 8 = 9 to help you cho[...] a compatible number.

Think: 720 ÷ 8 = 90

The team needs to earn about $90 each week.

More Examples

A Estimate: 409 ÷ 6
Think: 42 ÷ 6 = 7
420 ÷ 6 = 70

B Estimate: 192 ÷ 5
Think: 20 ÷ 5 = 4
200 ÷ 5 = 40

Check Out the Glossar[...]
estimate
compatible numbers
See page 544.

CHECK

Check for Understanding

Estimate. Show the compatible numbers you used.

1. 57 ÷ 3 — 60 ÷ 3 = 20
2. 98 ÷ 5 — 100 ÷ 5 = 20
3. 312 ÷ 6 — 300 ÷ 6 = 50
4. 652 ÷ 8 — 640 ÷ 8 = 80
5. 787 ÷ 9 — 810 ÷ 9 = 90
6. 2,489 ÷ 4 — 2,400 ÷ 4 = 600
7. 4,809 ÷ 7 — 4,900 ÷ 7 = 700
8. 6,225 ÷ 9 — 6,300 ÷ 9 =

Critical Thinking: Analyze **Explain your reasoning.**

9. Show two different ways to estimate the quotient using compatible numbers. Which estimate will be closer to the exact answer?
a. 292 ÷ 4 **b.** 2,234 ÷ 6

Meeting Individual Needs

Early Finishers

Have students use ex. 13–16 to decide whether the exact answer would be more than or less than the estimate. Have them use a calculator to check their answers.

Extra Support

As students work on exercises, have them identify compatible numbers they can use to estimate. If they have difficulty, give students possible compatible numbers, and ask why they would or would not use them.

Ongoing Assessment

Observation Checklist Determine if students understand how to estimate by observing if they are able to find compatible numbers to divide.

Follow Up Allow students who are unsure of how to find compatible numbers to refer to basic division facts to help them estimate. For additional help, assign **Reteach 67.**

Ask students who demonstrate mastery to find two sets of compatible numbers for each of ex. 1–16. You may also wish to assign **Extend 67.**

Students' graphs should reflect the data they collected.

ractice Estimates may vary. Possible estimates are given.

imate. Show the compatible numbers you used.

79 ÷ 4 80 ÷ 4 = 20	**2** 80 ÷ 3 90 ÷ 3 = 30	**3** 37 ÷ 2 40 ÷ 2 = 20	**4** 96 ÷ 5 100 ÷ 5 = 20
167 ÷ 2 160 ÷ 2 = 80	**6** 152 ÷ 8 160 ÷ 8 = 20	**7** 379 ÷ 4 360 ÷ 4 = 90	**8** 532 ÷ 6 540 ÷ 6 = 90
1,578 ÷ 5 1,500 ÷ 5 = 300	**10** 2,654 ÷ 3 2,700 ÷ 3 = 900	**11** 4,512 ÷ 5 4,500 ÷ 5 = 900	**12** 7,465 ÷ 8 7,200 ÷ 8 = 900
198 ÷ 4 200 ÷ 4 = 50	**14** 4,732 ÷ 6 4,800 ÷ 6 = 800	**15** 518 ÷ 7 490 ÷ 7 = 70	**16** 8,976 ÷ 9 9,000 ÷ 9 = 1,000

PRACTICE

XED APPLICATIONS

roblem Solving

17. $80; possible answer: estimate $320 ÷ 4 = $80.

A town has $324 for supplies for its 4 Little League teams. About how much can each team spend for supplies? Explain your thinking. See above.

What is the distance between the bases on a major league field? SEE INFOBIT. 90 ft

Major league bats cannot be longer than 42 inches. How much longer is this than the longest Little League bat? SEE INFOBIT. 9 in.

INFOBIT
Little League bats cannot be longer than 33 inches. The distance between the bases is 60 feet. This is 30 feet shorter than on a major league field.

Data Point Survey your classmates to find their favorite baseball team. Show your results on a graph. See above.

Little League coaches try out 488 children during 8 sessions. About how many children try out at each session? Possible answer: about 60 children

22 **Write a problem** that you can solve by estimating a quotient. Have others solve it. Students check each other's work by comparing problems and solutions.

mixed review • test preparation

$123.89 − $95.99 $27.90	**2** $912.43 + $0.99 + $1.79 $915.21	**3** 242 × 6 1,452
3 × 5,004 15,012	**5** $904.00 + $19.36 $923.36	**6** $307 − $249 $58

a Practice, page 512

Alternate Teaching Strategy

Have students read the problem on Student Book page 280. Then write the following division sentence on the chalkboard: 752 ÷ 8.

Remind students that they know how to divide multiples of ten, 640 ÷ 8, using basic division facts such as 64 ÷ 8. Students can use this method to estimate quotients. The numbers they use are called compatible numbers.

Have a volunteer draw a ring around the digits 7 and 5 in the dividend 752. Then have the student write 75 ÷ 8 under the original example. Ask:

- **What basic fact does 75 ÷ 8 make you think of?** *[Possible answer: 72 ÷ 8 = 9]*
- **How can you use this fact to estimate the quotient?** *[720 ÷ 8 = 90]*

Repeat the activity with other division examples, such as 656 ÷ 8, and 4,409 ÷ 7.

PRACTICE • 67

HOMEWORK

Practice 67

Name:

MENTAL MATH: ESTIMATE QUOTIENTS

Estimate by using compatible numbers.
Explain your method. Estimates may vary. Possible estimates are given.

1. 41 ÷ 2	40 ÷ 2 = 20	**2.** 70 ÷ 3	60 ÷ 3 = 20
3. 70 ÷ 4	80 ÷ 4 = 20	**4.** 362 ÷ 9	360 ÷ 9 = 40
5. 279 ÷ 3	270 ÷ 3 = 90	**6.** 237 ÷ 8	240 ÷ 8 = 30
7. 349 ÷ 7	350 ÷ 7 = 50	**8.** 430 ÷ 9	450 ÷ 9 = 50
9. 470 ÷ 6	480 ÷ 6 = 80	**10.** 563 ÷ 8	560 ÷ 8 = 70
11. 730 ÷ 9	720 ÷ 9 = 80	**12.** 642 ÷ 8	640 ÷ 8 = 80
13. 1,815 ÷ 6	1,800 ÷ 6 = 300	**14.** 3,255 ÷ 4	3,200 ÷ 4 = 800
15. 2,523 ÷ 5	2,500 ÷ 5 = 500	**16.** 5,511 ÷ 7	5,600 ÷ 7 = 800
17. 8,321 ÷ 9	8,100 ÷ 9 = 900	**18.** 5,420 ÷ 6	5,400 ÷ 6 = 900
19. 2,045 ÷ 3	2,100 ÷ 3 = 700	**20.** 1,209 ÷ 5	1,000 ÷ 5 = 200
21. 6,234 ÷ 7	6,300 ÷ 7 = 900	**22.** 2,978 ÷ 4	2,800 ÷ 4 = 700
23. 7,389 ÷ 9	7,200 ÷ 9 = 800	**24.** 5,005 ÷ 7	4,900 ÷ 7 = 700

Solve.

25. Your family travels a total of 94 miles to El Paso, Texas, every week for shopping. If you go 3 times a week, about how many miles is each round trip to El Paso?
about 30 mi

26. Your parents once took a bike trip of 183 miles to Jasper, Wyoming. It took them 9 days. About how many miles did they travel each day?
about 20 mi a day

McGraw-Hill School Division

RETEACH • 67

Reteach 67

Name:

MENTAL MATH: ESTIMATE QUOTIENTS

Compatible numbers are numbers you can divide easily. You can use compatible numbers to estimate quotients.

Estimate: 321 ÷ 4

Think:
321 is close to 320.
320 ÷ 4 should make you think of 32 ÷ 4.
32 ÷ 4 = 8
320 ÷ 4 = 80
So, 321 ÷ 4 is about 80.

Think of a division fact that is like the numbers you are dividing.

Complete.

1. Estimate: 453 ÷ 9
Division fact: 45 ÷ 9 = 5
Estimate: 450 ÷ 9 = 50

2. Estimate: 213 ÷ 7
Division fact: 21 ÷ 7 = 3
Estimate: 210 ÷ 7 = 30

3. Estimate: 299 ÷ 6
Division fact: 30 ÷ 6 = 5
Estimate: 300 ÷ 6 = 50

4. Estimate: 319 ÷ 4
Division fact: 32 ÷ 4 = 8
Estimate: 320 ÷ 4 = 80

Estimate. Ring the letter of the division sentence with the compatible number. Then complete the division.

5. 123 ÷ 4	(a.) 120 ÷ 4 = 30	b. 100 ÷ 4 = ____
6. 319 ÷ 8	a. 300 ÷ 8 = ____	(b.) 320 ÷ 8 = 40
7. 147 ÷ 5	(a.) 150 ÷ 5 = 30	b. 100 ÷ 5 = ____
8. 2,355 ÷ 8	(a.) 2,400 ÷ 8 = 300	b. 2,000 ÷ 8 = ____
9. 4,529 ÷ 9	a. 4,900 ÷ 9 = ____	(b.) 4,500 ÷ 9 = 500

McGraw-Hill School Division

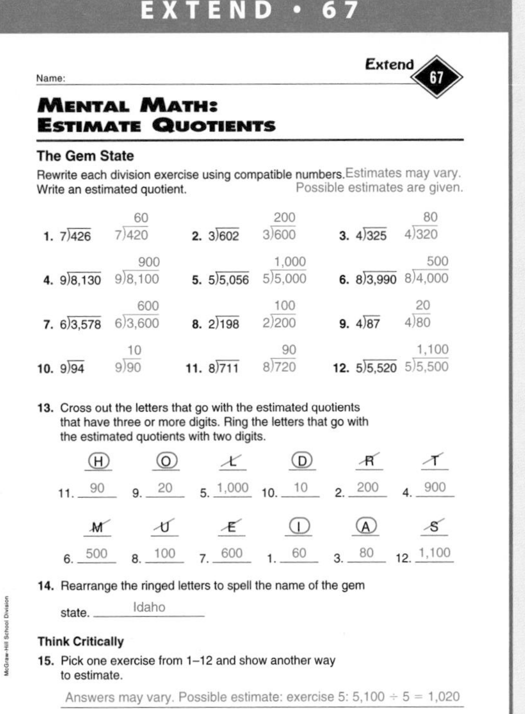

EXTEND • 67

Extend 67

Name:

MENTAL MATH: ESTIMATE QUOTIENTS

The Gem State

Rewrite each division exercise using compatible numbers. Write an estimated quotient. Estimates may vary. Possible estimates are given.

1. 7)426 — 7)420 = 60	**2.** 3)602 — 3)600 = 200	**3.** 4)325 — 4)320 = 80
4. 9)8,130 — 9)8,100 = 900	**5.** 5)5,056 — 5)5,000 = 1,000	**6.** 8)3,990 — 8)4,000 = 500
7. 6)3,578 — 6)3,600 = 600	**8.** 2)198 — 2)200 = 100	**9.** 4)87 — 4)80 = 20
10. 9)94 — 9)90 = 10	**11.** 8)711 — 8)720 = 90	**12.** 5)5,520 — 5)5,500 = 1,100

13. Cross out the letters that go with the estimated quotients that have three or more digits. Ring the letters that go with the estimated quotients with two digits.

(H)	(O)	~~L~~	(D)	~~R~~	~~T~~
11. 90	9. 20	5. 1,000	10. 10	2. 200	4. 900

~~M~~	~~U~~	~~E~~	(I)	(A)	~~S~~
6. 500	8. 100	7. 600	1. 60	3. 80	12. 1,100

14. Rearrange the ringed letters to spell the name of the gem state. Idaho

Think Critically

15. Pick one exercise from 1–12 and show another way to estimate.
Answers may vary. Possible estimate: exercise 5: 5,100 ÷ 5 = 1,020

McGraw-Hill School Division

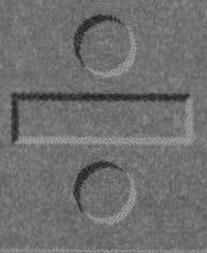

EXPLORE ACTIVITY

Divide by 1-Digit Numbers

OBJECTIVE Use models to explore dividing 2-digit numbers by 1-digit numbers.

Teaching with Technology
See alternate computer lesson, pp. 285A–285B.

RESOURCE REMINDER
Math Center Cards 68
Practice 68, Reteach 68, Extend 68

SKILLS TRACE

GRADE 3	• Use place-value models to explore dividing 2-digit numbers by 1-digit numbers. *(Chapter 12)*
GRADE 4	• Use place-value models to explore dividing 2-digit numbers by 1-digit numbers.
GRADE 5	• Divide 2- and 3-digit numbers by 1-digit numbers. *(Chapter 5)*

MANIPULATIVE WARM-UP

Cooperative Pairs — Kinesthetic

OBJECTIVE Use models to show multiplication and division sentences.

Materials per pair: place-value models—9 tens, 20 ones; two 4-part spinners (TA 2)—one labeled 15, 24, 21, and 19, the other labeled 2, 3, 4, and 3

▶ Display the following arrangement of place-value models:

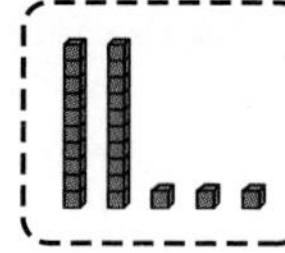
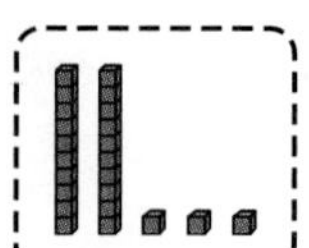
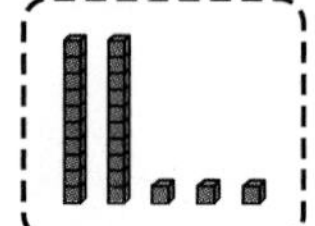
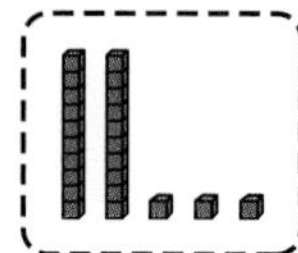

▶ Have a volunteer write a multiplication sentence and a division sentence with a 1-digit divisor that the models could represent. *[4 × 23 = 92; 92 ÷ 4 = 23]*

▶ Pairs spin the spinners and use models to show multiplying the two numbers. They then write a multiplication sentence and a division sentence with a 1-digit divisor, which the models represent.

▶ Students repeat the activity until they have written five pairs of multiplication and division sentences.

ESL APPROPRIATE

STATISTICS CONNECTION

Cooperative Pairs — Visual/Spatial

OBJECTIVE Connect estimating quotients to interpreting data in statistics.

▶ Display the following:

Students and Classes in Grades 3–5, Pine Elementary

Grade	Total Number of Students	Number of Classes
3	88	4
4	78	3
5	96	4

▶ Have pairs divide to find the average number of students in each class. *[Grade 3, 22 students; Grade 4, 26 students; Grade 5, 24 students]* Have each pair make a bar graph to display the average number of students in the class of each grade.

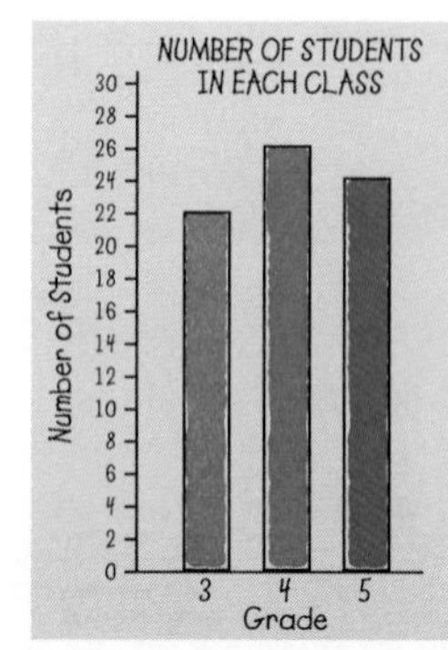

Daily Review

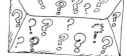

PREVIOUS DAY QUICK REVIEW

Estimate by using compatible numbers.

1. 98 ÷ 5 *[20]*
2. 172 ÷ 4 *[40]*
3. 1,793 ÷ 6 *[300]*
4. 3,105 ÷ 3 *[1,000]*

FAST FACTS

1. 5 × 3 *[15]*
2. 1 × 9 *[9]*
3. 6 × 0 *[0]*
4. 8 × 4 *[32]*

Problem of the Day • 68

Juan collects baseball cards. He puts the cards in separate pockets on plastic pages. Each page has 4 rows and each row holds 2 cards. How many pages does Juan need for 96 baseball cards? *[12 pages]*

TECH LINK

Math Van

MATH VAN

Activity You may wish to use *Shooting the Grand Canyon* to teach this lesson.

MATH FORUM

Management Tip I allow pairs of students to share place-value models and work through division exercises together. This way, they often coach and encourage each other.

Visit our Resource Village at http://www.mhschool.com to see more of the Math Forum.

MATH CENTER

Practice

OBJECTIVE Use models to divide.

Materials per student: 8 paper cups, 99 counters, Math Center Recording Sheet (TA 31 optional)

Students use paper cups and counters to divide 2-digit numbers by 1-digit divisors. *[Check students' work.]*

PRACTICE ACTIVITY 68 — MATH CENTER, On Your Own

Manipulatives • Paper Cup Division

- Grab a handful of counters. Count them and write down the total. This number is your dividend.
- Pick any number of paper cups. This number is your divisor. Write a division sentence, and then estimate the quotient. Will there be a remainder?
- Use the paper cups to divide the counters into equal groups. Do you have any counters left over? Write your final answer.
- Repeat this activity several times with different numbers of counters and paper cups.

YOU NEED
- 8 paper cups
- 99 counters (or connecting cubes or ones models)

Grade Level 4 · McGraw-Hill School Division

Chapter 8, Lesson 3, pages 282–285 — Division

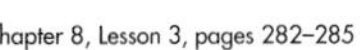
ESL APPROPRIATE

NCTM Standards
- ✓ Problem Solving
- Communication
- ✓ Reasoning
- Connections

Problem Solving

OBJECTIVE Explore divisibility patterns.

Students solve a riddle that relates to the remainder of each division problem. They then create riddles of their own. *[24]*

PROBLEM-SOLVING ACTIVITY 68 — MATH CENTER, On Your Own

Logical Reasoning • Division Riddles

Who am I?

- When you divide me by 1, you get a remainder of 0.
- When you divide me by 2, you get a remainder of 0.
- When you divide me by 3, you get a remainder of 0.
- When you divide me by 4, you get a remainder of 0.
- When you divide me by 5, you get a remainder of 4.
- When you divide me by 6, you get a remainder of 0.
- When you divide me by 7, you get a remainder of 3.

Make up two riddles of your own and ask another student to solve them.

Grade Level 4 · McGraw-Hill School Division

Chapter 8, Lesson 3, pages 282–285 — Division

NCTM Standards
- ✓ Problem Solving
- Communication
- ✓ Reasoning
- Connections

EXPLORE ACTIVITY

Divide by 1-Digit Numbers

OBJECTIVE Use models to explore dividing 2-digit numbers by 1-digit numbers.

Materials per group: connecting cubes; paper bags; 1–9 spinner (TA 2)

Vocabulary dividend, divisor, quotient, regroup, remainder

Introduce

To give a context to the numbers in the table on page 282, present this problem:

Bob's mother has collected 59 postcards from around the United States. She wants to give the same number of cards to each of her 4 children. How many postcards should she give each child?

- **What operation would you use to solve this problem?** *[division]*
- **What quotient would you have to find?** *[59 ÷ 4]*
- **About how many postcards should Bob's mother give to each child? Explain.** *[about 14 postcards; 71 ÷ 4 = 17 R3]*

Teach *Cooperative Groups*

LEARN Work Together To help students think creatively about different ways to divide the cubes so that each person gets the same number, ask:

- **How can you divide the trains in the pile equally into different groups?** *[Possible answer: Take the trains apart and use single cubes.]*
- **How can you use estimation to help you make equal numbers of cubes for each person?** *[Possible answer: The estimate tells you about how many cubes each person will get.]*
- **When will some cubes be left over?** *[when there are not enough cubes to give an equal group to each person]*
- **Can the number left over be greater than the number of people who share the cubes? Explain.** *[No; possible answer: it must be less or each person would get another cube.]*

Talk It Over Allow groups to explain when they decided to regroup and how they used estimation. Have them compare methods for ease of use and for accuracy.

EXPLORE ACTIVITY • DIVISION

Divide by 1-Digit Numbers

LEARN

You can use cubes to help you divide by 1-digit numbers.

Work Together

Work in a group to share cubes.

You will need
- *1–9 spinner*
- *connecting cubes*

Make a pile of 9 trains that each have 10 cubes. Make another pile with 9 single cubes.

Take a handful of trains and single cubes. Record the total in a table like the one below.

Spin the spinner to see how many people will share the cubes.

Divide the cubes so that each person gets an equal number. Record your work.

Repeat the activity five times.

KEEP IN MIND
▶ Be prepared to expla[in] your answers and methods.

Total	Number of People	Number of Cubes for Each Person	Number Left Over
59	4		

Question 1. Possible answer: If there were enough trains to sha equally among the students, then the tr were broken apart in single cubes and the shared.

Talk It Over

▶ How did you decide when to **regroup?**
See above.

▶ How can you use estimation to check your answers?
Possible answer: Use compatible numbers to find an estimate and see if the exact answer is close to the estimate.

Meeting Individual Needs

Extra Support

Choose exercises from ex. 5–28. Have students use models to demonstrate and explain each step of the process. Ask:

- **Do you need to break a ten into ones?**
- **Are all the groups equal?**

Language Support

Help these students with the division vocabulary necessary to answer the first item in **Make Connections.**

ESL APPROPRIATE

Ongoing Assessment

Anecdotal Report Note if students connect the number of equal groups to the divisor in a division sentence, and the number in each group to the quotient.

Follow Up If students have difficulty, give them more work with models using **Reteach 68.**

Have students who are ready for a challenge complete **Extend 68.**

stion 1. Possible answer: The dividend is the total, the divisor is the number of people groups), the quotient is the number of cubes for each person (or the number in each p), and the remainder is the number left over.

ke Connections

a's group shared 59 cubes among eople. They recorded it like this.

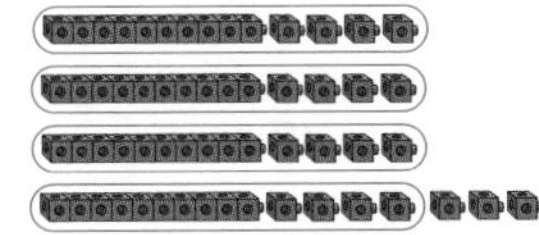

al	Number of People	Number of Cubes for Each Person	Number Left Over
)	4	14	3

stion 2. Possible answer: Total—61 ÷ Number of People—5 = 12 cubes R1

can also use a division sentence to record what done.

Check Out the Glossary
For vocabulary words
See page 544.

59 ÷ 4 = 14 R3 ← **remainder**

↑ **dividend** ↑ **divisor** ↑ **quotient**

Explain what each part of the division sentence means. See above.

Write division sentences for each row in your table. See above.

eck for Understanding

nplete the division sentence for the picture.

36 ÷ 4 = ■ 9

2 43 ÷ 6 = ■ 7 R1

de. You may use place-value models.

51 ÷ 3 17 **4** 75 ÷ 5 15 **5** 98 ÷ 7 14 **6** 76 ÷ 4 19

39 ÷ 6 6 R3 **8** 88 ÷ 9 9 R7 **9** 87 ÷ 2 43 R1 **10** 99 ÷ 8 12 R3

tical Thinking: Generalize **Explain your reasoning.**

How are remainders related to divisors in the division sentences below? What is the greatest possible remainder for a given divisor? the least possible remainder?

26 ÷ 2 = 13
77 ÷ 2 = 38 R1

57 ÷ 3 = 19
73 ÷ 3 = 24 R1
29 ÷ 3 = 9 R2

88 ÷ 4 = 22
61 ÷ 4 = 15 R1
34 ÷ 4 = 8 R2
55 ÷ 4 = 13 R3

Possible answer: Remainders are always less than the divisor because *remainder* means the number left over that cannot be e into a group as large as the divisor; the greatest sible remainder is 1 less than the divisor; the least sible remainder is 0.

Turn the page for Practice.

MAKE CONNECTIONS

The division sentence provides another way of recording the information from the table. Students should connect each number in the table with a part of the division sentence.

To make sure that students understand the relationship between the division sentences and the models, write a division sentence from each group on the chalkboard. Then have students from other groups explain how each division sentence could be demonstrated using the models. If possible, have a few volunteers identify the entire procedure, starting with the number spun and ending with the connection to the division sentence.

Encourage students to check their quotients after writing each division sentence. Ask:

- **How can you use multiplication and addition to check your answer?** *[Multiply quotient by divisor, then add the remainder.]*

Remind students of the importance of using compatible numbers to estimate as they review their quotients.

3 Close

Check for Understanding using items 1–11, page 283.

Critical Thinking

In item 11, students relate remainders to divisors. To make sure that they understand the generalization, ask:

- **What should you do if you have a remainder greater than the divisor?** *[Increase the quotient.]*

Practice See pages 284–285.

▶ PRACTICE

Materials have available: place-value models; calculators

Options for assigning exercises:
A—All ex. 1–4; odd ex. 5–27; all ex. 29–34; **More to Explore**
B—All ex. 1–4; even ex. 6–28; all ex. 29–34; **More to Explore**

- Being able to visualize groups of numbers is important in understanding division. For ex. 1–4, students use number sense to help them develop the division sentences that are represented by the models.
- Suggest that students use mental math and basic division facts to solve ex. 5–8 and ex. 17–20.
- Encourage students to use estimation to help them divide in ex. 5–28. Some students will be able to divide using only estimation and mental math.
- For **Make It Right** (ex. 29), see **Common Error** below.
- For ex. 33, students may use the problem-solving strategy, Interpret Data, to solve.

Problem/Solution For ex. 34, invite students to share their problems and solutions. Ask volunteers to identify the problem. Then invite the class to suggest other solutions where possible.

More to Explore Read the words *prime number* and *composite number* aloud, together with their definitions. Then have volunteers suggest a prime number and a composite number between 3 and 10. *[prime: 3, 5, 7; composite: 4, 6, 8, 9, 10] Tell students that the numbers that a number is divisible by are its factors. The factors of 15 are 1, 3, 5, and 15.*

Have pairs work together. For each exercise, suggest that students list the two numbers that the prime numbers are divisible by and some of the numbers that the composite numbers are divisible by. *[1, 13; 1, 3, 7, 21; 1, 19; 1, 7; 1, 2, 7, 14]* After students have completed the exercises, ask:

- **Can an even number greater than 2 ever be prime? Explain.** *[No; an even number is always divisible by 2.]*

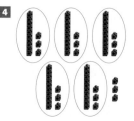

Practice

Write a division sentence to represent the models.

1 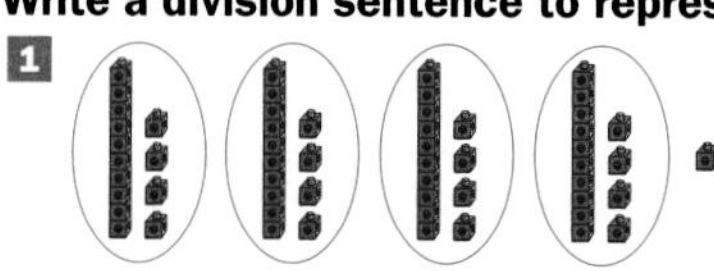
57 ÷ 4 = 14 R1

2 24 ÷ 6 = 4 or 24 ÷ 4 = 6

3 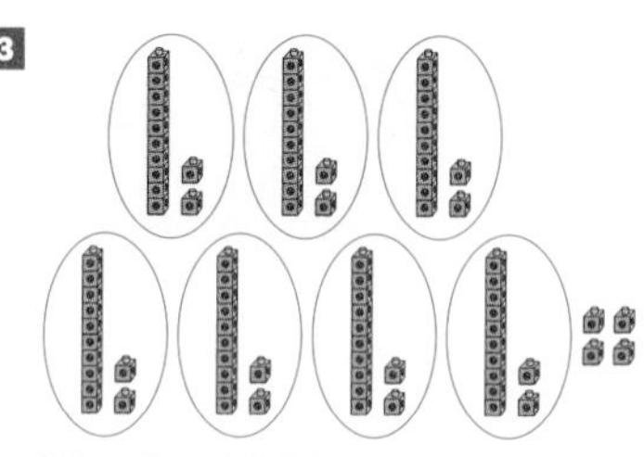
88 ÷ 7 = 12 R4

4 68 ÷ 5 = 13 R3

Divide. You may use place-value models.

5 49 ÷ 8 **6 R1**	6 37 ÷ 4 **9 R1**	7 31 ÷ 7 **4 R3**	8 26 ÷ 3 **8**
9 91 ÷ 6 **15 R1**	10 70 ÷ 5 **14**	11 49 ÷ 2 **24 R1**	12 77 ÷ 5 **15 R2**
13 97 ÷ 7 **13 R6**	14 99 ÷ 2 **49 R1**	15 87 ÷ 8 **10 R7**	16 47 ÷ 3 **15 R2**
17 89 ÷ 9 **9 R8**	18 84 ÷ 4 **21**	19 69 ÷ 7 **9 R6**	20 46 ÷ 6 **7**
21 47 ÷ 5 **9 R2**	22 46 ÷ 2 **23**	23 74 ÷ 3 **24 R2**	24 44 ÷ 8 **5**
25 64 ÷ 3 **21 R1**	26 19 ÷ 3 **6 R1**	27 91 ÷ 8 **11 R3**	28 67 ÷ 5 **13 R2**

Make It Right

29 Explain what mistake was made. Show the correct answer.

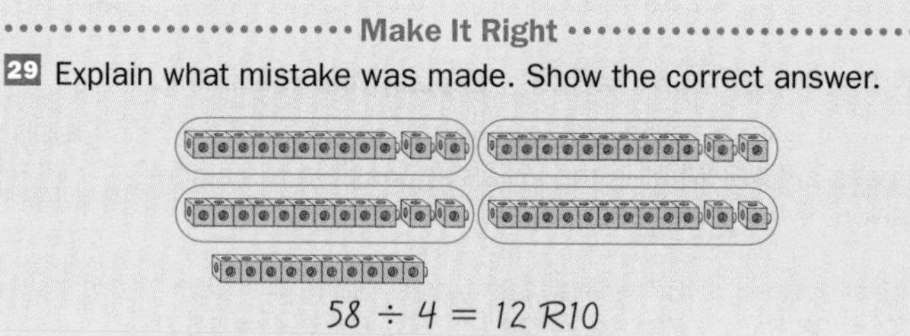

58 ÷ 4 = 12 R10

Did not regroup the tens model into 10 ones and show 4 groups of 1 ten and 4 on and 2 ones left over; the division sentence should be 58 ÷ 4 = 14 R2.

Meeting Individual Needs

Early Finishers

Have students extend the activity on page 282 to 3-digit dividends using 10 and 20 ten-cube trains and a handful of cubes. Have students write a division sentence to record what they do.

ESL APPROPRIATE

Gifted And Talented

Present this problem: If I separate a stack of cards into groups of 6, I have 3 left over. If I separate them into groups of 8, there are 5 left over. How many cards are in the stack? *[45 cards]*

Common Error

As in **Make It Right** on page 284, when there are not enough tens models for each group, some students may treat the leftover tens models as part of the remainder rather than regrouping the tens as ones. Remind students to compare the remainder to the divisor, or the number to the number of groups. If the remainder is greater than the divisor, they will have to regroup to divide.

XED APPLICATIONS

roblem Solving

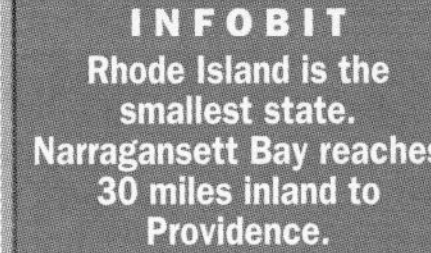

Each column in front of the Supreme Court in Washington, D.C., is 3 stories high. If you created a single column from all the columns, it would be 48 stories high! How many columns are there? **16 columns**

You can travel from Providence down Narragansett Bay and then to Block Island. A boat sails this distance in 2 hours. It covers a mile in about 3 minutes. How far is Block Island from Narragansett Bay? **SEE INFOBIT. 10 mi**

INFOBIT
Rhode Island is the smallest state. Narragansett Bay reaches 30 miles inland to Providence.

the bar graph for problems 32–34.

In 1994, about how many more people lived in Washington, D.C., than Wyoming? **Possible answer: about 100,000 people**

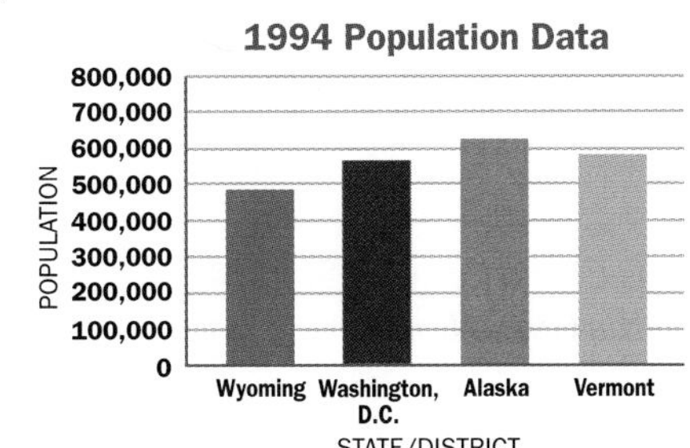

One of these states was the least populated state in the country in 1994. Which state was it? **Wyoming**

Problem/Solution Write another problem based on the graph. Tell how to solve the problem. **Students should compare problems and solutions.**

more to explore

me and Composite Numbers

rime number is divisible by only numbers, itself and 1.

÷ 1 = 17 17 ÷ 17 = 1

is divisible by 1 and 17 only.

A *composite number* is divisible by more than two numbers.

15 ÷ 1 = 15 15 ÷ 5 = 3
15 ÷ 15 = 1 15 ÷ 3 = 5

15 is divisible by 1, 3, 5, and 15.

if the number is prime or composite.

13 **prime** **2** 21 **composite** **3** 19 **prime** **4** 7 **prime** **5** 14 **composite**

a Practice, page 512

Alternate Teaching Strategy

Materials per pair: place-value models—9 tens, 20 ones

Present this problem:

There are 63 sheets of drawing paper and 5 friends. If each friend gets the same number of sheets, how many sheets does each friend get?

Ask:

- **What operation can you use to solve the problem?** *[division]*
- **What quotient do you want to find? What is an estimate using compatible numbers?** *[63 ÷ 5; possible estimate: 50 ÷ 5 = 10]*
- **How can you use the estimate to divide 63 into 5 equal groups?** *[Possible answer: Start with 10 in each group.]*

Have students work in pairs and use the place-value models to show 63. Have them put 1 ten in 5 different groups. Ask:

- **How much is left after you put 1 ten in each of 5 groups?** *[13, or 1 ten 3 ones]*
- **How many ones can you put in each of the 5 groups so each group has the same amount? How many are left?** *[2 ones; 3 ones]*
- **How many are in each group? What is the quotient? What is the remainder?** *[12, or 1 ten 2 ones; 12; 3]*

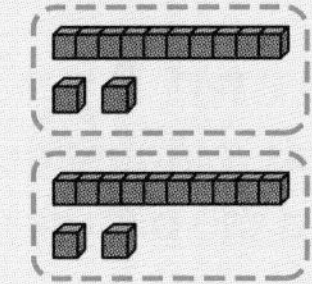

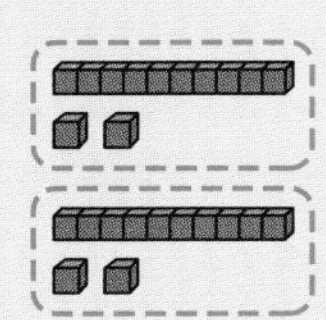

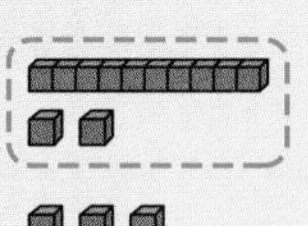

63 ÷ 5 = 12R3

PRACTICE • 68

Practice 68

Name:

Division by 1-Digit Numbers

Write a division sentence to represent the models.

1. 28 ÷ 7 = 4
2. 67 ÷ 5 = 13 R2
3. 15 ÷ 2 = 7 R1
4. 51 ÷ 4 = 12 R3
5. 35 ÷ 3 = 11 R2
6. 26 ÷ 8 = 3 R2

Divide. You may use place-value models.

7. 19 ÷ 6 = 3 R1	**8.** 35 ÷ 4 = 8 R3	**9.** 29 ÷ 8 = 3 R5
10. 32 ÷ 9 = 3 R5	**11.** 40 ÷ 9 = 4 R4	**12.** 60 ÷ 9 = 6 R6
13. 49 ÷ 4 = 12 R1	**14.** 64 ÷ 5 = 12 R4	**15.** 79 ÷ 6 = 13 R1
16. 82 ÷ 7 = 11 R5	**17.** 98 ÷ 6 = 16 R2	**18.** 99 ÷ 7 = 14 R1
19. 53 ÷ 2 = 26 R1	**20.** 97 ÷ 2 = 48 R1	**21.** 89 ÷ 3 = 29 R2
22. 59 ÷ 7 = 8 R3	**23.** 28 ÷ 3 = 9 R1	**24.** 38 ÷ 5 = 7 R3
25. 17 ÷ 2 = 8 R1	**26.** 41 ÷ 9 = 4 R5	**27.** 20 ÷ 6 = 3 R2
28. 29 ÷ 5 = 5 R4	**29.** 62 ÷ 7 = 8 R6	**30.** 53 ÷ 6 = 8 R5

McGraw-Hill School Division

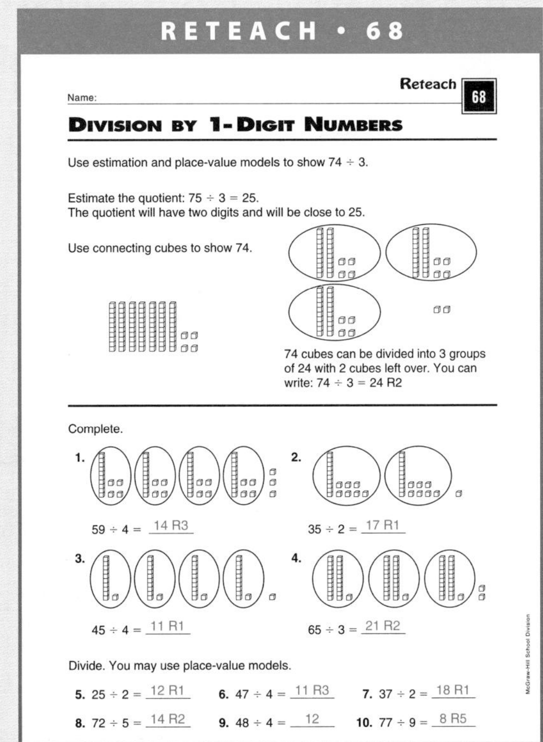

RETEACH • 68

Reteach 68

Name:

Division by 1-Digit Numbers

Use estimation and place-value models to show 74 ÷ 3.

Estimate the quotient: 75 ÷ 3 = 25.
The quotient will have two digits and will be close to 25.

Use connecting cubes to show 74.

74 cubes can be divided into 3 groups of 24 with 2 cubes left over. You can write: 74 ÷ 3 = 24 R2

Complete.

1. 59 ÷ 4 = 14 R3
2. 35 ÷ 2 = 17 R1
3. 45 ÷ 4 = 11 R1
4. 65 ÷ 3 = 21 R2

Divide. You may use place-value models.

5. 25 ÷ 2 = 12 R1	**6.** 47 ÷ 4 = 11 R3	**7.** 37 ÷ 2 = 18 R1
8. 72 ÷ 5 = 14 R2	**9.** 48 ÷ 4 = 12	**10.** 77 ÷ 9 = 8 R5

McGraw-Hill School Division

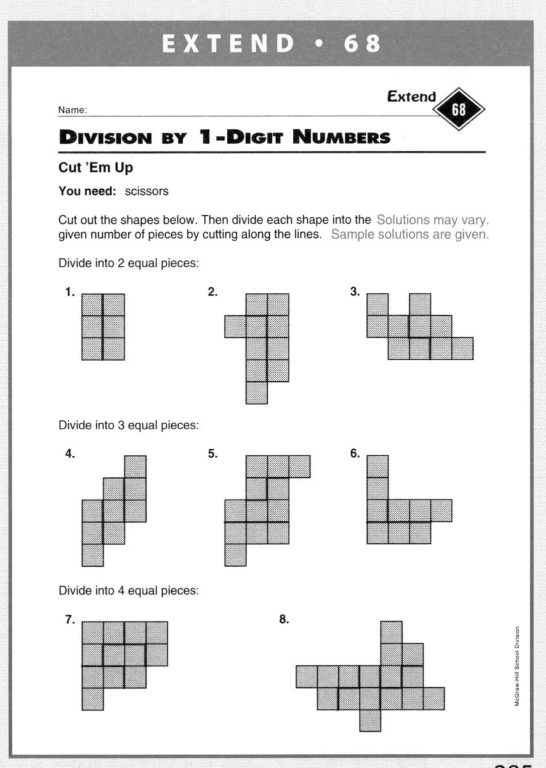

EXTEND • 68

Extend 68

Name:

Division by 1-Digit Numbers

Cut 'Em Up

You need: scissors

Cut out the shapes below. Then divide each shape into the given number of pieces by cutting along the lines. Solutions may vary. Sample solutions are given.

Divide into 2 equal pieces:

1. 2. 3.

Divide into 3 equal pieces:

4. 5. 6.

Divide into 4 equal pieces:

7. 8.

McGraw-Hill School Division

Teaching With Technology

Divide by 1-Digit Numbers

OBJECTIVE Students learn to divide by 1-digit numbers using models.

Resource Math Van Activity: *Shooting the Grand Canyon*

SET UP

Provide students with the activity card for *Shooting the Grand Canyon.* Start ***Math Van*** and click the *Activities* button. Click the *Shooting the Grand Canyon* activity on the Fax Machine.

USING THE MATH VAN ACTIVITY

1 **Getting Started** Students use a Division Mat and Place-Value Models to help plan the photography and arrange a photo album for a rafting trip through the Grand Canyon.

2 **Practice and Apply** Students use a Division Mat and Place-Value Models to figure out how many photo album pages they will need to hold the pictures of the Grand Canyon.

3 **Close** Have students discuss how they used the Place-Value Models to represent division and share their work with other students.

Extend Students use a Division Mat and Place-Value Models to figure out how much film they will need for a trip. They use Place-Value Models to plan how to put the pictures in a photo album.

TIPS FOR TOOLS

If the workspace is crowded, students may be able to use the *Trade Up* button to combine groups of Place-Value Models.

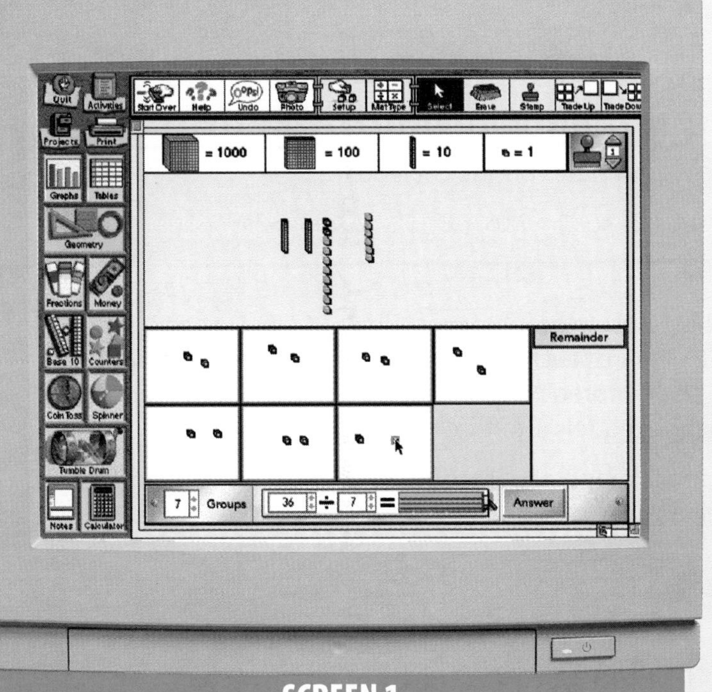

SCREEN 1

Students use Place-Value Models to figure out how many pictures can be taken a day with one roll of film.

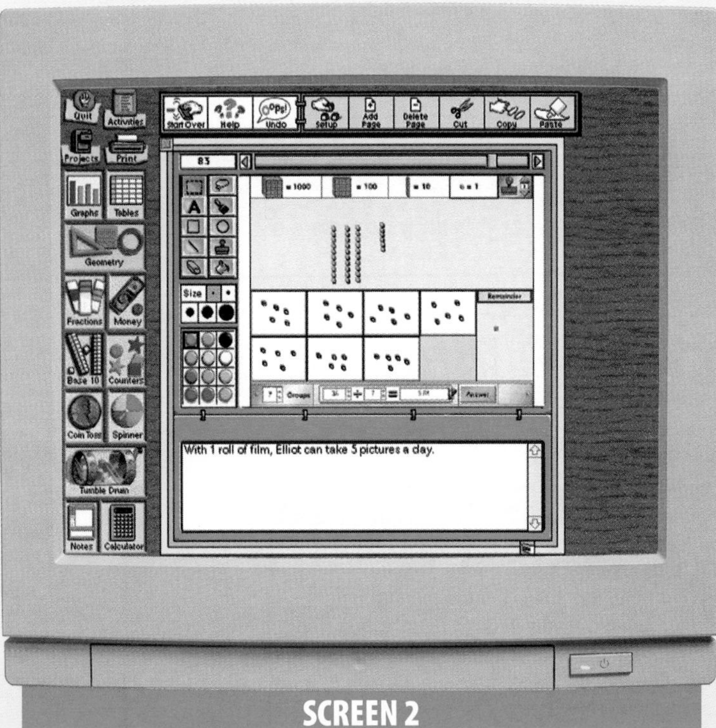

SCREEN 2

Students answer questions about how many pictures they can take each day with one roll of film.

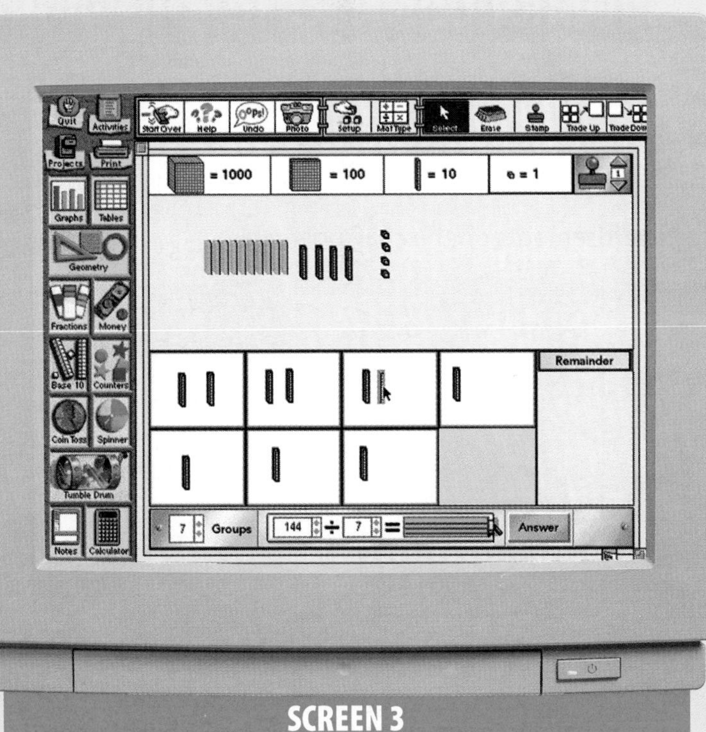

SCREEN 3

Students find how many pictures they can take each day if they buy two, three, or four rolls of film.

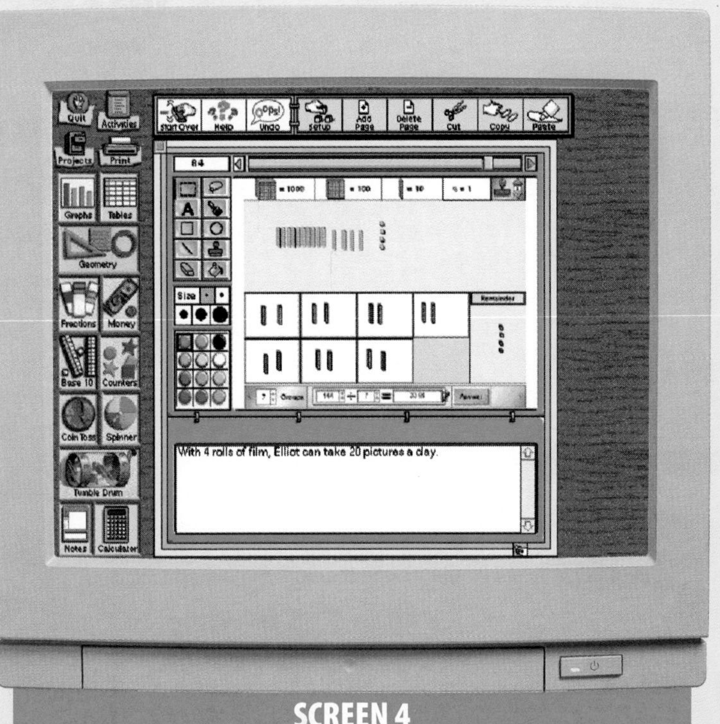

SCREEN 4

Students take a photo of their work and type their final answers in their Notes.

LESSON 8.4

Divide by 1-Digit Numbers

OBJECTIVE Divide 2- and 3-digit numbers by 1-digit numbers.

RESOURCE REMINDER
Math Center Cards 69
Practice 69, Reteach 69, Extend 69

SKILLS TRACE

GRADE 3	• Use place-value models to explore dividing 2-digit numbers by 1-digit numbers. *(Chapter 12)*
GRADE 4	• Divide 2- and 3-digit numbers by 1-digit numbers.
GRADE 5	• Divide 2- and 3-digit numbers by 1-digit numbers. *(Chapter 5)*

MANIPULATIVE WARM-UP

Cooperative Groups — **Visual/Spatial**

OBJECTIVE Divide 3-digit numbers by 1-digit numbers.

Materials per group: centimeter graph paper (TA 7), scissors

▶ Write these division examples on the chalkboard:

144 ÷ 3 *[48]*　216 ÷ 8 *[27]*　198 ÷ 3 *[66]*

168 ÷ 4 *[42]*　217 ÷ 7 *[31]*　486 ÷ 6 *[81]*

▶ Demonstrate 144 ÷ 3 using graph paper. Show 144 by cutting a 10-by-10 square, 4 strips of 10 squares each, and 4 single squares. Then show the division by cutting the hundred into ten 10-strips, and tens into ones as necessary, to divide the models into three equal groups.

▶ Ask groups to use the graph paper to find the remaining quotients. Have them compare their answers.

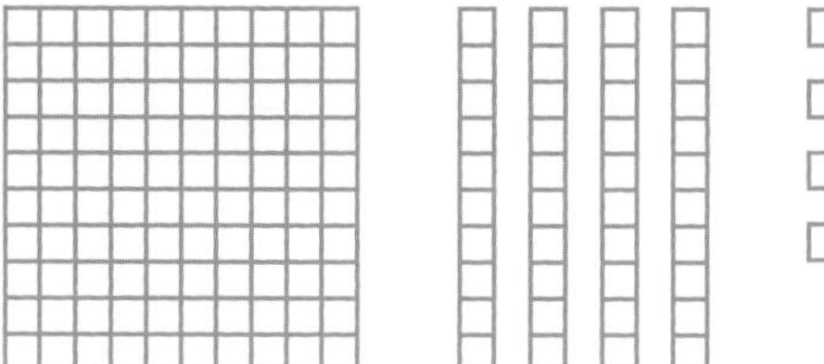

CONSUMER CONNECTION

Cooperative Pairs — **Kinesthetic**

OBJECTIVE Connect division to consumer purchases.

Materials per pair: play money—9 ten-dollar bills, 20 one-dollar bills (TA 11)

Prepare Copy these advertisements on the chalkboard:

▶ Have students use play money to determine how much one of each of the advertised items costs. *[Each hammer is $19, each book is $15, each chair is $28.]* Remind them that they may have to trade some $10 bills for $1 bills. If more play money is needed, have students use index cards to make it.

▶ Repeat the activity with other advertisements.

Daily Review

PREVIOUS DAY QUICK REVIEW

1. 37 ÷ 2 *[18 R1]*
2. 65 ÷ 4 *[16 R1]*
3. 92 ÷ 8 *[11 R4]*
4. 59 ÷ 6 *[9 R5]*

FAST FACTS

1. 35 ÷ 7 *[5]*
2. 24 ÷ 8 *[3]*
3. 16 ÷ 4 *[4]*
4. 72 ÷ 9 *[8]*

Problem of the Day • 69

Kim went to Water World Park with her family for a family reunion. Admission to the park cost a total of $172. There were 8 children and 9 adults. A child's admission cost $8.00. How much was the adult admission? *[$12]*

TECH LINK

Math Van

MATH VAN

Activity You may wish to use *Shooting the Grand Canyon* to practice and extend skills and concepts.

MATH FORUM

Idea I allow my students to use a calculator to check their answers. They receive the calculator after they have completed all of their assigned exercises.

Visit our Resource Village at http://www.mhschool.com to see more of the Math Forum.

MATH CENTER

Practice

OBJECTIVE Use estimation and paper-and-pencil division to find a given remainder.

Materials per student: 0-9 spinner (TA 2), counter, Math Center Recording Sheet (TA 31 optional)

Students play a self-checking game by writing division exercises to get remainders as a way of moving on a game board. They may move back and forth as they play. *[Check students' work.]*

PRACTICE ACTIVITY 69 — MATH CENTER — On Your Own

Number Sense • Remainder Row

YOU NEED
- spinner (0–9)
- counter

- Copy the strip. Put a different digit in each square.
- Spin the spinner four times. Use the numbers to make a 1-digit divisor and a 3-digit dividend. Find the quotient. If there is a remainder that is the same number as one of the boxes in the strip, move your counter to that box. Write the problem out.
- Repeat. Make more divisors and dividends. Use the same four numbers or spin for four new ones. Play until you have landed on each box once or reached the remainder on the last box before *End*.

Start								End

McGraw-Hill School Division — Grade Level 4

Chapter 8, Lesson 4, pages 286–289 — Division

ESL APPROPRIATE

NCTM Standards
- Problem Solving
- ✓ Communication
- ✓ Reasoning
- Connections

Problem Solving

OBJECTIVE Explore the pattern of remainders when dividing by 9.

Materials per student: Math Center Recording Sheet (TA 31 optional)

Students explore the patterning of numbers divisible by 9. They add all the digits of a number together and repeat until they have a 1-digit sum. If that number is 9 then the original number is divisible by 9. Otherwise, the number is the remainder when the original number is divided by 9. *[Check students' work.]*

PROBLEM-SOLVING ACTIVITY 69 — MATH CENTER — Partners

Patterning • Mystery Remainders

- Write a 3-digit number. Add the three digits. If you get a single digit, stop. If you get a 2-digit number, add the 2 digits until you have a single digit.
- Write the digit on a piece of paper. If the digit is 9, write zero. Put the paper in your pocket.
- Ask your partner to divide the original 3-digit number by 9 and then read the remainder. Compare the remainder to the number in your pocket. Show the number in your pocket to your partner.

Repeat several times to see if this mystery math works with any number you divide by 9.

McGraw-Hill School Division — Grade Level 4

Chapter 8, Lesson 4, pages 286–289 — Division

NCTM Standards
- ✓ Problem Solving
- ✓ Communication
- ✓ Reasoning
- Connections

Divide by 1-Digit Numbers

OBJECTIVE Divide 2- and 3-digit numbers by 1-digit numbers.

Materials per pair: 4 hundreds, 10 tens, 10 ones place-value models

1 Introduce

Present the following problem:

Jamal's class has 456 flowers. The class plants the same number of flowers on each of the 4 sides of the school. How many flowers do they plant on each side? *[114]*

- **What division sentence would you use to solve the problem?** *[456 ÷ 4]*

Have students work in pairs and use place-value models to find the quotient. Ask a pair of students to show and explain how they used their models.

2 Teach *Whole Class*

LEARN Have students use place-value models to show each division step shown in the book.

- **Why are 1 ten and 7 ones outside the groups in the second diagram?** *[Possible answer: The 1 ten was left over and the 7 ones have not yet been put into groups.]*
- **Why is the 1 ten regrouped?** *[Possible answer: so it can be put into equal groups]*
- **How many ones are left? How is this recorded in the division sentence?** *[3; R3]*

Discuss the paper-and-pencil method for division.

- **How do you know that the quotient has two digits?** *[Possible answer: The estimate shows that the first digit of the quotient is in the tens place.]*

Go through each step of the algorithm with students. Make sure they understand how the description below each step corresponds to the way it is recorded in the algorithm.

Before reviewing how to check the answer, remind students to compare the answer to the estimate to determine if the answer is reasonable. Then discuss why it is important to check the answer.

Talk It Over Extend the discussion by asking:

- **What should you do if the difference is greater than the divisor?** *[Possible answer: Increase the quotient.]*

Divide by 1-Digit Numbers

LEARN

In the last lesson, you snapped apart cubes to find the answer. Here are some other ways to divide.

Divide: 87 ÷ 7

You can divide using place-value models.

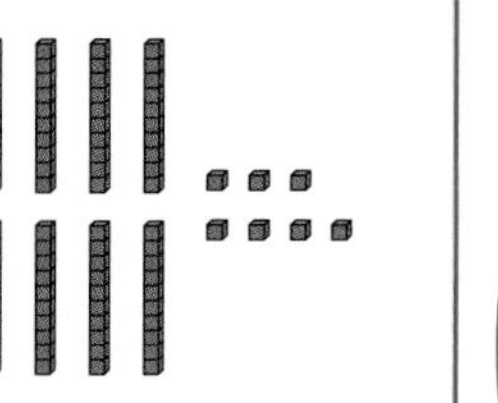

8 tens 7 ones

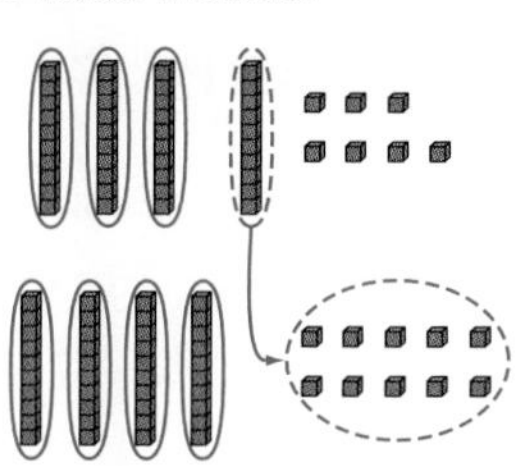

Put 1 ten in each of 7 groups. Regroup 1 ten as 10 ones. Divide the ones equally among the 7 groups.

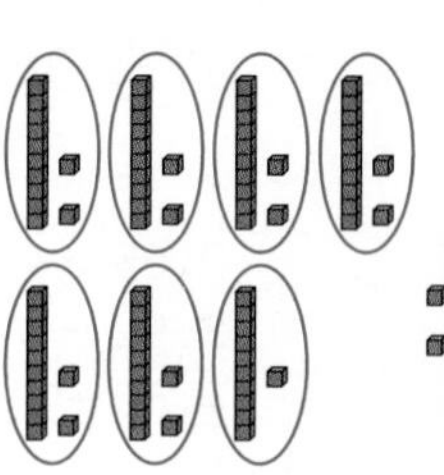

Each of the 7 groups has 1 ten 2 ones. There are 3 ones left over.

87 ÷ 7 = 12 R3

You can also divide using pencil and paper.

Estimate to place the first digit of the quotient.

Estimate: 87 ÷ 7 **Think:** 70 ÷ 7 = 10 The first digit is in the tens place.

Step 1	Step 2
Divide the tens.	**Bring down the ones. Divide the ones. Write the remainder.**
$\begin{array}{r} 1 \\ 7\overline{)87} \\ -7 \\ \hline 1 \end{array}$ **Think:** $7\overline{)8}$ → 1 Multiply: 1 × 7 = 7 Subtract: 8 − 7 = 1 Compare: 1 < 7	$\begin{array}{r} 12 \text{ R3} \\ 7\overline{)87} \\ -7\downarrow \\ \hline 17 \\ -14 \\ \hline 3 \end{array}$ **Think:** $7\overline{)17}$ → 2 Multiply: 2 × 7 = 14 Subtract: 17 − 14 = 3 Compare: 3 < 7 **Check:** 7 × 12 = 84 84 + 3 = 87

So 87 ÷ 7 = 12 R3.

Talk It Over

▶ Why is it a good idea to compare the difference with the divisor at each step? **Possible answer: If the difference is greater than the divisor, then another group could have been made, so the quotient that was used is less than it should be.**

Meeting Individual Needs

Early Finishers

Have students write two word problems that can be solved by using division. Students present the problems they wrote to the class and have classmates solve them.

Extra Support

Help children to verbalize each step of the algorithm. For example, as they start in the hundreds place, have them tell if there are enough hundreds to divide. Then they compute, record in that place, and continue.

Ongoing Assessment

Observation Checklist Determine if students understand dividing by 1-digit numbers by observing them as they record each step of the division process for one of the exercises in the lesson.

Follow Up Allow students who need additional help to work with place-value models and record each step as they group the models, or assign **Reteach 69.**

For students who demonstrate understanding, assign **Extend 69.**

ivide: 800 ÷ 7

stimate to place the first digit of the quotient.

stimate: 800 ÷ 7 **Think:** 700 ÷ 7 = 100
The first digit is in the hundreds place.

tep 1	Step 2	Step 3
vide the hundreds.	**Bring down the tens. Divide the tens.**	**Bring down the ones. Divide the ones. Write the remainder.**
1)800 −7 1 **Think:** 7)8 (1) Multiply: 1 × 7 = 7 Subtract: 8 − 7 = 1 Compare: 1 < 7	11 7)800 −7↓ 10 −7 3 **Think:** 7)10 (1) Multiply: 1 × 7 = 7 Subtract: 10 − 7 = 3 Compare: 3 < 7	114 R2 7)800 −7↓ 10 −7↓ 30 −28 2 **Think:** 7)30 (4) Multiply: 4 × 7 = 28 Subtract: 30 − 28 = 2 Compare: 2 < 7 **Check:** 7 × 114 = 798; 798 + 2 = 800

o, 800 ÷ 7 = 114 R2.

ore Examples

A 4)$52 = $13; −4↓ 12 −12 0

B 5)327 = 65 R2; −30↓ 27 −25 2

C 4)340 = 85; −32↓ 20 −20 0

heck for Understanding

ivide.

1. 6)82 **13 R4**
2. 4)97 **24 R1**
3. 5)429 **85 R4**
4. 4)$692 **$173**
5. 8)968 **121**
6. 57 ÷ 5 **11 R2**
7. 77 ÷ 3 **25 R2**
8. $384 ÷ 4 **$96**
9. 743 ÷ 6 **123 R5**
10. 987 ÷ 7 **141**

ritical Thinking: Summarize

11. Write the steps you would use to find 794 ÷ 3. Explain how to check the answer. **Possible answer: divide 7 by 3, 19 by 3, then 14 by 3 for an answer of 264 R2. You can check your answer by multiplying 264 by 3 then adding 2.**

CHECK

Turn the page for Practice.

Language Support

Make sure these students understand the steps in the algorithm. This algorithm may be different than ones students have used in their countries.

ESL APPROPRIATE

Discuss the estimate. Have students identify the method used for the estimate. *[compatible numbers]* Then ask:

- **How does the estimate help you divide?** *[Possible answer: It tells you the first digit is in the hundreds place.]*

Go through the steps of the algorithm. Have students explain how the steps in the **Think** correspond to the way the division is recorded. In Step 3, ask:

- **What does the arrow mean in the division?** *[Bring down the tens.]*

Elicit that the answer is reasonable since it is close to the estimate. Then have students use multiplication and addition to check the answer. *[114 × 7 = 798; 798 + 2 = 800]*

More Examples Point out that in Examples B and C, the answer begins in the tens place rather than the hundreds place.

Ask students how they could determine this if they were doing the division themselves. *[Possible answers: Use compatible numbers to estimate and find that the answer begins in the tens place; compare the hundreds digit to the divisor and determine that since the hundreds digit is less, you must regroup hundreds as tens to divide.]*

3 Close

Check for Understanding using items 1–11, page 287.

Encourage students to estimate the quotients before dividing and to check their answers after dividing for ex. 1–10.

Critical Thinking

Encourage students to comment on each step they record so that when they look back in their journals, they will have a clear idea of how they divided.

Practice See pages 288–289.

PRACTICE

Materials have available: calculators

Options for assigning exercises:

A—Odd ex. 1–27; all ex. 29–36; **Remainders Game; Mixed Review**

B—Even ex. 2–28; all ex. 29–36; **Remainders Game; Mixed Review**

- To reinforce students' estimation skills, encourage them to record the compatible numbers they use to estimate in ex. 9–28.
- Check that students remember to record the dollar sign in their answers for ex. 14 and 26.
- For ex. 32–35, have students explain each of their choices.
- For **Make It Right** (ex. 36), see **Common Error** below.

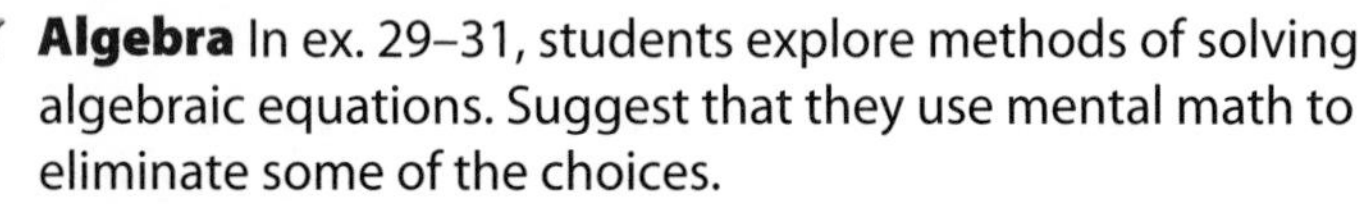

Algebra In ex. 29–31, students explore methods of solving algebraic equations. Suggest that they use mental math to eliminate some of the choices.

Remainders Game Have students work in cooperative groups to play the Remainders Game. As they play, students may develop the strategy of arranging the cards to give the greatest remainder to increase their points. As this happens, students may write the same dividends to divide.

You may want to place the game in a math center so that students have easy access to it. Repeatedly playing the game, or a variation of the game, will provide practice in dividing and in developing division strategies. Variations include trying to get the least possible remainder (zero) or targeting a specific remainder.

Mixed Review/Test Preparation Students use addition and multiplication properties, concepts they learned in Chapters 2 and 6. Have students identify each property they use to find the value of the missing number.

Practice

Divide mentally.

1. 60 ÷ 6 **10**
2. 80 ÷ 4 **20**
3. 81 ÷ 9 **9**
4. 90 ÷ 3 **30**
5. 280 ÷ 7 **40**
6. 720 ÷ 9 **80**
7. 630 ÷ 7 **90**
8. 350 ÷ 5 **70**

Divide. Remember to estimate.

9. 5)85 **17**
10. 2)79 **39 R1**
11. 8)89 **11 R1**
12. 7)99 **14 R1**
13. 6)74 **12 R2**
14. 9)$855 **$95**
15. 2)38 **19**
16. 9)876 **97 R3**
17. 6)68 **11 R2**
18. 7)380 **54 R2**
19. 4)948 **237**
20. 6)919 **153 R1**
21. 8)914 **114 R2**
22. 5)659 **131 R4**
23. 4)944 **236**
24. 3)176 **58 R2**
25. 5)96 **19 R1**
26. 2)$496 **$248**
27. 3)95 **31 R2**
28. 4)776 **194**

ALGEBRA Write the letter of the missing number.

29. 347 ÷ ■ = 69 R2 **b** a. 4 b. 5 c. 6 d. 7
30. 158 ÷ ■ = 52 R2 **c** a. 5 b. 6 c. 3 d. 8
31. 720 ÷ 8 = ■ **c** a. 9 b. 80 c. 90 d. 8

Write the letter of the correct answer.

32. If the divisor is 7, which cannot be a remainder? **c** a. 0 b. 6 c. 9 d. 4
33. If the remainder is 6, which cannot be a divisor? **a** a. 4 b. 9 c. 7 d. 8
34. If the dividend is 42, the quotient will have 2 digits if the divisor is ■. **d** a. 6 b. 5 c. 7 d. 3
35. If the dividend is 42, the quotient will have 1 digit if the divisor is ■. **a** a. 5 b. 4 c. 3 d. 2

Make It Right

36. Here is how Karl divided 334 by 3. Explain what mistake was made. Show how to correct it. **Possible answer: He did not divide the hundreds place.**

```
   11 R1
3)334
 -3
  04
 - 3
   1
```

```
  111 R1
3)334
 -3↓
  03
 - 3↓
   04
  - 3
    1
```


Meeting Individual Needs

Common Error

As in the **Make It Right** on page 288, some students may forget to divide one or more places in a 3-digit dividend. Encourage them to estimate the quotient first to find the number of digits in the quotient.

Inclusion

Ask students who have trouble aligning digits when subtracting to use an index card to cover the digits of lesser place values.

Gifted And Talented

Challenge students with this problem, where each letter stands for a different number.

```
   7A
A)2BC
 -2D
   1C
 - 1C
    0
```

[A = 4, B = 9, C = 6, D = 8]

ESL APPROPRIATE

Remainders Game!

First, make three sets of index cards labeled 0 through 9. Create a scorecard like the one shown.

Next, mix up the cards and have each player choose three cards.

Play the Game

- Spin the spinner once to get a divisor.

Note: Do not use zero as a divisor.

- Each player arranges the three cards as a 3-digit dividend and finds the quotient and remainder. Record the remainder as the player's score.
- Replace the cards and mix them up. Choose new cards and then spin the spinner for a new divisor.
- Continue playing until a player has 20 points.

What strategy could you use to help you get the most points? **Arrange the cards to give the greatest remainder.**

mixed review • test preparation

1. 752 + 0 = ■ **752**
2. (2 × 9) × 5 = (2 × ■) × 9 **5**
3. 24 × ■ = 24 **1**
4. 68 + 57 = 57 + ■ **68**
5. ■ × 95 = 0 **0**
6. 33 × 56 × ■ = 0 **0**
7. 6 × 26 = (3 × 26) + (■ × 26) **3**
8. ■ × 42 = (4 × 42) + (4 × 42) **8**

Extra Practice, page 513

Alternate Teaching Strategy

Materials place-value chart (TA 4)

Read the following problem:

Ms. Holly puts 248 plants in boxes. Each box holds 9 plants. How many boxes will Ms. Holly fill? How many plants will be left over?

Ask students what division sentence they can use to solve the problem. *[248 ÷ 9]* Then have students write 248 ÷ 9 on a place-value chart, leaving room at the top to write the quotient. Ask:

- **Are there enough hundreds to divide? Why?** *[No; the number of hundreds is less than the divisor.]*
- **Circle the digits in the hundreds and tens places. This is the number of tens. How many tens are there? Are there enough tens to divide?** *[24; yes.]*

Have students divide the tens, then divide the ones, and use the quotient to solve the problem

	hundreds	tens	ones
		2	7 R5
9)	2	4	8
	1	8	
		6	8
		6	3
			5

Continue the activity with other division exercises.

PRACTICE • 69

Practice 69

Name:

DIVISION BY 1-DIGIT NUMBERS

Divide. Remember to estimate.

1. 2)80 **40**	2. 3)210 **70**	3. 5)450 **90**	4. 9)810 **90**
5. 3)47 **15 R2**	6. 2)31 **15 R1**	7. 4)53 **13 R1**	8. 2)79 **39 R1**
9. 2)93 **46 R1**	10. 7)96 **13 R5**	11. 6)69 **11 R3**	12. 3)91 **30 R1**
13. 6)473 **78 R5**	14. 5)364 **72 R4**	15. 4)290 **72 R2**	16. 6)299 **49 R5**
17. 4)$375 **$93 R$3**	18. 7)$646 **$92 R$2**	19. 9)$872 **$96 R$8**	20. 4)$896 **$224**
21. 5)665 **133**	22. 8)453 **56 R5**	23. 3)265 **88 R1**	24. 2)625 **312 R1**

Algebra Ring the letter of the missing number.

25. 85 ÷ □ = 12 R 1	a. 6	**(b.) 7**	c. 8	d. 9
26. □ ÷ 9 = 50	a. 45	**(b.) 450**	c. 400	d. 540
27. 46 ÷ □ = 15 R1	a. 2	b. 5	c. 6	**(d.) 3**
28. □ ÷ 8 = 7 R5	a. 65	b. 56	c. 51	**(d.) 61**
29. 67 ÷ □ = 6 R1	a. 9	b. 10	**(c.) 11**	d. 12

Solve.

30. Ann has a roll of 159 stickers. She pastes an equal number in 7 different notebooks. How many does Ann put in each notebook? How many are left over? **22 stickers; 5 stickers**

31. Ann's story notebook has 215 pages. If she fills it with 4-page stories, how many stories will she have? How many pages will be left over? **53 stories; 3 pages**

McGraw-Hill School Division

RETEACH • 69

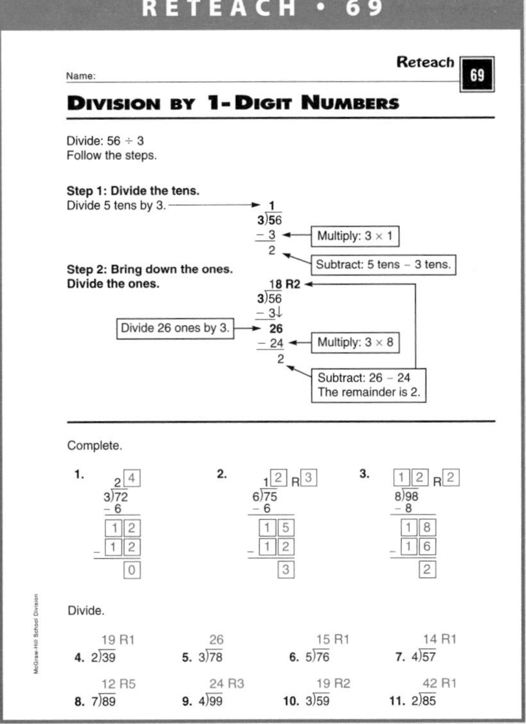

Reteach 69

Name:

DIVISION BY 1-DIGIT NUMBERS

Divide: 56 ÷ 3
Follow the steps.

Step 1: Divide the tens.
Divide 5 tens by 3. → 1; 3)56; − 3 ← Multiply: 3 × 1; 2 ← Subtract: 5 tens − 3 tens.

Step 2: Bring down the ones. Divide the ones.
18 R2; 3)56; − 3↓; 26 ← Divide 26 ones by 3.; − 24 ← Multiply: 3 × 8; 2 ← Subtract: 26 − 24. The remainder is 2.

Complete.

1. 3)72 = 24; − 6; 12; − 12; 0
2. 6)75 = 12 R3; − 6; 15; − 12; 3
3. 8)98 = 12 R2; − 8; 18; − 16; 2

Divide.

4. 2)39 **19 R1**	5. 3)78 **26**	6. 5)76 **15 R1**	7. 4)57 **14 R1**
8. 7)89 **12 R5**	9. 4)99 **24 R3**	10. 3)59 **19 R2**	11. 2)85 **42 R1**

McGraw-Hill School Division

EXTEND • 69

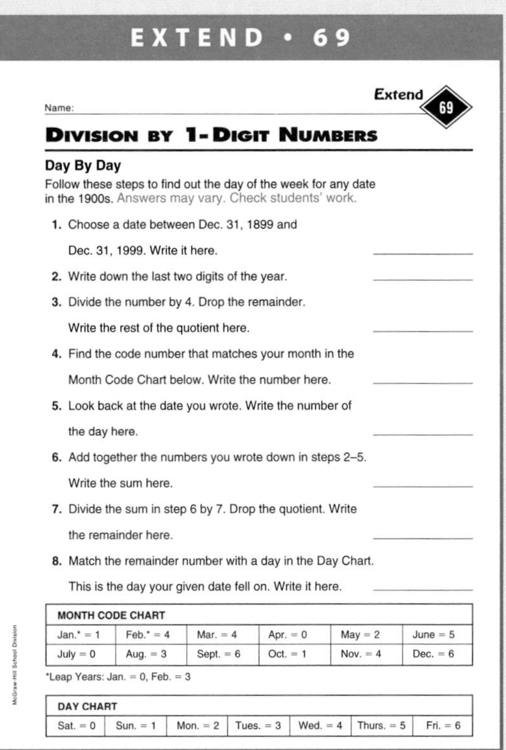

Extend 69

Name:

DIVISION BY 1-DIGIT NUMBERS

Day By Day

Follow these steps to find out the day of the week for any date in the 1900s. **Answers may vary. Check students' work.**

1. Choose a date between Dec. 31, 1899 and Dec. 31, 1999. Write it here. ______
2. Write down the last two digits of the year. ______
3. Divide the number by 4. Drop the remainder. Write the rest of the quotient here. ______
4. Find the code number that matches your month in the Month Code Chart below. Write the number here. ______
5. Look back at the date you wrote. Write the number of the day here. ______
6. Add together the numbers you wrote down in steps 2–5. Write the sum here. ______
7. Divide the sum in step 6 by 7. Drop the quotient. Write the remainder here. ______
8. Match the remainder number with a day in the Day Chart. This is the day your given date fell on. Write it here. ______

MONTH CODE CHART					
Jan.* = 1	Feb.* = 4	Mar. = 4	Apr. = 0	May = 2	June = 5
July = 0	Aug. = 3	Sept. = 6	Oct. = 1	Nov. = 4	Dec. = 6

*Leap Years: Jan. = 0, Feb. = 3

DAY CHART						
Sat. = 0	Sun. = 1	Mon. = 2	Tues. = 3	Wed. = 4	Thurs. = 5	Fri. = 6

McGraw-Hill School Division

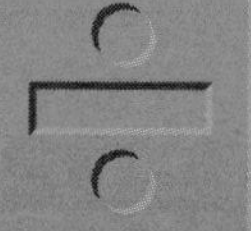

Zeros in the Quotient

OBJECTIVE Divide 2- and 3-digit numbers by 1-digit numbers with zeros in the quotient.

RESOURCE REMINDER
Math Center Cards 70
Practice 70, Reteach 70, Extend 70

SKILLS TRACE

GRADE 3	• Use place-value models to explore dividing 2-digit numbers by 1-digit numbers. *(Chapter 12)*
GRADE 4	• Divide 2- and 3-digit numbers by 1-digit numbers with zeros in the quotient.
GRADE 5	• Divide up to 5-digit numbers by 1-digit numbers with/without zeros in the quotient. *(Chapter 5)*

MANIPULATIVE WARM-UP

Cooperative Pairs — Visual/Spatial

OBJECTIVE Explore creating and completing division exercises.

Materials per pair: 2 sets of number cards for 1–9

▶ Pairs of students mix the number cards and place them in a pile face-down. Each student draws four cards from the pile.

▶ Each student uses the four number cards to make a 3-digit dividend and 1-digit divisor that will produce the greatest possible quotient. Students use paper and pencil to find the quotients.

▶ The student with the greater quotient wins one point. Students mix the cards and repeat the activity until one player reaches five points.

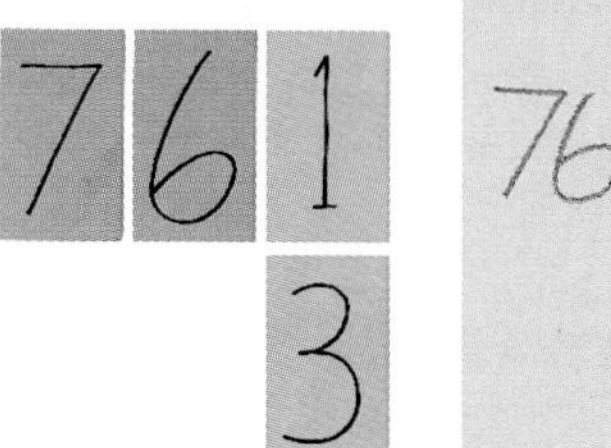

ALGEBRA CONNECTION

Cooperative Pairs — Logical/Analytical

OBJECTIVE Connect completing division sentences to algebra.

Materials have available: place-value models—hundreds, tens, and ones

Prepare Copy the following table on the chalkboard:

Dividend	Divisor	Quotient	Remainder
417	*[5]*	83	2
[805]	6	134	1
[249]	9	27	6
649	3	*[216]*	*[1]*
604	*[4]*	151	0

▶ Have pairs of students work together to complete the table, using place-value models if they wish. Discuss what operations were used.

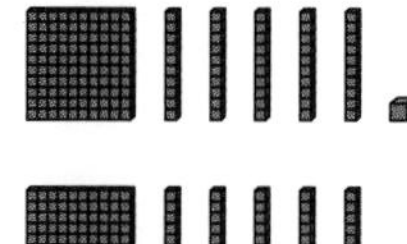
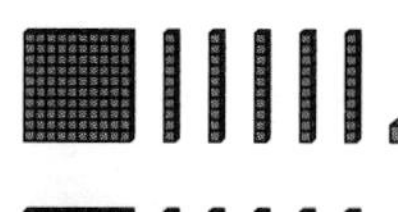

604 ÷ 4 = 151

Daily Review

PREVIOUS DAY QUICK REVIEW

Divide. Remember to estimate.

1. 93 ÷ 5 *[18 R3]*
2. 227 ÷ 9 *[25 R2]*
3. 204 ÷ 3 *[68]*
4. 557 ÷ 4 *[139 R1]*

FAST FACTS

1. 6 × 5 *[30]*
2. 1 × 4 *[4]*
3. 7 × 7 *[49]*
4. 8 × 9 *[72]*

Problem of the Day • 70

Mr. Auguste makes 3 models in an hour. He works on the models 2 hours each day. How many days did Mr. Auguste work to make 720 models? *[120 days]*

TECH LINK

MATH VAN

Tool You may wish to use the Calculator with this lesson.

MATH FORUM

Cultural Diversity Students from other cultures may be familiar with different methods of division, such as using an abacus. Encourage students to demonstrate these methods.

Visit our Resource Village at http://www.mhschool.com to see more of the Math Forum.

MATH CENTER

Practice

OBJECTIVE Determine if a quotient will contain a 0.

Materials per student: Math Center Recording Sheet (TA 31 optional)

Students try to determine mentally which quotients will contain zeros. Then they check their answers using paper and pencil. *[No zeros: 5)673 (134 R3), 8)96 (12); 1 zero: 3)906 (302), 4)843 (210 R3), 5)536 (107 R1), 7)75 (10 R5); 2 zeros: 3)301 (100 R1), 4)802 (200 R2)]*

MATH CENTER
On Your Own

PRACTICE ACTIVITY 70

Algebra Sense • What's the Dividend?

Study the division problems below. Without actually dividing, sort them in a chart like the one shown below. Then find the quotients with paper and pencil to see if you sorted them correctly.

3)906 3)301 4)802 4)843
5)536 5)673 7)75 8)96

Write two division problems of your own for each column of the chart. Then divide to check.

Quotients with—		
No Zeros	1 Zero	2 Zeros

Grade Level 4 McGraw-Hill School Division

Chapter 8, Lesson 5, pages 290–291 Division

ESL APPROPRIATE

NCTM Standards

- Problem Solving
- ✓ Communication
- ✓ Reasoning
- ✓ Connections

Problem Solving

OBJECTIVE Write division sentences that have a quotient containing a zero.

Materials per student: number cards for 0-9 (TA 29), Math Center Recording Sheet (TA 31 optional)

Students arrange number cards to make division sentences with 1-digit divisors and quotients containing zeros.

MATH CENTER
On Your Own

PROBLEM-SOLVING ACTIVITY 70

Logical Reasoning • Zero Search

YOU NEED
- number cards (0–9)

Mix up the number cards. Pick four cards without looking.

- Arrange the cards to make a division sentence with a 1-digit divisor and a 3-digit dividend. You want the quotient to have one or more zeros in it.
- Use the same cards to make another division sentence that has a quotient with one or more zeros in it.

Repeat the activity five times. Record your work.

0 5 8 4

Grade Level 4 McGraw-Hill School Division

Chapter 8, Lesson 5, pages 290–291 Division

ESL APPROPRIATE

NCTM Standards

- ✓ Problem Solving
- ✓ Communication
- ✓ Reasoning
- Connections

Zeros in the Quotient

OBJECTIVE Solve division problems with zero in the quotient.

Materials per pair: place-value models—3 hundreds, 10 tens, 10 ones

1 Introduce

Write the following on the chalkboard: 315 ÷ 3.

Have students use place-value models to find the quotient. *[105]* Point out that when there are not enough tens to divide, students write 0 in the tens place in the quotient.

2 Teach *Whole Class*

Cultural Connection Read the **Cultural Note.** Tell students that the Statue of Liberty was a gift from France to celebrate America's Centennial.

▶ **LEARN** After the introductory problem is read, review the estimate. Then work through each of the steps to find the exact answer. Have students use their own words to explain why a zero is recorded in the quotient in Step 2. After Step 3, ask:

- **Can you use mental math to check the answer? Explain.** *[Possible answer: Yes; 101 × 3 = 303, 303 + 2 = 305.]*

3 Close

▶ **Check for Understanding** using items 1–6, page 290.

Critical Thinking
In item 6, students are asked to analyze when there will be a zero in the tens place of a quotient. Continue by asking:

- **When do you get a zero in the ones place of a quotient? In both the tens and ones place?** *[Possible answers: when there are not enough ones to divide; when there are not enough tens or ones to divide]*

▶ **PRACTICE**
Materials have available: calculators

Options for assigning exercises:
A—Ex. 1–10, 19–25; **Mixed Review**
B—Ex. 11–25; **Mixed Review**

- For ex. 1–18, encourage students to use mental math when they can. Remind them to check their answers.
- Students must interpret the meaning of the remainder to solve ex. 22–23.
- For ex. 24, students may use the problem-solving strategy, Estimation, to solve.

Mixed Review/Test Preparation In ex. 1–4, students review addition, subtraction, and multiplication, learned in Chapters 2, 5, and 6. Students select units of measurement in ex. 5–7, a skill learned in Chapter 7. Have them explain their choices.

Zeros in the Quotient

LEARN

The Statue of Liberty stands 305 feet high above New York Bay on Liberty Island. A class is making a 3-foot model of the statue. How many times larger is the actual statue?

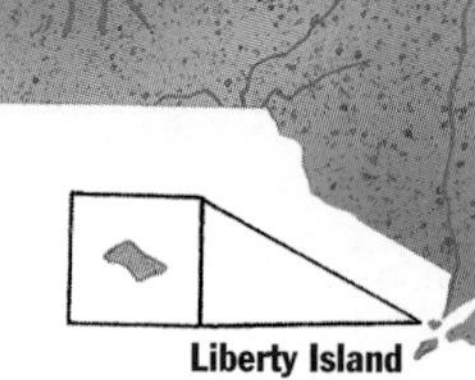

Cultural Note
The words at the bottom of the Statue of Liberty were written by the American poet Emma Lazarus. They include, "Give me your tired, your poor, your huddled masses yearning to breathe free."

Estimate to place the first digit of the quotient.

Estimate: 305 ÷ 3 **Think:** 300 ÷ 3 = 100
The first digit is in the hundreds place.

Step 1	Step 2	Step 3
Divide the hundreds.	**Bring down the tens. Divide the tens.**	**Bring down the ones. Divide the ones. Write the remainder.**
1 3)305 −3 0 **Think:** 3)3 Multiply: 1 × 3 = 3 Subtract: 3 − 3 = 0 Compare: 0 < 3	10 3)305 −3↓ 00 **Think:** 0 < 3 Not enough tens. Write 0 in the quotient.	101 R2 3)305 −3↓↓ 005 − 3 2 **Think:** 3)5 Multiply: 1 × 3 = Subtract: 5 − 3 = Compare: 2 < 3

The actual statue is over 101 times larger than the model.

CHECK

Check for Understanding

Divide.

1 6)425 **70 R5** **2** 2)211 **105 R1** **3** 8)833 **104 R1** **4** 4)842 **210 R2** **5** 3)902 **300 R2**

Critical Thinking: Analyze **Explain your reasoning.**

6 When do you get a zero in the tens place of a quotient? **Possible answer: when there are not enough tens to divide the divisor into**

Meeting Individual Needs

Early Finishers

Have students write and solve problems similar to problem 22, using different numbers of students and buses with different capacities.

Extra Support

Some students may make the common error of skipping a place instead of writing a zero in the quotient. Have them write division exercises on graph paper to help them focus on the division process, place by place.

Ongoing Assessment

Anecdotal Report Make notes on whether students are able to correctly write quotients when one or more of the digits is zero.

Follow Up Allow students who need additional help to continue to use place-value models to divide. Assign **Reteach 70** for more practice.

Have students who are ready for a challenge try **Extend 70.**

Possible answer: about 20,000 more; by rounding and estimating the difference

22. No; 387 ÷ 7 = 55 R2, which means each bus would have to hold 56 students.
23. Yes; 387 ÷ 9 = 43, which means you could place 43 students on each bus—43 < 44.

PRACTICE

Practice

Divide.

4)429 107 R1 | 2 3)614 204 R2 | 3 8)322 40 R2 | 4 5)518 103 R3 | 5 7)146 20 R6

3)$912 $304 | 7 7)846 120 R6 | 8 2)814 407 | 9 6)$660 $110 | 10 4)837 209 R1

62 ÷ 3 20 R2 | 12 82 ÷ 8 10 R2 | 13 153 ÷ 5 30 R3 | 14 732 ÷ 7 104 R4

$412 ÷ 4 $103 | 16 $850 ÷ 5 $170 | 17 $749 ÷ 7 $107 | 18 $418 ÷ 2 $209

How many:

$5 are in $100? 20 | 20 $9 are in $954? 106 | 21 $1 are in $740? 740

MIXED APPLICATIONS

Problem Solving

Use this information for problems 22–23:

387 students and teachers want to visit the Statue of Liberty. The school hires buses that hold 44 people each.

Will 7 buses be enough to hold all of the students and teachers? Why or why not? See above.

23 **What if** there are 9 buses. Will they be able to go to the Statue of Liberty? Why or why not? See above.

In 1993, New York City was listed as the place where 128,434 immigrants intended to live. Los Angeles was listed by 106,703 immigrants. About how many more immigrants listed New York than Los Angeles? Explain your thinking. See above.

25 The ferry to the Statue of Liberty has benches that each hold up to 8 people. If 240 people sit at the same time, what is the fewest number of benches needed to hold all the people? Explain your thinking. See below.

mixed review • test preparation

768 + 625 1,393 | 2 6,520 − 129 6,391 | 3 3,109 × 5 15,545 | 4 5,675 × 27 153,225

Choose the letter of the best unit to measure.

mass of a child a — a. kg b. mg c. g | 6 capacity of a bottle c — a. mL b. g c. L | 7 height of a door b — a. cm b. m c. g

25. 30 benches; 240 ÷ 8 = 30, so 30 benches each with 8 people will hold 240 people.

Extra Practice, page 513

Alternate Teaching Strategy

Materials per pair: place-value models—9 hundreds, 19 tens, 19 ones

Have students work in pairs to show 615 using the place-value models. Have them put the models into 6 equal groups. Ask:

- **What quotient are you trying to find when you put 615 into 6 equal groups?** *[615 ÷ 6]*
- **Are there enough hundreds to divide?** *[Yes.]*
- **Are there enough tens to divide? How can you record this?** *[No; 0 tens.]*
- **Are there enough ones to divide?** *[Yes.]*

Have students give their answer as 1 hundred 0 tens 2 ones with 3 left. Then have them record 102 R3.

Repeat the activity for other quotients.

1 hundred 0 tens 2 ones
with 3 ones left

PRACTICE • 70

Practice 70

Name:

Zeros in the Quotient

Divide.

1. 4)418 104 R2 2. 6)616 102 R4 3. 2)405 202 R1 4. 2)603 301 R1
5. 5)526 105 R1 6. 2)817 408 R1 7. 6)241 40 R1 8. 7)762 108 R6
9. 3)319 106 R1 10. 4)835 208 R3 11. 5)$550 $110 12. 3)$902 $300 R$2
13. 2)340 170 14. 4)423 105 R3 15. 2)617 308 R1 16. 7)768 109 R5
17. 8)853 106 R5 18. 7)710 101 R3 19. 9)985 109 R4 20. 6)584 97 R2
21. 3)925 308 R1 22. 8)562 70 R2 23. 4)814 203 R2 24. 5)654 130 R4

How many:

25. $5 are in $200? 40 26. $5 are in $450? 90
27. $6 are in $618? 103 28. $7 are in $735? 105
29. $3 are in $306? 102 30. $2 are in $406? 203
31. $2 are in $960? 480 32. $3 are in $609? 203

Solve.

33. Francis earns $535 in 5 months by selling maps and guidebooks to tourists. If divided evenly, how much is that a month? $107

34. A family of 4 spends $436 during their vacation. How much money does one person spend if they all spend the same amount? $109

RETEACH • 70

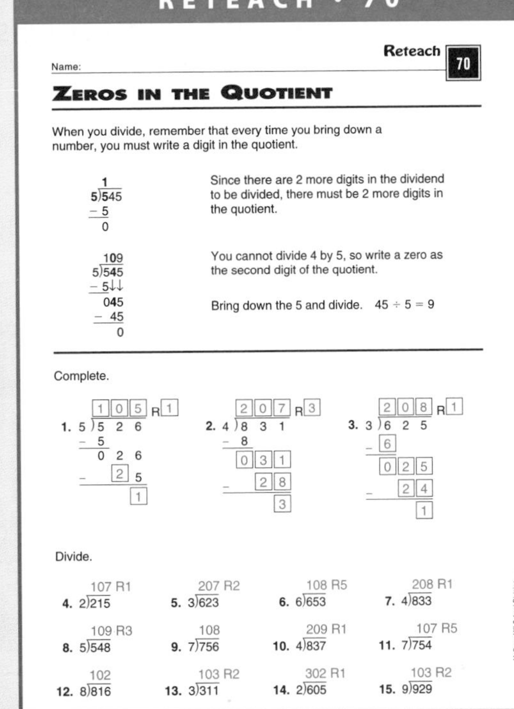

Reteach 70

Name:

Zeros in the Quotient

When you divide, remember that every time you bring down a number, you must write a digit in the quotient.

Since there are 2 more digits in the dividend to be divided, there must be 2 more digits in the quotient.

You cannot divide 4 by 5, so write a zero as the second digit of the quotient.

Bring down the 5 and divide. 45 ÷ 5 = 9

Complete.

1. 5)526 105 R1 2. 4)831 207 R3 3. 3)625 208 R1

Divide.

4. 2)215 107 R1 5. 3)623 207 R2 6. 6)653 108 R5 7. 4)833 208 R1
8. 5)548 109 R3 9. 7)756 108 10. 4)837 209 R1 11. 7)754 107 R5
12. 8)816 102 13. 3)311 103 R2 14. 2)605 302 R1 15. 9)929 103 R2

EXTEND • 70

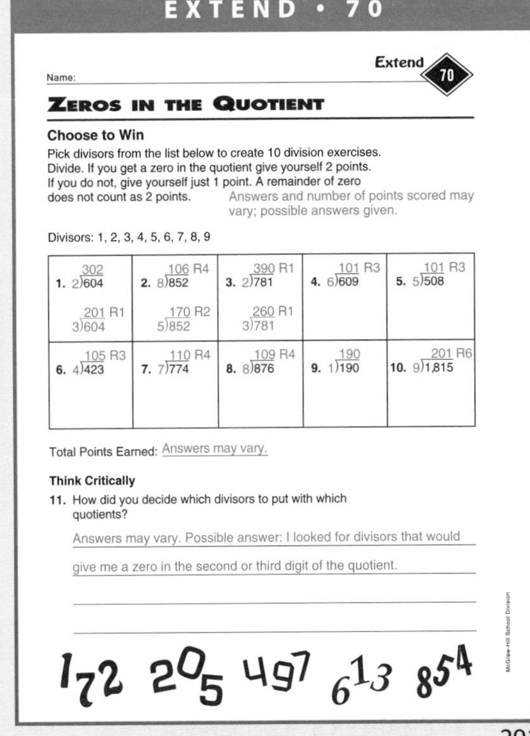

Extend 70

Name:

Zeros in the Quotient

Choose to Win

Pick divisors from the list below to create 10 division exercises. Divide. If you get a zero in the quotient give yourself 2 points. If you do not, give yourself just 1 point. A remainder of zero does not count as 2 points. Answers and number of points scored may vary; possible answers given.

Divisors: 1, 2, 3, 4, 5, 6, 7, 8, 9

1. 2)604 302; 3)604 201 R1	2. 8)852 106 R4; 5)852 170 R2	3. 2)781 390 R1; 3)781 260 R1	4. 6)609 101 R3	5. 5)508 101 R3
6. 4)423 105 R3	7. 7)774 110 R4	8. 8)876 109 R4	9. 1)190 190	10. 9)1,815 201 R6

Total Points Earned: Answers may vary.

Think Critically

11. How did you decide which divisors to put with which quotients?
Answers may vary. Possible answer: I looked for divisors that would give me a zero in the second or third digit of the quotient.

172 205 497 613 854

LESSON 8.6

Divide Greater Numbers

OBJECTIVE Divide up to 5-digit numbers by 1-digit numbers.

RESOURCE REMINDER
Math Center Cards 71
Practice 71, Reteach 71, Extend 71

SKILLS TRACE

GRADE 3	• Use place-value models to explore dividing 2-digit numbers by 1-digit numbers. *(Chapter 12)*
GRADE 4	• Divide up to 5-digit numbers by 1-digit numbers.
GRADE 5	• Divide up to 5-digit numbers by 1-digit numbers. *(Chapter 5)*

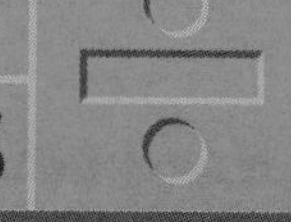

MANIPULATIVE WARM-UP

Cooperative Pairs — **Logical**

OBJECTIVE Estimate division of greater numbers.

Materials per pair: play money—25 hundred-dollar bills, 20 ten-dollar bills, 20 one-dollar bills (TA 11)

Prepare Write this table on the chalkboard:

FANTASTIC FURNITURE

Chairs for Sale			
A: 4 for $1,680	B: 6 for $516	C: 5 for $1,520	D: 3 for $630
E: 8 for $584	F: 6 for $1,230	G: 9 for $2,295	H: 8 for $1,840

▶ Have pairs of students work together to estimate the cost of a single chair in each of these sets. *[A: $400; B: $80; C: $300; D: $200; E: $70; F: $200; G: $200; H: $200]*

▶ Have pairs use play money to show if they underestimate or overestimate the price. Allow time for some pairs to present their methods to the class.

ALGEBRA CONNECTION

Cooperative Groups — **Logical/Analytical**

OBJECTIVE Connect division to algebra.

Materials per pair: 0–9 spinner (TA 2); 9 number cards labeled 1,000–9,000

▶ Have groups place the number cards in a pile facedown. One student spins the spinner and draws a card. The group uses the numbers to find the greatest multiple. For example, if the student spins a 7 and draws an 8,000, the group finds the greatest multiple of 7 that is less than 8,000.

▶ Groups continue the activity until each member has a chance to spin the spinner and draw a number card.

▶ Have each group explain how they find the greatest multiple. *[Possible answers: Use trial and error combined with estimation, use division.]*

Daily Review

PREVIOUS DAY QUICK REVIEW

1. 877 ÷ 8 *[109 R5]*
2. 841 ÷ 4 *[210 R1]*
3. 901 ÷ 3 *[300 R1]*
4. 800 ÷ 5 *[160]*

FAST FACTS

1. 17 − 8 *[9]*
2. 11 − 6 *[5]*
3. 13 − 5 *[8]*
4. 12 − 3 *[9]*

Problem of the Day • 71

Every seat in Torch Stadium was filled for each of 6 gymnastics demonstrations. If 19,290 tickets were sold, how many people attended each demonstration? *[3,215 people]*

TECH LINK

Math Van

MATH VAN

Tool You may wish to use the Calculator with this lesson.

MATH FORUM

Multi-Age Classes I have younger students show division with money or other models, as partners with more experience dividing larger numbers record the division process on paper.

Visit our Resource Village at http://www.mhschool.com to see more of the Math Forum.

MATH CENTER

Practice

OBJECTIVE Divide greater numbers.

Materials per student: blank spinner (TA 3), Math Center Recording Sheet (TA 31 optional)

Prepare Have students make a 9-part spinner labeled 1 through 9.

Students plan city-to-city trips across the United States. They spin a spinner to find the number of days they have to travel and divide the distance by the number of days to find the number of miles to travel each day. *[Check students' work.]*

PRACTICE ACTIVITY 71 — MATH CENTER, On Your Own

Spatial Sense • Measuring Map Miles

YOU NEED
- spinner (1–9)

Plan some trips in the United States.

- Choose two cities from the chart. Find the distance between them. For example, the distance from New York to Dallas is about 1,450 miles.
- Spin the spinner to determine the number of days it will take to travel from one city to the other.
- Divide to find the number of miles you will travel each day.
- Record your work. Try a trip to 2 or 3 cities—for example, New York to Chicago, then to Dallas.

MILEAGE TABLE

	New York	Dallas	Chicago	Los Angeles
New York		1,450	800	2,450
Dallas	1,450		750	1,150
Chicago	800	750		1,500
Los Angeles	2,450	1,150	1,500	

Grade Level 4 — McGraw-Hill School Division

Chapter 8, Lesson 6, pages 292–293 — Division

ESL APPROPRIATE

NCTM Standards
- ✓ Problem Solving
- Communication
- Reasoning
- ✓ Connections

Problem Solving

OBJECTIVE Formulate division sentences with 4- and 5-digit dividends.

Materials per student: number cube, 0–9 spinner (TA 2), Math Center Recording Sheet (TA 31 optional)

Students use randomly generated numbers to form division sentences with 4- and 5-digit dividends and quotients with and without remainders. You may want to point out to students that sometimes they cannot complete the task given the randomly selected digits.

PROBLEM-SOLVING ACTIVITY 71 — MATH CENTER, On Your Own

Logical Reasoning • What's the Problem?

YOU NEED
- number cube
- spinner (0–9)

Record your work at each step.

- Spin the spinner four times. You will use these numbers to make a dividend.
- Toss the number cube. Use this number as the divisor.
- Try to arrange the four digits to make a dividend that will give you a quotient *without* a remainder.
- Now arrange the same four digits to make a dividend that when divided by your divisor will give you a quotient *with* a remainder.
- Repeat, but spin five digits for the dividend.

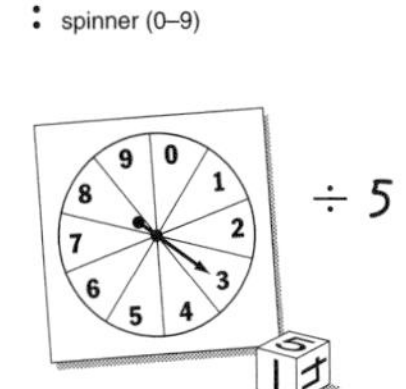

Grade Level 4 — McGraw-Hill School Division

Chapter 8, Lesson 6, pages 292–293 — Division

ESL APPROPRIATE

NCTM Standards
- ✓ Problem Solving
- Communication
- Reasoning
- ✓ Connections

Divide Greater Numbers

OBJECTIVE Divide 4- and 5-digit numbers by 1-digit numbers.

Materials per student: calculators

1 Introduce

Write the following on the chalkboard: 4,001 ÷ 2. Then ask:

- **What compatible numbers can you use to estimate the quotient? What is the estimate?** *[4,000 ÷ 2 = 2,000]*
- **How can you use mental math to find the exact answer?** *[Possible answer: Find 2,000 × 2 = 4,000—since the dividend is 4,001, the quotient is 2,000 R1.]*

2 Teach *Whole Class*

LEARN After the introductory problem is read, review the estimate. Work through each division step with the class. Ask:

- **Why do you begin by dividing the hundreds and not the thousands?** *[Possible answer: The estimate shows the first digit in the quotient will be in the hundreds place. Also, since 1 < 9, you must regroup the thousands as hundreds.]*

When reviewing calculator keying, explain that the *Int* key shows the answer as a whole number quotient and a remainder. The division key gives a decimal answer if there is a remainder.

3 Close

Check for Understanding using items 1–5, page 292.

CRITICAL THINKING
For item 5, students are asked to determine if an answer is reasonable. Ask students to explain alternate methods for determining if an answer is reasonable.

PRACTICE

Materials have available: calculators

Options for assigning exercises:
A—Ex. 1–8, 13–22; **Cultural Connection**
B—Ex. 5–22; **Cultural Connection**

- For ex 1–12, remind students to include the dollar sign for the exercises that divide money amounts.
- For ex. 21, students may use the problem-solving strategy, Solve a Multistep Problem, to solve.

Cultural Connection Tell students that Babylonia was an ancient empire in southwestern Asia. Babylonia was prominent between 2000 and 1000 BC.

Divide Greater Numbers

LEARN

In Florida, the Olympic torch was carried 1,148 miles in 9 days. If the same distance was covered each day, how many miles was the torch carried each day?

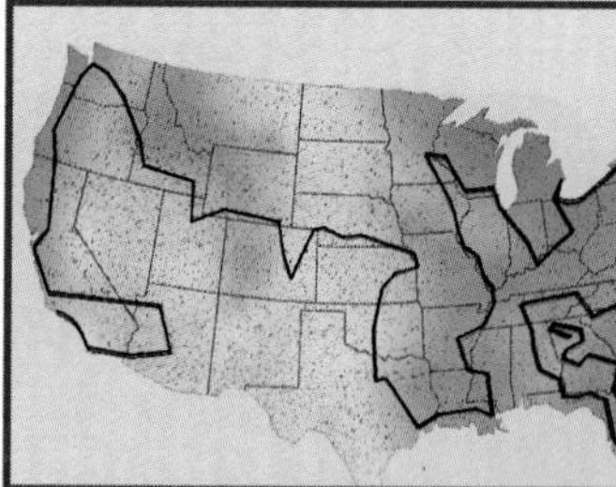

1996 Olympic Torch Route

Estimate to place the first digit of the quotient.

Estimate: 1,148 ÷ 9

Think: 900 ÷ 9 = 100
The first digit is in the hundreds place.

Step 1	Step 2	Step 3
Divide the hundreds.	**Bring down the tens. Divide the tens.**	**Bring down the ones. Divide the ones. Write the remainder.**
9)1,148 = 1; − 9; 2	9)1,148 = 12; − 9↓; 24; − 18; 6	9)1,148 = 127 R5; − 9↓; 24; − 18↓; 68; − 63; 5
Think: 9)11 = 1 Multiply: 1 × 9 = 9 Subtract: 11 − 9 = 2 Compare: 2 < 9	**Think:** 9)24 = 2 Multiply: 2 × 9 = 18 Subtract: 24 − 18 = 6 Compare: 6 < 9	**Think:** 9)68 = 7 Multiply: 7 × 9 = 6 Subtract: 68 − 63 = Compare: 5 <

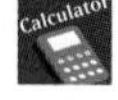

You can also use a calculator.
Press: 1,148 ÷R 9 = 127 R5

The torch was carried about 128 miles each day.

CHECK

Check for Understanding

Divide.

1. 4,257 ÷ 3 **1,419**
2. $7,368 ÷ 8 **$921**
3. 3,278 ÷ 3 **1,092 R2**
4. 61,721 ÷ 2 **30,860 R1**

Critical Thinking: Analyze

5. Kim used a calculator to find 1,245 ÷ 7. Her answer was 1,779 R2. Is this answer reasonable? How can you check? What might Kim have done? **No; possible answer: check by estimating—1,400 ÷ 7 = 200—therefore the answer should be close to 200; Kim probably pressed an extra key when using the calculator—she pressed 12455 ÷ 7.**

Meeting Individual Needs

Early Finishers

Show students how to use four 9s and any of the four operations to make the number 1. For example, (9 − 9) + (9 ÷ 9) = 1. Challenge students to use four nines to make the number 2. *[Possible answer: (9 ÷ 9) + (9 ÷ 9)]*

Extra Support

Give students pairs of similar problems with 3-digit and greater dividends, such as 216 ÷ 6 and 2,160 ÷ 6, and 345 ÷ 3 and 3,450 ÷ 3. Have them use the first problem to help them complete the second.

Ongoing Assessment

Observation Checklist Determine if students understand how to divide 4- and 5-digit numbers by observing how they divide 27,145 ÷ 9. *[3,016 R1]* Check that they record the quotient correctly.

Follow Up You may want to give students more practice dividing greater numbers using **Reteach 71.**

For students who would enjoy a challenge, assign **Extend 71.**

California; 1,208 ÷ 6 = 201 R2, which is about 201 d, while the torch traveled about 128 d in Florida.

actice

de.

6)$738 $123	2 7)712 101 R5	3 4)4,275 1,068 R3	4 5)3,154 630 R4
7)75,214 10,744 R6	6 6)14,567 2,427 R5	7 8)$320 $40	8 9)$9,144 $1,016
912 ÷ 9 101 R3	10 $2,040 ÷ 4 $510	11 1,054 ÷ 3 351 R1	12 38,606 ÷ 6 6,434 R2

only those quotients that are greater than 800.

$3,975 ÷ 5 less than 800	14 12,562 ÷ 7 1,794 R4	15 4,175 ÷ 3 1,391 R2	16 $4,368 ÷ 6 less than 800
7,345 ÷ 4 1,836 R1	18 1,121 ÷ 3 less than 800	19 1,605 ÷ 2 802 R1	20 $80,325 ÷ 9 $8,925

PRACTICE

XED APPLICATIONS

roblem Solving

Pencil & Paper · Calculator · Mental Math

In 1996, the Olympic torch was carried across California for 6 days and covered 1,208 miles. Did the torch travel more miles each day in Florida (see page 292) or California? Explain.
See above.

22 During the Summer Olympic Games, some athletes try to eat about 8,000 calories each day. If an athlete eats 6 meals each day, about how many calories should she eat at each meal?
about 1,333 Cal

ltural Connection Babylonian Division

ient Babylonians divided by 5 ng a method similar to the one wn below.

de: 340 ÷ 5

p 1
iply the dividend by 2.
340 = 680

Step 2
Divide the product by 10.
680 ÷ 10 = 68

340 ÷ 5 = 68.

IRAQ
Babylon

Babylonian division to divide. Then use a culator to check your answer.

260 ÷ 5 52	2 720 ÷ 5 144	3 180 ÷ 5 36	4 370 ÷ 5 74	5 480 ÷ 5 96

a Practice, page 513

Alternate Teaching Strategy

Write the following on the chalkboard:

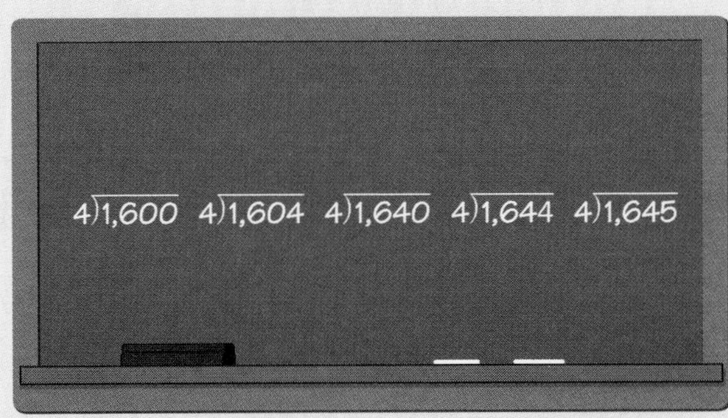

Have students compare each of the problems. Then ask:

- **What is the first quotient? How do you know?** *[400; you can use division patterns.]*
- **By how much does the second dividend differ from the first dividend? How can you use this to find the quotient?** *[4; possible answer: since the divisor is 4, the quotient will be 1 more than the first quotient, or 401.]*

Continue this process of questioning to find the third and fourth quotients by comparing them to the first quotient. *[410; 411]* Compare the last quotient to the fourth quotient to find the answer. *[411 R1]*

Record the division process to show how to find each quotient.

Repeat the activity having student volunteers complete the quotients on the chalkboard.

PRACTICE • 71

Practice 71

Name:

Divide Greater Numbers

Divide.

1. 7)892 127 R3	2. 9)733 81 R4	3. 5)615 123	4. 8)868 108 R4
5. 4)279 69 R3	6. 7)3,546 506 R4	7. 5)1,205 241	8. 7)3,026 432 R2
9. 6)6,094 1,015 R4	10. 3)$3,019 $1,006 R$1	11. 4)8,704 2,176	
12. 3)28,602 9,534	13. 8)40,969 5,121 R1	14. 9)70,235 7,803 R8	

Find only those quotients that are greater than 600.

15. 4)2,432 608	16. 9)6,246 694	17. 9)5,290 less than 600	18. 2)1,628 814
19. 6)2,562 less than 600	20. 5)3,567 713 R2	21. 3)2,587 862 R1	22. 4)2,527 631 R3
23. 8)6,016 752	24. 7)4,196 less than 600	25. 8)4,992 624	26. 6)2,927 less than 600
27. 7)5,613 801 R6	28. 9)5,321 less than 600	29. 6)4,002 667	30. 8)5,760 720
31. 6)4,535 755 R5	32. 5)3,013 602 R3	33. 4)2,244 less than 600	34. 9)5,596 621 R7

Solve.

35. Your family collects 1,071 photographs from 7 summers together. If you took the same number of photographs each year, how many photographs are there for each summer?
153 photographs

36. During 3 summers, your family travels 2,052 miles going to and from the same camping area. How many miles did you travel in one summer? How many miles is it one way?
684 mi; 342 mi

McGraw-Hill School Division

RETEACH • 71

Reteach 71

Name:

Divide Greater Numbers

When dividing greater numbers, the first step is to decide where to place the first digit of the quotient.

Divide: 1,872 ÷ 2

Think: You can't divide 1 by 2. Divide 18 by 2. Write 9 in the quotient above the 8.

2)1,872 — 9

You can see that there will be 3 digits in the quotient.

Divide: 7,804 ÷ 3

Think: You can divide 7 by 3. Write 2 in the quotient above the 7.

3)7,804 — 2

You can see that there will be 4 digits in the quotient.

Complete.

1. 4)1,266 = 3 1 6 R 2
− 1 2 → 6; − 4 → 2 6; − 2 4 → 2

2. 3)4,169 = 1 3 8 9 R 2
− 3 → 1 1; − 9 → 2 6; − 2 4 → 2 9; − 2 7 → 2

3. 6)7,235 = 1 2 0 5 R 5
− 6 → 1 2; − 1 2 → 0 3 5; − 3 0 → 5

Divide.

4. 2)1,572 786	5. 3)1,394 464 R2	6. 7)8,572 1,224 R4	7. 5)7,693 1,538 R3
8. 6)3,219 536 R3	9. 4)8,763 2,190 R3	10. 6)9,467 1,577 R5	11. 4)9,930 2,482 R2

McGraw-Hill School Division

EXTEND • 71

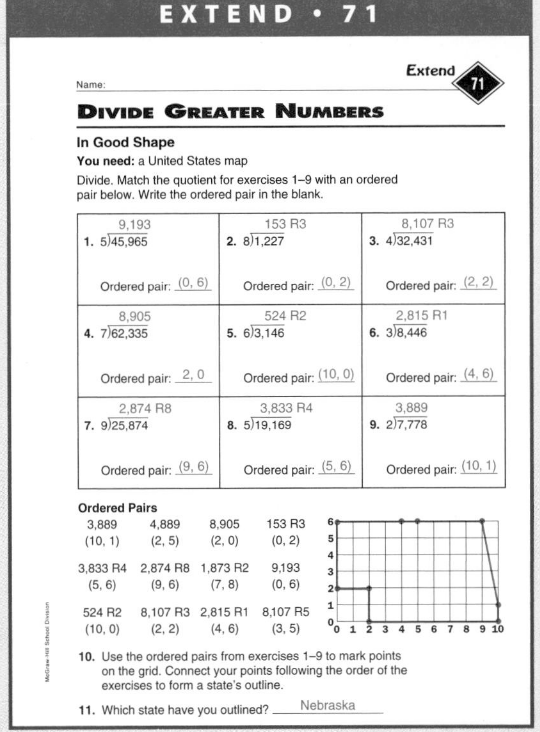
Extend 71

Name:

Divide Greater Numbers

In Good Shape

You need: a United States map

Divide. Match the quotient for exercises 1–9 with an ordered pair below. Write the ordered pair in the blank.

1. 5)45,965 9,193 Ordered pair: (0, 6)	2. 8)1,227 153 R3 Ordered pair: (0, 2)	3. 4)32,431 8,107 R3 Ordered pair: (2, 2)
4. 7)62,335 8,905 Ordered pair: 2, 0	5. 6)3,146 524 R2 Ordered pair: (10, 0)	6. 3)8,446 2,815 R1 Ordered pair: (4, 6)
7. 9)25,874 2,874 R8 Ordered pair: (9, 6)	8. 5)19,169 3,833 R4 Ordered pair: (5, 6)	9. 2)7,778 3,889 Ordered pair: (10, 1)

Ordered Pairs

3,889 (10, 1)	4,889 (2, 5)	8,905 (2, 0)	153 R3 (0, 2)
3,833 R4 (5, 6)	2,874 R8 (9, 6)	1,873 R2 (7, 8)	9,193 (0, 6)
524 R2 (10, 0)	8,107 R3 (2, 2)	2,815 R1 (4, 6)	8,107 R5 (3, 5)

10. Use the ordered pairs from exercises 1–9 to mark points on the grid. Connect your points following the order of the exercises to form a state's outline.

11. Which state have you outlined? Nebraska

McGraw-Hill School Division

Problem-Solving Strategy: Guess, Test, and Revise

OBJECTIVE Solve problems using a guess, test, and revise strategy.

RESOURCE REMINDER
Math Center Cards 72
Practice 72, Reteach 72, Extend 72

SKILLS TRACE

GRADE 3	• Solve problems using the guess, test, and revise strategy. *(Chapter 5)*
GRADE 4	• Solve problems using the guess, test, and revise strategy.
GRADE 5	• Solve problems using the guess, test, and revise strategy. *(Chapter 6)*

MANIPULATIVE WARM-UP

Cooperative Groups — Logical/Analytical

OBJECTIVE Explore using and revising clues to solve a problem.

Materials per group: paper bag, 50 counters

▶ One student in each group takes up to 50 counters while the other students are not looking. The student counts them and puts the counters in the bag.

▶ Other students take turns asking the first student questions about the number that can be answered either *Yes* or *No*. Each student can ask up to three questions. They then guess the number.

▶ Have students repeat the activity until each student has selected.

DISCRETE MATH CONNECTION

Cooperative Pairs — Visual/Spatial

OBJECTIVE Connect using clues about figures to discrete math.

▶ Have each student work independently to draw a flag with four different geometric figures. The flag should be divided into four equal sections.

▶ Divide students into pairs. One student names the four different geometric figures he or she used. The other student asks questions about each figure's location on the flag until she or he is able to reproduce it.

▶ Have students reverse roles. Vary the activity by allowing different numbers of questions.

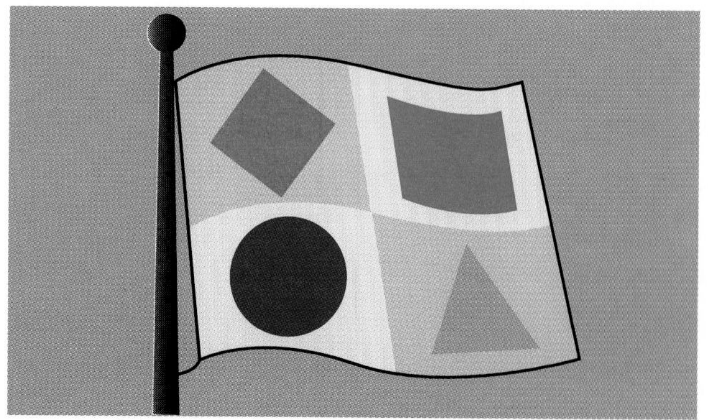

Daily Review

PREVIOUS DAY QUICK REVIEW

1. 1,294 ÷ 6 *[215 R4]*
2. 3,663 ÷ 3 *[1,221]*
3. 1,550 ÷ 5 *[310]*
4. 8,018 ÷ 8 *[1,002 R2]*

FAST FACTS

1. 18 ÷ 3 *[6]*
2. 24 ÷ 6 *[4]*
3. 63 ÷ 7 *[9]*
4. 8 ÷ 8 *[1]*

Problem of the Day • 72

At the Summer River Festival, 126 people rented canoes and kayaks. Twice as many people rented canoes as kayaks. How many people rented canoes? Kayaks? *[84 people; 42 people]*

TECH LINK

MATH FORUM

Idea My students enjoy working in small groups to solve guess, test, and revise problems. Students take turns in the roles of Guesser, Tester, and Reviser.

Visit our Resource Village at http://www.mhschool.com to see more of the Math Forum.

MATH CENTER

Practice

OBJECTIVE Formulate problems with the least possible answer.

Materials per student: Math Center Recording Sheet (TA 31 optional)

Students place 5 numbers to find the answer with the least value. They may use the guess, test, and revise strategy. *[**1.** 248 + 69 = 317; **2.** 246 − 98 = 148; **3.** 269 × 48 = 12,912; **4.** 2468 ÷ 9 = 274 R 2]*

PRACTICE ACTIVITY 72 — MATH CENTER On Your Own

Logical Reasoning • Least Number Puzzle

For each problem, find the least number that can be the answer. Use the numbers 2, 4, 6, 8, and 9 only once in each problem.

1. □□□ + □□ 2. □□□ − □□ 3. □□□ × □□

4. Find the lowest possible quotient for this division problem: □)□□□□

Chapter 8, Lesson 7, pages 294–295 — Problem Solving

ESL APPROPRIATE

NCTM Standards
✓ Problem Solving
Communication
✓ Reasoning
Connections

Problem Solving

OBJECTIVE Explore combinations.

Students write all possible vote combinations to decide whether a voting method is fair or unfair. This activity is a good application of the strategy make an organized list. *[**1.** 1,1,1; 2,2,2; 3,3,3; 1,1,2; 1,1,3; 2,2,1; 2,2,3; 3,3,1; 3,3,2; 1,2,3; **2.** Answers may vary. Possible answer: It is not fair, because there are 4 possible combinations that will result in a vote for the mountains, 4 for the ocean, and only 2 for the lake.]*

PROBLEM-SOLVING ACTIVITY 72 — MATH CENTER On Your Own

Decision Making • Vacation Voting

Here is how one family decides where to go on vacation.

Each of the three family members secretly writes a number—1, 2, or 3—on a slip of paper.

Then they look at the numbers. If the sum is 3, 4, or 5, the family goes to the mountains. If the sum is 6 or 7, they go to the ocean. If the sum is 8 or 9, they go to the lake.

- Write all the possible vote combinations to get a sum for the mountains; for the ocean; for the lake.
- Do you think this is a fair voting method? Explain.

Chapter 8, Lesson 7, pages 294–295 — Problem Solving

NCTM Standards
✓ Problem Solving
✓ Communication
✓ Reasoning
Connections

Problem-Solving Strategy: Guess, Test, and Revise

OBJECTIVE Solve problems using a guess, test, and revise strategy.

Present the following problem:

> Mr. Cooper has a stack of 5 index cards. The product of the top 3 cards is 60. If the cards are marked with the numbers 3, 6, 5, 4, and 2, what are the top 3 cards?

Have students suggest methods to solve the problem. *[Possible answer: Pick three numbers and multiply. Compare the product to 60. If not 60, try again.]* Then have them solve it. *[6, 5, 2]*

Whole Class

LEARN After reading the problem on page 294, have students use their own words to explain what they know and what they are trying to find. Then guide students through the problem-solving process. Ask:

- **How can you use your first guess to help make your second guess?** *[Possible answer: You can compare the results of your first guess to the target number. Since the answer is too high, your second guess should use numbers that will make the second answer lower.]*

Encourage students to find other ways to solve the problem.

Check for Understanding using items 1 and 2, page 294.

CRITICAL THINKING
Have students use examples from the lesson to explain how they guessed and then revised guesses.

PRACTICE

Materials have available: calculators

Assign ex. 1–11 as independent work.

- For ex. 1 and 6, students may use the strategy, Guess, Test, and Revise, to solve.
- Have students check their answer for ex. 4 by making a model that corresponds to the problem.

Problem-Solving Strategy

Read | Plan | Solve | Look Back

Guess, Test, and Revise

LEARN

Read **Eighteen students in a science class sign up to collect water samples from Lake Michigan on one day during the week. A group of either 3 or 4 students will go each day. On how many days will a group of 3 collect samples? a group of 4?**

MICHIGAN
Lake Michigan

Plan List the information you know.
a. The sum of the days with 3 students and the days with 4 students is 5 days.
b. 18 students will collect samples.

Sign Up to Collect Water Samples

Day	Your Initials			
1	KG.	JM	HS.	
2	AM.	CJ.	SL.	TT.
3				
4				

Solve

Guess Start with two numbers whose sum is 5. Try 1 and 4.

Then find the number of students.

Think: 1 day—3 students $1 \times 3 = 3$
4 days—4 students $4 \times 4 = 16$

Test $3 + 16 = 19$ students Too high

Revise Choose two other numbers whose sum is 5.

Guess Try 2 and 3. **Think:** $2 \times 3 = 6$
$3 \times 4 = 12$

Test $6 + 12 = 18$ students

There will be 3 students on 2 days and 4 students on 3 days.

Look Back How can you solve this problem a different way? **Possible answers: Use models, make a table.**

CHECK

Check for Understanding

1 **What if** there are 17 students instead of 18. On how many days will there be 3 students? 4 students? **3 d; 2 d**

Critical Thinking: Summarize

2 Explain how the test answer helps you to make a new guess. **Possible answer: the answer to the test is too high, then change the guess to get a lower answer, an if the answer to the test is too low, then change the guess to get a higher answer.**

294 Lesson 8.7

Meeting Individual Needs

Early Finishers

Challenge students to solve this problem: Two numbers have a sum of 21 and a difference of 9. What are the numbers? *[15 and 6]*

Extra Support

Help students to complete problem 1 on page 295. Remind them that they can start by making any guess. Then ask:

- **How can you change your guess to make the answer higher (or lower)?**

Ongoing Assessment

Anecdotal Report Make notes on how students use each guess to revise their next guesses.

Follow Up Help students who are having difficulty organizing information in a problem, by having them verbalize what they need to find and how they can use a guess to help solve. Assign **Reteach 72.**

For students who are able to guess, test, and revise to solve problems, assign **Extend 72.**

o; possible answer: 3 is an odd number, nd if an odd number is multiplied by an dd number, the answer is an odd number.

7. 40 trailers; possible answer: 320 ÷ 8 = 40—put as many cars on each trailer as possible in order to find the least number of trailers.

KED APPLICATIONS

oblem Solving

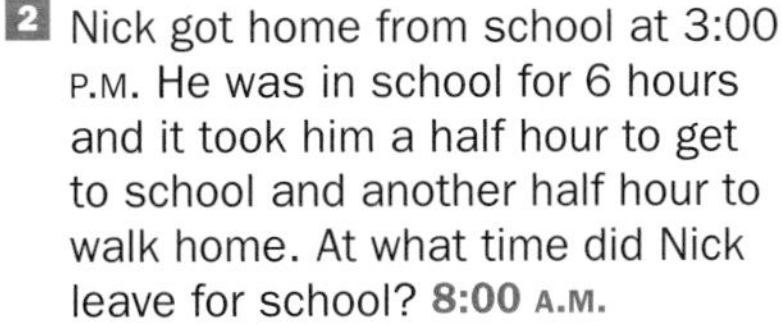

Jenny is making sand art. A bottle holds 8 inches of sand. Jenny wants to have 2 inches more of red sand than blue sand. How many inches of each color will she pour? **3 in. of blue and 5 in. of red**

You have $80. You already have groceries that cost $73.22. Can you buy a box of cereal for $3.95? Explain. **Yes; overestimate to get $74 + $4 = $78 < $80.**

Logical reasoning If you multiply a number by 3, you get an even number. Can the number be odd? Explain. **See above.**

Mrs. Kelly stores 120 books in a small bookcase and a large bookcase. Each large shelf holds 20 books. Each small shelf holds 15 books. How many shelves are in the large bookcase? The small bookcase? **3 shelves; 4 shelves**

In 1851, there were only 3 schools in Minnesota to teach 250 students. If each school had about the same number of students, were there more than 80 students in each school? Explain your answer. **See below.**

the table for problems 9–11.

Which city has about five times as many people as Grand Rapids? **Detroit**

Which two cities are closest in population? **Warren and Flint**

About how many more people does the most populated city have than Lansing? **about 900,000 more people**

2 Nick got home from school at 3:00 P.M. He was in school for 6 hours and it took him a half hour to get to school and another half hour to walk home. At what time did Nick leave for school? **8:00 A.M.**

4 **Spatial reasoning** The sheet of paper was folded in half and then holes were punched through it. Show what it will look like unfolded.

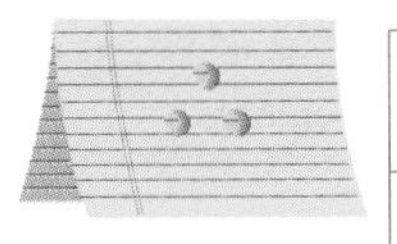

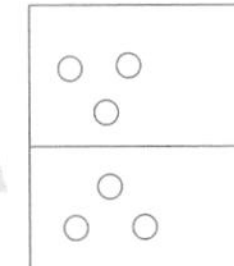

7 Detroit, Michigan, is famous for making cars. One factory has 320 cars to deliver on trailers. Each trailer holds 8 cars. What is the least number of trailers needed to deliver the cars? Explain your answer. **See above.**

Population of Largest Cities in Michigan	
Detroit	1,027,974
Grand Rapids	189,126
Warren	144,864
Flint	140,761
Lansing	127,321

8. Possible answer: 3 × 80 = 240, and since 250 > 240, there must have been more than 80 students in each class.

a Practice, page 514

PRACTICE

Alternate Teaching Strategy

Read the problem on Student Book page 294. To help students understand how the guess, test, and revise method can simplify problem solving, make a table as shown. The table lists all the possible combinations of three students and four students in the five-day total.

NUMBER OF DAYS

3 students (per day)	1 day	2 days	3 days	4 days
4 students (per day)	4 days	3 days	2 days	1 day
Total Number of Students	3 × 1 = 3 4 × 4 = 16 3 + 16 = 19	3 × 2 = 6 4 × 3 = 12 6 + 12 = 18	3 × 3 = 9 4 × 2 = 8 9 + 8 = 17	3 × 4 = 12 4 × 1 = 4 12 + 4 = 16

Lead students through the completion of the first column. Then have them work on their own to complete the other columns. Have a volunteer point out the column with the information that solves the problem. *[column with 2 days of 3 students and 3 days of 4 students—6 + 12 = 18]*

PRACTICE • 72

HOMEWORK

Practice 72

Name:

Problem-Solving Strategy: Guess, Test, and Revise

✔ Read ✔ Plan ✔ Solve ✔ Look Back

Solve using the guess, test, and revise strategy.

1. Your family bikes and camps in Vermont for 5 days. You cover 22 miles by going either 4 or 5 miles a day. On how many days do you travel 4 miles? 5 miles?
   4 mi on 3 days; 5 mi on 2 days
2. Your brother has the task of dividing 20 snacks between you and 3 friends. He wants you to have twice as many as any of the others. How many snacks do you get? How many do the others get?
   8 snacks; 4 snacks
3. While biking, you drink 19 ounces of a juice and water mixture that you prepared. It contains 3 more ounces of water than juice. How many ounces of water do you drink?
   11 oz
4. You spent $3 or $4 a day on snacks in small towns while on the bike trip. If you spent $17 during the 5 days, on how many days did you spend $3? $4?
   $3 on 3 days; $4 on 2 days

Solve using any method. 

5. A forest ranger tells you that about 1,300 cars used a nearby highway over a recent 4-day holiday weekend. Estimate the number of cars per day.
   Possible answer: 300 cars per day
6. You stop at a bookstore in a small town to buy a Bike Traveler's Manual. It has 1,035 pages. You plan to read 5 pages a night. How many nights will it take?
   207 nights
7. By saving all year, your family has $1,002 to spend on this vacation trip. By the third night, you have spent $499. How much is left to spend? How much is that for each of 2 days?
   $503; $251.50
8. To plan for next year's vacation, your parents have decided to save $140 each month for 9 months. Your brother will save $3.75 and you will save $0.35 each month. How much is that in all?
   $1,296.90

McGraw-Hill School Division

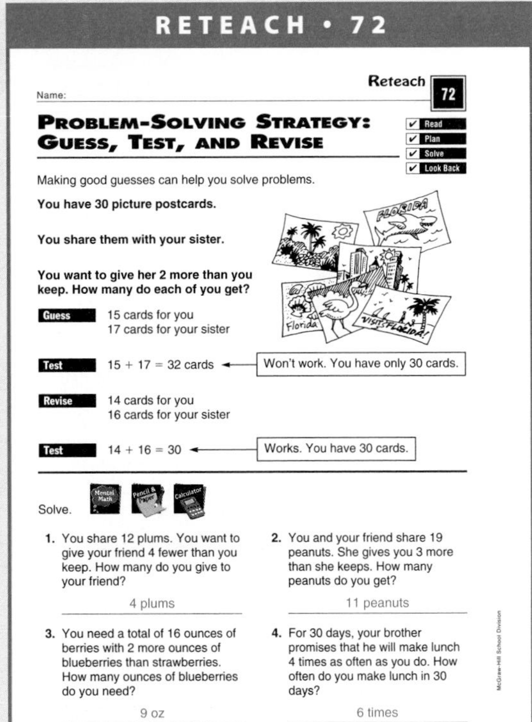

RETEACH • 72

Reteach 72

Name:

Problem-Solving Strategy: Guess, Test, and Revise

✔ Read ✔ Plan ✔ Solve ✔ Look Back

Making good guesses can help you solve problems.

You have 30 picture postcards.

You share them with your sister.

You want to give her 2 more than you keep. How many do each of you get?

Guess 15 cards for you
17 cards for your sister

Test 15 + 17 = 32 cards ← Won't work. You have only 30 cards.

Revise 14 cards for you
16 cards for your sister

Test 14 + 16 = 30 ← Works. You have 30 cards.

Solve.

1. You share 12 plums. You want to give your friend 4 fewer than you keep. How many do you give to your friend?
   4 plums
2. You and your friend share 19 peanuts. She gives you 3 more than she keeps. How many peanuts do you get?
   11 peanuts
3. You need a total of 16 ounces of berries with 2 more ounces of blueberries than strawberries. How many ounces of blueberries do you need?
   9 oz
4. For 30 days, your brother promises that he will make lunch 4 times as often as you do. How often do you make lunch in 30 days?
   6 times

McGraw-Hill School Division

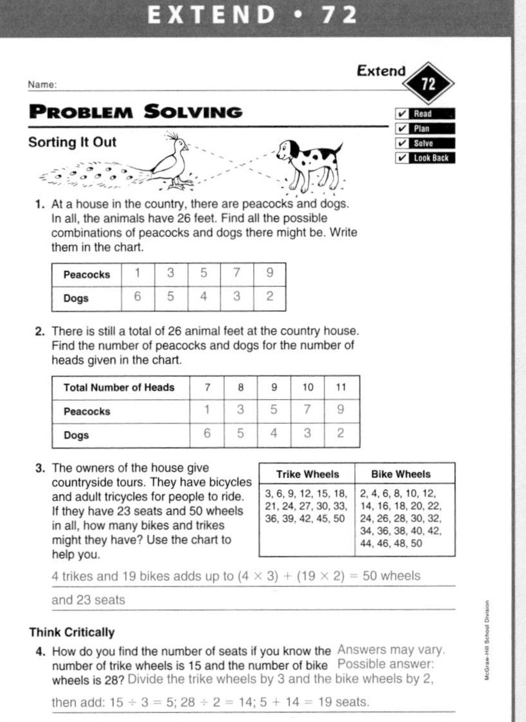

EXTEND • 72

Extend 72

Name:

Problem Solving

✔ Read ✔ Plan ✔ Solve ✔ Look Back

Sorting It Out

1. At a house in the country, there are peacocks and dogs. In all, the animals have 26 feet. Find all the possible combinations of peacocks and dogs there might be. Write them in the chart.

Peacocks	1	3	5	7	9
Dogs	6	5	4	3	2

2. There is still a total of 26 animal feet at the country house. Find the number of peacocks and dogs for the number of heads given in the chart.

Total Number of Heads	7	8	9	10	11
Peacocks	1	3	5	7	9
Dogs	6	5	4	3	2

3. The owners of the house give countryside tours. They have bicycles and adult tricycles for people to ride. If they have 23 seats and 50 wheels in all, how many bikes and trikes might they have? Use the chart to help you.

Trike Wheels	Bike Wheels
3, 6, 9, 12, 15, 18, 21, 24, 27, 30, 33, 36, 39, 42, 45, 50	2, 4, 6, 8, 10, 12, 14, 16, 18, 20, 22, 24, 26, 28, 30, 32, 34, 36, 38, 40, 42, 44, 46, 48, 50

4 trikes and 19 bikes adds up to (4 × 3) + (19 × 2) = 50 wheels and 23 seats

Think Critically

4. How do you find the number of seats if you know the number of trike wheels is 15 and the number of bike wheels is 28? Answers may vary. Possible answer: Divide the trike wheels by 3 and the bike wheels by 2, then add: 15 ÷ 3 = 5; 28 ÷ 2 = 14; 5 + 14 = 19 seats.

McGraw-Hill School Division

PURPOSE Maintain and review concepts, skills, and strategies that students have learned thus far in the chapter.

Materials per student: calculator (optional)

Using the Midchapter Review

Have students complete the **Midchapter Review** independently or use it with the whole class.

 **Algebra: Patterns** In ex. 1, students understand the relationship between numbers by finding division patterns.

For ex. 4–7, students need to get information from the table before estimating. They should use compatible numbers to estimate.

For ex. 18–20, students should be able to use mental math to solve.

Students can approach this open-ended problem at their own levels.

Possible methods include:
–a model (counters, connecting cubes, or place-value)
–a paper-and-pencil method
–a calculator
–mental math

Vocabulary Review

Write the following words on the chalkboard:

compatible numbers	**divisor**	**regroup**
dividend	**estimate**	**remainder**
divisible	**quotient**	

Ask for volunteers to explain the meanings of these words and to give examples.

ALGEBRA: PATTERNS Complete.

1. 12 ÷ 4 = ■ **3**
120 ÷ 4 = ■ **30**
1,200 ÷ 4 = ■ **300**

2. ■ ÷ 6 = 4 **24**
■ ÷ 6 = 40 **240**
■ ÷ 6 = 400 **2,400**

3. 42 ÷ 7 = ■ **6**
420 ÷ 7 = ■ **60**
4,200 ÷ 7 = ■ **6(**

Estimate how many are in each box if the boxes have the same number in them.

4. 7 boxes of pens **about 40 pens**
5. 4 boxes of binders **about 30 binders**
6. 6 boxes of scissors **about 50 pairs of scissors**
7. 8 boxes of erasers **about 90 erasers**

Item	Total
Pens	287
Binders	121
Erasers	693
Scissors	321

Divide.

8. 4)532 **133**
9. 7)95 **13 R4**
10. 3)314 **104 R2**
11. 6)61 **10 R1**
12. 8)29 **3 R5**
13. 6)713 **118 R5**
14. 7)372 **53 R1**
15. 4)427 **106 R3**
16. 4)1,961 **490 R1**
17. 2)$88,' **$44,06.**

Find the missing number.

18. 3,200 ÷ 8 = ■ **400**
19. 900 ÷ ■ = 300 **3**
20. 2,000 ÷ ■ = 500 **4**

Solve. Use mental math when you can.

21. The Rainbow Bridge in Utah is 200 ft high. It is the largest natural arch in the world. Gateway Arch in Missouri is the tallest monument in the United States. It is 430 ft taller than the Rainbow Bridge. How tall is it? **630 ft**

22. The Hershey Plant in Pennsylvani is the world's largest chocolat factory. Some candy bars are divided into 8 squares each. If you had 872 squares, how many chocolate bars would you have? **109 chocolate bars**

23. One of the largest stock exchanges in the United States is the Philadelphia Stock Exchange. Mr. Morris bought $552 worth of stocks. He paid $8 for each share. How many shares did he buy? **69 shares**

24. **What if** Mr. Morris paid $9 for each share and bought $864 worth of stocks. About how mar shares would he own? **Possible answer: about 100 shares**

25. Journal: Describe two different methods you could use to find 482 ÷ 4. **Students may suggest using mental math or compatible numbers following the 3-step method.**

296 Midchapter Review

Reinforcement and Remediation

CHAPTER OBJECTIVES	MIDCHAPTER REVIEW ITEMS	STUDENT BOOK PAGES	TEACHER'S EDITION PAGES: Activities	TEACHER'S EDITION PAGES: Alternate Teaching Strategy	TEACHER RESOURCES: Reteach
*8A	4–7	280–281	279A	281	67
*8B	8–17	282–293	281A, 285, 289A, 291A	285, 289, 291, 293	68–71
*8C	1–3, 18–20	278–279	277A	279	66
*8E	21–25	294–295	293A	295	72

*8A Estimate quotients of whole numbers and money amounts
*8B Divide by 1-digit divisors
*8C Divide by multiples of 10
*8E Solve problems, including those that involve division and guessing, testing, and revising

developing algebra sense

MATH CONNECTION

Explore Divisibility Rules

agine hiking along a trail that starts Maine and goes all the way to Georgia. can do it on the Appalachian Trail. at if a hiker starts in New York and es 135 miles in 9 days. Can she hike same distance each day?

can use a divisibility rule to find out if re will be a remainder when you divide.

e: If there is no remainder when you divide, the dividend is divisible by the divisor.

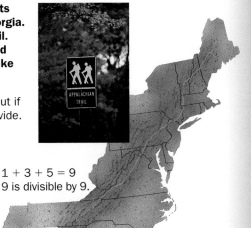

umber is divisible by 9 if the n of its digits is divisible by 9.

$1 + 3 + 5 = 9$
9 is divisible by 9.

5 is divisible by 9.

eck your answer: $135 \div 9 = 15$.

e can travel 15 miles each day.

re are more divisibility rules. umber is divisible by:

f the ones digit is 0, 2, 4, 6, or 8.
f the sum of its digits is divisible by 3.
f the ones digit is 0 or 5.
6 if it is divisible by both 2 and 3.
10 if the ones digit is 0.

e divisibility rules to answer mentally. Explain your thinking.

A tour company donates 1,456 tickets for a tour to Niagara Falls to 3 schools. Can you divide the tickets equally among the schools? **See above.**

1. **No, the sum of the digits is 16, which is not divisible by 3.**

2 A group of 459 students are marching in a parade in New York City. Can they march in equal rows of 9 students across? **Yes; 4 + 5 + 9 = 18, which is divisible by 9.**

Can 657 jelly beans be divided equally among 2 classes? **No; 7 is not divisible by 2.**

4 Can you divide 354 counters into groups of 2? 3? 5? 6? 9? 10? **See above.**

4. 354 counters can be divided into groups of 2, 3, and 6; 354 ends in 4 so it is divisible by 2, the sum of its digits 12 so it is divisible by 3, and since it is divisible by 2 and 3 it is also divisible by 6.

Make a decision You want to share cookies evenly among 6 of your friends. Would you buy a box that had 47, 98, or 102 cookies? **Possible answer: Box of 102 cookies; it is the only number that can be divided evenly by 6.**

6 **Write a problem** that can be solved by using a divisibility rule. Solve it. Trade it with a classmate. Solve each other's problem. **Students should compare problems and solutions.**

OBJECTIVE Explore divisibility rules.

Materials calculator (optional)

Using Algebra Sense

Math Connection In Lesson 3, students used divisibility to determine if numbers were prime numbers or composite numbers. Here students explore rules about divisibility to help solve division problems.

After students read the opening problem, discuss what they need to find out to solve the problem. *[if 135 ÷ 9 has a remainder]* Then discuss the divisibility rule for 9 and how it is used to solve the problem.

Review the divisibility rules for 2, 3, 5, 6, and 10. Then ask:

- **What is a divisibility rule?** *[Possible answer: a rule that tells you whether division by a particular divisor will have a remainder]*

Let students use the divisibility rules to answer each of the following:

- **Which number is divisible by 3,132 or 133? Explain.** *[132; 1 + 3 + 2 = 6 is divisible by 3.]*
- **Is 168 divisible by 6? Explain.** *[Yes; 168 is divisible by 2, 1 + 6 + 8 = 15 and 15 is divisible by 3, so 168 is divisible by 6.]*
- **Which number is divisible by 9: 108 or 118? Explain.** *[108; 1 + 0 + 8 = 9 and 9 is divisible by 9.]*

Students may work in pairs or on their own to complete ex. 1–6.

Applying Division

OBJECTIVE Apply division by 1- and 2-digit numbers in a social studies context.

Materials per group: travel brochures, hotel flyers, restaurant flyers, airline advertisements, train schedules, bus schedules, and road maps that relate to your state

1 Engage

Using the Group Discussion (with Round Robin) Strategy, in a small group, students take turns in a clockwise fashion sharing memorable travel experiences. Students may say "pass" when they do not wish to contribute for that round. They continue until everyone has contributed at least once. Ask them to be as specific as possible about places, modes of transportation, and entrance fees. Then begin a class list of places students would like to visit.

2 Investigate *Cooperative Groups*

Make some suggestions to prepare groups for practical decision making, such as trying to see sites that are near one another.

Remind students that the trip is a group trip, so they will have to make compromises.

Planning the Tour It may be helpful to give groups a budget of $200 per student. If time allows, have students suggest ways they could raise the money. As an alternative, have them imagine that they have won a trip around the state with unlimited funding.

You might also set a time limit for the trip. Consider a two-day trip as a minimum.

3 Reflect and Share

Materials have available: calculators

Report Your Findings Have students describe how they were able to agree upon places to visit, stay, and eat. As you discuss student reports, compare costs associated with different trips.

Students should use calculators to find the cost per person each day and then find the total cost for the trip.

Revise your work Students can check their schedules by choosing three dates and times at random and deciding whether or not the schedule clearly tells them where they will be and what they will be doing.

real-life investigation

APPLYING DIVISION

A State Tour

Where would you want to go if you and your friends could take a tour of places in your state? In this activity, you will work with a group to take a tour of special places you choose and then split the cost.

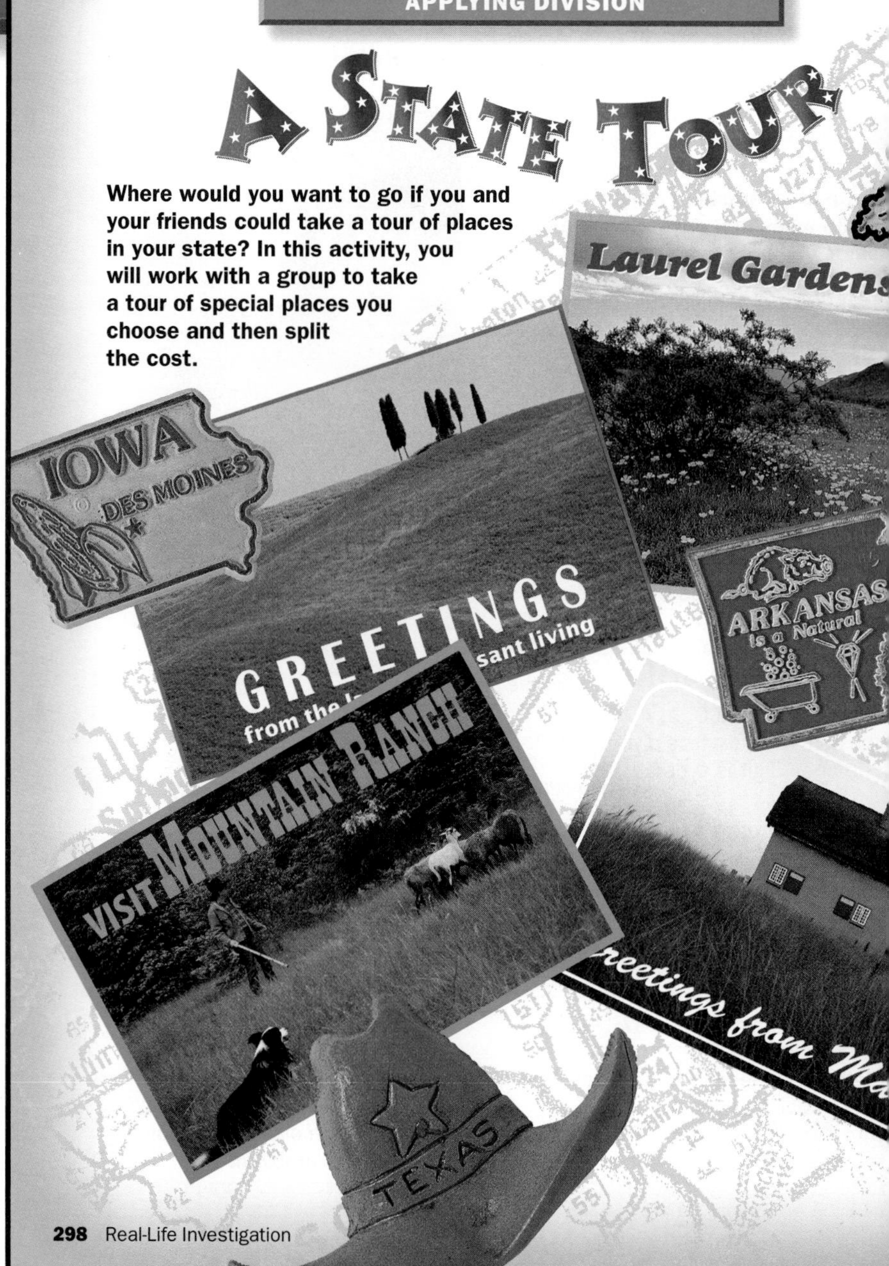

298 Real-Life Investigation

More To Investigate

Predict Possible locations: zoos, historical sites, national parks, caves, state parks, state capital. Possible reasons: fun, interesting, educational, important

Explore Possible answer: Use a map to plan a trip to the state capital.

Find Possible answer: They receive information from airlines, cruise ship lines, railroads, car rental agencies, and hotels that their customers use.

Bibliography Students who wish to learn more about different places of interest to visit can read:

Museums, by Jason Cooper. Vero Beach, FL: Rourke Corporation, 1992. ISBN 0–86593–209–3.

Our National Parks, by Michael Weber. Brookfield, CT: Middlebrook Press, 1994. ISBN 1–56294–438–X.

swers may vary.
eck students' work.

See Teacher's Edition
for sample of student work.

DECISION MAKING

Planning the Tour

1 Work with a group. Collect travel information about interesting places in your state.

2 Decide what places you and your group will tour and how long you will spend at each place.

3 Estimate the total amount you will spend for each of the following:
a. transportation from your home to the places on the tour. You need to decide if you will use an airplane, a train, or a bus.
b. motels or hotels for overnight stays.
c. meals.
d. tickets for the places on the tour.

4 Decide how you will split the cost of the tour among your group. For each person, find:
a. the cost each day.
b. the total amount to pay.

Reporting Your Findings

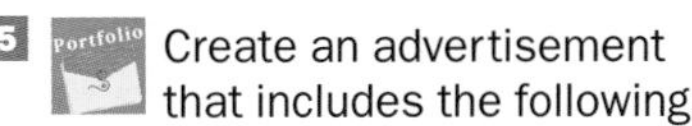

5 Create an advertisement that includes the following:

- a description of the tour and all that is included.
- a list that shows the cost each day for hotels, meals, entertainment, and transportation for one person.
- an explanation of how the costs were divided and why.

6 Compare your tour with those of other groups.

Revise your work.

- Did you provide all the information that was asked for?
- Is the advertisement organized and easy to follow?

MORE TO INVESTIGATE

PREDICT which locations in your state would be the most popular. Tell why.

EXPLORE other places of interest in your state and the distance you would travel each day to get there from your home.

FIND out how travel agents plan trips. Where do they get their information?

Students' Work

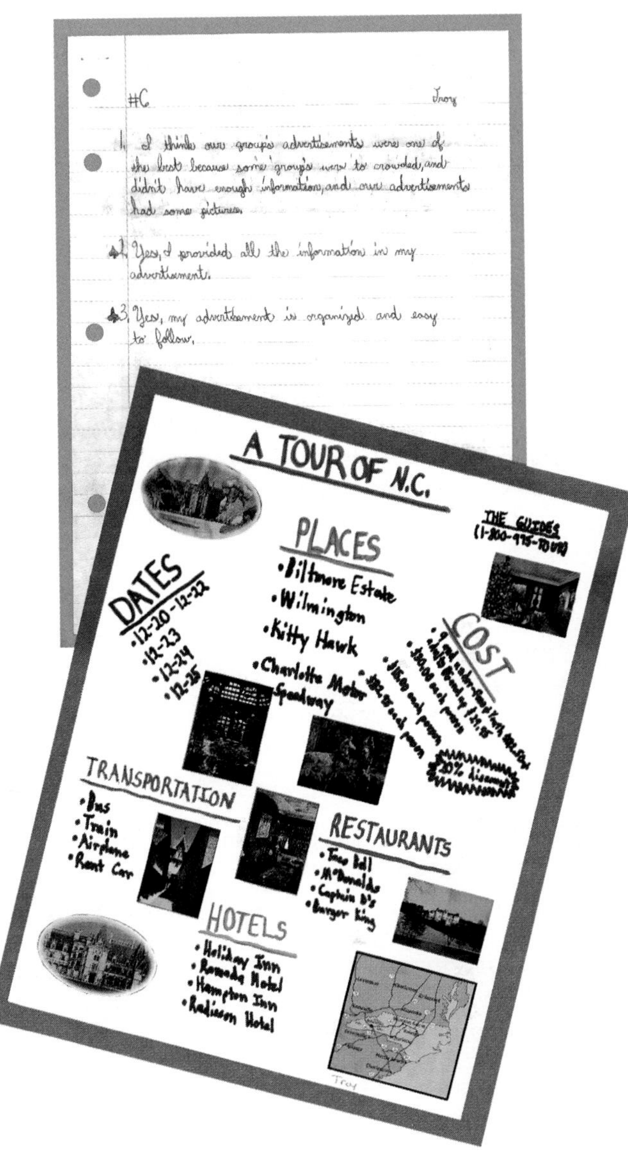

Building A Portfolio

This investigation will allow you to evaluate a student's ability to organize data, create a schedule, and to divide in order to solve a problem.

Allow students to revise their work for the portfolio. Each student's portfolio piece should consist of a copy of his or her schedule of the team's tour and a description of the tour. This includes a list with travel, lodging, and food expenses, and an explanation of how the costs were calculated.

You may use the Holistic Scoring Guide to assess this task. See page 27 in Teacher's Assessment Resources.

EXPLORE ACTIVITY
Average

OBJECTIVE Explore finding the average for a set of data.

RESOURCE REMINDER
Math Center Cards 73
Practice 73, Reteach 73, Extend 73

SKILLS TRACE

GRADE 3	• Introduced at grade 4.
GRADE 4	• Explore finding the average of a set of numbers.
GRADE 5	• Explore finding the mean for a set of data. *(Chapter 5)*

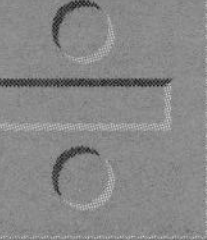

LESSON 8.8 RESOURCES

WARM-UP

Cooperative Groups — Kinesthetic

OBJECTIVE Review the concept of median and mode.

Materials per group: metric measuring tape

▶ Have students work in groups, using the tape to measure and record each others' heights in centimeters.

▶ Have them find the median height. Remind them to put the numbers in order from least to greatest before finding the median.

▶ Ask students if they can think of any other way of describing a "middle" or typical height for members of the group. If no one mentions it, review the idea of mode. Ask students to find the mode of their group's height.

STATISTICS CONNECTION

Cooperative Groups — Logical/Analytical

OBJECTIVE Connect different ways of describing data to choosing the most appropriate statistical measure.

Materials per group: calculators

▶ Write this chart on the chalkboard:

Salaries Paid by the Zeta Company	
President	$95,000
Salesperson A	$35,000
Salesperson B	$30,000
Assistant A	$25,000
Assistant B	$25,000

▶ Have students find the mean, median, and mode for the set of data, using calculators if they wish. *[mean, $42,000; median, $30,000; mode, $25,000]*

▶ Have students discuss which statistic gives the best idea of the company's typical salary, and why. *[Possible answer: the median, because it is in the middle. The president's high salary makes the average too high to describe a typical salary.]*

Daily Review

PREVIOUS DAY QUICK REVIEW

1. 3,624 ÷ 6 *[604]*
2. 1,125 ÷ 4 *[281 R1]*
3. 5,018 ÷ 5 *[1,003 R3]*
4. 28,246 ÷ 2 *[14,123]*

FAST FACTS

1. 7 + 9 *[16]*
2. 8 + 5 *[13]*
3. 3 + 7 *[10]*
4. 6 + 6 *[12]*

Problem of the Day • 73

There are 5 classes at the sports center. There are 8 students in the first class and a total of 27 students in classes 2–4. The last class has 2 more students than the first. What is the average number of students in each class?
[9 students]

TECH LINK

Math Van

MATH VAN

Tool You may wish to use the Counters tool and the Calculator with this lesson.

MATH FORUM

Management Tip If there are not enough snap cubes for the Explore activity, counters or other countable objects such as play coins may be used.

Visit our Resource Village at http://www.mhschool.com to see more of the Math Forum.

MATH CENTER

Practice

OBJECTIVE Collect data and find an average.

Materials per pair: 6 paper cups, marker; per student: 8 counters, Math Center Recording Sheet (TA 31 optional)

Students play a game in which they toss 8 counters into scored cups. They find their average scores, and the higher average score wins.

PRACTICE ACTIVITY 73 — MATH CENTER — Partners

Game • Average Tosses

YOU NEED
- 6 paper cups
- marker
- 8 counters

- Use the marker to label each cup with a score from 10 to 20.
- Arrange the cups on the desk in two rows of three.
- Stand about a yard away. Toss your counters one by one. Add up the scores on the cups that you hit.
- Your partner takes a turn.
- Each of you determines your average. The one with the higher average wins.

Grade Level 4 — McGraw-Hill School Division

Chapter 8, Lesson 8, pages 300–301 — Division

ESL APPROPRIATE

NCTM Standards
- ✓ Problem Solving
- Communication
- Reasoning
- ✓ Connections

Problem Solving

OBJECTIVE Collect data and find the average.

Materials per student: paper, paper clip, yardstick, Math Center Recording Sheet (TA 31 optional)

Students create and fly a paper airplane. Then they measure the flight distance to the nearest foot. After 5 trials, students find the average distance flown. Students need a 10-yard-long flying space.

PROBLEM-SOLVING ACTIVITY 73 — MATH CENTER — On Your Own

Using Data • Aerodynamic Averages

YOU NEED
- paper clip
- yardstick or tape measure

- Carefully fold a paper plane. Put a paper clip where one is shown in the picture.
- Fly your plane in as straight a line as possible. Measure and record the distance flown to the nearest foot using the yardstick or tape measure.
- After 5 flights, find the average distance flown. Show your work.

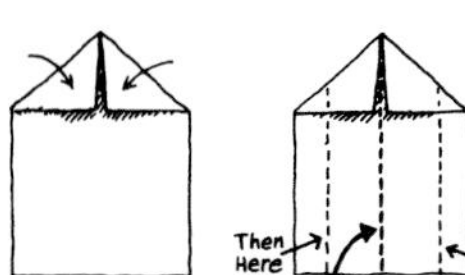

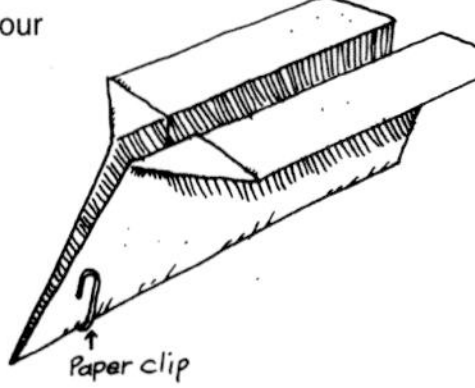

Grade Level 4 — McGraw-Hill School Division

Chapter 8, Lesson 8, pages 300–301 — Division

ESL APPROPRIATE

NCTM Standards
- ✓ Problem Solving
- ✓ Communication
- Reasoning
- ✓ Connections

EXPLORE ACTIVITY
Average

OBJECTIVE Find the mean of a set of numbers.

Vocabulary average

1 Introduce

Materials per pair: 85 connecting cubes

Present the following problem:

Andrew ran 21 kilometers last week. He ran about the same number of kilometers each day. About how many kilometers did he run each day?

Have students suggest ways they could use connecting cubes to solve the problem. *[Possible answer: Show 21 snap cubes, then divide them into 7 groups. Andrew ran about three kilometers each day.]*

2 Teach *Cooperative Pairs*

LEARN Work Together After reading the problem on page 300, ask students why they might want to find an average. *[Possible answer: to get an idea of the typical number in a group]*

After groups complete the activity, have them share their answers for each of the sets of data.

MAKE CONNECTIONS

After reviewing each of the steps, have students use addition and division to find the average of other groups of numbers.

As the first **What if?** question is discussed, ask how the average would have been affected if Emmitt had scored 15 touchdowns in 1993. *[It would have increased, because more touchdowns are divided by the same number of years.]*

3 Close

Check for Understanding using items 1–3, page 301.

CRITICAL THINKING
In item 3, students are asked to explain how zero affects an average. Have students further analyze the data by having them find the median and discuss which measure they think best describes the data, the mean or the median. *[Answers may vary.]*

PRACTICE

Materials have available: calculators

Assign ex. 1–6 as independent work.

- Allow students to use calculators to complete ex. 1–6.
- In ex. 6, students interpret a line graph. Point out the broken scale.

EXPLORE ACTIVITY • DIVISION

Average

LEARN

For three years in a row, Emmitt Smith of the Dallas Cowboys won the NFL rushing title. In addition, he scored 12 touchdowns in 1991, 18 in 1992, and 9 in 1993. How many touchdowns did he average each year?

The Dallas Cowboys have won the Super Bowl five times.

Work Together
Work with a partner.

You will need
- *connecting cubes*

Let each cube stand for a touchdown. Use stacks of cubes to show the number of touchdowns for each year.

Rearrange the cubes so that the stacks are all the same height. The number of cubes in each stack is the **average** number of touchdowns.

Record your work in a table like the one shown.

Number of Stacks	Total Number of cubes	Avera
3	12+18+9=39	

Use cubes to help you find the average of these numbers. Record your work.

a. 15, 8, 17, 9, 6 **11**
b. 17, 7, 12, 3, 2, 13 **9**
c. 25, 19, 16, 24 **21**

Make Connections
Look at your table. First, you found the total number of cubes. Then, you separated the total into equal groups.

Check Out the Glossary
average
See page 544.

You can use addition and division to find the average of any group of numbers, such as Emmitt Smith's touchdowns.

Step 1	Step 2
Add all the numbers.	**Divide the sum by the number of addends.**
12 + 18 + 9 = 39	39 ÷ 3 = 13

Emmitt scored an average of 13 touchdowns.

Meeting Individual Needs

Early Finishers

Have students think of some other data for which they might like to find means, such as gasoline mileage or hours of TV watching. Then have them find the means.

Extra Support

Since finding the mean, or average, of a set of numbers requires the use of two operations, encourage students to identify each operation as they use it. Then have them state what the average is.

Ongoing Assessment

Observation Checklist Determine if students understand how to find the mean of a set of numbers by observing the steps they follow in the Practice exercises. You may wish to have them explain these steps.

Follow Up Have students who need additional help computing the average of a set of numbers, try **Reteach 73.**

Have students who demonstrate mastery, find the mean for sets of data with five-digit numbers. You may also wish to assign **Extend 73.**

estion 2. The average would be the same—13 touchdowns each year; there are
re touchdowns scored, but the number of years has also increased, so the average
52 ÷ 4 = 13.

What if Emmitt had scored only 3 touchdowns in 1993. How would this change the average? Explain. See below.

What if Emmitt had scored 13 touchdowns in 1994. How would this change the average? Explain. See above.

heck for Understanding

d the average.

Number of minutes spent with each customer: 21, 42, 15, 35, 9, 22 **24 min**

2 Number of kilometers driven each day: 101, 92, 119, 85, 123 **104 km**

itical Thinking: Analyze
plain your reasoning.

Find the average math score for the first 4 weeks and then for the 5 weeks. How does one zero affect the grade? Explain. See below.

Week	Math Quiz Scores
1	98
2	94
3	61
4	87
5	0

CHECK

ractice

d the average.

3. 4 wk—85, 5 wk—68; possible answer: a zero lowers the average since the same total is being divided equally among more weeks.

Number of cousins each student has: 2, 6, 10 **6 cousins**

2 Number of tickets sold for each play: 11, 33, 55, 202, 101, 6 **68 tickets**

Number of umbrellas sold each day: 35, 46, 17, 119, 75, 14 **51 umbrellas**

4 Number of meals served at each school: 752, 864, 328 **648 meals**

Find the average number of votes for each state. **average of 7 votes for Florida and 8 votes for California**

6 Find the average number of tickets sold for the six months. **1,000 tickets**

Where Would You Like to Live?

lass	Florida	California
A	𝍸 III	𝍸 I
B	𝍸 𝍸	𝍸 III
C	IIII	𝍸 II
D	𝍸 I	𝍸 𝍸 I

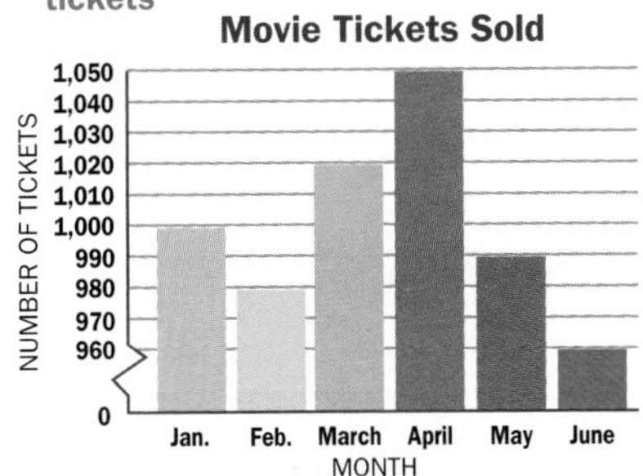

PRACTICE

estion 1. The average would be less—11 touchdowns each year; fewer
uchdowns are divided by the same number of years.

tra Practice, page 514

Alternate Teaching Strategy

Materials per group: 50 counters

Read the problem on Student Book page 300. Ask:

- **How many touchdowns did Emmitt Smith have each year?** *[12, 18, and 9]*
- **What is the sum of the numbers?** *[39]*

Have small groups of students take 39 counters and place the counters into 3 equal groups. Then ask:

- **What operation is used when you put the 39 counters in 3 groups?** *[division]*
- **What division sentence can you write to show the operation?** *[39 ÷ 3 = 13]*
- **The quotient of the division sentence is the average number of touchdowns. What is Smith's average for each year?** *[13 touchdowns]*
- **What two operations did you use to find the average?** *[addition and division]*

Repeat the activity, asking similar questions for the other sets of numbers on page 300 in the **Work Together** section.

PRACTICE • 73

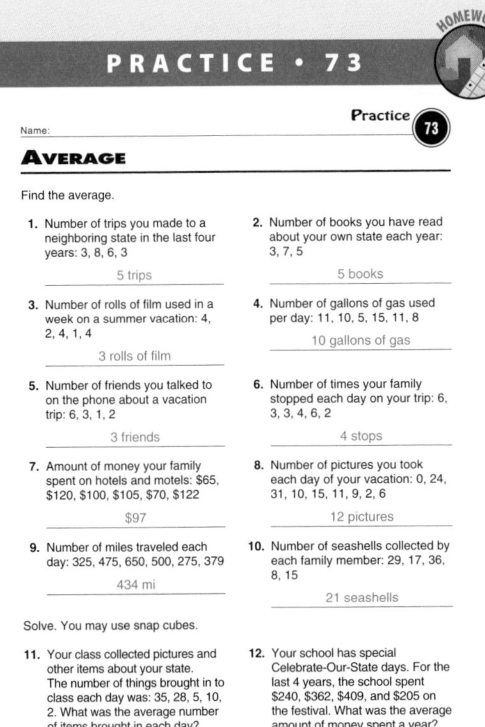

Practice 73

Name:

AVERAGE

Find the average.

1. Number of trips you made to a neighboring state in the last four years: 3, 8, 6, 3 — 5 trips
2. Number of books you have read about your own state each year: 3, 7, 5 — 5 books
3. Number of rolls of film used in a week on a summer vacation: 4, 2, 4, 1, 4 — 3 rolls of film
4. Number of gallons of gas used per day: 11, 10, 5, 15, 11, 8 — 10 gallons of gas
5. Number of friends you talked to on the phone about a vacation trip: 6, 3, 1, 2 — 3 friends
6. Number of times your family stopped each day on your trip: 6, 3, 3, 4, 6, 2 — 4 stops
7. Amount of money your family spent on hotels and motels: $65, $120, $100, $105, $70, $122 — $97
8. Number of pictures you took each day of your vacation: 0, 24, 31, 10, 15, 11, 9, 2, 6 — 12 pictures
9. Number of miles traveled each day: 325, 475, 650, 500, 275, 379 — 434 mi
10. Number of seashells collected by each family member: 29, 17, 36, 8, 15 — 21 seashells

Solve. You may use snap cubes.

11. Your class collected pictures and other items about your state. The number of things brought in to class each day was: 35, 28, 5, 10, 2. What was the average number of items brought in each day? — 16 items
12. Your school has special Celebrate-Our-State days. For the last 4 years, the school spent $240, $362, $409, and $205 on the festival. What was the average amount of money spent a year? — $304

RETEACH • 73

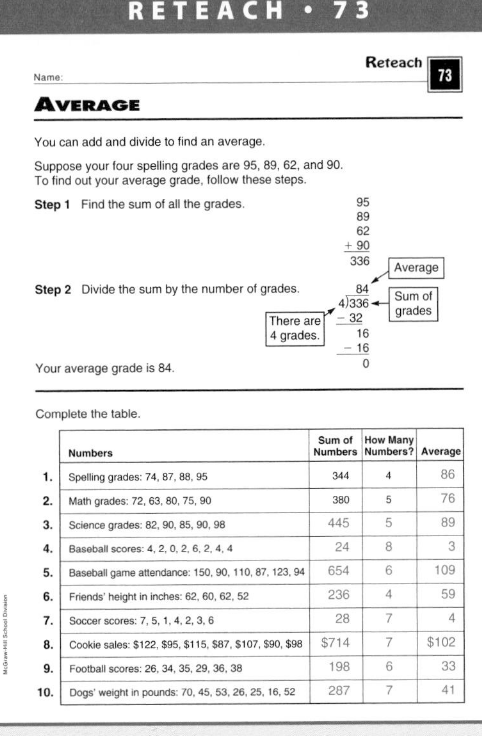

Reteach 73

Name:

AVERAGE

You can add and divide to find an average.

Suppose your four spelling grades are 95, 89, 62, and 90. To find out your average grade, follow these steps.

Step 1 Find the sum of all the grades.

$$95 + 89 + 62 + 90 = 336$$

Step 2 Divide the sum by the number of grades.

$$336 \div 4 = 84$$

(There are 4 grades. 336 = Sum of grades. 84 = Average)

Your average grade is 84.

Complete the table.

	Numbers	Sum of Numbers	How Many Numbers?	Average
1.	Spelling grades: 74, 87, 88, 95	344	4	86
2.	Math grades: 72, 63, 80, 75, 90	380	5	76
3.	Science grades: 82, 90, 85, 90, 98	445	5	89
4.	Baseball scores: 4, 2, 0, 2, 6, 2, 4, 4	24	8	3
5.	Baseball game attendance: 150, 90, 110, 87, 123, 94	654	6	109
6.	Friends' height in inches: 62, 60, 62, 52	236	4	59
7.	Soccer scores: 7, 5, 1, 4, 2, 3, 6	28	7	4
8.	Cookie sales: $122, $95, $115, $87, $107, $90, $98	$714	7	$102
9.	Football scores: 26, 34, 35, 29, 36, 38	198	6	33
10.	Dogs' weight in pounds: 70, 45, 53, 26, 25, 16, 52	287	7	41

EXTEND • 73

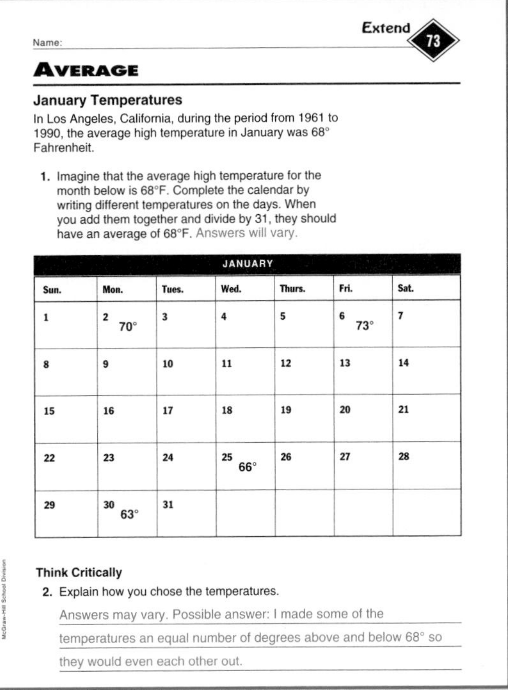

Extend 73

Name:

AVERAGE

January Temperatures

In Los Angeles, California, during the period from 1961 to 1990, the average high temperature in January was 68° Fahrenheit.

1. Imagine that the average high temperature for the month below is 68°F. Complete the calendar by writing different temperatures on the days. When you add them together and divide by 31, they should have an average of 68°F. Answers will vary.

JANUARY

Sun.	Mon.	Tues.	Wed.	Thurs.	Fri.	Sat.
1	2 70°	3	4	5	6 73°	7
8	9	10	11	12	13	14
15	16	17	18	19	20	21
22	23	24	25 66°	26	27	28
29	30 63°	31				

Think Critically

2. Explain how you chose the temperatures.
Answers may vary. Possible answer: I made some of the temperatures an equal number of degrees above and below 68° so they would even each other out.

MENTAL MATH

Divide by Multiples of Ten

OBJECTIVE Use mental math strategies to divide multiples of 10 by multiples of 10.

RESOURCE REMINDER
Math Center Cards 74
Practice 74, Reteach 74, Extend 74

SKILLS TRACE

GRADE 3	• Use mental math strategies to divide multiples of 10 and 100 by 1-digit numbers. *(Chapter 12)*
GRADE 4	• Use mental math strategies to divide multiples of ten by multiples of ten.
GRADE 5	• Use mental math strategies to divide whole numbers by multiples of ten. *(Chapter 6)*

LESSON 8.9 RESOURCES

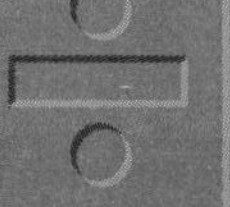

WARM-UP

Cooperative Pairs — **Logical/Analytical**

OBJECTIVE Review multiplication patterns.

Materials have available: calculator

▶ Write this multiplication pattern on the board:

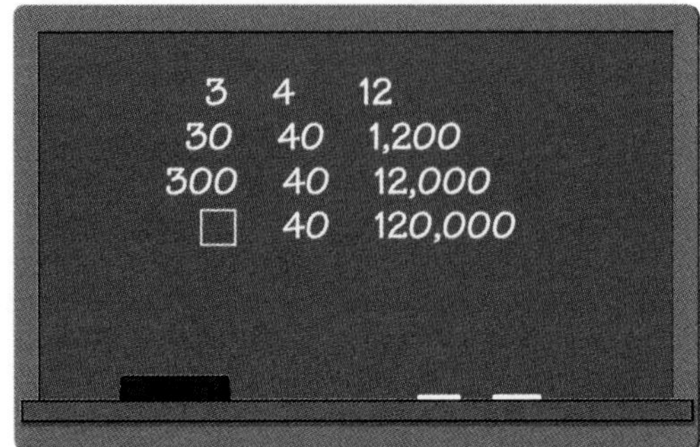

▶ Have a volunteer find the missing number *[3,000]* and explain how she or he found it.

▶ Have pairs work together to find the missing numbers below.

2 × 5 = 10	6 × 4 = 24	■ × 5 = 20 *[4]*
20 × 50 = ■ *[1,000]*	60 × 4 = 240	■ × 50 = 2,000 *[40]*
200 × 50 = 10,000	■ × 4 = 2,400 *[600]*	■ × 50 = 20,000 *[400]*
■ × 50 = 100,000 *[2,000]*	6,000 × 4 = ■ *[24,000]*	■ × 50 = 200,000 *[4,000]*

CONSUMER CONNECTION

Cooperative Groups — **Social**

OBJECTIVE Connect using division to packaging.

Materials have available: calculators

▶ Have groups use mental math or calculator to complete:

Total Number of Cans	Number of Cans in Each Box	Number of Boxes Needed
400	20	*[20]*
4,000	*[10]*	400
6,000	*[200]*	*[30]*
[60,000]	300	*[200]*

▶ Then have students write a division sentence to show each packaging.
[400 ÷ 20 = 20, 4,000 ÷ 10 = 400, 6,000 ÷ 200 = 30, 60,000 ÷ 300 = 200]

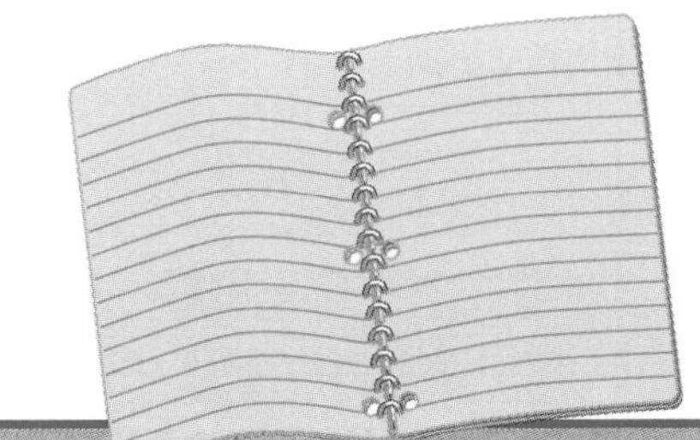

Daily Review

PREVIOUS DAY QUICK REVIEW

Find the average.

1. 7, 12, 5 *[8]*
2. 9, 6, 3, 6 *[6]*
3. 15, 19, 26 *[20]*
4. 5, 2, 7, 1, 10 *[5]*

FAST FACTS

1. 9 × 3 *[27]*
2. 6 × 7 *[42]*
3. 7 × 2 *[14]*
4. 5 × 7 *[35]*

Problem of the Day • 74

Students at Lincoln School print 2,600 flyers. They print 500 more flyers than each class will have to distribute outside of school. How many flyers will each class have if there are 30 classes at their school and each class receives the same number of flyers? *[70 flyers]*

TECH LINK

MATH VAN

Tool You may wish to use the Table and Graph tool for the Data Point in this lesson.

MATH FORUM

Idea My students enjoy playing a game using cards with exercises similar to those in this lesson. They respond by telling the basic fact used, the zero pattern shown, and the answer.

Visit our Resource Village at http://www.mhschool.com to see more of the Math Forum.

MATH CENTER

Practice

OBJECTIVE Divide by multiples of ten.

Materials per pair: 4-part spinner (TA 2); per student: Math Center Recording Sheet (TA 31 optional)

Prepare Have students make a 4-part spinner labeled zero through 3.

Students use a spinner to determine how many zeros are in the divisor and quotient. They write a division sentence based on the spin. *[Check students' work.]*

PRACTICE ACTIVITY 74 — MATH CENTER, Partners

Spatial Sense • How Many Zeros?

YOU NEED: spinner (0–3)

- Spin the spinner. Use the following rules to make up division sentences for your partner to solve. Make up at least 3 per spin.

Spin 0 Neither divisor nor quotient has a zero at the end.
Spin 1 Divisor has 1 zero, quotient has none.
Spin 2 Divisor and quotient have 1 zero each.
Spin 3 Divisor has 1 zero, quotient has 2.

Take turns and repeat the activity five times.

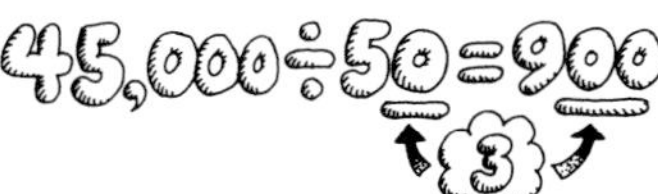

Grade Level 4 · McGraw-Hill School Division

Chapter 8, Lesson 9, pages 302–303 — Division

NCTM Standards
- Problem Solving
- ✓ Communication
- ✓ Reasoning
- Connections

Problem Solving

OBJECTIVE Explore division patterns.

Materials per student: Math Center Recording Sheet (TA 31 optional)

Students complete division sentences that follow a doubling pattern. They discover that if the dividend and the divisor are both doubled, the quotient remains the same. They make up their own divisions following the same pattern. *[**1.** 9; 360 ÷ 40 = 9; **2.** 9; 504 ÷ 56 = 9; **3.** 7; 448 ÷ 64 = 7; **4.** 8; 384 ÷ 48 = 8; **5.** 6; 432 ÷ 72 = 6; **6.** 8; 512 ÷ 64 = 8.]*

PROBLEM-SOLVING ACTIVITY 74 — MATH CENTER, Partners

Patterning • Halves and Doubles

Work together to complete each group of division sentences. Find the pattern and use it to write the next division sentence.

1. 45 ÷ 5 = ?
90 ÷ 10 = ?
180 ÷ 20 = ?

2. 63 ÷ 7 = ?
126 ÷ 14 = ?
252 ÷ 28 = ?

3. 56 ÷ 8 = ?
112 ÷ 16 = ?
224 ÷ 32 = ?

4. 48 ÷ 6 = ?
96 ÷ 12 = ?
192 ÷ 24 = ?

5. 54 ÷ 9 = ?
108 ÷ 18 = ?
216 ÷ 36 = ?

6. 64 ÷ 8 = ?
128 ÷ 16 = ?
256 ÷ 32 = ?

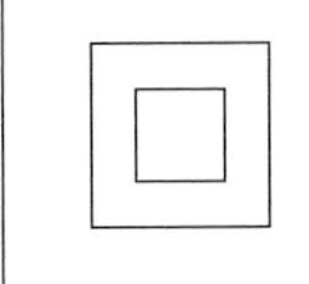

On your own, make up division sentences that follow the same pattern. Trade with your partner and solve. Discuss why the pattern works.

Grade Level 4 · McGraw-Hill School Division

Chapter 8, Lesson 9, pages 302–303 — Division

NCTM Standards
- ✓ Problem Solving
- ✓ Communication
- ✓ Reasoning
- Connections

MENTAL MATH
Divide by Multiples of Ten

OBJECTIVE Use mental math strategies to divide multiples of 10 by multiples of 10.

1 Introduce

Materials per student: crayons; centimeter graph paper (TA 7)

Have students draw a 4-by-20 grid on a sheet of graph paper and color each row of 20 squares a different color.

- **What two division sentences can you write to describe the equal groups?** *[80 ÷ 20 = 4, 80 ÷ 4 = 20]*
- **What division facts do these two sentences remind you of?** *[Possible answer: 8 ÷ 2 = 4, 8 ÷ 4 = 2]*

2 Teach — *Whole Class*

LEARN Read the introductory problem.

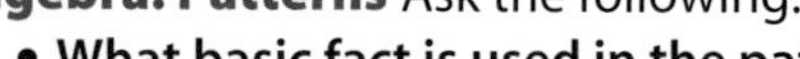

Algebra: Patterns Ask the following:

- **What basic fact is used in the pattern?** *[45 ÷ 9]*
- **Why does 450 ÷ 50 have the same quotient as 45 ÷ 5?** *[Possible answer: Since the quotient and the divisor are both ten times greater, the quotient remains the same.]*

More Examples For Examples A and C, students should note the patterns are the same as those discussed.

3 Close

Check for Understanding using items 1–8, page 302.

Algebra: Patterns In items 1–3, students understand the relationship between numbers by finding division patterns.

CRITICAL THINKING

Accept any answer as long as it shows understanding of the pattern of zeros in the dividend, divisor, and quotient.

PRACTICE

Materials have available: calculators

Options for assigning exercises:
A—Odd ex. 1–15; all ex. 17–28; **Mixed Review**
B—Even ex. 2–16; all ex. 17–28; **Mixed Review**

- For ex. 26, students may use the problem-solving strategy Solve a Multistep Problem, to solve.

Algebra In ex. 17–22, students gain experience solving informal algebraic equations.

Mixed Review/Test Preparation In ex. 1–4, students review addition, subtraction, and multiplication, learned in Chapters 2 and 6. Students order measurements in ex. 5 and 6, a skill they learned in Chapter 7.

Divide by Multiples of Ten

LEARN

Have you ever said, "Are we there yet?" when traveling with your family?

The distance from Toledo, Ohio, to Washington, D.C., is 450 miles. If you drive 50 miles each hour, how long will the trip take?

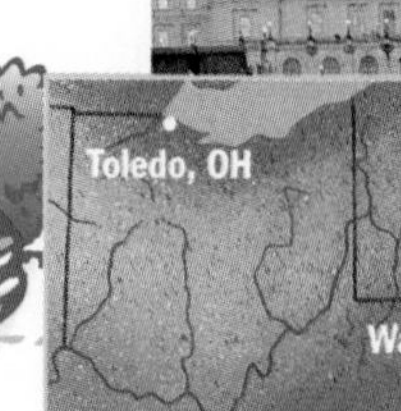

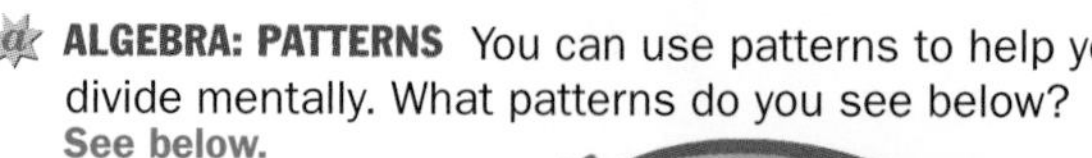

ALGEBRA: PATTERNS You can use patterns to help you divide mentally. What patterns do you see below? **See below.**

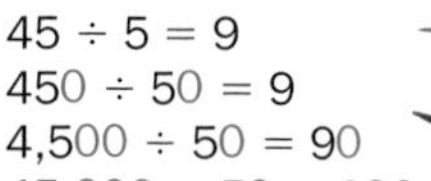

45 ÷ 5 = 9
450 ÷ 50 = 9
4,500 ÷ 50 = 90
45,000 ÷ 50 = 900

The trip will take 9 hours.

More Examples

A 6 ÷ 2 = 3
60 ÷ 20 = 3
600 ÷ 20 = 30
6,000 ÷ 20 = 300

B \$28 ÷ 7 = \$4
\$280 ÷ 70 = \$4
\$2,800 ÷ 70 = \$40
\$28,000 ÷ 70 = \$400

C 20 ÷ 5 = 4
200 ÷ 50 = 4
2,000 ÷ 50 = 40
20,000 ÷ 50 = 40

CHECK

Check for Understanding

Check students' descriptior

ALGEBRA: PATTERNS Describe and complete the pattern.

1 15 ÷ 3 = 5
150 ÷ 30 = ■ **5**
1,500 ÷ 30 = ■ **50**
15,000 ÷ 30 = ■ **500**

2 40 ÷ 5 = 8
400 ÷ 50 = ■ **8**
4,000 ÷ 50 = ■ **80**
40,000 ÷ 50 = ■ **800**

3 8 ÷ 4 = 2
80 ÷ 40 = ■ **2**
800 ÷ 40 = ■ **20**
8,000 ÷ 40 = ■ **2**

Divide mentally.

4 540 ÷ 90 **6** **5** 90 ÷ 30 **3** **6** \$3,000 ÷ 60 **\$50** **7** 64,000 ÷ 8 **800**

Critical Thinking: Generalize

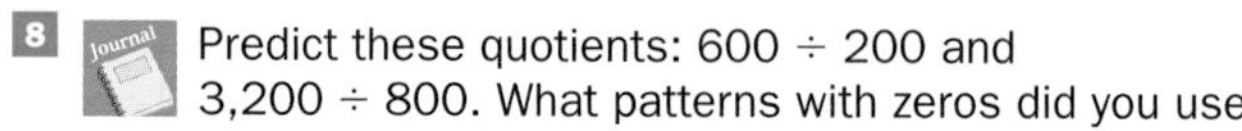

8 Predict these quotients: 600 ÷ 200 and 3,200 ÷ 800. What patterns with zeros did you use?

Use a calculator to check your answer. **Possible answer: 3, 4; the divisor and dividend have the same number of zeros, so there are no zeros in the quotient.**

Question 1. Possible answer: Make new division sentences by starting with a basic fact, multiplying the divisor by 10, and multiplying the dividend by 10, 100, or 1,000.

Meeting Individual Needs

Early Finishers

In the exercises with one-digit quotients, have students continue the pattern and write the related two- and three-digit quotients.

Extra Support

When using division patterns, students may forget to check if the dividend in the basic fact ended in zero. Have them circle the basic division fact, then cross out zeros in the divisor and the matching zeros in the dividend.

Ongoing Assessment

Interview Determine if students can use division patterns. Ask:

- **How could you use a basic fact and a pattern of zeros to find 6,400 ÷ 80?** *[Possible answer: 64 ÷ 8 = 8; the dividend has one more zero than the divisor, so the quotient has one zero, and is 80.]*

Follow Up If students need help, have them use basic facts as they divide. Assign **Reteach 74.**

For students who are ready for a challenge using mental math, assign **Extend 74.**

. 345 mi; find the average: 304 + 450 + 280 = 1,035 and 1,035 ÷ 3 = 345.
. Students' bar graphs should reflect the populations given in the Databank, as well as the population of their own town or city.

ractice

ide mentally.

630 ÷ 90 **7**	2 160 ÷ 20 **8**	3 600 ÷ 30 **20**	4 300 ÷ 60 **5**
1,000 ÷ 50 **20**	6 2,100 ÷ 30 **70**	7 $8,000 ÷ 20 **$400**	8 4,000 ÷ 80 **50**
5,600 ÷ 70 **80**	10 $7,200 ÷ 90 **$80**	11 4,000 ÷ 50 **80**	12 $3,600 ÷ 40 **$90**
16,000 ÷ 40 **400**	14 35,000 ÷ 50 **700**	15 32,000 ÷ 80 **400**	16 21,000 ÷ 30 **700**

EBRA Find the missing number.

60 ÷ 30 = ■ **2**	18 160 ÷ 20 = ■ **8**	19 300 ÷ ■ = 60 **5**
420 ÷ ■ = 6 **70**	21 800 ÷ ■ = 40 **20**	22 ■ ÷ 70 = 70 **4,900**

PRACTICE

IXED APPLICATIONS
roblem Solving

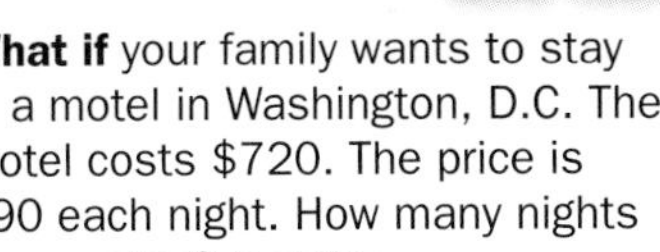

What if your family wants to stay in a motel in Washington, D.C. The motel costs $720. The price is $90 each night. How many nights do you stay? **8 nights**

24 **What if** your family finds a motel in another part of town that charges $80 each night. How many nights can you and your family stay and still pay $720? **9 nights**

In three days, Mr. Garcia drove 305 miles, 450 miles, and 280 miles. What is the average number of miles that he drove each day? Explain your method. **See above.**

26 Michael practiced for a marathon by running 37 miles each week for 7 weeks. He then ran 49 miles each week for 20 weeks. How many miles did he run altogether? **1,239 mi**

Write a problem that you could solve mentally using division. Solve it. Share your problem and solution with the class. **Students should compare problems and solutions.**

28 **Data Point** Use the Databank on page 539. Make a bar graph to show the populations. Add the population of your city. **See above.**

mixed review • test preparation

65,842 + 16,625 **82,467**	2 138,615 − 56,124 **82,491**	3 5,600 × 40 **224,000**	4 15 × 249 **3,735**

der the measurements from least to greatest.

300 cm, 2 m, 100 cm, 250 mm **250 mm, 100 cm, 2 m, 300 cm**

6 50 in., 2 yd, 5 ft, 1 yd **1 yd, 50 in., 5 ft, 2 yd**

tra Practice, page 515

Alternate Teaching Strategy

Materials per group: calculator; place-value models—20 ones and 20 tens

Write the following on the chalkboard.

12 ÷ 3   120 ÷ 30   1,200 ÷ 30

Have students find 12 ÷ 3 *[4]*, and use this basic fact to predict the quotient of 120 ÷ 30. Ask them to explain their predictions. *[Possible answer: 120 ÷ 3 is the same as 12 tens ÷ 3tens, so the answer is 4.]* Then have them use models to find the quotient.

Have students use the quotient for 120 ÷ 30 to predict the quotient for 1,200 ÷ 30 and explain their predictions. *[Possible answer: The dividend is ten times greater, but the divisor remains the same, so the quotient will be ten times greater—40.]* Then have them use calculators to find the quotient.

PRACTICE • 74

HOMEWORK

Practice 74

Name:

Mental Math: Divide by Multiples of Ten

Divide mentally.

1. 160 ÷ 4 = 40	2. 120 ÷ 40 = 3	3. 1,200 ÷ 40 = 30
4. 90 ÷ 30 = 3	5. 60 ÷ 10 = 6	6. 600 ÷ 30 = 20
7. 350 ÷ 70 = 5	8. 560 ÷ 70 = 8	9. 3,500 ÷ 70 = 50
10. 720 ÷ 80 = 9	11. 360 ÷ 60 = 6	12. 7,200 ÷ 80 = 90
13. 270 ÷ 90 = 3	14. 810 ÷ 90 = 9	15. 300 ÷ 50 = 6
16. $360 ÷ 90 = $4	17. $200 ÷ 50 = $4	18. 540 ÷ 90 = 6
19. 1,800 ÷ 20 = 90	20. 3,000 ÷ 50 = 60	21. 30,000 ÷ 50 = 600
22. $4,000 ÷ 50 = $80	23. 54,000 ÷ 60 = 900	24. $2,800 ÷ 70 = $40
25. 49,000 ÷ 70 = 700	26. $2,000 ÷ 40 = $50	27. $20,000 ÷ 50 = $400
28. 6,300 ÷ 70 = 90	29. 14,000 ÷ 70 = 200	30. 48,000 ÷ 60 = 800

Algebra Find the missing number.

31. 80 ÷ 40 = 2	32. 450 ÷ 90 = 5	33. 320 ÷ 80 = 4
34. 240 ÷ 60 = 4	35. 490 ÷ 70 = 7	36. 400 ÷ 50 = 8
37. 180 ÷ 60 = 3	38. 600 ÷ 20 = 30	39. 3,600 ÷ 40 = 90

Solve.

40. The teachers have 270 animal picture cards to be divided among 30 fourth graders. How many does each student get? 9 cards

41. There are 3,200 "Save the Rain Forests" pins given to 80 different school classes. How many pins does each class get? 40 pins

McGraw-Hill School Division

RETEACH • 74

Reteach 74

Name:

Mental Math: Divide by Multiples of Ten

To divide mentally, you can use basic division facts and look for patterns. Count the zeros on both sides of the ÷ sign.

The basic fact is 8 ÷ 2 = 4.

80 ÷ 20 = 4
1 zero − 1 zero = 0 zeros
800 ÷ 20 = 40
2 zeros − 1 zero = 1 zero
8,000 ÷ 20 = 400
3 zeros − 1 zero = 2 zeros

The basic fact is 30 ÷ 5 = 6.

300 ÷ 50 = 6
1 extra zero − 1 zero = 0 zeros
3,000 ÷ 50 = 60
2 extra zeros − 1 zero = 1 zero
30,000 ÷ 50 = 600
3 extra zeros − 1 zero = 2 zeros

Complete the pattern. You can count zeros.

1. 18 ÷ 3 = 6
   180 ÷ 30 = 6
   1,800 ÷ 30 = 60
   18,000 ÷ 30 = 600

2. 9 ÷ 3 = 3
   90 ÷ 30 = 3
   900 ÷ 30 = 30
   9,000 ÷ 30 = 300

3. 56 ÷ 7 = 8
   560 ÷ 70 = 8
   5,600 ÷ 70 = 80
   56,000 ÷ 70 = 800

4. 20 ÷ 4 = 5
   200 ÷ 40 = 5
   2,000 ÷ 40 = 50
   20,000 ÷ 40 = 500

Divide mentally.

5. 12 ÷ 4 = 3	6. 120 ÷ 40 = 3	7. 1,200 ÷ 40 = 30
8. 18 ÷ 6 = 3	9. 180 ÷ 60 = 3	10. 1,800 ÷ 60 = 30
11. 35 ÷ 5 = 7	12. 350 ÷ 50 = 7	13. 3,500 ÷ 50 = 70

McGraw-Hill School Division

EXTEND • 74

Extend 74

Name:

Mental Math: Divide by Multiples of Ten

Moving Right Along

For each exercise, ring the correct answer. Use mental math. Then use the remaining answers to write the next division exercise. Repeat those steps until you have finished the page. The first two exercises have been started for you.

1. 9,000 ÷ 10 = 900
   a. 2,700 (b.) 900 c. 90
2. 2,700 ÷ 90 = 30
   (a.) 30 b. 3,000 c. 50
3. 3,000 ÷ 50 = 60
   a. 90 (b.) 60 c. 3,600
4. 3,600 ÷ 90 = 40
   a. 4,000 b. 80 (c.) 40
5. 4,000 ÷ 80 = 50
   (a.) 50 b. 2,000 c. 40
6. 2,000 ÷ 40 = 50
   (a.) 50 b. 2,400 c. 60
7. 2,400 ÷ 60 = 40
   a. 48,000 b. 60 (c.) 40
8. 48,000 ÷ 60 = 800
   (a.) 800 b. 80 c. 64,000
9. 64,000 ÷ 80 = 800
   a. 800,000 (b.) 800 c. 80
10. 800,000 ÷ 80 = 10,000
    a. 1,000 b. 10 (c.) 10,000
11. 1,000 ÷ 10 = 100
    (a.) 100 b. 10,000 c. 50
12. 10,000 ÷ 50 = 200
    a. 2,000 (b.) 200 c. 20

Think Critically

13. Look at exercise 10. How did you decide how many zeros were in the quotient?
    Answers may vary. Possible answer: There are 4 more zeros in 800,000 than in 80, so I know the quotient has 4 zeros.

McGraw-Hill School Division

LESSON 8.10

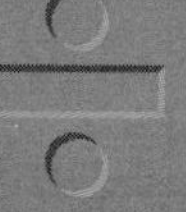

LESSON 8.10 RESOURCES

EXPLORE ACTIVITY

Divide by Tens

OBJECTIVE Use models to explore division by multiples of 10 with remainders.

RESOURCE REMINDER
Math Center Cards 75
Practice 75, Reteach 75, Extend 75

SKILLS TRACE

GRADE 3	• Use place-value models to explore dividing 2-digit numbers by 1-digit numbers. *(Chapter 12)*
GRADE 4	• Use place-value models to explore division by multiples of ten with remainders.
GRADE 5	• Use place-value models to explore dividing whole numbers by 2-digit numbers. *(Chapter 6)*

WARM-UP

Cooperative Pairs — Logical/Analytical

OBJECTIVE Explore using compatible numbers to estimate quotients with 2-digit divisors.

Materials per pair: two sets of number cards for 1–9 (TA 29),

▶ Pairs of students mix the number cards and place them in a pile facedown. Each student draws five cards from the pile.

▶ Each student uses the five number cards to make a three-digit dividend and two-digit divisor. Students then use compatible numbers and mental math to estimate the quotient. For example, if they are estimating 381 ÷ 46, they might use the numbers 360 ÷ 40 or 400 ÷ 50.

▶ Students check each others' work. If they can think of a different pair of compatible numbers to use, they suggest it.

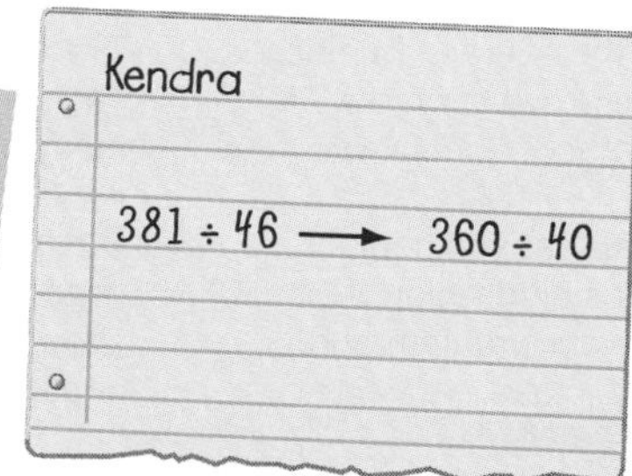

LITERATURE CONNECTION

Cooperative Pairs — Linguistic

OBJECTIVE Connect division clues to poetry.

Resource Read-Aloud Anthology, p. 40–41

▶ Read "One Hundred Hungry Ants" aloud.

▶ Have students work with a partner to list the four ways into which one hundred ants divided. *[2 lines of 50, 4 lines of 25, 5 lines of 20, 10 lines of 10]*

▶ Give students a different number of ants and have them list all the way the ants could divide.

Daily Review

PREVIOUS DAY QUICK REVIEW

Divide mentally.

1. 80 ÷ 40 *[2]*
2. 360 ÷ 90 *[4]*
3. 400 ÷ 80 *[5]*
4. 1,800 ÷ 60 *[30]*

FAST FACTS

1. 7 × 5 *[35]*
2. 3 × 8 *[24]*
3. 6 × 9 *[54]*
4. 9 × 2 *[18]*

Problem of the Day • 75

There are 144 cartons of juice in the cafeteria. There are 36 cartons of each kind of juice. How many kinds of juice are there? *[4 kinds]*

TECH LINK

Math Van

MATH VAN

Tool You may wish to use the Place-Value Models tool with this lesson.

MATH FORUM

Management Tip I have my students work in pairs to solve division exercises. One student uses models to divide while the other uses paper and pencil. They compare, check, and alternate roles.

Visit our Resource Village at http://www.mhschool.com to see more of the Math Forum.

MATH CENTER

Practice

OBJECTIVE Divide by multiples of ten.

Materials per student: calculator, Math Center Recording Sheet (TA 31 optional)

Students learn how to use repeated subtraction on the calculator to find a quotient and remainder. *[**1.** 4 R25; **2.** 2 R57; **3.** 7 R16; **4.** 6 R24; **5.** 5 R39; **6.** 6 R31; **7.** 7 R16; **8.** 8 R18]*

PRACTICE ACTIVITY 75 — MATH CENTER, On Your Own

Calculator • Key Patterns

YOU NEED: calculator

How can you divide on a calculator without pressing [÷]? Here is a way.

176 ÷ 40 = ?

Enter 176 [−] 40 [=]. Repeat [=] until the display shows a number less than 40. 176 [−] 40 [=] 136 [=] 96 [=] 56 [=] 16.

The quotient is the number of times you press [=], in this case 4. The remainder is the display less than the divisor, or 16.

So, 176 ÷ 40 = 4 R16.

Use this method to find the quotients and remainders.

1. 40)185 2. 90)237 3. 30)226 4. 70)444
5. 50)289 6. 60)391 7. 80)576 8. 20)178

Chapter 8, Lesson 10, pages 304–307 — Division

McGraw-Hill School Division — Grade Level 4

ESL APPROPRIATE

NCTM Standards
- Problem Solving
- Communication
- ✓ Reasoning
- Connections

Problem Solving

OBJECTIVE Use logical reasoning to form divisions that have remainders.

Materials per pair: number cube; per student: Math Center Recording Sheet (TA 31 optional)

Students roll a number cube to get a divisor. Then they choose a dividend to get a quotient with remainder. The goal is to get the greatest possible remainder. *[Check students' work.]*

PROBLEM-SOLVING ACTIVITY 75 — MATH CENTER, Partners

Logical Reasoning • Pick Your Dividend

YOU NEED: number cube

Solve. Use play money if you like.

- Each player rolls the number cube. Multiply that number by 10 to get a divisor.
- Choose a number from the chart. Find the quotient in any way you choose. The player with the greater remainder gets 1 point. In case of a tie, both players get a point.
- The first person to get 7 points is the winner.

118	123	146	152	167	171	184	190

Chapter 8, Lesson 10, pages 304–307 — Division

McGraw-Hill School Division — Grade Level 4

ESL APPROPRIATE

NCTM Standards
- ✓ Problem Solving
- ✓ Communication
- ✓ Reasoning
- Connections

EXPLORE ACTIVITY
Divide by Tens

OBJECTIVE Use models to explore division by multiples of 10 with remainders.

Materials per group: 8-part spinner labeled 20, 30, 40, 50, 60, 70, 80, 90 (TA 2); place-value models—5 hundreds, 19 tens, and 19 ones

Present the following problem:

There are 26 students in Natalie's art class and 89 tubes of paint. Each student gets the same number of tubes. About how many tubes does each student get? *[about 3 tubes]*

Ask:

- **How could you use compatible numbers to estimate the quotient and solve the problem?** *[Possible answer: Use 90 ÷ 30 = 3—each student gets about 3 tubes of paint.]*
- **How could you use multiplication to check your estimate? Will the exact quotient have a remainder?** *[Possible answer: Multiply 26 × 3 = 78; since 78 is less than 90, the exact quotient will have a remainder.]*
- **How can you find the remainder?** *[Subtract: 89 − 78 = 11]*
- **Does the remainder change your answer to the problem? Explain.** *[Possible answer: No; since the remainder is less than 26, there will not be enough tubes left over for each student to get a fourth tube of paint.]*

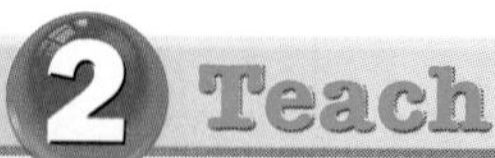

Cooperative Groups

LEARN Work Together Review the steps of the activity with students. Have them identify which number is the dividend and which the divisor. *[total; number spun]* Point out that if the two-digit number they spin is greater than the total, students must spin again for a lesser two-digit number.

Have students repeat the activity at least five times.

Talk It Over Extend the discussion by asking:

- **Why does a remainder have to be smaller than a divisor?** *[If a remainder is greater than a divisor, there will be enough numbers to make another group or to add one to each group.]*

Divide by Tens

LEARN

You used models to divide by 1-digit numbers. You can also use them to divide by tens.

Work Together
Work in a group.

Place 9 tens models in a pile. Place 9 ones models in another pile. Take a handful of models from each pile to get the total.

Spin the spinner to get the number in each group. Separate the total to find how many groups.

Record your results in a table. Write a division sentence or example.

Total	Number in Each Group	Number of Equal Groups	Number Left Over	Division Sentence or Example
97	40	2	17	97 ÷ 40 = 2 R17

You will need
- *spinner*
- *place-value models*

Take turns spinning, dividing, and recording.

Talk It Over

▶ Compare the remainder to the divisor in each line of your table. What do you notice? **Possible answer: The number left over is always less than the number in each group.**

304

Meeting Individual Needs

Extra Support

Work with students to help them use models to complete Check for Understanding items 1, 3, and 5. Have them verbalize each step of the process.

Gifted And Talented

Challenge students to extend their division abilities by having them find the quotients of up to four-digit dividends divided by multiples of ten.

Ongoing Assessment

Observation Checklist
Observe if students are able to divide numbers by multiples of ten by having them explain how to divide one of the Practice exercises, with or without the use of models.

Follow Up Have students who need additional help dividing with two-digit divisors use models to demonstrate division examples generated by class groups or try **Reteach 75.**

For students who are able to solve division examples with two-digit divisors easily, assign **Extend 75.**

ke Connections
lly's group divided by tens this way and labeled their results.

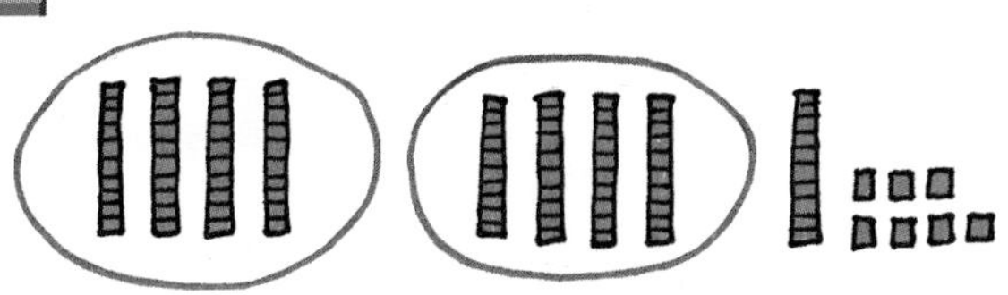

$$\begin{array}{r} 2 \leftarrow \text{number of groups} \\ \text{number in each group} \rightarrow 40\overline{)97} \leftarrow \text{total} \\ -80 \\ \hline 17 \leftarrow \text{amount left over} \end{array}$$

u can also use this method with greater numbers.

vide: 128 ÷ 40

timate to place the first digit of the quotient.

timate: 128 ÷ 40 **Think:** 120 ÷ 40 = 3
The first digit is in the ones place.

$$\begin{array}{r} 3\text{ R8} \\ 40\overline{)128} \\ -120 \\ \hline 8 \end{array}$$

Think: $40\overline{)128}$ → 3
Multiply: 3 × 40 = 120
Subtract: 128 − 120 = 8
Compare: 8 < 40

Check:
3 × 40 = 120
120 + 8 = 128

heck for Understanding

vide using any method.

1 $10\overline{)79}$ 7 R9
2 $20\overline{)60}$ 3
3 $30\overline{)167}$ 5 R17
4 $20\overline{)109}$ 5 R9
5 $80\overline{)488}$ 6 R8

ritical Thinking: Generalize

Suppose you divide 158 by 40. What compatible numbers would you use to estimate? Would your estimate be the actual quotient? Why or why not? **Possible answer: 160 ÷ 40 = 4; no; 4 cannot be the quotient since 4 × 40 = 160 and 160 > 158, so the quotient would be 1 less, or 3.**

Turn the page for Practice.

Language Support

Stress that the division process for two-digit numbers is the same as for one-digit numbers. Pair these students with native speakers to facilitate the identification.

ESL APPROPRIATE

MAKE CONNECTIONS

Copy the models from Molly's group on the chalkboard. Then have a volunteer explain how the models in Molly's group correspond to the way the group recorded the results.

To give a context to the division example using greater numbers, read the following:

Mr. Burke has 128 buttons. He puts 40 buttons in a box. How many boxes can Mr. Burke fill? How many buttons will be left?

Have students identify the division needed to solve the problem. *[128 ÷ 40]* Then guide them through each step of the division process. Ask:

- **How does the estimate help you place the first digit of the quotient?** *[Possible answer: The estimate tells you whether to start the quotient in the hundreds, tens, or ones place.]*
- **Why do you multiply after you place the first digit of the quotient?** *[Possible answer: to record how many in all are in the groups]*
- **Why don't you continue to divide after comparing?** *[Possible answer: Because there are not enough left to put in equal groups of 40.]*
- **Why should you check the answer?** *[Possible answer: to make sure you have divided correctly]*

Point out that the process of dividing with a two-digit divisor is the same as dividing with a one-digit divisor.

3 Close

Check for Understanding using items 1–6, page 303.

CRITICAL THINKING
In item 6, students are asked to compare an estimate to the exact quotient. Have them compute the exact quotient to compare.

Practice See pages 306–307.

PRACTICE

Materials have available: place-value models—hundreds, tens, and ones

Options for assigning exercises:
A—Odd ex. 1–27; all ex. 28–34; **More to Explore**
B—Even ex. 2–26; all ex. 28–34; **More to Explore**

- For ex. 1–2, allow students to use models to correspond to the models pictured to help them solve the division sentences.
- For ex. 3–22, allow students to use models if they wish. Remind students to check their answers.
- For **Make It Right** (ex. 28), see Common Error below.
- Guess, Test, and Revise and Make a Table are good strategies to use for ex. 29, 31, and 33.

Algebra Students continue to explore methods of solving algebraic equations in ex. 1–2 and ex. 23–27. This provides ongoing preparation for more formal work with algebra.

More to Explore Discuss why it is important to change smaller units of measurement into larger units. Ask:

- **Why would you want to think of 108 inches as 9 feet?** *[Possible answer: It is easier to visualize 9 ft than 108 in.]*

Review equivalent units for length, capacity, and weight in the customary system by having students come to the board to list equivalencies. Then ask:

- **Why do you divide by 12 when changing inches to feet?** *[Possible answer: You must make groups of 12 inches since 12 in. = 1 ft.]*

Have students summarize how to change units of length, weight, and capacity by asking:

- **How do you change feet to yards?** *[divide the number of feet by 3]*
- **How do you change ounces to pounds?** *[divide the number of ounces by 16]*
- **How do you change cups to pints? pints to quarts? quarts to gallons?** *[Divide the number of cups by 2; divide the number of pints by 2; divide the number of quarts by 4.]*
- **Could you change inches to yards? Explain.** *[Yes; divide the number of inches by 12 to find feet, then divide the number of feet by 3 to find yards.]*

Have students work independently to complete the exercises.

Practice

Complete the division sentence.

1 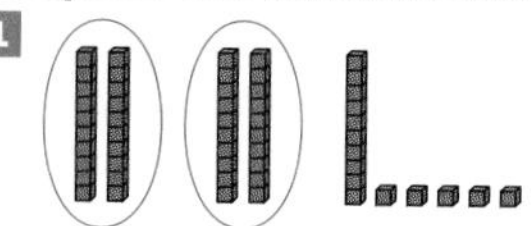

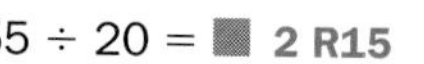

55 ÷ 20 = ■ 2 R15

2 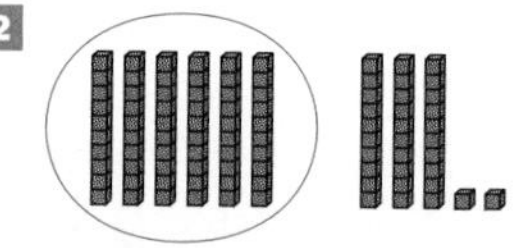

92 ÷ 60 = ■ 1 R32

Divide using any method.

3. 20)93 4 R13
4. 10)69 6 R9
5. 20)31 1 R11
6. 30)68 2 R8
7. 40)94 2 R14
8. 20)183 9 R3
9. 70)222 3 R12
10. 50)265 5 R15
11. 60)$240 $4
12. 80)58… 7 R28
13. 128 ÷ 30 4 R8
14. $540 ÷ 60 $9
15. 374 ÷ 50 7 R24
16. 495 ÷ 80 6 R15
17. 300 ÷ … 4 R20
18. 468 ÷ 90 5 R18
19. 354 ÷ 40 8 R34
20. $630 ÷ 70 $9
21. 356 ÷ 60 5 R56
22. 859 ÷ … 9 R49

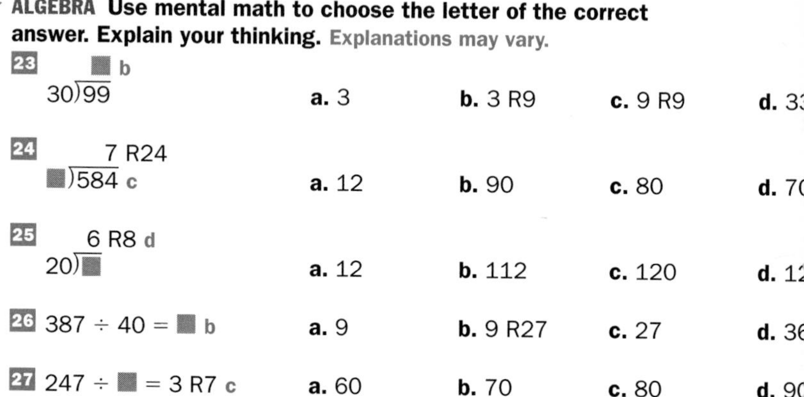

ALGEBRA Use mental math to choose the letter of the correct answer. Explain your thinking. Explanations may vary.

23. 30)99 = ■ b — a. 3 b. 3 R9 c. 9 R9 d. 3…
24. ■)584 = 7 R24 c — a. 12 b. 90 c. 80 d. 7…
25. 20)■ = 6 R8 d — a. 12 b. 112 c. 120 d. 1…
26. 387 ÷ 40 = ■ b — a. 9 b. 9 R27 c. 27 d. 3…
27. 247 ÷ ■ = 3 R7 c — a. 60 b. 70 c. 80 d. 9…

Make It Right

28. Here is how Kerry found 48 ÷ 30. Tell what mistake was made. Explain how to correct it.
48 ÷ 30 = 18
She used the remainder as the quotient: 48 ÷ 30 = 1 R18.

Meeting Individual Needs

Early Finishers

Have students use the method on page 304 to write three division examples. Then have them use the paper-and-pencil method to solve each example.

Inclusion

You may wish to have students comfortable with the division algorithm help those who are having difficulty.

Common Error

As in **Make It Right** on page 306, some students may incorrectly identify the remainder as the quotient when using models to divide. Remind students that the number that is not in any of the equal groups is the remainder.

). 4 slices; add the calories for milk and 1 egg, subtract that sum from 515, divide the difference by 70.

33. 2 that seat 2 and 4 that seat 3 or 5 that seat 2 and 2 that seat 3

MIXED APPLICATIONS

Problem Solving

Pencil & Paper · Calculator · Mental Math

se the table for problems 29–31.

Food	Quantity	Calories
Eggs	1	85
Milk	1 cup	150
Bread	1 slice	70

] There were 280 calories in the bread Leslie ate for breakfast. How many slices did she have? 4 slices

] Russell had a cup of milk, one egg, and some bread for breakfast. If he had a total of 515 calories for breakfast, how many slices of bread did he have? Explain your method. See above.

] Kelly ate 600 calories at breakfast. What combination of eggs, milk, and bread could she have eaten? 2 eggs, 4 slices of bread, and 1 cup of milk

] Ralph's Breakfast Nook seats 16 people. Some booths seat 2 and others seat 3. How many of each type of booth does Ralph have in his restaurant? See above.

32 A farmer buys chicken feed for \$74.70. She gives the clerk four \$20 bills and three quarters. What is her change? \$6.05

34 **Write a problem** that can be solved using multiplication or division. Solve it both ways. Share your problem and solutions with the class. Students should compare problems and solutions.

more to explore

hanging Measurements

ou can divide to change smaller units of easurement into larger units of measurement.

hange 108 inches into feet.

hink: 12 in. = 1 ft
108 in. ÷ 12 = ■ ft

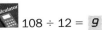

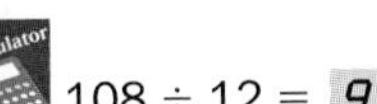

108 ÷ 12 = 9

08 in. = 9 ft

Length	Weight	Capacity
12 in. = 1 ft	16 oz = 1 lb	2 c = 1 pt
3 ft = 1 yd		2 pt = 1 qt
		4 qt = 1 gal

onvert the measurement to the unit shown. ou may use a calculator.

] 1,728 ft = ■ yd 576 2 72 in. = ■ ft 6 3 128 oz = ■ lb 8 4 1,236 qt = ■ gal 309

xtra Practice, page 515

Alternate Teaching Strategy

Materials per pair: 72 counters

Present the following problem:

Shauna has 72 beads. She needs 30 beads to make a necklace. How many necklaces can she make? How many beads will be left?

Have students work with a partner to solve. Guide them through the process by asking:

- **What operation must you use to solve the problem? What do you want to divide?** *[division, 72 ÷ 30; total number of beads into groups of 30]*
- **How can you use counters to show 72 ÷ 30?** *[Make equal groups of 30 from 72 counters.]*
- **Show the division using your counters. How many groups of 30 did you make? How many counters are left?** *[2 groups; 12 counters]*
- **How many necklaces can Shauna make? How many beads will she have left?** *[2 necklaces; 12 beads]*

Repeat with other examples.

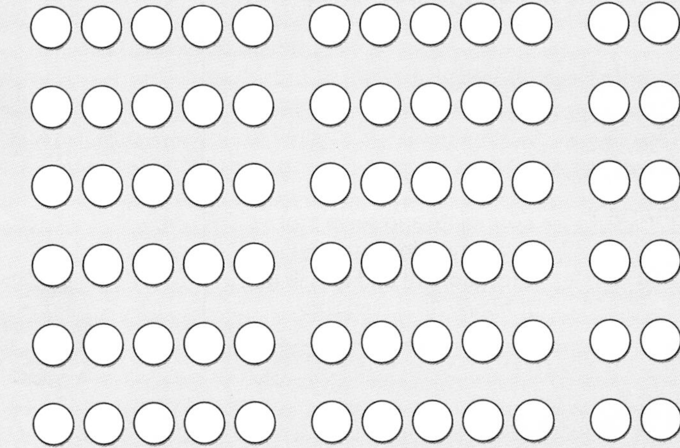

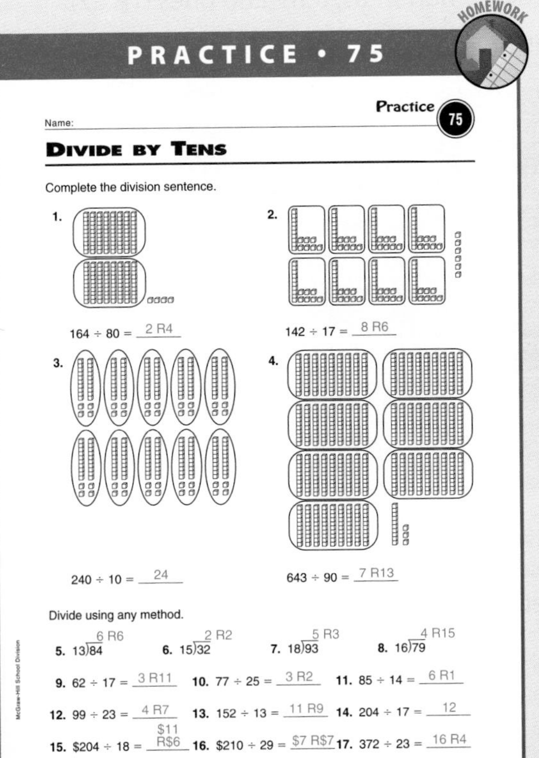

PRACTICE • 75

HOMEWORK

Practice 75

Name:

DIVIDE BY TENS

Complete the division sentence.

1. 164 ÷ 80 = 2 R4
2. 142 ÷ 17 = 8 R6
3. 240 ÷ 10 = 24
4. 643 ÷ 90 = 7 R13

Divide using any method.

5. 13)84 6 R6
6. 15)32 2 R2
7. 18)93 5 R3
8. 16)79 4 R15
9. 62 ÷ 17 = 3 R11
10. 77 ÷ 25 = 3 R2
11. 85 ÷ 14 = 6 R1
12. 99 ÷ 23 = 4 R7
13. 152 ÷ 13 = 11 R9
14. 204 ÷ 17 = 12
15. \$204 ÷ 18 = \$11 R\$6
16. \$210 ÷ 29 = \$7 R\$7
17. 372 ÷ 23 = 16 R4

McGraw-Hill School Division

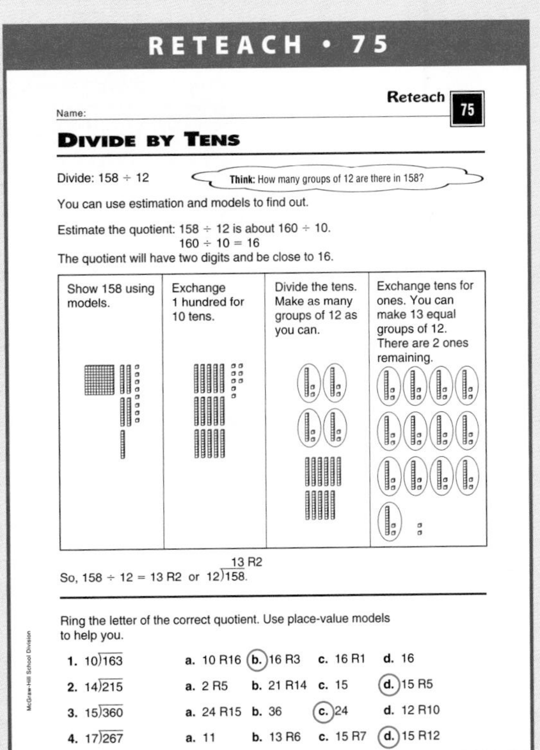

RETEACH • 75

Reteach 75

Name:

DIVIDE BY TENS

Divide: 158 ÷ 12

Think: How many groups of 12 are there in 158?

You can use estimation and models to find out.

Estimate the quotient: 158 ÷ 12 is about 160 ÷ 10.
160 ÷ 10 = 16
The quotient will have two digits and be close to 16.

Show 158 using models.	Exchange 1 hundred for 10 tens.	Divide the tens. Make as many groups of 12 as you can.	Exchange tens for ones. You can make 13 equal groups of 12. There are 2 ones remaining.

So, 158 ÷ 12 = 13 R2 or 12)158 = 13 R2.

Ring the letter of the correct quotient. Use place-value models to help you.

1. 10)163 a. 10 R16 (b.) 16 R3 c. 16 R1 d. 16
2. 14)215 a. 2 R5 b. 21 R14 c. 15 (d.) 15 R5
3. 15)360 a. 24 R15 b. 36 (c.) 24 d. 12 R10
4. 17)267 a. 11 b. 13 R6 c. 15 R7 (d.) 15 R12

McGraw-Hill School Division

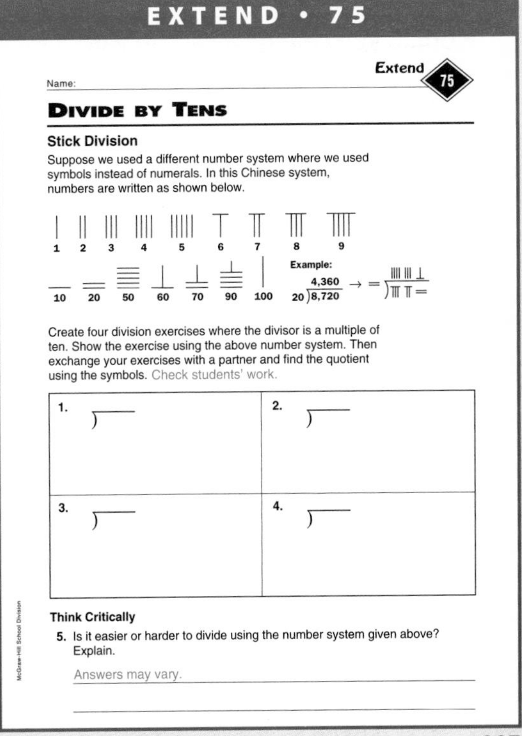

EXTEND • 75

Extend 75

Name:

DIVIDE BY TENS

Stick Division

Suppose we used a different number system where we used symbols instead of numerals. In this Chinese system, numbers are written as shown below.

1 2 3 4 5 6 7 8 9

10 20 50 60 70 90 100

Example: 20)8,720 = 4,360

Create four division exercises where the divisor is a multiple of ten. Show the exercise using the above number system. Then exchange your exercises with a partner and find the quotient using the symbols. Check students' work.

1.	2.
3.	4.

Think Critically

5. Is it easier or harder to divide using the number system given above? Explain.

Answers may vary.

McGraw-Hill School Division

LESSON 8.11

Problem Solvers at Work

OBJECTIVE Solve/write problems by interpreting the quotient and remainder.

RESOURCE REMINDER
Math Center Cards 76
Practice 76, Reteach 76, Extend 76

SKILLS TRACE

GRADE 3	• Formulate and solve problems involving interpreting the quotient and remainder. *(Chapter 12)*
GRADE 4	• Formulate and solve problems involving interpreting the quotient and remainder.
GRADE 5	• Formulate and solve problems involving interpreting the quotient and remainder. *(Chapter 5)*

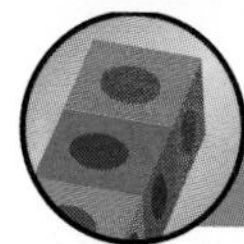

MANIPULATIVE WARM-UP

Cooperative Groups — Kinesthetic

OBJECTIVE Interpret quotients and remainders using models.

Materials per group: 60 beans and 5 paper cups.

▶ Present this problem on the chalkboard:
Brenda and Lauren need to place 60 basketballs in bins. They can put 16 balls in each bin. How many bins will they fill? How many basketballs will be left?

▶ Ask students what division sentence will solve this problem. Then have them use models to show and write the solution. *[60 ÷ 16 = 3 R12]* Then ask:
- **Which groups of models represent the full bins?** *[the 3 cups of 16 beans]*
- **Which models represent the balls that are left?** *[the 12 beans left]*

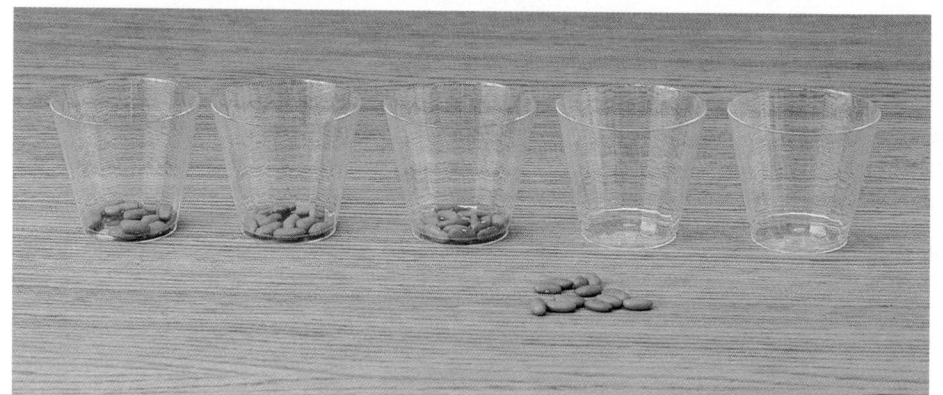

LOGICAL REASONING CONNECTION

Cooperative Pairs — Logical/Analytical

OBJECTIVE Connect logical reasoning to division.

Materials per pair: place-value models—hundreds, tens, and ones (TA 22)

▶ Copy the following onto the chalkboard:

Dividend	Quotient and Remainder	Divisor
135	2 R15	50
105	5 R15	21
156	3 R6	60
146	3 R20	30
132	4 R12	18
125	5 R20	42

▶ Have students work with a partner to write division sentences that match the dividend and quotient and remainder to the correct divisor. They may use place-value models. Discuss the methods students used. *[Possible answers: compatible numbers; mental math; multiplication; 135 ÷ 60 = 2 R15; 105 ÷ 18 = 5 R15; 156 ÷ 50 = 3 R6; 146 ÷ 42 = 3 R20; 132 ÷ 30 = 4 R12; 125 ÷ 21 = 5 R20]*

Daily Review

PREVIOUS DAY QUICK REVIEW

1. 189 ÷ 20 *[9 R9]*
2. 100 ÷ 40 *[2 R20]*
3. 258 ÷ 50 *[5 R8]*
4. 280 ÷ 30 *[9 R10]*

FAST FACTS

1. 49 ÷ 7 *[7]*
2. 15 ÷ 3 *[5]*
3. 54 ÷ 6 *[9]*
4. 48 ÷ 8 *[6]*

Problem of the Day • 76

Each flower arrangement takes up at least 16 inches on a display table. How many flower arrangements can be displayed on a table that is 108 inches long? *[6 flower arrangements]*

TECH LINK

Math Van

MATH VAN

Aid You may wish to use the Electronic Teacher Aid in the Math Van with this lesson.

MATH FORUM

Idea My students enjoy making a data center where they display family data such as those that were gathered in problem 9 on page 311.

Visit our Resource Village at http://www.mhschool.com to see more of the Math Forum.

MATH CENTER

Practice

OBJECTIVE Interpret remainders.

Materials per student: Math Center Recording Sheet (TA 31 optional)

Students find the number of vehicles needed to transport people attending a conference. *[12 buses, or 43 mini-vans, or 69 cars, or 86 rowboats, or 171 tandem bikes. If you completely fill 5 buses first, you also need either 7 more buses, or 24 mini-vans, or 39 cars, or 48 row-boats, or 96 tandem bikes]*

MATH CENTER
On Your Own

PRACTICE ACTIVITY 76

Logical Reasoning • Getting There From Here

A group of 342 people are going to a conference across the lake. How many buses will you need to transport everyone? minivans? cars? rowboats? bicycles?

How many of each other kind of vehicle would you need if you completely fill 5 buses first? Record your findings.

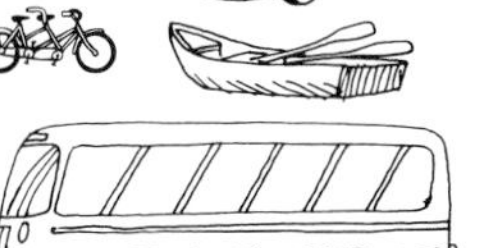

Type of Vehicle	People It Can Hold
Bus	30 people
Minivan	8 people
Car	5 people
Rowboat	4 people
Bicycle Built for Two	2 people

Grade Level 4 · McGraw-Hill School Division

Chapter 8, Lesson 11, pages 308–311 · Problem Solving

NCTM Standards

- ✓ Problem Solving
- Communication
- ✓ Reasoning
- Connections

Problem Solving

OBJECTIVE Use an organized list to solve problems about football scores.

Materials per student: number cube, Math Center Recording Sheet (TA 31 optional)

Students toss a number cube to get a 2-digit football score. Then they find out what ways that number of points could have been scored. *[Answers may vary. Possible answer: Score of 12: 2 touchdowns; 1 touchdown, 1 point after touchdown, 2-point conversion, 1 field goal]*

MATH CENTER
On Your Own

PROBLEM-SOLVING ACTIVITY 76

Logical Reasoning • Football Fun

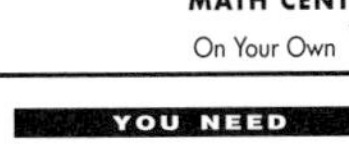

Football teams can score points in the following ways:

Touchdown	6 points
Point after touchdown	1 point
Two-point conversion	2 points
Safety	2 points
Field goal	3 points

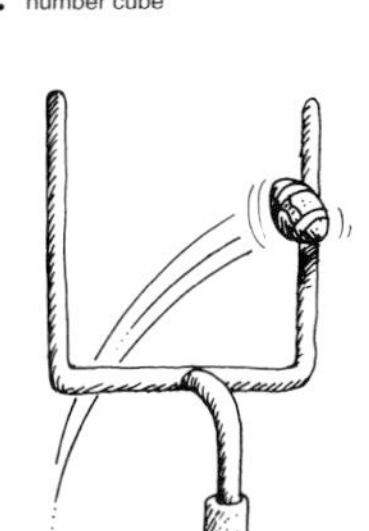

- Roll the number cube twice. Write down the numbers you rolled as a 2-digit football score.
- How could a team score this number of points? Find as many different ways as you can.
- Roll again and repeat the activity.

Grade Level 4 · McGraw-Hill School Division

Chapter 8, Lesson 11, pages 308–311 · Problem Solving

NCTM Standards

- ✓ Problem Solving
- ✓ Communication
- ✓ Reasoning
- Connections

Problem Solvers at Work

OBJECTIVE Solve/write problems by interpreting the quotient and remainder.

Materials Have available: calculators; hundreds, tens, and ones place-value models

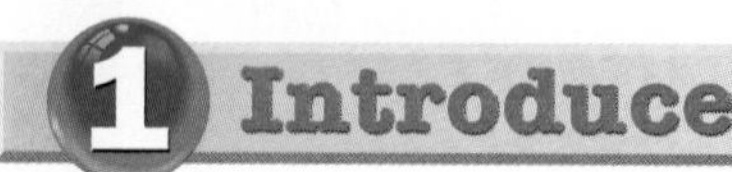

1 Introduce

Cultural Connection Read the **Cultural Note.** George Washington Carver (1864–1943) was a great innovator in the agricultural sciences. He developed many industrial uses for sweet potatoes and soy beans, as well as peanuts. He even developed a new type of cotton that is named after him, "Carver's Hybrid."

2 Teach *Cooperative Groups*

Part 1 Interpret the Quotient and Remainder

LEARN Have students read the problem at the top of page 308.

Work Together Because some of the division examples have two-digit divisors, let students use place-value models to solve. Remind them to read each problem carefully to identify the divisor and to use compatible numbers to estimate.

For item 1, you may wish to point out that students will have to use the information at the top of the page.

After students solve item 3, ask:

- **How does interpreting the remainder help you solve the problem?** *[Possible answer: The remainder means an additional jar of peanut butter was needed to make all the sandwiches.]*

For item 4, students may find it helpful to draw a diagram to help them organize the extra sandwiches into the boxes.

Problem Solvers at Work

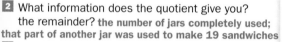

Read · Plan · Solve · Look Back

LEARN

Part 1 Interpret the Quotient and Remainder

Did you know that almost all the peanut butter that is made is eaten in the United States? You can make about 20 sandwiches from an 8-oz jar of peanut butter.

Work Together

Solve. Explain your thinking.

1. A student makes a total of 179 sandwiches for a picnic. Write the division sentence you would use to find the number of 8-oz jars of peanut butter he uses. **179 ÷ 20 = 8 R19**
2. What information does the quotient give you? the remainder? **the number of jars completely used; that part of another jar was used to make 19 sandwiches**
3. How many jars of peanut butter does he need to make 179 sandwiches? **9 jars; 8 jars would be used completely, and 1 jar would be partially used.**
4. **What if** the student packs the same number of sandwiches in each of 8 boxes. He then places the leftover sandwiches one at a time into some of the boxes. How many sandwiches will be in each box? **22 sandwiches in 5 boxes and 23 sandwiches in 3 boxes; 179 ÷ 8 = 22 R3**
5. **Make predictions** Predict whether there will be more or fewer sandwiches in a box if the sandwiches are separated equally into 9 boxes with leftovers added one at a time to different boxes. Explain. **Possible answer: There will be fewer sandwiches in each box since the same number of sandwiches are placed in more boxes.**

Cultural Note

George Washington Carver, born in Diamond, Missouri, was a chemist and inventor who developed hundreds of products from peanuts and other plants.

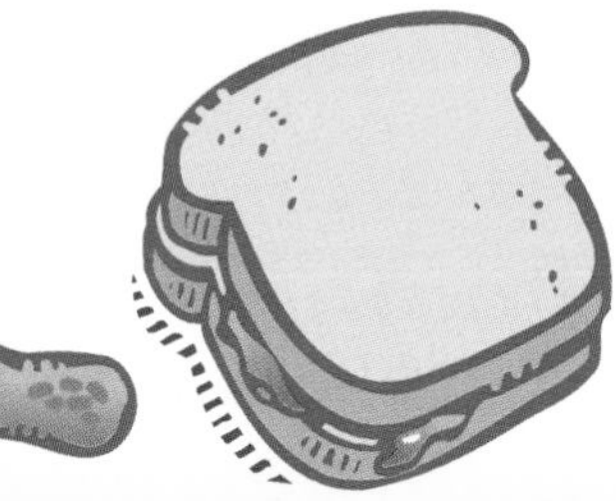

308 Lesson 8.11

Meeting Individual Needs

Extra Support

Have students solve a simpler problem:

There are 26 people taking a trip. 4 people can fit in a car.

- **How many cars will they fill?** *[6]*
- **Will they need a seventh car? Explain.** *[Yes; 2 people are left.]*

Ongoing Assessment

Anecdotal Report Make notes on students' ability to use the quotient and remainder to answer the questions posed by the problems.

Follow Up Encourage students who are having difficulty interpreting the remainder to use models or diagrams. Have them compare models, division sentence, and problem before solving. Assign **Reteach 76**

For students who successfully complete the lesson, assign **Extend 76.**

. Students should explain how changing the amount of peanuts will change the dividend in Scott's problem, and the amount of sandwiches Mrs. Jones can make.

art 2 Write and Share Problems

cott used the information about the eanuts to write his own problem.

Did you know that it takes 13 peanuts to make the peanut butter for one sandwich?

CHECK

Mrs. Jones has 218 peanuts to make peanut butter. She needs to make as many peanut butter sandwiches as she can to take to the banquet tomorrow. How many sandwiches can she make?

6 Solve Scott's problem using division. 218 ÷ 13 = 16 R10, 16 sandwiches

7 Change the information about peanuts that was used. Explain how the change affects the answer to Scott's problem. See above.

8 **Write a problem** that uses division. The answer should include a remainder. For problems 8–11, see Teacher's Edition.

9 **Problem/Solution** Explain why the problem can be solved with division. Explain what the remainder means.

10 Trade problems. Solve at least three problems written by your classmates.

11 What was the most interesting problem that you solved?

Scott Horton
Piney Grove Elementary School
Charlotte, NC

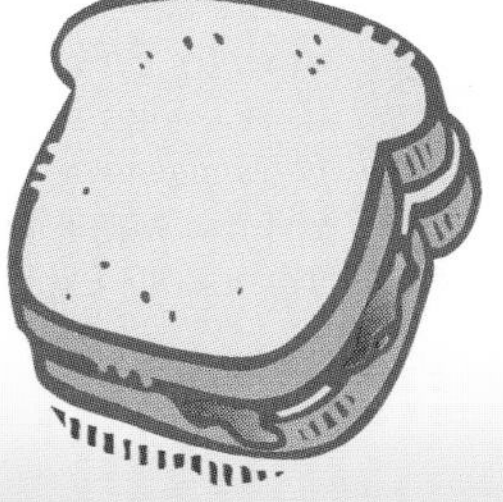

Turn the page for Practice Strategies.

Part 2 Write and Share Problems

Check Item 7 allows students to change the information. Tell students to assume that the given information is realistic and to use this fact to make a reasonable change when they alter the information. Ask them to explain how and why they chose to make their changes. Did they consider how the change would affect Scott's problem before or after they made the change?

For item 8, students can write any type of division problem.

Problem/Solution Have volunteers share the problems they wrote for item 8 and their explanations for item 9. Discuss students' explanations. Students should recognize that identifying the problem helps them choose the operation necessary to solve it.

For items 10 and 11, encourage students to discuss the problems they solved and their reasons why a problem was most interesting.

3 Close

Have students discuss how they wrote their division problems and how they decided to use the remainders.

Practice See pages 310–311.

PART 3 PRACTICE STRATEGIES

Materials have available: calculators

Students have the option of choosing any five problems from ex. 1–8, and any two problems from ex. 9–12. They may choose to do more problems if they wish.

- Students must interpret the remainder and the quotient to solve ex. 1 and 5.
- Guess, Test, and Revise is a good strategy to use for ex. 2.
- Working Backward is a good strategy to use in ex. 4.
- For ex. 11, point out that the time taken for the activity in the chart is the total time for the day. Students must take this into account as they write their schedules. Encourage them to be realistic in scheduling their days.

At the Computer If computers are not available, students can make a table and use a calculator to do ex. 12. Make sure that students understand how to use the spreadsheet to find the averages. To find the average of four test scores in cell F2, on page 311, they can use these rules: (B2 + C2 + D2 + E2)/4 or Sum (B2:E2)/4 or Average (B2:E2). Encourage students to try a score of 0 and to comment on how the average changes. *[It decreases significantly.]*

Math Van Have students use the Table tool to make a spreadsheet. They can record their data on the spreadsheet. A project electronic teacher aid has been provided.

PRACTICE

Menu

Choose five problems and solve them. Explain your methods. Explanations may vary.

Pencil & Paper · Calculator · Mental Math

1. Rhonda has a 130-ounce bottle of juice. She pours all the juice into 8-ounce glasses. She fills each glass and pours any leftover juice into an extra glass. How many glasses has she used? Explain your answer. **17 glasses; 16 filled glasses and a glass with 2 oz.**

2. There were 178 people at a restaurant. There were 16 more men than women. How many men were there? How many women were there? **97 men; 81 women**

3. **Logical reasoning** Eight fourth graders have been on the roller coaster and the parachute drop. Six have only been on the roller coaster. Five have only been on the parachute drop. How many have been on the parachute drop? **13 fourth graders**

4. Mr. Ruiz must be at work by 9:00 A.M. Trains leave his tow[n] at 8:00, 8:15, 8:30, a[nd] 8:45 A.M. It takes him 5 minutes to walk fro[m] his house to the train. He rides the train a half hour and then walks another 5 minutes to his office. What is the latest time he can leave his house and get t[o] work on time? Why? **See above.**

4. 8:10; he will get the 8:15 train, ride until 8:45, and walk 5 minutes to arrive at 8:50.

5. Mrs. Teng wants to share 164 crayons equally among her 9 grandchildren. What is the greatest number of crayons she can give each grandchild? Explain how you got your answer. **See below.**

6. Sweaters sell for \$25 each at Willmett's Department Store. At Buy Low's the same sweaters are 2 for \$48. How much more do you have to spend at Willmett['s] for the 2 sweaters? **\$2 more**

7. Cashews cost \$4 a pound. Pistachios cost \$3 a pound. Suppose you want to buy an equal number of pounds of each kind of nut. What is the greatest number of pounds of each you can buy for \$30? **4 lb of each**

8. Alberto carries a 70-ounce container of water on a hike. If he drinks about 6 ounces every hou[r], will the water last f[or] 14 hours? Explain. **No; 70 ÷ 6 = 11 R4, so the water will be finished in less tha[n] 12 h.**

5. 18 crayons; 164 ÷ 9 = 18 R2, so the most each grandchild can get is 18 crayons.

310 Lesson 8.11

Meeting Individual Needs

Early Finishers

Have students check one or more of the problems they solved using a strategy that is different from the one they originally used.

Inclusion

Encourage older students to share how they use word clues in problems to suggest strategies and how they use the strategies to solve problems.

Language Support

Remind students that they can use the pictures to help identify vocabulary in the word problems on page 310.

ESL APPROPRIATE

Gifted And Talented

Have students prepare a report on George Washington Carver and present it to the class.

. Students' averages should reflect the data they collected.
. Students budget their time according to the time it takes for each activity.

oose two problems and solve them. Explain your methods. Explanations may vary.

Data Point Choose five classmates or family members. Find out how many hours each week they each watch television, do homework, talk on the phone, and sleep. Show the data in a table or graph. Use the data to find the average number of hours for each activity. See above.

10 Tom will plant several rows of corn, beans, squash, and cabbage seeds. He plans to have corn in the 2nd row, 6th row, and 10th row. If he continues this pattern, how many rows of corn will he plant in the first 20 rows? Design a pattern to plant 30 rows while keeping the same pattern for corn.
5 rows of corn; check students' work.

Write a schedule for your next school day. Include information from the chart on the left. See above.

ctivity	Time Taken
eals	45 minutes
ravel time	30 minutes
chool	6 hours 15 minutes
leep	7 hours 45 minutes

School-Day Schedule

Activity	Time Start	Time End
Breakfast	6:30 AM	7:15 AM
Get Dressed	7:15 AM	7:30 AM
Travel to School		

At the Computer You can use a spreadsheet program to keep track of your grade averages. Check students' work.

a. Choose three subject areas. Keep track of the grades for your next four tests. Find the average for each subject.

b. Add a column for Test 5 and change the rule for the averages to include the new tests. Experiment to see what grade you need on Test 5 to raise the average for each subject by 1 point.

c. Predict how your next test will actually affect your average. Then check your prediction by putting your actual grade in the spreadsheet under Test 5.

ubject	Test 1	Test 2	Test 3	Test 4	Average
1ath					
cience					
1usic					

Alternate Teaching Strategy

Materials place-value models—1 hundred, 19 tens, and 19 ones

Present the following problem:

There are 180 test tubes in the science lab. Each test-tube rack holds 24 tubes. How may test tubes are in an unfilled rack?

Have pairs use models to show the division sentence that can be used to solve the problem. *[180 ÷ 24 = 7 R12]* Ask:

- **What does the quotient tell you?** *[the number of full test-tube racks]*
- **What does the remainder tell you?** *[the number of test tubes in an unfilled rack]*
- **How many more test tubes would be needed to fill the rack? Explain.** *[12 test tubes; 24 − 12 = 12]*
- **If each test-tube rack is put into a box, how many boxes would be needed for the 180 test tubes? Explain.** *[8 boxes; there are 8 racks.]*

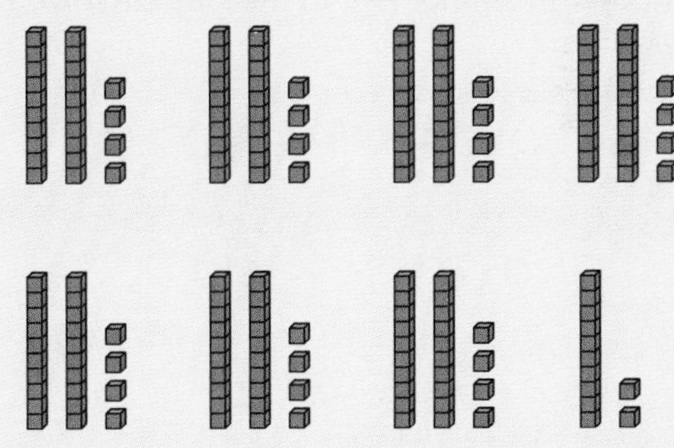

PRACTICE • 76

HOMEWORK

Name: Practice 76

PROBLEM SOLVING: INTERPRET THE QUOTIENT AND REMAINDER

✔ Read ✔ Plan ✔ Solve ✔ Look Back

Solve.

1. A charity organization delivers boxes of apples. Each box can hold 35 apples. If someone donates 180 apples, how many boxes can be completely filled? How many apples will be left over?
   5 boxes; 5 apples left over
2. People volunteer to deliver the boxes of apples to different locations. Each car can carry 4 boxes. How many cars are needed to deliver 122 boxes? How many boxes will be in the last car?
   31 cars; 2 boxes in the last car
3. Each location receives 8 boxes of apples. If there are 219 boxes, how many locations will receive 8 boxes? How many boxes are left over?
   27 locations; 3 boxes left over
4. There are 34 locations for the deliveries. Six out of 7 cars make 5 deliveries each. How many deliveries does the 7th car make?
   4 deliveries

Solve using any method. Mental Math / Pencil & Paper / Calculator

5. A school bus uses 1 gallon of gasoline to travel 9 miles. How many gallons does it use to travel 180 miles?
   20 gal
6. A school bus uses 1 tank of gasoline to travel 200 miles. About how many tanks does it use to travel 760 miles?
   about 4 tanks
7. A school bus travels 150 miles in 5 days. How many miles does it travel in 1 day if it travels the same number of miles each day?
   30 mi
8. If a school bus travels 600 miles each month, how many miles does it travel in 6 months?
   3,600 mi

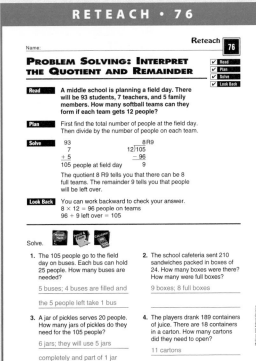

McGraw-Hill School Division

RETEACH • 76

Name: Reteach 76

PROBLEM SOLVING: INTERPRET THE QUOTIENT AND REMAINDER

✔ Read ✔ Plan ✔ Solve ✔ Look Back

Read **A middle school is planning a field day. There will be 93 students, 7 teachers, and 5 family members. How many softball teams can they form if each team gets 12 people?**

Plan First find the total number of people at the field day. Then divide by the number of people on each team.

Solve 93 + 7 + 5 = 105 people at field day

$12\overline{)105}$ = 8 R9; 105 − 96 = 9

The quotient 8 R9 tells you that there can be 8 full teams. The remainder 9 tells you that people will be left over.

Look Back You can work backward to check your answer.
8 × 12 = 96 people on teams
96 + 9 left over = 105

Solve. Mental Math / Pencil & Paper / Calculator

1. The 105 people go to the field day on buses. Each bus can hold 25 people. How many buses are needed?
   5 buses; 4 buses are filled and the 5 people left take 1 bus
2. The school cafeteria sent 210 sandwiches packed in boxes of 24. How many boxes were there? How many were full boxes?
   9 boxes; 8 full boxes
3. A jar of pickles serves 20 people. How many jars of pickles do they need for the 105 people?
   6 jars; they will use 5 jars completely and part of 1 jar
4. The players drank 189 containers of juice. There are 18 containers in a carton. How many cartons did they need to open?
   11 cartons

McGraw-Hill School Division

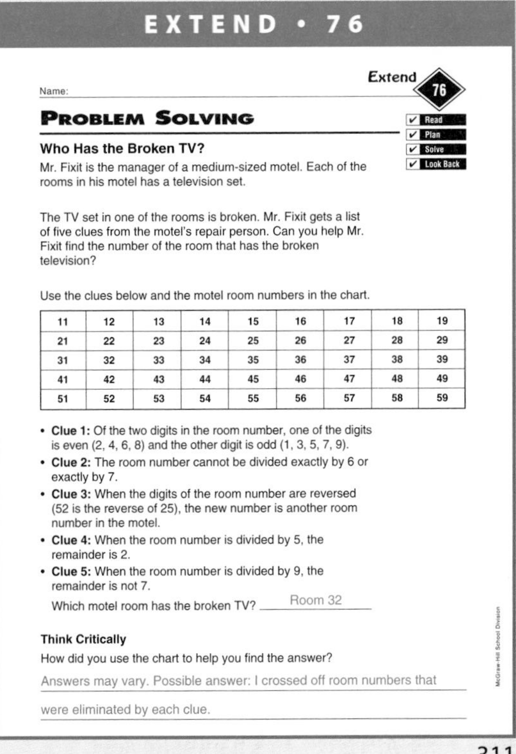

EXTEND • 76

Name: Extend 76

PROBLEM SOLVING

✔ Read ✔ Plan ✔ Solve ✔ Look Back

Who Has the Broken TV?

Mr. Fixit is the manager of a medium-sized motel. Each of the rooms in his motel has a television set.

The TV set in one of the rooms is broken. Mr. Fixit gets a list of five clues from the motel's repair person. Can you help Mr. Fixit find the number of the room that has the broken television?

Use the clues below and the motel room numbers in the chart.

11	12	13	14	15	16	17	18	19
21	22	23	24	25	26	27	28	29
31	32	33	34	35	36	37	38	39
41	42	43	44	45	46	47	48	49
51	52	53	54	55	56	57	58	59

- **Clue 1:** Of the two digits in the room number, one of the digits is even (2, 4, 6, 8) and the other digit is odd (1, 3, 5, 7, 9).
- **Clue 2:** The room number cannot be divided exactly by 6 or exactly by 7.
- **Clue 3:** When the digits of the room number are reversed (52 is the reverse of 25), the new number is another room number in the motel.
- **Clue 4:** When the room number is divided by 5, the remainder is 2.
- **Clue 5:** When the room number is divided by 9, the remainder is not 7.

Which motel room has the broken TV? Room 32

Think Critically

How did you use the chart to help you find the answer?

Answers may vary. Possible answer: I crossed off room numbers that were eliminated by each clue.

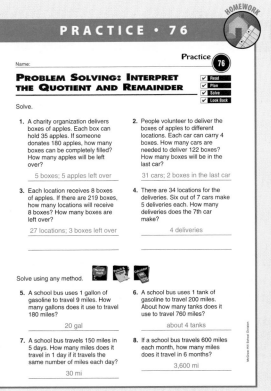

McGraw-Hill School Division

PURPOSE Review and assess concepts, skills, and strategies that students have learned in this chapter.

Materials per student: calculator (optional)

Chapter Objectives

- **8A** Estimate quotients of whole numbers and money amounts
- **8B** Divide by 1-digit divisors
- **8C** Divide by multiples of 10
- **8D** Find the average of a group of numbers
- **8E** Solve problems, including those that involve division and guessing, testing, and revising

Using the Chapter Review

The **Chapter Review** can be used as a review, practice test, or chapter test.

Think Critically Students' explanations for ex. 42–43 will indicate whether they understand the steps involved in dividing numbers.

Language and Mathematics

Complete the sentence.
Use a word in the chart. (pages 278–307)

Vocabulary
dividend
divisor
quotient
compatible
remainder
average

1. The ■ of 720 ÷ 8 is 90. **quotient**
2. To estimate 169 ÷ 4, use ■ numbers. **compatible**
3. The ■ of 35, 45, and 52 is 44. **average**
4. If you divide 754 by 8, the ■ must be less than 8. **remainder**

Concepts and Skills

Divide mentally. (page 278)

5. 80 ÷ 2 **40**
6. 420 ÷ 7 **60**
7. 200 ÷ 4 **50**
8. 3,000 ÷ 5 **600**
9. 80 ÷ 20 **4**
10. 350 ÷ 70 **5**
11. 7,200 ÷ 90 **80**
12. 4,000 ÷ 5 **80**

Estimates may vary. Possible estimates are given.

Estimate. Show the compatible numbers you used. (page 280)

13. 827 ÷ 9 **810 ÷ 9 = 90**
14. 143 ÷ 5 **150 ÷ 5 = 30**
15. 1,427 ÷ 4 **1,600 ÷ 4 = 400**
16. 5,376 ÷ 8 **5,600 ÷ 8 = 7**
17. 209 ÷ 40 **200 ÷ 40 = 5**
18. 365 ÷ 60 **360 ÷ 60 = 6**
19. 484 ÷ 70 **490 ÷ 70 = 7**
20. 848 ÷ 90 **810 ÷ 90 =**

Find the average. (page 300)

21. 20, 32, 18, 26 **24**
22. 231, 124, 512 **289**
23. 154, 23, 129, 400 **143**

Divide. (page 282)

24. 9)37 **4 R1**
25. 4)85 **21 R1**
26. 2)75 **37 R1**
27. 5)94 **18 R4**
28. 8)93 **11 R5**
29. 9)$657 **$73**
30. 6)421 **70 R1**
31. 3)157 **52 R1**
32. 7)$742 **$106**
33. 3)765 **255**
34. 2,437 ÷ 6 **406 R1**
35. 1,534 ÷ 8 **191 R6**
36. 4,578 ÷ 3 **1,526**
37. 4,431 ÷ 4 **1,107 R3**
38. 360 ÷ 10 **36**
39. 184 ÷ 20 **9 R4**
40. 227 ÷ 30 **7 R17**
41. 182 ÷ 40 **4 R22**

Think critically. (page 282)

42. Analyze. Explain what the mistake is, then correct it. **Brought down the ones incorrectly.**

```
  11 R3          12 R1
7)85           7)85
 -75            -7
  10             15
  -7            -14
   3              1
```


Reinforcement and Remediation

CHAPTER OBJECTIVES	CHAPTER REVIEW ITEMS	STUDENT BOOK PAGES		TEACHER'S EDITION PAGES		TEACHER RESOURCES
		Lessons	Midchapter Review	Activities	Alternate Teaching Strategy	Reteach
8A	2, 13–20, 43	280–281	296	279A,	281	67
8B	1, 4, 27–37, 42–43	282–293	296	281A, 285C, 289A, 291A	285, 289, 291, 293	68–71
8C	5–12, 38–41	278–279, 302–307	296	277A, 301A, 303A	279, 303, 307	66, 74–75
8D	3, 21–23, 43	300–301		299A	301	73
8E	44–50	294–295, 308–311	296	293A 307A	295, 311	72, 76

b. **False; examples like 1,675 ÷ 5 = 355 show this is not always true.**

Generalize. Write *true* or *false*. Explain why.

a. To find the average of a set of data, add the data and divide the sum by 5. **False; divide by the number of items.**

b. When you divide a 4-digit number by a 1-digit divisor, the quotient must always have at least 4 digits. **See above.**

c. When you use compatible numbers to estimate the quotient, the estimate is sometimes greater than the exact answer. **See below.**

44. No; possible answer: 2,340 ÷ 9 = 260, so they would have to travel about 260 mi each day.

IXED APPLICATIONS
roblem Solving

(pages 294, 308)

The longest river in the United States is the Mississippi River. It is 2,340 miles long. A family travels about 200 miles along the river each day. Can they travel along the entire length in 9 days? Explain. **See above.**

45 A local charity group has collected 23 boxes of food to give to 5 shelters. Some of the shelters will get 4 boxes and others will get 5. How many shelters will get 4 boxes? **2 shelters**

Use the diagram. How many feet of fencing are needed to go around the pool? **234 ft**

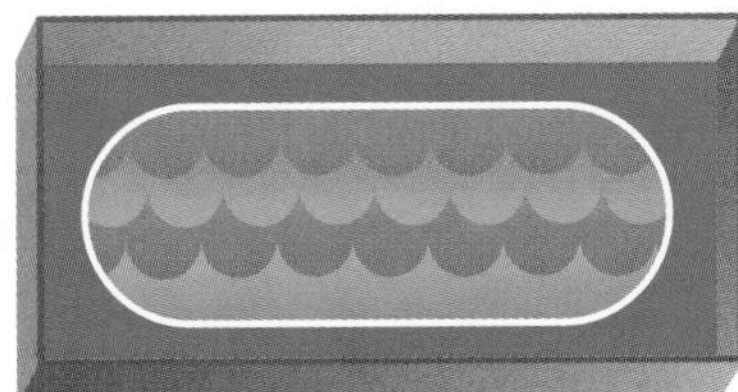

It takes Juan a half hour to clean each of the 8 kennels in the dog shelter. At what time must he begin cleaning the kennels in order to be done by 4:00 P.M.? **12 noon**

se the table for problems 48–50.

How much larger is the largest state than the fifth-largest state? **534,826 sq mi**

About how many times larger than California is Alaska? **about 4 times**

Which two states are about half as large as Texas? **New Mexico, Montana**

Area of the Five Largest States	
State	**Area (in square miles)**
California	163,707
Alaska	656,424
Texas	268,601
New Mexico	121,598
Montana	147,046

c. True; examples like the following show this is true: 124 ÷ 5 estimates to 100 ÷ 5 = 20 < exact answer, and 191 ÷ 5 estimates to 200 ÷ 5 = 40 > exact answer.

CHAPTER TEST

PURPOSE Assess the concepts, skills, and strategies students have learned in this chapter.

Chapter Objectives

- **8A** Estimate quotients of whole numbers and money amounts
- **8B** Divide by 1-digit divisors
- **8C** Divide by multiples of 10
- **8D** Find the average of a group of numbers
- **8E** Solve problems, including those that involve division and guessing, testing, and revising

Using the Chapter Test

The **Chapter Test** can be used as a practice test, a chapter test, or as an additional review. The **Performance Assessment** on Student Book page 315 provides an alternate means of assessing students' understanding of division by 1- and 2-digit numbers.

The table below correlates the test items to the chapter objectives and to the Student Book pages on which the skills are taught.

Assessment Resources

Test Masters

The Testing Program Blackline Masters provide three forms of the Chapter Test to assess students' understanding of the chapter concepts, skills, and strategies. Form C uses a free-response format. Forms A and B use a multiple-choice format.

Computer Test Generator

The Computer Test Generator supplies abundant multiple-choice and free-response test items, which you may use to generate tests and practice work sheets tailored to the needs of your class.

Teacher's Assessment Resources

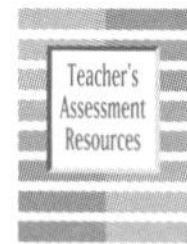

Teacher's Assessment Resources provides resources for alternate assessment. It includes guidelines for Building a Portfolio, page 6, and the Holistic Scoring Guide page 27.

chapter test

Estimates may vary. Possible estimates are giv

Estimate. Show the compatible numbers you used.

1. 731 ÷ 90 **720 ÷ 90 = 8**
2. 308 ÷ 50 **300 ÷ 50 = 6**
3. $417 ÷ 7 **$420 ÷ 7 = $60**
4. 1,397 ÷ 20 **1,400 ÷ 20 = 70**
5. $5,567 ÷ 9 **$5,400 ÷ 9 = $600**
6. 6,298 ÷ 70 **6,300 ÷ 70 = 90**

Find the average.

7. 75, 54, 31, 12 **43**
8. 312, 154, 89 **185**
9. 19, 549, 32, 100 **175**

Divide. Use mental math when you can.

10. $312 ÷ 6 **$52**
11. 560 ÷ 7 **80**
12. 3,457 ÷ 8 **432 R1**
13. 4,324 ÷ 3 **1,441 R1**
14. 638 ÷ 70 **9 R8**
15. 360 ÷ 6 **60**
16. 291 ÷ 40 **7 R11**
17. 2,000 ÷ 50 **40**
18. $612 ÷ 6 **$102**
19. 9)25 **2 R7**
20. 7)82 **11 R5**
21. 4)3,413 **853 R1**

Solve.

22. Alley is standing in a line. She is 12th from the left and 17th from the right. How many people are standing in line? **28 people**
23. Twice as many adults as children visited the town hall in one day. If 456 people visited the town hall, how many were children? **152 children**
24. The road distance between Los Angeles and Atlanta is 2,182 miles. Suppose you average 50 miles an hour and you drive for 8 hours each day. Could you drive from Los Angeles to Atlanta in 5 days? Why or why not? **No; in 5 d, distance driven wo be 2,000 mi, another day would be needed to complete the trip.**
25. Los Angeles is 2,451 air miles from New York. If an airplane takes 5 hours to make this trip, about how many miles each hour is the plane flying? **Possible answer: about 500 mi each hour**

314 Chapter 8 Test

Test Correlation

CHAPTER OBJECTIVES	TEST ITEMS	TEXT PAGES
8A	1–6	280–281
8B	10–21	282–293
8C	11, 15, 17	278–279
8D	7–9	300–301
8E	22–25	294–295, 308–311

ee Teacher's Assessment Resources for samples of student work. Check students' work.

What Did You Learn?

town wants to hire buses to take 389 tudents to visit the dinosaur exhibits at the niversity of Nebraska State Museum. Each us holds 45 students. Will 9 buses hold all he students?

- Solve this problem in two different ways. How could you use division? multiplication? See below.
- Which way for solving this problem do you prefer? Explain why. Accept any reasonable explanation of preference.

A Good Answer
- sets up the correct division and multiplication problems
- clearly shows the steps for solving the problem using each operation

You may want to place your work in your portfolio.

What Do You Think

See Teacher's Edition.

1. How do you know how to interpret the remainder when you solve a problem?
2. How have you used averages in the past? Was finding the average helpful? Explain.
3. What method do you use to find the first digit in the quotient?
   - Estimate using compatible numbers.
   - Choose a quotient by thinking of a fact and then use multiplication and addition to check your guess.
   - Other. Explain.

Question 1. Check students' work. Possible answer: The 9 buses will hold all the students; $389 \div 9 = 43$ R2, so 9 buses that hold 44 or more students can take the 389 students; $9 \times 45 = 405$, so 9 buses will hold 405 students, which is more than the 389 students that the town wants to take to the exhibits.

Reviewing A Portfolio

Have students review their portfolios. Consider including these items:
- Finished work on the Chapter Project (p. 275F) or **Investigation** (pp. 298–299).
- Selected math journal entries, pp. 277, 287, 296, 302.
- Finished work on the nonroutine problem in **What Do You Know?** (p. 277) and problems from the Menu (pp. 310–311).
- Each student's self-selected "best piece" from work completed during the chapter. Have each student attach a note explaining why he or she chose that piece.
- Any work you or an individual student wishes to keep for future reference.

You may take this opportunity to conduct conferences with students. The Portfolio Analysis Form can help you report students' progress. See Teacher's Assessment Resources, page 33.

PURPOSE Review and assess the concepts, skills, and strategies learned in this chapter.

Materials have available: place-value models, calculators (optional)

Using the Performance Assessment

Have students read and restate the problems in their own words.

Point out the section on the student page headed "A Good Answer." Make sure students understand that you will use these points to evaluate their answers.

Evaluating Student Work

As you read students' papers, look for the following:
- *Does the student know the basic multiplication and division facts or have strategies for finding them?*
- *Can the student solve the problem using multiplication? using division?*
- *Can the student explain why he or she prefers one of the methods?*

The Holistic Scoring Guide and annotated samples of students' work can be used to assess this task. See pages 27–32 and 37–72 in Teacher's Assessment Resources.

Using the Self-Assessment

What Do You Think? Assure students that there are no right or wrong answers. Tell them the emphasis is on what they think and how they justify their answers.

Follow-Up Interviews

These questions can be used to gain insight into students' thinking:
- **How did you solve the problem using multiplication?**
- **How did you solve the problem using division?**
- **What do you do with the remainder? (Ask of students who divided by 9 and of students who divided by 45.)**
- **Which way of solving the problem do you prefer? Why?**

MATH • SCIENCE • TECHNOLOGY CONNECTION

OBJECTIVE Investigate maps in a math and science context.

Materials compasses (optional)

Resources drawing program or Math Van Tools

Science

Cultural Connection Read the **Cultural Note** on page 316. After looking at the maps and discussing the questions, point out how maps have changed over the years. Ask:

- **How is the ancient Babylonian map on page 316 different from modern maps?** *[Possible answers: On the Babylonian map, Babylonia is at the center of the world; it doesn't show the rest of the world.]*
- **How do you think maps were made before satellite photographs were available?** *[Possible answers: People would fly in airplanes to see what the land looked like; people made maps of what they saw as they explored by ship or on land]*

Math

Have students work in pairs to complete items 1–3. Discuss the answers as a class. Have volunteers explain their reasoning for each answer.

For item 1, students can draw a line that is 2 centimeters long and divide it into 4 equal parts representing the 4-meter-long chalkboard. They can use this line to see that each centimeter stands for 2 meters.

Point out the importance of a map's scale. Ask:

- **Why must maps be drawn to scale?** *[Possible answer: You couldn't draw a map that is the actual size of a town, you need to draw it to scale.]*
- **What are some things you can tell from a map if you understand its scale?** *[Possible answers: how far away places are from each other; how large or small lakes or rivers are.]*

math science technology CONNECTION

Question 1. Possible answer: Road maps; drawings that represent real things but were much smaller and keys that explain the symbols; the maps were useful because they gave information in a short format.

Cultural Note

The oldest known map of the world is from about 600 B.C. It was found in Mesopotamia, an area that held some of the earliest civilizations. It is carved on a clay tablet about the size of your hand. At the center of the map is the city of Babylon. The makers of most early maps put their own cities at the center.

Modern maps are very accurate because they are made from satellite photographs of Earth.

- ▶ What types of maps have you seen or made? What was shown on the maps? Why were they useful? **See above.**
- ▶ Why do you think it might be helpful to place a landmark familiar to you as the center of your map? This is similar to what was done on the Babylonian map. **See below.**
- ▶ How are the maps you have seen similar to each other? How are they different? **Possible answer: Similar—they all show something in a smaller size; different—they show different things and may have more or fewer details on them.**

Question 2. Possible answer: It can help users find other locations on the map.

Extending The Activity

Show students how to use a compass to find north, south, east, and west. Have students use compasses to make "treasure maps" to a secret location within the school. Students can work in groups to create their maps, then exchange and follow each other's directions.

Possible answer: The chalkboard would be smaller; anything that was 1 cm on the map would be 100 times smaller.

lassroom Maps

aps show real objects or distances at smaller size. They use scales to tell w much larger the real objects are.

e scale 1 cm = 1 m tells you that centimeter stands for 1 meter. ything shown on the map that is cm long is actually 1 m long.

A map shows a chalkboard that is 2 cm long. The chalkboard is actually 4 m long. What scale is on the map? **1 cm = 2 m**

What if you drew a similar map but used a different scale, 1 cm = 200 m. Would the chalkboard be smaller or larger on the map? Explain. **See above.**

What if you wanted to draw a map of your state. Which scale would you use? Explain your reasoning.

a. 1 cm = 1 m **b.** 1 cm = 10 m
c. 1 cm = 1 km **d.** 1 cm = 10 km

ssible answer: 1 cm = 10 km; in der to show a large area, a scale ust be used that will make the map on a sheet of paper.

4. For problems 4–5, students' maps should be accurate to scale.

At the Computer

Check students' work.

4 Use a drawing or graphics program to make a map of your school, neighborhood, or town. **See above.**

5 Change the scale of the map to see how this affects how clear and useful the map is. Tell what you notice.
Students should see how increasing the scale will make the map smaller on the grid, while decreasing the scale makes it larger.

Technology

Have students work in pairs to complete the activity at the computer. First have them sketch their map using pencil and paper. Remind them that they will need to choose a scale for their map.

For item 5, students may realize that if they make their scale too big (1 cm = 1 m) they won't be able to fit their map on the paper. If they make it too small (1 cm = 1 km) the map will be too small to see.

Math Van Students may use the Drawing tool in Math Van Tools to draw their maps.

Interesting Facts

- **Atlases are named after the Greek god Atlas,** who was required to carry Earth on his shoulders as a punishment.
- **Map comes from the Latin word *mappa*,** which means cloth. Many early maps were drawn on cloth.
- **Only four different colors are needed** to color countries on a map so that no two adjacent countries are the same color. This idea from the 19th century was proven in 1976 by two mathematicians.

Bibliography

Be Your Own Map Expert, by Barbara Taylor. New York: Sterling Publishing Co., Inc. 1994. ISBN 0-8069-0664-2.

Getting From Here to There, by Harvey Weiss. Boston, MA: Houghton Mifflin Co., 1991. ISBN: 0-395-56264-2.

Maps: Plotting Places on the Globe, by Paula Pratt. San Diego, CA: Lucent Books, Inc., 1995. ISBN 0-56006-255-X.

CHAPTER 9 AT A GLANCE:

Geometry

Theme: Art and Nature

Suggested Pacing: 13–16 days

WEEK ONE

DAY 1 — PREASSESSMENT

Introduction p. 318

What Do You Know? p. 319

CHAPTER OBJECTIVES: 9A, 9B, 9C, 9D, 9E

RESOURCES Read-Aloud Anthology pp. 43–44
Pretest: Test Master Form A, B, or C
Diagnostic Inventory

Portfolio Journal

NCTM STANDARDS: 1, 2, 3, 4, 9

DAY 2 — LESSON 9.1

EXPLORE ACTIVITY

3-Dimensional Figures pp. 320–323

CHAPTER OBJECTIVES: 9A

MATERIALS 3-dimensional figure patterns (TA 23–25), scissors, tape, newspapers, magazines

RESOURCES Reteach/Practice/Extend: 77
Math Center Cards: 77
Extra Practice: 516

Daily Review TE p. 319B

Technology Link

NCTM STANDARDS: 4, 9

DAY 3 — LESSON 9.2

2-Dimensional Figures and Polygons pp. 324–327

CHAPTER OBJECTIVES: 9A

MATERIALS calculators (opt.)

RESOURCES Reteach/Practice/Extend: 78
Math Center Cards: 78
Extra Practice: 516

Daily Review TE p. 323B

Journal

Technology Link

NCTM STANDARDS: 9

WEEK TWO

DAY 1 — LESSON 9.5

EXPLORE ACTIVITY

Angles pp. 332–335

CHAPTER OBJECTIVES: 9A

MATERIALS calculators (opt.)

RESOURCES Reteach/Practice/Extend: 81
Math Center Cards: 81
Extra Practice: 517

Daily Review TE p. 331B

Technology Link

NCTM STANDARDS: 4, 9

DAY 2 — MIDCHAPTER ASSESSMENT

Midchapter Review p. 336

CHAPTER OBJECTIVES: 9A

Developing Spatial Sense p. 337

MATERIALS place-value models (TA 22)

REAL-LIFE INVESTIGATION:

Applying Geometry pp. 338–339

Portfolio Journal

NCTM STANDARDS: 1, 2, 3, 4, 9

DAY 3 — LESSON 9.6

EXPLORE ACTIVITY

Congruency and Similarity pp. 340–343

CHAPTER OBJECTIVES: 9D

MATERIALS centimeter dot paper (TA 9), scissors, rulers (TA 18)

RESOURCES Reteach/Practice/Extend: 82
Math Center Cards: 82
Extra Practice: 517

Daily Review TE p. 339B

Technology Link

NCTM STANDARDS: 4, 9

WEEK THREE

DAY 1 — LESSON 9.9

EXPLORE ACTIVITY

Area pp. 348–351

CHAPTER OBJECTIVES: 9B

MATERIALS inch graph paper (TA 8), calculators (opt.)

RESOURCES Reteach/Practice/Extend: 85
Math Center Cards: 85
Extra Practice: 518

Daily Review TE p. 347D

Technology Link

NCTM STANDARDS: 4, 9, 10

DAY 2 — LESSON 9.10

EXPLORE ACTIVITY

Volume pp. 352–353

CHAPTER OBJECTIVES: 9B

MATERIALS boxes, centimeter cubes, centimeter graph paper (TA 7), rulers (TA 18)

RESOURCES Reteach/Practice/Extend: 86
Math Center Cards: 86
Extra Practice: 519

Daily Review TE p. 351B

Technology Link

NCTM STANDARDS: 4, 9, 10

DAY 3 — LESSON 9.11

PROBLEM SOLVERS AT WORK

Use Diagrams pp. 354–357

CHAPTER OBJECTIVES: 9E

MATERIALS rope or string, masking tape, calculators (opt.)

RESOURCES Reteach/Practice/Extend: 87
Math Center Cards: 87
Extra Practice: 519

Daily Review TE p. 353B

Algebraic Thinking

Technology Link

NCTM STANDARDS: 1, 2, 3, 4, 9, 13

DAY 4

LESSON 9.3

EXPLORE ACTIVITY

Line Segments, Lines, and Rays pp. 328–329

CHAPTER OBJECTIVES: 9A

RESOURCES Reteach/Practice/Extend: 79
Math Center Cards: 79
Extra Practice: 516

Daily Review TE p. 327B

Technology Link

NCTM STANDARDS: 4, 9

LESSON 9.7

Symmetry pp. 344–345

CHAPTER OBJECTIVES: 9D

MATERIALS calculators (opt.)

RESOURCES Reteach/Practice/Extend: 83
Math Center Cards: 83
Extra Practice: 518

Daily Review TE p. 343B

Technology Link

NCTM STANDARDS: 9

DAY 5

LESSON 9.4

PROBLEM-SOLVING STRATEGY

Make an Organized List pp. 330–331

CHAPTER OBJECTIVES: 9E

MATERIALS calculators (opt.)

RESOURCES Reteach/Practice/Extend: 80
Math Center Cards: 80
Extra Practice: 517

Daily Review TE p. 329B

Algebraic Thinking

Technology Link

NCTM STANDARDS: 1, 2, 3, 4, 9, 13

LESSON 9.8

EXPLORE ACTIVITY

Slides, Flips, and Turns pp. 346–347

CHAPTER OBJECTIVES: 9C

MATERIALS centimeter graph paper (TA 7), rulers (TA 18), calculators (opt.)

RESOURCES Reteach/Practice/Extend: 84
Math Center Cards: 84
Extra Practice: 518

TEACHING WITH TECHNOLOGY
Alternate Lesson TE pp. 347A–347B

Daily Review TE p. 345B

Technology Link

NCTM STANDARDS: 4, 9

CHAPTER ASSESSMENT

Chapter Review pp. 358–359

MATERIALS calculators (opt.)

Chapter Test p. 360

RESOURCES Posttest: Test Master Form A, B, or C

Performance Assessment p. 361

RESOURCES Performance Task: Test Master

Math • Science • Technology Connection pp. 362–363

Cumulative Review pp. 364–365

MATERIALS calculators (opt.)

Portfolio

NCTM STANDARDS: 1, 4, 9

Assessment Options

FORMAL

Chapter Tests

STUDENT BOOK
- Midchapter Review, p. 336
- Chapter Review, pp. 358–359
- Chapter Test, p. 360
- Cumulative Review, pp. 364–365

BLACKLINE MASTERS
- Test Master Form A, B, or C
- Diagnostic Inventory

COMPUTER TEST BANK
- Available on disk

TAAS Preparation and Practice
- Chapter Test

Performance Assessment
- What Do You Know? p. 319
- Performance Assessment, p. 361
- Holistic Scoring Guide, Teacher's Assessment Resources, pp. 27–32
- Follow-Up Interviews, p. 361
- Performance Task, Test Masters

Teacher's Assessment Resources
- Portfolio Guidelines and Forms, pp. 6–9, 33–35
- Holistic Scoring Guide, pp. 27–32
- Samples of Student Work, pp. 37–72

INFORMAL

Ongoing Assessment
- Observation Checklist, pp. 324, 344, 346, 348, 352, 354
- Interview, pp. 320, 330
- Anecdotal Report, pp. 328, 332, 340

Portfolio Opportunities
- Chapter Project, p. 317F
- What Do You Know? p. 319
- Investigation, pp. 338–339
- Journal Writing, pp. 319, 325, 336
- Performance Assessment, p. 361
- Self-Assessment: What Do You Think? p. 361

Chapter Objectives		Standardized Test Correlations
9A	Identify 2-dimensional and 3-dimensional figures and their parts	MAT, CAT, SAT, ITBS, CTBS
9B	Find area and volume	MAT, CAT, ITBS, CTBS, TN*
9C	Identify how a figure is transformed	SAT, TN*
9D	Identify congruent and symmetric figures	MAT, CAT, SAT, CTBS, TN*
9E	Solve problems, including those that involve geometry and making an organized list	MAT, CAT, SAT, ITBS, CTBS, TN*

*Terra Nova

NCTM Standards Grades K–4	
1 Problem Solving	8 Whole Number Computation
2 Communication	9 Geometry and Spatial Sense
3 Reasoning	10 Measurement
4 Connections	11 Statistics and Probability
5 Estimation	12 Fractions and Decimals
6 Number Sense and Numeration	13 Patterns and Relationships
7 Concepts of Whole Number Operations	

Meeting Individual Needs

LEARNING STYLES

- AUDITORY/LINGUISTIC
- **LOGICAL/ANALYTICAL**
- **VISUAL/SPATIAL**
- **MUSICAL**
- KINESTHETIC
- **SOCIAL**
- **INDIVIDUAL**

Students who are talented in art, language, and physical activity may better understand mathematical concepts when these concepts are connected to their areas of interest. Use the following activities to stimulate the different learning styles of some of your students.

Kinesthetic Learners

Have a pair of students draw a line down the middle of a sheet of paper. One student draws a simple picture along one side of the center line. The other student draws the other side to make the entire picture symmetrical.

Auditory/Linguistic Learners

Play a game by displaying a number of polygons on a geoboard. Choose a shape without telling students. They can ask yes or no questions about the shape. As students eliminate shapes, cover them with an index card.

See Lesson Resources, pp. 319A, 323A, 327A, 329A, 331A, 339A, 343A, 345A, 347C, 351A, 353A.

GIFTED AND TALENTED

Challenge students to investigate the angles of clock hands. Ask students to name a time and set an analog clock to that time. Have students list the time and the degree of the angles formed by the hands.

See also Meeting Individual Needs, pp. 322, 324, 334, 348, 355.

3:00
90° angle

EXTRA SUPPORT

Some students may need to have models of geometric terms and figures throughout the chapter. As they become more familiar with these terms, they will rely less on concrete aids.

Specific suggestions for ways to provide extra support to students appear in every lesson in this chapter.

See Meeting Individual Needs, pp. 324, 328, 330, 332, 340, 344, 346, 348, 352, 354.

EARLY FINISHERS

Students who complete their class work early may make invitations in geometric shapes asking another class to see the art show. (See *Chapter Project,* p. 317F.)

See also Meeting Individual Needs, pp. 322, 326, 328, 330, 334, 342, 344, 346, 350, 352, 356.

LANGUAGE SUPPORT

On cards, list attributes of shapes. Draw pictures of polygons on another set of cards. Have students pick an attribute card and choose the polygon card that matches it.

The name of the polygons can be written on the back of the picture cards, so students can check their answers.

See also Meeting Individual Needs, pp. 321, 333, 356.

ESL APPROPRIATE

INCLUSION

- **For inclusion ideas, information, and suggestions, see pp. 320, 326, 334, 342, 349, 356, T15.**
- **For gender fairness tips, see pp. 355, T15.**

USING MANIPULATIVES

Building Understanding Have students use a geoboard to explore polygons, open and closed figures, lines, line segments, rays, and angles. Students can make examples of these on the geoboard. They can then copy them onto dot paper, label, and list characteristics.

Draw a shape on the chalkboard. Students can practice making congruent shapes on a geoboard. Or they can draw and cut out the shapes and test for congruency by laying the pieces on top of each other.

Easy-to-Make Manipulatives If a geoboard is not available, cut a $7\frac{1}{2}$-inch by $7\frac{1}{2}$-inch square from $\frac{1}{2}$-inch or thicker plywood. Use 1-inch finishing nails to make the grid.

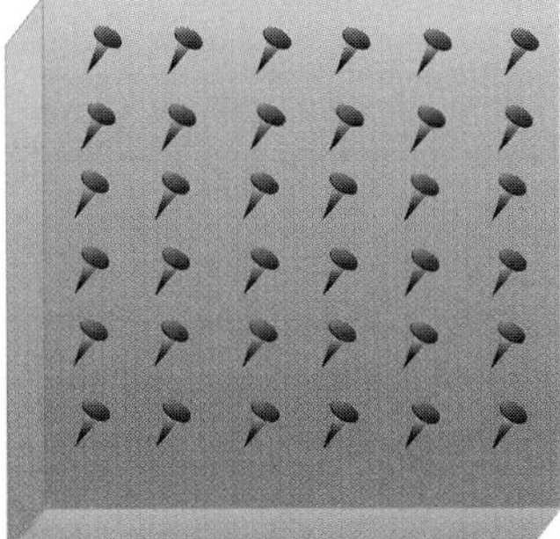

ESL APPROPRIATE

USING COOPERATIVE LEARNING

Group Product This strategy develops teamwork by having students work together to produce a product or report.

- **Students work together in groups of three, four, or five.**
- **Jobs or roles are assigned to the group by the teacher.**
- **The group organizes the work, and comes to an agreement on what the final product or project will include.**
- **The group completes their product, and presents it to another group, several groups, or the whole class.**

USING LITERATURE

Use the selection *A Short Walk Around the Pyramids & Through the World of Art* to introduce the chapter theme, Art and Nature. This selection is reprinted on pages 43–44 of the Read-Aloud Anthology.

Also available in the Read-Aloud Anthology is the poem "Shapes," page 45.

GEOMETRY

Linking Technology

This integrated package of programs and services allows students to explore, develop, and practice concepts; solve problems; build portfolios; and assess their own progress. Teachers can enhance instruction, provide remediation, and share ideas with other educational professionals.

CD-ROM ACTIVITY

In *Flustered Flag Maker,* students use the geometry tool to make the national flag of a country. Students can use the online notebook to write about how they moved the various geometric shapes. To extend the activity, students use the Math Van tools to make a picture using geometric shapes. **Available on CD-ROM.**

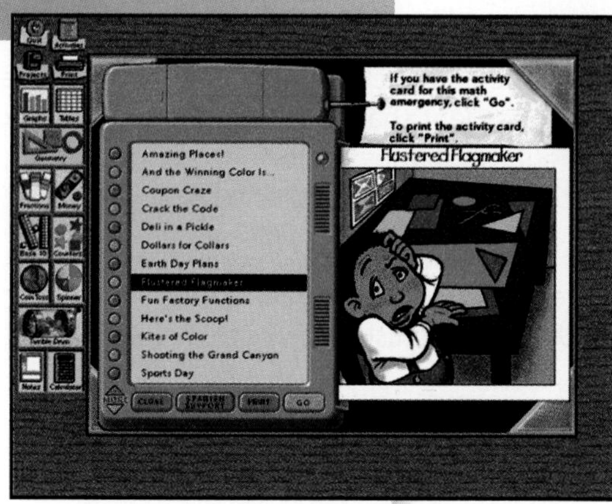

CD-ROM TOOLS

Students can use Math Van's geometry tool to explore the concept of geometric shapes. The Tech Links on the Lesson Resources pages highlight opportunities for students to use this and other tools such as tables, online notes, and calculator to provide additional practice, reteaching, or extension. **Available on CD-ROM.**

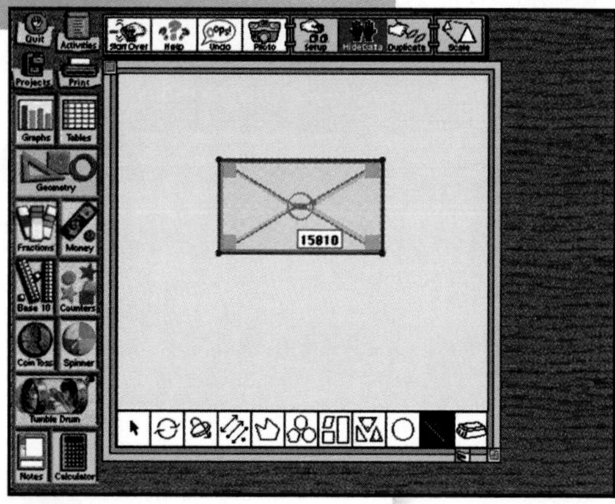

WEB SITE http://www.mhschool.com

Teachers can access the McGraw-Hill School Division World Wide Web site for additional curriculum support at http://www.mhschool.com. Click on our Resource Village for specially designed activities linking Web sites to geometry. Motivate children by inviting them to explore Web sites that develop the chapter theme of "Art and Nature." Exchange ideas on classroom management, cultural diversity, and other areas in the Math Forum.

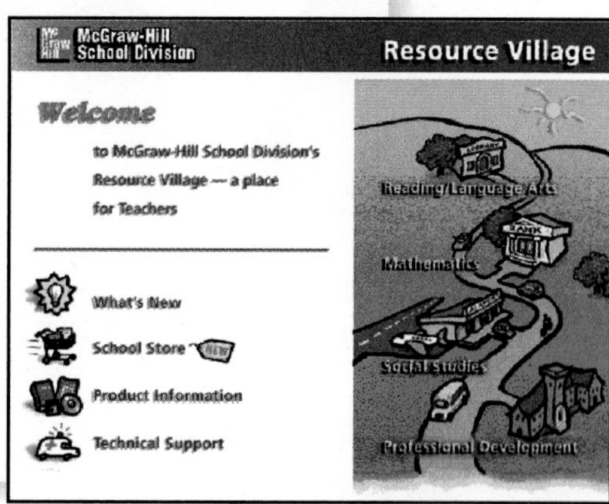

Chapter Project GEOMETRY-IN-NATURE ART SHOW

Highlighting the Math

- identify geometric shapes/terms
- describe and define geometric shapes/terms
- relate geometric shapes/terms to objects of nature

1 Starting the Project

Introduce the idea of an art show called Geometry in Nature. Begin by making three columns on the chalkboard or on chart paper and labeling them with the following column heads:

Geometric Shapes/Terms Description/Attributes Nature Connection

Have students brainstorm a list of geometric shapes. Record the list on the chart, allowing ample space between items. Continue in a similar way with the second column.

Tell students that they will create a nature art show using the information they've listed in the first two columns. Consider how family and community members can participate.

2 Continuing the Project

- Individually or with a partner, students show geometric shapes found in nature.
- Students prepare their presentation for the class art show: a snapshot, drawing or painting, a model made of clay or found materials. Assist students in filling in the third column of the chart.
- Students also provide an information card to place beside their finished product.

Object name:
Presented by:
Medium:
Geometric Relationship:

3 Finishing the Project

Hold the art show, having children place their display tables around the room. Each child makes a presentation to the class, using the information from his or her display cards and any other additional information he or she thinks appropriate. If possible, have parent volunteers tape record the presentations.

Community Involvement

Invite another class to visit Geometry in Nature. Or you may wish to invite a ranger or guide from a nearby nature preserve to speak to the class.

BUILDING A PORTFOLIO

Each student's portfolio piece should include a photo, photocopy, or original drawing of their nature object, the display card accompanying the object, and a brief summary describing all geometric relationships found within the nature object.

To assess students' work, refer to the Holistic Scoring Guide on page 27 in the Teacher's Assessment Resources.

PURPOSE Introduce the theme of the chapter.

Resources Read-Aloud Anthology, pages 43–44

Using Literature

Read "A Short Walk Through the Pyramids and Through the World of Art" from the Read-Aloud Anthology to introduce the theme of the chapter, "Art and Nature."

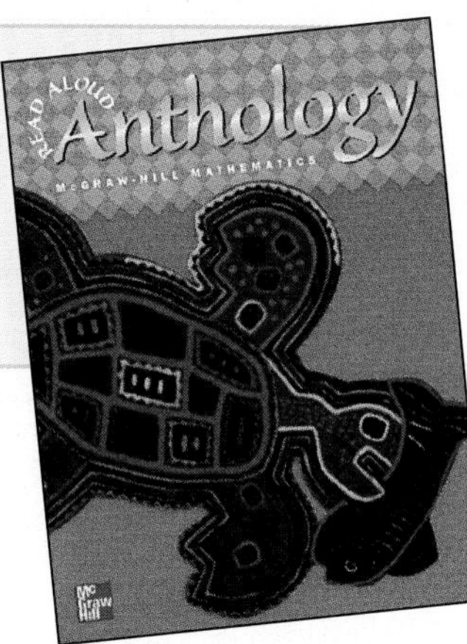

Developing the Theme

Ask students what geometry is. They may have unusual answers that are partially correct. Considering their partial definitions, have students look at pictures in the classroom and nature outside the window or on this page. Ask students how they think art and nature are connected with geometry.

Students may see the shapes that play intricate roles in art and nature. Encourage students to share as much as they know about geometry and its connection to art and nature.

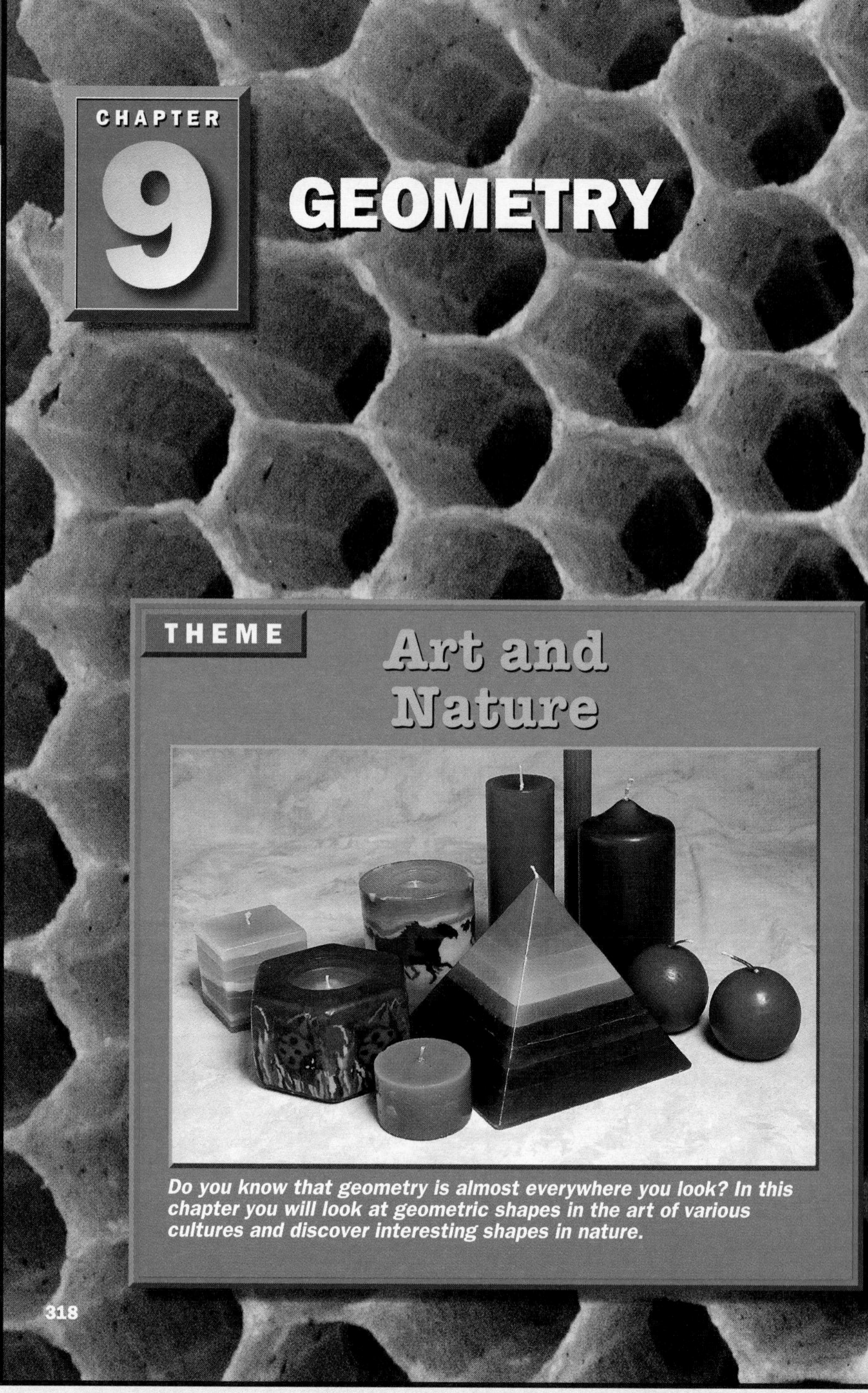

CHAPTER
9
GEOMETRY
THEME
Art and Nature
Do you know that geometry is almost everywhere you look? In this chapter you will look at geometric shapes in the art of various cultures and discover interesting shapes in nature.
318

Chapter Bibliography

And So They Build by Bert Kitchen. Cambridge, MA: Candlewick Press, 1993. ISBN 1–56402–217–X.

Animal Architecture by Jennifer Owings Dewey. New York, NY: Orchard Books, 1991. ISBN 0–531–05930–8.

Nature in Art by Anthea Peppin. Brookfield, CT: The Millbrook Press, 1992. ISBN 1–56294–173–9.

Community Involvement

Have small groups of students design a fountain or other water feature for their community. In preparation, the class might visit local fountains to gather ideas, take photographs, sketch, and make measurements. Small groups can build models of their fountains, using foil or aluminum wire to represent water. They can then write a proposal for installation and a letter to a local landscape architect about display of the models and proposals.

1. Possible answers: the globe is a sphere, and the math book is a rectangular prism.

What Do You Know?

Look at the objects around you in the classroom. Create a table that lists the objects and their shapes. Check students' work.

1 What shapes did you list? Explain how you recognize each shape. See above.

2 Describe at least three shapes that you can see in nature or in art. See below.

3 Portfolio Choose three shapes from the list below. Sketch each shape. Then describe the shape in as many ways as you can.

triangle	**rectangle**	**circle**
kite	**cylinder**	**cube**

2. Possible answers: the moon is a sphere; a picture of a building is a rectangle; and the tree trunk is a cylinder.

Categories **Look at the table you made of objects and their shapes. Put the shapes you found in your classroom into three different groups or categories.** Check students' work.

Sometimes it is helpful to group things that are alike. When you put things into categories, you can compare them more easily.

1 What groups of shapes did you make? Describe each group. Possible answers: a group of shapes with straight edges and those with rounded edges

2 How are your categories different? Possible answers: in color, size, shape, use

Vocabulary*

*partial list

3-dimensional, p. 320	**polygon,** p. 324	**diagonal,** p. 330	**slide,** p. 346
edge, p. 321	**line,** p. 328	**angle,** p. 332	**turn,** p. 346
face, p. 321	**ray,** p. 328	**congruent,** p. 340	**area,** p. 348
vertex, p. 321	**intersecting,** p. 328	**similar,** p. 340	**square unit,** p. 348
2-dimensional, p. 324	**parallel,** p. 328	**line of symmetry,** p. 344	**volume,** p. 352
open, p. 324	**perpendicular,** p. 328	**flip,** p. 346	**cubic unit,** p. 352
closed, p. 324			

Reading, Writing, Arithmetic

Categories Invite students to think of ways to group other things. Examples may include the numbers 1–20, books in the classroom, items in their desks, food they eat for lunch. Encourage students to think of as many different groups as they can. Use their work to point out that there are usually different possibilities for categorizing the same objects.

Vocabulary

Students may record new words in their journals. Encourage them to show examples and draw diagrams to help them tell what the words mean.

PURPOSE Assess students' ability to apply prior knowledge of geometry.

Assessing Prior Knowledge

Draw a triangle and a rectangle on the board.

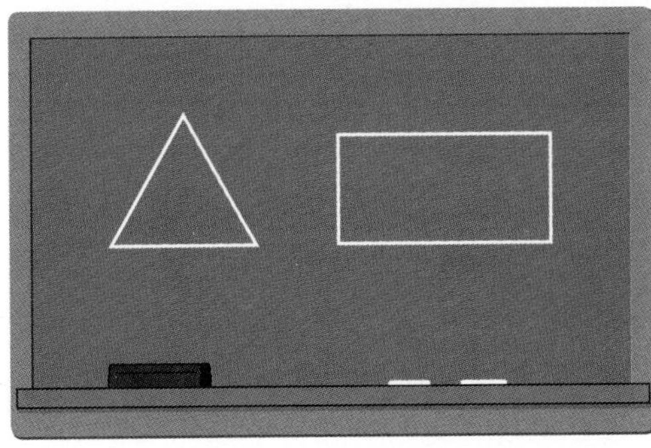

Ask how they are alike and how they are different. *[possible answers: alike-both are polygons, both are made up of line segments; different-the triangle has 3 sides and 3 angles; the rectangle has 4 sides and 4 angles]*

Encourage students to use whatever methods they wish to answer items 1–3. Observe students as they work. Look at the ways they describe the shapes they sketch for item 3. Discuss the answers that students gave for items 1–3. In particular, let them share their explanations for item 1 and their descriptions for item 3.

Building a Portfolio

Item 3 can be used as a benchmark to show where students are in their understanding of geometry.

A Portfolio Checklist for Students and a Checklist for Teachers are provided in Teacher's Assessment Resources, pp. 33–34.

Prerequisite Skills

- *Can students identify common shapes?*
- *Can students multiply whole numbers?*

Assessment Resources

Diagnostic Inventory

Use this blackline master to assess prerequisite skills that students will need in order to be successful in this chapter.

Test Masters

Use the multiple choice format (form A or B) or the free response format (form C) as a pretest of the skills in this chapter.

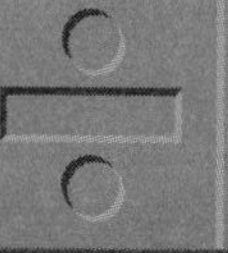

EXPLORE ACTIVITY

3-Dimensional Figures

OBJECTIVE Explore identifying and analyzing 3-dimensional figures by their attributes.

RESOURCE REMINDER
Math Center Cards 77
Practice 77, Reteach 77, Extend 77

SKILLS TRACE

GRADE 3	• Explore identifying and sorting 3-dimensional figures in the real world by their attributes. *(Chapter 10)*
GRADE 4	• Explore identifying and analyzing 3-dimensional figures.
GRADE 5	• Explore making models of 3-dimensional figures and identifying their attributes. *(Chapter 12)*

MANIPULATIVE WARM-UP

Whole Class — Logical/Analytical

OBJECTIVE Explore using attributes to sort 2- and 3-dimensional shapes.

Materials 3-dimensional shapes (sphere, cone, rectangular prism, cube, or objects that have these shapes) and cutouts of 2-dimensional shapes (circle, triangle, square, rectangle)

▶ Display 3-dimensional figures and cutouts of 2-dimensional figures. Invite groups of students to inspect the shapes.

▶ Have students discuss ways for sorting the shapes into two groups.

▶ Continue the activity until students have suggested sorting the objects into two groups: one group of 2-dimensional figures and one group of 3-dimensional figures. Discuss with students the difference between a 2-dimensional and a 3-dimensional figure.

ART CONNECTION

Cooperative Pairs — Visual/Spatial

OBJECTIVE Connect 3-dimensional figures and artwork.

Materials per pair: geometric figure patterns (TA 23–25), crayons or colored markers, index cards

▶ Have students use 3-dimensional shapes to make a city of the future. Explain that they will use patterns to make the shapes. Before constructing the shapes, they can draw on the sides of the patterns to show windows, doors, and any other details they wish.

▶ Next to each building, have students put an index card which lists the name of the shape or combination of shapes that was used to make the building, and what kind of building it is in the student's city of the future.

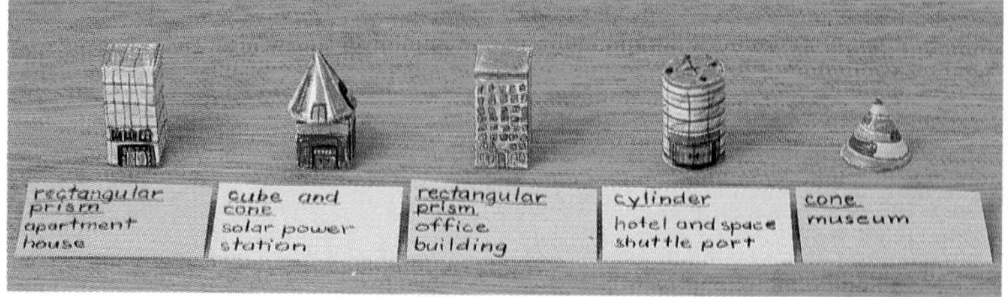

Daily Review

PREVIOUS DAY QUICK REVIEW

1. 17 ÷ 3 *[5 R2]*
2. 29 ÷ 7 *[4 R1]*
3. 39 ÷ 6 *[6 R3]*
4. 58 ÷ 8 *[7 R2]*

FAST FACTS

1. 6 × 3 *[18]*
2. 2 × 7 *[14]*
3. 8 × 8 *[64]*
4. 6 × 5 *[30]*

Problem of the Day • 77

The product of three numbers is 1. The sum of these numbers is 3. What are the three numbers? *[1, 1, 1]*

TECH LINK

ONLINE EXPLORATION

Use our Web-linked activities and lesson plans to connect your students to the real world of art and nature.

MATH FORUM

Idea Since there are many new terms to learn with geometry, I have my students make their own illustrated dictionary.

Visit our Resource Village at http://www.mhschool.com to access the Online Exploration and the Math Forum.

MATH CENTER

Practice

OBJECTIVE Describe 3-dimensional figures.

Materials per pair: 2 small objects, 1 counter; per student: Math Center Recording Sheet (TA 31 optional)

Students describe 3-dimensional figures as they travel around a game board. *[Students check each others' work.]*

PRACTICE ACTIVITY 77 — MATH CENTER — Partners

Game • Figure Facts

YOU NEED
- 2 ones models (as markers)
- 1 two-color counter

- Make a copy of the game board. Put markers at START. On every turn, a player tosses the counter. Yellow means, "Move 1 space." Red means, "Move 2 spaces."
- Copy the name of the figure in the space. Write one fact about that figure, such as its number of vertices, edges, and flat faces. You may not repeat your own facts.
- When both players have reached HOME, compare your written facts. Decide which are correct. Revise any that are not.

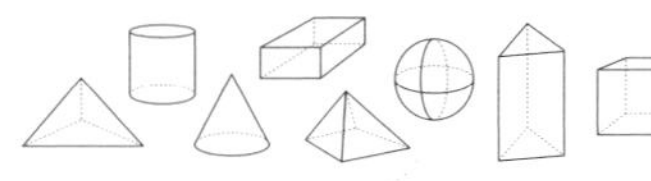

START | rectangular prism | cylinder | cube | triangular prism | square pyramid | triangular prism | cone | rectangular prism | cylinder | cube | triangular pyramid | square prism | triangular prism | cone | sphere | HOME

Grade Level 4 — McGraw-Hill School Division

Chapter 9, Lesson 1, pages 320–323 — Geometry

NCTM Standards
- ✓ Problem Solving
- ✓ Communication
- ✓ Reasoning
- ✓ Connections

Problem Solving

OBJECTIVE Analyze 3-dimensional figures.

Materials per student: centimeter graph paper (TA 7), scissors, tape, markers, Math Center Recording Sheet (TA 31 optional)

Students redraw 2 nets to change them into nets for different space figures. *[Figure A becomes a rectangular prism if the 4 squares in a row become rectangles drawn vertically. Figure B is a square pyramid; it becomes a triangular pyramid if the center figure becomes a triangle surrounded by three triangles.]*

PROBLEM-SOLVING ACTIVITY 77 — MATH CENTER — On Your Own

Patterning • Nets, Nets, and More Nets

YOU NEED
- graph paper
- scissors
- tape
- markers

- Figure A is a net for a cube. See for yourself. Trace it, cut it out, and fold it. How can you change this net to make it into a net for a rectangular prism? Try to draw one on graph paper. Cut it out and see if it works.
- Look at Figure B. What figure will this net make? How can you change this net to make a net for a triangular pyramid?
- Try making a net for a triangular prism. You need three rectangles and two triangles.

Figure A

Figure B

Grade Level 4 — McGraw-Hill School Division

Chapter 9, Lesson 1, pages 320–323 — Geometry

ESL APPROPRIATE

NCTM Standards
- ✓ Problem Solving
- ✓ Communication
- ✓ Reasoning
- ✓ Connections

EXPLORE ACTIVITY

3-Dimensional Figures

OBJECTIVE Explore identifying and analyzing 3-dimensional figures by their attributes.

Materials per pair: shape nets (TA 23), scissors, tape, newspapers, magazines

Vocabulary cone, cube, cylinder, edge, face, rectangular prism, sphere, square pyramid, 3-dimensional, triangular prism, triangular pyramid, vertex

1 Introduce

Ask students to name things they have made by using a pattern. Students might suggest airplanes or kites. Have students describe how the pattern helped them make the items. They might suggest that a pattern guides them so they are sure to get the item they are trying to make.

Have students look at the shape nets. Ask volunteers to guess and describe what the shapes might look like after folding and taping.

2 Teach *Cooperative Pairs*

LEARN Work Together Have students work in pairs to make each 3-dimensional figure. Suggest that students carefully cut out, fold, and tape the pattern so their finished figure is as accurate a model as possible.

Give each pair newspapers and magazines. Have them search for pictures showing examples of the 3-dimensional figures they made. Have them cut out at as many examples of each figure as they can find.

Talk It Over Discuss the questions with the class once all the pairs have finished. For item 1, students might suggest that the figures are all 3-dimensional; accept any other resonable suggestions. For item 2, you might discuss the figure students had the most difficulty finding.

EXPLORE ACTIVITY • GEOMETRY

3-Dimensional Figures

LEARN

You can fold paper to make 3-dimensional figures.

You can also fold patterns to make 3-dimensional figures. This pattern can be folded to make a box.

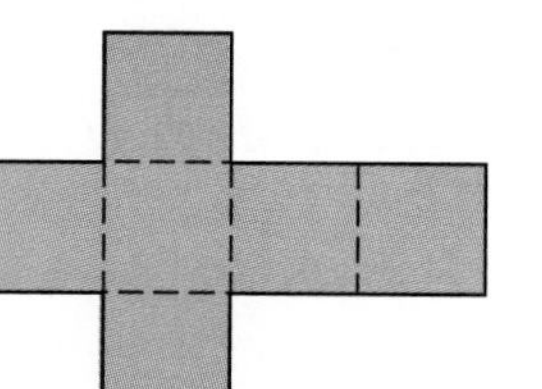

Question 1. Students may compare sizes and any variations in the shapes.

Work Together

Work with a partner. Copy and cut out patterns along the solid lines. Fold each pattern at the dotted lines. Tape the sides together to make the 3-dimensional figure.

Note: A 3-dimensional figure has length, width, and height.

Look at newspapers and magazines. Find pictures of objects that have the same shape as your 3-dimensional figures.

You will need
- *patterns for figures*
- *scissors*
- *tape*
- *newspapers, magazines*

Talk It Over

- How would you describe each figure? How are the figures alike? How are they different? See above.
- What figure did you find the most pictures of? Why do you think this is so? See below.

Check Out the Glossary
For vocabulary words
See page 544.

Question 2. Answers may vary. Possible answer: Cylinder; most of the pictures were of cans of food that are usually cylinders.

Meeting Individual Needs

Early Finishers

Have students try to draw other patterns from which they can make 3-dimensional shapes, such as triangular prisms or pyramids. Students should describe the characteristics successful patterns share.

Inclusion

For visually impaired students, ask volunteers to pre-assemble each of the 3-dimensional figures. Let students use these models to answer questions based on what they feel with their hands.

Ongoing Assessment

Interview Determine if students can identify 3-dimensional figures by showing students any one of the figures they made. Ask each student to name the figure they are shown and tell how many vertices, edges, and faces it has.

Follow Up For more practice with 3-dimensional figures, assign **Reteach 77.**

For students who need a greater challenge, assign **Extend 77.**

ke Connections

ok at these figures. Think about ways to describe them describing their parts.

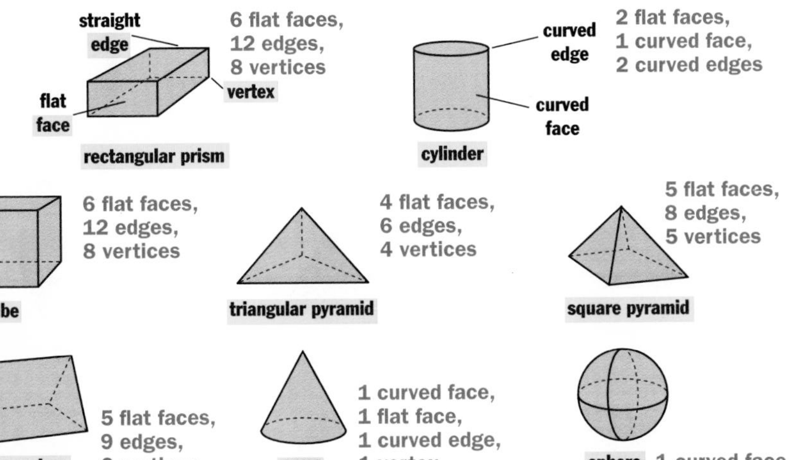

Which figures have flat faces and straight edges? How many vertices, faces, and edges does each have? See above.

Which figures have curved edges or curved faces? See above.

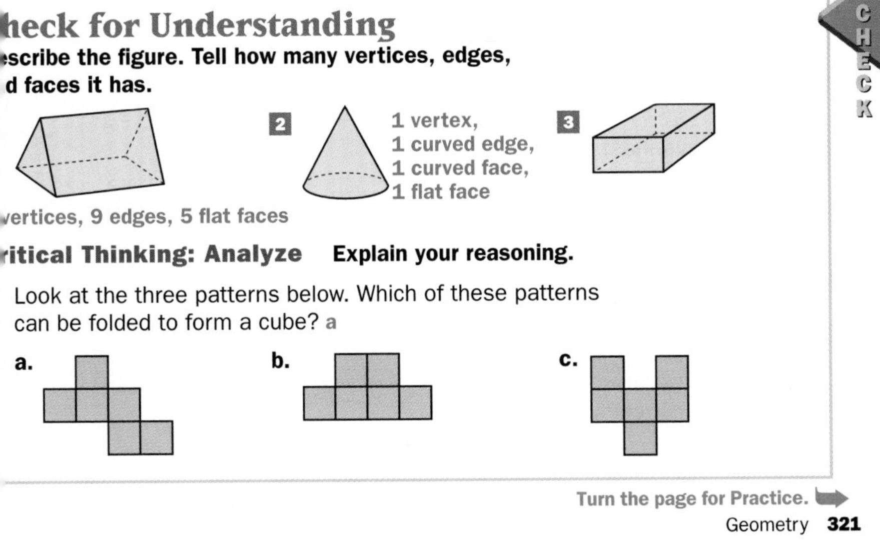

heck for Understanding

scribe the figure. Tell how many vertices, edges, d faces it has.

vertices, 9 edges, 5 flat faces

2 1 vertex, 1 curved edge, 1 curved face, 1 flat face

3

itical Thinking: Analyze **Explain your reasoning.**

Look at the three patterns below. Which of these patterns can be folded to form a cube? a

a. b. c.

Turn the page for Practice.

MAKE CONNECTIONS

Have students compare the 3-dimensional figures they made to the ones shown in the text. Say aloud a name of one of the figures, and have students hold up the corresponding model.

For each figure, have students point out the faces, edges, and vertices. Ask students to describe the shape of each of the faces. For the cylinder and cone, ask students to describe the shape of the curved surface before it was cut out and assembled. *[cylinder: rectangle; cone: sector of a circle or pie wedge]*

3 Close

Check for Understanding using items 1–4, page 321.

Critical Thinking

Have students describe how they know whether the patterns can be folded into cubes. Let students describe all the methods they can use to determine this. Students may benefit from making each pattern on dot paper, cutting it out, folding, and taping it together to see whether the pattern forms a cube.

Practice See pages 322–323.

Language Support

This lesson involves the use of many new words. Have students make a set of flash cards in which each card illustrates and defines each new word in this lesson to help them learn the vocabulary.

ESL APPROPRIATE

PRACTICE

Materials have available: calculators

Each student completes ex. 1–22 and the **Mixed Review** as independent work.

- In ex. 1–9, ask students to try to name the figures without referring to p. 321. After writing all their answers, suggest that students turn to p. 321 to check.
- For ex. 10–13, you may want students to describe the edges and faces as flat or curved.
- For **Make It Right** (ex. 14), see Common Error below.
- For ex. 16, Drawing a Picture is a good strategy to use.
- In ex. 18, students solve a multistep problem.

Mixed Review/Test Preparation Students review addition, subtraction, multiplication, and division, learned in Chapters 2, 6, and 7.

PRACTICE

Practice

Name the 3-dimensional figure the object looks like.

1  sphere

2  cube

3  rectangular prism

4 

cylinder

5 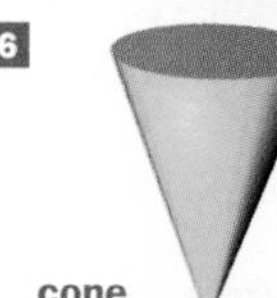 square or triangular pyramid

6  cone

7  cone

8  sphere

9  triangular prism

Describe the figure. Tell how many edges, vertices, and faces it has.

10 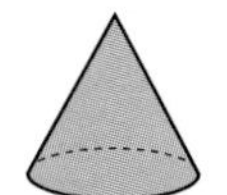 1 curved edge, 1 vertex, 1 flat face, 1 curved face

11 no edges, no vertices, 1 curved face

12 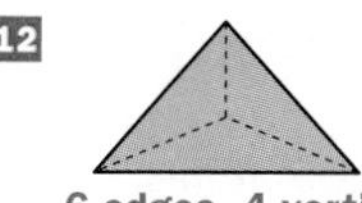 6 edges, 4 vertices, 4 flat faces

13 What figure has:

a. 1 curved face and no edges? sphere

b. only 4 flat faces with all faces the same shape? triangular pyramid

Make It Right

14 Marcos described this figure. Tell what the error is and correct it.

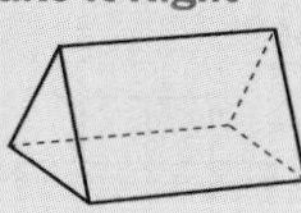

4 flat faces
6 vertices
9 edges

Marcos forgot to count one of the faces—5 flat faces, 6 vertices, 9 edges.

Meeting Individual Needs

Early Finishers

Have each student make two different 3-dimensional figures using straws and clay as connectors. Have them describe how the figures are alike and how they are different.

Common Error

Students can incorrectly count the number of faces, vertices, or edges of 3-dimensional figures as in **Make It Right** on page 322. Have them keep models handy as they mark each edge, vertex, or face as they count.

Gifted And Talented

Show students pictures of several different pyramids and prisms. Ask students to write their own definition of pyramid and prism. Students should recognize that pyramids have one base face of any shape and any number of triangular faces that meet at one vertex. Prisms have two identical base faces and any number of rectangles connecting the bases.

. Possible answer: 1 hundred-dollar bill, 60 one-dollar bills; 6 ten-dollar bills equal $60, which is the same as 60 one-dollar bills, so both combinations show $160.

IXED APPLICATIONS

roblem Solving

INFOBIT
The pyramid of Khufu at Giza in Egypt is the world's largest pyramid. Each side of its base measures 230 m.

There are 35 marbles in a jar. If 8 children each get the same number of marbles, how many marbles will be left over? **3 marbles**

Spatial reasoning Sheila built a 3-dimensional figure out of straws. Her figure has 8 vertices, 12 edges, and 6 faces. What could her figure be? **cube or rectangular prism**

The Khufu pyramid is a square pyramid. About how long is the perimeter of its base? SEE INFOBIT. **Possible answer: about 800 m**

Marlena saved $33.61 to buy her mother and father each a present. She bought her father a sweater for $16.55 and her mother a purse for $13.87. How much money does Marlena have left? **$3.19**

Flyers from two different supermarkets were sent to you. Shopfirst has 9 oranges on sale for 81¢. ValueFood has 3 oranges on sale for 24¢. Where would you buy oranges? Explain why. **See below.**

Data Point Copy the table on the right. Use the categories shown to sort the objects in the Databank on page 540. Complete the table by listing the object beside each category it fits.

19 Rory bought a bicycle for $160. He paid for it with 1 hundred-dollar bill and 6 ten-dollar bills. What other combinations of one-, ten-, and hundred-dollar bills could he have used? Explain. **See above.**

21 **Write a problem** about a 3-dimensional figure. Ask for a description of the figure, including the number of vertices, faces, and edges. Ask someone to solve the problem.

Sorting Objects	
a. even number of faces	See below.
b. odd number of faces	
c. straight edges only	
d. curved edges only	

2. a. jewelry box, seashell, basket
b. paint jar, glass beads, purse
c. jewelry box, glass beads, basket, purse
d. paint jar, seashell

mixed review • test preparation

2,623 + 845 **3,468**	**2** 983 − 217 **766**	**3** 286 × 419 **119,834**	**4** 17,600 × 43 **756,800**
84 ÷ 6 **14**	**6** 184 ÷ 30 **6 R4**	**7** 288 ÷ 9 **32**	**8** 482 ÷ 70 **6 R62**

0. Possible answer: ValueFood; the cost of each orange at ValueFood is 8¢, while the cost at Shopfirst is 9¢.

xtra Practice, page 516

Alternate Teaching Strategy

Materials cereal box, number cube, ball, can, pictures of a pup tent and a pyramid, ice cream cone

Display the 3-dimensional objects and the pictures of 3-dimensional objects for students.

Begin by discussing the box, cube, pup tent, and pyramid, pointing out their similarities and differences. Then follow with the ice cream cone, can, and ball. Note that all the objects are 3-dimensional.

Tell students the name of each of the objects and demonstrate the meanings of face, edge, and vertex. Have students use these words to point out the number of faces, edges, and vertices of the 3-dimensional figures you have shown.

Then have students name examples of each 3-dimensional figure they have been shown as you list them on the chalkboard.

PRACTICE • 77

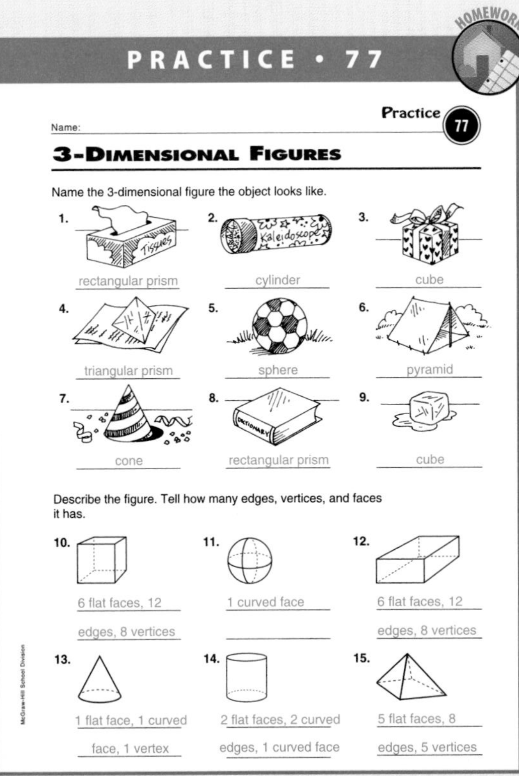

Practice 77

Name:

3-Dimensional Figures

Name the 3-dimensional figure the object looks like.

1. rectangular prism
2. cylinder
3. cube
4. triangular prism
5. sphere
6. pyramid
7. cone
8. rectangular prism
9. cube

Describe the figure. Tell how many edges, vertices, and faces it has.

10. 6 flat faces, 12 edges, 8 vertices
11. 1 curved face
12. 6 flat faces, 12 edges, 8 vertices
13. 1 flat face, 1 curved face, 1 vertex
14. 2 flat faces, 2 curved edges, 1 curved face
15. 5 flat faces, 8 edges, 5 vertices

RETEACH • 77

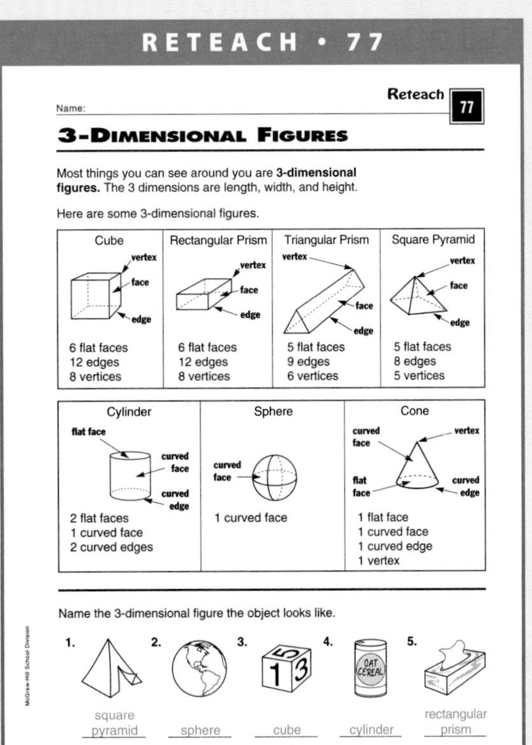

Reteach 77

Name:

3-Dimensional Figures

Most things you can see around you are **3-dimensional figures.** The 3 dimensions are length, width, and height.

Here are some 3-dimensional figures.

Cube	Rectangular Prism	Triangular Prism	Square Pyramid
6 flat faces 12 edges 8 vertices	6 flat faces 12 edges 8 vertices	5 flat faces 9 edges 6 vertices	5 flat faces 8 edges 5 vertices

Cylinder	Sphere	Cone
2 flat faces 1 curved face 2 curved edges	1 curved face	1 flat face 1 curved face 1 curved edge 1 vertex

Name the 3-dimensional figure the object looks like.

1. square pyramid
2. sphere
3. cube
4. cylinder
5. rectangular prism

EXTEND • 77

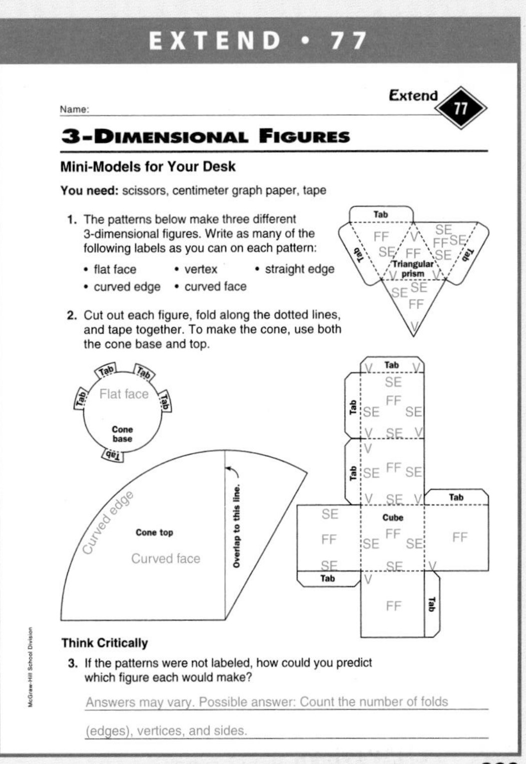

Extend 77

Name:

3-Dimensional Figures

Mini-Models for Your Desk

You need: scissors, centimeter graph paper, tape

1. The patterns below make three different 3-dimensional figures. Write as many of the following labels as you can on each pattern:
• flat face • vertex • straight edge
• curved edge • curved face

2. Cut out each figure, fold along the dotted lines, and tape together. To make the cone, use both the cone base and top.

Think Critically

3. If the patterns were not labeled, how could you predict which figure each would make?
Answers may vary. Possible answer: Count the number of folds (edges), vertices, and sides.

LESSON 9.2

2-Dimensional Figures and Polygons

OBJECTIVE Identify 2-dimensional figures and polygons.

RESOURCE REMINDER
Math Center Cards 78
Practice 78, Reteach 78, Extend 78

SKILLS TRACE	
GRADE 3	• Explore identifying and sorting 2-dimensional figures by their attributes. *(Chapter 10)*
GRADE 4	• Identify 2-dimensional figures and polygons.
GRADE 5	• Explore identifying plane figures as open or closed. *(Chapter 8)* • Explore identifying and classifying plane figures as polygons. *(Chapter 8)*

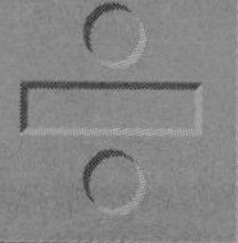

LESSON 9.2 RESOURCES

WARM-UP

Cooperative Pairs — Logical/Analytical

OBJECTIVE Review 3-dimensional and 2-dimensional figures.

▶ Have each pair list ten 3-dimensional objects and identify any 2-dimensional shapes they see in the objects. Remind students that 2-dimensional shapes have length and width but no depth or height.

▶ For example, tell students that their math book is a 3-dimensional object in the shape of a rectangular prism, but the front cover of their book is 2-dimensional in the shape of a rectangle.

▶ Have pairs of students share their lists.

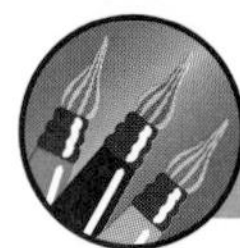

ART CONNECTION

Cooperative Pairs — Visual/Spatial

OBJECTIVE Connect 2-dimensional shapes to art.

Materials per pair: tangram shapes (TA 21), scissors, markers, glue

▶ Have students cut apart their tangram shapes and identify all the shapes—triangles, parallelogram, and square.

▶ Explore using the shapes to make other shapes, such as using two triangles to make a square. Then challenge students to make a dog using the shapes.

▶ Have pairs make animals of their own creation using the tangram pieces. When pairs come to an agreement, have them paste down their shapes, and color their animals. Display students' tangram animals.

ESL APPROPRIATE

Daily Review

PREVIOUS DAY QUICK REVIEW

Tell the number of vertices, edges, and faces each figure has.

1. triangular pyramid *[4, 6, 4]*
2. cube *[8, 12, 6]*
3. cone *[1, 1, 2]*
4. sphere *[none]*

FAST FACTS

1. 8 × 9 *[72]*
2. 6 × 9 *[54]*
3. 4 × 5 *[20]*
4. 7 × 8 *[56]*

Problem of the Day • 78

Tabitha earned $3.50 per hour helping Mrs. Longo with yard work. Tabitha worked four weeks for the following number of hours: 15 h, 8 h, 10 h, and 5 h. Make a line graph showing how much she earned each week. *[Check students' graphs.]*

TECH LINK

Math Van

MATH VAN

Tool You may wish to use the Geometry tool with this lesson.

MATH FORUM

Multi-Age Classes I let my older students who know about polygons help younger students distinguish between the various kinds of polygons, especially the quadrilaterals.

Visit our Resource Village at http://www.mhschool.com to see more of the Math Forum.

MATH CENTER

Practice

OBJECTIVE Identify and draw 2-dimensional figures.

Materials per pair: geoboard, rubber bands; per student: centimeter dot paper (TA 9), Math Center Recording Sheet (TA 31 optional)

Students construct models of polygons on a geoboard for each other to name and then make a different version of the same polygon. *[Check students' drawings.]*

PRACTICE ACTIVITY 78 — MATH CENTER — Partners

Manipulatives • Geo-"Mates"

- One partner makes a polygon on a geoboard.
- The other partner names the polygon and draws it on dot paper. Then that partner tries to make a different version of the same polygon. The sides may have different lengths. It may have a different look, as long as the number of sides is the same.
- Reverse roles and play again. Start with a new figure each time.

YOU NEED
- geoboard
- rubber bands
- centimeter dot paper

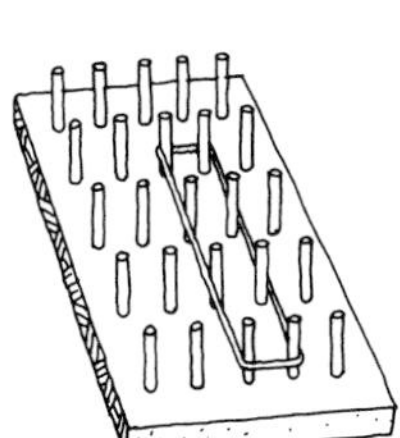

Grade Level 4 — McGraw-Hill School Division

Chapter 9, Lesson 2, pages 324–327 — Geometry

NCTM Standards
- ✓ Problem Solving
- ✓ Communication
- ✓ Reasoning
- Connections

Problem Solving

OBJECTIVE Construct polygons from other polygons.

Materials per student: pattern blocks (TA 17), Math Center Recording Sheet (TA 31 optional)

Students use three kinds of regular polygons to construct others. *[**1.** rhombus, trapezoid, hexagon; **2.** hexagon and parallelogram; **3.** parallelogram; **4.** hexagon]*

PROBLEM-SOLVING ACTIVITY 78 — MATH CENTER — On Your Own

Manipulatives • Polygon Puzzles

1. What figure can you make from two triangles? three triangles? six triangles?
2. What two figures can you make from two trapezoids?
3. What figure can you make from a trapezoid and a triangle?
4. What figure can you make from a trapezoid, a triangle, and a rhombus?

YOU NEED
- cutouts of the figures below or pattern blocks

Grade Level 4 — McGraw-Hill School Division

Chapter 9, Lesson 2, pages 324–327 — Geometry

NCTM Standards
- ✓ Problem Solving
- Communication
- ✓ Reasoning
- ✓ Connections

2-Dimensional Figures and Polygons

OBJECTIVE Identify 2-dimensional figures and polygons.

Vocabulary closed, decagon, heptagon, hexagon, kite, octagon, open, parallelogram, pentagon, polygon, quadrilateral, rectangle, rhombus, square, trapezoid, triangle

Give each group a 3-dimensional object shaped like a rectangular prism, a triangular prism, a cube, a cone, a square pyramid, or a triangular pyramid. Have groups name the shape of their object. Then ask them to describe each side of the shape.

Whole Class

LEARN Using the picture at the top of page 324, distinguish between 2- and 3-dimensional figures. Also use the picture to point out the difference between open and closed figures. Tell students that polygons are 2-dimensional closed figures with straight sides.

Have students draw examples of open and closed figures. Then have students draw 2-dimensional figures that are not polygons. Ask students to explain why they are not polygons.

Have students study the six polygons illustrated on page 324, and ask how the figures are alike. Students might suggest that some of the shape names end with *-gon.*

Talk It Over

READING ARITHMETIC WRITING

Categories Make a table on the chalkboard with headings 3, 4, 5, and so on. Have each student draw a polygon on a stick-on note. As you call out a number of corners, each student with a polygon with that number of corners places the stick-on note in the correct column.

Then ask students if they arrange the polygons by sides would they have to rearrange any of the stick-on notes. Students should see that there is no rearranging to be done.

2-Dimensional Figures and Polygons

LEARN

What 2-dimensional figures do you see when you look at these objects?

The sides of many 3-dimensional objects show 2-dimensional figures.

Note: A 2-dimensional figure has length and width only.

You can describe a 2-dimensional figure as **open** or **closed.**

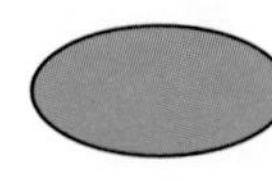

Closed figures

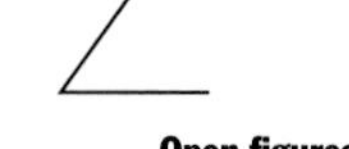

Open figures

Polygons are closed 2-dimensional figures made up of straight sides. A square is a polygon. A circle is not.

You can group polygons by the number of sides that they have.

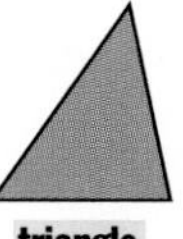

triangle
3 sides

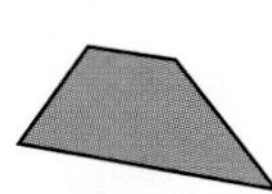

quadrilateral
4 sides

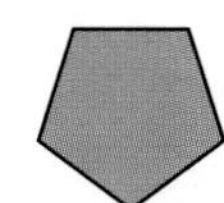

pentagon
5 sides

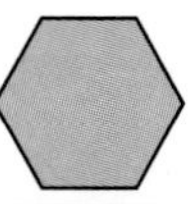

hexagon
6 sides

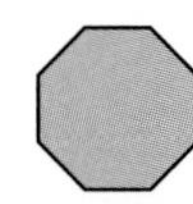

octagon
8 sides

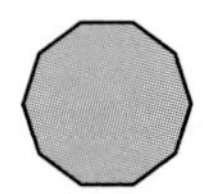

decagon
10 sides

Talk It Over

▶ **Categories** Do you think that you can group polygons by the number of corners that they have? Why or why not?

Yes; possible answer: polygons have equal numbers of sides and corners, so they can be grouped using either their sides or their corners.

Check Out the Glossar
For vocabulary words
See page 544.

Meeting Individual Needs

Extra Support

Have students make index cards showing each of the 2-dimensional figures with their respective names and descriptions on the backs of the cards to help students recall all of the figures.

Gifted And Talented

Have students use as many 2-dimensional figures as they can to make a drawing. Have them identify all the 2-dimensional figures they used and how many of each.

Ongoing Assessment

Observation Checklist Determine if students can identify polygons by showing them several polygons and an open figure. Ask them to name each. Students should recognize an open figure is not a polygon. Ask them to explain why.

Follow Up For more practice with 2-dimensional figures, have students draw a picture using just polygons and identify each of the shapes. Assign **Reteach 78.**

For students who need a challenge, assign **Extend 78.**

estion 1. Possible answer: They all have 4 sides and 4 corners; a square has all 4 corners equal and all sides equal, while a trapezoid does not.

You can group quadrilaterals by the length of their sides and the size of their corners.

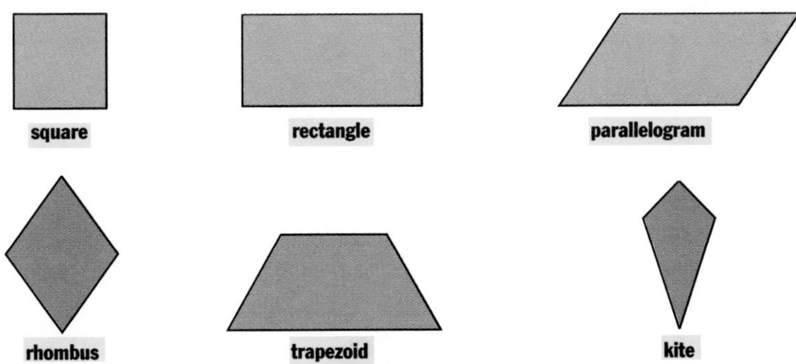

How are all quadrilaterals alike? How is a square different from a trapezoid? See above.

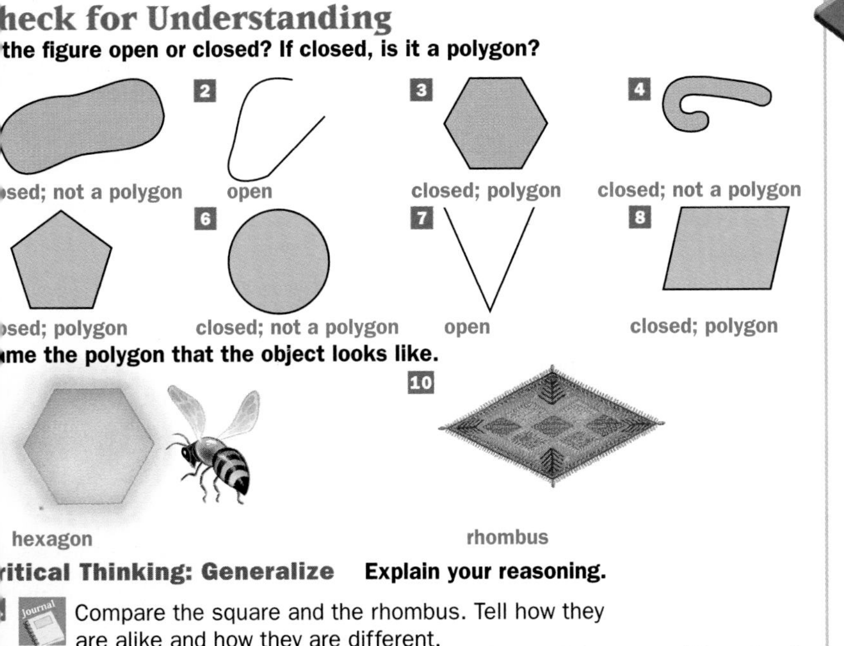

heck for Understanding

the figure open or closed? If closed, is it a polygon?

osed; not a polygon

2 open

3 closed; polygon

4 closed; not a polygon

osed; polygon

6 closed; not a polygon

7 open

8 closed; polygon

me the polygon that the object looks like.

hexagon

10 rhombus

ritical Thinking: Generalize **Explain your reasoning.**

Compare the square and the rhombus. Tell how they are alike and how they are different.

ssible answer: Alike—both have 4 equal straight sides and 4 corners; different—all e corners in a square are the same, while only the pairs of posite corners are the same in a rhombus.

Turn the page for Practice.

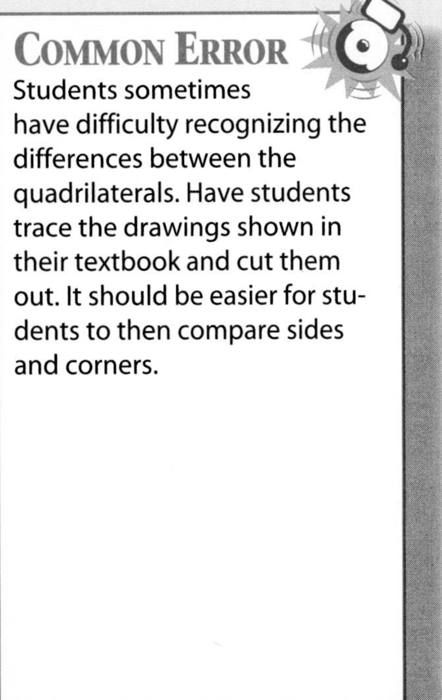

COMMON ERROR

Students sometimes have difficulty recognizing the differences between the quadrilaterals. Have students trace the drawings shown in their textbook and cut them out. It should be easier for students to then compare sides and corners.

Discuss the different kinds of quadrilaterals shown at the top of page 325. Have students describe each and tell the number of sides and corners. Write students' descriptions on the chalkboard. Lead students to make sure each description distinguishes one kind of quadrilateral from another.

3 Close

Check for Understanding using items 1–11, page 325.

Critical Thinking

For item 11, ask students to also compare the rectangle and the parallelogram. They should recognize that these figures have the same similarities and differences as the square and the rhombus.

Practice See pages 326–327.

PRACTICE

Materials have available: calculators

Options for assigning exercises:
A—Ex. 1–25; choice of two from ex. 26–30; **Cultural Connection**
B—Ex. 1–11; even ex. 12–30; **Cultural Connection**

- For ex. 9–11, have students name each polygon.
- For ex. 12–17, tell students to name the type of quadrilateral shown whenever possible.
- For ex. 26, students can use the problem-solving strategy of Drawing a Picture.
- For ex. 30, some students may need to review the meaning of perimeter.

Cultural Connection After reading the **Cultural Connection** on page 327, have students describe the types of kites they have flown or seen flown. After answering the question in the text, ask students to draw the shape of a kite they have flown or seen. Have them identify any polygons and any similar or congruent figures in their drawings.

24. Check that students draw a figure with 7 sides using the measurements for the given 6 sides. The length of the seventh side may vary.

Practice

Tell if the figure is open or closed.

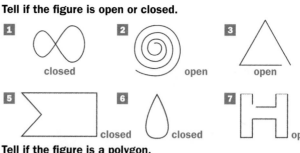

1 closed
2 open

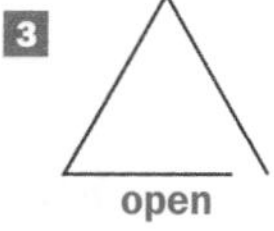

3 open

4 closed

5 closed
6 closed

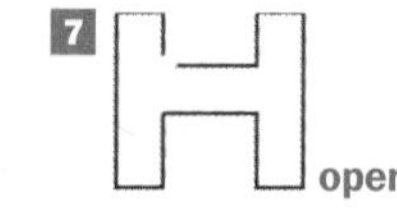

7 open

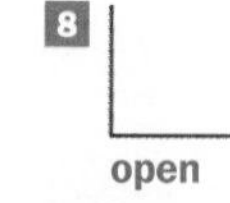

8 open

Tell if the figure is a polygon.

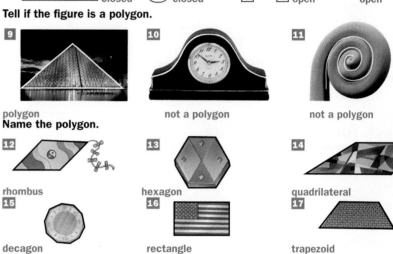

9 polygon

10 not a polygon

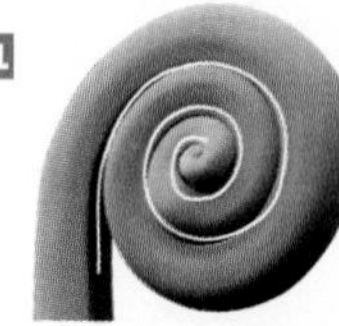

11 not a polygon

Name the polygon.

12 rhombus

13 hexagon

14 quadrilateral

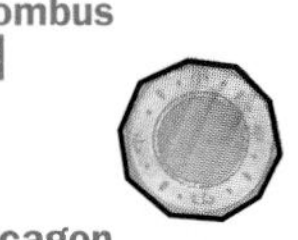

15 decagon

16 rectangle

17 trapezoid

18 a quadrilateral with all sides equal in length **rhombus or square**

19 a polygon with 10 sides **decagon**

Draw the figure and name it. Check students' drawings.

20 a 4-sided polygon **quadrilateral**

21 a 3-sided polygon **triangle**

22 a 6-sided polygon **hexagon**

23 a 5-sided polygon **pentagon**

24 A **heptagon** is a polygon with 7 sides. Draw one that has the following measurements for 6 of its sides: 3 cm, 5 cm, 7 cm, 7 cm, 9 cm, and 11 cm. **See above.**

25 Draw a pentagon and label the sides to show a perimeter of 25 cm. **Students may draw and label a pentagon with 5 cm sides.**

Check Out the Glossar
heptagon
See page 544.

Meeting Individual Needs

Early Finishers

Working in pairs, have each student draw "footprints" of any 3-dimensional figure and exchange with their partner. Each partner names the 3-dimensional shape based on the "footprints."

Inclusion

For the visually-impaired student, cut out models of each of the polygons discussed in this lesson. Label each polygon with its name in Braille.

MIXED APPLICATIONS

Problem Solving

6 Marla used toothpicks to make the following: 3 triangles, 4 pentagons, 5 quadrilaterals, and 6 octagons. How many toothpicks did she need? **97 toothpicks**

8 **Logical reasoning** Use a table like the one at the right to help you find the shape. **parallelogram**
Clue 1: I have four sides.
Clue 2: My sides are not equal lengths.
Clue 3: My opposite sides are equal.

9 **Write a problem** similar to problem 27 for a shape other than a square. Solve it. Then have others solve it. **Students should compare problems and solutions.**

Possible answers: cube, rectangular prism, square pyramid

27 **Spatial reasoning** When you look at the bottom of a 3-dimensional figure, you see a square. What figure could you be looking at?

	Clue 1	Clue 2	Clue 3
Square	Y	N	N
Circle	N	N	N
Parallelogram	Y	Y	Y
Rhombus	Y	Y	N
Trapezoid	Y	Y	N

30 Each side of a hexagon measures 6 cm. What is the perimeter of the hexagon? **36 cm**

Cultural Connection

Kites from Different Cultures

he first kites were built over 3,000 years ago in China. These kites had bamboo pipes attached to hem. The pipes made loud whistling sounds when he kites were flown. The Chinese used these kites n battle to frighten their enemies.

n Japan, there are kites that are larger than umans. They are flown in a festival that has een celebrated for over 400 years.

Modern kites are flown for fun by adults and hildren around the world.

- Name the shapes you see in the kite shown. **hexagon, triangle, rhombus, trapezoid**

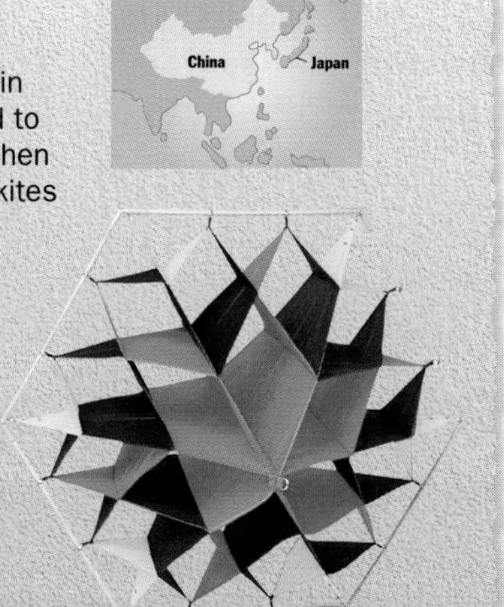

xtra Practice, page 516

Alternate Teaching Strategy

Materials per student: straws, clay, scissors

Tell students that a polygon is a closed 2-dimensional figure made up of straight sides. Demonstrate a non-polygon by showing an open figure and one with a curved side. Note that polygons are named by the number of sides—triangle (3 sides), quadrilateral (4 sides), and pentagon (5 sides).

List *square, rectangle, parallelogram, rhombus, trapezoid,* and *kite* on the chalkboard. Describe each quadrilateral using sides and angles.

Show students how to make a model of any polygon such as a hexagon using the straws and clay to hold the vertices together. Then have students make any polygon of their choice to share with the class.

ESL APPROPRIATE

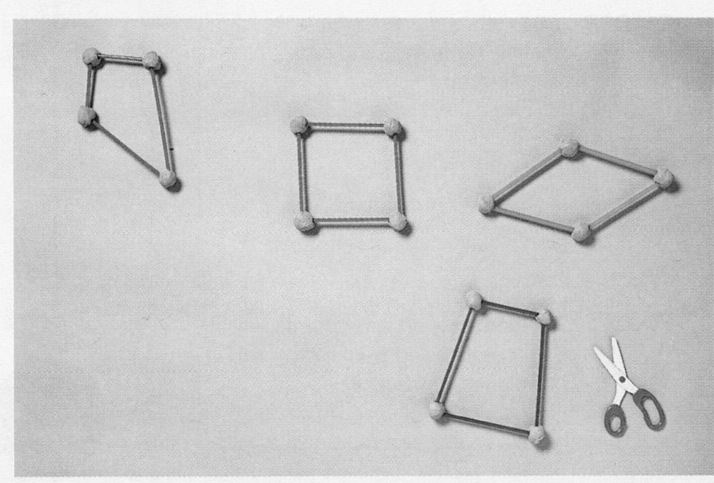

PRACTICE • 78

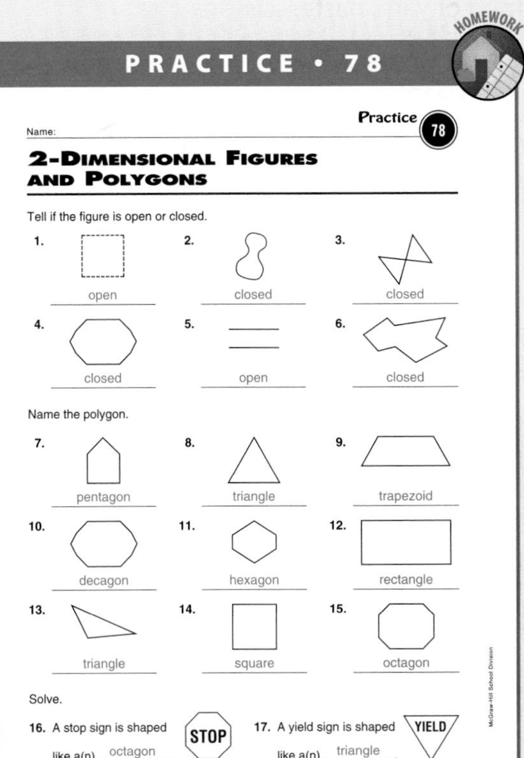

Practice 78

Name:

2-DIMENSIONAL FIGURES AND POLYGONS

Tell if the figure is open or closed.

1. open
2. closed
3. closed
4. closed
5. open
6. closed

Name the polygon.

7. pentagon
8. triangle
9. trapezoid
10. decagon
11. hexagon
12. rectangle
13. triangle
14. square
15. octagon

Solve.

16. A stop sign is shaped like a(n) octagon.
17. A yield sign is shaped like a(n) triangle.

RETEACH • 78

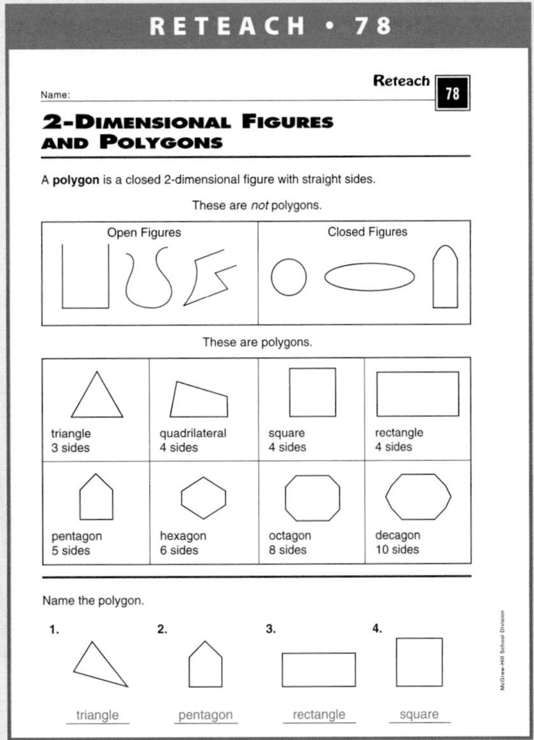

Reteach 78

Name:

2-DIMENSIONAL FIGURES AND POLYGONS

A **polygon** is a closed 2-dimensional figure with straight sides.

These are *not* polygons.

Open Figures	Closed Figures

These are polygons.

triangle 3 sides	quadrilateral 4 sides	square 4 sides	rectangle 4 sides
pentagon 5 sides	hexagon 6 sides	octagon 8 sides	decagon 10 sides

Name the polygon.

1. triangle
2. pentagon
3. rectangle
4. square

EXTEND • 78

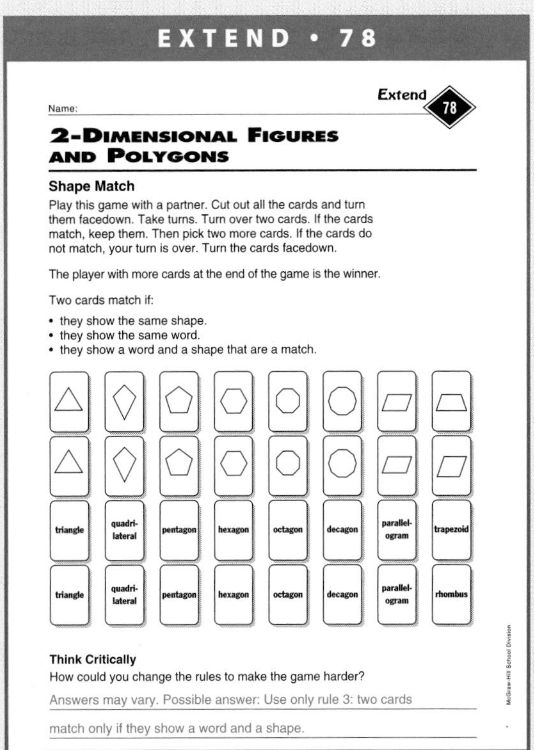

Extend 78

Name:

2-DIMENSIONAL FIGURES AND POLYGONS

Shape Match

Play this game with a partner. Cut out all the cards and turn them facedown. Take turns. Turn over two cards. If the cards match, keep them. Then pick two more cards. If the cards do not match, your turn is over. Turn the cards facedown.

The player with more cards at the end of the game is the winner.

Two cards match if:
- they show the same shape.
- they show the same word.
- they show a word and a shape that are a match.

triangle	quadrilateral	pentagon	hexagon	octagon	decagon	parallelogram	trapezoid
triangle	quadrilateral	pentagon	hexagon	octagon	decagon	parallelogram	rhombus

Think Critically

How could you change the rules to make the game harder?

Answers may vary. Possible answer: Use only rule 3: two cards match only if they show a word and a shape.

EXPLORE ACTIVITY

Line Segments, Lines, and Rays

OBJECTIVE Explore identifying lines, line segments, rays, and line relationships.

RESOURCE REMINDER
Math Center Cards 79
Practice 79, Reteach 79, Extend 79

SKILLS TRACE	
GRADE 3	• Explore identifying lines, line segments, and rays. *(Chapter 10)*
GRADE 4	• Identify lines, line segments, rays, and line relationships.
GRADE 5	• Identify and name points, lines, line segments, rays, and planes. *(Chapter 8)*

LESSON 9.3 RESOURCES

MANIPULATIVE WARM-UP

Cooperative Groups — Visual/Spatial

OBJECTIVE Review 2-dimensional figures.

Materials per group: colored paper, scissors

▶ Have groups make a number of each of the several kinds of 2-dimensional figures and cut them out of the colored paper. Have each student in the group take turns sorting the shapes into categories of his or her own choosing, such as all red 4-sided figures. Be sure students record their results after each turn.

▶ As an extension, have one student make a pattern with the figures and have group members describe the pattern.

ART CONNECTION

Cooperative Pairs — Kinesthetic

OBJECTIVE Connect line segments and student artwork.

Materials per pair: colored paper, string or yarn, paste, scissors

▶ Have partners work together to make their own string art design by gluing line segments of string or yarn to colored paper.

▶ Remind students that a line is always straight and never curved. Suggest that students try to make the line segments (string or yarn) intersect in various ways.

▶ When pairs have finished their artwork, have them share their string art with the rest of the class. Then ask students to point out similarities and differences between the examples of string art.

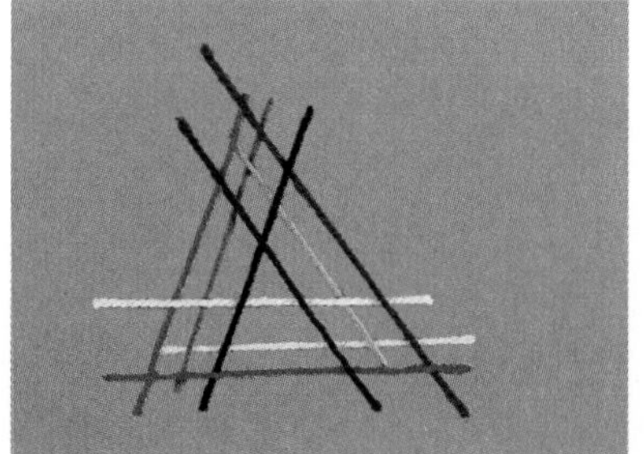

Daily Review

PREVIOUS DAY QUICK REVIEW

Name the polygon with:

1. five sides *[pentagon]*
2. three sides *[triangle]*
3. six sides *[hexagon]*
4. eight sides *[octagon]*

FAST FACTS

1. 54 ÷ 6 *[9]*
2. 72 ÷ 8 *[9]*
3. 81 ÷ 9 *[9]*
4. 56 ÷ 8 *[7]*

Problem of the Day • 79

The fourth-grade class of Holman Middle School is going on a field trip. Each student may bring up to two guests. Fifty-nine students signed up for the trip. What are the least and greatest number of buses they will need if one bus holds 60 people? *[1 bus for 59 people and 3 buses for 177 people]*

TECH LINK

Math Van

MATH VAN

Tool You may wish to use the Geometry tool with this lesson.

MATH FORUM

Management Tip I keep dot paper, paste, colored paper, yarn, and string on a shelf in the classroom so students have ready access to the materials they need to draw and construct geometric figures.

Visit our Resource Village at http://www.mhschool.com to see more of the Math Forum.

MATH CENTER

Practice

OBJECTIVE Identify lines, line segments, and rays.

Materials per student: graph paper, ruler, Math Center Recording Sheet (TA 31 optional)

Students use a diagram made from perpendicular, parallel, and intersecting line segments to answer questions. Then they draw their own figure and write questions for it. *[**1.** Line segment DC; or line segments AB and AF; **2.** Line segments DG and AF; **3.** Line segments FE, EH, AB, CH and BC; **4.** Line segments AF, FE, DG, and GH. Check students' figures and questions.]*

PRACTICE ACTIVITY 79 — MATH CENTER, On Your Own

Spatial Sense • Seeing Segments

YOU NEED: graph paper, ruler

- Use this figure to answer problems 1–4.
  1. Line segment *AD* is perpendicular to which line segments?
  2. Line segment *GD* is parallel to which line segments?
  3. Line segment *BE* intersects which line segments?
  4. Line segment *GF* is perpendicular to which line segments?
- Draw your own figure using parallel, intersecting, and perpendicular line segments. Label all the endpoints and write 4 questions about your figure for your classmates to answer.

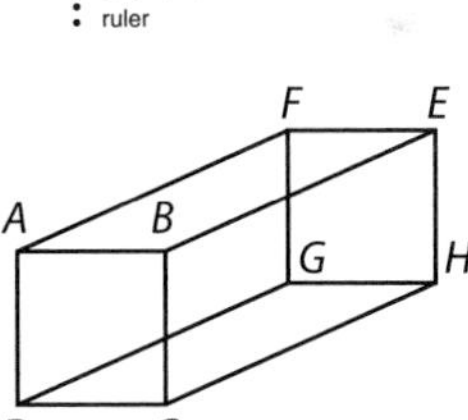

Chapter 9, Lesson 3, pages 328–329 — Geometry

NCTM Standards
✓ Problem Solving
✓ Communication
✓ Reasoning
Connections

Problem Solving

OBJECTIVE Use line segments in problem solving.

Materials per student: cup, ruler, Math Center Recording Sheet (TA 31 optional)

Students look for a pattern as they cut a circle with an ever increasing number of line segments and look to see how many pieces they can create. *[There is a pattern. Each cut after the second cut creates an additional number of pieces equal to the number of the cut: 1 cut = 2 pieces, 2 cuts = 4 pieces, 3 cuts = 7 pieces, 4 cuts = 11 pieces, 5 cuts = 16 pieces, 6 cuts = 22 pieces]*

PROBLEM-SOLVING ACTIVITY 79 — MATH CENTER, Partners

Formulating Problems • Slice It Up

YOU NEED: cup for tracing circles, ruler

- If you cut a pancake with one straight line you get 2 pieces of pancake.
- If you cut a pancake with two straight lines that intersect at one point, you get 4 pieces of pancake.
- If you cut a pancake with three straight lines that do not intersect at the same point, you get 7 cuts.
- How many pieces do you get with 4, 5, and 6 cuts if none of the cuts intersect at the same points? Is there a pattern?

Chapter 9, Lesson 3, pages 328–329 — Geometry

NCTM Standards
✓ Problem Solving
✓ Communication
✓ Reasoning
Connections

EXPLORE ACTIVITY
Line Segments, Lines, and Rays

OBJECTIVE Explore identifying lines, line segments, rays, and line relationships.

Vocabulary endpoint, intersecting, line, line segment, parallel, perpendicular, ray

1 Introduce

Ask students to name different types of artists such as painters and sculptors. Then have students describe how they think these artists use geometric ideas in their work. Accept any reasonable answers.

2 Teach *Cooperative Pairs*

LEARN Use the differences students have pointed out in the picture at the top of page 328 to introduce each definition in the Student Book. For each term, have volunteers point out as many examples in the painting as they can find.

Work Together Have students refer to the definitions on page 328 to check and revise their descriptions of each other's sketches. Suggest that students make their sketches as clear as possible to help their partners describe them.

Talk It Over Have students share their discoveries or observations. Have them describe the ways their partners made their sketches easier to describe.

MAKE CONNECTIONS

Remind students that parallel lines do not meet and that perpendicular lines meet at square corners. Discuss why it is important to identify each line in the pair by name (letters).

3 Close

Check for Understanding using items 1–5, page 329.

CRITICAL THINKING
Remind students that a cube has square faces. For students who have difficulty visualizing item 5, have them use a number cube.

PRACTICE

Options for assigning exercises:
A—Ex. 1–6
B—Ex. 3–6

- In ex. 1–4, remind students to use the labels in the pictures to describe the parallel, perpendicular, and intersecting lines they see.
- For ex. 6, encourage students to think of as many examples as they can.

EXPLORE ACTIVITY • GEOMETRY

Line Segments, Lines, and Rays

LEARN

Artists use geometric ideas in their work.

"METROPOLITAN PORT," 1935–1939, JOSEPH STELLA, NATIONAL MUSEUM OF AMERICAN ART

A **line** is a straight figure that goes on forever in both directions.

A **ray** is another straight figure. It has one **endpoint** and goes on forever in just one direction.

A **line segment** is a straight figure with two endpoints.

Line segments that stay the same distance apart from each other are **parallel.**

Line segments that meet or cross each other are called **intersecting** line segments.

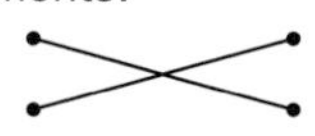

Intersecting line segments that form square corners are **perpendicular** to each other.

Work Together
Work with a partner to sketch your own designs.

Without showing your partner, sketch a design using the geometric figures above. Then exchange sketches.

Describe your partner's sketch using the words *line*, *ray*, *line segment*, *parallel*, *intersecting*, and *perpendicular*.

Talk It Over
- What could your partner have added to the sketch to make it easier to describe? **Possible answers: Made each figure a different color, placed labels on the figures.**

Check Out the Glossary
For vocabulary words
See page 544.

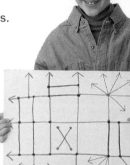

Meeting Individual Needs

Early Finishers

Have students use the notation to describe the line relationships in the following figure.

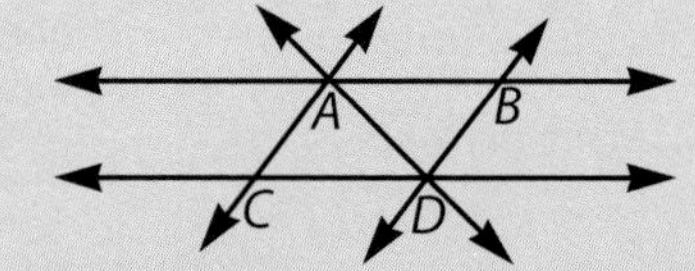

Extra Support

Have students draw each figure from page 328 on an index card, and write a description on the back of each to help the students remember the figures.

Ongoing Assessment

Anecdotal Report Make notes on students' abilities to recognize types of lines and line relationships in sketches and in real-world examples.

Follow Up If students need more practice with lines, have them draw the examples they named in ex. 6. Assign **Reteach 79.**

For students who understand lines, line segments, and rays, assign **Extend 79.**

ake Connections

metimes it is easier to describe geometric figures hey are labeled.

ne segment *AB* is parallel to line segment *CD*.

ne *HJ* is perpendicular to line segment *AB*.

y *EG* intersects line *LH*.

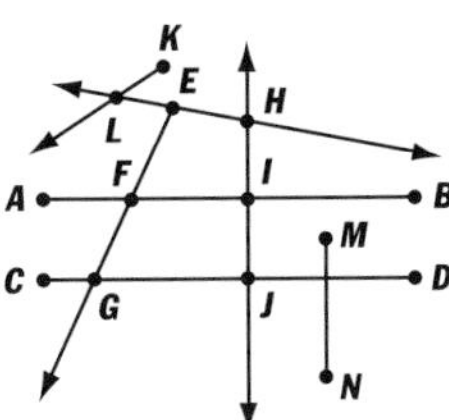

heck for Understanding

e the figures above for ex. 1–4. **Possible answers are given.**

List three line segments. **line segments *AB*, *CD*, *MN***

2 List two rays. **rays *EG*, *KL***

List two intersecting line segments. Are they perpendicular? Explain.

4 Are there any parallel lines? **There are no parallel lines.**

e segments *CD* and *MN*; yes; they meet to form square corners.

itical Thinking: Generalize **Explain your reasoning.**

Explain why you agree or disagree with each statement.

a. The opposite faces of a cube are perpendicular.

b. The corner of a cube is formed by three perpendicular faces.

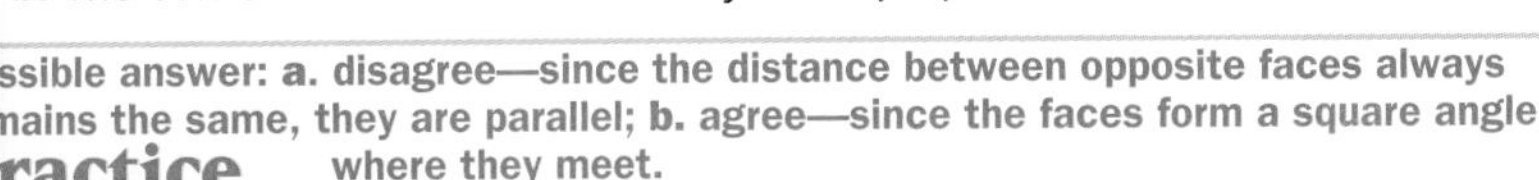

ssible answer: a. disagree—since the distance between opposite faces always mains the same, they are parallel; b. agree—since the faces form a square angle where they meet.

ractice

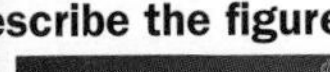

scribe the figure.

parallel line segments *KL* and *MN*

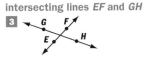

2 **line segment *AB***

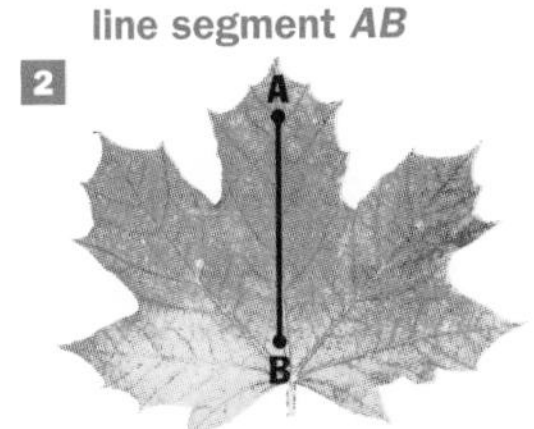

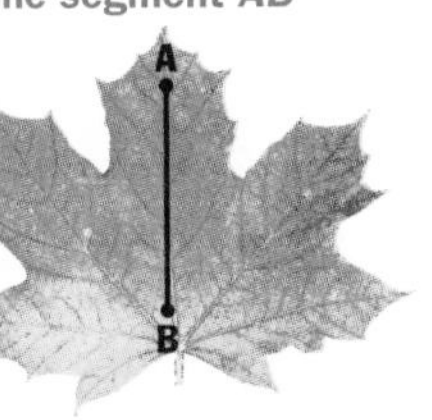

3 **intersecting lines *EF* and *GH***

4 **ray *CD***

Sketch some polygons. Describe them using the terms *line segment*, *parallel lines*, and *intersecting lines*. **Possible answer: A trapezoid has 2 sides that are parallel and is made up of 4 line segments.**

6 The horizon is a real-world example of a line. List a real-world example of a *line segment*, *parallel lines*, and *intersecting lines*. **Possible answer: line segment—edge of a book; parallel lines—edges of a box; intersecting lines—tree branches**

tra Practice, page 516

Alternate Teaching Strategy

Draw a line on the chalkboard. Tell students that a line goes on forever in opposite directions and that it has no endpoints.

Explain to students that part of a line with one endpoint is called a ray. Ask students why the light from the sun is considered a ray. Students should conclude that the ray of light has one end point at the sun.

Explain to students that a part of a line with two endpoints is called a line segment. Ask students if the edge of the chalkboard is a line, a ray, or a line segment. Students should conclude that this is part of a line that has two endpoints.

Ask students to consider all the possible ways two lines could intersect or not intersect. Have volunteers draw pairs of lines to show the possibilities. Use their drawings to introduce parallel, perpendicular, and intersecting lines.

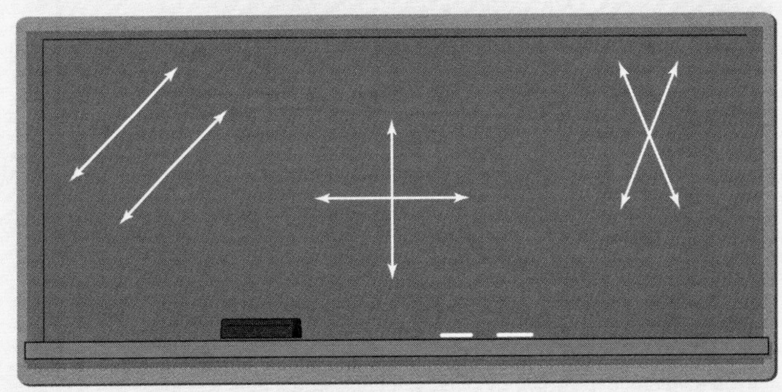

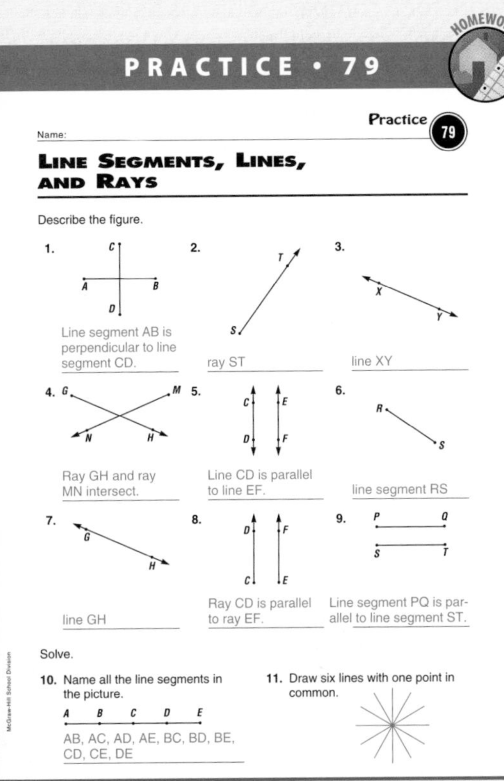

PRACTICE • 79

Practice 79

Name:

LINE SEGMENTS, LINES, AND RAYS

Describe the figure.

1. Line segment AB is perpendicular to line segment CD.
2. ray ST
3. line XY
4. Ray GH and ray MN intersect.
5. Line CD is parallel to line EF.
6. line segment RS
7. line GH
8. Ray CD is parallel to ray EF.
9. Line segment PQ is parallel to line segment ST.

Solve.

10. Name all the line segments in the picture. AB, AC, AD, AE, BC, BD, BE, CD, CE, DE
11. Draw six lines with one point in common.

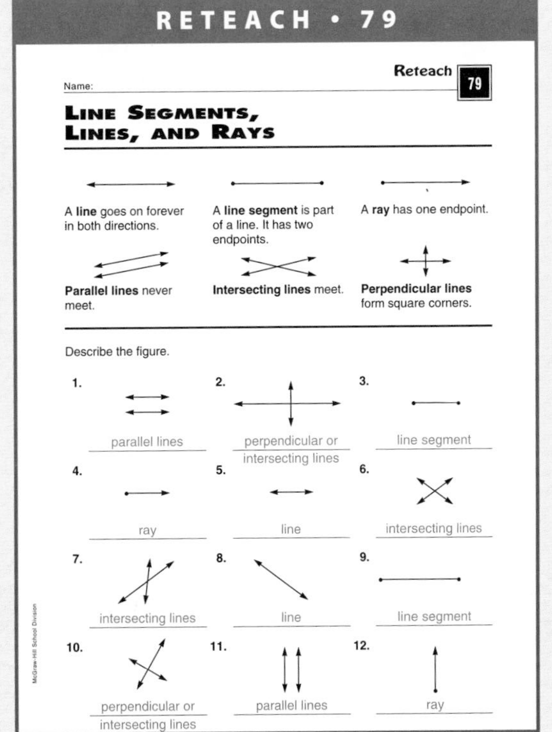

RETEACH • 79

Reteach 79

Name:

LINE SEGMENTS, LINES, AND RAYS

A **line** goes on forever in both directions.

A **line segment** is part of a line. It has two endpoints.

A **ray** has one endpoint.

Parallel lines never meet.

Intersecting lines meet.

Perpendicular lines form square corners.

Describe the figure.

1. parallel lines
2. perpendicular or intersecting lines
3. line segment
4. ray
5. line
6. intersecting lines
7. intersecting lines
8. line
9. line segment
10. perpendicular or intersecting lines
11. parallel lines
12. ray

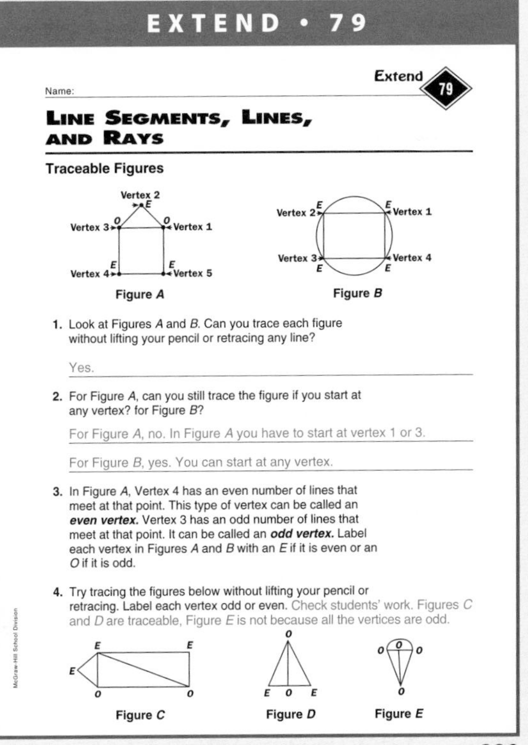

EXTEND • 79

Extend 79

Name:

LINE SEGMENTS, LINES, AND RAYS

Traceable Figures

Figure A — Vertex 1, Vertex 2, Vertex 3, Vertex 4, Vertex 5

Figure B — Vertex 1, Vertex 2, Vertex 3, Vertex 4

1. Look at Figures *A* and *B*. Can you trace each figure without lifting your pencil or retracing any line? Yes.
2. For Figure *A*, can you still trace the figure if you start at any vertex? for Figure *B*? For Figure *A*, no. In Figure *A* you have to start at vertex 1 or 3. For Figure *B*, yes. You can start at any vertex.
3. In Figure *A*, Vertex 4 has an even number of lines that meet at that point. This type of vertex can be called an ***even vertex***. Vertex 3 has an odd number of lines that meet at that point. It can be called an ***odd vertex***. Label each vertex in Figures *A* and *B* with an *E* if it is even or an *O* if it is odd.
4. Try tracing the figures below without lifting your pencil or retracing. Label each vertex odd or even. Check students' work. Figures *C* and *D* are traceable, Figure *E* is not because all the vertices are odd.

Figure C   Figure D   Figure E

Problem-Solving Strategy: Make an Organized List

OBJECTIVE Solve problems by making an organized list.

RESOURCE REMINDER
Math Center Cards 80
Practice 80, Reteach 80, Extend 80

SKILLS TRACE

GRADE 3	• Solve problems by making an organized list. *(Chapter 7)*
GRADE 4	• Solve problems by making an organized list.
GRADE 5	• Solve problems by making an organized list. *(Chapter 9)*

LESSON 9.4 RESOURCES

MANIPULATIVE WARM-UP

Cooperative Pairs — Kinesthetic

OBJECTIVE Use play coins to find all possible solutions for a problem.

Materials per pair: play coins—quarters, dimes, nickels

▶ Tell students that trail mix in a snack machine costs 45¢. The machine takes quarters, dimes, and nickels. A flashing light on the machine indicates that at this time, the machine cannot give change; it can only take exact change.

▶ Have pairs of students use the play coins to find all the possible combinations of coins that would make the exact change they need to buy the trail mix. Have them record their results. *[1 quarter, 2 dimes; 1 quarter, 1 dime, 2 nickels; 1 quarter, 4 nickels; 1 dime, 7 nickels; 2 dimes, 5 nickels; 3 dimes, 3 nickels; 4 dimes, 1 nickel; 9 nickels]*

▶ Pairs can share their results with the class.

CONSUMER CONNECTION

Cooperative Groups — Logical/Analytical

OBJECTIVE Connect consumer buying and making an organized list.

▶ Ask students to imagine that they work for a company which is designing a grocery list that requires a consumer to simply check off the items they need.
- **How could the company arrange the list of food items?**

▶ Have the groups design a grocery list. If students have trouble getting started, ask them to think about the categories of grocery items such as breads, fresh vegetables, and so forth. Remind groups that the list cannot be too long or too complicated because then it would be too difficult to use.

▶ Compare the differences and similarities in the categories and design of the lists from the groups.

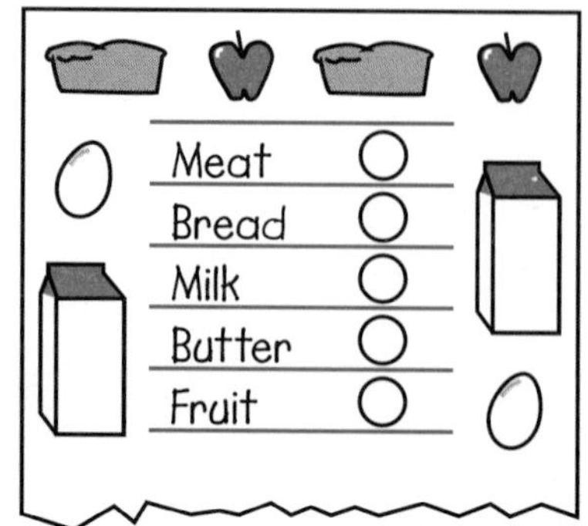

Daily Review

PREVIOUS DAY QUICK REVIEW

Draw each.

1. ray *AD*
2. parallel lines *AD* and *BC*
3. perpendicular line segments *XY* and *PQ* *[Check students' drawings.]*

FAST FACTS

1. 6×6 *[36]*
2. 8×9 *[72]*
3. 7×5 *[35]*
4. 3×8 *[24]*

Problem of the Day • 80

Wylan used 4 carnival tickets on food, 8 tickets on rides, and 6 tickets on games. If each ticket cost $0.75, how much money did Wylan spend? *[$13.50]*

TECH LINK

Math Van

MATH VAN

Tool You may wish to use the Geometry tool with this lesson.

MATH FORUM

Cultural Diversity I ask my students to write a problem based on a cultural tradition. This gives students an opportunity to share a little about their own cultures.

Visit our Resource Village at http://www.mhschool.com to see more of the Math Forum.

MATH CENTER

Practice

OBJECTIVE Complete a table to solve a problem.

Materials per student: Math Center Recording Sheet (TA 31 optional)

Students fill in a table to explore relationships between space figures. *[triangular pyramid—4 vertices, 6 edges, 4 faces; square pyramid—5 vertices, 8 edges, 5 faces; triangular prism—6 vertices, 9 edges, 5 faces; cube/rectangular prism—8 vertices, 12 edges, 6 faces; the edges and flat faces increase; a cube and rectangular prism are most alike.]*

PRACTICE ACTIVITY 80 — MATH CENTER, On Your Own

Logical Reasoning • 3-D Facts Table

- Look at these 3-dimensional figures. As the number of vertices increases, what happens to the number of edges? of faces? Which figures have the most in common?
- Copy the table below on a separate sheet of paper. Write the number of vertices, edges, and faces.

Space Figure	Vertices	Edges	Faces
triangular pyramid			
square pyramid			
triangular prism			
cube			
rectangular prism			

square pyramid
triangular pyramid
triangular prism
cube
rectangular prism

Grade Level 4 · McGraw-Hill School Division

Chapter 9, Lesson 4, pages 330–331 — Problem Solving

NCTM Standards
- ✓ Problem Solving
- ✓ Communication
- ✓ Reasoning
- Connections

Problem Solving

OBJECTIVE Make an organized list.

Materials per student: Math Center Recording Sheet (TA 31 optional)

Students look for all the possible ways they can seat four people at a table. Student lists should have the headings A, B, C, D and indicate which friend is at each lettered place. *[There are 24 possible arrangements.]*

PROBLEM-SOLVING ACTIVITY 80 — MATH CENTER, On Your Own

Patterning • Who Sits Where?

You are having four friends over for dinner. You have set the table for dinner.

- What if you are sitting at the head of the table? Using the names of 4 of your friends, make an organized list to show the different ways your dinner guests can be seated.

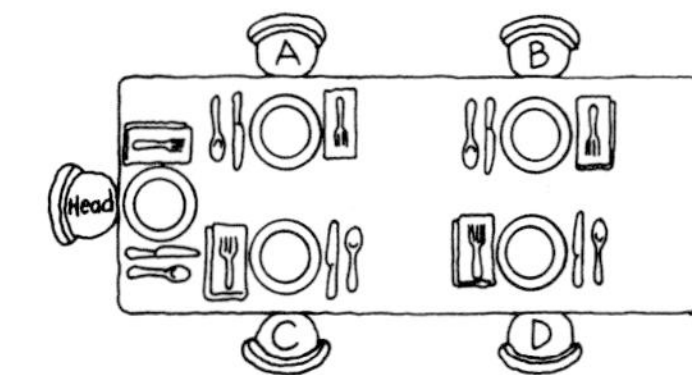

Grade Level 4 · McGraw-Hill School Division

Chapter 9, Lesson 4, pages 330–331 — Problem Solving

NCTM Standards
- ✓ Problem Solving
- ✓ Communication
- ✓ Reasoning
- Connections

Problem-Solving Strategy: Make an Organized List

OBJECTIVE Solve problems by making an organized list.

Vocabulary diagonal

1 Introduce

Ask students what *diagonal* means. Accept all reasonable answers. Have students use the word *diagonal* in a sentence and draw a picture of a diagonal.

2 Teach *Cooperative Pairs*

LEARN Review the names of polygons. Have volunteers draw examples of each on the chalkboard and tell the number of sides and corners each has.

Go over the **Read** and **Plan** sections as a class. Have students give definitions of the following: *line segment, diagonal, polygon,* and *octagon.* Have students work in pairs to complete the table and answer the question.

Discuss the table and the discoveries students made. Let students share the methods they used to determine the number of diagonals in an octagon.

Have students determine the number of diagonals in a polygon with 11 sides. *[44 diagonals in an 11-sided figure]*

3 Close

Check for Understanding using items 1–2, page 330.

CRITICAL THINKING
Ask students if they could organize the shapes by the number of corners. Students should recognize that they could because the number of sides and number of corners in any polygon are the same.

PRACTICE
Materials have available: calculators

Each student should choose seven exercises from ex. 1–11.

- In ex. 2, students can use the problem-solving strategy of Working Backward.
- In ex. 1, 5, and 6, students can use the problem-solving strategy of Making an Organized List.

Algebra: Patterns In ex. 5, students find a pattern to solve the word problem. Finding patterns in word problems encourages algebraic thinking skills.

Problem-Solving Strategy

Read | Plan | Solve | Look Back

Make an Organized List

PRACTICE

Read **Compare the number of sides and the number of diagonals of different polygons. How can you use this relationship to predict the number of diagonals in an octagon?**

A line segment that connects two vertices, but is not a side, is called a **diagonal.** In the string figure on the right, a diagonal connects vertex *A* to vertex *C* and another diagonal connects vertex *B* to vertex *D*.

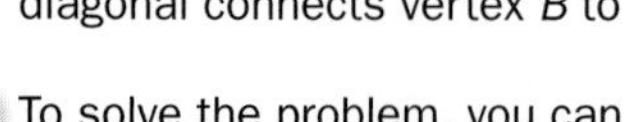

Plan To solve the problem, you can make a table to help you compare the numbers and to find a pattern.

Check Out the Glossary
diagonal
See page 544.

Solve Order the shapes in the table according to the number of sides. Look for a pattern.

Polygon	Number of Sides	Number of Diagonals
Quadrilateral	4	2
Pentagon	5	5
Hexagon	6	9
Heptagon	7	14

+ 3, + 4, + 5

An octagon has one more side than a heptagon, so the octagon has $14 + 6 = 20$ diagonals.

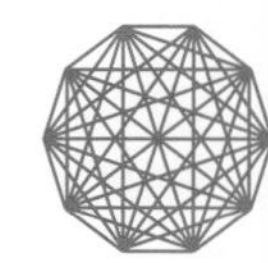
A decagon has 35 diagonals.

Look Back Can the pattern be used to predict the number of diagonals in other polygons? Show an example. **Yes; check students' work.**

CHECK

Check for Understanding

1. Alberto claims that a 12-sided polygon, or dodecagon, has 54 diagonals. Is he correct? How did he get this number without drawing the shape? **Yes; possible answer: he followed the pattern using the diagonals of an octagon to get $20 + 7 + 8 + 9 + 10 = 54$ diagonals.**

Critical Thinking: Summarize

2. Why is it a good idea to organize the shapes in the table according to the number of sides they have? **Possible answer: The number of sides is known, so it is easier to organize the list this way and then find a pattern.**

Meeting Individual Needs

Early Finishers

Have students make a geometric pattern. Have students share their patterns with other students.

Extra Support

Students will often make long lists to find a solution. While this eventually gives them the answer, encourage students to look for patterns in their lists before exhausting all of the possibilities.

Ongoing Assessment

Interview Determine if students understand how to make a list to solve a problem by asking them to describe how they solved ex. 5 on page 331.

Follow Up If students need more practice with making an organized list, assign **Reteach 80.**

If students need a greater challenge, assign **Extend 80.**

Start with 1 in the first week and write 2 more than the first week in the second week, 3 more than the second week in the third week, then 4 more than the third week in the fourth week.

MIXED APPLICATIONS

Problem Solving

The first day of camp is July 8th, which falls on a Monday. The last day of camp is July 31. What day is that? **Wednesday**

2 Melinda drew a polygon that had 27 diagonals. How many sides are in her polygon? **9 sides**

Make a decision You are visiting an amusement park. Use the list at the right. How would you spend 50 tickets at the park? **Students' answers should reflect the data provided.**

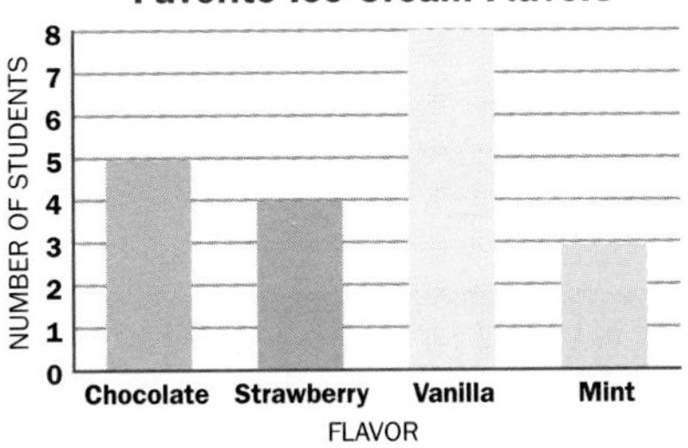

RIDES..............................4 TICKETS
TILT A WHIRL
FERRIS WHEEL
GAMES.............................5 TICKETS
BASKETBALL SHOOT
PONY RIDE
COIN TOSS
WATER RACE
FOOD/DRINK................3 TICKETS
COTTON CANDY
HOT DOGS
SODA

A student saved the same amount of money each week for 7 weeks. He saved a total of $84.00. How much money did he save each week? **$12.00**

ALGEBRA: PATTERNS Terry's goal is to write to at least 50 sports stars to ask for autographs. She wrote 1 letter the first week, 3 letters the second, 6 letters the third, and 10 letters the fourth week. What pattern is Terry following? **See above.**

6 Students are playing telephone. The first player gives a message to 2 other players. Each of these players gives the message to 2 other players. If each of these players then tells 3 more players, how many players will have given or heard the message? **19 players**

An African giant frog measures 31 in. with its legs outstretched. When it is sitting normally, it measures 14 in. How much more does it measure when its legs are outstretched? **17 in.**

8 **Write a problem** that describes a polygon and asks for its name. Ask others to solve your problem. If they cannot, ask them to suggest ways you can describe the polygon more clearly. **Students check each other's work by comparing questions and solutions.**

se the bar graph for problems 9–11.

How many students were surveyed? **20 students**

Which flavor was the favorite of 4 students? **strawberry**

How many more students prefer vanilla to chocolate ice cream? **3 students**

Favorite Ice Cream Flavors

NUMBER OF STUDENTS: 0 1 2 3 4 5 6 7 8

Chocolate Strawberry Vanilla Mint

FLAVOR

xtra Practice, page 517

PRACTICE

Alternate Teaching Strategy

Materials per student: dot paper (TA 7)

Have students draw a quadrilateral, pentagon, hexagon, and heptagon on the dot paper. Then have them draw the diagonals in each. Tell students that a diagonal is a line segment connecting two vertices but it is not a side.

Then have students tell the number of diagonals for each polygon as you record the results in a table on the chalkboard. Students should have 2 diagonals for the quadrilateral, 5 for the pentagon, 9 for the hexagon, and 14 for the heptagon.

Have students look for a pattern to predict the number of diagonals in an octagon. *[Possible answer: The pentagon has 3 more diagonals than the quadrilateral, the hexagon has 4 more diagonals than the pentagon, the heptagon has 5 more diagonals than the hexagon, so the octagon will have 6 more diagonals than the heptagon. The octagon will have 6 + 14 = 20 diagonals.]*

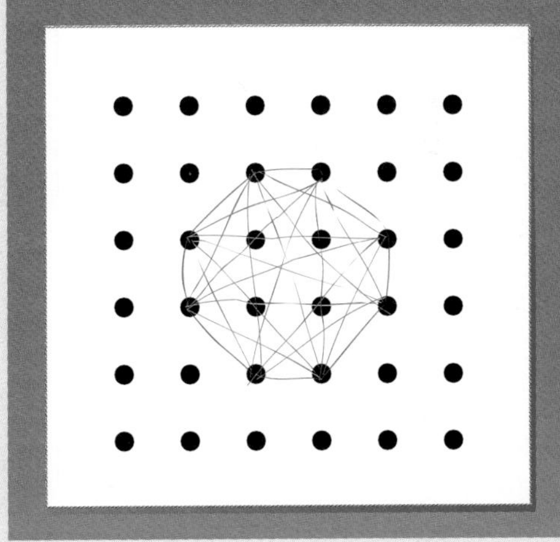

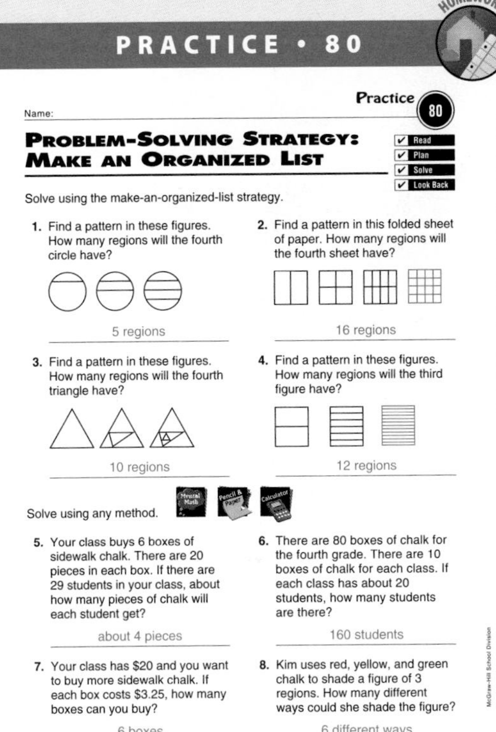

PRACTICE • 80

HOMEWORK

Practice 80

Name:

PROBLEM-SOLVING STRATEGY: MAKE AN ORGANIZED LIST

✔ Read ✔ Plan ✔ Solve ✔ Look Back

Solve using the make-an-organized-list strategy.

1. Find a pattern in these figures. How many regions will the fourth circle have? 5 regions
2. Find a pattern in this folded sheet of paper. How many regions will the fourth sheet have? 16 regions
3. Find a pattern in these figures. How many regions will the fourth triangle have? 10 regions
4. Find a pattern in these figures. How many regions will the third figure have? 12 regions

Solve using any method. (Mental Math, Pencil & Paper, Calculator)

5. Your class buys 6 boxes of sidewalk chalk. There are 20 pieces in each box. If there are 29 students in your class, about how many pieces of chalk will each student get? about 4 pieces
6. There are 80 boxes of chalk for the fourth grade. There are 10 boxes of chalk for each class. If each class has about 20 students, how many students are there? 160 students
7. Your class has $20 and you want to buy more sidewalk chalk. If each box costs $3.25, how many boxes can you buy? 6 boxes
8. Kim uses red, yellow, and green chalk to shade a figure of 3 regions. How many different ways could she shade the figure? 6 different ways

McGraw-Hill School Division

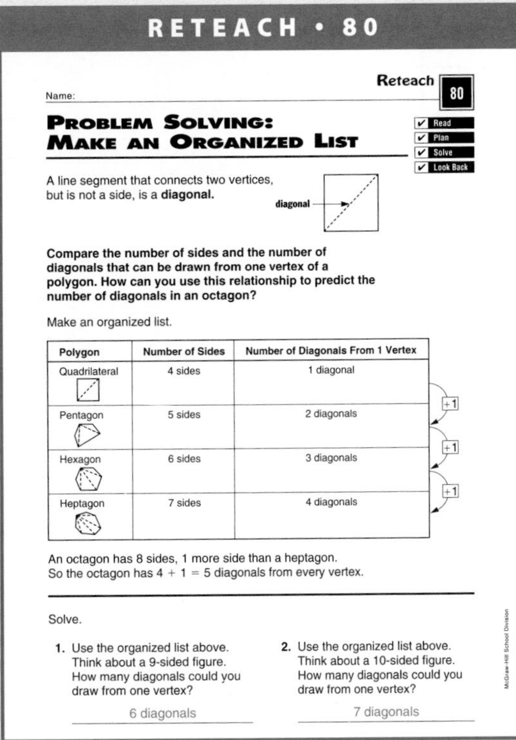

RETEACH • 80

Reteach 80

Name:

PROBLEM SOLVING: MAKE AN ORGANIZED LIST

✔ Read ✔ Plan ✔ Solve ✔ Look Back

A line segment that connects two vertices, but is not a side, is a **diagonal.**

diagonal

Compare the number of sides and the number of diagonals that can be drawn from one vertex of a polygon. How can you use this relationship to predict the number of diagonals in an octagon?

Make an organized list.

Polygon	Number of Sides	Number of Diagonals From 1 Vertex
Quadrilateral	4 sides	1 diagonal
Pentagon	5 sides	2 diagonals
Hexagon	6 sides	3 diagonals
Heptagon	7 sides	4 diagonals

+1 +1 +1

An octagon has 8 sides, 1 more side than a heptagon. So the octagon has 4 + 1 = 5 diagonals from every vertex.

Solve.

1. Use the organized list above. Think about a 9-sided figure. How many diagonals could you draw from one vertex? 6 diagonals
2. Use the organized list above. Think about a 10-sided figure. How many diagonals could you draw from one vertex? 7 diagonals

McGraw-Hill School Division

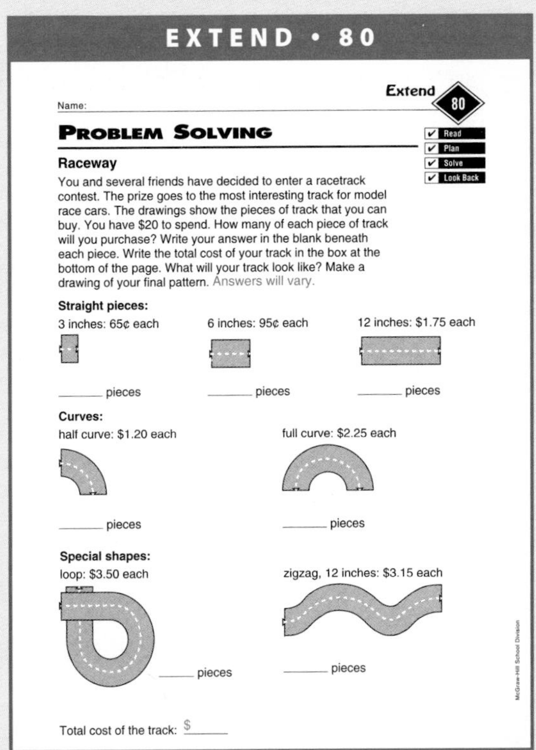

EXTEND • 80

Extend 80

Name:

PROBLEM SOLVING

✔ Read ✔ Plan ✔ Solve ✔ Look Back

Raceway

You and several friends have decided to enter a racetrack contest. The prize goes to the most interesting track for model race cars. The drawings show the pieces of track that you can buy. You have $20 to spend. How many of each piece of track will you purchase? Write your answer in the blank beneath each piece. Write the total cost of your track in the box at the bottom of the page. What will your track look like? Make a drawing of your final pattern. Answers will vary.

Straight pieces:

3 inches: 65¢ each ______ pieces

6 inches: 95¢ each ______ pieces

12 inches: $1.75 each ______ pieces

Curves:

half curve: $1.20 each ______ pieces

full curve: $2.25 each ______ pieces

Special shapes:

loop: $3.50 each ______ pieces

zigzag, 12 inches: $3.15 each ______ pieces

Total cost of the track: $______

McGraw-Hill School Division

LESSON 9.5 RESOURCES

EXPLORE ACTIVITY

Angles

OBJECTIVE Explore identifying and classifying angles.

RESOURCE REMINDER

Math Center Cards 81
Practice 81, Reteach 81, Extend 81

SKILLS TRACE	
GRADE 3	• Explore identifying angles. *(Chapter 10)*
GRADE 4	• Explore identifying angles and classifying triangles.
GRADE 5	• Identify an angle and its parts. • Explore classifying triangles by the length of the sides and by the measure of the angles. *(Chapter 8)*

MANIPULATIVE WARM-UP

Cooperative Pairs — **Logical/Analytical**

OBJECTIVE Review lines, line segments, and rays.

Materials per pair: 12 index cards

▶ Each pair makes two sets of cards—one set of 6 cards with the names listed below, and one set of 6 cards with drawings that correspond to the names:

line, line segment, ray, intersecting lines that are not perpendicular, perpendicular lines, and parallel lines

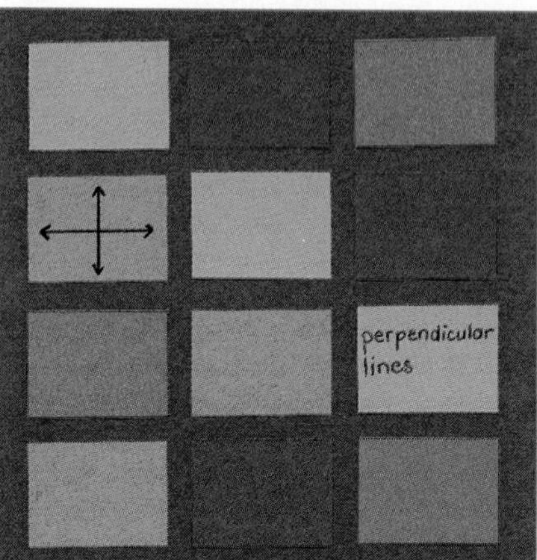

▶ Partners mix the cards and place them facedown in an array. They then take turns picking pairs of cards. If the cards match, the player keeps them. If not, the player returns them facedown to the array.

▶ Play continues until all of the cards are matched.

LITERATURE CONNECTION

Whole Class — **Visual/Spatial**

OBJECTIVE Find angles formed in letters of the alphabet.

▶ Write the alphabet in block letters on the chalkboard.

▶ Students copy the letters. They then circle the letters that have angles and tell what kind of angle each angle in the letter is: acute, obtuse, or right.

▶ Have students compare their work.

Daily Review

PREVIOUS DAY QUICK REVIEW

Give the name of each.

1. a pair of lines that meet at square corners *[perpendicular]*
2. a straight figure with one endpoint *[ray]*

FAST FACTS

1. 42 ÷ 6 *[7]*
2. 64 ÷ 8 *[8]*
3. 56 ÷ 7 *[8]*
4. 36 ÷ 4 *[9]*

Problem of the Day • 81

Tell how many angles there are in the diagram shown. *[24]*

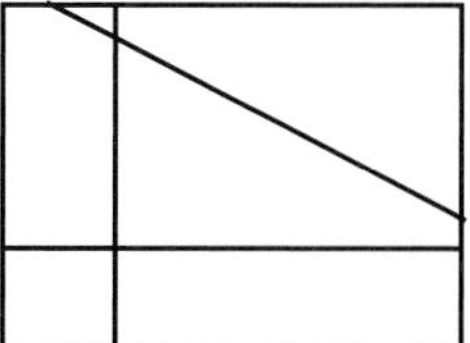

TECH LINK

MATH VAN

Tools You may wish to use the Geometry tool with this lesson.

MATH FORUM

Multi-Age Classes I have my older students help younger students learn to identify acute, obtuse, and right angles by making drawings of angles and have the younger students name the angles.

Visit our Resource Village at http://www.mhschool.com to see more of the Math Forum.

MATH CENTER

Practice

OBJECTIVE Identify acute and obtuse angles.

Materials per student: paper, ruler, Math Center Recording Sheet (TA 31 optional)

Students use a sheet of paper to determine if the angles in a figure are obtuse, acute, or right angles. Then they create a new 6-sided figure with obtuse, acute, and right angles. *[Students may name the angles using only the vertices. **1.** angles FED, AFE; **2.** angles ABC, CDE, FAB; **3.** angle BCD; Check students' drawings.]*

PRACTICE ACTIVITY 81 — MATH CENTER On Your Own

Manipulatives • Angle Sense

YOU NEED: sheet of paper, ruler

The corner of a sheet of paper is a right angle.

- Use a corner of a sheet of paper to identify the inner angles of this 6-sided figure. Name each angle by the letter nearest to it.
  1. Name the angles that are obtuse.
  2. Name the angles that are acute.
  3. Which angles are right angles?
- Make an 8-sided figure that has obtuse, acute, and right angles.

F E B A C D

Chapter 9, Lesson 5, pages 332–335 — Geometry

NCTM Standards
- ✓ Problem Solving
- ✓ Communication
- ✓ Reasoning
- Connections

Problem Solving

OBJECTIVE Explore angles in letters.

Materials per student: three different colors of markers, Math Center Recording Sheet (TA 31 optional)

Students identify angles in capital letters of the alphabet and answer questions based on them. *[A, E, F, H, I, K, L, M, N, T, V, W, X, Y, and Z are made only from line segments; yes, obtuse angles appear below the horizontal line segment in A as well as the side angles of K, X, and Y; E, F, H, L, T can be drawn with only right angles]*

PROBLEM-SOLVING ACTIVITY 81 — MATH CENTER On Your Own

Spatial Reasoning • Alphabet Angles

YOU NEED: two or three different-colored crayons or markers

- Write every capital letter that is made only of line segments; for example, K and L—but not O or D. Make each letter large. Look closely at the angles. Use one color of crayon or marker to shade in acute angles. Use another color to shade in the right angles. Will you need another color for the obtuse angles?
- Which letters can you make using only right angles?

Chapter 9, Lesson 5, pages 332–335 — Geometry

NCTM Standards
- ✓ Problem Solving
- ✓ Communication
- ✓ Reasoning
- ✓ Connections

EXPLORE ACTIVITY
Angles

OBJECTIVE Explore identifying and classifying angles.

Vocabulary acute angle, angle, obtuse angle, right angle

1 Introduce

Have students draw a stick figure of their hand and fingers. Tell students that you want them to draw only line segments to represent their fingers and a polygon to represent the palm of their hand.

Ask students to describe what they drew.

- **What shape did you use for your palm?** *[Answers may vary.]*
- **What did you draw for your fingers?** *[line segments]*

2 Teach *Cooperative Pairs*

LEARN Introduce your students to the term *angles*. Have them point out the angles in the drawings of their hands.

Ask a volunteer to read the definition of a right angle. Then have students check their drawings to see if they included any right angles.

Work Together Have students write *R* next to angles on their drawings that are right angles. If the angle is smaller than a right angle, have students write *SR*. If an angle is larger than a right angle, have students write *LR*.

Talk It Over As a class, have students share items from their drawings. Ask students how they decided whether an angle was smaller than or larger than a right angle. Some students may suggest that the size of an angle depends on how wide the sides are open.

Angles

LEARN

Maybe you noticed that if you draw intersecting line segments or rays, you create angles.

Check Out the Glossar
For vocabulary words
See page 544.

Angles are formed when two line segments or rays meet or cross.

You can find angles everywhere in nature.

A **right angle** is formed by perpendicular lines. A right angle forms a square.

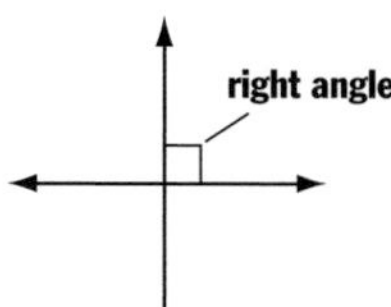

Artists, architects, and builders use a right angle as a measuring tool.

Work Together
Work with a partner to make a list of angles that you see in your classroom.

Use a corner of a sheet of paper, which is a right angle, as a paper tool.

Find angles in your classroom. Use your paper tool to compare them to right angles. Then choose categories to help you sort the angles.

Talk It Over
▶ What does the size of an angle depend on? **the distance between the rays or line segments**

Meeting Individual Needs

Extra Support

Have students use index cards to cut out an example of each kind of angle. Be sure students include the name and a brief description of each angle. They can use the cards to help them identify angles.

Ongoing Assessment

Anecdotal Report Make notes on whether students can tell if angles are smaller than or larger than a right angle, and whether they are able to use the terms acute and obtuse to describe these angles.

Follow Up For more practice with angles, have students write riddles describing an item in the classroom by its angles. Let students swap riddles and solve. Assign **Reteach 81.**

For students who can classify angles and name them, assign **Extend 81.**

ake Connections
ıgles that are not right angles also have special names.

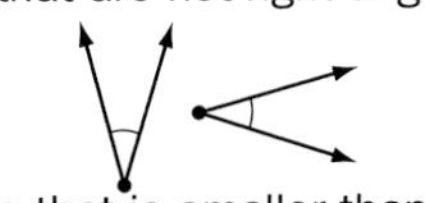

ı angle that is smaller than a right ıgle is called an **acute angle.**

An angle that is larger than a right angle is called an **obtuse angle.**

Use *acute*, *obtuse*, and *right angle* to describe the angles on your list.

:heck for Understanding

ɪrite *acute*, *obtuse*, or *right* for the angle.

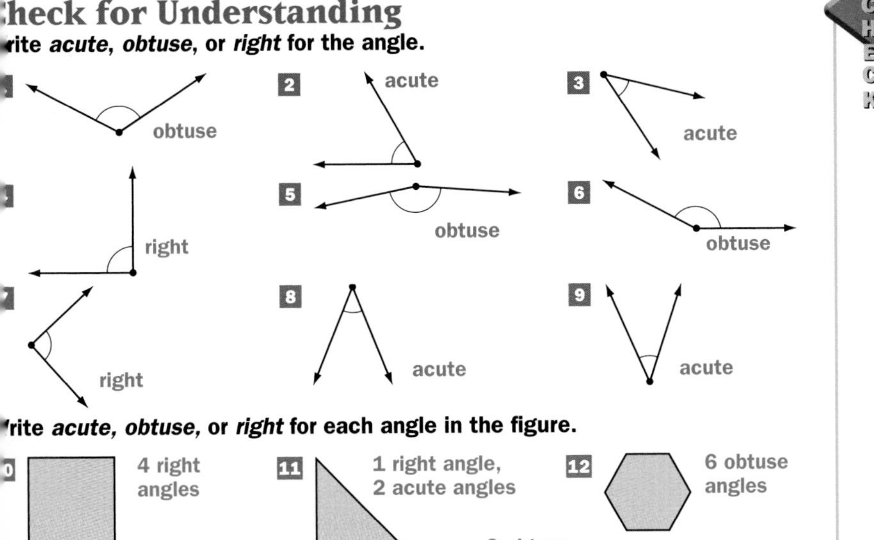

'rite *acute*, *obtuse*, or *right* for each angle in the figure.

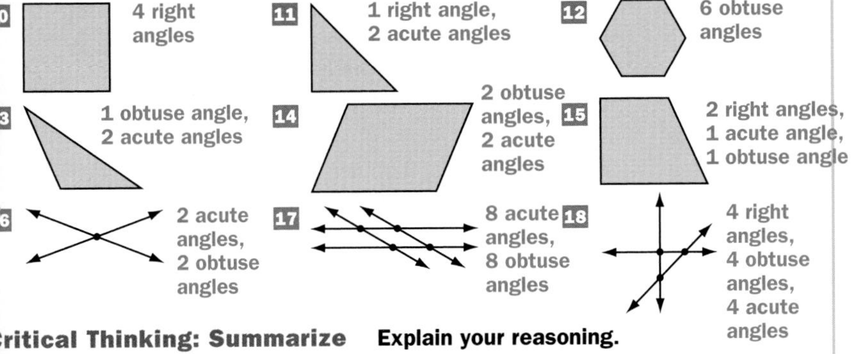

:ritical Thinking: Summarize **Explain your reasoning.**

19 Explain the difference between a right angle, an acute angle, and an obtuse angle. Give an example of each.
heck students' drawings. Possible answer: A right angle forms a square corner, an cute angle is less than a right angle, and an obtuse angle s larger than a right angle.

Turn the page for Practice.

MAKE CONNECTIONS

Ask a volunteer to read the definitions of acute and obtuse angles. Then have students point out examples of acute and obtuse angles in the classroom. They should be able to use their drawings as a guide.

Ask students:

- **What do you call an angle that has rays that are perpendicular?** *[right angle]*
- **What do you call an angle that is smaller than a right angle?** *[acute angle]*
- **What do you call an angle that is larger than a right angle?** *[obtuse angle]*
- **How can you tell if an angle is smaller or larger than a right angle?** *[Possible answer: Use a corner of a piece of paper to check the size of the angle. If the angle is completely under the paper, the angle is acute. If one side sticks out, the angle is obtuse.]*

3 Close

Check for Understanding using items 1–19, page 333.

CRITICAL THINKING
Be sure students clearly distinguish between acute, right, and obtuse angles and use the corner of their paper to check their drawings of each.

Practice See pages 334–335.

Language Support

To help students remember the difference between an acute and an obtuse angle, have them think of the angle formed by a capital A to remember acute for angles less than a right angle.

ESL APPROPRIATE

PRACTICE

Materials have available: calculators

Options for assigning exercises:
A—Odd ex. 1–15; **More to Explore**
B—All ex. 1–15; **More to Explore**

- For ex. 7, tell students there may be more than one right answer.
- For the **Make It Right** (ex. 11), see Common Error below.
- For ex. 12, students can use the problem-solving strategy of Drawing a Picture.

More to Explore Have students read over the definitions of the three types of triangles. Ask them if they think there are triangles that are not acute, right, or obtuse. Have students attempt to draw such a triangle. Students should soon discover that any other type of triangle is impossible.

Suggest that students make drawings to help them answer item 5.

Practice

Write *acute*, *obtuse*, or *right* for the angle.

1 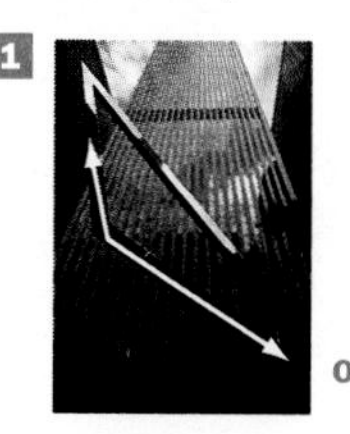 obtuse

2  acute

3 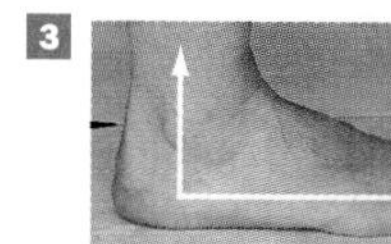 right

4  acute

5  right

6 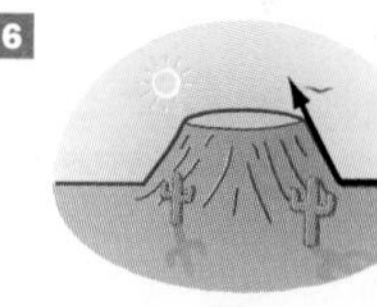 obtuse

7 Which of these polygons have right angles? b and c

a. 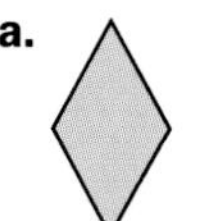
b. 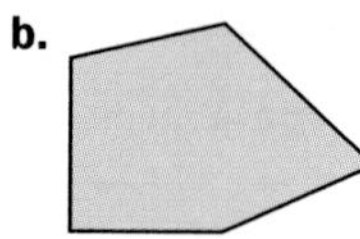
c. 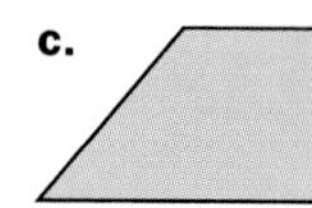
d. 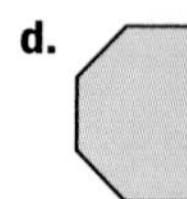

Write the letter that best describes the polygon.

8 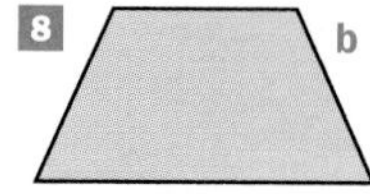 b
a. 2 acute angles, 2 right angles, 1 pair of parallel angles
b. 2 acute angles, 2 obtuse angles, 1 pair of parallel lines

9 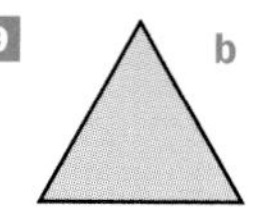 b
a. 2 acute angles, 1 obtuse angle, 2 pairs of perpendicular lines
b. 3 acute angles, 3 intersecting lines

10 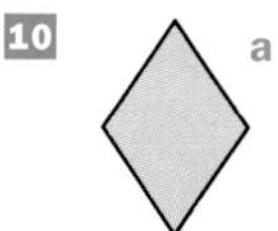 a
a. 2 acute angles, 2 obtuse angles, 2 pairs of parallel lines
b. 4 obtuse angles, 2 pairs of intersecting lines

Make It Right

11 Todd says this triangle has 3 right angles. Write him a note explaining what error was made.

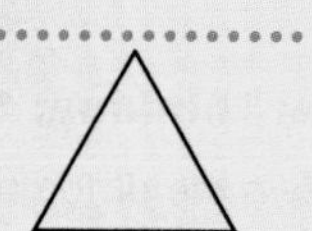

Todd identified the acute angles as right angles.

334 Lesson 9.5

Meeting Individual Needs

Early Finishers

Have students label the angles in the drawing of their hand with R, A, or O for right, acute, or obtuse. Let students share their drawings with a partner. The partner should check the labels to see if he or she agrees.

Common Error

Sometimes students incorrectly identify equal angles in a triangle as right angles as in the **Make It Right** on page 334. Remind students that right angles make square corners.

Inclusion

For students who are visually impaired, have them make angles with 2 straws. To test their knowledge have them show examples of right, obtuse, and acute angles.

Gifted And Talented

Have students fold a sheet of paper to make a paper airplane. Then have them unfold the airplane and identify all the types of angles created by the fold lines.

XED APPLICATIONS

roblem Solving

Logical reasoning What polygon am I? **pentagon**
I have 1 pair of parallel lines.
I have more than 1 right angle.
I have 2 obtuse angles and 1 acute angle.

13 **Spatial reasoning** Veronica bought a collector's doll. The box it came in was in the shape of a triangular prism. What are the shapes of the faces of the box? **2 triangles, 3 rectangles**

the line plot for problems 14–15.

How many students spend 3 or more hours on the Internet each month? **7 students**

Do more students spend 1 hour or 4 hours on the Internet each month? How many more students? **1 hour; 2 students**

Hours Spent on the Internet Each Month by Students

0	1	2	3	4	5
	x				
	x				
	x		x	x	
x	x		x	x	
x	x	x	x	x	x

HOURS

more to explore

iangles

u can describe triangles using their angle sizes.

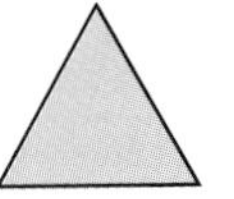

acute triangle has
acute angles.

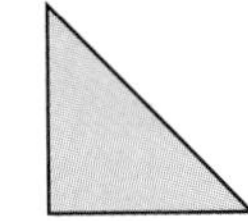

A right triangle has 1 right angle and 2 acute angles.

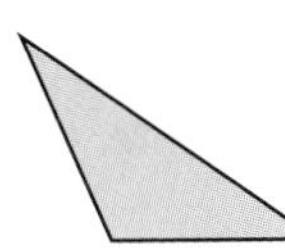

An obtuse triangle has 1 obtuse angle and 2 acute angles.

l if the triangle is an acute, obtuse, or right triangle.

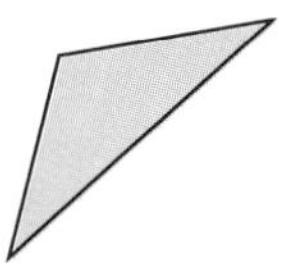

obtuse

2

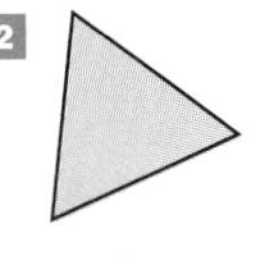

acute

3

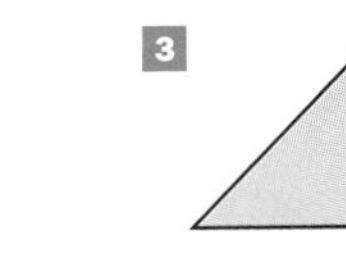

right

4

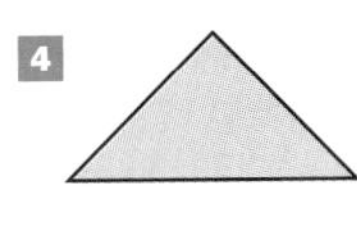

right

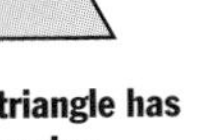

Can you have a triangle with all right angles? with all obtuse angles? with 2 obtuse angles? Why or why not? **No; no; no; possible answer: these angles cannot be connected with 3 lines.**

tra Practice, page 517

Alternate Teaching Strategy

Tell students that an angle is formed when two rays or line segments cross or meet.

Ask students to stand and make the capital letter "L" with their arms. Tell students they have made a right angle because their arms have formed a square corner.

Then have students make a capital "V" with their arms. Tell students that this angle is smaller than a right angle and is called an acute angle.

Finally have students make an angle larger than a right angle with their arms. Tell them this angle is called an obtuse angle.

Have students make and label drawings of each kind of angle.

HOMEWORK

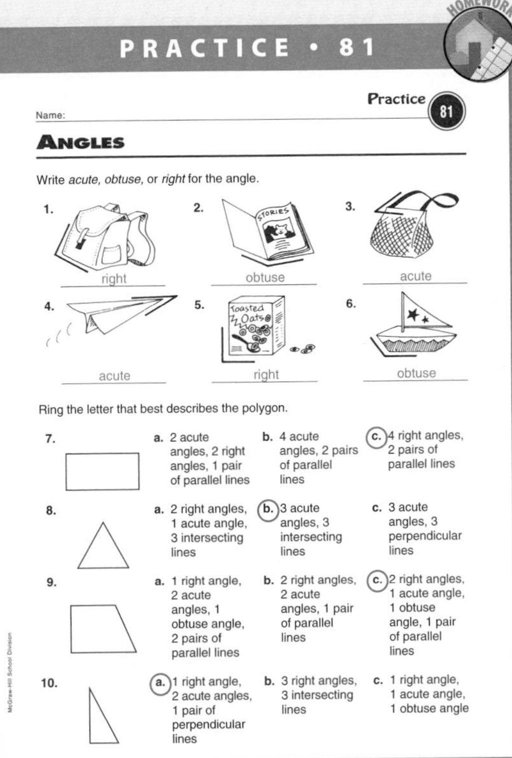

PRACTICE • 81

Practice 81

Name:

ANGLES

Write *acute, obtuse,* or *right* for the angle.

1. right
2. obtuse
3. acute
4. acute
5. right
6. obtuse

Ring the letter that best describes the polygon.

7. a. 2 acute angles, 2 right angles, 1 pair of parallel lines b. 4 acute angles, 2 pairs of parallel lines **(c.)** 4 right angles, 2 pairs of parallel lines
8. a. 2 right angles, 1 acute angle, 3 intersecting lines **(b.)** 3 acute angles, 3 intersecting lines c. 3 acute angles, 3 perpendicular lines
9. a. 1 right angle, 2 acute angles, 1 obtuse angle, 2 pairs of parallel lines b. 2 right angles, 2 acute angles, 1 pair of parallel lines **(c.)** 2 right angles, 1 acute angle, 1 obtuse angle, 1 pair of parallel lines
10. **(a.)** 1 right angle, 2 acute angles, 1 pair of perpendicular lines b. 3 right angles, 3 intersecting lines c. 1 right angle, 1 acute angle, 1 obtuse angle

McGraw-Hill School Division

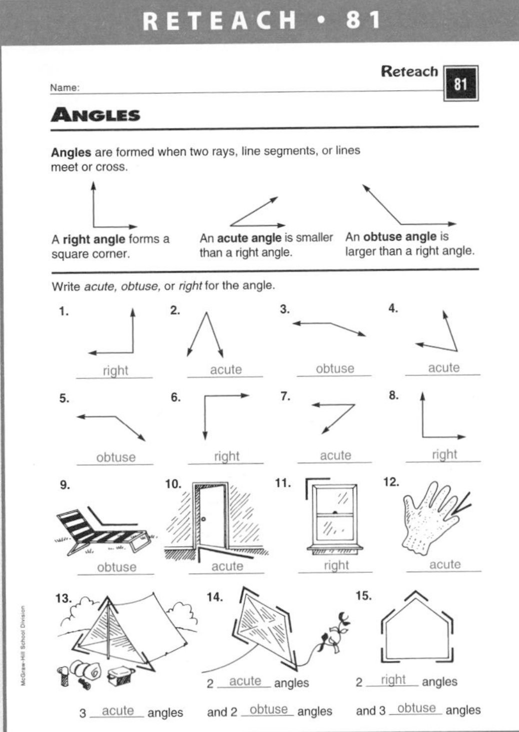

RETEACH • 81

Reteach 81

Name:

ANGLES

Angles are formed when two rays, line segments, or lines meet or cross.

A **right angle** forms a square corner. An **acute angle** is smaller than a right angle. An **obtuse angle** is larger than a right angle.

Write *acute, obtuse,* or *right* for the angle.

1. right
2. acute
3. obtuse
4. acute
5. obtuse
6. right
7. acute
8. right
9. obtuse
10. acute
11. right
12. acute
13. 3 acute angles
14. 2 acute angles and 2 obtuse angles
15. 2 right angles and 3 obtuse angles

McGraw-Hill School Division

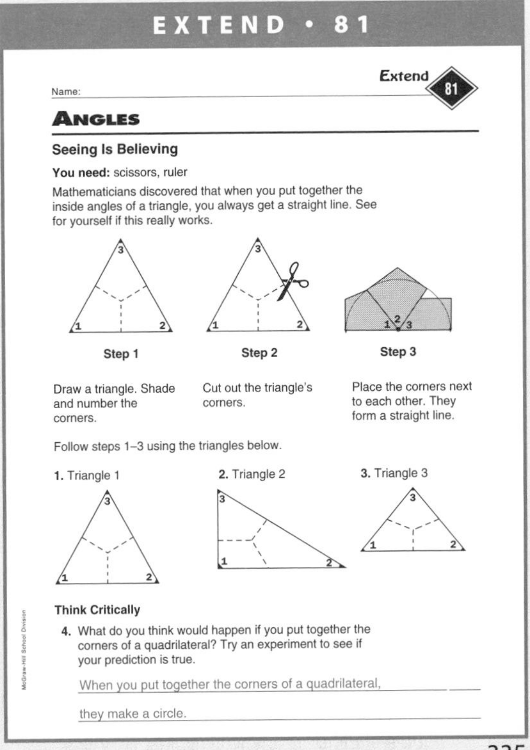

EXTEND • 81

Extend 81

Name:

ANGLES

Seeing Is Believing

You need: scissors, ruler

Mathematicians discovered that when you put together the inside angles of a triangle, you always get a straight line. See for yourself if this really works.

Step 1 Draw a triangle. Shade and number the corners.

Step 2 Cut out the triangle's corners.

Step 3 Place the corners next to each other. They form a straight line.

Follow steps 1–3 using the triangles below.

1. Triangle 1
2. Triangle 2
3. Triangle 3

Think Critically

4. What do you think would happen if you put together the corners of a quadrilateral? Try an experiment to see if your prediction is true.
When you put together the corners of a quadrilateral, they make a circle.

McGraw-Hill School Division

PURPOSE Maintain and review concepts, skills, and strategies that students have learned thus far in the chapter.

Using the Midchapter Review

Have students complete the **Midchapter Review** independently or use it with the whole class.

These exercises will help students review and integrate the terms they have learned thus far in this chapter. Since students will learn even more geometric terms in future lessons, this is a good time to make sure students have a firm grasp on the ones already taught.

Students should know that parallel lines do not intersect. Students should see that perpendicular lines are intersecting lines that form right angles.

Vocabulary Review

Write the following words on the chalkboard:

acute angle	**intersecting**	**ray**
angle	**kite**	**rectangle**
closed figure	**line**	**rhombus**
cone	**line segment**	**right angle**
cube	**obtuse angle**	**sphere**
cylinder	**octagon**	**square**
decagon	**open figure**	**square pyramid**
diagonal	**parallel**	**trapezoid**
edge	**parallelogram**	**triangle**
endpoint	**pentagon**	**triangular prism**
face	**perpendicular**	**triangular pyramid**
heptagon	**polygon**	**vertex**
hexagon	**quadrilateral**	

Ask for volunteers to explain, show, or act out the meaning of these words.

Name the figure the object looks like.

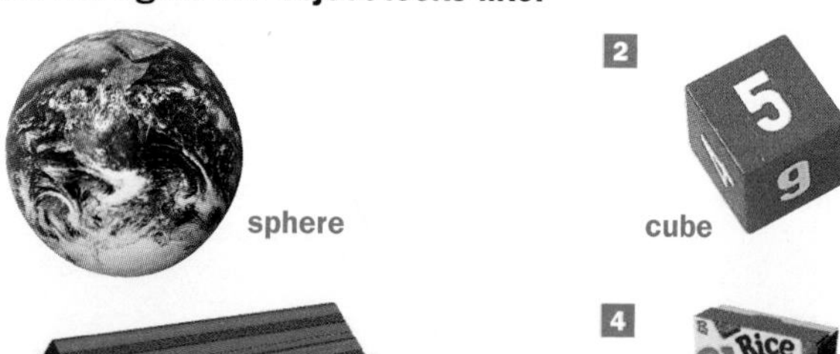

1 sphere

2 cube

3 a triangular prism

4 rectangular prism

Is the figure open or closed? If closed, is it a polygon?

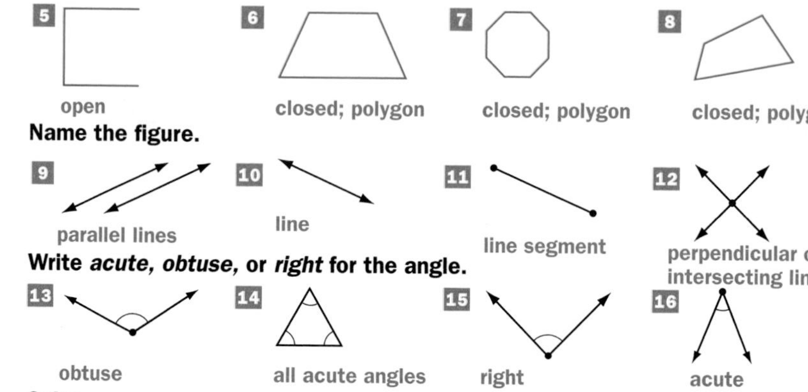

5 open

6 closed; polygon

7 closed; polygon

8 closed; polyg

Name the figure.

9 parallel lines

10 line

11 line segment

12 perpendicular or intersecting line

Write *acute, obtuse,* or *right* for the angle.

13 obtuse

14 all acute angles

15 right

16 acute

Solve.

17 Find the number of faces, edges, and vertices in a rectangular prism. Make an organized list to help find the answer. 6 faces, 12 edges, 8 vertices

18 I am a 4-sided polygon. All my sides are equal in length. I have acute angles and 2 obtuse angle What am I? rhombus

19 Compare the following:
a. a line and a line segment
b. a line and a ray
c. an acute and an obtuse angle
a. a line segment has 2 endpoints, while a line has no endpoints; b. a ray has one endpoint, while a line has none; c. an acute angle is less than a right angle, while an obtuse angle is greater than a right angle.

20 Describe how you tell the difference between paralle perpendicular, and intersecting lines. Possible answer: Parallel lin always stay the same distance aw from each other, perpendicular line have a right angle between them, a intersecting lines meet each other

Reinforcement and Remediation

CHAPTER OBJECTIVE	MIDCHAPTER REVIEW ITEMS	STUDENT BOOK PAGES	TEACHER'S EDITION PAGES		TEACHER RESOURCES
			Activities	Alternate Teaching Strategy	Reteach
*9A	1–20	320–329, 332–335	319A, 323A, 327A, 331A	323, 327, 329, 335	77, 78, 79, 81

*9A Identify 2-dimensional and 3-dimensional figures and their parts

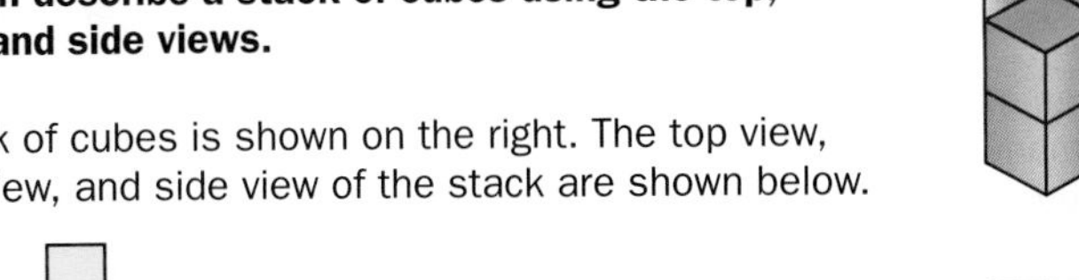

Use Perspective

ou can describe a stack of cubes using the top, ont, and side views.

stack of cubes is shown on the right. The top view, ont view, and side view of the stack are shown below.

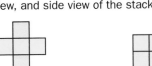

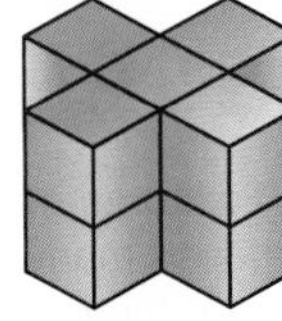

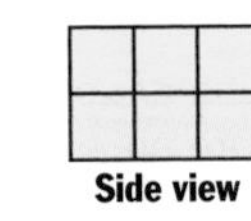

Top view Front view Side view

se centimeter cubes to build each stack of cubes. hen draw the three views for each.

1 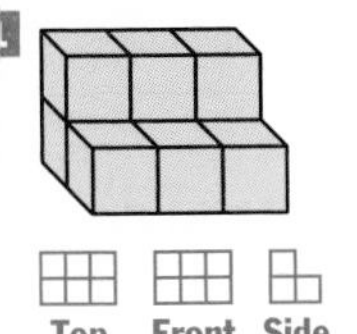
Top Front Side

2 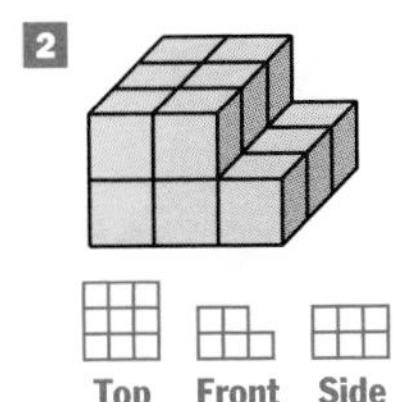
Top Front Side

3 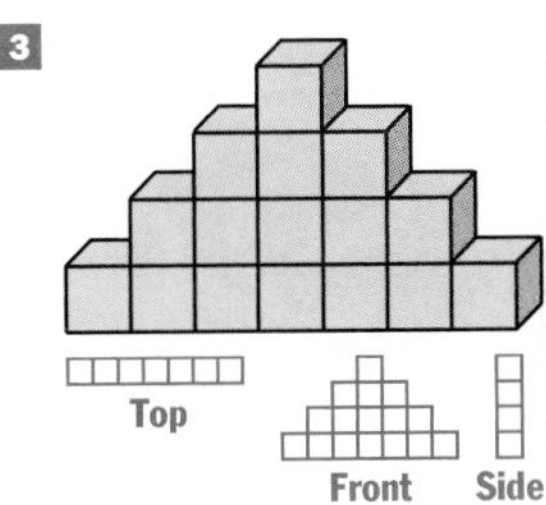
Top Front Side

se the three views to build the stack. Tell how nany cubes you used. 10 or 11 cubes

4 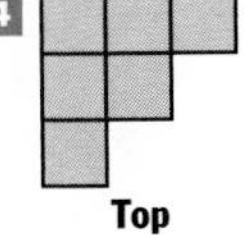
Top

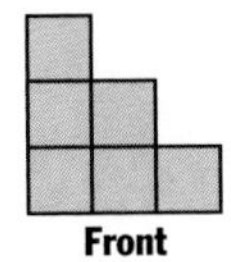
Front

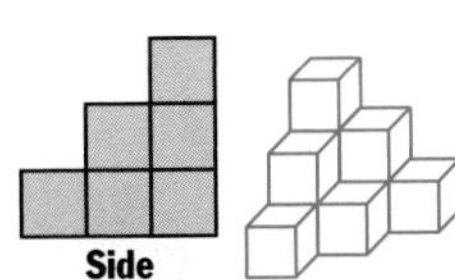
Side

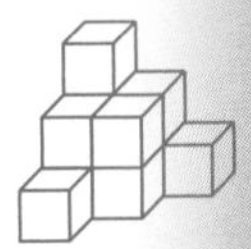

5 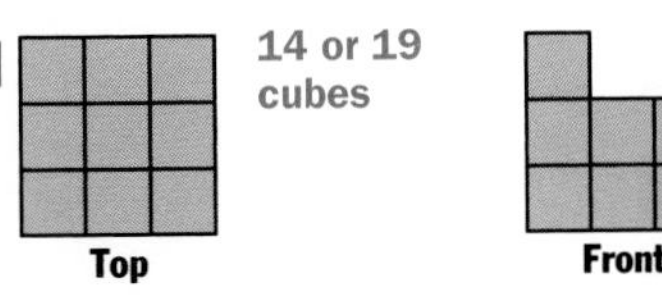
14 or 19 cubes
Top

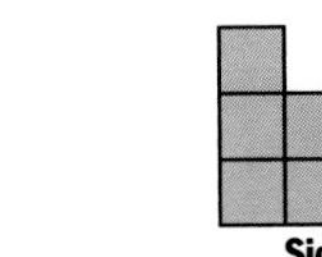
Front

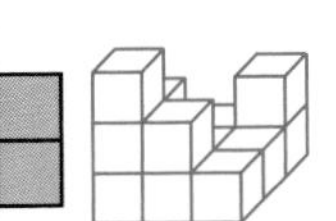
Side

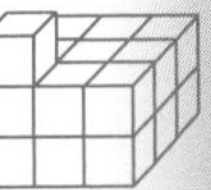

OBJECTIVE Develop spatial sense.

Materials have available: place-value models—ones

Using Spatial Sense

Math Connection Use ones place-value models for centimeter cubes to make the first stack of cubes. If students have difficulty understanding the top, front, and side views shown, let them study the stack of cubes. Ask them to draw the layout of the squares they see from each view.

Ask students:

- **Is a stack of cubes a 3-dimensional or 2-dimensional figure?** *[3-dimensional]*
- **Is the view that you see from each direction 2-dimensional or 3-dimensional?** *[2-dimensional]*
- **How do the top, front, and side views compare to the actual stack of blocks?** *[The top, front, and side views are of the faces on one side of the cubes.]*

Students may work in small groups to complete ex. 1–5. If a group completes the exercises before the others, have them make their own stack of blocks and draw the three views. Groups can exchange their drawings and try to make each others' stack of cubes.

Applying Geometry

OBJECTIVE Explore congruent polygons in an art context.

Materials pattern blocks, tracing paper, scissors

Vocabulary tessellation

Have students describe different designs made with kitchen tiles, bathroom tiles, or mosaics they may have seen. Discuss how shape and color are used in these designs.

- **Why are tiles often square?** *[Possible answer: to fully cover a given area, which is most often square or rectangular]*
- **What happens to the designs printed on the tiles?** *[They often match up and create different patterns.]*

2 Investigate *Cooperative Groups*

Point out the **Cultural Note** on page 338. Dutch artist M.C. Escher (1898–1972) used color symmetry, geometric shapes, and a "regular division of the plane" to make pictures with interlocking designs. A graphic artist and designer, Escher created works that are particularly interesting to mathematicians and scientists because of their symmetry. Some of the figures used in Escher's interlocking designs include fish, birds, lizards, crabs, moths, flowers, leaves, and frogs.

Using the Group Product Strategy, have students work together in groups to create a tessellation using pattern blocks. Jobs or roles are assigned to the group by the teacher. The group organizes the work, and comes to an agreement on what the final product will include. The group completes their product, and presents their product to another group, several groups, or the whole class.

Creating Tessellations Have students work in teams to make a tessellation using pattern blocks. As an alternative, have them draw congruent geometric shapes and cut them out.

3 Reflect and Share

Materials have available: calculators; computer spreadsheet program (optional)

Report Your Findings As students present their tessellations, invite others to compare and contrast them to other tessellations made in class. Encourage students to think about how both regular and irregular polygons can be used to make tessellations.

TESSELLATIONS

In many cultures, people create designs by repeating one or more shapes many times. The shapes are fitted together without overlapping and with no spaces between them. The design is called a **tessellation.**

Tessellations are often used to cover floors, walls, or other places where an area has to be filled.

Find out what shapes you can tessellate to create your own designs!

Cultural Note
One of the most famous uses of tessellations in modern times was by M. C. Escher, a Dutch graphic artist. He tessellated animals in several works to create very interesting images.

Symmetry Drawing E15 by M. C. Escher

Bobst Library at New York University

Alhambra Palace in Granada, Spain

tessellation Related shapes that cover a flat surface without leaving any gaps.

More To Investigate

Predict Possible approaches: Students will succeed with different sized squares, rhombi, quadrilaterals, equilateral triangles, scalene triangles, irregular pentagons, regular and irregular hexagons, and irregular octagons. They may also discover that tessellations of irregular polygons can be broken down into tessellations of quadrilaterals and/or triangles.

Explore Possible answers: S-shapes and C-shapes.

Find Possible examples: fish scales, butterfly wings, turtle shells, and sunflower seeds. Sample answer: Most snakes have scales that overlap, but the patterns of color on those scales often tessalate.

Bibliography Students who wish to learn more about Escher or different types of tessellations can read:

Let's Investigate Shape Patterns, by Marion Smoothey. Tarrytown, NY: Marshall Cavendish, 1993. ISBN 1–85435–465–5.

Visions of Symmetry: Notebooks, Periodic Drawings & Related Work of M. C. Escher, by Doris Schattschneider. New York: W. H. Freeman & Company, 1995. ISBN 0–7167–2352–2.

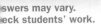

swers may vary.
eck students' work.

See Teacher's Edition for sample of student work.

DECISION MAKING

Creating Tessellations

1 Work with a partner. You may use pattern blocks, objects that you trace, or cut out shapes.

2 Decide on the following things:
- ▶ what shape or shapes to use
- ▶ what kind of paper you will use
- ▶ where on the paper you will start the design
- ▶ what colors you will use

3 Create a tessellation. Lay out and trace the shapes until your entire paper is filled. Use at least three colors to complete your design.

4 Now try another one.

Reporting Your Findings

5 Portfolio Prepare to present your tessellations. Include the following:
- ▶ Finished tessellations.
- ▶ A description of the shapes you used.
- ▶ Any discoveries you made about the types of shapes that tessellate.

6 Compare your tessellations with those of your classmates. How are they alike? How are they different?

Revise your work.
- ▶ Do your shapes fit together without overlapping and without space between them?
- ▶ Did you include a written description of the polygons and colors you used?

MORE TO INVESTIGATE

See Teacher's Edition.

PREDICT which polygons, other than the ones you used, will tessellate. Try them out.

EXPLORE ways to create a curved shape that will tessellate.

FIND more examples of tessellations in art and nature. What is tessellated on a snake?

Students' Work

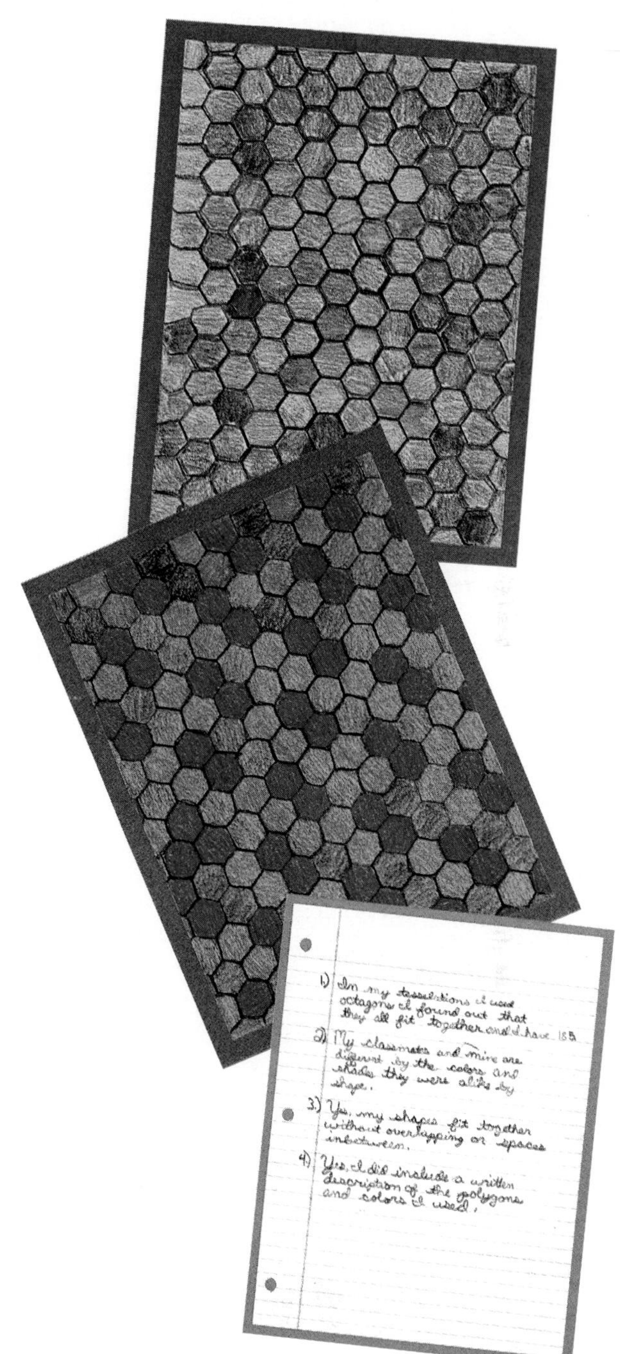

Building A Portfolio

This investigation will allow you to evaluate a student's ability to use patterns and geometry to solve a problem.

Allow students to revise their work for the portfolio. Each student's portfolio piece should consist of a copy of his or her tessellation and a description of the polygon(s) used in the tessellation. It should also include any observations or discoveries the team made about types of polygons that tessellate or that can be found in a tessellation.

You may wish to use the Holistic Scoring Guide to assess this task. See page 27 in Teacher's Assessment Resources.

EXPLORE ACTIVITY

Congruency and Similarity

OBJECTIVE Explore identifying congruent and similar figures.

RESOURCE REMINDER
Math Center Cards 82
Practice 82, Reteach 82, Extend 82

SKILLS TRACE

GRADE 3	• Explore using slides, flips, and turns and combinations of them to identify congruent figures. *(Chapter 10)*
GRADE 4	• Explore identifying congruent and similar figures.
GRADE 5	• Identify congruent figures and their corresponding parts. • Identify slide, flip, and turn motions. Explore identifying similar figures. *(Chapter 8)*

LESSON 9.6 RESOURCES

MANIPULATIVE WARM-UP

Cooperative Pairs — **Visual/Spatial**

OBJECTIVE Find polygons that are alike and different.

Materials per pair: centimeter dot paper (TA 9), scissors

▶ Have each pair use dot paper to draw and cut out a polygon made of five equal squares. Then have pairs compare their polygons with other pairs and try to find two or more that are exactly alike. Students should show this by placing one polygon on top of the other.

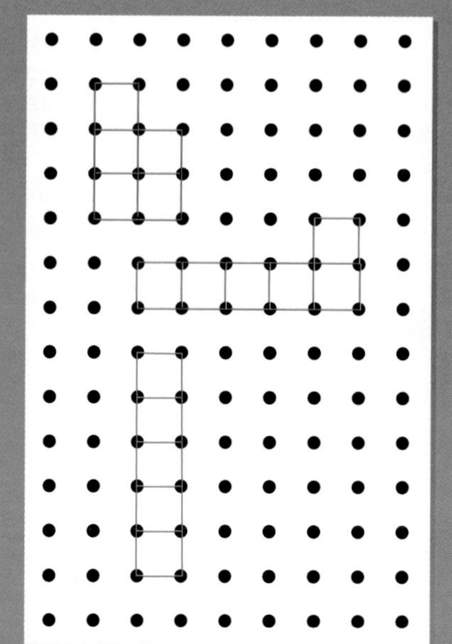

▶ Then ask:
How do the other polygons compare? *[They are different or they have a different shape.]*

▶ Have students display the possible variations in the arrangement of the five squares on the bulletin board.

CULTURAL CONNECTION

Cooperative Groups — **Kinesthetic**

OBJECTIVE Connect tangrams and similar and congruent figures.

Materials per group: tangram (TA 21)

▶ Tell students that the ancient Chinese made a puzzle called a *tangram.* The puzzle consists of 1 large square divided into 7 pieces: 5 triangles, 1 square, and 1 parallelogram.

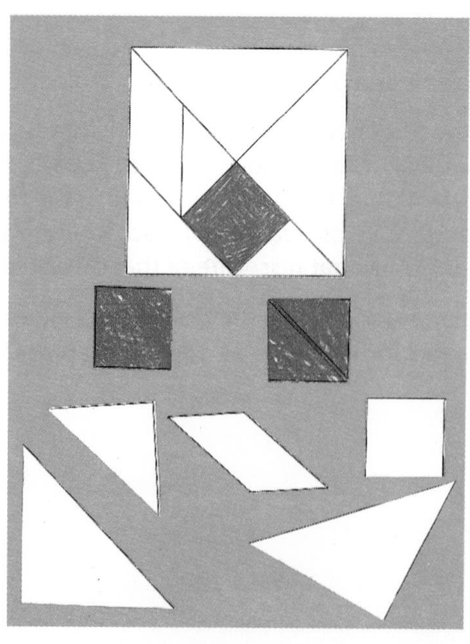

▶ Have groups use the tangram pieces to show two equal triangles, two equal squares, and two equal parallelograms. Have groups discuss other shapes and sizes in the tangram.

▶ You may wish to have students explore using the tangram pieces to make other shapes.

Daily Review

PREVIOUS DAY QUICK REVIEW

Name each.

1. an angle greater than a right angle *[obtuse]*
2. a triangle with one right angle *[right triangle]*

FAST FACTS

1. 9 × 7 *[63]*
2. 7 × 5 *[35]*
3. 4 × 8 *[32]*
4. 8 × 7 *[56]*

Problem of the Day • 82

Fill this square with the numbers 0 to 8 so that the sum in each row, column, and diagonal is 12. Use each number just once.

[7]	*[0]*	*[5]*
[2]	*[4]*	*[6]*
[3]	*[8]*	*[1]*

TECH LINK

Math Van

MATH VAN

Tools You may wish to use the Geometry tool with this lesson.

MATH FORUM

Multi-Age Classes I use this lesson as an opportunity to introduce my older students to corresponding parts of similar and congruent figures.

Visit our Resource Village at http://www.mhschool.com to see more of the Math Forum.

MATH CENTER

Practice

OBJECTIVE Identify congruent and similar figures.

Materials per student: centimeter graph paper, ruler, 2-color counter

Students draw similar congruent polygons depending on the flip of a 2-color counter. *[Students check each other's work.]*

PRACTICE ACTIVITY 82 — MATH CENTER, Small Group

Game • Look-Alike Game

- One player draws a polygon on graph paper. The rest of the group studies it for several minutes. Then the player puts it away.
- Each of the other players tosses a counter. If it lands red side up, the player must draw on graph paper a congruent figure. If it lands yellow side up, the player must draw a similar figure.
- Compare the finished drawings with the original. Each successful drawing earns 1 point. Keep playing so that each group member gets to draw the original figure at least once.

YOU NEED
- centimeter graph paper
- 1 two-color counter per player
- ruler

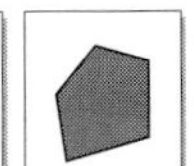
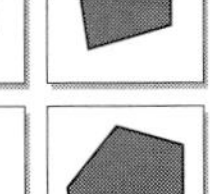

Chapter 9, Lesson 6, pages 340–343 — Geometry

ESL APPROPRIATE

NCTM Standards
- ✓ Problem Solving
- ✓ Communication
- ✓ Reasoning
- Connections

Problem Solving

OBJECTIVE Solve a problem involving congruent and similar figures.

Materials per student: graph paper (TA 7), ruler

Students solve an area problem and then decide whether the figures in their answers are congruent or similar to each other. *[Some students may divide the land into rectangular sections; other solutions will involve non-rectangular sections. Solutions that contain congruent figures would be: five 4 × 10 areas; five 2 × 20 areas; four 5 × 8 areas and one 2 × 20]*

PROBLEM-SOLVING ACTIVITY 82 — MATH CENTER, On Your Own

Decision Making • Similar or Congruent?

A queen wants to divide some land fairly among five people. She is using a map to help her decide how to divide the land. The map is a rectangle, 20 units by 10 units.

- Draw as many ways as possible to divide the land equally using figures that are all congruent.
- Draw as many ways as possible to divide the land equally using noncongruent figures.
- Are any of the shapes created by your solutions similar to or congruent with the original rectangle?

YOU NEED
- graph paper
- ruler

Chapter 9, Lesson 6, pages 340–343 — Geometry

ESL APPROPRIATE

NCTM Standards
- ✓ Problem Solving
- ✓ Communication
- ✓ Reasoning
- Connections

EXPLORE ACTIVITY

Congruency and Similarity

OBJECTIVE Explore identifying congruent and similar figures.

Materials per pair: centimeter dot paper (TA 9), scissors

Vocabulary congruent, similar

1 Introduce

Point out the photo of the Navajo rug at the top of page 340. Ask students to identify the shapes they see in the rug. Have students compare the shapes and patterns they see in the Navajo rug to other rugs and fabrics they have seen.

Discuss with students how hand-woven rugs are made and what the weaver does to create the shapes and patterns.

2 Teach *Cooperative Pairs*

LEARN Have a volunteer read the definitions for congruent and similar. Then ask students to find pairs of congruent and similar figures in the Navajo rug pattern.

Work Together Be sure students use the dots as vertices for their figure. This will make it easier for them to make congruent and similar figures.

Talk It Over Have pairs answer these questions and share their answers with the class.

It may be more difficult for students to make similar figures. Suggest they use the dots on the dot paper to help them. If a rectangle, for example, is 3 units by 2 units they can make a similar rectangle, 6 units by 4 units, by doubling the sides.

LEARN

Congruency and Similarity

IN THE WORKPLACE
Priscilla Warren, Navajo rug weaver, Shiprock, NM

Many Navajo blankets have patterns that are made up of congruent and similar figures.

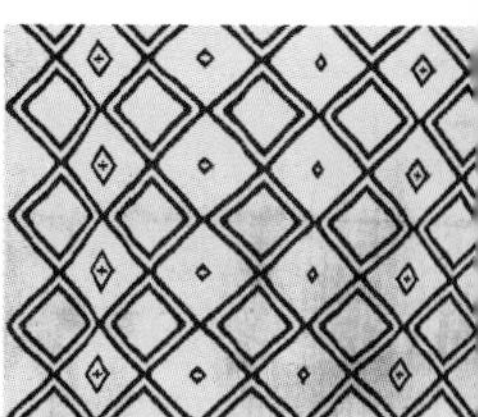

Figures that are the same shape and size are **congruent.**

Figures that are the exact same shape but are different sizes are **similar.**

Work Together
Work with a partner. One partner creates a figure on dot paper.

You will need
- *dot paper*

The other partner uses dot paper to create two figures, one that is congruent to the original figure and one that is similar.

Change roles and continue making new figures as well as figures that are similar and congruent.

Check Out the Glossary
congruent
similar
See page 544.

Talk It Over
- ▶ What method did you use to create a figure congruent to your partner's original figure? one that is similar? **Possible answer: Placed the band over the original figure; made sure the figures look alike even though one is smaller.**
- ▶ How could you prove the figures are congruent? **Possible answer: Cut out a sheet of paper the same shape as the original figure and match it to the congruent figure.**

Meeting Individual Needs

Extra Support

Some students may have difficulty determining similar figures. Have them cut out figures from dot paper and check if the figures are exactly alike. If not, have them check to see if the angles are the same; if they are, the figures are similar.

Ongoing Assessment

Anecdotal Report Make notes on students' ability to recognize a congruent and a similar figure. Students should be able to visually recognize similarity and congruence.

Follow Up For more practice with congruency and similarity, have students draw a pair of figures—one similar, one congruent—for some of the figures shown on pages 324–325. Assign **Reteach 82.**

For students who understand congruent and similar figures, assign **Extend 82.**

ake Connections

ckie and Don used dot paper to show how they created a ure and then created congruent and similar figures.

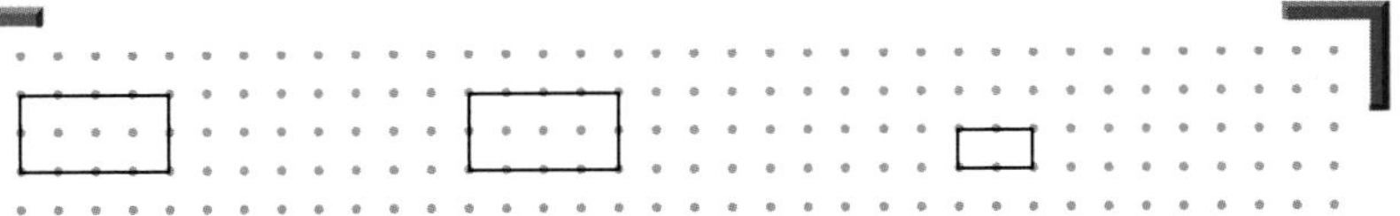

First, I make a drawing of a rectangle on my dot paper.

To make a congruent rectangle, I draw another rectangle with the same width and length.

To make a similar rectangle, I draw a rectangle that is half as wide and half as long.

Would ink on a stamp create a congruent or similar shape to the figure on the stamp? **congruent**

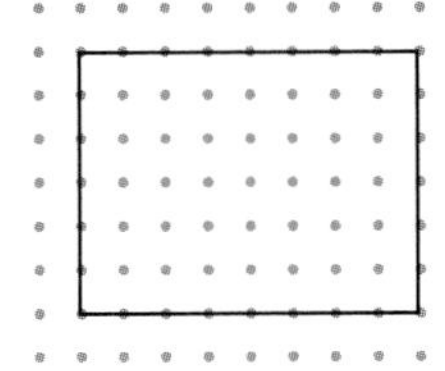

The rectangle on the right is not similar to Jackie and Don's rectangle because the length is twice as long but the width is three times as wide. Draw another rectangle that is not similar to their rectangle. **Check students' work.**

heck for Understanding

e the figures congruent? If not, are they similar?

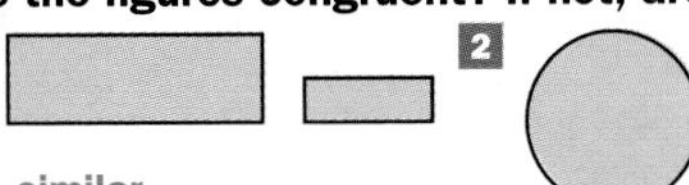

similar

2 **congruent**

3 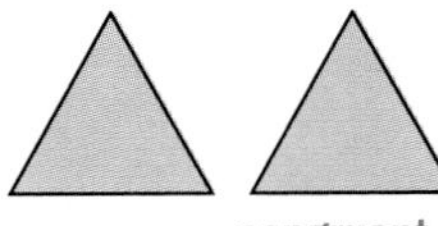

congruent

aw the figure on dot paper. Then draw one figure that is ngruent and one that is similar to the original. **Check students' drawings.**

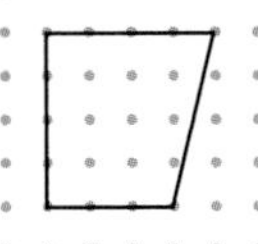

5 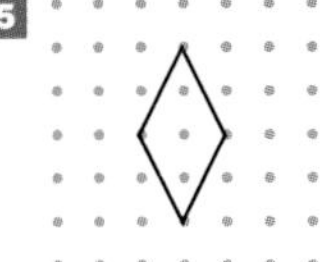

6 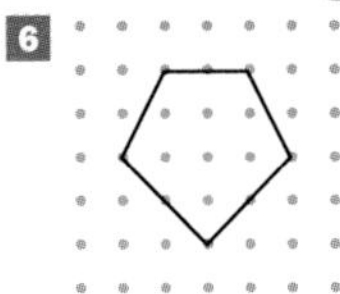

itical Thinking: Analyze **Explain your reasoning.**

Hannah believes that if you can fit one shape exactly over another, then the shapes are congruent. Explain why you agree or disagree with her. **Possible answer: If the figures fit exactly over each other, they are the same shape and size, so they are congruent.**

Turn the page for Practice.

MAKE CONNECTIONS

Have pairs of students review Jackie and Don's drawings and methods for making congruent and similar figures. Ask pairs to answer the questions, then go over them as a class. Ask students:

- **If you multiply the length and width of a rectangle by the same number, will the new rectangle always be a similar figure?** *[Yes.]*
- **If you divide the length and width of a rectangle by the same number, will the new rectangle always be a similar figure?** *[Yes.]*
- **Will this hold true with all shapes, or does it only work with rectangles?** *[all shapes]*

3 Close

Check for Understanding using items 1–7, page 341.

Critical Thinking

Ask students if they can always fit one shape exactly over another when the shapes are similar. Have students draw and cut out similar shapes to support their reasoning.

Practice See pages 342–343.

PRACTICE

Materials have available: centimeter dot paper (TA 9), rulers, cardboard barriers

Options for assigning exercises:
A—All ex. 1–13; **Draw My Shape Game!; More to Explore**
B—Odd ex. 1–7; all ex. 8–13; **Draw My Shape Game!; More to Explore**

- For ex. 1–3, students should find one similar and one congruent figure among each of the four options.
- For ex. 8–11, point out that students are drawing two figures, one that is congruent and one that is similar.

Draw My Shape Game! Give each pair time to read over the directions for the game. Then work through an example. Draw a figure on the chalkboard. Ask students to tell how they might describe the shape to their partner.

Either you or a student could play the part of the partner and draw only what was said. Have students refine their descriptions as necessary.

Give students a set time to play the game, then come back again as a class to discuss strategies.

More to Explore Go over the directions with the class. Tell students that the diameter of a circle is the distance between opposite sides of the circle through the center. Students can measure round objects such as paper cups, paper plates, cans, bottle and jar caps, and so forth.

PRACTICE

Practice

Is each figure *congruent* or *similar* to the original figure?

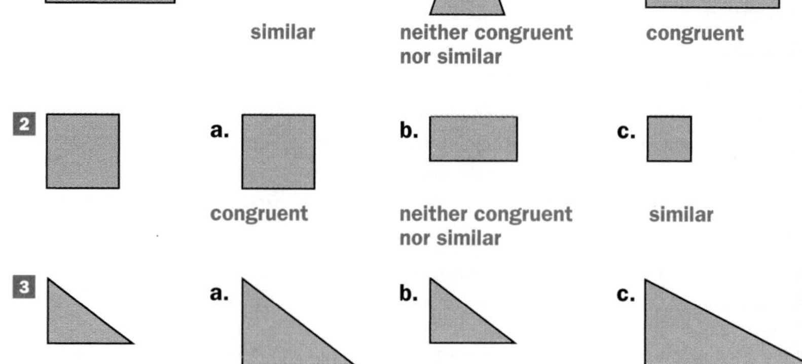

Are the figures congruent? If not, are they similar?

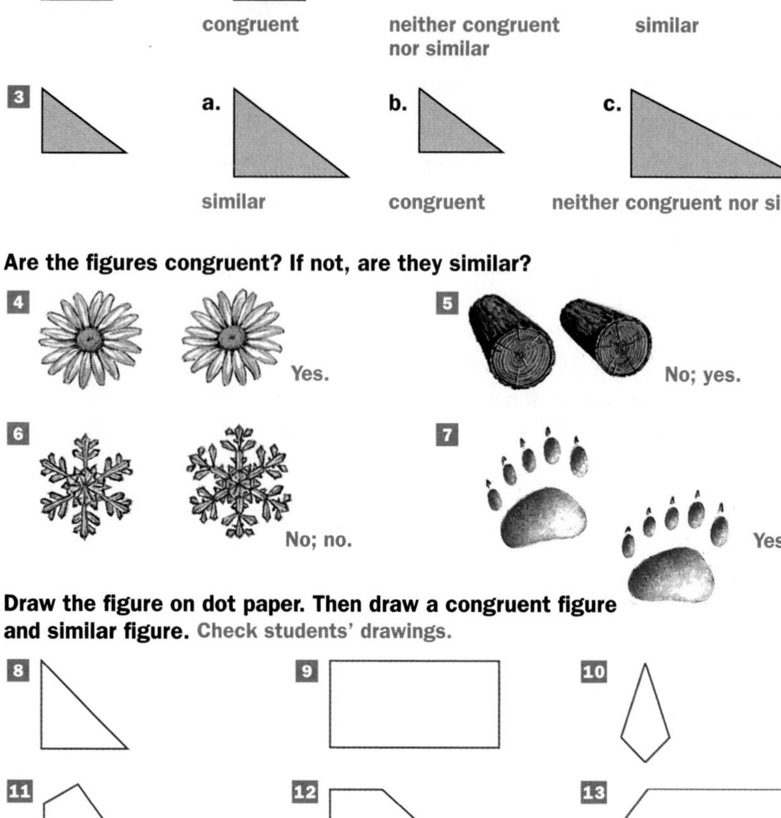

Draw the figure on dot paper. Then draw a congruent figure and similar figure. Check students' drawings.

8 9 10 11 12 13

Meeting Individual Needs

Early Finishers

Have students create a pattern or design on dot paper with similar and congruent figures. Limit students to two or three shapes and require that all remaining shapes be congruent or similar to the three.

Language Support

You may wish to have an English-speaking student be an extra partner to a student acquiring English for the first time through the game.

ESL APPROPRIATE

Inclusion

Some students will be able to determine similarity visually. Others will need to check dimensions to see if one set is a multiple of the other. Encourage students to always check the dimensions if they are not sure.

y with a partner.
ce a barrier on a desk between the players. The rier should be tall enough so that it prevents one yer from seeing the other player's work.

You will need
- *dot paper*
- *rulers*
- *cardboard barriers*

ay the Game

The first player draws a figure on dot paper and describes the figure.

The second player follows the directions and draws a congruent figure. Then both players compare the figures to see if they are congruent.

If the figures are not congruent, then the players discuss better ways to describe the figure.

If the figures are congruent, the players trade roles and continue to play.

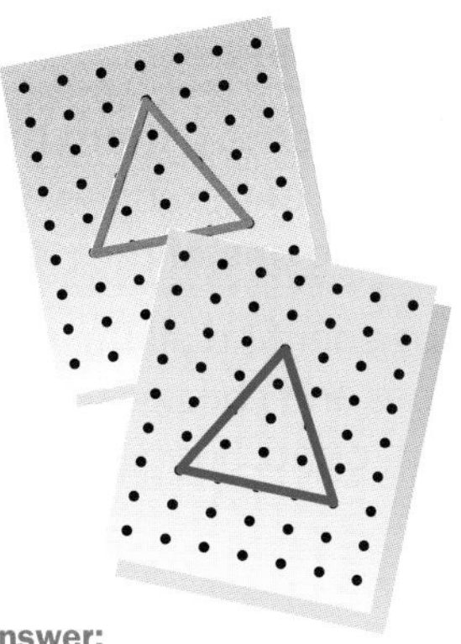

at strategies did you use to make sure your ections were complete and easy to follow? **Possible answer: ed shapes that were familiar and described each part of the shape carefully.**

more to explore

rcle Measurements

w does the distance around a circle compare to diameter?

You will need
- *string*
- *scissors*

easure the outside of the circle on the right with a ce of string. Then measure the diameter with a ce of string.

mpare the lengths. What do you notice? **See below.**

e circular containers or objects such as cans draw circles of different sizes. Compare the stance around each circle to its diameter. at pattern do you see?

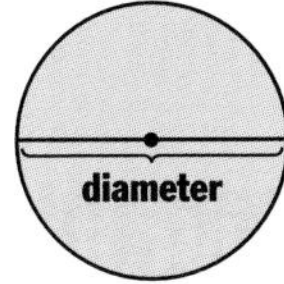

e distance around the circle is about 3 times as long as the diameter.

tra Practice, page 517

Alternate Teaching Strategy

Materials cardboard triangle

Set up the overhead projector so that it shines onto the chalkboard. Place the triangle on the overhead projector and have a volunteer trace around the image on the chalkboard.

Move the triangle to another spot and have another volunteer trace the new image. Ask students how these triangles compare. Tell them since they are exactly the same shape and size, these triangles are called *congruent.*

Move the overhead closer to the chalkboard. Have a third student trace the new image. Ask students how this triangle compares to the previous pair of triangles.

- **Is it the same size?** *[No.]* **Is it the same shape?** *[Yes.]*

Tell students that since it is the same shape and has the same size angles, this figure is *similar* to the previous two.

PRACTICE • 82

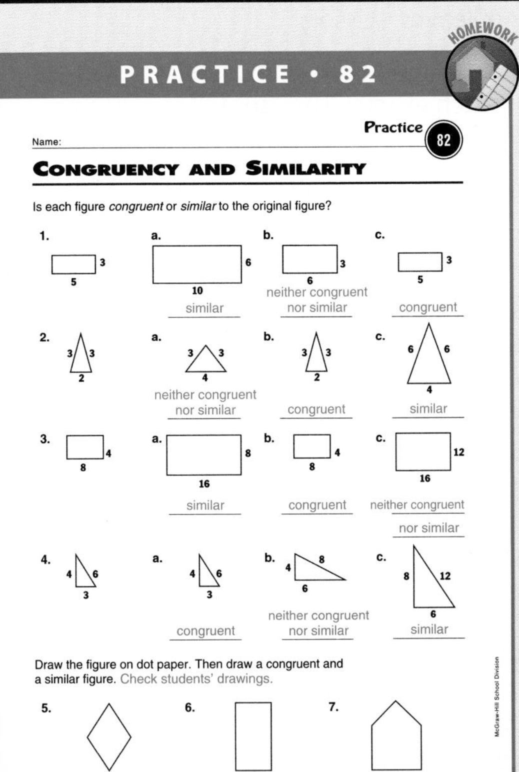

HOMEWORK

Practice 82

Name:

Congruency and Similarity

Is each figure *congruent* or *similar* to the original figure?

1. (5 by 3) a. (10 by 6) similar b. (6 by 3) neither congruent nor similar c. (5 by 3) congruent
2. (3, 3, 2) a. (3, 3, 4) neither congruent nor similar b. (3, 3, 2) congruent c. (6, 6, 4) similar
3. (8 by 4) a. (16 by 8) similar b. (8 by 4) congruent c. (16 by 12) neither congruent nor similar
4. (4, 6, 3) a. (4, 6, 3) congruent b. (4, 8, 6) neither congruent nor similar c. (8, 12, 6) similar

Draw the figure on dot paper. Then draw a congruent and a similar figure. Check students' drawings.

5. 6. 7.

RETEACH • 82

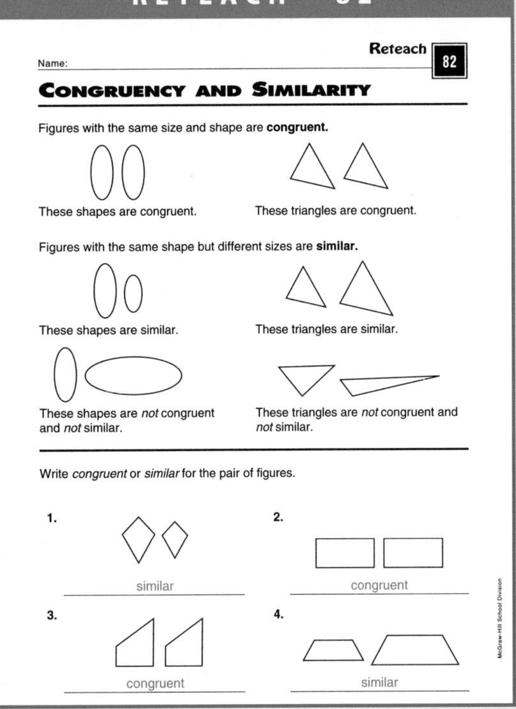

Reteach 82

Name:

Congruency and Similarity

Figures with the same size and shape are **congruent.**

These shapes are congruent. These triangles are congruent.

Figures with the same shape but different sizes are **similar.**

These shapes are similar. These triangles are similar.

These shapes are *not* congruent and *not* similar. These triangles are *not* congruent and *not* similar.

Write *congruent* or *similar* for the pair of figures.

1. similar
2. congruent
3. congruent
4. similar

EXTEND • 82

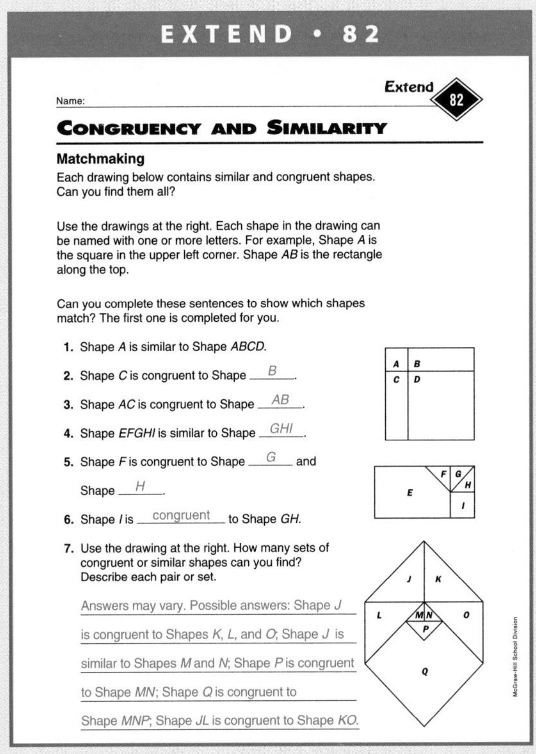

Extend 82

Name:

Congruency and Similarity

Matchmaking

Each drawing below contains similar and congruent shapes. Can you find them all?

Use the drawings at the right. Each shape in the drawing can be named with one or more letters. For example, Shape *A* is the square in the upper left corner. Shape *AB* is the rectangle along the top.

Can you complete these sentences to show which shapes match? The first one is completed for you.

1. Shape *A* is similar to Shape *ABCD.*
2. Shape *C* is congruent to Shape B.
3. Shape *AC* is congruent to Shape AB.
4. Shape *EFGHI* is similar to Shape GHI.
5. Shape *F* is congruent to Shape G and Shape H.
6. Shape *I* is congruent to Shape *GH.*
7. Use the drawing at the right. How many sets of congruent or similar shapes can you find? Describe each pair or set.
Answers may vary. Possible answers: Shape *J* is congruent to Shapes *K, L,* and *O;* Shape *J* is similar to Shapes *M* and *N;* Shape *P* is congruent to Shape *MN;* Shape *Q* is congruent to Shape *MNP;* Shape *JL* is congruent to Shape *KO.*

McGraw-Hill School Division

LESSON 9.7

Symmetry

OBJECTIVE Identify symmetric figures and draw lines of symmetry.

RESOURCE REMINDER
Math Center Cards 83
Practice 83, Reteach 83, Extend 83

SKILLS TRACE

GRADE 3	• Explore identifying lines of symmetry. *(Chapter 10)*
GRADE 4	• Identify symmetric figures and draw lines of symmetry.
GRADE 5	• Identify lines of symmetry and complete symmetric figures. *(Chapter 8)*

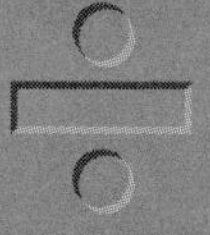

LESSON 9.7 RESOURCES

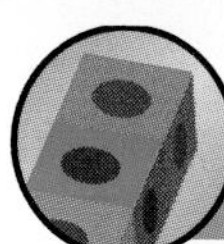

MANIPULATIVE WARM-UP

Cooperative Pairs | **Kinesthetic**

OBJECTIVE Explore lines of symmetry.

Materials per pair: pattern blocks (TA 16), scissors

▶ Have pairs cut out the pattern blocks. Then have them fold each shape in half so that one half of the shape matches the other half exactly. Demonstrate the procedure using one of the pattern blocks.

▶ Have each partner find all the possible folds for one shape. Partners exchange shapes and check each other's shapes to see if all of the possible folds have been found. Suggest students draw over the fold lines with a pen or pencil. *[trapezoid—1, triangle—3, square—4, parallelogram—1, rhombus—2, hexagon—6]*

▶ As a class, have students compare shapes and their fold lines.

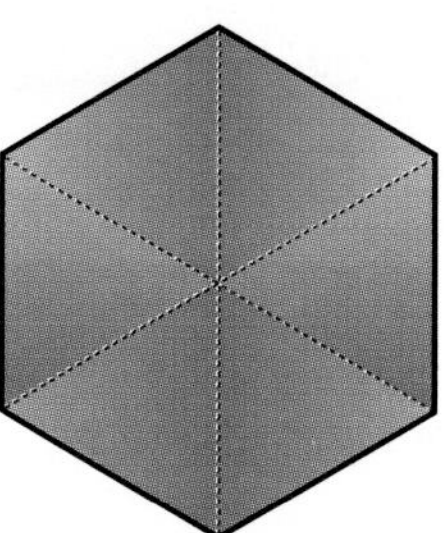

SCIENCE CONNECTION

Cooperative Groups | **Visual/Spatial**

OBJECTIVE Finding symmetry or approximations of symmetry in nature.

Materials per group: different kinds of leaves, scissors

▶ Have students work together to trace around each kind of leaf, cut it out, and fold it in half to see if the halves match exactly. They should record their results in a table.

▶ Have groups compare their results with the class. Discuss with students that in nature the two parts of the leaves may not exactly match up because the leaves are not ideal geometric shapes.

▶ Have students review their results to see if the halves are close to being a match. Students should conclude that most of the leaves can be folded to show parts that match or are close to matching.

Daily Review

PREVIOUS DAY QUICK REVIEW

Draw each on dot paper. *[Check students' drawings.]*

1. two congruent rectangles
2. two congruent triangles
3. two similar squares
4. two similar rectangles

FAST FACTS

1. 27 ÷ 3 *[9]*
2. 45 ÷ 5 *[9]*
3. 8 ÷ 8 *[1]*
4. 21 ÷ 3 *[7]*

Problem of the Day • 83

Use the clues to find the name of the teacher in Room 220. *[Mr. Chen]*

Room 218	Room 220	Room 222	Room 224

- Mr. Yen's room is number 224.
- Ms. O'Brien's room is next to Mr. Yen's room.
- Mr. Wilson's room is not to the right of Mr. Chen's room.

TECH LINK

Math Van

MATH VAN

Tools You may wish to use the Geometry tool with this lesson.

MATH FORUM

Idea I have my students each draw half of a shape and its line of symmetry and exchange with another student to finish the shape.

Visit our Resource Village at http://www.mhschool.com to see more of the Math Forum.

MATH CENTER

Practice

OBJECTIVE Identify lines of symmetry.

Materials per student: ruler, paper, scissors, tape, Math Center Recording Sheet (TA 31 optional)

Students trace and cut out figures to find lines of symmetry. *[Figures with No Lines of Symmetry: B; 1–2 Lines of Symmetry: F; 3 or More Lines of Symmetry: A, C, D, E]*

PRACTICE ACTIVITY 83 — MATH CENTER, On Your Own

Spatial Sense • Lines of Symmetry

- Draw six figures like the ones shown.
- Fold to find all the possible lines of symmetry.
- Draw each line of symmetry on the figures.
- Draw three columns on a sheet of paper and label them as below:

No lines of Symmetry	1 or 2 lines of Symmetry	3 or more lines of Symmetry

- Sort and then tape figures *A* to *F* to the columns of your chart.

YOU NEED: ruler, paper, scissors, tape

McGraw-Hill School Division — Grade Level 4

Chapter 9, Lesson 7, pages 344–345 — Geometry

ESL APPROPRIATE

NCTM Standards

- Problem Solving
- ✓ Communication
- ✓ Reasoning
- Connections

Problem Solving

OBJECTIVE Create a symmetrical design pattern.

Materials per student: pattern blocks (TA 17), Math Center Recording Sheet (TA 31 optional)

Students use simple plane figures to draw symmetrical designs and show lines of symmetry. *[Check students' drawings.]*

PROBLEM-SOLVING ACTIVITY 83 — MATH CENTER, On Your Own

Patterning • Symmetrical Designs

- Copy the figures shown here. Make a symmetrical design with them. Use any figures you like, but there must be a line of symmetry.
- When you finish, draw an outline of the design and draw the line of symmetry.

YOU NEED: cutouts of these figures or pattern blocks

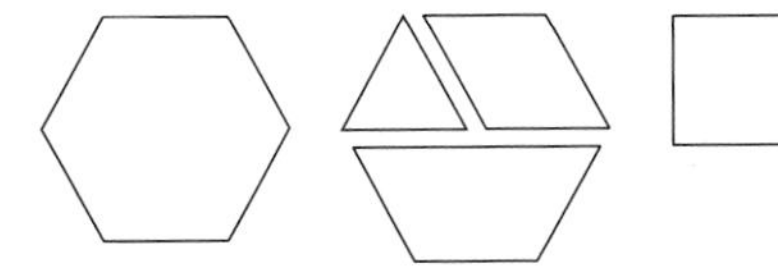

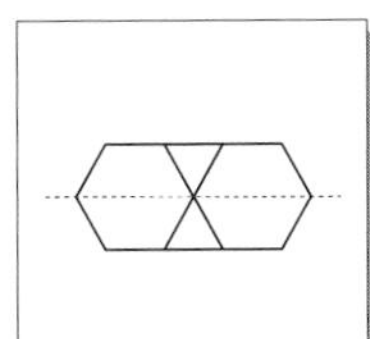

McGraw-Hill School Division — Grade Level 4

Chapter 9, Lesson 7, pages 344–345 — Geometry

APPROPRIATE

NCTM Standards

- ✓ Problem Solving
- ✓ Communication
- ✓ Reasoning
- Connections

Symmetry

OBJECTIVE Identify symmetric figures and draw lines of symmetry.

Vocabulary line of symmetry

1 Introduce

With students working in pairs, have them look at each other's faces. Have them imagine a vertical line down the middle of their partner's face along which their partner's face is folded in half.

- **Would one half of your partner's face match up exactly with the other half?** *[Possible answer: Yes—the match may not be as exact as in geometric figures, but it is close enough to be called a match.]*

2 Teach *Whole Class*

LEARN To show students the meanings of *symmetrical figure* and *line of symmetry,* choose an item in the classroom to show its line(s) of symmetry.

Point out the photos of the honeycomb on page 344. Ask students if there is more than one line of symmetry for the hexagon in the honeycomb. Draw a regular hexagon on the chalkboard and have volunteers come to the board to each draw one line of symmetry. Students should find 6 lines of symmetry.

Students may think the rectangle has a line of symmetry along its diagonal. Have students fold a sheet of paper along its diagonal to show that this is not a line of symmetry.

3 Close

Check for Understanding using items 1–4, page 344.

Critical Thinking
For item 3, have students experiment with irregular shapes cut out from paper before they answer. For item 4, have students trace an object on a piece of paper. Flip the object then trace it again. Have students compare the two shapes.

PRACTICE
Materials have available: calculators

Each student may choose ten exercises from ex. 1–12 and the **Mixed Review.**

- For ex. 9, students can use the Guess, Test, and Revise problem-solving strategy.
- For ex. 12, encourage students to find a shape that has several lines of symmetry.

Mixed Review/Test Preparation Students review estimating sums, differences, products, and quotients, learned in Chapters 2, 6, and 8.

Symmetry

LEARN

You probably see examples of symmetry every day. A figure that can be folded to make equal parts is a symmetrical figure. The fold line is a **line of symmetry.**

Check Out the Glossary
line of symmetry
See page 544.

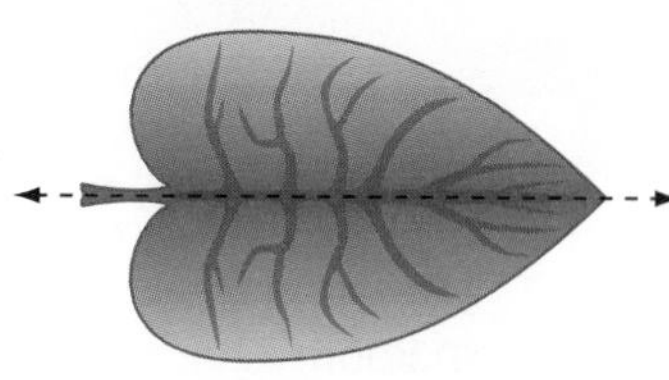
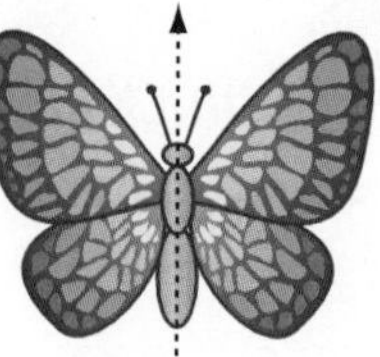

If you have ever seen a cell in a bee's honeycomb, you may have noticed that its shape is similar to a hexagon. A hexagon has 6 lines of symmetry.

Here are other pattern block shapes and their lines of symmetry.

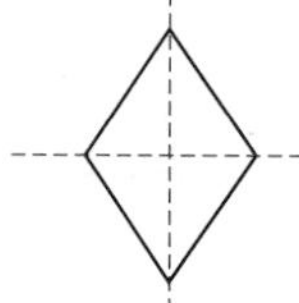
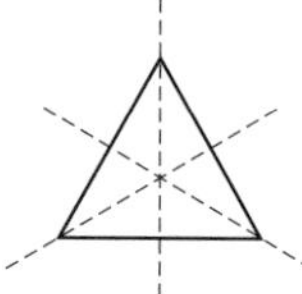
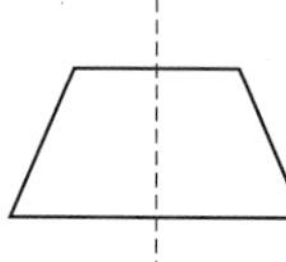
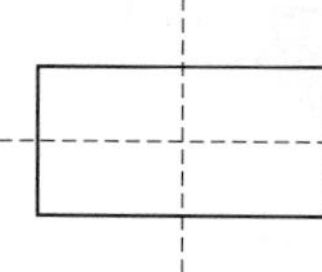

CHECK

Check for Understanding

1. Show eight capital letters that are symmetrical. How many lines of symmetry does each of them have? **Possible answer: A, B, C, D, E, I, K, M; lines of symmetry—1, 1, 1, 1, 1, 2, 1, and 1**

2. Which numbers from 1 to 10 are symmetrical? How many lines of symmetry does each of these numbers have? **1, 3, 8, 10; lines of symmetry—2, 1, 2, 1**

Critical Thinking: Analyze **Explain your reasoning.**

3. Can you find lines of symmetry for every shape? If not, show examples of figures that do not have lines of symmetry. **No; possible answer: triangles with corners of different sizes do not have lines of symmetry.**

4. If a figure is flipped across a line of symmetry to get another figure, will the two figures be congruent?

Meeting Individual Needs

Early Finishers

Have students write block numbers for the numbers 1–9 and find the lines of symmetry for each.

Extra Support

Have students trace the drawings and illustrations in ex. 1–8 on page 345, cut them out, and fold them in half to help them find the lines of symmetry.

Ongoing Assessment

Observation Checklist Determine if students understand symmetry by observing if they can find all the lines of symmetry for a given figure. Students should also be able to complete shapes when given one half of the shape and the line of symmetry.

Follow Up If students need more practice with symmetry, assign **Reteach 83.**

For students who understand symmetry, assign **Extend 83.**

Check students' drawings. Possible answers: A seesaw is symmetrical around the center, the length of the seesaw on either side is equal, the seesaw is even when there are equal weights on either side, the seesaw makes an acute angle when one person is up and the other is down.

ractice

he dashed line a line of symmetry?

No.

2 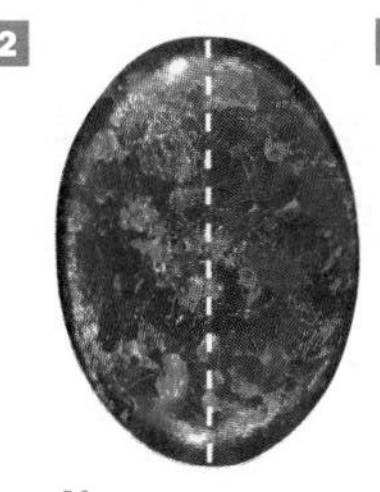
Yes.

3 
Yes.

4 
No.

he figure symmetrical? If yes, draw its lines of symmetry.

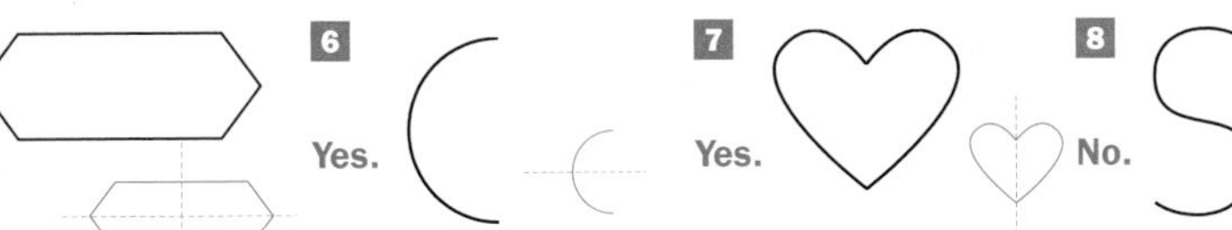
Yes. 6 Yes. 7 No. 8

IXED APPLICATIONS

roblem Solving

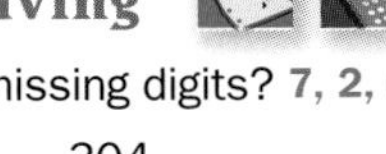

What are the missing digits? 7, 2, 0

$$\begin{array}{r} 304 \\ \times\ 1\blacksquare \\ 21\blacksquare 8 \\ +\ 3\blacksquare 40 \\ \hline 5{,}168 \end{array}$$

Describe a seesaw using as many geometric and measurement words as you can. Include drawings with your descriptions. See above.

10. Students should draw a rectangle that is 9 squares by 7 squares.

11 **Logical reasoning** A rectangle drawn on graph paper has 63 small squares inside. The length of the rectangle is 2 squares longer than the width. Draw the rectangle on graph paper and label its sides. See above.

12 **Write a problem** that asks for the lines of symmetry of a figure. Solve it and have others solve it. Students should compare problems and solutions.

mixed review • test preparation

timate. Estimates may vary. Possible estimates are given.

346 + 128 400	2 163 ÷ 4 40	3 781 − 302 500	4 38 × 41 1,600
536 − 292 200	6 87 × 21 1,800	7 479 + 826 1,300	8 3,402 ÷ 50 70

ra Practice, page 518

PRACTICE

Alternate Teaching Strategy

Materials per group: a small mirror

Give each group a mirror and have them turn to the polygons on pages 324 and 325 in the Student Book.

For each polygon, have students find at least one place where they can place the mirror so that the half of the polygon on the page and the half reflected in the mirror make up one whole polygon. Work with students to show them how to do this.

Ask students to draw polygons like the ones shown and draw the lines where they placed the mirror to make a whole polygon. Explain to students that the lines they drew are called *lines of symmetry*.

Have students share their results.

ESL APPROPRIATE

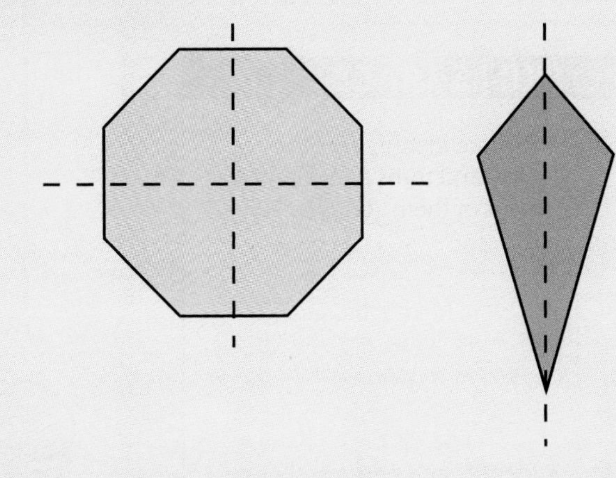

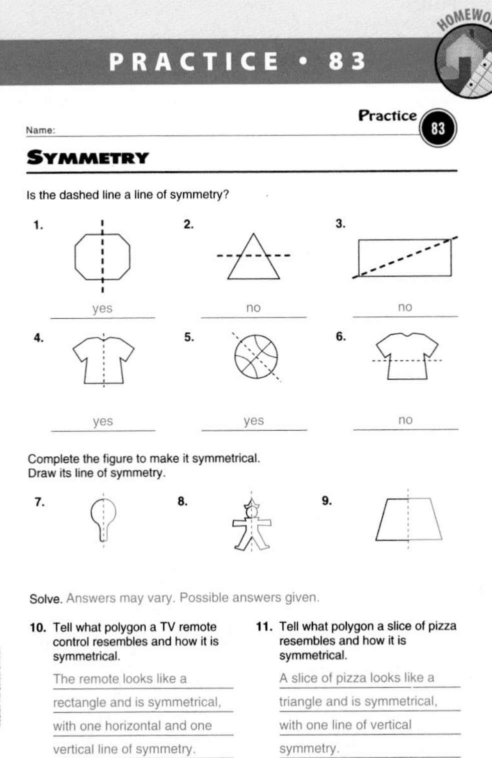

PRACTICE • 83

HOMEWORK

Name: Practice 83

SYMMETRY

Is the dashed line a line of symmetry?

1. yes
2. no
3. no
4. yes
5. yes
6. no

Complete the figure to make it symmetrical. Draw its line of symmetry.

7. 8. 9.

Solve. Answers may vary. Possible answers given.

10. Tell what polygon a TV remote control resembles and how it is symmetrical. The remote looks like a rectangle and is symmetrical, with one horizontal and one vertical line of symmetry.

11. Tell what polygon a slice of pizza resembles and how it is symmetrical. A slice of pizza looks like a triangle and is symmetrical, with one line of vertical symmetry.

McGraw-Hill School Division

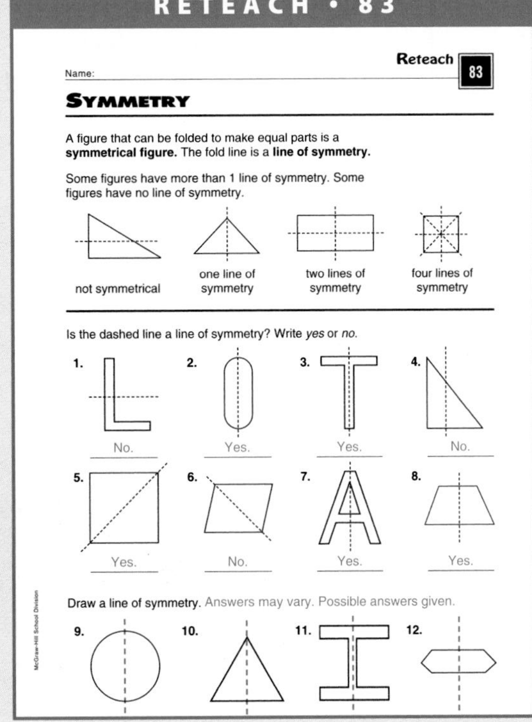

RETEACH • 83

Name: Reteach 83

SYMMETRY

A figure that can be folded to make equal parts is a **symmetrical figure.** The fold line is a **line of symmetry.**

Some figures have more than 1 line of symmetry. Some figures have no line of symmetry.

not symmetrical | one line of symmetry | two lines of symmetry | four lines of symmetry

Is the dashed line a line of symmetry? Write *yes* or *no*.

1. No.
2. Yes.
3. Yes.
4. No.
5. Yes.
6. No.
7. Yes.
8. Yes.

Draw a line of symmetry. Answers may vary. Possible answers given.

9. 10. 11. 12.

McGraw-Hill School Division

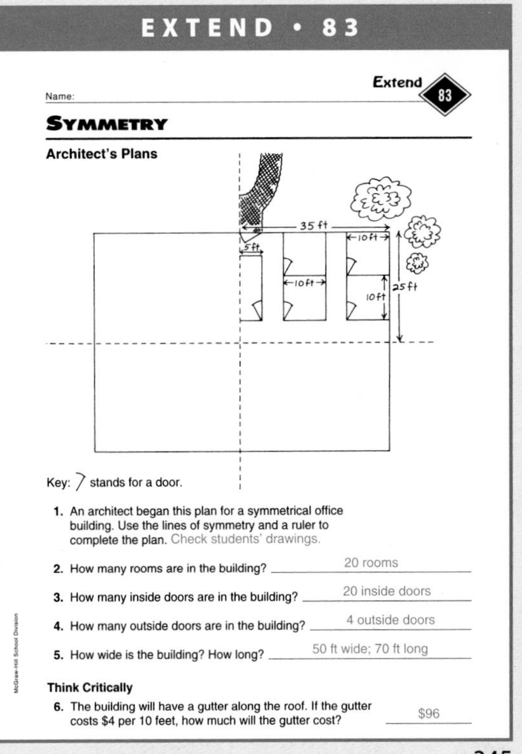

EXTEND • 83

Name: Extend 83

SYMMETRY

Architect's Plans

Key: stands for a door.

1. An architect began this plan for a symmetrical office building. Use the lines of symmetry and a ruler to complete the plan. Check students' drawings.
2. How many rooms are in the building? 20 rooms
3. How many inside doors are in the building? 20 inside doors
4. How many outside doors are in the building? 4 outside doors
5. How wide is the building? How long? 50 ft wide; 70 ft long

Think Critically

6. The building will have a gutter along the roof. If the gutter costs $4 per 10 feet, how much will the gutter cost? $96

McGraw-Hill School Division

EXPLORE ACTIVITY

Slides, Flips, and Turns

OBJECTIVE Explore identifying and performing transformations.

Teaching With Technology
See alternate computer lesson, pp. 347A–347B.

RESOURCE REMINDER
Math Center Cards 84
Practice 84, Reteach 84, Extend 84

SKILLS TRACE

GRADE 3	• Explore identifying slides, flips, and turns and combinations of them. *(Chapter 10)*
GRADE 4	• Explore identifying and performing slides, flips, and turns and combinations of them.
GRADE 5	• Identify and perform slides, flips, and turns and combinations of them. *(Chapter 8)*

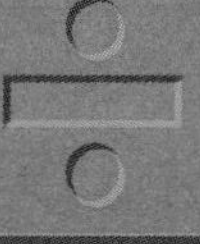

LESSON 9.8 RESOURCES

MANIPULATIVE WARM-UP

Whole Class — Visual/Spatial

OBJECTIVE Explore transformations.

Materials per student: triangle

▶ Put the triangle shown in figure 1 on the overhead projector. Slide the triangle to the right. Have students describe how you moved the triangle and tell what happened to the B. *[The triangle was slid to the right; the B is facing the same way.]*

▶ Turn the triangle as shown in figure 2. Have students describe how you moved the triangle, and tell what happened to the B. *[The triangle was turned; the B turned on its side.]*

▶ Flip the triangle as shown in figure 3. Have students describe how you moved the triangle, and tell what happened to the B. *[The triangle was flipped; the B got reversed.]*

Figure 1

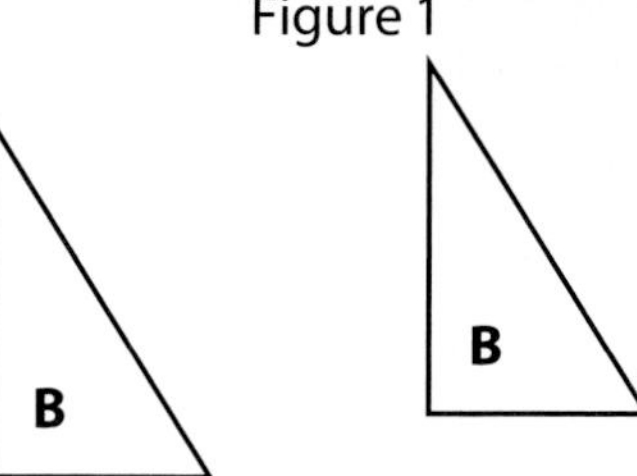

Figure 2

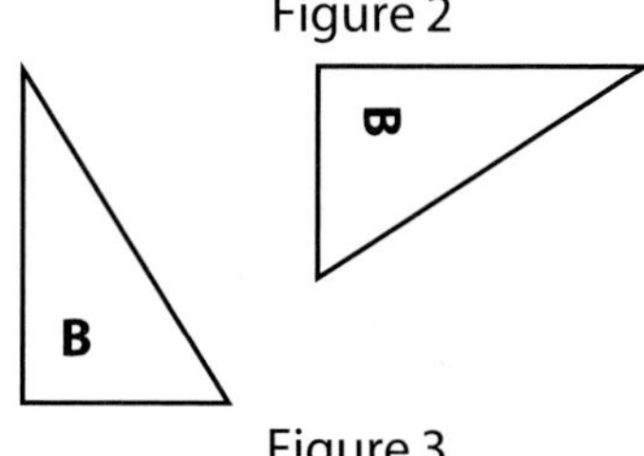

Figure 3

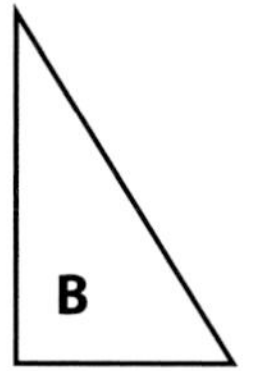

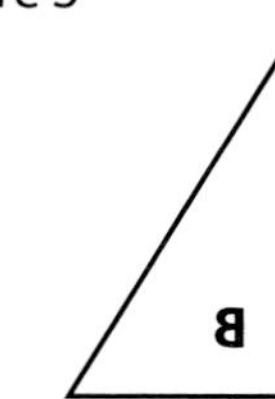

▶ Have students repeat the three maneuvers using their triangles.

SPATIAL REASONING CONNECTION

Whole Class — Visual/Spatial

OBJECTIVE Connect letters of the alphabet to transformations.

Materials per pair: cardboard, scissors, ruler

▶ Write the alphabet in block letters on the chalkboard.

▶ Have students copy the letters. Then have them circle the letters that would look the same if they were flipped.

ESL APPROPRIATE

Daily Review

PREVIOUS DAY QUICK REVIEW

How many lines of symmetry does each figure have?

1. H *[2]*
2. I *[2]*
3. T *[1]*
4. M *[1]*

FAST FACTS

1. 6 × 7 *[42]*
2. 2 × 8 *[16]*
3. 6 × 6 *[36]*
4. 3 × 4 *[12]*

Problem of the Day • 84

Gwen made a pictograph that shows the number of students who like different flavors of ice cream. Each ice cream cone represents 8 students. How many ice cream cones should Gwen draw to represent 20 students? *[$2\frac{1}{2}$]*

TECH LINK

Math Van

MATH VAN

Activity You may wish to use *Flustered Flagmaker* to teach this lesson.

Tool You may wish to use the Geometry tool with this lesson.

MATH FORUM

Cultural Diversity I have my students share designs from their countries of origin that show slides, flips, and turns.

Visit our Resource Village at http://www.mhschool.com to see more of the Math Forum.

MATH CENTER

Practice

OBJECTIVE Move letters over a line of symmetry.

Materials per student: centimeter graph paper (TA 7), a small mirror, markers

Students use a mirror to turn, flip, and slide a simple figure as part of the process of creating a symmetrical design pattern. *[Check students' drawings. Ask them to show all the lines of symmetry in their final design patterns.]*

PRACTICE ACTIVITY 84 — MATH CENTER — On Your Own

Patterning • Mirror Mosaics

The pattern below shows the simple figure "N" moved into different positions to create a symmetrical pattern.

- Choose another letter of the alphabet.
- Use the mirror to help you draw how your pattern will look depending on where you place the line of symmetry. Draw a dotted line through the line of symmetry.

YOU NEED
- graph paper
- a small mirror
- colored pencils or markers

Grade Level 4 — McGraw-Hill School Division

Chapter 9, Lesson 8, pages 346–347 — Geometry

ESL APPROPRIATE

NCTM Standards
- ✓ Problem Solving
- ✓ Communication
- Reasoning
- ✓ Connections

Problem Solving

OBJECTIVE Explore slides, flips and turns of a figure.

Materials graph paper, pattern blocks (TA 17)

Students play a game sliding, flipping, and turning cutout shapes. Then they try to describe the methods they used so that the rest of the group can attempt to recreate their movements. *[Students' check each other's work.]*

PROBLEM-SOLVING ACTIVITY 84 — MATH CENTER — Small Group

Logical Reasoning • Move and Match

- Take turns being the leader. The leader picks a pattern block for everyone to trace.
- The leader then draws three movements of the original figure, showing a slide, a turn, or a flip. The leader then explains how to move and trace the blocks so that the rest of the players can draw the same picture. Be as specific as possible about slide lines, turning points, and flip possibilities.
- At the end of the leader's explanation, compare drawings. If there are any matches, both players get a point. After each person gets to be a leader, the person with the most points wins.

YOU NEED
- graph paper
- pattern blocks

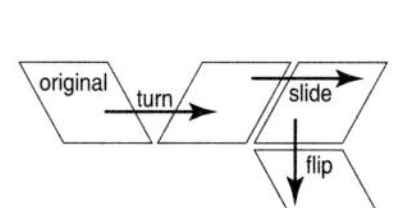

Grade Level 4 — McGraw-Hill School Division

Chapter 9, Lesson 8, pages 346–347 — Geometry

NCTM Standards
- ✓ Problem Solving
- ✓ Communication
- ✓ Reasoning
- Connections

EXPLORE ACTIVITY
Slides, Flips, and Turns

OBJECTIVE Explore identifying and performing transformations.

Materials per pair: centimeter graph paper (TA 7), rulers

Vocabulary flip, slide, turn

1 Introduce

Have students identify the shapes on the items in the photograph at the top of page 346. Ask students if the shapes are congruent or similar. Let students use rulers if they wish.

2 Teach *Cooperative Pairs*

LEARN Point out the examples of a flip, slide, and turn. You may wish to point out that flips, slides, and turns are also known as refractions, translations, and rotations, respectively.

Work Together Have students work in pairs to complete this activity. Allow students time to draw several figures for their partners. Ask students:

- **How did you know when your partner flipped his or her figure?** *[Possible answer: The flipped figure looked like a mirror image.]*
- **How did you know when your partner slid his or her figure?** *[Possible answer: The second figure was just moved right or left on the paper.]*
- **How did you know when your partner turned his or her figure?** *[Possible answer: The second figure was not facing in the same direction.]*

MAKE CONNECTIONS
With their partners, have students look over Toya's design and answer the questions.

3 Close

Check for Understanding using items 1–7, page 347.

CRITICAL THINKING
Ask students if it is possible to use slides, flips, or turns to create a figure that is not congruent to the original figure. Students should see that this is impossible.

PRACTICE
Materials have available: calculators

Options for assigning exercises:
A—All ex. 1–9
B—Choice of 6 exercises from ex. 1–9

EXPLORE ACTIVITY • GEOMETRY

Slides, Flips, and Turns

LEARN

Many patterns are created by moving figures in different ways.

You can **flip** a figure over a line.

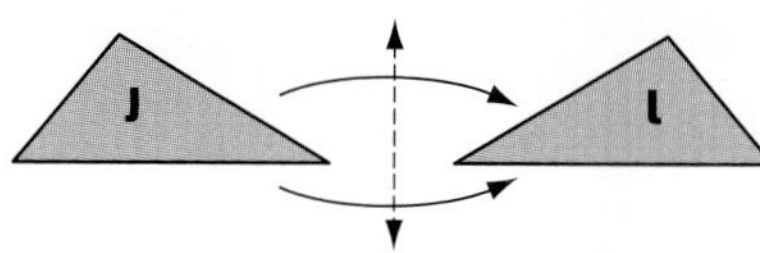

You can **slide** a figure across a line.

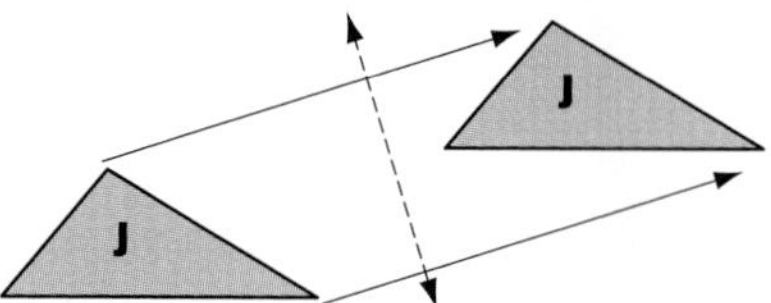

You can **turn** a figure around a point on a line.

Work Together
Work with a partner. Draw a geometric figure on graph paper. Now draw another figure by either flipping, sliding, or turning the original figure.

You will need
- graph paper
- rulers

Exchange drawings with your partner. Have your partner tell whether your figure shows a flip, a slide, or a turn.

Check Out the Glossary
For vocabulary words
See page 544.

Change places and follow the same steps.

Make Connections
You can combine flips, slides, and turns to create a pattern.

Toya took her shape and made a pattern by using a flip.

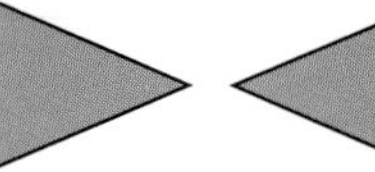

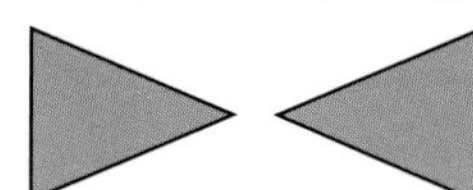

▶ What would Toya's pattern look like if she had used a slide instead?

346 Lesson 9.8

Meeting Individual Needs

Early Finishers
Have students draw each kind of quadrilateral and then draw a slide, flip, and turn of each. Have them exchange drawings to verify them.

Extra Support
Have students trace a cardboard cutout of a polygon on a sheet of paper. Have students make at least one example of slides, flips, and turns to ensure understanding.

Ongoing Assessment
Observation Checklist Determine whether students understand transformations by having them verbalize the movements as they slide, flip, and turn a figure.

Follow Up If students need more practice with slides, flips, and turns, assign **Reteach 84.**

If they need a greater challenge, assign **Extend 84.**

Check for Understanding

Write *flip, slide,* or *turn* to tell how the figure was moved.

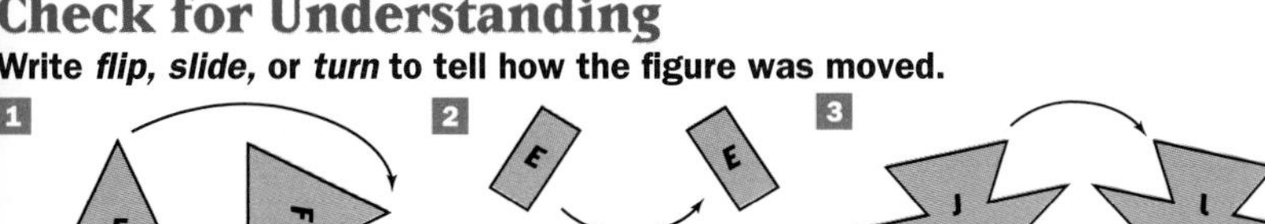

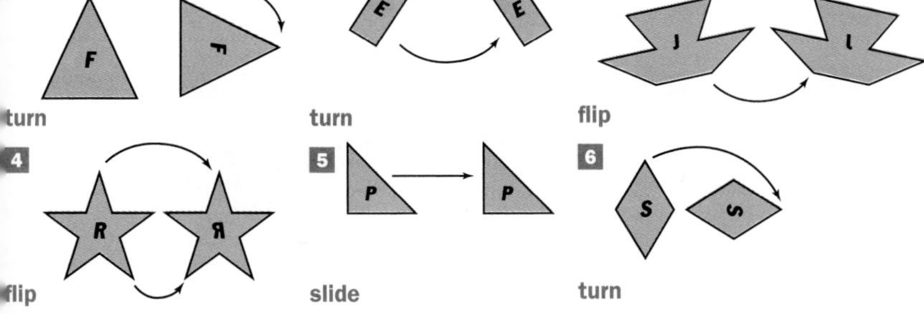

1 turn 2 turn 3 flip

4 flip 5 slide 6 turn

Critical Thinking: Analyze **Explain your reasoning.**

7 How can you use flips, slides, and turns to show that two figures are congruent? **Possible answer: If a figure is moved using flips, slides, or turns so that it fits directly over another figure, then the figures are congruent.**

Practice

Tell how the figure was moved. Write *flip, slide,* or *turn.*

1 
turn

2 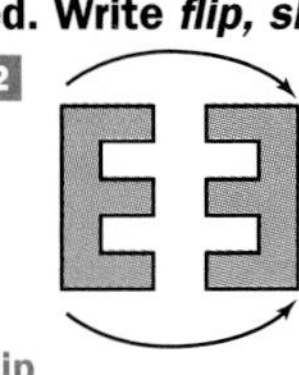
flip

3 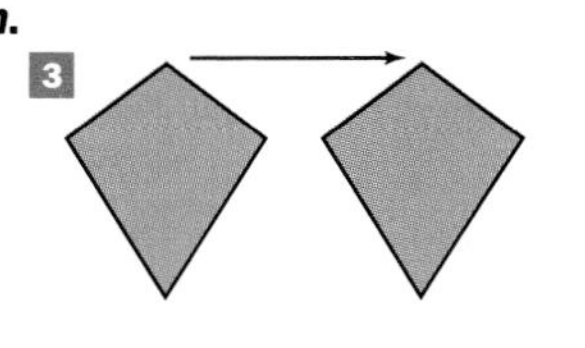
slide

Copy the figure onto graph paper. Move the figure in the way indicated. **Check students' work. Students should draw the sizes of the figures consistently.**

4 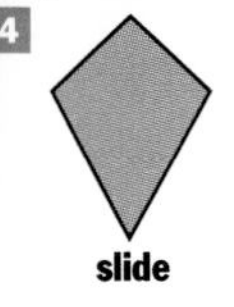
slide

5 
turn

6 
slide

7 **flip**

8 
slide

9 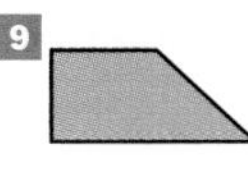
flip, then turn

Extra Practice, page 518

Alternate Teaching Strategy

Materials per student: pencil, book

Demonstrate a flip by flipping a pencil over a vertical line drawn on the chalkboard as students do the same with a pencil at their desks. Tell students that this movement is called a *flip*. Point out that the eraser end of the pencil is now facing the opposite direction.

Demonstrate a *slide* in the same manner by sliding the pencil along a horizontal line as students do the same at their desks. Point out that the eraser end of the pencil is still facing the same direction as it was but the pencil has moved right or left.

Finally demonstrate a *turn* by turning the pencil a $\frac{1}{4}$ turn or 90°. Tell students that the position of the pencil has changed by turning it, and the eraser end of the pencil is now facing a different direction.

Have students demonstrate a slide, flip, and turn using a book.

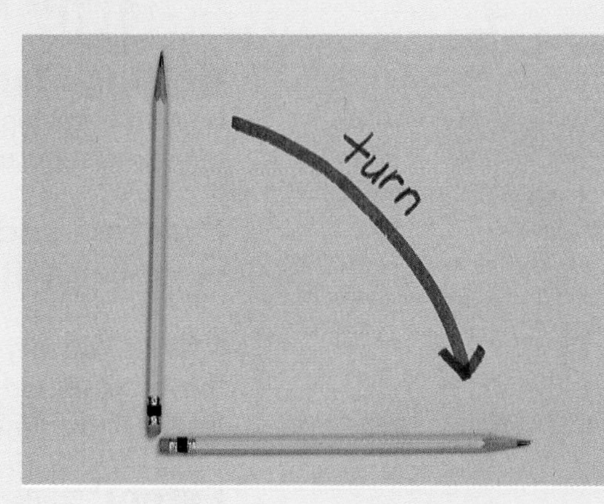

PRACTICE • 84

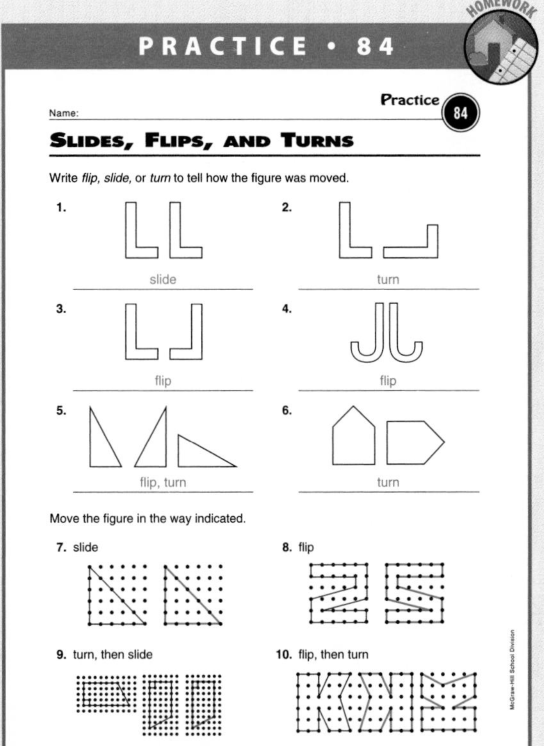

Practice 84

Name:

SLIDES, FLIPS, AND TURNS

Write *flip, slide,* or *turn* to tell how the figure was moved.

1. slide
2. turn
3. flip
4. flip
5. flip, turn
6. turn

Move the figure in the way indicated.

7. slide
8. flip
9. turn, then slide
10. flip, then turn

RETEACH • 84

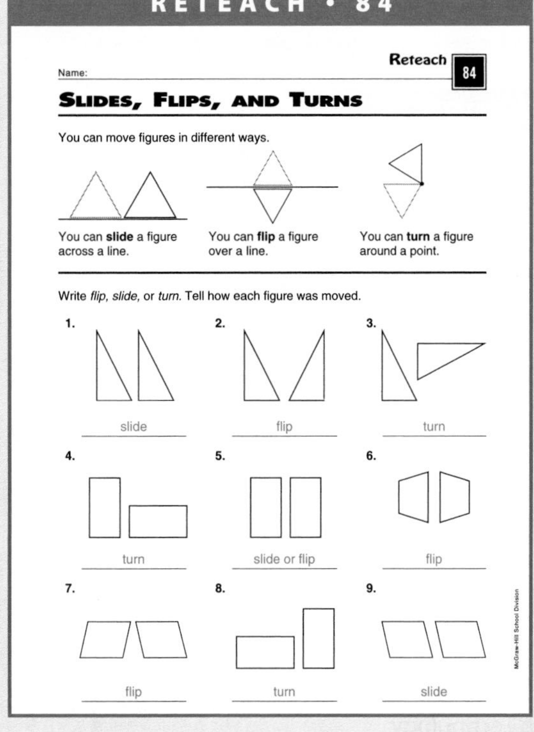

Reteach 84

Name:

SLIDES, FLIPS, AND TURNS

You can move figures in different ways.

You can **slide** a figure across a line. You can **flip** a figure over a line. You can **turn** a figure around a point.

Write *flip, slide,* or *turn*. Tell how each figure was moved.

1. slide
2. flip
3. turn
4. turn
5. slide or flip
6. flip
7. flip
8. turn
9. slide

EXTEND • 84

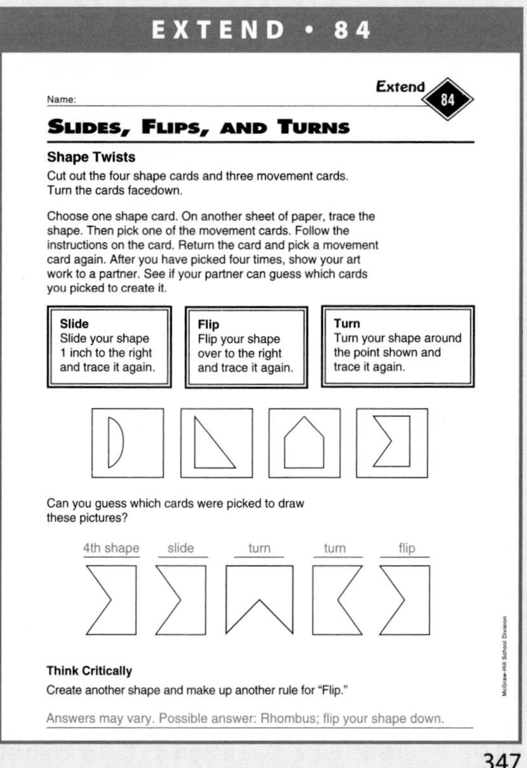

Extend 84

Name:

SLIDES, FLIPS, AND TURNS

Shape Twists

Cut out the four shape cards and three movement cards. Turn the cards facedown.

Choose one shape card. On another sheet of paper, trace the shape. Then pick one of the movement cards. Follow the instructions on the card. Return the card and pick a movement card again. After you have picked four times, show your art work to a partner. See if your partner can guess which cards you picked to create it.

Slide	Flip	Turn
Slide your shape 1 inch to the right and trace it again.	Flip your shape over to the right and trace it again.	Turn your shape around the point shown and trace it again.

Can you guess which cards were picked to draw these pictures?

4th shape slide turn turn flip

Think Critically

Create another shape and make up another rule for "Flip."

Answers may vary. Possible answer: Rhombus; flip your shape down.

Teaching With Technology

Slides, Flips, and Turns

OBJECTIVE Students explore using transformations to manipulate geometric shapes.

Resource Math Van Activity: *Flustered Flagmaker*

SET UP

Provide students with the activity card for *Flustered Flagmaker.* Start ***Math Van*** and click the *Activities* button. Click the *Flustered Flagmaker* activity on the Fax Machine.

Using the Math Van Activity

1 **Getting Started** Students learn to use the *Slide, Flip,* and *Turn* buttons to manipulate geometric shapes and place them correctly in the rectangular outline to make a flag of Grenada.

2 **Practice and Apply** Students use what they have learned to create the initial of their first or last name by manipulating shapes.

3 **Close** You may wish to have the students discuss how they moved shapes to the desired places. Be sure they use correct terms for the transformations.

Extend Students continue to use what they have learned about manipulating shapes to create their own picture. They use the Geometry tools to slide, flip, and turn the shapes to make their picture.

TIPS FOR TOOLS

Remind the students to use the *Undo* button if they make a mistake, and continue to explore transformations using the Geometry tools.

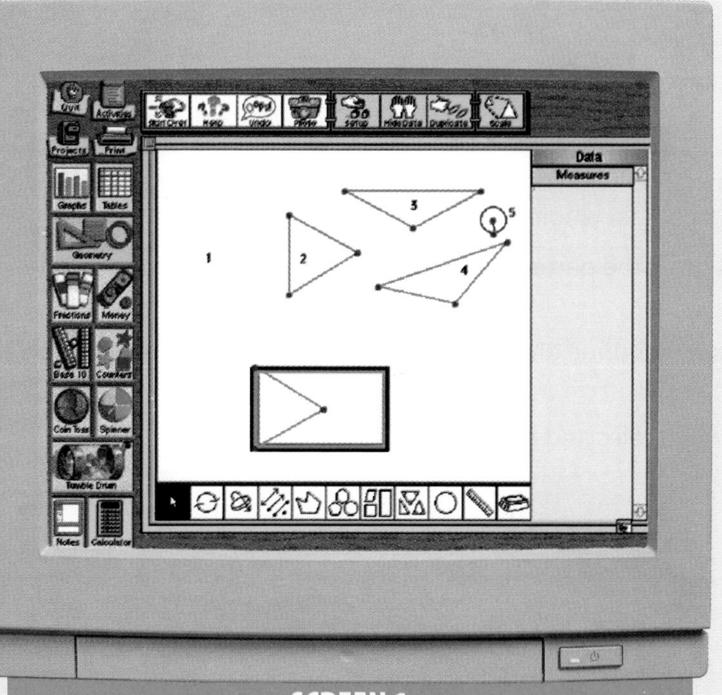

SCREEN 1

Students use the Geometry buttons to slide the shapes to make the flag of Grenada.

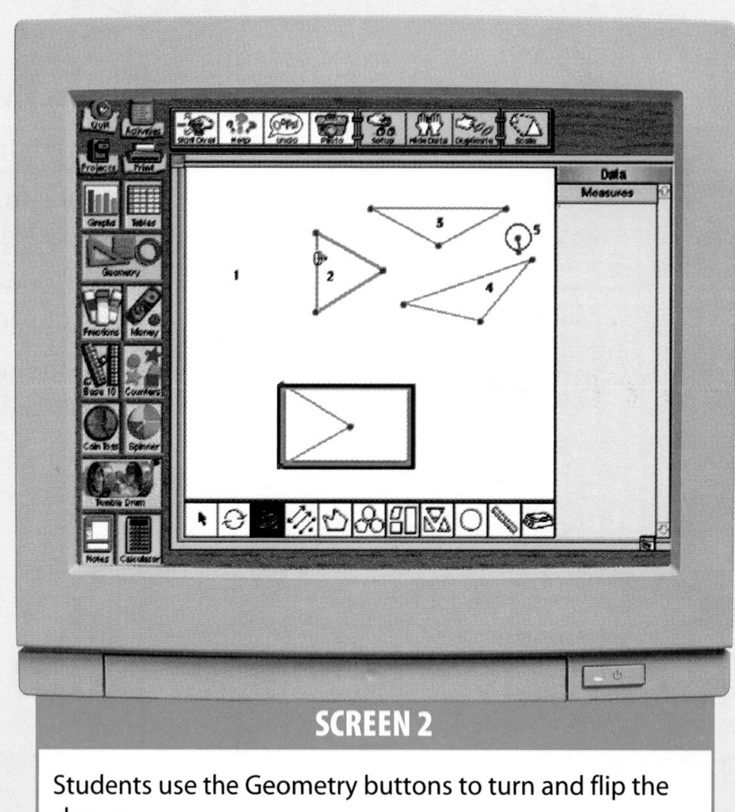

SCREEN 2

Students use the Geometry buttons to turn and flip the shapes.

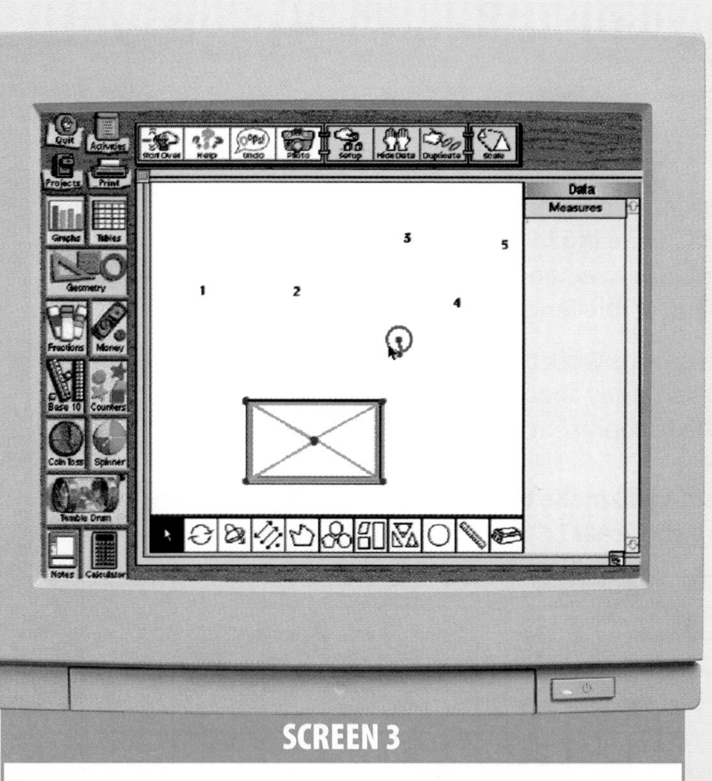

SCREEN 3

Students continue to move the shapes to complete the flag.

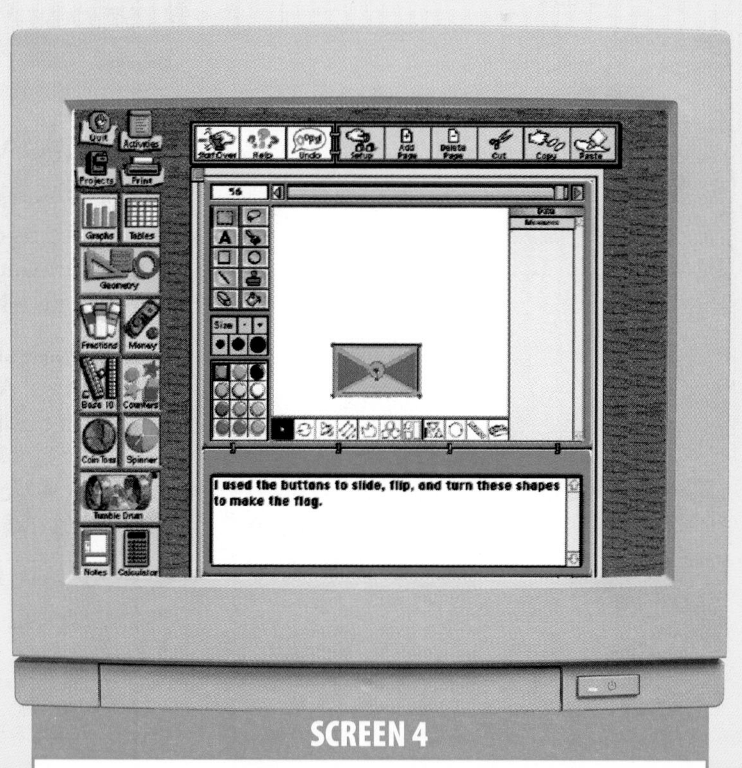

SCREEN 4

Students take a photo of their work and write in their Notes how they moved the shapes to make the flag.

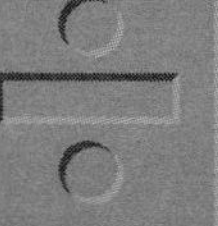

EXPLORE ACTIVITY

Area

OBJECTIVE Explore finding the area of rectangular regions and estimating the area of irregular shapes.

RESOURCE REMINDER
Math Center Cards 85
Practice 85, Reteach 85, Extend 85

SKILLS TRACE

GRADE 3	• Explore estimating and measuring the area of rectangular regions. *(Chapter 9)*
GRADE 4	• Explore finding the area of rectangular regions and estimating the area of irregular shapes using a grid.
GRADE 5	• Explore finding the area of a rectangle and estimating the area of irregular shapes. *(Chapter 12)*

MANIPULATIVE WARM-UP

Cooperative Pairs — Logical/Analytical

OBJECTIVE Draw polygons of a specific area.

Materials per pair: centimeter graph paper (TA 7)

▶ One student draws a polygon on graph paper without the partner seeing it. The polygon should contain whole squares.

▶ The first student gives the partner clues about the figure so that the partner can duplicate it.

▶ The student should continue giving clues until the partner is able to duplicate the drawing.

▶ Have partners switch roles and repeat the activity.

CONSUMER CONNECTION

Cooperative Groups — Visual/Spatial

OBJECTIVE Connect consumer purchases and possible perimeters.

▶ Present the following problem:
Amos can purchase fencing in 36-foot lengths. He wants to buy only one length to enclose a rectangular garden. If he uses all of the fencing, what are the possible lengths and widths of his garden?

▶ Have students in groups work together to find all of the possible dimensions of Amos's garden. They should draw the possible rectangles on graph paper using 1 square to represent 1 foot. *[Possible answers: 1 by 17, 2 by 16, 3 by 15, 4 by 14, 5 by 13, 6 by 12, 7 by 11, 8 by 10, 9 by 9]*

- **Which dimension will make the greatest area of the garden? the least? What are the areas?** *[9 × 9; 1 × 17; 81 square feet, 17 square feet]*

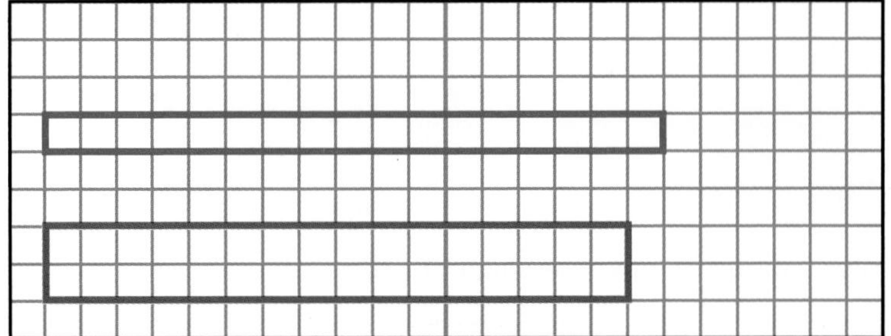

Daily Review

PREVIOUS DAY QUICK REVIEW

Show the following motions for a circle. What can you conclude?

1. a slide **2.** a flip **3.** a turn

[A slide, flip, and turn of a circle are the same as the original circle.]

FAST FACTS

1. 27 ÷ 3 *[9]*
2. 24 ÷ 4 *[6]*
3. 42 ÷ 6 *[7]*
4. 18 ÷ 2 *[9]*

Problem of the Day • 85

Carrie is making a picture frame for a print that measures 36 inches long and 18 inches wide. The frame is $2\frac{1}{2}$ inches wide. What will the dimensions of the picture with frame be when completed? *[41 inches long by 23 inches wide]*

TECH LINK

Math Van

MATH VAN

Tool You may wish to use the Geometry tool with this lesson.

MATH FORUM

Management Tip I have students keep graph paper handy to help them find areas of rectangles and squares.

Visit our Resource Village at http://www.mhschool.com to see more of the Math Forum.

MATH CENTER

Practice

OBJECTIVE Find the area of rectangular regions.

Materials per student: metric ruler, 3 textbooks, Math Center Recording Sheet (TA 31 optional)

Students measure the length and width of different textbooks and list the books in order of increasing area. *[Answers will vary depending on the size of the textbooks.]*

PRACTICE ACTIVITY 85 — MATH CENTER, On Your Own

Spatial Reasoning • Classroom Areas

YOU NEED: metric ruler; 3 textbooks

- Measure the length and width of the front cover of a textbook to the nearest centimeter. Calculate its area.
- Repeat with two other books. List the books by name in order from least to greatest area.

Grade Level 4 · McGraw-Hill School Division

Chapter 9, Lesson 9, pages 348–351 — Geometry

NCTM Standards
- ✓ Problem Solving
- ✓ Communication
- ✓ Reasoning
- Connections

Problem Solving

OBJECTIVE Find the area of irregular-shaped figures.

Materials per student: centimeter graph paper (TA 7), Math Center Recording Sheet (TA 31 optional)

Students estimate the area of boxstyle letters. *[Check students' work.]*

PROBLEM-SOLVING ACTIVITY 85 — MATH CENTER, On Your Own

Logical Reasoning • Area Alphabet?

YOU NEED: centimeter graph paper

- Draw capital letters on graph paper. Use only straight-line segments.
- Find the area inside each letter. For example, the H shown here has an area of 32 square centimeters.
- Spell a name or a word on graph paper with straight-line capital letters. What is the total area?

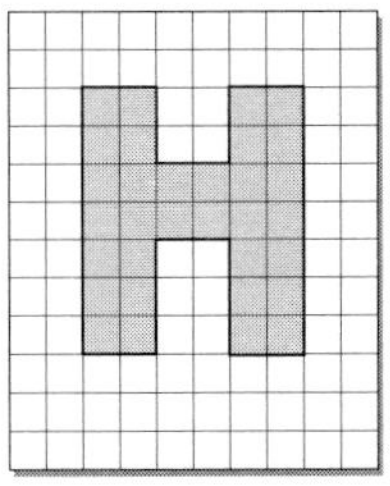

Grade Level 4 · McGraw-Hill School Division

Chapter 9, Lesson 9, pages 348–351 — Geometry

ESL APPROPRIATE

NCTM Standards
- ✓ Problem Solving
- ✓ Communication
- ✓ Reasoning
- ✓ Connections

Lesson 9.9

EXPLORE ACTIVITY
Area

OBJECTIVE Explore finding the area of rectangular regions and estimating the area of irregular shapes.

Materials per pair: inch graph paper (TA 8)

Vocabulary area, square unit

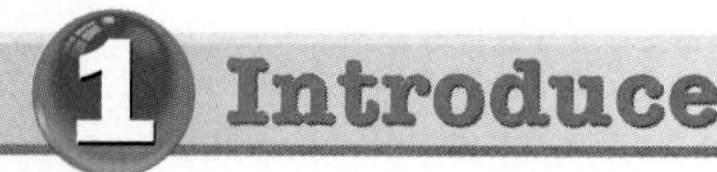

1 Introduce

Ask students when knowing the area of a shape is necessary, such as when tiling or carpeting a floor or painting a wall. Ask students to help you think of other ways in which area can be used.

2 Teach *Cooperative Pairs*

LEARN After discussing the introductory example and the information on area, use a yardstick to draw a square with an area of one square foot on the chalkboard. Ask students to estimate the area of the chalkboard in square feet. Record their estimates. Then ask how they could find the exact area of the chalkboard. Accept any reasonable answers.

Work Together Have students complete this activity in pairs. Encourage students to vary the sizes of their rectangles as much as possible.

Talk It Over Ask students to use the data in their tables to answer the first question. Then have students attempt to find all the possible rectangles with an area of 24 square inches. Pairs should write a description of the method they used.

As a class, let students share their results and any observations they have made.

Area

LEARN

The **area** of a 2-dimensional figure is the number of square units needed to cover the figure.

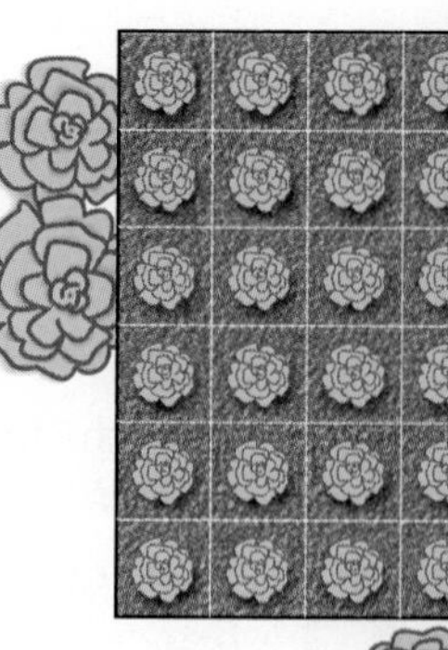

This garden is the size of 24 squares. Each square has sides that are 1 foot long. The garden has an area of 24 **square units,** or 24 square feet.

You can find the area of other rectangles by using graph paper.

Work Together
Work with a partner. Draw different-size rectangles on graph paper. Find the area of each rectangle in square inches.

Record the length, width, and area of each rectangle in a table. Organize your table from least to greatest area.

You will need
- *1-inch graph paper*

Length	Width	Area
6 inches	4 inches	24 square inches

Talk It Over
- **What if** you increase either the length or width of the rectangle. How does the area change? What if you decrease either the length or the width? **The area increases; the area decreases.**
- What strategy would you use to find all the possible rectangles with an area of 24 square inches? **See above.**

Possible answer: Start with a width of 1 in. and find all the rectangles, increasing the width until no new rectangles are found.

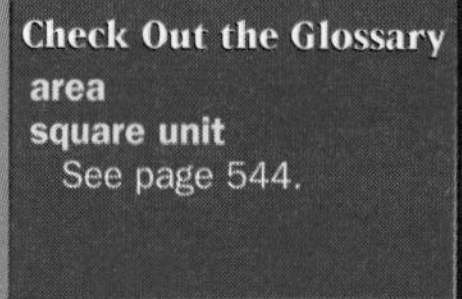

Check Out the Glossary
area
square unit
See page 544.

Meeting Individual Needs

Extra Support

Students sometimes confuse *area* and *perimeter*. It may help to review perimeter during this lesson. Have students find the perimeter of each of the rectangles in the practice exercises.

Gifted And Talented

Have students calculate the area of a rectangular table top or desk in the classroom. Have students measure each dimension of the surface to the nearest inch.

ESL APPROPRIATE

Ongoing Assessment

Observation Checklist Determine if students understand area by observing them and questioning them about calculation methods as they find the areas of shapes in this lesson.

Follow Up For more practice with area, have students draw a picture of a figure that covers an area of 50 square inches. Assign **Reteach 85.**

For students who understand area, assign **Extend 85.**

ke Connections

y and Elizabeth used graph er to find all the possible tangles with an area of square inches. They wrote lengths and widths of the tangles in a table. They iced that for the first tangle, if they multiplied gth times width, they the area.

Width (in inches)	Length (in inches)	Area (in square inches)
1	24	24
2	12	24
3	8	24
4	6	24

Would this work for the other rectangles in the table? **Yes.**

Why didn't they list the rectangle with a width of 6 inches and a length of 4 inches? **It is the same as the rectangle with a width of 4 in. and length of 6 in.**

Did they list all the possible rectangles? How do you know? **Yes; possible answer: the list includes all the factors of 24 as either a width or length.**

heck for Understanding

d the area for the figure.

square units

2 10 square units

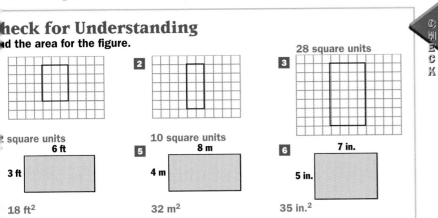

3 28 square units

6 ft, 3 ft — 18 ft^2

5 8 m, 4 m — 32 m^2

6 7 in., 5 in. — 35 in.^{2}

ritical Thinking: Generalize **Explain your reasoning.**

How many possible rectangles are there with an area of 20 square units? How can you tell without drawing them? **three possible rectangles; possible answer: from the factors of 20, which are 1×20, 2×10, and 4×5**

Kurt says that if you know the length of one side of a square, all you have to do to find the area is multiply the length times itself. Why is he correct? **All the sides of a square have equal lengths, so multiplying the length by the width is the same as multiplying the length by itself.**

Turn the page for Practice.

CHECK

MAKE CONNECTIONS

Have students compare their method of finding all the rectangles with an area of 24 square inches to Cory and Elizabeth's method. Did they find the same rectangles as Cory and Elizabeth? *[Answers may vary.]*

Ask students to answer the questions in this section with their partners. Have students use Cory and Elizabeth's method to find all the rectangles having an area of 30.

Let students discuss their answers as a class. Ask all students with different results for the final question to share their methods. Make sure that students fully understand that multiplying the length and width of a rectangle is an easy way to find its area.

3 Close

Check for Understanding using items 1–8, page 349.

CRITICAL THINKING

For item 7, remind students when they are finding the factors of 20 to remember to include 1×20. For item 8, some students may benefit from drawing squares on graph paper.

Practice See pages 350–351.

Inclusion

For students who are visually impaired, have them make rectangles on geoboards for the Explore activity. For the practice exercises, students should be able to determine answers by multiplying the length and width.

PRACTICE

Materials have available: graph paper (TA 8), calculators

Options for assigning exercises:
A—Odd ex. 1–23; **More to Explore**
B—Even ex. 2–22; **More to Explore**

- In ex. 21, remind students that 8 pints = 1 gallon.

More to Explore If students have difficulty estimating area, have them make a 5-by-5 grid on graph paper. Have them shade 15 whole squares, 4 half squares, 2 squares that are a little less than half, 2 squares that are a little more than half, and 2 squares that are almost whole squares. They can use their grids to help them when estimating area.

PRACTICE

Practice

Find the area of the rectangle.

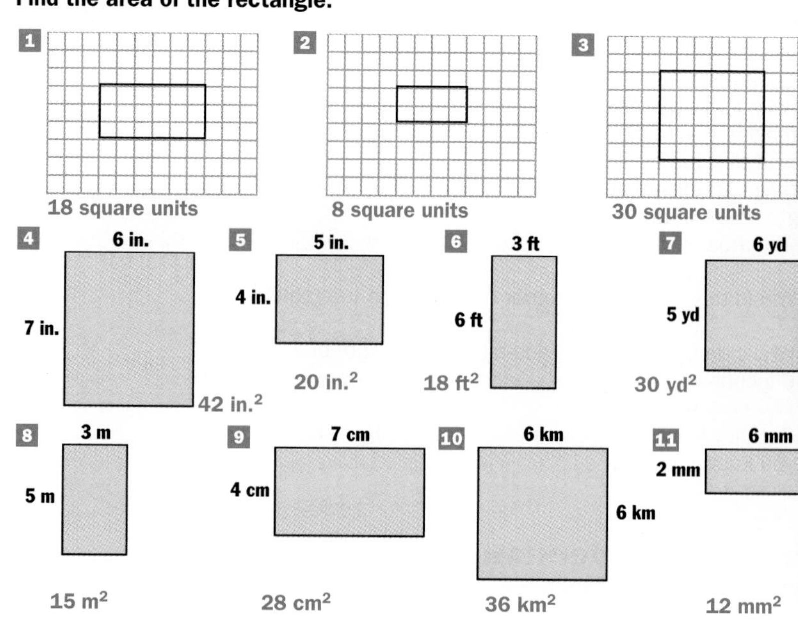

Use graph paper to draw rectangles with the following areas. How many rectangles are possible for each?

12 14 square units **two possible rectangles: 1 × 14, 2 × 7**

13 18 square units **three possible rectangles: 1 × 18, 2 × 9, 3 × 6**

14 22 square units **two possible rectangles: 1 × 22, 2 × 11**

15 25 square units **two possible rectangles: 1 × 25, 5 × 5**

16 28 square units **three possible rectangles: 1 × 28, 2 × 14, 4 × 7**

17 36 square units **five possible rectangles: 1 × 36, 2 × 18, 3 × 4 × 9, 6 × 6**

Solve.

18 The dimensions of four rectangles are given below. Use graph paper to draw each rectangle. Then list the areas from least to greatest.
a. length, 4 cm; width, 5 cm
b. length, 8 cm; width, 2 cm
c. length, 5 cm; width, 6 cm
d. length, 3 cm; width, 9 cm
Check students' drawings; 16 cm², 20 cm², 27 cm², 30 cm².

19 Which figure has the greater area? **They are both 16 in.².**
a. a rectangle with a length of 8 in. and a width of 2 in.
b. a square with 4-in. sides

Meeting Individual Needs

Early Finishers

Ask students to find a value for the area of a rectangle for which there are more than 4 possible rectangles having that area. Possible answers include rectangles with an area of 60 or 100 square units.

ESL APPROPRIATE

Common Error

Some students may forget to label the answer to area problems with square units. Remind them that area is a measure and should always have a square unit as part of the answer.

20. Possible answer: 6 ft by 8 ft; the fencing for this area will cost the least, $28.

MIXED APPLICATIONS

Problem Solving

20 **Make a decision** Mr. East wants to fence in 48 square feet of his yard for a garden. The fencing he wants costs $1.00 for each foot. He has $50.00 to spend. What dimensions should he choose? Why? See above.

21 Mrs. McCarthy's class is going on a field trip. She thinks that her 32 students and 6 parents will each drink about 1 pint of lemonade at lunch. How many gallons of lemonade should she plan to bring? 5 gal

INFOBIT
The omnitheater screen at the Liberty Science Center in New Jersey is about 88 feet across and 65 feet high.

22 Tamika is comparing two trees. One tree measures 42 ft and another measures 14 yds. Which is taller? How do you know?
They are the same height; 3 ft is 1 yd, so 42 ft = 42 ÷ 3 = 14 yd.

23 About how large is the area of the omnitheater screen at the Liberty Science Center? SEE INFOBIT.
Possible answer: about 6,300 ft^2

more to explore

Estimating the Area of Irregular Shapes

You can estimate the area of irregular shapes by using a grid. Count the whole squares first. Then look at the parts of squares and estimate how many whole squares they would make. Add to estimate the total area.

Scientists measure paw prints to learn more about animals. This badger paw print is about 38 square units.

Set a sheet of graph paper on the floor. Trace around your shoe on the graph paper. Estimate how many square units your shoe fits. Then count.

Extra Practice, page 518

Geometry **351**

Alternate Teaching Strategy

Materials per group: ads for carpeting, yardstick or measuring tape

Ask students to imagine that they are to choose carpeting for the classroom. After giving each group ads for carpeting, tell them that carpeting is sold by the square yard (area).

Explain area and show how the area of a rectangle can be calculated by multiplying length by width.

Ask volunteers to measure the length and width of the classroom to the nearest yard. In groups, have students use this data to determine the area, the amount of carpeting needed, and the cost based on the ads.

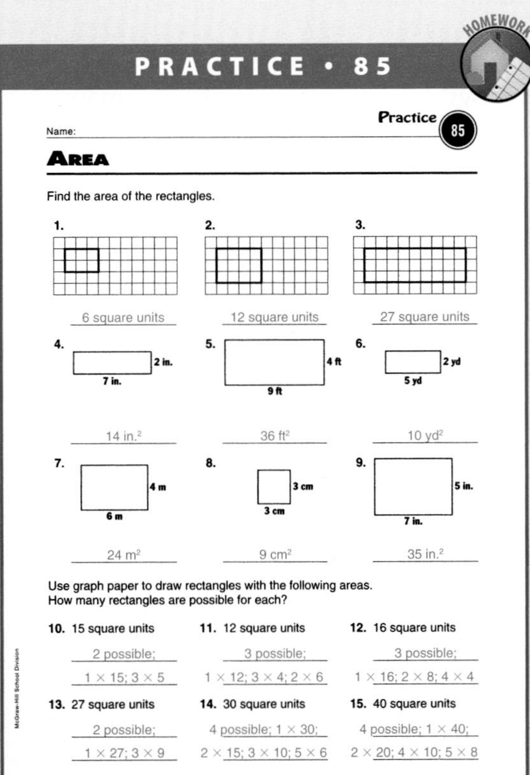

PRACTICE • 85

HOMEWORK

Practice 85

Name:

AREA

Find the area of the rectangles.

1. 6 square units
2. 12 square units
3. 27 square units
4. 7 in. × 2 in. — 14 in.^{2}
5. 9 ft × 4 ft — 36 ft^2
6. 5 yd × 2 yd — 10 yd^2
7. 6 m × 4 m — 24 m^2
8. 3 cm × 3 cm — 9 cm^2
9. 7 in. × 5 in. — 35 in.^{2}

Use graph paper to draw rectangles with the following areas. How many rectangles are possible for each?

10. 15 square units — 2 possible; 1 × 15; 3 × 5
11. 12 square units — 3 possible; 1 × 12; 3 × 4; 2 × 6
12. 16 square units — 3 possible; 1 × 16; 2 × 8; 4 × 4
13. 27 square units — 2 possible; 1 × 27; 3 × 9
14. 30 square units — 4 possible; 1 × 30; 2 × 15; 3 × 10; 5 × 6
15. 40 square units — 4 possible; 1 × 40; 2 × 20; 4 × 10; 5 × 8

McGraw-Hill School Division

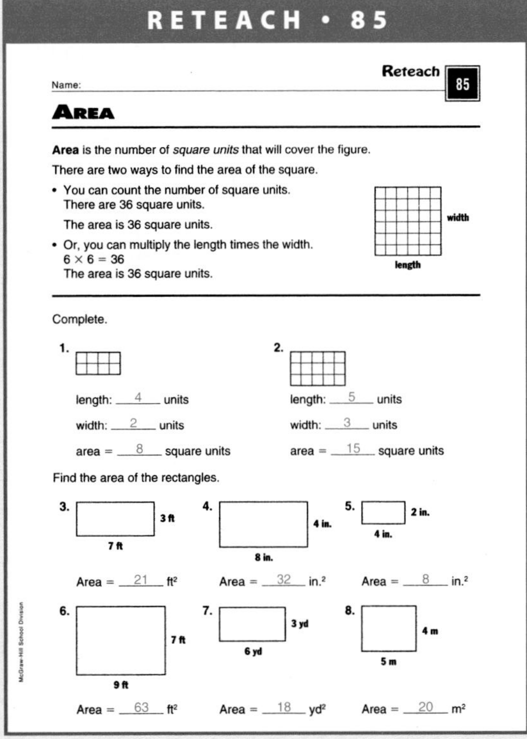

RETEACH • 85

Reteach 85

Name:

AREA

Area is the number of *square units* that will cover the figure.

There are two ways to find the area of the square.

- You can count the number of square units. There are 36 square units.
  The area is 36 square units.
- Or, you can multiply the length times the width.
  6 × 6 = 36
  The area is 36 square units.

width
length

Complete.

1. length: 4 units; width: 2 units; area = 8 square units
2. length: 5 units; width: 3 units; area = 15 square units

Find the area of the rectangles.

3. 7 ft × 3 ft — Area = 21 ft^2
4. 8 in. × 4 in. — Area = 32 in.^{2}
5. 4 in. × 2 in. — Area = 8 in.^{2}
6. 9 ft × 7 ft — Area = 63 ft^2
7. 6 yd × 3 yd — Area = 18 yd^2
8. 5 m × 4 m — Area = 20 m^2

McGraw-Hill School Division

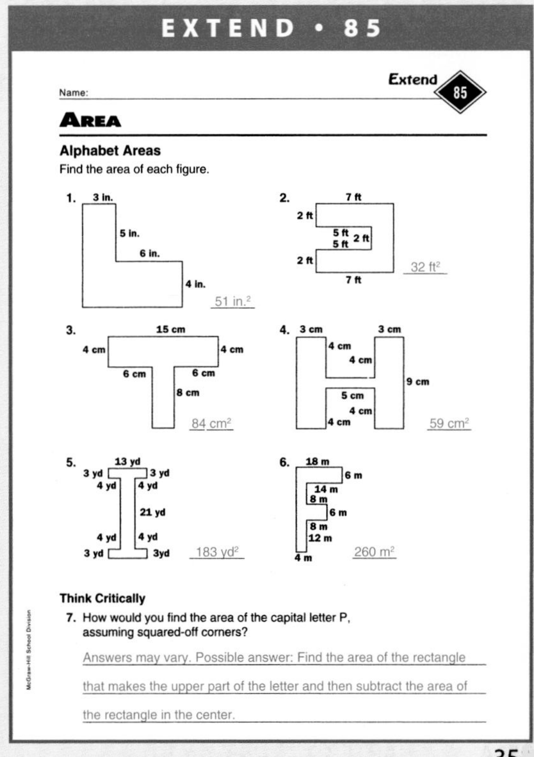

EXTEND • 85

Extend 85

Name:

AREA

Alphabet Areas

Find the area of each figure.

1. 51 in.^{2}
2. 32 ft^2
3. 84 cm^2
4. 59 cm^2
5. 183 yd^2
6. 260 m^2

Think Critically

7. How would you find the area of the capital letter P, assuming squared-off corners?
Answers may vary. Possible answer: Find the area of the rectangle that makes the upper part of the letter and then subtract the area of the rectangle in the center.

McGraw-Hill School Division

EXPLORE ACTIVITY

Volume

OBJECTIVE Explore estimating and finding the volume of rectangular prisms.

RESOURCE REMINDER
Math Center Cards 86
Practice 86, Reteach 86, Extend 86

SKILLS TRACE

GRADE 3	• Explore estimating and measuring the volume of rectangular prisms using stacked area. *(Chapter 9)*
GRADE 4	• Explore estimating and finding the volume of rectangular prisms using stacked area.
GRADE 5	• Explore estimating and finding the volume of rectangular prisms. *(Chapter 12)*

MANIPULATIVE WARM-UP

Whole Class — Logical/Analytical

OBJECTIVE Review attributes of 3-dimensional shapes.

Materials 3-dimensional shapes (sphere, cone, rectangular prism, cube, or objects that have these shapes)

▶ Display some 3-dimensional figures. The figures should include a cube and a rectangular prism.

▶ As volunteers name the figures, record the names on the chalkboard.

▶ Ask students to describe what makes the cube and the rectangular prism different from other 3-dimensional figures. Students should mention that a rectangular prism has faces that are either rectangles or squares, and that in a cube, all edges have the same length.

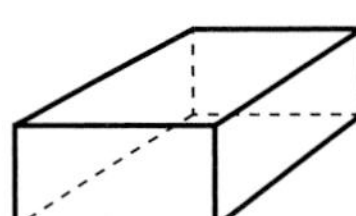 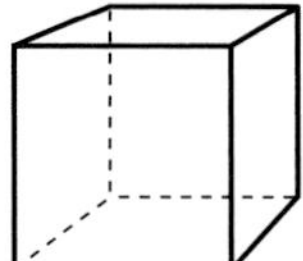 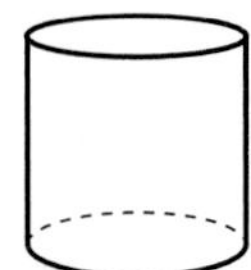 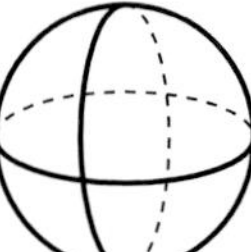 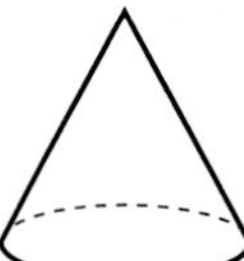

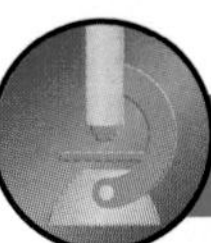

SCIENCE CONNECTION

Whole Class — Logical/Analytical

OBJECTIVE Connect metric volume, capacity, and mass, and use the connection to calculate the mass of a given volume of water.

Materials have available: calculators

▶ Explain to students that in the metric system, volume, capacity, and mass are related: 1 cubic cm holds 1 mL of water, which has a mass of 1 g.

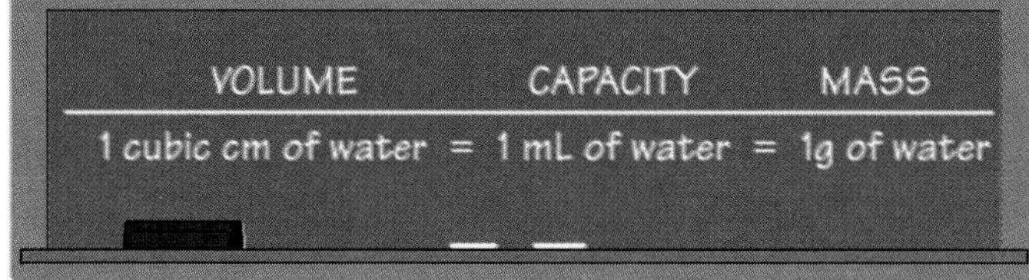

VOLUME CAPACITY MASS
1 cubic cm of water = 1 mL of water = 1g of water

▶ Write the table below on the chalkboard. Explain that it gives the dimensions of some aquariums. Have students find the mass of the water that fills these dimensions. Remind students that 1,000 g = 1 kg.

Length	Width	Height	Mass of the Water that Fills the Aquarium
30 cm	30 cm	30 cm	*[27 kg]*
40 cm	40 cm	30 cm	*[48 kg]*
60 cm	60 cm	60 cm	*[216 kg]*

Daily Review

PREVIOUS DAY QUICK REVIEW

Find the area of the rectangle.

1. length, 7 in.; width, 9 in.
[63 in.^{2}]

2. length, 16 cm; width, 22 cm
[352 cm^2]

FAST FACTS

1. 3 × 6 *[18]*
2. 5 × 7 *[35]*
3. 2 × 9 *[18]*
4. 8 × 5 *[40]*

Problem of the Day • 86

Ben, Maggie, and Kurt collect marbles. Ben has 5 more marbles than Maggie. Kurt has 8 less marbles than Ben. Maggie has 38 marbles. How many marbles do Ben and Kurt have?
[Ben—43, Kurt—35]

TECH LINK

MATH FORUM

Idea To make clear the relationship between perimeter, area, and volume, I give students a set of problems involving all three.

Visit our Resource Village at http://www.mhschool.com to see more of the Math Forum.

MATH CENTER

Practice

OBJECTIVE Build models and find the volume of 3-dimensional figures.

Materials per group: 30 ones models; per student: Math Center Recording Sheet (TA 31 optional)

Students may use ones place-value models if centimeter cubes are not available. Students find the volume, length, width, or height by building models of 3-dimensional figures. *[Table: 30, 48, 2, 3; multiply the length by the width by the height.]*

PRACTICE ACTIVITY 86 — MATH CENTER, Small Group

Algebra Sense • Missing Measures

YOU NEED
- 30 ones models (centimeter cubes)

- Build rectangular prisms with ones models for each of the examples in the chart. Copy the chart on a separate sheet of paper. Fill in the missing numbers.

	Length	Width	Height	Volume
1.	2 cm	5 cm	3 cm	☐ cubic cm
2.	6 cm	4 cm	2 cm	☐ cubic cm
3.	2 cm	2 cm	☐ cm	8 cubic cm
4.	2 cm	☐ cm	4 cm	24 cubic cm

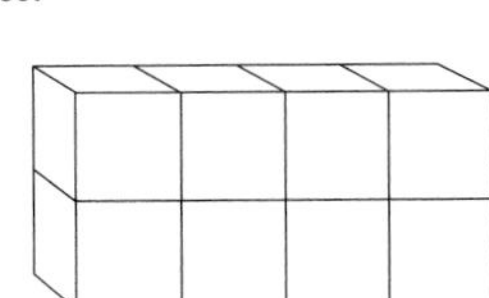

- How do you find the volume of a figure?

Grade Level 4 — McGraw-Hill School Division

Chapter 9, Lesson 10, pages 352–353 — Geometry

NCTM Standards
- ✓ Problem Solving
- ✓ Communication
- ✓ Reasoning
- Connections

Problem Solving

OBJECTIVE Solve problems involving volume.

Students use volume to find which shed can store more boxes.

[Shed A can store 90 boxes, shed B can store 80 boxes; Shed A can store more boxes; Shed A will have 120 square feet left over, Shed B will have 210 square feet left over. Note that the volume for Shed A is 840 cubic feet and the volume for Shed B is 850 cubic feet, but when students make a model to solve they will find that the dimensions of Shed A allows for more boxes to be stored inside.]

PROBLEM-SOLVING ACTIVITY 86 — MATH CENTER, On Your Own

Decision Making • Storing Boxes

You have two sheds in which you want to store some boxes for your new business. Each box is 2 feet by 2 feet by 2 feet.

- How many boxes does each shed store?
- Which shed stores the most boxes?
- Will there be any leftover space in either of the sheds? If so, how much space?

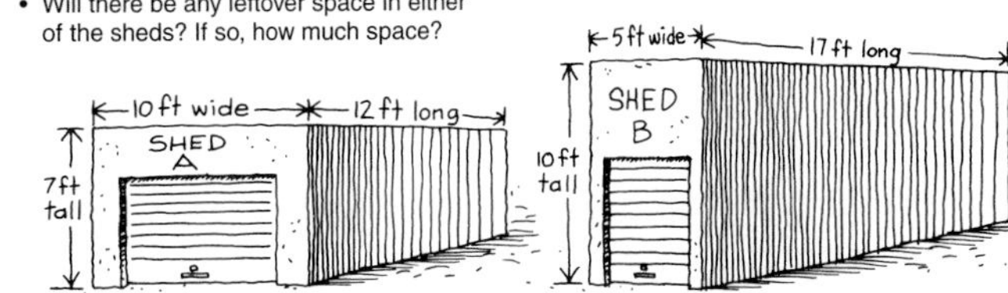

Grade Level 4 — McGraw-Hill School Division

Chapter 9, Lesson 10, pages 352–353 — Geometry

NCTM Standards
- ✓ Problem Solving
- Communication
- ✓ Reasoning
- Connections

EXPLORE ACTIVITY
Volume

OBJECTIVE Explore estimating and finding the volume of rectangular prisms.

Materials different-size boxes; per pair: ones place-value models, centimeter graph paper (TA 7), rulers (TA 18)

Vocabulary cubic unit, volume

1 Introduce

Ask students when knowing the volume of a figure is necessary, such as when filling a fish tank or packaging a box. Ask students to help you think of other ways in which volume can be used.

2 Teach *Cooperative Pairs*

LEARN Ask a volunteer to make a prism using 24 ones place-value models, or centimeter cubes, if available. Tell students that this prism has a volume of 24 cubic cm. Have volunteers make other prisms with the same number of cubes. *[1 × 3 × 8, 1 × 2 × 12, 2 × 2 × 6, and 2 × 4 × 3]*

Work Together Have students work in pairs. Be sure they try to find all the prisms with a volume of 36 cubic cm.

Record the data in a table on the chalkboard. Have students share ways in which they discovered some of their prisms.

MAKE CONNECTIONS

Compare the class table with the one in the text. If the class missed any of the prisms, have students verify them by building them with their cubes.

Discuss the questions. Be sure students understand that volume is the product of the length, width, and height of a prism.

3 Close

Check for Understanding using items 1–4, page 353.

CRITICAL THINKING
Ask students to name measures that indicate volume. Students might suggest gallon, liter, pint, quart, and so forth.

PRACTICE

Options for assigning exercises:
A—Odd ex. 1–7
B—Even ex. 2–8

- For ex. 1–3, tell students to find their answer by multiplying. Students can check their answers by building their own prism of the same dimensions and counting the cubes.
- For ex. 8, suggest that students draw each prism.

EXPLORE ACTIVITY • GEOMETRY

Volume

LEARN

Volume is the amount of space that a 3-dimensional figure takes up. The volume of an object is measured in **cubic units.**

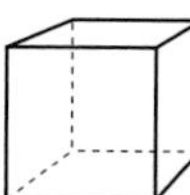
1 cubic unit

These rectangular prisms are made up of centimeter cubes. Each one has a volume of 24 cubic centimeters (cubic cm).

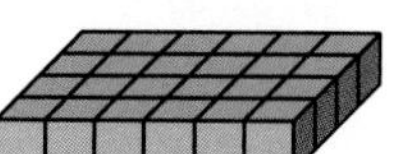
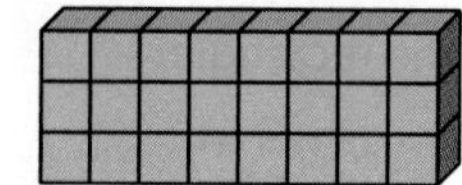

How many different rectangular prisms with a volume of 36 cubic cm can you make?

Work Together
Work with a partner. Use centimeter cubes to create rectangular prisms with a volume of 36 cubic cm.

You will need
- *centimeter cubes*

Start with a prism that is one layer high. Then build a prism that is two layers high, three layers high, and so on.

Record the height, length, width, and volume of each rectangular prism in a table like the one shown.

Height	Width	Length	Volume
1 cm	3 cm	12 cm	36 cubic cm

Check Out the Glossary
volume
cubic unit
See page 544.

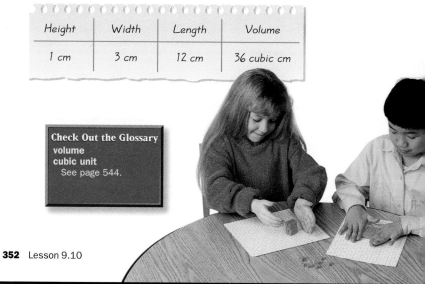

Meeting Individual Needs

Early Finishers

Have students find the volume of an item in the classroom. Students can measure the dimensions with a ruler to the nearest inch or centimeter, or use centimeter cubes.

Extra Support

For students who have difficulty finding volume when given three measurements, have them draw a rectangular prism to help them visualize the meanings of the dimensions.

Ongoing Assessment

Observation Checklist
Determine if students understand volume by observing if they can find volume using multiplication.

Follow Up To help students bridge the gap from counting to multiplying to find volume, have them complete a table that includes the three dimensions of the prism, the number of cubes they counted, and the product of the three dimensions. Assign **Reteach 86.**

For students who understand volume, assign **Extend 86.**

lake Connections

tacey and Gary made rectangular risms that were 1 layer, 2 layers, layers, and 4 layers high. They corded their work in a table.

Height (cm)	Width (cm)	Length (cm)	Area (square cm)	Volume (cubic cm)
1	2	18	36	36
2	2	9	18	36
3	2	6	12	36
4	3	3	9	36

What happens when you multiply the height by the area?
You get 36 cm^3, the volume.

How can you find the volume of a rectangular prism without counting the cubes?
Possible answer: Find the product of the height, length, and width.

heck for Understanding

ind the volume for the rectangular prism.

40 cm^3

2 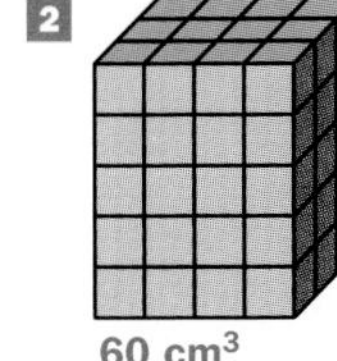

60 cm^3

3 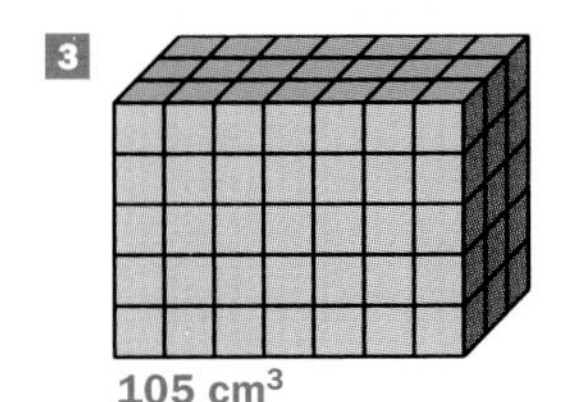

105 cm^3

ritical Thinking: Generalize **Explain your reasoning.**

For what objects might it be important to know the volume?
Possible answer: containers for liquids

CHECK

ractice

ind the volume for the rectangular prism.

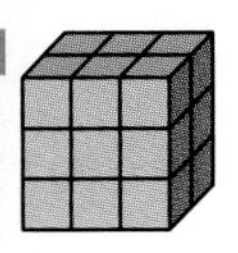

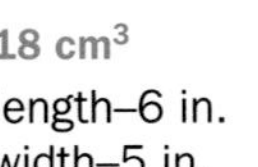

18 cm^3

2 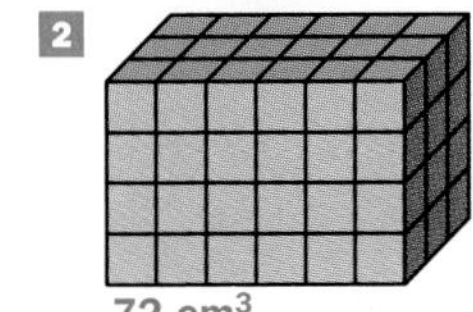

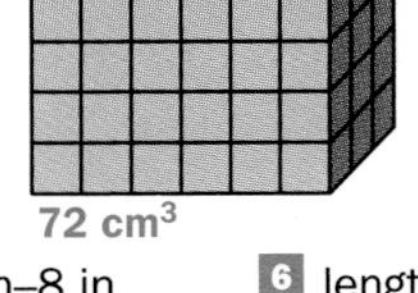

72 cm^3

3 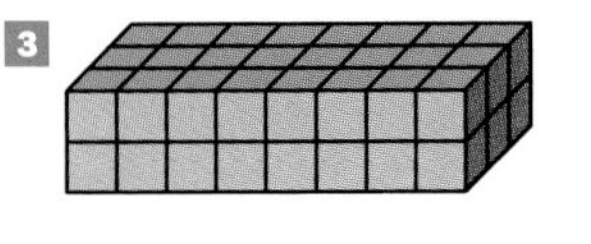

48 cm^3

length–6 in.
width–5 in.
height–4 in.
120 in.^{3}

5 length–8 in.
width–6 in.
height–5 in.
240 in.^{3}

6 length–3 in.
width–12 in.
height–5 in.
180 in.^{3}

7 length–7 in.
width–11 in.
height–6 in.
462 in.^{3}

List the volumes in ex. 4–7 from least to greatest. 120 in.^{3}, 180 in.^{3}, 240 in.^{3}, 462 in.^{3}

PRACTICE

xtra Practice, page 519

Alternate Teaching Strategy

Materials per group: ones place-value models, small rectangular containers

Give each group two or three small containers and enough ones place-value models, or centimeter cubes, if available, to fill the largest one. Ask students to fill the containers with as many cubes as possible and record their results.

Tell students that the *volume* of their containers is measured by the number of cubes it holds. If some of the containers are slightly shorter or taller than the top stack of cubes, tell students to estimate the number of whole cubes in the top layer.

Then tell students that volume can also be found by multiplying the length, width, and height of the container. Ask students to measure their containers and find the volume. Have them compare their results when using these two methods.

ESL APPROPRIATE

PRACTICE • 86

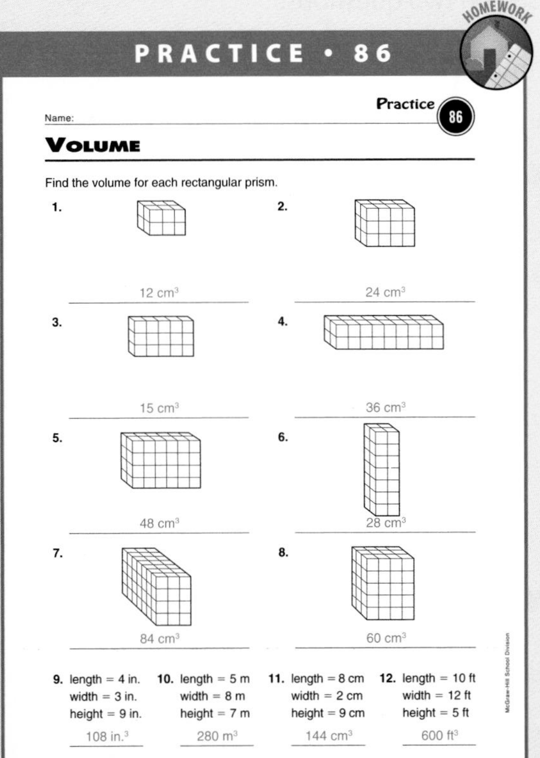

Practice 86

Name:

VOLUME

Find the volume for each rectangular prism.

1. 12 cm^3
2. 24 cm^3
3. 15 cm^3
4. 36 cm^3
5. 48 cm^3
6. 28 cm^3
7. 84 cm^3
8. 60 cm^3
9. length = 4 in. width = 3 in. height = 9 in. 108 in.^{3}
10. length = 5 m width = 8 m height = 7 m 280 m^3
11. length = 8 cm width = 2 cm height = 9 cm 144 cm^3
12. length = 10 ft width = 12 ft height = 5 ft 600 ft^3

RETEACH • 86

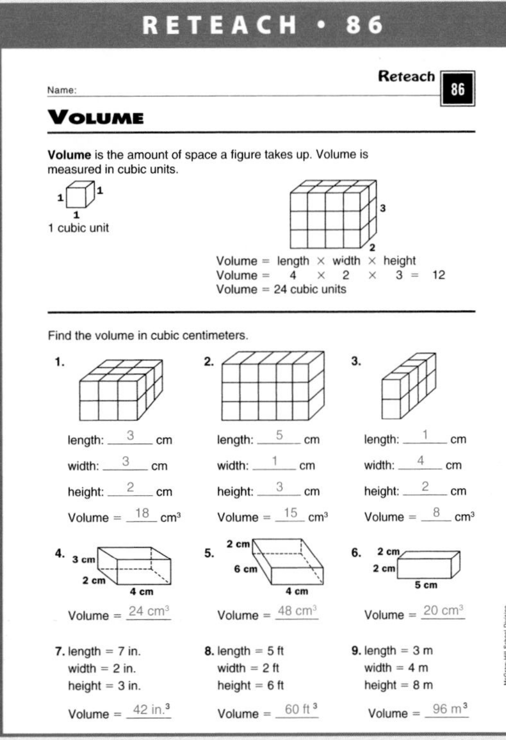

Reteach 86

Name:

VOLUME

Volume is the amount of space a figure takes up. Volume is measured in cubic units.

1 cubic unit

Volume = length × width × height
Volume = 4 × 2 × 3 = 12
Volume = 24 cubic units

Find the volume in cubic centimeters.

1. length: 3 cm width: 3 cm height: 2 cm Volume = 18 cm^3
2. length: 5 cm width: 1 cm height: 3 cm Volume = 15 cm^3
3. length: 1 cm width: 4 cm height: 2 cm Volume = 8 cm^3
4. Volume = 24 cm^3
5. Volume = 48 cm^3
6. Volume = 20 cm^3
7. length = 7 in. width = 2 in. height = 3 in. Volume = 42 in.^{3}
8. length = 5 ft width = 2 ft height = 6 ft Volume = 60 ft^3
9. length = 3 m width = 4 m height = 8 m Volume = 96 m^3

EXTEND • 86

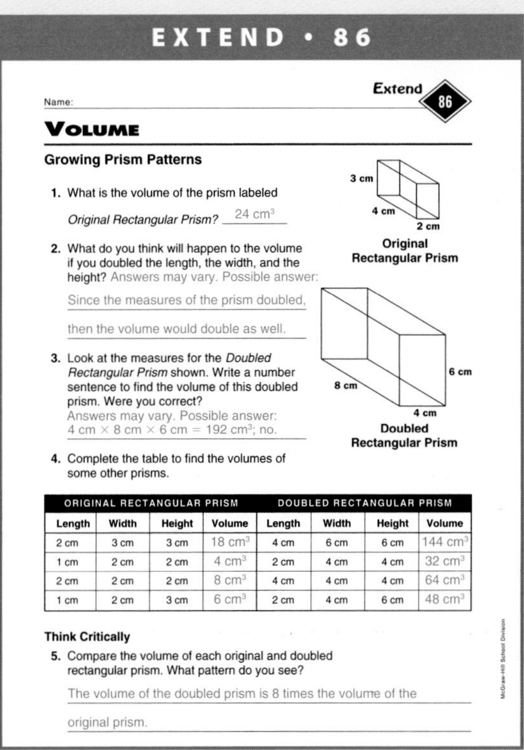

Extend 86

Name:

VOLUME

Growing Prism Patterns

1. What is the volume of the prism labeled *Original Rectangular Prism?* 24 cm^3
2. What do you think will happen to the volume if you doubled the length, the width, and the height? Answers may vary. Possible answer: Since the measures of the prism doubled, then the volume would double as well.
3. Look at the measures for the *Doubled Rectangular Prism* shown. Write a number sentence to find the volume of this doubled prism. Were you correct? Answers may vary. Possible answer: 4 cm × 8 cm × 6 cm = 192 cm^3; no.
4. Complete the table to find the volumes of some other prisms.

Original Rectangular Prism; Doubled Rectangular Prism

ORIGINAL RECTANGULAR PRISM				DOUBLED RECTANGULAR PRISM			
Length	Width	Height	Volume	Length	Width	Height	Volume
2 cm	3 cm	3 cm	18 cm^3	4 cm	6 cm	6 cm	144 cm^3
1 cm	2 cm	2 cm	4 cm^3	2 cm	4 cm	4 cm	32 cm^3
2 cm	2 cm	2 cm	8 cm^3	4 cm	4 cm	4 cm	64 cm^3
1 cm	2 cm	3 cm	6 cm^3	2 cm	4 cm	6 cm	48 cm^3

Think Critically

5. Compare the volume of each original and doubled rectangular prism. What pattern do you see? The volume of the doubled prism is 8 times the volume of the original prism.

Problem Solvers at Work

OBJECTIVE Solve and write problems by using a diagram.

RESOURCE REMINDER
Math Center Cards 87
Practice 87, Reteach 87, Extend 87

SKILLS TRACE

GRADE 3	• Formulate and solve problems involving using/drawing a diagram. *(Chapter 10)*
GRADE 4	• Formulate and solve problems involving using/drawing a diagram.
GRADE 5	• Formulate and solve problems involving using/drawing a diagram. *(Chapter 12)*

MANIPULATIVE WARM-UP

Cooperative Pairs — Kinesthetic

OBJECTIVE Explore sorting objects.

Materials per pair: a handful of buttons, beads, or attribute blocks

▶ Have pairs sort the objects into three or more different categories and record the number of objects in each category. The categories may relate to size, shape, color, and so forth.

▶ Have each pair sort the objects again using different categories and again record their results. Pairs may continue doing this for as many categories as they can think of.

▶ Have pairs share results with the class.

ESL APPROPRIATE

STATISTICS CONNECTION

Cooperative Groups — Auditory/Linguistic

OBJECTIVE Connect using categories and classifications with statistics.

▶ Have each group take surveys based on two questions:
- **Do you like watching sports?**
- **Do you like listening to classic music?**

▶ After taking the survey, have groups display their results in a Venn diagram.

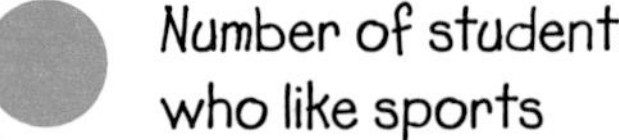

Number of students who like classical music

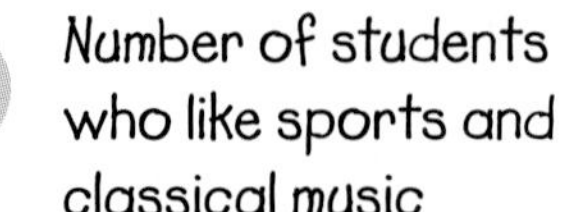

Daily Review

PREVIOUS DAY QUICK REVIEW

Find the volume.

1. length: 8 cm; width: 4 cm; height: 3 cm *[96 cm^3]*
2. length: 14 cm; width: 8 cm; height: 12 cm *[1,344 cm^3]*

FAST FACTS

1. 42 ÷ 7 *[6]*
2. 36 ÷ 6 *[6]*
3. 24 ÷ 8 *[3]*
4. 4 ÷ 4 *[1]*

Problem of the Day • 87

Austin lives 5 miles from school, 2 miles from the library, and 4 miles from the airport. He is drawing a map where one inch represents a half mile. On the map, how far should his house be from the airport? *[8 in.]* Sketch the map using inch graph paper. *[Check students' work.]*

TECH LINK

MATH VAN

Aid You may wish to use the Electronic Teacher Aid in the Math Van with this lesson.

MATH FORUM

Idea To reinforce the connection of problem solving and the real world, I often have my students pose math problems that they or their family encounter.

Visit our Resource Village at http://www.mhschool.com to see more of the Math Forum.

MATH CENTER

Practice

OBJECTIVE Use Venn diagrams to identify line relationships.

Students describe and sort the line segments in capital letters. *[Answers may vary depending on how letters are drawn.]*

PRACTICE ACTIVITY 87 — MATH CENTER On Your Own

Spatial Reasoning • Letters

- Use the letters E, F, H, K, L, M, N, T, V, W, X, Y, and Z to answer these questions.
  1. Which letters contain parallel line segments?
  2. Which letters contain perpendicular line segments?
  3. Which letters contain intersecting line segments that are not parallel or perpendicular?

Copy and complete this Venn diagram. Place your answers in the appropriate part of the ovals.

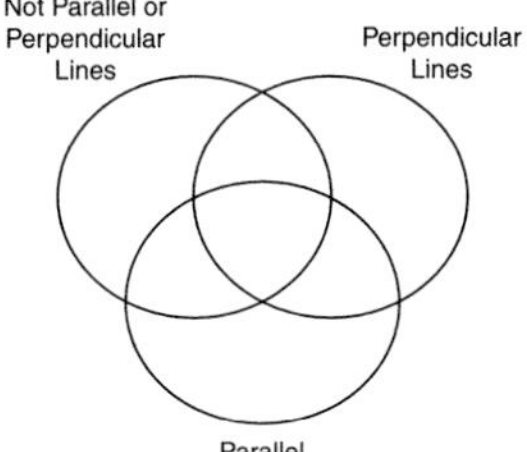

Chapter 9, Lesson 11, pages 354–357 — Problem Solving

NCTM Standards
- ✓ Problem Solving
- ✓ Communication
- ✓ Reasoning
- Connections

Problem Solving

OBJECTIVE Use problem solving to build a display room.

Materials per student: centimeter graph paper (TA 7), ruler

Students calculate the area of a sculpture and use the answer to create a custom room to display it. They draw floor plans and different views of the room. *[Answers may vary. Check students' work.]*

PROBLEM-SOLVING ACTIVITY 87 — MATH CENTER On Your Own

Spatial Reasoning • Designing a Display Room

YOU NEED: graph paper, ruler

- Design a display room for a sculpture. The sculpture has a square base with 5-foot sides. It is 12 feet tall.
- Decide what shape the room should be. It should have enough space both to hold the sculpture and to allow someone to walk around it and view it from all sides. You may want to make the room large enough to hold a group of people for the grand unveiling party.
- Draw plans that show the dimensions of the floor, walls, and ceiling. Substitute centimeters for feet. Draw front, back, side, top, and bottom views of the room.

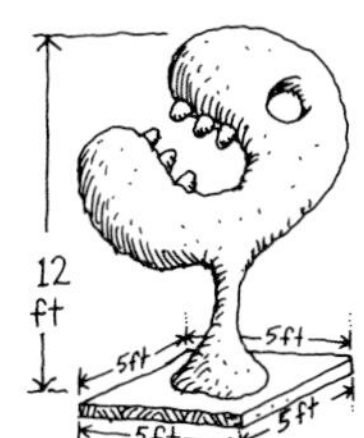

Chapter 9, Lesson 11, pages 354–357 — Problem Solving

NCTM Standards
- ✓ Problem Solving
- ✓ Communication
- ✓ Reasoning
- Connections

ESL APPROPRIATE

Problem Solvers at Work

OBJECTIVE Solve and write problems by using a diagram.

Materials enough rope or string to make two circles that are each big enough for 6 students to stand in, masking tape

1 Introduce

Use rope or string and masking tape to make two overlapping circles, each large enough for 6 students, on the floor.

Choose 6 volunteers. Have the volunteers who are wearing something black stand in one circle, but not in the part where it overlaps the other. Have volunteers who are wearing something blue stand in the other circle, but not in the part where it overlaps the first.

- **Where should you stand if you are wearing something black and something blue?** *[in the part where the two circles overlap]*

2 Teach *Cooperative Pairs*

PART 1 USE DIAGRAMS

LEARN Work Together Have students answer these questions in pairs. Discuss the answers together as a class.

Categories Make a list on the chalkboard of all the categories students thought of in question 5.

Ask students:

- **What if the two categories had been "Polygons with an even number of sides" and "Polygons with an odd number of sides." Would there ever be any shape in the overlapping section? Explain your reasoning.** *[No; a polygon has either an even number or an odd number of sides, it can't have both.]*

Problem Solvers at Work

Read | Plan | Solve | Look Back

Part 1 Use Diagrams

LEARN

Some scientists use Venn diagrams like the one on the right to help them organize and sort their work.

How can a Venn diagram help you organize your work?

Where Animals Live

Animals that live in water | Animals that live on land

jellyfish | frog | elephant

Work Together

Categories Copy the Venn diagram below. Use it to help you organize the shapes.

1. Why was the parallelogram placed in the area where the two circles overlap? **It fits both categories.**
2. Where would you place a rectangle? Why? **See below.**
3. Where would you place a figure that is not a polygon? Why? **Outside the circles; only polygons should be placed in the circles.**
4. **What if** the category labeled *Polygons with at least 1 acute angle* was changed to *Polygons with at least 1 right angle*? Show how the Venn diagram you drew would change. **See page T17.**
5. **Make a decision** Choose other categories that can be used to sort the shapes. Create a Venn diagram to organize your work. **See above.**

5. Students' decisions should reflect the data provided.

Shapes

Polygons with at least 1 acute angle | Polygons with even number of sides

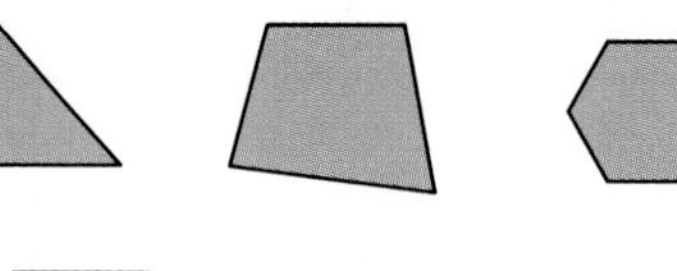

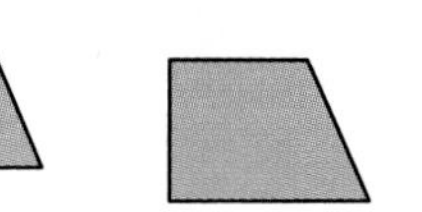

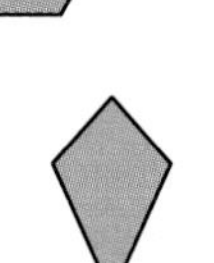

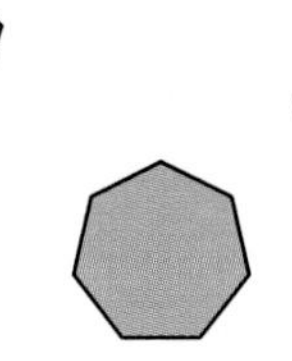

2. In the right circle for polygons with even number of sides; it does not have any acute angles.

Meeting Individual Needs

Extra Support

Have students make two large intersecting circles to help them solve problems using Venn diagrams. The larger circles will give them the space to enter the items and to erase or remove items as needed.

ESL APPROPRIATE

Ongoing Assessment

Observation Checklist Determine whether students understand how to use Venn diagrams to solve problems by observing whether they can explain the meaning of the overlapping section, and whether they can sort items into the three separate categories on the diagram.

Follow Up For more practice using diagrams, assign **Reteach 87.**

For a greater challenge, assign **Extend 87.**

·dents in Mrs. Jule's Class

Students with brothers | Students with sisters

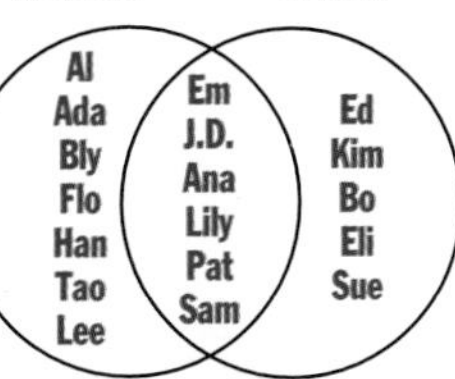

Ann, Cam, Sal, Amy

STUDENT TO STUDENT
CHECK
Lee's mom just had a baby girl. Where should you move Lee's name on the diagram?

Erin McCormick
St. Gabriel School
Riverdale, NY

· wrote this problem about the ·rmation in the Venn diagram.

Solve Erin's problem. **Lee should be placed where the circles overlap.**

Write a problem where you need to sort words or numbers using a Venn diagram. **For problems 7–10, see Teacher's Edition.**

Solve the new problem.

Trade problems. Solve at least three problems written by your classmates.

What was the most interesting problem you solved? Why?

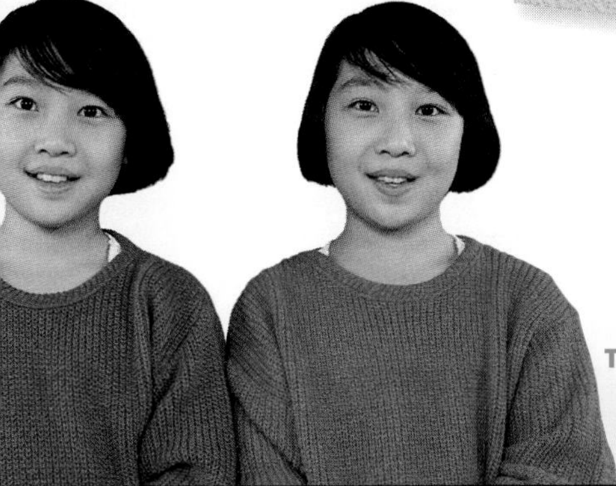

Turn the page for Practice Strategies.

PART 2 WRITE AND SHARE PROBLEMS

Check Let students work in pairs to complete item 6. Invite volunteers to explain how they solved this student's problem.

Item 7 provides an opportunity for students to write their own problems using Venn diagrams.

After students have exchanged and solved the problems written by their classmates, invite them to share the problems they found most challenging with the whole class.

For items 9 and 10, encourage students to discuss the problems they solved and their reasons why a problem was most interesting.

 Close

Have students discuss how they used the Venn diagram to write their own problems. Have them discuss what types of data and problems are best suited to Venn diagrams.

Practice See pages 356–357.

Gifted And Talented

Have students draw a Venn diagram with three overlapping circles and draw at least one polygon in each section. The categories are as follows: At least 3 acute angles, At least 1 right angle, and 4 or more sides.

Gender Fairness

If there are shy boys or girls in the class, speak to them individually before class "warning" them that they will be called on that day. Then discuss with students how to respond or review a question that will be asked.

Lesson 9.11 *continued*

Part 3 Practice Strategies

Materials have available: calculators

Students have the option of choosing any five problems from ex. 1–8 and any two problems from ex. 9–13. They may choose to do more problems if they wish.

- For ex. 1, some students may benefit from using ones place-value models or centimeter cubes to make a model.
- For ex. 2, remind students to subtract the previous number from the subsequent number and see if there is a pattern.
- For ex. 9, tell students that their drawing does not need to be to scale.
- For ex. 12, have students check each other's examples.

At the Computer If a computer is not available, students can build cubes using centimeter cubes. This may even be helpful when drawing the cubes with a drawing program.

If a drawing program is not available, students can use a spreadsheet program to create the chart or make one by hand.

Math Van Have students use the Drawing tool to draw the cubes. A project electronic teacher aid has been provided.

---

2. Start by adding 1 and then add on twic[e] what was added before to get the next number; 33, 65, 129.

Part 3 Practice Strategies

PRACTICE

Menu

Choose five problems and solve them. Explain your methods.

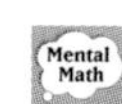

Explanations may v[ary].

1 How many cubes are in this rectangular prism? **192 cubes**

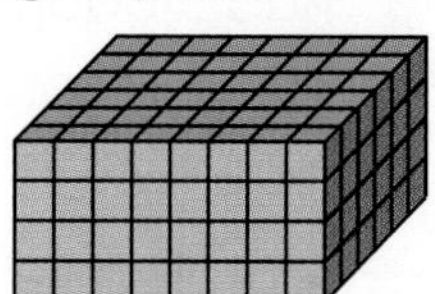

2 Helen used a calculator to creat[e a] number pattern. Find the patter[n]. Then give the next three numbe[rs]. 2, 3, 5, 9, 17, ■, ■, ■
See above.

3 Gordy's family ate 6 granola bars on Wednesday. That was twice as many as they ate on Monday but 3 less than they ate on Tuesday. How many granola bars are left from a box of 24?
6 granola bars

4 Jeffrey wants to buy a paintbrus[h] set for $8.95 and as many bott[les] of paint as he can. Each bottle [of] paint costs $1.25. If he has $20.00, how many bottles of paint can he buy and still get the paintbrush set?
8 bottles

5 Antonio claims he can write his name 35 times in a minute. It takes him 3 seconds to write his name once. Is his claim reasonable? If not, about how long will it actually take him?
No; possible answer: about 2 min.

Antonio Antonio Antonio
Antonio Antonio Antonio

6 Stacy, Phil, Millie, and Theresa w[ent] to a movie. Millie sat next to St[acy] who was on Phil's left. If Theres[a] sat next to Phil, who were sitting in the middle?
Stacy and Phil

7 Use the figure to give an example of a line segment, line, ray, parallel lines, perpendicular lines, and intersecting lines.

Possible answers: line segment *BC*, line *AC*, ray *IC*, parallel lines *FB* and *AD*, perpendicular lines *AC* and *BD*, intersecting lines *AC* and *FB*

8 Sheila has a rectangular-shaped section in her yard where she tra[ins] her dog. What is the area?
108 ft²

12 ft.

Fence around = 42 ft.

Meeting Individual Needs

Early Finishers

Have students make a Venn diagram showing the number of students who play basketball, play baseball, and play both basketball and baseball. Then have them write a problem about their diagram.

Inclusion

Some students may benefit by having physical models of the objects they are categorizing for Venn diagrams.

Language Support

Pair students acquiring English with English-speaking students. Have them work together so that any unfamiliar words can be explained. Remind students that the art or photos with each problem can help with vocabulary.

ESL APPROPRIATE

Common Error

Some students often forget to erase or remove items from one part of a Venn diagram when they have made a change.

9. Check students' work. Possible answer: The volume of the box is 500 in.^{3}, so it holds 500 cubes with 1-in. sides.

12. Check students' work. Possible answers: peep, otto, toot, 75357, 626

Choose two problems and solve them. Explain your methods. Explanations may vary.

9 Draw the bottom and sides of a transparent box that would hold 500 wooden cubes with 1-inch sides. Your box should waste as little space as possible. Label the length and width of the bottom and sides.

Explain how you know that your box would hold all 500 cubes.
See above.

10 **Spatial reasoning** What is the volume of this figure? How many cubes would you need to add to make this a rectangular prism?
88 cubic units; 8 cubes

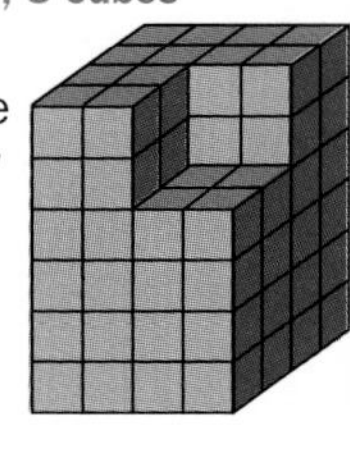

11 Choose different categories that you can use to sort the toys, games, or puzzles that you know or have heard about. Make Venn diagrams to show your work.
Check students' work.

12 A **palindrome** is a word or number that is the same if you read it forward or backward. The word *noon* is a palindrome. Find as many other palindromes as you can.
See above.

13 **At the Computer** You can make cubes out of smaller cubes as shown on the right.

Use a drawing program to create the next three larger cubes.

Record the measurements of the cubes in a table like the one below. Write about any patterns you see.

Length	Width	Height	Number of Cubic Units
1	1	1	1
2	2	2	8
3	3	3	27
4	4	4	64
5	5	5	125
6	6	6	216

13. Possible answer: Length, width, and height are the same, and the number of cubic units = length × width × height.

Alternate Teaching Strategy

Materials per group: pattern blocks (TA 16), yarn, scissors, index cards

Have students make two large intersecting circles with the yarn. Tell them that they are going to sort the pattern blocks into two categories: *3 or more equal sides* and *at least 2 acute angles.* The categories are written on index cards and each card placed over one of the circles.

Tell groups to sort the pattern blocks into the appropriate regions of the circles. After they have finished, tell students they have made a model of a *Venn diagram.*

For class discussion, ask:

- **Which pattern blocks are in each category?**
- **Are there any pattern blocks in the overlapping section? If so, what are they?**

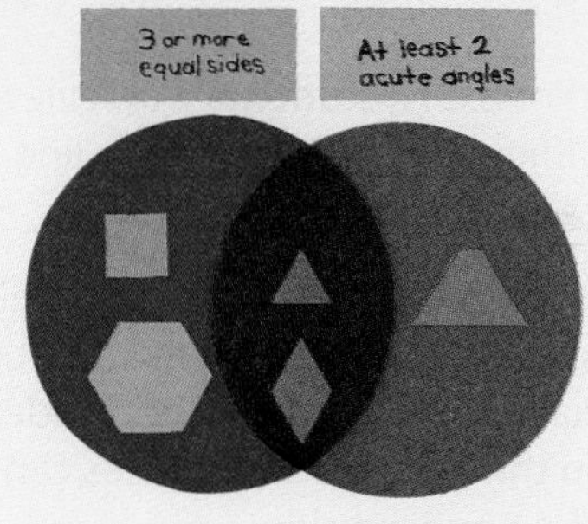

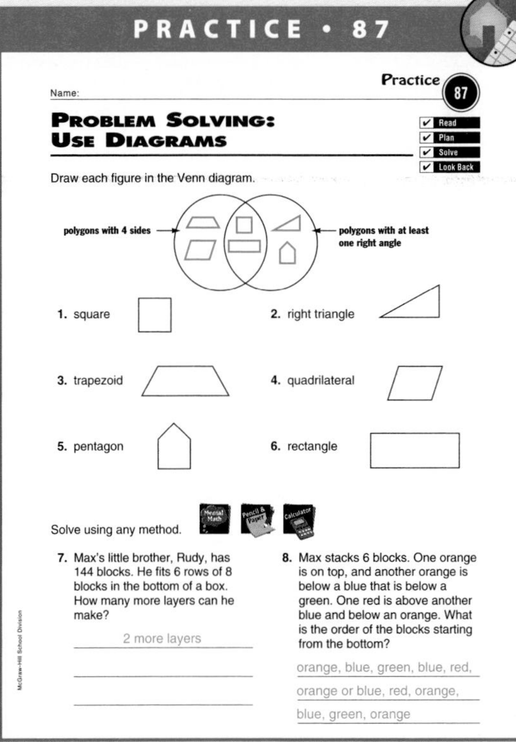

PRACTICE • 87

Practice 87

Name:

PROBLEM SOLVING: USE DIAGRAMS

✔ Read ✔ Plan ✔ Solve ✔ Look Back

Draw each figure in the Venn diagram.

polygons with 4 sides — polygons with at least one right angle

1. square
2. right triangle
3. trapezoid
4. quadrilateral
5. pentagon
6. rectangle

Solve using any method.

7. Max's little brother, Rudy, has 144 blocks. He fits 6 rows of 8 blocks in the bottom of a box. How many more layers can he make?
2 more layers

8. Max stacks 6 blocks. One orange is on top, and another orange is below a blue that is below a green. One red is above another blue and below an orange. What is the order of the blocks starting from the bottom?
orange, blue, green, blue, red, orange or blue, red, orange, blue, green, orange

McGraw-Hill School Division

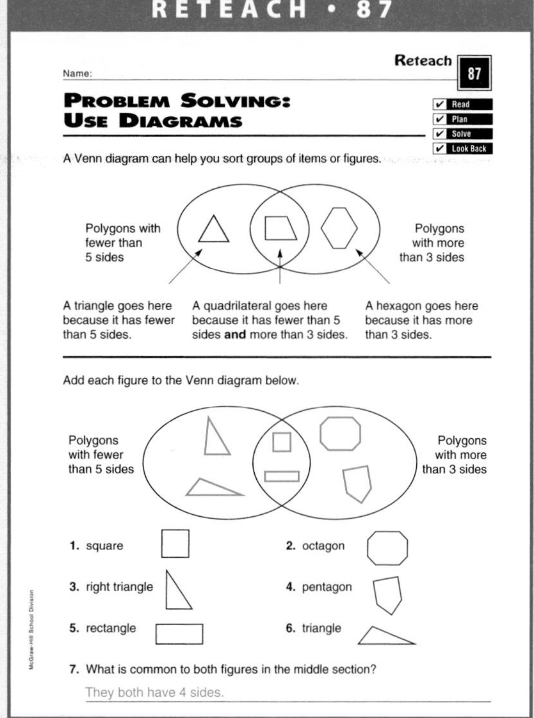

RETEACH • 87

Reteach 87

Name:

PROBLEM SOLVING: USE DIAGRAMS

✔ Read ✔ Plan ✔ Solve ✔ Look Back

A Venn diagram can help you sort groups of items or figures.

Polygons with fewer than 5 sides — Polygons with more than 3 sides

A triangle goes here because it has fewer than 5 sides.

A quadrilateral goes here because it has fewer than 5 sides **and** more than 3 sides.

A hexagon goes here because it has more than 3 sides.

Add each figure to the Venn diagram below.

Polygons with fewer than 5 sides — Polygons with more than 3 sides

1. square
2. octagon
3. right triangle
4. pentagon
5. rectangle
6. triangle
7. What is common to both figures in the middle section?
They both have 4 sides.

McGraw-Hill School Division

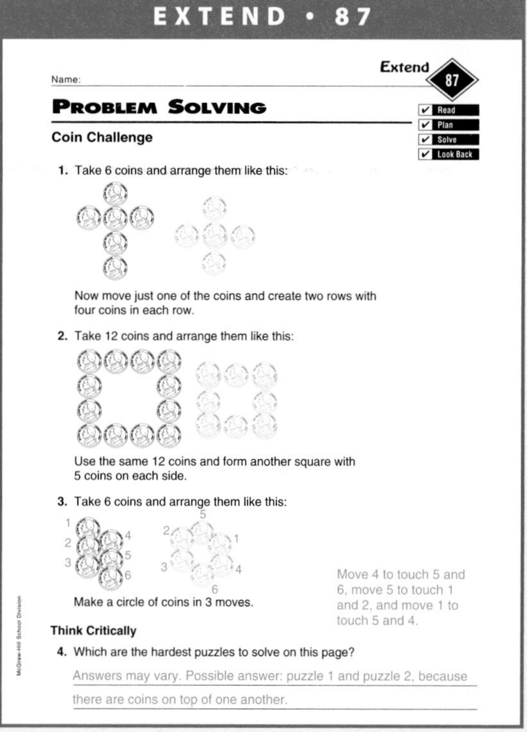

EXTEND • 87

Extend 87

Name:

PROBLEM SOLVING

✔ Read ✔ Plan ✔ Solve ✔ Look Back

Coin Challenge

1. Take 6 coins and arrange them like this:

Now move just one of the coins and create two rows with four coins in each row.

2. Take 12 coins and arrange them like this:

Use the same 12 coins and form another square with 5 coins on each side.

3. Take 6 coins and arrange them like this:

Make a circle of coins in 3 moves.

Move 4 to touch 5 and 6, move 5 to touch 1 and 2, and move 1 to touch 5 and 4.

Think Critically

4. Which are the hardest puzzles to solve on this page?
Answers may vary. Possible answer: puzzle 1 and puzzle 2, because there are coins on top of one another.

McGraw-Hill School Division

CHAPTER REVIEW

PURPOSE Review and assess concepts, skills, and strategies that students have learned in this chapter.

Materials per student: calculator (optional)

Chapter Objectives

9A Identify 2-dimensional and 3-dimensional figures and their parts
9B Find area and volume
9C Identify how a figure is transformed
9D Identify congruent and symmetric figures
9E Solve problems, including those that involve geometry and making an organized list

Using the Chapter Review

The **Chapter Review** can be used as a review, practice test, or chapter test.

Think Critically For ex. 17, students will review their understanding of the differences between lines, line segments, and rays. Ask students to define the three terms.

For ex. 18, students may want to draw a capital *j* on a slip of paper to use to help them see the transformation that took place. The *J* will have to be drawn on both sides of the paper. Draw it heavily on the first side so the lines can be followed to reproduce it on the opposite side.

Language and Mathematics

Complete the sentence. Use a word in the chart. (pages 320–353)

1. An ■ angle is one that measures less than a right angle. acute
2. A 6-sided ■ is called a hexagon. polygon
3. Two figures that are exactly the same shape and size are said to be ■. congruent
4. Lines that are ■ never intersect. parallel
5. The ■ of a rectangle can be found if you know its length and width. area

Vocabulary
parallel
area
polygon
acute
congruent
perpendicular

Concepts and Skills

Name the figure. (pages 320, 324)

6. 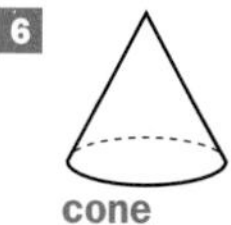
cone

7. 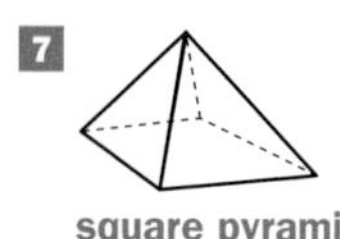
square pyramid

8. 
pentagon

Describe the angle. (page 332)

9. 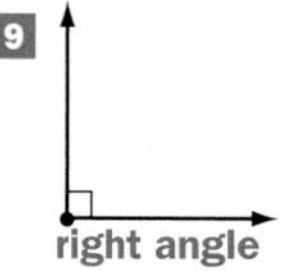
right angle

10. 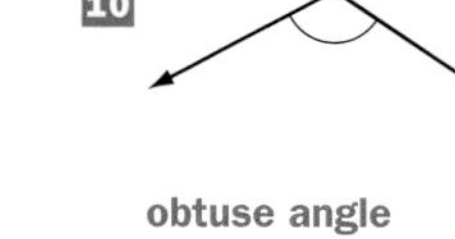
obtuse angle

11. 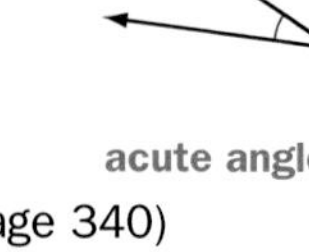
acute angle

Are the figures congruent? If not, are they similar? (page 340)

12. 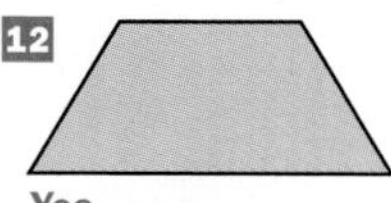 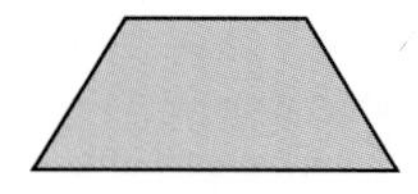
Yes.

13. 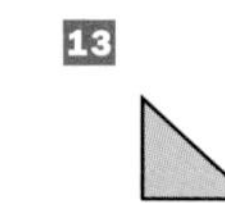 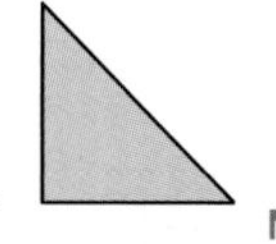
No; yes.

Tell whether or not the dotted line is a line of symmetry. (page 344)

14. 
No.

15. 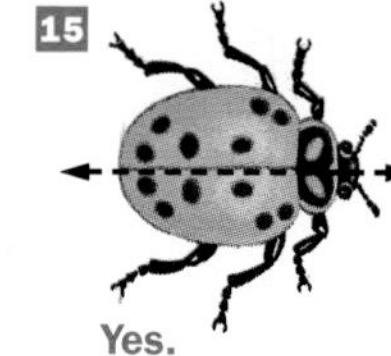
Yes.

16. 
Yes.

Reinforcement and Remediation

CHAPTER OBJECTIVES ITEMS	CHAPTER REVIEW	STUDENT BOOK PAGES		TEACHER'S EDITION PAGES		TEACHER RESOURCES
		Lessons	Midchapter Review	Activities	Alternate Teaching Strategy	Reteach
9A	1–2, 4, 6–11, 17	320–329, 332–335	332	319A, 323A, 327A, 331A	323, 327, 329, 335	77, 78, 79, 81
9B	5, 24	348–351, 352–353		347C, 351A	351, 353	85, 86
9C	18	346–347		345A	347	84
9D	3, 12–16	340–345		339A, 343A	343, 345	82, 83
9E	19–25	330–331, 354–357		329A, 353A	331, 357	80, 87

. Possible answer: Buy 2 packages for $34, since buying 300 loose sheets is much more expensive, $45, and buying 1 package and 100 loose sheets costs about the same amount, $32.

ink critically. (pages 328, 346)

Analyze. Explain what the mistakes are, then correct them. **They are not all lines, since *BD* is a line segment and *CD* is a ray.**

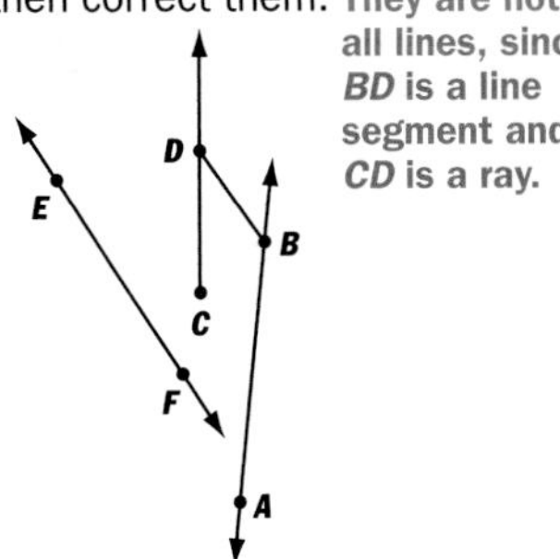

Lines: AB, BD, CD, EF

18 Analyze. Use the terms *flip, slide,* and *turn* to describe how the square has been moved.

a.  **turn**

b.  **slide**

c.  **flip**

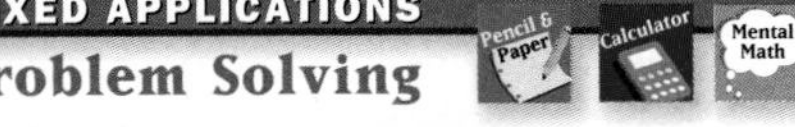

IXED APPLICATIONS
roblem Solving (pages 330, 354)

The perimeter of a rectangle measures 40 meters. The width measures 6 meters. What is the length of the rectangle? **14 m**

What is the volume of each rectangular prism on the right? What pattern do you see? What would be the volume of the sixth rectangular prism in this pattern? **See below.**

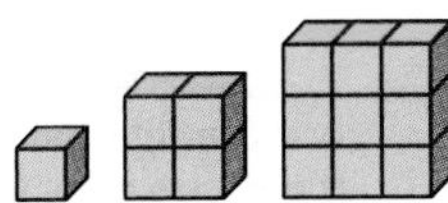

Draw a figure that has 3 or more lines of symmetry. Label each vertex with a letter. Use five different mathematical terms you learned in this chapter to describe your figure. **Check students' descriptions. Students may choose any shapes from the chapter.**

Make a decision An art store sells sheets of drawing paper for 15¢. You can buy a package of 200 sheets of the same type of paper for $17.00. What would you buy if you needed 300 sheets of paper? Make an organized list to help find the answer. **See above.**

e the figure for problems 23–25. **Possible answers are given.**

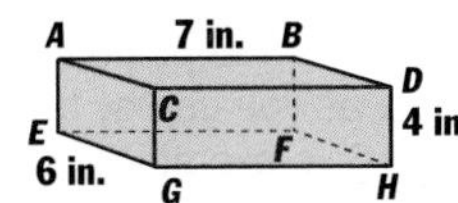

Name one pair of parallel line segments. **line segments *AB* and *CD***

Find the area of the largest face. **42 in.^{2}**

Name one pair of perpendicular line segments. **line segments *AE* and *AB***

. **1 cubic unit, 4 cubic units, 9 cubic units; possible answer: if you multiply the position of the rectangular prism in the pattern by itself, you get the volume in cubic units; 36 cubic units.**

CHAPTER TEST

PURPOSE Assess the concepts, skills, and strategies students have learned in this chapter.

Chapter Objectives

- **9A** Identify 2-dimensional and 3-dimensional figures and their parts
- **9B** Find area and volume
- **9C** Identify how a figure is transformed
- **9D** Identify congruent and symmetric figures
- **9E** Solve problems, including those that involve geometry and making an organized list

Using the Chapter Test

The **Chapter Test** can be used as a practice test, a chapter test, or as an additional review. The **Performance Assessment** on Student Book page 361 provides an alternate means of assessing students' understanding of geometry.

Assessment Resources

Test Masters

The Testing Program Blackline Masters provide three forms of the Chapter Test to assess students' understanding of the chapter concepts, skills, and strategies. Form C uses a free-response format. Forms A and B use a multiple-choice format.

Computer Test Generator

The Computer Test Generator supplies abundant multiple-choice and free-response test items, which you may use to generate tests and practice worksheets tailored to the needs of your class.

Teacher's Assessment Resources

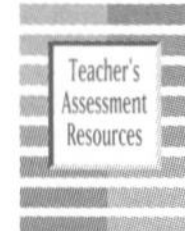

Teacher's Assessment Resources provides resources for alternate assessment. It includes guidelines for Building a Portfolio, page 6 and the Holistic Scoring Guide, page 27.

Are the figures intersecting, parallel, or perpendicular?

1 intersecting

2 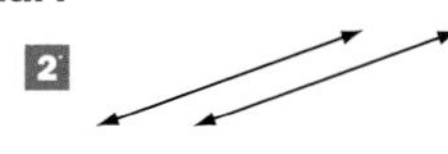 parallel

Tell if the angle is obtuse, acute, or a right angle.

3  obtuse

4  right

Name the figure.

5  cylinder

6 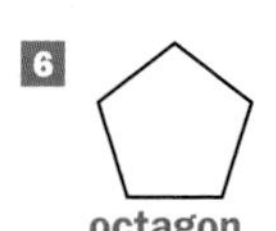  octagon

7 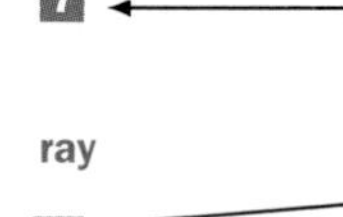 ray

8 triangular pyramid

9 line

10  triangular prism

Tell if the figure is symmetric.

11 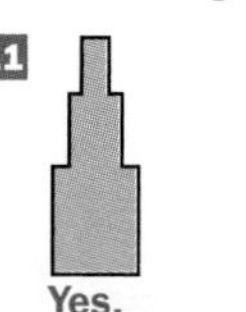 Yes.

12  No.

Find the area.

13 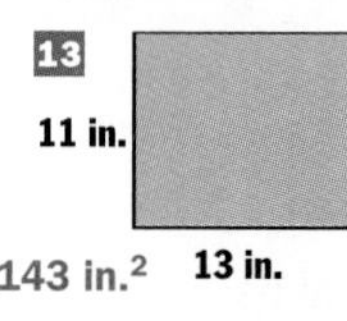

143 in.^{2}

14 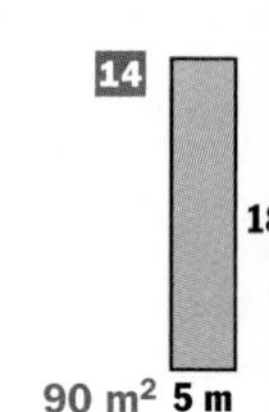

90 m^2

Are the figures congruent? If not, are they similar?

15 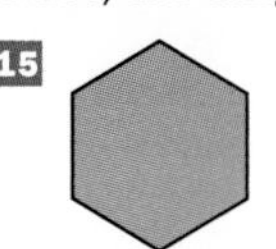 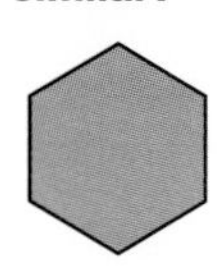 congruent

Find the volume.

16 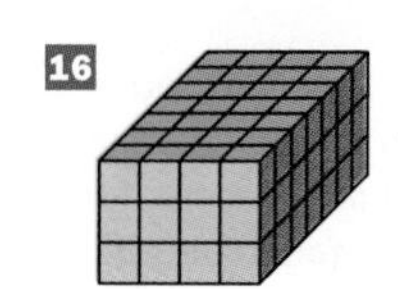 84 cubic units

Solve.

17 An artist is arranging four paintings of Tampa, Los Angeles, Houston, and Dayton along a wall. How many different ways can she arrange the four paintings? **24 different ways**

18 Classrooms 101, 102, 103, 104 and 105 have one computer eac All 5 computers are connected b wires to all of the others. How many connections are there in a **10 connections**

19 Can you get the same position by flipping a kite as you can by turning it? sliding it? Give examples. **Yes; yes; check students' work.**

20 Is it possible to have parallel line that intersect? perpendicular line that intersect? Explain.

No, parallel lines stay the same distance from each other so th never meet; yes, perpendicular lines intersect at right angles.

360 Chapter 9 Test

Test Correlation

CHAPTER OBJECTIVES	TEST ITEMS	TEXT PAGES
9A	1–10	320–329, 332–335
9B	13–14, 16	348–353
9C	19	346–347
9D	11–12, 15	340–345
9E	17–20	330–331, 354–357

ee Teacher's Assessment Resources for mples of student work.

Vhat Did You Learn?

"LE REMORGUEUR," FERNAND LEGER, GRENOBLE MUSEE

rnand Leger is a famous artist. Look at is photograph of one of his paintings.

Describe three geometric figures you see in the painting. Describe each figure in as many ways as you can. See below.

Draw and label three geometric figures that are not in the painting. Use the three figures you drew to create a picture of your own. The picture should show examples of slides, flips, and turns.

You will need
- *dot paper*
- *colored pencil*

ssible answer: kite, triangle, rhombus; check students' work.

A Good Answer
- accurately describes figures in the paintings using geometric terms
- identifies geometric figures that are not in the painting and correctly shows slides, flips, and turns

You may want to place your work in your portfolio.

What Do You Think?

See Teacher's Edition.

1 Do you look at the parts of a figure if you are unsure about how to name it? Why or why not?

2 List all the ways you might use to help you name a 3-dimensional figure:
- Use the shape of the faces.
- Use the angles in the figure.
- Think of real-life objects.
- Other. Explain.

3 Are you always able to determine how a figure has been moved? What method do you use?

uestion 1. Possible answer: Circle is a closed figure, has no edges or angles; rectangle as 4 sides, 4 right angles, perpendicular adjacent sides, parallel opposite sides; apezoid has 4 sides, 1 pair of parallel opposite sides, 1 obtuse angle, acute angle, and 2 right angles.

Reviewing A Portfolio

Have students review their portfolios. Consider including these items:
- Finished work on the Chapter Project (p. 317F) or **Investigation** (pp. 338–339).
- Selected math journal entries, pp. 319, 325, 336, 341.
- Finished work on the nonroutine problem in **What Do You Know?** (p. 319) and problems from the Menu (pp. 356–357).
- Each student's self-selected "best piece" from work completed during the chapter. Have each student attach a note explaining why he or she chose that piece.
- Any work you or an individual student wishes to keep for future reference.

You may take this opportunity to conduct conferences with students. The Portfolio Analysis Form can help you report students' progress. See Teacher's Assessment Resources, p. 33.

PURPOSE Review and assess the concepts, skills, and strategies learned in this chapter.

Materials have available: rulers

Using the Performance Assessment

Have students read and restate the problems in their own words.

Point out the section on the student page headed "A Good Answer." Make sure students understand that you will use these points to evaluate their answers.

Evaluating Student Work

As you read students' papers, look for the following:
- *Does the student describe three geometric figures in the painting using geometric terms?*
- *Do the descriptions name the parts of the figures as well as the entire figures?*
- *Does the student identify three geometric figures that are not in the painting?*
- *Does the student correctly use those figures to show examples of slides, flips, and turns?*

The Holistic Scoring Guide and annotated samples of students' work can be used to assess this task. See pages 27–32 and 37–72 in Teacher's Assessment Resources.

Using the Self-Assessment

What Do You Think? Assure students that there are no right or wrong answers. Tell them the emphasis is on what they think and how they justify their answers.

Follow-Up Interviews

These questions can be used to gain insight into students' thinking:
- **What are some geometric figures in the painting?**
- **How else can you describe the parts of this figure? (Ask as you point to one of the figures.)**
- **How else can you describe this figure as a whole? (Ask as you point to one of the figures.)**
- **What are some 2-dimensional geometric figures that are not in the painting?**
- **What is a slide? a flip? a turn?**

OBJECTIVE Apply geometric concepts to mosaics.

Materials colored construction paper, glue, cardboard (optional)

Resources drawing program or Math Van Tools

Science

Cultural Connection Read the **Cultural Note** on page 363. Encourage students to share descriptions of mosaics they have seen. After looking at the pictures and discussing the questions, guide students to see how the concepts they learned in geometry are related to mosaics.

Then write the geometrical terms lines, polygons, angles, congruency, similarity, rays, and area on the chalkboard. Have students find examples of each in the pictures of mosaics shown on page 362.

Math

Have students work in pairs or small groups to complete items 1–4.

Before students begin item 3, have them measure the area of a single grid square; each square measures 1 cm by 1 cm.

math science technology
CONNECTION

From Bits and Pieces

1

Mosaics are made of small pieces of stone, glass, or tile cemented onto objects.

2 Some mosaics are geometric designs. Others are pictures.

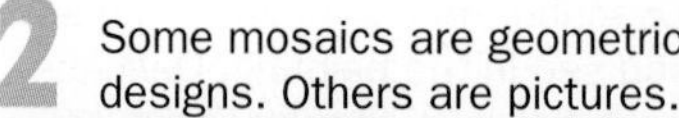

3 Some of the oldest mosaics were made with colored stones cemented into walkways to make pictures and designs.

4

A volcano buried the ancient Roman of Pompeii with ash in A.D. 79. Scier learned about what life was like in Pompeii from mosaics, and other th they uncovered.

- ▶ What geometric shapes are found in the mosaics that are shown? **Possible answer: triangle, trapezoid, rectangle**
- ▶ What other things do you think scientists uncovered in Pompeii? What might still be there after centuries have passed? **Possible answer: pottery, metal tools, walls**

Extending The Activity

Have students work in pairs or small groups to create mosaics that represent their school, town, or family in some way, using pieces of construction paper. Have students sketch the outline of the mosaic on cardboard, then cut out pieces of colored construction paper to fill in each shape.

. Possible answer: The mosaic on page 363 has squares and triangles.
. Possible answer: The mosaic on page 363 has 3 different polygons—squares, rhombi, and triangles.

Studying Mosaics

Study the mosaics on pages 362–363 and then answer the questions.
Check students' work.

1 What different figures do you see in the mosaics? **See above.**

2 How many different kinds of polygons can you find in the mosaics? **See above.**

3 Use the centimeter grid to estimate the area of each section in the mosaic below. **Each section is 1 square cm.**

4 What colors are used in the mosaic below? How much area of the mosaic does each color cover? Use the centimeter grid to estimate the area of each color. **See below.**

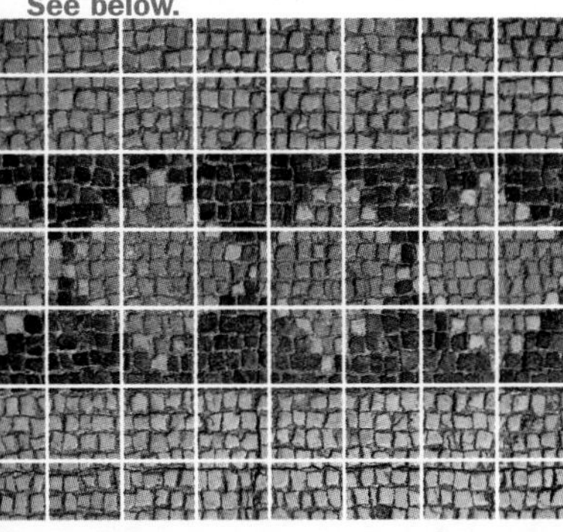

4. **Possible answers: light, medium, and dark browns; light brown covers about 32 square cm, medium brown covers about 11 square cm, dark brown covers about 10 square cm**

At the Computer

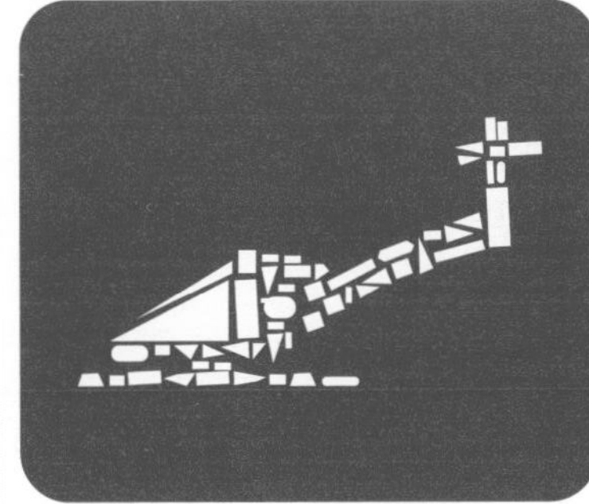

5 Use a drawing program to make your own mosaic. Decide whether you want to make a mosaic that is a geometric design, one that pictures something, or one that combines a picture and a geometric design. Use your computer program to repeat different shapes and use different colors.

6 Write a description of your mosaic using geometric terms.

Cultural Note

People in different cultures have created mosaic art pieces. The Greeks taught the Romans how to make them. Muslims in India made mosaics. The Mayan and Aztec Indians of Central America also made them.

Bibliography

Piece by Piece: Mosaics of the Ancient World, by Michael Avi-Yonah. Minneapolis, MN: Lerner Publications Co., 1993. ISBN 0–8225–3204–2.

Technology

Before students begin designing their mosaics have them brainstorm ideas about what the mosaic will include. Encourage them to include pictures that represent their culture or family or themselves. For example, if they enjoy music have them include instruments, musical notes, and dancers in their mosaics.

For item 6, students can describe the shapes, area of different colors, and shapes that make up their mosaic.

If you have a color printer available, print out students' mosaics for an art display in your classroom. Invite other classes to visit. Allow students to make brief presentations to the classes about their individual mosaics.

Math Van Students may use the Geometry tool in Math Van Tools to help create their mosaic.

Interesting Facts

- **The eruption of Mt. Vesuvius** destroyed the city of Pompeii in the year 62 A.D. and again in 79 A.D. About 20,000 people lived in Pompeii.
- **The word graffiti** was originally used by archaeologists to describe the drawings found on walls in Pompeii.
- **The first archaeologist to study the Pompeii ruins** to learn about its civilization was Giuseppe Fiorelli in 1860. Before this time explorers were only interested finding treasure.

CUMULATIVE REVIEW

PURPOSE Review and assess the concepts, skills, and strategies that students have already learned.

Materials per student: calculators (optional)

Using the Cumulative Review

The **Cumulative Review** is presented in a multiple-choice format to provide practice in taking a standardized test.

The table below correlates the review items to the text pages on which the skills are taught.

Assessment Resources

Test Masters

There are multiple-choice Cumulative Tests and a Year-End Test that provides additional opportunities for students to practice taking standardized tests.

Computer Test Generator

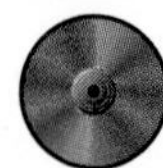

The Computer Test Generator supplies abundant multiple-choice and free-response test items, which you may use to generate tests and practice worksheets tailored to the needs of your class.

TEST PREPARATION

Choose the letter of the correct answer.

1 If you have $2.60, what is the greatest number of quarters you could have? B
A 8
B 10
C 12
D 15

2 Jerry's class recycled 69 pounds of aluminum cans. They got $0.33 for each pound of cans. Which is the best estimate of how much money they got? H
F $2.10
G $18.00
H $21.00
J $210.00

3 What do the letters A, H, M, T, and X have in common? They are all ■. B
A closed figures
B symmetrical
C similar
D congruent

4 What number when added to 28,863 gives a number between 34,000 and 35,000? G
F 8,000
G 6,000
H 5,000
J 4,000

5 Complete the sentence.
$48 \times 6 = 6 \times$ ■ $= 288$ B
A 6
B 48
C 54
D 288

6 The perimeter of a square is 36 cm. What is the length of one side? J
F 6 cm
G 7 cm
H 8 cm
J 9 cm

7 Albert has $1.53 worth of coins in his pocket. Which combination of coins can he *not* have? C
A 6 quarters, 3 pennies
B 3 quarters, 5 dimes, 4 nickels, 8 pennies
C 4 quarters, 3 dimes, 5 nickels, 3 pennies
D 5 quarters, 2 dimes, 1 nickel, 3 pennies

8 Ada bought 4 licorice ropes that each measured 36 inches in length. If she gives a 5-inch piece to each of her 28 classmates, how much will she have left? H
F 8 in.
G 5 in.
H 4 in.
J 3 in.

9 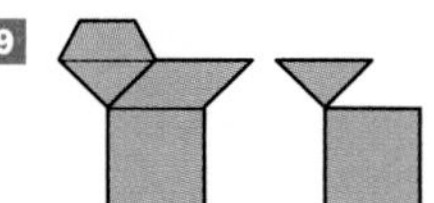

Which pattern blocks would you need to complete the design on the right to match the one on the left? B
A 1 square and 1 trapezoid
B 1 trapezoid and 1 parallelogram
C 2 trapezoids
D 1 triangle and 1 square

Cumulative Review Correlation

REVIEW ITEMS	TEXT PAGES	REVIEW ITEMS	TEXT PAGES
1, 7	40–41	11	8–11
2	42–43	12	256–259
3	344–345	13	138–139
4	48–51	14	282–289
5	140–141	15	210–217
6	250–251	16	48–51, 62–65
8	182–183	17	262–265
9	138–139, 324–327	18	90–93
10	308–311	19	328–329

10 A parent must accompany each group of 6 students on a trip. If 32 students are going, how many parents will be needed? G

- **F** 3
- **G** 6
- **H** 7
- **J** 32

11 What is the value of the digit 3 in the number 134,927? C

- **A** 300
- **B** 3,000
- **C** 30,000
- **D** 300,000

12 Marcus fills a pitcher with 3 qt of water. This is the same as ■. H

- **F** 1 gal
- **G** 8 pt
- **H** 12 c
- **J** 84 c

13 What are the next three numbers in this pattern: 1, 3, 6, 10? D

- **A** 13, 16, 20
- **B** 20, 30, 40
- **C** 15, 20, 25
- **D** 15, 21, 28

14 Carol has $10.00. She buys 2 notebooks for $0.99 each and a box of crayons for $2.25. The tax is $0.31. How much change will she get? J

- **F** $3.55
- **G** $4.23
- **H** $4.54
- **J** $5.46

15 43 × 16 D

- **A** 59
- **B** 201
- **C** 658
- **D** 688

16 547 ÷ 6 J

- **F** 9 R11
- **G** 91
- **H** 90 R1
- **J** 91 R1

17 Which is the most reasonable answer? During the day, Hector drank a ■ of water. A

- **A** liter
- **B** meter
- **C** milliliter
- **D** gram

18 Of the following data, 84 is the ■.
97, 59, 65, 97, 102. J

- **F** range
- **G** median
- **H** mode
- **J** average

19 What is *not* shown in the diagram? D

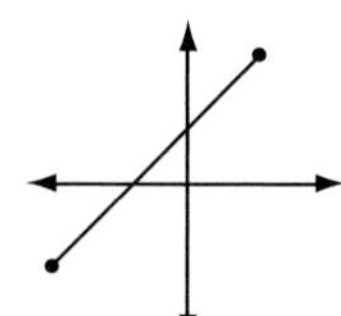

- **A** perpendicular lines
- **B** intersecting lines
- **C** line segment
- **D** parallel lines

TEST PREPARATION

CHAPTER 10 AT A GLANCE:

Theme: Fun for Rainy Days Suggested Pacing: 14–17 days

Fractions and Probability

	DAY 1	DAY 2	DAY 3
WEEK ONE	**PREASSESSMENT** Introduction **p. 366** What Do You Know? **p. 367** **CHAPTER OBJECTIVES:** 10A, 10B, 10C, 10D, 10E **RESOURCES** Read-Aloud Anthology pp. 46–47 Pretest: Test Master Form A, B, or C Diagnostic Inventory Portfolio Journal **NCTM STANDARDS:** 1, 2, 3, 4, 11, 12	**LESSON 10.1** Part of a Whole **pp. 368–371** **CHAPTER OBJECTIVES:** 10A **MATERIALS** inch rulers (TA 18), graph paper (TA 8), crayons, calculators (opt.) **RESOURCES** Reteach/Practice/Extend: 88 Math Center Cards: 88 Extra Practice: 520 Daily Review TE p. 367B Technology Link **NCTM STANDARDS:** 12	**LESSON 10.2** Part of a Group **pp. 372–373** **CHAPTER OBJECTIVES:** 10A **MATERIALS** calculators (opt.) **RESOURCES** Reteach/Practice/Extend: 89 Math Center Cards: 89 Extra Practice: 520 Daily Review TE p. 371B Journal Technology Link **NCTM STANDARDS:** 12
WEEK TWO	**LESSON 10.5** Simplify Fractions **pp. 380–381** **CHAPTER OBJECTIVES:** 10B **MATERIALS** counters (TA 13), calculators (opt.) **RESOURCES** Reteach/Practice/Extend: 92 Math Center Cards: 92 Extra Practice: 521 **TEACHING WITH TECHNOLOGY** Alternate Lesson TE pp. 381A–381B Daily Review TE p. 379B Technology Link **NCTM STANDARDS:** 4, 12	**LESSON 10.6** Compare Fractions **pp. 382–383** **CHAPTER OBJECTIVES:** 10B **MATERIALS** fractions strips (TA 26), inch rulers (TA 18), calculators (opt.) **RESOURCES** Reteach/Practice/Extend: 93 Math Center Cards: 93 Extra Practice: 521 Daily Review TE p. 381D Technology Link **NCTM STANDARDS:** 12	**LESSON 10.7** Mixed Numbers **pp. 384–385** **CHAPTER OBJECTIVES:** 10A **MATERIALS** calculators (opt.) **RESOURCES** Reteach/Practice/Extend: 94 Math Center Cards: 94 Extra Practice: 522 Daily Review TE p. 383B Technology Link **NCTM STANDARDS:** 12
WEEK THREE	**LESSON 10.9** Fractions and Probability **pp. 392–393** **CHAPTER OBJECTIVES:** 10D **MATERIALS** calculators (opt.) **RESOURCES** Reteach/Practice/Extend: 96 Math Center Cards: 96 Extra Practice: 522 Daily Review TE p. 391B Journal Technology Link **NCTM STANDARDS:** 11, 12	**LESSON 10.10** PROBLEM-SOLVING STRATEGY Conduct an Experiment **pp. 394–395** **CHAPTER OBJECTIVES:** 10E **MATERIALS** number cubes (opt.), calculators (opt.) **RESOURCES** Reteach/Practice/Extend: 97 Math Center Cards: 97 Extra Practice: 523 Daily Review TE p. 393B Technology Link **NCTM STANDARDS:** 1, 2, 3, 4, 11	**LESSON 10.11** EXPLORE ACTIVITY Predict and Experiment **pp. 396–397** **CHAPTER OBJECTIVES:** 10D **MATERIALS** coins or 2-color counters (TA 13) **RESOURCES** Reteach/Practice/Extend: 98 Math Center Cards: 98 Extra Practice: 523 Daily Review TE p. 395B Technology Link **NCTM STANDARDS:** 4, 11

DAY 4

LESSON 10.3

EXPLORE ACTIVITY

Find a Fraction of a Number pp. 374–375

CHAPTER OBJECTIVES: 10C

MATERIALS straws or sticks, marbles or number cubes, calculators (opt.)

RESOURCES Reteach/Practice/Extend: 90
Math Center Cards: 90
Extra Practice: 520

Daily Review TE p. 373B

Technology Link

NCTM STANDARDS: 4, 12

MIDCHAPTER ASSESSMENT

Midchapter Review p. 386

CHAPTER OBJECTIVES: 10A, 10B, 10C, 10E

MATERIALS calculators (opt.)

Developing Technology Sense p. 387

REAL-LIFE INVESTIGATION:

Applying Fractions pp. 388–389

 Portfolio 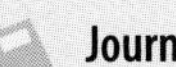  Journal

NCTM STANDARDS: 1, 2, 3, 4, 12

LESSON 10.12

PROBLEM SOLVERS AT WORK

Solve Multistep Problems pp. 398–401

CHAPTER OBJECTIVES: 10E

MATERIALS calculators (opt.), computer probability program (opt.), graphing program (opt.)

RESOURCES Reteach/Practice/Extend: 99
Math Center Cards: 99
Extra Practice: 523

Daily Review TE p. 397B

 Technology Link

NCTM STANDARDS: 1, 2, 3, 4, 8

DAY 5

LESSON 10.4

EXPLORE ACTIVITY

Equivalent Fractions pp. 376–379

CHAPTER OBJECTIVES: 10B

MATERIALS fraction strips (TA 26), calculators (opt.)

RESOURCES Reteach/Practice/Extend: 91
Math Center Cards: 91
Extra Practice: 521

Daily Review TE p. 375B

 Algebraic Thinking

 Technology Link

NCTM STANDARDS: 4, 12

LESSON 10.8

EXPLORE ACTIVITY

Probability pp. 390–391

CHAPTER OBJECTIVES: 10D

MATERIALS spinners (TA 2–3)

RESOURCES Reteach/Practice/Extend: 95
Math Center Cards: 95
Extra Practice: 522

Daily Review TE p. 389B

 Technology Link

NCTM STANDARDS: 4, 11

CHAPTER ASSESSMENT

Chapter Review pp. 402–403

MATERIALS calculators (opt.)

Chapter Test p. 404

RESOURCES Posttest: Test Master Form A, B, or C

Performance Assessment p. 405

RESOURCES Performance Task: Test Master

Math • Science • Technology Connection pp. 406–407

Portfolio

NCTM STANDARDS: 1, 4, 10

Assessment Options

FORMAL

Chapter Tests

STUDENT BOOK
- Midchapter Review, p. 386
- Chapter Review, pp. 402–403
- Chapter Test, p. 404

BLACKLINE MASTERS
- Test Master Form A, B, or C
- Diagnostic Inventory

COMPUTER TEST GENERATOR
- Available on disk

TAAS Preparation and Practice
- Chapter Test

Performance Assessment
- What Do You Know? p. 367
- Performance Assessment, p. 405
- Holistic Scoring Guide, Teacher's Assessment Resources, pp. 27–32
- Follow-Up Interviews, p. 405
- Performance Task, Test Masters

Teacher's Assessment Resources
- Portfolio Guidelines and Forms, pp. 6–9, 33–35
- Holistic Scoring Guide, pp. 27–32
- Samples of Student Work, pp. 37–72

INFORMAL

Ongoing Assessment
- Observation Checklist, pp. 368, 372, 374, 376, 382, 384, 392, 394, 396, 398
- Interview, p. 380
- Anecdotal Report, p. 390

Portfolio Opportunities
- Chapter Project, p. 365F
- What Do You Know? p. 367
- Investigation, pp. 388–389
- Journal Writing, pp. 367, 372, 386, 392
- Performance Assessment, p. 405
- Self-Assessment: What Do You Think? p. 405

Chapter Objectives		Standardized Test Correlations
10A	Read and write fractions and mixed numbers	MAT, CAT, SAT, ITBS, CTBS, TN*
10B	Compare and order fractions and find equivalent fractions	MAT, CAT, SAT, ITBS, CTBS, TN*
10C	Find the fraction of a number	MAT, CAT, SAT, ITBS, CTBS, TN*
10D	Find the probability of an event	MAT, CAT, SAT, ITBS, CTBS, TN*
10E	Solve problems, including those that involve fractions, probability, and conducting an experiment	MAT, CAT, SAT, ITBS, CTBS, TN*

*Terra Nova

NCTM Standards Grades K–4

1 Problem Solving
2 Communication
3 Reasoning
4 Connections
5 Estimation
6 Number Sense and Numeration
7 Concepts of Whole Number Operations
8 Whole Number Computation
9 Geometry and Spatial Sense
10 Measurement
11 Statistics and Probability
12 Fractions and Decimals
13 Patterns and Relationships

Meeting Individual Needs

LEARNING STYLES

- AUDITORY/LINGUISTIC
- LOGICAL/ANALYTICAL
- VISUAL/SPATIAL
- MUSICAL
- KINESTHETIC
- SOCIAL
- INDIVIDUAL

Students who are talented in art, language, and physical activity may better understand mathematical concepts when these concepts are connected to their areas of interest. Use the following activity to stimulate the different learning styles of some of your students.

Kinesthetic Learners

Students may need to manipulate fraction bars or pieces when solving problems involving fractions. Play a game called, "Show Me." Write a fraction or mixed number on the board. Students show the fraction using fraction bars.

Ask students which is more, $\frac{1}{2}$ or $\frac{1}{4}$. Have them explain why using fraction bars.

See Lesson Resources, pp. 367A, 371A, 373A, 375A, 379A, 381C, 383A, 389A, 391A, 393A, 395A, 397A.

GIFTED AND TALENTED

Some students may be able to explore the relationship between division and fractional parts of larger numbers. Have them find $\frac{1}{4}$, $\frac{2}{4}$, $\frac{3}{4}$, and $\frac{4}{4}$ of numbers that are divisible by four (24, 48, 60, 360, and so on).

Have students find fractional parts of common objects. For example, have them figure out how many days equal one half of a year.

See also Meeting Individual Needs, pp. 370, 378, 398.

EXTRA SUPPORT

Have available fraction strips for students who need practice with fractions.

Specific suggestions for ways to provide extra support to students appear in every lesson in this chapter.

See Meeting Individual Needs, pp. 368, 372, 374, 376, 380, 382, 384, 390, 392, 394, 396, 398.

EARLY FINISHERS

Students who finish their class work early may write an article for the school newspaper about the math games they have been playing. (See *Chapter Project*, p. 365F.)

See also Meeting Individual Needs, pp. 370, 372, 374, 378, 380, 382, 384, 390, 392, 394, 396, 400.

LANGUAGE SUPPORT

Be sure students are not mixing up the words *hole* and *whole.* Write the two words and discuss their meanings.

In addition, write the words *one whole, one half, two halves,* when referring to fractions. Reading the words and seeing the number and a model may help students say the fraction names.

See also Meeting Individual Needs, pp. 368, 376, 400.

ESL APPROPRIATE

INCLUSION

- **For inclusion ideas, information, and suggestions, see pp. 378, T15.**
- **For gender fairness tips, see pp. 377, T15.**

USING MANIPULATIVES

Building Understanding Students can use pattern blocks to explore halves, thirds, and sixths. Have them use only the yellow, red, and green shapes, with the yellow hexagon representing one whole. Students can show how many red pieces and how many green pieces make a whole. Have students find different ways to make a whole yellow piece. They can record their findings.

Easy-to-Make Manipulatives Paper fraction strips can be made and used to reinforce the concept of fractions. Students can have multiple sets to show fractions greater than one. Have students label the fraction parts in order to identify the pieces. Use a different color for each fraction.

ESL APPROPRIATE

USING COOPERATIVE LEARNING

Huddle This strategy develops teamwork by having students work together to confer about an answer.

- **Students form huddles, in groups of three to five.**
- **Students count off within their group.**
- **The teacher asks a simple factual question and the huddle confers quietly.**
- **The teacher randomly chooses a spokesperson for the group (i.e. ask all the Number 3's to stand and call on specific ones to represent the group).**

USING LITERATURE

Use the story *It Happened in America* to introduce the chapter theme, Fun for Rainy Days. This story is reprinted on pages 46–47 of the Read-Aloud Anthology.

Also available in the Read-Aloud Anthology is the folktale *The Divided Students,* page 48.

Linking Technology

This integrated package of programs and services allows students to explore, develop, and practice concepts; solve problems; build portfolios; and assess their own progress. Teachers can enhance instruction, provide remediation, and share ideas with other educational professionals.

CD-ROM ACTIVITY

In *Kites of Color,* students use the fraction mat to design kite colors. Students can use the online notebook to write about the various ways they used fractions. To extend the activity, students use the Math Van tools to complete an open-ended problem related to the concept. In the activity *And the Winning Color Is...,* students use a bar graph to help them predict how a spinner will land. **Available on CD-ROM.**

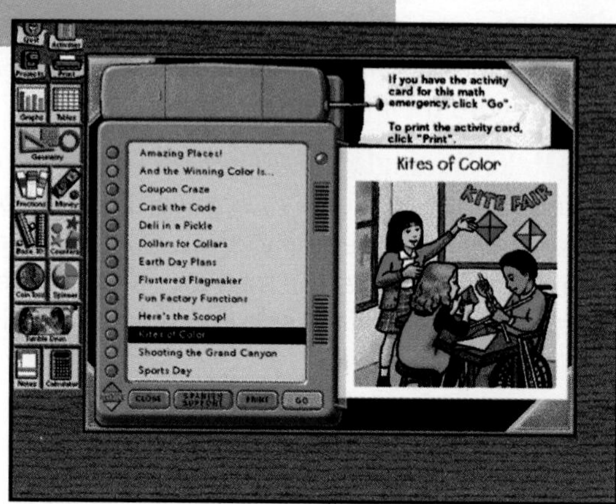

CD-ROM TOOLS

Students can use Math Van's fraction strips to explore the concept of fractions, and they can use graphs and the probability tools (coin toss, spinners, and tumble drum) to investigate probability. The Tech Links on the Lesson Resources pages highlight opportunities for students to use these and other tools such as counters, tables, online notes, and calculator to provide additional practice, reteaching, or extension. **Available on CD-ROM.**

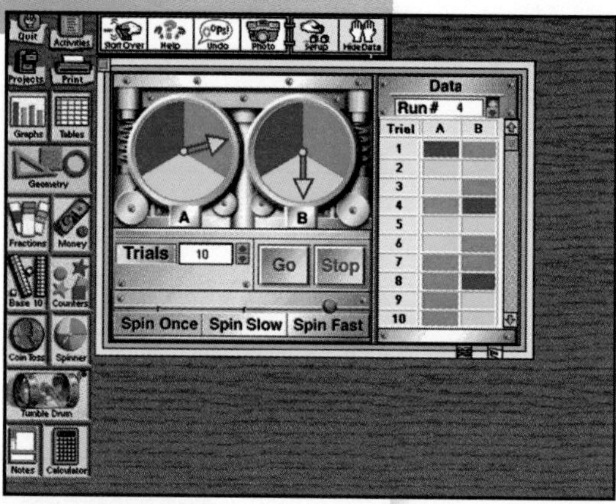

WEB SITE http://www.mhschool.com

Teachers can access the McGraw-Hill School Division World Wide Web site for additional curriculum support at http://www.mhschool.com. Click on our Resource Village for specially designed activities linking Web sites to fractions and probability. Motivate children by inviting them to explore Web sites that develop the chapter theme of "Fun for a Rainy Day." Exchange ideas on classroom management, cultural diversity, and other areas in the Math Forum.

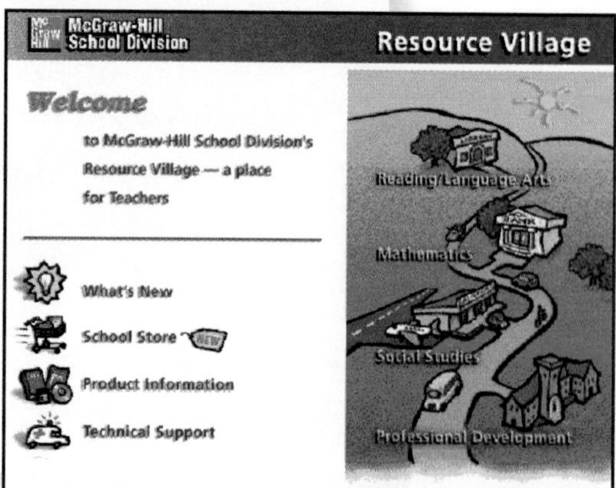

Chapter Project TAKE YOUR TURN

Highlighting the Math

- determine probability
- make adjustments to attain equal probability
- use number sense and problem-solving skills to create fair games

1 Starting the Project

Groups of students will design and play games, with each group using a coin, a spinner, or number cube. (*At the beginning of the chapter:* have students play the games. *Beginning with Lesson 8:* discuss what makes a game fair and how to express the "probability of winning" as a fraction.) Assign students to groups and assign each group a game: Flip a Coin, Spin a Spinner, or Toss a Cube.

2 Continuing the Project

- Each group designs its game using the following structure: Materials, Number of Players, How to Determine Who Goes First, Rules, How to Win. Each group makes a score card.
- Each group plays its game.
- Each group makes a booklet describing how to play its game.

3 Finishing the Project

The groups present their booklets to the class. Then groups take turns playing each others' games.

Community Involvement

Make copies of the activity books and donate them to a local hospital for the children's ward. Students can donate number cubes, coins, and spinners to be included with each booklet.

BUILDING A PORTFOLIO

Each student's portfolio piece should include a copy of the group's booklet, along with an explanation of how the group determined the fairness of each game. Students can also include an opinion of which game is their favorite and why.

To assess students' work, refer to the Holistic Scoring Guide on page 27 in the Teacher's Assessment Resources.

PURPOSE Introduce the theme of the chapter.

Resource Read-Aloud Anthology, pages 46–47.

Using Literature

Read "It Happened in America" from the Read-Aloud Anthology to introduce the theme of the chapter, "Fun for Rainy Days."

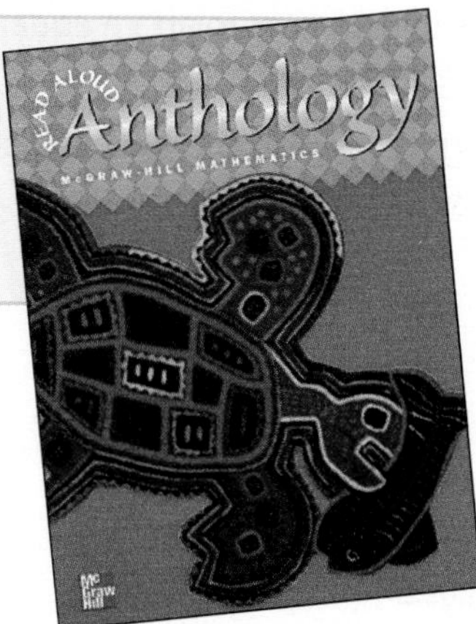

Developing the Theme

Let students describe their favorite games. Encourage them by suggesting different types of games such as board games, video games, computer games, card games, jacks, marbles, and so on. Have them explain the goals, strategies, and rules of games they suggest. Ask them why they enjoy playing particular games.

Differentiate between games of chance and games of strategy and skill. Have students tell which type they prefer and why. Chess is a game of strategy and skill that some fourth graders play. Discuss games that involve both chance and strategy such as Monopoly.

In addition to games, have students describe other activities that they enjoy, such as solving puzzles and making crafts. Discuss different types of puzzles and crafts and why they are fun to do.

These games, puzzles, and crafts are discussed in this chapter:

puzzles	p. 366	board games	pp. 376–377, 392–393, 398–399
crafts	pp. 368–369	Lu-lu	pp. 380–381
chess	pp. 372–373	computer games	pp. 382–383
pick-up sticks	pp. 374–375	Dish It Up	pp. 384–385

On pages 388–389, students explore word games.

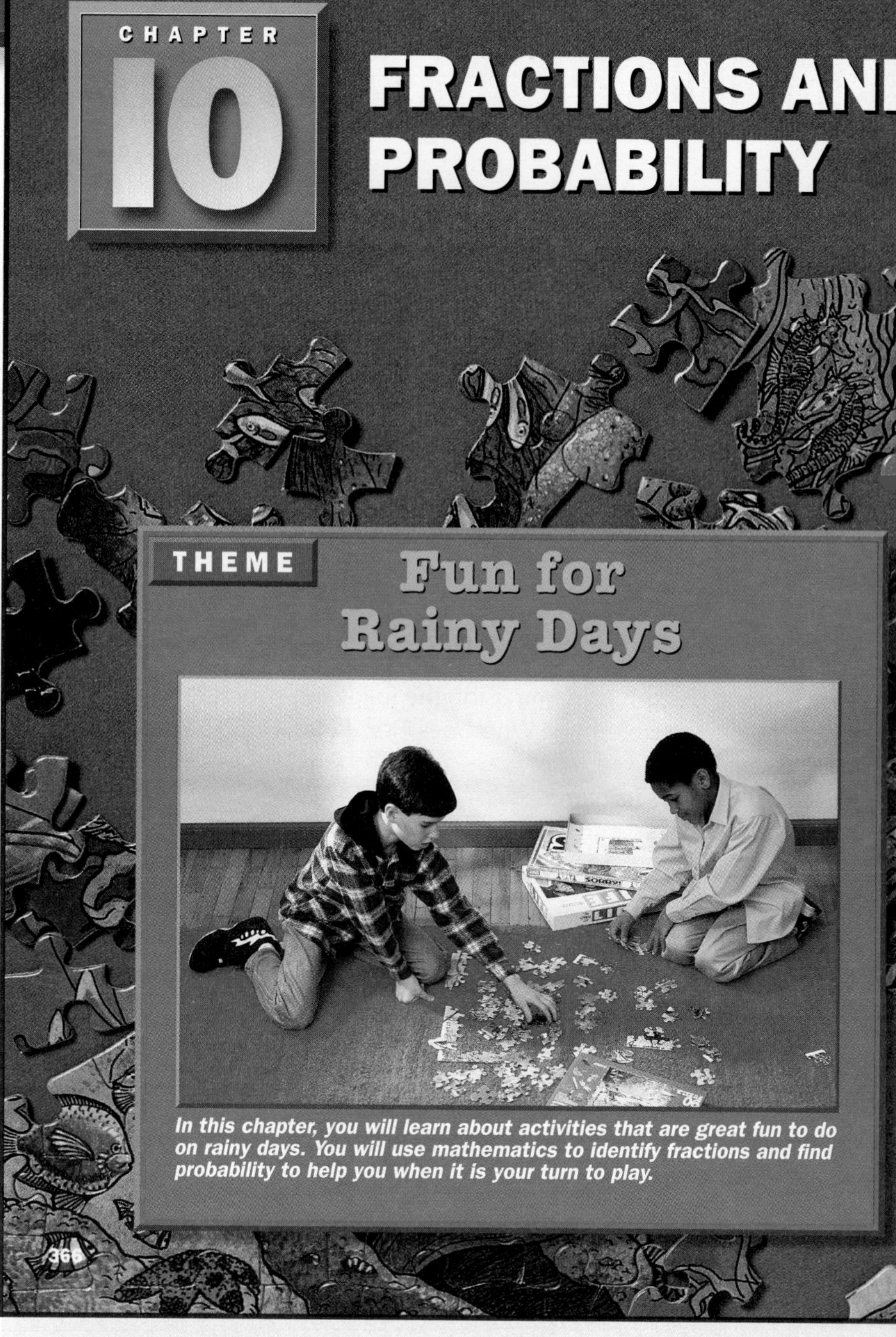
CHAPTER 10

FRACTIONS AN
PROBABILITY

THEME

Fun for Rainy Days

In this chapter, you will learn about activities that are great fun to do on rainy days. You will use mathematics to identify fractions and find probability to help you when it is your turn to play.

366

Chapter Bibliography

Anno's Math Games II by Mitsumasa Anno. New York: Philomel Books, 1989. ISBN 0–399–21615–4.

Fractions are Parts of Things by J. Richard Dennis. New York: HarperCollins Children's Books, 1972. ISBN 0–690–31521–X.

A Young Painter: The Life and Paintings of Wang Yani—China's Extraordinary Young Artist by Zheng Zhensun and Alice Low. New York: Scholastic, Inc., 1991. ISBN 0–590–44906–0.

Community Involvement

Have students write a Rainy Day Game Book to sell as a fundraiser in the neighborhood. As a class, list games and activities that can be played indoors at home. Groups of students can brainstorm ideas for games, write out a set of rules, then use drawings to show how the game is played. As a class, decide the order the games will appear in the book and a reasonable price for its purchase.

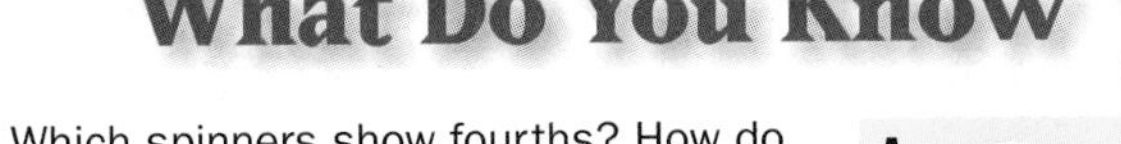

What Do You Know?

1 Which spinners show fourths? How do you know? **See above.**

2 Which spinner shows eighths? How do you know? **See above.**

3 Which spinner would give you the best chance of winning a game by spinning red? Explain your reasoning. **See below.**

4 Draw a spinner that is divided into equal parts. Color the spinner using different colors. Describe it using words or fractions. **Accept any reasonable answers.**

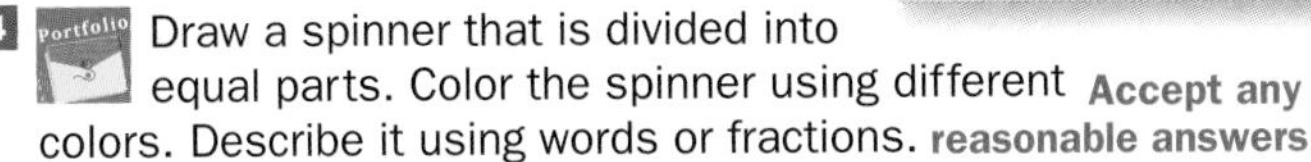

Make Predictions **Each player in a basketball game has taken 10 shots. Mia has made 8 baskets, James 4, and Toshi 6. To win, a player must get 20 baskets. Predict who will be the winner.** **3. Possible answer: Spinner B has the greatest part of the spinner colored red, so it gives the best chance of spinning red.**

When you make a prediction, you use what you already know to make a guess about what comes next.

1 Which player did you predict to win? to come in last? Why? **Mia—she has made the most baskets; James—he has made the fewest baskets.**

2 What fraction of the 20 baskets has each player made so far? **Mia—$\frac{8}{20}$ or $\frac{2}{5}$; James—$\frac{4}{20}$ or $\frac{1}{5}$; Toshi—$\frac{6}{20}$ or $\frac{3}{10}$**

Vocabulary

fraction, p. 368
numerator, p. 368
denominator, p. 368
equivalent fraction, p. 376
simplest form, p. 380
improper fraction, p. 384
mixed number, p. 384
possible outcome, p. 390
probability, p. 391
favorable outcome, p. 392

Reading, Writing, Arithmetic

Make Predictions Students may point out that sometimes players do come from behind to win a game. Explain that a prediction is not always correct but is a "best guess" based on available information. Have students make other predictions based on data. For example, you may wish to provide class attendance records for the past week and ask for predictions about the coming week. Have students check the accuracy of their predictions, then discuss the results.

Vocabulary

Students may record new words in their journals. Encourage them to show examples and draw diagrams to help them tell what the words mean.

PURPOSE Assess students' ability to apply prior knowledge of fractions and probability.

Materials have available: spinner blanks, color pencils or crayons

Assessing Prior Knowledge

Draw a spinner on the board divided into thirds. Shade one of the thirds white.

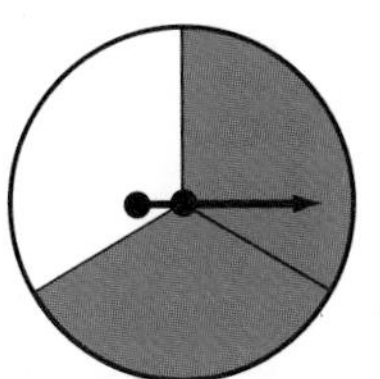

Ask these questions.

- **What fraction of the spinner is white?** *[$\frac{1}{3}$]*
- **What fraction is green (or whatever the color of the board is)?** *[$\frac{2}{3}$]*
- **Suppose I was going to spin a spinner like this one time and you were going to get a prize if you predicted correctly whether it would stop on white or green. Which would you predict and why?** *[Answers may vary. Possible answer: green, because there is more green than white.]*

Encourage students to use whatever methods they wish to answer items 1–3.

Building a Portfolio

Item 4 can be used as a benchmark to show where students are in their understanding of fractions.

A Portfolio Checklist for Students and a Checklist for Teachers are provided in Teacher's Assessment Resources, pp. 33–34.

Prerequisite Skills

- *Do students recognize parts of a whole?*
- *Do students recognize parts of a group?*
- *Can students identify equal and unequal parts of a whole?*

Assessment Resources

Diagnostic Inventory

Use this blackline master to assess prerequisite skills that students will need in order to be successful in this chapter.

Test Masters

Use the multiple choice format (form A or B) or the free response format (form C) as a pretest of the skills in this chapter.

Part of a Whole

OBJECTIVE Identify, read, and write fractions for parts of regions.

RESOURCE REMINDER
Math Center Cards 88
Practice 88, Reteach 88, Extend 88

SKILLS TRACE

GRADE 3	• Explore fractions as equal parts of regions. *(Chapter 11)* • Explore reading and writing fractions for parts of regions. *(Chapter 11)*
GRADE 4	• Read and write fractions for parts of regions.
GRADE 5	• Read, write, and draw fractions for parts of regions. *(Chapter 9)*

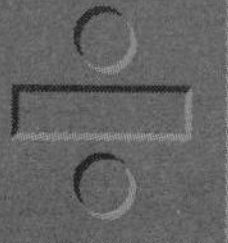

MANIPULATIVE WARM-UP

Cooperative Pairs — Visual/Spatial

OBJECTIVE Explore making fractions using parts of a whole.

Materials per pair: crayons

▶ Draw 10 squares of the same size. Have students divide 3 squares into fourths and 7 squares into eighths as shown below:

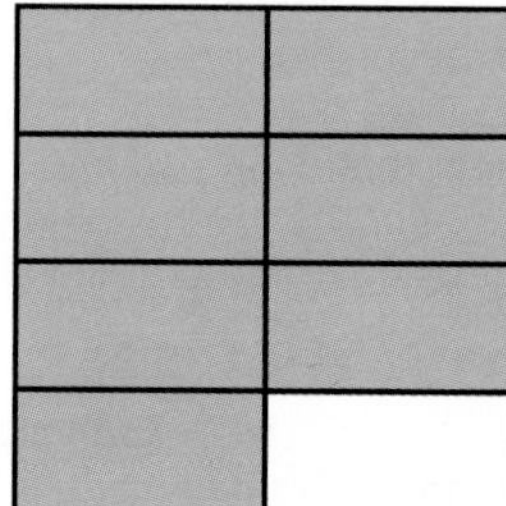

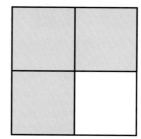

▶ Of the squares divided into fourths, have students use a crayon to color one part of one square, two parts of a second square, and three parts of a third square.

▶ Of the squares divided into eighths, have students color one part of one square, two parts of a second square, repeating this pattern until they color seven parts of a seventh square.

▶ Have pairs compare diagrams. Match the squares that were colored in the same parts.

ESL APPROPRIATE

LANGUAGE ARTS CONNECTION

Cooperative Pairs — Auditory/Linguistic

OBJECTIVE Connect fractions to the concept of sharing as depicted in a folktale.

Resource Read-Aloud Anthology, pp. 48–49

▶ With a partner, have each student read *The Divided Students* and discuss the outcome.

▶ Have students divide several different sheets of rectangular paper into quarters. Suggest that students fold the papers to make each part of the whole equal. Have pairs display some of their quarters.

▶ Discuss why dividing a piece of bread into equal quarters would be more difficult than dividing a piece of rectangular paper. *[Possible answer: because sometimes breads have irregular shapes]*

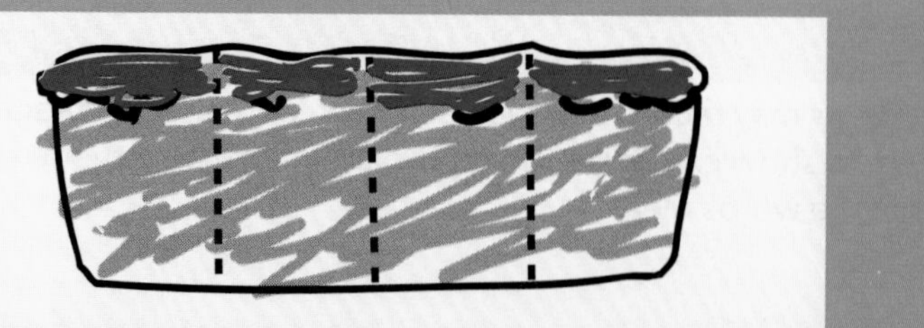

Daily Review

PREVIOUS DAY QUICK REVIEW

Find the volume.

1. 1 cm by 2 cm by 2 cm
2. 2 cm by 3 cm by 3 cm
3. 3 cm by 2 cm by 2 cm
[1. 4 cu cm; 2. 18 cu cm; 3. 12 cu cm]

FAST FACTS

1. 3 × 4 *[12]*
2. 2 × 8 *[16]*
3. 7 × 3 *[21]*
4. 9 × 6 *[54]*

Problem of the Day • 88

The Samson family is having pizza for dinner. The pizza has 8 equal slices. Two slices have pepperoni and three slices have pepperoni and mushrooms. The rest of the pizza is cheese. What fraction of the pizza is only cheese? *[$\frac{3}{8}$ pizza]*

TECH LINK

ONLINE EXPLORATION

Use our Web-linked activities and lesson plans to connect your students to the real world of games and puzzles.

MATH FORUM

Cultural Diversity My students enjoy using crafts and foods to represent fractions. To stimulate ideas and discussions, I have students list their fractions on the chalkboard with word descriptions.

Visit our Resource Village at http://www.mhschool.com to access the Online Exploration and the Math Forum.

MATH CENTER

Practice

OBJECTIVE Identify fractions as part of a whole.

Materials per student: marker, ruler, Math Center Recording Sheet (TA 31 optional)

Students draw the hands of a clock to show fractional parts of a whole. They draw and label each fraction. If the students have trouble with the time aspect, you may want to provide a clock with movable hands. *[Answers may vary. Possible answers: **1.** 6:00; **2.** 3:00; **3.** 4:00; **4.** 8:00; **5.** 9:00]*

PRACTICE ACTIVITY 88 — MATH CENTER, On Your Own

Spatial Sense • Fraction Hours

YOU NEED: drawing paper; marker; straightedge ruler

Draw 5 circles to use as clock faces. Then draw in the hands and shade the clock face to show each fraction. Write the time that fraction shows.

1. $\frac{1}{2}$ of the clock face
2. $\frac{1}{4}$ of the clock face
3. $\frac{1}{3}$ of the clock face
4. $\frac{2}{3}$ of the clock face
5. $\frac{3}{4}$ of the clock face

Grade Level 4 — McGraw-Hill School Division

Chapter 10, Lesson 1, pages 368–371 — Fractions

ESL APPROPRIATE

NCTM Standards
✓ Problem Solving
Communication
✓ Reasoning
Connections

Problem Solving

OBJECTIVE Write and solve problems involving fractional parts of a whole.

Materials per student: pattern blocks (TA 17), Math Center Recording Sheet (TA 31 optional)

Students solve problems involving different pattern blocks and different numbers of pattern blocks. They then write and exchange problems. *[**1.** trapezoid = $\frac{1}{2}$, rhombus = $\frac{1}{3}$, triangle = $\frac{1}{6}$; **2.** trapezoid would be = $\frac{1}{4}$; **3.** triangle = $\frac{1}{2}$; Possible answer: If two rhombuses stand for 1, what does one triangle stand for? $\frac{1}{4}$]*

PROBLEM-SOLVING ACTIVITY 88 — MATH CENTER, On Your Own

Formulating Problems • Pattern Block Fractions

YOU NEED: cutouts of the shapes shown or pattern blocks (optional)

1. If the hexagon equals 1, what does the trapezoid equal? the rhombus? the triangle?
2. If two hexagons equal 1, what does one trapezoid equal?
3. Suppose the rhombus equals 1. What does the triangle equal?

Experiment with different kinds and quantities of shapes equalling 1. Write problems like the ones above. Give your problems to a classmate to solve.

hexagon
trapezoid
triangle
rhombus

Grade Level 4 — McGraw-Hill School Division

Chapter 10, Lesson 1, pages 368–371 — Fractions

NCTM Standards
✓ Problem Solving
Communication
✓ Reasoning
Connections

Part of a Whole

OBJECTIVE Identify, read, and write fractions for parts of regions.

Materials per student: inch ruler (TA 18)

Vocabulary denominator, fraction, numerator

1 Introduce

Draw a circular pie divided into halves on the chalkboard. Tell students that you want to eat half the pie. Have a volunteer erase half of the circle. Ask:

- **What part of the pie is eaten? not eaten?** [$\frac{1}{2}$; $\frac{1}{2}$]

Repeat with circular pies where you tell students to identify $\frac{1}{4}$ and $\frac{1}{8}$ of the pie as well as identify the fractions $\frac{3}{4}$ and $\frac{3}{8}$.

2 Teach — *Whole Class*

LEARN Direct students to read the introductory problem. Point out that when a whole object such as the bracelet is divided into equal parts, you can use a *fraction* to show part of the whole. Have students suggest other situations that use fractions.

As students look at how to write a fraction, help them read and identify the *numerator* and *denominator.* Stress that the denominator always shows the number of equal parts that make up the whole.

After students have identified the fractions of the bracelet that are blue and white, ask:

- **What if the entire bracelet was made of blue beads. What fraction of the bracelet would be blue? red?** [$\frac{8}{8}$; $\frac{0}{8}$]

Point out that in the first fraction, the numerator shows 8 blue parts which is all the beads; and in the second fraction, it shows zero red beads. The denominators for both fractions are 8 since the total number of parts in the bracelet is still 8.

Talk It Over To encourage discussion, suggest that students draw diagrams to rearrange the color pattern on the bracelet.

Make sure that students understand that either red, blue, white, or yellow refers to all of the colors in the bracelet. To have them identify fractions of other combinations of colors, ask:

- **What part of the bracelet is red and yellow? red and white?** [$\frac{4}{8}$, $\frac{3}{8}$]
- **What part of the bracelet is not red? not white?** [$\frac{6}{8}$, $\frac{7}{8}$]
- **What fraction of the bracelet is either red, blue, or yellow?** [$\frac{7}{8}$]
- **What fraction of the bracelet is green? not green?** [$\frac{0}{8}$, $\frac{8}{8}$]

Part of a Whole

LEARN

This bracelet was designed on a loom from a Native American craft kit. What part of the whole bracelet is red?

You can describe the part of the bracelet that is red using words: 2 red parts out of eight equal parts.

You can also write a **fraction.**

Write: $\frac{2}{8}$ ← **numerator** / ← **denominator**

Read: Two eighths of the bracelet is red.

Talk It Over 1. Possible answer: No; no; no; no; the equal parts and whole remain the same even though the parts are arranged differently.

What fraction of the whole bracelet is blue? white?

$\frac{3}{8}$ ← blue parts / ← parts in all

Three eighths of the bracelet is blue.

$\frac{1}{8}$ ← white part / ← parts in all

One eighth of the bracelet is white.

Talk It Over

▶ **What if** you rearrange the color pattern on the bracelet. Will the fraction that is red change? the fraction that is blue? white? yellow? Explain. **See above.**

▶ How would you describe the fraction of the bracelet that is *either* red, blue, white, *or* yellow? Explain. **Possible answer: $\frac{8}{8}$; all the 8 equal parts of the bracelet are red, blue, white, or yellow.**

Check Out the Glossary
fraction
numerator
denominator
See page 544.

Meeting Individual Needs

Extra Support

Provide students with additional opportunities to write fractions. Have students use multicolor cubes to make their own patterned bracelets. Have them write fractions for each color in their bracelets.

Language Support

Help students who are unfamiliar with ordinal numbers and their pronunciation by sounding out several denominator names. Make a list of the most common denominators. Point out the *th* at the end of most of the names.

ESL APPROPRIATE

Ongoing Assessment

Observation Checklist Determine if students understand how to read and write fractions by having them identify different fractional parts of a circle divided into sixths.

Follow Up Some students may benefit by explaining how they identify the numerator and denominator of a fraction shown in a picture. For additional help, assign **Reteach 88.**

For students who understand how to read and write fractions, assign **Extend 88.**

can also measure fractions of an inch using a ruler.

bracelet is 1 in. wide. What part n inch do the rows of blue and red ds make up?

a ruler that shows eighths easure.

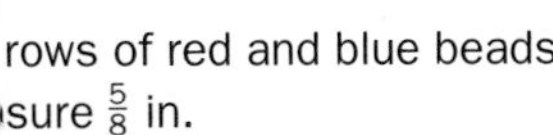

rows of red and blue beads sure $\frac{5}{8}$ in.

e Examples

of the bracelet is yellow.

B

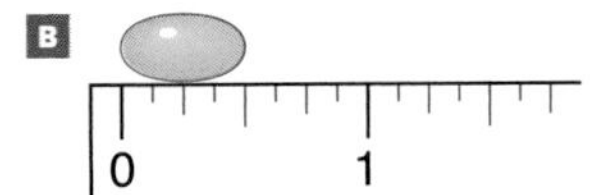

The bead is $\frac{4}{8}$ in., $\frac{2}{4}$ in., or $\frac{1}{2}$ in. long.

eck for Understanding

e a fraction for the part that is shaded.

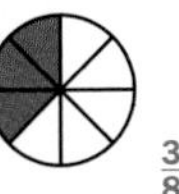
$\frac{3}{8}$

2 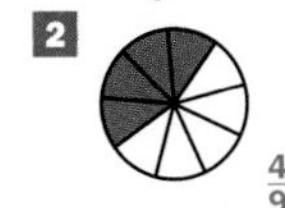
$\frac{4}{9}$

3 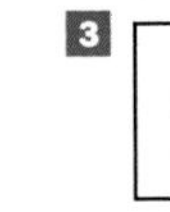
$\frac{1}{3}$

4 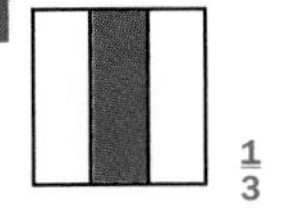

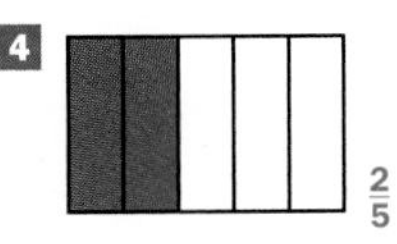
$\frac{2}{5}$

sure the segment to the nearest $\frac{1}{8}$, $\frac{1}{4}$, and $\frac{1}{2}$ inch.

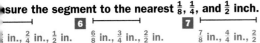

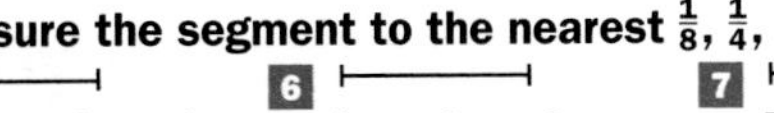
in., $\frac{2}{4}$ in., $\frac{1}{2}$ in.

6 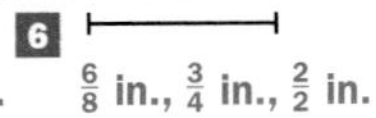
$\frac{6}{8}$ in., $\frac{3}{4}$ in., $\frac{2}{2}$ in.

7 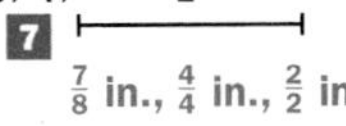
$\frac{7}{8}$ in., $\frac{4}{4}$ in., $\frac{2}{2}$ in.

8 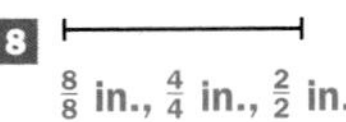
$\frac{8}{8}$ in., $\frac{4}{4}$ in., $\frac{2}{2}$ in.

tical Thinking: Analyze **Explain your reasoning.**

Which of these squares does *not* show $\frac{1}{4}$ red? **b; the parts are not equal.**

. 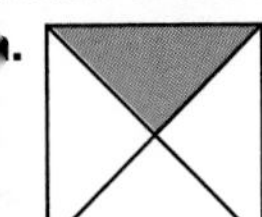

b. 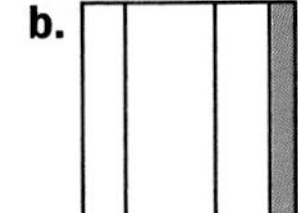

c. 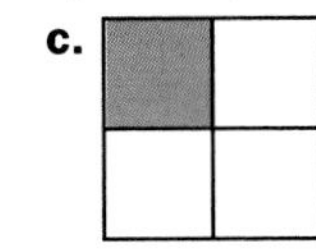

d. 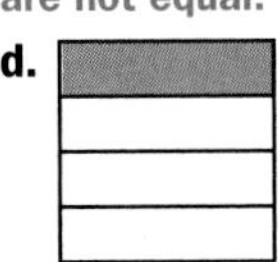

What if $\frac{1}{3}$ of an object is blue. What part is *not* blue? How can you tell?

sible answer: $\frac{2}{3}$; the whole contains 3 parts, so if 1 part ue, there are 2 parts that are not.

Turn the page for Practice.

CHECK

To solve the problem, students need to know how to read fractions of an inch on the ruler. Have students identify those segments of the ruler that represent a half, fourths, and eighths.

After a volunteer reads the problem, have the class use rulers to measure the thickness. Remind them that care must be taken to ensure accuracy with such small measurements. Elicit that the zero must be aligned with the left end of the object to be measured.

More Examples Have volunteers read each of the fractions aloud. For Example B, elicit that the fractions $\frac{4}{8}$ in., $\frac{2}{4}$ in., and $\frac{1}{2}$ in. measure the same length; the fractions look different because one fraction is in eighths, another fraction is in fourths, and the other is in halves.

3 Close

Check for Understanding using items 1–10, page 369.

For items 5–8, encourage students to write more than one fraction if they are able to do so.

Critical Thinking

For item 8, have students explain how they determined that the parts in item b are not equal. Then ask:

- **How could you redraw the vertical lines to show $\frac{1}{4}$ red in b?** *[Answers may vary.]*

For item 10, have students use a diagram to support their reasoning.

Practice See pages 370–371.

PRACTICE

Materials have available: calculators, graph paper, crayons

Options for assigning exercises:
A—Choice of ten exercises from ex. 1–18; all ex. 19–25; **Fraction Colors Game!; Mixed Review**
B—Choice of five exercises from ex. 1–12; all ex. 13–25; **Fraction Colors Game!; Mixed Review**

- It may be helpful to students to use grid paper for ex. 7–18.
- Students may want to compare actual rulers to the pictures in ex. 19–21.
- For ex. 22–24, point out that the total number of squares on the checkerboard can be found using multiplication: $8 \times 8 = 64$.
- For ex. 25, students may use the problem-solving strategy, Choose an Operation.

Fraction Colors Game! Have students work with a partner to play this game. Some students may have difficulty drawing squares that can be divided into equal parts for each fraction. Suggest that students use a 2×2 square to find a half, a 3×3 square to find thirds, a 4×4 square to find fourths, and so on, and a 12×12 square to find twelfths. Some students may opt to use other size squares where the number of units in the square is a multiple of the denominator of the fraction sought.

Mixed Review/Test Preparation In ex. 1–4, students review addition, subtraction, multiplication, and division, learned in Chapters 2, 6, and 8. Students review finding the area of rectangles and squares in ex. 5–8, a skill learned in Chapter 9.

Cultural Connection Read the **Cultural Note** on page 370. Ask students if they play checkers. Tell them that the rules for the 16th-century game were different than the rules used today. About 1800, modern game rules became widely accepted. All play is on black squares and black always moves first.

Practice

Write the fraction for the part that is white.

1 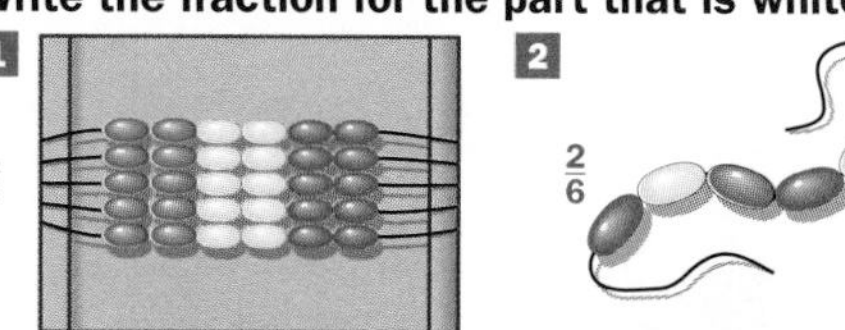 $\frac{1}{3}$

2 $\frac{2}{6}$

3 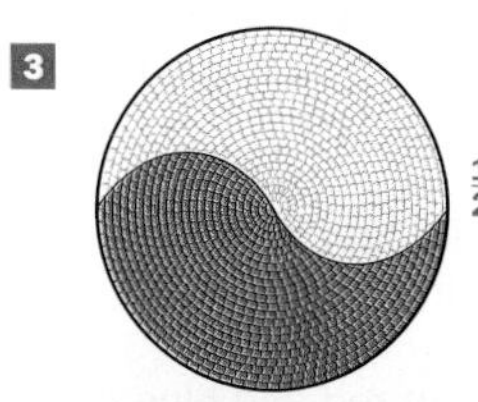 $\frac{1}{2}$

4 $\frac{5}{9}$

5 $\frac{1}{6}$

6 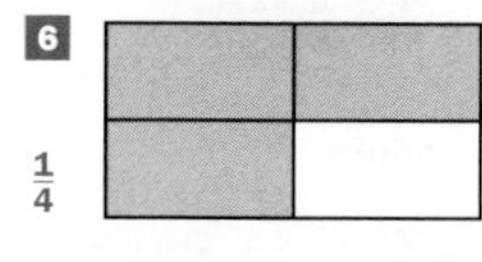 $\frac{1}{4}$

Draw a rectangle with the fraction shaded. Check students' work.

7 $\frac{2}{3}$ 8 $\frac{1}{4}$ 9 $\frac{5}{8}$ 10 $\frac{3}{5}$ 11 $\frac{1}{2}$ 12 $\frac{5}{9}$

13 $\frac{1}{5}$ 14 $\frac{1}{6}$ 15 $\frac{4}{7}$ 16 $\frac{4}{5}$ 17 $\frac{7}{8}$ 18 $\frac{2}{9}$

Measure the segment to the nearest $\frac{1}{8}$, $\frac{1}{4}$, and $\frac{1}{2}$ inch.

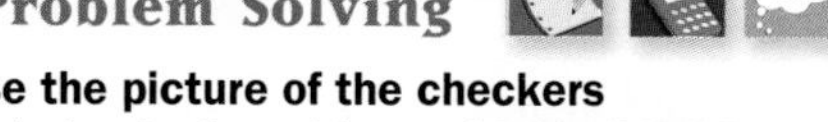

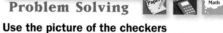

19 $\frac{5}{8}$ in., $\frac{3}{4}$ in., $\frac{1}{2}$ in.

20 $\frac{2}{8}$ in., $\frac{1}{4}$ in., $\frac{1}{2}$ in.

21 $\frac{3}{8}$ in., $\frac{2}{4}$ in., $\frac{1}{2}$ in.

MIXED APPLICATIONS
Problem Solving

Pencil & Paper | Calculator | Mental Math

Use the picture of the checkers and checkerboard for problems 22–24.

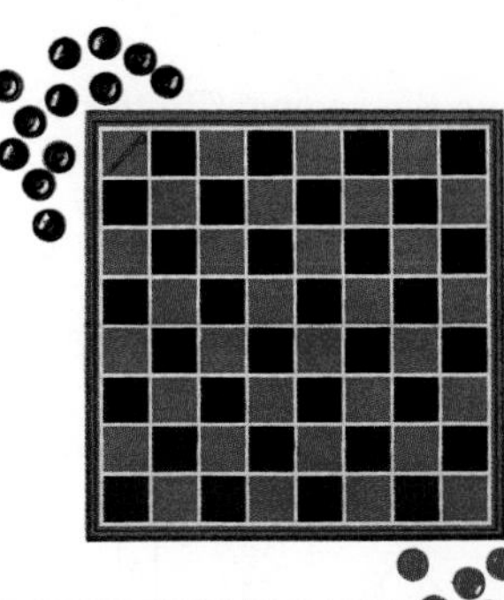

22 What fraction of the board is black squares? $\frac{32}{64}$ of the board

23 What fraction of the board is red squares? $\frac{32}{64}$ of the board

24 What fraction of the board is squares that touch the edges? $\frac{28}{64}$ of the board

25 Uri is playing a card game with 3 other players. She deals out all 52 cards. Everyone gets the same number of cards. How many cards does each player get? 13 cards

Cultural Note
In Britain, checkers is called *draughts*. Records show it was played during the 1500s.

Meeting Individual Needs

Early Finishers

Have pairs of students draw designs for several fractions. Then have them guess what fraction each other's designs show. Students may realize that showing $\frac{1}{4}$ red is the same as showing $\frac{3}{4}$ not red.

Common Error

Some students may name the incorrect fractional part on diagrams. Have them first write the denominator, stressing that the total number of parts is the denominator. Then have them count and record the numerator.

Gifted And Talented

Challenge these students to make drawings that show equivalent fractions. For example, they can show $\frac{2}{4}$ and $\frac{1}{2}$ as equivalent on a circle divided into fourths by outlining the half.

ESL APPROPRIATE

raction Colors Game!

st, write each of the following fractions on index card:

$\frac{2}{3}, \frac{1}{4}, \frac{3}{4}, \frac{3}{5}, \frac{1}{6}, \frac{5}{8}, \frac{7}{8}, \frac{3}{10}, \frac{11}{12}$.

xt, write each of the following colors on index card: blue, green, yellow, red.

You will need
- *pencils or crayons*
- *graph paper*

ay the Game

y with a partner.

Place the cards in separate stacks. Mix up each stack.

Choose a card from each stack. Each player draws a square or rectangle on graph paper and shows the fraction in the color chosen.

If both players correctly show the same design, they each score 2 points. If both players correctly show different designs, they each score 4 points. If only one player shows the correct design, the player scores 4 points.

	Round 1	Round 2
Katie	4	
Lolita	4	

Continue until a player has more than 20 points.

mixed review • test preparation

2,658 + 562 **3,220**

2. 7,543 − 921 **6,622**

3. 3,000 × 25 **75,000**

4. 89 ÷ 3 **29 R2**

d the area.

5. cm; 14 cm — **140 cm²**

6. 32 in.; 24 in. — **768 in.²**

7. 7 ft — **49 ft²**

8. 42 cm — **1,764 cm²**

ra Practice, page 520

Alternate Teaching Strategy

Draw a circle divided into eighths on the chalkboard. Shade $\frac{1}{8}$ of the circle. Ask:

- **What is the total number of parts in the circle?** *[8]*
- **How many parts of the circle are shaded?** *[1 part]*

Tell students that you can use a fraction to represent the number of shaded parts out of the total number of parts. The numerator tells the number of parts that are shaded and the denominator tells the total number of parts. Ask:

- **What fraction of the circle is shaded?** *[$\frac{1}{8}$ of the circle]*

Continue the activity by having volunteers shade an additional section of the circle. The newly shaded section does not have to be adjacent to the previously shaded section(s). Repeat until all of the circle is shaded so that students identify the fractions $\frac{1}{8}, \frac{2}{8}, \frac{3}{8}, \frac{4}{8}, \frac{5}{8}, \frac{6}{8}, \frac{7}{8}$ and $\frac{8}{8}$.

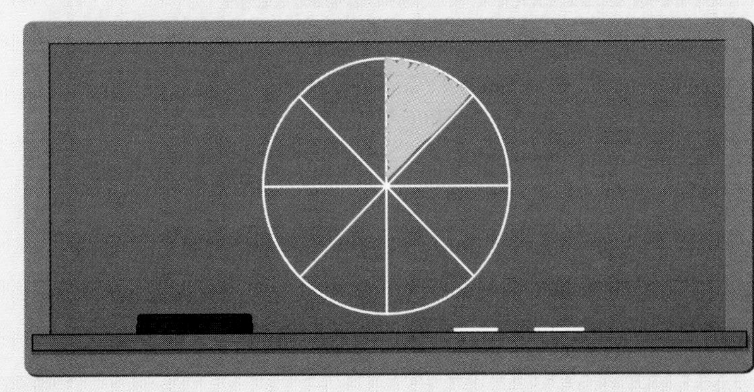

PRACTICE • 88

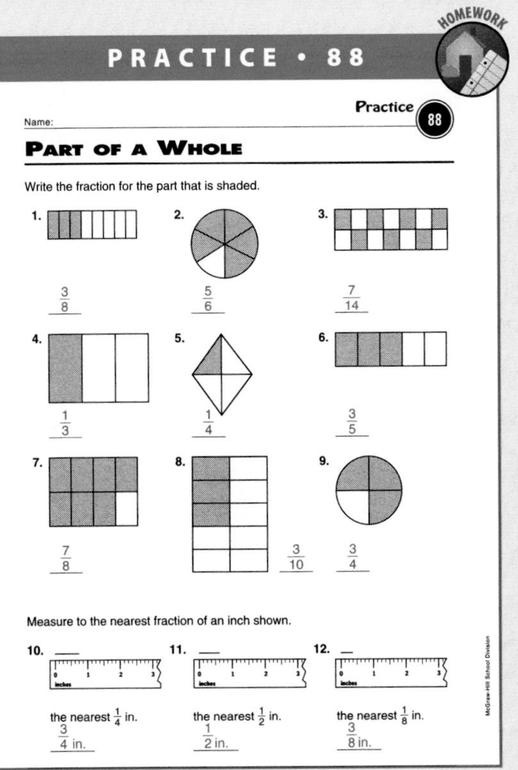

Practice 88

Name:

Part of a Whole

Write the fraction for the part that is shaded.

1. $\frac{3}{8}$ 2. $\frac{5}{6}$ 3. $\frac{7}{14}$

4. $\frac{1}{3}$ 5. $\frac{1}{4}$ 6. $\frac{3}{5}$

7. $\frac{7}{8}$ 8. $\frac{3}{10}$ 9. $\frac{3}{4}$

Measure to the nearest fraction of an inch shown.

10. the nearest $\frac{1}{4}$ in. $\frac{3}{4}$ in.

11. the nearest $\frac{1}{2}$ in. $\frac{1}{2}$ in.

12. the nearest $\frac{1}{8}$ in. $\frac{3}{8}$ in.

RETEACH • 88

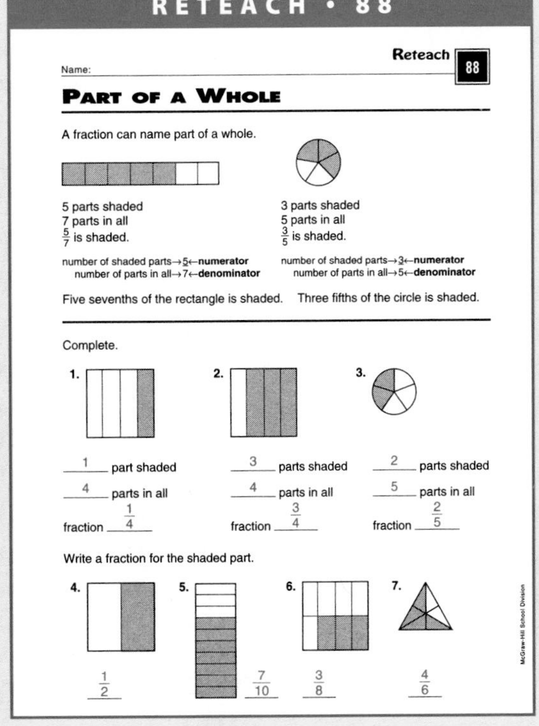

Reteach 88

Name:

Part of a Whole

A fraction can name part of a whole.

5 parts shaded
7 parts in all
$\frac{5}{7}$ is shaded.

number of shaded parts → 5 ← **numerator**
number of parts in all → 7 ← **denominator**

Five sevenths of the rectangle is shaded.

3 parts shaded
5 parts in all
$\frac{3}{5}$ is shaded.

number of shaded parts → 3 ← **numerator**
number of parts in all → 5 ← **denominator**

Three fifths of the circle is shaded.

Complete.

1. 1 part shaded; 4 parts in all; fraction $\frac{1}{4}$
2. 3 parts shaded; 4 parts in all; fraction $\frac{3}{4}$
3. 2 parts shaded; 5 parts in all; fraction $\frac{2}{5}$

Write a fraction for the shaded part.

4. $\frac{1}{2}$ 5. $\frac{7}{10}$ 6. $\frac{3}{8}$ 7. $\frac{4}{6}$

EXTEND • 88

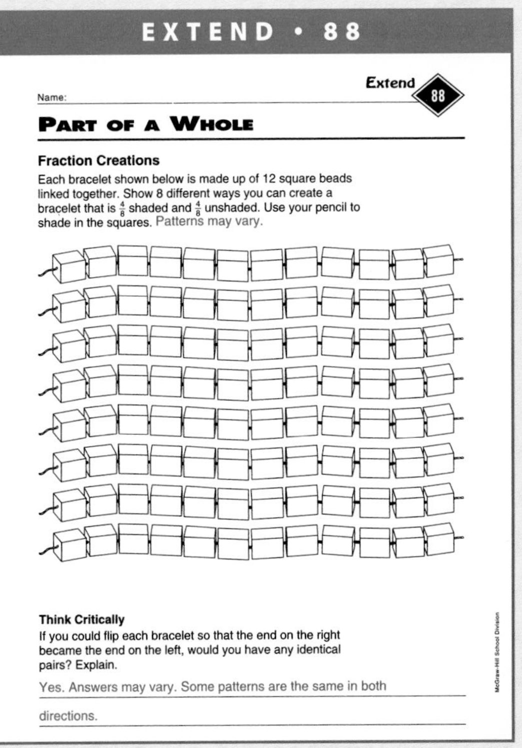

Extend 88

Name:

Part of a Whole

Fraction Creations

Each bracelet shown below is made up of 12 square beads linked together. Show 8 different ways you can create a bracelet that is $\frac{4}{6}$ shaded and $\frac{4}{6}$ unshaded. Use your pencil to shade in the squares. Patterns may vary.

Think Critically

If you could flip each bracelet so that the end on the right became the end on the left, would you have any identical pairs? Explain.

Yes. Answers may vary. Some patterns are the same in both directions.

LESSON 10.2

Part of a Group

OBJECTIVE Identify, read, and write fractions for parts of sets.

RESOURCE REMINDER
Math Center Cards 89
Practice 89, Reteach 89, Extend 89

SKILLS TRACE

GRADE 3	• Explore fractions as equal parts of sets. *(Chapter 11)* • Explore reading and writing fractions for parts of sets. *(Chapter 11)*
GRADE 4	• Read and write fractions for parts of sets.
GRADE 5	• Read, write, and draw fractions for parts of sets. *(Chapter 9)*

LESSON 10.2 RESOURCES

MANIPULATIVE WARM-UP

Cooperative Pairs — Visual/Spatial

OBJECTIVE Explore identifying fractions.

Materials per pair: number cube

▶ Draw a circle divided into sixths on the chalkboard. Have students draw several of these divided circles. For greater accuracy and less time, you may prefer to draw the circles on a page in advance for students.

▶ Each student tosses a number cube and records the number tossed as the numerator of a fraction with a denominator of 6. Then students shade a circle to show the fraction. Have them repeat the activity several times.

▶ Discuss different designs that show the same fraction. Point out that parts of the fraction may or may not be adjacent as long as their total area is the same.

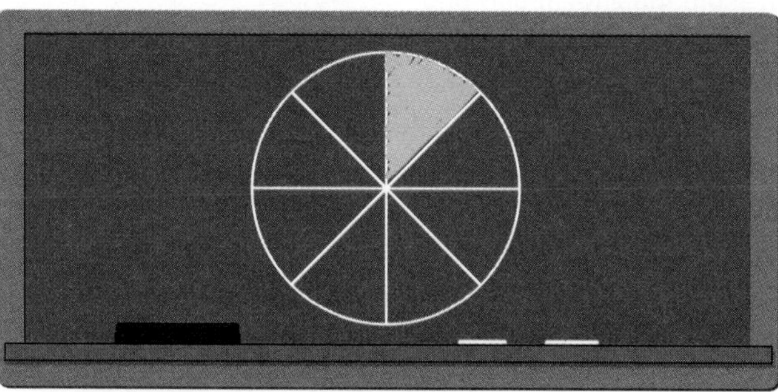

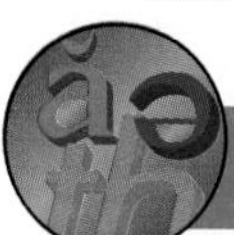

LANGUAGE ARTS CONNECTION

Cooperative Groups — Auditory/Linguistic

OBJECTIVE Connect fractions to making decisions in folktales.

Resource Read-Aloud Anthology, pp. 48–49

Materials per group: fraction circle (TA 27)

▶ Have students work in a small group to read *The Divided Students* and discuss how the priest benefited from the students' unwillingness to share the bread. Encourage students to share comments and insights.

▶ Then have students work together to simulate what happened in the story. Students use a fraction circle and divide the circle into 4 equal parts. Have them repeat what the priest had done in the story, dividing each subsequent part into two equal parts, until almost nothing is left.

▶ Discuss the moral of the story.

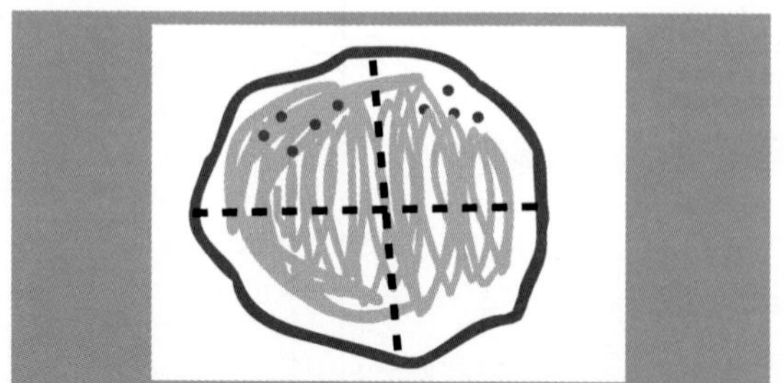

Daily Review

PREVIOUS DAY QUICK REVIEW

Shade a rectangle to show each fraction. *[Check students' work.]*

1. $\frac{1}{3}$ **2.** $\frac{3}{4}$
3. $\frac{2}{5}$ **4.** $\frac{5}{7}$

FAST FACTS

1. 6 ÷ 6 *[1]*
2. 9 ÷ 3 *[3]*
3. 45 ÷ 5 *[9]*
4. 56 ÷ 8 *[7]*

Problem of the Day • 89

John and Karen are playing a card game. John is holding 8 cards. There are two kings, two queens, and one jack in his hand. What fraction of John's cards are kings, queens, or jacks? *[$\frac{5}{8}$]*

TECH LINK

Math Van

MATH VAN

Tool You may wish to use the Counter tool with this lesson.

MATH FORUM

Idea My students enjoy quizzing each other on fractions of sets using items in the classroom.

Visit our Resource Village at http://www.mhschool.com to see more of the Math Forum.

MATH CENTER

Practice

OBJECTIVE Identify fractions as parts of a set.

Materials per student: 30 pennies or two-color counters, paper bag, connecting cubes or paper clips

Students use pennies or counters as a whole group and identify parts as the items that are heads or tails and covered by markers. *[Answers will vary. Check students' work.]*

PRACTICE ACTIVITY 89 — MATH CENTER On Your Own

Manipulatives • Parts of a Group

YOU NEED
- 30 pennies or 2-color counters in paper bag
- connecting cubes or paper clips

Spill 20 pennies or counters from the bag onto a table. Some will be tails up (red side of counters) and some will be heads up (yellow side of counters).

Put paper clips or cubes on some of the counters or pennies. Then answer these questions:

1. What fraction are heads up? tails up?
2. What fraction are covered?
3. What fraction of the heads-up pennies or counters are covered?

Repeat with 30 counters or pennies.

Grade Level 4 McGraw-Hill School Division

Chapter 10, Lesson 2, pages 372–373 Fractions

ESL APPROPRIATE

NCTM Standards
- Problem Solving
- ✓ Communication
- ✓ Reasoning
- Connections

Problem Solving

OBJECTIVE Solve fraction problems.

Materials per student: Math Center Recording Sheet (TA 31 optional)

Students think of words to fit fraction descriptions. *[Answers may vary. Possible answers: **1.** people; **2.** place; **3.** Oregon; **4.** tooth; **5.** tent; **6.** hill; **7.** eerie]*

PROBLEM-SOLVING ACTIVITY 89 — MATH CENTER On Your Own

Logical Reasoning • Alphabet Soup

Think of a word as a group of letters. Find a word whose letters fit the description. There are many possible answers to each.

1. $\frac{3}{6}$ of the letters are vowels. around $\frac{3}{6}$
2. $\frac{2}{5}$ of the letters are vowels.
3. $\frac{1}{6}$ of the letters are capitals.
4. $\frac{2}{5}$ of the letters are *o*s.
5. $\frac{2}{4}$ of the letters are *t*s.
6. $\frac{3}{4}$ of the letters are tall consonants (like the letter *h*).
7. $\frac{3}{5}$ of the letters are the same.

Grade Level 4 McGraw-Hill School Division

Chapter 10, Lesson 2, pages 372–373 Fractions

NCTM Standards
- ✓ Problem Solving
- Communication
- ✓ Reasoning
- ✓ Connections

Part of a Group

OBJECTIVE Identify, read, and write fractions for parts of sets.

1 Introduce

Materials bag containing 3 pencils and 2 pens

Show students the contents of a bag: 3 pencils and 2 pens. Ask:

- **What is the total number of writing tools in the bag?** *[5 writing instruments]*
- **How many of the 5 writing tools are pencils?** *[3 pencils]*
- **What fraction of the writing tools are pencils?** *[$\frac{3}{5}$]*

Have students help you create another similar problem.

2 Teach *Whole Class*

Cultural Connection Read the **Cultural Note.** Tell students that *chaturanga* is a Sanskrit word. It refers to the four divisions of an Indian army: elephants, cavalry, chariots, and infantry. The pieces of modern chess are based on these divisions. Ask if any students play chess, and discuss why they like to play it.

LEARN Have a volunteer read the introductory problem. Explain that the words *either* and *or* indicate that the king and all of the pawns are included in the numerator.

Differentiate between a fraction that shows part of a *group* and a fraction that shows part of a *whole*. Part of a group consists of objects or members of a group, whereas part of a whole consists of equal-sized parts of a divided whole.

More Examples Ask students to identify the game for each set of game pieces: A—Checkers, B—Risk, and C—Chinese checkers. Point out other fractions shown.

3 Close

Check for Understanding using items 1–5, page 372.

CRITICAL THINKING

For item 5, students may use a diagram to explain their reasoning. They can draw 16 squares and label 9 out of 16 squares with a K (king) or P (pawn). Then they can count the remaining squares (7) to show that $\frac{7}{16}$ of the pieces are neither a king nor a pawn.

PRACTICE

Materials have available: calculators

Options for assigning exercises:

A—Odd ex. 1–11; ex. 12–13

B—Even ex. 2–10; ex. 12–13

- It may be useful to supply cubes for ex. 4–6.

Part of a Group

LEARN

What fraction of the chess pieces are *either* a king *or* a pawn?

Using words or a fraction, you can describe the part of the chess pieces that are either a king or a pawn.

There are 9 king or pawn pieces out of 16 total pieces.

king or pawn pieces → 9 ← numerator
total pieces → 16 ← denominator

$\frac{9}{16}$ of the pieces are either a king or a pawn.

Cultural Note
Chess was first played in India. It was called *chaturanga* (CHUH-tuh-ran-gah).

More Examples

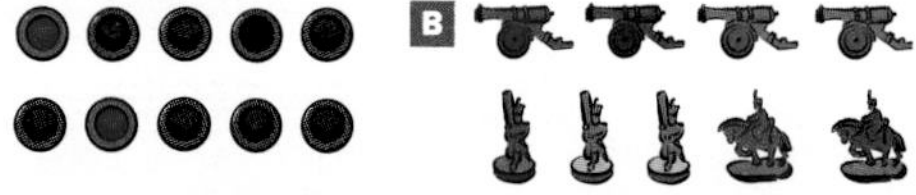

A $\frac{8}{10}$ are black.

B $\frac{5}{9}$ are blue or red.

C $\frac{4}{6}$ are not white or yellow.

CHECK

Check for Understanding

Write a fraction that names the part.

1 red $\frac{2}{10}$

2 white $\frac{1}{10}$

3 blue or black $\frac{5}{10}$

4 not black $\frac{8}{10}$

Critical Thinking: Analyze **Explain your reasoning.**

5 If you know that 9 out of 16 pieces are either a king or a pawn, how can you use this to find the fraction of the pieces that are neither a king nor a pawn? **If 9 out of 16 are either a king or a pawn, then the rest are neither a king nor a pawn, so 7 out of 16 pieces are neither a king nor a pawn.**

Meeting Individual Needs

Extra Support

Some students may confuse the numerator and the denominator. Encourage them to count the total first and write the denominator. Then they can focus on the part for the numerator.

Early Finishers

Using games of their choice, have students write fractions involving the game pieces. Then have them write problems about the pieces using fractions. Students can trade and solve each others' problems.

Ongoing Assessment

Observation Checklist Observe if students understand how to read and write fractions for parts of a group by asking them to use a fraction to identify the number of blue marbles out of a group of 2 red, 3 blue, and 4 white marbles. *[$\frac{3}{9}$]*

Follow Up For students who need additional help identifying the fractional part of a group, assign **Reteach 89.**

Have students who understand how to find the fraction of a group try **Extend 89.**

ractice

oose the fraction that tells which part is blue.

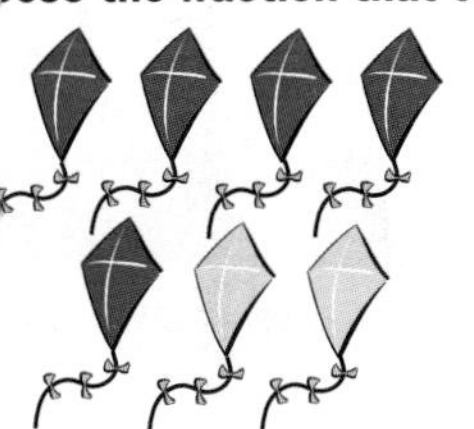

a. $\frac{5}{7}$ b. $\frac{2}{7}$ c. $\frac{7}{2}$ a

2 

a. $\frac{3}{11}$ b. $\frac{3}{7}$ c. $\frac{3}{14}$ c

3

a. $\frac{2}{9}$ b. $\frac{2}{7}$ c. $\frac{2}{4}$ a

e the number cubes for ex. 4–6.

What part of the green cubes show 1? $\frac{3}{5}$

What part of all the cubes show 3? $\frac{3}{10}$

What part of the blue cubes show 5? $\frac{0}{3}$, or 0

w a picture, then write the fraction. Check students' work.

Five out of seven students are not wearing hats. $\frac{5}{7}$

8 One out of four people are smiling. $\frac{1}{4}$

Three out of eleven pets are dogs. $\frac{3}{11}$

10 All of the six beanbags are red. $\frac{6}{6}$

In ex. 7–10, how did the descriptions help you write the fractions? Possible answer: The numerator shows the number out of the total that is described, and the denominator shows the total.

IXED APPLICATIONS

roblem Solving

The time allowed for each move during the Internet chess game was 7 min. What is the longest time this game could have taken? SEE INFOBIT. 455 min, or 7 h 35 min

INFOBIT
On August 26, 1996, Anatoly Karpov played the first open chess game on the Internet. The game ended after 65 moves.

Write a problem in which you name a fractional part of a group. Solve your problem. Have others solve it. Share and compare problems with other classmates. Students check each other's work by comparing problems and solutions.

tra Practice, page 520

Alternate Teaching Strategy

Fold a piece of paper in half. Shade one half. Ask:

- **What fraction of the page is shaded?** *[$\frac{1}{2}$]*

Cut the paper in half. Ask:

- **What fraction of the pages is shaded?** *[$\frac{1}{2}$]*

Discuss how the fractions are similar and different. *[Similar—they are the same fraction; different—one shows the part of a whole while the other shows the part of a group.]*

Have pairs of students repeat the process by cutting pictures that show parts of a whole into parts of a group. Have them use thirds, quarters, sixths, and eighths. Students should identify several different sets of fractions.

PRACTICE • 89

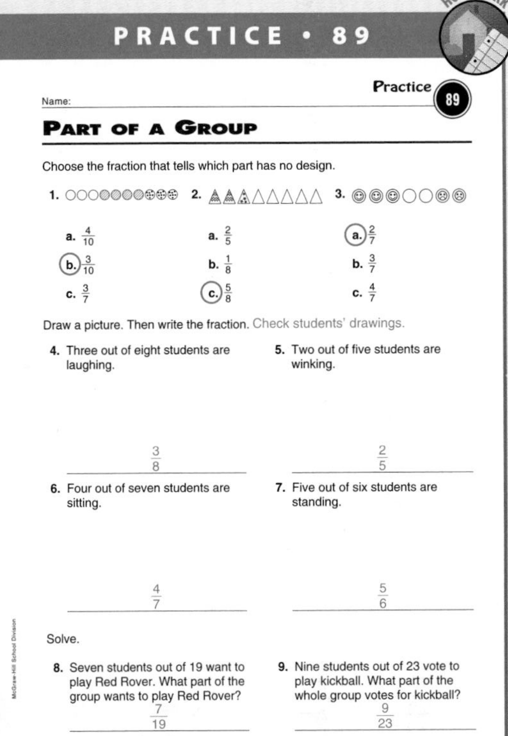

RETEACH • 89

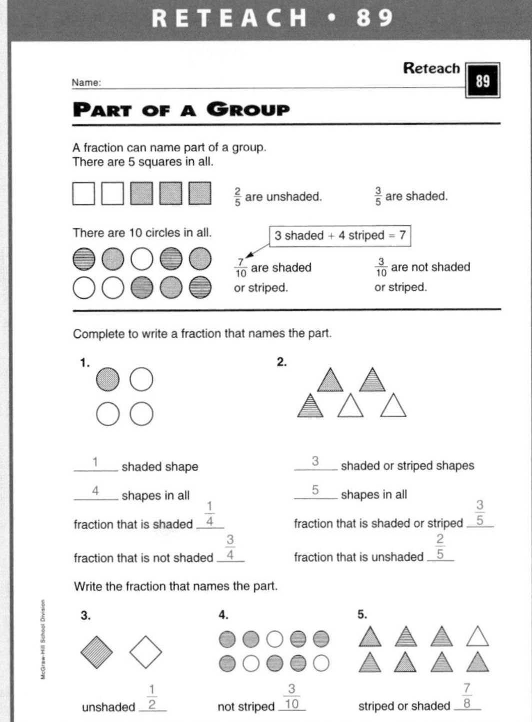

EXTEND • 89

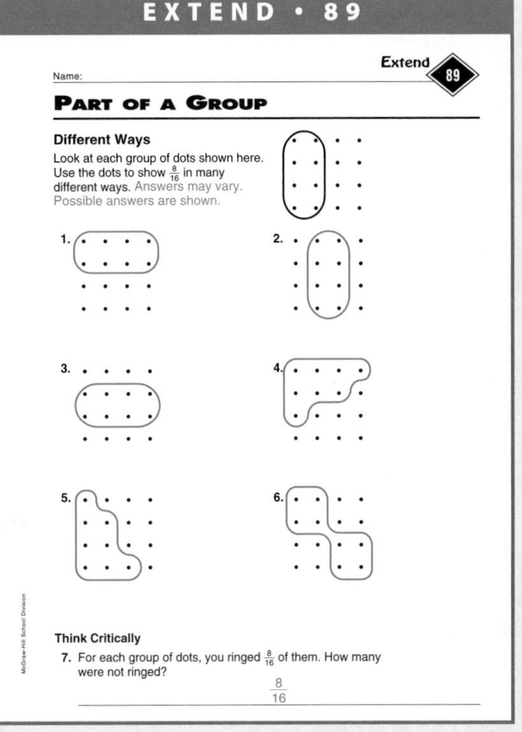

EXPLORE ACTIVITY

Find a Fraction of a Number

OBJECTIVE Explore finding a fractional part of a set.

RESOURCE REMINDER
Math Center Cards 90
Practice 90, Reteach 90, Extend 90

SKILLS TRACE

GRADE 3	• Explore finding parts of a set. *(Chapter 11)*
GRADE 4	• Explore finding a fractional part of a set.
GRADE 5	• Multiply whole numbers by fractions. *(Chapter 11)*

MANIPULATIVE WARM-UP

Cooperative Pairs — Logical/Analytical

OBJECTIVE Explore making equal groups.

Materials per pair: 18 counters

▶ Have pairs work together to find as many equal groups as they can using 10, 12, 15, and 18 counters. *[10: 2 groups of 5 and 5 of 2; 12: 2 groups of 6, 6 of 2, 3 of 4, and 4 of 3; 15: 3 groups of 5 and 5 of 3; 18: 2 groups of 9, 9 of 2, 3 of 6, and 6 of 3]*

▶ Encourage students to use drawings to demonstrate their results. Then have them suggest ways to record the parts of equal groups.

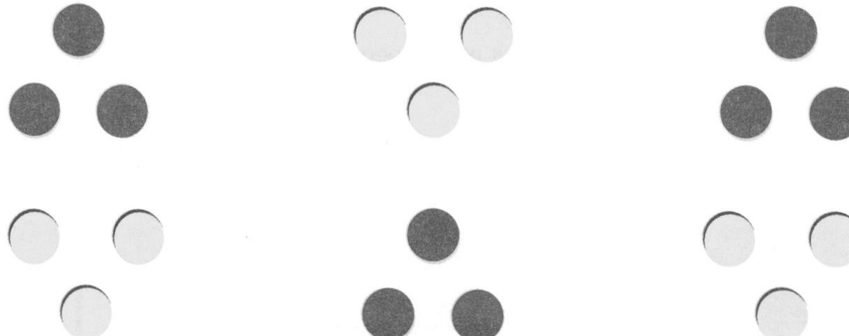

ESL APPROPRIATE

CONSUMER CONNECTION

Cooperative Pairs — Visual/Spatial

OBJECTIVE Connect sale prices to fractions.

Materials per pair: 24 index cards, 3 markers: blue, red, yellow

Prepare On index cards write the Regular price with a colored circle or the Sale price as shown.

▶ Mix cards and display for students to make their own set.

▶ Tell students that a store is having a sale. A blue sticker item is $\frac{1}{4}$ off, a red sticker item is $\frac{1}{2}$ off, and a yellow sticker item is $\frac{3}{4}$ off. Students match the regular prices with the sale prices. *[Matches are shown above.]*

▶ Discuss how students made their matches.

Reg.	Sale	Reg.	Sale	Reg.	Sale
$12	$9	$8	$4	$4	$1
$20	$15	$16	$8	$32	$8
$4	$3	$24	$12	$28	$7
$32	$24	$48	$24	$64	$16

Daily Review

PREVIOUS DAY QUICK REVIEW

Draw stars and shade to show each fraction. *[Check students' work.]*

1. $\frac{1}{5}$ **2.** $\frac{3}{8}$

3. $\frac{2}{3}$ **4.** $\frac{4}{9}$

FAST FACTS

1. 2 × 0 *[0]*
2. 3 × 5 *[15]*
3. 6 × 6 *[36]*
4. 9 × 8 *[72]*

Problem of the Day • 90

Martha and Donna are playing jacks. Each girl has 10 jacks. Martha picks up $\frac{2}{5}$ of her jacks and Donna picks up $\frac{1}{2}$ of her jacks. Who picks up more jacks? Explain. *[Donna: $\frac{1}{2}$ of 10 = 5; $\frac{2}{5}$ of 10 = 4]*

TECH LINK

Math Van

MATH VAN

Tool You may wish to use the Counter tool with this lesson.

MATH FORUM

Combination Classes My students work through the exercises together. One student uses division and multiplication and the other uses models to find the fraction of a number. They alternate roles.

Visit our Resource Village at http://www.mhschool.com to see more of the Math Forum.

MATH CENTER

Practice

OBJECTIVE Find the fraction of a number.

Materials per student: 48 counters, Math Center Recording Sheet (TA 31 optional)

Students solve a problem involving fractional parts of 4 dozen rice cakes. *[**1.** Kelly, 4 rice cakes; Hope, 16 rice cakes; Jules, 12 rice cakes; Ray, 8 rice cakes; Orzi, 8 rice cakes. **2.** Answer may vary. Possible answer: $4.80 ÷ 48 rice cakes = $.10 per rice cake, so that Kelly pays $.40; Hope, $1.60; Jules, $1.20; Ray, $0.80; Orzi, $0.80]*

PRACTICE ACTIVITY 90 — MATH CENTER, On Your Own

Number Sense • Rice Cake Crunch

YOU NEED: 48 counters

Use counters to show how many rice cakes each person will get. Draw a picture of your models.

1. Five friends share 4 dozen rice cakes that they just bought.
   Kelly would like $\frac{1}{12}$ of the rice cakes.
   Hope would like $\frac{1}{3}$ of the rice cakes.
   Jules would like a quarter of the rice cakes.
   Ray and Orzi each would like $\frac{1}{6}$ of the rice cakes.
2. If the rice cakes cost $5.00, about how much money should each person pay for the cost of their rice cakes?

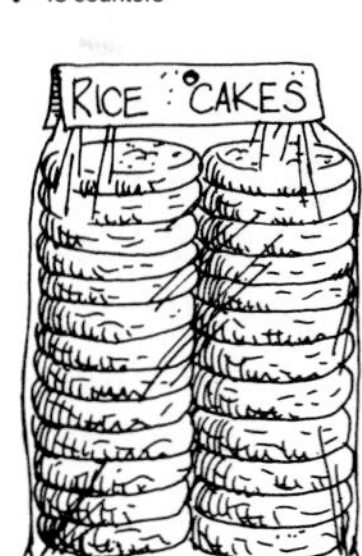

Grade Level 4 · McGraw-Hill School Division

Chapter 10, Lesson 3, pages 374–375 · Fractions

NCTM Standards
- Problem Solving
- ✓ Communication
- ✓ Reasoning
- Connections

Problem Solving

OBJECTIVE Solve multistep problems involving fractions.

Materials per student: Math Center Recording Sheet (TA 31 optional)

Students find fractional parts of sets. *[**1.** $\frac{1}{7}, \frac{1}{9}, \frac{1}{6}, \frac{1}{8}, \frac{1}{5}$; **2.** Carmen can build 4 more identical baskets; **3.** 2 grapefruit, 6 plums, 6 apples **4.** Check students' problems.]*

PROBLEM-SOLVING ACTIVITY 90 — MATH CENTER, On Your Own

Using Data • Fruit Baskets

Carmen will make a fruit basket with 2 grapefruit, 1 cantaloupe, 3 plums, 2 peaches, and 2 apples. She will use the fruit from these boxes.

1. What fraction of the box of grapefruit will Carmen use in the fruit basket? of the box of cantaloupes? of the box of plums? of the box of peaches? of the box of apples?
2. How many more identical baskets can Carmen make? Explain.
3. How much more of each fruit will she need to make 8 identical baskets altogether?
4. Write a similar problem. Use different numbers of fruit.

Grade Level 4 · McGraw-Hill School Division

Chapter 10, Lesson 3, pages 374–375 · Fractions

NCTM Standards
- ✓ Problem Solving
- ✓ Communication
- ✓ Reasoning
- Connections

EXPLORE ACTIVITY
Find a Fraction of a Number

OBJECTIVE Explore finding a fractional part of a set.

Materials per pair: 24 straws or pick-up sticks; have available: 30 marbles or number cubes

1 Introduce

Present the following problem:

Matthew has 30 marbles. He gives half of them to his little brother. How many marbles does each boy have?

Have students suggest ways to solve the problem. *[15 marbles]*

2 Teach *Cooperative Pairs*

LEARN Read the introductory problem and review the steps to find $\frac{1}{3}$ of 24. You may suggest students make their own models with straws, paper strips, etc. to show that $\frac{1}{3}$ of 24 is 8.

Work Together Discuss any patterns students see in the fractions of numbers they are asked to find. *[Possible answer: Each row shows fractions with the same denominator and numerators ranging from 1 to the number that is the denominator.]* After students find each fraction of a number, ask:

- **How did you find $\frac{2}{2}$ of 18, $\frac{2}{3}$ of 33, and $\frac{2}{5}$ of 20?** *[Answers may vary.]*
- **How can you use division to find $\frac{1}{8}$ of 24? $\frac{1}{6}$ of 24?** *[24 ÷ 8 = 3; 24 ÷ 6 = 4]*

MAKE CONNECTIONS

Review each of the steps with the class. Students may notice that the answer is the same if you change the order of the operations and multiply first, then divide: 2 × 20 = 40 and 40 ÷ 5 = 8. Point out that by dividing first and then multiplying, students work with smaller numbers.

Use the second question to help students understand why a fraction of a number is less than or equal to the number.

3 Close

Check for Understanding using items 1–14, page 375.

Critical Thinking
Accept any reasonable answer. Encourage students to draw diagrams to illustrate $\frac{1}{7}$ of 21, $\frac{2}{7}$ of 21, and $\frac{3}{7}$ of 21.

PRACTICE

Materials have available: calculators

Assign ex. 1–3 as independent work. Each student should select and complete five exercises from ex. 4–11.

- Encourage students to draw simple pictures, such as groups of stars or circles, to support their answers.

EXPLORE ACTIVITY • FRACTIONS

Find a Fraction of a Number

LEARN

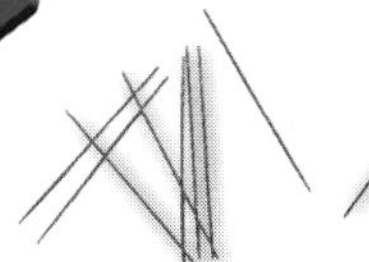

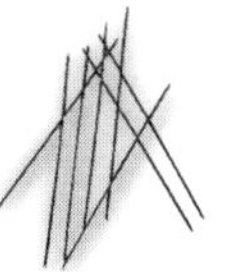

In the game of pick-up sticks, there are 24 sticks. What if you picked up of the sticks before you lost your tu How many sticks did you pick up?

You can use counters to find the fraction of a number.

Find $\frac{1}{3}$ of 24.

First, make 3 equal groups using 24 counters.
Then, find the number of counters in 1 group.

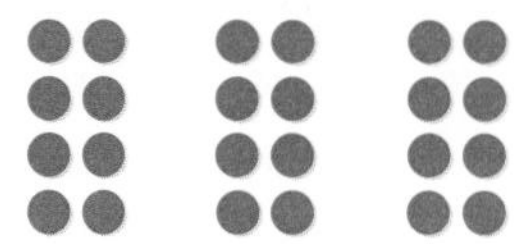

Think: 24 ÷ 3 = 8

So $\frac{1}{3}$ of 24 = 8.

You picked up 8 sticks.

Work Together
Work with a partner. Use counters to find the fraction of the number. **Check students' work.**

You will need
- counters

a. $\frac{1}{2}$ of 18 **9** $\quad$ $\frac{2}{2}$ of 18 **18**

b. $\frac{1}{3}$ of 33 **11** $\quad$ $\frac{2}{3}$ of 33 **22** $\quad$ $\frac{3}{3}$ of 33 **33**

c. $\frac{1}{5}$ of 20 **4** $\quad$ $\frac{2}{5}$ of 20 **8** $\quad$ $\frac{3}{5}$ of 20 **12** $\quad$ $\frac{4}{5}$ of 20 **16** $\quad$ $\frac{5}{5}$ of 20 **20**

Make Connections
You can use multiplication and division to find fractions of a number.

Find $\frac{2}{5}$ of 20.

Step 1	Step 2
Use the denominator. **Divide the total into that many groups.** 20 ÷ 5 = 4 **Think:** The denominator is 5.	**Use the numerator.** **Multiply the quotient by that number.** 2 × 4 = 8 **Think:** The numerator is 2.

So $\frac{2}{5}$ of 20 is 8.

Meeting Individual Needs

Early Finishers

Have students write their own problems where they find fractions of numbers such as $\frac{3}{8}$ of 24. Have them draw a diagram for each problem. Then they can exchange problems with a partner and solve.

Extra Support

Students may forget to multiply to find a fraction of a number with a numerator greater than 1. Have them make equal groups of red counters. Then turn over the needed number of groups (the numerator).

ESL APPROPRIATE

Ongoing Assessment

Observation Checklist Determine if students are able to find the fraction of a number by observing if they use division and multiplication to find $\frac{3}{4}$ of 12. *[12 ÷ 4 = 3; 3 × 3 = 9]*

Follow Up Have students who need additional help finding a fraction of a number try **Reteach 90.**

For students who are ready for a challenge, assign **Extend 90.**

2. Possible answer: The fraction of the number is the same as the number; the fraction of the number is less than the number.

How is the method you used with counters the same as dividing and multiplying? **See below.**

What do you notice about the fraction of the number when the numerator and denominator of the fraction are the same? when the numerator is less than the denominator? **See above.**

Check for Understanding

Find the answer. Use any method.

1. $\frac{1}{4}$ of 8 **2**
2. $\frac{1}{2}$ of 16 **8**
3. $\frac{1}{8}$ of 16 **2**
4. $\frac{1}{5}$ of 15 **3**
5. $\frac{2}{3}$ of 12 **8**
6. $\frac{3}{4}$ of 16 **12**
7. $\frac{1}{4}$ of 20 **5**
8. $\frac{1}{12}$ of 12 **1**
9. $\frac{2}{5}$ of 10 **4**
10. $\frac{1}{10}$ of 30 **3**
11. $\frac{5}{6}$ of 12 **10**
12. $\frac{3}{3}$ of 3 **3**

Critical Thinking: Analyze **Explain your reasoning.**

13. You know that $\frac{3}{5}$ of 15 counters are blue. How can you tell how many counters are not blue? **Possible answers: Subtract $\frac{3}{5}$ of 15, or 9, from 15 or find $\frac{2}{5}$ of 15.**

14. Journal Explain how to find $\frac{1}{7}$ of 21. How can you use the answer to find $\frac{2}{7}$ of 21? $\frac{3}{7}$ of 21?

Possible answer: Divide 21 by 7 to get 3; multiply 3 × 2; multiply 3 × 3.

CHECK

Practice

Use the picture to help you find the missing number or fraction.

1. 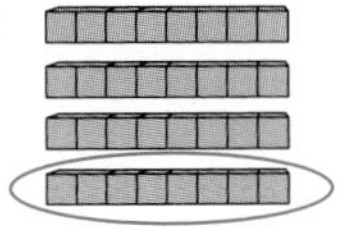

$\frac{1}{4}$ of 32 = ■ **8**

2. $\frac{3}{5}$ of 10 = ■ **6**

3. 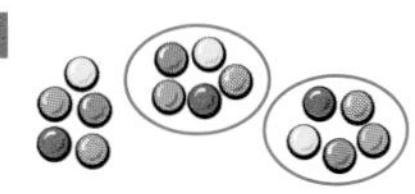

■ of 15 = 10 **$\frac{2}{3}$**

Find the answer. Use any method.

4. $\frac{1}{8}$ of 32 **4**
5. $\frac{1}{5}$ of 30 **6**
6. $\frac{3}{5}$ of 30 **18**
7. $\frac{1}{3}$ of 27 **9**
8. $\frac{2}{3}$ of 27 **18**
9. $\frac{4}{7}$ of 21 **12**
10. $\frac{5}{8}$ of 16 **10**
11. $\frac{2}{9}$ of 27 **6**

1. Possible answer: Separating into equal groups is the same as dividing, counting the number in several groups is the same as multiplying.

Extra Practice, page 520

PRACTICE

Alternate Teaching Strategy

Materials per pair: 24 two-color counters

Students work with a partner. Have them make two equal groups out of the 24 counters. Then have them turn one group over to show the other color. Ask:

- **How many counters are in each group?** *[12 counters]*
- **One group is half the total or $\frac{1}{2}$ of 24. What is $\frac{1}{2}$ of 24?** *[12]*

Next have them make 8 equal groups and turn the counters of one group over. Ask:

- **How many counters are in each group?** *[3 counters]*
- **The group is $\frac{1}{8}$ the total or $\frac{1}{8}$ of 24. What is $\frac{1}{8}$ of 24?** *[3]*

Turn over a second group of counters. Ask:

- **What is $\frac{2}{8}$ of 24?** *[6]*

Continue the activity to find $\frac{3}{8}$, $\frac{4}{8}$, $\frac{5}{8}$, $\frac{6}{8}$, $\frac{7}{8}$, and $\frac{8}{8}$ of 24. Then have students use counters to find $\frac{1}{4}$, $\frac{2}{4}$, and $\frac{3}{4}$ of 24.

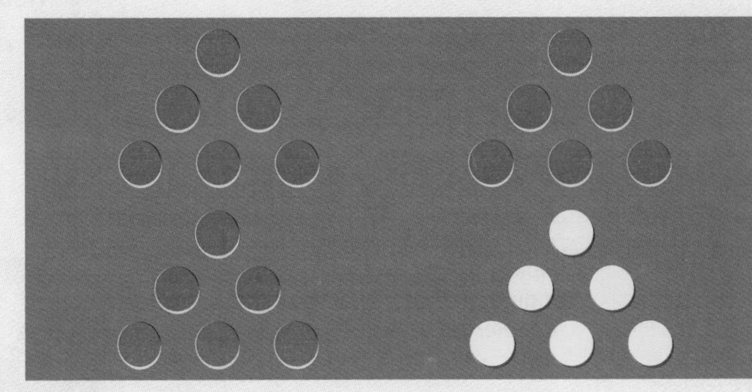

PRACTICE • 90

HOMEWORK

Name: Practice 90

FIND A FRACTION OF A NUMBER

Use the picture to help you find the missing number or fraction.

1. $\frac{1}{3}$ of 9 = 3
2. $\frac{3}{4}$ of 12 = 9
3. $\frac{6}{7}$ of 14 = 12
4. $\frac{2}{5}$ of 20 = 8
5. $\frac{1}{3}$ of 18 = 6
6. $\frac{5}{7}$ of 21 = 15

Find the answer. Use any method.

7. $\frac{2}{3}$ of 9 = 6
8. $\frac{3}{4}$ of 16 = 12
9. $\frac{2}{3}$ of 12 = 8
10. $\frac{5}{8}$ of 16 = 10
11. $\frac{2}{3}$ of 18 = 12
12. $\frac{1}{5}$ of 15 = 3
13. $\frac{9}{10}$ of 20 = 18
14. $\frac{4}{7}$ of 21 = 12
15. $\frac{1}{3}$ of 27 = 9

Solve. You may use counters.

16. Keisha wins 30 games of Flash Card Race. She played $\frac{2}{5}$ of those games with fifth graders. How many games is that? 12 games
17. Of the 21 fourth graders, $\frac{1}{3}$ like to play football. How many students is that? 7 students

McGraw-Hill School Division

RETEACH • 90

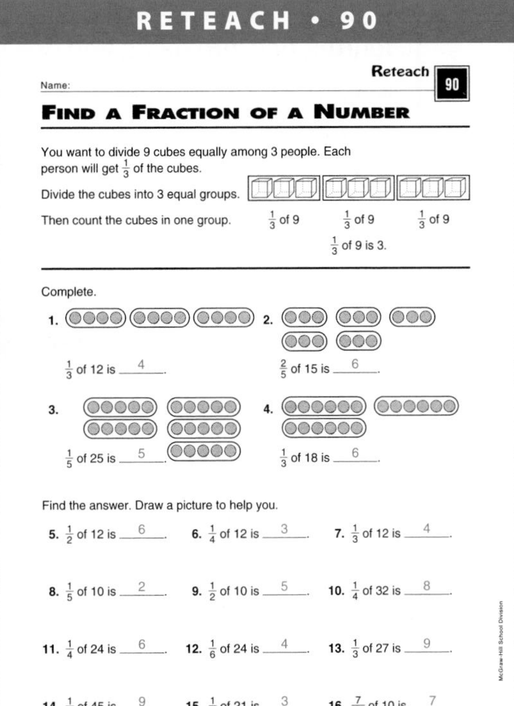

Name: Reteach 90

FIND A FRACTION OF A NUMBER

You want to divide 9 cubes equally among 3 people. Each person will get $\frac{1}{3}$ of the cubes.

Divide the cubes into 3 equal groups.

Then count the cubes in one group. $\frac{1}{3}$ of 9 $\frac{1}{3}$ of 9 $\frac{1}{3}$ of 9

$\frac{1}{3}$ of 9 is 3.

Complete.

1. $\frac{1}{3}$ of 12 is 4.
2. $\frac{2}{5}$ of 15 is 6.
3. $\frac{1}{5}$ of 25 is 5.
4. $\frac{1}{3}$ of 18 is 6.

Find the answer. Draw a picture to help you.

5. $\frac{1}{2}$ of 12 is 6.
6. $\frac{1}{4}$ of 12 is 3.
7. $\frac{1}{3}$ of 12 is 4.
8. $\frac{1}{5}$ of 10 is 2.
9. $\frac{1}{2}$ of 10 is 5.
10. $\frac{1}{4}$ of 32 is 8.
11. $\frac{1}{4}$ of 24 is 6.
12. $\frac{1}{6}$ of 24 is 4.
13. $\frac{1}{3}$ of 27 is 9.
14. $\frac{1}{5}$ of 45 is 9.
15. $\frac{1}{7}$ of 21 is 3.
16. $\frac{7}{10}$ of 10 is 7.

McGraw-Hill School Division

EXTEND • 90

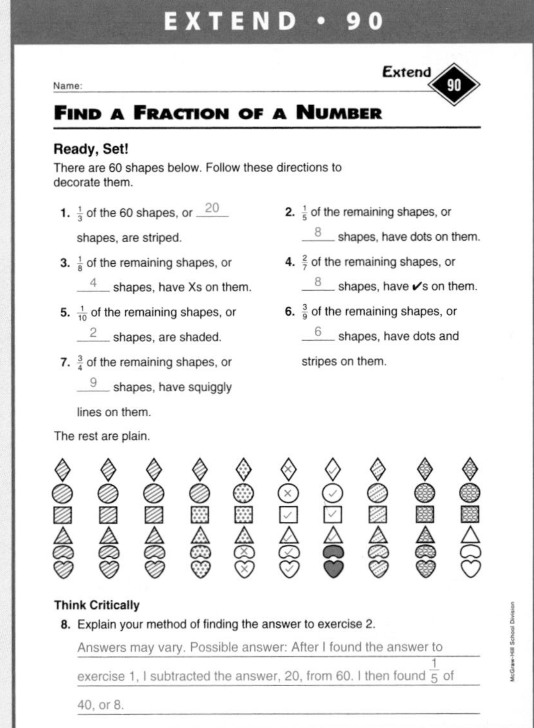

Name: Extend 90

FIND A FRACTION OF A NUMBER

Ready, Set!

There are 60 shapes below. Follow these directions to decorate them.

1. $\frac{1}{3}$ of the 60 shapes, or 20 shapes, are striped.
2. $\frac{1}{5}$ of the remaining shapes, or 8 shapes, have dots on them.
3. $\frac{1}{8}$ of the remaining shapes, or 4 shapes, have Xs on them.
4. $\frac{2}{7}$ of the remaining shapes, or 8 shapes, have ✔s on them.
5. $\frac{1}{10}$ of the remaining shapes, or 2 shapes, are shaded.
6. $\frac{1}{3}$ of the remaining shapes, or 6 shapes, have dots and stripes on them.
7. $\frac{3}{4}$ of the remaining shapes, or 9 shapes, have squiggly lines on them.

The rest are plain.

Think Critically

8. Explain your method of finding the answer to exercise 2.

Answers may vary. Possible answer: After I found the answer to exercise 1, I subtracted the answer, 20, from 60. I then found $\frac{1}{5}$ of 40, or 8.

McGraw-Hill School Division

EXPLORE ACTIVITY

Equivalent Fractions

OBJECTIVE Explore finding equivalent fractions.

RESOURCE REMINDER
Math Center Cards 91
Practice 91, Reteach 91, Extend 91

SKILLS TRACE

GRADE 3	• Explore finding equivalent fractions. *(Chapter 11)*
GRADE 4	• Explore finding equivalent fractions.
GRADE 5	• Explore identifying and finding equivalent fractions. *(Chapter 9)*

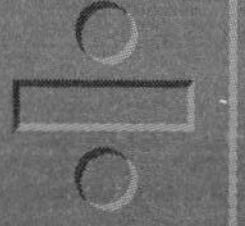

WARM-UP

Whole Class **Kinesthetic**

OBJECTIVE Review identifying fractions.

▶ Ask all students wearing red anywhere on their clothing or shoes to stand in one corner of the room. Have students identify the fraction of the class that are wearing red.

▶ Then ask the boys wearing red to stand apart from the girls wearing red. Have students identify the fraction of girls in class wearing red and the fraction of boys in class wearing red.

▶ Compare the numbers of girls and boys wearing red. Compare the fractions for girls and boys in the class wearing red. Ask:

- **Are the same number of girls and boys wearing red?**
- **Are the fractions the same?**
  [Answers may vary.]

ART CONNECTION

Whole Class **Visual/Spatial**

OBJECTIVE Connect equivalent fractions to geometric designs.

Materials per student: crayons

▶ Draw four circles on the chalkboard. Divide one circle into halves, one into fourths, one into sixths, and one into eighths.

▶ Students copy the circles and color half of each circle. Then have them write the fraction for each design that they have shaded. $[\frac{1}{2}, \frac{2}{4}, \frac{3}{6}, \frac{4}{8}]$

▶ Elicit that each fraction shows the same area of the circle.

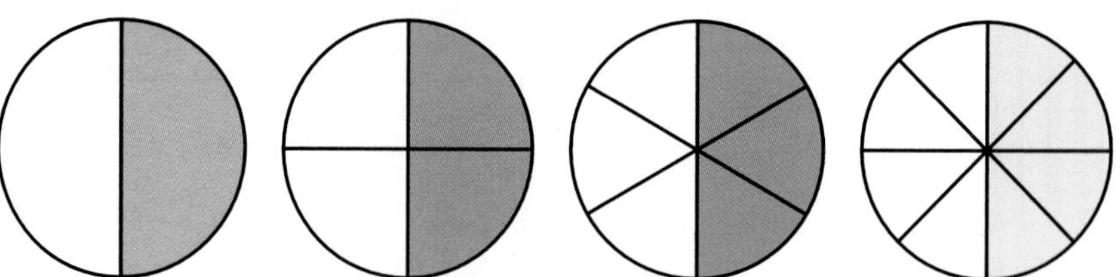

ESL APPROPRIATE

Daily Review

PREVIOUS DAY QUICK REVIEW

1. $\frac{1}{3}$ of 18 *[6]*
2. $\frac{1}{4}$ of 20 *[5]*
3. $\frac{2}{3}$ of 9 *[6]*
4. $\frac{3}{5}$ of 15 *[9]*

FAST FACTS

1. 3 × 2 *[6]*
2. 4 × 7 *[28]*
3. 7 × 6 *[42]*
4. 9 × 5 *[45]*

Problem of the Day • 91

Erica painted $\frac{2}{3}$ of her poster while Renee painted $\frac{5}{12}$ of her poster. Janet painted $\frac{1}{2}$ of her poster and Teresa painted $\frac{4}{6}$ of her poster. Which girls painted the same amount of their posters? *[Erica and Teresa]*

TECH LINK

Math Van

MATH VAN

Tool You may wish to use the Fraction Models tool and the Graph tool for Data Point with this lesson.

MATH FORUM

Management Tip I have my students work through the exercises in pairs. They alternate using fraction strips and dividing or multiplying to compare methods and answers.

Visit our Resource Village at http://www.mhschool.com to see more of the Math Forum.

MATH CENTER

Practice

OBJECTIVE Draw models of equivalent fractions.

Materials per pair: two-color counters; per student: crayons, Math Center Recording Sheet (TA 31 optional)

Students play a game by starting with a drawn model of a fraction. The partners pass the drawing back and forth to show different equivalent fractions.

PRACTICE ACTIVITY 91 — MATH CENTER, Partners

Manipulatives • Equivalent Art

YOU NEED
- 2-color counters
- markers or crayons

- Draw a diagram of counters to show a fraction of a group. For example, draw 1 red counter and 2 yellow counters to show $\frac{1}{3}$ (1 out of 3).
- Pass the drawing to your partner. Your partner changes the drawing to show an equivalent fraction.
- Check your partner's work and change the drawing to show still another equivalent fraction.
- Now let your partner draw a new fraction. Repeat the activity.

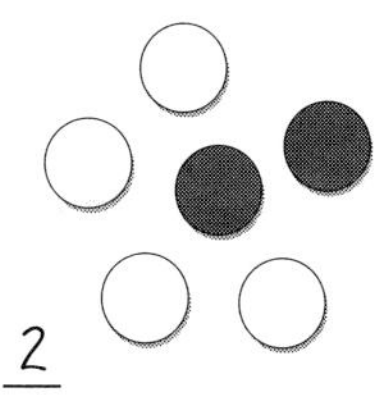

Grade Level 4 · McGraw-Hill School Division

Chapter 10, Lesson 4, pages 376–379 — Fractions

ESL APPROPRIATE

NCTM Standards
- Problem Solving
- ✓ Communication
- ✓ Reasoning
- Connections

Problem Solving

OBJECTIVE Compare equivalent fractions.

Materials per pair: fraction circles (TA 27), fraction strips (TA 26)

Students play a game where they use manipulatives to make equivalent fractions.

PROBLEM-SOLVING ACTIVITY 91 — MATH CENTER, Partners

Spatial Reasoning • Round the Circle

YOU NEED
- fraction circles (halves, thirds, fourths, sixths, eighths) or fraction strips

- Put all the fraction pieces in a paper bag. Partners take turns choosing a fraction piece without showing it. Continue until all the pieces are passed out.
- By turns, each partner names one of the fractions they have chosen. The other tries to make an equivalent fraction with one or more of their own pieces. Players get 1 point for each equivalent fraction they make.
- Set aside the matched set of fractions. Continue playing until no more equivalent fractions can be made.

Grade Level 4 · McGraw-Hill School Division

Chapter 10, Lesson 4, pages 376–379 — Fractions

NCTM Standards
- ✓ Problem Solving
- ✓ Communication
- ✓ Reasoning
- Connections

EXPLORE ACTIVITY

Equivalent Fractions

OBJECTIVE Explore finding equivalent fractions.

Materials per group: fraction strips (TA 26)

Vocabulary equivalent fractions

1 Introduce

Copy the following circle on the chalkboard:

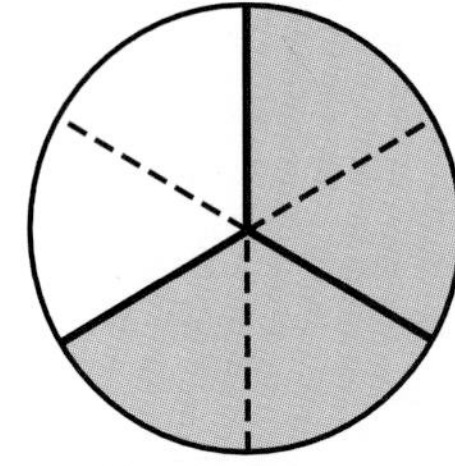

Ask:

- **How many thirds are shaded? sixths?** *[$\frac{2}{3}$, $\frac{4}{6}$]*

Elicit that both fractions refer to the same amount.

2 Teach

Cooperative Groups

LEARN Read the introductory problem. Point out that the term *equivalent fractions* refers to the other fractions Jason could have used. Stress that equivalent fractions all name the same part of the whole or group and thus are equivalent.

Work Together Encourage students to try as many of the fraction strips as they can to find equivalent fractions. Tell them to look for patterns that they can identify, such as factors or multiples of numbers. Encourage students to find more than one equivalent fraction for $\frac{4}{8}$, $\frac{1}{3}$, and $\frac{2}{8}$. To help students think creatively, tell them that numerators and denominators may both increase or both decrease.

Make sure students are able to align the fraction strips to correctly identify the equivalent fractions.

Talk It Over Allow groups to explain how they found their equivalent fractions. Discuss if and when they recognized any patterns between equivalent fractions. Have students explain how they may have used these patterns to find other equivalent fractions. Ask:

- **How did the denominator help you find equivalent fractions?** *[Possible answer: Look for multiples or factors of the denominator, then divide (multiply) both numerator and denominator by the same number.]*
- **How did comparing the numerator and denominator of a fraction help you find equivalent fractions?** *[Possible answer: If the denominator is 4 times the numerator, you can find equivalent fractions by looking for other fractions where the denominator is 4 times the numerator.]*

LEARN

Equivalent Fractions

Jason is playing Monopoly. He has 4 houses and 4 hotels, so he says that $\frac{4}{8}$ of his properties are hotels. What other fractions could Jason have used to tell what part are hotels?

You can use fraction strips to find other fractions that name the same number as $\frac{4}{8}$. These are called **equivalent fractions**.

Work Together

Work in a group. Use fraction strips.

You will need
- *fraction strips*

Use eighths to show $\frac{4}{8}$.

$\frac{1}{8}$	$\frac{1}{8}$	$\frac{1}{8}$	$\frac{1}{8}$

Check each type of fraction strip. Which ones can you use to show an amount that is the same as $\frac{4}{8}$?

How many sections of each type of strip do you need to use?

Copy the table and record your work.

Equivalent Fraction for $\frac{4}{8}$

Fraction Strip Used	Number of Sections	Equivalent Fractions
$\frac{1}{8}$	4	$\frac{4}{8}$
$\frac{1}{2}$		

Use the same method to find equivalent fractions for $\frac{2}{3}$, $\frac{2}{8}$, $\frac{5}{10}$, and $\frac{2}{12}$.

Talk It Over

- How is the denominator in $\frac{4}{8}$ related to the numerator? **Possible answer: The denominator is 2 times the numerator.**
- How are the denominators in all of the fractions that are equivalent to $\frac{4}{8}$ related to their numerators? **All of the denominators are 2 times their numerators.**

Meeting Individual Needs

Extra Support

On centimeter graph paper, have students draw two 6-by-4 rectangles. Have them shade $\frac{8}{24}$ of one and $\frac{4}{12}$ of another. Students should see that these are equivalent fractions because they show the same area.

Language Support

Stress to students that equivalent means the fractions are equal. Encourage them to use fraction strips to reinforce the concept and visualize the process of identification.

ESL APPROPRIATE

Ongoing Assessment

Observation Checklist Determine if students can find equivalent fractions by observing if they multiply or divide the numerator and denominator of a fraction by the same number.

Follow Up You may want to give students more work with fraction strips using **Reteach 91.**

Have students who are ready for a challenge list five fractions and then name four equivalent fractions for each fraction in their list. Assign **Extend 91.**

1. Yes; possible answer: the result is $\frac{2}{3}$, which was shown to be equivalent to $\frac{4}{6}$ in the example above.

ake Connections

ou used fraction models to find quivalent fractions.

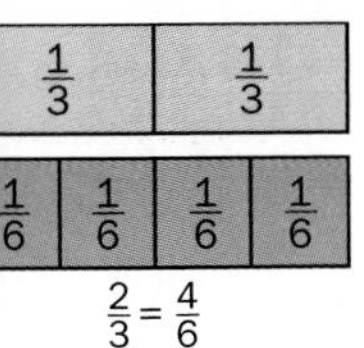

$\frac{2}{3} = \frac{4}{6}$

o $\frac{2}{3}$ and $\frac{4}{6}$ are equivalent fractions.

You can also multiply to find equivalent fractions.

To find an equivalent fraction for $\frac{2}{3}$, multiply the numerator and denominator by the same number.

$\frac{2 \times 2}{3 \times 2} = \frac{4}{6}$

What if you divide the numerator and denominator of $\frac{4}{6}$ by the same number, 2. Does this give you an equivalent fraction? How do you know? **See above.**

Multiply or divide to check that the fractions you found are equivalent. **Check students' work.**

Check Out the Glossary
equivalent fractions
See page 544.

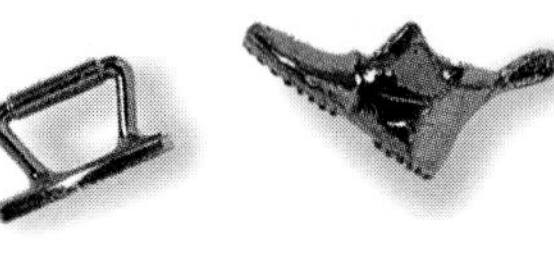

heck for Understanding

Possible answers are given. Explanations may vary.

ame three equivalent fractions for the fraction.

1 $\frac{2}{3}$ $\frac{4}{6}, \frac{6}{9}, \frac{8}{12}$ 2 $\frac{1}{4}$ $\frac{2}{8}, \frac{3}{12}, \frac{4}{16}$ 3 $\frac{1}{5}$ $\frac{2}{10}, \frac{3}{15}, \frac{4}{20}$ 4 $\frac{4}{5}$ $\frac{8}{10}, \frac{12}{15}, \frac{16}{20}$ 5 $\frac{1}{2}$ $\frac{3}{6}, \frac{4}{8}, \frac{9}{18}$ 6 $\frac{1}{3}$ $\frac{2}{6}, \frac{3}{9}, \frac{4}{12}$

omplete to name the equivalent fractions.

7
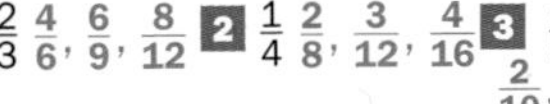

$\frac{2}{4} = \frac{■}{8}$ 4

8
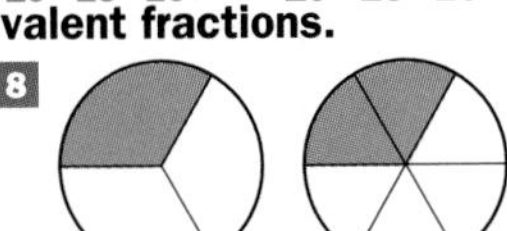
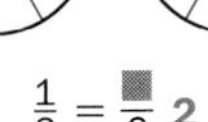

$\frac{1}{3} = \frac{■}{6}$ 2

9
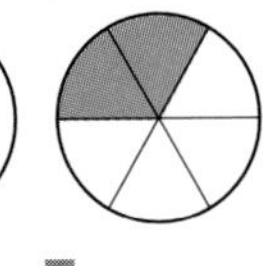
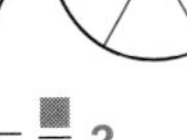
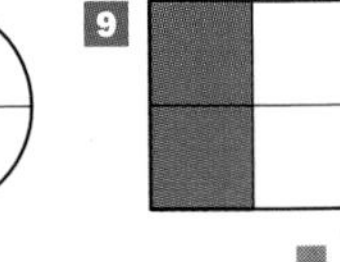

$\frac{■}{4} = \frac{1}{2}$ 2

ritical Thinking: Analyze **Explain your reasoning.**

0 John says that no unit fraction (a fraction with a numerator of 1) is equivalent to a different unit fraction. Do you agree or disagree? **Agree; possible answer: the numerator of all unit fractions is 1, and 1 can only be multiplied by itself to get 1, so the denominator would have to be multiplied by 1 also, which gives the same unit fraction.**

Turn the page for Practice.

CHECK

Gender Fairness

Check that students do different tasks when working in a group. For example, the girls and boys should alternate the job of recording the group's work.

MAKE CONNECTIONS

Allow students to use their own fraction models to show $\frac{2}{3} = \frac{4}{6}$. Then focus on how to use multiplication and division to find equivalent fractions. To help students understand why multiplying or dividing the numerator and denominator by the same number makes equivalent fractions, ask:

- **What whole number is $\frac{2}{2}$ equal to? What whole number is any fraction with the same numerator and denominator equal to?** *[1; 1]*

Discuss why multiplying and dividing the numerator and denominator by the same number works. *[It is the same as multiplying or dividing by 1.]*

Explain to students that they cannot multiply or divide by zero when finding equivalent fractions. Elicit that $\frac{0}{0}$ does not equal 1.

3 Close

Check for Understanding using items 1–10, page 377.

CRITICAL THINKING

JOURNAL To help students understand the meaning of unit fractions, have them include a definition in their journals with several examples such as $\frac{1}{2}, \frac{1}{3}, \frac{1}{4}$, and so on. Suggest students use diagrams to support their reasoning.

Practice See pages 378–379.

▶ PRACTICE

Materials have available: fraction strips (TA 26); calculators

Options for assigning exercises:
A—Odd ex. 1–25; all ex. 27–33; **Cultural Connection**
B—Even ex. 2–26; all ex. 27–33; **Cultural Connection**

- Encourage students to use mental math for ex. 7–14.
- Remind students to use both multiplication and division in ex. 18–23.
- Have students explain their methods for ex. 24–26.
- For the **Make It Right** (ex. 27), see Common Error below.
- For ex. 28, students must find an equivalent fraction to solve.
- For ex. 30–33, students may use the problem-solving strategy, Interpret Data, to solve.

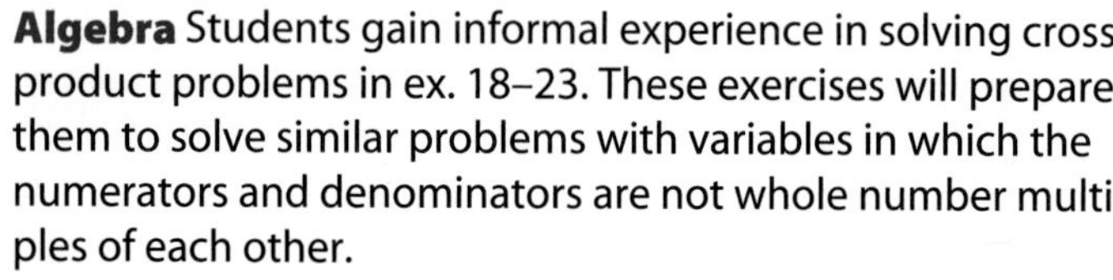

Algebra Students gain informal experience in solving cross product problems in ex. 18–23. These exercises will prepare them to solve similar problems with variables in which the numerators and denominators are not whole number multiples of each other.

Cultural Connection Have students describe any old coins they have seen and where they have seen them. Then have them read about "pieces of eight."

Tell students that the Spanish name for piece of eight was *peso.* Point out that the peso remains a unit of currency in some Spanish-speaking countries such as Colombia, Cuba, and Mexico. The *pesata* is the unit of currency now used in Spain. Pieces of eight were also used as currency in the United States until 1857.

Before assigning ex. 1–4, point out that each fraction is a fraction of a dollar or 100 cents.

PRACTICE

Practice

Complete to name the equivalent fraction.

1 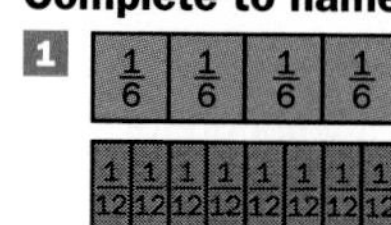

$\frac{4}{6} = \frac{■}{12}$ 8

2 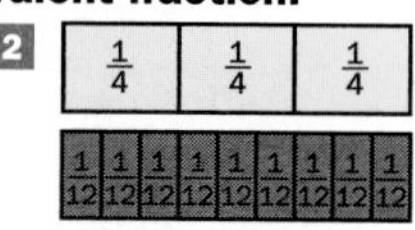

$\frac{3}{4} = \frac{■}{12}$ 9

3 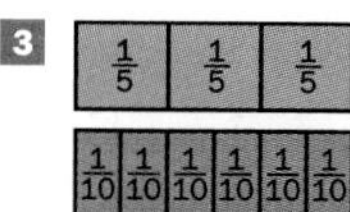

$\frac{■}{5} = \frac{6}{10}$ 3

4 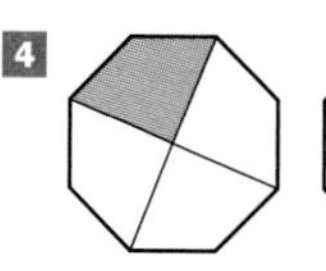 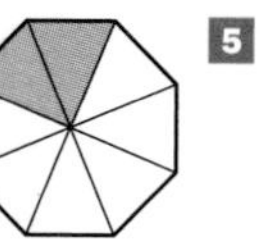

$\frac{1}{4} = \frac{■}{8}$ 2

5 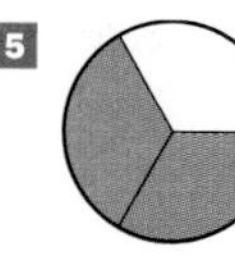 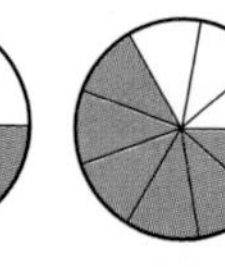

$\frac{2}{3} = \frac{■}{9}$ 6

6 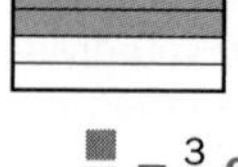

$\frac{■}{8} = \frac{3}{4}$ 6

7 $\frac{1}{2} = \frac{■}{14}$ 7 **8** $\frac{8}{24} = \frac{■}{3}$ 1 **9** $\frac{1}{5} = \frac{3}{■}$ 15 **10** $\frac{2}{3} = \frac{8}{■}$ 12

11 $\frac{10}{35} = \frac{■}{7}$ 2 **12** $\frac{3}{8} = \frac{■}{16}$ 6 **13** $\frac{6}{18} = \frac{2}{■}$ 6 **14** $\frac{9}{27} = \frac{3}{■}$ 9

Complete.

15 $\frac{1 \times ■}{2 \times ■} = \frac{5}{10}$ 5; 5 **16** $\frac{3 \times ■}{5 \times ■} = \frac{9}{15}$ 3; 3 **17** $\frac{1 \times ■}{4 \times ■} = \frac{3}{12}$ 3; 3

ALGEBRA: PATTERNS Complete the equivalent fractions.

18 $\frac{1}{2} = \frac{■}{4} = \frac{■}{6} = \frac{4}{■} = \frac{5}{■} = \frac{■}{12}$ 2; 3; 8; 10; 6

19 $\frac{1}{5} = \frac{■}{10} = \frac{■}{15} = \frac{4}{■} = \frac{5}{■} = \frac{■}{30}$ 2; 3; 20; 25; 6

20 $\frac{3}{4} = \frac{■}{8} = \frac{■}{12} = \frac{12}{■} = \frac{15}{■} = \frac{■}{24}$ 6; 9; 16; 20; 18

21 $\frac{2}{3} = \frac{■}{6} = \frac{■}{9} = \frac{8}{■} = \frac{10}{■} = \frac{■}{18}$ 4; 6; 12; 15; 12

22 $\frac{2}{5} = \frac{■}{10} = \frac{6}{■} = \frac{8}{■} = \frac{■}{25}$ 4; 15; 20; 10

23 $\frac{3}{7} = \frac{■}{14} = \frac{■}{21} = \frac{12}{■} = \frac{15}{■}$ 6; 9; 28; 35

Choose the letter of the equivalent fraction.

24 $\frac{5}{8}$ c a. $\frac{5}{12}$ b. $\frac{10}{15}$ c. $\frac{10}{16}$ d. $\frac{8}{16}$

25 $\frac{1}{5}$ b a. $\frac{5}{10}$ b. $\frac{5}{25}$ c. $\frac{2}{20}$ d. $\frac{3}{12}$

26 $\frac{16}{20}$ d a. $\frac{10}{15}$ b. $\frac{4}{8}$ c. $\frac{8}{12}$ d. $\frac{4}{5}$

Make It Right

27 Here is how Miki found equivalent fractions.
Find the mistake and correct it.

$\frac{12 \div 3}{20 \div 4} = \frac{4}{5}$ $\frac{12}{20}$ *and* $\frac{4}{5}$ *are equivalent fractions.*

Miki did not divide the numerator and denominator by the same number, and $\frac{12 \div 4}{20 \div 4} = \frac{3}{5}$, so $\frac{12}{20}$ and $\frac{3}{5}$ are equivalent fractions.

378 Lesson 10.4

Meeting Individual Needs

Early Finishers

Have students use their own methods to find two equivalent fractions each for $\frac{5}{6}, \frac{3}{8}, \frac{3}{6}$, and $\frac{6}{8}$.
[Possible answers: $\frac{10}{12}, \frac{15}{18}; \frac{6}{16}, \frac{9}{24}; \frac{1}{2}, \frac{6}{12}; \frac{3}{4}, \frac{12}{16}$]

Common Error

Some students may not divide (or multiply) the numerator and the denominator by the same number. Have them circle the divisor (multiplier) in both the numerator and denominator and check that it is the same.

Inclusion

Some students may need a review of multiplication and division facts to help find equivalent fractions.

Gifted And Talented

Challenge students to write pairs of fractions that are equivalent. For example, $\frac{6}{8}$ and $\frac{9}{12}$ are equivalent since both are equivalent to $\frac{3}{4}$.

28. No; possible answer: $\frac{2}{10}$ is equivalent to $\frac{1}{5}$, and 1 out of 5 is not the same as 3 out of 5.

IXED APPLICATIONS
roblem Solving

Ricki and Mort are playing jacks. Ricki has picked up $\frac{2}{10}$ of the jacks. Mort has picked up $\frac{3}{5}$ of the jacks. Have they picked up the same number of jacks? Explain. See above.

29 What fraction of each is made up of vowels? consonants?
a. your first name
b. your last name
c. your whole name
Check students' work.

se the graph for problems 30–32.

What fraction of the class picked chess as their favorite game? $\frac{4}{24}$ or $\frac{1}{6}$ of the class

How many more votes did Clue get than Monopoly? 2 more votes

What game got $\frac{1}{3}$ of the class votes? Clue

Data Point Survey your classmates about their favorite games. Graph your findings. Write a summary of the results. Students' outcomes should reflect their data.

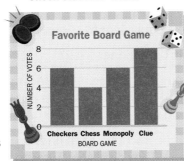

Favorite Board Game
NUMBER OF VOTES: 0, 2, 4, 6, 8
Checkers Chess Monopoly Clue
BOARD GAME

ultural Connection Pieces of Eight

undreds of years ago, a Spanish silver coin orth 8 *reales* (ray-AH-lez) was used. If people eeded a smaller unit of money, they cut the coin.

ften, they cut the coin into 4 equal parts. How uch was each part worth?

ink: The coin was worth 8 reales. $\frac{1}{4}$ of 8 reales is 2 reales.

ach part was worth 2 reales.

Spain

ame the United States coin that is worth the fraction f a dollar.

ote: 1 United States dollar = 100 cents

1 $\frac{10}{100}$ dime
2 $\frac{25}{100}$ quarter
3 $\frac{1}{100}$ penny
4 $\frac{5}{100}$ nickel

Alternate Teaching Strategy

Materials colored chalk

With pink chalk, draw a circle divided into eighths on the chalkboard. With green chalk, divide the circle into fourths. With blue chalk, divide the circle into halves. Line segments should overlap.

Shade $\frac{1}{2}$ of the circle. Show that $\frac{1}{2} = \frac{2}{4} = \frac{4}{8}$. Tell students that these are equivalent fractions.

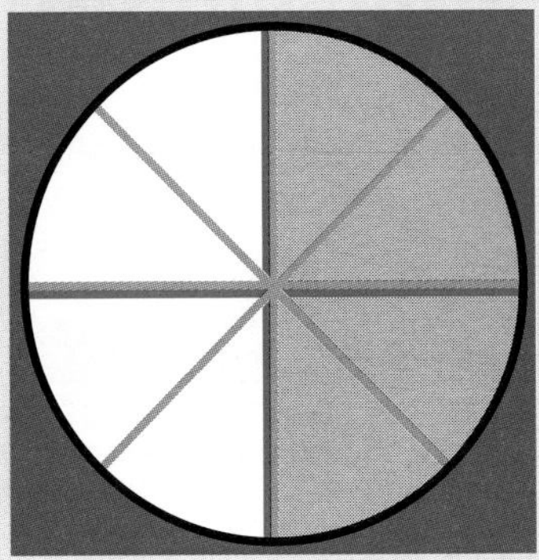

Then shade the circle to show that $\frac{1}{4} = \frac{2}{8}$ and $\frac{3}{4} = \frac{6}{8}$.

Then draw a square divided into eighths and have volunteers repeat the activity to identify and record the equivalent fractions.

Continue the activity using rectangles divided into tenths and twelfths. Have students find as many equivalent fractions as they can using the diagrams.

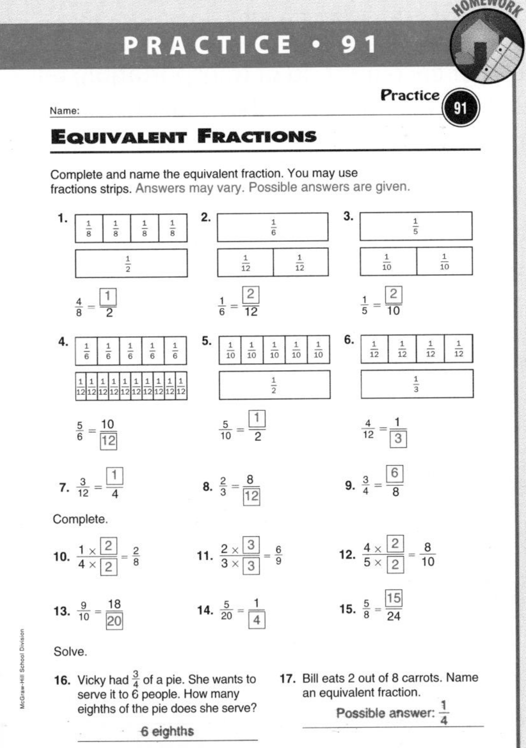

PRACTICE • 91

Practice 91

Name:

EQUIVALENT FRACTIONS

Complete and name the equivalent fraction. You may use fractions strips. Answers may vary. Possible answers are given.

1. $\frac{4}{8} = \frac{1}{2}$ 2. $\frac{1}{6} = \frac{2}{12}$ 3. $\frac{1}{5} = \frac{2}{10}$

4. $\frac{5}{6} = \frac{10}{12}$ 5. $\frac{5}{10} = \frac{1}{2}$ 6. $\frac{4}{12} = \frac{1}{3}$

7. $\frac{3}{12} = \frac{1}{4}$ 8. $\frac{2}{3} = \frac{8}{12}$ 9. $\frac{3}{4} = \frac{6}{8}$

Complete.

10. $\frac{1 \times 2}{4 \times 2} = \frac{2}{8}$ 11. $\frac{2 \times 3}{3 \times 3} = \frac{6}{9}$ 12. $\frac{4 \times 2}{5 \times 2} = \frac{8}{10}$

13. $\frac{9}{10} = \frac{18}{20}$ 14. $\frac{5}{20} = \frac{1}{4}$ 15. $\frac{5}{8} = \frac{15}{24}$

Solve.

16. Vicky had $\frac{3}{4}$ of a pie. She wants to serve it to 6 people. How many eighths of the pie does she serve? 6 eighths

17. Bill eats 2 out of 8 carrots. Name an equivalent fraction. Possible answer: $\frac{1}{4}$

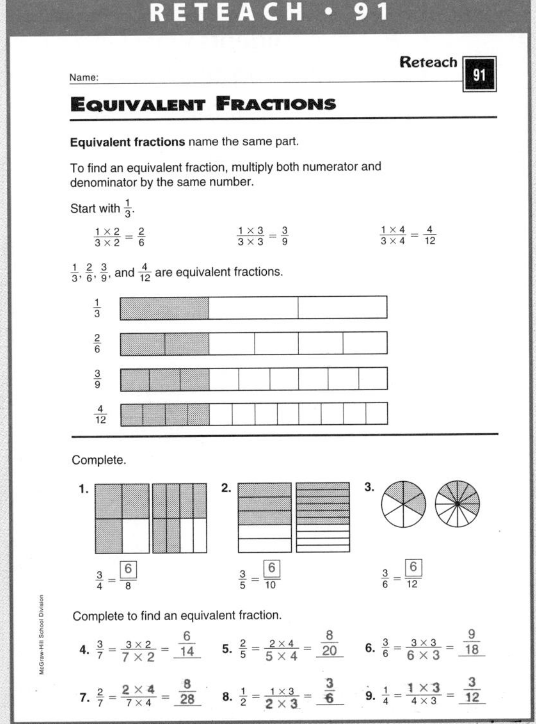

RETEACH • 91

Reteach 91

Name:

EQUIVALENT FRACTIONS

Equivalent fractions name the same part.

To find an equivalent fraction, multiply both numerator and denominator by the same number.

Start with $\frac{1}{3}$.

$\frac{1 \times 2}{3 \times 2} = \frac{2}{6}$ $\frac{1 \times 3}{3 \times 3} = \frac{3}{9}$ $\frac{1 \times 4}{3 \times 4} = \frac{4}{12}$

$\frac{1}{3}, \frac{2}{6}, \frac{3}{9}$, and $\frac{4}{12}$ are equivalent fractions.

Complete.

1. $\frac{3}{4} = \frac{6}{8}$ 2. $\frac{3}{5} = \frac{6}{10}$ 3. $\frac{3}{6} = \frac{6}{12}$

Complete to find an equivalent fraction.

4. $\frac{3}{7} = \frac{3 \times 2}{7 \times 2} = \frac{6}{14}$ 5. $\frac{2}{5} = \frac{2 \times 4}{5 \times 4} = \frac{8}{20}$ 6. $\frac{3}{6} = \frac{3 \times 3}{6 \times 3} = \frac{9}{18}$

7. $\frac{2}{7} = \frac{2 \times 4}{7 \times 4} = \frac{8}{28}$ 8. $\frac{1}{2} = \frac{1 \times 3}{2 \times 3} = \frac{3}{6}$ 9. $\frac{1}{4} = \frac{1 \times 3}{4 \times 3} = \frac{3}{12}$

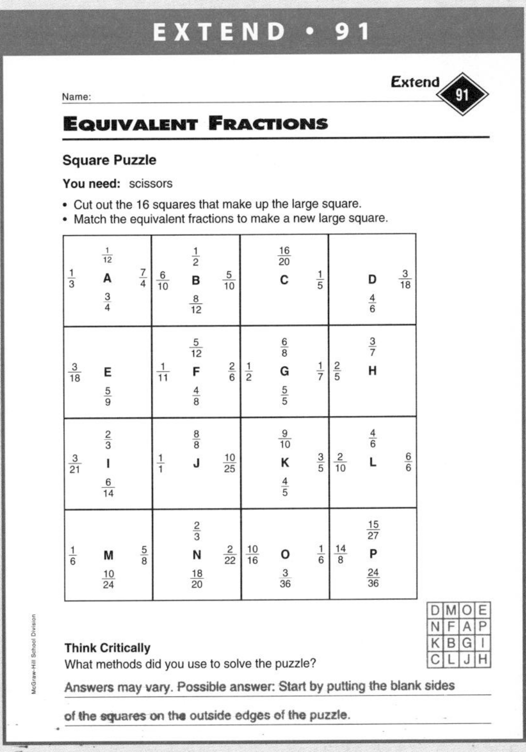

EXTEND • 91

Extend 91

Name:

EQUIVALENT FRACTIONS

Square Puzzle

You need: scissors

- Cut out the 16 squares that make up the large square.
- Match the equivalent fractions to make a new large square.

A	B	C	D
E	F	G	H
I	J	K	L
M	N	O	P

D	M	O	E
N	F	A	P
K	B	G	I
C	L	J	H

Think Critically
What methods did you use to solve the puzzle?
Answers may vary. Possible answer: Start by putting the blank sides of the squares on the outside edges of the puzzle.

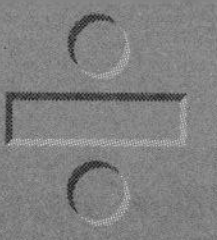

Simplify Fractions

OBJECTIVE Write fractions in simplest form.

Teaching With Technology
See alternate computer lesson, pp. 381A–381B.

RESOURCE REMINDER
Math Center Cards 92
Practice 92, Reteach 92, Extend 92

SKILLS TRACE

GRADE 3	• Explore finding equivalent fractions. *(Chapter 11)*
GRADE 4	• Write fractions in simplest form.
GRADE 5	• Write fractions in simplest form. *(Chapter 9)*

MANIPULATIVE WARM-UP

Cooperative Pairs — Logical/Analytical

OBJECTIVE Review equivalent fractions.

Materials per pair: 0–9 spinner (TA 2)

▶ Each student spins the spinner twice to write a fraction. The lesser number is the numerator and the greater number is the denominator. A student who spins a zero spins again.

▶ Students exchange fractions. Each finds an equivalent fraction and shows it by drawing a picture. They display pictures to their partners, and each student tells what fraction their partner illustrated.

▶ Have them repeat the activity several times.

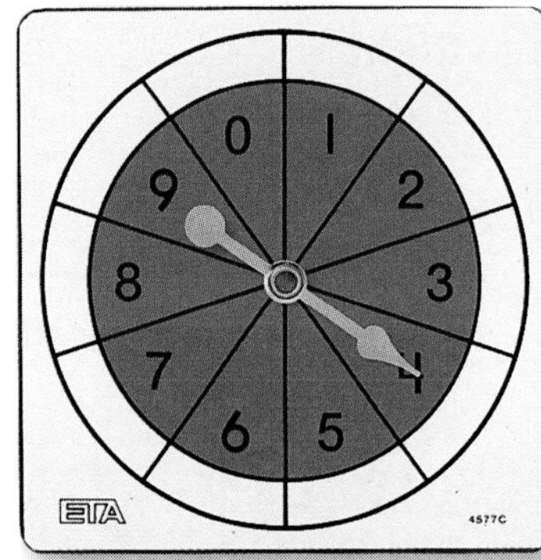

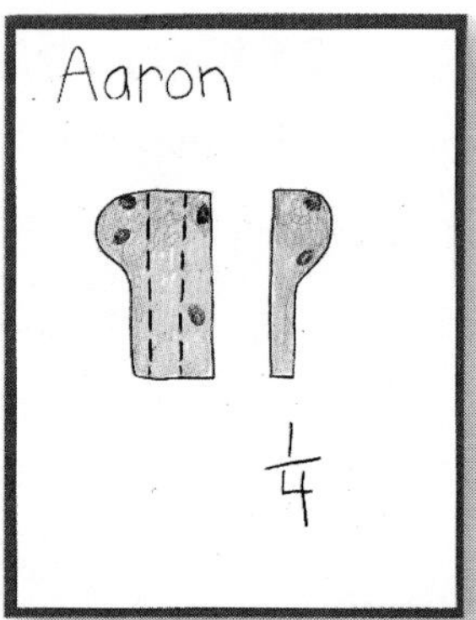

ESL APPROPRIATE

SOCIAL STUDIES CONNECTION

Cooperative Pairs — Visual/Spatial

OBJECTIVE Connect fractions and circle graphs to social studies.

▶ On the chalkboard, write the survey results on methods of transportation to Springs Elementary School: 12 students ride the bus, 6 walk, and 6 ride bikes.

▶ Have students work with a partner. For each method of transportation, tell students to write a fraction that shows the number of students taking that method out of the total number of students. [$\frac{12}{24}$, $\frac{6}{24}$, $\frac{6}{24}$]

▶ For each fraction have students write in its simplest form. [$\frac{1}{2}$, $\frac{1}{4}$, and $\frac{1}{4}$]

▶ Next have them make a circle graph to show the survey results. Students can divide a circle into one half and two fourths as shown below:

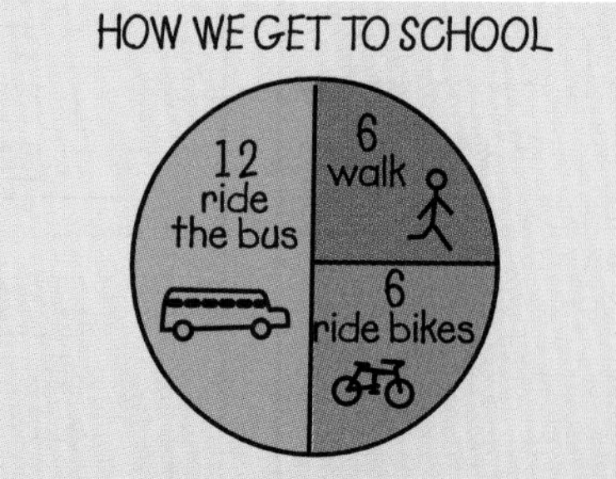

Daily Review

PREVIOUS DAY QUICK REVIEW

Complete.

1. $\frac{2}{3} = \frac{n}{6}$ *[4]* **2.** $\frac{3}{5} = \frac{9}{n}$ *[15]*

3. $\frac{9}{18} = \frac{n}{2}$ *[1]* **4.** $\frac{12}{16} = \frac{3}{n}$ *[4]*

FAST FACTS

1. 1 × 8 *[8]*
2. 3 × 3 *[9]*
3. 4 × 6 *[24]*
4. 9 × 7 *[63]*

Problem of the Day • 92

Clark has 36 geograph cards. Nine of the cards are about South American countries. What fraction of the cards are about South American countries? *[$\frac{1}{4}$ of the cards]*

TECH LINK

MATH VAN

Activity You may wish to use *Kites of Color* to teach this lesson.

Tool You may wish to use the Fraction Models tool with this lesson.

MATH FORUM

Idea I allow my students to use fraction strips to help them find fractions in simplest form.

Visit our Resource Village at http://www.mhschool.com to see more of the Math Forum.

MATH CENTER

Practice

OBJECTIVE Match equivalent fractions.

Materials per student: crayons, or markers, Math Center Recording Sheet (TA 31 optional)

Students determine how shapes in a pattern can be expressed as a fraction of a whole. They then make a fraction-shape pattern of their own. *[squares = $\frac{5}{12}$, triangles = $\frac{1}{3}$, circles = $\frac{1}{4}$]*

PRACTICE ACTIVITY 92 — MATH CENTER — On Your Own

Patterning • Fraction Patterns

YOU NEED
- crayons or markers

- Look at the pattern of shapes. How can each different kind of shape be expressed as a fraction of a whole? There are 24 shapes in all. Express your final answers in simplest form.

- Make a fraction-shape pattern of your own. Draw 30 to 50 shapes. Describe each shape as a fraction of a whole in simplest form.

Grade Level 4 — McGraw-Hill School Division

Chapter 10, Lesson 5, pages 380–381 — Fractions

NCTM Standards
- Problem Solving
- ✓ Communication
- ✓ Reasoning
- Connections

Problem Solving

OBJECTIVE Solve a puzzle involving equivalent fractions.

Students form equivalent fractions with given numbers and give the simplest form. Then they make up a puzzle to give to a classmate. *[$\frac{8}{12}, \frac{10}{15}, \frac{12}{18}, \frac{14}{21}; \frac{2}{3}$; Check students' puzzles.]*

PROBLEM-SOLVING ACTIVITY 92 — MATH CENTER — On Your Own

Patterning • Equivalent Puzzle

- Use the numbers below to make four equivalent fractions. You may use some numbers more than once.

8, 10, 12, 14, 15, 18, 21

$\frac{\square}{\square} = \frac{\square}{\square} = \frac{\square}{\square} = \frac{\square}{\square}$

What is the simplest form of these fractions?

- Make a similar puzzle for your classmates. Think about working backward to make up the puzzle.

$\frac{20}{25} = \frac{16}{20} = \frac{12}{15} = \frac{8}{10} = \frac{4}{5}$

Grade Level 4 — McGraw-Hill School Division

Chapter 10, Lesson 5, pages 380–381 — Fractions

NCTM Standards
- ✓ Problem Solving
- Communication
- ✓ Reasoning
- Connections

Simplify Fractions

OBJECTIVE Write fractions in simplest form.

Materials have available: counters

Vocabulary simplest form

1 Introduce

Show the rectangle that is shaded as shown below. Ask:

- **What fractions show the shaded part?** *[$\frac{8}{20}$; $\frac{4}{10}$; $\frac{2}{5}$]*
- **Which of these fractions has the least value in the numerator and the denominator? How did you find this fraction?** *[$\frac{2}{5}$; possible answer: divided until the numerator and denominator had no common factor.]*

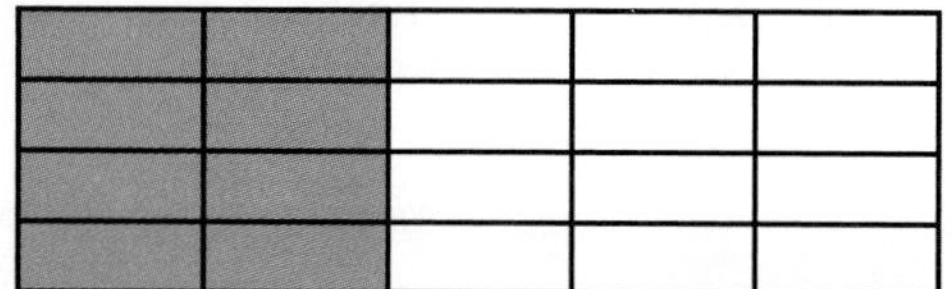

2 Teach — *Whole Class*

LEARN Read the introductory problem. Tell students the Hawaiian game Lu-Lu, meaning to shake, is a game of chance played on the beach.

Have students give some examples of fractions already in simplest form. Review the steps for simplifying a fraction.

3 Close

Check for Understanding using items 1–7, page 380.

CRITICAL THINKING
Algebra: Patterns For item 7, ask students to identify the type of fractions listed. *[unit fractions]*

PRACTICE
Materials have available: calculators

Options for assigning exercises:
A—Odd ex. 1–23; all ex. 25–28; **Mixed Review**
B—Even ex. 2–24; all ex. 25–28; **Mixed Review**

- For ex. 13–24, remind students that they can divide more than once to write the fraction in simplest form if they cannot identify the factor that is greatest.
- Point out the **Cultural Note** on page 381. Students may be interested to find out that several board games are based on Pachisi—Parchessi™, ...Sorry!™, and Trouble™.

Mixed Review/Test Preparation In ex. 1–3, students review addition, subtraction, and multiplication, learned in Chapters 2 and 5. Students review dividing in ex. 4 and 5, a skill learned in Chapter 8. Encourage students to use estimation to check answers.

FRACTIONS

Simplify Fractions

LEARN

Hallie is playing Lu-lu with her friends. On her first toss, 2 out of the 4 game pieces land blank side up. Write the fraction of the pieces that land blank side up in simplest form.

Check Out the Glossary
simplest form
See page 544.

A fraction is in **simplest form** when the numerator and denominator have no common factor greater than 1.

You can simplify $\frac{2}{4}$ by dividing the numerator and denominator by the common factor that is greatest.

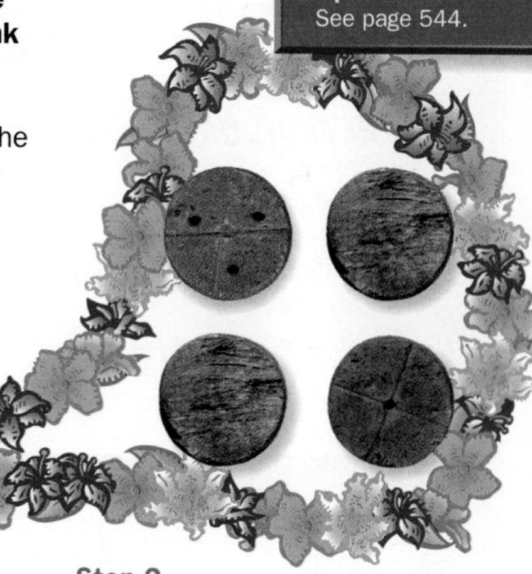

Step 1
Find the common factors.

Factors of 2: 1, 2
Factors of 4: 1, 2, 4
Common factors: 1 and 2

The simplest form of $\frac{2}{4}$ is $\frac{1}{2}$.

Step 2
Divide the numerator and denominator by the common factor that is greatest.

$\frac{2}{4} = \frac{2 \div 2}{4 \div 2} = \frac{1}{2}$

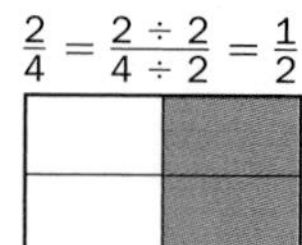

CHECK

Check for Understanding

Write the fraction in simplest form. Show your method. See below.

1 $\frac{6}{15}$ **2** $\frac{2}{26}$ **3** $\frac{12}{18}$ **4** $\frac{10}{20}$ **5** $\frac{12}{15}$ **6** $\frac{64}{88}$

Critical Thinking: Generalize

7 **ALGEBRA: PATTERNS** Is each fraction in simplest form? Write *yes* or *no*. What pattern do you see? **Possible answer: They are all in simplest form; any fraction with a numerator of 1 is in simplest form.**

a. $\frac{1}{2}$ **b.** $\frac{1}{3}$ **c.** $\frac{1}{4}$ **d.** $\frac{1}{5}$ **e.** $\frac{1}{7}$ **f.** $\frac{1}{9}$

1–6. $\frac{6 \div 3}{15 \div 3} = \frac{2}{5}$, $\frac{2 \div 2}{26 \div 2} = \frac{1}{13}$, $\frac{12 \div 6}{18 \div 6} = \frac{2}{3}$, $\frac{10 \div 10}{20 \div 10} = \frac{1}{2}$, $\frac{12 \div 3}{15 \div 3} = \frac{4}{5}$, $\frac{64 \div 8}{88 \div 8} = \frac{8}{11}$

Meeting Individual Needs

Early Finishers

Have students draw rectangles on graph paper and shade parts of them. Encourage students to make creative designs. Then have them write the fraction in simplest form that tells what part of the rectangle is shaded.

ESL APPROPRIATE

Extra Support

Some students may have difficulty following the steps in simplifying fractions. Have them make a list of factors and circle common factors. Next have them box the factor that is greatest and then divide.

Ongoing Assessment

Interview Have students simplify $\frac{16}{24}$ using the common factor that is greatest. *[$\frac{2}{3}$; 8]*

Follow Up Ask students who are having difficulty identifying the common factor that is greatest to use repeated division to simplify fractions. After the fraction is in simplest form, have them try to identify the common factor from the original fraction that is greatest. Assign **Reteach 92.**

Have students who are adept at simplifying fractions try **Extend 92.**

ractice

mplete to show the simplest form.

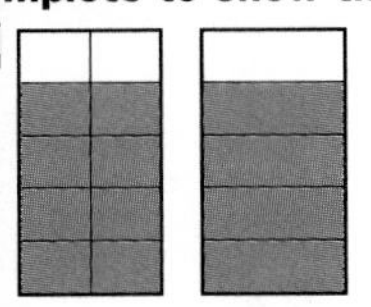

$\frac{8}{10} = \frac{■}{■}$ 4/5

2 $\frac{4}{6} = \frac{■}{■}$ 2/3

3 $\frac{2}{8} = \frac{■}{■}$ 1/4

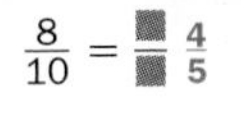

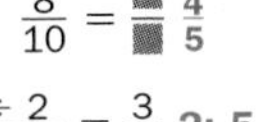
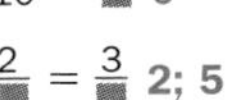

$\frac{6 \div 2}{10 \div ■} = \frac{3}{■}$ 2; 5

5 $\frac{9 \div ■}{15 \div 3} = \frac{■}{5}$ 3; 3

6 $\frac{8 \div ■}{12 \div 4} = \frac{■}{3}$ 4; 2

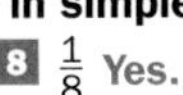

the fraction in simplest form? Write *yes* or *no*.

$\frac{4}{10}$ No. 8 $\frac{1}{8}$ Yes. 9 $\frac{9}{15}$ No. 10 $\frac{8}{9}$ Yes. 11 $\frac{6}{21}$ No. 12 $\frac{6}{10}$ No.

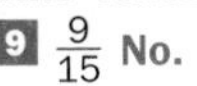

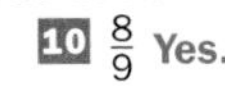
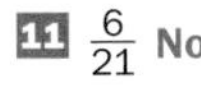

rite the fraction in simplest form. Show your method. Methods may vary.

$\frac{7}{21}$ $\frac{1}{3}$ 14 $\frac{2}{10}$ $\frac{1}{5}$ 15 $\frac{6}{8}$ $\frac{3}{4}$ 16 $\frac{4}{16}$ $\frac{1}{4}$ 17 $\frac{9}{18}$ $\frac{1}{2}$ 18 $\frac{3}{27}$ $\frac{1}{9}$

$\frac{14}{16}$ $\frac{7}{8}$ 20 $\frac{15}{18}$ $\frac{5}{6}$ 21 $\frac{10}{35}$ $\frac{2}{7}$ 22 $\frac{24}{28}$ $\frac{6}{7}$ 23 $\frac{15}{24}$ $\frac{5}{8}$ 24 $\frac{12}{40}$ $\frac{3}{10}$

IXED APPLICATIONS

roblem Solving

e the game board for problems 25–28.

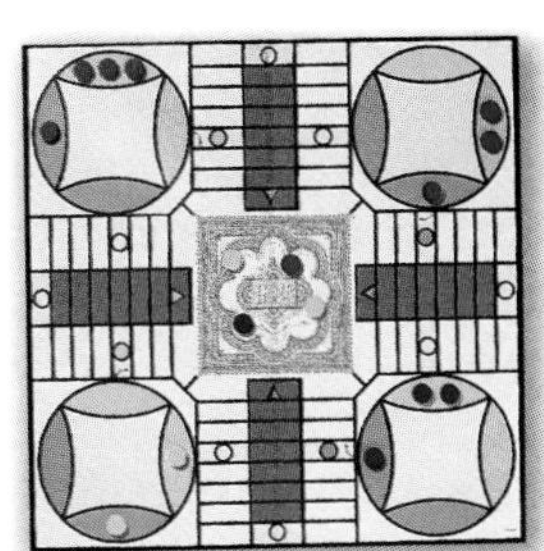

Sari was playing pachisi. In one toss, she scored 12 points. If the highest possible score on each toss is 25, how many more points could she have scored? 13 points

What fraction of the blue counters are on the green space? $\frac{1}{4}$ of the blue counters

What fraction of the red counters are on the yellow space? $\frac{3}{4}$ of the red counters

What fraction of all the counters are in the center square? $\frac{4}{16}$, or $\frac{1}{4}$, of all the counters

Cultural Note

Pachisi (puh-CHEE-zee), which is considered the national game of India, has been played there for over 1,000 years. The game was played originally with cowrie shells.

mixed review • test preparation

258 + 625 883 | 2 847 − 290 557 | 3 4,582 × 3 13,746 | 4 8)804 100 R4 | 5 10)775 77 R5

tra Practice, page 521

PRACTICE

Alternate Teaching Strategy

Copy the following fractions on the chalkboard: $\frac{4}{10}, \frac{2}{5}, \frac{20}{50}, \frac{8}{20}$, and $\frac{6}{15}$. Ask:

- **What do these fractions have in common?** *[They are equivalent.]*
- **If you divide the numerator and denominator of $\frac{4}{10}$ by 2, what is the equivalent fraction? $\frac{20}{50}$ by 10? $\frac{8}{20}$ by 4? $\frac{6}{15}$ by 3?** *[$\frac{2}{5}, \frac{2}{5}, \frac{2}{5}, \frac{2}{5}$]*
- **Can you divide the numerator and denominator of $\frac{2}{5}$ by any whole number other than 1 to find an equivalent fraction?** *[No.]*

Explain that the fraction $\frac{2}{5}$ is in simplest form.

Repeat with other sets of equivalent fractions. Allow students to tell when the fraction is in simplest form.

PRACTICE • 92

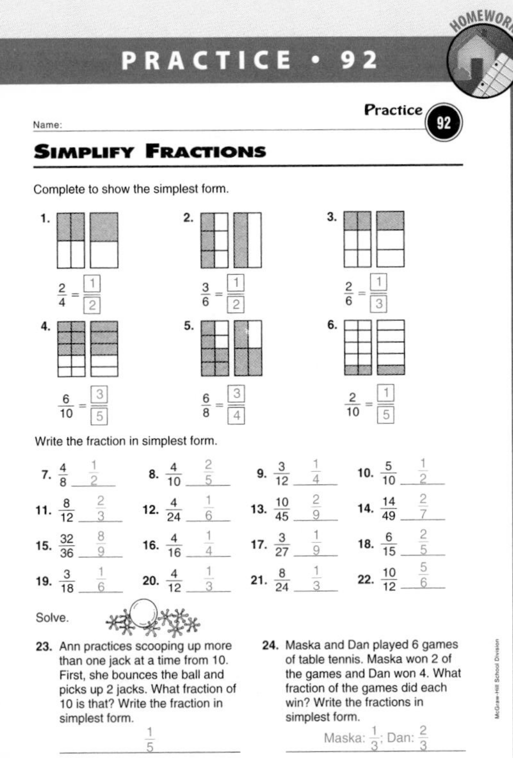

Name: Practice 92

SIMPLIFY FRACTIONS

Complete to show the simplest form.

1. $\frac{2}{4} = \frac{1}{2}$ 2. $\frac{3}{6} = \frac{1}{2}$ 3. $\frac{2}{6} = \frac{1}{3}$

4. $\frac{6}{10} = \frac{3}{5}$ 5. $\frac{6}{8} = \frac{3}{4}$ 6. $\frac{2}{10} = \frac{1}{5}$

Write the fraction in simplest form.

7. $\frac{4}{8}$ $\frac{1}{2}$ 8. $\frac{4}{10}$ $\frac{2}{5}$ 9. $\frac{3}{12}$ $\frac{1}{4}$ 10. $\frac{5}{10}$ $\frac{1}{2}$

11. $\frac{8}{12}$ $\frac{2}{3}$ 12. $\frac{4}{24}$ $\frac{1}{6}$ 13. $\frac{10}{45}$ $\frac{2}{9}$ 14. $\frac{14}{49}$ $\frac{2}{7}$

15. $\frac{32}{36}$ $\frac{8}{9}$ 16. $\frac{4}{16}$ $\frac{1}{4}$ 17. $\frac{3}{27}$ $\frac{1}{9}$ 18. $\frac{6}{15}$ $\frac{2}{5}$

19. $\frac{3}{18}$ $\frac{1}{6}$ 20. $\frac{4}{12}$ $\frac{1}{3}$ 21. $\frac{8}{24}$ $\frac{1}{3}$ 22. $\frac{10}{12}$ $\frac{5}{6}$

Solve.

23. Ann practices scooping up more than one jack at a time from 10. First, she bounces the ball and picks up 2 jacks. What fraction of 10 is that? Write the fraction in simplest form. $\frac{1}{5}$

24. Maska and Dan played 6 games of table tennis. Maska won 2 of the games and Dan won 4. What fraction of the games did each win? Write the fractions in simplest form. Maska: $\frac{1}{3}$; Dan: $\frac{2}{3}$

RETEACH • 92

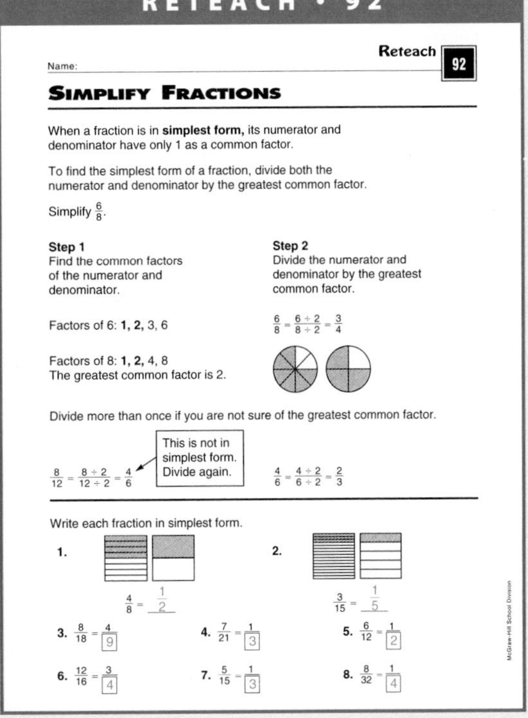

Name: Reteach 92

SIMPLIFY FRACTIONS

When a fraction is in **simplest form**, its numerator and denominator have only 1 as a common factor.

To find the simplest form of a fraction, divide both the numerator and denominator by the greatest common factor.

Simplify $\frac{6}{8}$.

Step 1: Find the common factors of the numerator and denominator.

Step 2: Divide the numerator and denominator by the greatest common factor.

Factors of 6: **1, 2,** 3, 6

$\frac{6}{8} = \frac{6 \div 2}{8 \div 2} = \frac{3}{4}$

Factors of 8: **1, 2,** 4, 8
The greatest common factor is 2.

Divide more than once if you are not sure of the greatest common factor.

$\frac{8}{12} = \frac{8 \div 2}{12 \div 2} = \frac{4}{6}$ — This is not in simplest form. Divide again. — $\frac{4}{6} = \frac{4 \div 2}{6 \div 2} = \frac{2}{3}$

Write each fraction in simplest form.

1. $\frac{4}{8} = \frac{1}{2}$ 2. $\frac{3}{15} = \frac{1}{5}$

3. $\frac{8}{18} = \frac{4}{9}$ 4. $\frac{7}{21} = \frac{1}{3}$ 5. $\frac{6}{12} = \frac{1}{2}$

6. $\frac{12}{16} = \frac{3}{4}$ 7. $\frac{5}{15} = \frac{1}{3}$ 8. $\frac{8}{32} = \frac{1}{4}$

EXTEND • 92

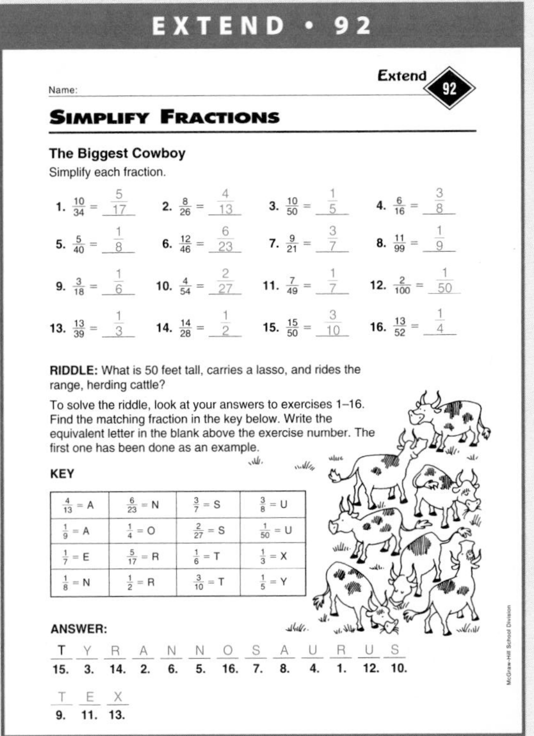

Name: Extend 92

SIMPLIFY FRACTIONS

The Biggest Cowboy

Simplify each fraction.

1. $\frac{10}{34} = \frac{5}{17}$ 2. $\frac{8}{26} = \frac{4}{13}$ 3. $\frac{10}{50} = \frac{1}{5}$ 4. $\frac{6}{16} = \frac{3}{8}$

5. $\frac{5}{40} = \frac{1}{8}$ 6. $\frac{12}{46} = \frac{6}{23}$ 7. $\frac{9}{21} = \frac{3}{7}$ 8. $\frac{11}{99} = \frac{1}{9}$

9. $\frac{3}{18} = \frac{1}{6}$ 10. $\frac{4}{54} = \frac{2}{27}$ 11. $\frac{7}{49} = \frac{1}{7}$ 12. $\frac{2}{100} = \frac{1}{50}$

13. $\frac{13}{39} = \frac{1}{3}$ 14. $\frac{14}{28} = \frac{1}{2}$ 15. $\frac{15}{50} = \frac{3}{10}$ 16. $\frac{13}{52} = \frac{1}{4}$

RIDDLE: What is 50 feet tall, carries a lasso, and rides the range, herding cattle?

To solve the riddle, look at your answers to exercises 1–16. Find the matching fraction in the key below. Write the equivalent letter in the blank above the exercise number. The first one has been done as an example.

KEY

$\frac{4}{13}$ = A	$\frac{6}{23}$ = N	$\frac{3}{7}$ = S	$\frac{3}{8}$ = U
$\frac{1}{9}$ = A	$\frac{1}{4}$ = O	$\frac{2}{27}$ = S	$\frac{1}{50}$ = U
$\frac{1}{7}$ = E	$\frac{5}{17}$ = R	$\frac{1}{6}$ = T	$\frac{1}{3}$ = X
$\frac{1}{8}$ = N	$\frac{1}{2}$ = R	$\frac{3}{10}$ = T	$\frac{1}{5}$ = Y

ANSWER:

T Y R A N N O S A U R U S
15. 3. 14. 2. 6. 5. 16. 7. 8. 4. 1. 12. 10.

T E X
9. 11. 13.

Teaching With Technology

Simplify Fractions

OBJECTIVE Students use Fraction Strips to learn about equivalent and simpler fractions.

Resource Math Van Activity: *Kites of Color*

SET UP

Provide students with the activity card for *Kites of Color*. Start ***Math Van*** and click the *Activities* button. Click the *Kites of Color* activity on the Fax Machine.

USING THE MATH VAN ACTIVITY

1 **Getting Started** Students use fractions to make kites according to specifications and to describe the colors of kites.

2 **Practice and Apply** Students figure out what fraction of the kite is red by reducing fractions to their simplest forms.

3 **Close** You may wish to discuss the pattern that can be seen in equivalent fractions with your students.

Extend Students design a kite using triangles and lines on the Geometry Mat and describe the colors of the kite using fractions.

TIPS FOR TOOLS

Remind students that they can Trade Up several Fraction Strips at one time by clicking *Trade Up* and then selecting a group of strips.

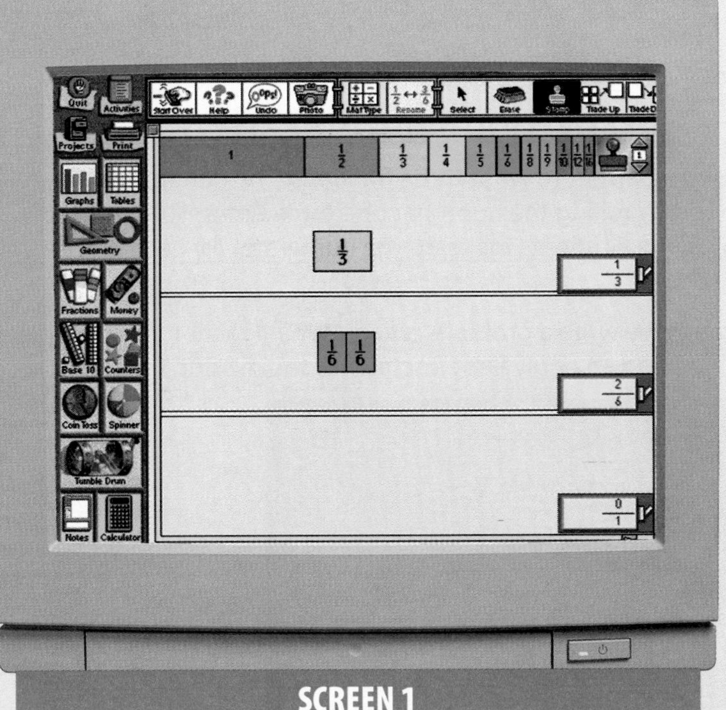

SCREEN 1

Students figure out how many $\frac{1}{6}$ strips it will take to make a kite $\frac{1}{3}$ green.

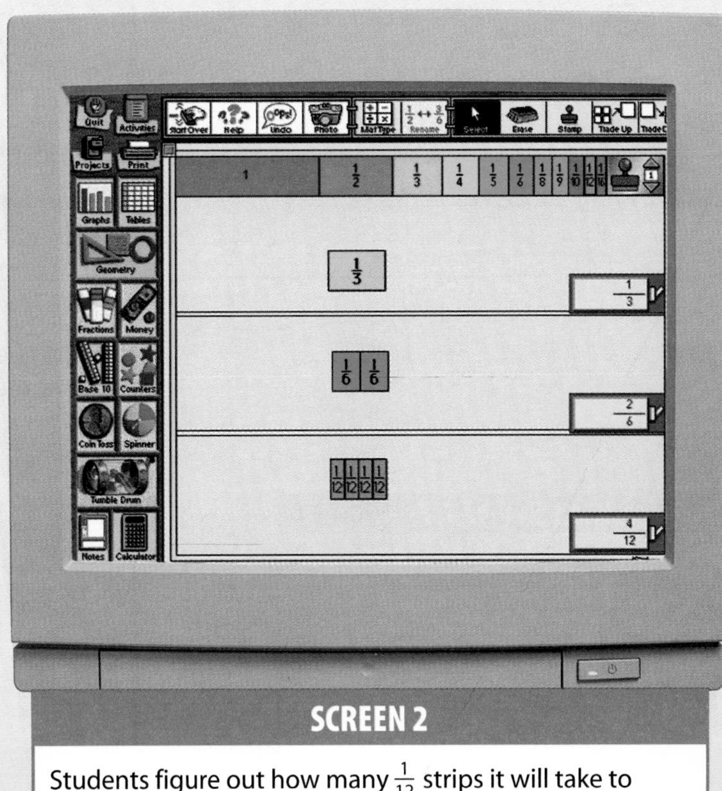

SCREEN 2

Students figure out how many $\frac{1}{12}$ strips it will take to make a kite $\frac{1}{3}$ green.

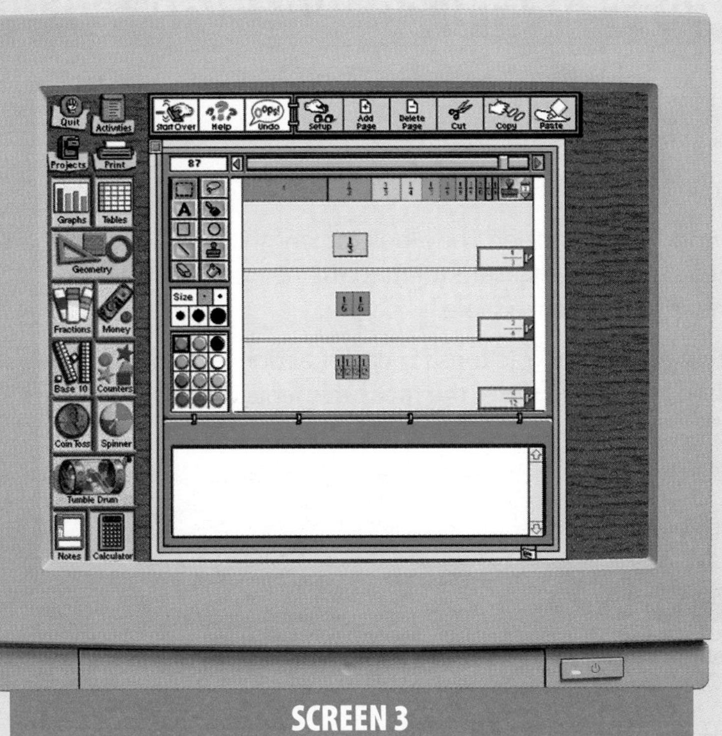

SCREEN 3

Students take a photo of the Fractions Mat they have worked on.

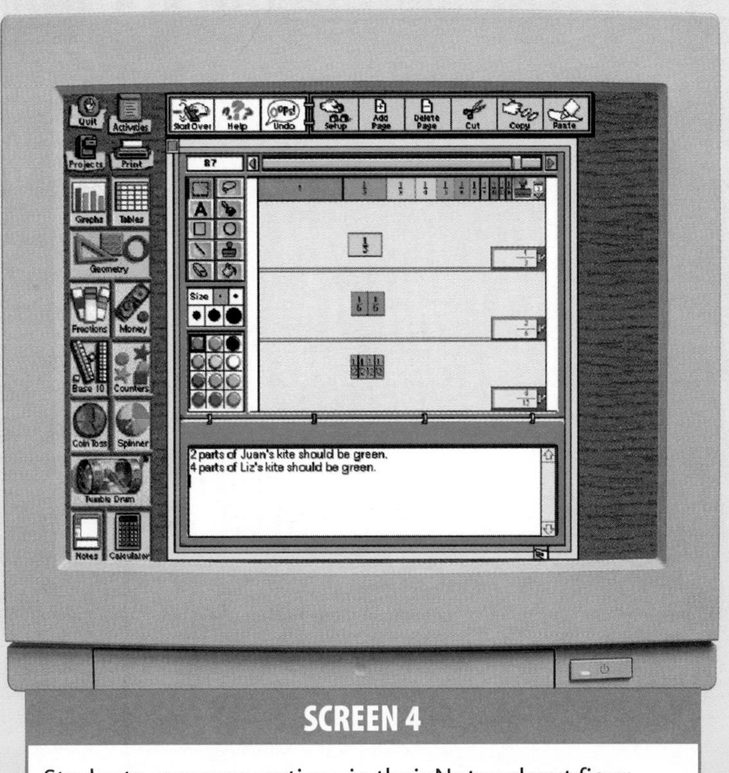

SCREEN 4

Students answer questions in their Notes about figuring out the color fractions of kites.

Compare Fractions

OBJECTIVE Compare and order fractions.

RESOURCE REMINDER
Math Center Cards 93
Practice 93, Reteach 93, Extend 93

SKILLS TRACE

GRADE 3	• Explore comparing fractions. *(Chapter 11)*
GRADE 4	• Compare fractions.
GRADE 5	• Use the LCD to compare and order fractions. *(Chapter 9)*

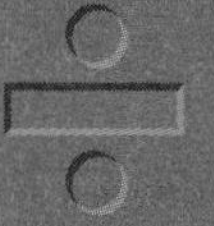

LESSON 10.6 RESOURCES

WARM-UP

Cooperative Pairs **Logical/Analytical**

OBJECTIVE Explore making equivalent fractions.

Materials per pair: 3 index cards, number cube

▶ Students work with a partner to write three fractions. The denominators of the fractions are found by rolling the number cube three times. Students may roll again if they roll a one. Students make up the numerator for each of the three fractions.

▶ On each index card they write a problem called, "What Fraction Am I?" The card should give a clue and an equivalent fraction for the missing fraction.

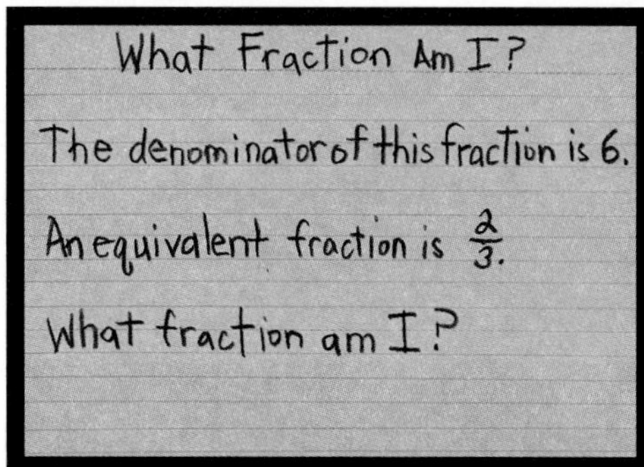

What Fraction Am I?
The denominator of this fraction is 6.
An equivalent fraction is 2/3.
What fraction am I?

▶ Pairs exchange cards and find the missing fractions.

DISCRETE MATH CONNECTION

Cooperative Pairs **Kinesthetic**

OBJECTIVE Connect fractions to measurement.

Materials per pair: inch ruler (TA 18)

▶ Have students work with a partner. They look for lengths or widths less than one inch within their reach and measure them to the nearest $\frac{1}{8}$ inch. Have them record the measurements in a table.

▶ Have students find equivalent fractions for each fraction in eighths, quarters, and halves. Then have them order the measurements in their table from least to greatest. *[Check students' work.]*

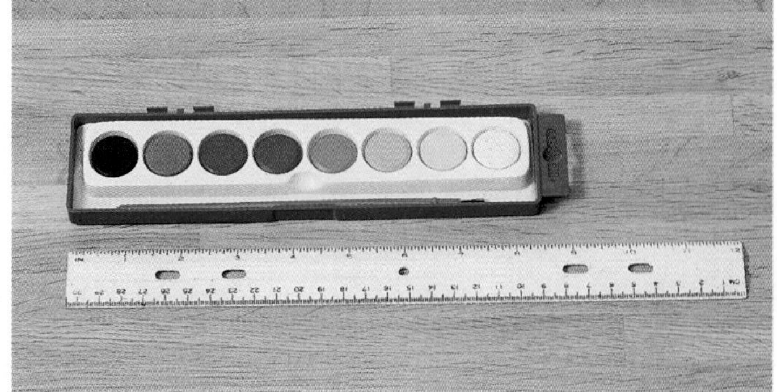

Daily Review

PREVIOUS DAY QUICK REVIEW

Write in simplest form.

1. $\frac{4}{12}$ [$\frac{1}{3}$]
2. $\frac{6}{8}$ [$\frac{3}{4}$]
3. $\frac{9}{15}$ [$\frac{3}{5}$]
4. $\frac{12}{14}$ [$\frac{6}{7}$]

FAST FACTS

1. 10 ÷ 2 [5]
2. 32 ÷ 4 [8]
3. 42 ÷ 6 [7]
4. 64 ÷ 8 [8]

Problem of the Day • 93

Sean, Darla, and Jose each have 36 marbles. Half of Sean's marbles are blue while $\frac{5}{12}$ of Darla's marbles are blue and $\frac{3}{4}$ of Jose's marbles are blue. Who has the most blue marbles? the least? *[Jose; Darla]*

TECH LINK

Math Van

MATH VAN

Tool You may wish to use the Fraction Models tool and the Graph tool for the Data Point with this lesson.

MATH FORUM

Idea My students make large zero to 1 number lines showing equivalent fractions. They are kept readily available for practice in comparing and ordering fractions.

Visit our Resource Village at http://www.mhschool.com to see more of the Math Forum.

MATH CENTER

Practice

OBJECTIVE To compare fractions.

Materials per pair: fraction strips, 20 index cards

Students arrange fractions in order from least to greatest. *[Students check each other's work.]*

MATH CENTER
Partners

PRACTICE ACTIVITY 93

Number Sense • Last But Not Least

- Each partner writes 10 different common fractions on 10 cards or slips of paper.
- Exchange fractions.
- Arrange the fractions in order from least to greatest. Use fraction strips when they help. If you find equivalent fractions, place one above the other.
- Check each other's work when you are finished.
- Now combine the two sets of fractions and order all 20 of them from least to greatest.

YOU NEED

fraction strips

20 index cards (or 5 sheets of paper folded and torn in quarters to make 20 slips of paper)

1/4, 1/3, 1/8, 3/8, 5/6

Grade Level 4

McGraw-Hill School Division

Chapter 10, Lesson 6, pages 382–383 — Fractions

ESL APPROPRIATE

NCTM Standards

Problem Solving
✓ Communication
✓ Reasoning
Connections

Problem Solving

OBJECTIVE Compare fractions.

Materials per student: Math Center Recording Sheet (TA 31 optional)

Students use fractions to describe how much time they spend on different activities. Partners compare lists to find which of them spends the greater fraction of their day doing various activities.

MATH CENTER
Partners

PROBLEM-SOLVING ACTIVITY 93

Using Data • Comparing Schedules

How do you spend your day?

- On your own, make a list of things you do in a typical school day. Use fractions to describe how much of your day you spend on different activities. For example, how much of a day is spent in school? how much eating? (A day has 24 hours, 48 half hours, and 96 quarter hours.)
- Discuss your list with your partner. Compare your fractions. Which of you spends the greater fraction of your day reading? doing homework? playing a sport?

Grade Level 4

McGraw-Hill School Division

Chapter 10, Lesson 6, pages 382–383 — Fractions

NCTM Standards

✓ Problem Solving
✓ Communication
✓ Reasoning
Connections

Lesson 10.6 *continued*

Compare Fractions

OBJECTIVE Compare and order fractions.

Materials per student: fractions strips (TA 26)

1 Introduce

Materials per student: inch ruler (TA 18)

Have students look at their rulers. Focus attention on the $\frac{1}{2}$-inch segment from zero to $\frac{1}{2}$-inch. Ask:

- **Is $\frac{1}{8}$ to the left or right of $\frac{1}{2}$?** *[left]*
- **Is $\frac{1}{8}$ greater than or less than $\frac{1}{2}$? Explain.** *[Less than; possible answer: distance is less.]*

2 Teach *Whole Class*

LEARN After the introductory problem is read, focus attention on the number line and the fraction strips. To make sure students understand how to compare fractions using the number line or the fraction strips, ask questions such as:

- **Is $\frac{7}{8}$ greater than or less than $\frac{1}{4}$? Why?** *[Greater than; it is to the right of $\frac{1}{4}$ on the number line.]*
- **Why are $\frac{1}{4}$ and $\frac{2}{8}$, $\frac{2}{4}$, and $\frac{4}{8}$, $\frac{3}{4}$ and $\frac{6}{8}$ at the same place on the number line?** *[They are equivalent fractions.]*

Then discuss why equivalent fractions with like denominators can be used to order fractions. Ask:

- **When ordering fractions, why find fractions with like denominators?** *[Possible answer: With like denominators, you just order numerators.]*

3 Close

Check for Understanding using items 1–6, page 382.

CRITICAL THINKING

Algebra: Patterns For item 5, students use numerators to compare and order fractions. For item 6, students use denominators to compare and order fractions. Encourage students to use models or diagrams to support their reasoning.

PRACTICE

Materials have available: calculators

Options for assigning exercises:
A—Ex. 1–9;14–23; **More to Explore**
B—Ex. 1–5; 10–23; **More to Explore**

- Encourage students to use mental math to find equivalent fractions to compare and order in ex. 14–21.

More to Explore Review how to interpret a circle graph. To reinforce the link between the fractions in eighths and how the circle is divided, have pairs of students create the circle graph by cutting out a circle and folding it in half three times.

Compare Fractions

LEARN

You are trying to reach the eighth level of a computer game. On your first try, you finish $\frac{3}{4}$ of the game. On your next try, you finish $\frac{5}{8}$ of the game. Which try was better?

You can use a number line or fraction strips to compare and order fractions.

0, $\frac{1}{8}$, $\frac{1}{4}$, $\frac{3}{8}$, $\frac{1}{2}$, $\frac{5}{8}$, $\frac{3}{4}$, $\frac{7}{8}$, 1

$\frac{1}{4}$	$\frac{1}{4}$	$\frac{1}{4}$	$\frac{3}{4}$

$\frac{1}{8}$	$\frac{1}{8}$	$\frac{1}{8}$	$\frac{1}{8}$	$\frac{1}{8}$	$\frac{5}{8}$

Since $\frac{3}{4} > \frac{5}{8}$, you did better on your first try.

You can also use equivalent fractions to order.

Order $\frac{1}{2}$, $\frac{1}{4}$, and $\frac{3}{8}$ from least to greatest.

5. Possible answer: When the denominators are the same, fractions can be ordered from least to greatest by ordering their numerators.

Step 1	**Step 2**
Write equivalent fractions with the same denominator.	**Compare the numerators.**
$\frac{1}{2} = \frac{1 \times 4}{2 \times 4} = \frac{4}{8}$	$\frac{4}{8}$ **Think:** 2 is the least. 4 is the greatest.
$\frac{1}{4} = \frac{1 \times 2}{4 \times 2} = \frac{2}{8}$	$\frac{2}{8}$
$\frac{3}{8}$	$\frac{3}{8}$ From least to greatest: $\frac{1}{4}$, $\frac{3}{8}$, $\frac{1}{2}$

CHECK

Check for Understanding

Write the fractions in order from least to greatest.

1 $\frac{5}{12}, \frac{7}{12}, \frac{1}{12}$ $\frac{1}{12}, \frac{5}{12}, \frac{7}{12}$ **2** $\frac{2}{5}, \frac{4}{5}, \frac{1}{5}$ $\frac{1}{5}, \frac{2}{5}, \frac{4}{5}$ **3** $\frac{1}{2}, \frac{3}{4}, \frac{3}{8}$ $\frac{3}{8}, \frac{1}{2}, \frac{3}{4}$ **4** $\frac{1}{10}, \frac{1}{8}, \frac{1}{6}, \frac{1}{4}$ $\frac{1}{10}, \frac{1}{8}, \frac{1}{6}, \frac{1}{4}$

Critical Thinking: Compare

ALGEBRA: PATTERNS Each group of fractions in ex. 5 and 6 is in order from least to greatest. Describe any patterns.

5 **a.** $\frac{1}{6}, \frac{2}{6}, \frac{3}{6}$ **b.** $\frac{1}{7}, \frac{2}{7}, \frac{3}{7}$ **6** **a.** $\frac{1}{10}, \frac{1}{8}, \frac{1}{6}$ **b.** $\frac{2}{9}, \frac{2}{5}, \frac{2}{4}$

6. Possible answer: When the numerators are the same, fractions can be ordered from greatest to least by ordering the denominators from least to greatest.

Meeting Individual Needs

Early Finishers

Challenge students to write five fractions, some with denominators that are multiples of each other and some that are not. Then have them order the fractions from least to greatest.

Extra Support

Some students may only compare numerators of fractions to order, even when denominators differ. Have students use fraction strips and write all of the fractions with the same denominator before comparing.

Ongoing Assessment

Observation Checklist Determine if students can compare fractions by observing if they write equivalent fractions with like denominators and then compare the numerators.

Follow Up Some students may need additional help comparing fractions. Have available several number lines for them to use for comparing fractions. Assign **Reteach 93.**

Have students who understand how to compare and order fractions try **Extend 93.**

ractice

te >, <, or =. Use mental math when you can.

$\frac{}{} \bullet \frac{3}{4}$ < **2** $\frac{7}{8} \bullet \frac{3}{4}$ > **3** $\frac{2}{3} \bullet \frac{5}{6}$ < **4** $\frac{1}{2} \bullet \frac{3}{8}$ > **5** $\frac{2}{5} \bullet \frac{2}{3}$ >

te in order from least to greatest.

$\frac{3}{8}, \frac{7}{8}, \frac{1}{8}$ $\frac{1}{8}, \frac{3}{8}, \frac{7}{8}$ **7** $\frac{4}{5}, \frac{1}{5}, \frac{3}{5}$ $\frac{1}{5}, \frac{3}{5}, \frac{4}{5}$ **8** $\frac{1}{4}, \frac{1}{8}, \frac{1}{2}$ $\frac{1}{8}, \frac{1}{4}, \frac{1}{2}$ **9** $\frac{1}{16}, \frac{1}{8}, \frac{1}{4}$ $\frac{1}{16}, \frac{1}{8}, \frac{1}{4}$

$\frac{5}{8}, \frac{3}{8}, \frac{3}{4}$ $\frac{3}{8}, \frac{5}{8}, \frac{3}{4}$ **11** $\frac{1}{3}, \frac{5}{6}, \frac{1}{6}$ $\frac{1}{6}, \frac{1}{3}, \frac{5}{6}$ **12** $\frac{4}{5}, \frac{3}{10}, \frac{1}{2}$ $\frac{3}{10}, \frac{1}{2}, \frac{4}{5}$ **13** $\frac{1}{3}, \frac{5}{7}, \frac{4}{21}$ $\frac{4}{21}, \frac{1}{3}, \frac{5}{7}$

te in order from greatest to least.

$\frac{4}{7}, \frac{2}{7}, \frac{6}{7}$ $\frac{6}{7}, \frac{4}{7}, \frac{2}{7}$ **15** $\frac{1}{3}, \frac{1}{2}, \frac{1}{6}$ $\frac{1}{2}, \frac{1}{3}, \frac{1}{6}$ **16** $\frac{3}{4}, \frac{1}{3}, \frac{5}{6}$ $\frac{5}{6}, \frac{3}{4}, \frac{1}{3}$ **17** $\frac{3}{8}, \frac{1}{2}, \frac{1}{4}$ $\frac{1}{2}, \frac{3}{8}, \frac{1}{4}$

$\frac{5}{7}, \frac{3}{7}, \frac{12}{21}$ $\frac{5}{7}, \frac{12}{21}, \frac{3}{7}$ **19** $\frac{1}{10}, \frac{2}{5}, \frac{1}{2}$ $\frac{1}{2}, \frac{2}{5}, \frac{1}{10}$ **20** $\frac{7}{8}, \frac{13}{16}, \frac{1}{4}$ $\frac{7}{8}, \frac{13}{16}, \frac{1}{4}$ **21** $\frac{1}{9}, \frac{5}{18}, \frac{11}{36}$ $\frac{11}{16}, \frac{5}{18}, \frac{1}{9}$

XED APPLICATIONS

roblem Solving

Pencil & Paper · Calculator · Mental Math

Three sisters each want to save $30 to buy board games. Jen has $\frac{1}{5}$ of the amount, Jackie has $\frac{3}{10}$, and Jill has $\frac{4}{10}$. Who has the most? the least? **Jill; Jen**

23 **Data Point** Use the Databank on page 541. Make a graph to show what fourth-grade students like to do. Write two statements that describe the data in your graph. **Students' graphs should reflect the data provided by the Databank.**

more to explore

cle Graph

rcle graph was used to show the data from a survey.

Did more students choose Super Mario or NBA Jam? How do you know? **See below.**

Which video is the favorite of about half the class? How do you know? **Ridge Racer; it covers about half the area of the circle.**

The fraction of the graph showing Zelda is $\frac{2}{8}$. How many students chose Zelda? Explain. **tudents; check students' explanations.**

Favorite Video Games

NBA Jam · Ridge Racer · Super Mario · Zelda

Voted on by 24 students in the class

Super Mario; possible answer: the fraction of the circle that shows Super Mario is greater.

a Practice, page 521

Alternate Teaching Strategy

Materials per student: fraction strips (TA 26)

Have students align their fraction strips for thirds and sixths. Ask:

- **Is $\frac{1}{3}$ or $\frac{1}{6}$ greater? Explain.** *[$\frac{1}{3}$; the fraction strip is longer.]*
- **Compare $\frac{1}{3}$ and $\frac{2}{6}$. Can you write an equivalent fraction in sixths for $\frac{1}{3}$?** *[Yes, they are equal—$\frac{1}{3} = \frac{2}{6}$.]*

Continue using the fraction strips to compare $\frac{2}{3}$ to other fractions in sixths such as $\frac{1}{6}, \frac{2}{6}$, and $\frac{5}{6}$. Then ask:

- **What fraction in sixths is equivalent to $\frac{2}{3}$?** *[$\frac{2}{3} = \frac{4}{6}$]*
- **How can you use the equivalent fractions to order the fractions: $\frac{1}{3}, \frac{1}{6}, \frac{2}{3}, \frac{5}{6}$?** *[Compare the numerators of the fractions with like denominators—in this case, sixths: $\frac{1}{6}, \frac{1}{3} = \frac{2}{6}, \frac{2}{3} = \frac{4}{6}, \frac{5}{6}$.]*

Repeat the activity with other fractions.

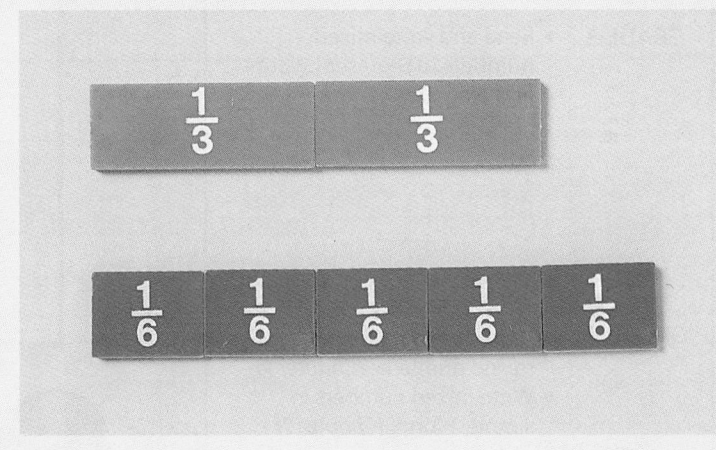

PRACTICE • 93

HOMEWORK

Practice 93

Name:

COMPARE FRACTIONS

Write >, <, or =. Use mental math when you can.

1. $\frac{1}{2} = \frac{5}{10}$ 2. $\frac{3}{4} > \frac{1}{2}$ 3. $\frac{2}{3} > \frac{3}{9}$
4. $\frac{8}{16} < \frac{3}{4}$ 5. $\frac{15}{30} = \frac{10}{20}$ 6. $\frac{1}{4} > \frac{2}{12}$
7. $\frac{2}{4} < \frac{6}{8}$ 8. $\frac{2}{3} = \frac{8}{12}$ 9. $\frac{3}{5} < \frac{14}{20}$
10. $\frac{5}{8} > \frac{1}{4}$ 11. $\frac{2}{3} > \frac{1}{6}$ 12. $\frac{3}{7} > \frac{8}{21}$
13. $\frac{3}{10} < \frac{2}{5}$ 14. $\frac{5}{6} = \frac{10}{12}$ 15. $\frac{6}{20} = \frac{3}{10}$
16. $\frac{3}{4} = \frac{9}{12}$ 17. $\frac{2}{20} < \frac{1}{5}$ 18. $\frac{8}{14} > \frac{1}{2}$

Write in order from greatest to least.

19. $\frac{5}{8}, \frac{1}{4}, \frac{1}{2}$ $\frac{5}{8}, \frac{1}{2}, \frac{1}{4}$ 20. $\frac{1}{2}, \frac{1}{8}, \frac{5}{8}$ $\frac{5}{8}, \frac{1}{2}, \frac{1}{8}$
21. $\frac{3}{8}, \frac{1}{8}, \frac{1}{2}$ $\frac{1}{2}, \frac{3}{8}, \frac{1}{8}$ 22. $\frac{1}{2}, \frac{3}{4}, \frac{1}{8}$ $\frac{3}{4}, \frac{1}{2}, \frac{1}{8}$
23. $\frac{3}{7}, \frac{1}{7}, \frac{5}{7}$ $\frac{5}{7}, \frac{3}{7}, \frac{1}{7}$ 24. $\frac{1}{9}, \frac{1}{3}, \frac{2}{3}$ $\frac{2}{3}, \frac{1}{3}, \frac{1}{9}$
25. $\frac{1}{2}, \frac{3}{4}, \frac{1}{4}$ $\frac{3}{4}, \frac{1}{2}, \frac{1}{4}$ 26. $\frac{1}{9}, \frac{7}{9}, \frac{2}{9}$ $\frac{7}{9}, \frac{2}{9}, \frac{1}{9}$
27. $\frac{1}{4}, \frac{1}{8}, \frac{3}{8}$ $\frac{3}{8}, \frac{1}{4}, \frac{1}{8}$ 28. $\frac{2}{3}, \frac{1}{6}, \frac{1}{3}$ $\frac{2}{3}, \frac{1}{3}, \frac{1}{6}$

Solve.

29. Nate ate $\frac{3}{8}$ of the pizza and Jane ate $\frac{1}{4}$ of the pizza. Who ate more pizza? Nate

30. Paul had $\frac{1}{2}$ of a bowl of soup. Tim had $\frac{2}{3}$ of a bowl, and Kelly had $\frac{3}{4}$ of a bowl. Order the amount from least to greatest. $\frac{1}{2}, \frac{2}{3}, \frac{3}{4}$

McGraw-Hill School Division

RETEACH • 93

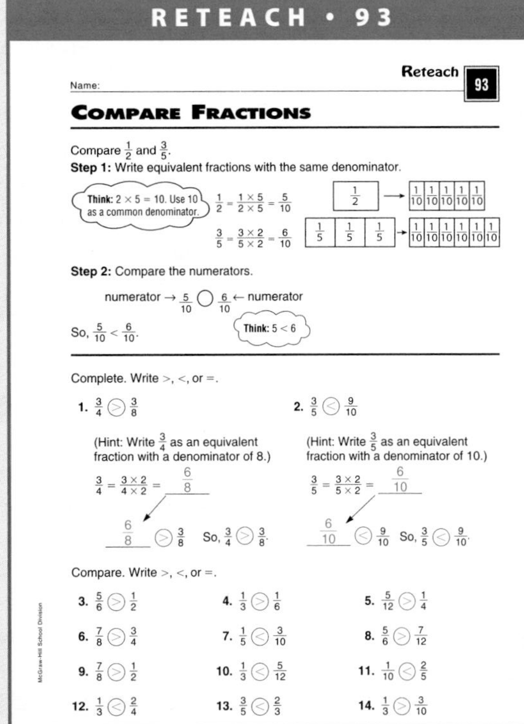
Reteach 93

Name:

COMPARE FRACTIONS

Compare $\frac{1}{2}$ and $\frac{3}{5}$.

Step 1: Write equivalent fractions with the same denominator.

Think: $2 \times 5 = 10$. Use 10 as a common denominator.

$\frac{1}{2} = \frac{1 \times 5}{2 \times 5} = \frac{5}{10}$

$\frac{3}{5} = \frac{3 \times 2}{5 \times 2} = \frac{6}{10}$

Step 2: Compare the numerators.

numerator $\rightarrow \frac{5}{10} \bigcirc \frac{6}{10} \leftarrow$ numerator

So, $\frac{5}{10} < \frac{6}{10}$. **Think:** $5 < 6$

Complete. Write >, <, or =.

1. $\frac{3}{4} > \frac{3}{8}$ (Hint: Write $\frac{3}{4}$ as an equivalent fraction with a denominator of 8.) $\frac{3}{4} = \frac{3 \times 2}{4 \times 2} = \frac{6}{8}$; $\frac{6}{8} > \frac{3}{8}$ So, $\frac{3}{4} > \frac{3}{8}$.

2. $\frac{3}{5} < \frac{9}{10}$ (Hint: Write $\frac{3}{5}$ as an equivalent fraction with a denominator of 10.) $\frac{3}{5} = \frac{3 \times 2}{5 \times 2} = \frac{6}{10}$; $\frac{6}{10} < \frac{9}{10}$ So, $\frac{3}{5} < \frac{9}{10}$.

Compare. Write >, <, or =.

3. $\frac{5}{6} > \frac{1}{2}$ 4. $\frac{1}{3} > \frac{1}{6}$ 5. $\frac{5}{12} > \frac{1}{4}$
6. $\frac{7}{8} > \frac{3}{4}$ 7. $\frac{1}{5} < \frac{3}{10}$ 8. $\frac{5}{6} > \frac{7}{12}$
9. $\frac{7}{8} > \frac{1}{2}$ 10. $\frac{1}{3} < \frac{5}{12}$ 11. $\frac{1}{10} < \frac{2}{5}$
12. $\frac{1}{3} < \frac{2}{4}$ 13. $\frac{3}{5} < \frac{2}{3}$ 14. $\frac{1}{3} > \frac{3}{10}$

McGraw-Hill School Division

EXTEND • 93

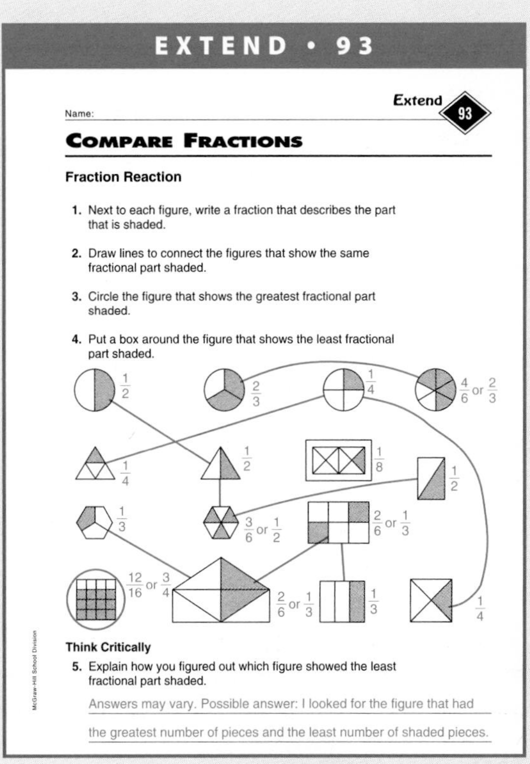
Extend 93

Name:

COMPARE FRACTIONS

Fraction Reaction

1. Next to each figure, write a fraction that describes the part that is shaded.
2. Draw lines to connect the figures that show the same fractional part shaded.
3. Circle the figure that shows the greatest fractional part shaded.
4. Put a box around the figure that shows the least fractional part shaded.

Think Critically

5. Explain how you figured out which figure showed the least fractional part shaded.

Answers may vary. Possible answer: I looked for the figure that had the greatest number of pieces and the least number of shaded pieces.

McGraw-Hill School Division

LESSON 10.7 Mixed Numbers

OBJECTIVE Read and write mixed numbers to represent words and diagrams.

RESOURCE REMINDER
Math Center Cards 94
Practice 94, Reteach 94, Extend 94

SKILLS TRACE	
GRADE 3	• Read and write mixed numbers to represent words and diagrams. *(Chapter 11)*
GRADE 4	• Read and write mixed numbers to represent words and diagrams.
GRADE 5	• Write improper fractions or mixed numbers. *(Chapter 9)* • Write mixed numbers in simplest form. *(Chapter 9)*

MANIPULATIVE WARM-UP

Cooperative Groups **Visual/Spatial**

OBJECTIVE Explore writing mixed numbers.

Materials per group: inch ruler (TA 18)

▶ Divide the class into 5 groups. Assign each group a different range: 1–2, 2–3, 3–4, 4–5, and 5–6.

▶ Students examine their rulers. They identify and record the whole numbers and whole numbers with halves, quarters, and eighths within their assigned range. For example, the group with 1–2 lists the quarters as 1, $1\frac{1}{4}$, $1\frac{2}{4}$, $1\frac{3}{4}$, 2.

▶ Discuss with the class how to read and write several of the measures recorded from each group.

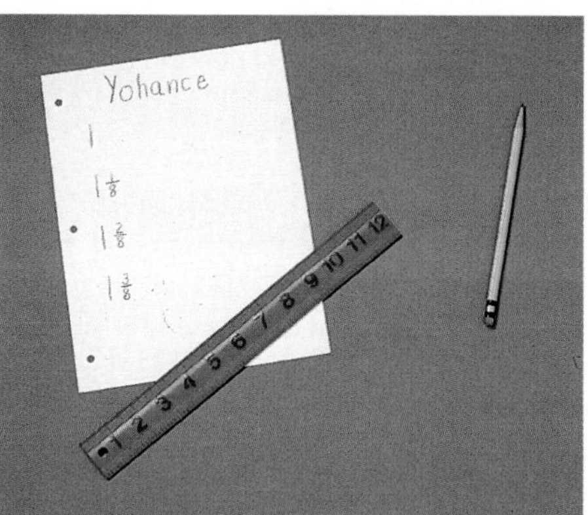

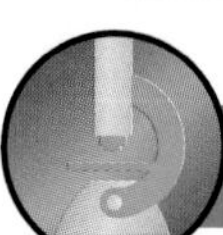

SCIENCE CONNECTION

Cooperative Pairs **Logical/Analytical**

OBJECTIVE Connect fractions to science.

Materials per pair: inch ruler (TA 18)

▶ Tell students that snowfall is recorded in inches. The table shows the snowfall for a week recorded at Fields Airport.

Snowfall at Fields Airport						
SUN	MON	TUES	WED	THURS	FRI	SAT
$1\frac{1}{8}$ in.	$1\frac{2}{8}$ in.	1 in.	$1\frac{1}{2}$ in.	$1\frac{1}{4}$ in.	$1\frac{1}{8}$ in.	$1\frac{3}{8}$ in.

▶ Have students work with a partner to determine which days had the most snow, the least snow, and the same amount of snow. *[Wednesday; Tuesday; Sunday and Friday, Monday and Thursday]*

▶ Discuss other ways the data could be displayed. *[Possible answers: bar graph, line graph]*

Daily Review

PREVIOUS DAY QUICK REVIEW

Compare. Use >, <, or =.

1. $\frac{3}{5}$ ■ $\frac{1}{5}$ *[>]*
2. $\frac{5}{8}$ ■ $\frac{1}{4}$ *[>]*
3. $\frac{1}{6}$ ■ $\frac{5}{12}$ *[<]*
4. $\frac{2}{3}$ ■ $\frac{5}{6}$ *[<]*

FAST FACTS

1. 3 × 7 *[21]*
2. 5 × 8 *[40]*
3. 6 × 4 *[24]*
4. 8 × 7 *[56]*

Problem of the Day • 94

Carol has $3\frac{3}{4}$ feet of ribbon. John has $3\frac{5}{8}$ feet of ribbon. Do they have the same amount of ribbon? Explain. *[No; $3\frac{3}{4} = 3\frac{6}{8}$, $3\frac{6}{8} > 3\frac{5}{8}$, so $3\frac{3}{4} > 3\frac{5}{8}$.]*

TECH LINK

Math Van

MATH VAN

Tool You may wish to use the Fraction Models tool with this lesson.

MATH FORUM

Idea I like to keep fraction strips available to help students simplify fractions when writing mixed numbers. This helps them focus on the process of finding mixed numbers.

Visit our Resource Village at http://www.mhschool.com to see more of the Math Forum.

MATH CENTER

Practice

OBJECTIVE Write mixed numbers.

Materials per student: bag of counters or roll of pennies, Math Center Recording Sheet (TA 31 optional)

Students make a plane figure using counters. They take a large handful of counters and create as many of the original figure as possible. They then write mixed numbers, fractions, or whole numbers to describe the number of figures.

PRACTICE ACTIVITY 94

MATH CENTER
On Your Own

Manipulatives • Figure It Out

YOU NEED
- counters or 1 roll of pennies

- Use 4–16 counters or pennies to make a figure such as a square or a triangle. Call this figure *A*.
- Pick up a big handful of counters. Make as many copies of figure *A* with them as you can. Make a partial figure with any remaining counters.
- Write a fraction and a mixed number to describe the number of figures you made as copies. For example, if your original figure *A* is made with 8 pennies and you used 18 to make copies, you may have $\frac{18}{8}$, or $2\frac{2}{8}$ copy figures.
- Repeat with 5 to 12 counters or pennies and make another figure.

Grade Level 4 · McGraw-Hill School Division

Chapter 10, Lesson 7, pages 384–385 · Fractions

ESL APPROPRIATE

NCTM Standards
- ✓ Problem Solving
- Communication
- ✓ Reasoning
- Connections

Problem Solving

OBJECTIVE Create visual representations of mixed numbers.

Materials per student: paper cup, scissors, Math Center Recording Sheet (TA 31 optional)

Students cut apart circles into fractional pieces and remove a few pieces. The remaining pieces are assembled into a model of a mixed number. *[Students check other's work as they do the activity.]*

PROBLEM-SOLVING ACTIVITY 94

MATH CENTER
Partners

Spatial Reasoning • Mixed-Number Puzzles

YOU NEED
- paper cup
- scissors

- On a sheet of paper, trace around the rim of a paper cup to make a circle. Repeat to make five circles in all. Cut them out. Carefully fold each circle in half. You may fold in half twice to make quarters or three times to make eighths.
- Unfold and cut apart the halves, quarters, and eighths. Remove 1 or 2 pieces. Give the rest to your partner to assemble. Record the finished puzzle as a mixed number—the whole number of circles plus the fraction of incomplete circles.

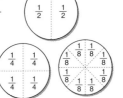

Grade Level 4 · McGraw-Hill School Division

Chapter 10, Lesson 7, pages 384–385 · Fractions

ESL APPROPRIATE

NCTM Standards
- ✓ Problem Solving
- ✓ Communication
- ✓ Reasoning
- Connections

Lesson 10.7 *continued*

Mixed Numbers

OBJECTIVE Read and write mixed numbers to represent words and diagrams.

Vocabulary improper fraction, mixed number

1 Introduce

Present the following problem for students to solve:

Andy ordered two large pizzas for his party. A large pizza had 8 slices. Twelve people were at his party and each ate 1 slice. How many eighths were eaten? How many pies were eaten? *[$1\frac{4}{8}$ or $1\frac{1}{2}$ pies.]*

2 Teach — *Whole Class*

LEARN After reading the definition of an improper fraction, ask:

- **If a fraction is greater than 1, is the fraction improper? Explain.** *[Yes; when a fraction is greater than 1, the numerator is greater than the denominator.]*

Help students read the mixed number as "two and one quarter." Point out that "and" separates the whole number and the fraction part of the mixed number when it is read aloud.

Then compare the fraction and the mixed number. Ask:

- **How are the improper fraction and the mixed number similar? different?** *[Possible answers: Similar—both name the same amount and use fourths; different—numerator of fraction is larger than denominator, mixed number has a whole number part.]*

After students work through Steps 1–2, discuss why the denominator is divided into the numerator to find the mixed number. *[Possible answer: to group the parts to make a whole]*

3 Close

Check for Understanding using items 1–7, page 384.

CRITICAL THINKING
For item 7, encourage students to include whole numbers other than just 1 in their examples, such as $\frac{10}{2} = 5$ or $\frac{10}{5} = 2$.

PRACTICE

Materials have available: calculators

Options for assigning exercises:
A—Ex. 1–9; 16–17; **More to Explore**
B—Ex. 1–3; 10–17; **More to Explore**

- Have students use multiplication to check their division for the mixed numbers in ex. 4–15.

More to Explore Suggest that students draw number lines to help them solve the exercises.

Mixed Numbers

LEARN

Dish It Up is a game where you fill in guest checks with 4 pictures to earn tips. The diagram below represents 3 guest checks. Describe how many guest checks have been filled.

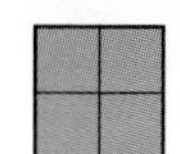
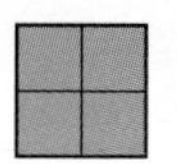
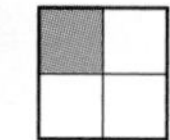

You can use an improper fraction to tell how many guest checks have been filled. An **improper fraction** has a numerator that is equal to or greater than the denominator.

Think: Each check has 4 sections.

$\frac{9}{4}$ guest checks have been filled.

You can rename an improper fraction as a whole number or a **mixed number,** which is a whole number with a fraction.

IN THE WORKPLACE
Monty and Anne Stambler are the game inventors who created Dish It Up.

Check Out the Glossary
improper fraction
mixed number
See page 544.

Step 1	Step 2
Divide the numerator by the denominator.	**Write the quotient as the whole number part. Write the remainder over the divisor as the fraction part.**
$4\overline{)9}$ = 2 R1; -8; 1	$2\frac{1}{4}$ **Think:** $\frac{1}{4}$ is in simplest form.

$2\frac{1}{4}$ guest checks have been filled.

CHECK

Check for Understanding

Rename as a whole number or as a mixed number in simplest form.

1 $\frac{8}{8}$ 1 **2** $\frac{12}{6}$ 2 **3** $\frac{15}{2}$ $7\frac{1}{2}$ **4** $\frac{11}{4}$ $2\frac{3}{4}$ **5** $\frac{13}{6}$ $2\frac{1}{6}$ **6** $\frac{11}{3}$ $3\frac{2}{3}$

Critical Thinking: Summarize **Explain your reasoning.**

7 Explain how to change a fraction that is greater than 1 to a whole or mixed number. Give examples. **Possible answer: Divide the numerator by the denominator, so that the quotient gives the whole number and the remainder over the denominator gives the fraction; for $\frac{35}{4}$, find 35 ÷ 4 = 8 R3, then rewrite as a mixed number, $8\frac{3}{4}$.**

Meeting Individual Needs

Early Finishers

Challenge students to write 5 mixed numbers and then write them as improper fractions. You may wish to show them an example, such as $2\frac{3}{5} = \frac{(2 \times 5) + 3}{5} = \frac{13}{5}$.

Extra Support

Some students may forget to divide when renaming a fraction as a mixed number. Post several examples with pictures in a math corner to help them remember the procedure for writing mixed numbers.

ESL APPROPRIATE

Ongoing Assessment

Observation Checklist Observe if students are able to read and write mixed numbers by having them write $\frac{8}{6}$ as a mixed number and read it aloud. *[$1\frac{1}{3}$]*

Follow Up Suggest students show fractions and mixed numbers with visual models such as gridded rectangles. Have students who need additional help with mixed numbers try **Reteach 94.**

For students who understand how to read and write mixed numbers, assign **Extend 94.**

ractice

scribe the colored or filled part as a fraction and as a ole or a mixed number.

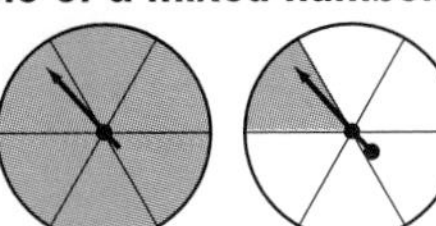
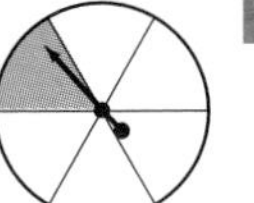
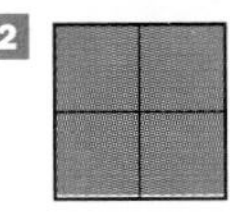
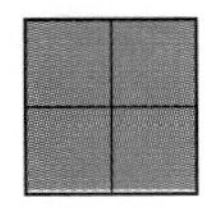
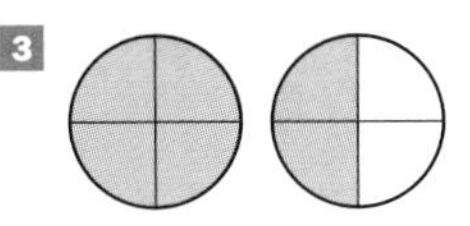

$\frac{7}{6}, 1\frac{1}{6}$ **2** $\frac{8}{4}, 2$ **3** $\frac{6}{4}, 1\frac{1}{2}$

ame as a whole number or as a mixed number in simplest form.

$\frac{13}{4}$ $3\frac{1}{4}$ **5** $\frac{12}{12}$ 1 **6** $\frac{15}{5}$ 3 **7** $\frac{16}{6}$ $2\frac{2}{3}$ **8** $\frac{14}{10}$ $1\frac{2}{5}$ **9** $\frac{68}{8}$ $8\frac{1}{2}$

$\frac{11}{7}$ $1\frac{4}{7}$ **11** $\frac{29}{3}$ $9\frac{2}{3}$ **12** $\frac{48}{9}$ $5\frac{1}{3}$ **13** $\frac{21}{14}$ $1\frac{1}{2}$ **14** $\frac{45}{11}$ $4\frac{1}{11}$ **15** $\frac{85}{2}$ $42\frac{1}{2}$

XED APPLICATIONS

roblem Solving

You watched $1\frac{1}{2}$ hours of TV. If all were $\frac{1}{2}$-hour shows, how many shows did you watch? three $\frac{1}{2}$-h shows

17 **Spatial reasoning** Suppose you have $2\frac{1}{2}$ circles. What do you need to make 3 whole circles? $\frac{1}{2}$ circle

more to explore

unding Mixed Numbers

can use a number line to help you round a mixed number he nearest whole number.

If the fraction part is less than $\frac{1}{2}$, round down.

▶ If the fraction is $\frac{1}{2}$ or greater, round up.

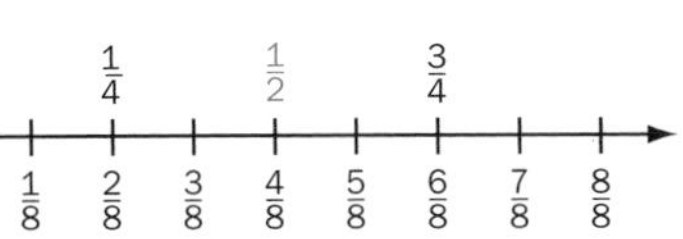
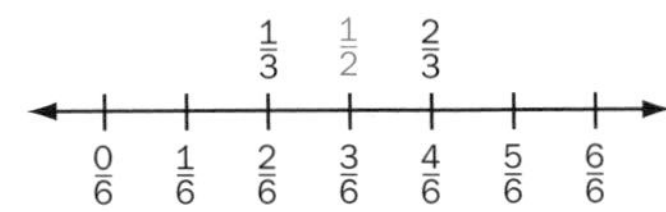

und $2\frac{1}{4}$.

nk: $\frac{1}{4}$ is less than $\frac{1}{2}$.
rounds down to 2.

Round $4\frac{5}{6}$.

Think: $\frac{5}{6}$ is more than $\frac{1}{2}$.
$4\frac{5}{6}$ rounds up to 5.

imate by rounding to the nearest whole number.

$1\frac{1}{8}$ 1 **2** $3\frac{3}{4}$ 4 **3** $1\frac{7}{8}$ 2 **4** $1\frac{1}{6}$ 1 **5** $4\frac{2}{3}$ 5 **6** $5\frac{1}{2}$ 6

ra Practice, page 522

PRACTICE

Alternate Teaching Strategy

Draw three circles divided into fourths on the chalkboard. Shade $2\frac{1}{4}$ of the circles.

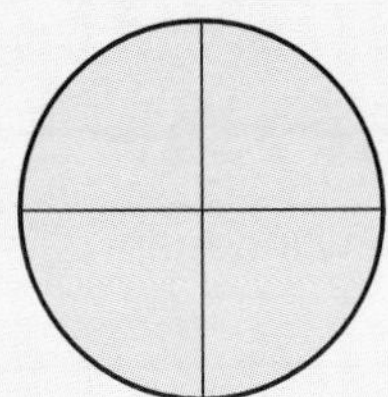
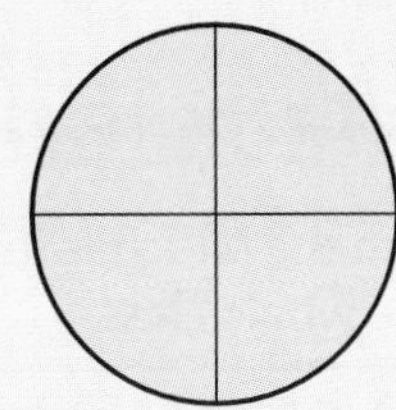
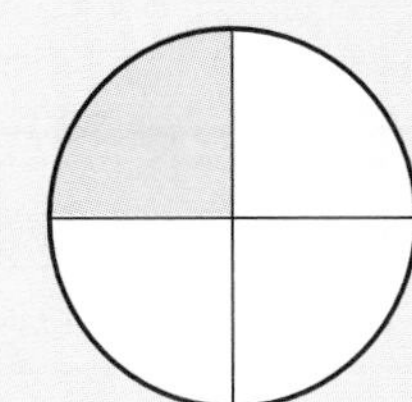

Ask: .

- **When you write the whole number and the fraction for the shaded circles, the number is called a mixed number. What mixed number do the circles show?** *[$2\frac{1}{4}$]*
- **How many total fourths are shaded?** *[$\frac{9}{4}$]*

Write on the chalkboard $2\frac{1}{4} = \frac{9}{4}$ under the diagrams.

Tell students that an improper fraction has a numerator that is greater than or equal to the denominator. By dividing the numerator by the denominator, the improper fraction can be written as a whole number or a mixed number.

Repeat the activity with other mixed numbers.

PRACTICE • 94

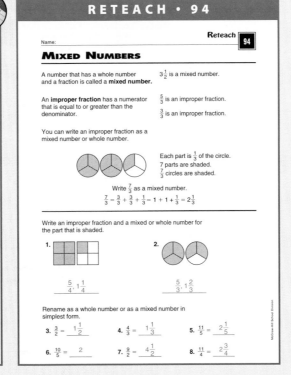

HOMEWORK

Practice 94

Name:

MIXED NUMBERS

Describe the shaded part as a fraction and as a whole or a mixed number.

1. $\frac{8}{5}, 1\frac{3}{5}$
2. $\frac{4}{3}, 1\frac{1}{3}$
3. $\frac{9}{4}, 2\frac{1}{4}$
4. $\frac{13}{6}, 2\frac{1}{6}$

Rename as a whole number or as a mixed number in simplest form.

5. $\frac{3}{3}$ 1	6. $\frac{5}{5}$ 1	7. $\frac{6}{5}$ $1\frac{1}{5}$	8. $\frac{9}{7}$ $1\frac{2}{7}$
9. $\frac{7}{7}$ 1	10. $\frac{6}{3}$ 2	11. $\frac{9}{3}$ 3	12. $\frac{10}{3}$ $3\frac{1}{3}$
13. $\frac{24}{6}$ 4	14. $\frac{25}{6}$ $4\frac{1}{6}$	15. $\frac{13}{4}$ $3\frac{1}{4}$	16. $\frac{31}{5}$ $6\frac{1}{5}$
17. $\frac{21}{14}$ $1\frac{1}{2}$	18. $\frac{24}{18}$ $1\frac{1}{3}$	19. $\frac{36}{18}$ 2	20. $\frac{27}{3}$ 9
21. $\frac{30}{7}$ $4\frac{2}{7}$	22. $\frac{48}{9}$ $5\frac{1}{3}$	23. $\frac{50}{8}$ $6\frac{1}{4}$	24. $\frac{75}{9}$ $8\frac{1}{3}$

Solve.

25. Wanda used $\frac{5}{3}$ cups of sugar in a cake recipe she was making. Write this as a whole or a mixed number. $1\frac{2}{3}$ c

26. Ben used $\frac{16}{4}$ cups of milk in a dessert he was making. Write this as a whole or a mixed number. 4 c

McGraw-Hill School Division

RETEACH • 94

Reteach 94

Name:

MIXED NUMBERS

A number that has a whole number and a fraction is called a **mixed number.** $3\frac{1}{2}$ is a mixed number.

An **improper fraction** has a numerator that is equal to or greater than the denominator. $\frac{5}{3}$ is an improper fraction. $\frac{3}{3}$ is an improper fraction.

You can write an improper fraction as a mixed number or whole number.

Each part is $\frac{1}{3}$ of the circle.
7 parts are shaded.
$\frac{7}{3}$ circles are shaded.

Write $\frac{7}{3}$ as a mixed number.

$\frac{7}{3} = \frac{3}{3} + \frac{3}{3} + \frac{1}{3} = 1 + 1 + \frac{1}{3} = 2\frac{1}{3}$

Write an improper fraction and a mixed or whole number for the part that is shaded.

1. $\frac{5}{4}, 1\frac{1}{4}$
2. $\frac{5}{3}, 1\frac{2}{3}$

Rename as a whole number or as a mixed number in simplest form.

3. $\frac{3}{2} = 1\frac{1}{2}$	4. $\frac{4}{3} = 1\frac{1}{3}$	5. $\frac{11}{5} = 2\frac{1}{5}$
6. $\frac{10}{5} = 2$	7. $\frac{9}{2} = 4\frac{1}{2}$	8. $\frac{11}{4} = 2\frac{3}{4}$

McGraw-Hill School Division

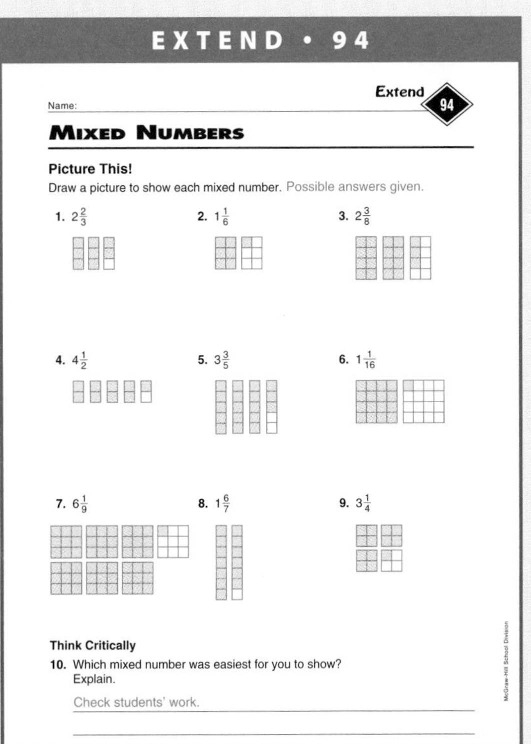

EXTEND • 94

Extend 94

Name:

MIXED NUMBERS

Picture This!

Draw a picture to show each mixed number. Possible answers given.

1. $2\frac{2}{3}$
2. $1\frac{1}{6}$
3. $2\frac{3}{8}$
4. $4\frac{1}{2}$
5. $3\frac{3}{5}$
6. $1\frac{1}{16}$
7. $6\frac{1}{9}$
8. $1\frac{6}{7}$
9. $3\frac{1}{4}$

Think Critically

10. Which mixed number was easiest for you to show? Explain.
Check students' work.

McGraw-Hill School Division

MIDCHAPTER REVIEW

PURPOSE Maintain and review concepts, skills, and strategies that students have learned thus far in the chapter.

Materials per student: calculator (optional)

Using the Midchapter Review

Have students complete the **Midchapter Review** independently or use it with the whole class.

For ex. 1–4, students need to refer to the diagrams to answer.

For ex. 5–7, students may find it helpful to draw diagrams to help solve.

For ex. 8–12, students should be able to use mental math to solve.

Students may want to include diagrams such as gridded rectangles to illustrate the fractions.

Vocabulary Review

Write the following words on the chalkboard:

denominator	**mixed number**
equivalent fractions	**numerator**
fraction	**simplest form**
improper fraction	

Ask for volunteers to explain the meanings of these words and to give examples.

Write the fraction for the part that is green.

1 $\frac{5}{8}$ 2 $\frac{5}{16}$

Complete.

3 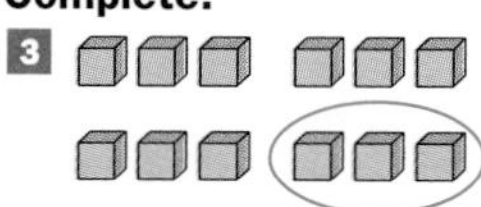

$\frac{1}{4}$ of 12 = ■ 3

4 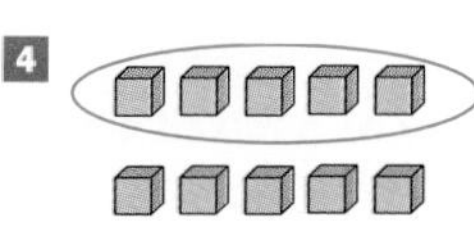

$\frac{1}{2}$ of 10 = ■ 5

24. Yes; $\frac{3}{4}$ and $\frac{6}{8}$ are equivalent fracti[ons] and both classes have the same t[otal] number of stude[nts] so the fraction o[f] each class is the same.

Find the answer.

5 $\frac{1}{3}$ of 9 3 6 $\frac{2}{5}$ of 15 6 7 $\frac{1}{6}$ of 18 3

Write in simplest form.

8 $\frac{10}{16}$ $\frac{5}{8}$ 9 $\frac{7}{14}$ $\frac{1}{2}$ 10 $\frac{12}{19}$ $\frac{12}{19}$ 11 $\frac{10}{18}$ $\frac{5}{9}$ 12 $\frac{2}{14}$ $\frac{1}{7}$

Write the fractions in order from least to greatest.

13 $\frac{7}{9}, \frac{2}{9}, \frac{5}{9}$ $\frac{2}{9}, \frac{5}{9}, \frac{7}{9}$ 14 $\frac{5}{6}, \frac{2}{3}, \frac{1}{3}$ $\frac{1}{3}, \frac{2}{3}, \frac{5}{6}$ 15 $\frac{3}{4}, \frac{11}{12}, \frac{2}{3}$ $\frac{2}{3}, \frac{3}{4}, \frac{11}{12}$

Complete to name the equivalent fraction.

16 $\frac{1}{2} = \frac{9}{■}$ 18 17 $\frac{4}{5} = \frac{■}{25}$ 20 18 $\frac{3}{■} = \frac{1}{8}$ 24

Rewrite as a whole number or as a mixed number in simplest form.

19 $\frac{4}{3}$ $1\frac{1}{3}$ 20 $\frac{15}{5}$ 3 21 $\frac{12}{8}$ $1\frac{1}{2}$ 22 $\frac{26}{7}$ $3\frac{5}{7}$

Solve. Use any method.

23 Jan, Hank, and Phil were in a long-distance race. Jan finished in $\frac{3}{4}$ of an hour. Hank took $\frac{1}{2}$ an hour to finish, and Phil took $\frac{7}{8}$ of an hour. Who finished first? last?
Hank; Phil

24 Of the 24 students in Class 4A, $\frac{3}{4}$ are 10 years old. Of the 24 students in Class 4B, $\frac{6}{8}$ are 10 years old. Do both classes have the same number of 10-year-old[s]? Explain. **See above.**

25 Journal Order the following fractions from least to greatest. Explain your method.
$\frac{1}{4}, \frac{5}{6}, \frac{2}{3}, \frac{5}{12}$ $\frac{1}{4}, \frac{5}{12}, \frac{2}{3}, \frac{3}{4}, \frac{5}{6}$; **possible answer: find equivalent fractions with common denominators for all the fractions, then compare the numerators.**

Reinforcement and Remediation

CHAPTER OBJECTIVES	MIDCHAPTER REVIEW ITEMS	STUDENT BOOK PAGES	TEACHER'S EDITION PAGES		TEACHER RESOURCES
			Activities	Alternate Teaching Strategy	Reteach
*10A	1–2, 19–22	368–373, 384–385	367A, 371A, 383A	371, 373, 385	88–89, 94
*10B	8–18	376–383	375A, 379A, 381C	379, 381, 383	91–93
*10C	3–7	374–375	373A	375	90
*10E	23–25	374–375, 376–383	373A, 375A, 379A, 381C	375, 379, 381, 383	90, 91–93

*10A Read and write fractions and mixed numbers
*10B Compare and order fractions and find equivalent fractions
*10C Find the fraction of a number
*10E Solve problems, including those that involve fractions, probability, and conducting an experiment

developing technology sense

MATH CONNECTION

Use Fraction Tools

Computer-based fraction strips let you model problems the same way you do with the actual fraction strips.

- You can use the stamp tool to stamp out the fraction strips that you want.
- You can compare fraction strips and find equivalent fractions.
- You can then save your work and print it out when you want.

Work with a partner. Use actual fraction strips if you can. Then use the computer fraction strips to solve.

1. Which fraction is greater, $\frac{5}{6}$ or $\frac{3}{8}$? $\frac{5}{6}$
2. Order the fractions from greatest to least: $\frac{3}{4}$, $\frac{9}{16}$, $\frac{7}{8}$. $\frac{7}{8}$, $\frac{3}{4}$, $\frac{9}{16}$
3. Are $\frac{8}{12}$ and $\frac{6}{9}$ equivalent fractions? Yes.
4. What is $\frac{12}{8}$ as a mixed number in simplest form? $1\frac{1}{2}$
5. Choose three fractions. Use the computer to help you find equivalent fractions. Check students' work.

Critical Thinking: Generalize

6. What are the advantages of using computer fraction strips rather than actual strips? Answers may vary. Possible answer: Many different types are available and many of them can be created very easily, equivalent fractions can be found quickly.

OBJECTIVE Compare and order fractions and decide whether two fractions are equivalent.

Resources software program with fraction strips, or Math Van Tools

Using Technology Sense

Math Connection In prior lessons students have used fraction strips to compare and order fractions and so on. Computer tools allow students to do these tasks and save and print their results. Here, students compare and order fractions, decide whether two fractions are equivalent, find equivalent fractions, and change an improper fraction to a mixed number in simplest form, by making fraction strips using a computer.

At the Computer Allow students to explore the creating fraction strips on the computer before beginning the activities. Have a volunteer demonstrate how to make fraction strips and move them.

Have students work individually or with a partner to complete the bulleted tasks and items 1–5. Discuss the Critical Thinking question with them.

Extending the Activity Have students make up a list of fractions and then order them from least to greatest using fraction strips.

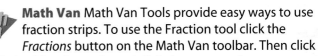

Math Van Math Van Tools provide easy ways to use fraction strips. To use the Fraction tool click the *Fractions* button on the Math Van toolbar. Then click the desired fraction strip and click the mouse where you want the fraction strip to appear. If you want more than one copy of the fraction strip, click the up arrow next to the picture of a stamp at the end of the Fraction toolbar after clicking the fraction strip. To move a fraction strip, click the *Select* button and then move the pointer over the fraction strip. Click and drag to move the hand and the fraction strip to the desired location.

Applying Fractions

OBJECTIVE Use fraction words to create a crossword puzzle.

Materials have available: calculators

1 Engage

To prepare students for making their own crossword puzzles, review how a crossword puzzle works. Then give students the clues they need to complete the following crossword puzzle. You may want to discuss how clues are used to complete it.

School Schedule Crossword

ACROSS
1. We have this subject before lunch. We use numbers to solve problems.

DOWN
2. We have this subject on Tuesdays and Thursdays. We use paint, clay, and found objects.

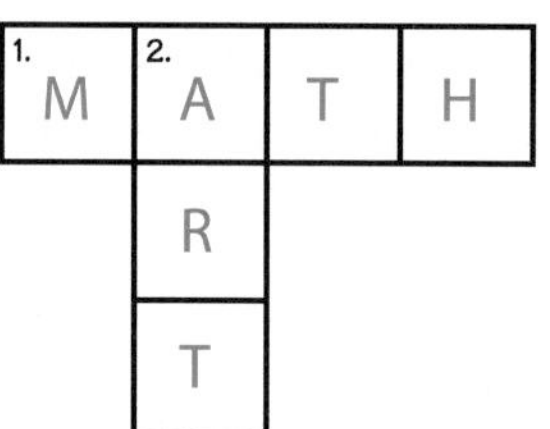

2 Investigate *Cooperative Groups*

Encourage students' creativity by allowing a wide variety of clues. Students may wish to write descriptions or short problems whose solutions correspond to a fraction in the puzzle. Others may want to use pictures, diagrams, or other visual aids to make the clues. You might even suggest they use combinations of words and diagrams in a single clue.

Using the Huddle Strategy, have students form a huddle, in groups of three to five, discuss the advantages and disadvantages of both easy and difficult clues.

3 Reflect and Share

Report Your Findings Have each group display a copy of their puzzle to the class. Select several clues and see if volunteers can identify the fractions. Discuss advantages and disadvantages of both easy and difficult clues.

- **What are some disadvantages of clues that are unclear?** *[Answers may vary. Possible answer: It may be difficult to complete the puzzle correctly.]*

The class may enjoy compiling a class puzzle using some of the clues from different groups.

After completing the group puzzle, students can use calculators to help them add the fractions in their puzzle. On a calculator that does not show fractions, demonstrate how to convert a fraction to a decimal amount, dividing numerator by denominator. They can then find a place in the puzzle to include this word name.

Fraction Crossword Puzzle

Solving word puzzles is a wonderful way to spend a rainy day. In fact, crossword puzzles are so much fun, you may want to do them when it is sunny outside!

In this investigation, you and your group will write the clues for your own fraction crossword puzzle.

Here is an example to help you when you create your own puzzle.

388 Real-life Investigation

More To Investigate

Predict Possible answer: Sketched clues may be more difficult to use, especially if they are poorly drawn.

Explore Possible approaches: Students may wish to research anagrams or word searches. Students may also be interested in using number clues to solve mathematical riddles, puzzles, or mysteries.

Find A precursor of the crossword puzzle designed for children appeared in England in the 19th century. The first puzzle to be called a crossword was printed in the Sunday supplement to *The New York World* in December 1913.

Bibliography Students who wish to complete more crossword puzzles or learn more about different types of puzzles can try:

Crosswords. New York: Dover, 1994. 0–486–28139–6

The Missing Clue, by G. Waters. Tulsa, OK: EDC Publishing Corporation, 1994. ISBN 0–88110–523–6

swers may vary.
eck students' work.

See Teacher's Edition
for sample of student work.

DECISION MAKING

Making Fraction Puzzles

1 Work in a group. Create the puzzle solution that contains all the fractions you will use.

2 Decide what hints you will use for each clue and the types of drawings or descriptions that will describe the fractions.

3 Include clues that use parts of a whole, parts of a group, and equivalent fractions.

4 Create a copy of the puzzle that other students can complete. Exchange your puzzles with other groups.

Reporting Your Findings

5 Prepare a report on what you learned. Include the following:

- a copy of your puzzle and its solution
- a list of your clues and their answers
- a description of how you decided on the clues to use and what kinds of clues are the hardest to solve

6 Compare your report with the reports of other groups.

Revise your work.

- Are the puzzle, clues, and diagrams clear?
- Did you check your solutions to make sure that they are accurate?
- Check to see if your work is neat.

MORE TO INVESTIGATE

See Teacher's Edition.

PREDICT which clues are the most difficult, then survey your classmates to check your prediction. Explain how to improve the clues so that they are easily understood.

EXPLORE other types of crossword puzzles or number puzzles in newspapers and magazines.

FIND when and where the earliest crossword puzzle was printed.

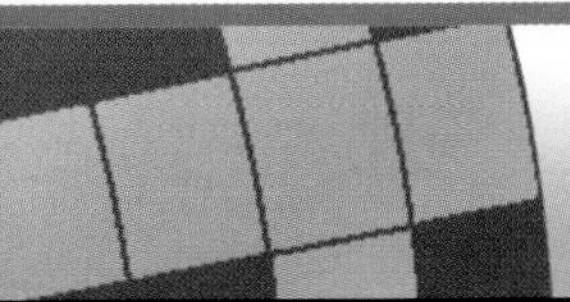

Building A Portfolio

This investigation will allow you to evaluate students' ability to describe and use fractions to write and solve problems.

Allow students to revise their work for the portfolio. Each student's portfolio piece should consist of a copy of his or her written report about how the team made the crossword puzzle. It will include a copy of the crossword puzzle and its solution, a list of clues and their answers, and a statement of how the team decided on appropriate clues for their fraction crossword puzzle.

You may wish to use the Holistic Scoring Guide to assess this task. See page 27 in Teacher's Assessment Resources.

Students' Work

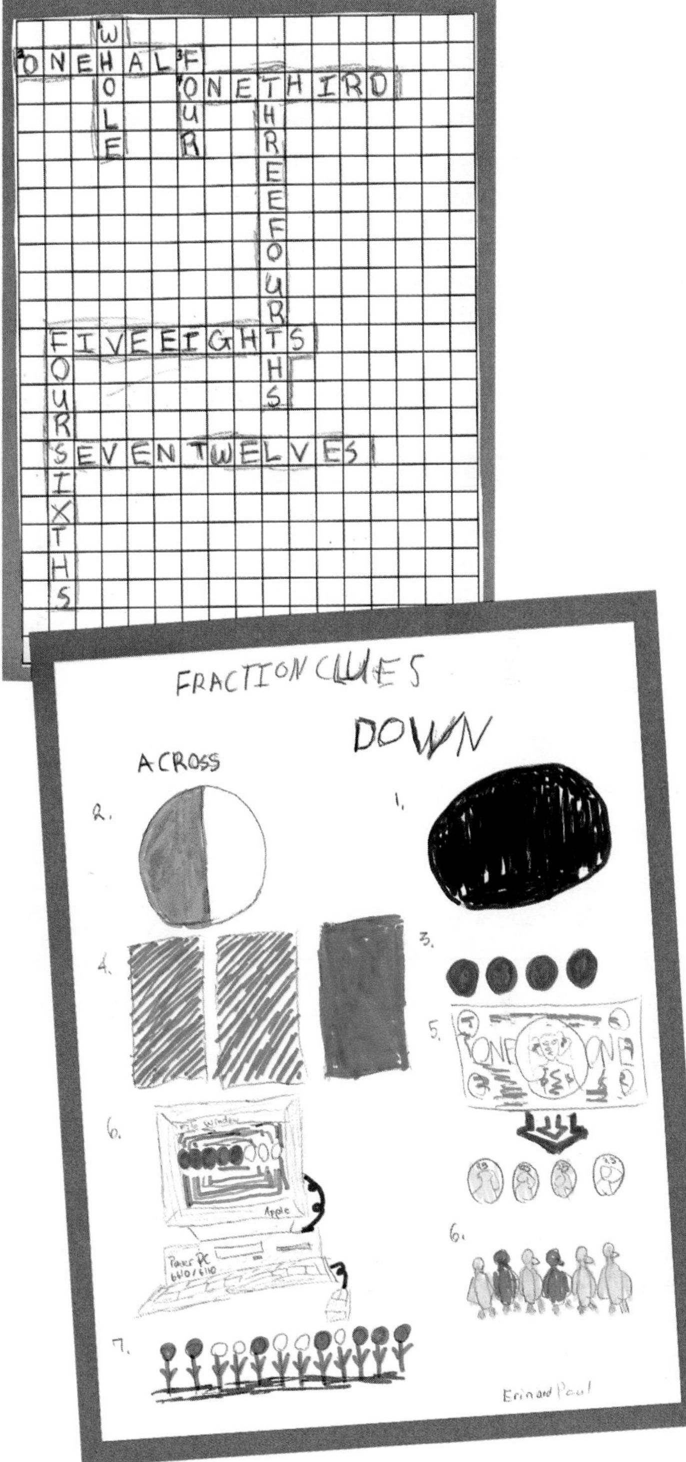

EXPLORE ACTIVITY

Probability

OBJECTIVE Explore probability and making predictions using simple experiments.

RESOURCE REMINDER
Math Center Cards 95
Practice 95, Reteach 95, Extend 95

SKILLS TRACE

GRADE 3	• Explore probability and making predictions using simple experiments. *(Chapter 11)*
GRADE 4	• Explore probability and making predictions using simple experiments.
GRADE 5	• Explore finding the probability of simple events. *(Chapter 13)*

MANIPULATIVE WARM-UP

Cooperative Pairs — Visual/Spatial

OBJECTIVE Review writing fractions for parts of a set.

Materials 10 straws (or markers): 3 red, 2 green, 4 blue, 1 yellow

▶ Display the 10 straws to the class. Write each color and its number on the chalkboard.

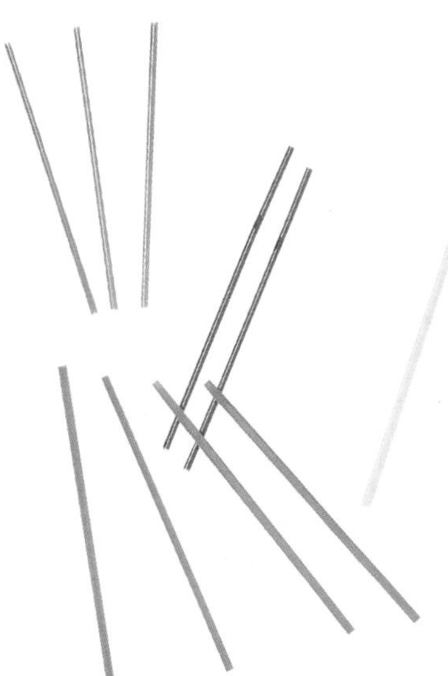

▶ Have each pair of students write as many fractions as they can think of for the parts of the set. For example: red out of total $[\frac{3}{10}]$; not green out of total $[\frac{8}{10}]$; blue and green out of total $[\frac{6}{10}]$. Have them record the fractions and the words describing the fractions in a table.

▶ List and discuss some of the different fractions described by each pair.

ESL APPROPRIATE

STATISTICS CONNECTION

Cooperative Pairs — Logical/Analytical

OBJECTIVE Connect making predictions to statistics.

▶ Have pairs predict something about their classmates that they can verify by observation or by taking a survey. Things students might predict include the color of classmates' socks, shoe color, favorite lunch food, favorite television program, etc.

▶ Allow students only several minutes to decide on their topic and make the predictions. Have them record the predictions as fractions of a whole. For example, they may predict $\frac{1}{2}$ class has white socks.

▶ Then have students use observation or take a survey to find the exact results. Discuss how the predictions compare to the exact results and why predictions are useful.

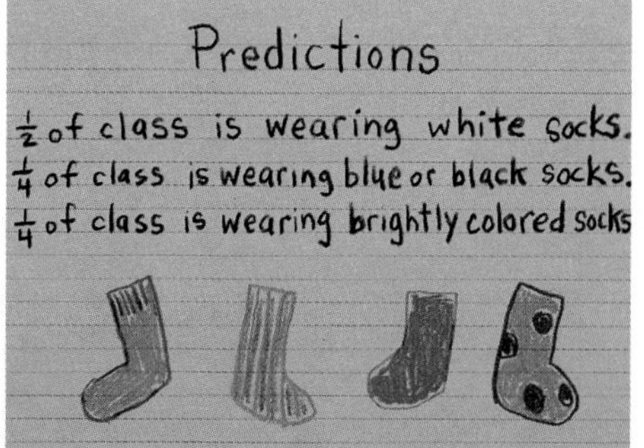

Daily Review

PREVIOUS DAY QUICK REVIEW

Rename.

1. $\frac{12}{12}$ [1]
2. $\frac{16}{8}$ [2]
3. $\frac{11}{5}$ [$2\frac{1}{5}$]
4. $\frac{18}{8}$ [$2\frac{1}{4}$]

FAST FACTS

1. 18 ÷ 9 [2]
2. 32 ÷ 8 [4]
3. 48 ÷ 6 [8]
4. 81 ÷ 9 [9]

Problem of the Day • 95

Lyle has a 6-sided number cube with the numbers 1, 2, 3, 2, 4, 2. One number is on each side of the cube. Find the likelihood of Lyle rolling a 2, a 1, and a 5. Explain. *[more likely; less likely; impossible]*

TECH LINK

Math Van

MATH VAN

Activity You may wish to use And the Winner Is . . . to practice and extend skills and concepts.

MATH FORUM

Cultural Diversity I have my students describe different games that they play, or that they are familiar with, that are played with number cubes.

Visit our Resource Village at http://www.mhschool.com to see more of the Math Forum.

MATH CENTER

Practice

OBJECTIVE Explore probability.

Materials per student: number cube, Math Center Recording Sheet (TA 31 optional)

Students toss a number cube 50 times and make a chart of the outcomes. Then they use the information to answer questions about probability. *[**1.** equally likely; **2.** equally likely; **3.** less likely; **4.** more likely]*

MATH CENTER
On Your Own

PRACTICE ACTIVITY 95

Number Sense • Is It Likely?

YOU NEED
number cube

Toss the number cube at least 50 times. Make a table to keep track of the numbers that come up. Look at your table and at the faces of the number cube. Then, before you toss the number cube, tell whether the chance of **a** is *more likely*, *equally likely*, or *less likely* than the chance of **b**.

1. **a.** a 1 comes up — **b.** a 5 comes up
2. **a.** an even number comes up — **b.** an odd number comes up
3. **a.** a number less than 3 — **b.** the number 3 or higher
4. **a.** the number 5 or less — **b.** a prime number

Number	1	2	3	4	5	6
Tally	|||	||||	||||	~~||||~~ |	||||	|||
Total						

Grade Level 4 McGraw-Hill School Division

Chapter 10, Lesson 8, pages 390–391 — Probability

NCTM Standards
- ✓ Problem Solving
- ✓ Communication
- ✓ Reasoning
- Connections

Problem Solving

OBJECTIVE Collect and interpret data.

Materials per student: three different types of books, Math Center Recording Sheet (TA 31 optional)

Students take a sampling from three different books to see if E, T, A, O, I, N, S, H, R, D, L, U are the most frequently used letters.

MATH CENTER
On Your Own

PROBLEM-SOLVING ACTIVITY 95

Using Data • The Printer's Helper

YOU NEED
three different types of books (for example, a mystery, biography, and science book)

- Once there was a man who helped printers set type. His name was ETAOIN SHRDLU (*pronounced ee-TAY-oh-inn SHURD-loo*). His name shows the most frequently used letters in the alphabet. *E* is the most frequently used letter, *T* is the second most frequently used letter, followed by *A*, and so on.
- Copy the table. Use three different types of books. Pick two pages from each book and tally how many times each letter appears.
- Were the letters *E*, *T*, and *A* the most frequently used letters? Explain.

E	T	A	O	I	N		S	H	R	D	L	U

Grade Level 4 McGraw-Hill School Division

Chapter 10, Lesson 8, pages 390–391 — Probability

NCTM Standards
- ✓ Problem Solving
- Communication
- ✓ Reasoning
- ✓ Connections

EXPLORE ACTIVITY
Probability

OBJECTIVE Explore probability and making predictions using simple experiments.

Materials per pair: 4 spinners (TA 2)

Vocabulary possible outcomes, probability

1 Introduce

Present the following problem:

Larry has 5 blue marbles and 2 red marbles. He puts all of the marbles in a paper bag. George picks a marble without looking.

Ask:

- **Would you expect George to pick a blue or a red marble? Explain.** *[Possible answer: Blue; there are more blue than red.]*

2 Teach *Cooperative Pairs*

▶ **LEARN Work Together** Review the rules of the game with students. Point out that each pair will play this game four times, each time with a different spinner.

Make Predictions Remind students to predict a winner for each game before they play. Ask:

- **How can the divisions for the colors on the spinners affect the outcome of a game?** *[Answers may vary. Possible answer: Colors with a greater area on the spinner have a greater chance of winning.]*

After students have played the games using all four spinners, discuss the results. Compare the results to their predictions.

MAKE CONNECTIONS

Go over each of the possible outcomes for each spinner. On Spinners 1 and 2, there are four possible outcomes: red, blue, green, and yellow. For Spinner 3, there are three possible outcomes: blue, green, and yellow. For Spinner 4, there is just one possible outcome: red.

3 Close

▶ **Check for Understanding** using items 1–9, page 391.

CRITICAL THINKING
Accept a wide variety of responses for items 7–9. Have students justify their answers. Then have them suggest events that are more likely, less likely, certain, and impossible.

▶ **PRACTICE**
Assign ex. 1–5 as independent work.

Probability

LEARN

What if you and three friends are playing a game. Each time you spin the spinner and your color appears, you score a point. Each time your color does not appear, another player takes a turn. What type of spinner would you want?

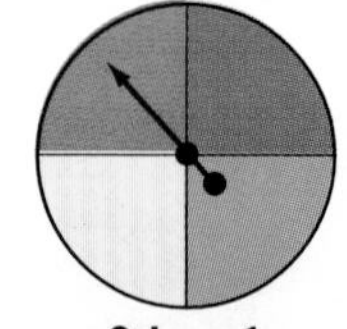

Spinner 1

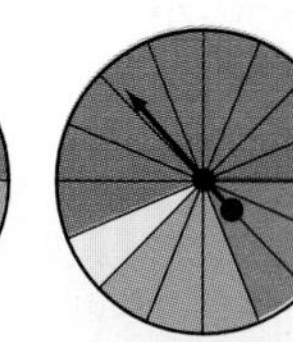
Spinner 2

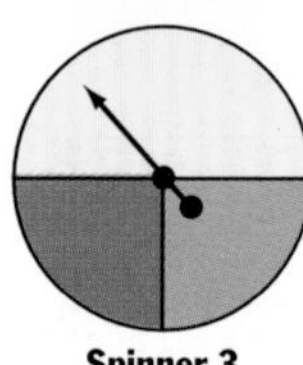
Spinner 3

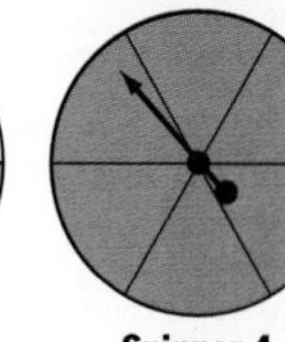
Spinner 4

Work Together

Work with a group to play the game using different spinners.

Each member of the group chooses a different color: red, blue, green, or yellow.

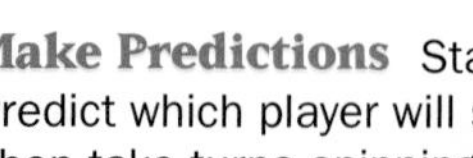

Make Predictions Start with Spinner 1. Predict which player will score the most points. Then take turns spinning until a player gets 5 points.

You will need
- *spinners*

Play other rounds using a different spinner each time. Record the results in a table.

	Red	Blue	Green	Yellow
Spinner 1				
Spinner 2				

▶ Explain the results of each round. How did your prediction compare to the actual results? **See page T17.**

▶ Did each player have the same chance of spinning his or her color in each round? Explain. **See below.**

Check Out the Glossary
possible outcomes
probability
See page 544.

Make Connections

Raman's group used the **possible outcomes** to help them predict the chance of spinning each color.

Spinner 1 is divided into 4 equal parts with all four colors shown. The possible outcomes are red, blue, green, or yellow and the chance of spinning each color is the same.

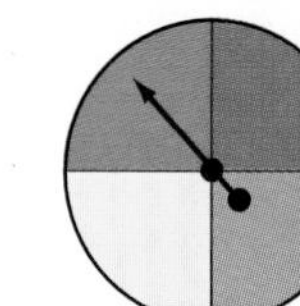

No; possible answer: the chance depends on the size of the section for a color.

Meeting Individual Needs

Early Finishers

Have students play the games again using each of the spinners. Have them compare the results found in the second set of games to those in the first set. Are there differences? What are possible reasons for these differences?

Extra Support

Give students time to work in pairs to name situations where probability is involved. For each situation, suggest students give examples of events that are more likely, less likely, equally likely, certain, and impossible to occur.

Ongoing Assessment

Anecdotal Report Note if students can identify different likelihoods by having them predict and compare the probability of picking a red, a white, and a black marble from a bag that contains 2 red, 4 white, and 8 black marbles.

Follow Up For students who need additional help with probability, assign **Reteach 95.**

For students who are ready for a challenge, assign **Extend 95.**

ssible answer: Choose the spinner that has the greatest
obability of spinning the color that the player wants.

e chance, or likeliness, that something happens is called its **obability.** You can describe the probability using special words.

In Spinner 1, there is an *equally likely* probability of spinning each color.

In Spinner 2, it is *more likely* to spin blue than any other color. It is *less likely* to spin red or green. It is *unlikely* that yellow will appear.

In Spinner 3, it is *impossible* to spin red.

In Spinner 4, it is *certain* that red will appear.

w does knowing the probability of spinning each color lp you to choose the spinner you would like to play with? **e above.**

heck for Understanding

e the words *likely, not likely, impossible,* or *certain* to scribe the probability of spinning:

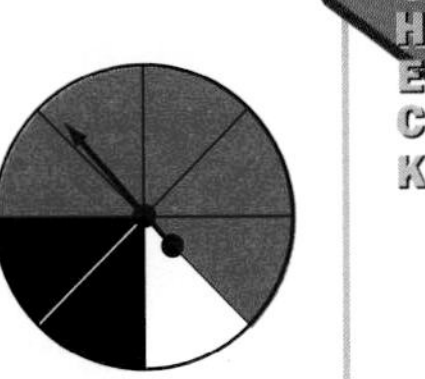

red. **likely** | **2** white. **not likely** | **3** pink. **impossible**

blue. **impossible** | **5** black. **not likely** | **6** purple. **impossible**

CHECK

itical Thinking: Generalize **Give examples how you would use the statement to help you make a cision.** **Answers may vary. Possible answers are given.**

It is very likely that it will rain today. **Take an umbrella to school.**

It is impossible to get to the museum in less than an hour. **Leave home at least one hour before the museum opens.**

It is certain that the hurricane will reach this town by tomorrow. **Buy extra food and water.**

ractice

e the words *more likely, less likely, equally likely, certain, impossible* to describe the probability.

picking a red ball **more likely**

picking a yellow ball **less likely**

picking a striped ball **impossible**

spinning white **less likely**

compare spinning black to *not* spinning black **equally likely**

PRACTICE

tra Practice, page 522

Alternate Teaching Strategy

Materials 4 index cards

Prepare Draw and color a circle on each card—3 with blue circles and 1 red circle.

Show students the index cards.

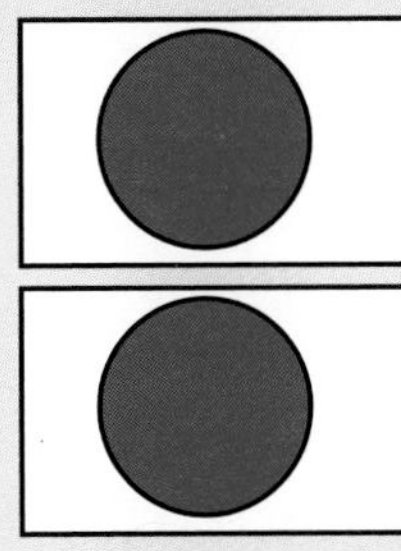

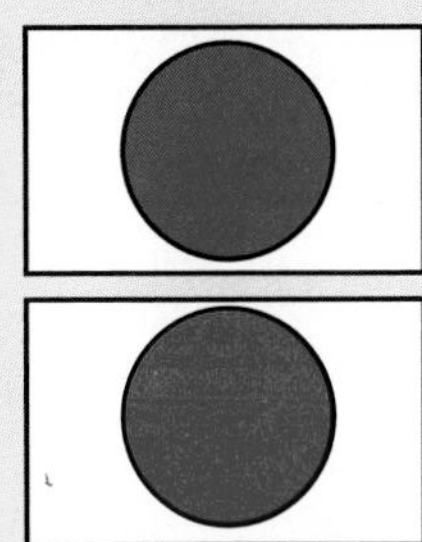

Then ask them the following:

- **If the cards are mixed and placed facedown, what color would you predict to be picked? Explain.** *[Blue; there are more of them.]*
- **The possible outcomes are blue and red. The probability of picking blue is more likely than picking red. Is the probability of picking red more or less likely than picking blue?** *[less likely]*
- **What is an impossible outcome when picking the index cards? a certain outcome?** *[Possible answer: picking green; picking red or blue]*

Have students refer to Student Book page 391 for a list of probability terms and examples. Then repeat the activity with other cards and colors.

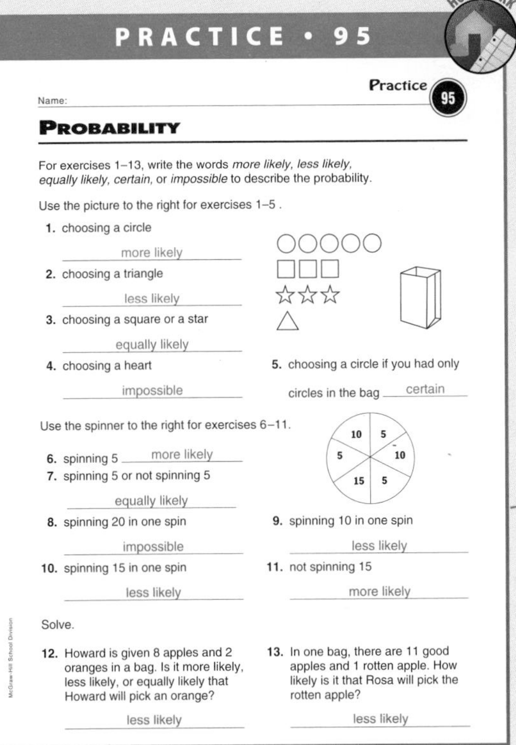

PRACTICE • 95

HOMEWORK

Name: Practice 95

PROBABILITY

For exercises 1–13, write the words *more likely, less likely, equally likely, certain,* or *impossible* to describe the probability.

Use the picture to the right for exercises 1–5 .

1. choosing a circle more likely
2. choosing a triangle less likely
3. choosing a square or a star equally likely
4. choosing a heart impossible
5. choosing a circle if you had only circles in the bag certain

Use the spinner to the right for exercises 6–11.

6. spinning 5 more likely
7. spinning 5 or not spinning 5 equally likely
8. spinning 20 in one spin impossible
9. spinning 10 in one spin less likely
10. spinning 15 in one spin less likely
11. not spinning 15 more likely

Solve.

12. Howard is given 8 apples and 2 oranges in a bag. Is it more likely, less likely, or equally likely that Howard will pick an orange? less likely
13. In one bag, there are 11 good apples and 1 rotten apple. How likely is it that Rosa will pick the rotten apple? less likely

McGraw-Hill School Division

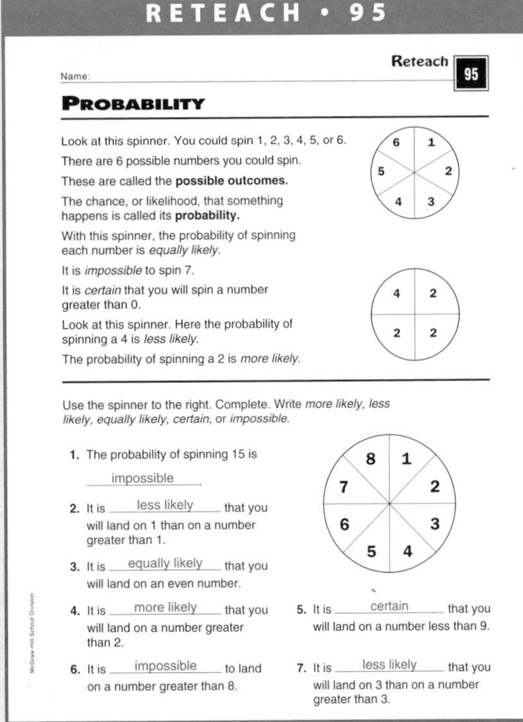

RETEACH • 95

Name: Reteach 95

PROBABILITY

Look at this spinner. You could spin 1, 2, 3, 4, 5, or 6.

There are 6 possible numbers you could spin.

These are called the **possible outcomes.**

The chance, or likelihood, that something happens is called its **probability.**

With this spinner, the probability of spinning each number is *equally likely*.

It is *impossible* to spin 7.

It is *certain* that you will spin a number greater than 0.

Look at this spinner. Here the probability of spinning a 4 is *less likely*.

The probability of spinning a 2 is *more likely*.

Use the spinner to the right. Complete. Write *more likely, less likely, equally likely, certain,* or *impossible.*

1. The probability of spinning 15 is impossible.
2. It is less likely that you will land on 1 than on a number greater than 1.
3. It is equally likely that you will land on an even number.
4. It is more likely that you will land on a number greater than 2.
5. It is certain that you will land on a number less than 9.
6. It is impossible to land on a number greater than 8.
7. It is less likely that you will land on 3 than on a number greater than 3.

McGraw-Hill School Division

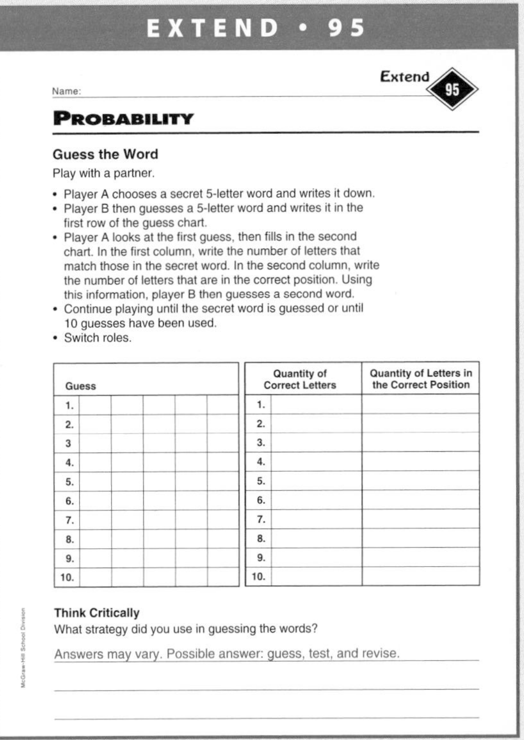

EXTEND • 95

Name: Extend 95

PROBABILITY

Guess the Word

Play with a partner.

- Player A chooses a secret 5-letter word and writes it down.
- Player B then guesses a 5-letter word and writes it in the first row of the guess chart.
- Player A looks at the first guess, then fills in the second chart. In the first column, write the number of letters that match those in the secret word. In the second column, write the number of letters that are in the correct position. Using this information, player B then guesses a second word.
- Continue playing until the secret word is guessed or until 10 guesses have been used.
- Switch roles.

Guess					
1.					
2.					
3					
4.					
5.					
6.					
7.					
8.					
9.					
10.					

	Quantity of Correct Letters	Quantity of Letters in the Correct Position
1.		
2.		
3.		
4.		
5.		
6.		
7.		
8.		
9.		
10.		

Think Critically

What strategy did you use in guessing the words?

Answers may vary. Possible answer: guess, test, and revise.

McGraw-Hill School Division

LESSON 10.9

Fractions and Probability

OBJECTIVE Find the probability of simple events.

RESOURCE REMINDER
Math Center Cards 96
Practice 96, Reteach 96, Extend 96

SKILLS TRACE

GRADE 3	• Explore probability and making predictions using simple experiments. *(Chapter 11)*
GRADE 4	• Use notation to describe the outcomes of an experiment.
GRADE 5	• Explore finding the probability of simple events. *(Chapter 13)*

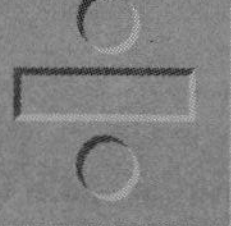

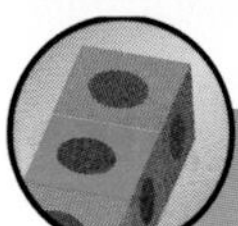

MANIPULATIVE WARM-UP

Cooperative Groups — **Kinesthetic**

OBJECTIVE Explore fractions and probability.

Materials per group: blank spinner (TA 2)

▶ Students divide and number six equal sections of the spinner 1, 2, 3, 2, 4, and 2.

▶ Have them use a fraction to identify the part of the spinner showing sections with 1; with 2; with 3; and with 4. *[$\frac{1}{6}$; $\frac{3}{6}$ or $\frac{1}{2}$; $\frac{1}{6}$; $\frac{1}{6}$]*

▶ Students use *more likely, equally likely,* and *less likely* to describe the probability of spinning a 1; of spinning a 2; of spinning a 3; of spinning a 4. *[Possible answer: less likely; more likely; less likely; less likely]* Discuss how students found their answers.

▶ Extend the activity by having students spin the spinner and compare the outcomes with their predictions.

PROBABILITY CONNECTION

Cooperative Pairs — **Logical/Analytical**

OBJECTIVE Connect fractions to probability.

▶ On the chalkboard write the following fractions:

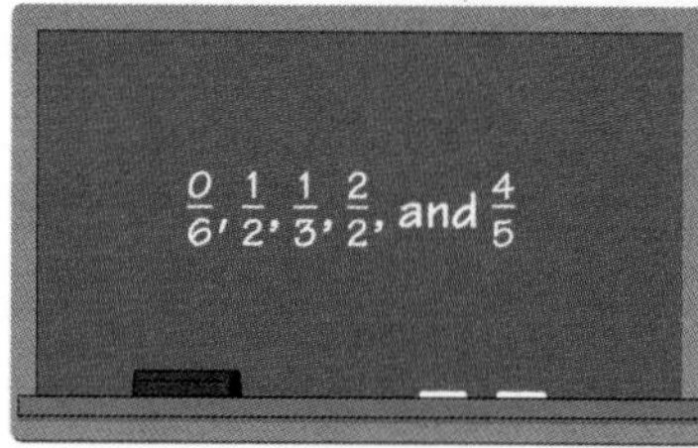

▶ Have students work in pairs to match these fractions with events that are more likely, less likely, equally likely, certain, and impossible to occur.
[$\frac{0}{6}$: impossible; $\frac{1}{3}$: less likely; $\frac{1}{2}$: equally likely; $\frac{4}{5}$: more likely; $\frac{2}{2}$: certain]

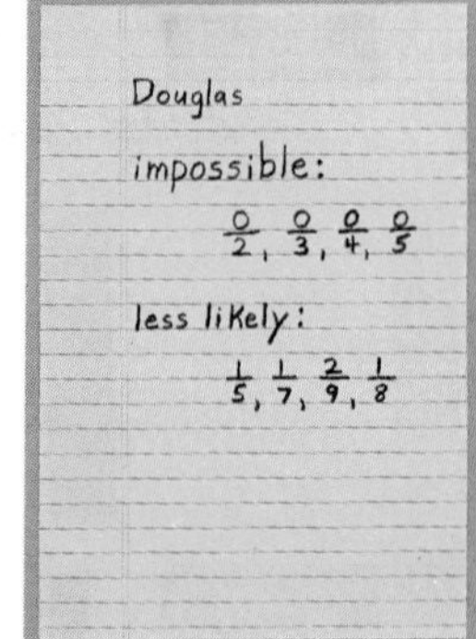

▶ Then have students write their own fractions that could correspond to events that are *more likely, less likely, equally likely, certain,* and *impossible.*

Daily Review

PREVIOUS DAY QUICK REVIEW

Find the likelihood of picking the letter:

1. c in clue *[less likely]*
2. b in by *[equally likely]*
3. o in tool *[more likely]*

FAST FACTS

1. 12 ÷ 3 *[4]*
2. 28 ÷ 4 *[7]*
3. 42 ÷ 7 *[6]*
4. 54 ÷ 9 *[6]*

Problem of the Day • 96

Maria has 6 red beads, 4 yellow beads, and 2 blue beads in a bag. If she picks one bead without looking, what is the probability that she picks a yellow or a blue bead? not a blue bead? *[$\frac{6}{12}$ or $\frac{1}{2}$; $\frac{10}{12}$ or $\frac{5}{6}$]*

TECH LINK

Math Van

MATH VAN

Tool You may wish to use the Probability tool with this lesson.

MATH FORUM

Management Tip I have my students work in pairs to solve probability problems. Working with a partner helps them to read carefully and focus on the desired probability.

Visit our Resource Village at http://www.mhschool.com to see more of the Math Forum.

MATH CENTER

Practice

OBJECTIVE Determine the probability of events.

Materials per student: paper bag, pattern blocks, Math Center Recording Sheet (TA 31 optional)

Students determine the probability of picking a shape from a grab bag. *[**a.** 1:3, **b.** 1:6, **c.** 1:2, **d.** 0:12; Answers may vary. Check students' work.]*

PRACTICE ACTIVITY 96 — MATH CENTER, On Your Own

Number Sense • Grab Bag

YOU NEED
- paper bag
- assorted pattern blocks such as triangles, hexagons, and squares

First, look at the diagram. If all the shapes were in the bag, and you picked one without looking, what would be the probability of choosing each?

a. triangle **b.** hexagon
c. square **d.** circle

Next, pick out some pattern blocks and put them in a bag. Record the shapes you put in. Shake the bag well. Tell the probability of picking each shape. Test your estimates of the probabilities.

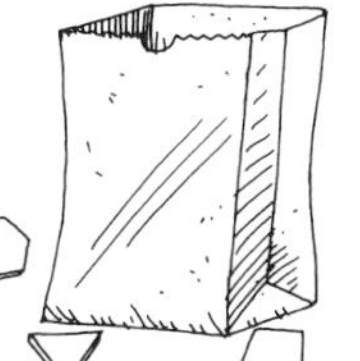

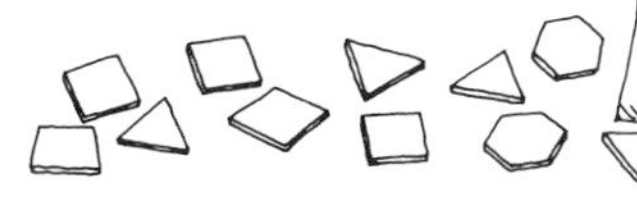

Chapter 10, Lesson 9, pages 392–393 — Probability

Grade Level 4 — McGraw-Hill School Division

NCTM Standards
- ✓ Problem Solving
- Communication
- ✓ Reasoning
- ✓ Connections

Problem Solving

OBJECTIVE Describe sets of number cards that result in various probabilities.

Materials per student: number cards for 0–9 (TA 29), Math Center Recording Sheet (TA 31 optional)

Students write directions for putting a set of number cards into a bag so that there is a given probability of choosing a card with given characteristics. *[Answers may vary. Possible answers: **1.** 3, 6, 9; **2.** 1, 2, 3, 4, 6; **3.** 4, 5, 6, 7, 8, 9; **4.** 1, 2, 3, 4, 5; **5.** 1, 3, 5, 7, 9; **6.** 1, 2, 3, 4, 5, 6, 7, 8]*

PROBLEM-SOLVING ACTIVITY 96 — MATH CENTER, On Your Own

Using Data • Exploring Outcomes

YOU NEED
- number cards (0–9)

You are putting number cards into a bag for someone to pick from. Choose a group of number cards that will give each probability. For example, to get a $\frac{1}{5}$ probability of picking an odd number, you might put the cards shown into the bag. Write down your choices.

1. $\frac{2}{3}$ probability of picking a number less than 7
2. $\frac{3}{5}$ probability of picking an even number
3. $\frac{2}{3}$ probability of picking a number greater than 5
4. $\frac{0}{5}$ chance of picking a 7
5. $\frac{3}{3}$ probability of picking an odd number
6. $\frac{1}{4}$ probability of picking a 3 or a 6

$\frac{1}{5}$ probability of getting an odd number

Chapter 10, Lesson 9, pages 392–393 — Probability

Grade Level 4 — McGraw-Hill School Division

NCTM Standards
- Problem Solving
- ✓ Communication
- ✓ Reasoning
- Connections

Fractions and Probability

OBJECTIVE Find the probability of simple events.

Vocabulary favorable outcomes

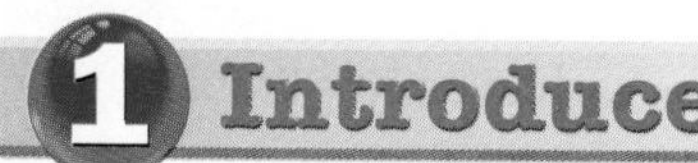

1 Introduce

Present the following problem:

Valerie is playing a game involving a coin and a bag of squares. She can win if she tosses a coin and it lands on heads or if she selects a blue square from a paper bag with 5 blue squares and 1 red square without looking.

Discuss which Valerie should choose, coin or bag, and why. *[Bag since picking blue is more likely; heads is equally likely.]*

2 Teach — *Whole Class*

LEARN Read the introduction and how the probability is found. Stress to students to read carefully to identify all of the favorable outcomes.

Connect the probability to equally likely, more or less likely, certain, and impossible by having students find other probabilities and then use the terms to describe the probabilities. Make sure they understand that they can simplify and use an equivalent fraction to write the probability. Elicit that $\frac{2}{6} = \frac{1}{3}$.

To conclude, ask:

- **Can the probability ever be greater than 1? Explain.** *[No; a certain outcome will have a probability with the numerator equal to the denominator, or 1.]*
- **When is the probability zero?** *[when the outcome is impossible]*

3 Close

Check for Understanding using items 1–5, page 392.

Critical Thinking

For item 5, have students identify outcomes that are certain and impossible. Then have them give other examples of certain and impossible outcomes and how the probabilities are recorded.

PRACTICE

Materials have available: calculators

Students may choose ten exercises from ex. 1–18, and all ex. 19 and 20, and the **Mixed Review.**

- Remind students to read carefully to identify all favorable outcomes, especially for *not*, in ex. 1–18.

Mixed Review/Test Preparation In ex. 1 and 2, students review averages, learned in Chapter 9. Students review the terms *vertices, faces,* and *edges,* in ex. 3–6 from Chapter 9.

Fractions and Probability

LEARN

Have you ever played a game where you need a certain number to win? What if you need to roll a 5 or 6 to win. What is the probability that you will win on your next roll?

Use a fraction to show the probability.

Think: Favorable outcomes: 5, 6
Possible outcomes: 1, 2, 3, 4, 5, 6

$$\textbf{Probability} = \frac{\text{number of favorable outcomes}}{\text{number of possible outcomes}} = \frac{2}{6}$$

The probability of winning is $\frac{2}{6}$.

Check Out the Glossary
favorable outcomes
See page 544.

CHECK

Check for Understanding

What is the probability of:

1 tossing a head? $\frac{1}{2}$

2 picking a white cube? a black cube? $\frac{4}{8}$, or $\frac{1}{2}$; $\frac{2}{8}$, or $\frac{1}{4}$

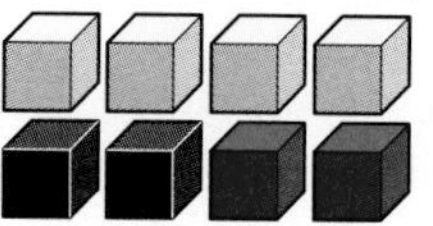

3 picking *W*? *E*? $\frac{1}{9}$; $\frac{4}{9}$

4 picking a number other than 11?

0	1	5	9	11	16	22	9

Critical Thinking: Synthesize **Explain your reasoning.**

5  Tell if you agree or disagree with the following statements:

a. The probability of flipping a coin and getting a head or a tail is $\frac{2}{2}$, or 1.

b. The probability of tossing a 7 on a 1–6 number cube is $\frac{0}{6}$, or 0. See page T17.

Meeting Individual Needs

Early Finishers

Have students write two probability problems using color cubes. They exchange problems and solve.

Extra Support

Students may not record all of the favorable outcomes in the numerator. Have them list all of the favorable outcomes and count them before writing the numerator of the fraction.

Ongoing Assessment

Observation Checklist Determine if students can find the probability of an event. When they write the probability as a fraction, observe if they include all favorable outcomes in the numerator and all possible outcomes in the denominator.

Follow Up Provide students who are having difficulty finding probabilities, with more hands-on practice with probability. Also, assign **Reteach 96.**

For students who would like a challenge, assign **Extend 96.**

9. The spinner with 10 numbers; the probability of spinning a number greater than 5 on the 1–10 spinner is $\frac{5}{10}$, or $\frac{1}{2}$, which is greater than the probability of spinning a number greater than 5 on the 1–6 spinner—$\frac{1}{6}$.

ractice

nd the probability of picking the color from the bag.

black marker $\frac{2}{11}$	2 white marker $\frac{6}{11}$
blue marker $\frac{1}{11}$	4 *not* a green marker $\frac{10}{11}$
purple marker $\frac{0}{11}$	6 *not* a white marker $\frac{5}{11}$

nd the probability of picking the color from the drawer.

one blue sock $\frac{2}{8}$, or $\frac{1}{4}$	8 one green sock $\frac{0}{8}$, or 0
not picking a red sock $\frac{6}{8}$, or $\frac{3}{4}$	10 *not* picking a yellow sock $\frac{8}{8}$, or 1
one white sock $\frac{2}{8}$, or $\frac{1}{4}$	12 one purple sock $\frac{0}{8}$, or 0

nd the probability of picking the color or shape.

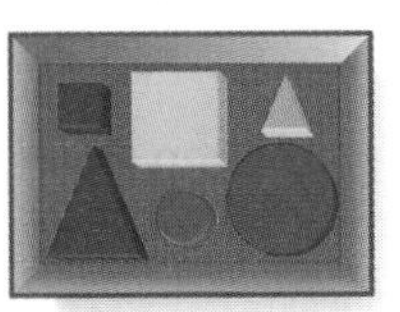

small shape $\frac{3}{6}$, or $\frac{1}{2}$	14 yellow shape $\frac{2}{6}$, or $\frac{1}{3}$
large blue triangle $\frac{1}{6}$	16 small yellow circle $\frac{0}{6}$, or 0
not picking a small shape $\frac{3}{6}$, or $\frac{1}{2}$	18 *not* picking a yellow shape $\frac{4}{6}$, or $\frac{2}{3}$

IXED APPLICATIONS

roblem Solving

Pencil & Paper · Calculator · Mental Math

Earth is about $\frac{3}{10}$ land and $\frac{7}{10}$ water. If a globe ball is thrown to you, what is the probability that your right thumb will land on water? $\frac{7}{10}$

20 **Make a decision** You need a number greater than 5 to win a game. You can spin either a 1–6 spinner or a 1–10 spinner. Which would you choose? Why? See above.

mixed review • test preparation

nd the average.

Number of hot dogs sold in a game: 125, 176, 146, 163, 135 149

2 Number of students in a fourth grade class: 29, 30, 28, 31, 32 30

ll how many vertices, faces, and edges the figure has.

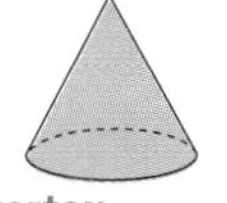

vertex, curved edge, curved face

4 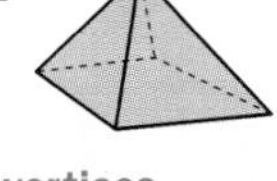

5 vertices, 5 faces, 8 edges

5 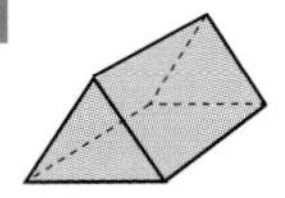

6 vertices, 5 faces, 9 edges

6 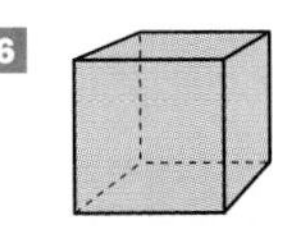

8 vertices, 6 faces, 12 edges

xtra Practice, page 522

Alternate Teaching Strategy

Materials glass jar; 4 marbles—1 red, 1 green, and 2 yellow

Put the marbles in the glass jar. Ask:

- **What fraction shows the red marble out of all the color marbles?** *[$\frac{1}{4}$]*

Tell students that the fraction $\frac{1}{4}$ also shows the probability of picking the red marble. *Probability* is the fraction showing the number of favorable outcomes over the total number of outcomes. The *favorable outcomes* are the desired results.

- **What is the probability of picking green? picking yellow?** *[$\frac{1}{4}$; $\frac{2}{4}$ or $\frac{1}{2}$]*
- **What is the probability of picking red or yellow?** *[$\frac{3}{4}$]*
- **What is the probability of picking not green? What are the favorable outcomes?** *[$\frac{3}{4}$; red or yellow]*

Repeat the activity using other colors. Continue having students identify the favorable outcomes.

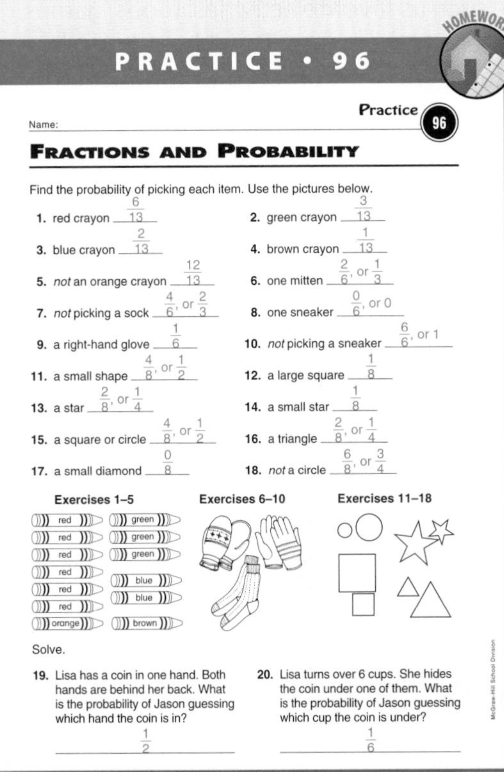

PRACTICE • 96

Practice 96

Name:

Fractions and Probability

Find the probability of picking each item. Use the pictures below.

1. red crayon $\frac{6}{13}$
2. green crayon $\frac{3}{13}$
3. blue crayon $\frac{2}{13}$
4. brown crayon $\frac{1}{13}$
5. *not* an orange crayon $\frac{12}{13}$
6. one mitten $\frac{2}{6}$, or $\frac{1}{3}$
7. *not* picking a sock $\frac{4}{6}$, or $\frac{2}{3}$
8. one sneaker $\frac{0}{6}$, or 0
9. a right-hand glove $\frac{1}{6}$
10. *not* picking a sneaker $\frac{6}{6}$, or 1
11. a small shape $\frac{4}{8}$, or $\frac{1}{2}$
12. a large square $\frac{1}{8}$
13. a star $\frac{2}{8}$, or $\frac{1}{4}$
14. a small star $\frac{1}{8}$
15. a square or circle $\frac{4}{8}$, or $\frac{1}{2}$
16. a triangle $\frac{2}{8}$, or $\frac{1}{4}$
17. a small diamond $\frac{0}{8}$
18. *not* a circle $\frac{6}{8}$, or $\frac{3}{4}$

Exercises 1–5 **Exercises 6–10** **Exercises 11–18**

Solve.

19. Lisa has a coin in one hand. Both hands are behind her back. What is the probability of Jason guessing which hand the coin is in? $\frac{1}{2}$
20. Lisa turns over 6 cups. She hides the coin under one of them. What is the probability of Jason guessing which cup the coin is under? $\frac{1}{6}$

McGraw-Hill School Division

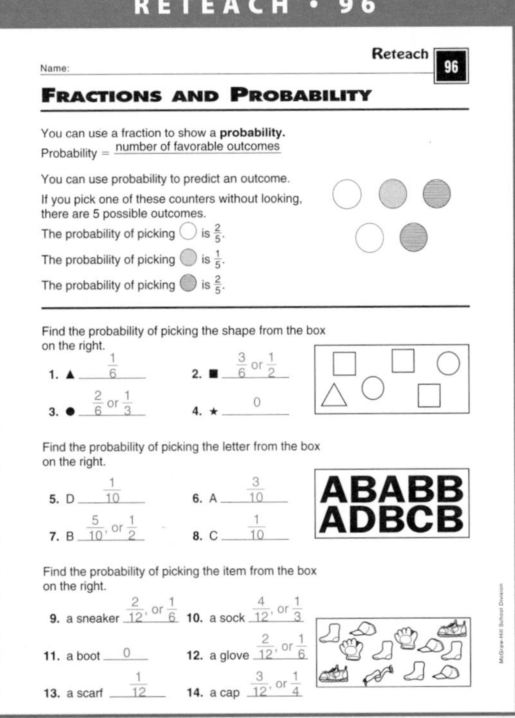

RETEACH • 96

Reteach 96

Name:

Fractions and Probability

You can use a fraction to show a **probability.**

Probability = number of favorable outcomes

You can use probability to predict an outcome.

If you pick one of these counters without looking, there are 5 possible outcomes.

The probability of picking ◯ is $\frac{2}{5}$.

The probability of picking ◯ is $\frac{1}{5}$.

The probability of picking ◯ is $\frac{2}{5}$.

Find the probability of picking the shape from the box on the right.

1. ▲ $\frac{1}{6}$
2. ■ $\frac{3}{6}$ or $\frac{1}{2}$
3. ● $\frac{2}{6}$ or $\frac{1}{3}$
4. ★ 0

Find the probability of picking the letter from the box on the right.

5. D $\frac{1}{10}$
6. A $\frac{3}{10}$
7. B $\frac{5}{10}$, or $\frac{1}{2}$
8. C $\frac{1}{10}$

Find the probability of picking the item from the box on the right.

9. a sneaker $\frac{2}{12}$, or $\frac{1}{6}$
10. a sock $\frac{4}{12}$, or $\frac{1}{3}$
11. a boot 0
12. a glove $\frac{2}{12}$, or $\frac{1}{6}$
13. a scarf $\frac{1}{12}$
14. a cap $\frac{3}{12}$, or $\frac{1}{4}$

McGraw-Hill School Division

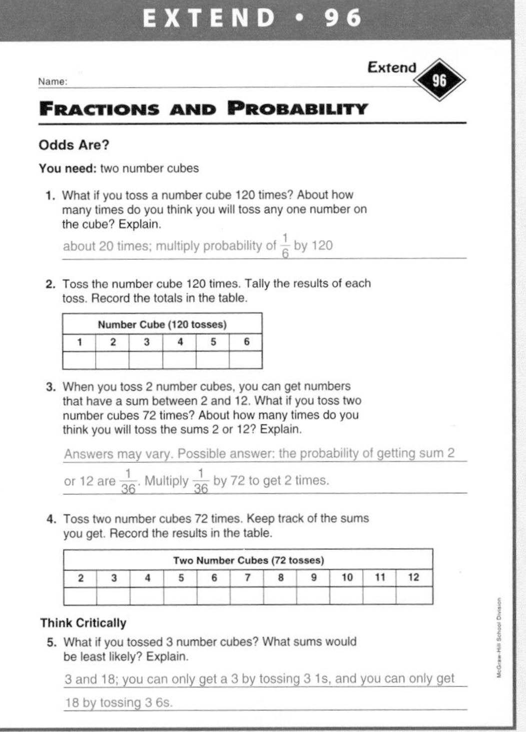

EXTEND • 96

Extend 96

Name:

Fractions and Probability

Odds Are?

You need: two number cubes

1. What if you toss a number cube 120 times? About how many times do you think you will toss any one number on the cube? Explain.

   about 20 times; multiply probability of $\frac{1}{6}$ by 120

2. Toss the number cube 120 times. Tally the results of each toss. Record the totals in the table.

Number Cube (120 tosses)					
1	2	3	4	5	6

3. When you toss 2 number cubes, you can get numbers that have a sum between 2 and 12. What if you toss two number cubes 72 times? About how many times do you think you will toss the sums 2 or 12? Explain.

   Answers may vary. Possible answer: the probability of getting sum 2 or 12 are $\frac{1}{36}$. Multiply $\frac{1}{36}$ by 72 to get 2 times.

4. Toss two number cubes 72 times. Keep track of the sums you get. Record the results in the table.

Two Number Cubes (72 tosses)										
2	3	4	5	6	7	8	9	10	11	12

Think Critically

5. What if you tossed 3 number cubes? What sums would be least likely? Explain.

   3 and 18; you can only get a 3 by tossing 3 1s, and you can only get 18 by tossing 3 6s.

McGraw-Hill School Division

LESSON 10.10

Problem-Solving Strategy: Conduct an Experiment

OBJECTIVE Solve problems by conducting an experiment.

RESOURCE REMINDER
Math Center Cards 97
Practice 97, Reteach 97, Extend 97

SKILLS TRACE

GRADE 3	• Solve problems by conducting an experiment. *(Chapter 11)*
GRADE 4	• Solve problems by conducting an experiment.
GRADE 5	• Solve problems by conducting an experiment. *(Chapter 13)*

LESSON 10.10 RESOURCES

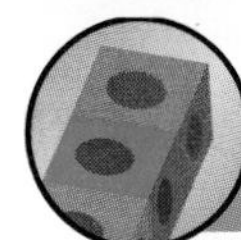

MANIPULATIVE WARM-UP

Cooperative Pairs **Kinesthetic**

OBJECTIVE Explore comparing probabilities and actual outcomes.

Materials per pair: number cube

▶ Have pairs find the probability of tossing an even number. *[$\frac{3}{6}$ or $\frac{1}{2}$]*

▶ Have each pair conduct an experiment by tossing a number cube 10 times. Students should record the number tossed on each roll. Have them identify:

a. the number of even numbers tossed, and
b. the fraction of even numbers out of all the numbers tossed.

▶ Have students comment on how the probability of tossing an even number compares to the fraction found in their experiment.

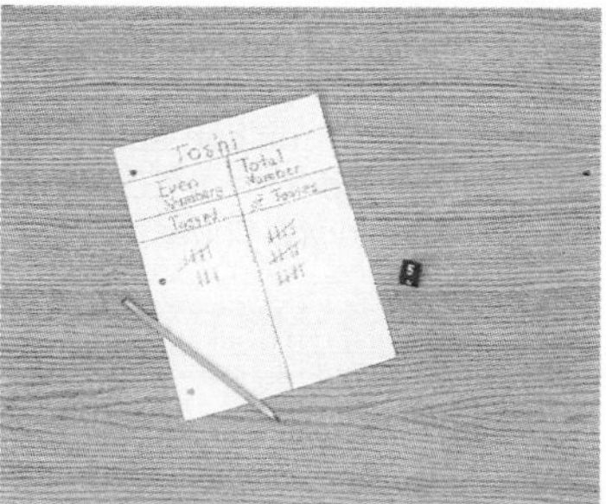

ESL APPROPRIATE

STATISTICS CONNECTION

Cooperative Groups **Auditory/Linguistic**

OBJECTIVE Connect recording data to statistics.

▶ Have each group decide on a topic such as favorite activities, foods, games, sports, or anything that particularly interests the group. They should plan how to survey their classmates about the topic and then proceed to conduct the survey.

▶ Students should show their survey results in a table. Have them write three or more sentences that describe their results and involve fractions. For example, $\frac{6}{17}$ of the students say chess is their favorite game.

▶ Have students comment on any surprises that they found in the results of the surveys.

What's Your Favorite Game?	
Chess	✓✓✓✓✓✓
Checkers	✓✓
Monopoly	✓✓✓✓✓
Scrabble	✓✓✓
Battle Ship	✓

Daily Review

PREVIOUS DAY QUICK REVIEW

Roll a 1–6 number cube. Find the probability.

1. rolling 2 *[$\frac{1}{6}$]*
2. rolling an odd number *[$\frac{3}{6}$ or $\frac{1}{2}$]*
3. not rolling 5 *[$\frac{5}{6}$]*

FAST FACTS

1. 7 × 0 *[0]*
2. 3 × 6 *[18]*
3. 9 × 4 *[36]*
4. 7 × 8 *[56]*

Problem of the Day • 97

There are 2 red cubes, 1 blue cube, and 1 yellow cube in a paper bag. Which color is most likely to be selected in 20 draws if the cube is drawn without looking and returned to the bag after each draw? Conduct an experiment to find out. *[Check students' work.]*

TECH LINK

Math Van

MATH VAN

Tool You may wish to use the Probability tool with this lesson.

MATH FORUM

Management Tip I find it useful to set up work stations for students to perform experiments, working together in small groups.

Visit our Resource Village at http://www.mhschool.com to see more of the Math Forum.

MATH CENTER

Practice

OBJECTIVE Conduct a probability experiment.

Materials per pair: nickel, penny, Math Center Recording Sheet (TA 31 optional)

Students play a game tossing two coins. They score points according to how many heads they tossed. They then discuss whether they think the game is fair or unfair. *[Answers may vary. This game is unfair because the probability of 2 heads is 1 out of 4 combinations, of 1 head is 2 out of 4, and of no heads is 1 out of 4.]*

MATH CENTER
Partners

PRACTICE ACTIVITY 97

Logical Reasoning • Fair or Unfair?

YOU NEED
- a nickel and a penny

- Take turns tossing the two coins and recording whether the coins show 2 heads, 1 head, or no heads. After each toss, record your results by making a tally mark. You each make 25 tosses.
- Player A gets 1 point each time the outcome is 2 heads (on the penny and the nickel). Player B gets 1 point each time the outcome is 1 head. No points are given when there are no heads.
- Do you think this is a fair game? Explain.

Outcomes	Player A Tally	Player B Tally
2 Heads		
1 Head		
No Heads		

McGraw-Hill School Division Grade Level 4

Chapter 10, Lesson 10, pages 394–395 Problem Solving

NCTM Standards
- ✓ Problem Solving
- ✓ Communication
- ✓ Reasoning
- Connections

Problem Solving

OBJECTIVE Solve problems involving spatial reasoning.

Materials per student: Math Center Recording Sheet (TA 31 optional), straightedge, compass or large jar.

Students find the greatest number of pieces into which a pie can be cut using 4 cuts and 5 cuts. *[The greatest number of pieces for 4 cuts is 11 pieces; for 5 cuts is 16 pieces]*

MATH CENTER
On Your Own

PROBLEM-SOLVING ACTIVITY 97

Spatial Reasoning • Any Way You Slice It

YOU NEED
- straightedge ruler
- compass or large jar

- Did you know that you can cut a pie into 7 pieces with just 3 straight cuts? The pieces will not be equal. Draw a circle and use a straightedge to show how you can get 7 pieces with 3 straight cuts. You may cut across the pie in different ways as shown.
- Draw two more circles. What is the greatest number of pie pieces you can make with 4 cuts? with 5 cuts?

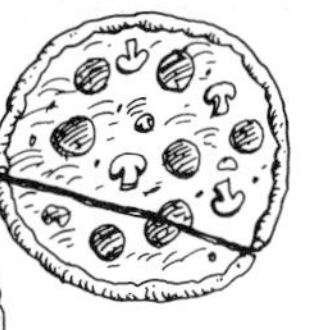

McGraw-Hill School Division Grade Level 4

Chapter 10, Lesson 10, pages 394–395 Problem Solving

NCTM Standards
- ✓ Problem Solving
- Communication
- ✓ Reasoning
- Connections

Problem-Solving Strategy: Conduct an Experiment

OBJECTIVE Solve problems by conducting an experiment.

Materials per pair: two number cubes

1 Introduce

Copy the circle onto the chalkboard.

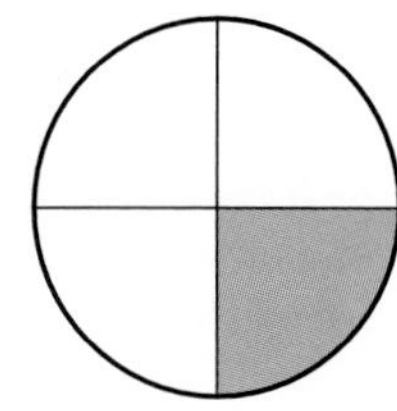

Ask:

- **If the circle represents a spinner, which outcome is more likely: shaded or unshaded?** *[unshaded]*
- **How can you find out the number of times the unshaded part will be the outcome in 10 spins? in 20 spins?** *[Conduct an experiment.]*

2 Teach *Whole Class*

▶ **LEARN** Read the problem on page 394. Ask:

- **What does it mean to conduct an experiment?** *[to try out or test in order to discover or prove something]*
- **How can conducting an experiment help you solve this problem?** *[Use results of experiment to identify and choose the outcome most likely to occur.]*

Review the results of an experiment. Point out that 5 can be obtained by tossing 4 and 1, 1 and 4, 2 and 3, or 3 and 2.

Then have students work with a partner, conduct their own experiment, and compare their results to those in the table. Have students comment on how their results are similar to or different from what they expected.

3 Close

▶ **Check for Understanding** using items 1–2, page 394.

Critical Thinking
Encourage students to conduct an experiment.

▶ **PRACTICE**

Materials have available: calculators

Assign ex. 1–9 as independent work.

- For ex. 3, students may list six possible sitting arrangements and use the list to find the probability.

Algebra: Patterns In ex. 1, finding patterns helps students recognize the relationship between numbers.

Problem-Solving Strategy — Read · Plan · Solve · Look Back

Conduct an Experiment

LEARN

Read **What if you are playing a game where you choose a number. Then you toss two number cubes 60 times. On each toss, you add the numbers that appear. If the sum is the same as the number you chose, you score a point. What number should you choose?**

Sum	Tally	Times Sum Appear
2		0
3	////	4
4	////	4
5	卌	5
6	卌 //	7
7	卌 卌	10
8	卌 卌	10
9	卌 ///	8
10	卌 ///	8
11	///	3
12	/	1

Plan To solve the problem, you can conduct an experiment.

Solve Toss the cubes and record how often the sums appear. A table with the results of one experiment is shown.

In this experiment, you should choose either 7 or 8.

Look Back How can you use probability to help you decide which number to choose? **Possible answer: Find the sum with the greatest probability of appearing, then choose that number.**

CHECK

Check for Understanding

1. **What if** you score a point each time your number does not appear. What number would you choose? Why? **Possible answer: 1; there is no chance that the sum will be 1, so it will never appear.**

Critical Thinking: Synthesize **Explain your reasoning.**

2. Kaitlin and Adam are playing a board game where they toss a 1–6 number cube. To get home first, Kaitlin needs a number greater than 2 to appear six times. Adam needs a number less than 5 to appear six times. What experiment could you do to predict who will win? **See below.**

394 Lesson 10.10 **2. Possible answer: Toss a number cube and see whether six numbers greater than 2 will appear before six numbers less tha**

Meeting Individual Needs

Early Finishers

Have students create a problem that can be solved by conducting an experiment using manipulatives of their choice: number cubes, spinners, coins, etc. Have them conduct the experiment and solve the problem.

Extra Support

Assign roles to students working in pairs to conduct an experiment. Have one student toss the number cubes and call out the sum; have the other student tally and record the sum. Together they analyze the results.

Ongoing Assessment

Observation Checklist Observe if students can perform experiments by noting whether they are able to record the results in an organized way so that they can draw a conclusion from the results.

Follow Up Help students who are having difficulty conducting an experiment to make a table to organize and record the results of their experiments. Assign **Reteach 97.**

For students who understand how to conduct an experiment, assign **Extend 97.**

17 stars; the number of stars in each row is the sum of the number of stars in the revious two rows.

IXED APPLICATIONS

roblem Solving

 whether or not you need to do an experiment. en solve.

ALGEBRA: PATTERNS Kaya's quilt has a star in the first row, 3 stars in the second row, 4 stars in the third, 7 stars in the fourth, and 11 stars in the fifth. How many stars will she have in the eighth row? Explain. **See above.**

There are 28 students playing word scramble. Each student gets 3 minutes to create new words from the word they are given. If students take turns, about how long will the game last? **Possible answer: bout 84 min, or 1 h 24 min**

Jordan, Ryan, and Bonita sit beside each other in a movie theater. What is the chance that the three of them sit in alphabetical order? **Possible answer: Find the probability; $\frac{1}{6}$.**

Randy puts 162 basketball trading cards into plastic holders. Some holders hold 10 cards and some hold 9 cards. If all the holders are filled, how many of each size holder does he have? **8 holders with 9 cards and 9 holders with 10**

What if you flip two coins 10 times. How often will you get two heads? **Possible answer: conduct an experiment; check students' results.**

4. **Students' decisions could be based on test results and averages.**

4 **Make a decision** Mr. Tallchief must send his best math student to the state math contest. If you were Mr. Tallchief, how would you determine who to send? **See above.**

6 Each of two spinners is divided into six equal parts with 3 on each part. If you spin both spinners and add the results 20 times, what sum will appear most often? **6 will always appear.**

8 Each number from 1 to 25 is written on index cards and mixed up. Which is most likely—picking a 1-digit number, a card with the digit 1 on it, or a card with the digit 2 on it? **Picking a card with the digit 1 on it is most likely.**

9 There are 17 red cubes, 54 blue cubes, and 13 yellow cubes. Use mental math to tell how many cubes there are in all. Explain your thinking. **84 cubes in all; possible answer: use the Order and Grouping Properties—(17 + 13) + 54 = 30 + 54 = 84**

tra Practice, page 523

PRACTICE

Alternate Teaching Strategy

Materials per pair: play money—coins

Show students two coins. Ask:

- **What are the possible outcomes if both coins are tossed?** *[2 heads; 2 tails; head and tail]*
- **If the coins are tossed, what outcome would you predict?** *[Possible answer: head and tail]*

Tell students that they are going to conduct an experiment. They work with a partner and toss their coins 20 times. They should record the results after each toss.

Discuss the results of the experiment.

PRACTICE • 97

HOMEWORK

Practice 97

Name:

PROBLEM-SOLVING STRATEGY: CONDUCT AN EXPERIMENT

✔ Read ✔ Plan ✔ Solve ✔ Look Back

Solve using the conduct-an-experiment strategy.

1. Which combinations of heads and tails will come up most often if you toss 2 coins 60 times? Will it be heads/heads, tails/tails, or heads/tails? All should be equally likely. Check students' results.

2. What if you place 1 red, 1 blue, and 2 green crayons in a bag? Then you have a friend take out one crayon, record the color, and put it back. What do you predict will happen if this is done several times? Check your prediction. Green will be picked more often.

3. You have 2 spinners. Each is numbered 4, 5, 6, 7, 10, 11, 14. If you spin both spinners 20 times and find the sum of each spin, which sums are likely to appear most often? 11, 15, 16, 17, 18, 21

4. If you toss 2 number cubes 20 times, how many times might you get multiples of 2 in each sum? How about 3? Make a prediction and check it. 10; about 6 or 7

Solve using any method.

5. Leroy wants to fix up 35 of his toy cars to give away. He paints 21 of them. Half of the remaining cars need new wheels. How many cars need new wheels? 7 cars

6. Leroy promises a day care center that he will help them collect 60 repaired toys. So far he has collected 2 toys each from 27 students. How far along is Leroy in keeping his promise? He is $\frac{9}{10}$ of the way done.

7. Leroy's neighbor gives him 9 boxes of 8 magic markers. He has enough to give 3 markers to each child at the day care center. How many children are there? 24 children

8. A business gives Leroy $1,000 to help with his day care center work. Leroy gives $500 to the day care center and spends $399 on books for the center. How much does he have left? $101

McGraw-Hill School Division

RETEACH • 97

Reteach 97

Name:

PROBLEM-SOLVING STRATEGY: CONDUCT AN EXPERIMENT

✔ Read ✔ Plan ✔ Solve ✔ Look Back

Sometimes you can solve a problem by doing an experiment.

About how many times can you fit the number 5 on a line that is 300 inches long?

Draw a line 3 inches long and write as many 5s as you can.

5 5 5 5 5 5 5 5 5 5 5 5 5 5 5

0 inches 1 2 3

Count the number of 5s that you drew. Since the problem above talks about a line 300 inches long, you can multiply the number of 5s you wrote on a 3-inch line by 100. That will help you predict how many 5s you can fit on a 300-inch line.

Describe an experiment you could do to solve the problem. Possible answers given.

1. How many times can you fit the letter M on a line 1,000 inches long? Write as many Ms as you can on a line 10 inches long and multiply that by 100.

2. How many breaths do you take in 5 minutes? Count number of breaths taken in 1 minute and multiply by 5.

3. If you toss a coin 500 times, how many times will you get tails? Toss a coin 50 times and multiply the result by 10.

4. How many times do you blink in 30 minutes? Count the number of blinks in 1 minute and multiply by 30.

5. If you toss a number cube 100 times, how many times will you toss a 2? Toss a number cube 20 times and multiply by 5.

McGraw-Hill School Division

EXTEND • 97

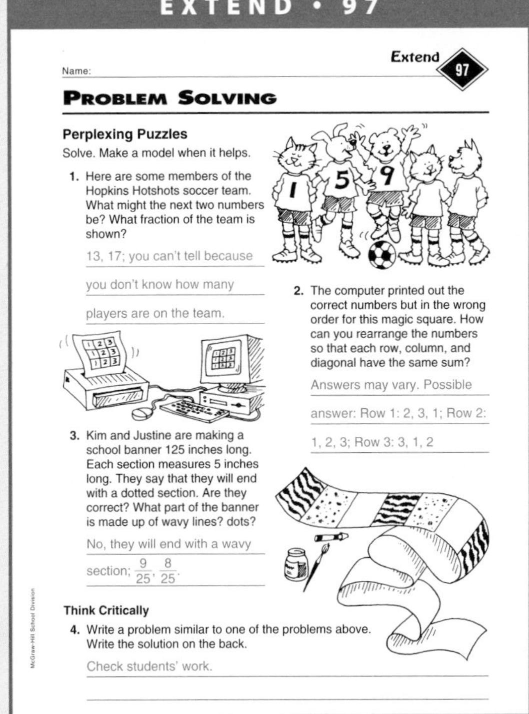
Extend 97

Name:

PROBLEM SOLVING

Perplexing Puzzles

Solve. Make a model when it helps.

1. Here are some members of the Hopkins Hotshots soccer team. What might the next two numbers be? What fraction of the team is shown? 13, 17; you can't tell because you don't know how many players are on the team.

2. The computer printed out the correct numbers but in the wrong order for this magic square. How can you rearrange the numbers so that each row, column, and diagonal have the same sum? Answers may vary. Possible answer: Row 1: 2, 3, 1; Row 2: 1, 2, 3; Row 3: 3, 1, 2

3. Kim and Justine are making a school banner 125 inches long. Each section measures 5 inches long. They say that they will end with a dotted section. Are they correct? What part of the banner is made up of wavy lines? dots? No, they will end with a wavy section; $\frac{9}{25}$, $\frac{8}{25}$.

Think Critically

4. Write a problem similar to one of the problems above. Write the solution on the back. Check students' work.

McGraw-Hill School Division

EXPLORE ACTIVITY

Predict and Experiment

OBJECTIVE Explore comparing theoretical versus experimental probability.

RESOURCE REMINDER
Math Center Cards 98
Practice 98, Reteach 98, Extend 98

SKILLS TRACE

GRADE 3	• Explore probability and making predictions using simple experiments. *(Chapter 11)*
GRADE 4	• Explore comparing theoretical versus experimental probability.
GRADE 5	• Explore comparing theoretical versus experimental probability. *(Chapter 13)*

MANIPULATIVE WARM-UP

Cooperative Pairs — Logical/Analytical

OBJECTIVE Review finding a fraction of a number using mental math.

Materials per pair: 3 index cards; blank spinner (TA 2)

Prepare Divide the spinner into 6 equal sections labeled 1 through 6.

▶ Write three problems, each on a separate index card.

▶ Have students use a 1–6 spinner to find the denominator and then write their own numerator and number. Pairs exchange problems and solve.

▶ Discuss the methods students used for determining which numerator and number to use. For example, "I chose a number that was a multiple of the denominator."

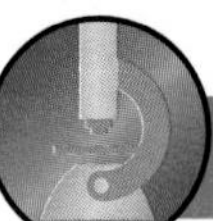

SCIENCE CONNECTION

Cooperative Groups — Kinesthetic

OBJECTIVE Connect designing an experiment to science.

Materials per group: paper bag; blue, red, and yellow connecting cubes

▶ Tell students that they are going to design their own experiment using the cubes and paper bag. They may select the number and color of cubes.

▶ After they decide on the experiment, have them work together to make a prediction about the outcome of their experiment. Then they conduct the experiment and record their results.

▶ Discuss the different types of experiments, how they were carried out, and the results of the experiments.

Daily Review

PREVIOUS DAY QUICK REVIEW

Use a 0–9 spinner. Find the probability of spinning:

1. zero *[$\frac{1}{10}$]*
2. not a zero *[$\frac{9}{10}$]*
3. an odd number *[$\frac{5}{10}$]*

FAST FACTS

1. 2 × 7 *[14]*
2. 5 × 4 *[20]*
3. 8 × 8 *[64]*
4. 7 × 9 *[63]*

Problem of the Day • 98

Jenny tosses a 1–6 number cube 60 times. How many times do you predict she will toss a 1 or a 2? an odd number? *[20 times; 30 times]*

TECH LINK

Math Van

MATH VAN

Tool You may wish to use the Probability tool with this lesson.

MATH FORUM

Combination Classes My students enjoy working with a partner to conduct experiments. They alternate roles performing the experiments and recording results.

Visit our Resource Village at http://www.mhschool.com to see more of the Math Forum.

MATH CENTER

Practice

OBJECTIVE Compare theoretical probability with experimental probability.

Materials per student: paper bag, connecting cubes—5 yellow, 5 red, 5 blue; Math Center Recording Sheet (TA 31 optional)

Students explore the probability of picking a cube out of a bag. If time allows have students repeat this experiment for 60 picks. *[Prediction: $\frac{5}{15}$, or $\frac{1}{3}$, or $\frac{1}{3}$ of 30 times is 10 times that yellow should be picked; actual results may vary; for 60 trials, the prediction should be 20 times.]*

PRACTICE ACTIVITY 98

MATH CENTER
On Your Own

Manipulatives • Half and Half?

YOU NEED
- paper bag
- 15 connecting cubes (5 red, 5 blue, 5 yellow)

- Make a table like the one shown. List up to 30 trials.
- Put the cubes into a paper bag. Predict how many times out of 30 you will pick yellow.
- Experiment by picking a cube, recording its color, and putting it back. Do this 30 times. Compare your results with your prediction.
- If you have time, do up to 60 trials. Did the results change?

Trial	Yellow	Blue	Red
1			
2			

Grade Level 4 McGraw-Hill School Division

Chapter 10, Lesson 11, pages 396–397 Probability

NCTM Standards
- ✓ Problem Solving
- ✓ Communication
- ✓ Reasoning
- Connections

Problem Solving

OBJECTIVE Predict the outcome of an experiment.

Materials per student: 9 index cards, paper bag, Math Center Recording Sheet (TA 31 optional)

Students use the words of a sentence as the basis for a simple probability experiment. Before they carry out the experiment, they predict its outcome. *[3 letters: $\frac{4}{9}$, 20; 4 letters: $\frac{2}{9}$, 10; 5 letters: $\frac{3}{9}$ or $\frac{1}{3}$, 15; **1.** $\frac{1}{9}$; $\frac{2}{9}$; **2.** 3 letters, because there are more 3-letter words than 5 letter words; **3.** Possible answer: No, but the results were close. If I did the experiment many more times, I would get closer.]*

PROBLEM-SOLVING ACTIVITY 98

MATH CENTER
On Your Own

Logical Reasoning • Word Predictions

YOU NEED
- 9 blank index cards
- paper bag

The quick brown fox jumps over the lazy dog.

Write each word in the sentence above on an index card. Count the number of letters in each word. Think about picking one of the cards out of the bag. Fill in the Probability column in the table.

Word Length	Probability	Prediction (out of 45 tries)
3 letters		
4 letters		
5 letters		

1. What is the probability of picking the word *dog*? of picking a 4-letter word?
2. At the end of the experiment, are you more likely to have picked more 3-letter words or 5-letter words?
3. Do the experiment by picking a card out of the bag 45 times. Do the results agree with your prediction? Explain.

Grade Level 4 McGraw-Hill School Division

Chapter 10, Lesson 11, pages 396–397 Probability

NCTM Standards
- ✓ Problem Solving
- ✓ Communication
- ✓ Reasoning
- ✓ Connections

EXPLORE ACTIVITY

Predict and Experiment

OBJECTIVE Explore comparing theoretical versus experimental probability.

Materials per pair: coin or two-color counter

1 Introduce

Ask students to name games they play that involve tossing a number cube. Ask:

- **What is the probability of tossing a 6 using a 1–6 number cube?** *[$\frac{1}{6}$]*
- **How can you conduct an experiment to compare the probability to an actual outcome?** *[Toss the number cube.]*

2 Teach *Cooperative Pairs*

LEARN Discuss situations in which students make predictions and the methods they use to make them.

Work Together Have students make a prediction about the results and then conduct the experiment. Discuss the predictions and the results.

MAKE CONNECTIONS

On the chalkboard, write the fraction that shows the number of heads out of the total number of flips found by the whole class. Compare this fraction to the fractional probability that gives the number of favorable outcomes out of the number of possible outcomes. The two fractions should be close in value.

Point out that using probability to make a prediction is like finding a fraction of a number. If the coin is flipped 30 times, find $\frac{1}{2}$ of 30 to predict 15 heads. Tell the class that if the coin is flipped many times, the fraction showing total heads out of total flips will get closer to $\frac{1}{2}$.

Discuss whether any pairs had exactly 15 heads and how this compares with what students might expect from the experiment. *[Possible answer: Number of heads should be close to 15 but unlikely that it will be exactly 15.]*

3 Close

Check for Understanding using items 1 and 2, page 397.

CRITICAL THINKING
Have students describe how they could make the game fair. *[Make cubes in bag 3 green, 3 blue, and 3 yellow.]*

PRACTICE
Assign ex. 1–9 as independent work.

- Remind students to pay attention to *not* and *never* when listing favorable outcomes in ex. 2–3.

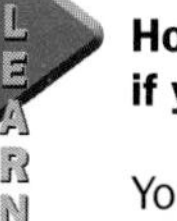

EXPLORE ACTIVITY • PROBABILITY

Predict and Experiment

LEARN

How many times will you get a head if you flip a coin 30 times?

You can solve this problem in two ways: by finding the probability of getting a head or by conducting an experiment.

Work Together
Work with a partner.

You will need
- *coin or two-color counter*

First, predict the number of heads in 30 flips.

Next, experiment by flipping a coin 30 times. Record your results in a table (use *H* for heads and *T* for tails). Compare your prediction with your results.

Continue until you have flipped the coin 60 times. Compare your prediction with the new results.

▶ How many times do you predict you will get heads after 80 flips? Why?

Make Connections
You can use probability to predict the outcome.

Think: Favorable outcome: H
Possible outcomes: H, T

$$\text{Probability} = \frac{\text{number of favorable outcomes}}{\text{number of possible outcomes}} = \frac{1}{2}$$

The probability of getting a head on each flip is $\frac{1}{2}$. Since the probability is $\frac{1}{2}$, predict that 1 out of every 2 flips will be a head.

If the coin is flipped 30 times, then you would predict that a head will appear 15 times.

▶ A coin is tossed 100 times. Is it reasonable to predict that heads will appear 89 times? Why or why not? **Possible answer: No; in 100 flips, a coin is expected to come up heads 50 times, so 89 times is unreasonable.**

Meeting Individual Needs

Early Finishers

Have students repeat the experiment on page 396 and compare their previous results. Numbers should be close but different. Discuss any differences in results and possible reasons for these differences.

Extra Support

Before students try the experiment with 30 flips, have them do the experiment with fewer total flips. Suggest they try the experiment with a total of 2 flips, 10 flips, and then 20 flips.

ESL APPROPRIATE

Ongoing Assessment

Observation Checklist Observe if students can make predictions by having them predict the number of tails they would expect in 50 tosses of a fair coin; 100 tosses. *[25 tails; 50 tails]*

Follow Up For students who need additional help, assign **Reteach 98.**

Challenge able students to create and conduct more difficult experiments. For example, toss two coins 20 times and predict the number of times two heads occur. *[probability of 2 heads = $\frac{1}{4}$; prediction—5 times]* Assign **Extend 98.**

No; possible answer: the probability of choosing green is $\frac{7}{10}$, so it is reasonable to predict that green will be chosen 7 times by each player, so there is a greater chance of picking green.

heck for Understanding

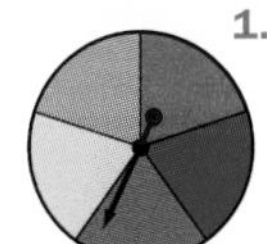

If you spin the spinner 50 times, is it reasonable to predict that you will spin red 10 times? Explain.

1. Yes; the probability of spinning red is $\frac{1}{5}$, so red would be expected to appear 10 times.

itical Thinking: Generalize **Explain your reasoning.**

Suppose you have a bag with 7 green, 1 blue, and 2 yellow cubes. Each player chooses a different color and tries to pick that color cube from the bag to score a point. Each player has 10 tries. Is this game fair? See above.

Possible answer: Yes; in 50 tosses, a quarter is expected to come up heads about 25 times.

ractice

e the spinner for problems 1–4. Write *true* or *false*. plain your reasoning.

7. Possible answer: No; in 30 rolls, a cube is expected to come up 2 about 5 times.

It is reasonable to predict that the spinner will land on red 6 out of 24 times. True; the probability of landing on red is $\frac{2}{8}$, and $\frac{2}{8}$ of 24 is 6 times.

The probability of *not* landing on white is $\frac{1}{4}$. False; the probability is $\frac{6}{8}$, or $\frac{3}{4}$.

8. Possible answer: Yes; in 30 rolls, a cube is expected to come up greater than 3 about 15 times.

You can never expect the spinner to land on green. True; the probability of getting green is 0.

4 You always expect the spinner to land on red, blue, black, or white. True; the probability of landing on any of these colors is 1.

A paper bag contains 25 cubes of one color, 10 cubes of another color, and 5 cubes of a third color. This chart shows the outcomes of 40 picks. Predict what is in the paper bag. Possible answer: 25 blue cubes, 10 green cubes, and 5 red cubes

Red	𝍸 II
Blue	𝍸 𝍸 𝍸 𝍸 I
Green	𝍸 𝍸 II

Suppose you toss a quarter 50 times. Is it reasonable to predict that it will land on heads at least 25 times? Explain. See above.

7 Suppose you roll a 1–6 number cube 30 times. Is it reasonable to predict that you will roll the number 2 at least 15 times? Explain. See above.

Suppose you roll a 1–6 number cube 30 more times. Is it reasonable to predict that you will roll a number greater than 3 at least 15 times? Explain. See above.

9 Pete has predicted that heads will appear 40 times if he flips a coin 80 times. How can he use this to predict the number of tails that will appear? Explain. See below.

Possible answer: There are only two possible outcomes, so if heads appear 40 times, then tails will appear the other 40 times.

tra Practice, page 523

Alternate Teaching Strategy

Materials six number cubes

Divide students into six small groups. Ask:

- **What is the probability of tossing a 2?** *[$\frac{1}{6}$]*
- **How many times do you think that you will toss a 2 in 60 tosses of the number cube?** *[Possible answer: 10 times]*

Tell students that they can use probability to predict the number of times that they will toss a 2 by finding the fraction of the number of tosses. The fraction they use is given by the probability. To predict the number of times a 2 will be tossed in 60 tosses find $\frac{1}{6}$ of 60. Predict 10 times.

Have groups toss their cubes 10 times and record their results. Pool the results of each group and discuss how the outcomes of the experiments compare with predictions for different combinations of numbers.

PRACTICE • 98

HOMEWORK

Name: Practice 98

Predict and Experiment

Use the spinner for problems 1–6. Write *true* or *false*. Explain your reasoning.

The probability of

1. landing on a shaded section is $\frac{2}{10}$. True; 2 out of 10 sections are shaded.
2. not landing on a shaded section is $\frac{2}{10}$. False; 8 out of 10 sections are not shaded.
3. not landing on white is $\frac{1}{5}$. False; it is $\frac{8}{10}$ or $\frac{4}{5}$.
4. landing on any of 3 designs is $\frac{3}{5}$. True; $\frac{6}{10} = \frac{3}{5}$.
5. landing on a red section is 0. True; there are no red sections.
6. landing on dots or stripes is $\frac{3}{5}$. False; $\frac{4}{10} = \frac{2}{5}$.

Use a number cube for problems 7–10. Explain your reasoning.

7. Predict the number of times a 4 will come up if you toss the number cube 30 times. About 5 times; the 4 can come up $\frac{1}{6}$ of the 30 times tossed.
8. What if you double the number of cube tosses from 30 to 60? How often might 4 come up? About 10 times; doubling the number of tosses doubles the results.
9. Is it reasonable to predict that you will toss a 6 on the number cube 2 out of 12 times? Yes; the probability of tossing a 6 is $\frac{1}{6}$, and $\frac{1}{6}$ of 12 is 2.
10. Can you predict exactly how many times 4 will come up when you toss a number cube? Why? No; we can only predict what probably will happen.

McGraw-Hill School Division

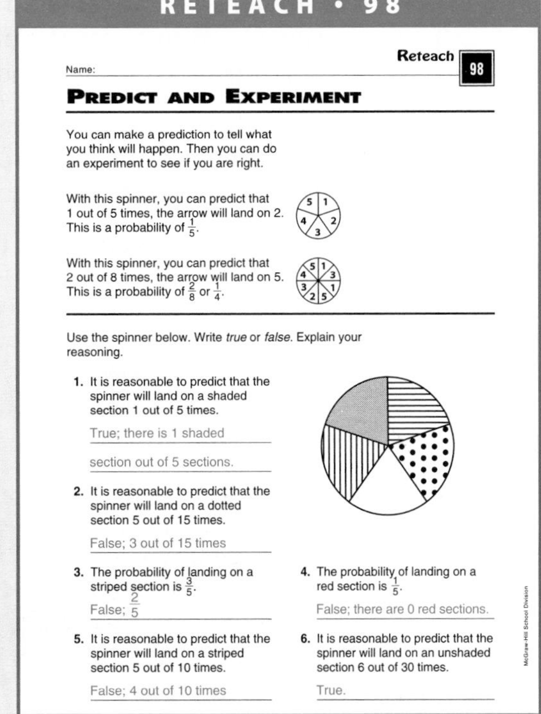

RETEACH • 98

Name: Reteach 98

Predict and Experiment

You can make a prediction to tell what you think will happen. Then you can do an experiment to see if you are right.

With this spinner, you can predict that 1 out of 5 times, the arrow will land on 2. This is a probability of $\frac{1}{5}$.

With this spinner, you can predict that 2 out of 8 times, the arrow will land on 5. This is a probability of $\frac{2}{8}$ or $\frac{1}{4}$.

Use the spinner below. Write *true* or *false*. Explain your reasoning.

1. It is reasonable to predict that the spinner will land on a shaded section 1 out of 5 times. True; there is 1 shaded section out of 5 sections.
2. It is reasonable to predict that the spinner will land on a dotted section 5 out of 15 times. False; 3 out of 15 times
3. The probability of landing on a striped section is $\frac{3}{5}$. False; $\frac{2}{5}$
4. The probability of landing on a red section is $\frac{1}{5}$. False; there are 0 red sections.
5. It is reasonable to predict that the spinner will land on a striped section 5 out of 10 times. False; 4 out of 10 times
6. It is reasonable to predict that the spinner will land on an unshaded section 6 out of 30 times. True.

McGraw-Hill School Division

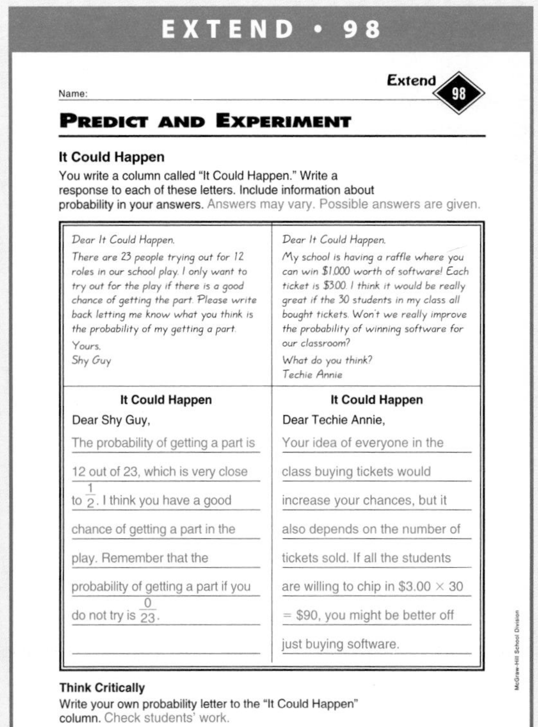

EXTEND • 98

Name: Extend 98

Predict and Experiment

It Could Happen

You write a column called "It Could Happen." Write a response to each of these letters. Include information about probability in your answers. Answers may vary. Possible answers are given.

Dear It Could Happen,
There are 23 people trying out for 12 roles in our school play. I only want to try out for the play if there is a good chance of getting the part. Please write back letting me know what you think is the probability of my getting a part.
Yours,
Shy Guy

Dear It Could Happen,
My school is having a raffle where you can win $1,000 worth of software! Each ticket is $3.00. I think it would be really great if the 30 students in my class all bought tickets. Won't we really improve the probability of winning software for our classroom?
What do you think?
Techie Annie

It Could Happen

Dear Shy Guy,

The probability of getting a part is 12 out of 23, which is very close to $\frac{1}{2}$. I think you have a good chance of getting a part in the play. Remember that the probability of getting a part if you do not try is $\frac{0}{23}$.

It Could Happen

Dear Techie Annie,

Your idea of everyone in the class buying tickets would increase your chances, but it also depends on the number of tickets sold. If all the students are willing to chip in $3.00 × 30 = $90, you might be better off just buying software.

Think Critically

Write your own probability letter to the "It Could Happen" column. Check students' work.

McGraw-Hill School Division

LESSON 10.12

Problem Solvers at Work

OBJECTIVE Solve and write multistep problems.

RESOURCE REMINDER
Math Center Cards 99
Practice 99, Reteach 99, Extend 99

SKILLS TRACE

GRADE 3	• Formulate and solve problems involving multisteps. *(Chapter 7)*
GRADE 4	• Formulate and solve problems involving multisteps.
GRADE 5	• Formulate and solve problems involving multisteps. *(Chapter 13)*

LESSON 10.12 RESOURCES

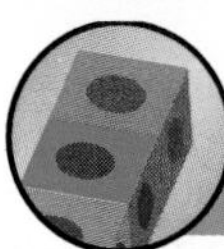

MANIPULATIVE WARM-UP

Cooperative Pairs — Visual/Spatial

OBJECTIVE Review using directions to find an object.

Materials per pair: 1 index card

▶ Students work with a partner to write a list of directions for a classmate to follow from a starting position in the classroom to an ending position. They may create a goal of the search such as a prize.

▶ Students write a list of directions to tell starting position and orientation, distances to travel, and turns to make until the search ends. They can record the directions on an index card.

▶ Pairs exchange cards and use the directions to make their search.

▶ Discuss directions that were particularly useful.

Directions Around the Classroom

Begin at the door. Face windows.
Proceed 4 steps. Turn left. Go 10 steps.
Turn right. Take 4 hops. You're here!

CONSUMER CONNECTION

Cooperative Pairs — Logical/Analytical

OBJECTIVE Connect solving multistep problems to consumer problems.

Materials per pair: 4 index cards

▶ Have students work together to write a problem that can be solved by finding the sum of two amounts of money. The sum should be less than $25. Have them record the problem on an index card.

▶ Then have them write and record related problems that can be solved by finding the difference, then the product, and then the quotient of two amounts. Each answer should be less than $25.

▶ Pairs exchange cards and solve the problems.

Daily Review

PREVIOUS DAY QUICK REVIEW

Toss a coin. Predict the number of times heads occur in:

1. 10 tosses *[5]*
2. 24 tosses *[12]*
3. 30 tosses *[15]*

FAST FACTS

1. 5 ÷ 1 *[5]*
2. 24 ÷ 3 *[8]*
3. 45 ÷ 9 *[5]*
4. 56 ÷ 7 *[8]*

Problem of the Day • 99

Jenny, Susan, Rosa, and Megan sat together for lunch on the same side of a picnic table. Jenny sat between Rosa and Susan. Rosa sat between Megan and Jenny. Which of the two girls sat on the ends? *[Megan and Susan]*

TECH LINK

Math Van

MATH VAN

Aid You may wish to use the Electronic Teacher Aid with this lesson.

MATH FORUM

Cultural Diversity My students enjoy telling stories about word games that they play with their families in which points are assigned for each letter.

Visit our Resource Village at http://www.mhschool.com to see more of the Math Forum.

MATH CENTER

Practice

OBJECTIVE Solve multistep problems.

Materials per student: Math Center Recording Sheet (TA 31 optional)

Students solve multistep problems about costs of computers. *[Answers may vary. Possible answer: **1.** The Thomsons will pay less money if they make 12 payments of $95. **2.** Martin needs 15 more months of saving $30 a month. If that's too long then Martin should consider buying it now and making monthly payments.]*

PRACTICE ACTIVITY 99 — MATH CENTER, On Your Own

Decision Making • By the Month

1. The Thomsons are thinking of buying a computer for $1,595. They can pay $500 and make 12 monthly payments of $95, or they can make 24 monthly payments of $70. What do you think they should do? Explain.
2. To save for a $600 computer, Martin puts aside $30 a month. He already has saved $150. How many more months does he have to go? If he needs the computer as soon as possible, what might he do?

McGraw-Hill School Division — Grade Level 4

Chapter 10, Lesson 12, pages 398–401 — Problem Solving

NCTM Standards

- ✓ Problem Solving
- ✓ Communication
- ✓ Reasoning
- Connections

Problem Solving

OBJECTIVE Solve a visual/spatial problem.

Materials per student: paper, ruler, scissors, Math Center Recording Sheet (TA 31 optional)

Students find how identical squares are placed in sequence to make a specific pattern. *[in order, first to last: D, E, F, G, C, B, A]*

PROBLEM-SOLVING ACTIVITY 99 — MATH CENTER, On Your Own

Spatial Reasoning • Eight Squares

YOU NEED: paper, ruler, scissors

Eight equal-sized squares are placed one on top of another as shown in the picture. The middle square was the last square to be placed. Figure out in what order the other 7 squares were placed so that they end up in the arrangement shown. Cut out 8 squares if it helps you find the solution to the problem.

A D H E B F C G

McGraw-Hill School Division — Grade Level 4

Chapter 10, Lesson 12, pages 398–401 — Problem Solving

NCTM Standards

- ✓ Problem Solving
- ✓ Communication
- ✓ Reasoning
- Connections

Problem Solvers at Work

OBJECTIVE Solve and formulate problems.

Materials have available: calculators; computer probability program and computer graphing program (optional)

1 Introduce

Present this problem:

There are 12 marbles in a box. One half of the marbles are blue, $\frac{1}{4}$ are clear, and $\frac{1}{4}$ are green. If Renzo picks all of the clear marbles and all of the green marbles, how many marbles does he pick?

Discuss different ways that the problem can be solved. *[Possible answers: Find the fraction of each color and then add to find the total or add the fractions and then find the fraction of the marbles that are clear and blue.]* Then have student solve the problem. *[6 marbles]*

2 Teach — *Whole Class*

PART 1 SOLVE MULTISTEP PROBLEMS

LEARN Encourage students to use counters, marbles, or squares of colored paper to make models to help solve the problems. Suggest that they draw diagrams to record their results. They may also want to use a table to keep track of their data.

After students have completed items 2–4, discuss what they had to find to solve each problem. Have them compare strategies and steps and explain their reasoning for ex. 4.

After students complete item 5, have them compare possible strategies that could be used to solve, such as Guess, Test, and Revise and Make a table. Discuss the different steps students must use to solve the problem with each strategy.

READING ARITHMETIC WRITING **Make Predictions** Item 6 is an enhanced problem in that students must use the available data to make a prediction about the most likely outcome. It will allow you to assess their understanding of the probability term *most likely outcome* as well as determine whether they can make reasonable predictions using a set of data. Elicit that groups can conduct an experiment to make or test their predictions.

Problem Solvers at Work

Read | Plan | Solve | Look Back

Part 1 Solve Multistep Problems

LEARN

Rainy-day recess can be fun when you play games you make up yourself. In this game, there are 18 beads in a bag. Of the beads in the bag, $\frac{1}{2}$ are red, $\frac{1}{3}$ are blue, and $\frac{1}{6}$ are yellow. What is the probability of choosing a red bead in a draw?

1. Possible answer: how many of each color bead are in the bag and the points for each color

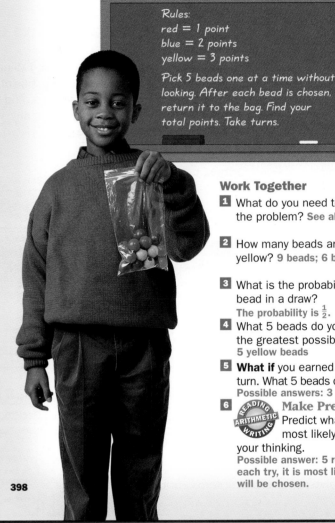

Rules:
red = 1 point
blue = 2 points
yellow = 3 points
Pick 5 beads one at a time without looking. After each bead is chosen, return it to the bag. Find your total points. Take turns.

Work Together

1. What do you need to know to solve the problem? **See above.**
2. How many beads are red? blue? yellow? **9 beads; 6 beads; 3 beads**
3. What is the probability of choosing a rec bead in a draw? **The probability is $\frac{1}{2}$.**
4. What 5 beads do you have to pick to ge the greatest possible score? **5 yellow beads**
5. **What if** you earned 12 points on your turn. What 5 beads could you have choser **Possible answers: 3 yellow, 1 blue, 1 red; 2 yellow,**
6. READING ARITHMETIC WRITING **Make Predictions** Predict what 5 beads you are most likely to pick. Explain your thinking. **Possible answer: 5 red beads since, on each try, it is most likely that a red bead will be chosen.**

398

Meeting Individual Needs

Extra Support

Ask students having difficulty solving multistep problems, to read each part of the problem carefully to decide how it affects the question.

Gifted And Talented

Have students who want an additional challenge write a multistep problem that involves finding the fraction of a number. Have them exchange and solve each others' problems.

Ongoing Assessment

Observation Checklist Note if students can solve problems involving mixed applications and strategies by observing if they are able to identify, organize, and solve the various steps in a multistep problem.

Follow Up Ask students who are having difficulty to list the information that is needed. Then have them write each step needed to find the information. Next students should rewrite the steps in order. Assign **Reteach 99.**

For students who understand, assign **Extend 99.**

rt 2 Write and Share Problems

ry used the game on page 398 to te his own problem.

Describe the steps that you would use to solve Gary's problem. See below.

Solve Gary's problem. See below.

Write a problem about the game on page 398 that can be solved in more than one step. For problems 8–11, see Teacher's Edition.

Explain the steps you would use to solve your problem, then solve it.

Trade problems. Solve at least three problems written by your classmates.

What was the most interesting problem that you solved? Why?

STUDENT TO STUDENT
CHECK
What color would you most likely not get? Why?

Gary Jones
Elephant's Fork Elementary School
Suffolk, VA

6. Possible answer: Find the number of beads of each color and choose the color that the fewest beads have.

7. $\frac{1}{2}$ of 18 = 9, $\frac{1}{3}$ of 18 = 6, and $\frac{1}{6}$ of 18 = 3, so yellow is the color that most likely will not be chosen.

Turn the page for Practice Strategies.

Part 2 Write and Share Problems

Check Discuss Gary's problem. When possible have different groups suggest alternate steps and stategies that could be used to solve the problem.

For item 10, have students select which steps/methods they prefer or think are simplest and explain why.

For items 11 and 12, encourage students to discuss the problems they solved and their reasons why a problem was most interesting.

3 Close

Before students write their own problem for item 8, discuss different strategies that can be used to make up a multistep problem about the game. Encourage a wide variety of problems by suggesting that some problems may require an experiment to solve, some may focus on predictions and outcomes, and some may refer to results after a round of the game has been completed.

Practice See pages 400–401.

PART 3 PRACTICE STRATEGIES

Materials have available: calculators

Students have the option of choosing any five problems from ex. 1–8, and any two problems from ex. 9–12. They may choose to do more problems if they wish. Have students describe how they solved their problems.

- For ex. 1, students will have to realize that $\frac{1}{10}$ of the students got a C. Then they can find the fraction of a number to solve. It may be helpful to suggest that they draw a diagram to find the missing fraction.
- For ex. 4, students may use the problem-solving strategy, Interpret the Remainder, to solve.
- Students should conduct an experiment to solve ex. 2. Have students who choose this exercise compare their results.
- For ex. 9, have students explain their choices. Encourage them to plan a balanced and nutritious meal.

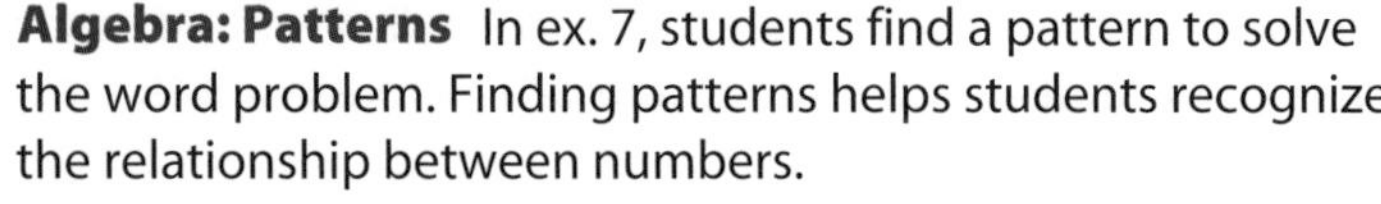

Algebra: Patterns In ex. 7, students find a pattern to solve the word problem. Finding patterns helps students recognize the relationship between numbers.

At the Computer If computers are not available, have 10 groups of students toss a coin 20 times. Then have them combine their results to find the number of heads in 200 tosses. For an alternate experiment, have students try tossing two coins at once. Make predictions for getting two heads and run the program for different numbers of tosses. Ask:

- **What probability did you use? What pattern do you see between the number of tosses and your prediction?** *[Possible answer: $\frac{1}{4}$; the more tosses, the closer the prediction is to the actual results.]*

Math Van Students may use the Graph tool to record the experiments.

4. 146 ÷ 15 = 9 R11, so he needs at least 10 crates.
6. Possible answer: She can underestimate the total—$3 + $2 + $2 = $7—to find that she does not have enough money, since the actual cost will be more than the estimate.

PRACTICE

Menu Explanations may vary.

Choose five problems and solve them. Explain your methods.

1 Of the 20 students in Mr. Mario's class, $\frac{3}{10}$ got an A in math, $\frac{6}{10}$ got a B, and the rest got a C. How many students got a C in math?
2 students

2 Hector wrote his first and last name as many times as he could in 2 minutes. Predict how many times he wrote it.
See below.

3 The Gordon twins rode their bikes for 45 minutes. Then, they played Clue for $2\frac{1}{2}$ hours. They finished playing at 7:30 P.M. What time did they begin riding?
4:15 P.M.

4 Paco works at the Fresh Fruit Packaging Company. He must put 146 oranges into crates that hold 15 oranges each. What is the least number of crates Paco will need to pack all of these oranges?
See above.

5 Mandy wants to call her cousin in London, England, at 7:00 P.M. London is 8 hours ahead. If the time on her watch is 8:30 A.M., how much longer should she wait before making the call? **$2\frac{1}{2}$ h**

6 Taylor has $7.00. A hamburger costs $3.95, a milk shake costs $2.75, and an apple pie costs $2.50. Explain how she can use estimation to find out if she has enough money to buy all three.
See above.

7 ALGEBRA: PATTERNS Gail's goal is to jog for 45 min each day. She jogs 10 min on the first day, 15 min on the second day, and 20 min on the third day. In how many more days will she reach her goal if she continues this pattern? How many days will it take in all?
5 more days; 8 days

8 **Logical reasoning** In a survey, 147 people saw Disney's *The Hunchback of Notre Dame* and 167 people saw *Harriet the Spy.* If 23 people saw both movies, how many people saw only *Harriet the Spy*? How many saw only *The Hunchback*...
144 people; 124 people

2. Possible answer: Students might divide the time it took to write the name once into two minutes; accept any reasonable answers.

Meeting Individual Needs

Early Finishers

Have pairs of students try Practice ex. 2. Have them predict how many times they can write their own names in two minutes. Then they can test their predictions. One student keeps time while the other writes.

Common Error

Students often forget to plan for all the steps when solving a multistep problem. Have them review the information and the question after each step.

Language Support

Pair these students with English-speaking students. Remind them that they can use the pictures to help identify vocabulary in the word problems on page 400.

ESL APPROPRIATE

ıoose two problems and solve them. Explanations may vary.
xplain your methods.

Food	Price
Chicken	$1.29 each pound
Hamburgers	$2.39 each pound
Potatoes	$0.69 each pound
Apples	$1.29 each pound
Lettuce (head)	$1.39 each
Peas	$0.99 each 10-oz bag
Milk (1 qt)	$1.49
Frozen yogurt ($\frac{1}{2}$ gal)	$3.99

Make a decision You have $20 to buy food to make a lunch for four. Use the chart to make a shopping list for your lunch. **Students' ıswers should reflect the chart's data.**

Make a decision You and three friends are planning a dinner. You will each contribute $7 to pay for dinner. Plan a dinner and estimate the cost. Do you have enough money? **Students' answers should reflect the chart's data.**

a. Make a table or chart showing all the possible products that you can get from multiplying the results of rolling two 1–6 number cubes.
b. Experiment to find the product of two cubes in each of 40 tosses. Record your results.
c. Use a graph to show the results.
d. Compare your graph to your table. **Check students' graphs and table.**

At the Computer You can use graphing and probability programs to conduct experiments that would otherwise take a very long time to do. **Check students' work.**

- Predict how many times you will get a head if you toss a coin 200 times. **Possible answer: 100 times**
- Run the program so that the computer does the experiment. How close were your predictions?
- Predict how many times you will get a head if you toss a coin 500 times. What probability did you use? **Possible answer: 250 times; $\frac{1}{2}$**
- Run the program again for 500 tosses. How close was your prediction this time?

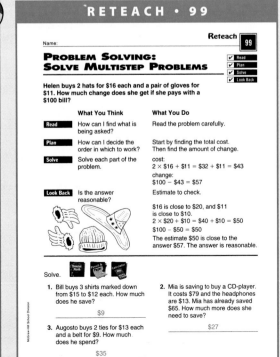

ıtra Practice, page 523

Alternate Teaching Strategy

Materials per pair; ruler, connecting cubes, index cards

Have students work with partners. Have them look at the opening problem on page 398. Each pair should write the value of each color on a separate index card. Then make three piles of cubes to model the situation in the opening problem.

Pairs can use their piles to answer questions 1–5. Then use them to conduct an experiment to test their prediction in question 6.

Students may use the cubes to answer problems 6–10 as needed.

PRACTICE • 99

HOMEWORK

Name: Practice 99

PROBLEM SOLVING: SOLVE MULTISTEP PROBLEMS

✔ Read ✔ Plan ✔ Solve ✔ Look Back

Solve.

1. The fourth grade has a bake sale. They sell chocolate chip cookies for $2 a bag. If the ingredients cost $22 and the students sell 40 bags, how much do they make on chocolate chip cookies? $58
2. The fourth grade sells 30 bags of brownies and 20 bags of oatmeal cookies. There are 3 brownies in a bag and 4 oatmeal cookies in a bag. How many brownies and oatmeal cookies are sold in all? 170 brownies and oatmeal cookies
3. The students bought 4 cases of 30 cartons of milk. If they sold 80 cartons, how many cases are left? $1\frac{1}{3}$ cases
4. Ten students brought 1 bottle of soda, and 3 students brought 2 bottles of soda. Aki brought the rest. If there were 19 bottles of soda in all, how many did Aki bring? 3 bottles

Solve using any method. 

5. Six students out of 18 in a class sing in the chorus after school. What fraction of the class sings in the chorus? $\frac{1}{3}$ of the class
6. One sixth of the students play in a baseball league after school. If there are 24 students in the class, how many play baseball? 4 students
7. Tino and Bernie ride their bicycles for 5 miles every day after school. About how many miles do they ride in one month? about 150 miles
8. Mary plays basketball for 2 hours after school. What fraction of one whole day does she spend playing basketball? $\frac{1}{12}$ of the day

McGraw-Hill School Division

RETEACH • 99

Name: Reteach 99

PROBLEM SOLVING: SOLVE MULTISTEP PROBLEMS

✔ Read ✔ Plan ✔ Solve ✔ Look Back

Helen buys 2 hats for $16 each and a pair of gloves for $11. How much change does she get if she pays with a $100 bill?

	What You Think	What You Do
Read	How can I find what is being asked?	Read the problem carefully.
Plan	How can I decide the order in which to work?	Start by finding the total cost. Then find the amount of change.
Solve	Solve each part of the problem.	cost: $2 \times \$16 + \$11 = \$32 + \$11 = \$43$ change: $\$100 - \$43 = \$57$
Look Back	Is the answer reasonable?	Estimate to check. $16 is close to $20, and $11 is close to $10. $2 \times \$20 + \$10 = \$40 + \$10 = \$50$ $\$100 - \$50 = \$50$ The estimate $50 is close to the answer $57. The answer is reasonable.

Solve.

1. Bill buys 3 shirts marked down from $15 to $12 each. How much does he save? $9
2. Mia is saving to buy a CD-player. It costs $79 and the headphones are $13. Mia has already saved $65. How much more does she need to save? $27
3. Augosto buys 2 ties for $13 each and a belt for $9. How much does he spend? $35

McGraw-Hill School Division

EXTEND • 99

Name: Extend 99

PROBLEM SOLVING

Guess the Number!

Play with a partner.

- Player A chooses a secret 5-digit number with no repeating digits.
- Player B then guesses a 5-digit number and writes it in the first row of the guess chart.
- Player A looks at the first guess, then fills in the second chart. In the first column, write how many numbers match those in the secret number. In the second column, write how many numbers are in the correct position. Using this information, player B then guesses a second number.
- Continue playing until the secret number is guessed or until 10 guesses have been used.
- Switch roles.

Guess					
1.					
2.					
3.					
4.					
5.					
6.					
7.					
8.					
9.					
10.					

	Quantity of Correct Letters	Quantity of Letters in the Correct Position
1.		
2.		
3.		
4.		
5.		
6.		
7.		
8.		
9.		
10.		

Think Critically

Is it easier to figure out a 5-digit number or a 5-letter word?

Answers may vary. Possible answer: Numbers; there are fewer choices because there are only 10 digits, but there are 26 letters.

McGraw-Hill School Division

CHAPTER REVIEW

PURPOSE Review and assess concepts, skills, and strategies that students have learned in this chapter.

Materials per student: calculator (optional)

Chapter Objectives

10A Read and write fractions and mixed numbers
10B Compare and order fractions and find equivalent fractions
10C Find the fraction of a number
10D Find the probability of an event
10E Solve problems, including those that involve fractions, probability, and conducting an experiment

Using the Chapter Review

The **Chapter Review** can be used as a review, practice test, or chapter test.

Think Critically Students' explanations for ex. 36 will indicate whether they understand the steps involved in finding a fraction of a number.

Language and Mathematics

Complete the sentence. Use a word in the chart. (pages 368–397)

Vocabulary
simplest form
numerator
equivalent
mixed number
denominator

1 You can write $\frac{4}{6}$ in ■ as $\frac{2}{3}$. simplest form

2 $\frac{4}{8}$ and $\frac{3}{6}$ are ■ fractions. equivalent

3 5 is the ■ in the fraction $\frac{5}{10}$. numerator

4 $3\frac{1}{2}$ is a ■. mixed number

Concepts and Skills

Name the part that is white. (page 368)

5 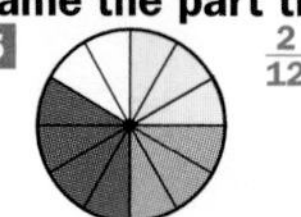 $\frac{2}{12}$, or $\frac{1}{6}$

6 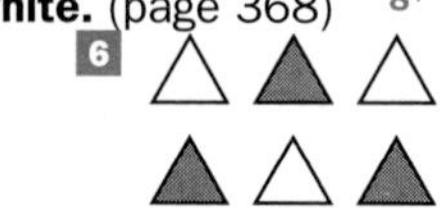 $\frac{4}{8}$, or $\frac{1}{2}$

7 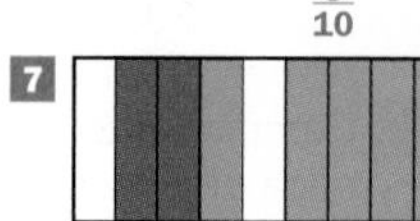 $\frac{3}{10}$

Write the letter of the equivalent fraction. (page 376)

8 $\frac{4}{5}$ b — **a.** $\frac{4}{10}$ **b.** $\frac{8}{10}$ **c.** $\frac{12}{16}$ **d.** $\frac{2}{10}$

9 $\frac{9}{12}$ d — **a.** $\frac{4}{8}$ **b.** $\frac{3}{9}$ **c.** $\frac{1}{4}$ **d.** $\frac{6}{8}$

Write in order from least to greatest. (page 382)

10 $\frac{1}{2}, \frac{1}{4}, \frac{1}{3}$ $\frac{1}{4}, \frac{1}{3}, \frac{1}{2}$

11 $\frac{3}{8}, \frac{1}{8}, \frac{5}{8}$ $\frac{1}{8}, \frac{3}{8}, \frac{5}{8}$

12 $\frac{3}{4}, \frac{1}{3}, \frac{5}{6}$ $\frac{1}{3}, \frac{3}{4}, \frac{5}{6}$

13 $\frac{1}{2}, \frac{7}{8}, \frac{3}{4}$ $\frac{1}{2}, \frac{3}{4}$

14 $\frac{1}{12}, \frac{5}{6}, \frac{2}{3}$ $\frac{1}{12}, \frac{2}{3}, \frac{5}{6}$

15 $\frac{3}{8}, \frac{1}{4}, \frac{3}{4}$ $\frac{1}{4}, \frac{3}{8}, \frac{3}{4}$

16 $\frac{1}{2}, \frac{3}{10}, \frac{1}{5}$ $\frac{1}{5}, \frac{3}{10}, \frac{1}{2}$

17 $\frac{1}{4}, \frac{2}{3}, \frac{11}{12}$ $\frac{1}{4}, \frac{2}{3}, \frac{11}{12}$

Write in order from greatest to least. (page 382)

18 $\frac{1}{3}, \frac{5}{8}, \frac{1}{2}$ $\frac{5}{8}, \frac{1}{2}, \frac{1}{3}$

19 $\frac{3}{10}, \frac{1}{5}, \frac{3}{5}$ $\frac{3}{5}, \frac{3}{10}, \frac{1}{5}$

20 $\frac{7}{8}, \frac{1}{3}, \frac{3}{4}$ $\frac{7}{8}, \frac{3}{4}, \frac{1}{3}$

21 $\frac{1}{3}, \frac{3}{6}, \frac{2}{3}$ $\frac{2}{3}, \frac{3}{6}$

Write the fraction as a whole number or mixed number. (page 384)

22 $\frac{17}{2}$ $8\frac{1}{2}$ **23** $\frac{15}{5}$ 3 **24** $\frac{56}{8}$ 7 **25** $\frac{26}{4}$ $6\frac{1}{2}$ **26** $\frac{14}{3}$ $4\frac{2}{3}$

27 $\frac{55}{6}$ $9\frac{1}{6}$ **28** $\frac{39}{9}$ $4\frac{1}{3}$ **29** $\frac{40}{7}$ $5\frac{5}{7}$ **30** $\frac{13}{2}$ $6\frac{1}{2}$ **31** $\frac{48}{5}$ $9\frac{3}{5}$

32 If you flip a coin 50 times, how many times would you predict that you will get heads? (page 396) Possible answer: 25 times

Reinforcement and Remediation

CHAPTER OBJECTIVES	CHAPTER REVIEW ITEMS	STUDENT BOOK PAGES		TEACHER'S EDITION PAGES		TEACHER RESOURCES
		Lessons	Midchapter Review	Activities	Alternate Teaching Strategy	Reteach
10A	1, 3–7, 22–31	368–373, 384–385	386	367A, 371A, 383A	371, 373, 385	88–89, 94
10B	2, 8–21	376–383	386	375A, 379A, 381C	379, 381, 383	91–93
10C	36–37	374–375	386	373A	375	90
10D	32–35	390–393, 396–397		389A, 391A, 395A	391, 393, 397	95–96, 98
10E	38–40	394–395, 398–401		393A, 397A	395, 401	97, 99

33 If you roll a 1–6 number cube 30 times, how many times would you predict that you will roll a 3 or 4? (page 396) **Possible answer: 10 times**

34 What is the probability of landing on red? (page 392) **$\frac{2}{12}$, or $\frac{1}{6}$**

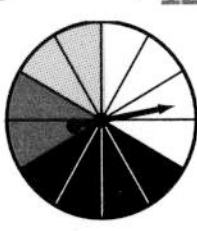

35 What is the probability of picking a white cube? (page 392) **$\frac{2}{6}$, or $\frac{1}{3}$**

Think critically. (page 374)

36 Analyze. Explain what mistake was made, and then correct it.
$8 \div 2 = 4$ should be $8 \times 2 = 16$.

$\frac{2}{4}$ of 32 $32 \div 4 = 8$
$8 \div 2 = 4$
So $\frac{2}{4}$ of $32 = 4$.

(pages 394, 398)

37 Dave put together $\frac{1}{4}$ of his 16 model airplanes. Bryan put together $\frac{1}{3}$ of his 15 model airplanes. Who needs to put together more model airplanes? How many?
Dave; 12 model airplanes

38 How long will it take you to write the name of your city and state 25 times? Make an estimate. Conduct an experiment to find the actual time. **Answers may vary according to the length of names and time it takes to write.**

39 Gus and Peter are almost finished playing Scrabble. There are only 8 tiles left to pick from. Gus needs the letter *E* to make a word. He sees that 10 *E*s have been used on the board. If there are 12 *E*s in all and Peter does not have any, what is the probability that Gus will pick an *E* next from the pile? Explain your reasoning. **See below.**

40 Jesse visits people in a nursing home for 30 minutes each week. She spends $\frac{1}{3}$ of the time with her favorite resident, Mr. Washington. If she visits the nursing home 40 weeks each year, how many minutes does she spend with Mr. Washington each year? **400 min**

39. There are 12 *E*s in all and 10 have been used, so of the 8 tiles that are left, 2 are *E*s—Gus has a 2 out of 8 chance, or $\frac{2}{8}$ probability, of getting an *E*.

CHAPTER TEST

PURPOSE Assess the concepts, skills, and strategies students have learned in this chapter.

Materials per student: calculator (optional)

Chapter Objectives

- **10A** Read and write fractions and mixed numbers
- **10B** Compare and order fractions and find equivalent fractions
- **10C** Find the fraction of a number
- **10D** Find the probability of an event
- **10E** Solve problems, including those that involve fractions, probability, and conducting an experiment

Using the Chapter Test

The **Chapter Test** can be used as a practice test, a chapter test, or as an additional review. The **Performance Assessment** on Student Book page 405 provides an alternate means of assessing students' understanding of fractions and probability.

Assessment Resources

Test Masters

The Testing Program Blackline Masters provide three forms of the Chapter Test to assess students' understanding of the chapter concepts, skills, and strategies. Form C uses a free-response format. Forms A and B use a multiple-choice format.

Computer Test Generator

The Computer Test Generator supplies abundant multiple-choice and free-response test items, which you may use to generate tests and practice work sheets tailored to the needs of your class.

Teacher's Assessment Resources

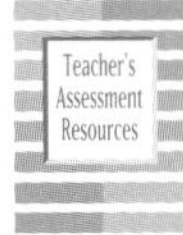

Teacher's Assessment Resources provide resources for alternate assessment. It includes guidelines for Building a Portfolio, page 6, and the Holistic Scoring Guide, page 27.

chapter test

Name the fraction or mixed number for the part that is white.

1 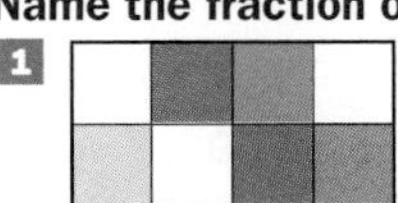 **$\frac{3}{8}$**

2 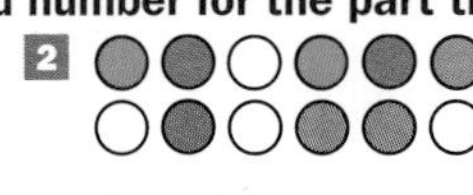 **$\frac{4}{12}$, or $\frac{1}{3}$**

3  **$2\frac{2}{6}$, or $2\frac{1}{3}$**

Write an equivalent fraction. **Answers may vary. Possible answers are given.**

4 $\frac{3}{8}$ **$\frac{6}{16}$**
5 $\frac{12}{18}$ **$\frac{2}{3}$**
6 $\frac{1}{3}$ **$\frac{9}{27}$**

Write in order from least to greatest.

7 $\frac{3}{7}, \frac{1}{7}, \frac{4}{7}$ **$\frac{1}{7}, \frac{3}{7}, \frac{4}{7}$**
8 $\frac{5}{6}, \frac{3}{4}, \frac{2}{3}$ **$\frac{2}{3}, \frac{3}{4}, \frac{5}{6}$**
9 $\frac{2}{3}, \frac{1}{4}, \frac{1}{8}$ **$\frac{1}{8}, \frac{1}{4}, \frac{2}{3}$**

Find the fraction of the number.

10 $\frac{1}{8}$ of 24 **3**
11 $\frac{3}{5}$ of 45 **27**
12 $\frac{2}{3}$ of 36 **24**
13 $\frac{3}{7}$ of 21 **9**

Write the fraction as a whole number or a mixed number.

14 $\frac{15}{7}$ **$2\frac{1}{7}$**
15 $\frac{32}{4}$ **8**
16 $\frac{71}{8}$ **$8\frac{7}{8}$**
17 $\frac{62}{9}$ **$6\frac{8}{9}$**
18 $\frac{42}{6}$ **7**

Use the spinner for ex. 19–21.

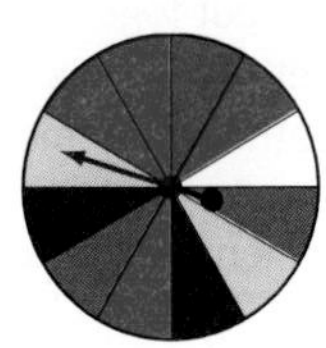

19 What is the probability of landing on blue? **$\frac{3}{12}$, or $\frac{1}{4}$**

20 Which color do you have the greatest probability of landing on? What is the probability? **red; $\frac{4}{12}$, or $\frac{1}{3}$**

21 What is the probability of landing on either black or white? **$\frac{3}{12}$, or $\frac{1}{4}$**

Solve. Conduct an experiment to solve if necessary.

22 Toyland sells 8 different brands of in-line skates. Last week, the store had 12 pairs of each brand. If the store sells 8 pairs, how many pairs will be left? **88 pairs; do not need to conduct an experiment.**

23 Of the 20 fourth graders, $\frac{1}{4}$ walk to school. Of the 24 third graders, $\frac{1}{6}$ walk to school. How many children walk to school from both grades combined? **9 students; do not need to conduct an experiment.**

24 If you close your eyes and point to a word in a textbook 20 times, how many times will you point to a word with the letter *e* in it? **Answers may vary. Need to conduct an experiment to solve this problem.**

25 Brad said the alphabet backwards. About how long did it take him? **Answers may vary. Need to conduct an experiment to solve this problem.**

Test Correlation		
CHAPTER OBJECTIVES	TEST ITEMS	TEXT PAGES
10A	1–6, 14–18	368–373, 384–385
10B	7–9	376–383
10C	10–13	374–375
10D	19–21	390–393, 396–397
10E	22–25	394–395, 398–401

e Teacher's Assessment Resources for samples of student work.

/hat Did You Learn? Check students' work.

ny used the counters to model that f the counters were red. Then, he w this diagram to prove that the ction $\frac{2}{3}$ is equivalent to $\frac{4}{6}$.

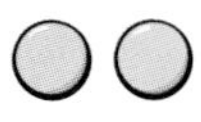

$\frac{4}{6} = \frac{2}{3}$

Use counters to model two different fractions that are equivalent to $\frac{2}{3}$.

Draw a diagram of your models to prove that they are equivalent to $\frac{2}{3}$. You may need to explain your diagrams.

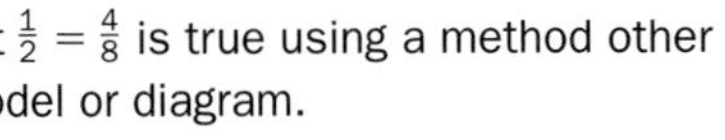

Prove that $\frac{1}{2} = \frac{4}{8}$ is true using a method other than a model or diagram.

A Good Answer

- names two different fractions that are equivalent to $\frac{2}{3}$
- shows a diagram with words or labels to prove that the fractions are equivalent
- uses a method other than a model or diagram to prove that $\frac{1}{2} = \frac{4}{8}$

folio You may want to place your work in your portfolio.

What Do You Think?

See Teacher's Edition.

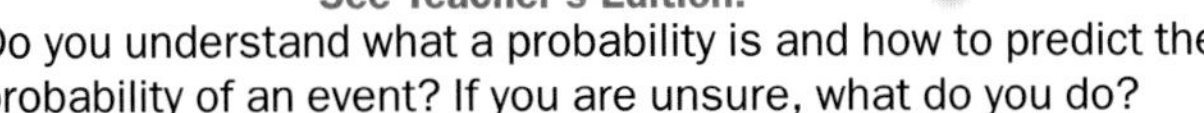

1 Do you understand what a probability is and how to predict the probability of an event? If you are unsure, what do you do?

2 List all the ways you might use to compare or order fractions.

- Use fraction models.
- Use a grid.
- Use a number line.
- Other. Explain.

Reviewing A Portfolio

Have students review their portfolios. Consider including these items:

- Finished work on the Chapter Project (p. 365F) or **Investigation** (pp. 388–389).
- Selected math journal entries, pp. 367, 377, 392.
- Finished work on the nonroutine problem in **What Do You Know?** (p. 367) and problems from the Menu (pp. 400–401).
- Each student's self-selected "best piece" from work completed during the chapter. Have each student attach a note explaining why he or she chose that piece.
- Any work you or an individual student wishes to keep for future reference.

You may take this opportunity to conduct conferences with students. The Portfolio Analysis Form can help you report students' progress. See Teacher's Assessment Resources, p. 33.

PERFORMANCE ASSESSMENT

PURPOSE Review and assess the concepts, skills, and strategies learned in this chapter.

Materials have available: counters

Using the Performance Assessment

Have students read and restate the problems in their own words. Make sure they understand how the diagram shows that $\frac{2}{3}$ is equivalent to $\frac{4}{6}$.

Point out the section on the student page headed "A Good Answer." Make sure students understand that you will use these points to evaluate their answers.

Evaluating Student Work

As you read students' papers, look for the following:

- *Can the student use counters to model two more fractions equivalent to $\frac{2}{3}$?*
- *Can the student use diagrams and explanations to show that her or his fractions are equivalent to $\frac{2}{3}$?*
- *What other methods can the student use to show that two fractions are equivalent?*

The Holistic Scoring Guide and annotated samples of students' work can be used to assess this task. See pages 27–32 and 37–72 in Teacher's Assessment Resources.

Using the Self-Assessment

What Do You Think? Assure students that there are no right or wrong answers. Tell them the emphasis is on what they think and how they justify their answers.

Follow-Up Interviews

These questions can be used to gain insight into students' thinking:

- **How do you know that these two fractions are equivalent?**
- **What is another way that you could show that these two fractions are equivalent?**
- **What patterns do you see in the numerators and denominators of the equivalent fractions you have written?**

OBJECTIVE Apply fractions in a sports context.

Materials basketballs, yardstick or meterstick, air pump (optional)

Resources graphing software, or Math Van Tools

Science

Cultural Connection Read the **Cultural Note.** You may wish to ask for volunteers to research and present information about many games.

Read the information about basketballs together with the class. Ask:

- **Why do referees want to make sure a basketball is properly inflated?** *[Possible responses: Game regulations; improper inflation can cause the ball to bounce either too high or too low and thus affect dribbling and shooting.*

Allow pairs to work independently. You may need to share basketballs among several pairs of students. Each pair should make their own data table.

Math

Have partners work together to complete items 1–4, then share and compare answers with the class.

For item 2, the more air the ball has the higher it will bounce.

For item 3, students can use the averages they found in item 1 as the numerators in their answers and the number 36 as the denominator. Have students write all fractions in lowest terms.

math science technology
CONNECTION

That's the way the Ball Bounces

Referees drop a ball from overhead to check if the ball has the correct amount of air. The ball should bounce back somewhere between their waist and shoulder.

Cultural Note

One of the most intricately decorated balls is the *temari* (te-MAH-ree), from Japan. In the 1800s, they were used to play *mari* games. Today, they are used mainly for decoration.

Try It Out

Work with a partner.

- Collect different basketballs to test. Make sure the amounts of air in the balls are different.
- Place a yardstick against the wall as shown.
- One partner holds the ball so that the bottom of the ball is at the same level as the top of the yardstick.
- The other partner watches how high the bottom of the ball reaches on the first bounce.
- Bounce each ball three times. Record your data in a table.

Do you think the height that the ball is dropped from also affects how it bounces? Check your answer by bouncing each ball from different heights. Record the data in a table. **See below.**

What else may affect the way the ball bounces? **Possible answers: the material that the ball is made from, the force that it is dropped with.**

Question 1. Possible answer: Yes; the closer the ball is to the ground, the shorter the bounce back will be.

Extending The Activity

1. Have students use only one basketball. Deflate it. Then add some air each time they record a new bounce.
2. Test the bouncing height of basketballs that cost different amounts.
3. Compare the bouncing height of balls when bounced at different temperatures. Students might seek permission to place a basketball (in a paper bag) inside a school refrigerator for an hour.

omparing Bounces

se the data you collected to answer ese questions. Check students' work.

What is the average height each ball bounced?

What can you say about the way the air in the ball affects the way it bounces?

The balls were all dropped from 36 in. On average, what fraction of that height did each ball reach on the first bounce?

What if a ball that is dropped from 36 in. bounces back 12 in. Would you predict that the ball had too little air or too much air? Explain. **Possible answer: Too little air; the less air there is in the ball, the lower the bounce will be.**

At the Computer

Check students' work.

- Use graphing software to make a table and a bar graph of your data.
- Write a short report that explains your findings about how well different basketballs bounce.
- Combine all of the class's data together and present the project to one of the school's physical education teachers.

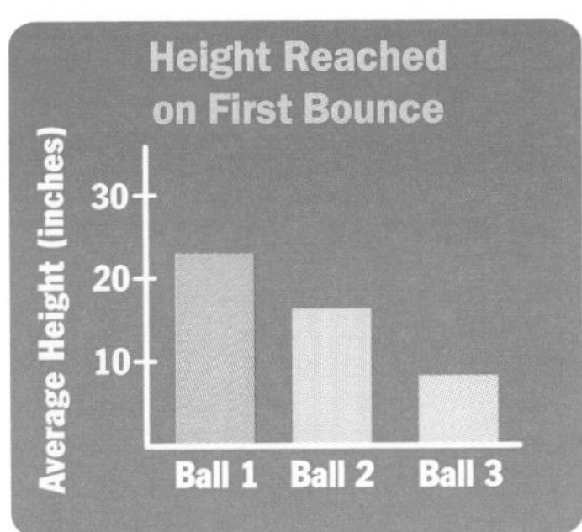

Technology

Have partners work together to create graphs and tables at the computer. They can use a word-processing program to write their reports.

Students can work together with the rest of the class to create a table and graph that combines the data from partners' graphs and tables.

Math Van Students may use the Graph and Table tools to make a table and bar graph. A project electronic teacher aid has been provided.

Interesting Facts

- **The one-handed jump shot** first became popular at colleges in the 1930s.
- **Professional basketball games** are 48 minutes long, college games are 40 minutes long, and high school games are 32 minutes long.
- **The National Basketball Association** (NBA) was formed in 1949. Until the 1970s there were only 9 teams in the NBA.

Bibliography

The *Basketball Hall of Fame,* by Terry Dunnahoo & Herma Silverstein. New York: Crestwood House, 1994. ISBN 0-89686-850-8.

Basketball Legends, by Paul Deegan. Edina, MN: Abdo & Daughters, 1990. ISBN 1-56239-006-6.

CHAPTER 11 AT A GLANCE:

Using Fractions

Theme: Food for Thought   Suggested Pacing: 11–14 days

CHAPTER 11 ORGANIZER

	DAY 1	DAY 2	DAY 3
WEEK ONE	**PREASSESSMENT** **Introduction** p. 408 **What Do You Know?** p. 409 **CHAPTER OBJECTIVES:** 11A, 11B, 11C, 11D **RESOURCES** Read-Aloud Anthology pp. 50–52; Pretest: Test Master Form A, B, or C; Diagnostic Inventory Portfolio Journal **NCTM STANDARDS:** 1, 2, 3, 4, 12	**LESSON 11.1** EXPLORE ACTIVITY **Add Fractions** pp. 410–413 **CHAPTER OBJECTIVES:** 11A **MATERIALS** fraction strips (TA 26), number cubes, pattern blocks (TA 16–17) **RESOURCES** Reteach/Practice/Extend: 100; Math Center Cards: 100; Extra Practice: 524 Daily Review TE p. 409B Algebraic Thinking Technology Link **NCTM STANDARDS:** 4, 12	**LESSON 11.2** **Add Fractions** pp. 414–415 **CHAPTER OBJECTIVES:** 11A **MATERIALS** brown sugar, white sugar, measuring cup, calculators (opt.) **RESOURCES** Reteach/Practice/Extend: 101; Math Center Cards: 101; Extra Practice: 524 Daily Review TE p. 413B Technology Link **NCTM STANDARDS:** 12
WEEK TWO	**MIDCHAPTER ASSESSMENT** **Midchapter Review** p. 422 **CHAPTER OBJECTIVES:** 11A, 11B, 11D **MATERIALS** calculators (opt.) **Developing Spatial Sense** p. 423 **MATERIALS** place-value models (TA 22) REAL-LIFE INVESTIGATION: **Applying Fractions** pp. 424–425 Portfolio Journal **NCTM STANDARDS:** 1, 2, 3, 4, 12	**LESSON 11.5** EXPLORE ACTIVITY **Find a Common Denominator** pp. 426–427 **CHAPTER OBJECTIVES:** 11A, 11B **MATERIALS** fraction strips (TA 26), blank number cubes **RESOURCES** Reteach/Practice/Extend: 104; Math Center Cards: 104; Extra Practice: 525 Daily Review TE p. 425B Technology Link **NCTM STANDARDS:** 4, 12	**LESSON 11.6** EXPLORE ACTIVITY **Add and Subtract Fractions with Unlike Denominators** pp. 428–431 **CHAPTER OBJECTIVES:** 11A, 11B **MATERIALS** fractions strips (TA 26), calculators (opt.) **RESOURCES** Reteach/Practice/Extend: 105; Math Center Cards: 105; Extra Practice: 526 TEACHING WITH TECHNOLOGY Alternate Lesson TE pp. 431A–431B Daily Review TE p. 427B Algebraic Thinking Technology Link **NCTM STANDARDS:** 4, 12
WEEK THREE	**LESSON 11.9** PROBLEM SOLVERS AT WORK **Choose the Operation** pp. 438–441 **CHAPTER OBJECTIVES:** 11D **MATERIALS** calculators (opt.), computer graphing program (opt.) **RESOURCES** Reteach/Practice/Extend: 108; Math Center Cards: 108; Extra Practice: 527 Daily Review TE p. 437B Technology Link **NCTM STANDARDS:** 1, 2, 3, 4, 12	**CHAPTER ASSESSMENT** **Chapter Review** pp. 442–443 **MATERIALS** calculators (opt.) **Chapter Test** p. 444 **RESOURCES** Posttest: Test Master Form A, B, or C **Performance Assessment** p. 445 **RESOURCES** Performance Task: Test Master **Math • Science • Technology Connection** pp. 446–447 Portfolio **NCTM STANDARDS:** 1, 4, 12	

DAY 4

LESSON 11.3

EXPLORE ACTIVITY

Subtract Fractions pp. 416–419

CHAPTER OBJECTIVES: 11B

MATERIALS fraction strips (TA 26), measuring cup, water, calculators (opt.)

RESOURCES Reteach/Practice/Extend: 102
Math Center Cards: 102
Extra Practice: 524

Daily Review TE p. 415B

Algebraic Thinking

Journal

Technology Link

NCTM STANDARDS: 4, 12

LESSON 11.7

PROBLEM-SOLVING STRATEGY

Draw a Picture pp. 432–433

CHAPTER OBJECTIVES: 11D

MATERIALS calculators (opt.)

RESOURCES Reteach/Practice/Extend: 106
Math Center Cards: 106
Extra Practice: 526

Daily Review TE p. 431D

Technology Link

NCTM STANDARDS: 1, 2, 3, 4, 12

DAY 5

LESSON 11.4

Subtract Fractions pp. 420–421

CHAPTER OBJECTIVES: 11B

MATERIALS calculators (opt.)

RESOURCES Reteach/Practice/Extend: 103
Math Center Cards: 103
Extra Practice: 525

Daily Review TE p. 419B

Algebraic Thinking

Technology Link

NCTM STANDARDS: 12

LESSON 11.8

EXPLORE ACTIVITY

Add and Subtract Mixed Numbers pp. 434–437

CHAPTER OBJECTIVES: 11C

MATERIALS index cards, fractions strips (TA 26), blank number cubes, calculators (opt.)

RESOURCES Reteach/Practice/Extend: 107
Math Center Cards: 107
Extra Practice: 527

Daily Review TE p. 433B

Algebraic Thinking

Technology Link

NCTM STANDARDS: 4, 12

Assessment Options

FORMAL

Chapter Tests

STUDENT BOOK
- Midchapter Review, p. 422
- Chapter Review, pp. 442–443
- Chapter Test, p. 444

BLACKLINE MASTERS
- Test Masters A, B, or C
- Diagnostic Inventory

COMPUTER TEST GENERATOR
- Available on disk

Performance Assessment
- What Do You Know? p. 409
- Performance Assessment, p. 445
- Holistic Scoring Guide, Teacher's Assessment Resources, pp. 27–32
- Follow-Up Interviews, p. 445
- Performance Task, Test Masters

Teacher's Assessment Resources
- Portfolio Guidelines and Forms, pp. 6–9, 33–35
- Holistic Scoring Guide, pp. 27–32
- Samples of Student Work, pp. 37–72

INFORMAL

Ongoing Assessment
- Observation Checklist, pp. 414, 420, 428, 432, 434
- Interview, p. 426
- Anecdotal Report, p. 410, 416, 438

Portfolio Opportunities
- Chapter Project, p. 407F
- What Do You Know? p. 409
- Investigation, pp. 424–425
- Journal Writing, pp. 409, 417, 422
- Performance Assessment, p. 445
- Self-Assessment: What Do You Think? p. 445

Chapter Objectives	Standardized Test Correlations
11A Add fractions with like and unlike denominators	MAT, CAT, CTBS,TN*
11B Subtract fractions with like and unlike denominators	MAT, CAT, CTBS,TN*
11C Add and subtract mixed numbers using models	MAT, CAT, CTBS,TN*
11D Solve problems, including those that involve fractions and drawing pictures	MAT, CAT, SAT, ITBS, CTBS,TN*

*Terra Nova

NCTM Standards Grades K–4

1 Problem Solving
2 Communication
3 Reasoning
4 Connections
5 Estimation
6 Number Sense and Numeration
7 Concepts of Whole Number Operations
8 Whole Number Computation
9 Geometry and Spatial Sense
10 Measurement
11 Statistics and Probability
12 Fractions and Decimals
13 Patterns and Relationships

Meeting Individual Needs

LEARNING STYLES

- AUDITORY/LINGUISTIC
- LOGICAL/ANALYTICAL
- VISUAL/SPATIAL
- MUSICAL
- KINESTHETIC
- SOCIAL
- INDIVIDUAL

Students who are talented in art, language, and physical activity may better understand mathematical concepts when these concepts are connected to their areas of interest. Use the following activity to stimulate the different learning styles of some of your students.

Visual/Spatial Learners

Some students may enjoy using real life problems involving fractions and pictures. Provide graph paper and encourage students to draw a picture when telling a fraction story such as the one below.

Mr. Soto had a vegetable garden.
The garden had twelve sections.
One half had carrots, one third had spinach, and one sixth had potatoes.

See Lesson Resources, pp. 409A, 413A, 415A, 419A, 425A, 427A, 431C, 433A, 437A.

GIFTED AND TALENTED

Students may enjoy looking for recipes and changing the measurements to accommodate more or less people. Have students double a recipe or cut it in half. If necessary, they can use models to help them change the fractions. For example, if they are doubling $\frac{2}{3}$, they can take two sets of $\frac{2}{3}$ and see how much that will be.

You may also wish to have students find fractional parts of common objects. For example, have them figure out how many minutes are in $\frac{2}{6}$ of an hour.

See also Meeting Individual Needs, pp. 412, 418, 430, 436, 440.

EXTRA SUPPORT

Have available fraction strips for students who need practice with fractions.

Specific suggestions for ways to provide extra support to students appear in every lesson in this chapter.

See Meeting Individual Needs, pp. 410, 414, 416, 420, 426, 428, 432, 434, 438.

EARLY FINISHERS

Students who finish their class work early may make menus to distribute at the class breakfast. (See *Chapter Project*, p. 407F.)

See also Meeting Individual Needs, pp. 412, 414, 418, 420, 426, 430, 432, 436, 440.

LANGUAGE SUPPORT

Some students may need to see visual models when working with fractions. Have students name the fractions as they are modeled. Write out the names of the fractions so students can see the written word. Help students read the words to name the fractions.

See also Meeting Individual Needs, pp. 418, 428, 434, 438.

ESL APPROPRIATE

INCLUSION

- **For inclusion ideas, information, and suggestions, see pp. 412, 416, 436, 440, T15.**
- **For gender fairness tips, see pp. 410, T15.**

USING MANIPULATIVES

Building Understanding Fraction bars can be used to model addition and subtraction of fractions. Students use the bars to find equivalent fractions when adding fractions with different denominators. Some students may need to lay the pieces showing the sum on top of a sheet with pictures of whole bars in order to help them convert improper fractions to mixed numbers. The bars can also be used to model addition and subtraction of mixed numbers.

Easy-to-Make Manipulatives Paper fraction rods can be made and used to reinforce the concept of fractions. Students can have multiple sets to show fractions greater than one. Be sure students label the fraction parts to make it easy for them to identify the pieces. Have students use a different color for each fraction.

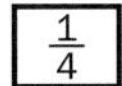

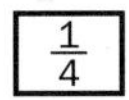

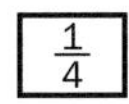

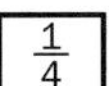

ESL APPROPRIATE

USING COOPERATIVE LEARNING

Jigsaw This strategy develops complex teamwork by having students divide the work to complete an assignment.

- **In groups of four, each member is responsible for a different segment of a question, problem, or group product.**
- **Each student is accountable for his or her part of the problem, and must teach it to the rest of the group.**
- **Parts must be integrated in order to form a whole problem, solution, or product.**

USING LITERATURE

Use the selection *Everybody Cooks Rice* to introduce the chapter theme, Food for Thought. This selection is reprinted on pages 50–52 of the Read-Aloud Anthology.

Also available in the Read-Aloud Anthology is the selection *The Kids' Multicultural Cookbook: Food & Fun Around the World,* page 53.

Linking Technology

This integrated package of programs and services allows students to explore, develop, and practice concepts; solve problems; build portfolios; and assess their own progress. Teachers can enhance instruction, provide remediation, and share ideas with other educational professionals.

CD-ROM ACTIVITY

In *Deli in a Pickle,* students use fraction models and tables to buy lunch for the entire band and choir. Students can use the online notebook to write about how they used common denominators. To extend the activity, students use the Math Van tools to complete an open-ended problem involving fractions. **Available on CD-ROM.**

CD-ROM TOOLS

Students can use Math Van's fraction models to explore the concept of fractions. The Tech Links on the Lesson Resources pages highlight opportunities for students to use this and other tools such as graphs, tables, online notes, and calculator to provide additional practice, reteaching, or extension. **Available on CD-ROM.**

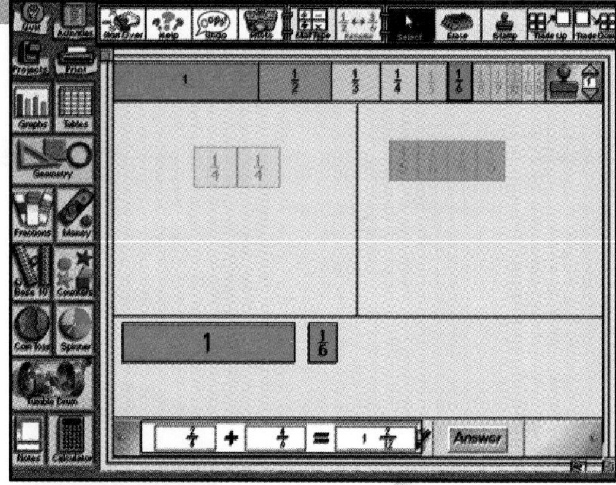

WEB SITE http://www.mhschool.com

Teachers can access the McGraw-Hill School Division World Wide Web site for additional curriculum support at http://www.mhschool.com. Click on our Resource Village for specially designed activities linking Web sites to using fractions. Motivate children by inviting them to explore Web sites that develop the chapter theme of "Food for Thought." Exchange ideas on classroom management, cultural diversity, and other areas in the Math Forum.

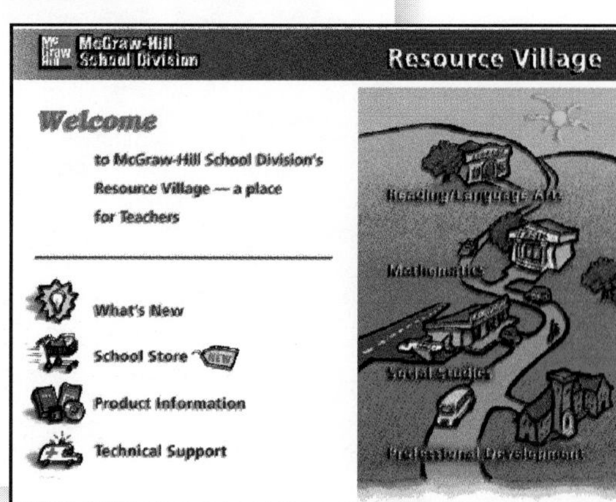

Chapter Project BREAKFAST RECIPE BOOK

Highlighting the Math

- determine fractional amounts
- add fractions and whole numbers to convert recipes
- collect and adjust data to fit specific needs

1 Starting the Project

Introduce the idea of a Breakfast Recipe Book as you display names of three categories of breakfast food. Brainstorm examples of each category and list each under the appropriate head. Tell students they will create one recipe for each category. Remind students to include the use of fractional amounts in the recipes. Consider how family and community members can participate.

2 Continuing the Project

- Groups create breakfast recipes by reading cookbooks to see how recipes are written.
- Groups choose ingredients from the display or add ingredients of their own as they write each recipe for 2 people and 4 people.
- Groups write recipes listing ingredients, amounts, and directions.

3 Finishing the Project

Have each group share its recipes with the class. Compile the recipes into two class Breakfast Recipe Books and allow each student to check a book out to take home for two days, or make a copy for each student.

Community Involvement

Have students choose favorite recipes from the book and prepare a class breakfast. Work together to figure out the amounts of ingredients needed. Invite parents to the breakfast.

Breakfast Drinks	Breakfast Foods (cold)	Breakfast Foods (Hot)
orange juice	fruit	oatmeal
apple juice	cereal	eggs
milk	bread	

BUILDING A PORTFOLIO

Each student's portfolio piece should include a copy of the group's three recipes and a description of how the group determined the amount of ingredients for 2 and then 4 people. Students may also write about a favorite recipe, and tell why it's the favorite.

To assess students' work, refer to the Holistic Scoring Guide on page 27 in the Teacher's Assessment Resources.

PURPOSE Introduce the theme of the chapter.

Resources Read-Aloud Anthology, page 50–52, newspapers

Using Literature

Read "Everybody Cooks Rice" from the Read-Aloud Anthology to introduce the theme of the chapter "Food for Thought."

Developing the Theme

Have students share descriptions of some of their favorite foods. Encourage them to bring in recipes or pictures. As the class examines the recipes, focus on some of the special ingredients that flavor the dishes, such as cinnamon, cloves, ginger, salt, and curry. Discuss how these spices were part of the incentive for exploration in the Age of Discovery.

Discuss the importance of food in fueling the body. Review the food pyramid and different food groups.

These food-related topics are discussed in this chapter:

pies	pp. 408–409	banana bread	p. 420
juices	p. 410	cookies	p. 422
ethnic dishes	pp. 414, 438	restaurants	p. 428
rice	p. 415	frozen foods	p. 432
bobotie	pp. 416–417		

On pages 424–425, students explore planning a class lunch.

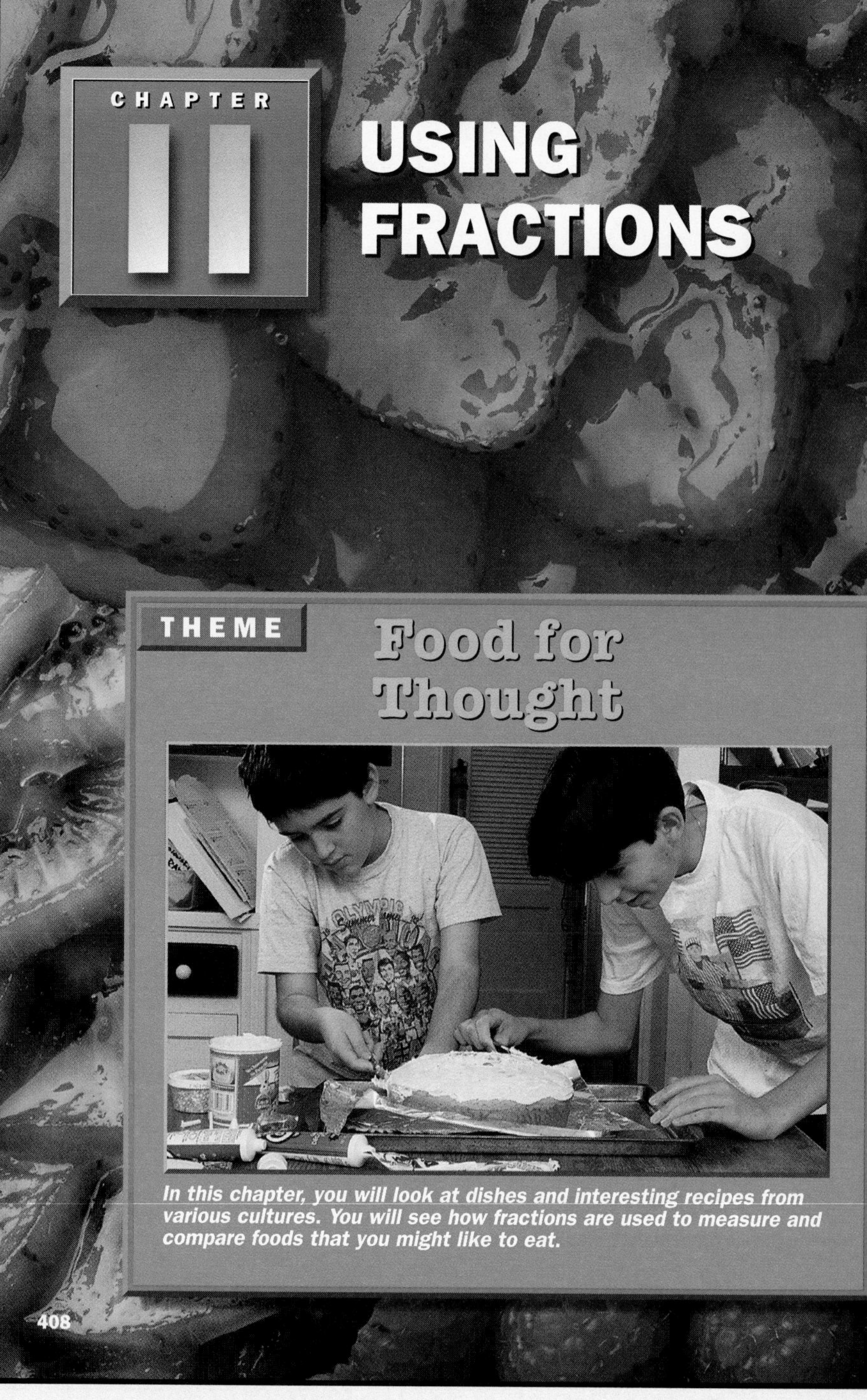

In this chapter, you will look at dishes and interesting recipes from various cultures. You will see how fractions are used to measure and compare foods that you might like to eat.

408

Chapter Bibliography

The Fun of Cooking by Jill Krementz. New York: Alfred A. Knopf, Inc., 1985. ISBN 0–394–54808–6.

A Good Soup Attracts Chairs: A First African Cookbook for American Kids by Fran Osseo-Asare. Gretna, PA: Pelican Publishing Company, Inc., 1993. ISBN 0–88289–816–7.

Community Involvement

Have students write a Kid's Guide to Spices to sell as a fundraiser in their community. Students can work in pairs to research a single spice and the history of its use. Partners can also make a drawing of the plant the spice comes from and trace the outlines of countries where the spice is used. Resources such as cookbooks and spice labels will help them write a list of foods in which the spice is customarily used.

Students should show the sugar, brown sugar, and salt used in both the filling and pie crust.

What Do You Know?

Use the recipe for problems 1–3.

1 Draw rectangles to represent fractions. Show the amounts of sugar and salt. See above.

2 A teaspoon is $\frac{1}{3}$ of a tablespoon. What fraction of a tablespoon is 2 teaspoons? $\frac{2}{3}$ tablespoon

3 Portfolio Double the recipe for the pie filling. Explain how you found the amounts for each ingredient. Use a drawing to help explain. Check tudents' work. Doubled amounts—$1\frac{1}{2}$ c sugar, tablespoons brown sugar, 2 teaspoons cinnamon, $\frac{1}{2}$ teaspoon salt, 12 apples

Apple Pie

Filling
3/4 CUP SUGAR
1 1/2 TABLESPOONS BROWN SUGAR
1 TEASPOON CINNAMON
1/4 TEASPOON SALT
6 APPLES, PEELED AND SLICED

Pie Crust
2 1/4 CUPS FLOUR
1/2 TEASPOON SALT
12 TABLESPOONS BUTTER
6 TABLESPOONS ICE WATER
MIX THE FILLING AND PLACE IN PIE CRUST.
BAKE AT 350°F FOR 45 MINUTES.

CINNAMON

Write a Report **Choose a favorite vegetable and write a short report about it. Describe it, tell how it tastes, what size it is, and how much it weighs. Find out how many classmates also like this vegetable.**

A report gives information about a subject. When you write a report, you usually do research first to learn more about the subject.

1 What fraction of students in your class like this vegetable? Answers depend on data collected.

2 What research did you do to answer question 1? Possible answer: took a survey

Vocabulary

fraction, p. 410
simplest form, p. 411
common denominator, p. 414
numerator, p. 414
mixed number, p. 434

Reading, Writing, Arithmetic

Write a Report Invite volunteers to read their reports to the class. Ask students to identify the vegetable's characteristics from the report. Follow up by having students compile data from the reports to create a table or chart showing favorite vegetables.

Vocabulary

Students may record new words in their journals. Encourage them to show examples and draw diagrams to help them tell what the words mean.

PURPOSE Assess students' ability to apply prior knowledge of adding fractions and mixed numbers.

Materials have available: fraction strips

Assessing Prior Knowledge

Draw a 10-by-10 grid like the one shown below and shade one fourth of the squares.

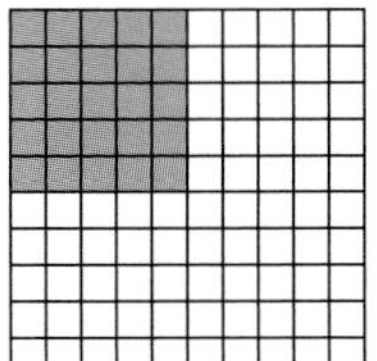

Ask these questions:

- **What fraction of the squares are shaded?** [$\frac{1}{4}$]
- **What fraction is not shaded?** [$\frac{3}{4}$]

Encourage students to use whatever methods they wish to answer items 1–3. Observe students as they work. Look at the drawings students use to explain how they found the amounts for each ingredient to answer item 3. Discuss the different methods students used to answer items 1–3. Let students show the drawings they made to help them explain how they doubled the recipe for the pie filling. Then you could ask students how they would triple the recipe for the pie filling.

Building a Portfolio

Item 3 can be used as a benchmark to show where students are in their understanding of adding fractions.

A Portfolio Checklist for Students and a Checklist for Teachers are provided in Teacher's Assessment Resources, pp. 33–34.

Prerequisite Skills

- *Can students identify equivalent fractions?*
- *Can students simplify fractions?*
- *Can students read and write fractions and mixed numbers?*

Assessment Resources

Diagnostic Inventory

Use this blackline master to assess prerequisite skills that students will need in order to be successful in this chapter.

Test Masters

Use the multiple choice format (form A or B) or the free response format (form C) as a pretest of the skills in this chapter.

EXPLORE ACTIVITY

Add Fractions

OBJECTIVE Explore adding fractions with like denominators.

RESOURCE REMINDER
Math Center Cards 100
Practice 100, Reteach 100, Extend 100

SKILLS TRACE

GRADE 3	• *Introduced at grade 4.*
GRADE 4	• Explore adding fractions with like denominators with sums less than or greater than 1.
GRADE 5	• Explore adding fractions with like denominators with sums less than or greater than 1. *(Chapter 10)*

MANIPULATIVE WARM-UP

Cooperative Pairs — Logical/Analytical

OBJECTIVE Review different ways to show fractions.

Materials per pair: construction paper; scissors

▶ Students work with a partner to make models showing different fractions. Have them use the same color of construction paper to show the same fraction different ways. For example, they can show fourths making fraction circles, fraction strips, on a number line, or on a grid. Encourage and accept a wide variety of models.

▶ Have students make models for several sets of fractions. Have the class compare and discuss the different models.

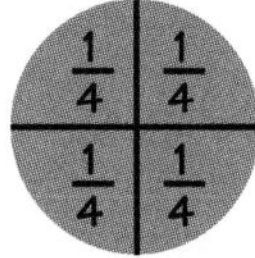

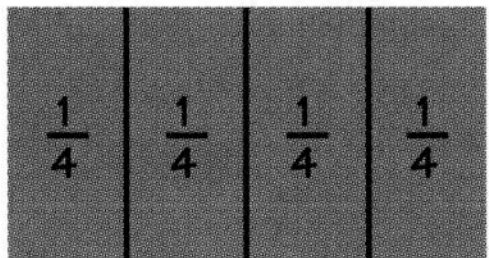

ESL APPROPRIATE

ART CONNECTION

Cooperative Pairs — Visual/Spatial

OBJECTIVE Connect making fractions to designs in art.

Materials per pair: six 6-inch squares, inch ruler, crayons

▶ Distribute the squares to each pair. Have students color each square a different color. Then students use rulers to divide several squares into the same kind of fraction either halves, thirds, fourths, or sixths. Students cut and label the parts of the squares.

▶ Have students create a design by combining like fractions of squares. Students can write an addition sentence to describe the design.

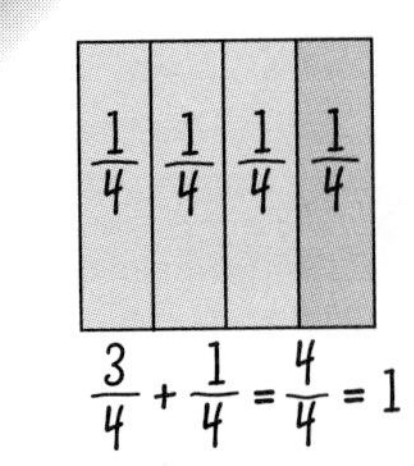

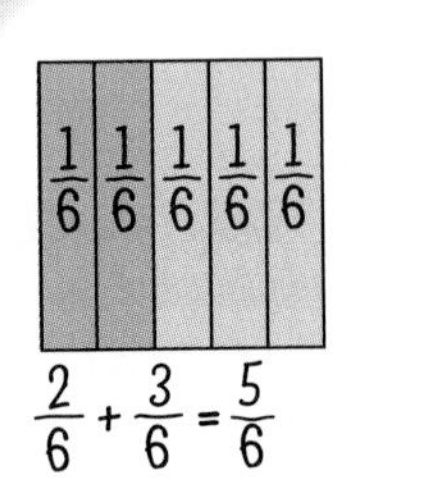

ESL APPROPRIATE

Daily Review

PREVIOUS DAY QUICK REVIEW

You toss a coin. Predict the number of times tails occur in:

1. 4 tosses *[2]*
2. 20 tosses *[10]*
3. 50 tosses *[25]*
4. 100 tosses *[50]*

FAST FACTS

1. 9×0 *[0]*
2. 6×3 *[18]*
3. 5×5 *[25]*
4. 9×7 *[63]*

Problem of the Day • 100

A pizza is divided into 8 equal slices. Betty and Bryan each eat $\frac{3}{8}$ of the pizza. What number sentence shows how much pizza they ate all together? What fraction of the pizza, in simplest form, did they eat? *[$\frac{3}{8} + \frac{3}{8} = \frac{6}{8}$; $\frac{3}{4}$ pizza]*

TECH LINK

ONLINE EXPLORATION

Use our Web-linked activities and lesson plans to connect your students to the real world of food.

MATH FORUM

Combination Classes I allow my students to work in pairs. They gain confidence in their abilities to add fractions as they alternate using models and recording number sentences.

Visit our Resource Village at http://www.mhschool.com to access the Online Exploration and the Math Forum.

MATH CENTER

Practice

OBJECTIVE Use fractions strips to add fractions with like denominators.

Materials per student: fraction strips (sixths, eighths, tenths, twelfths), blank number cube (labeled 1, 1, 2, 2, 3, 3), paper bag, Math Center Recording Sheet (TA 31 optional)

Students model fractions by rolling a number cube and picking fraction strips from a paper bag. They do this twice to make two fractions and then write an addition sentence, renaming as needed. *[Check students' work.]*

PRACTICE ACTIVITY 100 — MATH CENTER — On Your Own

Algebra Sense • It's in the Bag

- Put all the tenths strips in the bag. Roll the cube for a number from 1 to 3. Remove that number of strips from the bag. Line them up side by side to show a fraction.
- Do this again to show another fraction.
- Write an addition sentence using both fractions.
- Repeat, but this time use the eighths strips. Continue until you have tried all the denominators.

YOU NEED
- fraction strips for sixths, eighths, tenths, and twelfths
- paper bag
- number cube (1–3)

$\frac{1}{12}$ $\frac{1}{10}$ $\frac{1}{8}$ $\frac{1}{6}$

Grade Level 4 — McGraw-Hill School Division

Chapter 11, Lesson 1, pages 410–413 — Fractions

ESL APPROPRIATE

NCTM Standards
- Problem Solving
- Communication
- Reasoning
- ✓ Connections

Problem Solving

OBJECTIVE Write and solve problems with models.

Materials per student: fraction strips; Math Center Recording Sheet (TA 31 optional)

Students use manipulatives to add fractions. Then they write problems of their own. *[**1.** Julie had $1\frac{1}{5}$ fruit rolls. **2.** Henry had 1 fruit roll. **3.** Julie had $\frac{1}{5}$ of a fruit roll more; Check students' word problems.]*

PROBLEM-SOLVING ACTIVITY 100 — MATH CENTER — On Your Own

Decision Making • Which Is Greater?

Use fraction strips to solve these problems.

YOU NEED
- fraction strips

1. Julie ate $\boxed{\frac{2}{5}}$ of a fruit roll. Later she ate $\boxed{\frac{4}{5}}$ of another fruit roll. How much fruit roll did she eat?
2. Henry ate $\boxed{\frac{1}{4}}$ of a fruit roll. Later he ate $\boxed{\frac{3}{4}}$ of another fruit roll. How much fruit roll did he eat?
3. Who ate more fruit roll? How much more?

Replace the fractions in the boxes with other fractions. Be sure the denominators are the same in each sentence. Solve them.

CHERRY FRUIT ROLL — GRAPE FRUIT ROLL — STRAWBERRY FRUIT ROLL

Grade Level 4 — McGraw-Hill School Division

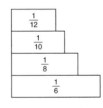

Chapter 11, Lesson 1, pages 410–413 — Fractions

NCTM Standards
- ✓ Problem Solving
- Communication
- ✓ Reasoning
- Connections

EXPLORE ACTIVITY
Add Fractions

OBJECTIVE Explore adding fractions with like denominators and sums less than or greater than 1.

Materials per pair: fraction strips (TA 26)

Vocabulary fraction, simplest form

1 Introduce

Draw a circle that is divided into eighths on the chalkboard or overhead projector. Shade $\frac{2}{8}$ of the circle.

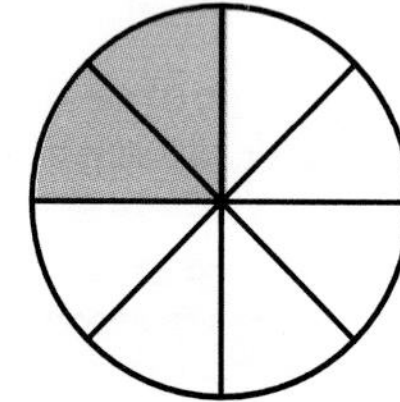

Ask:

- **What fraction of the circle is shaded?** *[$\frac{2}{8}$]*

Shade another $\frac{1}{8}$ of the circle. Ask:

- **What fraction of the circle is shaded now?** *[$\frac{3}{8}$]*
- **How can I record what we just did?** *[Possible answer: Use a number sentence—$\frac{2}{8} + \frac{1}{8} = \frac{3}{8}$.]*

Continue adding eighths and asking questions until the circle is completely shaded. Discuss ways of recording the process.

2 Teach — *Cooperative Pairs*

LEARN Work Together Encourage students to double check that their fraction strips reflect the fractions listed.

You may wish to have students actually pour $\frac{1}{3}$ cup of pineapple juice and $\frac{1}{3}$ cup of orange juice into a measuring container to verify that the mixture is $\frac{2}{3}$ cups.

Talk It Over Have students compare their answers. Some students may have different sums for the same addition phrase because they simplified their fraction answers. Discuss why they simplified and how. All students will have an opportunity to simplify their fractions in the Make Connections section.

Add Fractions

LEARN

You can mix $\frac{1}{3}$ cup of pineapple juice with $\frac{1}{3}$ cup of orange juice to make pineapple-orange drink. How much drink will this make?

To solve this problem, you need to add **fractions.**

Work Together

Work with a partner to explore adding fractions.

Use fraction strips to model the problem. Find $\frac{1}{3} + \frac{1}{3}$. Write a number sentence to show your work. **Q. 1 Possible answer: Found fraction strips to represent each fraction and added them together.**

Continue using fraction strips to add these fractions:

You will need
- *fraction strips*

a. $\frac{1}{2} + \frac{1}{2}$ **$\frac{2}{2}$, or 1**
b. $\frac{1}{5} + \frac{3}{5}$ **$\frac{4}{5}$**
c. $\frac{5}{8} + \frac{1}{8}$ **$\frac{6}{8}$, or $\frac{3}{4}$**
d. $\frac{3}{4} + \frac{1}{4}$ **$\frac{4}{4}$, or 1**
e. $\frac{3}{4} + \frac{3}{4}$ **$\frac{6}{4}$, or $1\frac{1}{2}$**
f. $\frac{3}{10} + \frac{7}{10}$ **$\frac{10}{10}$, or 1**
g. $\frac{5}{6} + \frac{5}{6}$ **$\frac{10}{6}$, or $1\frac{2}{3}$**
h. $\frac{7}{10} + \frac{9}{10}$ **$\frac{16}{10}$, or $1\frac{3}{5}$**
i. $\frac{7}{12} + \frac{11}{12}$ **$\frac{18}{12}$, or $1\frac{1}{2}$**

Check Out the Glossary
fraction
simplest form
See page 544.

Talk It Over

- ▶ What method did you use to find the sums? **See above.**
- ▶ How much drink will you make if you mix $\frac{1}{3}$ cup of pineapple juice with $\frac{1}{3}$ cup of orange juice? **$\frac{2}{3}$ c**
- ▶ How would you show $\frac{10}{6}$ in another way? **See below.**
- ▶ How would you show $\frac{10}{10}$ in another way? **Possible answer: Write it as a whole number, $\frac{10}{10} = 1$.**

Question 3. Possible answer: Divide the numerator by the denominator to rename it as a mixed number, $1\frac{4}{6}$, then simplify it to $1\frac{2}{3}$.

Meeting Individual Needs

Extra Support

Provide students with examples that show how to use fraction strips to add. Post these examples in front of the class for them to refer to as they add fractions on their own.

ESL APPROPRIATE

Gender Fairness

To make sure that both students in a pair explore the activity, have them alternate roles of recording and making models.

Ongoing Assessment

Anecdotal Report Observe how students use the fraction strips to add. Make sure that they differentiate between the numerators and denominators as they find a sum.

Follow Up For students who need additional practice with models, assign **Reteach 100.**

Have students who are ready for a challenge try **Extend 100.**

ake Connections

ive and Lisa added these fractions. They wrote
mber sentences to show what they did.

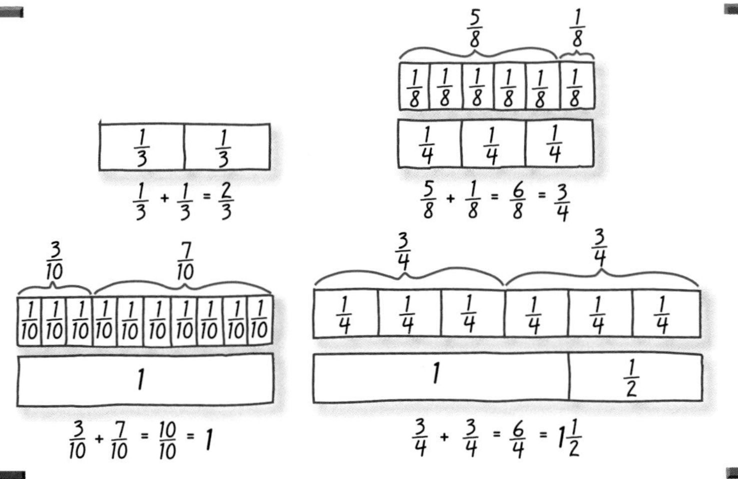

$\frac{5}{8}$ $\frac{1}{8}$
$\frac{1}{3}+\frac{1}{3}=\frac{2}{3}$
$\frac{5}{8}+\frac{1}{8}=\frac{6}{8}=\frac{3}{4}$
$\frac{3}{10}+\frac{7}{10}=\frac{10}{10}=1$
$\frac{3}{4}+\frac{3}{4}=\frac{6}{4}=1\frac{1}{2}$

Check if the sums in your number sentences are in **simplest form.** If not, write them in simplest form. **Check students' work. See answers on page 410.**

heck for Understanding

se the models to complete the number sentence.

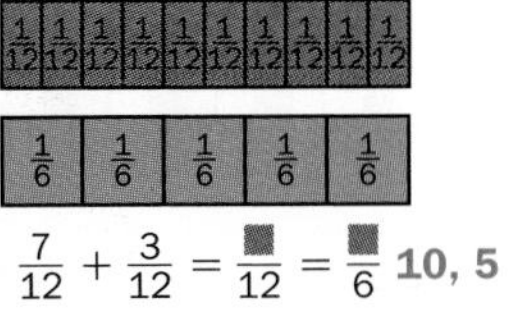

$\frac{7}{12}+\frac{3}{12}=\frac{■}{12}=\frac{■}{6}$ **10, 5**

2 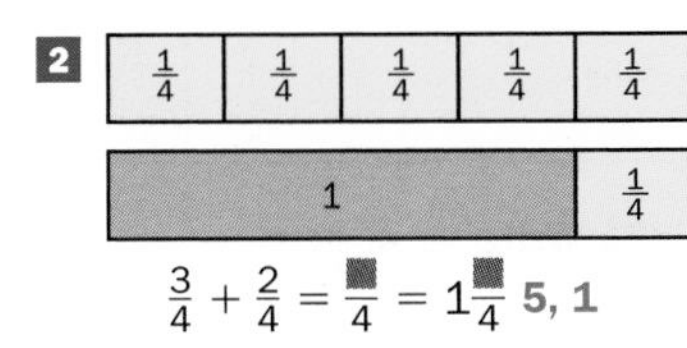

$\frac{3}{4}+\frac{2}{4}=\frac{■}{4}=1\frac{■}{4}$ **5, 1**

dd. Write the sum in simplest form.

$\frac{2}{3}+\frac{2}{3}$ **$1\frac{1}{3}$** **4** $\frac{3}{5}+\frac{4}{5}$ **$1\frac{2}{5}$** **5** $\frac{8}{10}+\frac{6}{10}$ **$1\frac{2}{5}$** **6** $\frac{9}{12}+\frac{11}{12}$ **$1\frac{2}{3}$** **7** $\frac{5}{8}+\frac{5}{8}$ **$1\frac{1}{4}$**

ritical Thinking: Generalize

Do you always need to simplify the sum after you add fractions? Why or why not? Give an example.

ssible answer: No; sometimes a sum is already in simplest rm; $\frac{1}{8}+\frac{2}{8}=\frac{3}{8}$, and $\frac{3}{8}$ does not need to be simplified.

Turn the page for Practice.

MAKE CONNECTIONS

Review each of Clive's and Lisa's sums. Discuss how to recognize that $\frac{10}{10}$ and $\frac{6}{4}$ are not in simplest form by asking:

- **How do you know that a fraction is not simplified?** *[Possible answers: The numerator is greater than or equal to the denominator, the numerator and denominator have a common factor.]*
- **How do you know that you can simplify $\frac{6}{4}$?** *[The numerator 6 is greater than the denominator 4, and the numerator and denominator have a common factor 2.]*
- **What are some ways you can simplify $\frac{6}{4}$?** *[Divide the numerator and denominator by 2 to get $\frac{3}{2}$ and divide 2 into 3 to get $1\frac{1}{2}$, or divide 4 into 6 to get $1\frac{2}{4}$ and divide the numerator and denominator by 2 to get $1\frac{1}{2}$.]*

After students simplify all the sums they found with fraction strips, have them list the steps for adding fractions with fraction strips and then simplifying the sum.

3 Close

Check for Understanding using items 1–8, page 411.

CRITICAL THINKING

In item 8, students are asked to make a generalization about when sums need to be simplified. Have them complete the analysis by asking:

- **What is an advantage to simplifying fraction sums?** *[Possible answer: Everyone will have the same correct fraction.]*

Practice See pages 412–413.

PRACTICE

Materials per pair: number cubes; triangle and hexagon pattern blocks (TA 17); have available: fraction strips (TA 26)

Options for assigning exercises:

A—Odd ex. 1–27; all ex. 29–37; **Hexagon Roll Game; Mixed Review**

B—Even ex. 2–28; all ex. 29–37; **Hexagon Roll Game; Mixed Review**

- For ex. 1–26, encourage students to write the sums in simplest form.
- For ex. 29–36, remind students to compare denominator to numerator to determine if the fraction is greater than 1 to help them compare.
- For **Make It Right** (ex. 37), see Common Error below.

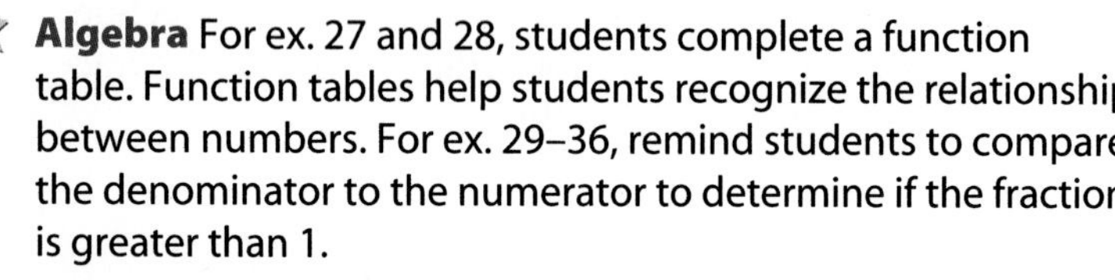

Algebra For ex. 27 and 28, students complete a function table. Function tables help students recognize the relationship between numbers. For ex. 29–36, remind students to compare the denominator to the numerator to determine if the fraction is greater than 1.

Hexagon Roll Game Have students play in pairs. Demonstrate how to form hexagons using the triangle pattern blocks before the game is played.

Mixed Review/Test Preparation In ex. 1–4, students review ordering fractions, learned in Chapter 10. Students describe situations using the probability terms *certain, likely, unlikely,* or *impossible* in ex. 5–8. Illustrate each term if students do not remember this terminology from Chapter 10.

Practice

Use models to complete the numbers sentences.

1 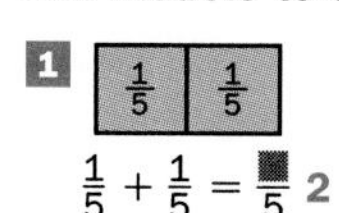

$\frac{1}{5} + \frac{1}{5} = \frac{■}{5}$ 2

2 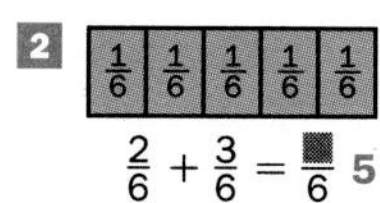

$\frac{2}{6} + \frac{3}{6} = \frac{■}{6}$ 5

3 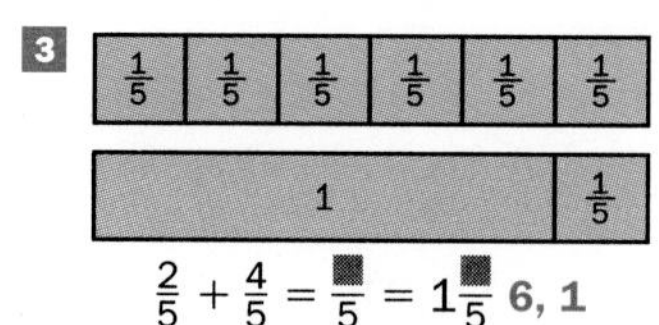

$\frac{2}{5} + \frac{4}{5} = \frac{■}{5} = 1\frac{■}{5}$ 6, 1

4 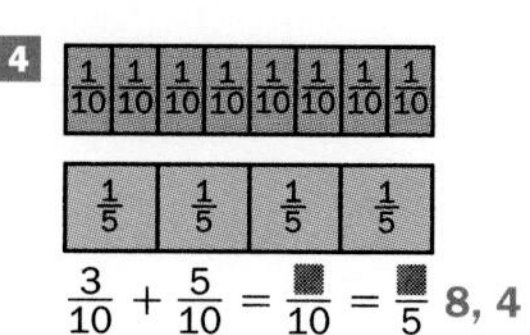

$\frac{3}{10} + \frac{5}{10} = \frac{■}{10} = \frac{■}{5}$ 8, 4

Add. You may use models if you wish.

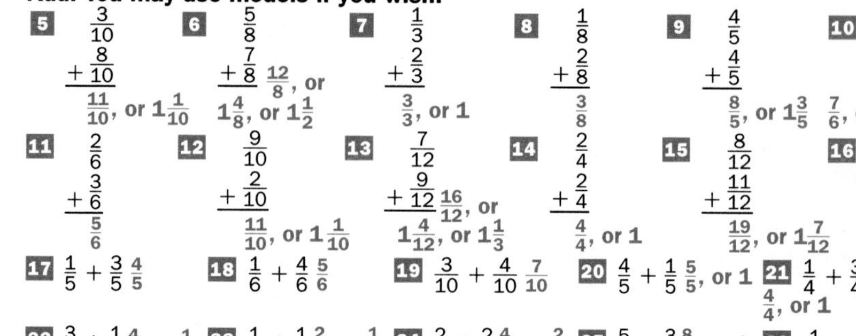

5 $\frac{3}{10} + \frac{8}{10}$ — $\frac{11}{10}$, or $1\frac{1}{10}$

6 $\frac{5}{8} + \frac{7}{8}$ — $\frac{12}{8}$, or $1\frac{4}{8}$, or $1\frac{1}{2}$

7 $\frac{1}{3} + \frac{2}{3}$ — $\frac{3}{3}$, or 1

8 $\frac{1}{8} + \frac{2}{8}$ — $\frac{3}{8}$

9 $\frac{4}{5} + \frac{4}{5}$ — $\frac{8}{5}$, or $1\frac{3}{5}$

10 $\frac{7}{6}$, o…

11 $\frac{2}{6} + \frac{3}{6}$ — $\frac{5}{6}$

12 $\frac{9}{10} + \frac{2}{10}$ — $\frac{11}{10}$, or $1\frac{1}{10}$

13 $\frac{7}{12} + \frac{9}{12}$ — $\frac{16}{12}$, or $1\frac{4}{12}$, or $1\frac{1}{3}$

14 $\frac{2}{4} + \frac{2}{4}$ — $\frac{4}{4}$, or 1

15 $\frac{8}{12} + \frac{11}{12}$ — $\frac{19}{12}$, or $1\frac{7}{12}$

16

17 $\frac{1}{5} + \frac{3}{5}$ $\frac{4}{5}$

18 $\frac{1}{6} + \frac{4}{6}$ $\frac{5}{6}$

19 $\frac{3}{10} + \frac{4}{10}$ $\frac{7}{10}$

20 $\frac{4}{5} + \frac{1}{5}$ $\frac{5}{5}$, or 1

21 $\frac{1}{4} + \frac{3}{4}$ $\frac{4}{4}$, or 1

22 $\frac{3}{8} + \frac{1}{8}$ $\frac{4}{8}$, or $\frac{1}{2}$

23 $\frac{1}{4} + \frac{1}{4}$ $\frac{2}{4}$, or $\frac{1}{2}$

24 $\frac{2}{6} + \frac{2}{6}$ $\frac{4}{6}$, or $\frac{2}{3}$

25 $\frac{5}{8} + \frac{3}{8}$ $\frac{8}{8}$, or 1

26 $\frac{1}{12} + $ … $\frac{3}{12}$, or $\frac{1}{4}$

ALGEBRA Complete the table.

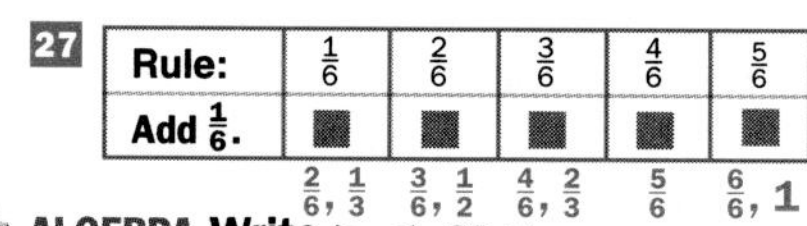

27

Rule:	$\frac{1}{6}$	$\frac{2}{6}$	$\frac{3}{6}$	$\frac{4}{6}$	$\frac{5}{6}$
Add $\frac{1}{6}$.	■	■	■	■	■
	$\frac{2}{6}$, $\frac{1}{3}$	$\frac{3}{6}$, $\frac{1}{2}$	$\frac{4}{6}$, $\frac{2}{3}$	$\frac{5}{6}$	$\frac{6}{6}$, 1

28

Rule:	$\frac{8}{12}$	$\frac{9}{12}$	$\frac{10}{12}$	$\frac{11}{12}$
Add $\frac{3}{12}$.	■	■	■	■
	$\frac{11}{12}$	$\frac{12}{12}$, 1	$\frac{13}{12}$, $1\frac{1}{12}$	$\frac{14}{12}$, 1…

ALGEBRA Write >, <, or =.

29 $\frac{1}{4} + \frac{2}{4}$ ● 1 <

30 $\frac{6}{12} + \frac{8}{12}$ ● 1 >

31 $\frac{3}{6} + \frac{3}{6}$ ● 1 =

32 $\frac{7}{8} + \frac{3}{8}$ ● 1

33 $\frac{4}{12} + \frac{8}{12}$ ● 1 =

34 $\frac{5}{10} + \frac{4}{10}$ ● 1 <

35 $\frac{3}{5} + \frac{3}{5}$ ● 1 >

36 $\frac{2}{6} + \frac{3}{6}$ ● 1

Make It Right

37 Megan used fraction strips to add $\frac{3}{4} + \frac{1}{4}$. Find the mistake, then correct it. $\frac{3}{4} + \frac{1}{4} = \frac{4}{16}$, or $\frac{1}{4}$

Megan added the numerators and denominators of all the fraction strips but she should have just added the numerators and used the common denominator—$\frac{3}{4} + \frac{1}{4} = \frac{4}{4} = 1$.

Meeting Individual Needs

Early Finishers

Have students write five different fraction addition sentences with sums of 1. *[Possible answers: $\frac{1}{2} + \frac{1}{2} = 1$; $\frac{1}{4} + \frac{3}{4} = 1$; $\frac{3}{8} + \frac{5}{8} = 1$; $\frac{2}{3} + \frac{1}{3} = 1$; $\frac{2}{5} + \frac{3}{5} = 1$]*

ESL APPROPRIATE

Common Error

Some students may add the numerators and the denominators as in **Make It Right** (ex. 37). Have these students circle the denominators of each addend. Then have them write the common denominator in the sum.

Inclusion

Students may not remember to write the sum in simplest form. Have them compare the numerator and denominator of the sum. Post a chart with the comparisons for students to refer to when necessary.

Gifted And Talented

Have students write several extended addition sentences using fractions where one addend is missing. For example: $\frac{1}{6} + \frac{3}{6} + \frac{2}{6} + ◆ = 1\frac{5}{6}$. *[$\frac{5}{6}$]* Students can exchange problems to find the missing addends.

Hexagon Roll Game!

rite the following numbers on each side of two number
bes: 0, $\frac{1}{6}$, $\frac{2}{6}$, $\frac{3}{6}$, $\frac{4}{6}$, $\frac{5}{6}$.

You will need
- *number cubes*
- *triangle and hexagon pattern blocks*

lay the Game

ay with a partner to form hexagons.
t each triangle pattern block stand
r $\frac{1}{6}$ and each hexagon stand for 1.

The first player rolls the two number cubes, then shows the fractions with the triangle pattern blocks.

Find the sum by combining the pattern blocks. Write a number sentence to show what you did.

$\frac{2}{6} + \frac{5}{6} = \frac{7}{6}$
$\frac{7}{6} = 1\frac{1}{6}$
HEXAGON!

If the triangle pattern blocks form a whole hexagon, call "Hexagon!" to score 1 point.

Take turns and continue playing for 5 rounds. The player with the most points is the winner.

$\frac{3}{6} + \frac{3}{6} = \frac{6}{6}$
$\frac{6}{6} = 1$
HEXAGON!

hich fractions would you like to roll
ach time? Explain. **Possible answer: Fractions**
at are $\frac{3}{6}$ or greater; the sum will always be 1 or greater.

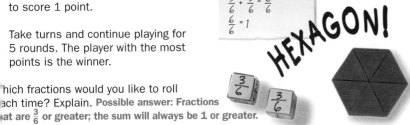

mixed review • test preparation

rite in order from least to greatest.

$\frac{2}{4}, \frac{2}{8}, \frac{2}{16}$ **$\frac{2}{16}, \frac{2}{8}, \frac{2}{4}$**

2 $\frac{5}{7}, \frac{2}{7}, \frac{6}{7}$ **$\frac{2}{7}, \frac{5}{7}, \frac{6}{7}$**

3 $\frac{1}{3}, \frac{11}{13}, \frac{1}{7}$ **$\frac{1}{7}, \frac{1}{3}, \frac{11}{13}$**

4 $\frac{2}{3}, \frac{5}{8}, \frac{5}{6}$ **$\frac{5}{8}, \frac{2}{3}, \frac{5}{6}$**

rite *certain, likely, unlikely,* or *impossible.*

spinning a number less than 8 on a 1–9 spinner **likely**

6 rolling a number greater than 9 on a 1–6 number cube **impossible**

choosing a blue cube from a bag that has seven blue cubes **certain**

8 flipping a head each time in 100 tries **unlikely**

xtra Practice, page 524

Alternate Teaching Strategy

Materials per student: centimeter graph paper (TA 7)

Have students make a border around four squares on the graph paper. Then have them repeat this for another four squares. Tell them that they will use the squares to find $\frac{3}{4} + \frac{3}{4}$.

Direct students to shade $\frac{3}{4}$ of each square. Then ask:

- **How many total squares are shaded?** *[6 squares]*
- **How many fourths in the squares are shaded?** *[6 fourths]*

Repeat the activity for each of the sums on Student Book page 410.

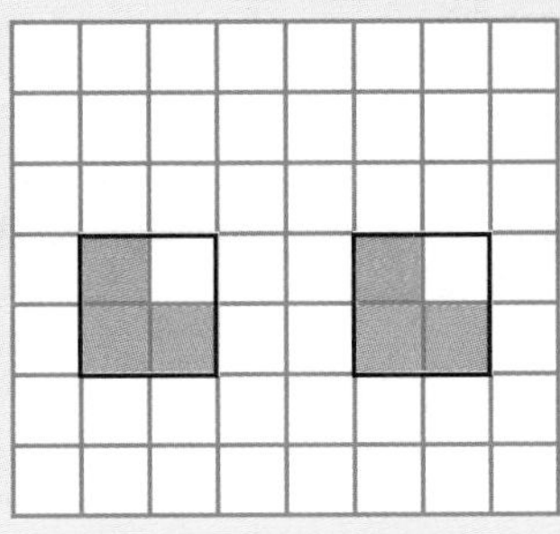

$\frac{3}{4} + \frac{3}{4} = \frac{6}{4}$, or $1\frac{1}{2}$

PRACTICE • 100

Practice 100

Name:

ADD FRACTIONS

Add. Write a number sentence for each model.

1. $\frac{1}{4} + \frac{2}{4} = \frac{3}{4}$
2. $\frac{2}{5} + \frac{1}{5} = \frac{3}{5}$
3. $\frac{3}{8} + \frac{5}{8} = \frac{8}{8}$, or 1
4. $\frac{2}{6} + \frac{2}{6} = \frac{4}{6}$, or $\frac{2}{3}$
5. $\frac{7}{10} + \frac{4}{10} = \frac{11}{10}$, or $1\frac{1}{10}$
6. $\frac{2}{6} + \frac{3}{6} = \frac{5}{6}$

Add. You may use models if you wish.

7. $\frac{3}{5} + \frac{1}{5} = \frac{4}{5}$
8. $\frac{1}{3} + \frac{1}{3} = \frac{2}{3}$
9. $\frac{2}{4} + \frac{1}{4} = \frac{3}{4}$
10. $\frac{4}{6} + \frac{1}{6} = \frac{5}{6}$
11. $\frac{3}{12} + \frac{5}{12} = \frac{8}{12}$, or $\frac{2}{3}$
12. $\frac{1}{10} + \frac{8}{10} = \frac{9}{10}$
13. $\frac{4}{8} + \frac{1}{8} = \frac{5}{8}$
14. $\frac{3}{8} + \frac{3}{8} = \frac{6}{8}$, or $\frac{3}{4}$
15. $\frac{5}{6} + \frac{5}{6} = \frac{10}{6}$, or $1\frac{2}{3}$
16. $\frac{5}{8} + \frac{9}{8} = \frac{14}{8}$, or $1\frac{3}{4}$
17. $\frac{2}{10} + \frac{6}{10} = \frac{8}{10}$, or $\frac{4}{5}$
18. $\frac{7}{12} + \frac{1}{12} = \frac{8}{12}$, or $\frac{2}{3}$
19. $\frac{2}{12} + \frac{4}{12} = \frac{6}{12}$, or $\frac{1}{2}$
20. $\frac{5}{6} + \frac{4}{6} = \frac{9}{6}$, or $1\frac{1}{2}$
21. $\frac{5}{8} + \frac{5}{8} = \frac{10}{8}$, or $1\frac{1}{4}$
22. $\frac{8}{12} + \frac{3}{12} = \frac{11}{12}$
23. $\frac{2}{8} + \frac{3}{8} = \frac{5}{8}$
24. $\frac{2}{3} + \frac{1}{3} = \frac{3}{3}$, or 1
25. $\frac{1}{6} + \frac{5}{6} = \frac{6}{6}$, or 1
26. $\frac{3}{8} + \frac{1}{8} = \frac{4}{8}$, or $\frac{1}{2}$
27. $\frac{3}{10} + \frac{5}{10} = \frac{8}{10}$, or $\frac{4}{5}$

McGraw-Hill School Division

RETEACH • 100

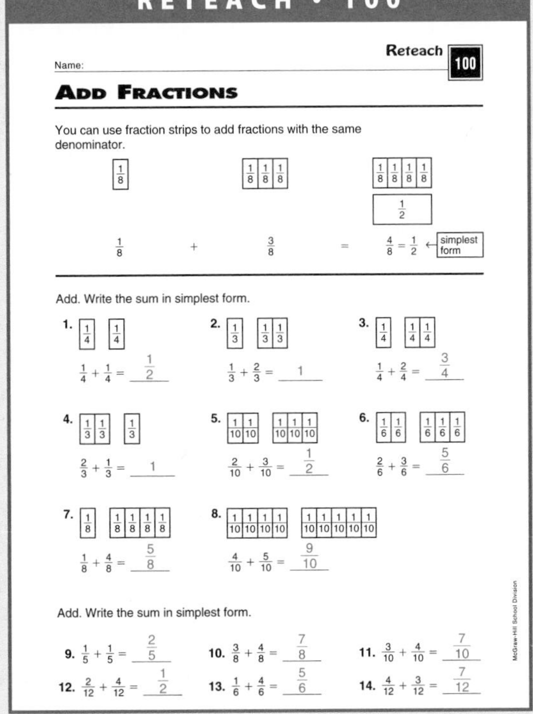

Reteach 100

Name:

ADD FRACTIONS

You can use fraction strips to add fractions with the same denominator.

$\frac{1}{8} + \frac{3}{8} = \frac{4}{8} = \frac{1}{2}$ ← simplest form

Add. Write the sum in simplest form.

1. $\frac{1}{4} + \frac{1}{4} = \frac{1}{2}$
2. $\frac{1}{3} + \frac{2}{3} = 1$
3. $\frac{1}{4} + \frac{2}{4} = \frac{3}{4}$
4. $\frac{2}{3} + \frac{1}{3} = 1$
5. $\frac{2}{10} + \frac{3}{10} = \frac{1}{2}$
6. $\frac{2}{6} + \frac{3}{6} = \frac{5}{6}$
7. $\frac{1}{8} + \frac{4}{8} = \frac{5}{8}$
8. $\frac{4}{10} + \frac{5}{10} = \frac{9}{10}$

Add. Write the sum in simplest form.

9. $\frac{1}{5} + \frac{1}{5} = \frac{2}{5}$
10. $\frac{3}{8} + \frac{4}{8} = \frac{7}{8}$
11. $\frac{3}{10} + \frac{4}{10} = \frac{7}{10}$
12. $\frac{2}{12} + \frac{4}{12} = \frac{1}{2}$
13. $\frac{1}{6} + \frac{4}{6} = \frac{5}{6}$
14. $\frac{4}{12} + \frac{3}{12} = \frac{7}{12}$

McGraw-Hill School Division

EXTEND • 100

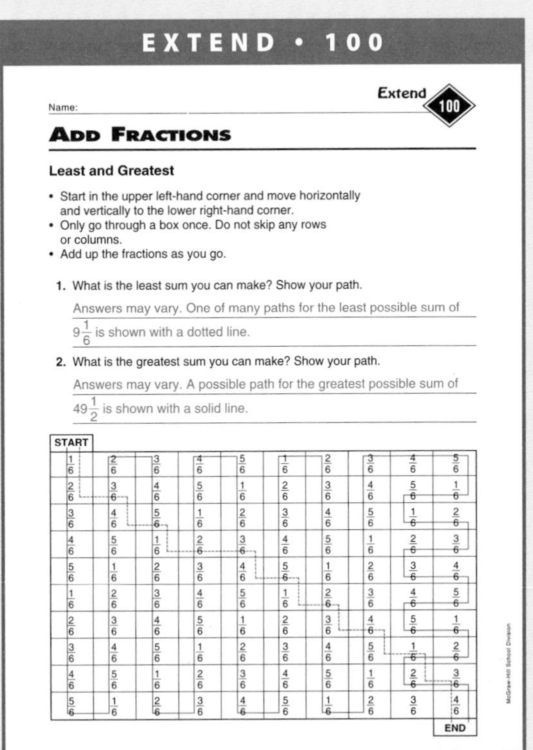

Extend 100

Name:

ADD FRACTIONS

Least and Greatest

- Start in the upper left-hand corner and move horizontally and vertically to the lower right-hand corner.
- Only go through a box once. Do not skip any rows or columns.
- Add up the fractions as you go.

1. What is the least sum you can make? Show your path.
Answers may vary. One of many paths for the least possible sum of $9\frac{1}{6}$ is shown with a dotted line.

2. What is the greatest sum you can make? Show your path.
Answers may vary. A possible path for the greatest possible sum of $49\frac{1}{2}$ is shown with a solid line.

START

$\frac{1}{6}$	$\frac{2}{6}$	$\frac{3}{6}$	$\frac{4}{6}$	$\frac{5}{6}$	$\frac{1}{6}$	$\frac{2}{6}$	$\frac{3}{6}$	$\frac{4}{6}$	$\frac{5}{6}$
$\frac{2}{6}$	$\frac{3}{6}$	$\frac{4}{6}$	$\frac{5}{6}$	$\frac{1}{6}$	$\frac{2}{6}$	$\frac{3}{6}$	$\frac{4}{6}$	$\frac{5}{6}$	$\frac{1}{6}$
$\frac{3}{6}$	$\frac{4}{6}$	$\frac{5}{6}$	$\frac{1}{6}$	$\frac{2}{6}$	$\frac{3}{6}$	$\frac{4}{6}$	$\frac{5}{6}$	$\frac{1}{6}$	$\frac{2}{6}$
$\frac{4}{6}$	$\frac{5}{6}$	$\frac{1}{6}$	$\frac{2}{6}$	$\frac{3}{6}$	$\frac{4}{6}$	$\frac{5}{6}$	$\frac{1}{6}$	$\frac{2}{6}$	$\frac{3}{6}$
$\frac{5}{6}$	$\frac{1}{6}$	$\frac{2}{6}$	$\frac{3}{6}$	$\frac{4}{6}$	$\frac{5}{6}$	$\frac{1}{6}$	$\frac{2}{6}$	$\frac{3}{6}$	$\frac{4}{6}$
$\frac{1}{6}$	$\frac{2}{6}$	$\frac{3}{6}$	$\frac{4}{6}$	$\frac{5}{6}$	$\frac{1}{6}$	$\frac{2}{6}$	$\frac{3}{6}$	$\frac{4}{6}$	$\frac{5}{6}$
$\frac{2}{6}$	$\frac{3}{6}$	$\frac{4}{6}$	$\frac{5}{6}$	$\frac{1}{6}$	$\frac{2}{6}$	$\frac{3}{6}$	$\frac{4}{6}$	$\frac{5}{6}$	$\frac{1}{6}$
$\frac{3}{6}$	$\frac{4}{6}$	$\frac{5}{6}$	$\frac{1}{6}$	$\frac{2}{6}$	$\frac{3}{6}$	$\frac{4}{6}$	$\frac{5}{6}$	$\frac{1}{6}$	$\frac{2}{6}$
$\frac{4}{6}$	$\frac{5}{6}$	$\frac{1}{6}$	$\frac{2}{6}$	$\frac{3}{6}$	$\frac{4}{6}$	$\frac{5}{6}$	$\frac{1}{6}$	$\frac{2}{6}$	$\frac{3}{6}$
$\frac{5}{6}$	$\frac{1}{6}$	$\frac{2}{6}$	$\frac{3}{6}$	$\frac{4}{6}$	$\frac{5}{6}$	$\frac{1}{6}$	$\frac{2}{6}$	$\frac{3}{6}$	$\frac{4}{6}$

END

McGraw-Hill School Division

Add Fractions

OBJECTIVE Add fractions with like denominators.

RESOURCE REMINDER
Math Center Cards 101
Practice 101, Reteach 101, Extend 101

SKILLS TRACE	
GRADE 3	• *Introduced at grade 4.*
GRADE 4	• Add fractions with like denominators with sums less than or greater than 1.
GRADE 5	• Add fractions with like or unlike denominators. *(Chapter 10)*

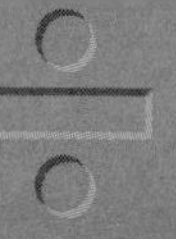

MANIPULATIVE WARM-UP

Cooperative Pairs — **Kinesthetic**

OBJECTIVE Using models to add fractions.

Materials per pair: fraction strips; 1–6 number cube

- ▶ Each student works with a partner. One student tosses the number cube.
- ▶ If the number tossed is 1, the partner finds two fractions with the same denominator whose sum is 1.
- ▶ If the number is 2, 3, 4, 5, or 6, the partner finds two fractions less than 1, each with the denominator tossed. Together, both students use fraction strips to find the sum of the fractions.
- ▶ Have students repeat the activity three more times, alternating roles.

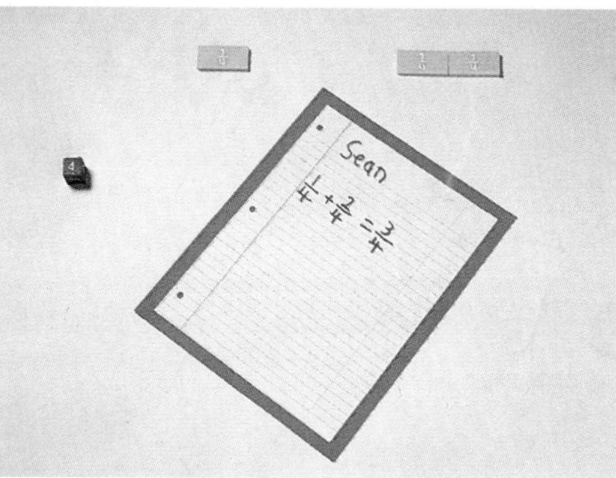

ESL APPROPRIATE

ALGEBRA CONNECTION

Cooperative Pairs — **Logical/Analytical**

OBJECTIVE Connect adding fractions to algebra.

Materials per pair: 1 index card; fraction strips (TA 26)

- ▶ Present the following problem:
  There are 12 peaches. Kim eats 3 peaches and Frank eats 2 peaches. What fraction of the peaches do Kim and Frank eat together?
- ▶ Have students work with a partner to solve the problem by writing a number sentence of fraction addition. They may use fraction strips to help solve. *[$\frac{3}{12} + \frac{2}{12} = \frac{5}{12}$ peaches]*
- ▶ Then have pairs work together to write a similar problem that can be solved by writing a number sentence of fraction addition. Pairs exchange problems and solve.
- ▶ Discuss how writing the number sentences helped solve the problems.

There are 18 students in my class. 4 boys and 6 girls are on the softball team. What fraction of the students in my class is on the softball team?

$$\frac{4}{18} + \frac{6}{18} = \frac{10}{18}, \text{ or } \frac{5}{9}$$

Daily Review

PREVIOUS DAY QUICK REVIEW

Find the sum.

1. $\frac{1}{3} + \frac{1}{3}$ *[$\frac{2}{3}$]*
2. $\frac{1}{4} + \frac{2}{4}$ *[$\frac{3}{4}$]*
3. $\frac{3}{8} + \frac{2}{8}$ *[$\frac{5}{8}$]*
4. $\frac{2}{5} + \frac{1}{5}$ *[$\frac{3}{5}$]*

FAST FACTS

1. 14 ÷ 7 *[2]*
2. 27 ÷ 9 *[3]*
3. 20 ÷ 4 *[5]*
4. 54 ÷ 9 *[6]*

Problem of the Day • 101

Lucy's plant grew $\frac{1}{16}$ inch the first week, $\frac{3}{16}$ inch the second week, and $\frac{5}{16}$ inch the third week. How much did the plant grow in 3 weeks? Did it grow more or less than $\frac{1}{2}$ inch? *[$\frac{9}{16}$ in.; more]*

TECH LINK

Math Van

MATH VAN

Tool You may wish to use the Fraction Models tool with this lesson.

MATH FORUM

Management Tip I keep sets of fraction strips available in a math corner for students to use as needed. Strips with the same denominator are separated and kept together in clearly marked envelopes.

Visit our Resource Village at http://www.mhschool.com to see more of the Math Forum.

MATH CENTER

Practice

OBJECTIVE Add fractions with like denominators.

Materials per pair: two-color counter; per student: connecting cube, Math Center Recording Sheet (TA 31 optional)

Partners move along a game board by adding fractions with like denominators and writing addition sentences. *[Students check each other's work.]*

MATH CENTER
Partners

PRACTICE ACTIVITY 101

Game • Adding to Go Home

YOU NEED
- 2 connecting cubes (as markers)
- two-color counter

- Copy the game board. Start on $\frac{1}{12}$. In turn, each player tosses the counter to move. Red side up means "+ $\frac{1}{12}$." Yellow side up means "+ $\frac{2}{12}$."
- Before you move, you must write an addition sentence for the space where you are and the amount of the move. Give the sum. If correct, you move to the space with that sum. If not, you lose that turn.
- The first player to reach $\frac{12}{12}$ or higher wins. Replay with a 16-box game board for sixteenths.

START	$\frac{1}{12}$	$\frac{2}{12}$	$\frac{3}{12}$	$\frac{4}{12}$	$\frac{5}{12}$	$\frac{6}{12}$	$\frac{7}{12}$	$\frac{8}{12}$	$\frac{9}{12}$	$\frac{10}{12}$	$\frac{11}{12}$	$\frac{12}{12}$	HOME

Grade Level 4 McGraw-Hill School Division

Chapter 11, Lesson 2, pages 414–415 Fractions

ESL APPROPRIATE

NCTM Standards
- Problem Solving
- Communication
- Reasoning
- ✓ Connections

Problem Solving

OBJECTIVE Explore fractional relationships among pattern blocks.

Materials per student: 0-9 spinner (TA 2), 2 number cubes, Math Center Recording Sheet (TA 31 optional)

Students write addition problems with like denominators, either 2, 4, or 8. Partners may use different denominators. They compare each other's problems to determine which has the greater sum.

MATH CENTER
Partners

PROBLEM-SOLVING ACTIVITY 101

Logical Reasoning • The 2–4–8 Game

YOU NEED
- 2 number cubes
- spinner (0–9)

Each of you works separately to make an addition problem of fractions.

- Roll the two number cubes. Use the two numbers to get the numerators. Then spin the spinner until you get 2, 4, or 8. If any other number comes up, spin again. That is your denominator for both fractions.
- Write your problems, but don't solve them. Decide who has the greater sum. The first player to name the greater sum correctly wins the round. Check by finding the sums and comparing them.

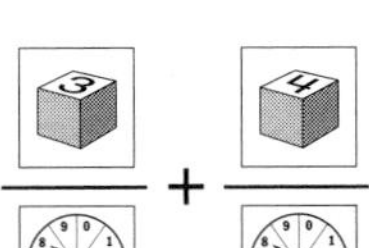
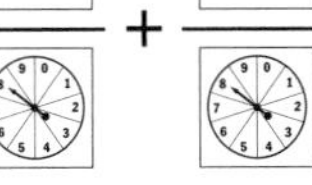

Grade Level 4 McGraw-Hill School Division

Chapter 11, Lesson 2, pages 414–415 Fractions

NCTM Standards
- ✓ Problem Solving
- ✓ Communication
- ✓ Reasoning
- Connections

Add Fractions

OBJECTIVE Add fractions with like denominators and sums less than or greater than 1.

Vocabulary common denominator, numerator

1 Introduce

Materials $\frac{1}{4}$ cup of brown sugar, $\frac{1}{4}$ cup of white sugar, measuring pitcher.

Present the sugar and pitcher to the class. Tell them:

A recipe for apple crisp uses $\frac{1}{4}$ cup of brown sugar and $\frac{1}{4}$ cup of white sugar. What is the total amount of sugar?

Have students suggest ways to solve the problem. Then have them find the total in simplest form. *[$\frac{1}{2}$ c sugar]*

2 Teach *Whole Class*

LEARN Compare the fraction strips to the steps listed for adding fractions. In Step 1, have students focus on the importance of a common denominator to add by asking:

- **Why do you need a common denominator to add?** *[Possible answer: to add like parts]*

More Examples Review the steps to find the sum for each example. Have students explain the additional steps they need to take to simplify answers in Examples B and C.

3 Close

Check for Understanding using items 1–5, page 414.

CRITICAL THINKING
In item 5, students are asked to determine if the Commutative Property of addition holds for fractions. Encourage them to extend the analysis to the Associative and Zero properties.

PRACTICE
Materials have available: calculators

Options for assigning exercises:
A—Odd ex. 1–13; all ex. 15–18; **Cultural Connection**
B—Even ex. 2–14; all ex. 15–18; **Cultural Connection**

- In ex. 17, students may need dot paper to help them find the answer.

Cultural Connection Liberia is a country in Western Africa. It was founded in the early 1800s.

Read through the **Cultural Note** with students. Suggest students order the units from least to greatest. Then have students work with a partner to complete the exercise.

Add Fractions

LEARN

Your class is creating a 12-month recipe calendar. You plan to have 4 main dish recipes, 3 appetizer recipes, and 5 dessert recipes. What fraction of the calendar contains recipes for appetizers and desserts?

Add: $\frac{3}{12} + \frac{5}{12}$ **Think:** $\frac{3}{12}$ are appetizers, $\frac{5}{12}$ are desserts.

Check Out the Glossary
common denominator
numerator
See page 544.

In the last lesson, you used fraction strips to add fractions with a **common denominator.**

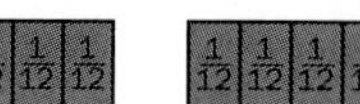
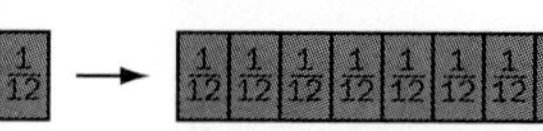
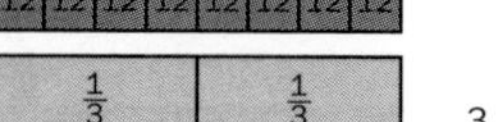

$\frac{3}{12} + \frac{5}{12} = \frac{8}{12}$, or $\frac{2}{3}$

Here is another method.

Step 1	Step 2	Step 3
Add the numerators. $\frac{3}{12} + \frac{5}{12} = \frac{8}{}$	**Use the common denominator.** $\frac{3}{12} + \frac{5}{12} = \frac{8}{12}$	**Write the sum in simplest fo** $\frac{8}{12} = \frac{8 \div 4}{12 \div 4} = \frac{2}{3}$

$\frac{2}{3}$ of the recipes are for appetizers and desserts.

More Examples

A $\frac{4}{16} + \frac{6}{16} + \frac{1}{16} = \frac{11}{16}$

B $\frac{3}{4} + \frac{2}{4} = \frac{5}{4}$
$\frac{5}{4} = 1\frac{1}{4}$

C $\frac{5}{6} + \frac{1}{6} = \frac{6}{6}$
$\frac{6}{6} = 1$

Check for Understanding

Add. Write the sum in simplest form.

1 $\frac{1}{6} + \frac{4}{6}$ $\frac{5}{6}$ **2** $\frac{1}{9} + \frac{2}{9}$ $\frac{1}{3}$ **3** $\frac{4}{12} + \frac{5}{12}$ $\frac{3}{4}$ **4** $\frac{3}{10} + \frac{1}{10} + \frac{8}{10}$

Critical Thinking: Analyze **Explain your reasoning.**

5 Does changing the order in which you add fractions change the sum? Why or why not? Give examples to support your answer.

No; the Commutative Property of addition holds; possible answer: $\frac{1}{4} + \frac{2}{4} = \frac{3}{4}$ and $\frac{2}{4} + \frac{1}{4} = \frac{3}{4}$.

Meeting Individual Needs

Early Finishers

Have students make up addition sentences each having three fractions with common denominators. Have them exchange number sentences with the sum missing so that they try to find the missing sums.

Extra Support

Some students make the common error of not simplifying the sum. Remind them to check if the numerator is greater than the denominator and to look for common factors after adding.

Ongoing Assessment

Observation Checklist
Observe if students can add fractions with like denominators by noting if they add the numerators and write the sum over a common denominator. Check that they remember to simplify the sum.

Follow Up Allow students who are having difficulty adding fractions to continue using fraction strips to find sums. Have them write the corresponding steps of the algorithm to record the sum. Assign **Reteach 101.**

For students who are ready for a challenge, assign **Extend 101.**

17.

ractice

1. Write the sum in simplest form.

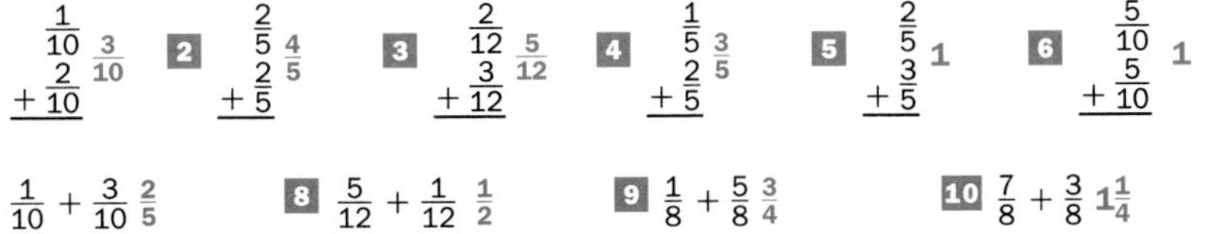

1 $\frac{1}{10} + \frac{2}{10}$ $\frac{3}{10}$ 2 $\frac{2}{5} + \frac{2}{5}$ $\frac{4}{5}$ 3 $\frac{2}{12} + \frac{3}{12}$ $\frac{5}{12}$ 4 $\frac{1}{5} + \frac{2}{5}$ $\frac{3}{5}$ 5 $\frac{2}{5} + \frac{3}{5}$ 1 6 $\frac{5}{10} + \frac{5}{10}$ 1

$\frac{1}{10} + \frac{3}{10}$ $\frac{2}{5}$ 8 $\frac{5}{12} + \frac{1}{12}$ $\frac{1}{2}$ 9 $\frac{1}{8} + \frac{5}{8}$ $\frac{3}{4}$ 10 $\frac{7}{8} + \frac{3}{8}$ $1\frac{1}{4}$

$\frac{1}{6} + \frac{1}{6} + \frac{3}{6}$ $\frac{5}{6}$ 12 $\frac{1}{9} + \frac{4}{9} + \frac{3}{9}$ $\frac{8}{9}$ 13 $\frac{1}{3} + \frac{2}{3} + \frac{2}{3}$ $1\frac{2}{3}$ 14 $\frac{2}{11} + \frac{5}{11} + \frac{6}{11}$ $1\frac{2}{11}$

PRACTICE

XED APPLICATIONS

roblem Solving

Pencil & Paper · Calculator · Mental Math

A basic muffin recipe for 12 muffins calls for $\frac{1}{4}$ cup of sugar and a $\frac{1}{2}$ cup of raisins. If you make 2 batches, how much sugar will you need? how many cups of raisins? $\frac{1}{2}$ **c sugar; 1 c raisins**

Spatial reasoning Is it possible to draw a triangle on dot paper that touches 8 dots but has no dots on the inside? Show an example. **Yes; see above for possible answer.**

16 **What if** you added $\frac{1}{8}$ cup of filberts and $\frac{1}{8}$ cup of hazelnuts to the recipe. How many cups of nuts is that? $\frac{1}{4}$ **c of nuts**

18 There are 12 muffins in each batch. How many muffins are there is 6 batches? **72 muffins**

ultural Connection

pelle Rice Measurement

e Kpelle (PE-lay) people of Liberia, Africa, measure e by using a *sâmo-ko* (sah-MOH-koh), or "salmon ." A sâmo-ko holds about 2 cups of rice.

rger amounts of rice may be measured with *ôke* (BAH-kee), or "bucket." A bôke is about sâmo-ko or $\frac{1}{2}$ of a *tin.* The largest Kpelle easure for rice is a *boro* (BAH-roh), or "bag." ôke is $\frac{1}{4}$ of a boro.

How are the units the Kpelle people use to measure rice related to each other?
sâmo-ko = 1 bôke, 2 bôke = 1 tin, 4 bôke = 1 boro, 2 tins = 1 boro

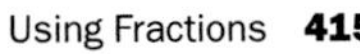

ra Practice, page 524

Alternate Teaching Strategy

Materials per student: fraction strips (TA 26)

Present the following problem:

Jeremy bought 6 granola bars. He ate 2 of the bars and gave one to his sister to eat.

Ask:

- **What fraction of the granola bars did Jeremy eat? his sister?** *[$\frac{2}{6}$; $\frac{1}{6}$]*
- **How many granola bars did Jeremy and his sister eat altogether?** *[3 granola bars]*
- **What fraction of the total did both eat?** *[$\frac{3}{6}$, or $\frac{1}{2}$]*

Have students use fraction strips to show each fraction and find the sum of $\frac{2}{6} + \frac{1}{6}$. *[$\frac{3}{6}$, or $\frac{1}{2}$]*

Point out that to find $\frac{2}{6} + \frac{1}{6}$, students add the numerators and write the sum over the common denominator. Then they simplify the sum.

Repeat the activity with other problems.

PRACTICE • 101

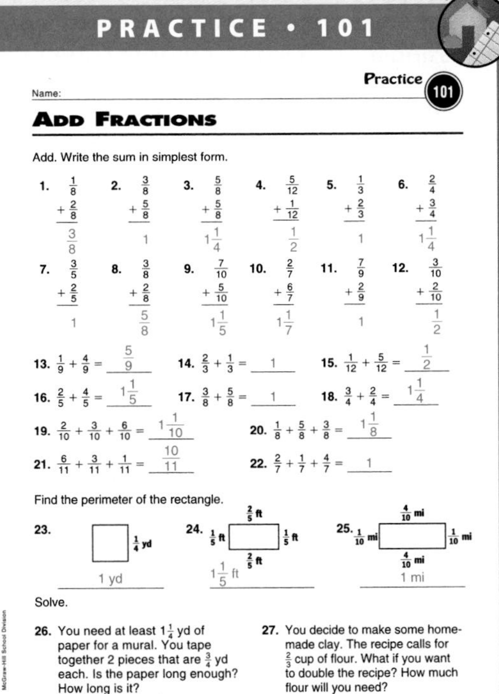

HOMEWORK

Practice 101

Name:

ADD FRACTIONS

Add. Write the sum in simplest form.

1. $\frac{1}{8} + \frac{2}{8}$ $\frac{3}{8}$
2. $\frac{3}{8} + \frac{5}{8}$ 1
3. $\frac{5}{8} + \frac{5}{8}$ $1\frac{1}{4}$
4. $\frac{5}{12} + \frac{1}{12}$ $\frac{1}{2}$
5. $\frac{1}{3} + \frac{2}{3}$ 1
6. $\frac{2}{4} + \frac{3}{4}$ $1\frac{1}{4}$
7. $\frac{3}{5} + \frac{2}{5}$ 1
8. $\frac{3}{8} + \frac{2}{8}$ $\frac{5}{8}$
9. $\frac{7}{10} + \frac{5}{10}$ $1\frac{1}{5}$
10. $\frac{2}{7} + \frac{6}{7}$ $1\frac{1}{7}$
11. $\frac{7}{9} + \frac{2}{9}$ 1
12. $\frac{3}{10} + \frac{2}{10}$ $\frac{1}{2}$
13. $\frac{1}{9} + \frac{4}{9} =$ $\frac{5}{9}$
14. $\frac{2}{3} + \frac{1}{3} =$ 1
15. $\frac{1}{12} + \frac{5}{12} =$ $\frac{1}{2}$
16. $\frac{2}{5} + \frac{4}{5} =$ $1\frac{1}{5}$
17. $\frac{3}{8} + \frac{5}{8} =$ 1
18. $\frac{3}{4} + \frac{2}{4} =$ $1\frac{1}{4}$
19. $\frac{2}{10} + \frac{3}{10} + \frac{6}{10} =$ $1\frac{1}{10}$
20. $\frac{1}{8} + \frac{5}{8} + \frac{3}{8} =$ $1\frac{1}{8}$
21. $\frac{6}{11} + \frac{3}{11} + \frac{1}{11} =$ $\frac{10}{11}$
22. $\frac{2}{7} + \frac{1}{7} + \frac{4}{7} =$ 1

Find the perimeter of the rectangle.

23. $\frac{1}{4}$ yd — 1 yd
24. $\frac{2}{5}$ ft, $\frac{1}{5}$ ft, $\frac{1}{5}$ ft, $\frac{2}{5}$ ft — $1\frac{1}{5}$ ft
25. $\frac{4}{10}$ mi, $\frac{1}{10}$ mi, $\frac{1}{10}$ mi, $\frac{4}{10}$ mi — 1 mi

Solve.

26. You need at least $1\frac{1}{4}$ yd of paper for a mural. You tape together 2 pieces that are $\frac{3}{4}$ yd each. Is the paper long enough? How long is it? Yes; $1\frac{1}{2}$ yd
27. You decide to make some home-made clay. The recipe calls for $\frac{2}{3}$ cup of flour. What if you want to double the recipe? How much flour will you need? $1\frac{1}{3}$ c

McGraw-Hill School Division

RETEACH • 101

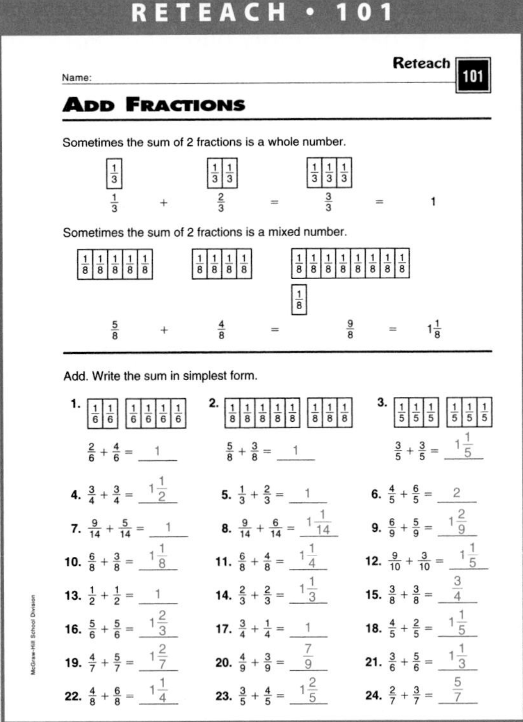

Reteach 101

Name:

ADD FRACTIONS

Sometimes the sum of 2 fractions is a whole number.

$\frac{1}{3} + \frac{2}{3} = \frac{3}{3} = 1$

Sometimes the sum of 2 fractions is a mixed number.

$\frac{5}{8} + \frac{4}{8} = \frac{9}{8} = 1\frac{1}{8}$

Add. Write the sum in simplest form.

1. $\frac{2}{6} + \frac{4}{6} =$ 1
2. $\frac{5}{8} + \frac{3}{8} =$ 1
3. $\frac{3}{5} + \frac{3}{5} =$ $1\frac{1}{5}$
4. $\frac{3}{4} + \frac{3}{4} =$ $1\frac{1}{2}$
5. $\frac{1}{3} + \frac{2}{3} =$ 1
6. $\frac{4}{5} + \frac{6}{5} =$ 2
7. $\frac{9}{14} + \frac{5}{14} =$ 1
8. $\frac{9}{14} + \frac{6}{14} =$ $1\frac{1}{14}$
9. $\frac{6}{9} + \frac{5}{9} =$ $1\frac{2}{9}$
10. $\frac{6}{8} + \frac{3}{8} =$ $1\frac{1}{8}$
11. $\frac{6}{8} + \frac{4}{8} =$ $1\frac{1}{4}$
12. $\frac{9}{10} + \frac{3}{10} =$ $1\frac{1}{5}$
13. $\frac{1}{2} + \frac{1}{2} =$ 1
14. $\frac{2}{3} + \frac{2}{3} =$ $1\frac{1}{3}$
15. $\frac{3}{8} + \frac{3}{8} =$ $\frac{3}{4}$
16. $\frac{5}{6} + \frac{5}{6} =$ $1\frac{2}{3}$
17. $\frac{3}{4} + \frac{1}{4} =$ 1
18. $\frac{4}{5} + \frac{2}{5} =$ $1\frac{1}{5}$
19. $\frac{4}{7} + \frac{5}{7} =$ $1\frac{2}{7}$
20. $\frac{4}{9} + \frac{3}{9} =$ $\frac{7}{9}$
21. $\frac{3}{6} + \frac{5}{6} =$ $1\frac{1}{3}$
22. $\frac{4}{8} + \frac{6}{8} =$ $1\frac{1}{4}$
23. $\frac{3}{5} + \frac{4}{5} =$ $1\frac{2}{5}$
24. $\frac{2}{7} + \frac{3}{7} =$ $\frac{5}{7}$

McGraw-Hill School Division

EXTEND • 101

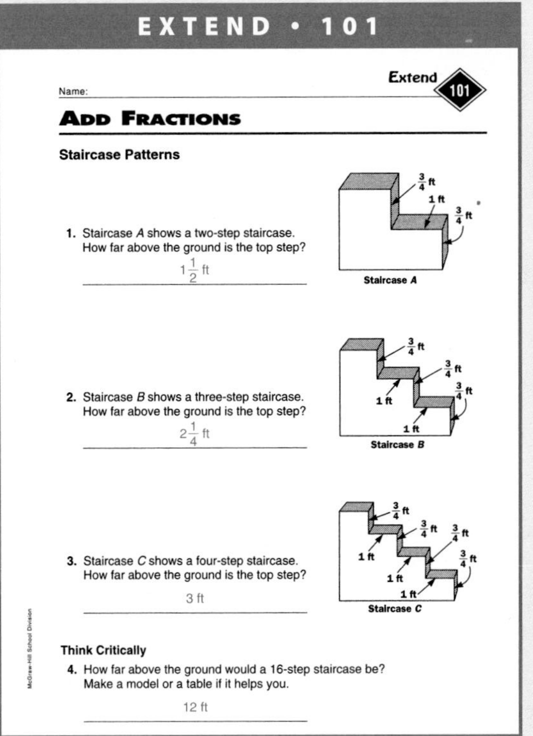

Extend 101

Name:

ADD FRACTIONS

Staircase Patterns

1. Staircase *A* shows a two-step staircase. How far above the ground is the top step? $1\frac{1}{2}$ ft
2. Staircase *B* shows a three-step staircase. How far above the ground is the top step? $2\frac{1}{4}$ ft
3. Staircase *C* shows a four-step staircase. How far above the ground is the top step? 3 ft

Think Critically

4. How far above the ground would a 16-step staircase be? Make a model or a table if it helps you. 12 ft

McGraw-Hill School Division

LESSON 11.3

EXPLORE ACTIVITY

Subtract Fractions

OBJECTIVE Explore subtracting fractions with like denominators.

RESOURCE REMINDER
Math Center Cards 102
Practice 102, Reteach 102, Extend 102

SKILLS TRACE

GRADE 3	• *Introduced at grade 4.*
GRADE 4	• Explore subtracting fractions with like denominators.
GRADE 5	• Explore subtracting fractions with like or unlike denominators. *(Chapter 10)*

MANIPULATIVE WARM-UP

Whole Class — **Individual**

OBJECTIVE Review finding fraction sums.

Materials have available: fraction strips (TA 26)

▶ Copy the following on the chalkboard:

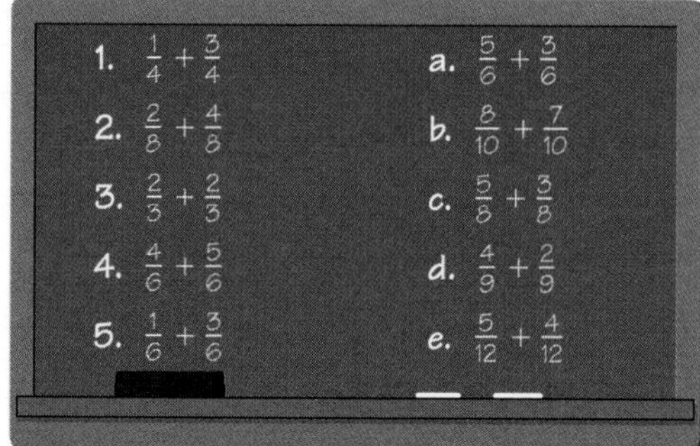

▶ Have students match the letters and numbers that have equal sums. *[**1.** c; **2.** e; **3.** a; **4.** b; **5.** d]* Students may use fraction strips to find the sums.

▶ Discuss how students found the equal sums. *[Possible answer: After adding, simplify each sum and look for equal sums.]*

PROBABILITY CONNECTION

Cooperative Groups — **Logical/Analytical**

OBJECTIVE Connect fraction sums to probability.

Materials per group: 2 index cards

▶ Have students work in small groups. First, tell them to think of an event that has 2 or more outcomes. For example, tossing a 2 or a 3 on a number cube.

▶ Then they write a problem about the event that can be solved by adding fractions. Students write the problem on an index card. See the example problem below.

▶ Have groups exchange index cards and work together to solve the problems.

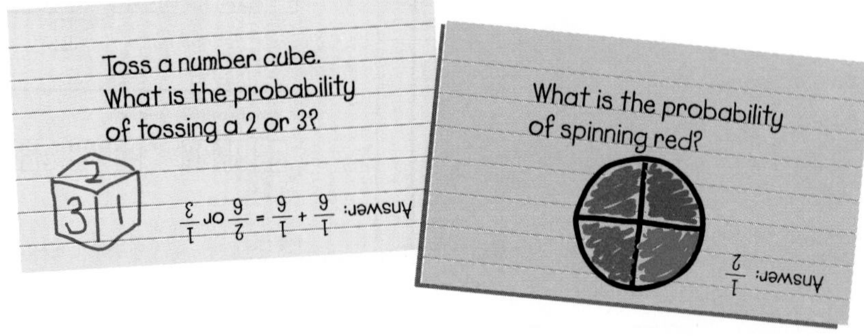

Toss a number cube.
What is the probability
of tossing a 2 or 3?
Answer: $\frac{1}{6}+\frac{1}{6}=\frac{2}{6}$ or $\frac{1}{3}$
What is the probability
of spinning red?
Answer: $\frac{1}{2}$

Daily Review

PREVIOUS DAY QUICK REVIEW

Find the sum and then simplify.

1. $\frac{3}{8} + \frac{3}{8}$ *[$\frac{3}{4}$]*
2. $\frac{2}{6} + \frac{5}{6}$ *[$1\frac{1}{6}$]*
3. $\frac{1}{4} + \frac{3}{4}$ *[1]*
4. $\frac{5}{8} + \frac{2}{8}$ *[$\frac{7}{8}$]*

FAST FACTS

1. 7 ÷ 1 *[7]*
2. 12 ÷ 2 *[6]*
3. 30 ÷ 6 *[5]*
4. 48 ÷ 8 *[6]*

Problem of the Day • 102

Clark has $\frac{7}{8}$ yard of blue ribbon and $\frac{3}{8}$ yard of red ribbon. How much more blue ribbon than red ribbon does Clark have? *[$\frac{4}{8}$, or $\frac{1}{2}$ yd]*

TECH LINK

Math Van

MATH VAN

Tool You may wish to use the Fraction Models tool and the Circle Graph tool with this lesson.

MATH FORUM

Idea I encourage my students to use addition to check each fraction difference. Writing addition sentences to check subtraction helps them gain facility in operations with fractions.

Visit our Resource Village at http://www.mhschool.com to see more of the Math Forum.

MATH CENTER

Practice

OBJECTIVE Use a model to subtract fractions with a common denominator.

Materials per student: Math Center Recording Sheet (TA 31 optional)

Students create a rectangle with a number of interior boxes equal to the denominator they are working with. They show the first fraction as unshaded boxes, and subtract the second fraction by crossing out unshaded boxes. *[1. $\frac{2}{9}$; 2. $\frac{1}{2}$; 3. $\frac{3}{11}$; 4. $\frac{3}{16}$; Check students' fraction boxes.]*

MATH CENTER On Your Own

PRACTICE ACTIVITY 102

Manipulatives • Fraction Box

You can make a fraction box to subtract like fractions. A fraction box is a long, thin rectangle divided into as many squares as the denominator has. Here is how to find the difference of $\frac{7}{12} - \frac{3}{12}$:

- First divide the rectangle into 12 boxes. Then count 7 squares (for $\frac{7}{12}$) and shade the rest.
- To subtract $\frac{3}{12}$, cross out 3 boxes and count what's left.

Draw a fraction box to find each difference.

1. $\frac{6}{9} - \frac{4}{9}$ 2. $\frac{8}{10} - \frac{3}{10}$
3. $\frac{9}{11} - \frac{6}{11}$ 4. $\frac{7}{16} - \frac{4}{16}$

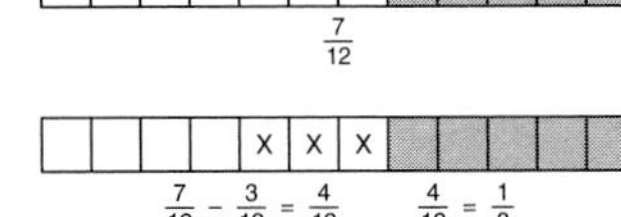

Grade Level 4 · McGraw-Hill School Division

Chapter 11, Lesson 3, pages 416–419 — Fractions

NCTM Standards
- ✓ Problem Solving
- ✓ Communication
- ✓ Reasoning
- Connections

Problem Solving

OBJECTIVE Subtract fractions using plane-figure shapes.

Materials per student: Math Center Recording Sheet (TA 31 optional)

Students subtract $\frac{2}{12}$ from a double-hexagon shape (10-sided polygon) equivalent to $\frac{12}{12}$. With each subtraction, students name and draw possible shapes for the newly formed polygon. *[Check students' work.]*

MATH CENTER On Your Own

PROBLEM-SOLVING ACTIVITY 102

Spatial Reasoning • Make a Polygon

- Put two hexagons together and you have a 10-sided polygon. Look closely and you can see that this new polygon is made up of 12 triangles. Each triangle equals $\frac{1}{12}$. The polygon itself equals $\frac{12}{12}$.
- Subtract $\frac{2}{12}$ from the polygon. What is left? Draw the possible shapes of the new polygon.
- Keep subtracting $\frac{2}{12}$ each time, drawing possible shapes for what is left.

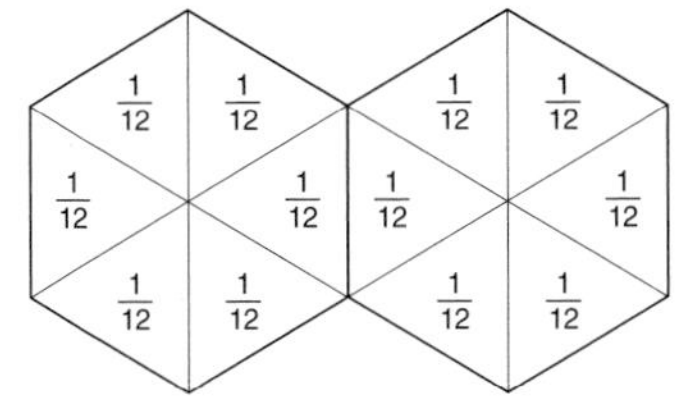

Grade Level 4 · McGraw-Hill School Division

Chapter 11, Lesson 3, pages 416–419 — Fractions

NCTM Standards
- ✓ Problem Solving
- Communication
- ✓ Reasoning
- Connections

EXPLORE ACTIVITY
Subtract Fractions

OBJECTIVE Explore subtracting fractions with like denominators.

Materials per pair: fraction strips (TA 26)

1 Introduce

Materials: clear plastic measuring cup with $\frac{1}{4}$ cup markings, 1 cup water

Pour $\frac{1}{4}$ cup water into a measuring cup and show students.

Then pour more water into the measuring cup until it shows $\frac{3}{4}$ cup full. Ask:

- **What number sentence can you use to show this process?** *[$\frac{1}{4}$ + _____ = $\frac{3}{4}$]*

Copy the following number sentence on the chalkboard:

$$\frac{1}{4} + \square = \frac{3}{4}.$$

Have students find the missing addend. *[$\frac{2}{4}$, or $\frac{1}{2}$]*
Then focus on the operation that can be used to find the missing fraction by asking:

- **What operation is the opposite of addition?** *[subtraction]*
- **How could you use subtraction to solve for the missing fraction?** *[$\frac{3}{4} - \frac{1}{4} = \blacksquare$]*
- **How much water was poured into the cup a second time?** *[$\frac{2}{4}$, or $\frac{1}{2}$ c]*

2 Teach *Cooperative Pairs*

Cultural Connection Read the **Cultural Note.** Southern Africa, dominated by the country of South Africa, includes the countries of Botswana, Zimbabwe, Namibia, Mozambique, Swaziland, and Lesotho. The main economic activity of Africa is agriculture. Rice, yams, cassava, okra, plantains, and bananas are among the crops raised for food. Ocean fishing and mining are also important activities in the economy of southern Africa.

LEARN Work Together Remind students to record all parts of a fraction as they record what the models show in number sentences.

Talk It Over Have students compare methods for subtracting and how they used the models. Have them comment on when they simplified their answers in the recording process.

Subtract Fractions

LEARN

Miko is making *bobotie* (BOH-boh-tī). She has a box of raisins in her cupboard that is $\frac{5}{8}$ filled. She will use $\frac{3}{8}$ of the box for her meal. What part of the box will be left?

To solve the problem, you need to subtract fractions.

Cultural Note
Bobotie is a spicy dish made in southe[rn] Africa. It is usually made in a cassero[le] dish with onions, bread, ground beef curry powder, almonds, and raisins.

Work Together
Work with a partner to explore subtracting fractions.

Use fraction strips to model the problem. Write a number sentence to show your work.

You will need
- *fraction strips*

Continue using fraction strips to subtract these fractions:

a. $\frac{2}{3} - \frac{1}{3}$ $\frac{1}{3}$ **b.** $\frac{4}{8} - \frac{3}{8}$ $\frac{1}{8}$ **c.** $\frac{3}{5} - \frac{1}{5}$ $\frac{2}{5}$

d. $\frac{5}{6} - \frac{1}{6}$ $\frac{4}{6}$, or $\frac{2}{3}$ **e.** $\frac{5}{10} - \frac{3}{10}$ $\frac{2}{10}$, or $\frac{1}{5}$ **f.** $\frac{11}{12} - \frac{5}{12}$ $\frac{6}{12}$, or $\frac{1}{2}$

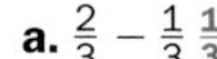

Talk It Over
- What part of the box of raisins is left? **$\frac{2}{8}$, or $\frac{1}{4}$, of the box**
- What method did you use to find the differences? **Possible answer: Found fraction strips to represent the total amount and took away strips to represent the amount used.**

Meeting Individual Needs

Extra Support

Remind students that they can use addition to check subtraction. If students prefer, have them check their differences using fraction strips.

Inclusion

Provide students with alternative ways to make models to subtract. For example, have them show $\frac{7}{12} - \frac{3}{12}$ using 7 marbles in an egg carton. Help them record the differences in number sentences.

Ongoing Assessment

Anecdotal Report Note if students are able to subtract fractions using fraction strips. Observe whether they write the difference over a common denominator.

Follow Up For students who would benefit by additional practice subtracting fractions with models, assign **Reteach 102.**

For students who successfully subtract fractions using models, assign **Extend 102.**

ake Connections

ndall and Lori drew fraction strips to show their work.

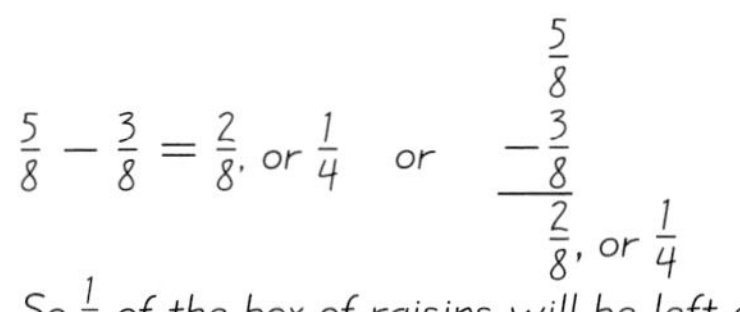

$\frac{5}{8} - \frac{3}{8} = \frac{2}{8}$, or $\frac{1}{4}$ or $\frac{5}{8} - \frac{3}{8} = \frac{2}{8}$, or $\frac{1}{4}$
So $\frac{1}{4}$ of the box of raisins will be left over.

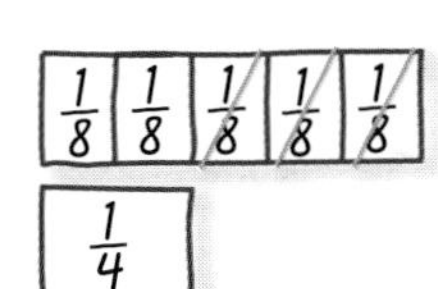

Check if the differences in your number sentences are in simplest form. If not, write them in simplest form. **Check students' work. See answers on page 416.**

heck for Understanding

se models to complete the number sentence.

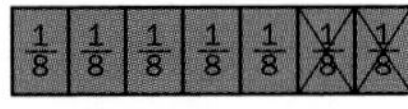

$\frac{7}{8} - \frac{2}{8} = \frac{■}{8}$ **5**

2 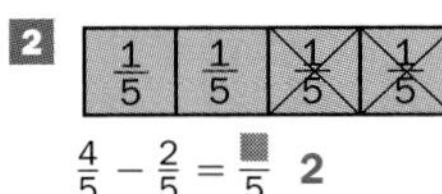

$\frac{4}{5} - \frac{2}{5} = \frac{■}{5}$ **2**

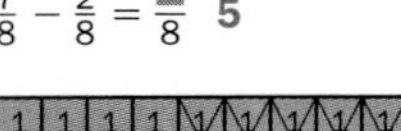

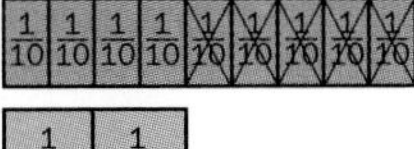

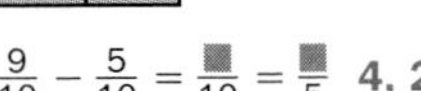

$\frac{9}{10} - \frac{5}{10} = \frac{■}{10} = \frac{■}{5}$ **4, 2**

4 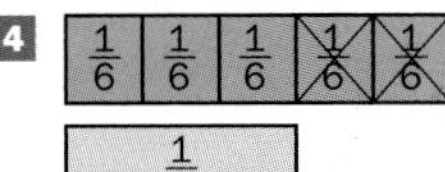

$\frac{5}{6} - \frac{2}{6} = \frac{■}{6} = \frac{■}{2}$ **3, 1**

ubtract using models. Write the difference in simplest form.

$\frac{7}{8} - \frac{5}{8}$ **$\frac{1}{4}$**	**6** $\frac{2}{4} - \frac{1}{4}$ **$\frac{1}{4}$**	**7** $\frac{4}{5} - \frac{1}{5}$ **$\frac{3}{5}$**	**8** $\frac{3}{4} - \frac{2}{4}$ **$\frac{1}{4}$**	**9** $\frac{5}{6} - \frac{3}{6}$ **$\frac{1}{3}$**	**10** $\frac{7}{8} - \frac{1}{8}$ **$\frac{3}{4}$**

$\frac{4}{8} - \frac{2}{8}$ **$\frac{1}{4}$** **12** $\frac{5}{8} - \frac{1}{8}$ **$\frac{1}{2}$** **13** $\frac{1}{2} - \frac{1}{2}$ **0** **14** $\frac{7}{10} - \frac{1}{10}$ **$\frac{3}{5}$** **15** $\frac{7}{12} - \frac{4}{12}$ **$\frac{1}{4}$**

ritical Thinking: Summarize

Describe how you would use fraction strips to subtract $\frac{7}{10} - \frac{5}{10}$. Tell how you would simplify the answer. **Possible answer: Show $\frac{7}{10}$ in strips, then take $\frac{5}{10}$ of them away and count the number of strips left; to simplify, see if there is another fraction strip that equals the $\frac{2}{10}$ that are left—$\frac{1}{5}$ equals $\frac{2}{10}$.**

Turn the page for Practice.

MAKE CONNECTIONS

Discuss how the number sentence $\frac{5}{8} - \frac{3}{8} = \frac{2}{8}$, or $\frac{1}{4}$, represents the fraction strips used to find the difference. As students complete number sentences using models, suggest they draw diagrams of their models. This will reinforce their understanding of the subtraction process and provide them with an alternative method for subtracting, if fraction strips are unavailable.

Encourage them to use alternative diagrams to find fraction differences such as rectangles divided into strips or grids, or circles divided into wedges.

3 Close

Check for Understanding using items 1–16, page 417.

CRITICAL THINKING

JOURNAL In item 16, students summarize how to use fraction strips to subtract. Accept a wide variety of responses. Encourage students to sketch the fraction strips beside the words that summarize their methods.

Practice See pages 418–419.

PRACTICE

Materials have available: fraction strips (TA 26); calculators

Options for assigning exercises:
A—Odd ex. 1–15; all ex. 17–21; ex. 22–26; **More to Explore**
B—Even ex. 2–16; all ex. 17–21; ex. 22–26; **More to Explore**

- For ex. 7–16, encourage students to use mental math when they can.
- In ex. 17–20, remind students that they can use the choices to help find the answer.
- For **Make It Right** (ex. 22), see Common Error below.
- In ex. 23, students use the problem-solving strategy, Interpret Data, to solve.

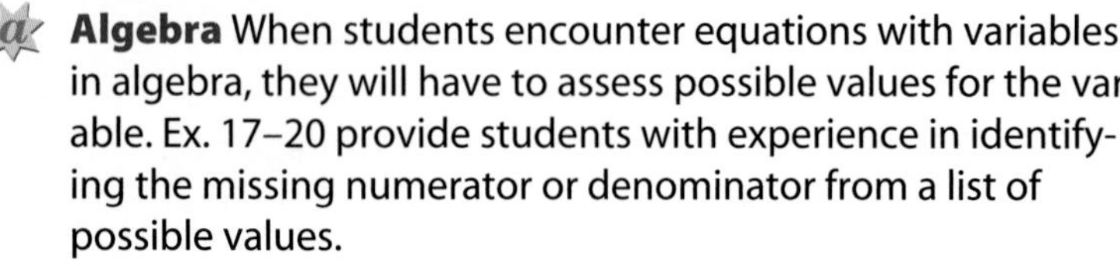

Algebra When students encounter equations with variables in algebra, they will have to assess possible values for the variable. Ex. 17–20 provide students with experience in identifying the missing numerator or denominator from a list of possible values.

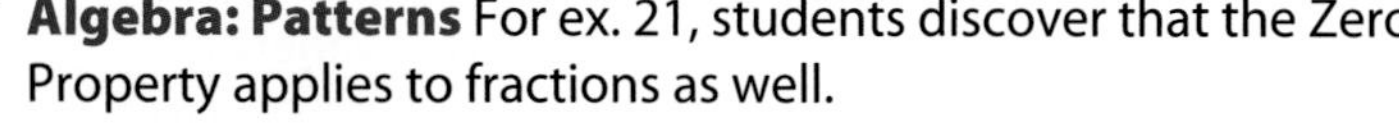

Algebra: Patterns For ex. 21, students discover that the Zero Property applies to fractions as well.

More to Explore Review how to read a circle graph. Make sure that students are able to interpret the graph with fractions by asking:

- **What fraction of the money spent is for dessert?** *[$\frac{3}{8}$]*

Then have students work in pairs to complete the exercises.

Practice

Use models to complete the number sentence.

1 $\frac{5}{10} - \frac{4}{10} = \frac{■}{10}$ 1

2 $\frac{6}{8} - \frac{3}{8} = \frac{■}{8}$ 3

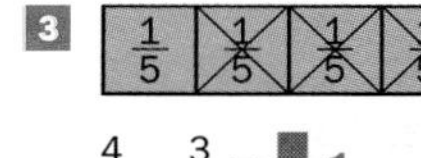

3 $\frac{4}{5} - \frac{3}{5} = \frac{■}{5}$ 1

4 $\frac{7}{12} - \frac{4}{12} = \frac{■}{12} = \frac{■}{4}$ 3, 1

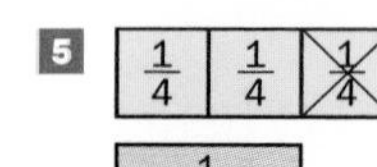

5 $\frac{3}{4} - \frac{1}{4} = \frac{■}{4} = \frac{■}{2}$ 2, 1

6 $\frac{4}{6} - \frac{1}{6} = \frac{■}{6} = \frac{■}{2}$ 3, 1

Subtract. Write the difference in simplest form.

7 $\frac{8}{12} - \frac{2}{12}$ $\frac{1}{2}$ **8** $\frac{4}{6} - \frac{3}{6}$ $\frac{1}{6}$ **9** $\frac{7}{10} - \frac{4}{10}$ $\frac{3}{10}$ **10** $\frac{5}{8} - \frac{2}{8}$ $\frac{3}{8}$ **11** $\frac{9}{12} -$

12 $\frac{4}{6} - \frac{2}{6}$ $\frac{1}{3}$ **13** $\frac{9}{12} - \frac{6}{12}$ $\frac{1}{4}$ **14** $\frac{8}{10} - \frac{2}{10}$ $\frac{3}{5}$ **15** $\frac{8}{12} - \frac{5}{12}$ $\frac{1}{4}$ **16** $\frac{3}{6} - \frac{1}{6}$

ALGEBRA Choose the letter of the number that completes the number sentence.

17 $\frac{3}{6} - \frac{2}{6} = ■$ b **a.** $\frac{8}{12}$ **b.** $\frac{1}{6}$ **c.** $\frac{5}{8}$ **d.** $\frac{1}{3}$

18 $\frac{8}{12} - \frac{■}{12} = \frac{1}{12}$ d **a.** 9 **b.** 1 **c.** 12 **d.** 7

19 $\frac{3}{8} - \frac{2}{■} = \frac{1}{8}$ c **a.** 3 **b.** 2 **c.** 8 **d.** 4

20 $\frac{■}{10} - \frac{3}{10} = \frac{3}{10}$ d **a.** 1 **b.** 2 **c.** 5 **d.** 6

a. If you subtract a fraction from itself, the difference is zero.

21 **ALGEBRA: PATTERNS** Find the difference. For each row, describe any patterns you see.

a. $\frac{2}{5} - \frac{2}{5}$ 0 $\frac{5}{6} - \frac{5}{6}$ 0 $\frac{1}{8} - \frac{1}{8}$ 0 $\frac{3}{10} - \frac{3}{10}$ 0

b. $\frac{1}{2} - 0$ $\frac{1}{2}$ $\frac{2}{3} - 0$ $\frac{2}{3}$ $\frac{3}{4} - 0$ $\frac{3}{4}$ $\frac{7}{12} - 0$ $\frac{7}{12}$

b. If you subtract zero from a fraction, the difference is the fraction.

Make It Right

22 Darren drew fraction strips to find $\frac{5}{8} - \frac{1}{8}$. Tell what the mistake is and correct it.

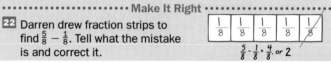

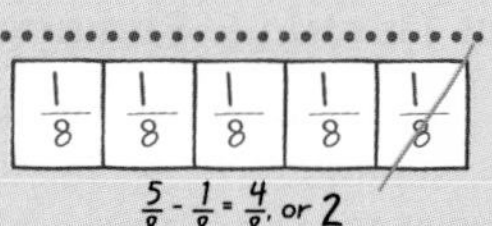

He counted the models—he should have written $\frac{5}{8} - \frac{1}{8} = \frac{4}{8} = \frac{1}{2}$.

Meeting Individual Needs

Early Finishers

Present this pattern of number sentences: $\frac{4}{5} - \frac{4}{5} = 0$, $\frac{4}{5} - \frac{3}{5} = \frac{1}{5}$, $\frac{4}{5} - \frac{2}{5} = \frac{2}{5}$. Ask students to write the next sentence. *[$\frac{4}{5} - \frac{1}{5} = \frac{3}{5}$]* Have students create similar patterns.

Common Error

Some students may not simplify fractions correctly, as in **Make It Right** (ex. 22). Have these students check that the simplified difference is less than or equal to the first fraction in the number sentence.

Language Support

As students work through the problems, discuss some of the foods listed. Promote cultural diversity by having students describe some of their favorite breakfast or lunch items.

ESL APPROPRIATE

Gifted And Talented

Have students write 5 to 10 number sentences that show finding the difference between 1 and some fraction. For example: $1 - \frac{3}{8} = \frac{5}{8}$. Have them identify any patterns they notice.

. No; students may have eaten more than one item in the pictograph for breakfast.

XED APPLICATIONS

roblem Solving

Pencil & Paper | Calculator | Mental Math

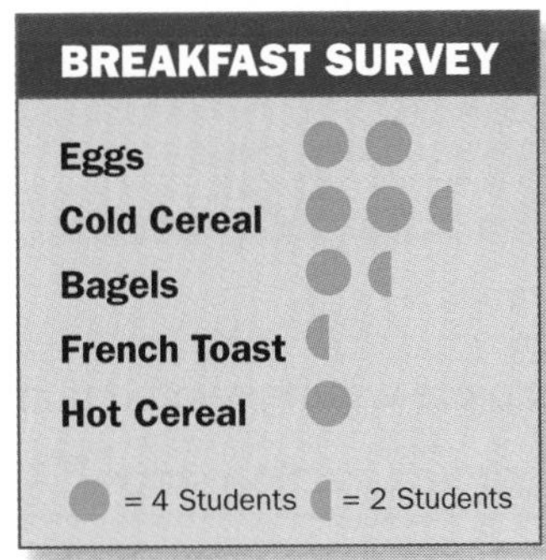

the pictograph for problem 23.

a. How many students ate eggs for breakfast? **8 students**

b. How many more students ate cold cereal than hot cereal? **6 students**

c. Can you tell how many students were surveyed? Why or why not? **See above.**

Ada needs $\frac{7}{8}$ cup of almonds for her bobotie. If she has $\frac{3}{8}$ cup, how many more cups does she need? **$\frac{4}{8}$ c, or $\frac{1}{2}$ c**

Mr. Hodges bought $\frac{3}{4}$ lb of roast beef. He used $\frac{1}{4}$ lb of roast beef for each of his two roast beef sandwiches. How much roast beef does he have left? **$\frac{1}{4}$ lb**

26 **Write a problem** that can be solved by subtracting fractions with like denominators. Solve it. Trade with a classmate and solve each other's problems. **Students should compare problems and solutions.**

more to explore

actions in Circle Graphs

can add and subtract fractions to solve blems using information from a circle graph.

circle graph shows what part of the total amount money was spent on different lunch items.

find the amount spent on andwich and fries, d the fractions.

Think: $\frac{3}{8} + \frac{1}{8} = \frac{4}{8}$, or $\frac{1}{2}$

$\frac{1}{2}$ the money was spent on a sandwich and fries.

Money Spent for Lunch

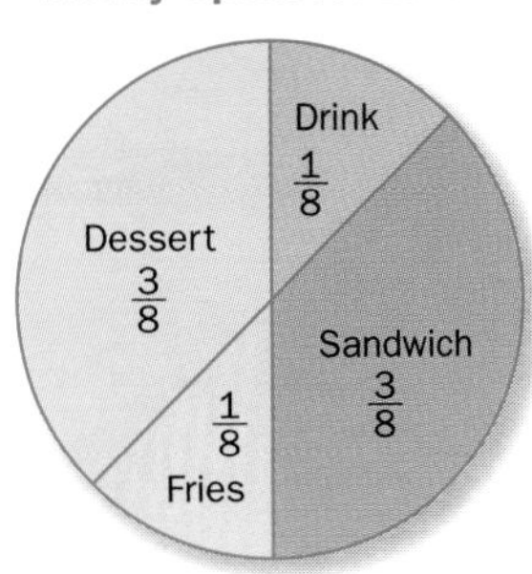

ve. Use the circle graph.

Was a greater fraction of the money spent for dessert or for fries? Explain. **Possible answer: For dessert; that part of the circle graph is larger than the part for fries.**

What if the drink was bought first. What part of the money was left after paying for it? $\frac{7}{8}$

ra Practice, page 524

Alternate Teaching Strategy

Materials per student: crayons

Have students copy the following circle divided into eighths:

Then read the problem on Student Book page 416. Have students color $\frac{5}{8}$ of the circle. Then have them cross out $\frac{3}{8}$ of the $\frac{5}{8}$ pieces. Ask:

- **What is $\frac{5}{8} - \frac{3}{8}$?** *[$\frac{2}{8}$, or $\frac{1}{4}$]*

Repeat the activity for each of the differences on Student Book page 416.

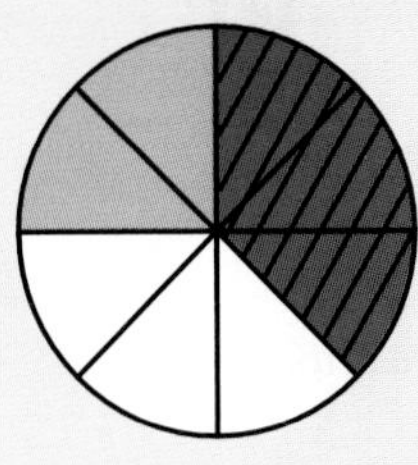

PRACTICE • 102

HOMEWORK

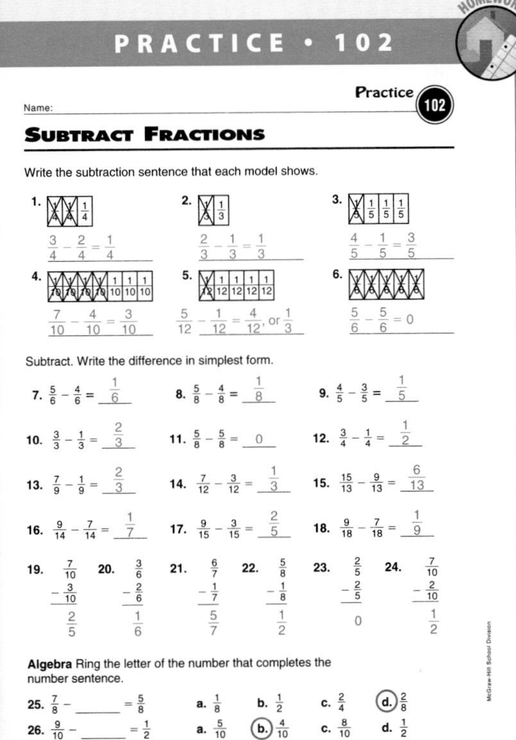

Practice 102

Name:

SUBTRACT FRACTIONS

Write the subtraction sentence that each model shows.

1. $\frac{3}{4} - \frac{2}{4} = \frac{1}{4}$
2. $\frac{2}{3} - \frac{1}{3} = \frac{1}{3}$
3. $\frac{4}{5} - \frac{1}{5} = \frac{3}{5}$
4. $\frac{7}{10} - \frac{4}{10} = \frac{3}{10}$
5. $\frac{5}{12} - \frac{1}{12} = \frac{4}{12}$, or $\frac{1}{3}$
6. $\frac{5}{6} - \frac{5}{6} = 0$

Subtract. Write the difference in simplest form.

7. $\frac{5}{6} - \frac{4}{6} = \frac{1}{6}$
8. $\frac{5}{8} - \frac{4}{8} = \frac{1}{8}$
9. $\frac{4}{5} - \frac{3}{5} = \frac{1}{5}$
10. $\frac{3}{3} - \frac{1}{3} = \frac{2}{3}$
11. $\frac{5}{8} - \frac{5}{8} = 0$
12. $\frac{3}{4} - \frac{1}{4} = \frac{1}{2}$
13. $\frac{7}{9} - \frac{1}{9} = \frac{2}{3}$
14. $\frac{7}{12} - \frac{3}{12} = \frac{1}{3}$
15. $\frac{15}{13} - \frac{9}{13} = \frac{6}{13}$
16. $\frac{9}{14} - \frac{7}{14} = \frac{1}{7}$
17. $\frac{9}{15} - \frac{3}{15} = \frac{2}{5}$
18. $\frac{9}{18} - \frac{7}{18} = \frac{1}{9}$
19. $\frac{7}{10} - \frac{3}{10} = \frac{2}{5}$
20. $\frac{3}{6} - \frac{2}{6} = \frac{1}{6}$
21. $\frac{6}{7} - \frac{1}{7} = \frac{5}{7}$
22. $\frac{5}{8} - \frac{1}{8} = \frac{1}{2}$
23. $\frac{2}{5} - \frac{2}{5} = 0$
24. $\frac{7}{10} - \frac{2}{10} = \frac{1}{2}$

Algebra Ring the letter of the number that completes the number sentence.

25. $\frac{7}{8} -$ ____ $= \frac{5}{8}$ a. $\frac{1}{8}$ b. $\frac{1}{2}$ c. $\frac{2}{4}$ (d.) $\frac{2}{8}$

26. $\frac{9}{10} -$ ____ $= \frac{1}{2}$ a. $\frac{5}{10}$ (b.) $\frac{4}{10}$ c. $\frac{8}{10}$ d. $\frac{1}{2}$

McGraw-Hill School Division

RETEACH • 102

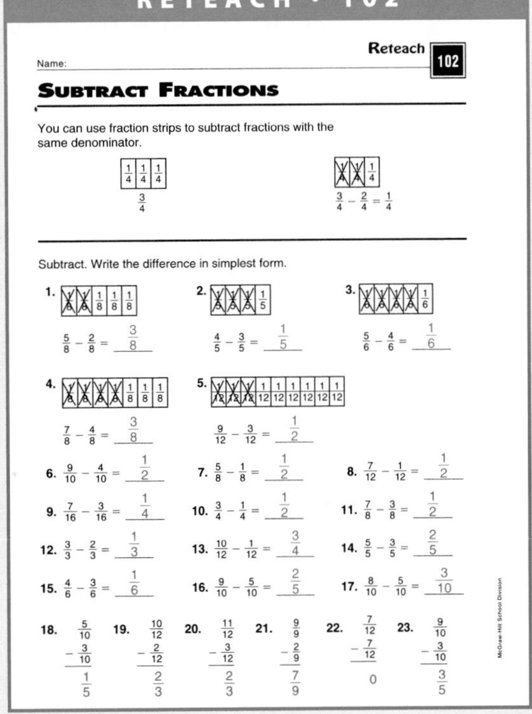

Reteach 102

Name:

SUBTRACT FRACTIONS

You can use fraction strips to subtract fractions with the same denominator.

$\frac{3}{4}$

$\frac{3}{4} - \frac{2}{4} = \frac{1}{4}$

Subtract. Write the difference in simplest form.

1. $\frac{5}{8} - \frac{2}{8} = \frac{3}{8}$
2. $\frac{4}{5} - \frac{3}{5} = \frac{1}{5}$
3. $\frac{5}{6} - \frac{4}{6} = \frac{1}{6}$
4. $\frac{7}{8} - \frac{4}{8} = \frac{3}{8}$
5. $\frac{9}{12} - \frac{3}{12} = \frac{1}{2}$
6. $\frac{9}{10} - \frac{4}{10} = \frac{1}{2}$
7. $\frac{5}{8} - \frac{1}{8} = \frac{1}{2}$
8. $\frac{7}{12} - \frac{1}{12} = \frac{1}{2}$
9. $\frac{7}{16} - \frac{3}{16} = \frac{1}{4}$
10. $\frac{3}{4} - \frac{1}{4} = \frac{1}{2}$
11. $\frac{7}{8} - \frac{3}{8} = \frac{1}{2}$
12. $\frac{3}{3} - \frac{2}{3} = \frac{1}{3}$
13. $\frac{10}{12} - \frac{1}{12} = \frac{3}{4}$
14. $\frac{5}{5} - \frac{3}{5} = \frac{2}{5}$
15. $\frac{4}{6} - \frac{3}{6} = \frac{1}{6}$
16. $\frac{9}{10} - \frac{5}{10} = \frac{2}{5}$
17. $\frac{8}{10} - \frac{5}{10} = \frac{3}{10}$
18. $\frac{5}{10} - \frac{3}{10} = \frac{1}{5}$
19. $\frac{10}{12} - \frac{2}{12} = \frac{2}{3}$
20. $\frac{11}{12} - \frac{3}{12} = \frac{2}{3}$
21. $\frac{9}{9} - \frac{2}{9} = \frac{7}{9}$
22. $\frac{7}{12} - \frac{7}{12} = 0$
23. $\frac{9}{10} - \frac{3}{10} = \frac{3}{5}$

McGraw-Hill School Division

EXTEND • 102

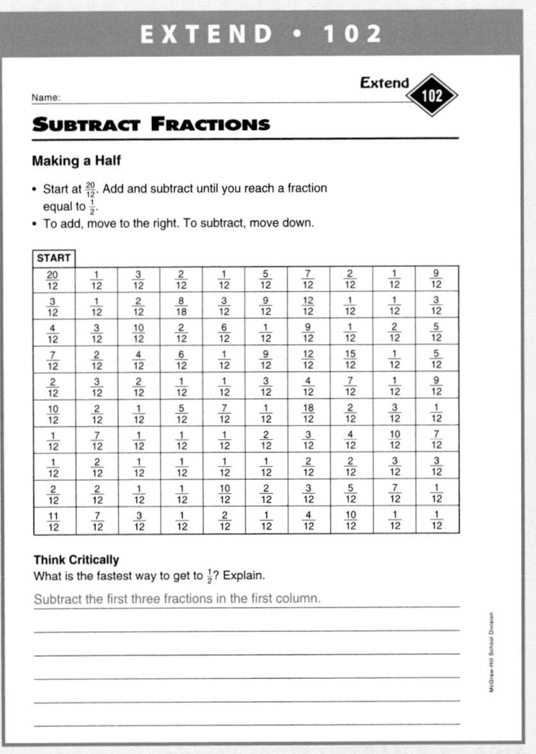

Extend 102

Name:

SUBTRACT FRACTIONS

Making a Half

- Start at $\frac{20}{12}$. Add and subtract until you reach a fraction equal to $\frac{1}{2}$.
- To add, move to the right. To subtract, move down.

START									
$\frac{20}{12}$	$\frac{1}{12}$	$\frac{3}{12}$	$\frac{2}{12}$	$\frac{1}{12}$	$\frac{5}{12}$	$\frac{7}{12}$	$\frac{2}{12}$	$\frac{1}{12}$	$\frac{9}{12}$
$\frac{3}{12}$	$\frac{1}{12}$	$\frac{2}{12}$	$\frac{8}{18}$	$\frac{3}{12}$	$\frac{9}{12}$	$\frac{12}{12}$	$\frac{1}{12}$	$\frac{1}{12}$	$\frac{3}{12}$
$\frac{4}{12}$	$\frac{3}{12}$	$\frac{10}{12}$	$\frac{2}{12}$	$\frac{6}{12}$	$\frac{1}{12}$	$\frac{9}{12}$	$\frac{1}{12}$	$\frac{2}{12}$	$\frac{5}{12}$
$\frac{7}{12}$	$\frac{2}{12}$	$\frac{4}{12}$	$\frac{6}{12}$	$\frac{1}{12}$	$\frac{9}{12}$	$\frac{12}{12}$	$\frac{15}{12}$	$\frac{1}{12}$	$\frac{5}{12}$
$\frac{2}{12}$	$\frac{3}{12}$	$\frac{2}{12}$	$\frac{1}{12}$	$\frac{1}{12}$	$\frac{3}{12}$	$\frac{4}{12}$	$\frac{7}{12}$	$\frac{1}{12}$	$\frac{9}{12}$
$\frac{10}{12}$	$\frac{2}{12}$	$\frac{1}{12}$	$\frac{5}{12}$	$\frac{7}{12}$	$\frac{1}{12}$	$\frac{18}{12}$	$\frac{2}{12}$	$\frac{3}{12}$	$\frac{1}{12}$
$\frac{1}{12}$	$\frac{7}{12}$	$\frac{1}{12}$	$\frac{1}{12}$	$\frac{1}{12}$	$\frac{2}{12}$	$\frac{3}{12}$	$\frac{4}{12}$	$\frac{10}{12}$	$\frac{7}{12}$
$\frac{1}{12}$	$\frac{2}{12}$	$\frac{1}{12}$	$\frac{1}{12}$	$\frac{1}{12}$	$\frac{1}{12}$	$\frac{2}{12}$	$\frac{2}{12}$	$\frac{3}{12}$	$\frac{3}{12}$
$\frac{2}{12}$	$\frac{2}{12}$	$\frac{1}{12}$	$\frac{1}{12}$	$\frac{10}{12}$	$\frac{2}{12}$	$\frac{3}{12}$	$\frac{5}{12}$	$\frac{7}{12}$	$\frac{1}{12}$
$\frac{11}{12}$	$\frac{7}{12}$	$\frac{3}{12}$	$\frac{1}{12}$	$\frac{2}{12}$	$\frac{1}{12}$	$\frac{4}{12}$	$\frac{10}{12}$	$\frac{1}{12}$	$\frac{1}{12}$

Think Critically

What is the fastest way to get to $\frac{1}{2}$? Explain.

Subtract the first three fractions in the first column.

McGraw-Hill School Division

Subtract Fractions

OBJECTIVE Subtract fractions with like denominators.

RESOURCE REMINDER
Math Center Cards 103
Practice 103, Reteach 103, Extend 103

SKILLS TRACE	
GRADE 3	• *Introduced at grade 4.*
GRADE 4	• Subtract fractions with like denominators.
GRADE 5	• Subtract fractions with like or unlike denominators. *(Chapter 10)*

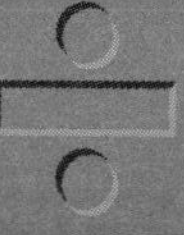

LESSON 11.4 RESOURCES

MANIPULATIVE WARM-UP

Cooperative Groups — Visual/Spatial

OBJECTIVE Explore writing related number sentences for fractions.

Materials per group: fraction strips (TA 26); number cube

▶ Students work in small groups. One student tosses the number cube. The number tossed is the numerator of a fraction in eighths. A second student repeats the process.

▶ The two fractions are the addends of a fraction sum. Have students find the sum using fraction strips. Then they write three other related number sentences for the fractions.

▶ Have students repeat the activity three more times for fractions with denominators of tenths and twelfths.

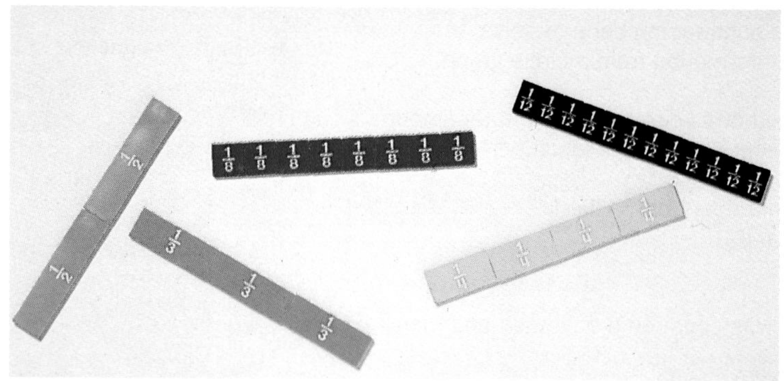

ESL APPROPRIATE

ALGEBRA CONNECTION

Cooperative Pairs — Logical/Analytical

OBJECTIVE Connect fraction sums and differences to algebra.

Materials per pair: fraction strips (TA 26)

▶ Have students work with a partner to solve for the fraction that completes each number sentence. They may use fraction strips to help solve.

1. $\frac{2}{3} + ■ = 1\frac{1}{3}$ [$\frac{2}{3}$]
2. $\frac{9}{12} - ■ = \frac{4}{12}$ [$\frac{5}{12}$]
3. $■ + \frac{5}{8} = \frac{6}{8}$ [$\frac{1}{8}$]
4. $■ - \frac{1}{6} = \frac{2}{6}$ [$\frac{3}{6}$]
5. $\frac{4}{10} + \frac{3}{10} = ■$ [$\frac{7}{10}$]
6. $\frac{7}{9} - \frac{2}{9} = ■$ [$\frac{5}{9}$]
7. $\frac{1}{5} + ■ = 1$ [$\frac{4}{5}$]
8. $\frac{11}{12} - ■ = \frac{11}{12}$ [0]
9. $■ + \frac{3}{4} = 1\frac{1}{4}$ [$\frac{2}{4}$]
10. $■ - \frac{7}{8} = 0$ [$\frac{7}{8}$]

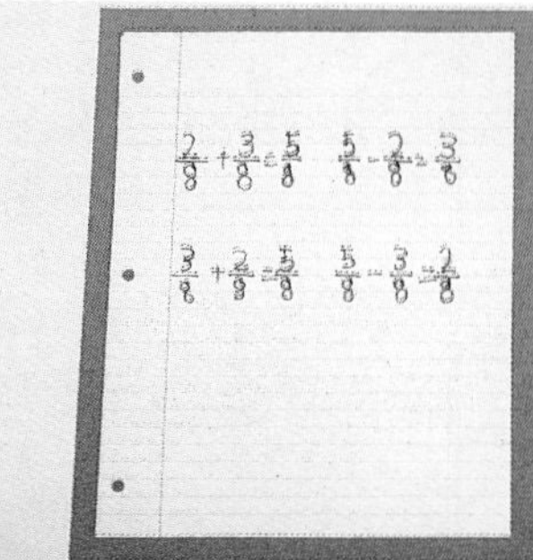

ESL APPROPRIATE

Daily Review

PREVIOUS DAY QUICK REVIEW

Find the difference.

1. $\frac{4}{5} - \frac{3}{5}$ *[$\frac{1}{5}$]*
2. $\frac{2}{3} - \frac{1}{3}$ *[$\frac{1}{3}$]*
3. $\frac{7}{8} - \frac{4}{8}$ *[$\frac{3}{8}$]*
4. $\frac{9}{10} - \frac{2}{10}$ *[$\frac{7}{10}$]*

FAST FACTS

1. $3 \div 3$ *[1]*
2. $8 \div 2$ *[4]*
3. $18 \div 6$ *[3]*
4. $42 \div 7$ *[6]*

Problem of the Day • 103

Jeff has $\frac{5}{8}$ yard of twine and $\frac{5}{6}$ yard of string. He uses $\frac{3}{8}$ yard of twine and $\frac{3}{6}$ yard of string. How much twine is left? string? Is there more twine or string left? *[$\frac{1}{4}$ yd; $\frac{1}{3}$ yd; string]*

TECH LINK

Math Van

MATH VAN

Tool You may wish to use the Fraction Models tool with this lesson.

MATH FORUM

Cultural Diversity I have students bring in recipes for some of their favorite foods. We use the recipes to compare amounts and to discuss different foods and different food groups.

Visit our Resource Village at http://www.mhschool.com to see more of the Math Forum.

MATH CENTER

Practice

OBJECTIVE Practice subtracting fractions.

Materials per group: number cube; per student: Math Center Recording Sheet (TA 31 optional)

Students play a game where they roll a number cube to generate numerators for fractions with denominators of 12. Then they subtract from a starting amount of $\frac{12}{12}$.

PRACTICE ACTIVITY 103

MATH CENTER
Small Group

Game • Getting to Zero

YOU NEED
- number cube

- Select one player to go first. Start the game by rolling the number cube. Write a fraction with a denominator of 12. Use the number rolled as the numerator. For example, 1 gives you $\frac{1}{12}$, 2 gives you $\frac{2}{12}$, and so on. Subtract the fraction from $\frac{12}{12}$.
- Then the second player rolls and makes another fraction with 12 as the denominator. Subtract again. Continue taking turns. The winner is the player who gets to zero first.
- Play again. Use a different number for the denominator.

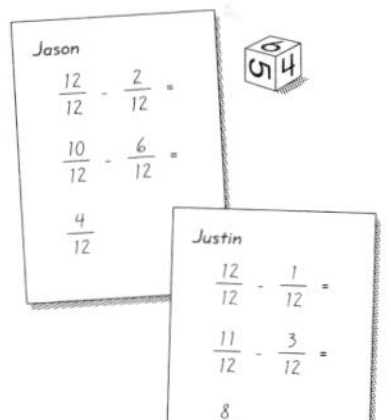

Grade Level 4 McGraw-Hill School Division

Chapter 11, Lesson 4, pages 420–421 Fractions

NCTM Standards
- Problem Solving
- Communication
- Reasoning
- ✓ Connections

Problem Solving

OBJECTIVE Complete number sequences.

Materials per student: fraction strips, Math Center Recording Sheet (TA 31 optional)

Students add and subtract fractions to find arithmetic sequences. *[**1.** Add $\frac{2}{12}$, subtract $\frac{1}{12}$: $\frac{5}{12}, \frac{4}{12}, \frac{6}{12}, \frac{5}{12}, \frac{7}{12}$; **2.** Subtract $\frac{1}{16}$, add $\frac{2}{16}$: $\frac{5}{16}, \frac{7}{16}, \frac{6}{16}, \frac{8}{16}, \frac{7}{16}$; **3.** Subtract $\frac{1}{10}$, subtract $\frac{1}{10}$, add $\frac{1}{10}$: $\frac{6}{10}, \frac{5}{10}, \frac{4}{10}, \frac{5}{10}, \frac{4}{10}$; **4.** Subtract $\frac{2}{8}$, add $\frac{1}{8}$: $\frac{7}{8}, \frac{8}{8}, \frac{6}{8}, \frac{7}{8}, \frac{5}{8}$; **5.** Subtract $\frac{4}{12}$, add $\frac{3}{12}$: $\frac{11}{12}, \frac{14}{12}, \frac{10}{12}, \frac{13}{12}, \frac{9}{12}$; **6.** Subtract $\frac{1}{3}$; 2, $1\frac{2}{3}$, $1\frac{1}{3}$, 1, $\frac{2}{3}$]*

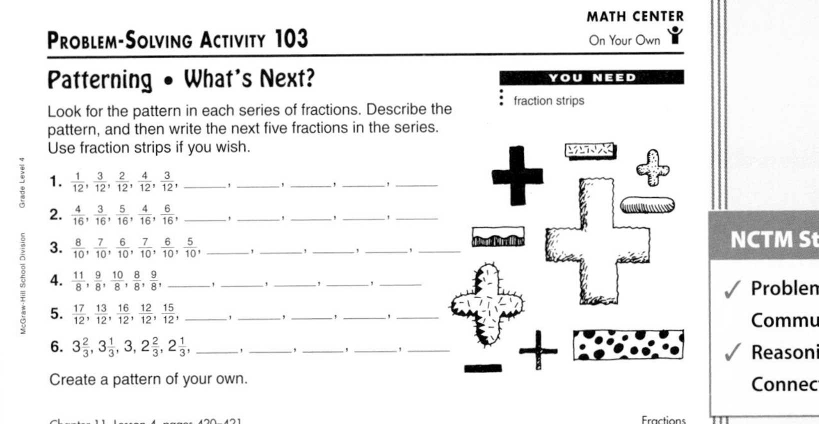

PROBLEM-SOLVING ACTIVITY 103

MATH CENTER
On Your Own

Patterning • What's Next?

YOU NEED
- fraction strips

Look for the pattern in each series of fractions. Describe the pattern, and then write the next five fractions in the series. Use fraction strips if you wish.

1. $\frac{1}{12}, \frac{3}{12}, \frac{2}{12}, \frac{4}{12}, \frac{3}{12}$, ____, ____, ____, ____, ____
2. $\frac{4}{16}, \frac{3}{16}, \frac{5}{16}, \frac{4}{16}, \frac{6}{16}$, ____, ____, ____, ____, ____
3. $\frac{8}{10}, \frac{7}{10}, \frac{6}{10}, \frac{7}{10}, \frac{6}{10}, \frac{5}{10}$, ____, ____, ____, ____, ____
4. $\frac{11}{8}, \frac{9}{8}, \frac{10}{8}, \frac{8}{8}, \frac{9}{8}$, ____, ____, ____, ____, ____
5. $\frac{17}{12}, \frac{13}{12}, \frac{16}{12}, \frac{12}{12}, \frac{15}{12}$, ____, ____, ____, ____, ____
6. $3\frac{2}{3}, 3\frac{1}{3}, 3, 2\frac{2}{3}, 2\frac{1}{3}$, ____, ____, ____, ____, ____

Create a pattern of your own.

Grade Level 4 McGraw-Hill School Division

Chapter 11, Lesson 4, pages 420–421 Fractions

NCTM Standards
- ✓ Problem Solving
- Communication
- ✓ Reasoning
- Connections

Subtract Fractions

OBJECTIVE Subtract fractions with like denominators.

1 Introduce

Present the following problem:

Marla colors $\frac{7}{10}$ of the rectangle blue. Then she colors 4 of the blue strips red so that the 4 strips become purple. What fraction of the rectangle is blue?

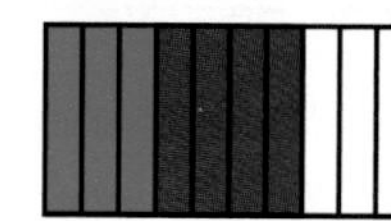

Have students tell what number sentence they could use to represent this problem. [$\frac{7}{10} - \frac{4}{10} = \frac{3}{10}$] Then have students solve the problem. Encourage them to create their own color mixing problems and then use markers to verify their answers.

2 Teach *Whole Class*

Cultural Connection Read the **Cultural Note.** The Caribbean is a popular resort area, characterized by a mild, tropical climate.

▶ **LEARN** After the introductory problem is read, have students explain why subtraction is needed to solve it.

3 Close

▶ **Check for Understanding** using items 1–11, page 420.

CRITICAL THINKING
In item 11, students are asked to analyze the Commutative Property. Check their understanding of the zero and inverse properties.

▶ **PRACTICE**
Materials have available: calculators

Options for assigning exercises:
A—Ex. 1–11; 17–26; **Mixed Review**
B—Ex. 7–26; **Mixed Review**

- Encourage students to use mental math in ex. 1–16.

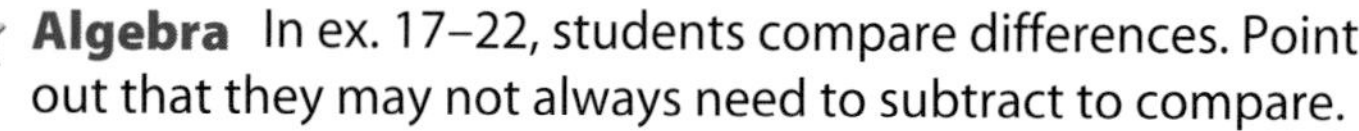

Algebra In ex. 17–22, students compare differences. Point out that they may not always need to subtract to compare.

Mixed Review/Test Preparation In ex. 1–4, students review addition, subtraction, multiplication, and division, learned in Chapters 2, 6, and 8. For ex. 5–8, students learned standard form in Chapter 2.

Subtract Fractions

LEARN

Are you cutting fat out of your diet? Many young people are. Two recipes for banana bread call for different amounts of margarine. How much more margarine is in the recipe that calls for $\frac{3}{4}$ cup than the one that calls for $\frac{1}{4}$ cup?

Subtract: $\frac{3}{4} - \frac{1}{4}$

In the last lesson, you used fraction strips to subtract fractions with a common denominator.

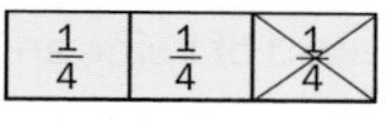

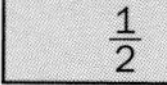

$\frac{3}{4} - \frac{1}{4} = \frac{2}{4} = \frac{1}{2}$

Cultural Note
In the Caribbean, bananas are used for many foods, such as banana bread. Even the leaves have uses. Sometimes, they are woven together to create shelter from the sun.

Here is another method.

Step 1	Step 2	Step 3
Subtract the numerators.	**Use the common denominator.**	**Write the difference in simplest form.**
$\frac{3}{4} - \frac{1}{4} = 2$	$\frac{3}{4} - \frac{1}{4} = \frac{2}{4}$	$\frac{2}{4} = \frac{2 \div 2}{4 \div 2} = \frac{1}{2}$

The second recipe has $\frac{1}{2}$ cup more margarine.

Check for Understanding

Subtract. Write the difference in simplest form.

1. $\frac{5}{7} - \frac{4}{7}$ $\frac{1}{7}$
2. $\frac{9}{11} - \frac{5}{11}$ $\frac{4}{11}$
3. $\frac{8}{9} - \frac{2}{9}$ $\frac{2}{3}$
4. $\frac{12}{12} - \frac{4}{12}$ $\frac{2}{3}$
5. $\frac{10}{16} - \frac{2}{16}$
6. $\frac{3}{7} - \frac{2}{7}$ $\frac{1}{7}$
7. $\frac{7}{16} - \frac{5}{16}$ $\frac{1}{8}$
8. $\frac{10}{14} - \frac{3}{14}$ $\frac{1}{2}$
9. $\frac{8}{10} - \frac{4}{10}$ $\frac{2}{5}$
10. $\frac{7}{8} - \frac{1}{8}$ $\frac{3}{4}$

Critical Thinking: Analyze **Explain your reasoning.**

11. Does changing the order in which you subtract fractions change the answer? Why or why not? Give examples to support your answer.

Yes; possible answer: the Order Property does not hold for subtraction; subtracting the numerators and using the common denominator, $\frac{5}{7} - \frac{1}{7} = \frac{4}{7}$, but $\frac{1}{7} - \frac{5}{7}$ does not equal $\frac{4}{7}$.

Meeting Individual Needs

Early Finishers

Have students use their answers to ex. 1–16 to create four problems similar to ex. 17–22. Then have them exchange problems and use mental math to compare and solve.

Extra Support

Some students may benefit by continuing to use fraction strips to subtract fractions. Or, you may suggest they draw diagrams of the strips.

Ongoing Assessment

Observation Checklist Check that students are able to subtract fractions with like denominators by having them explain how to find and record the difference of $\frac{7}{8} - \frac{5}{8}$. [$\frac{1}{4}$]

Follow Up Allow students who are having difficulty subtracting fractions to continue using fraction strips to find differences. Have them try **Reteach 103** for additional practice.

For students who understand how to subtract fractions, assign **Extend 103.**

They are the same distance from school; $\frac{7}{10} - \frac{3}{10} = \frac{4}{10} = \frac{2}{5}$, so Mel is $\frac{2}{5}$ mi from school, and $\frac{4}{5} - \frac{2}{5} = \frac{2}{5}$, so Shelley is $\frac{2}{5}$ mi from school.

ractice

btract. Write the difference in simplest form.

$\frac{7}{11} - \frac{4}{11} = \frac{3}{11}$ **2** $\frac{6}{7} - \frac{2}{7} = \frac{4}{7}$ **3** $\frac{9}{10} - \frac{9}{10} = 0$ **4** $\frac{4}{7} - \frac{1}{7} = \frac{3}{7}$ **5** $\frac{6}{9} - \frac{4}{9} = \frac{2}{9}$ **6** $\frac{8}{11} - \frac{5}{11} = \frac{3}{11}$

$\frac{8}{8} - \frac{5}{8}$ $\frac{3}{8}$ **8** $\frac{7}{12} - \frac{5}{12}$ $\frac{1}{6}$ **9** $\frac{8}{9} - \frac{5}{9}$ $\frac{1}{3}$ **10** $\frac{6}{12} - \frac{3}{12}$ $\frac{1}{4}$ **11** $\frac{5}{10} - \frac{3}{10}$ $\frac{1}{5}$

$\frac{5}{16} - \frac{1}{16}$ $\frac{1}{4}$ **13** $\frac{11}{12} - \frac{7}{12}$ $\frac{1}{3}$ **14** $\frac{7}{10} - \frac{2}{10}$ $\frac{1}{2}$ **15** $\frac{5}{8} - \frac{3}{8}$ $\frac{1}{4}$ **16** $\frac{5}{12} - \frac{1}{12}$ $\frac{1}{3}$

GEBRA Write >, <, or =.

$\frac{7}{11} - \frac{4}{11}$ ● $\frac{5}{11} - \frac{2}{11}$ = **18** $\frac{10}{16} - \frac{5}{16}$ ● $\frac{1}{4}$ > **19** $\frac{5}{8} - \frac{1}{8}$ ● $\frac{5}{6} - \frac{1}{6}$ <

$\frac{3}{4} - \frac{1}{4}$ ● $\frac{3}{4} - \frac{2}{4}$ > **21** $\frac{2}{3} - \frac{1}{3}$ ● $\frac{7}{9} - \frac{1}{9}$ < **22** $\frac{4}{5} - \frac{2}{5}$ ● $\frac{9}{10} - \frac{7}{10}$ >

IXED APPLICATIONS

roblem Solving

Pencil & Paper · Calculator · Mental Math

Rashid pours some milk from a full pint container. There are 12 ounces of milk left. What fraction of the container did he pour out? (Hint: 16 ounces = 1 pint) $\frac{1}{4}$ pt

24 The school cafeteria sold 1,212 chicken fingers at lunchtime. Each student who bought lunch got 3 chicken fingers. How many students bought lunch? 404 students

Mel walks $\frac{7}{10}$ mi to school. He walks $\frac{3}{10}$ mi in 5 minutes. Shelley walks $\frac{4}{5}$ mi to school. She walks $\frac{2}{5}$ mi in 5 minutes. Who is closer to school after walking for 5 minutes? Explain your thinking. See above.

26 **Data Point** Survey ten or more family members or friends to find out what their favorite food is. Display the data using a graph. Write a paragraph explaining what your graph shows. Students' graphs and explanations should reflect data.

mixed review • test preparation

876 + 364 1,240 **2** 627 − 429 198 **3** 583 × 24 13,992 **4** 563 ÷ 3 187 R2

ite the number in standard form.

four thousand, sixty-two 4,062 **6** one hundred ten thousand, six 110,006

thirty-two thousand, fourteen 32,014 **8** ninety-nine thousand, ninety-nine 99,099

tra Practice, page 525

Alternate Teaching Strategy

Materials per pair: fraction strips (TA 26)

Present the following problem:

Mario needs $\frac{7}{8}$ yard of fabric lengths to make a flag. He has $\frac{5}{8}$ yard of fabric. How many more yards of fabric does Mario need to make the flag?

Have students work with a partner to find the difference using fraction strips. Have them write a number sentence to show the difference [$\frac{7}{8} - \frac{5}{8} = \frac{2}{8}$] Then ask:

- **What do you notice about the denominators in the number sentence?** *[They are the same.]*
- **What is the difference of the numerators?** *[2]*
- **How can you use these observations to subtract fractions?** *[Subtract the numerators and write the difference over a common denominator.]*
- **What is $\frac{2}{8}$ in simplest form?** *[$\frac{1}{4}$]*
- **In simplest form, how many more yards of fabric does Mario need?** *[$\frac{1}{4}$ yd]*

Repeat the activity with other fractions.

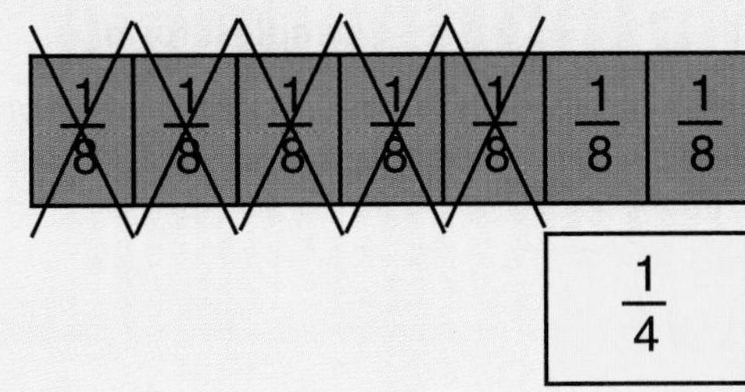

PRACTICE • 103

HOMEWORK

Practice 103

Name:

SUBTRACT FRACTIONS

Subtract. Write the difference in simplest form.

1. $\frac{3}{4} - \frac{2}{4} = \frac{1}{4}$ 2. $\frac{7}{11} - \frac{5}{11} = \frac{2}{11}$ 3. $\frac{6}{7} - \frac{1}{7} = \frac{5}{7}$ 4. $\frac{3}{4} - \frac{1}{4} = \frac{1}{2}$ 5. $\frac{6}{12} - \frac{6}{12}$ 6. $\frac{11}{12} - \frac{7}{12} = \frac{1}{3}$
7. $\frac{9}{10} - \frac{7}{10} = \frac{1}{5}$ 8. $\frac{9}{14} - \frac{2}{14} = \frac{1}{2}$ 9. $\frac{6}{12} - \frac{3}{12} = \frac{1}{4}$ 10. $\frac{8}{9} - \frac{5}{9} = \frac{1}{3}$ 11. $\frac{5}{8} - \frac{1}{8} = \frac{1}{2}$ 12. $\frac{9}{10} - \frac{3}{10} = \frac{3}{5}$
13. $\frac{11}{12} - \frac{3}{12} = \frac{2}{3}$ 14. $\frac{4}{5} - \frac{1}{5} = \frac{3}{5}$ 15. $\frac{7}{18} - \frac{1}{18} = \frac{1}{3}$
16. $\frac{5}{7} - \frac{1}{7} = \frac{4}{7}$ 17. $\frac{7}{12} - \frac{6}{12} = \frac{1}{12}$ 18. $\frac{7}{10} - \frac{6}{10} = \frac{1}{10}$
19. $\frac{9}{15} - \frac{1}{15} = \frac{8}{15}$ 20. $\frac{6}{7} - \frac{4}{7} = \frac{2}{7}$ 21. $\frac{9}{16} - \frac{9}{16} = 0$

Algebra Write <, >, or =.

22. $\frac{3}{4} - \frac{1}{4}$ (=) $\frac{1}{2}$ 23. $\frac{9}{10} - \frac{4}{10}$ (>) $\frac{1}{4}$ 24. $\frac{11}{12} - \frac{4}{12}$ (>) $\frac{1}{2}$
25. $\frac{6}{12} - \frac{3}{12}$ (<) $\frac{1}{2}$ 26. $\frac{4}{7} - \frac{2}{7}$ (<) $\frac{3}{7}$ 27. $\frac{8}{9} - \frac{2}{9}$ (>) $\frac{1}{3}$
28. $\frac{10}{12} - \frac{2}{12}$ (=) $\frac{2}{3}$ 29. $\frac{7}{8} - \frac{3}{8}$ (>) $\frac{1}{4}$ 30. $\frac{13}{16} - \frac{9}{16}$ (=) $\frac{1}{4}$
31. $\frac{4}{5} - \frac{1}{5}$ (<) $\frac{7}{8}$ 32. $\frac{8}{9} - \frac{5}{9}$ (=) $\frac{1}{3}$ 33. $\frac{5}{7} - \frac{4}{7}$ (<) $\frac{1}{2}$

Solve.

34. At lunch, you cut an apple into 4 parts and eat 3 of the parts. What fraction of the apple don't you eat? $\frac{1}{4}$

35 . For breakfast, lunch, and dinner, you will drink equal parts of a quart of milk. How much of the quart is left after lunch? $\frac{1}{3}$ qt

McGraw-Hill School Division

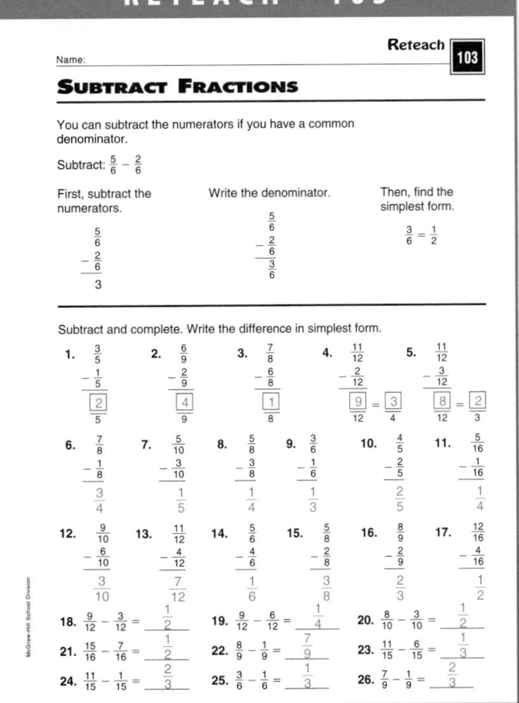

RETEACH • 103

Reteach 103

Name:

SUBTRACT FRACTIONS

You can subtract the numerators if you have a common denominator.

Subtract: $\frac{5}{6} - \frac{2}{6}$

First, subtract the numerators. $\frac{5}{6} - \frac{2}{6}$ → 3

Write the denominator. $\frac{5}{6} - \frac{2}{6} = \frac{3}{6}$

Then, find the simplest form. $\frac{3}{6} = \frac{1}{2}$

Subtract and complete. Write the difference in simplest form.

1. $\frac{3}{5} - \frac{1}{5} = \frac{\boxed{2}}{5}$ 2. $\frac{6}{9} - \frac{2}{9} = \frac{\boxed{4}}{9}$ 3. $\frac{7}{8} - \frac{6}{8} = \frac{\boxed{1}}{8}$ 4. $\frac{11}{12} - \frac{2}{12} = \frac{\boxed{9}}{12} = \frac{\boxed{3}}{4}$ 5. $\frac{11}{12} - \frac{3}{12} = \frac{\boxed{8}}{12} = \frac{\boxed{2}}{3}$
6. $\frac{7}{8} - \frac{1}{8} = \frac{3}{4}$ 7. $\frac{5}{10} - \frac{3}{10} = \frac{1}{5}$ 8. $\frac{5}{8} - \frac{3}{8} = \frac{1}{4}$ 9. $\frac{3}{6} - \frac{1}{6} = \frac{1}{3}$ 10. $\frac{4}{5} - \frac{2}{5} = \frac{2}{5}$ 11. $\frac{5}{16} - \frac{1}{16} = \frac{1}{4}$
12. $\frac{9}{10} - \frac{6}{10} = \frac{3}{10}$ 13. $\frac{11}{12} - \frac{4}{12} = \frac{7}{12}$ 14. $\frac{5}{6} - \frac{4}{6} = \frac{1}{6}$ 15. $\frac{5}{8} - \frac{2}{8} = \frac{3}{8}$ 16. $\frac{8}{9} - \frac{2}{9} = \frac{2}{3}$ 17. $\frac{12}{16} - \frac{4}{16} = \frac{1}{2}$
18. $\frac{9}{12} - \frac{3}{12} = \frac{1}{2}$ 19. $\frac{9}{12} - \frac{6}{12} = \frac{1}{4}$ 20. $\frac{8}{10} - \frac{3}{10} = \frac{1}{2}$
21. $\frac{15}{16} - \frac{7}{16} = \frac{1}{2}$ 22. $\frac{8}{9} - \frac{1}{9} = \frac{7}{9}$ 23. $\frac{11}{15} - \frac{6}{15} = \frac{1}{3}$
24. $\frac{11}{15} - \frac{1}{15} = \frac{2}{3}$ 25. $\frac{3}{6} - \frac{1}{6} = \frac{1}{3}$ 26. $\frac{7}{9} - \frac{1}{9} = \frac{2}{3}$

McGraw-Hill School Division

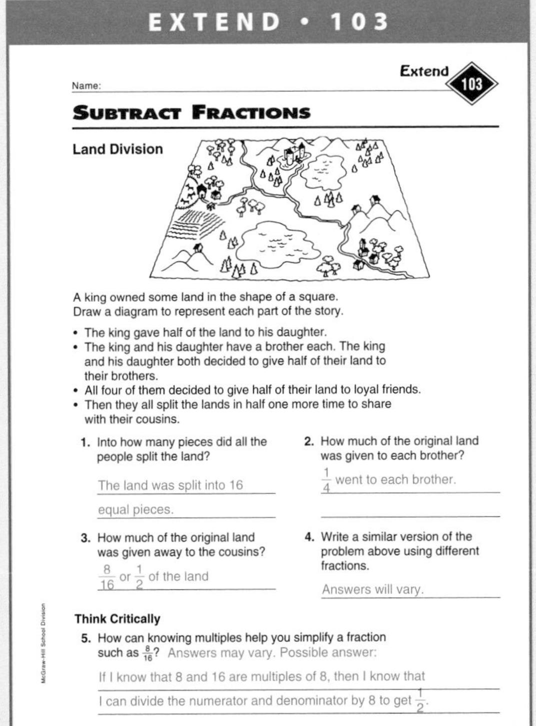

EXTEND • 103

Extend 103

Name:

SUBTRACT FRACTIONS

Land Division

A king owned some land in the shape of a square. Draw a diagram to represent each part of the story.

- The king gave half of the land to his daughter.
- The king and his daughter have a brother each. The king and his daughter both decided to give half of their land to their brothers.
- All four of them decided to give half of their land to loyal friends.
- Then they all split the lands in half one more time to share with their cousins.

1. Into how many pieces did all the people split the land? The land was split into 16 equal pieces.
2. How much of the original land was given to each brother? $\frac{1}{4}$ went to each brother.
3. How much of the original land was given away to the cousins? $\frac{8}{16}$ or $\frac{1}{2}$ of the land
4. Write a similar version of the problem above using different fractions. Answers will vary.

Think Critically

5. How can knowing multiples help you simplify a fraction such as $\frac{8}{16}$? Answers may vary. Possible answer: If I know that 8 and 16 are multiples of 8, then I know that I can divide the numerator and denominator by 8 to get $\frac{1}{2}$.

McGraw-Hill School Division

MIDCHAPTER REVIEW

PURPOSE Maintain and review concepts, skills, and strategies that students have learned thus far in the chapter.

Materials per student: calculator (optional)

Using the Midchapter Review

Have students complete the **Midchapter Review** independently or use it with the whole class.

For ex. 1–14, students may be able to use mental math to solve.

Students can approach this open-ended problem at their own levels. Most students should include subtracting numerators and using common denominators in their explanation of how subtracting fractions and whole numbers are alike or different.

Vocabulary Review

Write the following words on the chalkboard:

common denominator	**numerator**
fraction	**simplest form**

Ask for volunteers to explain the meanings of these words and to give examples.

Add. Write the sum in simplest form.

1. $\frac{2}{6}+\frac{4}{6}$ **1**
2. $\frac{3}{12}+\frac{6}{12}$ **$\frac{3}{4}$**
3. $\frac{5}{7}+\frac{5}{7}$ **$1\frac{3}{7}$**
4. $\frac{1}{6}+\frac{3}{6}+$ …
5. $\frac{7}{16}+\frac{4}{16}$ **$\frac{11}{16}$**
6. $\frac{3}{8}+\frac{3}{8}$ **$\frac{3}{4}$**
7. $\frac{3}{4}+\frac{2}{4}$ **$1\frac{1}{4}$**
8. $\frac{5}{10}+\frac{7}{10}$ **$1\frac{1}{5}$**

Subtract. Write the difference in simplest form.

9. $\frac{8}{12}-\frac{1}{12}$ **$\frac{7}{12}$**
10. $\frac{7}{11}-\frac{7}{11}$ **0**
11. $\frac{5}{6}-\frac{2}{6}$ **$\frac{1}{2}$**
12. $\frac{9}{10}-\frac{7}{10}$ **$\frac{1}{5}$**
13. $\frac{15}{16}-\frac{3}{16}$ **$\frac{3}{4}$**
14. $\frac{8}{8}-\frac{2}{8}$ **$\frac{3}{4}$**

Write >, <, or =.

15. $\frac{1}{2}+\frac{1}{2}$ ● 1 **=**
16. $\frac{9}{12}-\frac{3}{12}$ ● $\frac{5}{12}-\frac{1}{12}$ **>**
17. $\frac{4}{7}+\frac{6}{7}$ ● 1 **>**
18. $\frac{6}{10}-\frac{4}{10}$ ● $\frac{4}{10}$ **<**
19. $\frac{3}{4}+\frac{1}{4}$ ● $\frac{5}{8}+\frac{2}{8}$ **>**
20. $\frac{7}{8}-\frac{3}{8}$ ● $\frac{15}{16}-\frac{6}{16}$ **<**

Solve.

21. A pizza is cut into 12 equal pieces. Paco eats 3 of the pieces, Len and Ben eat 2 pieces each. What fraction of the pizza is left? **$\frac{5}{12}$**

22. Karen baked two batches of cookies. She used $\frac{3}{4}$ pound of dough for each batch. How mu… dough did she use altogether? …

23. Molly lives $\frac{7}{8}$ mi from the mall. She walked $\frac{3}{8}$ mi toward the mall before meeting a friend. She walked another $\frac{2}{8}$ mi before meeting another friend. How far away from the mall is Molly when she meets the second friend? **$\frac{1}{4}$ mi**

24. Dylan started cooking dinner at 3 P.M. He took $\frac{3}{4}$ h to make the tu… casserole, $\frac{1}{4}$ h to make biscuits, $\frac{1}{4}$ h to make soup, and $\frac{3}{4}$ h to make dessert. What time did Dylan finish cooking dinner? Explain your methods. **See belo…**

25. Journal: Explain how subtracting fractions less than one with like denominators and subtracting whole numbers are alike and are different. **Possible answer: Alike—taking away from or comparing one number to another; different—for fractions less than one with l… denominators, subtracting the numerators and using the common denominato… then simplifying if necessary, while for whole numbers, subtracting each place regrouping if necessary.**

24. 5 P.M.; possible answer: $\frac{3}{4}+\frac{1}{4}=1$, and $\frac{1}{4}+\frac{3}{4}$… so 1 + 1 = 2h—2 h after 3 P.M. is 5 P.M.

Reinforcement and Remediation

CHAPTER OBJECTIVES	MIDCHAPTER REVIEW ITEMS	STUDENT BOOK PAGES	TEACHER'S EDITION PAGES		TEACHER RESOURCES
			Activities	Alternate Teaching Strategy	Reteach
*11A	1–8, 15, 17, 19	410–413, 414–415	409A, 413A	413, 415	100, 101
*11B	9–14, 16, 18, 20, 25	416–419, 420–421	415A, 419A	419, 421	102, 103
*11D	21–24	415, 419, 421			

*11A Add fractions with like and unlike denominators
*11B Subtract fractions with like and unlike denominators
*11D Solve problems, including those that involve fractions and drawing pictures

developing spatial sense

MATH CONNECTION

Find Area Using Fractions of Shapes

ometimes, you can find the area of shape if it is a part of another shape ou know.

"ON THE POINTS," WASSILY KANDINSKY, MUSEE NATIONAL D'ART MODERNE, PARIS, FRANCE

he side of the square is 8 units ong. So the area of the square is 4 square units.

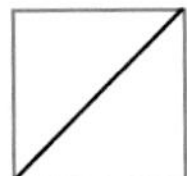

Each triangle is $\frac{1}{2}$ of the square.

o the area of each triangle is $\frac{1}{2}$ of 64, r 32 square units.

he square above is outlined in each figure. se fractions to help you find the area of the entire shape.

1 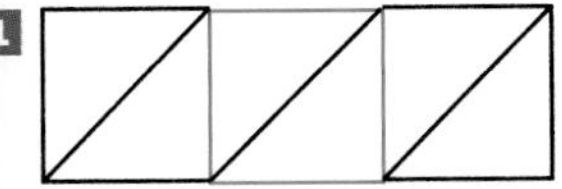

192 square units

2 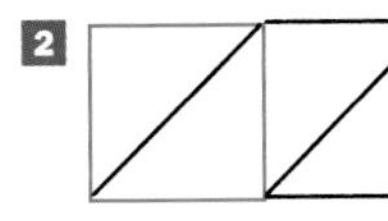

128 square units

3 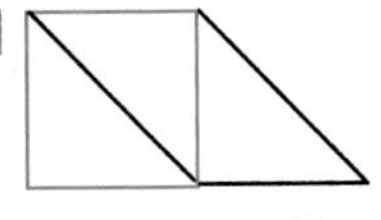

96 square units

4 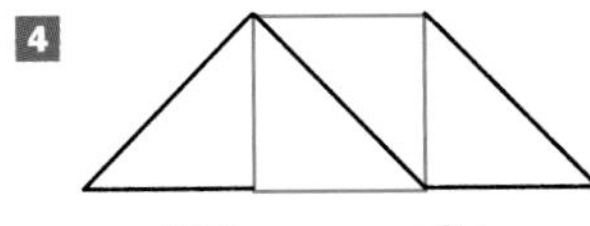

128 square units

5 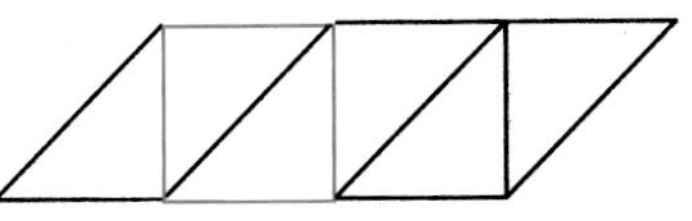

192 square units

6 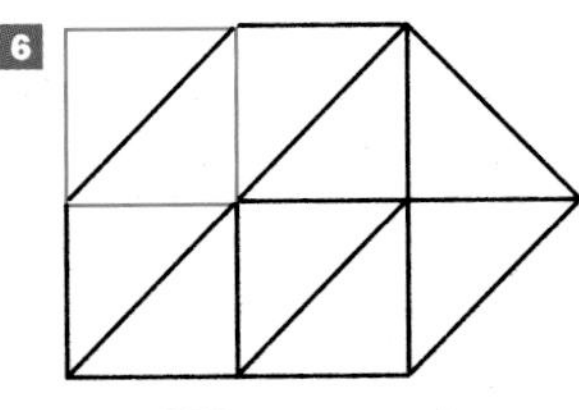

320 square units

Using Fractions **423**

DEVELOPING SPATIAL SENSE

PURPOSE Develop spatial sense.

Materials have available: graph paper

Using Spatial Sense

Math Connection Draw an 8-by-8 square on graph paper and then fold it into two triangular halves. Tell students when a shape is divided into equal parts, the area of its parts can be found by using fractions.

Ask students:

- **What is the area of an 8-by-8 square?** *[64 square units]*
- **What fraction is the triangular part of the square? How do you find the area of the triangular part?** *[$\frac{1}{2}$; find $\frac{1}{2}$ of 64 square units which is 32 square units]*
- **If the square is divided into four, equal, triangular parts, how do you find the area of each triangular part?** *[find $\frac{1}{4}$ of 64 square units which is 16 square units.]*

Students may work in small groups to complete ex. 1-6. If a group completes the exercises, have them draw three 4-by-4 squares on graph paper and cut each square into two equal triangles. Groups rearrange the triangles to form rectangles, parallelograms, or trapezoids. Have other groups find the area of the different shapes.

Applying Fractions

OBJECTIVE Collect data and use fractions to plan a meal.

Materials have available: calculators; spreadsheet program (optional)

1 Engage

Ask students to make a mental picture of their favorite dish.

- **Have you ever prepared your favorite dish by yourself?** *[Answers may vary.]*
- **What meals have you prepared by yourself?**

Have students discuss meals they have prepared at home.

2 Investigate *Cooperative Groups*

Encourage the class to think about food variety.

- **What would be some advantages of having a large selection of different foods on your menu?** *[Possible answers: There will be something for everyone.]*

Planning Lunch Using the Jigsaw Strategy, have students form groups of four, with each member responsible for a different segment of conducting the survey. A volunteer can record favorite foods on the chalkboard while another student keeps tally. If possible, provide students with sample containers or trays that are used in the school cafeteria to help them visualize portions.

Help students focus on fractions whenever they come up in the planning stages of preparing the meal. In addition to calculating fractions in each meal by weight (pounds) or area (square inches of serving tray covered), students can also work with volume.

3 Reflect and Share

Report Your Findings

Write a Report Students can use their calculators to help total the amounts of each type of food ordered, served, and left over, for use in their tables.

Discuss any differences that appear in the survey results, using two or more graphs as props. Computer-generated tables may also be displayed and compared. Then have each group compare their menus with those of other groups.

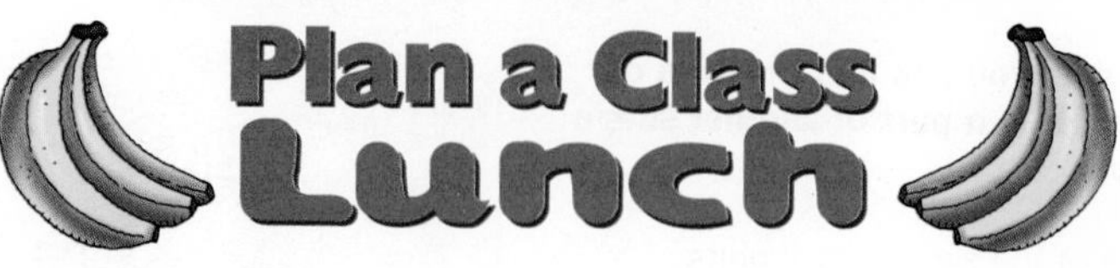

Plan a Class Lunch

Suppose you are in charge of preparing lunch for the students in your class. What kinds of decisions would you have to make? Here are just a few.

- What kinds of foods would you serve?
- How much of each food would you prepare?
- How would you decide if you needed to make more of one kind of food?

Write a Report In this activity, you will collect and combine information to prepare an imaginary lunch. You will use what you have learned about adding and subtracting fractions to help you collect and present the data in a report.

More To Investigate

Predict Possible answer: Kindergarten students would most likely eat smaller portions than the older students would eat. Their menus should include fewer "messy" foods, too.

Explore Possible approach: Compare the ratio of foods on the menu to those listed in the Food Pyramid, or simply make sure each menu includes lots of carbohydrates (such as bread or rice) and fruits and vegetables, but few dishes that are high in fat.

Find Possible answer: pizza, hamburgers, and french fries.

Bibliography Students looking for good recipes can try:

The Boxcar Children Cookbook, by Diane Blain, edited by Kathy Tucker. New York: Western Publishing Co., 1991. ISBN 0–8075–0859–4.

Kids in the Kitchen: One Hundred Delicious, Fun, and Healthy Recipes to Cook and Bake, by Micah Pulleyn and Sarah Bracken. New York: Sterling Publishers, Inc., 1993. ISBN 0–8069–0447–X.

Roald Dahl's Revolting Recipes, compiled by Roald Dahl and Felicity Dahl. New York: Viking Children's Books, 1994. ISBN 0–670–85836–6.

Answers may vary. Check students' work.

See Teacher's Edition for sample of student work.

DECISION MAKING

Planning Lunch

1 Work in a group to plan the class lunch. Survey your classmates to find out what they like to eat.

2 Use your data to decide:
- what food you will serve.
- what fraction of a pound or a serving tray you will use as a serving portion.
- the total amount of each type of food you will need to serve lunch.

3 Create a menu for your classmates to choose from. Have them order lunch. Keep track of how much food is served.

Reporting Your Findings

4 Prepare a report on what you learned. Include the following:
- a graph that shows the results of your survey
- statements about the results of the survey and how you used the results to decide what your menu would contain
- a table that shows the total amounts for each type of food, the amounts that were ordered, and the amounts that were left

5 Tell what changes you would make if you planned another lunch.

Revise your work.
- Did you include all of the data required?
- Did you add or subtract the fractions correctly?
- Is the table organized and accurate?

MORE TO INVESTIGATE

See Teacher's Edition.

PREDICT how the menu and the amounts served would change if you prepared lunch for kindergarten students.

EXPLORE whether your menu contains healthy, balanced meals. Explain how you can change it to be more healthy.

FIND what foods are most popular in your own school cafeteria. Interview the cafeteria staff or survey other grades. Report your findings to the class.

Students' Work

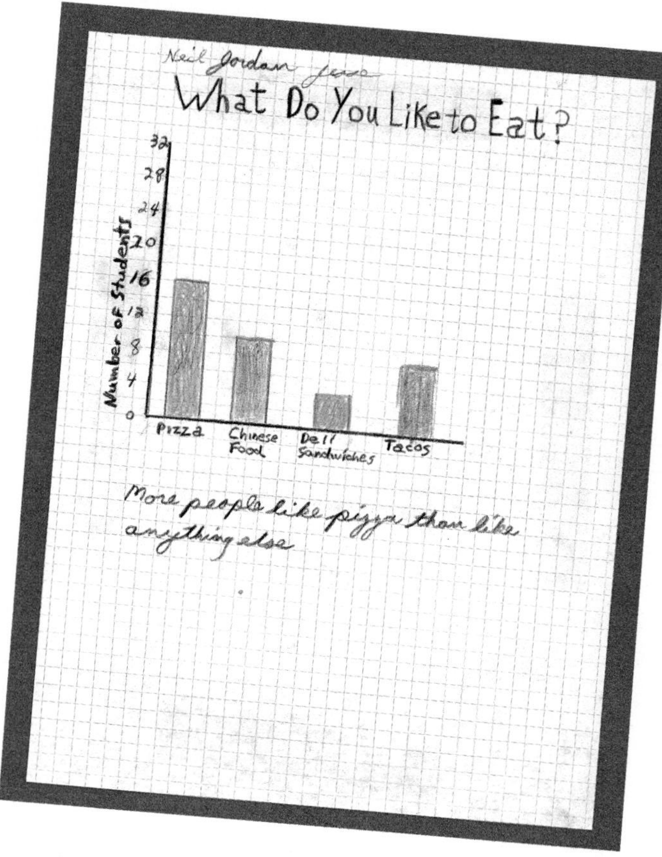

Building A Portfolio

This investigation will help you to evaluate a student's ability to organize data and use fractions to solve a problem.

Allow students to revise their work for the portfolio. Each student's portfolio piece should consist of a copy of his or her written report about the team's findings, which includes the results of the class survey and how the results were used. It also includes a graph showing the results of the survey and a table showing the amounts of the different types of foods for lunch.

You may wish to use the Holistic Scoring Guide to assess this task. See page 27 in Teacher's Assessment Resources.

EXPLORE ACTIVITY

Find a Common Denominator

OBJECTIVE Use fraction strips to explore finding a common denominator.

RESOURCE REMINDER
Math Center Cards 104
Practice 104, Reteach 104, Extend 104

SKILLS TRACE

GRADE 3	• *Introduced at grade 4.*
GRADE 4	• Use fraction models to explore finding the common denominator.
GRADE 5	• Find the least common denominator. *(Chapter 9)*

WARM-UP

Whole Class — **Individual**

OBJECTIVE Review finding equivalent fractions.

▶ Have students find the missing number by finding the equivalent fraction. Then have them decode the answers using the decoder to find the message.

1. $\frac{1}{3} = \frac{3}{■}$ *[9]*
2. $\frac{■}{4} = \frac{2}{8}$ *[1]*
3. $\frac{5}{6} = \frac{■}{12}$ *[10]*
4. $\frac{8}{■} = \frac{2}{3}$ *[12]*
5. $\frac{1}{2} = \frac{4}{■}$ *[8]*
6. $\frac{2}{3} = \frac{■}{6}$ *[4]*
7. $\frac{4}{6} = \frac{2}{■}$ *[3]*
8. $\frac{3}{■} = \frac{6}{10}$ *[5]*
9. $\frac{4}{6} = \frac{2}{■}$ *[3]*
10. $\frac{2}{6} = \frac{■}{3}$ *[1]*
11. $\frac{1}{5} = \frac{■}{10}$ *[2]*
12. $\frac{4}{■} = \frac{1}{3}$ *[12]*
13. $\frac{2}{3} = \frac{■}{9}$ *[6]*
14. $\frac{4}{5} = \frac{■}{10}$ *[8]*
15. $\frac{5}{■} = \frac{10}{14}$ *[7]*

Decoder	1	2	3	4	5	6	7	8	9	10	11	12
	A	C	E	F	H	I	N	O	P	R	S	T

What fractions are: *[P A R T OF THE ACTION]*

__ __ __ __   __ __   __ __ __   __ __ __ __ __ __

9 1 10 12   8 4   12 5 3   1 2 12 6 8 7

CONSUMER CONNECTION

Cooperative Pairs — **Logical/Analytical**

OBJECTIVE Connect comparing fractions to consumer comparisons.

▶ Copy the following sales items onto the chalkboard.

FRUITS
green apples $\frac{1}{2}$ lb for $0.59
red apples $\frac{5}{6}$ lb for $0.59
CEREALS
oatmeal $\frac{1}{4}$ lb for $0.29
farina $\frac{3}{8}$ lb for $0.29
VEGETABLES
salad tomatoes $\frac{3}{4}$ lb for $0.69
plum tomatoes $\frac{1}{2}$ lb for $0.69
PASTA
spaghetti $\frac{5}{8}$ lb for $0.49
macaroni $\frac{1}{2}$ lb for $0.49

▶ Have students work in pairs to find the better buy in each category. *[red apples, salad tomatoes, farina, spaghetti]*

▶ Discuss how students made their comparisons. *[Possible answer: Write equivalent fractions with like denominators and compare.]* Then have students suggest when the better buy might not be desired. *[Possible answer: when the other food items are needed or preferred]*

Daily Review

PREVIOUS DAY QUICK REVIEW

Find the difference.

1. $\frac{5}{6} - \frac{1}{6}$ *[$\frac{4}{6}$, or $\frac{2}{3}$]*
2. $\frac{3}{4} - \frac{1}{4}$ *[$\frac{2}{4}$, or $\frac{1}{2}$]*
3. $\frac{7}{8} - \frac{3}{8}$ *[$\frac{4}{8}$, or $\frac{1}{2}$]*
4. $\frac{9}{10} - \frac{3}{10}$ *[$\frac{6}{10}$, or $\frac{3}{5}$]*

FAST FACTS

1. 5 × 0 *[0]*
2. 4 × 3 *[12]*
3. 5 × 6 *[30]*
4. 7 × 7 *[49]*

Problem of the Day • 104

One piece of wood measures $\frac{5}{6}$ yard, another piece measures $\frac{2}{3}$ yard, and the last piece measures $\frac{3}{4}$ yard. What equivalent fractions can you write with a common denominator for the fractions? *[$\frac{10}{12}$ yd; $\frac{8}{12}$ yd; $\frac{9}{12}$ yd]*

TECH LINK

Math Van

MATH VAN

Tool You may wish to use the Fraction Models tool with this lesson.

MATH FORUM

Idea I have my students make a multiples chart that shows the multiples of the numbers 2 to 10. This is a good review of finding multiples of numbers and also helps them to identify common denominators for fractions.

Visit our Resource Village at http://www.mhschool.com to see more of the Math Forum.

MATH CENTER

Practice

OBJECTIVE Write equivalent fractions.

Materials per pair: 0–9 spinner (TA 2), fraction strips; per student: Math Center Recording Sheet (TA 31 optional)

Students write fractions from randomly generated numerators and denominators and find common denominators. Students may use fraction strips. *[Check students' work.]*

MATH CENTER
Partners

PRACTICE ACTIVITY 104

Number Sense • Common Denominators

YOU NEED
- spinner (0–9)
- fraction strips

- One player spins the spinner for four numbers and writes two fractions with unlike denominators. If you spin 1, make it a numerator. If you spin 0, use it as the denominator 10.
- The second player writes the denominators, and then lists at least five multiples of each denominator.
- The first player then picks a multiple that can be used as a common denominator and writes an equivalent fraction for each of the original fractions. Use fraction strips when you can.
- Players change roles.

EXAMPLE

$\frac{1}{2}$ $\frac{2}{3}$

2—4, 6, 8, 10, 12, . . .
3—6, 9, 12, 15, 18, . . .

6 and 12 are common denominators.

$\frac{1}{2} = \frac{3}{6}$ and

$\frac{2}{3} = \frac{4}{6}$

McGraw-Hill School Division Grade Level 4

Chapter 11, Lesson 5, pages 426–427 Fractions

NCTM Standards
- Problem Solving
- ✓ Communication
- Reasoning
- ✓ Connections

Problem Solving

OBJECTIVE Use common denominators to write words in code.

Materials per student: Math Center Recording Sheet (TA 31 optional)

This activity challenges students to write a message by coding each letter as a fraction using common denominators and then renaming the fractions with unlike denominators. Students strive not to give away the message as well as to code/decode accurately.

MATH CENTER
Partners

PROBLEM-SOLVING ACTIVITY 104

Logical Reasoning • Fraction Codes

- Think of a one- or two-word message with 6 to 12 different letters. Give each letter a fraction code number. Choose 6, 8, 10, or 12 as the common denominator for all. Keep a list of each fraction and the letter it stands for. Add extra letters and numbers to the list, as well.
- Write your message in fractions, but rename the fractions so they don't have a common denominator. You might write $\frac{6}{16}$ for H if your original fraction was $\frac{3}{8}$. Exchange coded messages and code lists with your partner. Decode the message you receive.

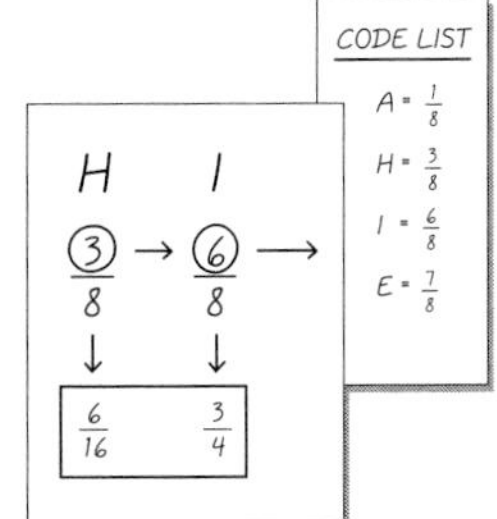

McGraw-Hill School Division Grade Level 4

Chapter 11, Lesson 5, pages 426–427 Fractions

NCTM Standards
- ✓ Problem Solving
- Communication
- ✓ Reasoning
- Connections

EXPLORE ACTIVITY

Find a Common Denominator

OBJECTIVE Use fraction strips to explore finding a common denominator.

Materials per pair: fraction strips (TA 26), blank number cube

1 Introduce

Ask students the following:

- **How would you compare two fractions with the same denominator?** *[Possible answers: Compare the numerators, use fraction strips.]*
- **How would you compare two fractions with unlike denominators?** *[Possible answers: Use fraction strips, draw a diagram, use a number line.]*

2 Teach *Cooperative Pairs*

LEARN **Work Together** Encourage students to use what they know about comparing fractions to show equivalent fractions using the fraction strips.

After pairs have completed the activity, elicit that a *common denominator* for $\frac{1}{2}$ and $\frac{5}{6}$ is 6 while another common denominator is 12. Discuss how students selected their common denominators for examples such as $\frac{1}{2}$ and $\frac{5}{6}$.

MAKE CONNECTIONS

After reviewing how Tom and Anne found a common denominator of 12 for $\frac{2}{3}$ and $\frac{3}{4}$, ask:

- **What common denominator would they use if they tossed $\frac{1}{2}$ and $\frac{3}{4}$? $\frac{3}{4}$ and $\frac{5}{6}$?** *[4; 12]*

Examine the list of multiples and ask:

- **Why do you use the least number in the list of common multiples?** *[Possible answers: It is easier to work with fractions with lesser denominators, you may avoid having to simplify later.]*

3 Close

Check for Understanding using items 1–8, page 427.

CRITICAL THINKING

In item 8, students are asked to find the common denominator of three fractions. Extend the analysis to fractions with three denominators where none of the denominators are the least common multiple by asking:

- **What is the common denominator for $\frac{1}{2}$, $\frac{1}{3}$, and $\frac{1}{4}$?** *[12]*

PRACTICE

Materials have available: fraction strips

Students may choose ten exercises from ex. 1–15 and complete all ex. 16–20.

EXPLORE ACTIVITY • FRACTIONS

Find a Common Denominator

LEARN

You can use fraction strips to help you find equivalent fractions with a common denominator.

Work Together

Work with a partner to compare fraction strips.

You will need
- *fraction strips*
- *number cube*

Write the following numbers on the faces of a number cube: $\frac{1}{2}$, $\frac{2}{3}$, $\frac{3}{4}$, $\frac{5}{6}$, $\frac{7}{12}$, $\frac{11}{12}$.

Toss the number cube twice to get two fractions. Show both fractions using fraction strips.

Find equivalent fractions for both fractions using only one type of fraction strip. Record the equivalent fractions you found.

Fractions	Equivalent Fractions
$\frac{2}{3}$	
$\frac{3}{4}$	

Continue tossing the number cube for other pairs of fractions.

▶ Explain how you decided which common fraction strips to use. **Students should choose strips showing the least common denominator.**

Making Connections

Tom and Anne showed equivalent fractions for both $\frac{2}{3}$ and $\frac{3}{4}$ using twelfth strips.

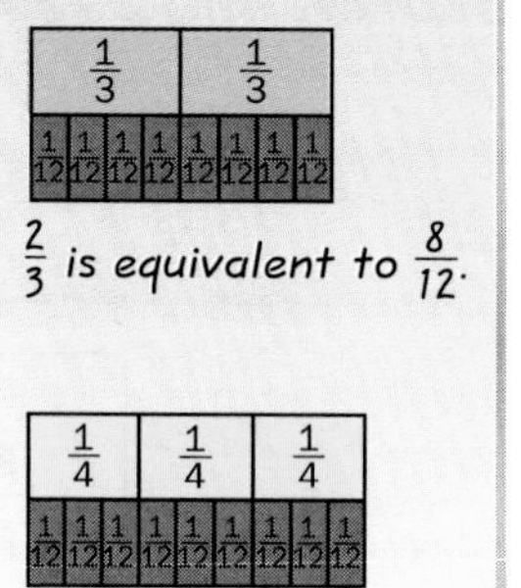

Meeting Individual Needs

Early Finishers

Have students write the equivalent fractions with the common denominators for ex. 1–10. *[$\frac{2}{6}$; $\frac{6}{8}$; $\frac{3}{12}$; $\frac{6}{12}$; $\frac{6}{9}$; $\frac{6}{15}$, $\frac{10}{15}$; $\frac{10}{12}$, $\frac{3}{12}$; $\frac{7}{14}$, $\frac{6}{14}$; $\frac{9}{12}$, $\frac{2}{12}$; $\frac{12}{14}$]*

Extra Support

Have students having difficulty identifying a common denominator show $\frac{1}{2}$ and $\frac{3}{4}$ on two grids, then change the grids so each has the same number of sections. They should see that $\frac{1}{2}$ is equivalent to $\frac{2}{4}$.

Ongoing Assessment

Interview Determine if students understand finding a common denominator. Ask:

- **What is a common denominator of $\frac{4}{5}$ and $\frac{1}{2}$? What are the fractions with the common denominator?** *[10; $\frac{8}{10}$ and $\frac{5}{10}$]*

Follow Up For students who need additional work with models, assign **Reteach 104.**

Have students who are ready for a challenge find the common denominator of three different fractions. Then have them try **Extend 104.**

ou can find a common denominator
y using multiples.

ompare the multiples of the
ncommon denominators.

has a denominator of 3. Multiples of 3: 3, 6, 9, **12**

has a denominator of 4. Multiples of 4: 4, 8, **12**

and $\frac{3}{4}$ can be written as equivalent fractions with 12
s the common denominator.

Are there different common denominators that you can use for fractions? Explain why or why not. **Yes; possible answer: the denominators have more than one common multiple, so there can be more than one common denominator.**

heck for Understanding

rite as equivalent fractions with common denominators.

1 $\frac{1}{4}$ and $\frac{4}{12}$ 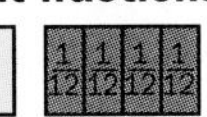 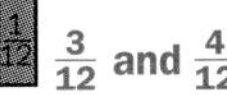 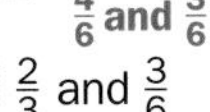 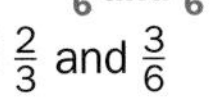 **$\frac{3}{12}$ and $\frac{4}{12}$**

2 $\frac{2}{5}$ and $\frac{3}{10}$ 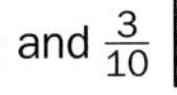 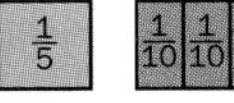 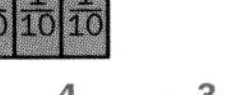 **$\frac{4}{10}$ and $\frac{3}{10}$**

3 $\frac{1}{4}$ and $\frac{3}{8}$ **and $\frac{3}{8}$**

4 $\frac{2}{3}$ and $\frac{3}{6}$ **$\frac{4}{6}$ and $\frac{3}{6}$**

5 $\frac{1}{6}$ and $\frac{1}{4}$ **$\frac{2}{12}$ and $\frac{3}{12}$**

 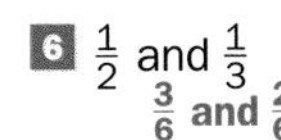 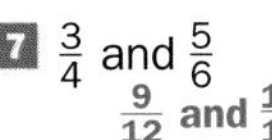

6 $\frac{1}{2}$ and $\frac{1}{3}$ **$\frac{3}{6}$ and $\frac{2}{6}$**

7 $\frac{3}{4}$ and $\frac{5}{6}$ **$\frac{9}{12}$ and $\frac{10}{12}$**

ritical Thinking: Analyze **Explain your reasoning.**

8 How would you use multiples to find the common denominator for these three fractions: $\frac{1}{3}, \frac{1}{2}, \frac{1}{6}$?

ist multiples of 2, 3, and 6 until the same one is found under all three denominators: 6.

ractice

ame the common denominator.

1 $\frac{1}{3}$ and $\frac{5}{6}$ **6** 2 $\frac{3}{4}$ and $\frac{5}{8}$ **8** 3 $\frac{1}{4}$ and $\frac{5}{12}$ **12** 4 $\frac{1}{2}$ and $\frac{5}{12}$ **12** 5 $\frac{2}{3}$ and $\frac{7}{9}$ **9**

6 $\frac{2}{5}$ and $\frac{2}{3}$ **15** 7 $\frac{5}{6}$ and $\frac{1}{4}$ **12** 8 $\frac{1}{2}$ and $\frac{3}{7}$ **14** 9 $\frac{3}{4}$ and $\frac{1}{6}$ **12** 10 $\frac{6}{7}$ and $\frac{1}{14}$ **14**

rite as equivalent fractions with common denominators.

11 $\frac{2}{3}$ and $\frac{1}{6}$ **$\frac{4}{6}$** 12 $\frac{1}{4}$ and $\frac{5}{8}$ **$\frac{2}{8}$** 13 $\frac{5}{6}$ and $\frac{5}{12}$ **$\frac{10}{12}$** 14 $\frac{9}{10}$ and $\frac{2}{5}$ **$\frac{4}{10}$** 15 $\frac{1}{2}$ and $\frac{3}{5}$ **$\frac{5}{10}, \frac{6}{10}$**

16 $\frac{1}{3}$ and $\frac{4}{5}$ **$\frac{5}{15}, \frac{12}{15}$** 17 $\frac{5}{6}$ and $\frac{1}{2}$ **$\frac{3}{6}$** 18 $\frac{1}{2}$ and $\frac{2}{5}$ **$\frac{5}{10}, \frac{4}{10}$** 19 $\frac{1}{4}$ and $\frac{2}{3}$ **$\frac{3}{12}, \frac{8}{12}$** 20 $\frac{1}{2}$ and $\frac{5}{8}$ **$\frac{4}{8}$**

xtra Practice, page 525

Alternate Teaching Strategy

Materials per student: fraction strips (TA 26)

Copy the following fractions on the chalkboard: $\frac{1}{2}, \frac{2}{3}, \frac{3}{4}, \frac{5}{6}$. Ask:

- **How would you compare $\frac{1}{2}$ and $\frac{3}{4}$?** *[Possible answer: Use a number line, use fraction strips, or write the fractions with like denominators and compare numerators.]*
- **What like denominator can you use to compare $\frac{1}{2}$ and $\frac{3}{4}$? What are the equivalent fractions?** *[4; $\frac{2}{4}, \frac{3}{4}$]*

Tell students that the like denominator is called a *common denominator*. Have them work in pairs to identify common denominators for $\frac{1}{2}$ and $\frac{2}{3}$, $\frac{2}{3}$ and $\frac{3}{4}$, $\frac{1}{2}$ and $\frac{5}{6}$, $\frac{3}{4}$ and $\frac{5}{6}$, and $\frac{2}{3}$ and $\frac{5}{6}$ using fraction strips. Have students write the equivalent fractions with the common denominator for each pair. *[6: $\frac{3}{6}, \frac{4}{6}$; 12: $\frac{8}{12}, \frac{9}{12}$; 6: $\frac{3}{6}, \frac{5}{6}$; 12: $\frac{3}{12}, \frac{10}{12}$; 6: $\frac{4}{6}, \frac{5}{6}$]*

PRACTICE • 104

HOMEWORK

Practice 104

Name:

Find a Common Denominator

Name the common denominator.

1. $\frac{1}{2}$ and $\frac{1}{4}$ 4
2. $\frac{1}{4}$ and $\frac{3}{8}$ 8
3. $\frac{3}{9}$ and $\frac{1}{3}$ 9
4. $\frac{5}{6}$ and $\frac{1}{3}$ 6
5. $\frac{5}{10}$ and $\frac{2}{5}$ 10
6. $\frac{1}{2}$ and $\frac{1}{8}$ 8
7. $\frac{3}{4}$ and $\frac{2}{8}$ 8
8. $\frac{3}{4}$ and $\frac{2}{3}$ 12
9. $\frac{3}{4}$ and $\frac{5}{6}$ 12
10. $\frac{1}{3}$ and $\frac{1}{2}$ 6
11. $\frac{1}{6}$ and $\frac{3}{4}$ 12
12. $\frac{5}{8}$ and $\frac{2}{3}$ 24
13. $\frac{1}{10}$ and $\frac{2}{5}$ 10
14. $\frac{2}{3}$ and $\frac{3}{9}$ 9
15. $\frac{1}{4}$ and $\frac{1}{5}$ 20
16. $\frac{3}{5}$ and $\frac{2}{3}$ 15
17. $\frac{2}{7}$ and $\frac{1}{3}$ 21
18. $\frac{1}{9}$ and $\frac{5}{6}$ 18
19. $\frac{1}{4}$ and $\frac{1}{7}$ 28
20. $\frac{2}{5}$ and $\frac{1}{15}$ 15
21. $\frac{3}{7}$ and $\frac{4}{5}$ 35

Write as equivalent fractions with common denominators. Possible answers are shown.

22. $\frac{1}{4}$ and $\frac{2}{8}$ $\frac{2}{8}, \frac{2}{8}$
23. $\frac{3}{6}$ and $\frac{2}{3}$ $\frac{3}{6}, \frac{4}{6}$
24. $\frac{1}{5}$ and $\frac{2}{10}$ $\frac{2}{10}, \frac{2}{10}$
25. $\frac{2}{5}$ and $\frac{10}{15}$ $\frac{6}{15}, \frac{10}{15}$
26. $\frac{5}{9}$ and $\frac{1}{3}$ $\frac{5}{9}, \frac{3}{9}$
27. $\frac{3}{8}$ and $\frac{1}{4}$ $\frac{3}{8}, \frac{2}{8}$
28. $\frac{1}{3}$ and $\frac{5}{12}$ $\frac{4}{12}, \frac{5}{12}$
29. $\frac{1}{2}$ and $\frac{3}{8}$ $\frac{4}{8}, \frac{3}{8}$
30. $\frac{3}{4}$ and $\frac{9}{12}$ $\frac{9}{12}, \frac{9}{12}$
31. $\frac{3}{5}$ and $\frac{6}{25}$ $\frac{15}{25}, \frac{6}{25}$
32. $\frac{1}{3}$ and $\frac{3}{5}$ $\frac{5}{15}, \frac{9}{15}$
33. $\frac{1}{3}$ and $\frac{1}{7}$ $\frac{7}{21}, \frac{3}{21}$
34. $\frac{1}{2}$ and $\frac{4}{5}$ $\frac{5}{10}, \frac{8}{10}$
35. $\frac{4}{9}$ and $\frac{1}{2}$ $\frac{8}{18}, \frac{9}{18}$
36. $\frac{1}{7}$ and $\frac{1}{2}$ $\frac{2}{14}, \frac{7}{14}$
37. $\frac{2}{9}$ and $\frac{5}{6}$ $\frac{4}{18}, \frac{15}{18}$
38. $\frac{3}{8}$ and $\frac{1}{6}$ $\frac{9}{24}, \frac{4}{24}$
39. $\frac{3}{4}$ and $\frac{5}{7}$ $\frac{21}{28}, \frac{20}{28}$

McGraw-Hill School Division

RETEACH • 104

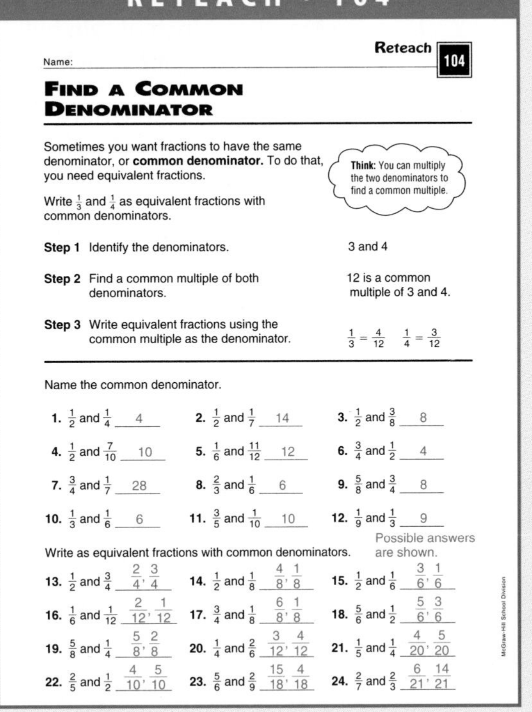

Reteach 104

Name:

Find a Common Denominator

Sometimes you want fractions to have the same denominator, or **common denominator.** To do that, you need equivalent fractions.

Think: You can multiply the two denominators to find a common multiple.

Write $\frac{1}{3}$ and $\frac{1}{4}$ as equivalent fractions with common denominators.

Step 1 Identify the denominators. 3 and 4

Step 2 Find a common multiple of both denominators. 12 is a common multiple of 3 and 4.

Step 3 Write equivalent fractions using the common multiple as the denominator. $\frac{1}{3} = \frac{4}{12}$ $\frac{1}{4} = \frac{3}{12}$

Name the common denominator.

1. $\frac{1}{2}$ and $\frac{1}{4}$ 4
2. $\frac{1}{2}$ and $\frac{1}{7}$ 14
3. $\frac{1}{2}$ and $\frac{3}{8}$ 8
4. $\frac{1}{2}$ and $\frac{7}{10}$ 10
5. $\frac{1}{6}$ and $\frac{11}{12}$ 12
6. $\frac{3}{4}$ and $\frac{1}{2}$ 4
7. $\frac{3}{4}$ and $\frac{1}{7}$ 28
8. $\frac{2}{3}$ and $\frac{1}{6}$ 6
9. $\frac{5}{8}$ and $\frac{3}{4}$ 8
10. $\frac{1}{3}$ and $\frac{1}{6}$ 6
11. $\frac{3}{5}$ and $\frac{1}{10}$ 10
12. $\frac{1}{9}$ and $\frac{1}{3}$ 9

Write as equivalent fractions with common denominators. Possible answers are shown.

13. $\frac{1}{2}$ and $\frac{3}{4}$ $\frac{2}{4}, \frac{3}{4}$
14. $\frac{1}{2}$ and $\frac{1}{8}$ $\frac{4}{8}, \frac{1}{8}$
15. $\frac{1}{2}$ and $\frac{1}{6}$ $\frac{3}{6}, \frac{1}{6}$
16. $\frac{1}{6}$ and $\frac{1}{12}$ $\frac{2}{12}, \frac{1}{12}$
17. $\frac{3}{4}$ and $\frac{1}{8}$ $\frac{6}{8}, \frac{1}{8}$
18. $\frac{5}{6}$ and $\frac{1}{2}$ $\frac{5}{6}, \frac{3}{6}$
19. $\frac{5}{8}$ and $\frac{1}{4}$ $\frac{5}{8}, \frac{2}{8}$
20. $\frac{1}{4}$ and $\frac{2}{6}$ $\frac{3}{12}, \frac{4}{12}$
21. $\frac{1}{5}$ and $\frac{1}{4}$ $\frac{4}{20}, \frac{5}{20}$
22. $\frac{2}{5}$ and $\frac{1}{2}$ $\frac{4}{10}, \frac{5}{10}$
23. $\frac{5}{6}$ and $\frac{2}{9}$ $\frac{15}{18}, \frac{4}{18}$
24. $\frac{2}{7}$ and $\frac{2}{3}$ $\frac{6}{21}, \frac{14}{21}$

McGraw-Hill School Division

EXTEND • 104

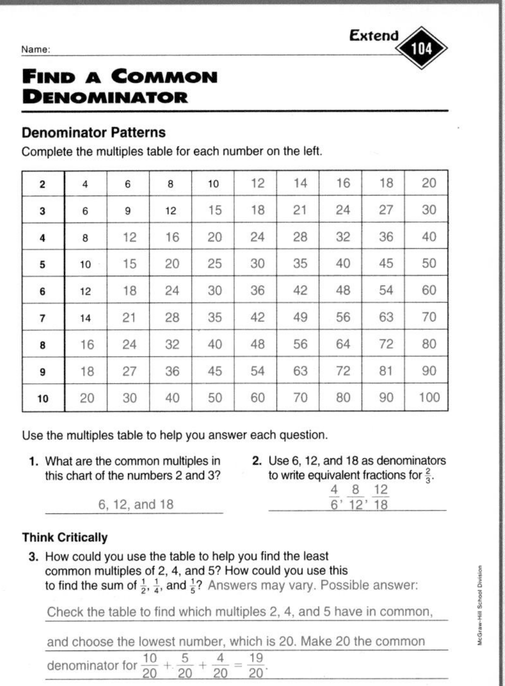

Extend 104

Name:

Find a Common Denominator

Denominator Patterns

Complete the multiples table for each number on the left.

2	4	6	8	10	12	14	16	18	20
3	6	9	12	15	18	21	24	27	30
4	8	12	16	20	24	28	32	36	40
5	10	15	20	25	30	35	40	45	50
6	12	18	24	30	36	42	48	54	60
7	14	21	28	35	42	49	56	63	70
8	16	24	32	40	48	56	64	72	80
9	18	27	36	45	54	63	72	81	90
10	20	30	40	50	60	70	80	90	100

Use the multiples table to help you answer each question.

1. What are the common multiples in this chart of the numbers 2 and 3? 6, 12, and 18
2. Use 6, 12, and 18 as denominators to write equivalent fractions for $\frac{2}{3}$. $\frac{4}{6}, \frac{8}{12}, \frac{12}{18}$

Think Critically

3. How could you use the table to help you find the least common multiples of 2, 4, and 5? How could you use this to find the sum of $\frac{1}{2}, \frac{1}{4}$, and $\frac{1}{5}$? Answers may vary. Possible answer: Check the table to find which multiples 2, 4, and 5 have in common, and choose the lowest number, which is 20. Make 20 the common denominator for $\frac{10}{20} + \frac{5}{20} + \frac{4}{20} = \frac{19}{20}$.

McGraw-Hill School Division

EXPLORE ACTIVITY

Add and Subtract Fractions with Unlike Denominators

OBJECTIVE Explore adding and subtracting fractions with unlike denominators.

Teaching with Technology
See alternate computer lesson, pp. 429A–429B.

RESOURCE REMINDER
Math Center Cards 105
Practice 105, Reteach 105, Extend 105

SKILLS TRACE

GRADE 3	• *Introduced at grade 4.*
GRADE 4	• Use fraction models to explore adding and subtracting fractions with unlike denominators.
GRADE 5	• Use fraction models to explore adding and subtracting fractions with unlike denominators. *(Chapter 10)*

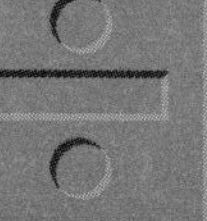

LESSON 11.6 RESOURCES

MANIPULATIVE WARM-UP

Cooperative Pairs — Logical/Analytical

OBJECTIVE Review finding equivalent fractions.

Materials per pair: fraction strips (TA 26)

▶ Students work with a partner to name as many equivalent fractions as they can using halves, thirds, fourths, sixths, eighths, and twelfths. Have students use fraction strips to show the equivalent fractions they wrote.

▶ Make a list of the equivalent fractions on the chalkboard. Have a pair of volunteers use fraction strips to show the equivalent fractions. *[Possible fractions: $1 = \frac{2}{2} = \frac{3}{3} = \frac{4}{4} = \frac{6}{6} = \frac{8}{8} = \frac{12}{12}$; $2 = \frac{4}{2} = \frac{12}{6}$; $\frac{1}{2} = \frac{2}{4} = \frac{3}{6} = \frac{4}{8} = \frac{6}{12}$; $\frac{1}{4} = \frac{2}{8} = \frac{3}{12}$; $\frac{1}{3} = \frac{2}{6} = \frac{4}{12}$; $\frac{1}{6} = \frac{2}{12}$]*

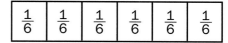

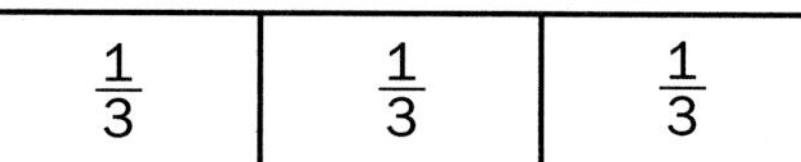

$\frac{1}{3}$	$\frac{1}{3}$	$\frac{1}{3}$

$\frac{1}{6}$	$\frac{1}{6}$	$\frac{1}{6}$	$\frac{1}{6}$	$\frac{1}{6}$	$\frac{1}{6}$

ESL APPROPRIATE

SCIENCE CONNECTION

Cooperative Pairs — Visual/Spatial

OBJECTIVE Connect adding and subtracting fractions to weather report.

Materials per pair: fraction strips (TA 26), inch ruler

▶ Present the following problem:
On Monday, $\frac{1}{4}$ inch of rain fell. On Tuesday, $\frac{3}{8}$ inch of rain fell. What total amount of rain fell? Which day did more rain fall? How much more?

▶ Students work with a partner to solve the problem. They may use fraction strips, number lines, inch ruler, or whatever method they desire to solve. *[$\frac{5}{8}$ in.; Tuesday; $\frac{1}{8}$ in.]*

▶ Discuss each solution with the class.

Daily Review

PREVIOUS DAY QUICK REVIEW

Write with common denominators.

1. $\frac{2}{3}, \frac{5}{6}$ *[$\frac{4}{6}, \frac{5}{6}$]*
2. $\frac{1}{4}, \frac{1}{2}$ *[$\frac{1}{4}, \frac{2}{4}$]*
3. $\frac{1}{2}, \frac{2}{5}$ *[$\frac{5}{10}, \frac{4}{10}$]*
4. $\frac{3}{4}, \frac{2}{3}$ *[$\frac{9}{12}, \frac{8}{12}$]*

FAST FACTS

1. 6 ÷ 2 *[3]*
2. 25 ÷ 5 *[5]*
3. 32 ÷ 8 *[4]*
4. 81 ÷ 9 *[9]*

Problem of the Day • 105

A serving of chicken noodle soup is $\frac{3}{4}$ cup at the cafeteria while a serving of tomato soup is $\frac{5}{8}$ cup. Which serving of soup is more? How much more? *[chicken noodle soup; $\frac{1}{8}$ c]*

TECH LINK

Math Van

MATH VAN

Tool You may wish to use the Fraction Models tool with this lesson.

Activity You may wish to use *Deli in a Pickle* to teach this lesson.

MATH FORUM

Combination Classes My students continue to work in pairs. They decide if they want to check using the opposite operation or use fraction strips.

Visit our Resource Village at http://www.mhschool.com to see more of the Math Forum.

MATH CENTER

Practice

OBJECTIVE Add and subtract fractions with unlike denominators.

Materials per student: fraction strips, paper bag, Math Center Recording Sheet (TA 31 optional)

Students pick out fraction strips from a paper bag, adding two and then subtracting a third from the sum. (They are told to make a sum is greater than the number they will subtract.) They repeat with the same strips in a different order as well as with three different strips. *[Check students' work.]*

PRACTICE ACTIVITY 105 — MATH CENTER — On Your Own

Manipulatives • Fraction Scramble

YOU NEED: fraction strips; paper bag

- Put fraction strips of several denominations in the bag. Without looking, take three or four strips out.
- Pick two to add. You might choose any two that have a common denominator. Then subtract a third strip from the sum. (Be sure to form a sum that is greater than the strip you will subtract from it.)
- Write an addition or subtraction sentence for each step. Use other strips from the box for help. Repeat with the same three strips, using different ones to add and subtract.
- Then play again with three new strips.

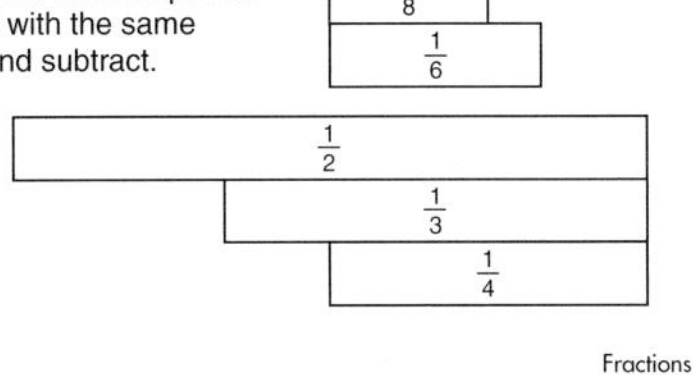

Grade Level 4 — McGraw-Hill School Division

Chapter 11, Lesson 6, pages 428–431 — Fractions

ESL APPROPRIATE

NCTM Standards

- ✓ Problem Solving
- Communication
- ✓ Reasoning
- Connections

Problem Solving

OBJECTIVE Write fractions to add and subtract to get the greatest estimated sum and the least estimated difference.

Materials per student: 0-9 spinner (TA 2), Math Center Recording Sheet (TA 31 optional)

Students spin for digits to write two fractions. They use the fractions to add and subtract. Students subtract the difference from the sum to get a score. Thus, the strategy is to get the greatest possible estimated sum and the least estimated difference.

PROBLEM-SOLVING ACTIVITY 105 — MATH CENTER — Partners

Logical Reasoning • Estimation Game

YOU NEED: spinner (0–9)

- Each player spins four times to make two fractions with unlike denominators. If you spin 0, use it as the denominator 10. If you spin 1, use it as a numerator. Be sure the numerator is less than the denominator.
- Estimate the sum and difference of the fractions. Your score is the estimated sum minus the estimated difference. Be sure you and your partner agree on the estimates. You may use fraction strips if you wish.
- Repeat until one player has 5 points.

Estimated Sum	Estimated Difference
2	0

Score: 2 − 0 = 2

Grade Level 4 — McGraw-Hill School Division

Chapter 11, Lesson 6, pages 428–431 — Fractions

ESL APPROPRIATE

NCTM Standards

- ✓ Problem Solving
- Communication
- ✓ Reasoning
- Connections

EXPLORE ACTIVITY

Add and Subtract Fractions with Unlike Denominators

OBJECTIVE Explore adding and subtracting fractions with unlike denominators.

Materials per pair: fraction strips (TA 26)

1 Introduce

Present the following problem with the circle divided into eighths:

Lou ate half the pie, and Sheila ate $\frac{1}{8}$ of the pie. How much of the pie did they eat in all? *[$\frac{5}{8}$]*

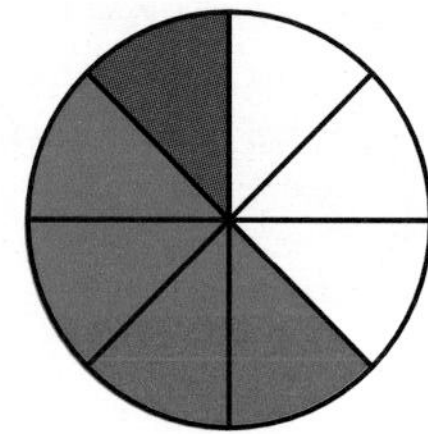

Have students create and solve similar problems.

2 Teach *Whole Class*

LEARN Read the opening paragraph and discuss why the chef tests recipes in small amounts. *[Possible answer: to see if people like the recipe]* Ask:

- **Why would you want to compare amounts in recipes?** *[Possible answer: to find a good mixture of different types of ingredients]*

Work Together Before students begin to add and subtract, review how to find a common denominator. Ask:

- **How can you find the common denominator between 2 numbers?** *[Possible answer: List multiples of the two numbers and find one common to both.]*

Encourage students to keep common denominators in mind as they begin to add and subtract fractions with unlike denominators using fraction strips.

Talk It Over Have students explain why common denominators were necessary to add and subtract fractions with unlike denominators. *[Possible answer: to add or subtract like parts of a whole]*

Add and Subtract Fractions with Unlike Denominators

LEARN

IN THE WORKPLACE
Chef, André Pierre Lincy, working in his kitchen

Have you ever thought about what it is like to cook for over 1,000 people a day? Part of a head chef's job is to create new recipes. You start by testing small amounts.

To work with recipes, you need to know how to add and subtract fractions with unlike denominators.

How much broth is used in this recipe?

How much more wild rice is used than orzo pasta?

Recipe for Wild Rice	
Liquids	**Dry Ingredients**
$\frac{3}{8}$ cup cider	$\frac{1}{3}$ cup wild rice
$\frac{1}{2}$ cup coconut milk	$\frac{1}{4}$ cup orzo pasta
$\frac{3}{4}$ cup chicken broth	$\frac{5}{12}$ cup basmati rice
$\frac{3}{8}$ cup beef broth	

Work Together

Work with a partner. Use fraction strips to model the problems.

You will need
- *fraction strips*

Add to find the total amount of broth. **$1\frac{1}{8}$ c**

Subtract to find the difference in the amounts of rice and pasta. **$\frac{1}{12}$c**

Use fraction strips to find the sum or difference:

a. $\frac{3}{8} + \frac{1}{2}$ $\frac{7}{8}$ **b.** $\frac{1}{2} + \frac{3}{4}$ $1\frac{1}{4}$ **c.** $\frac{1}{3} + \frac{1}{4}$ $\frac{7}{12}$ **d.** $\frac{1}{4} + \frac{5}{12}$ $\frac{8}{12} = \frac{2}{3}$

e. $\frac{5}{12} - \frac{1}{6}$ $\frac{3}{12} = \frac{1}{4}$ **f.** $\frac{3}{4} - \frac{3}{8}$ $\frac{3}{8}$ **g.** $\frac{5}{12} - \frac{1}{4}$ $\frac{2}{12} = \frac{1}{6}$ **h.** $\frac{5}{12} - \frac{1}{3}$ $\frac{1}{12}$

Talk It Over

▶ How did you use fraction strips to add and subtract fractions when their denominators were different?

Possible answer: Found a common denominator and used that type of fraction strip to make equivalent fractions with like denominators, then found the sum or difference.

Meeting Individual Needs

Extra Support

Have students make a list of multiples of 2, 3, 4, 5, 6, 8, 9, 10, and 12. Have them refer to this list to find common multiples, or denominators, as they write equivalent fractions to add or subtract fractions.

Language Support

Help students with the pronunciation of different food items with which they are unfamiliar. Describe any of the unfamiliar foods and give examples of how they are prepared or eaten.

ESL APPROPRIATE

Ongoing Assessment

Observation Checklist Observe if students are able to add and subtract fractions with unlike denominators by noting if they first find a common denominator and then find equivalent fractions before adding or subtracting.

Follow Up For students who need additional practice, assign **Reteach 105.**

For students who successfully add and subtract fractions using models, assign **Extend 105.**

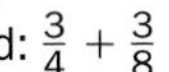

ake Connections

u can use what you know about adding and btracting fractions with like denominators to add d subtract fractions with unlike denominators.

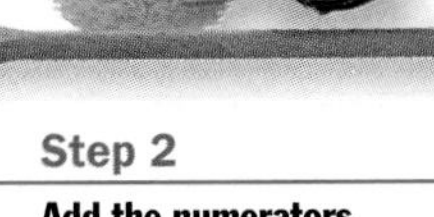

d: $\frac{3}{4} + \frac{3}{8}$

ep 1

d equivalent fractions with a common ominator.

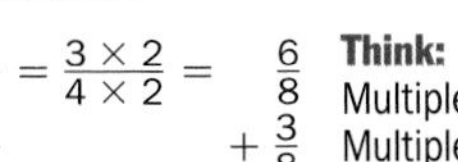

$\frac{3}{4} = \frac{3 \times 2}{4 \times 2} = \frac{6}{8}$

$\frac{3}{8} \quad + \frac{3}{8}$

Think:
Multiples of 4: 4, 8
Multiples of 8: 8
8 is the common denominator.

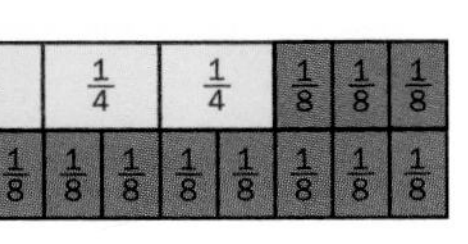

Step 2

Add the numerators.
Use the common denominator.

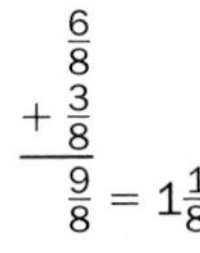

$\frac{6}{8} + \frac{3}{8} = \frac{9}{8} = 1\frac{1}{8}$

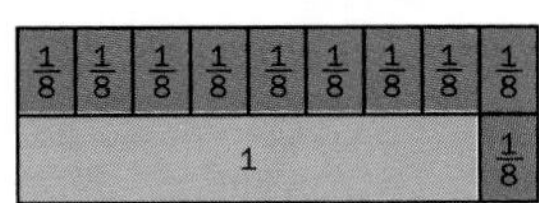

btract: $\frac{1}{3} - \frac{1}{4}$

ep 1

d equivalent fractions with a common ominator.

$\frac{1}{3} = \frac{1 \times 4}{3 \times 4} = \frac{4}{12}$

$\frac{1}{4} = \frac{1 \times 3}{4 \times 3} = -\frac{3}{12}$

Think:
Multiples of 3: 3, 6, 9, 12
Multiples of 4: 4, 8, 12
12 is the common denominator.

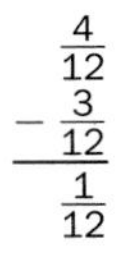

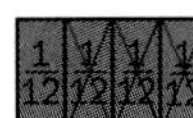

Step 2

Subtract the numerators.
Use the common denominator.

$\frac{4}{12} - \frac{3}{12} = \frac{1}{12}$

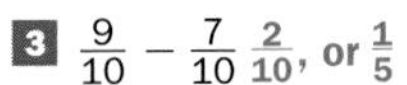

heck for Understanding

ld or subtract using any method.

$\frac{3}{8} + \frac{1}{4}$ $\frac{5}{8}$ **2** $\frac{2}{12} + \frac{4}{6}$ $\frac{10}{12}$, or $\frac{5}{6}$ **3** $\frac{9}{10} - \frac{7}{10}$ $\frac{2}{10}$, or $\frac{1}{5}$ **4** $\frac{5}{6} - \frac{1}{3}$ $\frac{3}{6}$, or $\frac{1}{2}$

ritical Thinking: Analyze **Explain your reasoning.**

Find $\frac{5}{6} - \frac{1}{3}$ in two ways, using 6, then 12, as the common denominator. What do you notice about the answers?

Possible answer: The answers are equivalent fractions.

Turn the page for Practice.

MAKE CONNECTIONS

Review the steps for adding fractions. For Step 1, ask:

- **How is a common denominator found in Step 1?** *[Possible answer: List multiples for each denominator until the same multiple shows in each list.]*
- **Why is 8 chosen in the list of multiples?** *[It is the least multiple common to both lists.]*
- **Why do you select the least multiple common to both lists?** *[Possible answers: to have the least possible common denominator, to minimize computations]*

For Step 2, ask:

- **Why don't you have to find an equivalent fraction for $\frac{3}{8}$?** *[It already has the common denominator of 8.]*
- **Why do you write $\frac{9}{8} = 1\frac{1}{8}$?** *[to write the answer in simplest form]*

Review the steps for subtracting fractions by asking similar questions.

3 Close

Check for Understanding using items 1–5, page 429.

Critical Thinking

Have students generalize about the differences in item 5. Ask:

- **Which difference is easier to find? Explain.** *[$\frac{5}{6} - \frac{2}{6} = \frac{3}{6} = \frac{1}{2}$; it involves fewer computations to solve and simplify—$\frac{10}{12} - \frac{4}{12} = \frac{6}{12} = \frac{1}{2}$.]*

Practice See pages 430–431.

PRACTICE

Materials have available: fraction strips (TA 26); calculators

Options for assigning exercises:
A—Odd ex. 1–27; ex. 28–32; **More to Explore**
B—Even ex. 2–26; ex. 28–32; **More to Explore**

- For ex. 12–26, encourage students to use mental math when they can.
- For **Make It Right** (ex. 28), see Common Error below.
- In ex. 29, students may use the problem-solving strategy, Solve a Multistep Problem, to find the answer.

More to Explore First, review how to round fractions less than 1 to zero, $\frac{1}{2}$, or 1 using a number line marked with zero, $\frac{1}{4}$, $\frac{1}{2}$, $\frac{3}{4}$, and 1. A number less than $\frac{1}{4}$ rounds to zero; a number greater than or equal to $\frac{1}{4}$ and less than $\frac{3}{4}$ rounds to $\frac{1}{2}$; and a number greater than or equal to $\frac{3}{4}$ rounds to 1. Point out that a single number line can be used if students use the equivalent fractions to compare to zero, $\frac{1}{2}$, or 1.

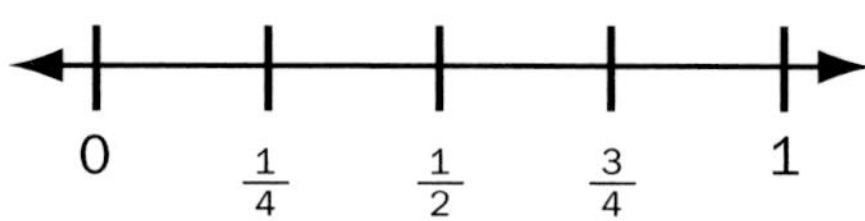

Summarize by asking:

- **Why would you want to estimate a fraction sum or difference?** *[Possible answer: to compare to an exact sum or difference to check the answer for reasonableness]*

Then have students work in pairs to complete the exercises. Encourage them to draw number lines to help them estimate.

Practice

Use the models to complete the number sentence.

1 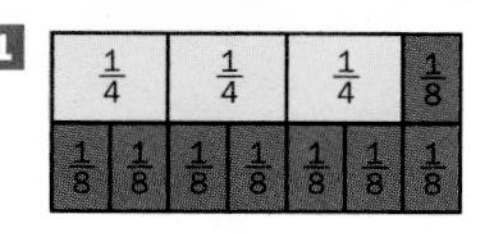

$\frac{3}{4} + \frac{1}{8} = ■$ $\frac{7}{8}$

2 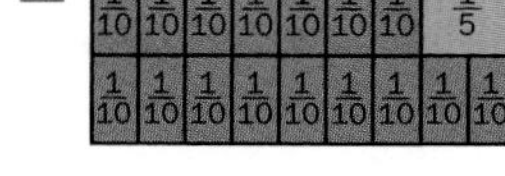

$\frac{7}{10} + \frac{1}{5} = ■$ $\frac{9}{10}$

3 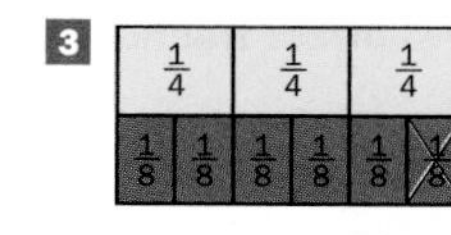

$\frac{3}{4} - \frac{1}{8} = ■$ $\frac{5}{8}$

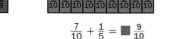

Find the equivalent fraction. Then add or subtract.

4 $\frac{2}{9} = \frac{■}{9}$ 2; $+\frac{2}{3} = \frac{■}{9}$ 6; $\frac{■}{9}$ 8

5 $\frac{1}{5} = \frac{■}{10}$ 2; $+\frac{4}{10} = \frac{■}{10}$ 4; $\frac{■}{10}$ 6

6 $\frac{3}{5} = \frac{■}{15}$ 9; $+\frac{1}{3} = \frac{■}{15}$ 5; $\frac{■}{15}$ 14

7 $\frac{2}{3} = \frac{■}{9}$ 6; $+\frac{5}{9} = \frac{■}{9}$ 5; $\frac{■}{9}$ 11

8 $\frac{4}{5} = \frac{■}{10}$ 8; $-\frac{5}{10} = \frac{■}{10}$ 5; $\frac{■}{10}$ 3

9 $\frac{5}{8} = \frac{■}{8}$ 5; $-\frac{1}{2} = \frac{■}{8}$ 4; $\frac{■}{8}$ 1

10 $\frac{5}{9} = \frac{■}{9}$ 5; $-\frac{1}{3} = \frac{■}{9}$ 3; $\frac{■}{9}$ 2

11 $\frac{1}{2} = \frac{■}{6}$ 3; $-\frac{1}{6} = \frac{■}{6}$ 1; $\frac{■}{6}$ 2

Add or subtract using any method.

12 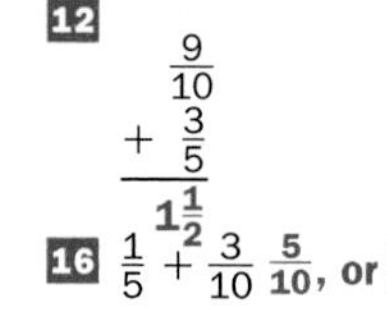

13 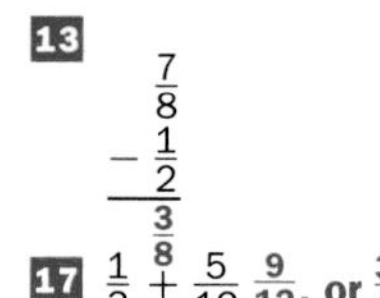

14 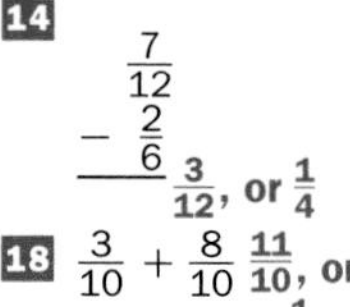

15 $\frac{1}{3} + \frac{5}{6}$ $\frac{7}{6}$, or $1\frac{1}{6}$

16 $\frac{1}{5} + \frac{3}{10}$ $\frac{5}{10}$, or $\frac{1}{2}$

17 $\frac{1}{3} + \frac{5}{12}$ $\frac{9}{12}$, or $\frac{3}{4}$

18 $\frac{3}{10} + \frac{8}{10}$ $\frac{11}{10}$, or $1\frac{1}{10}$

19 $\frac{3}{4} + \frac{2}{8}$ $\frac{8}{8}$, or

20 $\frac{7}{8} - \frac{1}{8}$ $\frac{6}{8}$, or $\frac{3}{4}$

21 $\frac{11}{12} - \frac{2}{3}$ $\frac{3}{12}$, or $\frac{1}{4}$

22 $\frac{5}{6} - \frac{1}{2}$ $\frac{2}{6}$, or $\frac{1}{3}$

23 $\frac{1}{2} - \frac{1}{6}$ $\frac{2}{6}$, or

24 $\frac{2}{3} - \frac{1}{6}$ $\frac{3}{6}$, or $\frac{1}{2}$

25 $\frac{2}{3} - \frac{5}{12}$ $\frac{3}{12}$, or $\frac{1}{4}$

26 $\frac{4}{5} - \frac{3}{10}$ $\frac{5}{10}$, or $\frac{1}{2}$

27 $\frac{7}{8} - \frac{3}{4}$ $\frac{1}{8}$

Make It Right

28 This is how Tamika found $\frac{5}{12} - \frac{1}{3}$. Tell what mistake was made, then correct it. $\frac{5}{12} - \frac{1}{3} = \frac{4}{9}$

She subtracted both the numerators and the denominators—she should have found equivalent fractions with like denominators, then subtracted the numerators and used the common denominator—$\frac{5}{12} - \frac{1}{3} = \frac{5}{12} - \frac{4}{12} = \frac{1}{12}$.

430 Lesson 11.6

Meeting Individual Needs

Early Finishers

Have students find the total amount of liquids and the total amount of dry ingredients listed in the table on Student Book page 428. *[2 c; 1 c]*

ESL APPROPRIATE

Gifted And Talented

Provide students with copies of several recipes. Have them find the amount of ingredients needed for doubling, tripling, and halving recipes. Encourage them to use number lines to find the halved ingredients.

Common Error

Students may add or subtract both numerators and denominators when adding or subtracting fractions, as in **Make It Right.** Have them use fraction strips, recording each step they use to find the answer.

. He brought home $\frac{1}{8}$ c; add $\frac{1}{2}+\frac{1}{4}=\frac{3}{4}$, subtract $\frac{7}{8}-\frac{3}{4}=\frac{1}{8}$.

30. She will put lace on her collar, skirt, and pants; change all fractions to twelfths, add the three lowest— $\frac{1}{6}+\frac{1}{2}+\frac{1}{4}=\frac{11}{12}$.

IXED APPLICATIONS

roblem Solving

lve. Use any method you choose.

Orville gave his little brother $\frac{7}{8}$ cup of raisins. His brother ate $\frac{1}{4}$ cup for a snack and $\frac{1}{2}$ cup for lunch. He brought the rest of the raisins home. How much did he bring home? Explain your thinking. **See above.**

Write a problem that has $\frac{7}{12}$ as the answer. Compare your problem with those of other classmates. How are they similar? different? **Students should compare problems and solutions.**

30 **Make a decision** Jan has $\frac{11}{12}$ yd of lace. She needs $\frac{1}{6}$ yd for her shirt collar, $\frac{1}{2}$ yd for her skirt, $\frac{3}{4}$ yd for her dress, and $\frac{1}{4}$ yd for her pants. She wants to add the lace to as many clothes as she can. Which should she add lace to? Explain. **See above.**

32 **Data Point** Use the Databank on page 542. Draw a graph to show the data. Explain how you decided what graph to choose. **Students' graphs should reflect data on number of apples picked by families.**

more to explore

stimating Sums and Differences of Fractions

u can use a number line to estimate the sum or ference of two fractions.

cide if the fraction is close to 0, $\frac{1}{2}$, or 1. en add or subtract your estimates.

timate: $\frac{3}{4}+\frac{1}{16}$

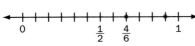

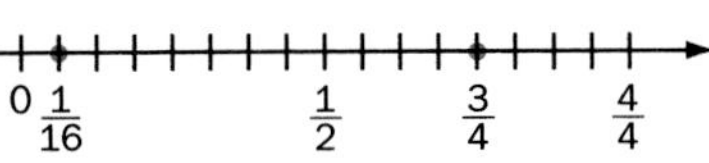

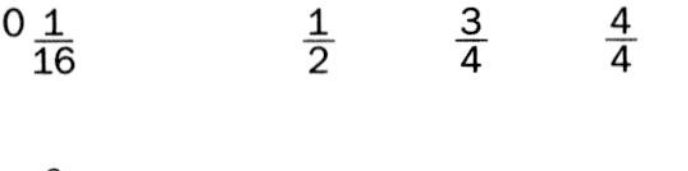

ink: $\frac{3}{4}$ is closer to 1.
$\frac{1}{16}$ is closer to 0.
$1+0=1$

$+\frac{1}{16}$ is about 1.

Estimate: $\frac{11}{12}-\frac{4}{6}$

0 $\frac{1}{2}$ $\frac{4}{6}$ 1

Think: $\frac{11}{12}$ is about 1.
$\frac{4}{6}$ is close to $\frac{1}{2}$.
$1-\frac{1}{2}=\frac{1}{2}$

$\frac{11}{12}-\frac{4}{6}$ is about $\frac{1}{2}$.

timate the sum or difference. **Estimates may vary. Possible estimates are shown.**

$\frac{14}{16}+\frac{7}{8}$ **2** 2 $\frac{3}{5}+\frac{4}{7}$ **1** 3 $\frac{4}{5}-\frac{3}{4}$ **close to 0** 4 $\frac{9}{10}-\frac{1}{16}$ **1**

Alternate Teaching Strategy

Materials per pair: centimeter graph paper (TA 7)

Present the following:

A recipe for applesauce bread uses $\frac{3}{4}$ cup applesauce and $\frac{1}{3}$ cup oil.

Ask:

- **How can you find the total amount of applesauce and oil in the recipe?** *[add $\frac{3}{4}+\frac{1}{3}$.]*
- **What is a common denominator for $\frac{3}{4}$ and $\frac{1}{3}$?** *[12]*

Direct students to make a box containing 12 squares on the grid paper. Then have them write each fraction with a common denominator. *[$\frac{9}{12}$, $\frac{4}{12}$]* Have them find the sum, using the grid paper. Ask:

- **What must you do to find the total using the grid paper? What is the total?** *[Draw another 12 squares; $1\frac{1}{12}$ c]*

Repeat the activity having students find how much more applesauce is used than oil. *[$\frac{5}{12}$c]*

Then repeat using both operations with other recipe amounts.

PRACTICE • 105

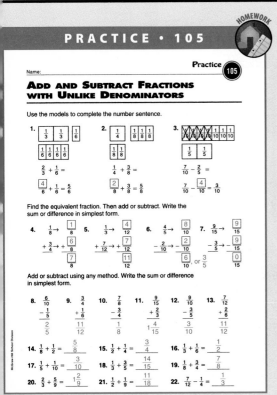

Practice 105

Name:

Add and Subtract Fractions with Unlike Denominators

Use the models to complete the number sentence.

1. $\frac{2}{3}+\frac{1}{6}=$
$\frac{4}{6}+\frac{1}{6}=\frac{5}{6}$

2. $\frac{1}{4}+\frac{3}{8}=$
$\frac{2}{8}+\frac{3}{8}=\frac{5}{8}$

3. $\frac{7}{10}-\frac{2}{5}=$
$\frac{7}{10}-\frac{4}{10}=\frac{3}{10}$

Find the equivalent fraction. Then add or subtract. Write the sum or difference in simplest form.

4. $\frac{1}{8}\to\frac{1}{8}$; $+\frac{3}{4}\to+\frac{6}{8}$; $\frac{7}{8}$
5. $\frac{1}{3}\to\frac{4}{12}$; $+\frac{7}{12}\to+\frac{7}{12}$; $\frac{11}{12}$
6. $\frac{4}{5}\to\frac{8}{10}$; $-\frac{2}{10}\to-\frac{2}{10}$; $\frac{6}{10}$, or $\frac{3}{5}$
7. $\frac{9}{15}\to\frac{9}{15}$; $-\frac{3}{5}\to-\frac{9}{15}$; $\frac{0}{15}$

Add or subtract using any method. Write the sum or difference in simplest form.

8. $\frac{6}{10}-\frac{1}{5}=\frac{2}{5}$
9. $\frac{3}{4}+\frac{1}{6}=\frac{11}{12}$
10. $\frac{7}{8}-\frac{3}{4}=\frac{1}{8}$
11. $\frac{9}{15}+\frac{2}{3}=1\frac{4}{15}$
12. $\frac{9}{10}-\frac{3}{5}=\frac{3}{10}$
13. $\frac{7}{12}+\frac{2}{6}=\frac{11}{12}$
14. $\frac{1}{8}+\frac{1}{2}=\frac{5}{8}$
15. $\frac{1}{2}+\frac{1}{4}=\frac{3}{4}$
16. $\frac{1}{3}+\frac{1}{6}=\frac{1}{2}$
17. $\frac{1}{5}+\frac{1}{10}=\frac{3}{10}$
18. $\frac{1}{3}+\frac{3}{5}=\frac{14}{15}$
19. $\frac{1}{8}+\frac{3}{4}=\frac{7}{8}$
20. $\frac{2}{3}+\frac{5}{9}=1\frac{2}{9}$
21. $\frac{1}{2}+\frac{1}{9}=\frac{11}{18}$
22. $\frac{7}{12}-\frac{1}{4}=\frac{1}{3}$

McGraw-Hill School Division

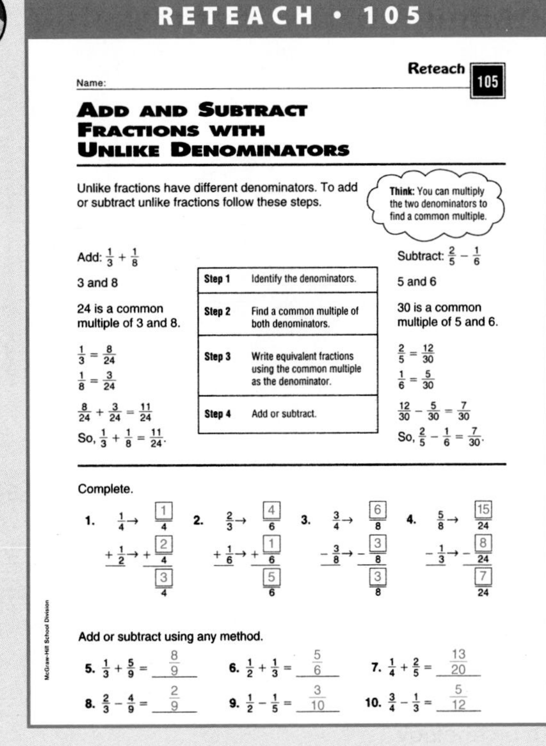

RETEACH • 105

Reteach 105

Name:

Add and Subtract Fractions with Unlike Denominators

Unlike fractions have different denominators. To add or subtract unlike fractions follow these steps.

Think: You can multiply the two denominators to find a common multiple.

Add: $\frac{1}{3}+\frac{1}{8}$			Subtract: $\frac{2}{5}-\frac{1}{6}$
3 and 8	Step 1	Identify the denominators.	5 and 6
24 is a common multiple of 3 and 8.	Step 2	Find a common multiple of both denominators.	30 is a common multiple of 5 and 6.
$\frac{1}{3}=\frac{8}{24}$, $\frac{1}{8}=\frac{3}{24}$	Step 3	Write equivalent fractions using the common multiple as the denominator.	$\frac{2}{5}=\frac{12}{30}$, $\frac{1}{6}=\frac{5}{30}$
$\frac{8}{24}+\frac{3}{24}=\frac{11}{24}$ So, $\frac{1}{3}+\frac{1}{8}=\frac{11}{24}$.	Step 4	Add or subtract.	$\frac{12}{30}-\frac{5}{30}=\frac{7}{30}$ So, $\frac{2}{5}-\frac{1}{6}=\frac{7}{30}$.

Complete.

1. $\frac{1}{4}\to\frac{1}{4}$; $+\frac{1}{2}\to+\frac{2}{4}$; $\frac{3}{4}$
2. $\frac{2}{3}\to\frac{4}{6}$; $+\frac{1}{6}\to+\frac{1}{6}$; $\frac{5}{6}$
3. $\frac{3}{4}\to\frac{6}{8}$; $-\frac{3}{8}\to-\frac{3}{8}$; $\frac{3}{8}$
4. $\frac{5}{8}\to\frac{15}{24}$; $-\frac{1}{3}\to-\frac{8}{24}$; $\frac{7}{24}$

Add or subtract using any method.

5. $\frac{1}{3}+\frac{5}{9}=\frac{8}{9}$
6. $\frac{1}{2}+\frac{1}{3}=\frac{5}{6}$
7. $\frac{1}{4}+\frac{2}{5}=\frac{13}{20}$
8. $\frac{2}{3}-\frac{4}{9}=\frac{2}{9}$
9. $\frac{1}{2}-\frac{1}{5}=\frac{3}{10}$
10. $\frac{3}{4}-\frac{1}{3}=\frac{5}{12}$

McGraw-Hill School Division

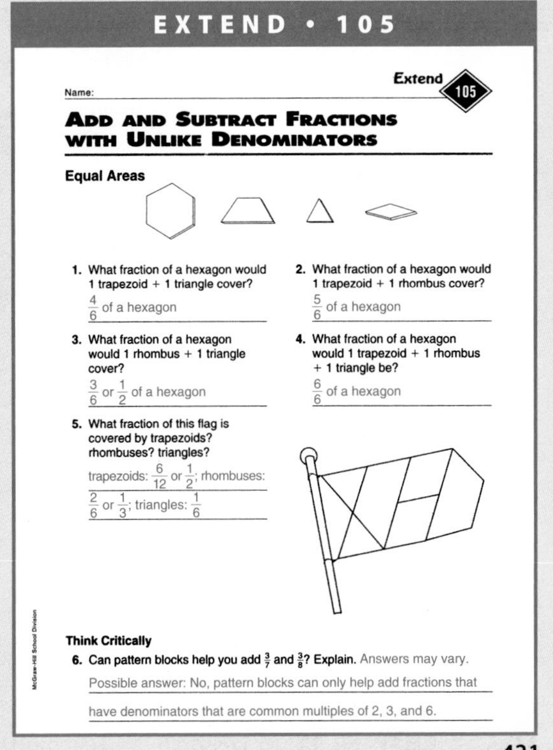

EXTEND • 105

Extend 105

Name:

Add and Subtract Fractions with Unlike Denominators

Equal Areas

1. What fraction of a hexagon would 1 trapezoid + 1 triangle cover? $\frac{4}{6}$ of a hexagon
2. What fraction of a hexagon would 1 trapezoid + 1 rhombus cover? $\frac{5}{6}$ of a hexagon
3. What fraction of a hexagon would 1 rhombus + 1 triangle cover? $\frac{3}{6}$ or $\frac{1}{2}$ of a hexagon
4. What fraction of a hexagon would 1 trapezoid + 1 rhombus + 1 triangle be? $\frac{6}{6}$ of a hexagon
5. What fraction of this flag is covered by trapezoids? rhombuses? triangles? trapezoids: $\frac{6}{12}$ or $\frac{1}{2}$; rhombuses: $\frac{2}{6}$ or $\frac{1}{3}$; triangles: $\frac{1}{6}$

Think Critically

6. Can pattern blocks help you add $\frac{3}{7}$ and $\frac{3}{8}$? Explain. Answers may vary. Possible answer: No, pattern blocks can only help add fractions that have denominators that are common multiples of 2, 3, and 6.

McGraw-Hill School Division

Teaching With Technology

Add and Subtract Fractions with Unlike Denominators

OBJECTIVE Students add and subtract fractions with unlike denominators using Fraction Strips.

Resource Math Van Activity: *Deli in a Pickle*

SET UP

Provide students with the activity card for *Deli in a Pickle.* Start ***Math Van*** and click the *Activities* button. Click the *Deli in a Pickle* activity on the Fax Machine.

USING THE MATH VAN ACTIVITY

1 **Getting Started** Students read tables and add and subtract fractions to figure out how much food they need to buy for the school band and choir.

2 **Practice and Apply** Students read a table with dessert orders for the band and choir. They add or subtract fractions to complete the table.

3 **Close** You may wish to have students share the methods they used to find the missing fractions in the Tables.

Extend Students create a table that shows a candy order that is incomplete. They have a partner add or subtract fractions to find the total order.

TIPS FOR TOOLS

Before students click the *Rename* button to rename a fraction, they must click the *Select* button and click the fraction they want to rename.

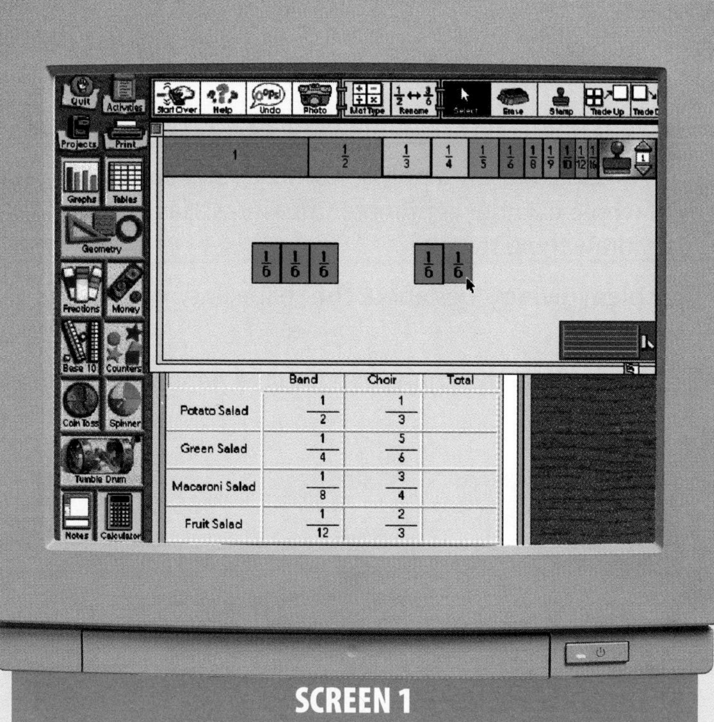

SCREEN 1

Students stamp and rename Fraction Strips to show how much potato salad the band needs to order. They add the fractions.

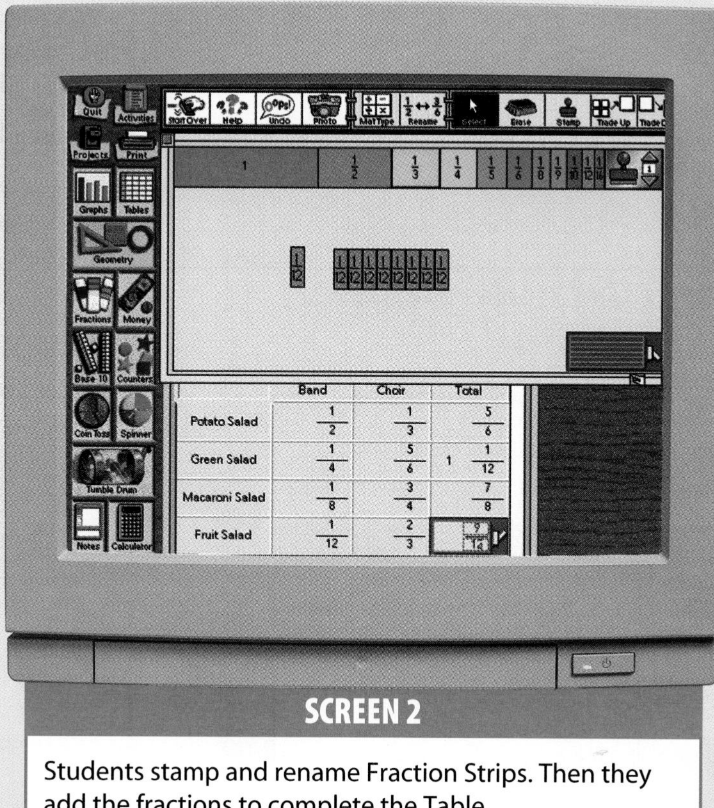

SCREEN 2

Students stamp and rename Fraction Strips. Then they add the fractions to complete the Table.

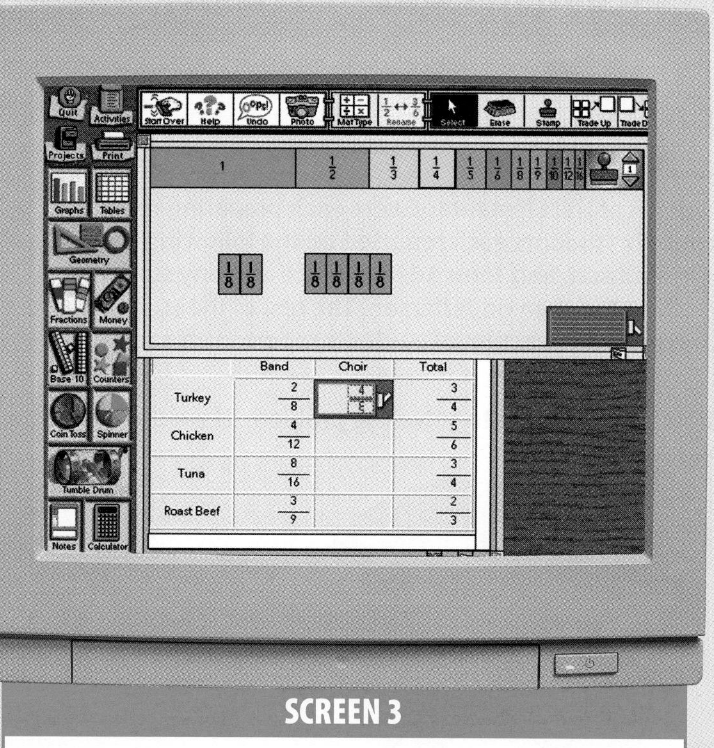

SCREEN 3

Students stamp Fraction Strips to show the total order. They rename fractions and find the missing fraction in the order.

SCREEN 4

Students take a photo of their completed Table and answer questions about adding and subtracting fractions.

LESSON 11.7

Problem-Solving Strategy: Draw a Picture

OBJECTIVE Solve problems by drawing a picture.

RESOURCE REMINDER
Math Center Cards 106
Practice 106, Reteach 106, Extend 106

SKILLS TRACE

GRADE 3	• Solve problems by drawing a picture. *(Chapter 3)*
GRADE 4	• Solve problems by drawing a picture.
GRADE 5	• Solve problems by drawing a picture. *(Chapter 3)*

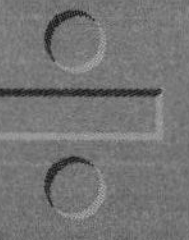

WARM-UP

Cooperative Groups — Visual/Spatial

OBJECTIVE Explore drawing diagrams to solve problems.

Materials per group: crayons or markers; centimeter rulers (TA 18)

▶ Students work in small groups to draw a polygon whose sides can be described as multiples of whole number centimeter measures. Have them measure the sides as they draw the polygon.

▶ The group writes a problem giving clues about the shape and measures of the polygon.

▶ Groups exchange problems, draw the figure, and find the perimeter of the polygon.

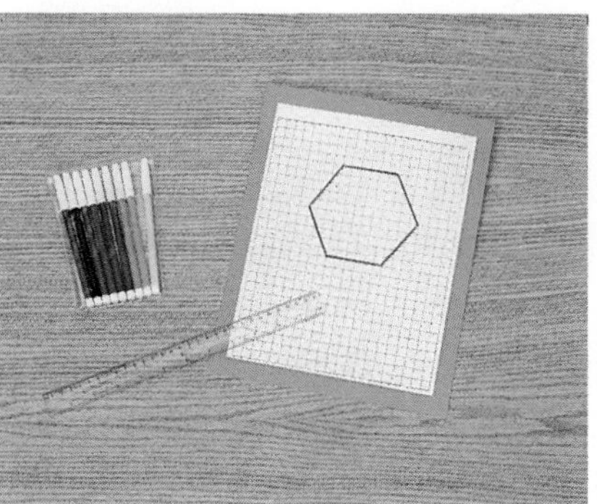

SOCIAL STUDIES CONNECTION

Cooperative Pairs — Logical/Analytical

OBJECTIVE Connect a circle graph to social studies.

▶ Present the following problem:

> **Forty-eight students at Hill Elementary were each preparing reports about presidents. Six students each reported on the following presidents: Jefferson, Madison, and John Adams. Twice as many students reported on Washington than on Jefferson. The rest of the students reported on Lincoln. What fraction of students reported on each president?**

▶ Have students draw a circle graph to solve the problem. Have them include the fractions for each part on the graph.

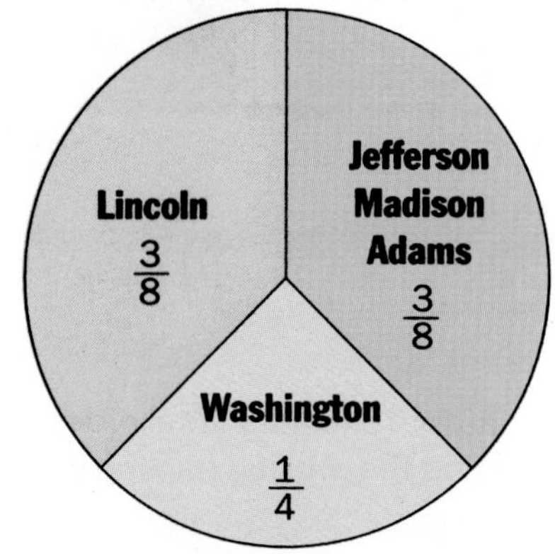

Daily Review

PREVIOUS DAY QUICK REVIEW

Add or subtract. Simplify.

1. $\frac{1}{4} + \frac{3}{4}$ *[1]*
2. $\frac{1}{6} + \frac{1}{3}$ *[$\frac{1}{2}$]*
3. $\frac{7}{8} - \frac{1}{8}$ *[$\frac{3}{4}$]*
4. $\frac{5}{6} - \frac{1}{2}$ *[$\frac{1}{3}$]*

FAST FACTS

1. 3 × 0 *[0]*
2. 8 × 3 *[24]*
3. 4 × 9 *[36]*
4. 7 × 6 *[42]*

Problem of the Day • 106

Half of a circle is blue and a third is red. The other two sections of the circle are equal in size. One of these sections is green; the other is yellow. What fraction of the circle is green?

[$\frac{1}{12}$ circle]

TECH LINK

MATH FORUM

Idea I have my students use graph paper to draw pictures for problems involving fractions. This allows them to make equal parts without worrying about the precision of the drawing.

Visit our Resource Village at http://www.mhschool.com to see more of the Math Forum.

MATH CENTER

Practice

OBJECTIVE Draw a picture to solve a problem that involves adding and subtracting fractions.

Materials per student: Math Center Recording Sheet (TA 31 optional)

Students find a common denominator for the fractional parts of a shelf that are filled to determine how much space is available. Although the denominator could be 12, the students use 36 to determine how many inches are available. *[$\frac{1}{3} + \frac{1}{4} + \frac{1}{4} = \frac{30}{36}; \frac{6}{36}$ is left; 6 inches will hold 12 CDs.]*

PRACTICE ACTIVITY 106 — MATH CENTER, On Your Own

Spatial Reasoning • Shelf Space

Your parents have a yard-long shelf that holds the family CDs. $\frac{1}{3}$ of the shelf is filled with country music. $\frac{1}{4}$ holds classical music. $\frac{1}{4}$ holds movie music. The rest of the shelf is open for your CDs. How many inches are open for you to use?

- To solve, use a common denominator of 36, the number of inches in a yard.
- Each inch of the shelf holds 2 CDs. How many CDs of your own can you fit on the shelf?

Grade Level 4 · McGraw-Hill School Division

Chapter 11, Lesson 7, pages 432–433 — Problem Solving

NCTM Standards
- ✓ Problem Solving
- ✓ Communication
- ✓ Reasoning
- Connections

Problem Solving

OBJECTIVE Draw a picture to solve a problem.

Materials per student: graph paper

Students follow directions to make a map. Then they add directions to get home. *[1. Check students' maps. 2. Go south 3 blocks, then west 1 block.]*

PROBLEM-SOLVING ACTIVITY 106 — MATH CENTER, On Your Own

Spatial Sense • How Far to Home?

YOU NEED: graph paper

Let each square on the graph paper equal one city block. Mark "home" in the center of the graph paper.

1. Follow the directions to draw Tamika's path. Label each location at which she stops.
   Start at home.
   Go 4 blocks south to the school, then
   go 5 blocks west to the soccer field, then
   go 6 blocks north to the bike shop, then
   go 2 blocks east to the pizza place, then
   go 3 blocks north to visit a friend, then
   go 4 blocks east to the library, then
   go 2 blocks south to visit another friend, then . . .
2. Write two more directions that Tamika can follow to get back home. Follow your directions on the map.

Grade Level 4 · McGraw-Hill School Division

Chapter 11, Lesson 7, pages 432–433 — Problem Solving

NCTM Standards
- ✓ Problem Solving
- Communication
- ✓ Reasoning
- ✓ Connections

Problem-Solving Strategy: Draw a Picture

OBJECTIVE Solve problems by drawing a picture.

Present the following problem:

Bobby made a square. He divided the square into quarters. Then he divided each quarter in half to make rectangles. How many rectangles did Bobby make? What fraction of the whole is half of the rectangles?

Have students draw a diagram to solve the problem. *[8 rectangles; $\frac{4}{8}$, or $\frac{1}{2}$]*

Whole Class

▶ **LEARN** After reading the problem on page 432, have students explain what they know and what they are trying to find.

As students review the Plan step, Ask:

- **What operations will you have to use to solve?** *[addition and subtraction]*

Work through the solution with students. Ask:

- **What is the least common denominator of any two fractions?** *[the least common multiple of the denominators of the fractions]*
- **How do you find the least common denominator of $\frac{1}{3}$, $\frac{3}{8}$, and $\frac{1}{12}$?** *[Multiples of 3: 3, 6, 9, 12, 15, 18, 21, 24; 8: 8, 16, 24; 12: 12, 24; LCD: 24]*

Discuss how to draw the picture to find the solution.

▶ **Check for Understanding** using items 1–2, page 432.

CRITICAL THINKING

In item 2, students are asked to generalize about the Drawing a Picture strategy. Have them analyze the usefulness of the strategy by asking:

- **Why can drawing a picture help you solve a problem?** *[Possible answer: It helps you to visualize and organize the information in the problem.]*

▶ **PRACTICE**

Materials have available: calculators (optional)

Assign ex. 1–9 as independent work.

- In ex. 2 and 8, students may use the strategy, Draw a Picture.
- For ex. 5 and 6, students may use the strategy, Make an Organized List.

Problem-Solving Strategy

Read · Plan · Solve · Look Back

Draw a Picture

LEARN

Read **Suppose you are designing packages for a new line of frozen dinners. The rectangular trays are divided into sections. Plan $\frac{1}{3}$ of the tray for potatoes, $\frac{3}{8}$ for a main course, $\frac{1}{12}$ for green beans, and $\frac{1}{12}$ for squash. How much of the tray is available for a dessert?**

Plan To solve the problem, you can draw a picture.

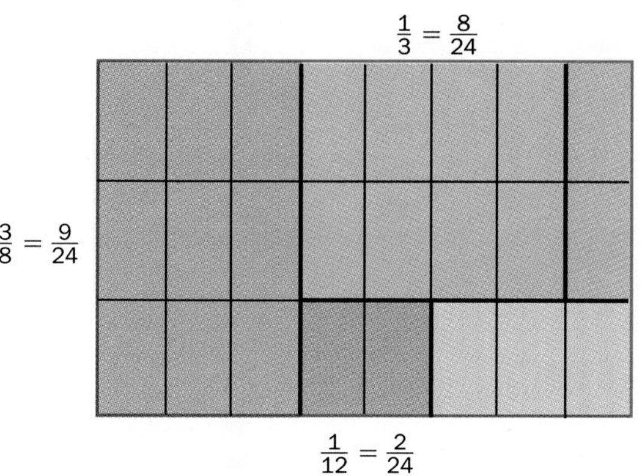

Solve A common denominator is 24, so divide the tray into 24 sections. When you fill in the portions, $\frac{3}{24}$, or $\frac{1}{8}$, is left empty.

$\frac{1}{8}$ of the tray is available for dessert.

Look Back What other way could you have solved this problem? **Possible answer: Add $\frac{1}{3}$, $\frac{3}{8}$, $\frac{1}{12}$, and $\frac{1}{12}$, then subtract the sum from 1.**

CHECK

Check for Understanding

1 **What if** the space for potatoes changes to $\frac{1}{4}$ of the tray. Now, how much will be left for the dessert? **$\frac{5}{24}$ of the tray**

Critical Thinking: Generalize

2 Which kinds of problems will you most likely solve by using the strategy of drawing a picture? **Possible answers: problems with too much information to remember, problems in which information changes, problems involving measurement**

432 Lesson 11.7

Meeting Individual Needs

Early Finishers

Have students write a problem that can be solved by drawing a picture. Then have them trade problems and solve each other's problems.

Extra Support

Some students may have difficulty drawing a picture to solve problems. Provide them with problems that show partial diagrams that they can use and complete to solve the problem.

Ongoing Assessment

Observation Checklist Check that students are able to solve problems involving mixed applications and strategies by noting if they can draw appropriate diagrams to solve problems.

Follow Up For students who are having difficulty using the Draw a Picture strategy, assign **Reteach 106.**

Have students who are ready for a challenge try **Extend 106.**

5 ways; 2 blues and 3 reds, 3 reds and 1
llow, 2 yellows, 2 blues and 1 yellow, 4 blues

IXED APPLICATIONS

roblem Solving

Pencil & Paper | Calculator | Mental Math

There are 175 students who want to see a play. The theater has rows of seats with 6 seats in each row. About how many rows will the students need to reserve to see the play? Explain your thinking. **out 30 rows; estimate: 180 ÷ 6 = 30**

Jacy writes the first ten letters of the alphabet on separate index cards. He turns them over and chooses one card. Which did he most likely choose: a vowel, a consonant that comes after *D*, or a consonant that comes before *D*? Explain your method. **See below.**

Ms. Hopkins is storing 205 baking pans in two cupboards. Each section of one cupboard holds 20 pans, and each section of the other cupboard holds 25 pans. She wants to fill each section that is used. How many sections in each cupboard will she use to store the pans? **See above.**

There are three food trays for a breakfast buffet. Each tray contains either eggs, potatoes, or fruit. The trays are placed in a row on the table. How many different ways can the trays be arranged on the table? **6 ways**

Suppose a serving bowl is divided into 12 equal sections. The first $\frac{1}{4}$ of the bowl is for olives, $\frac{1}{3}$ is for carrot sticks, $\frac{1}{6}$ for celery sticks, and $\frac{1}{12}$ is for radishes. How much of the bowl is left for the dip? **$\frac{1}{6}$ of the bowl**

. **Possible answer: a consonant that comes after *D*, since it has the greatest probability; explanations may vary.**

xtra Practice, page 526

5. **Possible answers: 4 sections that hold 20 pans and 5 sections that hold 25 pans, 9 sections that hold 20 pans and 1 section that holds 25 pans**

2 The Turners framed their family portrait. The framed portrait is 12 inches wide and 16 inches long. The frame is 1 inch wide all around. What is the area of the picture without the frame? **140 sq in.**

4 **What if** the principal arranges to buy popcorn for the 175 students. There are 30 boxes with 6 bags of popcorn in each box. Use mental math to determine if there is enough popcorn for each student to get a bag. Explain your methods. **There is enough; 30 × 6 = 180 > 175.**

6 The school fair has a game in which you must throw beanbags into different-color boxes. A bag in the red box is worth 8 points, blue is 12, and yellow is 24. To win, you must score exactly 48 points. You get up to 5 throws to win. How many different ways can you win? Explain your thinking. **See above.**

8 Cora, Kurt, Nathan, and Toni are sitting beside each other at a play. Nathan is between Cora and Kurt. Kurt is at the end of the row. In what order are they sitting? **Toni, Cora, Nathan, Kurt**

PRACTICE

Alternate Teaching Strategy

Materials fraction circles (TA 27)

Present the following problem:

A circular serving tray contains fruits in four sections. One quarter of the tray is for apple slices, $\frac{1}{3}$ is for orange slices, and $\frac{1}{6}$ is for pear slices. What fraction of the tray is for grapes?

Ask:

- **Are each of the sections in the circular tray the same size? Explain.** *[No; the fractions are different.]*
- **How can you use a common denominator to determine the size of each section in the circle?** *[Possible answer: Divide circle into 12 (common denominator) slices, then find the number of slices for each fruit section.]*

Have students divide each part of the 6-part circle in half to get a circle divided into twelfths. Have students write equivalent fractions with a common denominator to complete the diagram and solve the problem. *[$\frac{1}{4}$ tray]*

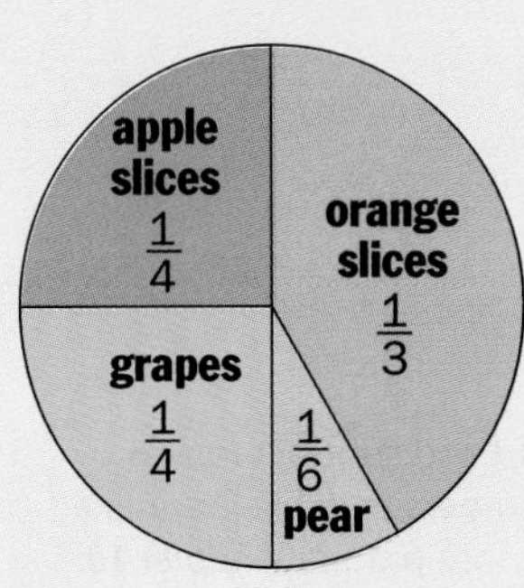

PRACTICE • 106

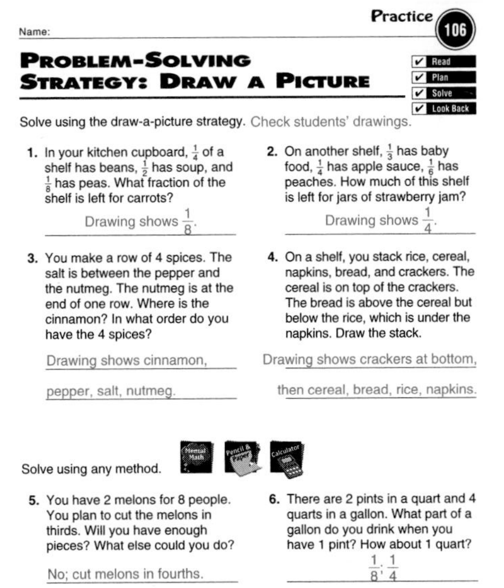

Name:

Practice 106

PROBLEM-SOLVING STRATEGY: DRAW A PICTURE

✔ Read ✔ Plan ✔ Solve ✔ Look Back

Solve using the draw-a-picture strategy. Check students' drawings.

1. In your kitchen cupboard, $\frac{1}{4}$ of a shelf has beans, $\frac{1}{2}$ has soup, and $\frac{1}{8}$ has peas. What fraction of the shelf is left for carrots? Drawing shows $\frac{1}{8}$.
2. On another shelf, $\frac{1}{3}$ has baby food, $\frac{1}{4}$ has apple sauce, $\frac{1}{6}$ has peaches. How much of this shelf is left for jars of strawberry jam? Drawing shows $\frac{1}{4}$.
3. You make a row of 4 spices. The salt is between the pepper and the nutmeg. The nutmeg is at the end of one row. Where is the cinnamon? In what order do you have the 4 spices? Drawing shows cinnamon, pepper, salt, nutmeg.
4. On a shelf, you stack rice, cereal, napkins, bread, and crackers. The cereal is on top of the crackers. The bread is above the cereal but below the rice, which is under the napkins. Draw the stack. Drawing shows crackers at bottom, then cereal, bread, rice, napkins.

Solve using any method. Mental Math | Pencil & Paper | Calculator

5. You have 2 melons for 8 people. You plan to cut the melons in thirds. Will you have enough pieces? What else could you do? No; cut melons in fourths.
6. There are 2 pints in a quart and 4 quarts in a gallon. What part of a gallon do you drink when you have 1 pint? How about 1 quart? $\frac{1}{8}$, $\frac{1}{4}$
7. You buy 25 cans of peaches at $1.22 a can. You have $30 in bills and 4 quarters. Will that be enough? Can you still buy 2 more cans? Yes; no.
8. There are 4 people in your family. They each eat an apple a day. Use mental math to estimate about how many apples that is in a month. about 120 apples

McGraw-Hill School Division

RETEACH • 106

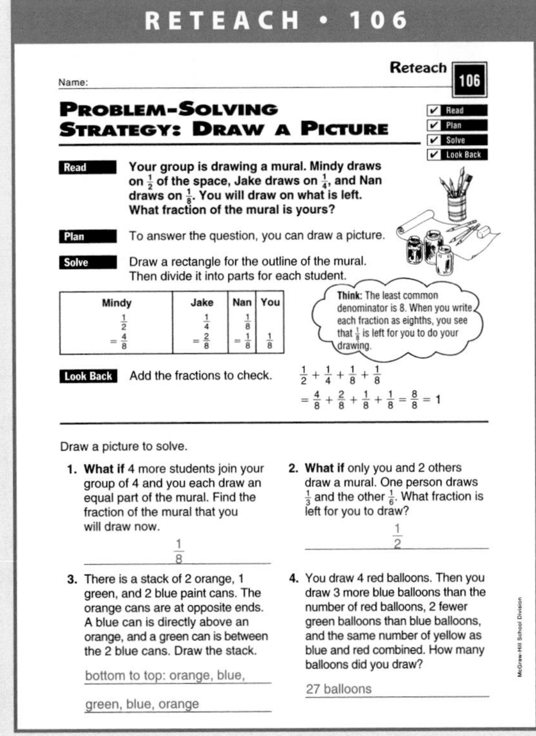

Name:

Reteach 106

PROBLEM-SOLVING STRATEGY: DRAW A PICTURE

✔ Read ✔ Plan ✔ Solve ✔ Look Back

Read **Your group is drawing a mural. Mindy draws on $\frac{1}{2}$ of the space, Jake draws on $\frac{1}{4}$, and Nan draws on $\frac{1}{8}$. You will draw on what is left. What fraction of the mural is yours?**

Plan To answer the question, you can draw a picture.

Solve Draw a rectangle for the outline of the mural. Then divide it into parts for each student.

Mindy	Jake	Nan	You
$\frac{1}{2} = \frac{4}{8}$	$\frac{1}{4} = \frac{2}{8}$	$\frac{1}{8} = \frac{1}{8}$	$\frac{1}{8}$

Think: The least common denominator is 8. When you write each fraction as eighths, you see that $\frac{1}{8}$ is left for you to do your drawing.

Look Back Add the fractions to check. $\frac{1}{2} + \frac{1}{4} + \frac{1}{8} + \frac{1}{8} = \frac{4}{8} + \frac{2}{8} + \frac{1}{8} + \frac{1}{8} = \frac{8}{8} = 1$

Draw a picture to solve.

1. **What if** 4 more students join your group of 4 and you each draw an equal part of the mural. Find the fraction of the mural that you will draw now. $\frac{1}{8}$
2. **What if** only you and 2 others draw a mural. One person draws $\frac{1}{3}$ and the other $\frac{1}{6}$. What fraction is left for you to draw? $\frac{1}{2}$
3. There is a stack of 2 orange, 1 green, and 2 blue paint cans. The orange cans are at opposite ends. A blue can is directly above an orange, and a green can is between the 2 blue cans. Draw the stack. bottom to top: orange, blue, green, blue, orange
4. You draw 4 red balloons. Then you draw 3 more blue balloons than the number of red balloons, 2 fewer green balloons than blue balloons, and the same number of yellow as blue and red combined. How many balloons did you draw? 27 balloons

McGraw-Hill School Division

EXTEND • 106

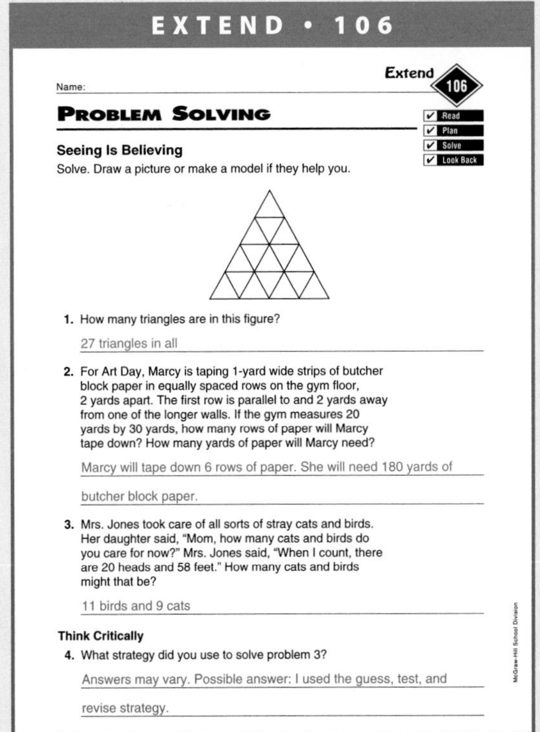

Name:

Extend 106

PROBLEM SOLVING

✔ Read ✔ Plan ✔ Solve ✔ Look Back

Seeing Is Believing

Solve. Draw a picture or make a model if they help you.

1. How many triangles are in this figure? 27 triangles in all
2. For Art Day, Marcy is taping 1-yard wide strips of butcher block paper in equally spaced rows on the gym floor, 2 yards apart. The first row is parallel to and 2 yards away from one of the longer walls. If the gym measures 20 yards by 30 yards, how many rows of paper will Marcy tape down? How many yards of paper will Marcy need? Marcy will tape down 6 rows of paper. She will need 180 yards of butcher block paper.
3. Mrs. Jones took care of all sorts of stray cats and birds. Her daughter said, "Mom, how many cats and birds do you care for now?" Mrs. Jones said, "When I count, there are 20 heads and 58 feet." How many cats and birds might that be? 11 birds and 9 cats

Think Critically

4. What strategy did you use to solve problem 3? Answers may vary. Possible answer: I used the guess, test, and revise strategy.

McGraw-Hill School Division

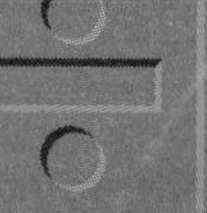

LESSON 11.8 RESOURCES

EXPLORE ACTIVITY

Add and Subtract Mixed Numbers

OBJECTIVE Explore adding and subtracting mixed numbers with like denominators.

RESOURCE REMINDER
Math Center Cards 107
Practice 107, Reteach 107, Extend 107

SKILLS TRACE

GRADE 3	• *Introduced at grade 4.*
GRADE 4	• Explore adding and subtracting mixed numbers with like denominators.
GRADE 5	• Add and subtract mixed numbers with like or unlike denominators. *(Chapter 10)*

MANIPULATIVE WARM-UP

Cooperative Pairs — **Logical/Analytical**

OBJECTIVE Review adding and subtracting fractions.

Materials have available: fraction strips (TA 26)

▶ Students work with a partner. Have them use the fractions below to write 5 addition sentences where the sum is greater than or equal to 1. *[Possible answers: $\frac{1}{2}+\frac{3}{4}=1\frac{1}{4}$; $\frac{1}{2}+\frac{5}{8}=1\frac{1}{8}$; $\frac{1}{2}+\frac{7}{8}=1\frac{3}{8}$; $\frac{7}{8}+\frac{1}{4}=1\frac{1}{8}$; $\frac{7}{8}+\frac{5}{8}=1\frac{1}{2}$]*

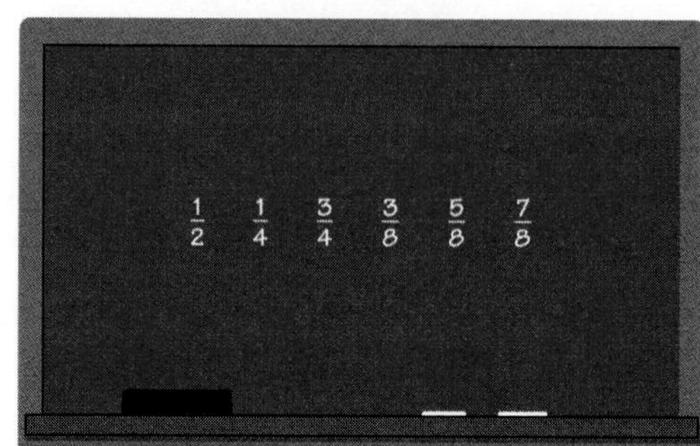

▶ Then have students use the same fractions to write at least 5 subtraction sentences with differences that are greater than 0 and less than or equal to $\frac{1}{2}$.

[Possible answers: $\frac{3}{4}-\frac{1}{2}=\frac{1}{4}$; $\frac{7}{8}-\frac{5}{8}=\frac{1}{4}$; $\frac{7}{8}-\frac{3}{8}=\frac{1}{2}$; $\frac{3}{8}-\frac{1}{4}=\frac{1}{8}$; $\frac{1}{2}-\frac{1}{4}=\frac{1}{4}$]

ESL APPROPRIATE

STATISTICS CONNECTION

Cooperative Pairs — **Visual/Spatial**

OBJECTIVE Connect fractions to finding the range of a set of data.

Materials per pair: inch ruler (TA 18)

▶ Copy the following table onto the chalkboard:

Student	Height (in inches)
Stuart	$43\frac{5}{8}$
Kimberly	$41\frac{2}{8}$
Rose	$42\frac{1}{8}$
Natalie	$41\frac{7}{8}$
Renzo	$44\frac{3}{8}$
Jeremy	$43\frac{4}{8}$

▶ Have students work with a partner to find the range of the heights in the table. *[$3\frac{1}{8}$ in.]* Students may use a ruler to help them solve. Then have students order the heights from least to greatest. *[$41\frac{2}{8}$, $41\frac{7}{8}$, $42\frac{1}{8}$, $43\frac{4}{8}$, $43\frac{5}{8}$, $44\frac{3}{8}$ in.]*

▶ Groups may continue this activity by measuring the lengths of classroom objects, finding the range, and ordering the lengths.

Daily Review

PREVIOUS DAY QUICK REVIEW

Find the sum or difference.

1. $\frac{2}{3} + \frac{2}{3}$ *[$1\frac{1}{3}$]*
2. $\frac{1}{4} + \frac{1}{8}$ *[$\frac{3}{8}$]*
3. $\frac{7}{8} - \frac{3}{8}$ *[$\frac{4}{8}$, or $\frac{1}{2}$]*
4. $\frac{9}{10} - \frac{1}{5}$ *[$\frac{7}{10}$]*

FAST FACTS

1. 15 ÷ 3 *[5]*
2. 16 ÷ 2 *[8]*
3. 63 ÷ 7 *[9]*
4. 40 ÷ 8 *[5]*

Problem of the Day • 107

Karin uses $1\frac{1}{4}$ cups of yogurt and $2\frac{3}{4}$ cups each of raspberries and orange juice to make some smoothies. How many total cups of yogurt, fruit, and juice does she use for the smoothies? *[$6\frac{3}{4}$ c]*

TECH LINK

Math Van

MATH VAN

Aid You may wish to use the Electronic Teacher Aid in the Math Van with this lesson.

MATH FORUM

Management Tip To ensure that there are enough fraction strips, I have pairs alternate sets. One pair uses quarters while another uses eighths. Then they exchange sets.

Visit our Resource Village at http://www.mhschool.com to see more of the Math Forum.

MATH CENTER

Practice

OBJECTIVE Add and subtract mixed numbers.

Materials per student: Math Center Recording Sheet (TA 31 optional)

Students write a list of directions for getting from one mixed number at the top of the grid to another mixed number at the bottom by adding or subtracting. Students may create a path to go in any direction, as long as it reaches the target. *[Check students' work.]*

PRACTICE ACTIVITY 107 — MATH CENTER, Partners

Formulating Problems • Make a Path

- Copy the table. Pick a box in the top row and a box in the bottom row. Write a set of directions to get from the top box to the bottom one by adding or subtracting. For example, if you started with $3\frac{5}{12}$, your first direction might be, "Subtract $1\frac{2}{12}$." This would tell your partner that your next box is $2\frac{3}{12}$.
- Don't tell your partner which boxes you have chosen. Just give the list of directions and the starting fraction.
- Exchange and follow each other's directions.

$3\frac{7}{12}$	$4\frac{1}{12}$	$2\frac{1}{12}$	$3\frac{5}{12}$
$2\frac{11}{12}$	$1\frac{4}{12}$	$1\frac{8}{12}$	$2\frac{3}{12}$
$1\frac{3}{12}$	$2\frac{6}{12}$	$2\frac{2}{12}$	$3\frac{2}{12}$
$1\frac{8}{12}$	$1\frac{9}{12}$	$3\frac{5}{12}$	$2\frac{2}{12}$
$2\frac{3}{12}$	$3\frac{1}{12}$	$4\frac{3}{12}$	$3\frac{9}{12}$
$3\frac{3}{12}$	$2\frac{11}{12}$	$3\frac{5}{12}$	$2\frac{6}{12}$

Grade Level 4 · McGraw-Hill School Division

Chapter 11, Lesson 8, pages 434–437 — Fractions

NCTM Standards

- ✓ Problem Solving
- ✓ Communication
- ✓ Reasoning
- Connections

Problem Solving

OBJECTIVE Describe and complete addition and subtraction patterns that use fractions.

Materials per student: Math Center Recording Sheet (TA 31 optional)

Students find the missing fraction operation and complete the input/output tables. They may choose to make up a table of their own. *[**1.** add $\frac{2}{3}$: 2, $2\frac{1}{3}$, $2\frac{2}{3}$; **2.** subtract $\frac{1}{5}$: 4, 4, $3\frac{4}{5}$; Check students' tables.]*

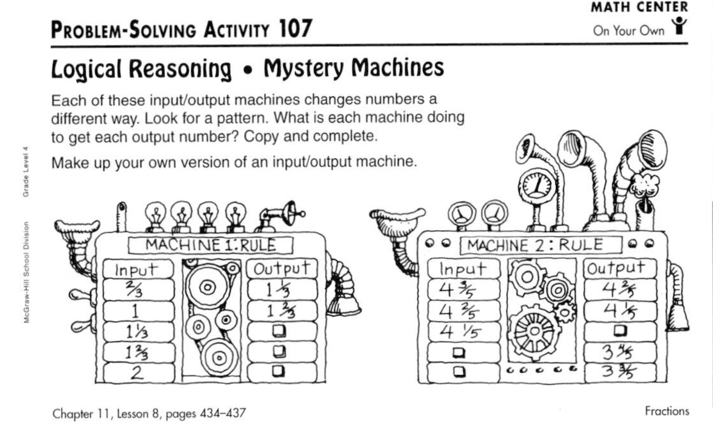

PROBLEM-SOLVING ACTIVITY 107 — MATH CENTER, On Your Own

Logical Reasoning • Mystery Machines

Each of these input/output machines changes numbers a different way. Look for a pattern. What is each machine doing to get each output number? Copy and complete.

Make up your own version of an input/output machine.

Grade Level 4 · McGraw-Hill School Division

Chapter 11, Lesson 8, pages 434–437 — Fractions

NCTM Standards

- ✓ Problem Solving
- Communication
- ✓ Reasoning
- Connections

EXPLORE ACTIVITY

Add and Subtract Mixed Numbers

OBJECTIVE Explore adding and subtracting mixed numbers.

Materials per pair: 5 index cards; fraction strips (TA 26); blank number cube

Vocabulary mixed number

1 Introduce

Copy the following circles onto the chalkboard:

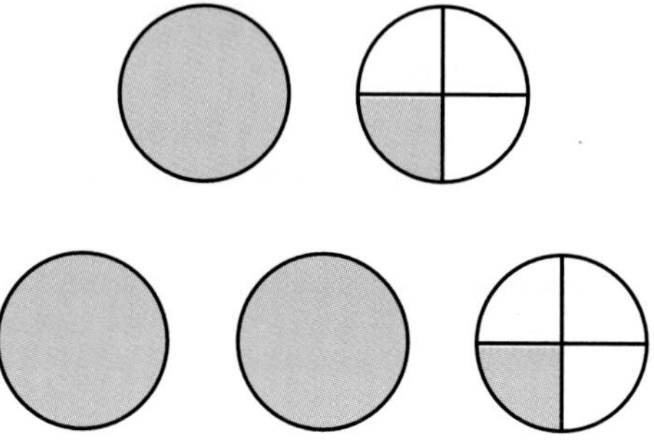

Ask:

- **What mixed number is represented by the first set of circles? the second set?** *[$1\frac{1}{4}$; $2\frac{1}{4}$]*
- **What mixed number shows the total?** *[$3\frac{2}{4}$, or $3\frac{1}{2}$]*
- **What number sentence shows the sum?** *[$1\frac{1}{4} + 2\frac{1}{4} = 3\frac{2}{4}$ or $3\frac{1}{2}$]*

2 Teach *Cooperative Pairs*

LEARN Work Together Guide students in preparing the materials for the activity. Encourage them to distinguish between the sums and differences as they repeat the activity. It may be useful to have them include another column in their tables that shows the sum or difference in a number sentence.

Talk It Over Have students compare the methods they used to add and subtract the mixed numbers. Some students may have used fraction strips only to add or subtract fraction parts, then added or subtracted whole numbers and combined whole number and fraction parts to find the answer. Other students may have changed the mixed numbers to improper fractions and then added or subtracted.

EXPLORE ACTIVITY • FRACTIONS

Add and Subtract Mixed Numbers

LEARN

Sometimes, when you add and subtract with fractions, the numbers you have to use are mixed numbers.

Work Together

Work with a partner to add and subtract mixed numbers.

You will need
- *fraction strips*
- *index cards*

Write these numbers on index cards:
$1\frac{1}{12}$, $1\frac{3}{12}$, $1\frac{5}{12}$, $1\frac{7}{12}$, $1\frac{11}{12}$, $2\frac{1}{12}$,

$2\frac{5}{12}$, $2\frac{7}{12}$, $2\frac{11}{12}$, $3\frac{5}{12}$, $3\frac{7}{12}$, $3\frac{11}{12}$.

Mix up the cards. Choose two cards. Use fraction strips to find the total. Record your work in a table.

Choose another pair of cards. Use fraction strips to find the difference. Record your work in another table.

Repeat the activity five times.

KEEP IN MIND
- You may have to find equivalent fractions.
- You may need to regroup whole numbers or fractions.

Card 1	Card 2	Total
$2\frac{5}{12}$	$2\frac{11}{12}$	

Card 1	Card 2	Difference
$2\frac{7}{12}$	$1\frac{5}{12}$	

Talk It Over

- What methods did you use to add and subtract mixed numbers? **Possible answer: Found fraction strips to represent each whole number and fraction on each number card and added them together or subtracted to find the difference.**
- How did you know when to regroup the fraction part of a mixed number? **Possible answer: If the fraction part had a numerator greater than the denominator, rewrote it as a mixed number, then added the whole number part of the original mixed number.**

mixed number A number that has a whole number and a fraction.

Meeting Individual Needs

Extra Support

Students having trouble operating with mixed numbers use egg cartons, cups, and 2-color counters. A cup represents a whole number and counters in a carton represent the fractional part.

Language Support

Have students discuss each step with their partners as they use models to add and subtract mixed numbers. Have them continue to practice saying mixed numbers to gain confidence in their pronunciation abilities.

ESL APPROPRIATE

Ongoing Assessment

Observation Checklist
Observe if students are able to add and subtract mixed numbers by noting if they perform the operations with the fractions before the whole number parts of the mixed numbers.

Follow Up Have students who are having difficulty finding sums and differences of mixed numbers start with numbers that are easy to operate such as $2\frac{1}{4} + 3\frac{2}{4}$ and $5\frac{2}{3} - 2\frac{1}{3}$. Assign **Reteach 107.**

For students who are ready for a challenge, assign **Extend 107.**

ake Connections

u can use fraction strips to add and subtract xed numbers.

d: $1\frac{7}{12} + 1\frac{3}{12}$

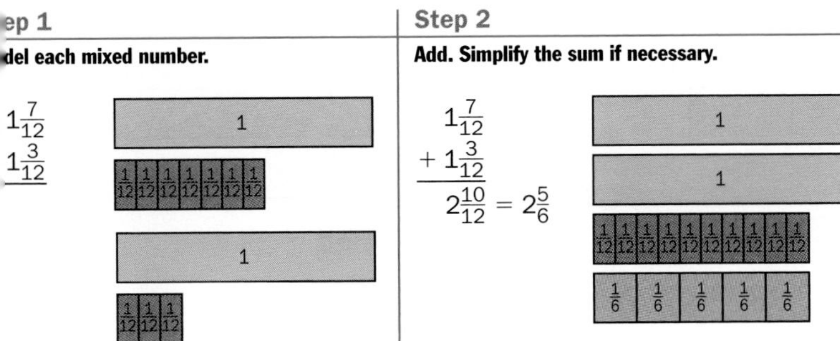

ep 1	Step 2
del each mixed number.	**Add. Simplify the sum if necessary.**
$1\frac{7}{12}$ $1\frac{3}{12}$	$1\frac{7}{12}$ $+ 1\frac{3}{12}$ $2\frac{10}{12} = 2\frac{5}{6}$

btract: $2\frac{7}{12} - 1\frac{5}{12}$

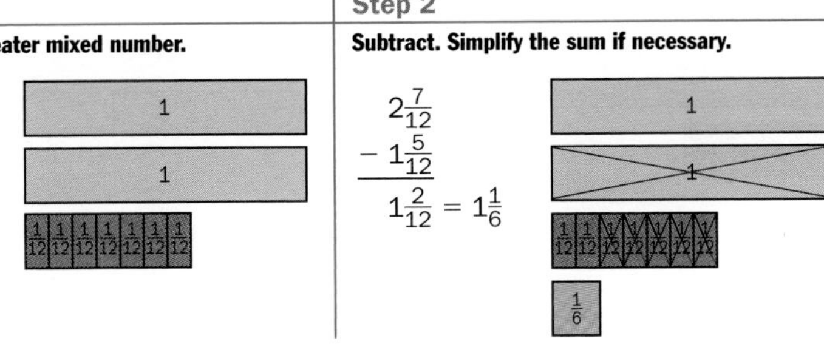

ep 1	Step 2
del the greater mixed number.	**Subtract. Simplify the sum if necessary.**
$2\frac{7}{12}$ $1\frac{5}{12}$	$2\frac{7}{12}$ $- 1\frac{5}{12}$ $1\frac{2}{12} = 1\frac{1}{6}$

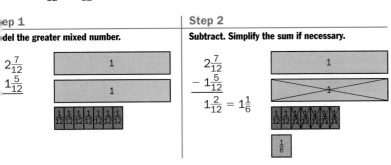

heck for Understanding

d or subtract.

$3\frac{3}{8} + 2\frac{1}{8}$ $5\frac{1}{2}$ | **2** $1\frac{5}{12} + 2\frac{3}{12}$ $3\frac{2}{3}$ | **3** $1\frac{4}{12} + 1\frac{10}{12}$ $3\frac{1}{6}$ | **4** $2\frac{4}{6} + 1\frac{2}{6}$ 4

$5\frac{9}{10} - 3\frac{6}{10}$ $2\frac{3}{10}$ | **6** $3\frac{5}{6} - 2\frac{2}{6}$ $1\frac{1}{2}$ | **7** $3\frac{5}{8} - 1\frac{1}{8}$ $2\frac{1}{2}$ | **8** $2\frac{3}{4} - 2\frac{1}{4}$ $\frac{1}{2}$

itical Thinking: Analyze **Explain your reasoning.**

Do you always need to rename when you add mixed numbers? Show an example.

Possible answer: Not if the two fraction parts of the mixed numbers do not equal a whole or more when combined; $4\frac{2}{5} + 2\frac{1}{5} = 6\frac{3}{5}$.

CHECK

Turn the page for Practice.

MAKE CONNECTIONS

Discuss how adding and subtracting mixed numbers is similar to and different from adding and subtracting fractions. *[Possible answer: Similar— need common denominators to add and subtract fraction parts; different— must add or subtract whole number part.]*

Discuss how to add and subtract mixed numbers, especially in vertical form, without using fraction strips.

3 Close

Check for Understanding using items 1–9, page 435.

Critical Thinking

In item 9, students are asked to analyze regrouping in the addition of mixed numbers. Have them extend the concept to subtraction by asking:

- **How can you use regrouping to find the difference $5 - 1\frac{2}{3}$?** *[$5 = 4\frac{3}{3}$; $4\frac{3}{3} - 1\frac{2}{3} = 3\frac{1}{3}$]*

Practice See pages 436–437.

PRACTICE

Materials have available: fraction strips (TA 26); calculators

Options for assigning exercises:
A—Ex. 1–2; 5–14; 15–21; **More to Explore**
B—Ex. 3–6; 11–14; 15–21; **More to Explore**

- For ex. 5 and 6, suggest that students write out the number sentence when completing the tables.
- Encourage students to use mental math when they can in ex. 7–14.
- For **Make It Right** (ex. 15), see Common Error below.
- For ex. 18, students may use the problem-solving strategy, Guess, Test, and Revise, to find the answer.

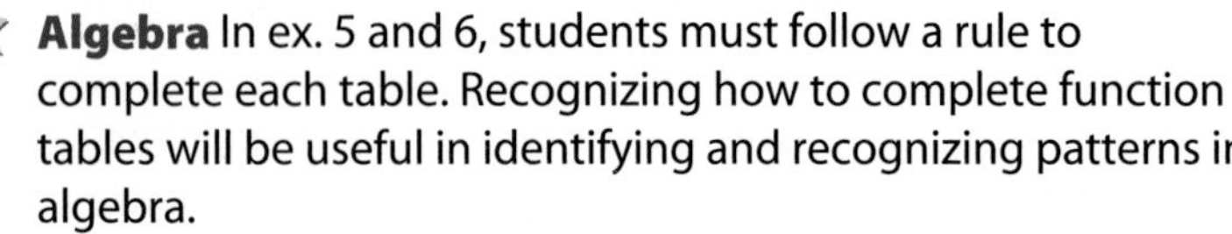

Algebra In ex. 5 and 6, students must follow a rule to complete each table. Recognizing how to complete function tables will be useful in identifying and recognizing patterns in algebra.

More to Explore Review how to round mixed numbers. Ask:

- **When do you round a mixed number down? up?** *[down if the fraction part is less than $\frac{1}{2}$; up if it is greater than or equal to $\frac{1}{2}$]*

Have students refer to number lines to help visualize how to round the fractional part, if necessary. Point out that the mixed numbers are rounded to whole numbers to estimate sums or differences to whole numbers.

Have students work in pairs to complete the exercises.

Practice

Complete the number sentence.

1 $2\frac{3}{5} + 1\frac{1}{5} = 3\frac{■}{5}$ 4

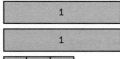

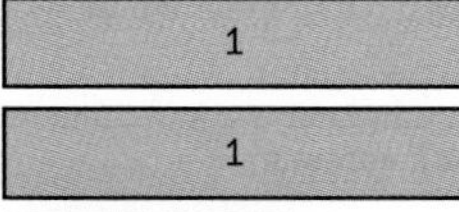

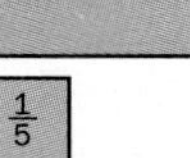

2 $3\frac{4}{10} - 3\frac{2}{10} = \frac{■}{10} = \frac{■}{5}$ 2, 1

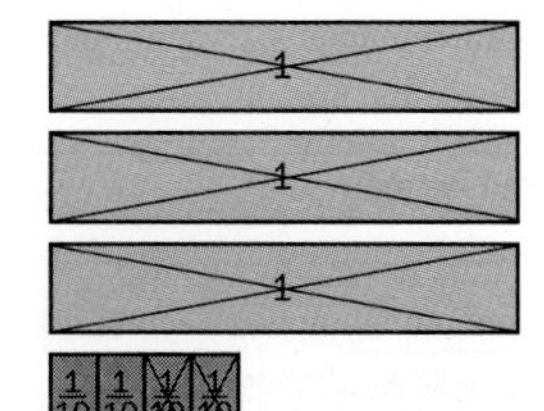

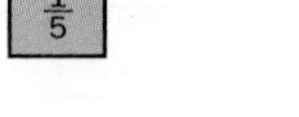

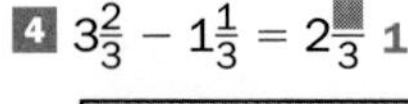

3 $1\frac{3}{8} + 1\frac{4}{8} = 2\frac{■}{8}$ 7

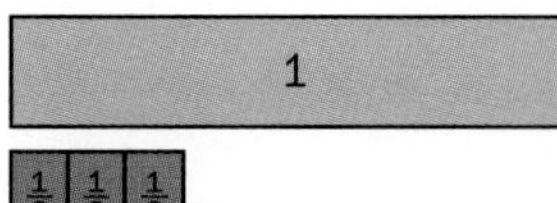

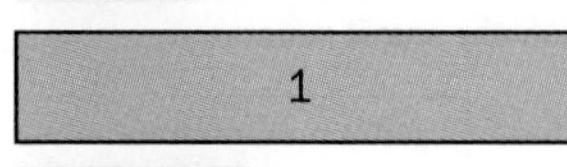

4 $3\frac{2}{3} - 1\frac{1}{3} = 2\frac{■}{3}$ 1

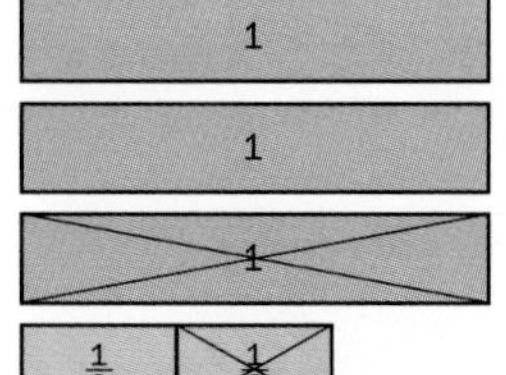

ALGEBRA Complete the table. Write the answers in simplest form.

5

Rule:	$1\frac{1}{6}$	$1\frac{2}{6}$	$1\frac{3}{6}$	$1\frac{4}{6}$
Add $1\frac{5}{6}$.	■	■	■	■

3 $3\frac{1}{6}$ $3\frac{1}{3}$ $3\frac{1}{2}$

6

Rule:	$3\frac{3}{8}$	$3\frac{4}{8}$	$3\frac{5}{8}$	$3\frac{6}{8}$
Subtract $1\frac{3}{8}$.	■	■	■	■

2 $2\frac{1}{8}$ $2\frac{1}{4}$ $2\frac{3}{8}$

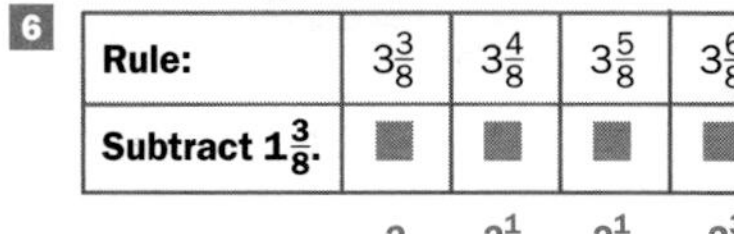

Add or subtract. Rename and simplify when necessary.

7 $2\frac{1}{5} + 1\frac{3}{5}$ $3\frac{4}{5}$ **8** $2\frac{4}{12} + 1\frac{5}{12}$ $3\frac{3}{4}$ **9** $1\frac{3}{10} + 2\frac{8}{10}$ $4\frac{1}{10}$ **10** $2\frac{7}{8} + 1\frac{7}{8}$ $4\frac{3}{4}$

11 $4\frac{6}{8} - 3\frac{1}{8}$ $1\frac{5}{8}$ **12** $4\frac{11}{12} - 2\frac{2}{12}$ $2\frac{3}{4}$ **13** $1\frac{5}{6} - 1\frac{3}{6}$ $\frac{1}{3}$ **14** $4\frac{3}{4} - 2\frac{1}{4}$ $2\frac{1}{2}$

Make It Right

15 Sid used fraction strips to add $3\frac{3}{4} + 2\frac{2}{4}$.
Explain what the mistake is, then correct it. $3\frac{3}{4} + 2\frac{2}{4} = 5\frac{1}{4}$

Possible answer: Sid didn't add the new whole to 5 when he regrouped, or he subtracted the numerators instead of adding—the correct answer is $6\frac{1}{4}$.

436 Lesson 11.8

Meeting Individual Needs

Early Finishers

Have students make their own function tables with a rule for adding or subtracting a mixed number. Have them exchange problems with a partner and solve each other's problems.

ESL APPROPRIATE

Common Error

Students may forget to regroup when simplifying mixed number sums, as in **Make It Right.** Have them record the sum in unsimplified form, then they can compare numerator and denominator to simplify the sum.

Inclusion

Provide students with alternative fraction aids to help them add and subtract mixed numbers. Students may use these to make models of fraction sums and differences.

Gifted And Talented

Have students find the perimeter of different rectangular items in the classroom by measuring the length and width to the nearest $\frac{1}{16}$ inch.

. $1\frac{1}{2}$ c of guacamole and 1 lb of ground beef
. George; George did homework for $1\frac{1}{2} + 1\frac{1}{2} = 3$ h, while Meg did homework for $1\frac{1}{4} + \frac{3}{4} = 2$ h.

IXED APPLICATIONS

roblem Solving

Pencil & Paper · Calculator · Mental Math

Pablo made $2\frac{3}{4}$ cups of guacamole and $3\frac{1}{2}$ pounds of ground beef. After his family ate, there were $1\frac{1}{4}$ cups of guacamole left and $2\frac{1}{2}$ pounds of ground beef. How much of each did his family eat? See above.

17 **Make a decision** George spent $1\frac{1}{2}$ h doing math homework and $1\frac{1}{2}$ h reading. Meg spent $1\frac{1}{4}$ h doing math and $\frac{3}{4}$ h reading. Who spent more time? Explain. See above.

Suppose vowels are worth 9¢, consonants are worth 4¢, and words beginning with *R* are worth an extra 7¢. Find three words that are worth more than 60¢. Possible nswer: mathematics, California, information

19 **Write a problem** in which you must either add or subtract mixed numbers with like denominators in order to solve it. Use fraction strips to solve it. Possible answer: $1\frac{1}{6} + 2\frac{3}{6} = 3\frac{4}{6}$, or $3\frac{2}{3}$

Rosalita is making a tropical fruit punch for a birthday party. She uses a recipe that mixes $6\frac{3}{4}$ cups of pineapple juice with $5\frac{1}{4}$ cups of guava juice. How many cups of tropical punch will there be for the party? 12 c

21 Michael is making a bowl of mixed nuts as a snack for family and friends. He has $3\frac{7}{8}$ pounds of peanuts and $2\frac{3}{8}$ pounds of Brazil nuts. Which type of nut does he have more of? How many more pounds of it does he have? peanuts; $1\frac{1}{2}$ pounds

more to explore

stimate Sums and Differences of Mixed Numbers

ou can round to estimate the sum or difference of two ixed numbers.

stimate: $3\frac{3}{4} + 2\frac{1}{7}$

hink: $\frac{3}{4} > \frac{1}{2}$ Round $3\frac{3}{4}$ up to 4.

$\frac{1}{7} < \frac{1}{2}$ Round $2\frac{1}{7}$ down to 2.

$\frac{3}{4} + 2\frac{1}{7}$ is about 4 + 2, or 6.

Estimate: $5\frac{3}{8} - 2\frac{1}{16}$

Think: $\frac{3}{8} < \frac{1}{2}$ Round $5\frac{3}{8}$ down to 5.

$\frac{1}{16} < \frac{1}{2}$ Round $2\frac{1}{16}$ down to 2.

$5\frac{3}{8} - 2\frac{1}{16}$ is about 5 − 2, or 3.

stimate the sum or difference. Estimates may vary. Possible estimates are shown.

$4\frac{12}{13} + 3\frac{5}{6}$ 9 **2** $1\frac{1}{15} + 2\frac{1}{7}$ 3 **3** $\frac{15}{16} + 3\frac{1}{12}$ 4 **4** $2\frac{8}{9} + \frac{1}{10}$ 3

$5\frac{4}{5} - \frac{6}{7}$ 5 **6** $4\frac{2}{3} - 1\frac{7}{8}$ 3 **7** $1\frac{8}{9} - 1\frac{1}{16}$ 1 **8** $3\frac{3}{4} - 1\frac{1}{16}$ 3

xtra Practice, page 527

Alternate Teaching Strategy

Copy the following number line divided into fourths on the chalkboard:

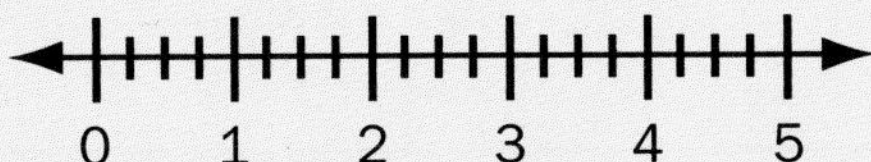

Direct students to copy the number line. Then have them work with a partner to show $1\frac{1}{4}$ on the number line. Then ask:

- **Where is 2 more than $1\frac{1}{4}$ on the number line?** *[$3\frac{1}{4}$]*
- **Where is $2\frac{2}{4}$ more than $1\frac{1}{4}$ on the number line?** *[$3\frac{3}{4}$]*

Summarize by having a volunteer come to the chalkboard to show how to use the number line to find $1\frac{1}{4} + 2\frac{2}{4}$.

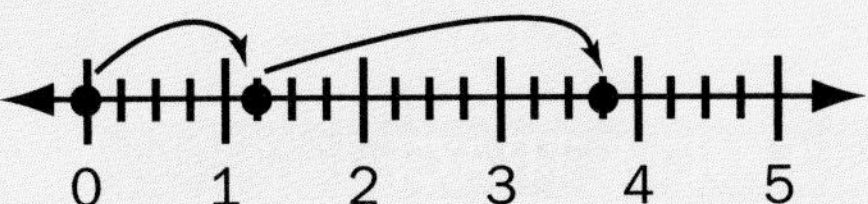

Repeat the activity for other mixed number sums and differences.

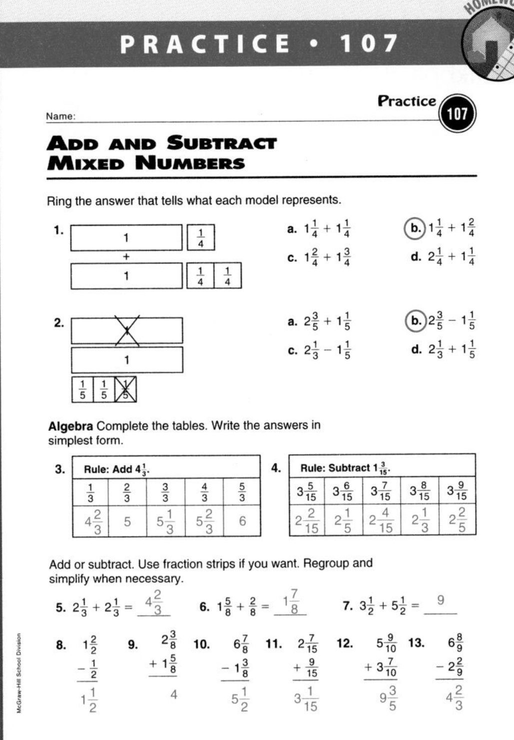

PRACTICE • 107

Practice 107

Name:

ADD AND SUBTRACT MIXED NUMBERS

Ring the answer that tells what each model represents.

1. a. $1\frac{1}{4} + 1\frac{1}{4}$ (b.) $1\frac{1}{4} + 1\frac{2}{4}$ c. $1\frac{2}{4} + 1\frac{3}{4}$ d. $2\frac{1}{4} + 1\frac{1}{4}$

2. a. $2\frac{3}{5} + 1\frac{1}{5}$ (b.) $2\frac{3}{5} - 1\frac{1}{5}$ c. $2\frac{1}{3} - 1\frac{1}{5}$ d. $2\frac{1}{3} + 1\frac{1}{5}$

Algebra Complete the tables. Write the answers in simplest form.

3. Rule: Add $4\frac{1}{3}$.

$\frac{1}{3}$	$\frac{2}{3}$	$\frac{3}{3}$	$\frac{4}{3}$	$\frac{5}{3}$
$4\frac{2}{3}$	5	$5\frac{1}{3}$	$5\frac{2}{3}$	6

4. Rule: Subtract $1\frac{3}{15}$.

$3\frac{5}{15}$	$3\frac{6}{15}$	$3\frac{7}{15}$	$3\frac{8}{15}$	$3\frac{9}{15}$
$2\frac{2}{15}$	$2\frac{1}{5}$	$2\frac{4}{15}$	$2\frac{1}{3}$	$2\frac{2}{5}$

Add or subtract. Use fraction strips if you want. Regroup and simplify when necessary.

5. $2\frac{1}{3} + 2\frac{1}{3} =$ $4\frac{2}{3}$ 6. $1\frac{5}{8} + \frac{2}{8} =$ $1\frac{7}{8}$ 7. $3\frac{1}{2} + 5\frac{1}{2} =$ 9

8. $1\frac{2}{2} - \frac{1}{2}$ = $1\frac{1}{2}$ 9. $2\frac{3}{8} + 1\frac{5}{8}$ = 4 10. $6\frac{7}{8} - 1\frac{3}{8}$ = $5\frac{1}{2}$ 11. $2\frac{7}{15} + \frac{9}{15}$ = $3\frac{1}{15}$ 12. $5\frac{9}{10} + 3\frac{7}{10}$ = $9\frac{3}{5}$ 13. $6\frac{8}{9} - 2\frac{2}{9}$ = $4\frac{2}{3}$

McGraw-Hill School Division

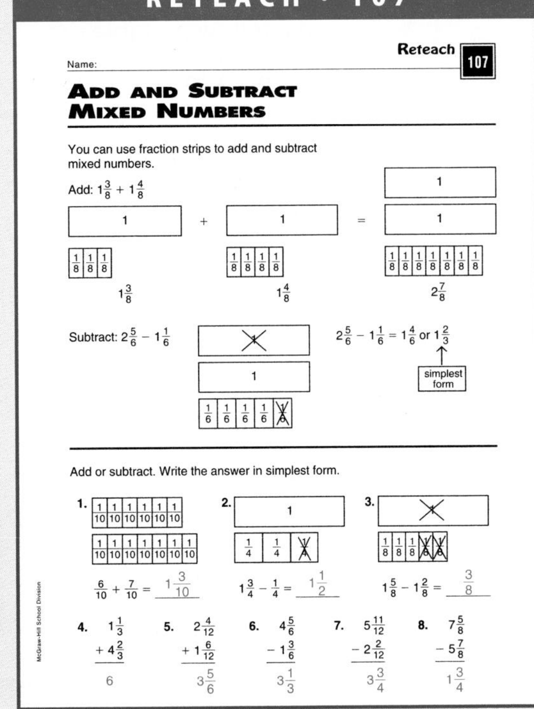

RETEACH • 107

Reteach 107

Name:

ADD AND SUBTRACT MIXED NUMBERS

You can use fraction strips to add and subtract mixed numbers.

Add: $1\frac{3}{8} + 1\frac{4}{8}$

$1\frac{3}{8}$ + $1\frac{4}{8}$ = $2\frac{7}{8}$

Subtract: $2\frac{5}{6} - 1\frac{1}{6}$

$2\frac{5}{6} - 1\frac{1}{6} = 1\frac{4}{6}$ or $1\frac{2}{3}$ ← simplest form

Add or subtract. Write the answer in simplest form.

1. $\frac{6}{10} + \frac{7}{10} =$ $1\frac{3}{10}$ 2. $1\frac{3}{4} - \frac{1}{4} =$ $1\frac{1}{2}$ 3. $1\frac{5}{8} - 1\frac{2}{8} =$ $\frac{3}{8}$

4. $1\frac{1}{3} + 4\frac{2}{3}$ = 6 5. $2\frac{4}{12} + 1\frac{6}{12}$ = $3\frac{5}{6}$ 6. $4\frac{5}{6} - 1\frac{3}{6}$ = $3\frac{1}{3}$ 7. $5\frac{11}{12} - 2\frac{2}{12}$ = $3\frac{3}{4}$ 8. $7\frac{5}{8} - 5\frac{7}{8}$ = $1\frac{3}{4}$

McGraw-Hill School Division

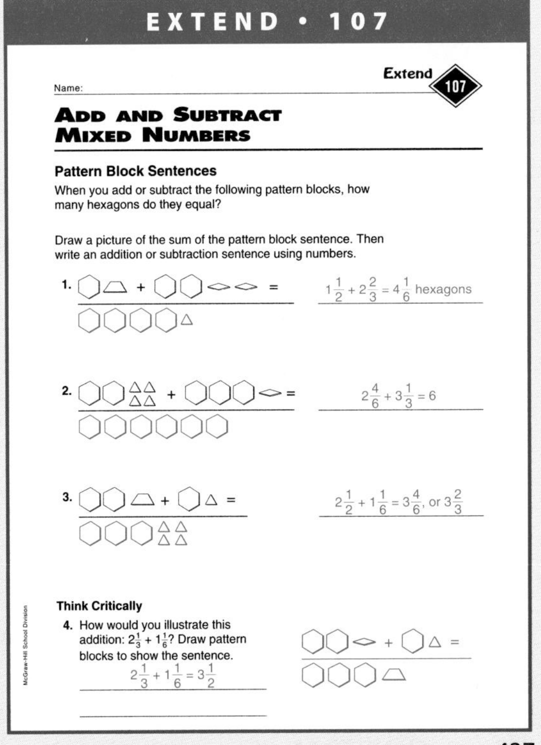

EXTEND • 107

Extend 107

Name:

ADD AND SUBTRACT MIXED NUMBERS

Pattern Block Sentences

When you add or subtract the following pattern blocks, how many hexagons do they equal?

Draw a picture of the sum of the pattern block sentence. Then write an addition or subtraction sentence using numbers.

1. $1\frac{1}{2} + 2\frac{2}{3} = 4\frac{1}{6}$ hexagons

2. $2\frac{4}{6} + 3\frac{1}{3} = 6$

3. $2\frac{1}{2} + 1\frac{1}{6} = 3\frac{4}{6}$, or $3\frac{2}{3}$

Think Critically

4. How would you illustrate this addition: $2\frac{1}{3} + 1\frac{1}{6}$? Draw pattern blocks to show the sentence. $2\frac{1}{3} + 1\frac{1}{6} = 3\frac{1}{2}$

McGraw-Hill School Division

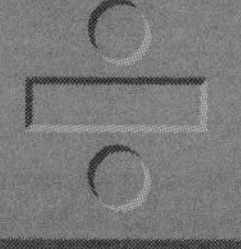

Problem Solvers at Work

OBJECTIVE Solve/write problems by choosing the operation.

RESOURCE REMINDER
Math Center Cards 108
Practice 108, Reteach 108, Extend 108

SKILLS TRACE

GRADE 3	• Formulate and solve problems by choosing the operation. *(Chapter 8)*
GRADE 4	• Formulate and solve problems by choosing the operation.
GRADE 5	• Formulate and solve problems by choosing the operation. *(Chapter 9)*

MANIPULATIVE WARM-UP

Cooperative Pairs — Visual/Spatial

OBJECTIVE Find fraction sums and differences.

Materials per pair: fraction strips (TA 26)

▶ Students work with a partner. They place the fraction strips on a desk. One student selects two fraction strips without looking. The students work together to find the sum and difference of the strips. Encourage them to use mental math when possible. Stress that accuracy is more important than speed.

▶ Have students repeat the activity two more times keeping the used fraction strips out.

▶ Then challenge students to mix up the strips and use the same procedure to find the sums of three and then four fractions.

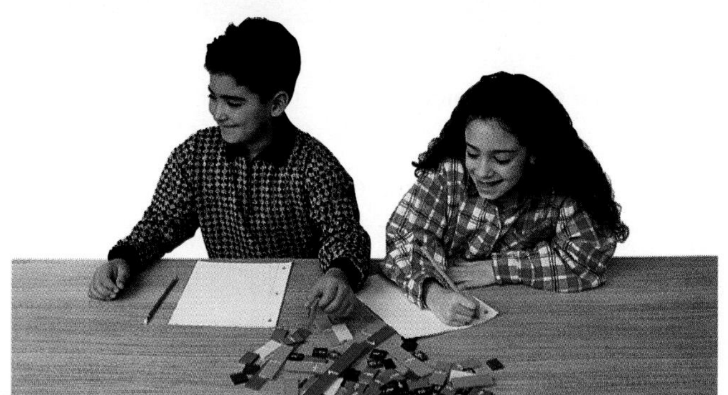

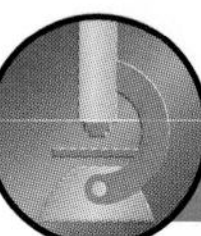

SCIENCE CONNECTION

Cooperative Pairs — Logical/Analytical

OBJECTIVE Connect adding and subtracting mixed numbers to problem solving in science.

Materials per pair: 2 index cards; fraction strips (optional)

▶ Copy the following table onto the chalkboard:

Month	Total Precipitation (in inches)
Jan.	$1\frac{1}{4}$
Feb.	$2\frac{1}{4}$
Mar.	$2\frac{2}{4}$
Apr.	$2\frac{3}{4}$

▶ Students work in pairs to write two problems using the data in the table. One problem should involve addition and the other subtraction.

▶ Students record each problem on an index card. Pairs exchange cards and solve. They may use fraction strips to help them solve.

What was the total precipitation for January - March?

How much more did it rain in April than in January?

Daily Review

PREVIOUS DAY QUICK REVIEW

Add or subtract.

1. $1\frac{2}{3} + 2$ [$3\frac{2}{3}$]
2. $2\frac{1}{6} + 1\frac{1}{6}$ [$3\frac{2}{6}$, or $3\frac{1}{3}$]
3. $4\frac{7}{8} - 2\frac{5}{8}$ [$2\frac{2}{8}$, or $2\frac{1}{4}$]
4. $5\frac{5}{6} - 1$ [$4\frac{5}{6}$]

FAST FACTS

1. $6 \div 1$ [6]
2. $7 \div 7$ [1]
3. $63 \div 9$ [7]
4. $72 \div 8$ [9]

Problem of the Day • 108

A small bookcase has a base and two shelves. The base and each shelf is $\frac{3}{8}$ in. thick. The distance from the base to the first shelf is $6\frac{5}{8}$ in. The distance from the first shelf to the top shelf is the same. What is the total height of the bookshelf? [$14\frac{3}{8}$ in.]

TECH LINK

MATH FORUM

Cultural Diversity As we review the different foods discussed in the lesson, I encourage my students to share descriptions of their own favorite foods from different countries.

Visit our Resource Village at http://www.mhschool.com to see more of the Math Forum.

MATH CENTER

Practice

OBJECTIVE Choose the operation and solve problems.

Materials per student: fraction strips (TA 26), Math Center Recording Sheet (TA 31 optional)

Students choose the operation needed to solve fraction problems. [**1.** subtraction, $\frac{5}{8}$ mi; **2.** addition and multiplication, 5 mi, \$10; **3.** addition; $6\frac{1}{12}$, or $5\frac{1}{12}$ mi]

MATH CENTER
On Your Own

PRACTICE ACTIVITY 108

Number Sense • Walk Away

Solve each problem, and write the operation you used.
Use fraction strips to help.

YOU NEED
- fraction strips

1. You begin a $\frac{7}{8}$-mile walk around a track after school to get ready for a Walkathon. You stop after $\frac{1}{4}$ mile to get some water. How much farther do you have to go?
2. Each student signs up to walk $2\frac{1}{2}$ miles. If each mile walked earns \$2.00, how much will you and a friend earn together?
3. You walk on three different days. On the first day, you walk $1\frac{1}{4}$ miles. On the second day, you walk $1\frac{1}{3}$ miles, and on the third day, you walk $2\frac{1}{2}$ miles. How far did you walk altogether?

Grade Level 4 · McGraw-Hill School Division

Chapter 11, Lesson 9, pages 438–441 — Problem Solving

NCTM Standards
- ✓ Problem Solving
- ✓ Communication
- ✓ Reasoning
- Connections

Problem Solving

OBJECTIVE Use data to solve problems.

Materials per student: Math Center Recording Sheet (TA 31 optional)

Students add and subtract fractions in a recipe setting. [**1.** $2\frac{1}{4}$ cups brown sugar; **2.** $\frac{3}{8}$ cup flour; **3.** 3 bars for each with 3 left over; **4.** margarine $3\frac{1}{4}$ cups, sugar $3\frac{1}{2}$ cups, granola $4\frac{1}{4}$ cups, flour 7 cups, baking powder $4\frac{1}{2}$ teaspoons]

MATH CENTER
On Your Own

PROBLEM-SOLVING ACTIVITY 108

Using Data • Baking Granola Bars

You are baking two dozen granola bars with the recipe shown.

1. You have 4 cups of brown sugar. How much brown sugar will be left over?
2. You have $3\frac{1}{8}$ cups flour. How much more flour do you need?
3. What if you give an equal number of granola bars to 6 teachers and the principal. How many granola bars will be in each package?
4. You want to make four dozen granola bars. How much of each ingredient will you need? Rewrite the recipe to show the amounts.

Granola Bars
(makes 2 dozen)

Ingredients	Amount
low-fat margarine	$1\frac{5}{8}$ cups
brown sugar	$1\frac{3}{4}$ cups
granola	$2\frac{1}{8}$ cups
flour	$3\frac{1}{2}$ cups
baking powder	$2\frac{1}{4}$ teaspoons

Grade Level 4 · McGraw-Hill School Division

Chapter 11, Lesson 9, pages 438–441 — Problem Solving

NCTM Standards
- ✓ Problem Solving
- Communication
- ✓ Reasoning
- ✓ Connections

Problem Solvers at Work

OBJECTIVE Solve/write problems by choosing the operation.

Resources graphing software, or Math Van Tools

1 Introduce

Present this problem:

Cecil has $5\frac{3}{4}$ cups of flour. She uses $2\frac{1}{4}$ cups to make pizza dough and $1\frac{1}{4}$ cups to make zucchini bread. How much flour does she have left?

Have students focus on the operations needed to solve the problem. *[addition and subtraction]*

Then discuss alternative ways to solve the problem. *[Find $5\frac{3}{4} - 2\frac{1}{4}$ and subtract $1\frac{1}{4}$ from the difference. Or add $2\frac{1}{4} + 1\frac{1}{4}$ and subtract the sum from the total.]*

Have students select a method and solve. [$2\frac{1}{4}$ c]

2 Teach *Cooperative Groups*

PART 1 CHOOSE THE OPERATION

LEARN Discuss the different foods in the table and where they are from. Encourage students to describe some of the foods with which they are familiar in the table. If necessary, provide descriptions or pictures of some of the foods.

Remind students to read the problems carefully to select the correct operation(s) needed to solve. Encourage them to use the table as needed. Not all of the problems involve addition and subtraction of fractions and mixed numbers.

Write a Report Encourage students to research the food they chose before they begin to write. Suggest that they include an illustration and a caption. Set aside time for students to share their reports with the class. You might compile the finished reports into a class book.

Problem Solvers at Work

Part 1 Choose the Operation

LEARN

This table shows some of the foods that were brought to a party to celebrate United Nations Day. Most of the food was eaten, but there were some leftovers.

Kind of Food/Country	Amount at Beginning of Party	Amount at End of Party
Taco salad/Mexico	2 bowls	$\frac{2}{3}$ bowl
Banana bread/Caribbean countries	3 loaves	$\frac{1}{2}$ loaf
Baked bananas/African countries	2 trays	$\frac{5}{8}$ tray
Paella/Spain	3 trays	$\frac{1}{8}$ tray
Vegetable rice/Japan	2 bowls	$\frac{1}{3}$ bowl

Work Together

Solve. Tell which operation you used.

1. How many bowls of taco salad and vegetable rice were eaten altogether? **3 bowls: $1\frac{1}{3}$ bowls of taco salad and $1\frac{2}{3}$ bowls of vegetable rice were eaten; addition.**
2. Next time, the party organizers will bring in twice as many loaves of banana bread. How many loaves will they bring in? **6 loaves; multiplication**
3. How much more baked bananas than paella was left at the end of the party? **$\frac{4}{8}$, or $\frac{1}{2}$, more of a tray; subtraction**
4. **What if** the banana bread was cut up into a total of 72 slices and there were 24 people. What is the greatest number of slices each person could eat if they all got the same amount? **3 slices; division**
5.  **Write a Report** Write a report about a food on the table. Tell what the food is like. Tell how much was served at the party and how much was eaten. **Check students' reports.**

Meeting Individual Needs

Extra Support

Suggest that students having difficulty identifying the operations needed to solve a problem read it without numbers. By ignoring fractions, they should be able to focus on the correct operation to solve.

Language Support

Encourage students to articulate how problems are solved with words. Students can often identify how to solve problems using key words.

Ongoing Assessment

Anecdotal Report Note if students are able to correctly identify the operation(s) needed to solve problems.

Follow Up Remind students who are having difficulty choosing the operation to ignore the fractional parts of mixed numbers as they decide how to solve. Then they solve with the mixed numbers. Have them try **Reteach 108.**

For students who successfully complete the lesson, assign **Extend 108.**

·t 2 Write and Share Problems

·rgan used the information ·he table to write a problem.

·od	Preparation Time	Cooking Time
·at loaf	$\frac{1}{2}$ hour	1 hour
·ili	$\frac{1}{2}$ hour	$2\frac{1}{2}$ hours
·za	$\frac{1}{4}$ hour	$\frac{1}{2}$ hour
·nato soup	$\frac{1}{4}$ hour	$1\frac{1}{4}$ hours

CHECK

How much longer does it take chili to cook than pizza?

Morgan McLuen
Piney Grove Elementary School
Charlotte, NC

Solve Morgan's problem. **2 h**

Change Morgan's problem so that you must use a different operation to solve it. **For problems 7–10, see Teacher's Edition.**

Solve your new problem. Explain why you must use a different operation to solve your problem than to solve Morgan's problem.

Write a problem of your own about foods from the table. Use foods other than those Morgan used. Solve your problem. Explain why you chose the operation you did to solve it.

Trade problems with another classmate. Solve each other's problems. Compare your solutions. Talk about why you chose the operations.

Turn the page for Practice Strategies.

PART 2 WRITE AND SHARE PROBLEMS

Check Before students solve item 6, discuss why it might be useful or necessary to compare cooking times for different foods.

In item 7, students must rewrite problem to use a different operation to solve. Most students will select the opposite operation, addition. Some students may extend the problem to a multistep problem.

For items 8 and 10, encourage students to discuss the problems they solved and their reasons for choosing the operation.

Encourage students to write multistep problems that involve more than one operation for item 9.

3 Close

Have students discuss how they recognize what operation(s) to use when solving problems.

Practice See pages 440–441.

▶ Part 3 Practice Strategies

Materials have available: calculators; computer graphing program (optional)

Students have the option of choosing any five problems from ex. 1–8, and any two problems from ex. 9–12. They may choose to do more problems if they wish. Have students describe how they made their choices.

- In ex. 2 and 7, students may use the problem-solving strategy, Choose the Operation, to find the answer.
- Encourage students to work with a partner to conduct the experiment in ex. 4.
- Students may use estimation to solve ex. 6.
- Students may want to Guess, Test, and Revise to solve ex. 9.
- Allow students to estimate some of the dimensions in ex. 10 by walking in "feet" around the classroom or parts of the classroom.

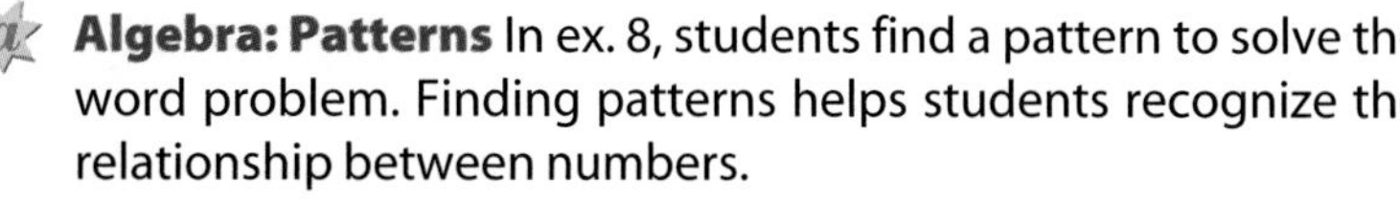

Algebra: Patterns In ex. 8, students find a pattern to solve the word problem. Finding patterns helps students recognize the relationship between numbers.

At the Computer Encourage students to sketch a circle graph of their estimates and then compare it to the computer generated graph.

If computers or software are unavailable, have students make graphs using their estimates to show the data.

Math Van Have students use the Graph tool to make a circle graph.

4. Answers may vary. Possible method: Conduct an experiment.

2. Mía's, $\frac{1}{2}$ lb heavier; possible method: find $2\frac{3}{8} + 1\frac{3}{8} = 3\frac{6}{8} = 3\frac{3}{4}$ and $2\frac{1}{4} + 1 =$ then find $3\frac{3}{4} - 3\frac{1}{4} = \frac{2}{4} = \frac{1}{2}$.

Part 3 Practice Strategies

PRACTICE

Menu

Choose five problems and solve them. Explain your methods. Explanations may vary.

1 Make a decision You have 3 h to do any activities you want. Create a schedule to show which activities you will do and how long they will take. Students' activities should equal 3 h.

ACTIVITY	TIME
Homework	
Baseball	

2 Mía is carrying $2\frac{3}{8}$ lb of apples and $1\frac{3}{8}$ lb of pears. Al is carrying $2\frac{1}{4}$ lb of nuts and 1 lb of grapes. Whose bag is heavier? How much heavier? See above.

3 Spatial reasoning How many different ways can you get three postage stamps from the post office so that they are all attached? 6 ways; possible method: make a drawing.

4 Brendan said the alphabet as quickly as he could. How many seconds did it take him to say it? See above.

A B C D E F G H I
J K L M N O P Q R
S T U V W X Y Z

5 Nathan woke up, took a shower for 15 min, got dressed in 15 min, ate breakfast in $\frac{1}{2}$ h, and then took $\frac{1}{2}$ h to walk to school. He got to school at 8:30 A.M. What time did he wake up? 7:00 A.M.; work backward.

6 A large pizza costs $8.95 for 8 slices. About how much will 4 large pies cost? If 16 students share them equally, how many slices will each student get? about $36 = 4 × $9;

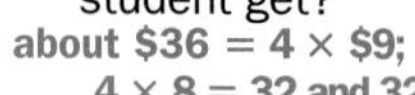

4 × 8 = 32 and 32 ÷ 16 = 2 slices

7 Logical reasoning Lena bought $2\frac{3}{4}$ lb of cold cuts. She bought $\frac{1}{4}$ lb bologna, $\frac{1}{2}$ lb ham, $\frac{1}{2}$ lb roast beef, and some turkey. How much turkey did she buy? $1\frac{1}{2}$ lb of turkey; possible method: first add $\frac{1}{4} + \frac{1}{2} + \frac{1}{2} = 1\frac{1}{4}$, then subtract $2\frac{3}{4} - 1\frac{1}{4} = 1\frac{1}{2}$.

8 ALGEBRA: PATTERNS In 1994, a school population was 300 students. The population was 30[?] in 1995, 315 in 1996, 330 in 1997, and 350 in 1998. If the same pattern continues, how many students will there be in this school in the year 2000? 405 students; possible method: find a pattern.

Meeting Individual Needs

Early Finishers

Have students find how much food was eaten from the table on Student Book page 438. Have them find the total cooking time using the table on page 439. *[$1\frac{1}{3}$ bowls; $2\frac{1}{2}$ loaves; $1\frac{3}{8}$ trays; $2\frac{7}{8}$ trays; $1\frac{2}{3}$ bowls; $4\frac{1}{2}$ h]*

ESL APPROPRIATE

Common Error

Have students who do not completely solve a multistep problem break the problem into separate parts. Then they can focus on the operation needed to solve each part.

Inclusion

Some students may not be able to focus on all of the numbers in the introductory problem. Provide these students with emblematic diagrams that correspond to some of the amounts.

Gifted And Talented

Have students who are ready for a challenge make a table that shows how much time they spend on different activities on an average weekday. Then have them make a circle graph to show the data.

Answers may vary. Possible answer: Fill the $1\frac{1}{2}$-qt container twice and empty it into the large container, then fill the $2\frac{1}{2}$-qt container twice and empty it into the large container—$1\frac{1}{2} + 1\frac{1}{2} + 2\frac{1}{2} + 2\frac{1}{2} = 8$ qt = 2 gal.

oose two problems and solve them.
plain your methods. Explanations may vary.

You have to fill a large container with exactly 2 gallons of water. The picture shows the containers you can use to measure. How will you use the containers to pour exactly 2 gallons of water?
(Hint: 4 quarts = 1 gallon)
See above.

What if you have to buy paint to paint your classroom walls and ceiling. The paint you plan to buy covers 200 sq ft per gallon. How many gallons should you buy?
Answers may vary depending on size of room.

Data Point Survey your class or another class to find out their opinion about a specific television program. Have them rate the show by telling you whether they like the show, neither like nor dislike the show, or dislike the show. Draw a graph or make a chart displaying the results of your survey. Then write a statement about what your graph or table shows.

Check students' work. To complete this problem, students will need to collect and interpret data.

At the Computer You can use a graphing program to make circle graphs to represent data.

Study your school lunch menu for 20 school days. Estimate how often each meal is served. Then estimate the fraction of the total number of meals for each type of meal.

Use a graphing program to draw a circle graph showing the fraction of the total number of meals each type of meal represents.

Compare your estimate with the graph. How close was your estimate? Check students' work.

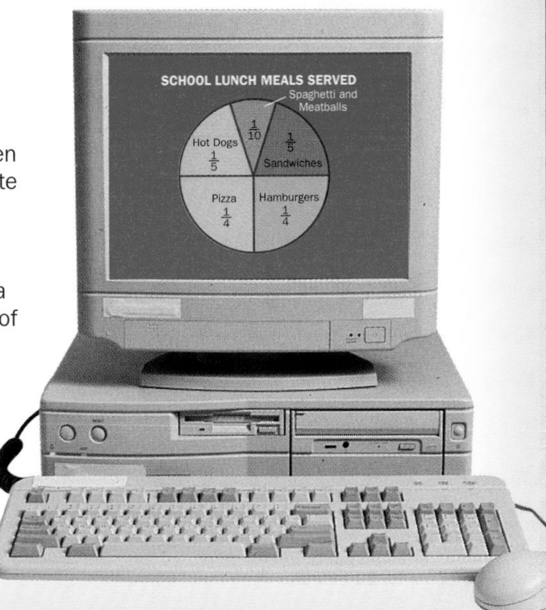

tra Practice, page 527

Alternate Teaching Strategy

Copy the following ingredients used in a vegetable soup recipe onto the chalkboard:

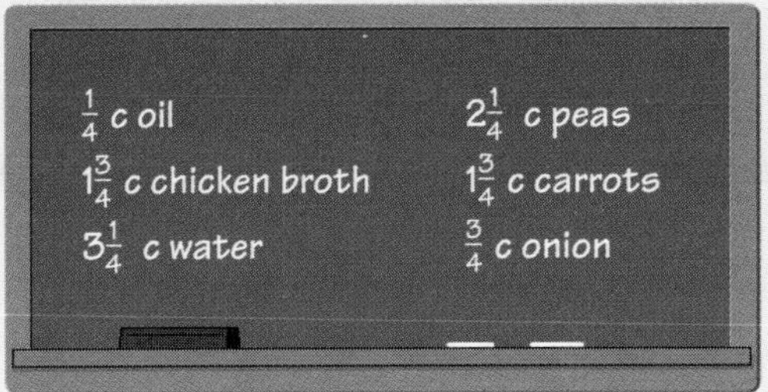

Ask:

- **What operation would you use to find the total amount of liquid ingredients in the recipe?** *[addition]*
- **What is the total? Explain.** *[$5\frac{1}{4}$ c: $\frac{1}{4} + 1\frac{3}{4} + 3\frac{1}{4} = 4\frac{5}{4} = 5\frac{1}{4}$]*
- **What operations would you use to find how many more cups of carrots and onion combined there are than peas?** *[addition and subtraction]*
- **How many more cups are there? Explain.** *[$\frac{1}{4}$ c; $1\frac{3}{4} + \frac{3}{4} = 1\frac{6}{4} = 2\frac{2}{4}$; $2\frac{2}{4} - 2\frac{1}{4} = \frac{1}{4}$]*
- **What if you double the recipe. How many cups of each ingredient would you need?** *[$\frac{1}{2}$ c oil, $3\frac{1}{2}$ c broth, $6\frac{1}{2}$ c water, $4\frac{1}{2}$ c peas, $3\frac{1}{2}$ c carrots, $1\frac{1}{2}$ c onion]*

Have students suggest other ingredients and quantities for the soup. Then ask similar questions, focusing on the operations used to solve.

PRACTICE • 108

Practice 108

Name:

Problem Solving: Choose the Operation

Read / Plan / Solve / Look Back

Solve. Tell which operation(s) you used.

1. Your class is writing notes using invisible ink. You write 4 notes each day. How many notes do you write by the fifth day? 20 notes; multiplication
2. It takes about $\frac{1}{4}$ c of invisible ink to write 3 notes. How much invisible ink would you use to write 12 notes? 1 c; division, addition
3. Your class is using baking powder and water to make the invisible ink. There is $\frac{1}{4}$ of one can of baking powder and $\frac{5}{6}$ of another can. How much more than one can is that? $\frac{1}{12}$; addition, subtraction
4. Thirteen students have each written 48 notes, 10 students have written 15, and 8 have written 12. If the class goal is 1,000 notes, how many more have to be written? 130 notes; multiplication, addition, subtraction

Solve using any method.

5. The fourth grade spends 25 minutes each day writing in a journal, 5 minutes for schedule writing, and 2 minutes for joke, riddle, or skit writing. How many minutes of writing is that in 38 school days? 1,216 min
6. You draw a poster for a writing contest. One fourth of the poster is for contest rules, $\frac{1}{12}$ is for previous winners, and $\frac{1}{6}$ for suggested titles. What fraction of the poster is still blank? Draw it. Drawing shows $\frac{1}{2}$ left over.
7. You fold paper to write one sentence in each section. Complete the table to show how many sections are created with each fold.

Folds	1	2	3	4	5
Sections	2	4	8	16	32

8. The PTA awards your class $100 for your writing program. You buy 16 boxes of colored pencils at $3.25 each and 8 packages of paper at $4.95. About how much of the $100 is left over? Possible answer: About $8

RETEACH • 108

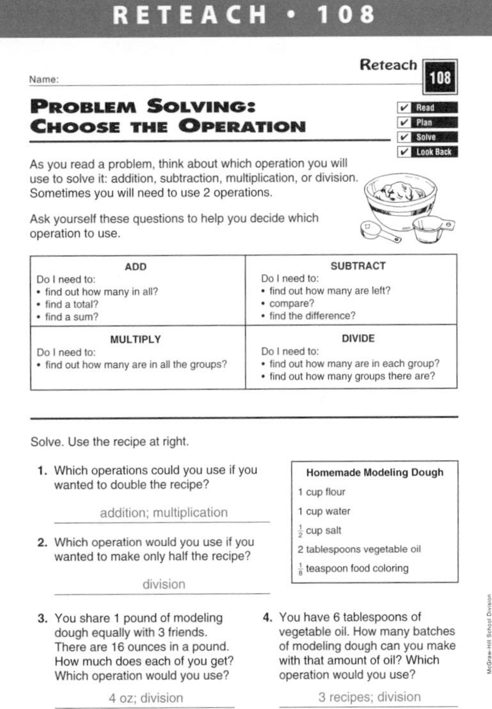

Reteach 108

Name:

Problem Solving: Choose the Operation

Read / Plan / Solve / Look Back

As you read a problem, think about which operation you will use to solve it: addition, subtraction, multiplication, or division. Sometimes you will need to use 2 operations.

Ask yourself these questions to help you decide which operation to use.

ADD	SUBTRACT
Do I need to: • find out how many in all? • find a total? • find a sum?	Do I need to: • find out how many are left? • compare? • find the difference?
MULTIPLY	**DIVIDE**
Do I need to: • find out how many are in all the groups?	Do I need to: • find out how many are in each group? • find out how many groups there are?

Solve. Use the recipe at right.

Homemade Modeling Dough
1 cup flour
1 cup water
$\frac{1}{2}$ cup salt
2 tablespoons vegetable oil
$\frac{1}{8}$ teaspoon food coloring

1. Which operations could you use if you wanted to double the recipe? addition; multiplication
2. Which operation would you use if you wanted to make only half the recipe? division
3. You share 1 pound of modeling dough equally with 3 friends. There are 16 ounces in a pound. How much does each of you get? Which operation would you use? 4 oz; division
4. You have 6 tablespoons of vegetable oil. How many batches of modeling dough can you make with that amount of oil? Which operation would you use? 3 recipes; division

EXTEND • 108

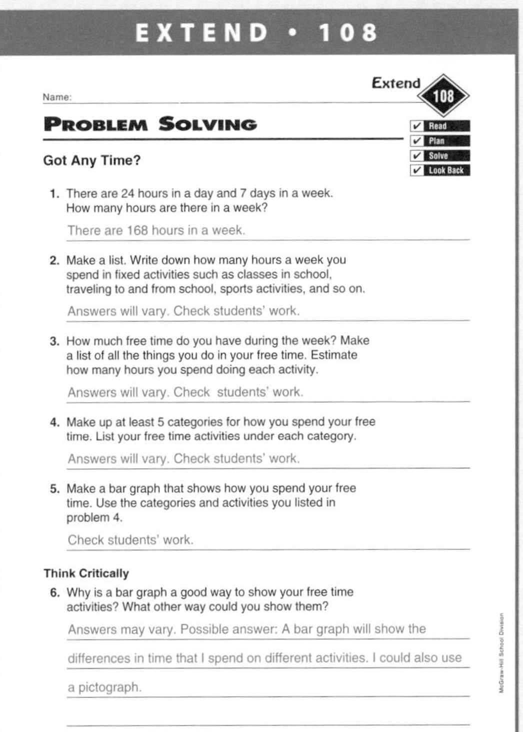

Extend 108

Name:

Problem Solving

Read / Plan / Solve / Look Back

Got Any Time?

1. There are 24 hours in a day and 7 days in a week. How many hours are there in a week? There are 168 hours in a week.
2. Make a list. Write down how many hours a week you spend in fixed activities such as classes in school, traveling to and from school, sports activities, and so on. Answers will vary. Check students' work.
3. How much free time do you have during the week? Make a list of all the things you do in your free time. Estimate how many hours you spend doing each activity. Answers will vary. Check students' work.
4. Make up at least 5 categories for how you spend your free time. List your free time activities under each category. Answers will vary. Check students' work.
5. Make a bar graph that shows how you spend your free time. Use the categories and activities you listed in problem 4. Check students' work.

Think Critically

6. Why is a bar graph a good way to show your free time activities? What other way could you show them? Answers may vary. Possible answer: A bar graph will show the differences in time that I spend on different activities. I could also use a pictograph.

PURPOSE Review and assess concepts, skills, and strategies that students have learned in this chapter.

Materials per student: calculator (optional)

Chapter Objectives

11A Add fractions with like and unlike denominators
11B Subtract fractions with like and unlike denominators
11C Add and subtract mixed numbers using models
11D Solve problems, including those that involve fractions and drawing pictures

Using the Chapter Review

The **Chapter Review** can be used as a review, practice test, or chapter test.

Think Critically Students' explanations for ex. 21 will indicate whether they understand the steps involved in adding fractions with a common denominator and simplifying the sum.

Language and Mathematics

Complete the sentence. Use a word in the chart. (pages 410–437)

Vocabulary
unlike
mixed number
improper
common
equivalent

1 To find $\frac{3}{4} - \frac{1}{8}$, you change $\frac{3}{4}$ and $\frac{1}{8}$ into fractions with ■ denominators. common

2 $\frac{2}{5}$ and $\frac{4}{10}$ are ■ fractions. equivalent

3 $1\frac{7}{9}$ is a ■. mixed number

4 $\frac{3}{5}$ and $\frac{3}{7}$ have ■ denominators. unlike

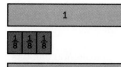

Concepts and Skills

Complete the number sentence. (page 410)

5 $2\frac{2}{5} + 2\frac{1}{5} = 4\frac{■}{5}$ 3

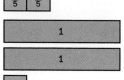

6 $1\frac{3}{8} + 1\frac{4}{8} = 2\frac{■}{8}$ 7

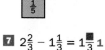

7 $2\frac{2}{3} - 1\frac{1}{3} = 1\frac{■}{3}$ 1

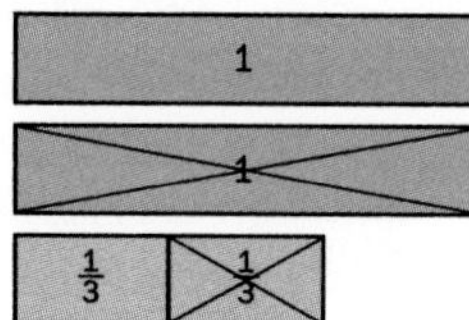

8 $2\frac{4}{5} - 1\frac{2}{5} = 1\frac{■}{5}$ 2

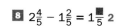

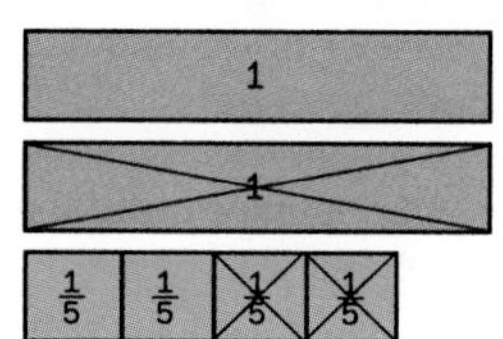

Reinforcement and Remediation

CHAPTER OBJECTIVES	CHAPTER REVIEW ITEMS	STUDENT BOOK PAGES: Lessons	STUDENT BOOK PAGES: Mid-chapter Review	TEACHER'S EDITION PAGES: Activities	TEACHER'S EDITION PAGES: Alternate Teaching Strategy	TEACHER RESOURCES: Reteach
11A	2, 4, 9–17, 21	410–413, 414–415, 426–427, 428–431	422	409A, 413A, 425A, 427A	413, 415, 427, 431	100–101, 104–105
11B	1, 18–20	416–419, 420–421, 428–431	422	415A, 419A, 427A	419, 421, 431	102–103, 105
11C	3, 5–8	434–437		433A	437	107
11D	22–25	432–433, 438–441		431C, 437A	433, 441	106, 108

23. The fractions add up to more than 1 whole, and only 1 whole class was surveyed.

rite as equivalent fractions with common denominators. (page 426)

$\frac{1}{3}$ and $\frac{1}{4}$ **$\frac{4}{12}$ and $\frac{3}{12}$**	**10** $\frac{2}{5}$ and $\frac{3}{10}$ **$\frac{4}{10}$ and $\frac{3}{10}$**	**11** $\frac{1}{6}$ and $\frac{3}{4}$ **$\frac{2}{12}$ and $\frac{9}{12}$**	**12** $\frac{2}{3}$ and $\frac{7}{12}$ **$\frac{8}{12}$ and $\frac{7}{12}$**

nd the sum or difference. Write the answer simplest form. (pages 410, 416)

$\frac{3}{8}+\frac{4}{8}$ **$\frac{7}{8}$**	**14** $\frac{1}{6}+\frac{3}{6}$ **$\frac{2}{3}$**	**15** $\frac{1}{12}+\frac{3}{12}+\frac{2}{12}$ **$\frac{1}{2}$**	**16** $\frac{2}{3}+\frac{2}{3}$ **$1\frac{1}{3}$**
$\frac{5}{6}-\frac{4}{6}$ **$\frac{1}{6}$**	**18** $\frac{10}{16}-\frac{5}{16}$ **$\frac{5}{16}$**	**19** $\frac{9}{10}-\frac{4}{10}$ **$\frac{1}{2}$**	**20** $\frac{11}{12}-\frac{3}{12}$ **$\frac{2}{3}$**

ink critically. (page 410)

Analyze. Explain what the mistake is, then correct it. **The sum was simplified incorrectly—$\frac{4}{3}=1\frac{1}{3}$.**

$\frac{2}{3}+\frac{2}{3}=\frac{4}{3}$

Simplify: $\frac{4}{3}=3\frac{1}{3}$

IIXED APPLICATIONS

Problem Solving

(pages 432, 438)

Rewrite the table so that the months are listed in order from least to greatest number of inches of precipitation. **February, January, April, March, May**

Average Monthly Precipitation for Albany, New York

Selected Months	Inches
January	$2\frac{2}{5}$
February	$2\frac{3}{10}$
March	3
April	$2\frac{9}{10}$
May	$3\frac{3}{10}$

Logical reasoning Eli surveyed his class to find out their favorite foods. He reported these results to his teacher: $\frac{1}{4}$ like pizza best, $\frac{2}{4}$ like hot dogs best, and $\frac{3}{4}$ like cheeseburgers best. His teacher told him that his results could not be correct. How could his teacher know this? **See above.**

Lonato must put a drape around the edge of a table for the science fair. The table is $3\frac{1}{4}$ ft long and $2\frac{3}{4}$ ft wide. How long a drape will Lonato need? **12 ft**

25 **What if** you start at the hiking station and hike 3 mi north, 5 mi east, 6 mi south, and 5 mi west. How far and in what direction would you have to hike to return to the station? **3 mi north**

CHAPTER TEST

PURPOSE Assess the concepts, skills, and strategies students have learned in this chapter.

Chapter Objectives

11A Add fractions with like and unlike denominators
11B Subtract fractions with like and unlike denominators
11C Add and subtract mixed numbers using models
11D Solve problems, including those that involve fractions and drawing pictures

Using the Chapter Test

The **Chapter Test** can be used as a practice test, a chapter test, or as an additional review. The **Performance Assessment** on Student Book page 445 provides an alternate means of assessing students' understanding of fractions and probability.

The table below correlates the test items to the chapter objectives and to the Student Book pages on which the skills are taught.

Assessment Resources

Test Masters

The Testing Program Blackline Masters provide three forms of the Chapter Test to assess students' understanding of the chapter concepts, skills, and strategies. Form C uses a free-response format. Forms A and B use a multiple-choice format.

Computer Test Generator

The Computer Test Generator supplies abundant multiple-choice and free-response test items, which you may use to generate tests and practice worksheets tailored to the needs of your class.

Teacher's Assessment Resources

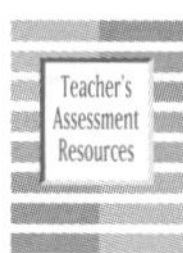

Teacher's Assessment Resources provides resources for alternate assessment. It includes guidelines for Building a Portfolio, page 6, and the Holistic Scoring Guide, page 27.

Find the sum or difference. Write the answer in simplest form.

1. $\frac{1}{8}+\frac{3}{8}$ $\frac{1}{2}$
2. $\frac{1}{6}+\frac{4}{6}$ $\frac{5}{6}$
3. $\frac{2}{10}+\frac{1}{10}+\frac{2}{10}$ $\frac{1}{2}$
4. $\frac{3}{4}+\frac{3}{4}$ $1\frac{1}{2}$
5. $\frac{10}{12}-\frac{8}{12}$ $\frac{1}{6}$
6. $\frac{5}{6}-\frac{2}{6}$ $\frac{1}{2}$
7. $\frac{7}{8}-\frac{1}{8}$ $\frac{3}{4}$
8. $\frac{11}{16}-\frac{1}{16}$ $\frac{5}{8}$
9. $\frac{3}{4}+\frac{5}{8}$ $1\frac{3}{8}$
10. $\frac{7}{12}+\frac{1}{3}$ $\frac{11}{12}$
11. $\frac{4}{5}-\frac{1}{10}$ $\frac{7}{10}$
12. $\frac{1}{2}-\frac{1}{6}$ $\frac{1}{3}$

Complete the number sentence.

13. $1\frac{5}{8}+1\frac{2}{8}=2\frac{■}{8}$ 7

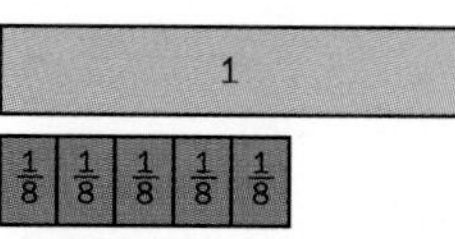

14. $1\frac{3}{12}+1\frac{4}{12}=2\frac{■}{12}$ 7

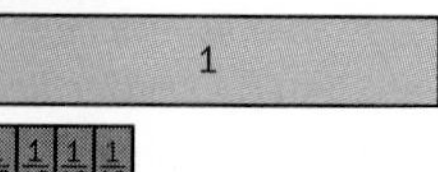

15. $2\frac{3}{4}-1\frac{2}{4}=1\frac{■}{4}$ 1

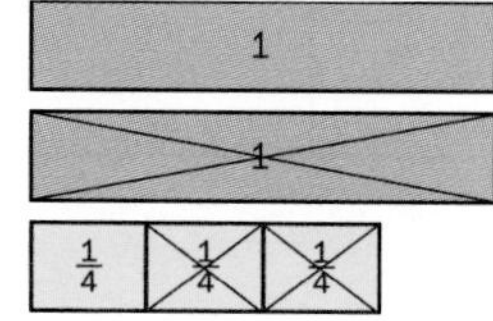

16. $2\frac{3}{5}-1\frac{1}{5}=1\frac{■}{5}$ 2

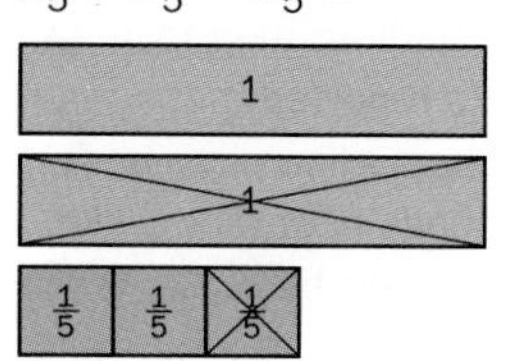

Solve.

17. The store has 6 more bags of unsalted corn chips than bags of salted corn chips. If there are 30 bags altogether, how many contain unsalted corn chips? 18 bags
18. Mrs. Gomez bought 5 lb of potatoes. She cooked $1\frac{1}{2}$ lb on Monday for dinner and $\frac{1}{2}$ lb on Tuesday for lunch. How many pounds of potatoes are left? 3 lb
19. The Wongs ordered 2 pizzas. Each of the 4 family members ate $\frac{3}{8}$ of a pizza. How much pizza was left over? $\frac{1}{2}$ pizza
20. Bo draws a rectangle that is 10 long and 8 in. wide. She draws lines to divide it into 4 rectangle What are the length and width o each of the smaller rectangles? 5 in. by 4 in.

444 Chapter 11 Test

Test Correlation		
CHAPTER OBJECTIVES	TEST ITEMS	TEXT PAGES
11A	1–4, 9–10	410–415, 426–431
11B	5–8, 11–12	416–421, 428–431
11C	13–16	434–437
11D	17–20	432–433, 438–441

Teacher's Assessment Resources for samples of student work. Check students' work.

'hat Did You Learn?

ɘ the chart to plan the meals for a day.

Find the total amount for each type of food. Use models or drawings to show your work.

Write two statements that compare the amounts of vegetables and fruits in your meals to the amount of cereal, rice, and pasta. Use fractions in your answer.

The meals should contain:
- 2-3 servings of milk or yogurt
- 2-3 servings of meat or beans
- 3-5 servings of vegetables
- 2-4 servings of fruit
- 6-11 servings of bread, cereal, rice, or pasta

Serving Size of Various Foods			
Milk or yogurt	1 cup	Bread	1 slice
Cooked beans	$1\frac{1}{2}$ cups	Chopped vegetables	$\frac{1}{2}$ cup
Meat, poultry, fish	2 ounces	Fruits	$\frac{1}{3}$ cup
Cereal, rice, pasta	$\frac{1}{2}$ cup	Fruit or vegetable juice	$\frac{3}{4}$ cup

;. Department of Agriculture

A Good Answer
- provides meals with the servings requested
- uses models or drawings to show the totals
- correctly compares the amounts

You may want to place your work in your portfolio.

What Do You Think?

See Teacher's Edition.

1. Can you add and subtract fractions as well as you add and subtract whole numbers? Explain.
2. What methods have you used to add and subtract fractions?
   - Models
   - Drawings
   - Mental math
   - Other. Explain.
3. Do you know when an answer can be simplified? Give examples.

Reviewing A Portfolio

Have students review their portfolios. Consider including these items:
- Finished work on the Chapter Project (p. 407F) or **Investigation** (pp. 424–425).
- Selected math journal entries, pp. 409, 417, 422.
- Finished work on the nonroutine problem in **What Do You Know?** (p. 409) and problems from the Menu (pp. 440–441).
- Each student's self-selected "best piece" from work completed during the chapter. Have each student attach a note explaining why he or she chose that piece.
- Any work you or an individual student wishes to keep for future reference.

You may take this opportunity to conduct conferences with students. The Portfolio Analysis Form can help you report students' progress. See Teacher's Assessment Resources, p. 33.

PURPOSE Review and assess the concepts, skills, and strategies learned in this chapter.

Materials have available: fraction strips, calculators

Using the Performance Assessment

Have students read and restate the problems in their own words. Make sure they understand they are to plan a breakfast, a lunch, and a dinner. Talk about what the requirements for servings of various kinds of food mean. For example, 3 slices of bread count as 3 servings of bread.

Point out the section on the student page headed "A Good Answer." Make sure students understand that you will use these points to evaluate their answers.

Evaluating Student Work

As you read students' papers, look for the following:
- *Does the student recognize that ordering the data will help him or her compare the data?*
- *Does the student realize that some of the data involves whole numbers and some of it involves fractions?*
- *Do the student's statements include numbers?*
- *Is each of the student's statements supported with a clear explanation, diagram or model?*

The Holistic Scoring Guide and annotated samples of students' work can be used to assess this task. See pages 27–32 and 37–72 in Teacher's Assessment Resources.

Using the Self-Assessment

What Do You Think? Assure students that there are no right or wrong answers. Tell them the emphasis is on what they think and how they justify their answers.

Follow-Up Interviews

These questions can be used to gain insight into students' thinking:
- **How did you organize the data to help you make comparisons?**
- **What methods or models did you use to help you organize the data?**
- **What is the basis for your conclusion? (Ask as you point to one of the students' conclusions.)**
- **What does this diagram show? (Ask as you point to one of the students' diagrams.)**

OBJECTIVE Apply fractions in a health context.

Materials small magnet, plastic bag, several food labels

Resources spreadsheet software, or Math Van Tools

Science

Cultural Connection Read the **Cultural Note** on page 446. Ask:

- **What conclusions can you make about how people got their vitamins in the 18th century?** *[Possible response: People had to get vitamins from the foods they ate.]*

Read and discuss the information presented in the table on page 446. Ask:

- **Which vitamins do you think are the most important or necessary? Why?** *[Answers may vary. Possible response: They all look important.]*
- **Based on the information in this table, which foods do you think you should add to your diet?** *[Answers may vary.]*

Math

Read the chart on page 447. You may wish to complete items 1–3 together as a class.

To answer item 3, remind students to use equivalent fractions to help them compare and order.

math science technology
CONNECTION

Eating Right

Cultural Note

In 1757, a British doctor, James Lind, discovered that eating fruits and vegetables rich in vitamin C could prevent the disease known as scurvy. The British navy then required sailors to eat lemons and limes each day.

Nutrients are substances in foods that are used by your cells to create energy and to help your cells grow and repair themselves. There are six groups of nutrients—proteins, carbohydrates, fats, vitamins, minerals, and water.

Fats give the body lasting energy and h the body store vitamins ar build tissue

Proteins are used by the body for growth and to build and repair cells. They keep muscles, skin, hair, and nails healthy.

Vitamins are needed by the bo grow and function.

Minerals are us by the body to bui new cells and control importa body process

Carbohydrates are used by the body as the main source of energy.

Water helps to keep the body temperature normal, dissolve some vitamins, a helps bring other nutrients to the cells in the body.

▶ Describe a healthy lunch. How is each group represented? **Answers may va Possible answer: chicken sandwich, baked potato, and fruit juice; carbohydrates— bread and potato, fat—butter, protein—chicken, vitamins and minerals—vegetabl and fruit juice, water—fruit juice**

446 Math • Science • Technology Connection

Extending The Activity

1. Have students work in groups to research vitamins or minerals not listed in the table on page 447, such as vitamin E (tocopherol), vitamin K, iodine, magnesium, potassium, selenium, and sodium. For each vitamin or mineral, groups can note one or two benefits to the human body and at least two sources for the nutrient.
2. Have students work in small groups to research the vitamin and mineral content of a specific breakfast cereal. Groups can then determine how much cereal a fourth grader would have to eat every day to get 100/100ths (100%) of his or her RDA (Recommended Daily Allowance) from cereal. As a class, estimate the cost of this approach when compared to that of taking a daily multi-vitamin or eating a balanced diet.

Balanced Meal

e table below shows the fraction the suggested amounts of iron, lcium, vitamin A, and vitamin C und in various foods.

se the table for problems 1–3.

Which of the foods supplies the greatest amount of iron in each serving? **cereal**

Which of the foods supplies the least amount of calcium? **spaghetti**

Order from greatest to least by the amounts shown the vitamins and minerals in green beans. **vitamin C, vitamin A, iron, calcium**

At the Computer

Check students' work.

4 Use a spreadsheet to keep track of the number of servings of each of the foods in the table you eat each day for a week. Also show the fraction of each type of vitamin and mineral.

5 Use a word processing program to write a short report that describes what the data shows.

Vitamins and Minerals in One Serving (fraction of suggested amount)

	Cereal	Spaghetti	Green Beans	Tomato Soup	Skimmed Milk
Iron	$\frac{2}{5}$	$\frac{1}{10}$	$\frac{1}{25}$	$\frac{1}{25}$	0
Calcium	$\frac{2}{25}$	0	$\frac{1}{50}$	$\frac{1}{50}$	$\frac{3}{10}$
Vitamin A	0	0	$\frac{2}{25}$	$\frac{1}{10}$	$\frac{1}{10}$
Vitamin C	0	0	$\frac{1}{10}$	$\frac{3}{10}$	$\frac{1}{25}$

Bibliography

Nutrition: What's in the Food We Eat, by Dorothy H. Patent. New York: Holiday House, 1992. ISBN: 0–8234–0968–6.

Vitamins and Minerals, by Dr. Alvin Silverstein, Virginia Silverstein, & Robert Silverstein. Brookfield, CT: The Millbrook Press, 1992. ISBN: 1–56294–206–9.

Technology

Before students begin their reports, you may wish to bring in several food labels for them to read. Point out how the look of the labels is the same, because the government requires certain information on every food label. Also point out that the labels show the RDA in percents. You can have students use the percents in their reports, or show them that they can change the percents to fractions simply by writing the number of the percent over 100 and dropping the % sign. (14% = $\frac{14}{100}$)

Math Van Students may use the Table tool to make the spreadsheet. A project electronic teacher aid has been provided.

Interesting Facts

- **For the body to make vitamin D,** ultraviolet light must strike the skin. Most window glass blocks this kind of light.
- **High doses of vitamin A** can be harmful. The liver of a polar bear is so rich in Vitamin A that it is poisonous.
- **Most multi-vitamin bottles are brown or opaque,** because sunlight quickly destroys riboflavin. Heat and moisture can destroy other vitamins, including Vitamin C and thiamine.

CHAPTER 12 AT A GLANCE:

Decimals

Theme: Communication   Suggested Pacing: 11–14 days

CHAPTER 12 ORGANIZER

	DAY 1	DAY 2	DAY 3
WEEK ONE	**PREASSESSMENT** Introduction p. 448 What Do You Know? p. 449 **CHAPTER OBJECTIVES:** 12A, 12B, 12C, 12D, 12E **RESOURCES** Read-Aloud Anthology pp. 56–57; Pretest: Test Master Form A, B, or C; Diagnostic Inventory Portfolio · Journal **NCTM STANDARDS:** 1, 2, 3, 4, 12	**LESSON 12.1** EXPLORE ACTIVITY Decimals Less Than 1 pp. 450–453 **CHAPTER OBJECTIVES:** 12A **MATERIALS** centimeter graph paper (TA 7), crayons or markers, calculators (opt.) **RESOURCES** Reteach/Practice/Extend: 109; Math Center Cards: 109; Extra Practice: 528 **TEACHING WITH TECHNOLOGY** Alternate Lesson TE pp. 453A–453B Daily Review TE p. 449B Technology Link **NCTM STANDARDS:** 4, 12	**LESSON 12.2** Decimals Greater Than 1 pp. 454–455 **CHAPTER OBJECTIVES:** 12A **MATERIALS** calculators (opt.) **RESOURCES** Reteach/Practice/Extend: 110; Math Center Cards: 110; Extra Practice: 528 Daily Review TE p. 453D Journal Technology Link **NCTM STANDARDS:** 12
WEEK TWO	**LESSON 12.4** PROBLEM-SOLVING STRATEGY Solve a Simpler Problem pp. 462–463 **CHAPTER OBJECTIVES:** 12E **MATERIALS** calculators (opt.) **RESOURCES** Reteach/Practice/Extend: 112; Math Center Cards: 112; Extra Practice: 529 Daily Review TE p. 461B Technology Link **NCTM STANDARDS:** 1, 2, 3, 4, 8	**LESSON 12.5** MENTAL MATH Estimate Sums and Differences pp. 464–465 **CHAPTER OBJECTIVES:** 12C **MATERIALS** play money (TA 10–11), calculators (opt.) **RESOURCES** Reteach/Practice/Extend: 113; Math Center Cards: 113; Extra Practice: 529 Daily Review TE p. 463B Technology Link **NCTM STANDARDS:** 5, 12	**LESSON 12.6** EXPLORE ACTIVITY Add and Subtract Decimals pp. 466–467 **CHAPTER OBJECTIVES:** 12D **MATERIALS** decimal squares (TA 30), crayons or markers, scissors, calculators (opt.) **RESOURCES** Reteach/Practice/Extend: 114; Math Center Cards: 114; Extra Practice: 530 Daily Review TE p. 465B Algebraic Thinking Technology Link **NCTM STANDARDS:** 4, 12
WEEK THREE	**LESSON 12.9** PROBLEM SOLVERS AT WORK Write a Number Sentence pp. 472–475 **CHAPTER OBJECTIVES:** 12E **MATERIALS** calculators (opt.), computer spreadsheet program (opt.) **RESOURCES** Reteach/Practice/Extend: 117; Math Center Cards: 117; Extra Practice: 531 Daily Review TE p. 471B Algebraic Thinking Technology Link **NCTM STANDARDS:** 1, 2, 3, 4, 12	**CHAPTER ASSESSMENT** Chapter Review pp. 476–477 **MATERIALS** calculators (opt.) Chapter Test p. 478 **RESOURCES** Posttest: Test Master Form A, B, or C Performance Assessment p. 479 **RESOURCES** Performance Task: Test Master Math • Science • Technology Connection pp. 480–481 Cumulative Review pp. 482–483 **MATERIALS** calculators (opt.) Portfolio **NCTM STANDARDS:** 1, 4, 12	

DAY 4

LESSON 12.3

Compare and Order Decimals
pp. 456–457

CHAPTER OBJECTIVES: 12B
MATERIALS calculators (opt.)
RESOURCES Reteach/Practice/Extend: 111
Math Center Cards: 111
Extra Practice: 528

Daily Review TE p. 455B
Technology Link

NCTM STANDARDS: 12

DAY 5

MIDCHAPTER ASSESSMENT

Midchapter Review **p. 458**
CHAPTER OBJECTIVES: 12A, 12B, 12E
MATERIALS calculators (opt.)

Developing Algebra Sense **p. 459**

REAL-LIFE INVESTIGATION:
Applying Decimals **pp. 460–461**

Algebraic Thinking
Portfolio
Journal

NCTM STANDARDS: 1, 2, 3, 4, 9, 10, 12, 13

LESSON 12.7

Add Decimals **pp. 468–469**

CHAPTER OBJECTIVES: 12D
MATERIALS calculators (opt.)
RESOURCES Reteach/Practice/Extend: 115
Math Center Cards: 115
Extra Practice: 530

Daily Review TE p. 467B
Technology Link

NCTM STANDARDS: 12

LESSON 12.8

Subtract Decimals **pp. 470–471**

CHAPTER OBJECTIVES: 12D
MATERIALS play money (TA 10–11), calculators (opt.)
RESOURCES Reteach/Practice/Extend: 116
Math Center Cards: 116
Extra Practice: 531

Daily Review TE p. 469B
Journal
Technology Link

NCTM STANDARDS: 12

Assessment Options

FORMAL

Chapter Tests

Student Book
- Midchapter Review, p. 458
- Chapter Review, pp. 476–477
- Chapter Test, p. 478
- Cumulative Review, pp. 482–483

Blackline Masters
- Test Master Form A, B, or C
- Diagnostic Invertory

Computer Test Generator
- Available on disk

Performance Assessment
- What Do You Know? p. 449
- Performance Assessment, p. 479
- Holistic Scoring Guide, Teacher's Assessment Resources, pp. 27–32
- Follow-Up Interviews, p. 479
- Performance Task, Test Masters

Teacher's Assessment Resources
- Portfolio Guidelines and Forms, pp. 6–9, 33–35
- Holistic Scoring Guide, pp. 27–32
- Samples of Student Work, pp. 37–72

INFORMAL

Ongoing Assessment
- Observation Checklist, pp. 450, 456, 462, 464, 468, 470
- Interview, p. 454
- Anecdotal Report, pp. 466, 472

Portfolio Opportunities
- Chapter Project, p. 447F
- What Do You Know? p. 449
- Investigation, pp. 460–461
- Journal Writing, pp. 449, 454, 458, 470
- Performance Assessment, p. 479
- Self-Assessment: What Do You Think? p. 479

Chapter Objectives		Standardized Test Correlations
12A	Read and write decimals to hundredths	MAT, CAT, SAT, ITBS, CTBS,TN*
12B	Compare and order decimals	MAT, CAT, SAT, ITBS, CTBS,TN*
12C	Estimate decimal sums and differences	MAT, CAT, SAT, CTBS,TN*
12D	Add and subtract decimals	MAT, CAT, SAT, CTBS,TN*
12E	Solve problems, including those that involve decimals and solving a simpler problem	MAT, CAT, SAT, ITBS, CTBS,TN*

*Terra Nova

NCTM Standards Grades K–4

1 Problem Solving
2 Communication
3 Reasoning
4 Connections
5 Estimation
6 Number Sense and Numeration
7 Concepts of Whole Number Operations
8 Whole Number Computation
9 Geometry and Spatial Sense
10 Measurement
11 Statistics and Probability
12 Fractions and Decimals
13 Patterns and Relationships

Meeting Individual Needs

LEARNING STYLES

- AUDITORY/LINGUISTIC
- LOGICAL/ANALYTICAL
- VISUAL/SPATIAL
- MUSICAL
- KINESTHETIC
- SOCIAL
- INDIVIDUAL

Students who are talented in art, language, and physical activity may better understand mathematical concepts when these concepts are connected to their areas of interest. Use the following activities to stimulate the different learning styles of some of your students.

Visual/Spatial Learners

Prepare graph paper by shading in parts of the whole. Assemble blank index cards, labeling half of the cards with the corresponding fractions and half with the decimals. Show the graph paper to students. Have them identify the number and then choose the correct index cards that correspond to the fraction and the decimal.

Individual Learners

Have students find examples of decimals in magazines, newspapers, or the media. Students can cut out the examples and glue them into a decimal book.

See Lesson Resources, pp. 449A, 453C, 455A, 461A, 463A, 467A, 469A, 471A.

GIFTED AND TALENTED

Some students may be able to manipulate decimals in a more abstract way. Provide students with a number spinner with the numbers zero to nine. With a partner, students take turns spinning and randomly placing the digits in the different place values on a recording sheet, including tenths, hundredths, and thousandths.

When they have finished, students compare their numbers. The student with the highest number is the winner. Students can play this game to practice adding and subtracting decimals.

See also Meeting Individual Needs, pp. 452, 474.

EXTRA SUPPORT

Some students may wish to use decimal squares throughout the chapter.

Specific suggestions for ways to provide extra support to students appear in every lesson in this chapter.

See Meeting Individual Needs, pp. 450, 454, 456, 462, 464, 466, 468, 470, 472.

EARLY FINISHERS

Students who finish their class work early may make a list of ways of communicating sports information, such as e-mail, television, fax, and the Internet. Have students choose one of these forms of communication to illustrate and comment on in a brief paragraph. (See *Chapter Project*, p. 447F.)

See also Meeting Individual Needs, pp. 452, 454, 456, 462, 464, 466, 468, 470, 474.

LANGUAGE SUPPORT

Write the names of the decimal places on cards. As students model the decimal or write the number, they can put the card over the correct place.

10	1	.01	.001	.0001
tens	ones	tenths	hundredths	thousandths

See also Meeting Individual Needs, pp. 450, 474.

ESL APPROPRIATE

INCLUSION

- **For inclusion ideas, information, and suggestions, see pp. 451, 474, T15.**
- **For gender fairness tips, see pp. 472, T15.**

USING MANIPULATIVES

Building Understanding Some students may be confused by place value models showing decimals. They may need to use a different model until they understand the concept. Make decimal models with hundreds paper. Cut out a block of squares that measure ten by ten centimeters, and write the number "1" on the blank side. Relate the "1" to one dollar. Tenths can be related to dimes. One hundredths can be related to one penny, and written as .01.

Easy-to-Make Manipulatives Make a decimal place-value mat to help students say the names and remember the value of the places.

10	1	.	.1	.01	.001
Tens	Ones	decimal point	Tenths	Hundredths	Thousandths

ESL APPROPRIATE

USING COOPERATIVE LEARNING

Jigsaw (with expert groupings) This strategy develops complex teamwork by having students divide the work to complete an assignment.

- **In groups of four, each member is accountable for a different segment of a problem.**
- **Individuals work with other students in the class who have the same segment of the assignment.**
- **Original groups meet to integrate all the parts to solve the problem.**

USING LITERATURE

Use the selection *Stories on Stone: Rock Art—Images from the Ancient Ones* to introduce the chapter theme, Communication. This selection is reprinted on pages 56–57 of the Read-Aloud Anthology.

Also available in the Read-Aloud Anthology is the selection *Signs of the Apes, Songs of the Whales: Adventures in Human-Animal Communication,* page 58.

DECIMALS

Linking Technology

This integrated package of programs and services allows students to explore, develop, and practice concepts; solve problems; build portfolios; and assess their own progress. Teachers can enhance instruction, provide remediation, and share ideas with other educational professionals.

CD-ROM ACTIVITY

In *Crack the Code,* students use place-value models to decipher secret messages. Students can use the online notebook to describe the number pattern in the coded message. To extend the activity, students use the Math Van tools to create their own alphabet code with decimals. **Available on CD-ROM.**

CD-ROM TOOLS

Students can use Math Van's place-value models to explore the concept of decimals. The Tech Links on the Lesson Resources pages highlight opportunities for students to use this and other tools such as drawing, graphs, tables, online notes, and calculator to provide additional practice, reteaching, or extension. **Available on CD-ROM.**

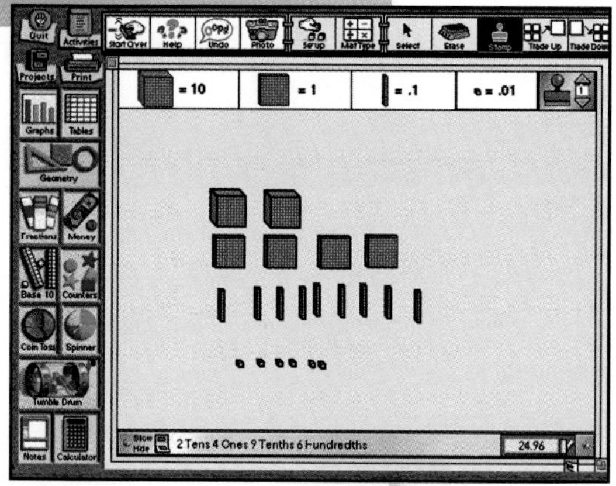

WEB SITE http://www.mhschool.com

Teachers can access the McGraw-Hill School Division World Wide Web site for additional curriculum support at http://www.mhschool.com. Click on our Resource Village for specially designed activities linking Web sites to decimals. Motivate children by inviting them to explore Web sites that develop the chapter theme of "Communication." Exchange ideas on classroom management, cultural diversity, and other areas in the Math Forum.

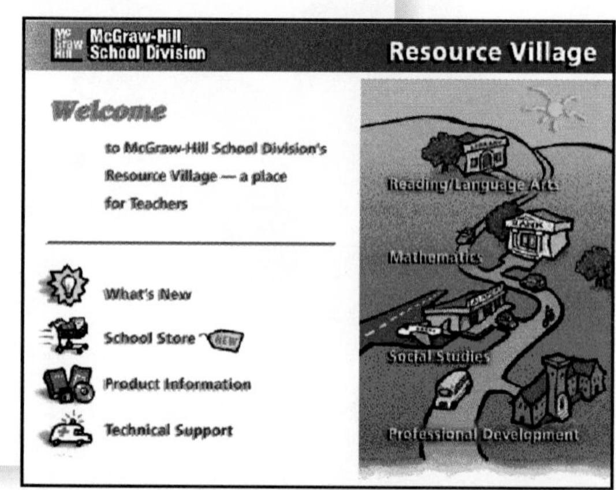

Chapter Project THE BEST OF THE BEST

Highlighting the Math

- collect, organize, and compare data
- compare decimals
- subtract decimals

1 Starting the Project

Introduce the idea of a radio broadcast or newsletter in which present-day Olympic running results are compared with those of the 1930s. Focus on men's and women's relays: 100 Meters, 200 Meters, and 400 Meters. Use an almanac as a source of information. Divide the class into groups and provide each group with an almanac. Consider ways in which family and community members can participate.

2 Continuing the Project

- Each group chooses a 1930s year to compare with the present year.
- Students research the results from both years and record their findings on a chart. Then they compare the record times from the 1930s with the record times of today.
- Each group writes and rehearses the "broadcast" of a radio script announcing the results of their comparisons. Encourage students to create props such as microphones. (Reminder: you may choose to have students create a newsletter instead of the radio broadcast.)

3 Finishing the Project

Each group presents its broadcast to the class. Call-in listeners may pose questions to the announcer. If possible, tape the sportscast and take pictures of the "radio studio."

Community Involvement

Invite a local radio announcer to speak with the class. Extend an invitation to parents to attend the talk.

BUILDING A PORTFOLIO

Each student's portfolio should include a copy of the group's script or a tape of it along with the data they used to create the script. Also include any pictures that may have been taken.

To assess students' work, refer to the Holistic Scoring Guide on page 27 in the Teacher's Assessment Resources.

PURPOSE Introduce the theme of the chapter.

Resources Read-Aloud Anthology, pages 56–57, newspapers

Using Literature

Read "Stories on Stone: Rock Art—Images from the Ancient Ones" from the Read-Aloud Anthology to introduce the theme of the chapter.

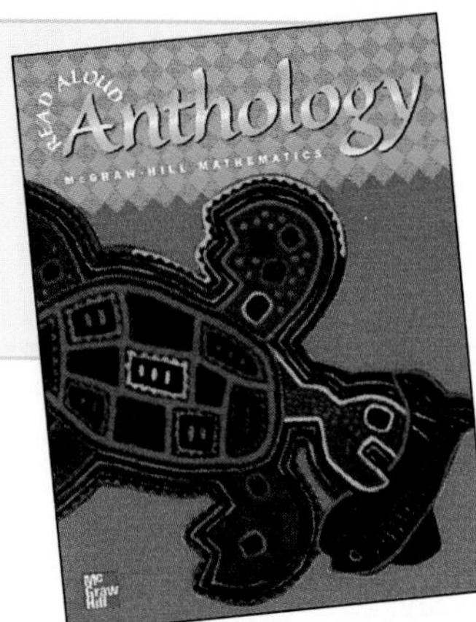

Developing the Theme

Have students describe as many different ways to communicate as they can think of. Encourage them to think creatively and describe modes of communication they use in play, in experiments, in books, in fantasy or science fiction programs or books, and from the past with which they are familiar.

These forms of communication are discussed in this chapter:

computer programs	pp. 450–453	mail	pp. 468–469
dolphin messages	p. 454	telescopes	pp. 470–471
Richter scale	pp. 456–457	weather reports	pp. 472–473
cable TV	p. 459	magazines	p. 474
newsletters	pp. 460–461	news program	p. 474
newspapers	pp. 462–463	radio station	p. 474
radio	pp. 464–465	CD	p. 474
TV sports	p. 465		

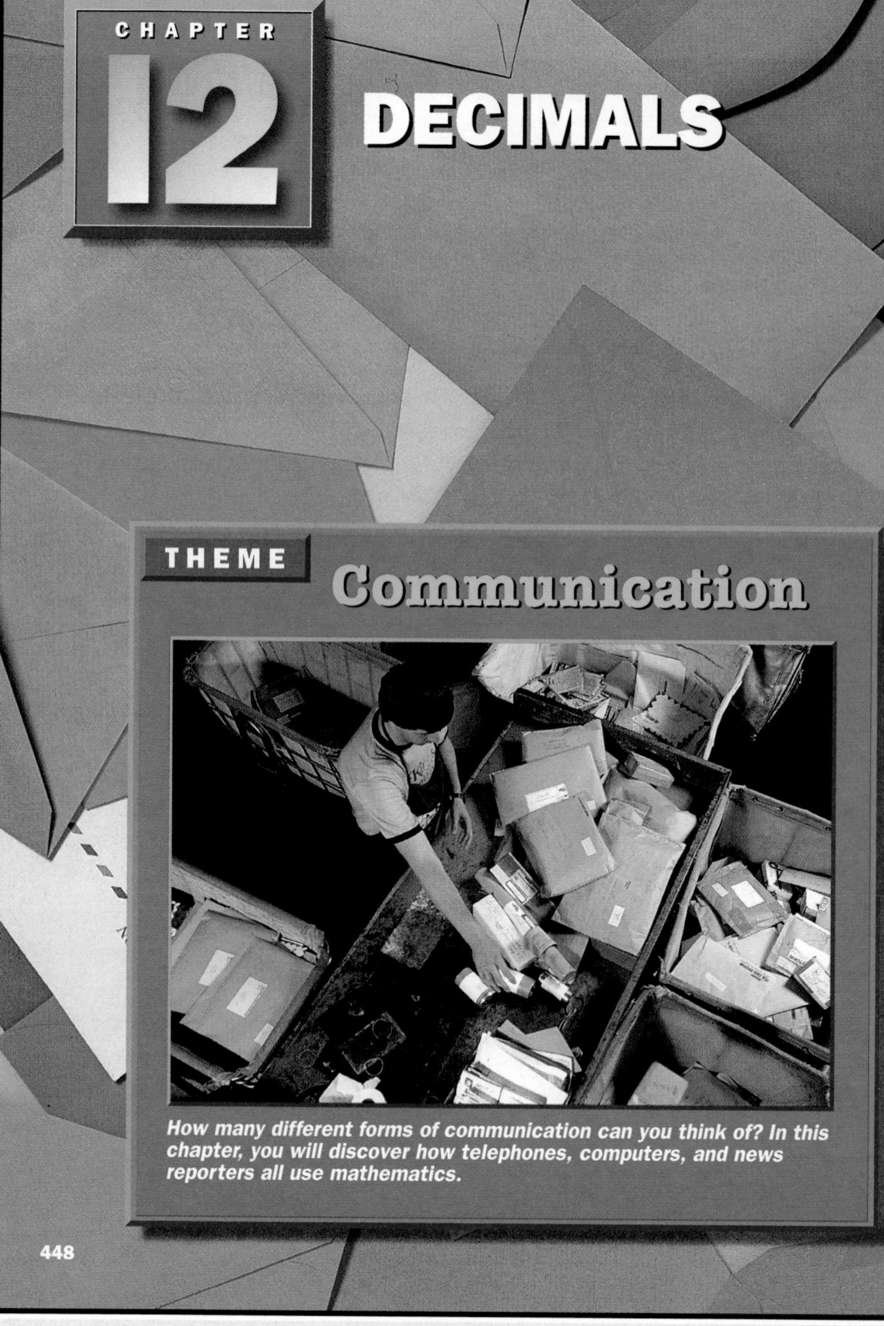

How many different forms of communication can you think of? In this chapter, you will discover how telephones, computers, and news reporters all use mathematics.

448

Chapter Bibliography

Bees Dance and Whales Sing: The Mysteries of Animal Communication by Margery Facklam. San Francisco: Sierra Club Books for Children, 1992. ISBN 0–87156–573–0.

The Indian Way: Learning to Communicate with Mother Earth by Gary McLain. Santa Fe, NM: John Muir Publications, 1990. ISBN 0–945465–73–4.

The Kids' Book of Secret Codes, Signals, and Ciphers by E. A. Grant. Philadelphia: Running Press, 1989. ISBN 0–89471–781–2.

Community Involvement

Have students make a Kids Yellow Pages phone directory for their community. Students can work in small groups to write dialing instructions, a list of phone rules and good manners, and a brief description of how the phone system works. Have students look at a neighborhood "yellow pages" directory for ideas. Students can distribute completed directories in their own neighborhoods and to listed businesses.

Possible answer: Less than 1 g; 0.75 is 75 hundredths, which is less than 100 hundredths, or 1.

What Do You Know?

There are many unique ways to provide information about products or services. However, advertising by mail is still very popular.

Use the mail advertisements for problems 1–3.

1. Does Wheat All give more or less than 1 g of extra cereal in each box? Explain. See above.

2. Wheat Chex gives $\frac{3}{10}$ g extra cereal in each box. How can you write $\frac{3}{10}$ as a decimal? Use a diagram to show your work.
   0.3 or 0.30; check students' diagrams.

3. Portfolio Choose at least two fractions from the advertisements. Then rename the fractions as decimals. Explain your work.
   See below.

9 OUT OF 10 doctors surveyed recommended Get Well!

We give you 0.75g more in each box of Wheat All Cereal

We'll finish the job in half the time!

We allow only a 1/100 cm error. NOW THAT'S CLOSE!

Write an Essay **Think about all the numbers in your life—your age, address, telephone number, and so on. Write an essay telling how these numbers give information about you.**

3. Students may choose from the following fractions: $\frac{9}{10} = 0.9$; $\frac{75}{100}$, or $\frac{3}{4} = 0.75$; $\frac{1}{2} = 0.5$; $\frac{1}{100} = 0.01$.

An essay presents ideas about a topic.

1. What are some things these numbers tell about you?
   Possible answers: where you live, how well you did on a test, your grade
2. Which of your numbers can you show as a decimal?
   Answers depend on the types of numbers used.

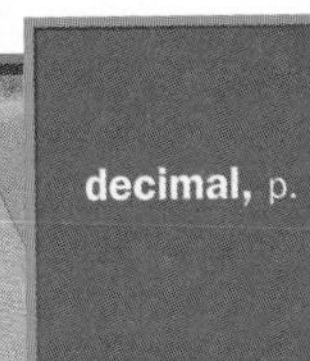

Vocabulary

decimal, p. 450 **decimal point,** p. 451 **mixed number,** p. 454

Decimals 449

Reading, Writing, Arithmetic

Write an Essay Before students begin writing, work as a class to brainstorm the kinds of numbers in their lives. Write suggestions on the chalkboard for students to use as a reference. You might use the finished essays as part of a bulletin board display entitled "Numbers in Our Lives."

Vocabulary

Students may record new words in their journals. Encourage them to show examples and draw diagrams to help them tell what the words mean.

PURPOSE Assess students' ability to apply prior knowledge of decimals.

Materials decimal squares

Assessing Prior Knowledge

Ask students to give examples of using decimals. *[possible answers: $4.12, 3.4 miles, 5.16 pounds, 0.5 liters, 2.614 gallons]* Make a 10 by 10 grid and shade 23 of the squares.

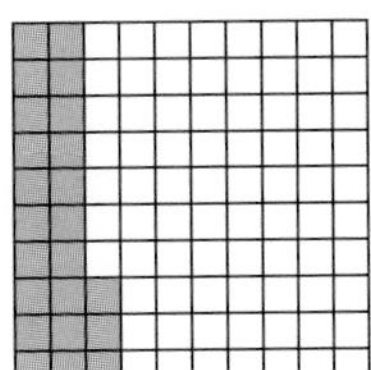

Ask these questions.

- **What fraction of the big square is shaded?** *[$\frac{23}{100}$]*
- **What decimal is represented by the shaded squares?** *[0.23]*

Encourage students to use whatever methods they wish to answer items 1–3. Observe students as they work.

BUILDING A PORTFOLIO

Item 3 can be used as a benchmark to show where students are in their understanding of the relationship between fractions and decimals.

A Portfolio Checklist for Students and a Checklist for Teachers are provided in Teacher's Assessment Resources, pp. 33–34.

Prerequisite Skills

- *Do students recognize representations of fractions?*
- *Do students recognize equivalent fractions?*
- *Can students add and subtract whole numbers?*

Assessment Resources

DIAGNOSTIC INVENTORY

Use this blackline master to assess prerequisite skills that students will need in order to be successful in this chapter.

TEST MASTERS

Use the multiple choice format (form A or B) or the free response format (form C) as a pretest of the skills in this chapter.

LESSON 12.1 RESOURCES

EXPLORE ACTIVITY

Decimals Less Than 1

OBJECTIVES Explore the concept of decimals; read and write decimals to hundredths.

Teaching With Technology
See alternate computer lesson, pp. 453A–453B.

RESOURCE REMINDER
Math Center Cards 109
Practice 109, Reteach 109, Extend 109

SKILLS TRACE

GRADE 3
- Explore the concept of decimals. *(Chapter 11)*
- Explore reading and writing decimals to hundredths. *(Chapter 11)*

GRADE 4
- Explore the concept of decimals.
- Explore reading and writing decimals to hundredths.

GRADE 5
- Explore reading and writing decimals to hundredths. Read and write decimals through thousandths. *(Chapter 1)*

WARM-UP

Cooperative Pairs — Auditory/Linguistic

OBJECTIVE Review place and value in numbers.

Materials per pair: 3 index cards

▶ Pairs work together to write three number riddles that each use the place and value of digits to describe a number. Numbers may vary from 1 to 9,999.

▶ Students can record each riddle on an index card. For example, a riddle for 236 is shown below.

▶ Have pairs exchange riddles and solve.

I am a 3-digit number. The digit in my greatest place is 2 and in my least is 6. The ones digit is the product of the tens and hundreds digits. What number am I?

DISCRETE MATH CONNECTION

Cooperative Pairs — Visual/Spatial

OBJECTIVE Connect writing fractions to geometry.

▶ Each student draws and colors 5 geometric shapes using the colors and shapes of their choice.

▶ Students work with a partner to write fractions and decimals describing their combined shapes. For example:

$\frac{5}{10}$ **or 0.5 of the figures are triangles.**

$\frac{2}{10}$ **or 0.2 of the figures are red.**

▶ Have them record as many observations as they can about color, shape, and color and shape combined.

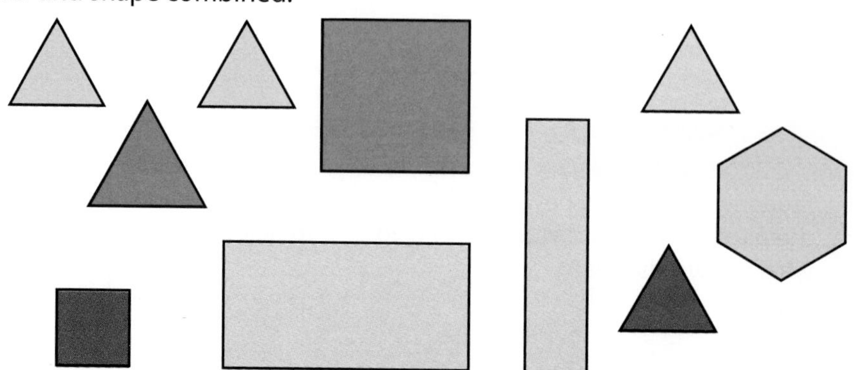

Daily Review

PREVIOUS DAY QUICK REVIEW

1. $\frac{2}{6} + \frac{3}{6}$ [$\frac{5}{6}$]
2. $\frac{3}{8} - \frac{1}{8}$ [$\frac{2}{8}$ or $\frac{1}{4}$]
3. $1\frac{1}{4} + 2\frac{1}{4}$ [$3\frac{2}{4}$ or $3\frac{1}{2}$]
4. $6\frac{1}{2} - 4$ [$2\frac{1}{2}$]

FAST FACTS

1. 8 ÷ 1 *[8]*
2. 36 ÷ 4 *[9]*
3. 72 ÷ 8 *[9]*
4. 63 ÷ 9 *[7]*

Problem of the Day • 109

A music store receives a shipment of 100 compact disks in a box. Half of the CDs are by one artist. What two decimals show how many CDs are by the artist? *[0.5; 0.50]*

TECH LINK

ONLINE EXPLORATION
Use our Web-linked activities and lesson plans to connect your students to the real world of communication.

MATH VAN
Activity You may wish to use *Crack the Code* to teach this lesson.

Visit our Resource Village at http://www.mhschool.com to access the Online Exploration.

MATH CENTER

Practice

OBJECTIVE Read and write decimals.

Materials per pair: 2 ones models, centimeter graph paper (TA 1), Math Center Recording Sheet (TA 31 optional)

Partners take turns showing decimals without shading—rather by indicating beginning and end squares. *[Students check each other's work.]*

PRACTICE ACTIVITY 109 — MATH CENTER, Partners

Spatial Sense • Begin-End Models

YOU NEED
- 2 ones models
- 10-by-10 grid drawn on centimeter graph paper

- Draw a 10-by-10 grid on graph paper. Label one edge TOP. Partners take turns modeling a decimal on the grid by placing two ones models on any two squares. These two squares *plus* all the squares between (going left to right across the grid, going down the grid) represent the decimal.
- The other partner names the decimal and writes it as a decimal and a fraction. The correct name earns a point. Play until one partner wins with 10 points.

Grade Level 4 · McGraw-Hill School Division

Chapter 12, Lesson 1, pages 450–453 — Decimals

NCTM Standards
- Problem Solving
- ✓ Communication
- ✓ Reasoning
- Connections

Problem Solving

OBJECTIVE Read and write decimals.

Materials per pair: 0–9 spinner (TA 2), centimeter graph paper (TA 1); per student: Math Center Recording Sheet (TA 31 optional)

Students use a spinner to decide how many squares to shade on a 10-by-10 grid as they take turns to fill in all the squares. Each time they fill in squares they name and write the corresponding decimal and score a point. The person who reaches 100 earns a bonus. *[Students check each other's work.]*

PROBLEM-SOLVING ACTIVITY 109 — MATH CENTER, Partners

Spatial Sense • Race to 1

YOU NEED
- spinner (0–9)
- 10-by-10 grid drawn on centimeter graph paper

- Players take turns spinning for a number. They decide to use the exact number or multiply it by 10. This is the number of squares they shade on the 10-by-10 grid.
- Each time a player shades in squares, that player names and writes the decimal for the total number of squares shaded so far. Players receive one point for every square they shade.
- Play until all 100 squares are shaded exactly to represent 1. (Any turn that goes beyond 100 does not count.) The player who shades the last square earns three points. The greater score wins.

Grade Level 4 · McGraw-Hill School Division

Chapter 12, Lesson 1, pages 450–453 — Decimals

NCTM Standards
- ✓ Problem Solving
- ✓ Communication
- ✓ Reasoning
- Connections

ESL APPROPRIATE

EXPLORE ACTIVITY
Decimals Less Than 1

OBJECTIVES Explore the concept of decimals; read and write decimals to hundredths.

Materials per pair: centimeter graph paper (TA 7), crayons, colored pencils, or markers

Vocabulary decimal, decimal point

1 Introduce

Draw the patterned rectangles below on the chalkboard or display them on the overhead projector:

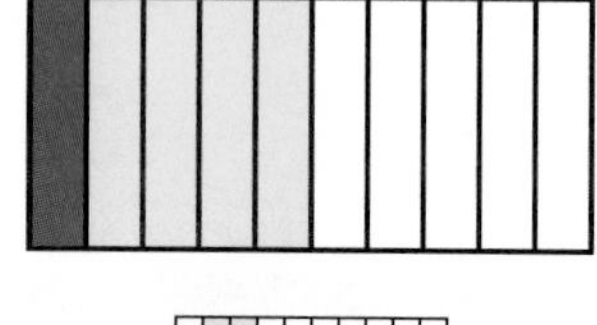

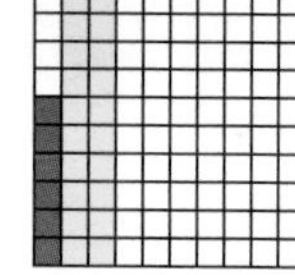

Have students identify different fractions of tenths and hundredths. Ask questions such as:

- **What part of the rectangle is shaded yellow? blue?** *[$\frac{4}{10}$; $\frac{1}{10}$]*
- **Write the fractions that describe the yellow and blue areas in the rectangle. How do you read these fractions?** *[$\frac{4}{10}$; $\frac{1}{10}$; four tenths; one tenth]*
- **What part of the square is shaded yellow? blue?** *[$\frac{20}{100}$; $\frac{6}{100}$]*
- **Write the fractions that describe the yellow and blue areas in the square. How do you read these fractions?** *[$\frac{20}{100}$; $\frac{6}{100}$; twenty hundredths or two tenths; six hundredths]*

2 Teach *Cooperative Pairs*

LEARN Read the introductory problem. Discuss how to express the striped and dotted sections of the program using fractions and decimals. Point to the table and have students read these fractions and decimals aloud.

Work Together To prepare students for identifying decimals, encourage them to keep their models simple. Elicit that it is easier to count the squares if they are grouped together. As students make their models for nine hundredths and ninety hundredths (e and f), encourage them to work independently and then compare their models.

Talk It Over Have pairs compare their models and comment on how they are similar and different. Discuss which models are easier to read and interpret as decimals. As students comment on how nine tenths and ninety hundredths compare, ask:

- **How do $\frac{90}{100}$ and $\frac{9}{10}$ compare? How do you know?** *[They are equivalent; $\frac{90}{100}$ simplifies to $\frac{9}{10}$.]*

EXPLORE ACTIVITY

Decimals Less Than 1

LEARN

Have you ever painted on a computer screen? Painting programs let you pick a style and a pattern.

What part of this 10-by-10 square is painted with stripes? with dots?

You can use a fraction or a **decimal** to name the parts that are striped and dotted.

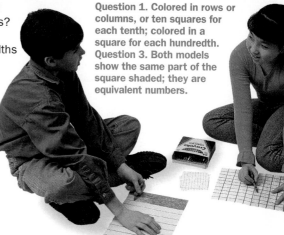

Part	Fraction	Decimal	Read
Stripes	$\frac{3}{10}$	0.3	three tenths
Dots	$\frac{45}{100}$	0.45	forty-five hundredths

Check Out the Glossary
decimal
decimal point
See page 544.

Work Together
Work with a partner to model these decimals. Use graph paper to create your own decimal squares.

a. two tenths
b. fifty-two hundredths
c. nine tenths
d. seventy-eight hundredths
e. nine hundredths
f. ninety hundredths

You will need
- *graph paper*
- *crayons, colored pencils, or markers*

Talk It Over
- How did you model tenths? hundredths? **See right.**
- How many hundredths are in a tenth? **10**
- How do your models for nine tenths and ninety hundredths compare? Why? **See right.**

Question 1. Colored in rows or columns, or ten squares for each tenth; colored in a square for each hundredth. Question 3. Both models show the same part of the square shaded; they are equivalent numbers.

Meeting Individual Needs

Extra Support

First, have students model decimals in tenths using a square divided into 10 strips. To show tenths, students shade a number of strips in the square. Have students model hundredths using 10-by-10 grids.

Language Support

Help students with the pronunciation of tenths and hundredths. Stress that the "th" sound is the same as is used in some fractions and ordinal numbers, such as fifths or sixths.

ESL APPROPRIATE

Ongoing Assessment

Observation Checklist
Observe if students are able to read and write decimals by noting if they can write decimals from fractions and word names.

Follow Up Have students who are having trouble reading decimals write the word names for the fractions before they read the decimal. You may want to give students more work with models using **Reteach 109.**

Have students who are ready for a challenge try **Extend 109.**

lake Connections

ou can use a model or a place-value chart to help you nderstand and write a decimal.

ote: The **decimal point** separates the ones from the tenths.

Ones		Tenths	Hundredths
0	•	9	

ead: nine tenths
/rite: 0.9

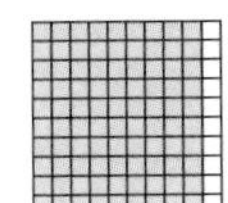

Ones		Tenths	Hundredths
0	•	7	8

Read: seventy-eight hundredths
Write: 0.78

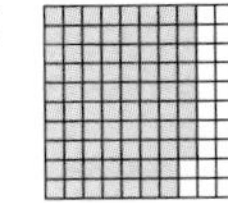

Ones		Tenths	Hundredths
0	•	0	9

ead: nine hundredths
/rite: 0.09

Ones		Tenths	Hundredths
0	•	9	0

Read: ninety hundredths
Write: 0.90

- When reading a decimal, which place name do you use? **Possible answer: the place value farthest to the right**
- What do the zeros mean in the decimal 0.09? **no ones, no tenths**

Check for Understanding

/rite a fraction and a decimal for the part that is shaded.

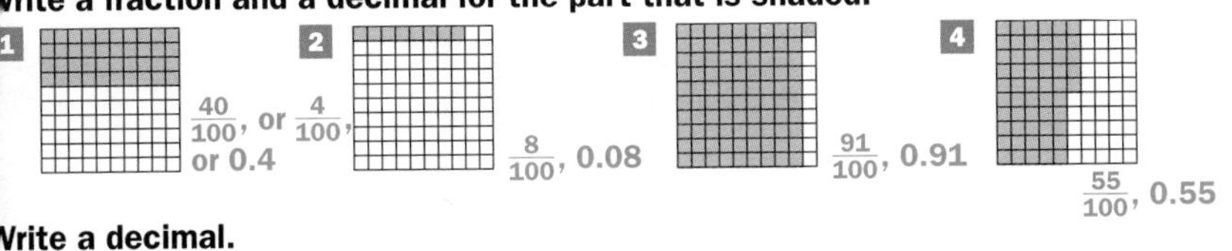

1 $\frac{40}{100}$, or $\frac{4}{100}$, or 0.4 2 $\frac{8}{100}$, 0.08 3 $\frac{91}{100}$, 0.91 4 $\frac{55}{100}$, 0.55

Vrite a decimal.

5 $\frac{1}{10}$ 0.1 6 $\frac{6}{10}$ 0.6 7 $\frac{60}{100}$ 0.60 8 $\frac{57}{100}$ 0.57 9 $\frac{98}{100}$ 0.98 10 $\frac{4}{100}$ 0.04

11 seven tenths 0.7 12 twelve hundredths 0.12 13 five hundredths 0.05

Critical Thinking: Analyze **Explain your reasoning.**

14 **What if** a decimal square stands for one dollar. Describe the models that would show one dime and one penny.

One dime—one tenth shaded, one penny—one hundredth shaded; one dime is one tenth of a dollar, one penny is one hundredth of a dollar.

Turn the page for Practice.

CHECK

Inclusion

Help students understand tenths by giving them 10 index cards. Have them position 3 cards vertically and 7 cards horizontally. Explain that 0.3 of the cards are vertical. Repeat with other decimals.

MAKE CONNECTIONS

Discuss how to use the decimal place-value chart. Stress that the decimal point always lies to the right of the ones place. Point out that the value of a digit depends upon its position or place.

For example, a 9 in the ones place has a value of 9, a 9 in the tenths place has a value of $\frac{9}{10}$, and a 9 in the hundredths place has a value of $\frac{9}{100}$. Ask:

- **Which place has the greatest value in the chart? least?** *[ones; hundredths]*
- **Which decimals in the chart name the same number?** *[0.9 and 0.90]*

3 Close

Check for Understanding using items 1–14, page 451.

CRITICAL THINKING

In item 14, students are asked to analyze the relationship between money and decimals. To extend the analysis, have them describe how they would use models to show one quarter and one nickel. Have them compare the ways the amounts are written as decimals and with dollar notation. *[Shade 25 out of 100 squares; shade 5 out of 100 squares; 0.25, $0.25; 0.05, $0.05; Notation is the same except for the dollar sign.]*

Practice See pages 452–453.

▶ PRACTICE

Materials have available: calculators

Options for assigning exercises:
A—Odd ex. 1–37; all ex. 39–44; **More to Explore**
B—Even ex. 2–38; all ex. 39–44; **More to Explore**

- For ex. 1–14, have students read aloud some of their answers.
- Encourage students to use number sense to match the amounts in ex. 33–37. They will have to extend tenths to hundredths to find some of the money amounts.
- For **Make It Right** (ex. 38), see Common Error below.
- For ex. 39–40, have students tell how much is not painted in addition to how much is painted. *[ex. 35: 0.48; ex. 36: 0.35]*
- In ex. 41, students may use the problem-solving strategies, Work Backward, or Guess, Test, and Revise, to find the answer.
- After completing ex. 43, have students compare their decisions and reasons. Discuss different local museums students may have visited.

More to Explore Review the place-value chart with students and read the thousandths. Point out that thousandths are one tenth of hundredths and therefore are to the right of hundredths in the place-value chart. Discuss how to read and write thousandths, including examples such as 0.015, 0.125, 0.203, 0.400 = 0.40 = 0.4, 0.160 = 0.16, and 0.080 = 0.08. Then ask:

- **Do you think that decimals stop at thousandths? Explain.** *[No; possible answer: they keep getting smaller.]*
- **When might thousandths be used?** *[Possible answer: for measurements of very small items]*

Have pairs of students work together to complete the exercises.

PRACTICE

Practice

7. eight hundredths
8. thirty-seven hundredths
9. seventeen hundredths
10. ninety-three hundredths

Write the word name.

1

Ones		Tenths	Hundredths
0	•	2	8

twenty-eight hundredths

2

Ones		Tenths	Hundredths
0	•	3	3

thirty-three hundredths

3

Ones		Tenths	Hundredths
0	•	7	

seven tenths

4

Ones		Tenths	Hundredths
0	•	0	5

five hundredths

5 0.5 five tenths
6 0.4 four tenths
7 0.08 See above.
8 0.37 See above.
9 0.17 See above.
10 0.93 See abo

Write a decimal for the part that is shaded.

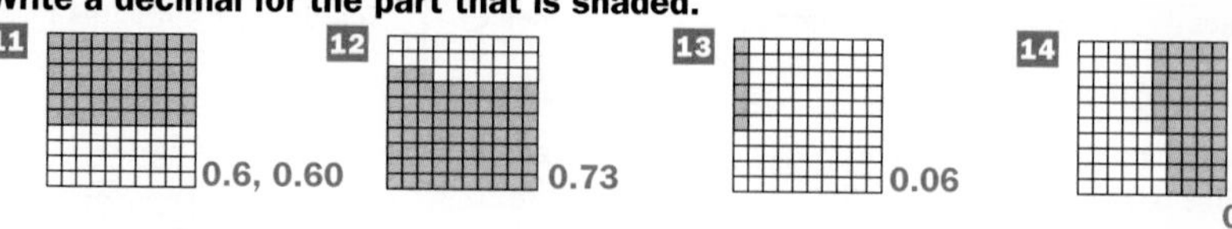

11 0.6, 0.60
12 0.73
13 0.06
14 0.

Write a decimal.

15 $\frac{7}{10}$ 0.7
16 $\frac{8}{10}$ 0.8
17 $\frac{49}{100}$ 0.49
18 $\frac{2}{100}$ 0.02
19 $\frac{93}{100}$ 0.93
20 $\frac{68}{100}$

21 $\frac{2}{10}$ 0.2
22 $\frac{9}{100}$ 0.09
23 $\frac{77}{100}$ 0.77
24 $\frac{5}{10}$ 0.5
25 $\frac{40}{100}$ 0.40
26 $\frac{7}{100}$

27 eight tenths 0.8
28 one tenth 0.1
29 twenty-one hundredths

30 seven hundredths 0.07
31 three tenths 0.3
32 ninety-nine hundredths

Match a money amount to its word name.

33 one tenth of a dollar c — **a.** $0.45
34 forty-five hundredths of a dollar a — **b.** $0.05
35 five tenths of a dollar e — **c.** $0.10
36 five hundredths of a dollar b — **d.** $0.25
37 one fourth of a dollar d — **e.** $0.50

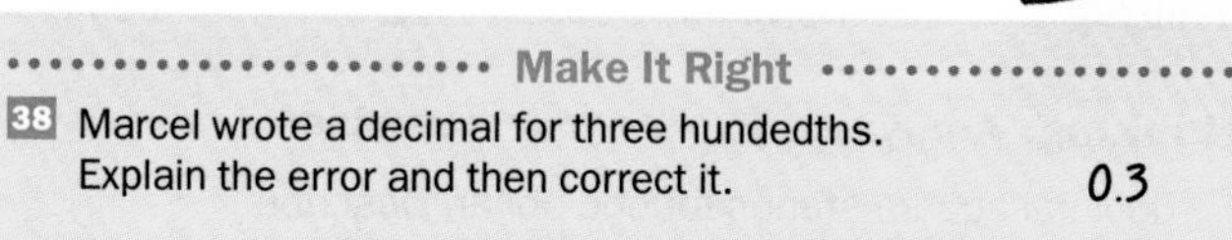

Make It Right

38 Marcel wrote a decimal for three hundedths. Explain the error and then correct it. 0.3

Marcel wrote the digit 3 in the tenths place instead of the hundredths place—0.03.

Meeting Individual Needs

Early Finishers

Have students write a fraction and a decimal for the unshaded or uncolored parts in each decimal square they made.

Gifted And Talented

Provide students with 10-by-10 graph paper to make a design of several colors. Then have them name the decimal for each color in the design. Discuss interesting designs and strategies for finding decimals in designs.

Common Error

Students may write decimal digits in the wrong place as in **Make It Right** (ex. 38). Have them use a place-value chart to write all their decimals. Tell them to use equivalent numbers and zeros so that all columns have an entry.

43. Answers may vary. Possible answer: The 3-h tour; it is a better buy—2 tours for $19—so each tour costs less than $10.

MIXED APPLICATIONS
Problem Solving

39 Susan painted this design on her computer screen. What decimal tells how much is painted with wavy lines? 0.52

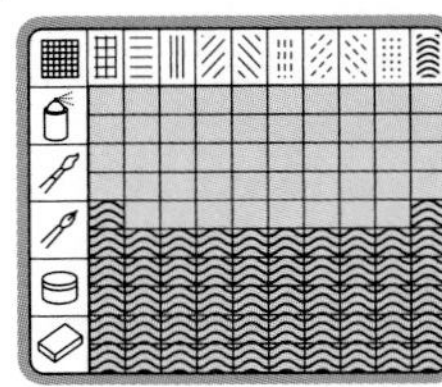

40 Calvin painted this design on his computer screen. What decimal tells how much he painted altogether? 0.65

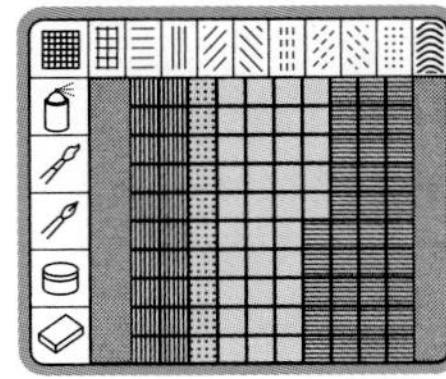

41 Marguerite is 3 years older than her sister, Janice. Janice is 6 years younger than her brother, Tommy, who is 1 year older than his best friend, Lee. If Lee is 14 years old, how old is Marguerite? 12 y old

42 Rosa bought a painting program and a morphing program for her computer. Each cost the same amount. The total bill was $159. How much did each software program cost? $79.50

43 **Make a decision** A 3-hour tour of two museums costs $19 and starts in 1 hour. A 2-hour tour on space communication costs $10. Which tour would you take? Why? See above.

44 **Write a problem** that is a set of directions for painting a 10-by-10 computer screen. Trade directions with a partner and draw each other's design. Students should compare problems and solutions.

more to explore

Thousandths

The first decimal square is divided into hundredths. Think of dividing each hundredth into 10 equal parts. So the second square shows thousandths.

Ones		Tenths	Hundredths	Thousandths
0	.	0	0	5

Read: five thousandths
Fraction: $\frac{5}{1,000}$
Decimal: 0.005

▸ What do the zeros mean in 0.005? no ones, no tenths, no hundredths

Write a decimal.

1 $\frac{7}{1,000}$ 0.007
2 $\frac{9}{1,000}$ 0.009
3 $\frac{10}{1,000}$ 0.010
4 $\frac{25}{1,000}$ 0.025
5 $\frac{115}{1,000}$ 0.115
6 $\frac{502}{1,000}$ 0.502

Extra Practice, page 528

Alternate Teaching Strategy

Materials centimeter graph paper (TA 7); markers

Draw a square on the chalkboard. Divide it into 10 equal sections:

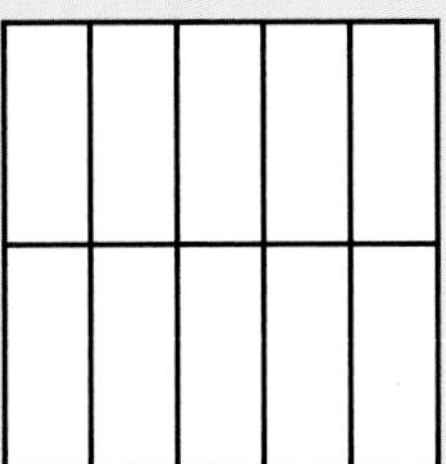

Shade one strip and ask:

- **What fraction of the square is shaded?** *[$\frac{1}{10}$]*

Tell students that another way to name the part shaded is with a decimal. Write 0.1 on the chalkboard and tell them that it is read the same way as the fraction: one tenth.

Shade another part of the square and have a volunteer write the decimal for the part shaded on the chalkboard. *[0.2]*

Repeat with other tenths. Then repeat the activity using grid paper to demonstrate hundredths.

PRACTICE • 109

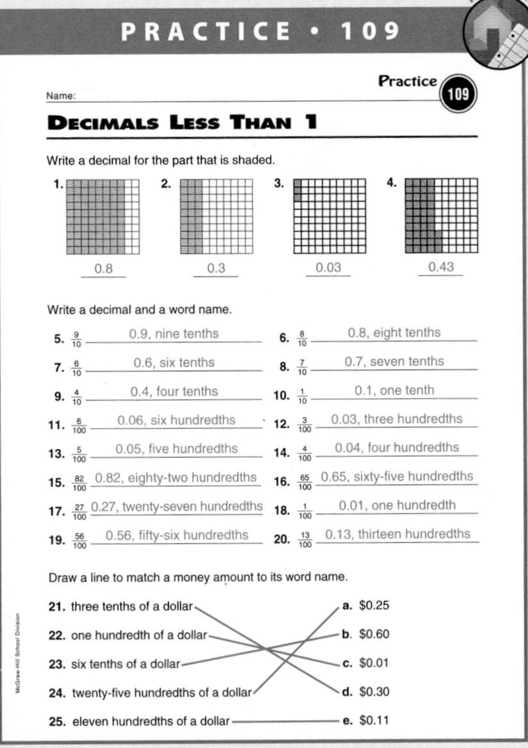

RETEACH • 109

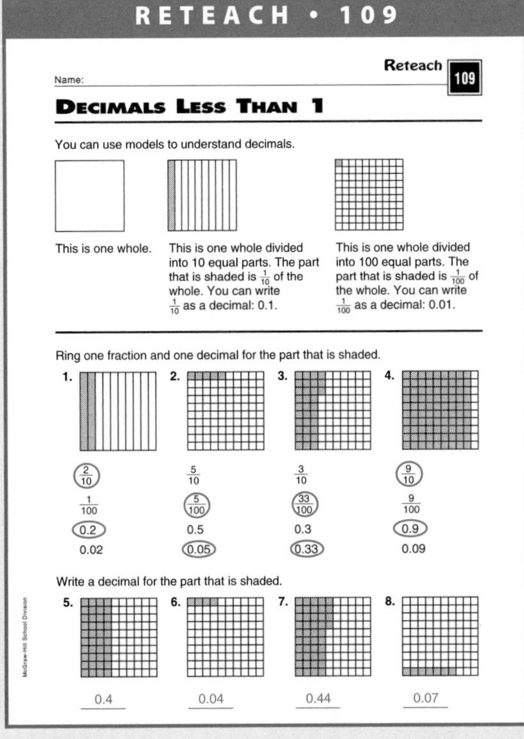

EXTEND • 109

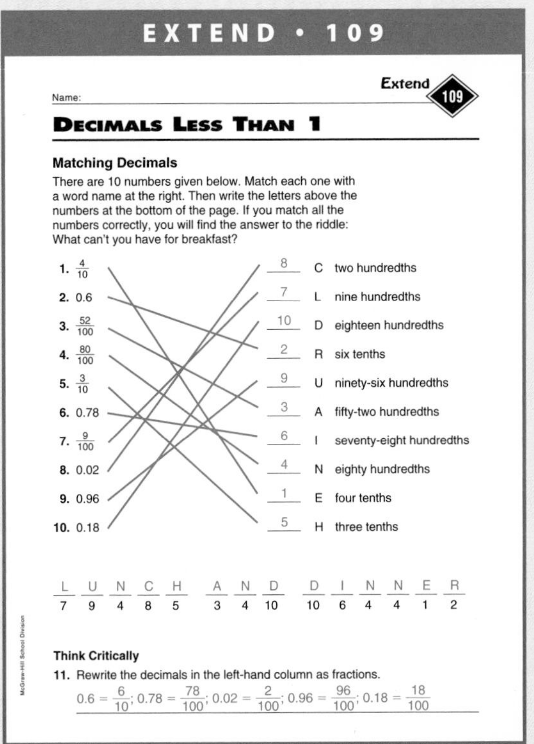

Teaching With Technology

Decimals Less Than 1

OBJECTIVE Students use models to show and compare decimal numbers to hundredths.

Resource Math Van Activity:
Crack the Code

SET UP

Provide students with the activity card for *Crack the Code*. Start ***Math Van*** and click the *Activities* button. Click the *Crack the Code* activity on the Fax Machine.

Using the Math Van Activity

1 **Getting Started** Students use Place-Value Models to help Dana Detective decipher a secret code and solve a mystery. Then they answer activity-related questions in their Notes.

2 **Practice and Apply** Students crack another code by deciphering decimal and number patterns. They use the cracked code to read a secret message and answer activity-related questions in their Notes.

3 **Close** Students may share the methods they used to crack the codes and discuss how the Place-Value Models were helpful in ordering the decimal numbers.

Extend Students create their own alphabet code with decimals and write a secret message for classmates to decipher.

TIPS FOR TOOLS

Encourage students to group blocks by tenths and hundredths on the mat.

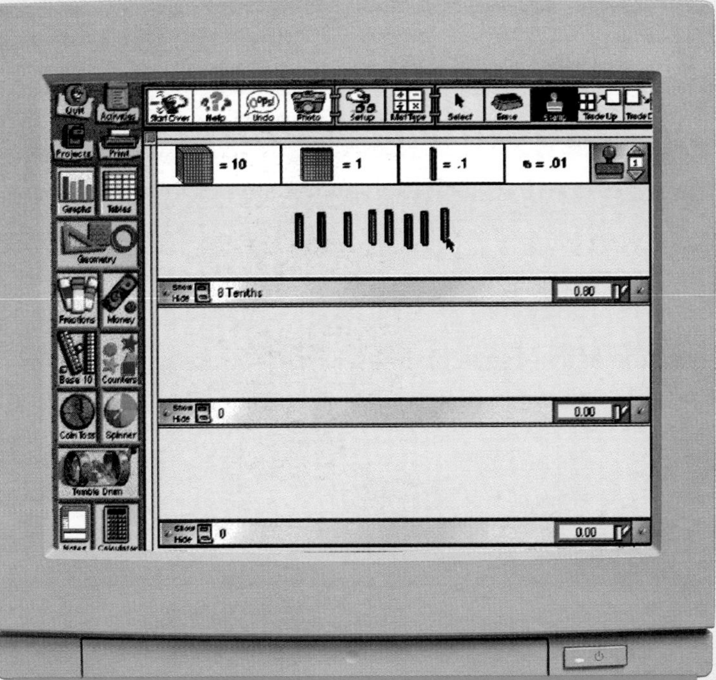

SCREEN 1

Students stamp Place-Value Models to show the first number from the secret message.

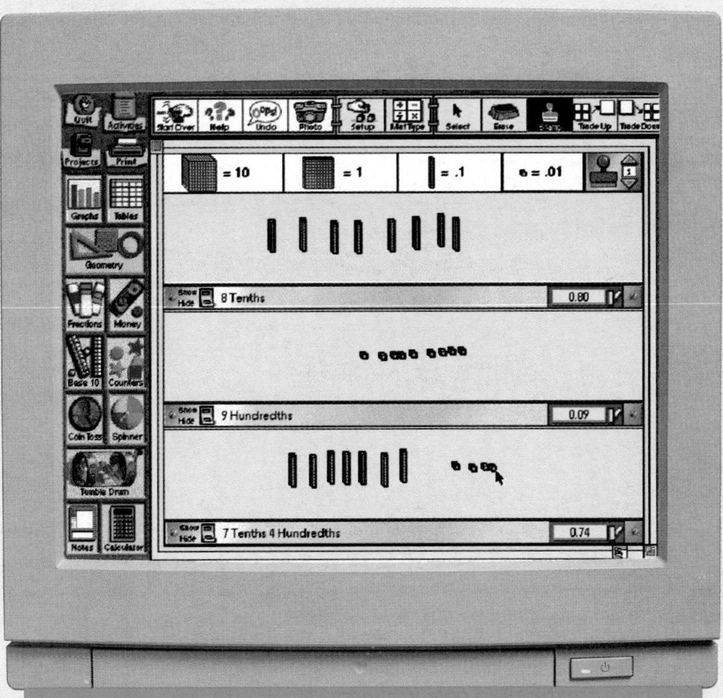

SCREEN 2

Students model the remaining numbers from the message.

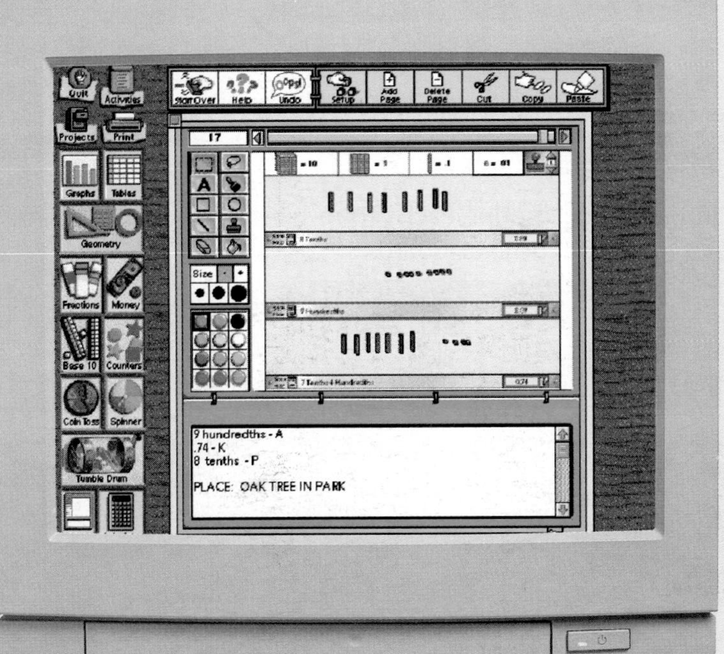

SCREEN 3

Using their understanding of place value, students order the numbers and crack the code.

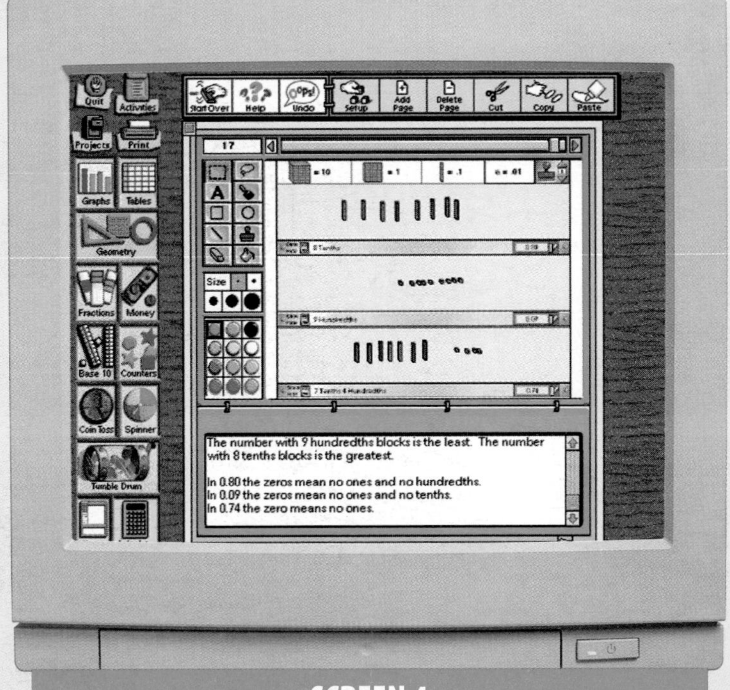

SCREEN 4

Students take a picture of their work and answer questions about determining the value of a decimal number.

Decimals Greater Than 1

OBJECTIVE Read and write decimals greater than 1.

RESOURCE REMINDER
Math Center Cards 110
Practice 110, Reteach 110, Extend 110

SKILLS TRACE

GRADE 3	• Read and write decimals greater than one. *(Chapter 11)*
GRADE 4	• Read and write decimals greater than one.
GRADE 5	• Read and write decimals through thousandths. *(Chapter 1)*

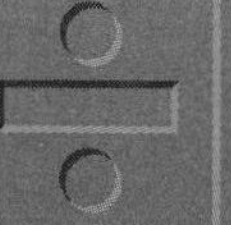

WARM-UP

Cooperative Pairs — Visual/Spatial

OBJECTIVE Explore identifying decimals from grid designs.

Materials per student: 3 sheets of centimeter graph paper (TA 7)

▶ Each student outlines a 10-by-10 square, then makes a block letter or other design.

▶ Students exchange papers and find the decimal that represents the shaded letter or design in the 10-by-10 square.

▶ Have students repeat the activity several times. Discuss strategies for identifying the decimals from the pictures.

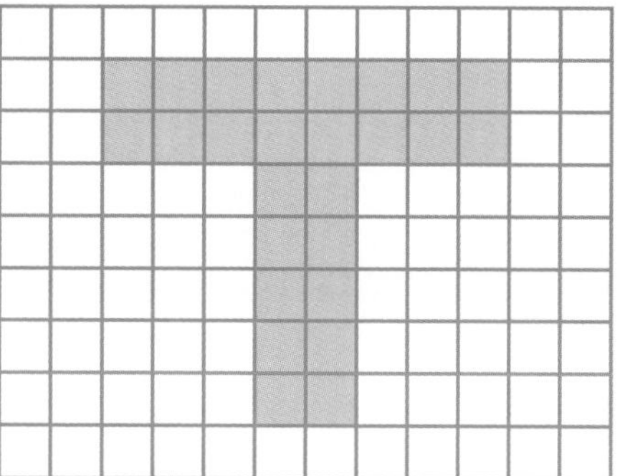

ESL APPROPRIATE

PROBABILITY CONNECTION

Cooperative Groups — Kinesthetic

OBJECTIVE Connect decimals to probability.

Materials per group: 0–9 spinner (TA 2)

▶ Divide the class into ten small groups. Each group spins its spinner 10 times and records results in a table on the chalkboard.

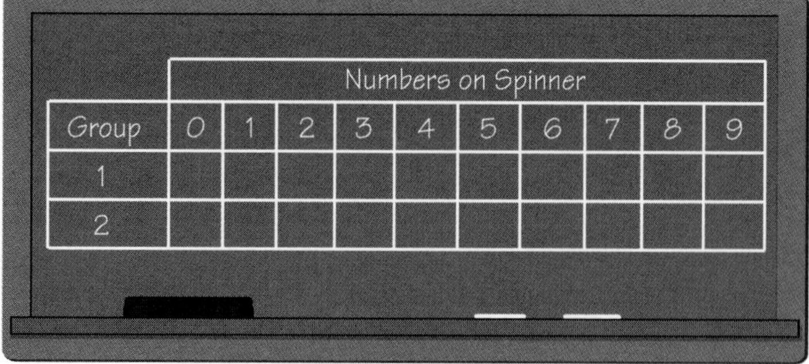

▶ Have volunteers compute the total number of times each number is spun by all groups. Then, for each number on the spinner, students write the decimal for the number of times the number is spun out of 100 spins. This is the experimental probability of spinning the number.

▶ Have students identify the theoretical probability of spinning each number, as a decimal. *[0.1]* Discuss how the experimental probability from the combined class results compares with the theoretical probability.

Daily Review

PREVIOUS DAY QUICK REVIEW

Write a decimal.

1. $\frac{9}{10}$ *[0.9]*
2. $\frac{49}{100}$ *[0.49]*
3. $\frac{76}{100}$ *[0.76]*
4. $\frac{3}{100}$ *[0.03]*

FAST FACTS

1. 9 ÷ 1 *[9]*
2. 14 ÷ 2 *[7]*
3. 35 ÷ 5 *[7]*
4. 40 ÷ 8 *[5]*

Problem of the Day • 110

A page of stamps has 100 stamps. Al has 3 full pages and a page that is missing 5 stamps. What decimal shows the number of pages of stamps that Al has? *[3.95]*

TECH LINK

Math Van

MATH VAN

Tool You may wish to use the Place-Value Models tool with this lesson.

MATH FORUM

Combination Classes To help students gain confidence with using decimals, I have them work with a partner. They alternate reading decimal names and writing the corresponding decimals.

Visit our Resource Village at http://www.mhschool.com to see more of the Math Forum.

MATH CENTER

Practice

OBJECTIVE Read and write decimals that are greater than 1.

Materials per student: 0–9 spinner (TA 4), Math Center Recording Sheet (TA 31 optional)

Students spin for three numbers to use in different orders for three different decimals greater than 1. They draw a model for each decimal. *[Check students' drawings.]*

MATH CENTER On Your Own

PRACTICE ACTIVITY 110

Number Sense • 3-Digit Draw

YOU NEED
- spinner (0–9)

- Spin for three different numbers. Fill the numbers in any order into a copy of the decimal grid. Draw a model of the decimal you made. Use a large square for ones, a narrow bar for tenths, and a very small square for hundredths.
- Change the order of the same three numbers in the decimal grid. Model the new decimal. Repeat to name, and model a third decimal using the same three numbers.
- Repeat by spinning for three new numbers.

ones	tenths	hundredths
2	3	4

ones	tenths	hundredths

Grade Level 4 McGraw-Hill School Division

Chapter 12, Lesson 2, pages 454–455 Decimals

ESL APPROPRIATE

NCTM Standards
- Problem Solving
- Communication
- ✓ Reasoning
- ✓ Connections

Problem Solving

OBJECTIVE Read and write decimals as money amounts.

Materials per student: play money (optional), markers, number cube, Math Center Recording Sheet (TA 31 optional)

Students use a number cube to select numbers of quarters, dimes, nickels and pennies. They exchange coins to express the total amount as dollars, dimes, and pennies.
[Check students' work.]

MATH CENTER On Your Own

PROBLEM-SOLVING ACTIVITY 110

Patterning • Dollars-Dimes-Pennies

YOU NEED
- play money (optional)
- markers or crayons
- number cube

- Roll the number cube four times. Copy the coin chart below, and write each number in one of the boxes. Take this total amount of play money (or draw pictures of the coins).
- Express the total amount of coins as dollars, dimes, and pennies. That is, find how many dollars you have in coins. Put that amount aside. How many dimes can you make from what is left? Express the amount left over as pennies. Write the dollars, dimes, and pennies as a decimal.
- Roll again and keep playing.

quarters	dimes	nickels	pennies
5	4	5	3

dollars	dimes	pennies
1	9	3

quarters	dimes	nickels	pennies

dollars	dimes	pennies

Grade Level 4 McGraw-Hill School Division

Chapter 12, Lesson 2, pages 454–455 Decimals

ESL APPROPRIATE

NCTM Standards
- ✓ Problem Solving
- Communication
- ✓ Reasoning
- ✓ Connections

Decimals Greater Than 1

OBJECTIVE Read and write decimals greater than 1.

Vocabulary mixed number

1 Introduce

Have students discuss places where they have heard echoes and how long it takes echoes to return. Then consider the echo in the introductory problem. Have students clap their hands and then estimate 1.45 seconds with another clap.

2 Teach *Whole Class*

LEARN Have students compare the model, mixed number, and decimal. Point out that "and" is read for the decimal point.

More Examples Review the place-value charts and how to read the decimals. In Example B, point out the importance of using zero as a placeholder by discussing the difference between 72.04 and 72.4.

3 Close

Check for Understanding using items 1–8, page 454.

CRITICAL THINKING

In item 8, students are asked to analyze how decimals name the same number. Extend the analysis to a generalization by asking:

- **Can you always write two decimals to name the same number such as 5.6? Explain.** *[Yes; writing 0s to the right of a given decimal number does not change the value of the number so that 5.6 = 5.60 = 5.600.]*

PRACTICE

Materials have available: calculators

Options for assigning exercises:
A—Odd ex. 1–27; all ex. 28–31; **Mixed Review**
B—Even ex. 2–26; all ex. 28–31; **Mixed Review**

- Have students read some of the decimals in ex. 3–17 aloud, especially ex. 16.
- In ex. 29, students may use the problem-solving strategy, Solve a Multistep Problem, to find the answer.

Mixed Review/Test Preparation Students review addition, subtraction, multiplication, and division of whole numbers, a skill learned in Chapters 2, 4, and 8. Encourage students to check their answers.

Decimals Greater Than 1

LEARN

Dolphins make clicking noises underwater that bounce back if the sound hits an object. Suppose an echo returns in one and forty-five hundredths seconds. How can you write this number?

You can write a **mixed number** as a decimal.

Model

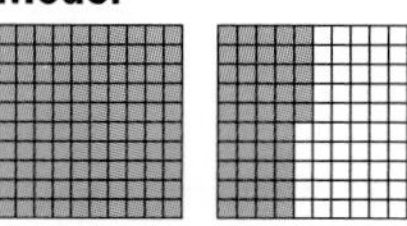

Decimal			
Ones		Tenths	Hundredths
1	•	4	5

mixed number A number that has a whole number and a fraction.

Mixed Number $1\frac{45}{100}$

Read: one *and* forty-five hundredths
Write: 1.45

More Examples

A $4\frac{7}{10}$

Decimal			
Ones		Tenths	Hundredths
4	•	7	

Read: four *and* seven tenths
Write: 4.7

B $72\frac{4}{100}$

Tens	Ones		Tenths	Hundredths
7	2	•	0	4

Read: seventy-two *and* four hundredths
Write: 72.04

CHECK

Check for Understanding

Write a mixed number and a decimal to tell how much is shaded.

1

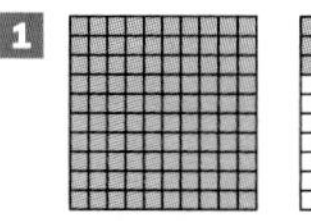

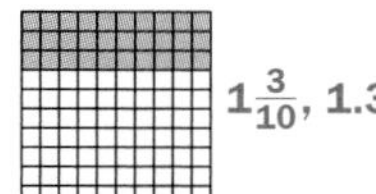

$1\frac{3}{10}$, 1.3

2

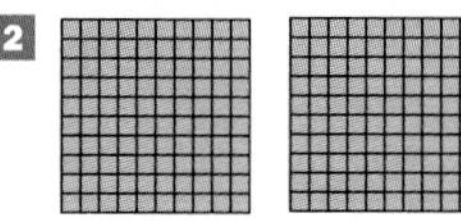

$2\frac{68}{100}$, 2.68

Write a decimal.

3 $8\frac{5}{10}$ 8.5 **4** $4\frac{18}{100}$ 4.18 **5** $1\frac{3}{100}$ 1.03 **6** $7\frac{8}{10}$ 7.8 **7** $12\frac{9}{100}$ 12.09

Critical Thinking: Analyze **Explain your reasoning.**

8 Do the two decimals name the same number? Include drawings of models with your explanations. **Check students' drawings.**
a. 3.5 and 3.05 **b.** 3.5 and 3.50

a. No; 3.5 is 3 and 5 tenths, 3.05 is 3 and 5 hundredths.

b. Yes; 5 tenths and 50 hundredths are equivalent decima

Meeting Individual Needs

Early Finishers

Have students write the word names of three decimals and then challenge other classmates to write each as a decimal. For example, if one student writes twenty-two and two hundredths, the other student writes 22.02.

Extra Support

Some students make the common error of mismatching word names and decimals, such as five and nine-hundredths and 5.9. Have these students use a place-value chart to help read the decimal.

Ongoing Assessment

Interview Determine if students understand how to read and write decimals by asking:

- **How do you read 4.06? How do you write two and sixteen hundredths?** *[four and six hundredths; 2.16]*

Follow Up Some students would benefit by additional practice. Assign **Reteach 110** to these students.

Have students who understand how to read and write decimals write several decimals to thousandths. Have them write the word name as well. Or have them try **Extend 110.**

ractice

rite a mixed number and a decimal to tell how much
shaded.

1 $1\frac{80}{100}$, $1\frac{8}{10}$, 1.8, 1.80

2 $3\frac{8}{100}$, 3.08

rite a decimal.

3 $9\frac{6}{10}$ 9.6 4 $6\frac{3}{100}$ 6.03 5 $42\frac{78}{100}$ 42.78 6 $6\frac{7}{10}$ 6.7 7 $15\frac{2}{10}$ 15.2

8 $\frac{24}{100}$ 0.24 9 $2\frac{50}{100}$ 2.50 10 $1\frac{8}{10}$ 1.8 11 $7\frac{4}{100}$ 7.04 12 $28\frac{5}{10}$ 28.5

13 $3\frac{18}{100}$ 3.18 14 $12\frac{1}{10}$ 12.1 15 $100\frac{3}{100}$ 100.03 16 $75\frac{99}{100}$ 75.99 17 $31\frac{43}{100}$ 31.43

18 nineteen and 9 tenths 19.9 19 sixty-one and three tenths 61.3

20 fifty-two and eight hundredths 52.08 21 two and seventeen hundredths 2.17

rite the word name.

22 7.2 even and wo tenths 23 9.07 nine and seven hundredths 24 12.32 twelve and thirty-two hundredths 25 4.6 four and six tenths 26 10.01 ten and one hundredth 27 75.8 seventy-five and eight tenths

MIXED APPLICATIONS

Problem Solving

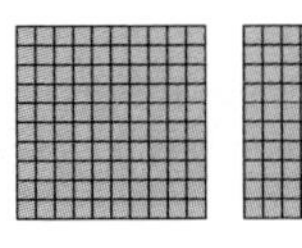

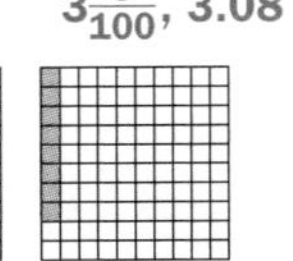

31. Students should compare problems and solutions.

28 When you used the computer spell-check for your 100-word paragraph on dolphins, you found 14 misspelled words. What decimal shows the part of the words that were misspelled? 0.14

29 Nicholas wants to buy a baseball for \$3.95 and a catcher's mitt for \$99.95. He has saved \$84.50. How much more money does he need? \$19.40

30 Fay watched a movie that lasted two and a half hours. What decimal shows how long the movie was? 2.5

31 **Write a problem** that uses one or more decimals greater than 1. Solve it and ask others to solve it. See above.

mixed review • test preparation

1 75 + 99 174 2 175 + 325 500 3 1,741 + 29 1,770 4 748 − 329 419 5 4,326 − 2,968 1,358

6 3 × 924 2,772 7 7 × 1,045 7,315 8 29 × 87 2,523 9 64 ÷ 8 8 10 1,800 ÷ 20 90

xtra Practice, page 528

Alternate Teaching Strategy

Prepare 3 pages each showing 100 stars and 1 page of 25 stars. All stars are the same size. These may be star stickers or ones you draw yourself.

Display 3 full pages of 100 stars and 1 page of 25 stars. Say:

- **A pack of stickers has pages of stars. Each page can hold 100 stars. There are 3 full pages in the pack and 1 page with 25 stars.**
- **What decimal can you write to represent the page with 25 stars?** *[0.25]*

Have a volunteer write the decimal in a place-value chart. Ask:

- **What decimal can you write to represent the number of pages of stars? Think of the mixed number that shows the number of pages.** *[3.25]*

Have a volunteer record 3.25 beneath 0.25 in the chart. Help students read 3.25 by having them write the mixed number $3\frac{25}{100}$ and then 3.25. Stress that "and" is read for the decimal point. Have students read and identify other decimals.

PRACTICE • 110

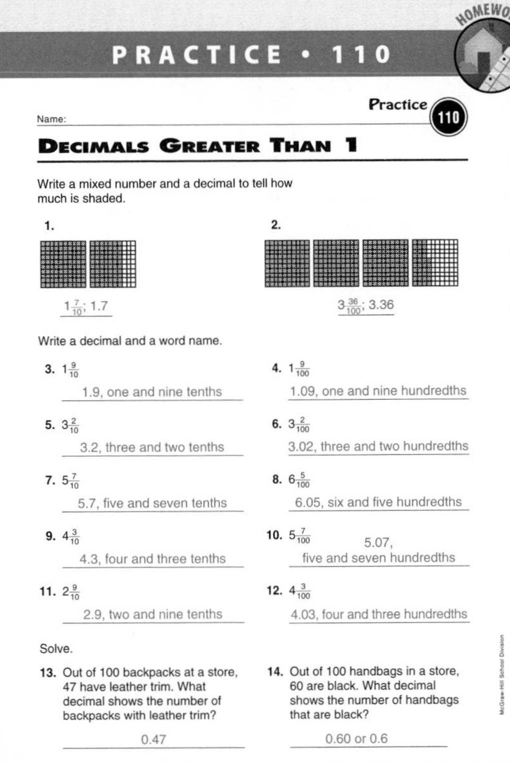
Practice 110

Name:

DECIMALS GREATER THAN 1

Write a mixed number and a decimal to tell how much is shaded.

1. $1\frac{7}{10}$; 1.7

2. $3\frac{36}{100}$; 3.36

Write a decimal and a word name.

3. $1\frac{9}{10}$ 1.9, one and nine tenths

4. $1\frac{9}{100}$ 1.09, one and nine hundredths

5. $3\frac{2}{10}$ 3.2, three and two tenths

6. $3\frac{2}{100}$ 3.02, three and two hundredths

7. $5\frac{7}{10}$ 5.7, five and seven tenths

8. $6\frac{5}{100}$ 6.05, six and five hundredths

9. $4\frac{3}{10}$ 4.3, four and three tenths

10. $5\frac{7}{100}$ 5.07, five and seven hundredths

11. $2\frac{9}{10}$ 2.9, two and nine tenths

12. $4\frac{3}{100}$ 4.03, four and three hundredths

Solve.

13. Out of 100 backpacks at a store, 47 have leather trim. What decimal shows the number of backpacks with leather trim? 0.47

14. Out of 100 handbags in a store, 60 are black. What decimal shows the number of handbags that are black? 0.60 or 0.6

RETEACH • 110

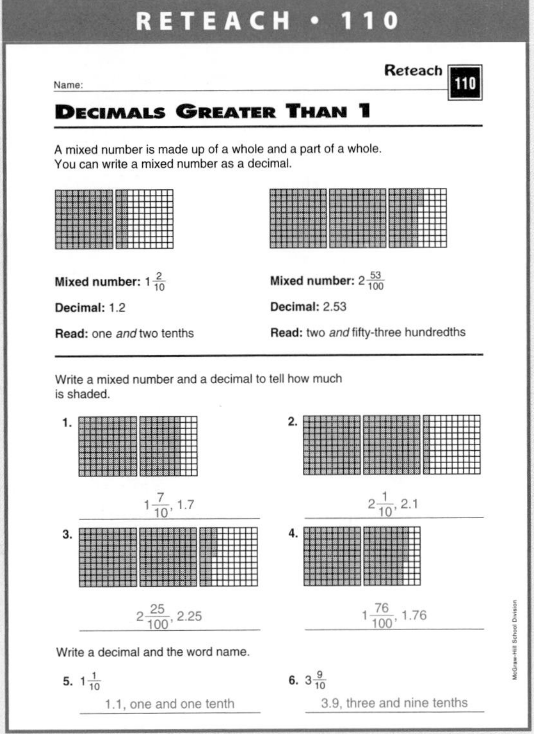
Reteach 110

Name:

DECIMALS GREATER THAN 1

A mixed number is made up of a whole and a part of a whole. You can write a mixed number as a decimal.

Mixed number: $1\frac{2}{10}$
Decimal: 1.2
Read: one *and* two tenths

Mixed number: $2\frac{53}{100}$
Decimal: 2.53
Read: two *and* fifty-three hundredths

Write a mixed number and a decimal to tell how much is shaded.

1. $1\frac{7}{10}$, 1.7

2. $2\frac{1}{10}$, 2.1

3. $2\frac{25}{100}$, 2.25

4. $1\frac{76}{100}$, 1.76

Write a decimal and the word name.

5. $1\frac{1}{10}$ 1.1, one and one tenth

6. $3\frac{9}{10}$ 3.9, three and nine tenths

EXTEND • 110

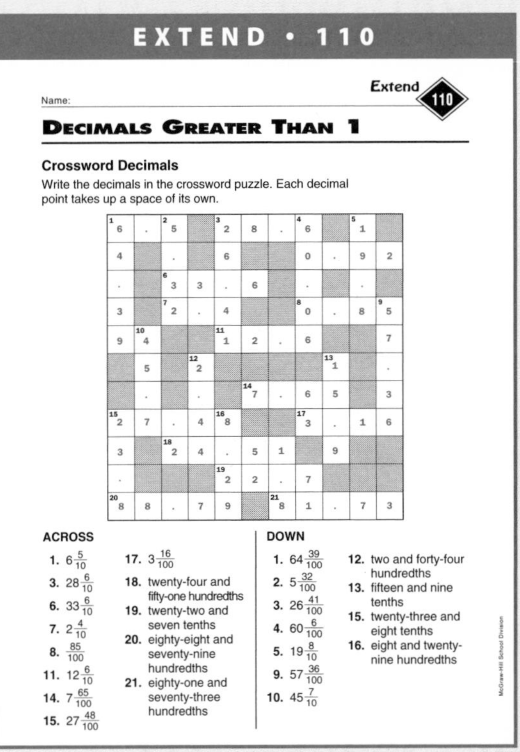
Extend 110

Name:

DECIMALS GREATER THAN 1

Crossword Decimals

Write the decimals in the crossword puzzle. Each decimal point takes up a space of its own.

ACROSS

1. $6\frac{5}{10}$
3. $28\frac{6}{10}$
6. $33\frac{6}{10}$
7. $2\frac{4}{10}$
8. $\frac{85}{100}$
11. $12\frac{6}{10}$
14. $7\frac{65}{100}$
15. $27\frac{48}{100}$
17. $3\frac{16}{100}$
18. twenty-four and fifty-one hundredths
19. twenty-two and seven tenths
20. eighty-eight and seventy-nine hundredths
21. eighty-one and seventy-three hundredths

DOWN

1. $64\frac{39}{100}$
2. $5\frac{32}{100}$
3. $26\frac{41}{100}$
4. $60\frac{6}{100}$
5. $19\frac{8}{10}$
9. $57\frac{36}{100}$
10. $45\frac{7}{10}$
12. two and forty-four hundredths
13. fifteen and nine tenths
15. twenty-three and eight tenths
16. eight and twenty-nine hundredths

LESSON 12.3

Compare and Order Decimals

OBJECTIVE Compare and order decimals.

RESOURCE REMINDER
Math Center Cards 111
Practice 111, Reteach 111, Extend 111

SKILLS TRACE	
GRADE 3	• *Introduced at grade 4.*
GRADE 4	• Compare and order decimals through hundredths.
GRADE 5	• Compare and order decimals through thousandths. *(Chapter 1)*

LESSON 12.3 RESOURCES

MANIPULATIVE WARM-UP

Cooperative Pairs — **Visual/Spatial**

OBJECTIVE Explore writing decimals with nonstandard units of measure.

Materials per pair: 10 paper clips

▶ Have pairs of students attach their paper clips. Tell them that 1 clip ruler = 10 paper clips or 1 paper clip = 0.1 clip ruler.

▶ Have them measure different objects on their desks using the clip ruler. They record the result as a decimal of the clip ruler. For example, a pencil might measure 0.8 clip ruler.

▶ Encourage students to measure objects that are greater than 1 clip ruler. Discuss how these objects were measured.

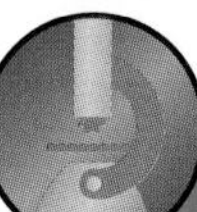

SCIENCE CONNECTION

Cooperative Pairs — **Logical/Analytical**

OBJECTIVE Connect decimals to telling stories.

▶ Write the table below on the chalkboard:

Normal Monthly Precipitation for Dallas-Fort Worth, Texas					
January	February	March	April	May	June
1.7 in.	1.9 in	2.4 in.	3.6 in.	4.3	2.6
July	August	September	October	November	December
2.0 in.	1.8 in	3.3 in.	2.5 in.	1.8 in.	1.7 in.

▶ Discuss the table. Explain that precipitation means rain or snow, and that the figures in the table were calculated by analyzing data reported for the 30-year period from 1951–1980.

▶ Have students create, exchange, and solve problems which require them to compare precipitation data for two or more months. For example:

- **Which month has greater normal precipitation, November or December?** *[November]*
- **Which month has the greatest normal precipitation? the least?** *[May; January and December]*

Daily Review

PREVIOUS DAY QUICK REVIEW

Write a decimal.

1. $5\frac{4}{10}$ *[5.4]*
2. $2\frac{35}{100}$ *[2.35]*
3. $86\frac{1}{10}$ *[86.1]*
4. $14\frac{7}{100}$ *[14.07]*

FAST FACTS

1. 18 ÷ 2 *[9]*
2. 24 ÷ 4 *[6]*
3. 28 ÷ 7 *[4]*
4. 42 ÷ 6 *[7]*

Problem of the Day • 111

Clarissa, Emma, and Beth each took a time test. Their times, in minutes, were: Clarissa—2.01, Emma—1.02, and Beth—1.20. Who had the fastest time? *[Emma]*

TECH LINK

MATH VAN

Tool You may wish to use the Calculator for the More to Explore and the Place-Value Model tool with this lesson.

MATH FORUM

Management Tip I keep copies of blank number lines in a math corner for students to use when comparing and ordering decimals. The number lines often help the students visualize the correct order.

Visit our Resource Village at http://www.mhschool.com to see more of the Math Forum.

MATH CENTER

Practice

OBJECTIVE Compare and order decimals.

Materials per group: 0–9 spinner (TA 4), per student: Math Center Recording Sheet (TA 31 optional)

Students use numbers from a spinner to create decimals. They combine results of group members to make a master list of decimals from least to greatest. *[Students check each other's work.]*

PRACTICE ACTIVITY 111 — MATH CENTER, Small Group

Number Sense • Master List

YOU NEED: spinner (0–9)

- Each player spins three times for three different digits. (If you repeat or spin zero, spin again.)
- Use the three digits to make a decimal with ones, tenths, and hundredths. Switch the numbers around to write two more decimals. List the three decimals in any order on a sheet that has your name at the top.
- Group members switch all lists with each other so that each person can copy all the numbers. Each group member tries to assemble a master list of all the decimal numbers in order from least to greatest.
- Check each other's lists when you are done.

Master List

Grade Level 4 — McGraw-Hill School Division

Chapter 12, Lesson 3, pages 456–457 — Decimals

NCTM Standards
- Problem Solving
- ✓ Communication
- ✓ Reasoning
- Connections

Problem Solving

OBJECTIVE Solve a logical reasoning problem.

Materials per student: 3 index cards, 3 slips of paper, Math Center Recording Sheet (TA 31 optional)

Students move decimals to another card, one at a time without placing a greater number over a lesser. *[The quickest solution takes 7 moves. Move the least amount to C, the middle amount to B, the least amount to the top of the middle amount on B, the greatest amount to C, the least amount to A, the middle amount on top of the greatest amount on C, the least amount on top of the middle amount on C.]*

PROBLEM-SOLVING ACTIVITY 111 — MATH CENTER, On Your Own

Logical Reasoning • Decimal Stacks

YOU NEED: 3 index cards; 3 slips of paper

- Write one letter—*A, B,* or *C*—on each card. Place the cards in order side-by-side.
- Write three decimal amounts greater than 1, each on a separate slip of paper. Stack the three slips on top of card *A* in order, the greatest number on the bottom and the least on the top.
- Your task is to move the slips to card *C*. You can move only one slip at a time. You may go from *A* to *C* (or *C* to *A*) in one move. You cannot place a greater number on top of a smaller number. You may place slips on card *B*.
- There are many solutions. Which way is the quickest?

2.53 1.75 1.22 A B C

Grade Level 4 — McGraw-Hill School Division

Chapter 12, Lesson 3, pages 456–457 — Decimals

NCTM Standards
- ✓ Problem Solving
- Communication
- ✓ Reasoning
- Connections

Compare and Order Decimals

OBJECTIVE Compare and order decimals.

1 Introduce

Present the following problem:

Jason has $1.86, Cameron has $2.14, and Jamal has $1.83. Who has the greatest amount of money? the least?

Have students solve the problem. *[Cameron; Jamal]* Then discuss how to order the amounts from least to greatest. *[$1.83, $1.86, $2.14]*

2 Investigate *Whole Class*

▶ **LEARN** Explain that seismology is the study of earthquakes which are caused by movements of the plates that make up the earth's crust. A worldwide network measures earthquakes.

Have students discuss and describe what happens during an earthquake. Then read the introductory problem.

- **How could you use the number line to compare 8.35 and 8.85?** *[Possible answer: You can approximate the locations of each number; 8.35 < 8.85.]*

Discuss the steps for ordering decimals without a number line.

- **In Step 2, why don't you include 7.27? Why don't you compare the tenths?** *[From Step 1, you know 7.27 is the greatest number; the tenths are the same.]*

3 Close

▶ **Check for Understanding** using items 1–4, page 456.

CRITICAL THINKING
For item 4, have students give examples that support and that disprove the statement.

▶ **PRACTICE**
Materials have available: calculators

Options for assigning exercises:
A—Odd ex. 1–13; all ex. 15–17; **More to Explore**
B—Even ex. 2–14; all ex. 15–17; **More to Explore**

- In ex. 15–17, students interpret data from a table to solve problems.

More to Explore Work through the example with students. Have students work individually to complete the exercises.

Compare and Order Decimals

LEARN

The San Francisco earthquake in 1994 had a Richter-scale rating of 6.8. Ratings give us information about the strengths of earthquakes.

Compare and order the ratings of these big earthquakes.

Richter-Scale Ratings	
Portugal in 1775	8.6
California in 1906	8.3
China in 1920	8.5

You can use a number line to compare and order decimal

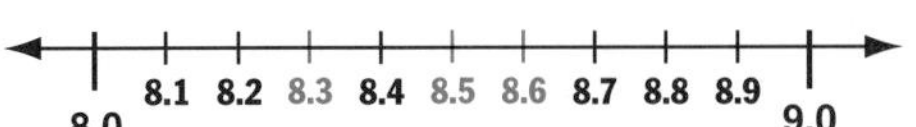

8.6 > 8.5, and 8.5 > 8.3

From greatest to least: 8.6, 8.5, 8
From least to greatest: 8.3, 8.5, 8

You can also compare and order decimals without a number line.

Compare and order 6.29, 7.27, and 6.25.

Step 1	Step 2	Step 3
Line up the decimal points.	**Compare the other two decimals.**	**Order the decimals.**
6.29 7.27 6.25	6.29 6.25	From greatest to least 7.27, 6.29, 6.25
Think: 7 > 6, so 7.27 is the greatest decimal.	**Think:** 0.2 = 0.2 Compare hundredths. 0.09 > 0.05, so 6.29 > 6.25.	From least to greatest 6.25, 6.29, 7.27

CHECK

Check for Understanding

Model each decimal. Then write in order from greatest to least.

1. 17.9, 18.6, 18.8 **18.8, 18.6, 17.9**
2. 4.64, 4.74, 4.7 **4.74, 4.7, 4.64**
3. $2.36, $2.28, $2. **$2.39, $2.36, $2.2**

Critical Thinking: Analyze **Explain your reasoning.**

4. If you compare two decimals, will the greater number always have more digits?

No; possible answer: a decimal like 1.2 has fewer digits than 1.09, but it is greater when the value of each place is compared.

Meeting Individual Needs

Early Finishers

Have students rewrite the table from page 457 so that it shows other major earthquakes that occurred between 1985 and the present.

Extra Support

For students who make the common error of incorrectly comparing digits in decimals, supply number lines. Helping them label the number lines may provide them with the confidence to order and compare decimals.

Ongoing Assessment

Observation Checklist Determine if students understand how to compare and order decimals by observing as they compare 2.01 and 2.1. Then name a decimal between them. *[2.01 < 2.1; Possible answer: 2.02]*

Follow Up Some students may have difficulty comparing decimals with only tenths to decimals with hundredths. Have them use place-value charts. Assign **Reteach 111.**

For students who are adept at comparing and ordering decimals, assign **Extend 111.**

ractice

mpare. Write >, <, or =.

0.5 ● 0.50 = **2** 3.2 ● 3.5 < **3** 0.67 ● 0.68 < **4** 3.9 ● 3.90 =

7.3 ● 7.37 < **6** $9.63 ● $9.36 > **7** 2.04 ● 2.4 < **8** 54.18 ● 45.81 >

ite in order from greatest to least.

0.43, 0.34, 0.40 **0.43, 0.40, 0.34** | **10** 0.77, 0.70, 0.07 **0.77, 0.70, 0.07** | **11** 13.8, 13.3, 18.3 **18.3, 13.8, 13.3**

ite in order from least to greatest.

3.61, 3.09, 3.9 **3.09, 3.61, 3.9** | **13** 0.9, 0.93, 0.85 **0.85, 0.9, 0.93** | **14** 5.53, 15.05, 5.3 **5.3, 5.53, 15.05**

PRACTICE

IXED APPLICATIONS

'roblem Solving

Pencil & Paper | Calculator | Mental Math

e the table for problems 15–17.

Which earthquake had a rating of six and nine tenths? **Armenia**

Which earthquake was weaker than Flores Island, Indonesia, but stronger than California, United States? **Kobe, Japan**

Write the locations of the three strongest earthquakes in order from greatest to least. **Mexico City, Mexico; Cabanatuan, Philippines; Flores Island, Indonesia**

Richter-Scale Ratings	
Kobe, Japan, in 1995	7.2
California, United States, in 1994	7.0
Flores Island, Indonesia, in 1992	7.5
Cabanatuan, Philippines, in 1990	7.5
Armenia in 1988	6.9
Mexico City, Mexico, in 1985	8.1

more to explore

'actions on a Calculator

e way to compare fractions is to rename them as decimals. vide the numerator by the denominator to find each decimal.

mpare $\frac{3}{10}$ and $\frac{6}{8}$.  $3 \div 10 =$ 0.3 $6 \div 8 =$ 0.75

nce $0.75 > 0.3$, $\frac{6}{8} > \frac{3}{10}$.

ename the fractions as decimals and then compare.

$\frac{6}{10}$ ● $\frac{12}{100}$ **nce 0.6 > 0.12, $> \frac{12}{100}$.**

2 $\frac{80}{100}$ ● $\frac{4}{5}$ **Since 0.8 = 0.8, $\frac{80}{100} = \frac{4}{5}$.**

3 $\frac{9}{12}$ ● $\frac{7}{10}$ **Since 0.75 > 0.7, $\frac{9}{12} > \frac{7}{10}$.**

4 $\frac{1}{4}$ ● $\frac{3}{10}$ **Since 0.25 < 0.3, $\frac{1}{4} < \frac{3}{10}$.**

tra Practice, page 528

Alternate Teaching Strategy

Materials per pair: decimal squares (TA 30)

Present the following problem:

Casey has two different running routes. She used her car to find the distance she runs on each route. Route A is 3.4 miles and route B is 3.7 miles. Which route is longer?

Have students work with a partner to show each number using the 10-by-10 decimal squares, as many as needed. Then have them compare the models to solve the problem. *[Route B]*

Repeat the activity for different distances. Include some distances with hundredths, such as comparing 2.46 and 2.6 or 1.09 and 1.23. *[2.46 < 2.6; 1.09 < 1.23]*

ESL APPROPRIATE

PRACTICE • 111

HOMEWORK

Practice 111

Name:

Compare and Order Decimals

Compare. Write >, <, or =.

1. 0.1 (>) 0.01 2. 9.09 (>) 0.90 3. 0.15 (<) 0.51 4. 6.2 (=) 6.20
5. 5.02 (<) 5.20 6. 0.93 (>) 0.39 7. 3.03 (<) 3.30 8. 7.64 (>) 7.46
9. 2.22 (>) 2.21 10. 1.11 (<) 11.11 11. 1.1 (=) 1.10 12. $1.01 (<) $1.10
13. $7.44 (>) $4.77 14. 1.00 (>) 0.11 15. 4.55 (<) 5.45 16. 16.11 (<) 61.11
17. 3.33 (>) 3.13 18. 4.04 (<) 4.14 19. 7.08 (<) 7.8 20. 8.07 (=) 8.07
21. 29.5 (>) 29.35 22. 0.38 (>) 0.33 23. 14.4 (>) 14.04 24. 5.12 (>) 2.15

Write in order from least to greatest.

25. 1.7, 1.0, 0.9 — 0.9, 1.0, 1.7
26. 0.7, 0.3, 1.3 — 0.3, 0.7, 1.3
27. 3.52, 3.25, 3.11 — 3.11, 3.25, 3.52
28. 5.07, 4.07, 6.07 — 4.07, 5.07, 6.07
29. 8.4, 8.04, 8.14 — 8.04, 8.14, 8.40
30. 2.60, 12.60, 2.66 — 2.60, 2.66, 12.60
31. 8.14, 9.62, 7.20 — 7.20, 8.14, 9.62
32. 2.19, 2.91, 2.09 — 2.09, 2.19, 2.91
33. 2.01, 2.00, 2.10 — 2.00, 2.01, 2.10
34. 1.04, 1.44, 1.24 — 1.04, 1.24, 1.44
35. 0.77, 0.07, 0.71 — 0.07, 0.71, 0.77
36. 0.99, 0.09, 0.90 — 0.09, 0.90, 0.99

Solve.

37. An oak tree is 9.2 meters tall. An elm tree is 9.6 meters tall. A maple tree is 9.4 meters tall. Which tree is the tallest? the elm tree

38. The maple tree grew 1.05 meters last year and 1.5 meters the year before. In which year did the tree grow more? the year before

McGraw-Hill School Division

RETEACH • 111

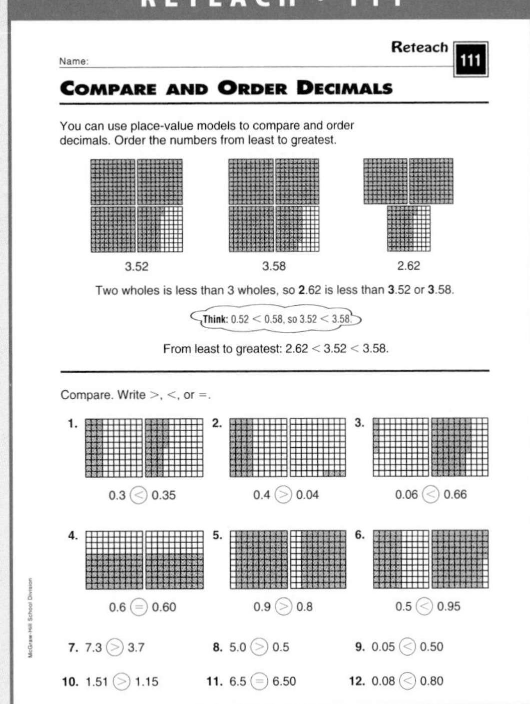

Reteach 111

Name:

Compare and Order Decimals

You can use place-value models to compare and order decimals. Order the numbers from least to greatest.

3.52 3.58 2.62

Two wholes is less than 3 wholes, so **2**.62 is less than **3**.52 or **3**.58.

Think: 0.52 < 0.58, so 3.52 < 3.58.

From least to greatest: 2.62 < 3.52 < 3.58.

Compare. Write >, <, or =.

1. 0.3 (<) 0.35 2. 0.4 (>) 0.04 3. 0.06 (<) 0.66
4. 0.6 (=) 0.60 5. 0.9 (>) 0.8 6. 0.5 (<) 0.95
7. 7.3 (>) 3.7 8. 5.0 (>) 0.5 9. 0.05 (<) 0.50
10. 1.51 (>) 1.15 11. 6.5 (=) 6.50 12. 0.08 (<) 0.80

McGraw-Hill School Division

EXTEND • 111

Extend 111

Name:

Compare and Order Decimals

Languages Spoken at Home

The list below shows the 18 most spoken languages (after English) in the United States, in millions. The languages are arranged in alphabetical order. Arrange the languages in order from greatest to lowest number of speakers in the table below.

LANGUAGES IN THE U.S.			
Language	Millions of Speakers	Language	Millions of Speakers
Arabic	0.36	Persian	0.20
Chinese	1.25	Polish	0.72
French	1.70	Portuguese	0.43
German	1.55	Russian	0.24
Greek	0.39	Spanish	17.34
Hindi & Urdu	0.33	Tagalog	0.84
Italian	1.31	Thai	0.21
Japanese	0.43	Vietnamese	0.51
Korean	0.63	Yiddish	0.21

LANGUAGES IN THE U.S.			
Language	Millions of Speakers	Language	Millions of Speakers
1. Spanish	17.34	10. Portuguese	0.43
2. French	1.70	11. Japanese	0.43
3. German	1.55	12. Greek	0.39
4. Italian	1.31	13. Arabic	0.36
5. Chinese	1.25	14. Hindi & Urdu	0.33
6. Tagalog	0.84	15. Russian	0.24
7. Polish	0.72	16. Yiddish	0.21
8. Korean	0.63	17. Thai	0.21
9. Vietnamese	0.51	18. Persian	0.20

McGraw-Hill School Division

PURPOSE Maintain and review concepts, skills, and strategies that students have learned thus far in the chapter.

Materials per student: calculator (optional)

Using the Midchapter Review

Have students complete the **Midchapter Review** independently or use it with the whole class.

For ex. 1–9, students should be able to identify the decimals from several different equivalent forms.

Students can approach this open-ended problem at their own levels. They should include comparing the digits from left to right in their explanation of ordering the decimals.

Vocabulary Review

Write the following words on the chalkboard:

decimal **mixed number**
decimal point

Ask for volunteers to explain the meanings of these words and to give examples.

Write a decimal.

1 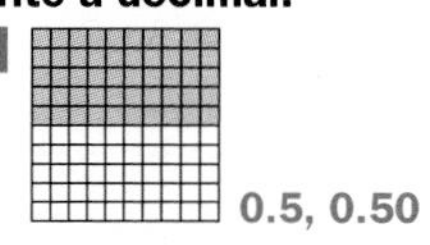 0.5, 0.50

2 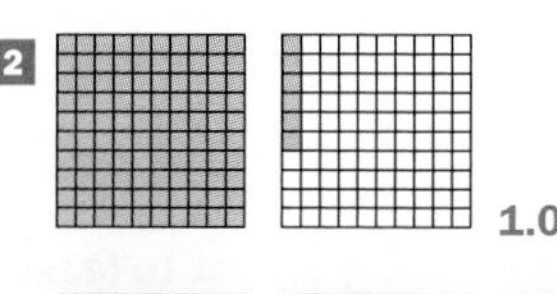 1.06

3 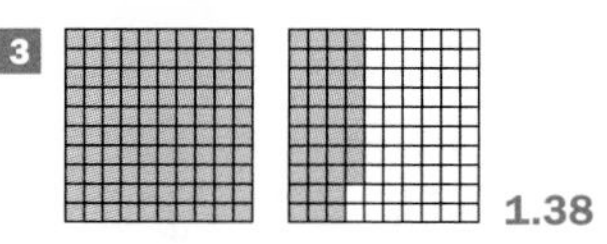 1.38

4 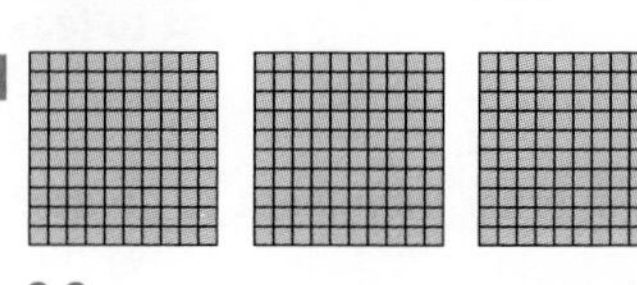 2.9

5 $\frac{46}{100}$ 0.46

6 $2\frac{7}{10}$ 2.7

7 $14\frac{93}{100}$ 14.93

8 four tenths 0.4

9 six and ninety-three hundredths 6.93

Write the word name.

10 0.83 eighty-three hundredths

11 2.6 two and six tenths

12 5.72 five and seventy-two hundredths

13 9.04 nine and fo[ur] hundredths

Compare. Write >, <, or =.

14 4.52 ● 4.25 >

15 3.08 ● 3.80 <

16 5.70 ● 5.7 =

17 2.23 ● 2.32 <

18 14.26 ● 4.62 >

19 9.2 ● 9.02 >

Write in order from greatest to least.

20 0.86, 0.83, 0.94 0.94, 0.86, 0.83

21 1.39, 1.93, 1.43 1.93, 1.43, 1.39

22 2.46, 2.44, 2.4 2.46, 2.44, 2.4

Solve.

23 Suppose your family phone bill shows that your brother's most expensive call cost $15.73. Your sister's most expensive call cost $14.92. Whose most expensive call cost more? your brother's

24 Six schools compare the average number of snow days they take each year: 3.3, 3.2, 3.5, 3.3, 3.6, and 3.4 days. List the averages from least to greatest. 3.2, 3.3, 3.3, 3.4, 3.5, 3.6

25 Write three different decimals using the digits 5, 0, and 8. Explain how you would order the decimals you wrote. Possible answer: 0.850, 0.805, 0.508; use place value to order from least to greatest: 0.508, 0.805, 0.850

Reinforcement and Remediation

CHAPTER OBJECTIVES	MIDCHAPTER REVIEW ITEMS	STUDENT BOOK PAGES	TEACHER'S EDITION PAGES		TEACHER RESOURCES
			Activities	Alternate Teaching Strategy	Reteach
*12A	1–13	450–453, 454–455	449A, 453A	453, 455	109–110
*12B	14–22, 25	456–457	455A	457	111
*12E	23–25	450–453, 454–455, 456–457			

*12A Read and write decimals to hundredths
*12B Compare and order decimals
*12E Solve problems, including those that involve decimals and solving a simpler problem

developing algebra sense

MATH CONNECTION

Graph a Function

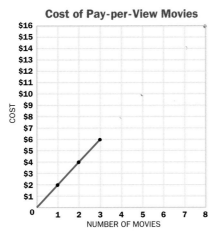

ave you watched cable TV? If so, ɒu probably know that your family ɑn order "Pay-per-View" movies.

ɑppose each movie costs $2. How uch would it cost a family to order movies? 5 movies?

.GEBRA You can multiply. You can also ɜe a function table and a graph to ,ee" what the function looks like.

Rule: Multiply by 2. Cost of Pay-per-View Movies)	
Input (Number of Movies)	Output (Cost)
1	$2
2	$4
3	$6
4	■ $8
5	■ $10

Cost of Pay-per-View Movies

raph the ordered pairs from the nction table. Then draw a line rough and beyond the points. se the line to find 1×2, 2×2, $\times 2$, 4×2, and 5×2.

ɔur movies cost $8, and 5 movies cost $10.

hat if the cost of each movie increases to $3. Make a nction table and graph to show what the function oks like.

How does your graph compare to the graph above? **The line is steeper.**

Predict what the graph of movies that each cost $1 would look like. Explain your reasoning. **Possible answer: The line would be less steep than the graph for movies that cost $2 each since the lower the cost, the less steep the line.**

OBJECTIVE Create function tables and graph the data.

Using Algebra Sense

Math Connection Students have used patterns to solve problems. Here students explore graphing functions by continuing a pattern and then using the coordinates from a function to graph the data.

Algebra After students read the opening problem, discuss how to complete the function table. Then explain that the coordinates of the ordered pairs are input and output where *input* = the horizontal coordinate and *output* = the vertical coordinate.

Review how to graph ordered pairs. After examining the graph with students, ask:

- **By how much does the cost increase for each increase in the number of movies?** *[As the number of movies increases by 1, the cost increases by $2.]*
- **How does the graph show this relationship?** *[As you move 1 unit right, you move 2 units up.]*
- **What will the next coordinate be on the graph?** *[(6, 12)]*
- **How can you find other coordinates on the graph?** *[Extend the line.]*

To summarize, have students describe what the graph of the function looks like. *[a straight line]*

Students may work in pairs or on their own to answer the questions at the bottom of the page. Students should realize that the greater the cost of each movie, the steeper the line of the graph that shows the function.

Applying Decimals

OBJECTIVE Add, subtract, and divide decimals while creating a newsletter.

Materials per group: paper; glue; scissors; centimeter ruler (TA 18); samples of newsletters.

1 Engage

Make sure that students understand what a newsletter is. Have them describe newsletters they may be familiar with.

- **What type of news was reported in the newsletters?** *[Possible answers: school news, sports games and/or scores, environmental news]*

Then show students some sample newsletters. Discuss a few topics that are covered. Then encourage students to suggest topics they think would be interesting in a newsletter.

2 Investigate *Cooperative Groups*

Discuss the kinds of content that can be included in a newsletter, such as articles, drawings, and cartoons.

- **What would a news article include?** *[factual information about recent events]* **an editorial?** *[opinions about recent events]* **a column?** *[information and opinions about specific topics]*

Creating a Newsletter Using the Jigsaw (with expert groupings) Strategy, have students form groups of four, with each member accountable for a different part of the newsletter (editor, art director, and so on). Individuals join with other students in the class who have the same part in the newsletter as they do. These "Expert Groups" discuss their parts, and plan how to share this information with other members of their original group. Original groups reconvene to integrate all of their parts in order to form the whole newsletter.

Review the newsletter layout in the Student Book. Remind students to keep the articles informative, interesting, and brief.

3 Reflect and Share

Materials have available: calculators

Reporting Your Findings Discuss what makes a newsletter interesting, fun, and easy to read. Tell students that readers generally move their eyes across a page from upper left to lower right. Then have students compare newsletters and layouts while using this new information. Also discuss measurement.

Write an Essay Review the purpose of newsletters before students begin writing. Remind students to support their essay theme with at least two reasons.

Revise your work Students can use calculators to check that the total length in centimeters of all text and art is not greater than the total length for all columns.

real-life investigation

APPLYING DECIMALS

Newsletter Layouts

A monthly newsletter is a great way to let people know about your classroom. Stories can cover what has happened as well as upcoming events. It is fun to put in cartoons, photos, and puzzles about your classmates.

You will need
- *paper*
- *glue*
- *scissors*
- *centimeter ruler*

You can plan the space needed for the columns, photos, and drawings by making a layout.

A layout shows:
- the length and width of the entire page.
- the length and width of each column, photo, or drawing on the page, and the spaces between them.
- the top, bottom, left, and right margins.

The Grand Canyon
Our trip to the Grand Canyon was terrific! We rode on the burros down the side of the canyon. Some of us were
0 1 2 3 4 5 6
centimeters

This column is 4.2 cm wide.

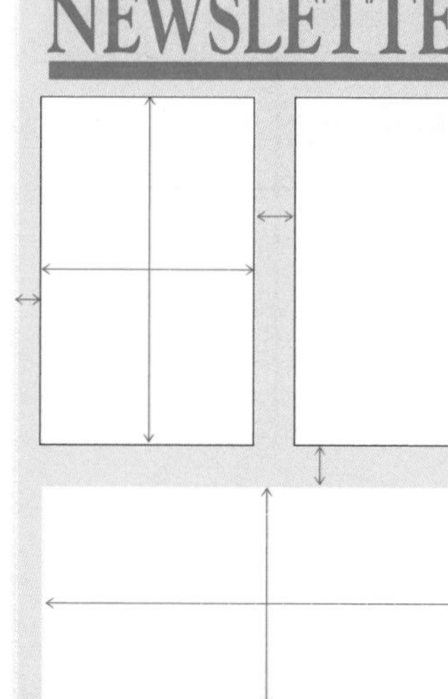

You need to think about:
- the title for the newsletter.
- what stories and other features you want in your paper.
- what size they can be so that everything fits on the page.

More To Investigate

Predict Possible answers: to report club news, sports news, or neighborhood events.

Explore Possible answer: length: $18\frac{3}{4}$ in. or 47 mm; width: $2\frac{1}{2}$ in. or 6.5 mm

Find Possible answer: Most likely, the layout was done on a computer with very little cutting and pasting by hand.

Bibliography Students who wish to learn more about newspapers and newsletters can read:

The Furry News: How to Make a Newspaper, by Loreen Leed. New York: Holiday House, Inc., 1990. ISBN 0–8234–0793–4.

How Newspapers Are Made, by Sarah Waters. New York: Facts on File, 1989. ISBN 0–8160–2042–6.

How to Do Leaflets, Newsletters, and Newspapers, 2nd edition, by Nancy Brigham et al. Detroit, MI: PEP Publishers, 1991. ISBN 0–9629067–6–X.

Make Your Own Newspaper, by Chris Harris and Ray Harris. Holbrook, MA: Adams Publishing, 1993. ISBN 1–55850–219–X.

Answers may vary. Check students' work.

See Teacher's Edition for sample of student work.

DECISION MAKING

Creating a Newsletter

1 Work with a group. Choose a page size for your newsletter. Measure its length and width to the nearest tenth of a centimeter. Then agree on the measurement of the columns, the space between the columns, and the margins.

2 Agree on the part of the newsletter each of you will contribute. Type or print your news items to fit the columns.

3 Measure and mark boxes on the page for any photos, drawings, or other items, such as a puzzle or cartoon.

4 When you have all your text and pictures, cut them out and paste them into your layout.

Reporting Your Findings

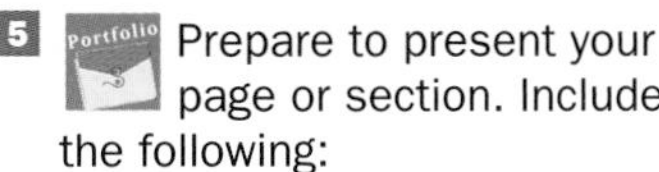

5 Prepare to present your page or section. Include the following:

- How you gathered your information and came up with your ideas.
- What measurements you used to do your layouts.
- Give a brief description of how you made all the items on the page fit together and why you put them in certain places on the page.

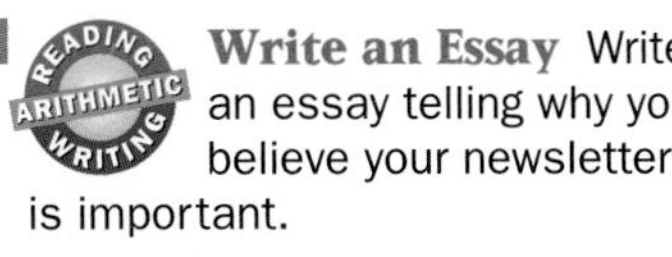

6 **Write an Essay** Write an essay telling why you believe your newsletter is important.

Revise your work.

- Are your measurements correct?
- Is your newsletter clear and organized? Is it easy to read?
- Did you proofread your work?

MORE TO INVESTIGATE

See Teacher's Edition.

PREDICT some different uses for newsletters.

EXPLORE the lengths and widths of columns in your local newspaper.

FIND how your local newspaper lays out its pages.

Building A Portfolio

This investigation will help you to evaluate a student's ability to organize data, take and use measurements, and use decimals to solve a problem.

Allow students to revise their work for the portfolio. Each student's portfolio piece should consist of a copy of his or her findings, which includes a copy of the newsletter page or section and a statement of how and why the information was gathered. It should also include a description of how the measurements were made and how the newsletter was put together using a layout.

You may wish to use the Holistic Scoring Guide to assess this task. See page 27 in Teacher's Assessment Resources.

Students' Work

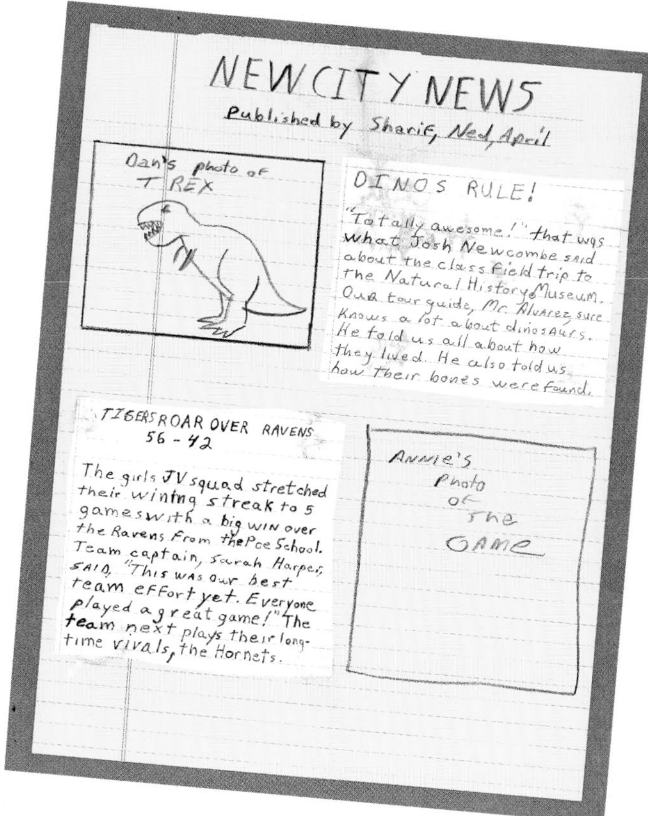

NEW CITY NEWS

Published by Sharif, Ned, April

Dan's photo of T REX

DINOS RULE!

"Totally awesome!" that was what Josh Newcombe said about the class field trip to the Natural History Museum. Our tour guide, Mr. Alvarez, sure knows a lot about dinosaurs. He told us all about how they lived. He also told us how their bones were found.

TIGERS ROAR OVER RAVENS 56 - 42

The girls JV squad stretched their wintng streak to 5 games with a big win over the Ravens from the Poe School. Team captain, Sarah Harper, said, "This was our best team effort yet. Everyone played a great game!" The team next plays their long-time rivals, the Hornets.

Annie's Photo of the Game

Lesson 12.4

Problem-Solving Strategy: Solve a Simpler Problem

OBJECTIVE Solve problems by solving a simpler problem.

RESOURCE REMINDER
Math Center Cards 112
Practice 112, Reteach 112, Extend 112

SKILLS TRACE

GRADE 3	• Solve problems by solving a simpler/similar problem. *(Chapter 12)*
GRADE 4	• Solve problems by solving a simpler/similar problem.
GRADE 5	• Solve problems by solving a simpler/similar problem. *(Chapter 11)*

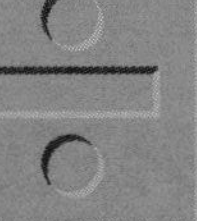

MANIPULATIVE WARM-UP

Cooperative Pairs — Logical/Analytical

OBJECTIVE Review solving multistep problems.

Materials per pair: 1–6 number cube; calculator (optional)

▶ Copy the following table onto the chalkboard:

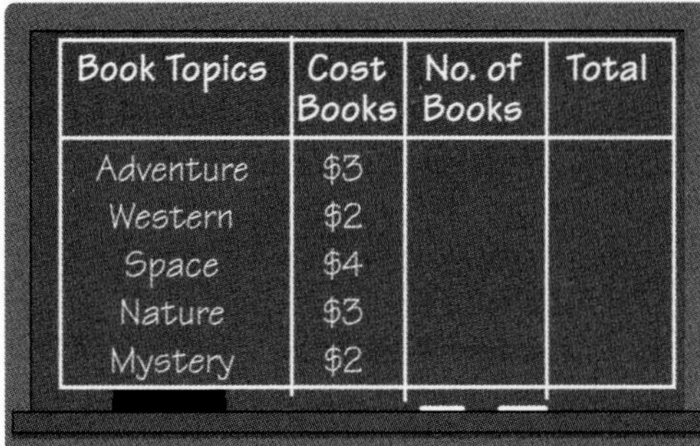

Book Topics	Cost Books	No. of Books	Total
Adventure	$3		
Western	$2		
Space	$4		
Nature	$3		
Mystery	$2		

▶ Students work with a partner. They toss the number cube to determine how many of each type of book they will order for a book fair. The first toss is for adventure books and so on.

▶ Have them find the total cost of all the books they order for the book fair, using a calculator if desired.

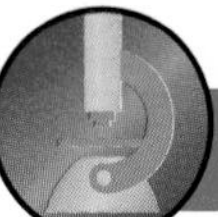

SCIENCE CONNECTION

Cooperative Pairs — Visual/Spatial

OBJECTIVE Connect measurement conversions to science.

Materials per pair: calculator (optional)

▶ Copy the following table onto the chalkboard:

PLANT GROWTH (IN CENTIMETERS)

Week	Fractional Height	Decimal Height
1	$\frac{3}{4}$	*[0.75]*
2	$\frac{4}{5}$	*[0.8]*
3	$1\frac{1}{4}$	*[1.25]*
4	$1\frac{7}{10}$	*[1.7]*
5	$1\frac{4}{5}$	*[1.8]*

▶ Have pairs work together to convert fractions to decimals, using a calculator if desired.

▶ Have students make a bar graph. Ask them to find the week with the greatest growth; with the least growth. *[between weeks 3 and 4 and weeks 2 and 3; between weeks 1 and 2]*

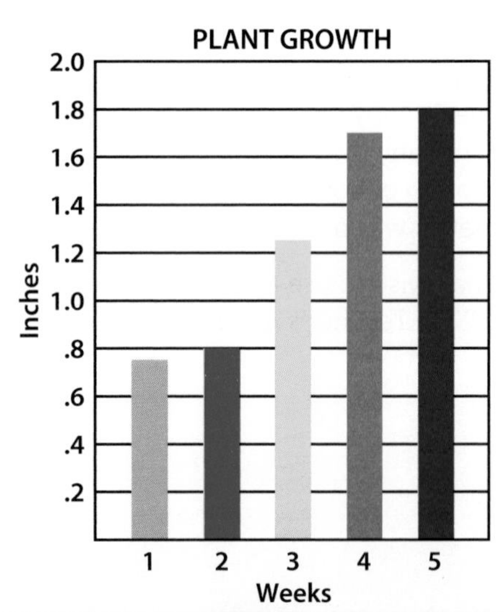

Daily Review

PREVIOUS DAY QUICK REVIEW

Compare. Write >, <, or =.

1. 5.9 □ 9.5 *[<]*
2. 3.26 □ 3.05 *[>]*
3. 2.64 □ 2.6 *[>]*
4. 1.8 □ 1.80 *[=]*

FAST FACTS

1. 21 ÷ 3 *[7]*
2. 36 ÷ 6 *[6]*
3. 56 ÷ 8 *[7]*
4. 72 ÷ 9 *[8]*

Problem of the Day • 112

There are 12 large oranges in one bag and 18 small oranges in another bag. In an order of 15 bags of small oranges and 28 bags of large oranges, how many more large oranges are there? *[66 large oranges]*

TECH LINK

Math Van

MATH VAN

Tool You may wish to use the Drawing tool for the Data Point in this lesson.

MATH FORUM

Management Tip I have my students work in pairs to write simpler problems, with each student providing a sample. They select the simpler problem and use it to solve the original problem.

Visit our Resource Village at http://www.mhschool.com to see more of the Math Forum.

MATH CENTER

Practice

OBJECTIVE Solve problems by using simpler numbers.

Materials per student: number cube, Math Center Recording Sheet (TA 31 optional)

Students use 1-digit numbers to find a way to solve a problem and then solve the same problem using decimal numbers that they generate by rolling a number cube. *[Larry's daily salary is multiplied by 5. Sara's hourly salary is multiplied twice—first by 2 hours, then by 5 days. The two products are added.]*

PRACTICE ACTIVITY 112

MATH CENTER
On Your Own

Formulating Problems • Find a Simpler Way

YOU NEED
- number cube

Larry earns $□.□□ a day delivering papers. His sister Sara earns $□.□□ an hour baby-sitting. She works 2 hours each afternoon. How much do they earn together in 5 days?

- Roll the cubes for two numbers. Copy the problem above. Then use each number to fill in the first box of each set. Use zeros in the rest of the boxes and solve the problem. Write out your solution.
- Then roll for new numbers to fill in *all* the boxes. Fill them in any order in a way that makes sense. Then solve the problem. Use the same method you used with simpler numbers.
- Try again, changing the number of hours and days as well as the money amounts.

Grade Level 4 · McGraw-Hill School Division

Chapter 12, Lesson 4, pages 462–463 — Problem Solving

NCTM Standards
- ✓ Problem Solving
- Communication
- ✓ Reasoning
- ✓ Connections

Problem Solving

OBJECTIVE Explore a pattern in numbers.

Materials per pair: 0–9 spinner (TA 1), play money (optional); per student; Math Center Recording Sheet (TA 31 optional)

Partners spin for three numbers each to write dollar and cents amounts. They determine the amounts that will give the greatest and least amount of tax at the rate of 1 penny tax per $0.10 of the amount. *[To determine the greatest tax, students must form the greatest possible cost from the three numbers, and the least cost will result in the least tax.]*

PROBLEM-SOLVING ACTIVITY 112

MATH CENTER
Partners

Patterning • Taxable Items

YOU NEED
- spinner (0–9)
- play money (optional)

In a certain town, there is a 1-cent sales tax on every $0.10 an item costs. If an item costs $0.20, the tax is 2 cents. If an item costs $0.50, the tax is 5 cents. If an item costs $1.00 the tax is 10 cents.

- Spin for three numbers. Each player uses the numbers in any order to make a 3-digit dollar amount under $10.00. This is the cost of an item. Write several costs for both sets of three numbers. What is the most sales tax you would pay on an item? the least?
- Play again with another set of three numbers. You might also raise the tax to 2 cents (or even 3 cents) on every $0.10.

Tax–1 penny on the dime

Grade Level 4 · McGraw-Hill School Division

Chapter 12, Lesson 4, pages 462-463 — Problem Solving

NCTM Standards
- ✓ Problem Solving
- Communication
- ✓ Reasoning
- ✓ Connections

Problem-Solving Strategy: Solve a Simpler Problem

OBJECTIVE Use the strategy, Solve a Simpler Problem, to solve problems.

1 Introduce

Present the following problem:

A large campground has 240 campsites. The campground fee is $7.00. How much money does the campground take in if it is half full?

Discuss the operations needed to solve the problem, without the numbers. *[division; multiplication]* Then have students use the numbers to solve the problem. *[$840]*

2 Teach *Whole Class*

LEARN After reading the problem on page 462, have students use their own words to tell what information is given and what they need to find in order to solve the problem.

As students review the Plan step, discuss why solving a similar but simpler problem can make solving the original problem easier. *[Possible answer: You can focus on the operations without being confused by the numbers.]*

Work through the solution with students. Elicit that mental math can be used to solve the simpler problem. After students solve the original problem, ask:

- **How does using the solution to the simpler problem help you in finding the exact solution?** *[Possible answer: use the solution of the simpler problem as an estimate to check if the exact answer is reasonable]*

3 Close

Check for Understanding using items 1 and 2, page 462.

CRITICAL THINKING
After discussing item 2, have students extend the analysis to a generalization by asking:

- **How can you use the simpler problem strategy to solve any problem?** *[Possible answer: Read the problem with simpler numbers to determine how it can be solved.]*

PRACTICE
Materials have available: calculators (optional)

Assign ex. 1–10 as independent work.

- For ex. 1, students may use the strategy, Solve a Simpler Problem, to solve.
- To solve ex. 2, students will have to select the information needed from the Infobit.
- Students will have to use the problem-solving strategy, Interpret Data, to solve ex. 6–10.

Problem-Solving Strategy — Read · Plan · Solve · Look Back

Solve a Simpler Problem

LEARN

Read **Suppose that you and your brother work at a local newspaper. You earn $6.40 an hour, and your brother earns $12.15 an hour. You both work an 8-hour day. How much do both of you earn each day altogether?**

Plan You can sometimes see how to solve a problem by first solving a simpler problem.

Solve Try using smaller or easier numbers instead of the numbers in the original problem.

A earns $5 an hour. B earns $10 an hour.

Now try the simpler problem.

A: $8 \times \$5 = \$40$ B: $8 \times \$10 = \$80$
Total Pay: $\$40 + \$80 = \$120$

Now solve the original problem the same way.

A: $8 \times \$6.40 = \$51.20$ B: $8 \times \$12.15 = \$97.20$
Total Pay: $\$51.20 + \$97.20 = \$148.40$

You both earn $148.40 each day altogether.

Look Back How could you solve the problem another way? **Possible answer: Add the two hourly amounts first and multiply that total by 8 h.**

CHECK

Check for Understanding

1. **What if** your sister starts to work at the paper. She earns $15.80 an hour. How much will the three of you earn each day? **$274.80**

Critical Thinking: Analyze **Accept any reasonable simpler problem. Possible answer: Multiply 8 × $15.80 and add that amount to the $148.40.**

2. Explain how you could use a simpler problem to solve problem 1.

462 Lesson 12.4

Meeting Individual Needs

Early Finishers

Have students write a problem that can be solved by solving a simpler problem. They should write the simpler problem first and extend it to write the more difficult problem. Have them solve and exchange problems.

Extra Support

Some students may have difficulty identifying the simpler problem. Review compatible numbers, in Ch. 8, with students. Help them find numbers they can work with mentally.

Ongoing Assessment

Observation Checklist Determine if students are able to solve problems involving mixed applications and strategies by observing how they organize the information from each problem to find a solution.

Follow Up For students who are having difficulty using the Solve a Simpler Problem strategy, assign **Reteach 112.**

Have students who are ready for a challenge try **Extend 112.**

IXED APPLICATIONS
roblem Solving

You have grown fruit to sell. There are 12 tomatoes for $0.40 each and 15 watermelons for $1.75 each. If you sell all your fruit, how much money will you have? **$31.05**

There are 192 countries in the world. In how many countries is *Peanuts* not published? **SEE INFOBIT. 117 countries**

INFOBIT
The cartoon strip *Peanuts* was first published in October 1950. It currently appears in 2,600 newspapers in 75 countries and in 21 languages.

Marcus scores 12 baskets for his team. Three of the baskets are worth 3 points, while the rest are worth 2 points. How many more 3-point baskets does he need to score 40 points? **five 3-point baskets**

Data Point Use the Databank on page 543. Show the story of the ballpoint pen by making and labeling a time line. **Check students' work.**

5 Helen rolls two 1–6 number cubes to get a factor. She rolls the cubes again to get another factor. What is the greatest product she can get? Explain your reasoning. **4,356; the greatest 2-digit number possible to roll is 66, so 66 × 66 = 4,356.**

e the tax table for problems 6–10.

What is the tax for an item that costs $6.90? **$0.54**

What is the tax for an item that costs $16.24? **$1.27**

What is the tax for an item that costs $54.96? **$4.32**

The price tag on an electronic diary is $28.99. What is the cost of the diary, with tax? **$31.27**

Write a problem using the tax table. Solve it and have others solve it. **Students should compare problems and solutions.**

Tax Table

Amount	Tax	Amount	Tax
6.49–6.57	0.50	9.24–9.32	0.72
6.58–6.66	0.51	9.33–9.41	0.73
6.67–6.75	0.52	9.42–9.50	0.74
6.76–6.84	0.53	9.51–9.59	0.75
6.85–6.93	0.54	9.60–9.68	0.76
6.94–7.01	0.55	9.69–9.77	0.77

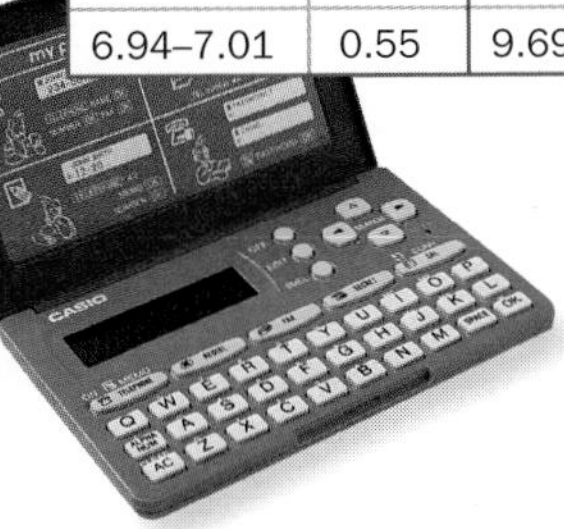

tra Practice, page 529

PRACTICE

Alternate Teaching Strategy

Materials have available: play money

Write the following problem on the chalkboard:

Justin and Henry earned money for their soccer team by washing cars and cleaning windows in their neighborhood. They charged $3.75 for each car and $1.25 for each window. They washed 7 cars and cleaned 8 windows. What was the total amount of money they earned?

Have a volunteer rewrite the second sentence of the problem using simpler numbers to estimate the solution. For example, point out that "about $1" for $1.25 and "about $4" for $3.75 make solving the problem easier. Have students estimate the solution. Then have them follow the same steps to solve the original problem. *[$36; $36.25]*

Repeat the activity by changing the numbers in the problem and having students find how much more money the boys earned washing cars than cleaning windows.

PRACTICE • 112

HOMEWORK

Practice 112

Name:

PROBLEM-SOLVING STRATEGY: SOLVE A SIMPLER PROBLEM

✔ Read ✔ Plan ✔ Solve ✔ Look Back

Solve by the solving-a-simpler-problem strategy. Explain how you could use a simpler problem.

1. Kenny baby-sits for $2\frac{3}{4}$ hours each Monday, Wednesday, and Friday. How many hours a week does he baby-sit?
   $8\frac{1}{4}$ hours; round up to 3 hours, multiply by 3
2. Joy baby-sits from 4:30 P.M. to 5:15 P.M. for 4 days each week. She is paid $3 an hour. How much is she paid in a week?
   $9; round 45 minutes to 1 hour
3. Joy buys 3 coloring books for $0.79 each, and 2 boxes of crayons for $1.19 each. How much does she spend?
   $4.75; round both prices to $1 and then multiply by 3 and 2
4. Joy will buy new boots when she has saved $50 from baby-sitting. So far, she has saved $3.50, $16.25, $7.90, and $12.25. How much more does she need?
   $10.10; round to nearest dollar first

Solve using any method.

5. Joy plans activities for 180 minutes of baby-sitting. She spends equal amounts of time on lunch, watching cartoons, napping, drawing, and playing games. How much time does she spend on each activity?
   36 min
6. Joy and Kenny compare the number of baby-sitting hours in one week. Joy says she baby-sat $4\frac{1}{2}$ hours. Kenny says he baby-sat 4 hours and 30 minutes. Write a number sentence to compare the hours they baby-sat.
   same amount; $4\frac{1}{2} = 4\frac{30}{60}$

McGraw-Hill School Division

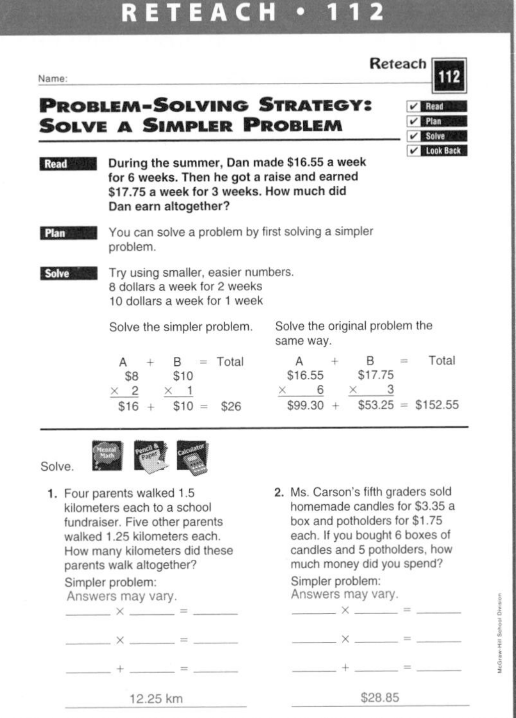

RETEACH • 112

Reteach 112

Name:

PROBLEM-SOLVING STRATEGY: SOLVE A SIMPLER PROBLEM

✔ Read ✔ Plan ✔ Solve ✔ Look Back

Read **During the summer, Dan made $16.55 a week for 6 weeks. Then he got a raise and earned $17.75 a week for 3 weeks. How much did Dan earn altogether?**

Plan You can solve a problem by first solving a simpler problem.

Solve Try using smaller, easier numbers.
8 dollars a week for 2 weeks
10 dollars a week for 1 week

Solve the simpler problem.

A + B = Total
$8 × 2 = $16; $10 × 1 = $10
$16 + $10 = $26

Solve the original problem the same way.

A + B = Total
$16.55 × 6 = $99.30; $17.75 × 3 = $53.25
$99.30 + $53.25 = $152.55

Solve.

1. Four parents walked 1.5 kilometers each to a school fundraiser. Five other parents walked 1.25 kilometers each. How many kilometers did these parents walk altogether?
   Simpler problem: Answers may vary.
   ___ × ___ = ___
   ___ × ___ = ___
   ___ + ___ = ___
   12.25 km
2. Ms. Carson's fifth graders sold homemade candles for $3.35 a box and potholders for $1.75 each. If you bought 6 boxes of candles and 5 potholders, how much money did you spend?
   Simpler problem: Answers may vary.
   ___ × ___ = ___
   ___ × ___ = ___
   ___ + ___ = ___
   $28.85

McGraw-Hill School Division

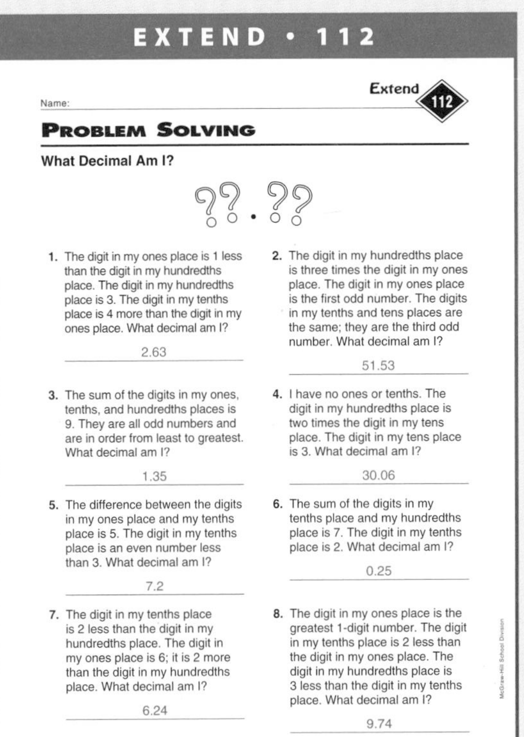

EXTEND • 112

Extend 112

Name:

PROBLEM SOLVING

What Decimal Am I?

??.??

1. The digit in my ones place is 1 less than the digit in my hundredths place. The digit in my hundredths place is 3. The digit in my tenths place is 4 more than the digit in my ones place. What decimal am I?
   2.63
2. The digit in my hundredths place is three times the digit in my ones place. The digit in my ones place is the first odd number. The digits in my tenths and tens places are the same; they are the third odd number. What decimal am I?
   51.53
3. The sum of the digits in my ones, tenths, and hundredths places is 9. They are all odd numbers and are in order from least to greatest. What decimal am I?
   1.35
4. I have no ones or tenths. The digit in my hundredths place is two times the digit in my tens place. The digit in my tens place is 3. What decimal am I?
   30.06
5. The difference between the digits in my ones place and my tenths place is 5. The digit in my tenths place is an even number less than 3. What decimal am I?
   7.2
6. The sum of the digits in my tenths place and my hundredths place is 7. The digit in my tenths place is 2. What decimal am I?
   0.25
7. The digit in my tenths place is 2 less than the digit in my hundredths place. The digit in my ones place is 6; it is 2 more than the digit in my hundredths place. What decimal am I?
   6.24
8. The digit in my ones place is the greatest 1-digit number. The digit in my tenths place is 2 less than the digit in my ones place. The digit in my hundredths place is 3 less than the digit in my tenths place. What decimal am I?
   9.74

McGraw-Hill School Division

MENTAL MATH

Estimate Sums and Differences

OBJECTIVE Estimate sums and differences of decimals by rounding.

RESOURCE REMINDER
Math Center Cards 113
Practice 113, Reteach 113, Extend 113

SKILLS TRACE

GRADE 3	• *Introduced at grade 4.*
GRADE 4	• Estimate decimal sums and differences by rounding.
GRADE 5	• Estimate decimal sums and differences by rounding. *(Chapter 2)*

MANIPULATIVE WARM-UP

Cooperative Pairs — Visual/Spatial

OBJECTIVE Explore writing greatest and least numbers

Materials per pair: 0–9 spinner (TA 21)

▶ One student spins the spinner three times while the other records the numbers.

▶ They work together to write two decimal numbers in the form □.□□. One number should be the greatest number possible and the other the least number possible.

▶ Students alternate roles and the activity three more times. Discuss strategies for forming each number.

8 . 4 1
1 . 4 8

CONSUMER CONNECTION

Cooperative Groups — Logical/Analytical

OBJECTIVE Connect estimating sums and differences of decimals to estimating and comparing costs of purchases.

Materials per group: advertisements showing similar items

▶ Provide each group with two advertisements showing similar items, such as food items, stationery, or school supplies. Most of the items should cost between $1.00 and $9.99.

▶ Give students a spending limit, such as $25. Have them choose items they would like to buy, and use estimation to find a combination of items that they can afford. Group members should check each other's work.

▶ Vary the activity by having students comparison shop. Students can estimate the difference in total cost a group of items would have if bought from one store rather than another.

Daily Review

PREVIOUS DAY QUICK REVIEW

Compare. Write >, <, or =.

1. 4.25 □ 4.31 *[<]*
2. 7.3 □ 7.6 *[<]*
3. 2.99 □ 2.89 *[>]*
4. 5.6 □ 5.49 *[>]*

FAST FACTS

1. 9 × 3 *[27]*
2. 6 × 8 *[48]*
3. 8 × 7 *[56]*
4. 7 × 9 *[63]*

Problem of the Day • 113

Jean buys 2 packs of baseball cards for $2.62 each and 1 bonus pack for $4.29. About how much money does Jean spend? *[$10]*

TECH LINK

MATH FORUM

Idea I use a calculator to demonstrate the exact sums and differences for some of the exercises. This stimulates a discussion on how the estimates compare with the exact answers.

Visit our Resource Village at http://www.mhschool.com to see more of the Math Forum.

MATH CENTER

Practice

OBJECTIVE Determine numbers that result in estimated sums and differences.

Materials per pair: 0–9 spinner (TA 4), two-color counter; per student: Math Center Recording Sheet (TA 31 optional)

Partners generate an estimated sum or difference. They list possible pairs of numbers that will result in that sum or difference. Then they compare lists. *[Students check each other's work.]*

PRACTICE ACTIVITY 113 — MATH CENTER — Partners

Algebra Sense • Esti-"mates"

- One partner spins for a number greater than 0. The other partner flips the counter—red side up means "sum" and yellow side up means "difference."
- The number that is spun is an estimated sum or difference (depending on the counter) of two decimals. Each partner lists pairs of decimals that result in the estimated sum or difference.
- Give yourselves a time limit. Then compare your list with your partner's. Play again to get at least two sums and two differences.

YOU NEED
- spinner (0–9)
- two-color counter

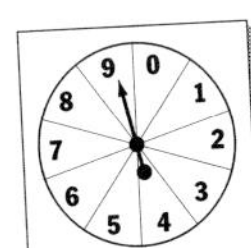

2.76 + 6.35

Grade Level 4 — McGraw-Hill School Division

Chapter 12, Lesson 5, pages 464–465 — Decimals

NCTM Standards
- ✓ Problem Solving
- ✓ Communication
- ✓ Reasoning
- Connections

Problem Solving

OBJECTIVE Estimate decimal sums and differences.

Materials per pair: 24 index cards; per student: Math Center Recording Sheet (TA 31 optional)

Students play a game where they estimate the sum or difference of two numbers. *[Answers may vary. Check students' work.]*

PROBLEM-SOLVING ACTIVITY 113 — MATH CENTER — Partners

Logical Reasoning • Less Is More

- Make 24 cards with the numbers listed below. Place them facedown in a pile.

33.4	4.7	27.8	45.3	22.1	40.6	31.9	10.2
7.5	5.8	46.2	29.3	0.8	0.9	3.2	19.8
9.3	3.6	13.7	47.4	58.3	7.2	35.5	24.3

- Take turns picking two numbers. Estimate either the sum or the difference, keeping in mind which will score more points.
- Use your answer and the table at right to find out how many points you receive.
- Play until there are no more cards left. The person with the greater score wins.

YOU NEED
- 24 index cards (or 3 sheets of paper, each folded in half 3 times and cut to make 8 slips apiece)

Answer: 0–20	Score: 3 points
Answer: 21–40	Score: 2 points
Answer: 41–60	Score: 3 points
Answer: 61–80	Score: 1.5 points
Answer: 81–100	Score: 1 point

Grade Level 4 — McGraw-Hill School Division

Chapter 12, Lesson 5, pages 464–465 — Decimals

NCTM Standards
- ✓ Problem Solving
- ✓ Communication
- ✓ Reasoning
- Connections

MENTAL MATH

Estimate Sums and Differences

OBJECTIVE Estimate sums and differences of decimals by rounding.

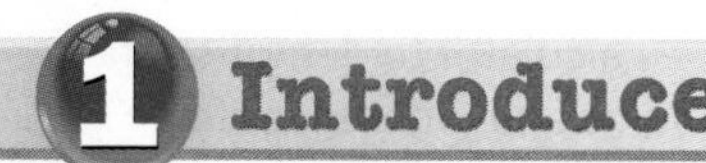

1 Introduce

Materials play money

Show students $2.15 in bills and coins and explain that you saved $2.15 last week. Then show $4.75 in bills and coins and explain that you saved $4.75 this week. Ask:

- **About how much is my total savings?** *[$7]*
- **About how much more did I save this week than last?** *[$3]*

Discuss methods students used to estimate the answers to these questions. *[Possible answers: round money amounts to the nearest dollar, then add or subtract.]*

2 Teach — *Whole Class*

LEARN Have students discuss why it is important to time television news stories. *[Possible answer: so the news program ends on time]* Then work through the introductory problem.

More Examples Have students explain the rounding shown in Examples A and B.

3 Close

Check for Understanding using items 1–4, page 464.

CRITICAL THINKING
In item 4, students are asked to compare estimating decimal sums and differences with money amounts. You may wish to have students compare estimated sums to exact sums. Ask:

- **When will the estimated sum be greater than the exact sum? less?** *[When both addends are overestimated; when both addends are underestimated.]*

PRACTICE

Materials have available: calculators

Options for assigning exercises:
A—Odd ex. 1–15; all ex. 16–17; **Cultural Connection**
B—Even ex. 2–14; all ex. 16–17; **Cultural Connection**

- In ex. 16–17, students interpret data from a table to find solutions.

Cultural Connection An abacus is a tool used to perform calculations. Most early civilizations used forms of the abacus. In medieval England, a table divided into squares represented the abacus.

Review how to use the schoty with students. Then have them work in pairs to complete the exercises.

Estimate Sums and Differences

LEARN

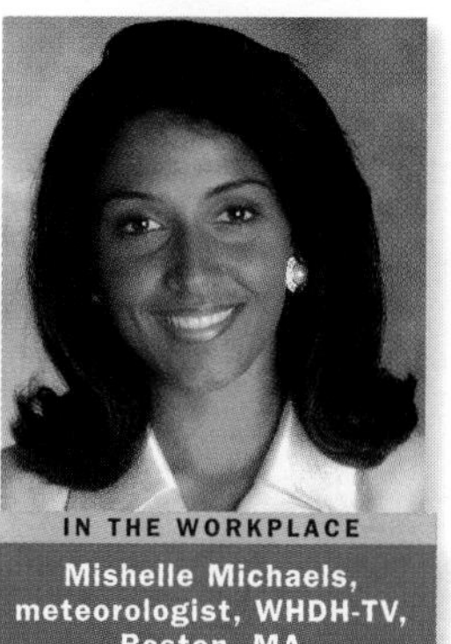

IN THE WORKPLACE
Mishelle Michaels, meteorologist, WHDH-TV, Boston, MA

How do you know what the weather is going to be like? Meteorologists, such as Mishelle Michaels, help you with their forecasts. Suppose Boston got 3.2 inches, 5.7 inches, and 4.6 inches of snow in one week. About how much snow would Mishelle say that Boston got?

You can round decimals to the nearest whole numbers to add or subtract mentally.

Estimate: 3.2 + 5.7 + 4.6

Read each addend. Look at the tenths place. Then estimate the sum.

3.2	+	5.7	+	4.6		
↓		↓		↓		
3	+	6	+	5	=	14
Think: $2 < 5$ Round down.		**Think:** $7 > 5$ Round up.		**Think:** $6 > 5$ Round up.		

She would say about 14 inches of snow fell that week.

More Examples

A Estimate: 2.57 + 8.08

2.57 + 8.08
↓ ↓
3 + 8 = 11

B Estimate: 12.50 − 5.76

12.50 − 5.76
↓ ↓
13 − 6 = 7

CHECK

Check for Understanding

Estimate. Round to the nearest whole number.

1 6.7 + 3.2 **10**
2 1.50 + 6.82 + 8.46 **17**
3 12.65 − 6.09

Critical Thinking: Compare **Explain your reasoning.**

4 How is estimating sums and differences with amounts of money similar to estimating with decimals? How is it different?

Possible answer: Similar—round the digit to the right of the decimal point to find the nearest dollar; different—need to remember to write the dollar sign in the estimate.

Meeting Individual Needs

Early Finishers

Have students use estimation to plan a 30-minute news broadcast. They can create sections of the show, such as news stories, sports, weather, and assign times for each that amounts to an estimated total of about 30 minutes.

Extra Support

Have students who do not round to the nearest whole number, use an index card to cover the digits to the right of the decimal point. Have them move the card to show the tenths digit, the digit they use to round.

Ongoing Assessment

Observation Checklist Determine if students are able to estimate decimal sums and differences by observing how they round and estimate. Make sure that they are rounding to the nearest whole number.

Follow Up Some students may benefit by using a visual tool such as a number line to help them round numbers for estimating sums and differences. Assign **Reteach 113.**

Have students who are adept at estimating decimal sums and differences try **Extend 113.**

ractice

timate. Round to the nearest whole number.

8.1 + 6.3 **14** | **2** 1.9 + 5.2 **7** | **3** 7.52 + 8.73 **17** | **4** 12.03 + 2.61 **15**

5.4 − 3.6 **1** | **6** 10.9 − 2.5 **8** | **7** 6.74 − 1.28 **6** | **8** 17.5 − 5.9 **12**

2.7 + 5.3 + 9.1 **17** | **10** 10.45 + 6.52 + 2.81 **20** | **11** 9.62 + 5.07 + 4.25 **19**

timate. Round to the nearest dollar.

$5.75 − $5.45 **$1** | **13** $8.89 + $3.75 **$13** | **14** $8.79 + $6.11 **$15** | **15** $12.05 − $7.50 **$4**

PRACTICE

IXED APPLICATIONS

roblem Solving

Pencil & Paper | Calculator | Mental Math

e the shot list for problems 16–17.

Round the time for each shot in the TV sports story. About how long is the sports story? **about 29 s**

Suppose there are 29.5 seconds to tell the story. The director decides to open with the sports replay. About how many seconds are left for other shots? **about 18 s**

Video Shot List
Description
Time (in seconds)
Coach talking
9.25
Sports replay
12.36
Player interview
7.52

ultural Connection The Russian Abacus

Russia, many salespeople lculate a customer's bill on a *hoty* (SHOH-tee). The schoty a kind of abacus. It can be ed to show decimal mbers.

millions
hundred-thousands
ten-thousands
thousands
hundreds
tens
ones
decimal point
tenths
hundredths
fractions

Russia

is schoty shows the number .05. Explain how you think e positions of the beads ow this number.
e page T17.

aw a picture of a schoty to show the decimal. See page T17.

8.14 | **2** 5.37 | **3** 21.03 | **4** 58.75

tra Practice, page 529

Alternate Teaching Strategy

Copy the following number line on the chalkboard:

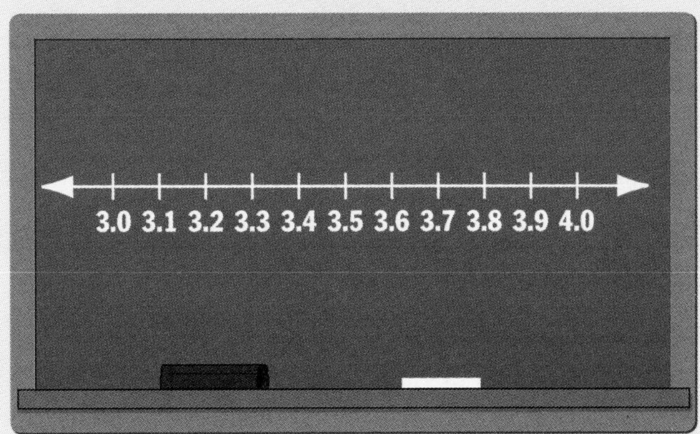

Have students read the introductory problem on Student Book page 464. Have them work with a partner to locate 3.2 on a number line. Encourage them to refer to the number line on the chalkboard. Ask:

- **Is 3.2 closer to 3 or to 4?** *[3]*
- **What is 3.2 rounded to the nearest whole number?** *[3]*

Repeat for the other numbers in the problem. Then have students use the rounded numbers to estimate the sum.

Continue the activity by having students use the tenths number lines for decimals to hundredths. They will have to estimate where the hundredths are between the tenths. Point out that they should continue to round the decimals to whole numbers to estimate sums and differences.

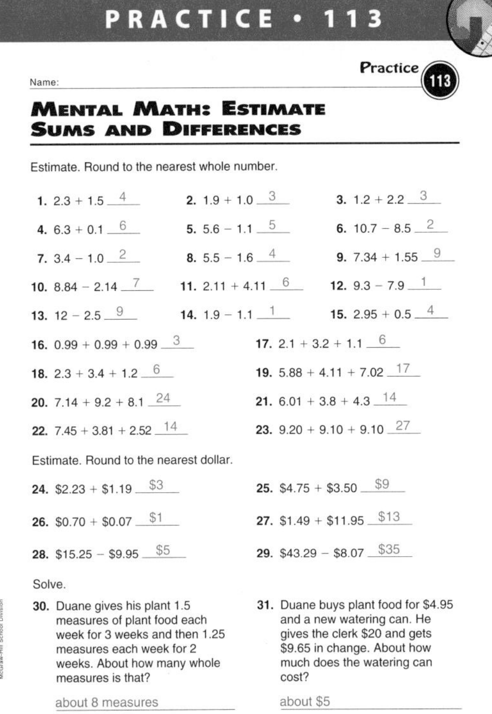

HOMEWORK

PRACTICE • 113

Practice 113

Name:

MENTAL MATH: ESTIMATE SUMS AND DIFFERENCES

Estimate. Round to the nearest whole number.

1. 2.3 + 1.5 4 | 2. 1.9 + 1.0 3 | 3. 1.2 + 2.2 3
4. 6.3 + 0.1 6 | 5. 5.6 − 1.1 5 | 6. 10.7 − 8.5 2
7. 3.4 − 1.0 2 | 8. 5.5 − 1.6 4 | 9. 7.34 + 1.55 9
10. 8.84 − 2.14 7 | 11. 2.11 + 4.11 6 | 12. 9.3 − 7.9 1
13. 12 − 2.5 9 | 14. 1.9 − 1.1 1 | 15. 2.95 + 0.5 4
16. 0.99 + 0.99 + 0.99 3 | 17. 2.1 + 3.2 + 1.1 6
18. 2.3 + 3.4 + 1.2 6 | 19. 5.88 + 4.11 + 7.02 17
20. 7.14 + 9.2 + 8.1 24 | 21. 6.01 + 3.8 + 4.3 14
22. 7.45 + 3.81 + 2.52 14 | 23. 9.20 + 9.10 + 9.10 27

Estimate. Round to the nearest dollar.

24. $2.23 + $1.19 $3 | 25. $4.75 + $3.50 $9
26. $0.70 + $0.07 $1 | 27. $1.49 + $11.95 $13
28. $15.25 − $9.95 $5 | 29. $43.29 − $8.07 $35

Solve.

30. Duane gives his plant 1.5 measures of plant food each week for 3 weeks and then 1.25 measures each week for 2 weeks. About how many whole measures is that? about 8 measures

31. Duane buys plant food for $4.95 and a new watering can. He gives the clerk $20 and gets $9.65 in change. About how much does the watering can cost? about $5

McGraw-Hill School Division

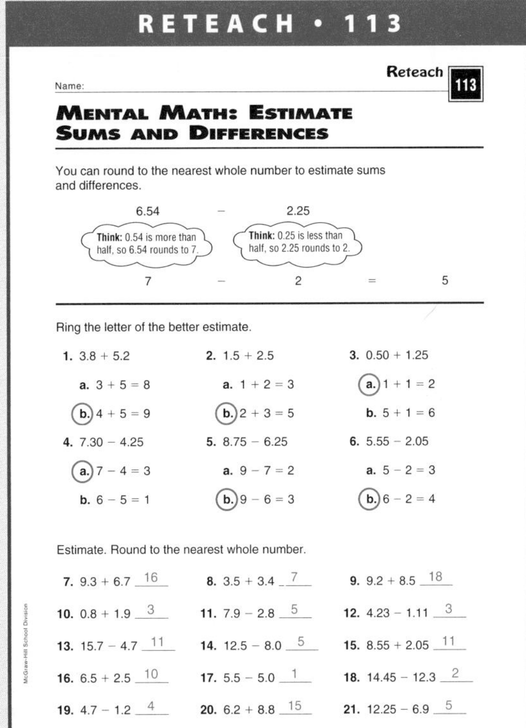

RETEACH • 113

Reteach 113

Name:

MENTAL MATH: ESTIMATE SUMS AND DIFFERENCES

You can round to the nearest whole number to estimate sums and differences.

6.54 − 2.25

Think: 0.54 is more than half, so 6.54 rounds to 7.

Think: 0.25 is less than half, so 2.25 rounds to 2.

7 − 2 = 5

Ring the letter of the better estimate.

1. 3.8 + 5.2 — a. 3 + 5 = 8 — (b.) 4 + 5 = 9
2. 1.5 + 2.5 — a. 1 + 2 = 3 — (b.) 2 + 3 = 5
3. 0.50 + 1.25 — (a.) 1 + 1 = 2 — b. 5 + 1 = 6
4. 7.30 − 4.25 — (a.) 7 − 4 = 3 — b. 6 − 5 = 1
5. 8.75 − 6.25 — a. 9 − 7 = 2 — (b.) 9 − 6 = 3
6. 5.55 − 2.05 — a. 5 − 2 = 3 — (b.) 6 − 2 = 4

Estimate. Round to the nearest whole number.

7. 9.3 + 6.7 16 | 8. 3.5 + 3.4 7 | 9. 9.2 + 8.5 18
10. 0.8 + 1.9 3 | 11. 7.9 − 2.8 5 | 12. 4.23 − 1.11 3
13. 15.7 − 4.7 11 | 14. 12.5 − 8.0 5 | 15. 8.55 + 2.05 11
16. 6.5 + 2.5 10 | 17. 5.5 − 5.0 1 | 18. 14.45 − 12.3 2
19. 4.7 − 1.2 4 | 20. 6.2 + 8.8 15 | 21. 12.25 − 6.9 5

McGraw-Hill School Division

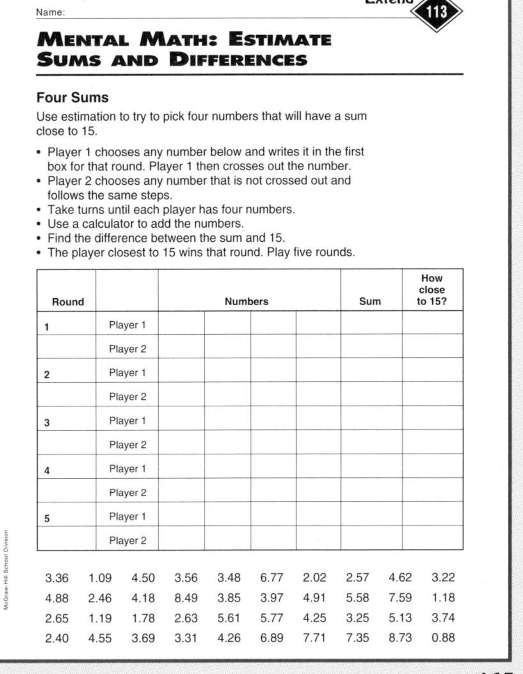

EXTEND • 113

Extend 113

Name:

MENTAL MATH: ESTIMATE SUMS AND DIFFERENCES

Four Sums

Use estimation to try to pick four numbers that will have a sum close to 15.

- Player 1 chooses any number below and writes it in the first box for that round. Player 1 then crosses out the number.
- Player 2 chooses any number that is not crossed out and follows the same steps.
- Take turns until each player has four numbers.
- Use a calculator to add the numbers.
- Find the difference between the sum and 15.
- The player closest to 15 wins that round. Play five rounds.

Round		Numbers				Sum	How close to 15?
1	Player 1						
	Player 2						
2	Player 1						
	Player 2						
3	Player 1						
	Player 2						
4	Player 1						
	Player 2						
5	Player 1						
	Player 2						

3.36	1.09	4.50	3.56	3.48	6.77	2.02	2.57	4.62	3.22
4.88	2.46	4.18	8.49	3.85	3.97	4.91	5.58	7.59	1.18
2.65	1.19	1.78	2.63	5.61	5.77	4.25	3.25	5.13	3.74
2.40	4.55	3.69	3.31	4.26	6.89	7.71	7.35	8.73	0.88

McGraw-Hill School Division

EXPLORE ACTIVITY

Add and Subtract Decimals

OBJECTIVE Explore adding and subtracting decimals.

RESOURCE REMINDER
Math Center Cards 114
Practice 114, Reteach 114, Extend 114

SKILLS TRACE

GRADE 3	• Explore adding and subtracting decimals through hundredths. *(Chapter 11)*
GRADE 4	• Explore adding and subtracting decimals through hundredths.
GRADE 5	• Explore adding and subtracting decimals through hundredths. *(Chapter 2)*

LESSON 12.6 RESOURCES

MANIPULATIVE WARM-UP

Cooperative Pairs — **Logical/Analytical**

OBJECTIVE Review estimating decimal sums and differences.

Materials per pair: 0–9 spinner (TA 2)

▶ Each student spins the spinner three times and uses the digits to make a decimal number in the form □.□□.

▶ Students work together to estimate the sum and difference of their numbers. Have them repeat this activity three or more times.

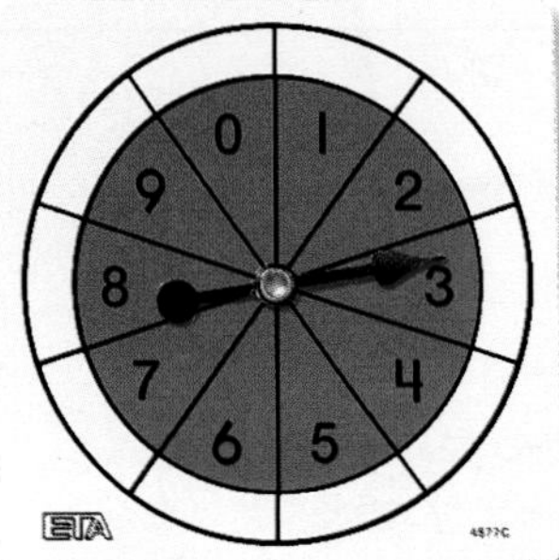

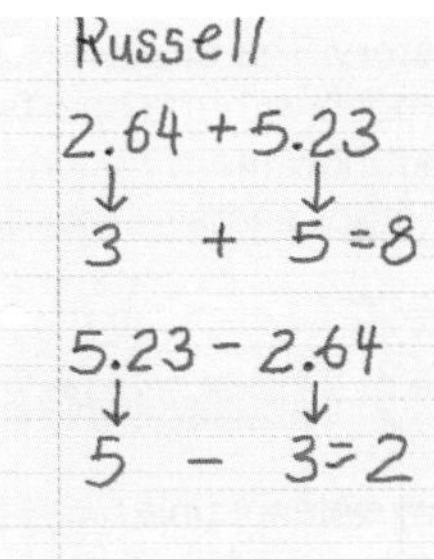

ESL APPROPRIATE

ALGEBRA CONNECTION

Whole Class — **Logical/Analytical**

OBJECTIVE Connect finding sums and differences to algebra.

▶ Copy the following table onto the chalkboard. Then have students complete the table, using the rules at the top of each column.

A	B	C (A + B)	D (A − B)	E (C + D)
5.6	2.1	*[7.7]*	*[3.5]*	*[11.2]*
4.3	1.9	*[6.2]*	*[2.4]*	*[8.6]*
12.8	5.4	*[18.2]*	*[7.4]*	*[25.6]*
2.65	1.34	*[3.99]*	*[1.31]*	*[5.30]*
4.29	2.83	*[7.12]*	*[1.46]*	*[8.58]*

▶ Discuss any patterns students may see in the table. *[Possible answer: E is twice A.]*

▶ Have students continue the pattern.

Daily Review

PREVIOUS DAY QUICK REVIEW

Estimate.

1. 7.1 + 4.8 *[12]*
2. 8.83 + 4.06 *[13]*
3. 9.7 − 2.2 *[8]*
4. 6.39 − 1.78 *[4]*

FAST FACTS

1. 9 ÷ 9 *[1]*
2. 30 ÷ 5 *[6]*
3. 27 ÷ 3 *[9]*
4. 64 ÷ 8 *[8]*

Problem of the Day • 114

Tina rides her bike 1.3 miles to the library. Then she rides 1.4 miles to Amy's house. How far does Tina ride altogether? *[2.7 mi]*

TECH LINK

Math Van

MATH VAN

Tool You may wish to use the Place-Value Model tool with this lesson.

MATH FORUM

Idea I keep some of the models students make together with the examples in a Math Corner. They are readily available for extra help and review.

Visit our Resource Village at http://www.mhschool.com to see more of the Math Forum.

MATH CENTER

Practice

OBJECTIVE Add and subtract decimals.

Materials per student: 2 sheets of centimeter graph paper (TA 1), crayons, scissors, straightedge, Math Center Recording Sheet (TA 31 optional)

Students color 10 by 10 grid to show decimals and solve addition and subtraction sentences. In a replay, they add two squares first to get a decimal greater than 1, then pick a third grid to write the sentence. *[Students check each others' work.]*

PRACTICE ACTIVITY 114 — MATH CENTER — Partners

Manipulatives • A Square Deal

YOU NEED
- 2 sheets of centimeter graph paper per person
- crayons
- scissors
- ruler

- Each partner outlines six 10-by-10 grids for each sheet of graph paper. Use two sheets to get 12 grids in all. Shade in each grid to show a decimal less than 1. Cut the grids apart.
- Mix the grids from both players together and spread them out facedown.
- Take turns choosing two grids and using the decimals to write an addition or subtraction number sentence. Then solve the number sentence. Place the grids aside. Continue taking turns until the squares are used up.
- Play again. First pick two grids to get a sum greater than 1. Then pick a third to write an addition or subtraction sentence.

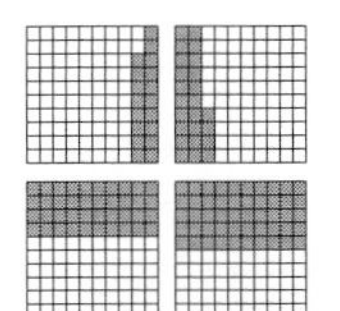

McGraw-Hill School Division Grade Level 4

Chapter 12, Lesson 6, pages 466–467 — Decimals

NCTM Standards
- Problem Solving
- ✓ Communication
- ✓ Reasoning
- Connections

Problem Solving

OBJECTIVE Add and subtract decimals.

Students organize the parts of a schedule by comparing, then adding and subtracting decimals. *[**1.** Mowing the lawn (1.5), visiting Aunt Oliana (1.25), soccer practice (1.2), cleaning out the fish tank (0.8), buying juice for the school picnic (0.2), returning books to the library (0.25), buying a gift for your brother's birthday (0.5), practicing the tuba (0.6); **2.** Answers will vary. Possible answer: Monday: return books, set up tables, practice tuba, buy juice; Tuesday: mow lawn, buy gift; Wednesday: soccer practice, clean fish tank; Thursday: practice tuba, visit aunt.]*

PROBLEM-SOLVING ACTIVITY 114 — MATH CENTER — On Your Own

Decision Making • Busy Schedule

The chart shows a list of tasks to be done on Monday through Thursday after school. You only have 2 hours free each afternoon. The time is expressed in decimals. Each 0.1 means 6 minutes; 0.2 means 12 minutes; 0.25 means 15 minutes; 0.5 means 30 minutes, and so on.

- Which 4 tasks take the greatest amount of time? the least amount of time?
- On which days would you complete each task?

After-School Tasks	Time (in hours)
Buy juice for the school picnic	0.2
Set up tables for the school picnic	0.75
Return books to the library	0.25
Visit Aunt Oliana	1.25
Buy a gift for your brother's birthday	0.5
Mow the lawn	1.5
Practice the tuba two times	0.6 each time
Clean out the fish tank	0.8
Soccer practice	1.2

McGraw-Hill School Division Grade Level 4

Chapter 12, Lesson 6, pages 466–467 — Decimals

NCTM Standards
- Problem Solving
- Communication
- ✓ Reasoning
- ✓ Connections

EXPLORE ACTIVITY

Add and Subtract Decimals

OBJECTIVE Explore adding and subtracting decimals.

Materials per pair: 10-by-10 decimal squares (TA 30); crayons, colored pencils, or markers; scissors

1 Introduce

Display the following diagram.

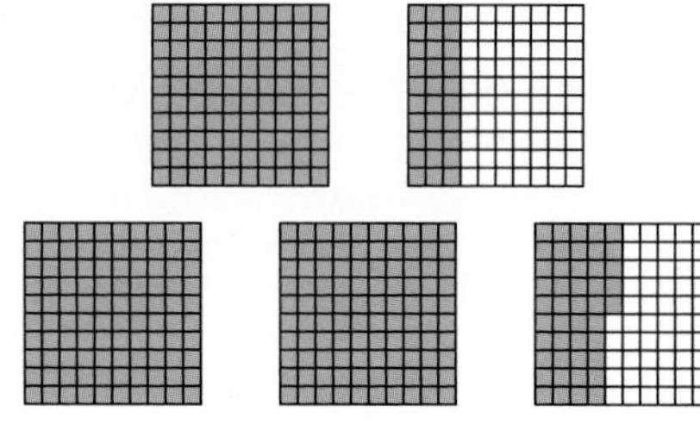

Ask students:

- **What decimals does each set of decimal squares show?** *[1.3, 2.45]*
- **What is their sum? difference?** *[3.75; 1.15]*

2 Teach *Cooperative Pairs*

LEARN Work Together Have students choose different digits for each square. Remind students to line up the decimal points when adding or subtracting vertically.

Have pairs use their models to explain some of their sums and differences to the class.

MAKE CONNECTIONS

Students should connect the models to the ways the sums and differences are recorded. Discuss the importance of regrouping when adding. Have a volunteer explain how to use the models to find 1.45 + 2.07 + 1.95.

3 Close

Check for Understanding using items 1–8, page 467.

Critical Thinking

In item 8, students are asked to generalize about regrouping for addition. Extend the generalization to subtraction. Ask:

- **When do you need to regroup when subtracting?** *[when a greater digit is being subtracted from a lesser digit]*

PRACTICE

Materials have available: calculators

Assign ex. 1-28 as independent work.

Add and Subtract Decimals

LEARN

You can use decimal squares to explore addition and subtraction with decimals.

Work Together

Work with a partner to add and subtract decimals.

You will need

- *decimal squares*
- *crayons, colored pencils, or markers*
- *scissors*

Choose any four digits from 0 to 9. Use the digits to complete the addition example and the subtraction example.

$$2.\square\square \qquad 2.\square\square$$
$$+1.\square\square \qquad -1.\square\square$$

Then use the decimal squares to find the exact answers. Color and cut them to find the sum and the difference. Record your answers.

Repeat the activity two more times.

▶ How did you use the decimal squares to add? to subtract?

Possible answer: Add—colored both addends, then cut and pasted the decimal parts to try to make one more whole or one more tenth; subtract—colored the greater number, then cut off the whole and decimal parts that represent the other number.

Make Connections

Here is how Mark and Sondra added.

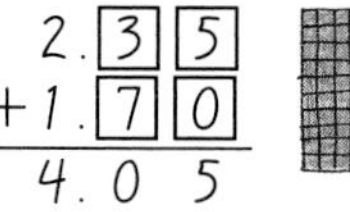

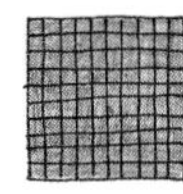
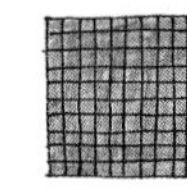
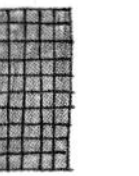
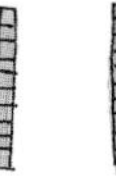
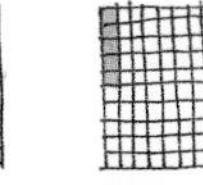

Here is how Mark and Sondra subtracted.

2.37
−1.50
0.87

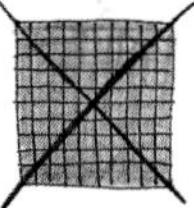
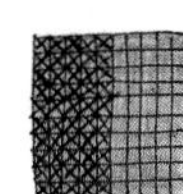
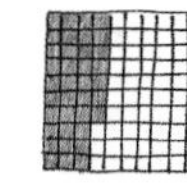

Meeting Individual Needs

Early Finishers

Have students repeat the opening activity one or more times. Encourage them first to find the sum and difference, and then to use models to check their answers.

Extra Support

Make sure that students having difficulty can add and subtract decimals to tenths before they attempt the operations for hundredths. Provide them with tenths strips, made on 10-by-10 grids, for their models.

Ongoing Assessment

Anecdotal Report Record how students use decimal squares to find decimal sums and differences. Note if they add and subtract the decimals like whole numbers.

Follow Up To provide more work with models for students who are having difficulty with decimal sums and differences, assign **Reteach 114.**

Have students who are ready for a challenge try **Extend 114.**

ssible answer: Added—colored each addend, regrouped 10 tenths to make another then added 3 + 1 + 0.05 = 4.05; subtracted—colored the greater number, then crossed off or cut off the amount named by the second number.

Explain how Mark and Sondra added and subtracted. See above.

How would you model 1.45 + 2.07 + 1.95? Check students' explanations—the sum is 5.47.

heck for Understanding

CHECK

se the models to complete the number sentence.

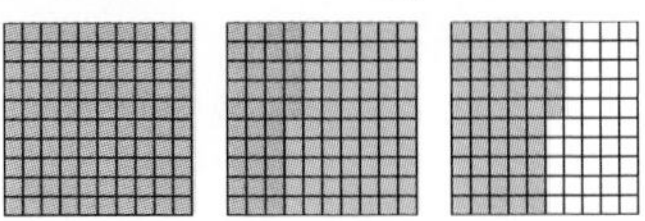

1.35 + 1.2 = ■ 2.55

2 1.08 − 0.2 = ■ 0.88

se decimal squares to add or subtract. Check students' models.

	4	**5**	**6**	**7**
0.8	1.5	1.6	2.15	3.06
+ 0.3	+ 1.8	− 0.2	− 1.73	− 0.89
1.1	3.3	1.4	0.42	2.17

ritical Thinking: Generalize Explain your reasoning.

When do you need to regroup when adding? when you have more than 10 hundredths or 10 tenths

ractice

PRACTICE

se the models to complete the number sentence.

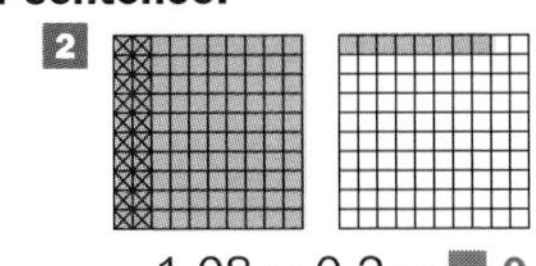

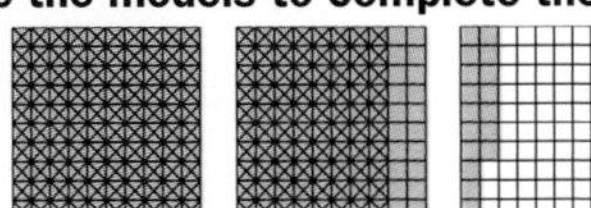

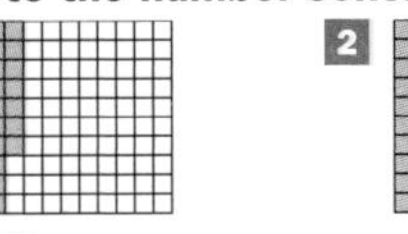

2.17 − 1.8 = ■ 0.37

2 1.4 + 0.29 = ■ 1.69

se decimal squares to add or subtract. Check students' models.

	4	**5**	**6**	**7**
0.4	0.8	1.42	1.66	2.09
+ 0.3	+ 0.5	+ 1.85	+ 0.45	+ 1.97
0.7	1.3	3.27	2.11	4.06

	9	**10**	**11**	**12**
0.7	1.4	1.28	2.07	3.45
− 0.1	− 0.5	− 0.40	− 1.45	− 1.96
0.6	0.9	0.88	0.62	1.49

1.5 + 1.7 3.2 **14** 1.50 + 1.25 2.75 **15** 1.8 + 0.29 2.09 **16** 1.33 + 1.9 3.23

2.7 − 1.9 0.8 **18** 1.3 − 0.4 0.9 **19** 2.11 − 1.03 1.08 **20** 2.09 − 1.64 0.45

0.9 + 0.07 0.97 **22** 0.9 − 0.3 0.6 **23** 1.85 + 0.11 1.96 **24** 3 − 1.09 1.91

2.2 − 0.8 1.4 **26** 1.16 + 2.8 3.96 **27** 2.04 − 0.38 1.66 **28** 1.3 + 1.83 3.13

tra Practice, page 530

Alternate Teaching Strategy

Materials per pair: decimal squares (TA 30); scissors

Copy the following examples on the chalkboard:

2.6	1.7	2.53	1.88
+ 1.3	+ 0.5	+ 1.22	+ 1.40

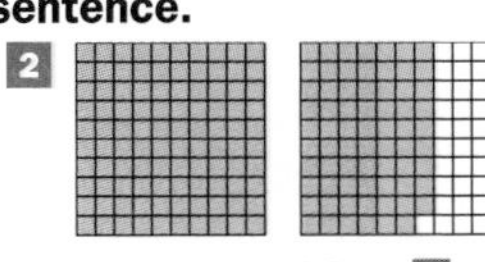

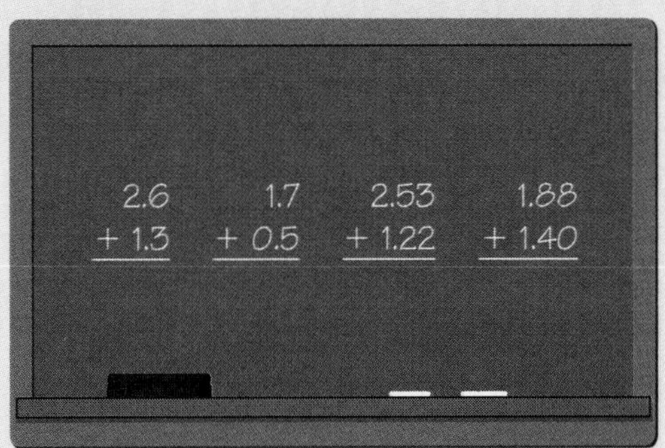

Students work with a partner. Each student in a pair uses the 10-by-10 decimal squares to model one of the addends in the first example. Then have them combine the models to find the sum. They may cut the models to combine them, if desired. Ask:

- **How many tenths are in the sum of the first exercise? How many ones?** *[9 tenths; 3 ones]*
- **What is the sum?** *[3.9]*

Have students continue this method to find the other sums. Remind them to regroup when necessary. *[2.2; 3.75; 3.28]*

Then extend the activity by having students find the differences of the numbers in each example, using the models. *[1.3; 1.2; 1.31; 0.48]*

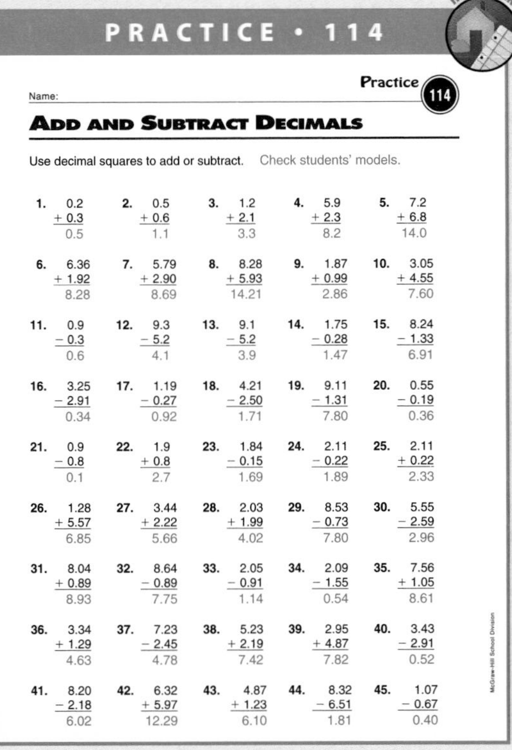

PRACTICE • 114

HOMEWORK

Name: Practice 114

Add and Subtract Decimals

Use decimal squares to add or subtract. Check students' models.

1.	2.	3.	4.	5.
0.2	0.5	1.2	5.9	7.2
+ 0.3	+ 0.6	+ 2.1	+ 2.3	+ 6.8
0.5	1.1	3.3	8.2	14.0

6.	7.	8.	9.	10.
6.36	5.79	8.28	1.87	3.05
+ 1.92	+ 2.90	+ 5.93	+ 0.99	+ 4.55
8.28	8.69	14.21	2.86	7.60

11.	12.	13.	14.	15.
0.9	9.3	9.1	1.75	8.24
− 0.3	− 5.2	− 5.2	− 0.28	− 1.33
0.6	4.1	3.9	1.47	6.91

16.	17.	18.	19.	20.
3.25	1.19	4.21	9.11	0.55
− 2.91	− 0.27	− 2.50	− 1.31	− 0.19
0.34	0.92	1.71	7.80	0.36

21.	22.	23.	24.	25.
0.9	1.9	1.84	2.11	2.11
− 0.8	+ 0.8	− 0.15	− 0.22	+ 0.22
0.1	2.7	1.69	1.89	2.33

26.	27.	28.	29.	30.
1.28	3.44	2.03	8.53	5.55
+ 5.57	+ 2.22	+ 1.99	− 0.73	− 2.59
6.85	5.66	4.02	7.80	2.96

31.	32.	33.	34.	35.
8.04	8.64	2.05	2.09	7.56
+ 0.89	− 0.89	− 0.91	− 1.55	+ 1.05
8.93	7.75	1.14	0.54	8.61

36.	37.	38.	39.	40.
3.34	7.23	5.23	2.95	3.43
+ 1.29	− 2.45	+ 2.19	+ 4.87	− 2.91
4.63	4.78	7.42	7.82	0.52

41.	42.	43.	44.	45.
8.20	6.32	4.87	8.32	1.07
− 2.18	+ 5.97	+ 1.23	− 6.51	− 0.67
6.02	12.29	6.10	1.81	0.40

McGraw-Hill School Division

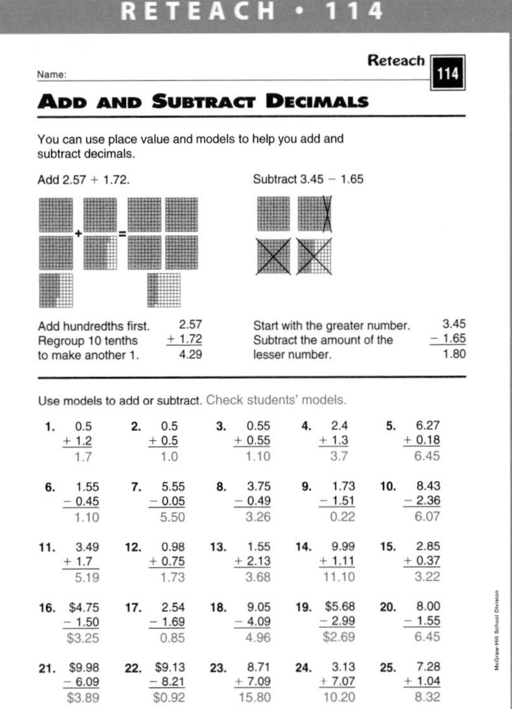

RETEACH • 114

Name: Reteach 114

Add and Subtract Decimals

You can use place value and models to help you add and subtract decimals.

Add 2.57 + 1.72.

Add hundredths first. Regroup 10 tenths to make another 1.

2.57
+ 1.72
4.29

Subtract 3.45 − 1.65

Start with the greater number. Subtract the amount of the lesser number.

3.45
− 1.65
1.80

Use models to add or subtract. Check students' models.

1.	2.	3.	4.	5.
0.5	0.5	0.55	2.4	6.27
+ 1.2	+ 0.5	+ 0.55	+ 1.3	+ 0.18
1.7	1.0	1.10	3.7	6.45

6.	7.	8.	9.	10.
1.55	5.55	3.75	1.73	8.43
− 0.45	− 0.05	− 0.49	− 1.51	− 2.36
1.10	5.50	3.26	0.22	6.07

11.	12.	13.	14.	15.
3.49	0.98	1.55	9.99	2.85
+ 1.7	+ 0.75	+ 2.13	+ 1.11	+ 0.37
5.19	1.73	3.68	11.10	3.22

16.	17.	18.	19.	20.
$4.75	2.54	9.05	$5.68	8.00
− 1.50	− 1.69	− 4.09	− 2.99	− 1.55
$3.25	0.85	4.96	$2.69	6.45

21.	22.	23.	24.	25.
$9.98	$9.13	8.71	3.13	7.28
− 6.09	− 8.21	+ 7.09	+ 7.07	+ 1.04
$3.89	$0.92	15.80	10.20	8.32

McGraw-Hill School Division

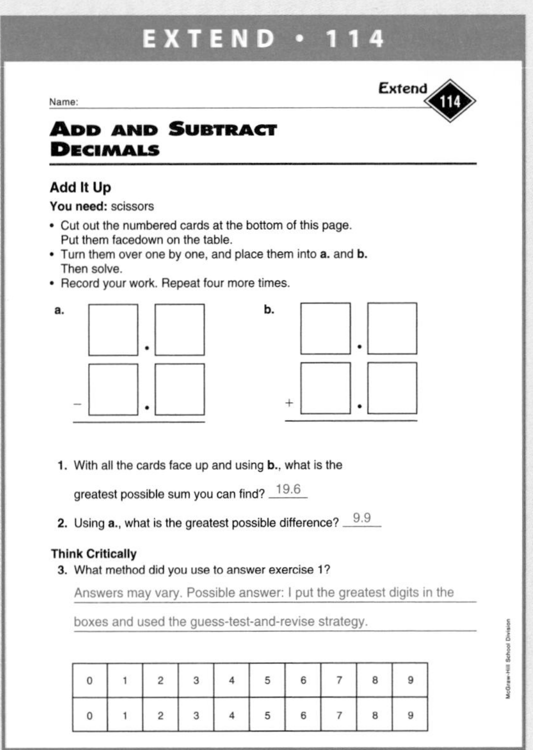

EXTEND • 114

Name: Extend 114

Add and Subtract Decimals

Add It Up

You need: scissors

- Cut out the numbered cards at the bottom of this page. Put them facedown on the table.
- Turn them over one by one, and place them into **a.** and **b.** Then solve.
- Record your work. Repeat four more times.

a. ☐.☐ − ☐.☐

b. ☐.☐ + ☐.☐

1. With all the cards face up and using **b.**, what is the greatest possible sum you can find? 19.6
2. Using **a.**, what is the greatest possible difference? 9.9

Think Critically

3. What method did you use to answer exercise 1?
Answers may vary. Possible answer: I put the greatest digits in the boxes and used the guess-test-and-revise strategy.

0	1	2	3	4	5	6	7	8	9
0	1	2	3	4	5	6	7	8	9

McGraw-Hill School Division

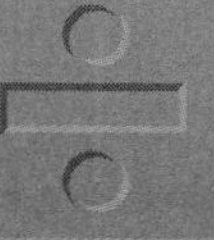

Add Decimals

OBJECTIVE Add decimals.

RESOURCE REMINDER
Math Center Cards 115
Practice 115, Reteach 115, Extend 115

SKILLS TRACE

GRADE 3	• Explore adding and subtracting decimals through hundredths. *(Chapter 11)*
GRADE 4	• Add decimals through hundredths.
GRADE 5	• Add decimals through thousandths. *(Chapter 2)*

MANIPULATIVE WARM-UP

Cooperative Pairs — Visual/Spatial

OBJECTIVE Explore finding decimal sums.

Materials per pair: number cube; decimal squares (TA 30)

▶ Each student tosses the number cube once and writes a decimal number that rounds to the number tossed.

▶ Students estimate the sum of their numbers. Then they find the exact sum with the decimal squares. Have students repeat this activity five times.

▶ Discuss how estimating the sum helped in finding the exact sum.

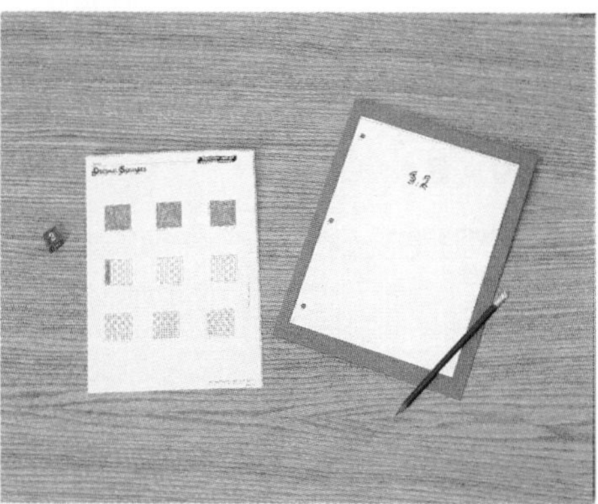

SPORTS CONNECTION

Cooperative Pairs — Logical/Analytical

OBJECTIVE Connect decimal sums to sports.

Materials per pair: decimal squares (TA 30) (optional)

▶ Tell students that Jackson keeps a log to record the time it takes for him to swim 10 laps in the pool. The following is an excerpt from his log.

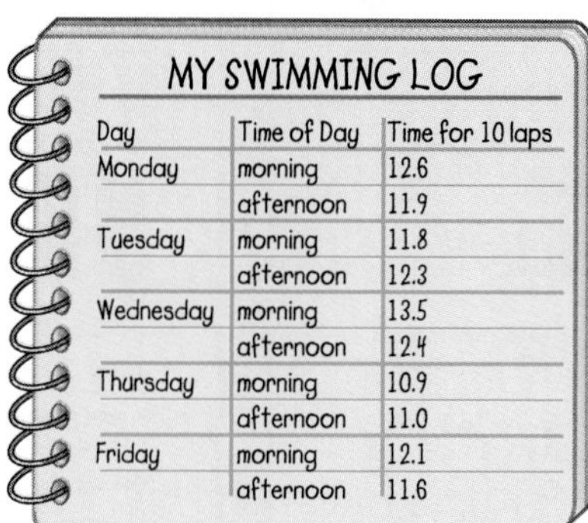

MY SWIMMING LOG

Day	Time of Day	Time for 10 laps
Monday	morning	12.6
	afternoon	11.9
Tuesday	morning	11.8
	afternoon	12.3
Wednesday	morning	13.5
	afternoon	12.4
Thursday	morning	10.9
	afternoon	11.0
Friday	morning	12.1
	afternoon	11.6

▶ Have students find Jackson's best time for the week. *[10.9 min]* Then have them find Jackson's total swimming time each day, using decimal squares if desired. *[24.5 min, 24.1 min, 25.9 min, 21.9 min, 23.7 min]*

Daily Review

PREVIOUS DAY QUICK REVIEW

Use decimal squares to add or subtract.

1. 0.3 + 0.2 *[0.5]*
2. 1.3 + 2.45 *[3.75]*
3. 0.9 − 0.5 *[0.4]*
4. 2.69 − 1.33 *[1.36]*

FAST FACTS

1. 4 × 8 *[32]*
2. 8 × 5 *[40]*
3. 9 × 9 *[81]*
4. 8 × 6 *[48]*

Problem of the Day • 115

Jackie's cactus garden is shaped like a quadrilateral. The measurements of the sides, in meters, are: 2.34, 2.62, 3.05, and 2.16. What is the perimeter of Jackie's garden? *[10.17 m]*

TECH LINK

MATH FORUM

Idea I have my students work in pairs to check their work. Students alternate estimating a sum and checking the sum on a calculator.

Visit our Resource Village at http://www.mhschool.com to see more of the Math Forum.

MATH CENTER

Practice

OBJECTIVE Add decimals.

Materials per student: 2 counters, 10 slips of paper, tape, Math Center Recording Sheet (TA 31 optional)

Students play a counter toss game to add decimals that the counters land on. They try to get as many different sums as possible. *[Answers may vary. Check students' work.]*

PRACTICE ACTIVITY 115 — MATH CENTER, On Your Own

Game • Counter Toss

- Write decimals greater than 1 on each of 10 slips of paper. Arrange the slips into 5 rows of two, with numbers increasing as they get farther from you. Tape them (on one edge only) to the desktop.
- Stand back about 1 yard and toss 2 counters at the numbers, one counter at a time. Add the 2 amounts that the counters land on.
- Keep playing. Try to get as many different sums as possible. You may also try to get the greatest sum possible by aiming for the farthest numbers.

YOU NEED
- 2 counters
- 10 slips of paper
- tape

4.32	5.71
3.85	4.02
2.95	3.45
2.12	2.75
1.51	2.01

McGraw-Hill School Division — Grade Level 4

Chapter 12, Lesson 7, pages 468–469 — Problem Solving

ESL APPROPRIATE

NCTM Standards
- Problem Solving
- Communication
- ✓ Reasoning
- Connections

Problem Solving

OBJECTIVE Solve problems that involve adding decimals.

Materials per student: calculator, Math Center Recording Sheet (TA 31 optional)

Students use currency rates to find United States currency exchanges equaling \$1, \$2, \$3, and so on. *[Answers may vary. Check students' work.]*

PROBLEM-SOLVING ACTIVITY 115 — MATH CENTER, On Your Own

Using Data • Current Currency

- The tables show the value of each currency in United States dollars. Add currencies from other countries together to equal 1 United States dollar.

For example,
1 Australian dollar = \$0.76 U.S.
1 Bolivian Boliviano = \$0.20 U.S.
+ 1 Thailand Baht = \$0.04 U.S.
\$1.00 U.S.

- Write more combinations for 1 U.S. dollar. Write others for \$2, \$3, and so on. You may have to add more than one unit of each currency.

YOU NEED
- calculator

Country	Currency
Albania	1 Lek = \$0.01
Australia	1 Australian dollar = \$0.76
Austria	1 Schilling = \$0.10
Bahrain	1 Dinar = \$2.65

Country	Currency
Bolivia	1 Boliviano = \$0.20
Botswana	1 Pula = \$0.34
China	1 Yuan = \$0.12
Egypt	1 Pound = \$0.29
El Salvador	1 Colón = \$0.11
Fiji	1 Fiji dollar = \$0.71
Germany	1 Mark = \$0.68
Malaysia	1 Ringgit = \$0.39
The Netherlands	1 Guilder = \$0.60
Qatar	1 Riyal = \$0.27
Thailand	1 Baht = \$0.04
Swaziland	1 Lilangeni = \$0.26

McGraw-Hill School Division — Grade Level 4

Chapter 12, Lesson 7, pages 468–469 — Problem Solving

NCTM Standards
- ✓ Problem Solving
- ✓ Communication
- Reasoning
- ✓ Connections

Add Decimals

OBJECTIVE Add decimals.

1 Introduce

On the chalkboard, draw a picture of a pen with a price tag of \$2.25 and a notebook with a price tag of \$1.75. Ask students:

- **What is the total cost of the pen and notebook?** *[\$4.00]*

Discuss methods students use to find the solution.

2 Teach *Whole Class*

LEARN After the introductory problem is read, discuss the estimate.

- **Why should you estimate the sum for both the paper and pencil method and using a calculator?** *[to check the reasonableness of the answer]*

Work through the algorithm with students. Stress that when adding decimals vertically, the decimal points of the addends are always lined up. After the decimal points are lined up, the addition is the same as for whole numbers. Remind students to line up the decimal point in the answer.

3 Close

Check for Understanding using items 1–11, page 468.

CRITICAL THINKING
In item 11, students are asked to add a number with tenths and a number with hundredths. After they have completed their analysis have them extend the analysis by asking:

- **Do you have to write 19.5 as 19.50 to add to 24.83? Explain.** *[No; as long as the decimal points are lined up and you know that there are 0 hundredths in 19.5, you can add.]*

PRACTICE
Materials have available: calculators

Options for assigning exercises:
A—Odd ex. 1–21; all ex. 22–26; **Mixed Review**
B—Even ex. 2–20; all ex. 22–26; **Mixed Review**

- Encourage students to use mental math to add when they can in ex. 1–15.
- For ex. 16–24, students should be able to write sums in vertical form, lining up the decimal points to add.
- For ex. 22–26, students will have to use a table to solve multistep problems.

Mixed Review/Test Preparation
Algebra: Patterns In ex. 9 and 10, students review equivalent fractions, learned in Chapter 10. Students review measurement conversions in ex. 1–8, a skill they learned in Chapter 7. Some students may need to look at the Table of Measures, page 553.

Add Decimals

LEARN

Do you love to get mail? Suppose you get a package. The gift inside th box weighs 5.85 oz and the box and wrapping weighs 2.38 oz. How much will the package weigh?

Estimate: 5.85 + 2.38 **Think:** 6 + 2

You have already used models to add decimals. You can also use pencil anc paper.

Add: 5.85 + 2.38

Think: Adding decimals is like adding whole numbers.

Whole Numbers	Decimals
$\begin{array}{r} ^{1\,1} \\ 585 \\ +\,238 \\ \hline 823 \end{array}$	$\begin{array}{r} ^{1\,1} \\ 5.85 \\ +\,2.38 \\ \hline 8.23 \end{array}$

↑ **Write the decimal point in the su**

You can also use a calculator. 5.85 + 2.38 = **8.23**

The package will weigh 8.23 oz.

CHECK

Check for Understanding

Estimates may vary. Estimates given are rounding to the nearest whole numbers.

Add using any method. Estimate to check that your answer is reasonable.

1 $\begin{array}{r} 0.47 \\ +\,0.59 \\ \hline \end{array}$ **1.06; 1**

2 $\begin{array}{r} 2.07 \\ +\,3.91 \\ \hline \end{array}$ **5.98; 6**

3 $\begin{array}{r} 6.98 \\ +\,4.50 \\ \hline \end{array}$ **11.48; 12**

4 $\begin{array}{r} 17.55 \\ 9.87 \\ +\;\;2.04 \\ \hline \end{array}$ **29.46; 30**

5 $\begin{array}{r} \$24.50 \\ 4.95 \\ +\;19.75 \\ \hline \end{array}$ **\$49.20; \$5**

6 $\begin{array}{r} 5.4 \\ +\,3.7 \\ \hline \end{array}$ **9.1**

7 $\begin{array}{r} \$3.05 \\ +\;\;2.31 \\ \hline \end{array}$ **\$5.36**

8 $\begin{array}{r} 26.27 \\ +\,12.80 \\ \hline \end{array}$ **39.07**

9 $\begin{array}{r} 23.25 \\ 1.60 \\ +\;\;4.08 \\ \hline \end{array}$ **28.93**

10 $\begin{array}{r} 38.50 \\ 21.36 \\ +\;\;3.54 \\ \hline \end{array}$ **63.40**

Critical Thinking: Analyze **Explain your reasoning.**

11 How would you estimate and add 19.5 and 24.83?

Possible answer: Estimate— round to nearest whole numbers (20 + 25 = 45) or n tens (20 + 20 = 40), add—to line up decimal points, write a zero 19.50 to get 19.50 + 24.83 = 44.33.

Meeting Individual Needs

Early Finishers

Write the following statement on the chalkboard: When you add two decimals, each greater than 0.5, the sum will always be greater than 1. Have students tell if they agree or disagree, and why. *[Agree; answers will vary.]*

Extra Support

Allow students to continue to use decimal squares to add. After they find a sum using models, have them find the sum using the algorithm. Then have them compare the steps in each method.

Ongoing Assessment

Observation Checklist Determine if students are able to add decimals by observing if they estimate, line up the decimal points, add, and write the decimal point in the sum.

Follow Up Have students write addends without the decimal points and add. Then have them find the original sum. Note that both addends must have the same number of decimal places for this to work. Assign **Reteach 115.**

For students who would like a challenge, assign **Extend 115.**

ractice

d using any method. Remember to estimate.

0.82 + 0.16 = **0.98**	2 0.8 + 0.5 = **1.3**	3 5.7 + 0.9 = **6.6**	4 6.4 + 2.9 = **9.3**	5 2.7 + 3.6 = **6.3**
0.52 + 0.98 = **1.50**	7 2.79 + 3.52 = **6.31**	8 5.82 + 8.34 = **14.16**	9 7.69 + 0.49 = **8.18**	10 $6.38 + 7.97 = **$14.35**
12.13 + 6.45 + 9.80 = **$28.38**	12 $24.25 + 9.06 + 1.45 = **$34.76**	13 49.72 + 3.74 + 10.07 = **63.53**	14 19.26 + 9.80 + 6.25 = **35.31**	15 35.30 + 7.74 + 20.80 = **63.84**

4.20 + 0.73 **4.93**

17 0.26 + 5.19 **5.45**

18 27.30 + 4.84 + 30.75 **62.89**

7.85 + 4.11 **11.96**

20 6.33 + 3.90 **10.23**

21 33.14 + 12.99 + 0.70 **46.83**

IXED APPLICATIONS

roblem Solving

Pencil & Paper · Calculator · Mental Math

e the price list for problems 22-26.

How much did it cost to send 3 packages that weigh 1 lb each? **$24.75**

How much did it cost to mail 2 paddles weighing 1 lb each and three 2-lb life preservers? **$45.00**

How much did it cost altogether to send 1-lb, 2-lb, 3-lb, 4-lb, and 5-lb boxes of chocolates? **$54.00**

What did it cost to send three 4-lb laptop computers and two 1-lb computer games? **$52.50**

Write a problem that uses information from the price list. Solve it and ask others to solve it. **Students should compare problems and solutions.**

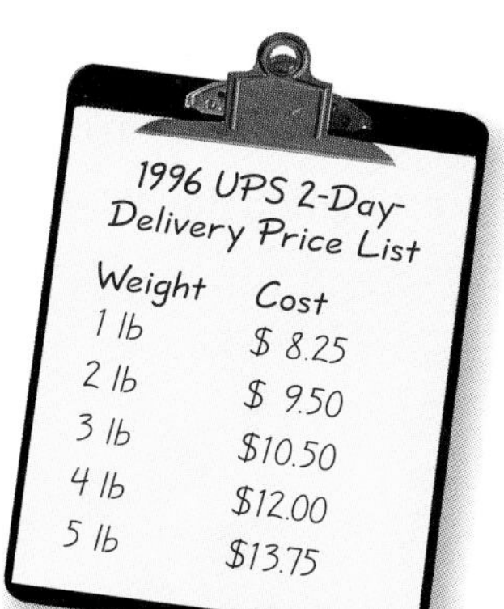

1996 UPS 2-Day Delivery Price List
Weight Cost
1 lb $ 8.25
2 lb $ 9.50
3 lb $10.50
4 lb $12.00
5 lb $13.75

mixed review • test preparation

8 ft = ■ in. **96**

2 2 mi = ■ yd **3,520**

3 6 gal = ■ qt **24**

4 16 oz = ■ lb **1**

3 cm = ■ mm **7**

6 7,000 m = ■ km **30**

7 10 kg = ■ g **10,000**

8 2,000 mL = ■ L **2**

GEBRA: PATTERNS Complete.

$\frac{1}{3} = \frac{■}{6} = \frac{■}{12} = \frac{8}{■} = \frac{16}{■} = \frac{■}{96}$ **2; 4; 24; 48; 32**

10 $\frac{1}{6} = \frac{2}{■} = \frac{3}{■} = \frac{■}{24} = \frac{■}{30} = \frac{6}{■}$ **12; 18; 4; 5; 36**

tra Practice, page 530

Alternate Teaching Strategy

Materials per student: decimal squares (TA 30)

Have students use decimal squares to solve the introductory problem on Student Book page 468. Then have them copy the addends into a table as follows:

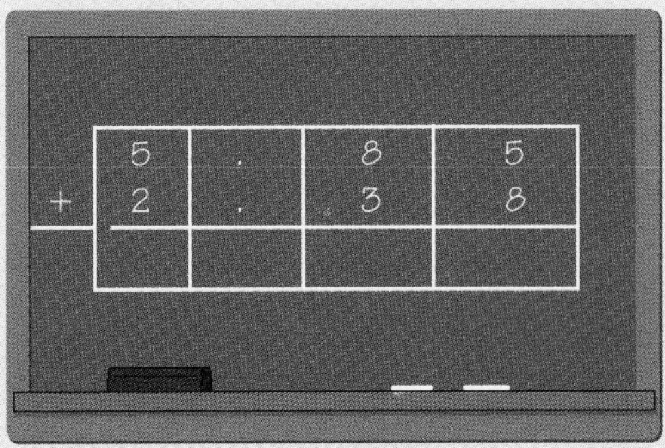

Have students add the numbers in each column as for whole numbers. They then place the decimal point in the sum. Have them compare the sum to the sum found using models.

Repeat the activity to find sums of other decimals.

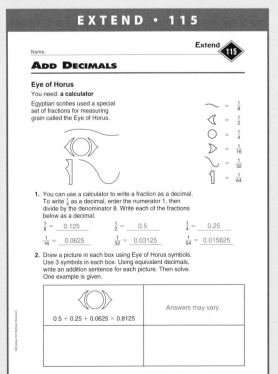

PRACTICE • 115

HOMEWORK

Practice 115

Name:

Add Decimals

Add using any method. Remember to estimate.

1. 0.28 + 0.19 = 0.47	2. 0.15 + 0.59 = 0.74	3. 0.50 + 0.50 = 1.00	4. 0.55 + 0.55 = 1.10	5. 1.50 + 1.50 = 3.00	6. 3.27 + 2.81 = 6.08
7. 5.77 + 1.33 = 7.10	8. 4.21 + 0.88 = 5.09	9. 3.21 + 0.59 = 3.80	10. $6.29 + 2.99 = $9.28	11. 18.05 + 7.29 = 25.34	12. 2.45 + 19.50 = 21.95
13. 0.94 + 21.6 = 22.54	14. 12.25 + 0.75 = 13.00	15. 23.55 + 9.4 = 32.95	16. 12.15 + 8.2 = 20.35	17. 16.05 + 4.15 = 20.20	18. 48.75 + 6.42 = 55.17
19. 1.17 + 29.97 = 31.14	20. 16.50 + 8.40 = 24.90	21. 5.27 + 13.05 + 9.8 = 28.12	22. $9.03 + 27.50 + 8.40 = $44.93	23. $1.50 + 0.05 + 15.95 = $17.50	24. $8.95 + 24.50 + 13.00 = $46.45

25. 6.5 + 0.42 = 6.92
26. 8.6 + 9.4 = 18.0
27. 12.25 + 12.55 = 24.80
28. 9.55 + 2.01 + 1.4 = 12.96
29. 1.50 + 1.50 + 1.50 = 4.50
30. 28.4 + 3.55 + 7.55 = 39.50
31. 1.72 + 2.27 + 7.12 = 11.11
32. 1.72 + 4.68 + 1.10 = 7.5
33. 9.57 + 4.51 + 6.3 = 20.38
34. 24.53 + 1.78 + 3.45 = 29.76

Solve.

35. At the post office, Lauren bought stamps for $2.47 and envelopes for $1.29. How much did she spend? $3.76

36. At the hardware store, Lauren bought packing tape for $1.97 and mailing cartons for $6.35. How much did she spend? $8.32

McGraw-Hill School Division

RETEACH • 115

Reteach 115

Name:

Add Decimals

You can add decimals in the same way that you add whole numbers.

Add 2.38 and 4.75.

Estimate first.
2.38 → 2
4.75 → + 5
7

Then follow these rules:
Line up the decimal points.
Add from right to left.
Regroup if necessary.
Write the decimal point in the sum.

2.38 + 4.75 = 7.13

Rewrite the problem and add.

1. 1.05 + 3.51 = 4.56
2. 4.60 + 0.49 = 5.09
3. 5.65 + 2.75 = 8.40
4. 2.55 + 0.90 + 3.25 = 6.70
5. 0.08 + 22.50 + 1.83 = 24.41
6. 10.65 + 0.67 + 4.83 = 16.15

Add using any method. Remember to estimate.

7. 0.63 + 0.17 = 0.80	8. 0.3 + 0.9 = 1.2	9. 3.23 + 1.99 = 5.22	10. 9.43 + 1.16 = 10.59	11. 2.87 + 0.33 = 3.20
12. 5.42 + 0.99 = 6.41	13. 8.20 + 1.02 = 9.22	14. 5.55 + 1.05 = 6.60	15. 2.45 + 2.55 = 5.00	16. 6.43 + 2.39 = 8.82

McGraw-Hill School Division

EXTEND • 115

Extend 115

Name:

Add Decimals

Eye of Horus

You need: **a calculator**

Egyptian scribes used a special set of fractions for measuring grain called the Eye of Horus.

Symbols: $= \frac{1}{8}$, $= \frac{1}{2}$, $= \frac{1}{4}$, $= \frac{1}{16}$, $= \frac{1}{32}$, $= \frac{1}{64}$

1. You can use a calculator to write a fraction as a decimal. To write $\frac{1}{8}$ as a decimal, enter the numerator 1, then divide by the denominator 8. Write each of the fractions below as a decimal.

$\frac{1}{8}$ = 0.125 $\frac{1}{2}$ = 0.5 $\frac{1}{4}$ = 0.25

$\frac{1}{16}$ = 0.0625 $\frac{1}{32}$ = 0.03125 $\frac{1}{64}$ = 0.015625

2. Draw a picture in each box using Eye of Horus symbols. Use 3 symbols in each box. Using equivalent decimals, write an addition sentence for each picture. Then solve. One example is given.

0.5 + 0.25 + 0.0625 = 0.8125	Answers may vary.

McGraw-Hill School Division

Subtract Decimals

OBJECTIVE Subtract decimals.

RESOURCE REMINDER
Math Center Cards 116
Practice 116, Reteach 116, Extend 116

SKILLS TRACE	
GRADE 3	• Explore adding and subtracting decimals through hundredths. *(Chapter 11)*
GRADE 4	• Subtract decimals through hundredths.
GRADE 5	• Subtract decimals through thousandths. *(Chapter 2)*

MANIPULATIVE WARM-UP

Cooperative Pairs **Visual/Spatial**

OBJECTIVE Explore finding decimal differences.

Materials per pair: 1–6 number cube; decimal squares (TA 30)

▶ Each student tosses the number cube once and writes a decimal number that rounds to the number tossed.

▶ Students estimate the difference of their numbers. Then they find the exact difference with the decimal squares.

▶ Have students repeat this activity five times.

▶ Discuss how estimating the difference helped in finding the exact difference.

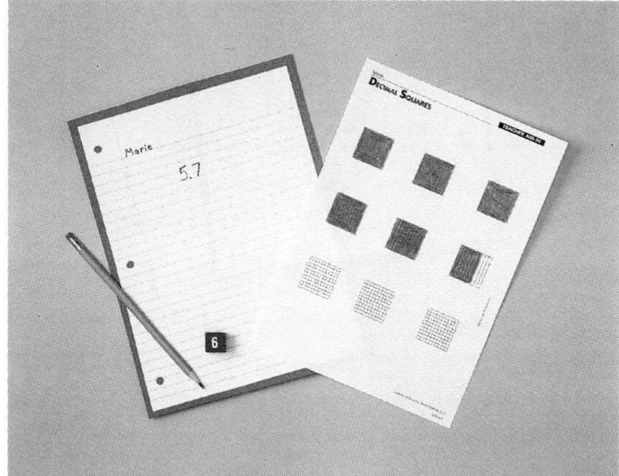

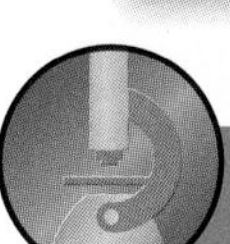

SCIENCE CONNECTION

Cooperative Pairs **Logical/Analytical**

OBJECTIVE Connect decimal difference to science.

Materials per pair: decimal squares (TA 30 optional)

▶ Copy the following table onto the chalkboard:

Beaker	Current Amount of Liquid (in liters)	Liquid Needed to Fill to Capacity (in liters)
A	4.3	*[1.2]*
B	2.1	*[3.4]*
C	1.9	*[3.6]*
D	0.8	*[4.7]*
E	3.5	*[2.0]*

▶ Tell students that each beaker holds 5.5 liters of liquid. Have them work with a partner to complete the table. They have to find how much more liquid can be put into each beaker before it is filled to capacity. They may use decimal squares to find each difference, if desired.

Daily Review

PREVIOUS DAY QUICK REVIEW

Add.

1. 0.9 + 0.7 *[1.6]*
2. 6.2 + 5.9 *[12.1]*
3. 0.73 + 0.11 *[0.84]*
4. 8.57 + 3.92 *[12.49]*

FAST FACTS

1. 16 ÷ 8 *[2]*
2. 36 ÷ 9 *[4]*
3. 49 ÷ 7 *[7]*
4. 54 ÷ 6 *[9]*

Problem of the Day • 116

Colin walked a total of 8.06 miles one week. The next week he walked a total of 7.5 miles. How many more miles did Colin walk the first week? *[0.56 mi]*

TECH LINK

Math Van

MATH VAN

Tool You may wish to use the Place-Value Model tool with this lesson.

MATH FORUM

Combination Classes I have my students work together to check their answers using a calculator. They alternate finding the differences and determine why there are any discrepancies.

Visit our Resource Village at http://www.mhschool.com to see more of the Math Forum.

MATH CENTER

Practice

OBJECTIVE Subtract decimals.

Materials per group: 0–9 spinner (TA 4), calculator; per student: Math Center Recording Sheet (TA 31 optional)

Students use numbers from a spinner to solve decimal subtraction exercises with paper and pencil and calculators. *[Answers may vary. Check students' work.]*

PRACTICE ACTIVITY 116 — MATH CENTER, Small Group

Calculator • Two Ways to Solve

YOU NEED
- spinner (0–9)
- calculator

- Race to subtract decimals quickly and accurately. Copy the boxes below. Then spin the spinner for six numbers and use the numbers to fill in the boxes.

□.□□
− □.□□

- One player uses a calculator to subtract the decimals. The other players solve the problem with pencil and paper and check their answers with the player using the calculator.
- All players with correct answers earn a point. The first player to give the correct answer earns an extra point. Take turns until each player has used the calculator for a round.

Grade Level 4 · McGraw-Hill School Division

Chapter 12, Lesson 8, pages 470-471 — Decimals

NCTM Standards
- ✓ Problem Solving
- ✓ Communication
- ✓ Reasoning
- Connections

Problem Solving

OBJECTIVE Solve problems that involve subtracting decimals.

Materials per student: Math Center Recording Sheet (TA 31 optional)

Students practice recording and subtracting purchases in a check register to spend a selected amount of money. *[Check students' work.]*

PROBLEM-SOLVING ACTIVITY 116 — MATH CENTER, On Your Own

Decision Making • Tracking Money

You have a checking account. The check register shows how you can keep track of money you spend and the table shows the prices of various items.

- Decide how much you want to keep in the account. Show several ways to spend the rest.

Date	Item Purchased	Total
		$33.00
5/12	2 granola bars	−$1.60 $31.40
5/13	1 mini-soccer ball	−$7.99 $23.41
5/14		

Item	Price
granola bar	$0.80
paperback book	$4.99
sports drink	$0.80
greeting card	$1.58
peanuts	$1.26
movie ticket	$4.00
mini-soccer ball	$7.99
top-ten CD	$5.99
salad & dessert	$3.67

Grade Level 4 · McGraw-Hill School Division

Chapter 12, Lesson 8, pages 470–471 — Decimals

NCTM Standards
- ✓ Problem Solving
- Communication
- ✓ Reasoning
- Connections

Subtract Decimals

OBJECTIVE Subtract decimals.

1 Introduce

Materials per group: play money—one \$10 bill, ten \$1 bills, 10 dimes, 10 pennies

Present the following problem:

- **Roger has \$10.00. He buys a video cassette for \$7.49. How much money does he have left?** *[\$2.51]*

Have the whole class discuss how to solve the problem.

2 Teach *Whole Class*

LEARN Have students discuss the uses of telescopes and times they have used them. Read the introductory problem. Then ask:

- **Why should you estimate the difference before subtracting?** *[Possible answer: To have an idea of what the answer should be.]*

After reviewing the algorithm, ask:

- **How is subtracting decimals different from whole numbers? How is it similar?** *[Possible answer: when subtracting decimals, you must line up decimal points and write a decimal point in the answer; in both, you line up the places, subtract, and regroup when necessary.]*

3 Close

Check for Understanding using items 1–6, page 470.

CRITICAL THINKING

For item 6, encourage a variety of responses. Have students provide examples in which they check different decimal additions and subtractions.

PRACTICE

Materials have available: calculators

Options for assigning exercises:
A—Ex. 1–10; all ex. 16–35; **Mixed Review**
B—Ex. 6–35; **Mixed Review**

- Encourage students to use mental math to subtract in ex. 1–5.
- Remind students to line up the decimal points when subtracting as they write ex. 16–31 in vertical form.
- For ex. 35, students should finish the code before writing their secret messages.

Mixed Review/Test Preparation Students add and subtract fractions, a skill they learned in Chapter 11. Remind them to simplify.

Subtract Decimals

LEARN

Telescopes allow us to see into space. The mirror of a large reflecting telescope at the Palomar Observatory in California is 5.08 m wide. The mirror on the Hubble space telescope is 4.29 m wide. Which mirror is wider? How much wider?

Above: Hubble space telescope. Left: Palomar Observatory.

Estimate: 5.08 − 4.29

Think: 5 − 4 = 1

You have already used models to subtract decimals. You can also use pencil and paper.

Subtract: 5.08 − 4.29

Think: Subtracting decimals is like subtracting whole numbers.

Whole Numbers	**Decimals**
4 10 18 (9)	4 10 18 (9)
5 0 8	5.0 8
− 4 2 9	− 4.2 9
7 9	0.7 9

Write the decimal point in the difference.

You can also use a calculator. 5.08 − 4.29 = 0.79

The mirror on the Palomar telescope is 0.79 m wider.

CHECK

Check for Understanding

Estimates may vary. Estimates given are by rounding to the nearest whole number.

Subtract using any method. Estimate to check that your answer is reasonable.

1. 0.8 − 0.3 **0.5; 1**
2. 9.3 − 6.5 **2.8; 2**
3. 6.75 − 4.03 **2.72; 3**
4. 12.91 − 7.48 **5.43; 6**
5. \$39.70 − 19.99 **\$19.71; \$2**

Critical Thinking: Generalize **Explain your reasoning.**

6.  Tell how you could check decimal sums and differences. **Possible answer: Sums—add up each column, differences—add difference to the number subtracted; the methods of checking whole numbers also work with decimals.**

Meeting Individual Needs

Extra Support

Have students who forget to line up the decimal points when subtracting in vertical form write the decimal points, including the one in the difference line, one under the other before writing the digits.

Early Finishers

Have students complete the magic square so that the sums are the same in all directions.

4.13	*[9.18]*	**2.11**
[3.12]	**5.14**	*[7.16]*
8.17	*[1.1]*	*[6.15]*

ESL APPROPRIATE

Ongoing Assessment

Observation Checklist
Observe if students can subtract decimals by noting if they line up the decimal points and write the decimal point in the difference.

Follow Up If students do not line up decimals, have them write the numbers on graph paper and then find the difference. Assign **Reteach 116.**

Have students who are ready for a challenge try **Extend 116.**

ᐧractice

ubtract using any method. Remember to estimate.

1 0.8 − 0.6 = **0.2**	2 4.9 − 0.3 = **4.6**	3 7.1 − 2.5 = **4.6**	4 9.4 − 3.8 = **5.6**	5 1.2 − 0.7 = **0.5**
6 0.63 − 0.12 = **0.51**	7 6.39 − 2.11 = **4.28**	8 2.43 − 1.36 = **1.07**	9 9.57 − 7.64 = **1.93**	10 4.02 − 1.67 = **2.35**
1 \$12.82 − 7.51 = **\$5.31**	12 \$27.25 − 4.06 = **\$23.19**	13 39.70 − 8.64 = **31.06**	14 15.21 − 1.50 = **13.71**	15 24.90 − 3.21 = **21.69**

6 9.6 − 7.2 **2.4**	17 4.5 − 2.8 **1.7**	18 3.50 − 1.06 **2.44**	19 \$5.08 − \$2.17 **\$2.91**
0 7.8 − 4.2 **3.6**	21 \$8.23 − \$3.04 **\$5.19**	22 9.31 − 4.56 **4.75**	23 11.42 − 4.02 **7.40**
4 6.2 − 1.5 **4.7**	25 5.06 − 2.40 **2.66**	26 \$8.41 − \$3.02 **\$5.39**	27 25.19 − 18.05 **7.14**
8 9.26 − 1.46 **7.80**	29 5.03 − 3.39 **1.64**	30 6.72 − 5.56 **1.16**	31 \$22.74 − \$7.38 **\$15.36**

MIXED APPLICATIONS

Problem Solving

Pencil & Paper · Calculator · Mental Math

2 **Logical reasoning** We are two numbers between 0 and 1. Our difference is 0.43. When you add us together, the sum is 1.53. When you subtract one of us from 1, the difference is 0.02. What numbers are we? **0.98 and 0.55**

33 Felipe created a secret code. The first ten letters in his code are:

A—0.1 *D*—0.13 *G*—0.22
B—0.11 *E*—0.2 *H*—0.23
C—0.12 *F*—0.21 *I*—0.3

Follow Felipe's pattern. What decimal would be used for *T*? **0.53**

4 The main body of the Hubble telescope is 13.12 m long and 4.27 m wide. How much longer is it than it is wide? **8.85 m**

35 **Write a problem** that is a message to a friend using Felipe's code in problem 33. Ask a friend to decode your message. **Students' codes should reflect data provided.**

mixed review • test preparation

1 $\frac{2}{3}+\frac{2}{3}$ **$1\frac{1}{3}$**	2 $\frac{3}{5}+\frac{4}{5}$ **$1\frac{2}{5}$**	3 $\frac{11}{12}+\frac{7}{12}$ **See below.**	4 $\frac{1}{6}+\frac{5}{6}$ **1**	5 $\frac{5}{8}+\frac{7}{8}$ **See below.**
6 $\frac{4}{5}-\frac{3}{5}$ **$\frac{1}{5}$**	7 $\frac{9}{10}-\frac{3}{10}$ **$\frac{6}{10}$, or $\frac{3}{5}$**	8 $\frac{14}{16}-\frac{10}{16}$ **$\frac{4}{16}$, or $\frac{1}{4}$**	9 $\frac{11}{12}-\frac{7}{12}$ **$\frac{4}{12}$, or $\frac{1}{3}$**	10 $\frac{3}{4}-\frac{3}{4}$ **0**

xtra Practice, page 531 **3. $1\frac{6}{12}$, or $1\frac{1}{2}$ 5. $1\frac{4}{8}$, or $1\frac{1}{2}$**

PRACTICE

Alternate Teaching Strategy

Materials per student: decimal squares (TA 30)

Have students use decimal squares to solve the introductory problem on Student Book page 470. Then have them copy the numbers into a table as follows:

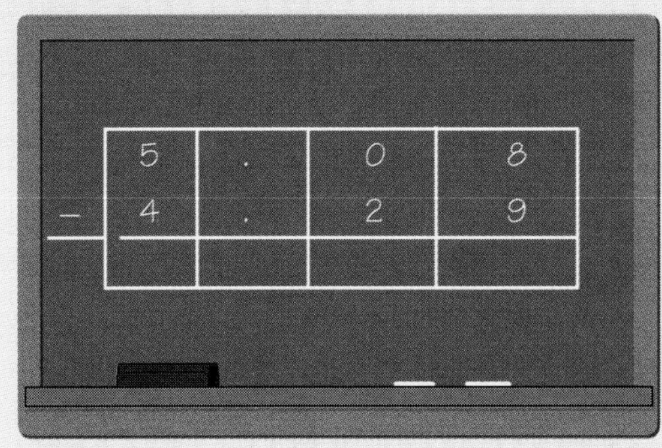

Have them subtract the numbers in each column as with whole numbers. Then have them compare the difference to the difference found using the models.

Repeat the activity to find differences between other decimals.

ESL APPROPRIATE

PRACTICE • 116

HOMEWORK

Practice 116

Name:

SUBTRACT DECIMALS

Subtract using any method. Remember to estimate.

1. 0.5 − 0.2 = 0.3	2. 5.7 − 0.9 = 4.8	3. 8.1 − 3.2 = 4.9	4. 7.3 − 2.7 = 4.6	5. 6.8 − 0.9 = 5.9	6. 0.57 − 0.18 = 0.39
7. 0.66 − 0.12 = 0.54	8. 5.00 − 2.55 = 2.45	9. 4.03 − 2.11 = 1.92	10. 2.00 − 0.65 = 1.35	11. 8.00 − 0.05 = 7.95	12. 8.00 − 3.50 = 4.50
13. 8.00 − 5.00 = 3.00	14. 8.00 − 1.5 = 6.50	15. 8.00 − 2.15 = 5.85	16. 7.43 − 3.5 = 3.93	17. 9.54 − 0.35 = 9.19	18. 6.97 − 1.5 = 5.47
19. 8.32 − 1.05 = 7.27	20. 5.09 − 0.05 = 5.04	21. \$9.37 − 6.28 = \$3.09	22. \$10.00 − 1.99 = \$8.01	23. \$5.35 − 1.75 = \$3.60	24. \$9.05 − 6.20 = \$2.85

25. 8.5 − 2.3 = 6.2
26. 9.4 − 1.05 = 8.35
27. 6.6 − 2.09 = 4.51
28. 7.01 − 2.55 = 4.46
29. 4.22 − 1.97 = 2.25
30. 7.61 − 6.99 = 0.62
31. \$5.75 − \$1.09 = \$4.66
32. \$3.57 − \$1.19 = \$2.38
33. \$7.75 − \$0.80 = \$6.95
34. \$25 − \$1.05 = \$23.95

Solve.

35. At a bookstore, you buy a small dictionary for \$6.15 and pay with a \$10 bill. What change do you get back? \$3.85

36. You buy books for \$2.05, \$7.50, and \$3.75, and pay \$0.87 in tax. What is your change from a \$20 bill? \$5.83

McGraw-Hill School Division

RETEACH • 116

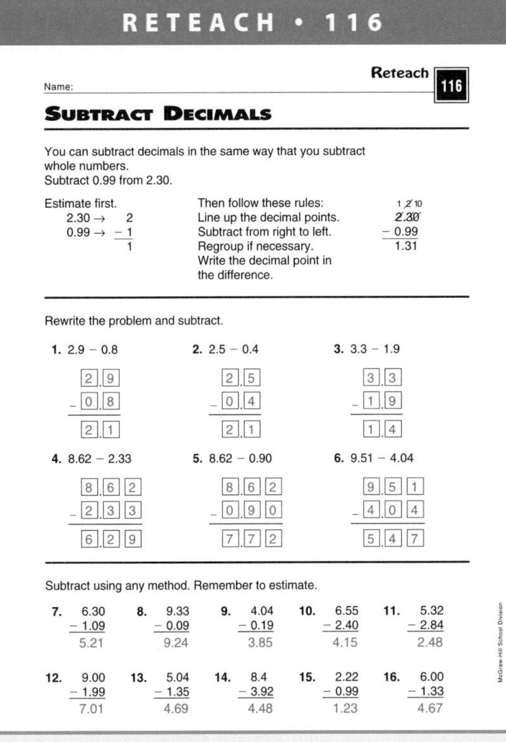

Reteach 116

Name:

SUBTRACT DECIMALS

You can subtract decimals in the same way that you subtract whole numbers.
Subtract 0.99 from 2.30.

Estimate first.
2.30 → 2
0.99 → − 1
1

Then follow these rules:
Line up the decimal points.
Subtract from right to left.
Regroup if necessary.
Write the decimal point in the difference.

2.30 − 0.99 = 1.31

Rewrite the problem and subtract.

1. 2.9 − 0.8 = 2.1
2. 2.5 − 0.4 = 2.1
3. 3.3 − 1.9 = 1.4
4. 8.62 − 2.33 = 6.29
5. 8.62 − 0.90 = 7.72
6. 9.51 − 4.04 = 5.47

Subtract using any method. Remember to estimate.

7. 6.30 − 1.09 = 5.21	8. 9.33 − 0.09 = 9.24	9. 4.04 − 0.19 = 3.85	10. 6.55 − 2.40 = 4.15	11. 5.32 − 2.84 = 2.48
12. 9.00 − 1.99 = 7.01	13. 5.04 − 1.35 = 4.69	14. 8.4 − 3.92 = 4.48	15. 2.22 − 0.99 = 1.23	16. 6.00 − 1.33 = 4.67

McGraw-Hill School Division

EXTEND • 116

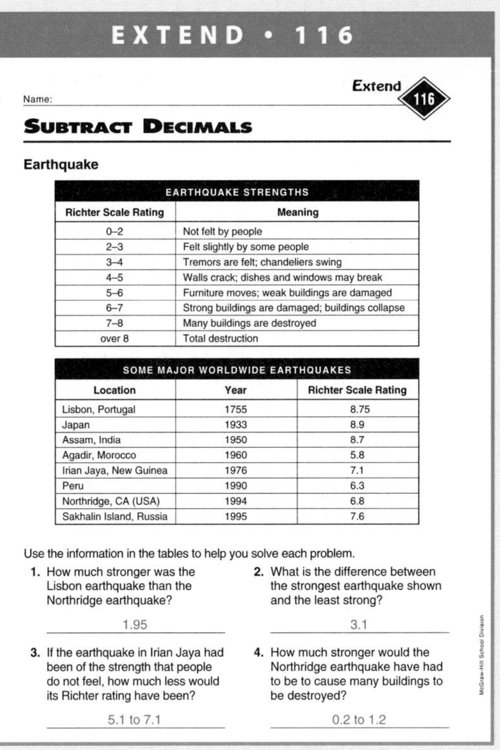

Extend 116

Name:

SUBTRACT DECIMALS

Earthquake

EARTHQUAKE STRENGTHS

Richter Scale Rating	Meaning
0–2	Not felt by people
2–3	Felt slightly by some people
3–4	Tremors are felt; chandeliers swing
4–5	Walls crack; dishes and windows may break
5–6	Furniture moves; weak buildings are damaged
6–7	Strong buildings are damaged; buildings collapse
7–8	Many buildings are destroyed
over 8	Total destruction

SOME MAJOR WORLDWIDE EARTHQUAKES

Location	Year	Richter Scale Rating
Lisbon, Portugal	1755	8.75
Japan	1933	8.9
Assam, India	1950	8.7
Agadir, Morocco	1960	5.8
Irian Jaya, New Guinea	1976	7.1
Peru	1990	6.3
Northridge, CA (USA)	1994	6.8
Sakhalin Island, Russia	1995	7.6

Use the information in the tables to help you solve each problem.

1. How much stronger was the Lisbon earthquake than the Northridge earthquake? 1.95
2. What is the difference between the strongest earthquake shown and the least strong? 3.1
3. If the earthquake in Irian Jaya had been of the strength that people do not feel, how much less would its Richter rating have been? 5.1 to 7.1
4. How much stronger would the Northridge earthquake have had to be to cause many buildings to be destroyed? 0.2 to 1.2

McGraw-Hill School Division

LESSON 12.9 RESOURCES

Write a Number Sentence

OBJECTIVE Solve/write problems by writing a number sentence.

RESOURCE REMINDER
Math Center Cards 117
Practice 117, Reteach 117, Extend 117

SKILLS TRACE

GRADE 3	• Formulate and solve problems by writing a number sentence. *(Chapter 8)*
GRADE 4	• Formulate and solve problems by writing a number sentence.
GRADE 5	• Formulate and solve problems by writing a number sentence. *(Chapter 2)*

MANIPULATIVE WARM-UP

Cooperative Pairs — Visual/Spatial

OBJECTIVE Explore finding decimal differences with money.

Materials per pair: 6 index cards; play money—dollars and quarters

▶ Students work with a partner. On each index card they write an amount of money less than \$8 in the form \$0.00, \$0.25, \$0.50, or \$0.75. They mix up the cards and place them facedown in a pile.

▶ Each student draws a card. They work together to find the difference between the amounts using play money. Have them record the difference in a subtraction sentence. Have students repeat the activity.

$4.75
$2.25

ESL APPROPRIATE

ALGEBRA CONNECTION

Cooperative Pairs — Logical/Analytical

OBJECTIVE Connect using algebra to solve problems.

Materials per pair: 2 index cards

▶ Have pairs of students work together. They write an addition or subtraction sentence using decimals or money amounts on one index card.

▶ Next, students write a problem on the other index card that can be solved using the number sentence. See sample cards below.

▶ Pairs exchange problems and solve. After solving, have students compare solutions with the original number sentence that solves the problem.

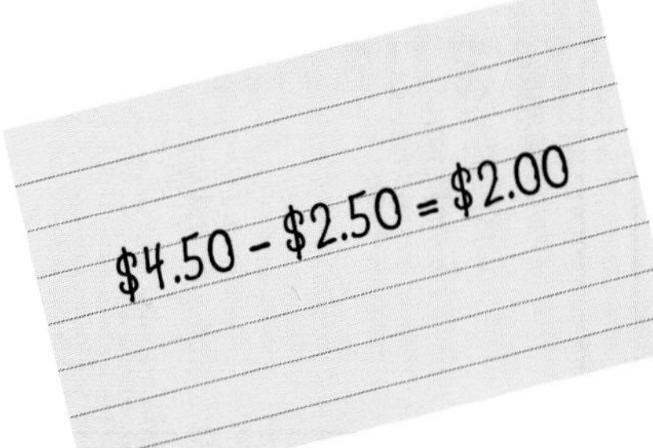
$4.50 - $2.50 = $2.00

Jack saved $4.50.
He bought baseball cards for $2.50.
How much did he have left?

Daily Review

PREVIOUS DAY QUICK REVIEW

1. 0.9 − 0.4 *[0.5]*
2. 8.6 − 2.7 *[5.9]*
3. 7.85 − 3.24 *[4.61]*
4. 5.43 − 2.36 *[3.07]*

FAST FACTS

1. 20 ÷ 5 *[4]*
2. 21 ÷ 7 *[3]*
3. 54 ÷ 6 *[9]*
4. 56 ÷ 8 *[7]*

Problem of the Day • 117

Candace jogged 3.2 km on Monday, 2.7 km on Wednesday, and 3.5 km on Friday. If she wants to jog a total of 12.5 km this week, how many more kilometers should she jog? *[3.1 km]*

TECH LINK

MATH VAN

Aid You may wish to use the Electronic Teacher Aid in the Math Van with this lesson.

MATH FORUM

Cultural Diversity My students enjoy using the precipitation data as a springboard to investigate the annual precipitation in different geographical areas, from their own to rain forests and deserts.

Visit our Resource Village at http://www.mhschool.com to see more of the Math Forum.

MATH CENTER

Practice

OBJECTIVE Solve problems.

Students write number sentences to answer problems about United States energy sources. *[**1.** 0.22 + 0.24 + 0.39 = 0.85; **2.** 0.11 + 0.04 = 0.15; **3.** 0.85 − 0.15 = 0.70]*

PRACTICE ACTIVITY 117 — MATH CENTER On Your Own

Using Data • Save Your Energy

Write a number sentence for each problem. Then solve the problem.

1. Coal, natural gas, and petroleum are all fossil fuels. How much of United States energy use relies on fossil fuels?
2. The category "other" includes solar power and wind power. These other sources combined with hydropower and nuclear power are all alternative sources of energy to fossil fuels. How much of United States energy is from alternative sources?
3. How much more of United States energy comes from fossil fuel sources than from alternative sources?

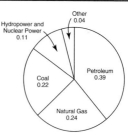

United States Energy Sources: Other 0.04; Hydropower and Nuclear Power 0.11; Coal 0.22; Petroleum 0.39; Natural Gas 0.24

McGraw-Hill School Division Grade Level 4

Chapter 12, Lesson 9, pages 472–475 — Problem Solving

NCTM Standards
- ✓ Problem Solving
- Communication
- ✓ Reasoning
- ✓ Connections

Problem Solving

OBJECTIVE Solve a logical reasoning problem.

Materials per student: 6 two-color counters, Math Center Recording Sheet (TA 31 optional)

Students try to switch positions of counters on a game board in the least number of moves possible. *[Answers may vary. One of the shortest methods for solving this puzzle takes 10 moves.]*

PROBLEM-SOLVING ACTIVITY 117 — MATH CENTER On Your Own

Spatial Reasoning • The Great Switcheroo

YOU NEED: 6 two-color counters

- Place the counters on a copy of the diagram below.
- Try to switch the position of three red-side-up counters and three yellow-side-up counters.
- You may make two kinds of moves—you can slide a counter one space left or right into the empty space; you can jump over one or more counters so that a counter lands in an empty space.
- Red counters can only move to the right, and yellow counters can only move to the left.
- What is the least number of moves you can make to completely switch the counters?

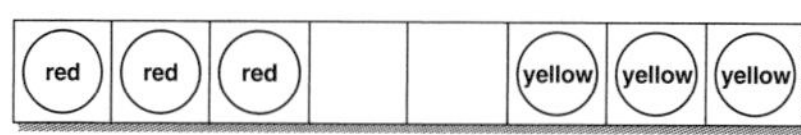

McGraw-Hill School Division Grade Level 4

Chapter 12, Lesson 9, pages 472–475 — Problem Solving

NCTM Standards
- ✓ Problem Solving
- ✓ Communication
- ✓ Reasoning
- Connections

Problem Solvers at Work

OBJECTIVE Solve and write problems by writing a number sentence.

Materials Have available: calculators

Resources spreadsheet program, or Math Van Tools

1 Introduce

Present this problem:

Kylie drove 12.6 miles from her home to a gas station. Then she drove 5.3 miles to work. How far did Kylie drive from her home to work?

Have students write a number sentence to solve the problem. *[12.6 + 5.3 mi = 17.9 mi]*

2 Teach *Cooperative Groups*

Cultural Connection Read the **Cultural Note.** Sirius is the brightest star in the sky. It is located in the constellation Canis Major. The ancient Egyptians thought of the star as a symbol of the rising Nile and of good harvest. They built many temples so that light from Sirius would shine inside. Sirius is one of the closest stars to the Earth, which is primarily why it is so bright. It is visible in both the Northern and Southern Hemispheres.

Part 1 Write a Number Sentence

LEARN Encourage students to focus on writing a complete number sentence to solve the problems. Allow them to use calculators to complete the number sentence. Versatility in writing number sentences will prepare them for solving for unknown variables in algebra. Stress that writing number sentences records the problem with numbers and symbols and provides a solution.

For item 3, students may write three number sentences to solve or they may combine the data to write fewer number sentences. Have the class compare the number sentences used to solve. Discuss what makes different number sentences easy to complete.

For item 4, students will have to compare data from part of item 3 with a new total provided in the problem.

Write an Essay Item 5 is an enhanced problem in that students will have to make their own assumptions about how they are able to solve the problem with or without a calculator. In their essay, they should explain their method of solution in contrast to or in agreement with Kristie's position. As students share their essays, they can compare and contrast their methods with each other's as well.

Problem Solvers at Work

Read | Plan | Solve | Look Back

Part 1 Write a Number Sentence

LEARN

Do weather reports ever catch your attention while you are channel surfing? It may be because meteorologists use interesting comparisons, unusual stories, and maps to capture your attention.

Cultural Note

During the days between July 3 and August 11, the ancient Egyptians noticed a star rising with the sun. They thought the star made the sun hotter. The star, Sirius, is part of a constellation shaped like a dog. Today, we call July 3–August 11 the "dog days of summer."

Rainfall

Date	This Year	Last Year
July 22	0.02 in.	0.00 in.
July 23	1.13 in.	0.18 in.
July 24	1.08 in.	0.84 in.
July 25	0.45 in.	2.62 in.
July 26	0.97 in.	3.09 in.

Work Together

Solve the problem. Write number sentences to record your work.

1. What is the difference between the greatest and least rainfalls from July 22 to July 26 this year? **1.13 − 0.02 = 1.11 in.**
2. What was the total rainfall from July 22 to July 26 this year? **0.02 + 1.13 + 1.08 + 0.45 + 0.97 = 3.65 in.**
3. Did it rain more altogether this year or last year on the dates given? How much more? **See below.**
4. **What if** the normal rainfall from July 22 to July 26 is 2.85 in. How much over this was the rainfall last year? **6.73 in. − 2.85 in. = 3.88 in. over**
5.  **Write an Essay** Kristie used a calculator to solve problem 3. She said that you have to use the MEMORY key to find the answer. Do you agree or disagree with her? Explain your reasoning in an essay. **Possible answer: Disagree; estimate to see that last year's total is greater, add to find this exact total, and then subtract each rainfall (from last week) one by one.**

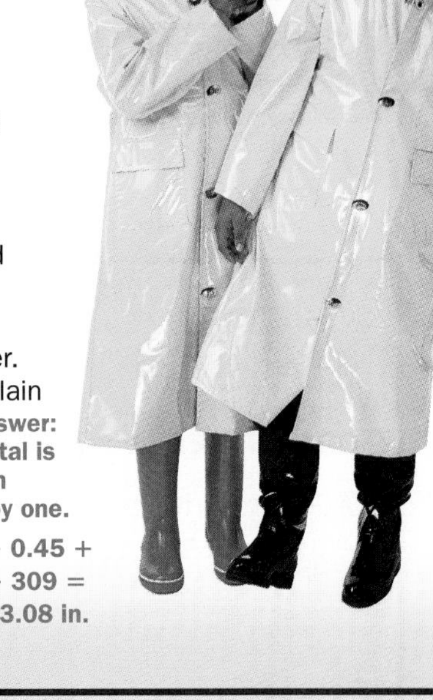

3. last year; 3.08 in. more; 0.02 + 1.13 + 1.08 + 0.45 + 0.97 = 3.65 in., 0.00 + 0.18 + 0.84 + 2.62 + 309 = 6.73 in., 6.73 in. − 3.65 in. = 3.08 in.

472 Lesson 12.9

Meeting Individual Needs

Extra Support

Encourage students to determine the operation needed to solve a problem before they write a number sentence. Have them use the numbers in the problem to solve. Remind them to check their solutions.

Gender Fairness

To reduce inhibitions, have students work in small same-sex groups to solve problems.

Ongoing Assessment

Anecdotal Report Note if students are able to solve problems by identifying the operations needed.

Follow Up Have students who are having difficulty writing number sentences try **Reteach 117.**

For students who successfully complete the lesson, assign **Extend 117.**

. Possible answer: What is the difference in precipitation between San Francisco, CA, and Albuquerque, NM?; 11.59 in.

art 2 Write and Share Problems

enya looked in an almanac to find information on e precipitation in several major United States ities. Kenya used the data to write a problem.

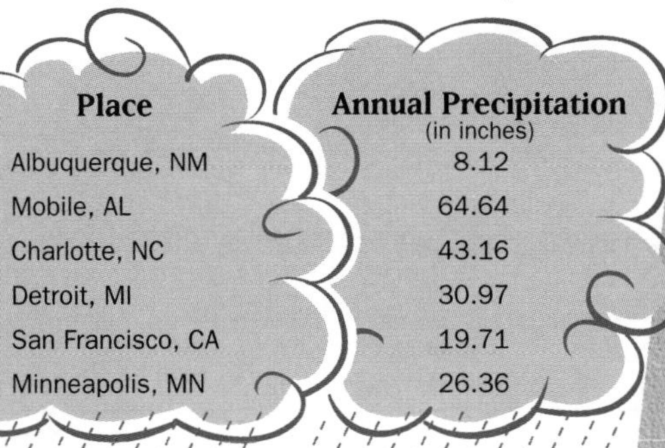

Place	Annual Precipitation (in inches)
Albuquerque, NM	8.12
Mobile, AL	64.64
Charlotte, NC	43.16
Detroit, MI	30.97
San Francisco, CA	19.71
Minneapolis, MN	26.36

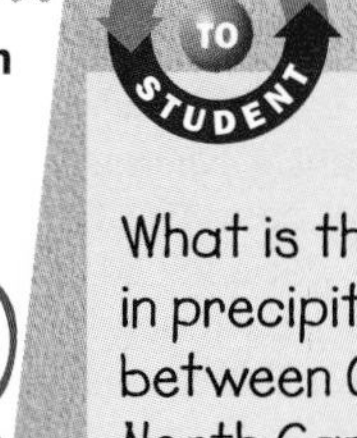

CHECK

What is the difference in precipitation between Charlotte, North Carolina, and Detroit, Michigan?

Kenya Smith
Elephant's Fork Elementary School
Suffolk, VA

6 Write a number sentence that will help you solve Kenya's problem. Then solve it. **43.16 − 30.97 = 12.19; 12.19 in.**

7 Change Kenya's problem so that you would complete this number sentence to solve it: 19.71 − 8.12 = ■. Then solve it. **See above.**

8 **Write a problem** of your own using the data in the table. **For problems 8–10, see Teacher's Edition.**

9 Trade problems. Solve at least three problems written by your classmates.

10 What was the most difficult problem that you solved? Why?

Turn the page for Practice Strategies.

PART 2 WRITE AND SHARE PROBLEMS

Check To make sure that students are able to interpret the data in the table, ask:

- **Which city was the driest?** *[Albuquerque]*
- **Which city had about 20 inches of precipitation?** *[San Francisco]*
- **Which city had between 20 and 30 inches of precipitation?** *[Minneapolis]*
- **Which cities had more than 40 inches of precipitation?** *[Charlotte and Mobile]*

For item 7, students must be able to compare and interpret the data in the table to work backward from solution to problem.

For item 8, students can write any type of problem. Encourage them to write problems that can be solved by writing a number sentence. Suggest that they write problems other than comparing the precipitation of two different cities.

For items 9 and 10, encourage students to discuss the problems they solved and their reasons why a problem was most interesting.

3 Close

Have students discuss how they used the data in the table to write their problems. Have them comment on how number sentences were used or could be used to solve the problems.

Practice See pages 474–475.

Part 3 Practice Strategies

Materials have available: calculators; computer spreadsheet program (optional)

Students have the option of choosing any five problems from ex. 1–8, and any two problems from ex. 9–12. They may choose to do more problems if they wish. Have students describe how they made their choices.

- Students should be able to use mental math to solve ex. 2.
- For ex. 3, students may use the problem-solving strategy, Make an Organized List, to find the answer.
- Have students identify the pattern they use to solve ex. 5. *[Add 7.]*
- For ex. 6, students may want to combine the Draw a Picture and Guess, Test, and Revise strategies to find the answer.
- To solve ex. 7, students may want to use the problem-solving strategy, Solve a Simpler Problem.
- For ex. 9, encourage students to explain how they planned each swim team and why.
- A diagram may help students with the logical reasoning for ex. 10.

At the Computer If computers are not available, have students use calculators to make the calculations. Point out that the numbers on the spreadsheet are entered in columns A–B but the computer calculates the total in column C.

Extend the activity by providing students with sales tax for column D; for example: D *[0.06 × C]*. Then have them use column E with the formula *C* + *D* to find the grand total.

Math Van Students may use the Table tool to make the spreadsheet. A project electronic teacher aid has been provided.

Part 3 Practice Strategies

PRACTICE

Menu

Choose five problems and solve them. Explain your methods. Explanations may vary.

1 Carol bought 4 concert tickets that cost $9.50 each. She got back $12 in change. How much did she give the cashier?
$50

2 Calvin says that the probability of choosing his favorite color is $\frac{3}{6}$. What is his favorite color?
blue

3 Annie has a red sweatshirt, a green sweatshirt, and a blue sweatshirt. She has white shorts and grey sweatpants. How many different combinations of outfits does she have?
6 outfits

4 You subscribe to 8 magazines. Yo[u] donate 1 out of every 4 magazine[s] to your classroom. How many magazines do you donate to your classroom?
2 magazines

5 **ALGEBRA: PATTERNS** John is watching a news program on TV. There are four parts to the program. The first three parts were shown on the 2nd, 9th, and 16th of the month. If this pattern continues, on what day will the fourth part be shown?
23rd day

6 Juan is buying plant food for his vegetable garden. He needs to know the area of the rectangular garden. One side of the garden measures 9 ft and the perimeter is 40 ft. What is the area?
99 ft^2

7 Roberto has $20.00. He wants to buy a CD for $8.99 and two cassettes for $3.00 each. How much change should he get back? Write one or more number sentences and solve them.

$5.01; possible answer: $20.00 − $8.99 = $11.01, $3.00 + $3.00 = $6.00, $11.01 − $6.00 = $5.01

8 A radio station plays 4 commercia[ls] every hour of a 24-hour day, excep[t] for Sundays on which it plays 2 commercials every hour. How many commercials does the station play in one week?
624 commercials

Meeting Individual Needs

Early Finishers

Have students use the table on page 472 to compare the amount rainfall increased or decreased each day from July 22–26 this year. *[increased 1.11 in.; decreased 0.05 in.; decreased 0.63 in.; increased 0.52 in.]*

Language Support

Pair students with English-speaking students. Point out that precipitation refers to rainfall and is measured in inches. Discuss the locations and pronunciations of the places listed in the table on page 473.

ESL APPROPRIATE

Inclusion

Some learning-disabled students may have difficulty finding extended sums. Have them find partial sums until they find the final sum, crossing off each addend as it is added to remember where they are in the sum.

Gifted And Talented

Have students make line graphs to show the precipitation data on page 472. Allow them to use a computer graphing program, if available. Have them comment on what the graphs show about the data.

Possible answer: Swimmer 1 and Swimmer 2 would have a team time of 86.93.

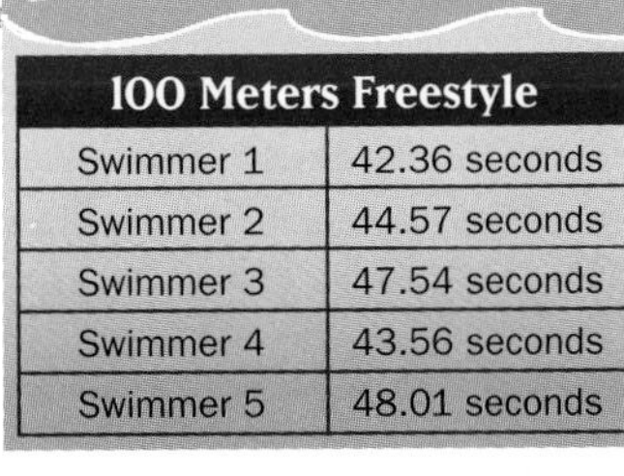

100 Meters Freestyle	
Swimmer 1	42.36 seconds
Swimmer 2	44.57 seconds
Swimmer 3	47.54 seconds
Swimmer 4	43.56 seconds
Swimmer 5	48.01 seconds

Choose two problems and solve them. Explain your methods. **Explanations may vary.**

9. Use the table to plan the possible combinations of two-person swim teams for the race. What would be the combined time for the two swimmers on each team? **See above.**

10. **Logical reasoning** There are three people standing in line to make purchases. Jon is not first in line. Ali is standing in front of Sandy. Sandy is not last in line. Who is first, second, and third in line? **Ali, Sandy, Jon**

11. Suppose you have 28 ft of picture-framing wood. Sketch and label the size of one picture you could frame. Now try using the 28 ft for two pictures. **See below.**

12. **At the Computer** A computer spreadsheet can arrange data in rows and columns and make calculations.

Telephone City is keeping track of the sales for its stores in Newport and Maple. They will use the information to decide how often to order the items listed on the spreadsheet.

Use a spreadsheet program to arrange the data below into rows and columns and make calculations.

Telephone City Sales
Sales for September 3, 1997

Item	A Sales for Newport	B Sales for Maple	C[A + B] Total	
Stick-on pad and pencil	$354.24	$75.75	$429.99	
Shoulder rest	$108.76	$104.89		**$213.65**
Long jack cord	$135.21	$199.45		**$334.66**
Earpiece amplifier	$91.00	$367.19		**$458.19**
30-ft expandable cord	$723.22	$605.60		**$1,328.82**

11. Answers may vary. Possible answer: 1 picture—rectangle 4 ft by 10 ft; 2 pictures—square 2 ft on each side and rectangle 2 ft by 8 ft

Extra Practice, page 531

Alternate Teaching Strategy

Refer to the data showing rainfall for the week of July 22–26 on Student Book page 472. Ask:

- **Did more rain fall on July 22 or July 23 of this year?** *[July 23]*
- **What number sentence can you write to show the difference?** *[1.13 − 0.02 = 1.11 in.]*
- **What number sentence can you write to find the total amount of rainfall for July 22–23 of this year?** *[1.13 + 0.02 = 1.15 in.]*
- **How much total rain fell on July 25 and 26 of this year? What number sentence shows the total?** *[1.42 in.; 0.45 + 0.97 = 1.42in.]*

Continue asking similar questions. Have students provide a number sentence for each of their answers. Use the data from last year, on Student Book page 472, for additional data if desired.

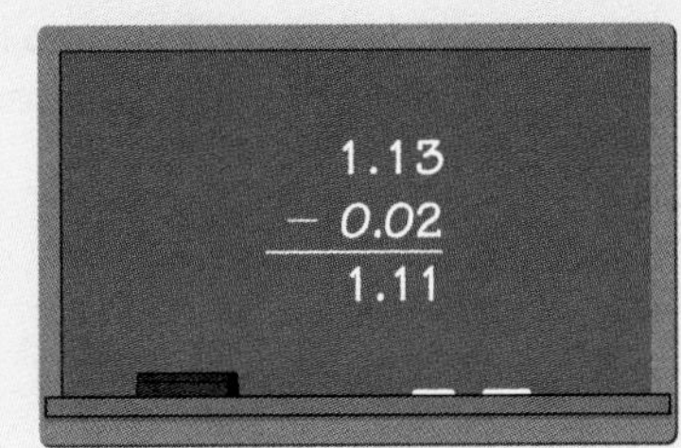

HOMEWORK

Practice 117

Name:

PROBLEM SOLVING: WRITE A NUMBER SENTENCE

✓ Read ✓ Plan ✓ Solve ✓ Look Back

Write a number sentence to solve.

SATURDAY HIKING CLUB	
Week 1	2.30 km
Week 2	2.05 km
Week 3	3.05 km
Week 4	4.50 km
Week 5	4.95 km
Week 6	5.50 km

1. Write a number sentence to show the total kilometers hiked by the club in 6 weeks. 2.3 + 2.05 + 3.05 + 4.50 + 4.95 + 5.50 = 22.35 km
2. Write a number sentence to show the difference between the greatest and least number of kilometers hiked. 5.50 − 2.05 = 3.45 km
3. The club wanted to hike $\frac{1}{2}$ kilometer more than they did in Week 4. Write a number sentence to show that total. 4.50 + 0.50 = 5.00 km
4. Between which 2 weeks did the hiking club increase their hike by one kilometer? Write a number sentence. Weeks 2 and 3; 3.05 − 2.05 = 1.00

Solve using any method.

5. During a long weekend, the club hiked $1\frac{1}{4}$ kilometers on Friday, $2\frac{1}{6}$ kilometers on Saturday, and $2\frac{1}{4}$ kilometers on Sunday. How many kilometers did they hike over the weekend? $5\frac{2}{3}$ km
6. The club plans to hike 10 kilometers in the winter. So far, they have hiked 3.5, 2.75, and 1.55 kilometers. How many more kilometers do they need to reach their goal? 2.20 km
7. By holding fundraisers the hiking club has made $195.25, $107.50, $83.25, and $66. What was the average amount of profit? $113
8. The fastest hiker in the club can travel 1.6 kilometers in 30 minutes. How far might she be able to travel in 90 minutes? 4.8 km

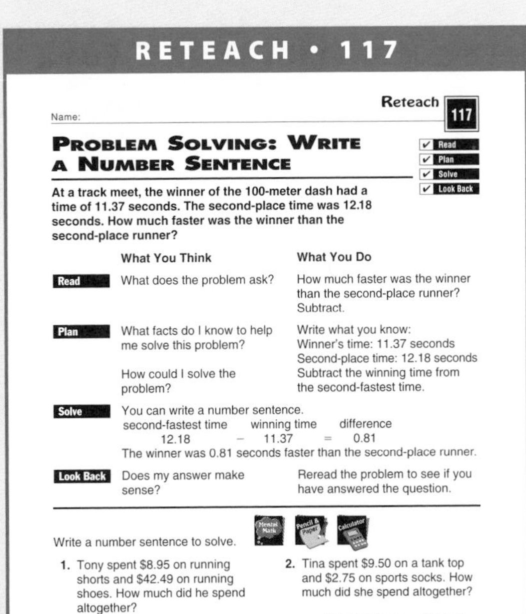

RETEACH • 117

Reteach 117

Name:

PROBLEM SOLVING: WRITE A NUMBER SENTENCE

✓ Read ✓ Plan ✓ Solve ✓ Look Back

At a track meet, the winner of the 100-meter dash had a time of 11.37 seconds. The second-place time was 12.18 seconds. How much faster was the winner than the second-place runner?

	What You Think	What You Do
Read	What does the problem ask?	How much faster was the winner than the second-place runner? Subtract.
Plan	What facts do I know to help me solve this problem?	Write what you know: Winner's time: 11.37 seconds Second-place time: 12.18 seconds
	How could I solve the problem?	Subtract the winning time from the second-fastest time.
Solve	You can write a number sentence. second-fastest time − winning time = difference; 12.18 − 11.37 = 0.81. The winner was 0.81 seconds faster than the second-place runner.	
Look Back	Does my answer make sense?	Reread the problem to see if you have answered the question.

Write a number sentence to solve.

1. Tony spent $8.95 on running shorts and $42.49 on running shoes. How much did he spend altogether? $8.95 + $42.49 = $51.44
2. Tina spent $9.50 on a tank top and $2.75 on sports socks. How much did she spend altogether? $9.50 + $2.75 = $12.25
3. The track team had $654.29 in its bank account. The team spent $162.50 to travel to a meet. How much does the team have left? $654.29 − $162.50 = $491.79
4. The team bought sweatshirts for $109.60 and hats for $24.98. How much more did they spend on sweatshirts than on hats? $109.60 − $24.98 = $84.62

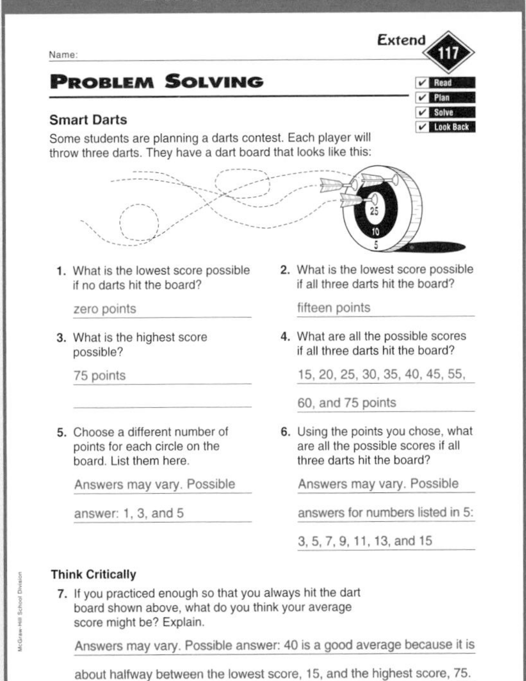

EXTEND • 117

Extend 117

Name:

PROBLEM SOLVING

✓ Read ✓ Plan ✓ Solve ✓ Look Back

Smart Darts

Some students are planning a darts contest. Each player will throw three darts. They have a dart board that looks like this:

1. What is the lowest score possible if no darts hit the board? zero points
2. What is the lowest score possible if all three darts hit the board? fifteen points
3. What is the highest score possible? 75 points
4. What are all the possible scores if all three darts hit the board? 15, 20, 25, 30, 35, 40, 45, 55, 60, and 75 points
5. Choose a different number of points for each circle on the board. List them here. Answers may vary. Possible answer: 1, 3, and 5
6. Using the points you chose, what are all the possible scores if all three darts hit the board? Answers may vary. Possible answers for numbers listed in 5: 3, 5, 7, 9, 11, 13, and 15

Think Critically

7. If you practiced enough so that you always hit the dart board shown above, what do you think your average score might be? Explain. Answers may vary. Possible answer: 40 is a good average because it is about halfway between the lowest score, 15, and the highest score, 75.

CHAPTER REVIEW

PURPOSE Review and assess concepts, skills, and strategies that students have learned in this chapter.

Materials per student: calculator (optional)

Chapter Objectives

12A Read and write decimals to hundredths
12B Compare and order decimals
12C Estimate decimal sums and differences
12D Add and subtract decimals
12E Solve problems, including those that involve decimals and solving a simpler problem

Using the Chapter Review

The **Chapter Review** can be used as a review, practice test, or chapter test.

Think Critically Students' explanations for ex. 44 and ex. 46 will indicate whether they understand the steps involved in estimating and finding decimal sums and differences.

Language and Mathematics

Complete the sentence. Use a word in the chart. (pages 450–471)

1. The ■ of two decimals will always be greater than either decimal. sum
2. In the decimal 0.08, the 8 is in the ■ place. hundredths
3. The ■ separates whole numbers from decimals. decimal point
4. There are 10 hundredths in 1 ■. tenth
5. You can estimate the sum of two or more decimals by ■. rounding

Vocabulary
decimal point
tenth
rounding
sum
hundredths
ten

Concepts and Skills

Write a decimal. (page 450)

6. 0.43
7. 1.9

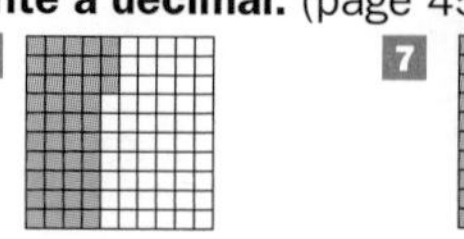

8. 1.07

9. $\frac{7}{100}$ 0.07
10. $3\frac{6}{10}$ 3.6
11. $7\frac{32}{100}$ 7.32
12. $\frac{54}{100}$ 0.54
13. $17\frac{3}{10}$ 17.3
14. $24\frac{74}{100}$ 24.74
15. four and six tenths 4.6
16. eight and thirty-two hundredths 8.32

Compare. Write >, <, or =. (page 456)

17. 2.76 ● 2.67 >
18. 6.56 ● 5.66 >
19. 9.30 ● 9.3 =

Write in order from least to greatest. (page 456)

20. 0.82, 0.88, 0.28 — 0.28, 0.82, 0.88
21. 1.93, 1.39, 1.79 — 1.39, 1.79, 1.93
22. 4.14, 4.04, 4.4 — 4.04, 4.14, 4.4

Write in order from greatest to least. (page 456)

23. 0.07, 0.70, 7.07 — 7.07, 0.70, 0.07
24. 2.28, 2.09, 2.25 — 2.28, 2.25, 2.09
25. 5.64, 5.90, 15.03 — 15.03, 5.90, 5.64

Estimate the sum or difference. (page 464)

26. 2.34 + 5.85 8
27. 12.08 + 3.50 16
28. 6.82 − 4.37 3
29. 13.70 − 6.9 7
30. 9.91 + 3.02 13
31. 20.39 + 0.77 21
32. 8.03 − 2.74 5
33. 38.71 − 4.0 35

Estimates may vary. Possible estimates are given.

Reinforcement and Remediation

CHAPTER OBJECTIVES	CHAPTER REVIEW ITEMS	STUDENT BOOK PAGES	TEACHER'S EDITION PAGES			TEACHER RESOURCES
		Lessons	Midchapter Review	Activities	Alternate Teaching Strategy	Reteach
12A	2–4, 6–16, 45	450–453, 454–455	458	449A, 453A	453, 455	109–110
12B	17–25	456–457	458	455A	457	111
12C	5, 26–33, 44	464–465		463A	465	113
12D	1, 34–43, 46	466–467, 468–469, 470–471		465A, 467A, 469A	467, 469, 471	114–116
12E	47–50	462–463, 472–475	458	461A, 471A	463, 475	112, 117

dd. (pages 466, 468)

4	35	36	37	38
0.26	4.5	14.62	2.20	$18.56
+ 0.44	+ 3.6	+ 0.94	+ 9.68	+ 57.39
0.70	**8.1**	**15.56**	**11.88**	**$75.95**

ubtract. (pages 466, 470)

9	40	41	42	43
0.43	13.2	23.15	64.35	$10.05
− 0.21	− 9.6	− 6.40	− 36.80	− 8.78
0.22	**3.6**	**16.75**	**27.55**	**$1.27**

hink critically. (pages 450, 464, 466)

4 Analyze. When Carla estimates decimal sums, she rounds each addend to the nearest whole number. What is the greatest amount she could be off by using this method to estimate the sum of two decimals? Give an example.
1; possible answer: 4.50 + 4.50—estimate is 10, and exact sum is 9.

5 Generalize. Explain how fractions help you to understand decimals. **Possible answer: Fractions and decimals both name parts of a whole or group, fractions can be changed to equivalent decimals.**

6 Generalize. Explain how adding and subtracting decimals is like adding and subtracting whole numbers. How is it different? **Possible answer: Add the numbers in the same place-values; insert the decimal point in the decimal answer.**

(pages 462, 472)

7 It rained 2.34 in. on Tuesday, 1.67 in. on Wednesday, and 0.43 in. on Thursday. What was the total rainfall for the three days? **4.44 in.**

8 Fernando's team swam the relay in 41.89 seconds. Mara's team swam it in 43.06 seconds. Who won? By how much?
Fernando's team; by 1.17 s

9 Cal is saving for a new microphone. It costs $39.95 plus $3.10 tax. So far he has saved $26.72. How much more does he need to buy the microphone? **$16.33**

0 Mrs. Kelly's class raised $147.58 in April for the Children's Hospital. They raised $23.18 the first week, $37.82 the second week, and $59.45 the third week. How much did the class raise during the fourth week in April? **$27.13**

CHAPTER TEST

PURPOSE Assess the concepts, skills, and strategies students have learned in this chapter.

Chapter Objectives

- **12A** Read and write decimals to hundredths
- **12B** Compare and order decimals
- **12C** Estimate decimal sums and differences
- **12D** Add and subtract decimals
- **12E** Solve problems, including those that involve decimals and solving a simpler problem

Using the Chapter Test

The **Chapter Test** can be used as a practice test, a chapter test, or as an additional review. The **Performance Assessment** on Student Book page 479 provides an alternate means of assessing students' understanding of fractions and probability.

The table below correlates the test items to the chapter objectives and to the Student Book pages on which the skills are taught.

Assessment Resources

Test Masters

The Testing Program Blackline Masters provide three forms of the Chapter Test to assess students' understanding of the chapter concepts, skills, and strategies. Form C uses a free-response format. Forms A and B use a multiple-choice format.

Computer Test Generator

The Computer Test Generator supplies abundant multiple-choice and free-response test items, which you may use to generate tests and practice work sheets tailored to the needs of your class.

Teacher's Assessment Resources

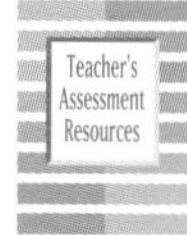

Teacher's Assessment Resources provides resources for alternate assessment. It includes guidelines for Building a Portfolio, page 6, and the Holistic Scoring Guide, page 27.

chapter test

Write the number as a decimal.

1 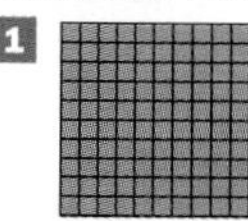 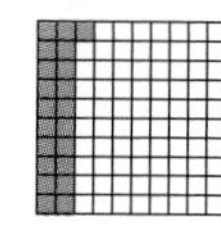 1.21

2 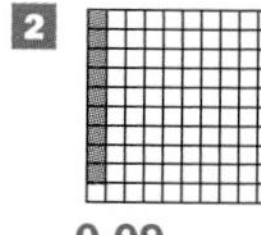 0.09

3 $\frac{1}{100}$ 0.01

4 $2\frac{7}{10}$ 2.7

5 eight and three hundredths 8.03

6 twelve and three tenths 12.3

Complete. Write >, <, or =.

7 1.13 ● 1.3 <

8 4.8 ● 4.80 =

9 1.50 ● 1.05 >

Write in order from least to greatest.

10 0.56, 0.65, 0.5 0.5, 0.56, 0.65

11 3.06, 2.99, 3.6 2.99, 3.06, 3.6

Estimate the sum or difference. Estimates may vary. Possible estimates are give

12 4.09 + 0.95 5

13 \$24.32 + \$6.75 \$31.00

14 7.82 − 2.09 6

15 5.12 − 2.23

Add.

16 0.67 + 0.43 = 1.10, or 1.1

17 3.60 + 5.46 = 9.06

18 62.35 + 0.48 = 62.83

Subtract.

19 0.52 − 0.10 = 0.42

20 \$10.00 − 0.09 = \$9.91

21 4.42 − 1.08 = 3.34

Solve.

22 Cary ran around a rectangular track one time. The track is 125.5 yd long and 85.5 yd wide. How far did she run? 422 yd

23 Lane walks 1.20 mi to a bus and rides another 7.25 mi to work. H boss drives 8.50 mi to work. Wh lives farther from work? How can you tell? the boss; 8.5 > 8.45

24 At the end of the summer Jed was riding his bike 264 mi each week. This was 8 times as far as he rode at the beginning of the summer. How far did he ride at the beginning of the summer? 33 mi each week

25 Walter bought a \$3.95 hamburge and \$1.75 fruit cup for lunch. He paid with a \$10 bill. The clerk ga him 4 one-dollar bills, 1 quarter, and 1 nickel for his change. Is th correct? Why or why not? Yes; \$3.95 + \$1.75 = \$5.70, \$10 − \$5.70 = \$4.30, \$4 + \$0.25 + \$0.05 = \$4.30.

478 Chapter 12 Test

Test Correlation

CHAPTER OBJECTIVES	TEST ITEMS	TEXT PAGES
12A	1–6	450–455
12B	7–11	456–457
12C	12–15	464–465
12D	16–21	466–471
12E	22–25	462–463, 472–475

e Teacher's Assessment Resources for samples of student work.

ʼhat Did You Learn?

eck students' work.

ı can communicate with people ›und the country or around the ʻrld by telephone.

Use the telephone bills. Write a paragraph comparing the cost of calls to three cities.

Compare the totals for all the calls on each bill. Use models or drawings to explain how you found the amounts.

SPEEDY TELEPHONE CARRIER

Calls to	Minutes	Total
Des Moines, Iowa	5	$0.45
Jackson, Mississippi	13	$1.17
Nashua, New Hampshire	22	$2.98
Norfolk, Virginia	5	$0.62
Kyoto, Japan	20	$10.68

RELIABLE TELEPHONE CARRIER

Calls to	Minutes	Total
Des Moines, Iowa	5	$0.34
Jackson, Mississippi	13	$1.09
Nashua, New Hampshire	22	$2.78
Norfolk, Virginia	5	$1.28
Kyoto, Japan	20	$9.68

A Good Answer

- gives accurate comparisons of the costs of calls to different cities
- uses models or drawings to find and compare the phone bills

You may want to place your work in your portfolio.

What Do You Think?

See Teacher's Edition.

1 Does it help to think about subtracting whole numbers when you subtract decimals? Why or why not?

2 How do you know which digits to add or subtract when you solve problems that include decimals?

- Line up the decimal points.
- Use 10-by-10 grids and group entire grids, rows, or single squares.
- Use place value to add digits in the same place.
- Other. Explain.

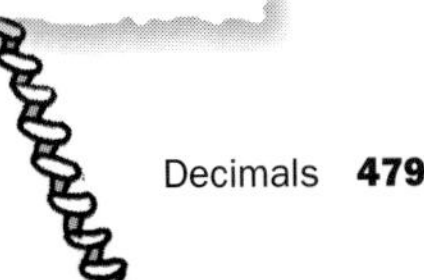

Reviewing A Portfolio

Have students review their portfolios. Consider including these items:

- Finished work on the Chapter Project (p. 447F) or **Investigation** (pp. 460–461).
- Selected math journal entries, pp. 449, 454, 458, 470.
- Finished work on the nonroutine problem in **What Do You Know?** (p. 449) and problems from the Menu (pp. 474–475).
- Each student's self-selected "best piece" from work completed during the chapter. Have each student attach a note explaining why he or she chose that piece.
- Any work you or an individual student wishes to keep for future reference.

You may take this opportunity to conduct conferences with students. The Portfolio Analysis Form can help you report students' progress. See Teacher's Assessment Resources, p. 33.

PURPOSE Review and assess the concepts, skills, and strategies learned in this chapter.

Materials have available: place-value models, calculators (optional)

Using the Performance Assessment

Have students read and restate the problems in their own words. Make sure they understand how to read the tables. Get them to notice that the calls on both bills are to the same cities and for the same lengths of time. Make sure they understand that they need to compare the costs for calls to three different cities and the totals for all the calls on each bill.

Point out the section on the student page headed "A Good Answer." Make sure students understand that you will use these points to evaluate their answers.

Evaluating Student Work

As you read students' papers, look for the following:

- *Does the student accurately compare the costs of calls to 3 cities?*
- *Does the student accurately compare the totals for each bill?*
- *How well does the student use models or drawings to explain how he or she found the totals?*

The Holistic Scoring Guide and annotated samples of students' work can be used to assess this task. See pages 27–32 and 37–72 in Teacher's Assessment Resources.

Using the Self-Assessment

What Do You Think? Assure students that there are no right or wrong answers. Tell them the emphasis is on what they think and how they justify their answers.

Follow-Up Interviews

These questions can be used to gain insight into students' thinking:

- **How did you compare the costs for the three cities you chose?**
- **How did you find the totals for each bill?**
- **How could you use models or drawings to find the totals?**
- **Were you surprised by which total was the lowest? Why or why not?**

OBJECTIVE Apply an understanding of decimals in the context of communication.

Materials newspaper, wallpaper paste, egg beater or electric mixer, cake pan, window screen, wax paper

Resource graphing program, or Math Van Tools

Science

Cultural Connection Read and discuss the **Cultural Note** and captions beneath the photographs. Discuss the question at the end of page 480 by encouraging students to share and compare other methods of communication they have known about. Ask:

- **What is the most common way you communicate with someone who lives far away?** *[Possible answer: by telephone]*
- **How is communicating by telephone the same as communicating by mail? different?** *[Possible answer: Same: You can communicate information using both methods; different: Unlike the mail, the phone can give you immediate oral responses to the person with whom you are communicating.]*

Math

Be sure students understand the information in the table before they begin working on items 1–3. Ask:

- **How much did a stamp cost in 1932? 1944? 1954?** *[$0.03]*
- **How can you tell?** *[Even though 1944 and 1954 are not listed on the table you can tell stamps were still $0.03 because according to the table there was no increase until 1958.]*

Students may realize that they can tell the cost of a stamp for any year from 1919 through 1995 using this table. If it didn't, they would not be able to answer item 3, since students' exact year of birth might not be listed.

math science technology CONNECTION

Communication and Technology

Humans have always looked for better and faster ways to communicate. Science and technology have influenced communication greatly.

Cultural Note

The Egyptians wrote message on a material made from a grasslike plant known as *papyrus* more than 5,000 yea ago. Before papyrus, people wrote on clay tablets or stone Paper was invented by the Chinese about 2,000 years ag

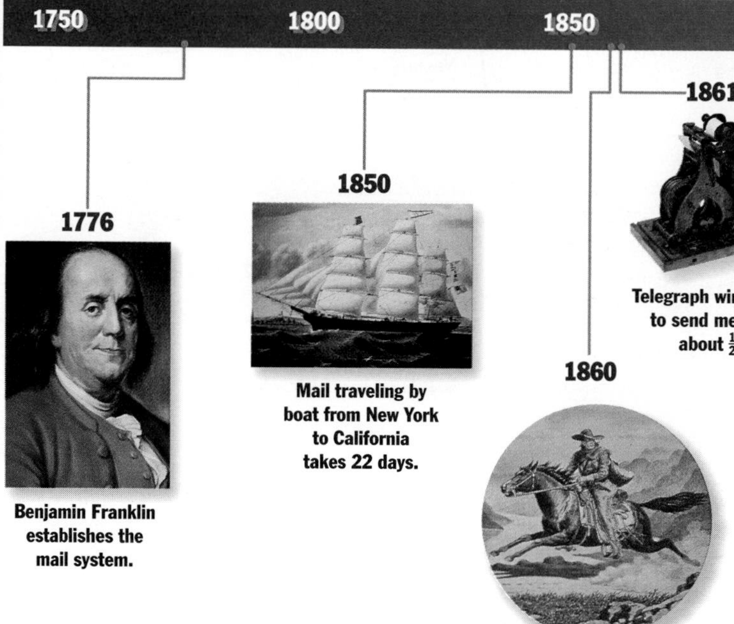

Benjamin Franklin establishes the mail system.

Mail traveling by boat from New York to California takes 22 days.

Telegraph wires are to send messages about $\frac{1}{2}$ hour.

Pony express riders carrying mail on horseback over a trail of almost 2,000 miles take 10 days.

- ▶ What other technologies do we use today to communicate? **Possible answers: computers, telephones**
- ▶ What are some of the advantages of today's communication technology? **Possible answer: It is possible to get a lot of information quickly so that decisions can be made.**

480 Math • Science • Technology Connection

Extending The Activity

Consider having students make recycled paper:

1. Tear a 12-inch sheet of paper into small pieces and soak it in water until it breaks up.
2. Add a teaspoon of wallpaper glue and mix in.
3. Place the window screen over a pan and pour the mixture over the screen. Cover with wax paper.
4. Use a rolling pin to squeeze as much of the water out as possible.
5. Allow the mixture to dry for several days, then peel off the wax paper.
6. Carefully remove the gray cardboard-like recycled paper from the screen.

ost of Stamps

e the table for problems 1–3.

Which increase in postage cost was greater, from 1968 to 1971 or from 1991 to 1995? **from 1991 to 1995**

During which years did postage cost increase by more than 2 cents? **1975, 1981, 1988, 1991, 1995**

Since you were born, how much has the cost of mailing a 1-ounce letter increased? **Answers may vary.**

Messages are sent almost instantaneously by transmitting information by way of communication satellites.

At the Computer

Check students' work.

4 Use a graphing program to make a bar graph that shows the cost of mailing for the years given.

5 Write two statements that describe the data in your bar graph.

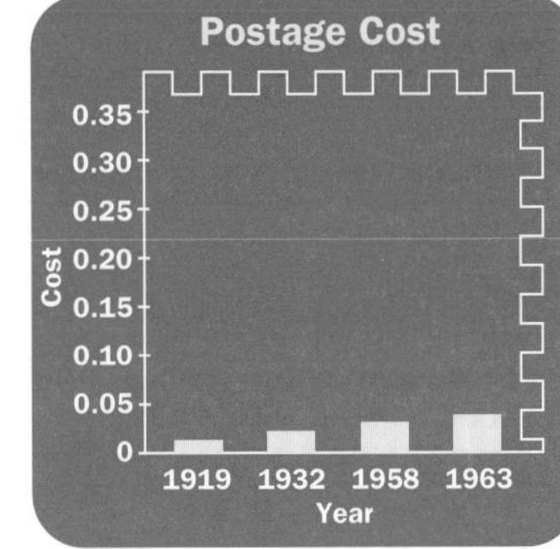

Postage Cost of Mailing a 1-ounce letter			
Year	**Cost**	**Year**	**Cost**
1919	$0.02	1978	$0.15
1932	$0.03	1981 (March)	$0.18
1958	$0.04	1981 (November)	$0.20
1963	$0.05	1985	$0.22
1968	$0.06	1988	$0.25
1971	$0.08	1991	$0.29
1974	$0.10	1995	$0.32
1975	$0.13		

Bibliography

Get the Message: Telecommunications in Your High-Tech World, by Gloria Skurzynski. New York: Bradbury Press, 1993. ISBN: 0–02–778071–6.

Stepping Through History: The Mail, by Peggy Burns. New York: Thomson Learning, 1994. ISBN: 1–56847–249–8.

Technology

Students can work in small groups at the computer. To help students who might have difficulty writing statements to describe the data, ask:

- **Did the price of stamps show any trend over the years?**
- **What part of the century showed more of an increase in the price of stamps than any other?**
- **What was the greatest or least increase in the price of stamps?**

Students can make a line graph or a bar graph with a graphing program.

Math Van Students may use the Graph tool from the Math Van Tools to create their graphs. A project electronic teacher aid has been provided.

Interesting Facts

- **The British were the first to charge postage to the sender,** in 1840. Until that time mail delivery was paid by the recipient of the letter.
- **The most valuable stamp in the world** is an 1856 one-cent stamp from British Guiana. There is only one known to exist in the world and it is estimated to be worth between one and four million dollars.
- **Greeting cards** make up about half of all personal mail. The three most popular holiday greeting cards are Christmas, Valentine's Day, and Easter.

CUMULATIVE REVIEW

PURPOSE Review and assess the concepts, skills, and strategies that students have already learned.

Materials per student: calculators (optional)

Using the Cumulative Review

The **Cumulative Review** is presented in a multiple-choice format to provide practice in taking a standarized test.

The table below correlates the review items to the text pages on which the skills are taught.

Assessment Resources

Test Masters

There are multiple-choice Cumulative Tests and a Year-End Test that provides additional opportunities for students to practice taking standardized tests.

Computer Test Generator

The Computer Test Generator supplies abundant multiple-choice and free-response test items, which you may use to generate tests and practice work sheets tailored to the needs of your class.

TEST PREPARATION

Choose the letter of the best answer.

1 What is the least number possible using the digits 1, 3, 4, and 0? **D**

A 3,104
B 1,340
C 1,304
D 1,034

2 Carter puts his baseball card collection in 14 shoe boxes with 488 cards in each box. How many cards does he have? **G**

F 8,712
G 6,832
H 6,382
J 502

3 Kim ran around the track in 65.19 seconds. Jenny ran around it in 71.04 seconds. How much faster was Kim's time? **A**

A 5.85 seconds
B 6.15 seconds
C 6.85 seconds
D 5.95 seconds

4 Jacob had $25. He spent $\frac{3}{5}$ of his money on a present for his mother. How much money does he have left? **H**

F $15.00
G $ 5.00
H $10.00
J $12.50

5 3,864 ÷ 8 **D**

A 408
B 438
C 480
D 483

6 Which numbers are ordered fro[m] least to greatest? **H**

F 0.48, 1.23, 1.05
G 1.01, 0.92, 0.50
H 0.02, 0.20, 2.00
J 8.08, 0.80, 0.88

7 Katie plans to build a fence around her garden. The garden measures 12 ft by 8 ft. How mu[ch] fencing will she need? **C**

A 96 ft
B 48 ft
C 40 ft
D 32 ft

8 Which subtraction is shown? **J**

$\frac{1}{10}$ $\frac{1}{10}$ $\frac{1}{10}$ $\frac{1}{10}$ $\frac{1}{10}$ $\frac{1}{10}$ $\frac{1}{10}$

F 0.7 − 0.5
G 7 − 2
H 0.5 − 0.2
J 0.7 − 0.2

9 7 × 1,765 **C**

A 13,355
B 12,553
C 12,355
D 8,925

10 Alan has $\frac{3}{4}$ cup of rice. He uses $\frac{1}{2}$ cup of rice. How much rice is le[ft]?

F $\frac{1}{4}$ cup
G $\frac{1}{2}$ cup
H $\frac{3}{4}$ cup
J 1 cup

Cumulative Review Correlation

REVIEW ITEMS	TEXT PAGES	REVIEW ITEMS	TEXT PAGES
1	8–11	10	428–431
2	224–225	11	84–87
3	470–471	12	450–453
4	374–375	13	454–455
5	292–293	14	320–329
6	456–457	15	344–345
7	250–251	16	8–11
8	470–471	17	376–379
9	188–191	18, 19	100–103

Jay finishes work at 4:00 P.M. If he works for 7 h 45 min each day, what time does he start? A

A 8:15 A.M

B 8:15 P.M.

C 9:15 A.M.

D 9:15 P.M.

The numbers 0.43, 0.65, 0.97, 0.74, and 0.31 are all ■. F

F less than 1

G greater than 1

H equal to 1

J less than $\frac{8}{10}$.

You can write 2.04 as ■. C

A two and four tenths

B twenty-four hundredths

C two and four hundredths

D not given

Which statement is true? J

F A circle is a polygon.

G Quadrilaterals always have a right angle.

H An obtuse angle is less than a right angle.

J Perpendicular lines meet at right angles.

Which letter has a line of symmetry? D

A F **B** G **C** R **D** T

Which is another way to write 4,065? G

F 40 tens 65 ones

G 406 tens 5 ones

H 4 thousands 65 tens

J 40 hundreds 65 tens

17 Which fractions are equivalent? C

A $\frac{1}{2}$ and $\frac{1}{12}$

B $\frac{1}{2}$ and $\frac{3}{9}$

C $\frac{1}{2}$ and $\frac{7}{14}$

D $\frac{1}{2}$ and $\frac{2}{2}$

Use the bar graph for problems 18–19.

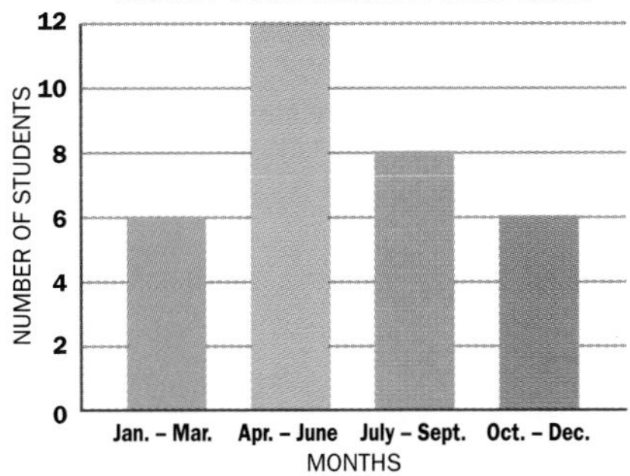

18 Which statement is *not* true about the number of students? H

F More than $\frac{1}{2}$ were born in months before July.

G $\frac{5}{8}$ were born in months between April and September.

H $\frac{3}{4}$ were born in months after September.

J $\frac{1}{4}$ were born in July through September.

19 Which can you find? B

A the number of students born in January

B the total number of students

C the birth date of each student

D the age of the students

TEST PREPARATION

PURPOSE Provide another opportunity for review and practice.

Materials have available: calculators

Using the Extra Practice

The **Extra Practice** can be used to provide further practice during a lesson or as a review later in the chapter.

Using the Additional Practice

The sections below provide additional practice that you can assign. You may wish to write these exercises on the chalkboard or put them on a reproducible master.

Length in Customary Units page 243
Write the letter of the best estimate.

	a.	b.	c.
1 width of a door b	a. 3 in.	b. 3 ft	c. 3 yd
2 length of a pencil a	a. 7 in.	b. 7 ft	c. 7 yd
3 length of a baseball bat c	a. 1 in.	b. 1 ft	c. 1 yd
4 width of a room b	a. 12 in.	b. 12 ft	c. 12 yd
5 speed limit on the highway c	a. 65 ft/h	b. 65 yd/h	c. 65 mi/h

Rename Customary Units of Length page 245
Complete.

1. 9 yd = ■ ft 27
2. 24 in. = ■ ft 2
3. 12 ft = ■ yd 4
4. 7 ft = ■ in. 8
5. 48 ft = ■ yd 16
6. 2 yd = ■ ft 6
7. 10 mi = ■ yd 17,600
8. 45 ft = ■ yd 15

Write >, <, or = .

9. 18 ft ● 5 yd >
10. 96 ft ● 35 yd <
11. 24 in. ● 2 ft =
12. 2,000 yd ● 1 mi >
13. 12 ft ● 132 in. >
14. 3 yd ● 48 ft <
15. 120 in. ● 12 ft <
16. 3 mi ● 6,000 yd <
17. 9 yd ● 36 ft <
18. 360 in. ● 25 ft >
19. 14 ft ● 168 in. =
20. 7,000 yd ● 4 mi <

Solve.

21. The length of a blue whale measures about 33 yards. The length of a finback whale measures about 84 feet. Which of these whales has a longer length? How much longer? **blue whale; 15 ft**

22. **Logical reasoning** The largest fish ever recorded was a whale shark over 41 ft long. It was about as long as: b
   a. a closet.
   b. a schoolroom.
   c. an ocean liner.

Additional Practice

p. 243 Write the letter of the best estimate.

	a.	b.	c.
1. length of a pencil *[c]*	a. 8 yd	b. 8 ft	c. 8 in.
2. height of a door *[b]*	a. 7 in.	b. 7 ft	c. 7 yd
3. length of a seal *[a]*	a. 6 ft	b. 6 yd	c. 6 in.
4. distance from Boston to Philadelphia *[b]*	a. 300 ft	b. 300 mi	c. 300 yd
5. depth of a swimming pool *[c]*	a. 9 yd	b. 9 in.	c. 9 ft

p. 245 Complete.

1. 18 yd = ◆ ft *[54]*
2. 10,560 yd = ◆ mi. *[6]*
3. 27 ft = ◆ yd. *[9]*
4. 60 in. = ◆ ft *[5]*
5. 3 mi = ◆ yd *[5,280]*
6. 9 ft = ◆ in. *[108]*
7. 21 ft = ◆ yd *[7]*
8. 48 in. = ◆ ft *[4]*
9. 7,040 yd = ◆ mi *[4]*
10. 2 mi = ◆ yd *[3,520]*
11. 14 yd = ◆ ft *[42]*
12. 7 ft = ◆ in. *[84]*

gth in Metric Units page 249
te the letter of the best estimate.

ieight of a woman **b**	**a.** 16 cm	**b.** 16 dm	**c.** 16 m
vidth of a teacher's desk **b**	**a.** 7 cm	**b.** 7 dm	**c.** 7 m
ength of a minivan **c**	**a.** 5 cm	**b.** 5 dm	**c.** 5 m
ieight of a dog **a**	**a.** 60 cm	**b.** 60 dm	**c.** 60 m
ength of a small boat **c**	**a.** 7 cm	**b.** 7 dm	**c.** 7 m

ve.

Write a problem that has this answer: Michelle traveled 1,987 km altogether. **Students should write problems that can be solved using lengths in metric units and addition.**

Ray buys 6 bags of lures packaged 12 in a bag. How many lures did he buy? **72 lures**

imeter page 251
d the perimeter.

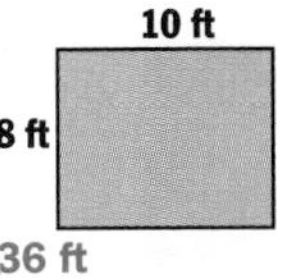

36 ft

2 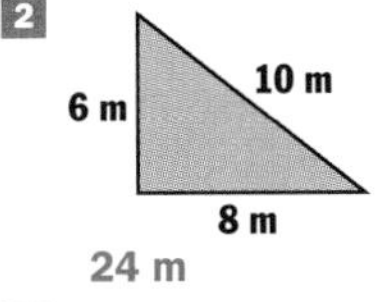
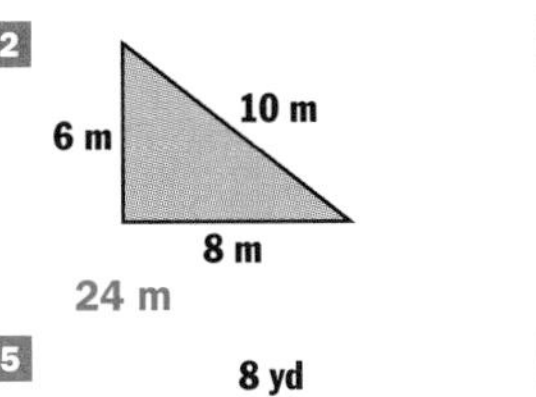

24 m

3 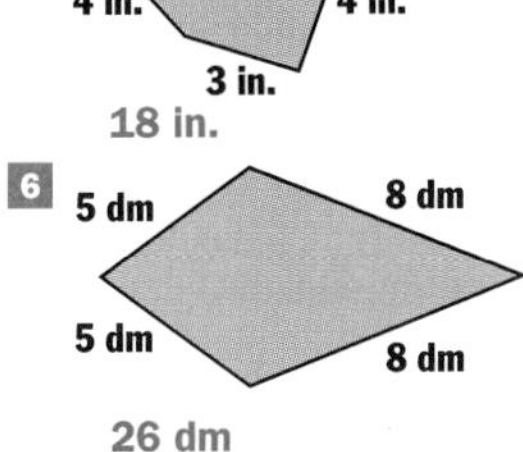

18 in.

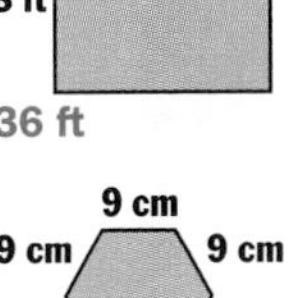
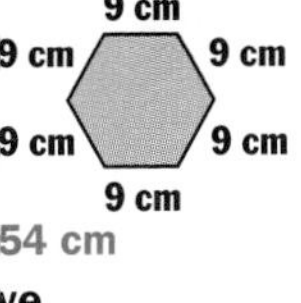

54 cm

5 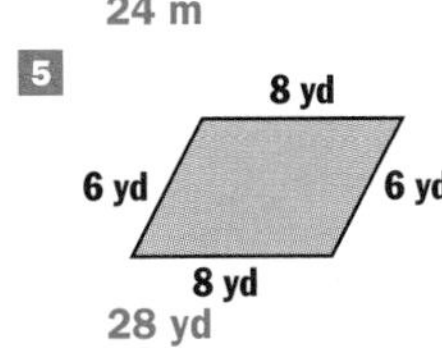
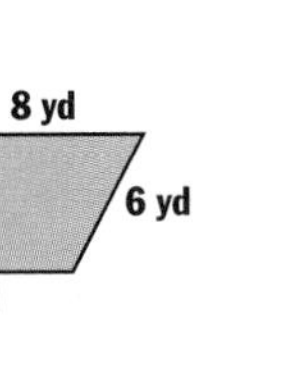

28 yd

6
5 dm 8 dm 5 dm 8 dm

26 dm

ve.

The perimeter of Jack's sand castle is 3 ft. Each side of Este's square sand castle measures 8 in. Whose castle has a greater perimeter? **Jack's**

A ship's captain ordered 218 cases of soda for the ship's crew. There are 24 cans of soda in each case. How many cans did he order? **5,232 cans**

Developing Algebra Sense

This section provides another opportunity for students to reinforce algebraic ideas.

Find the set of blocks that will balance the cube on the fourth scale. (Blocks of the same shape weigh the same amount.)

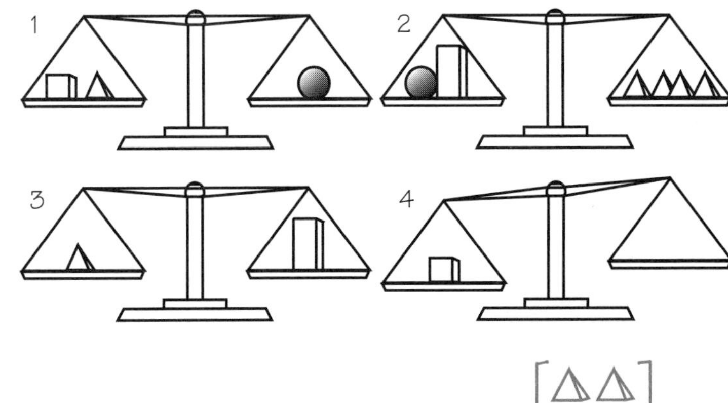

[△△]

p.249 Write the letter of the best estimate.

1. distance walked in an hour *[b]*	**a.** 5 cm	**b.** 5 km	**c.** 5 m
2. height of a table *[c]*	**a.** 60 m	**b.** 60 mm	**c.** 60 cm
3. length of a pencil *[a]*	**a.** 15 cm	**b.** 15 dm	**c.** 15 m
4. length of a swimming pool *[c]*	**a.** 25 cm	**b.** 25 dm	**c.** 25 m
5. length of a textbook *[b]*	**a.** 2 cm	**b.** 2 dm	**c.** 2 m

p.251 Find the perimeter.

1. 3 ft. 5 ft. 4 ft.

[12 ft]

2. 6 in. 6 in. 6 in. 6 in.

[24 in.]

3. 4 in. 3 in. 3 in. 5 in.

[15 in.]

p.251 Find the perimeter (continued).

4. 3 cm 3 cm 3 cm 3 cm 3 cm 3 cm 3 cm 3 cm

[24 cm]

5. 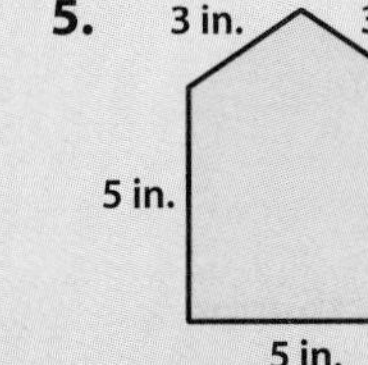
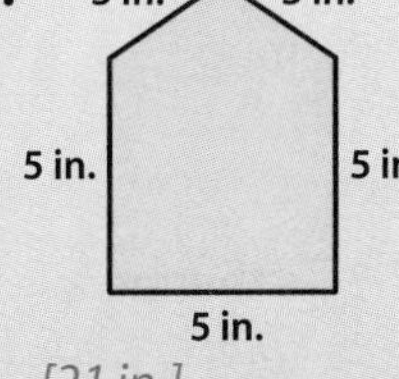

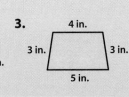

[21 in.]

6. 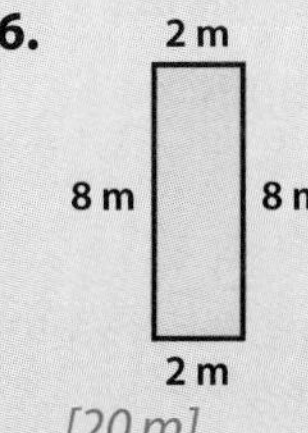

[20 m]

7. 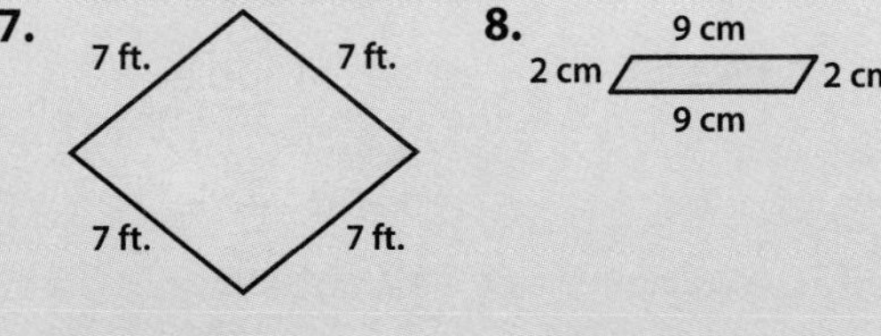

[28 ft]

8. 

[22 cm]

9. 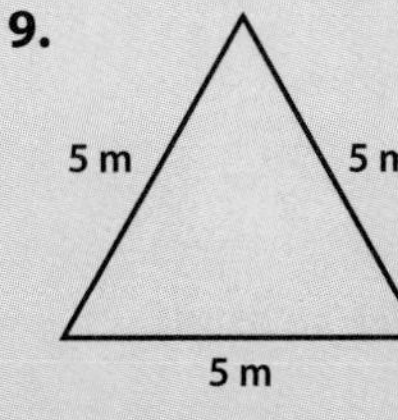

[15 m]

PURPOSE Provide another opportunity for review and practice.

Materials have available: calculators

Using the Extra Practice

The **Extra Practice** can be used to provide further practice during a lesson or as a review later in the chapter.

Using the Additional Practice

The sections below provide additional practice that you can assign. You may wish to write these exercises on the chalkboard or put them on a reproducible master.

Capacity and Weight in Customary Units page 259

Choose the best unit to measure capacity. Write *cup, pint, quart,* or *gallon.*

1. bathtub **gallon**
2. coffeepot **cup**
3. cocoa mug **cup**
4. auto gas **gallon**
5. juice box **cup or pint**
6. swimming pool **gallon**
7. saucepan **pint or quart**
8. water buc **quart or g**

Choose the better unit to measure weight. Write *ounce* or *pound.*

9. pair of skates **pound**
10. paper clip **ounce**
11. butter **ounce or pound**
12. thumbtac **ounce**
13. pencil **ounce**
14. bicycle **pound**
15. straight pin **ounce**
16. big dog **pound**

Solve.

17. Kristy's thermos bottle holds 3 gallons. How many quarts of lemonade can Kristy put in the bottle? **12 qt**
18. Denny spends $1.50 each sch day for lunch. How much will he spend for lunch in 4 weeks? **$3**

Problem-Solving Strategy: Use Logical Reasoning page 261

Solve. Explain your methods. Explanations may vary.

1. Copy the tangram at the right and try to arrange the pieces to make the pictures shown below. Then, try to make up your own picture using the pieces. Be sure to use all pieces and do not overlap them. **Check students' pictures.**

2. Jeffrey and his family took a boat ride from Medora to Sandy Point. They arrived at Sandy Point at 8:45 A.M. and left at 4:20 P.M. How much time did they spend at Sandy Point? **7 h 35 min**
3. Dennis is saving money to mak trip to Plant City's aquarium. Fo every $3 he saves, his mother gives him $2. How much money will his mother have given him when he has a total of $30? **$1**

Additional Practice

p. 259 Choose the best unit to measure capacity. Write *cup, pint, quart,* or *gallon.*

1. bathtub *[gallon]*
2. mug *[cup]*
3. bowl of soup *[cup or pint]*
4. large pot of water *[quart]*
5. a thermos *[pint or quart]*
6. an aquarium *[gallon]*

Choose the best unit to measure weight. Write *ounce* or *pound.*

7. tennis ball *[ounce]*
8. bike *[pound]*
9. an apple *[ounce]*
10. television *[pound]*
11. magazine *[ounce]*
12. whale *[pound]*

p. 261 Solve. Explain your methods. *[Explanations may vary.]*

1. **Logical reasoning** Sharon has 4 times as many seashells as Bob. Bob has 3 less than Tom. Tom has 8. How many do Bob and Sharon each have? *[Bob 5; Sharon 20]*
2. A swim club wants to retile the edge of the pool. It measures 15 ft by 60 ft. If each tile is 6 in. long, how many tiles should be ordered? *[300 tiles]*
3. Scott bought two books. They cost $9.95 and $12.95. If he gives the clerk $30, what will his change be? *[$7.10]*
4. When John went fishing, he threw back all his fish under 3 pounds He caught fish weighing 54 oz, 27 oz, and 36 oz. How many fish did he keep? *[1]*

acity and Mass in Metric Units page 265
ose the best unit to measure. Write *milliliter, liter, gram,* *ilogram.*

Iow much liquid does a teaspoon hold? **milliliter**

Iow much do you weigh? **kilogram**

Iow heavy is a paper clip? **gram**

Iow much water does a bathtub hold? **liter**

nplete.

,000 mL = ■ L **6**
6 9 L = ■ mL **9,000**
7 8 kg = ■ g **8,000**
8 3,000 g = ■ kg **3**

ve.

A pitcher contains 1 liter of juice. Rex uses the pitcher to fill three 100-mL containers and two 250-mL containers. Can he fill yet another 250-mL container? Explain. **No; he used 800 mL to fill the containers, so he has only 200 mL left.**

10 Luke uses 18 posters for his report on ocean life. Five posters show fish, and seven posters show plant life. The rest show other marine animals. How many posters show other marine animals? **6 posters**

blem Solvers at Work page 269
ve. Explain your methods. **Explanations may vary.**

Caroline said, "If the temperature is 95 degrees tomorrow, we will swim in the lake." Did she mean 95° Celsius or 95° Fahrenheit? Explain. **95° Fahrenheit; 95° Celsius is very near the boiling point.**

While scuba diving, Enrique saw 8 fish, each with 5 red stripes. He also saw 9 fish, each with 4 blue spots. How many fish did he see in all? **17 fish**

Logical reasoning A symbol in a pictograph stands for 2 students' responses. If 8 students respond they like to swim and 4 students respond they like to water ski, how many symbols will you use to record these responses? **6 symbols**

Logical reasoning Mei, Al, and Kay are wearing fishing hats. One is red, one is yellow, and one is orange. Neither girl is wearing a red hat. Mei wishes she had an orange hat. What color is each child wearing? **Kay—orange, Al—red, Mei—yellow**

Extra Practice **511**

Developing Number Sense

This section provides another opportunity for students to reinforce number sense.

Compare. Write > or <.

1. a stride ◆ 6 cm *[>]*
2. a fingernail ◆ 1 m *[<]*
3. arm length ◆ 2 mm *[>]*
4. your height ◆ 4 km *[<]*
5. foot length ◆ 1 dm *[>]*
6. length of your palm ◆ 2 cm *[>]*

p.265 Choose the best unit to measure. Write *milliliter, liter, gram, or kilogram.*

1. How heavy is a thumb tack? *[gram]*
2. How much soup can be held in a bowl? *[milliliter]*
3. How much punch does a punchbowl hold? *[liter]*
4. How heavy is a shark? *[kilogram]*

Complete.

5. 3 kg = ◆ g *[3,000]*
6. 6,000 mL = ◆ L *[6]*
7. 12 L = ◆ mL *[12,000]*
8. 15,000 g = ◆ kg *[15]*
9. 20 L = ◆ mL *[20,000]*
10. 428,000 g = ◆ kg *[428]*

p.269 Solve. Explain your methods. *[Explanations may vary.]*

1. Devon wants enough cider to serve 3 cups each to 16 people. How many gallons should he buy? *[3 gal]*
2. Ricky is going to Spain. The average temperature for the time he will be there is 29°C. What kind of clothes should he pack? *[summer clothes]*
3. **Write a problem** about temperature. Use information from a newspaper or almanac. Trade problems. Solve at least three problems written by classmates. *[Check students' problems.]*
4. Barry's mother told him to buy 2 pounds of cheddar cheese. It was sold in 12-oz packages. How many packages should be buy? *[3; 2 lbs = 32 oz; 12 × 3 = 36 oz; 36 > 32]*

Chapter 8 EXTRA PRACTICE

PURPOSE Provide another opportunity for review and practice.

Materials have available: calculators, place-value models

Using the Extra Practice

The **Extra Practice** can be used to provide further practice during a lesson or as a review later in the chapter.

Using the Additional Practice

The sections below provide additional practice that you can assign. You may wish to write these exercises on the chalkboard or put them on a reproducible master.

extra practice

Division Patterns page 279

Divide mentally.

1 50 ÷ 5 **10**	2 90 ÷ 3 **30**	3 40 ÷ 4 **10**	4 120 ÷ 2
5 280 ÷ 4 **70**	6 560 ÷ 8 **70**	7 3,500 ÷ 7 **500**	8 2,400 ÷

Solve.

9 Josie shares 480 pennies equally among 7 friends and herself. How many pennies will each have?
60 pennies

10 **ALGEBRA: PATTERNS** Write the next two numbers: 0, 3, 1, 4, 2, 5, ■, ■. Explain how you know. **3, 6; rule is add 3, subtract 2.**

Estimate Quotients page 281 **Estimates may vary. Possible estimates are given.**

Estimate by using compatible numbers.

1 62 ÷ 6 **60 ÷ 6 = 10**	2 57 ÷ 3 **60 ÷ 3 = 20**	3 178 ÷ 9 **180 ÷ 9 = 20**
4 275 ÷ 4 **280 ÷ 4 = 70**	5 556 ÷ 8 **560 ÷ 8 = 70**	6 368 ÷ 6 **360 ÷ 6 = 60**
7 432 ÷ 7 **420 ÷ 7 = 60**	8 215 ÷ 5 **200 ÷ 5 = 40**	9 3,545 ÷ 4 **3,600 ÷ 4 = 900**
10 4,193 ÷ 6 **4,200 ÷ 6 = 700**	11 3,125 ÷ 4 **3,200 ÷ 4 = 800**	12 6,441 ÷ 9 **6,300 ÷ 9 = 700**

Division by 1-Digit Numbers page 285

Divide. You may use place-value models.

1 45 ÷ 7 **6 R3**	2 76 ÷ 8 **9 R4**	3 34 ÷ 5 **6 R4**	4 53 ÷ 7 **7**
5 29 ÷ 4 **7 R1**	6 47 ÷ 8 **5 R7**	7 68 ÷ 9 **7 R5**	8 36 ÷ 7 **5**
9 35 ÷ 2 **17 R1**	10 85 ÷ 4 **21 R1**	11 98 ÷ 3 **32 R2**	12 58 ÷ 5 **1**

Solve.

13 Joe has 89 cubes. He groups them in piles of 5. How many piles of 5 can he make? How many cubes are left over?
17 piles; 4 cubes left over

14 **Logical reasoning** Al is standing in line between Joe and Mary. Minnie is directly in front of Joe. Two students are between Joe and Jeff. How are they lined up?
Minnie, Joe, Al, Mary, Jeff

Additional Practice

p.279 Divide mentally.

1. 80 ÷ 4 *[20]*	**2.** 360 ÷ 6 *[60]*	**3.** 180 ÷ 2 *[90]*
4. 3,500 ÷ 5 *[700]*	**5.** 2,800 ÷ 7 *[400]*	**6.** 2,400 ÷ 3 *[800]*

p.281 Estimate by using compatible numbers. *[Estimates may vary. Possible estimates are given.]*

1. 62 ÷ 6 *[60 ÷ 6 = 10]*	**2.** 477 ÷ 8 *[480 ÷ 8 = 60]*	**3.** 4,625 ÷ 5 *[4,500 ÷ 5 = 900]*
4. 8,029 ÷ 9 *[8,100 ÷ 9 = 900]*	**5.** 222 ÷ 3 *[210 ÷ 3 = 70]*	**6.** 5,714 ÷ 7 *[5,600 ÷ 7 = 800]*

p.285 Divide. You may use place-value models.

1. 55 ÷ 9 *[6 R1]*	**2.** 25 ÷ 2 *[12 R1]*	**3.** 83 ÷ 6 *[13 R5*
4. 77 ÷ 5 *[15 R2]*	**5.** 68 ÷ 4 *[17]*	**6.** 53 ÷ 2 *[26 R1*
7. 49 ÷ 3 *[16 R1]*	**8.** 94 ÷ 6 *[15 R4]*	**9.** 80 ÷ 5 *[16]*
10. 23 ÷ 8 *[2 R7]*	**11.** 38 ÷ 4 *[9 R2]*	**12.** 63 ÷ 3 *[21]*
13. 92 ÷ 8 *[11 R4]*	**14.** 48 ÷ 4 *[12]*	**15.** 39 ÷ 7 *[5 R4]*

sion by 1-Digit Numbers page 289

ide. Remember to estimate.

	4)92 **23**	2	3)57 **19**	3	5)84 **16 R4**	4	2)71 **35 R1**	5	4)$72 **$18**
	7)89 **12 R5**	7	6)95 **15 R5**	8	9)358 **39 R7**	9	8)579 **72 R3**	10	2)195 **97 R1**
	8)253 **31 R5**	12	9)$387 **$43**	13	6)513 **85 R3**	14	7)535 **76 R3**	15	4)513 **128 R1**
	5)128 **25 R3**	17	3)196 **65 R1**	18	7)501 **71 R4**	19	9)318 **35 R3**	20	4)145 **36 R1**

ve.

Jorge has 4 quarters, 3 dimes, and 2 nickels. How many 5-cent decals can he buy at the souvenir stand? **28 decals**

22 A roller coaster seats 36 people. Each seat holds 3 people. How many seats are on the ride? **12 seats**

os in the Quotient page 291

ide.

	8)854 **106 R6**	2	2)419 **209 R1**	3	9)960 **106 R6**	4	3)306 **102**	5	7)914 **130 R4**
	5)653 **130 R3**	7	4)682 **170 R2**	8	4)439 **109 R3**	9	8)879 **109 R7**	10	6)918 **153**

	91 ÷ 3 **30 R1**	12	83 ÷ 4 **20 R3**	13	$303 ÷ 3 **$101**	14	$847 ÷ 7 **$121**

ve.

Craig has 618 compact discs. He stores them in small boxes with 6 discs in each box. How many boxes does he fill? **103 boxes**

Jo leaves home and travels 3 blocks north, 2 blocks east, 5 blocks south, and 2 blocks west. How far is she from home? **2 blocks**

ide Greater Numbers page 293

ide.

	5)816 **163 R1**	2	6)$8,526 **$1,421**	3	4)9,741 **2,435 R1**	4	9)4,613 **512 R5**	5	6)$5,124 **$854**
	6)4,394 **732 R2**	7	3)1,152 **384**	8	9)4,559 **506 R5**	9	2)3,051 **1,525 R1**	10	8)40,445 **5,055 R5**

	2,945 ÷ 4 **736 R1**	12	4,995 ÷ 6 **832 R3**	13	1,672 ÷ 5 **334 R2**	14	$29,344 ÷ 7 **$4,192**

Developing Algebra Sense

This section provides another opportunity for students to reinforce algebraic ideas.

Use the divisibility rules to find the answer mentally.

1. Six friends want to share a bag of 132 marbles. Can they share the marbles evenly? *[Yes, 132 is even, and 1 + 3 + 2 = 6 and 6 is divisible by 3.]*

2. The cooking class baked 213 cookies. Can they divide the cookies evenly between two fourth grade classes if there are 20 students in each class? *[No, 213 is not an even number.]*

3. Ms. Ryan bought 45 balloons to decorate for a party. Can she divide them equally in groups of 2? 3? 5? 6? 9? 10? *[She can divide them into groups of 3, 5, and 9.]*

4. Mr. Taylor bought 245 trading cards to divide among his 3 children. Can he divide them equally among the children? *[No, 2 + 4 + 5 = 11; 11 is not divisible by 3.]*

p. 289 Divide. Remember to estimate.

1. 6)72 *[12]* **2.** 5)82 *[16 R2]* **3.** 3)61 *[20 R1]*

4. 4)615 *[153 R3]* **5.** 2)386 *[193]* **6.** 8)453 *[56 R5]*

7. 7)$725 *[$103 R4]* **8.** 3)417 *[139]* **9.** 9)372 *[41 R3]*

p. 291 Divide.

1. 5)521 *[104 R1]* **2.** 6)245 *[40 R5]* **3.** 4)$813 *[$203 R1]*

4. 720 ÷ 7 *[102 R6]* **5.** $924 ÷ 3 *[$308]* **6.** $619 ÷ 2 *[$309 R1]*

p. 293 Divide.

1. 4)$938 *[$234 R2]* **2.** 6)27,158 *[4,526 R2]* **3.** 5)$7,293 *[$1,458 R3]*

4. 3)6,237 *[2,079]* **5.** 8)5,814 *[726 R6]* **6.** 2)43,715 *[21,857 R1]*

7. $1,714 ÷ 3 *[$571 R1]* **8.** 32,524 ÷ 5 *[6,504 R4]* **9.** 814 ÷ 4 *[203 R2]*

10. $6,015 ÷ 8 *[$751 R7]* **11.** 2,127 ÷ 3 *[709]* **12.** 57,938 ÷ 6 *[9,656 R2]*

PURPOSE Provide another opportunity for review and practice.

Materials have available: calculators

Using the Extra Practice

The **Extra Practice** can be used to provide further practice during a lesson or as a review later in the chapter.

Using the Additional Practice

The sections below provide additional practice that you can assign. You may wish to write these exercises on the chalkboard or put them on a reproducible master.

Problem-Solving Strategy: Guess, Test, and Revise page 295

Solve. Explain your methods. Explanations may vary.

1. The sum of two dog-tag numbers is 57. Their difference is 33. What are the numbers? **12 and 45**
2. A ticket to the dog show costs $ Can Jake buy 14 tickets for $10 Explain. **No; 14 tickets cost $11**
3. Jean's collie weighs 25 pounds more than Dan's chihuahua and 62 pounds less than Joe's 97-pound rottweiler. How much does each dog weigh? **rottweiler—97 lb, collie—35 lb, chihuahua—10 lb**
4. The Kennedy Dog Association is going to spend $72 for dog coll It can buy either $6 or $9 collar How many more $6 collars can buy than $9 collars? **4 more**
5. Mindy spent $52 for 2 doggie sweaters. One sweater cost $6 more than the other. How much did each sweater cost? **$23 and $29**
6. Jay has twice as much money a Ruth. Ruth has twice as much money as Irene. Irene has 45¢. How much money does Jay have **180¢, or $1.80**

Average page 301

Find the average.

1. Number of miles to and from school: 7, 13, 21, 19 **15 miles**
2. Test scores: 88, 76, 91, 89 **86**
3. Number of minutes each student spends on homework: 35, 65, 80, 40, 30 **50 min**
4. Number of tickets sold for the school carnival: 235, 198, 206 **213 tickets**

Use the pictograph to find the answers to ex. 5–7.

5. How many rebounds were made in all? **24 rebounds**
6. Find the average number of rebounds. **6 rebounds**
7. How many more rebounds did Abby have than Lee? **4 rebounds**

Number of Rebounds	
Lee	🏀 ◐
Abby	🏀 🏀 🏀 ◐
Bo	🏀 🏀 🏀 🏀 🏀
Pat	🏀 🏀

Key: 🏀 represents 2 rebounds. ◐ represents 1 rebound.

Additional Practice

p. 295 Solve. Explain your methods. *[Explanations may vary.]*

1. Beth and her father plan to hike 85 miles in 6 days. If they walk 13 miles a day, will they complete their goal? *[No, 13 × 6 = 78]*
2. The sum of the digits of a two-digit number is 13. The product of the digits is 36. The tens digit is larger than the ones digit. What is the number? *[94]*
3. Jerry packs 32 model cars in 6 boxes. He puts 6 cars in some boxes and 5 in others. How many boxes have 6 cars and how many have 5 cars? *[2 boxes have 6 cars, 4 boxes have 5]*
4. Emil's baseball game is at 5:30 P.M. He must be at the field 30 minutes early. It takes him 15 minutes to get to the field. When should he leave? *[4:45 P.M.]*

p. 301 Find the average.

1. Number of players on sports teams: 28, 26, 30 *[28 players]*
2. Number of fish sold in pet store in five days: 8, 2, 12, 15, 13 *[10 fish]*
3. Number of miles hiked each day on a trip: 12, 10, 8, 10, 11, 9 *[10 miles]*
4. Number of minutes spent reading: 45, 52, 38, 57, 47, 50, 33 *[46 minutes]*
5. Number of miles driven each day: 85, 72, 69, 58, 41 *[65 miles]*
6. Number of people visiting the gallery: 32, 45, 48, 56, 74 *[51 people]*

de by Multiples of Ten page 303
de mentally.

720 ÷ 80 **9** | **2** 360 ÷ 60 **6** | **3** $560 ÷ 70 **$8**

210 ÷ 30 **7** | **5** $3,000 ÷ 50 **$60** | **6** 1,000 ÷ 20 **50**

3,100 ÷ 90 **90** | **8** 2,800 ÷ 70 **40** | **9** 6,300 ÷ 90 **70**

4,000 ÷ 80 **50** | **11** $9,000 ÷ 30 **$300** | **12** 8,000 ÷ 40 **200**

e.

The Rodriguez family spent $264 for food on their 8-day vacation. Find the average spent per day. **$33**

14 The Rodriguez family brought 8 boxes of cereal on the trip. One box makes 8 servings. How many boxes will be left after 48 servings? **2 boxes**

de by Tens page 307
de using any method.

10)91 **9 R1** | **2** 20)75 **3 R15** | **3** 20)159 **7 R19** | **4** 20)113 **5 R13** | **5** 30)256 **8 R16**

128 ÷ 20 **6 R8** | **7** 157 ÷ 30 **5 R7** | **8** $120 ÷ 30 **$4** | **9** 132 ÷ 40 **3 R12** | **10** 194 ÷ 40 **4 R34**

161 ÷ 50 **3 R11** | **12** $420 ÷ 70 **$6** | **13** 123 ÷ 60 **2 R3** | **14** 187 ÷ 20 **9 R7** | **15** 125 ÷ 90 **1 R35**

ve.

Jim has 150 marbles, 10 times as many as Ken. How many does Ken have? **15 marbles**

17 Alan drives 90 kilometers per hour. How many kilometers will he drive in 9 hours? **810 km**

blem Solvers at Work page 311
ve. Explain your methods. Explanations may vary.

Betty uses one ribbon to make 3 hair bows. She wants to make 115 bows in all. How many ribbons does she need? **39 ribbons**

2 The cows and ducks in the barnyard have a total of 7 heads and 20 feet. How many cows and ducks are there in all? **3 cows and 4 ducks**

Logical reasoning Tom's ride home is less than Jane's. Tami's ride is more than Harry's, but less than Tom's. Who has the longest ride? **Jane**

4 Ryan has a test score of 88. What does he need to score on his next test to have an average of 90? **92**

Extra Practice **515**

Developing Number Sense

This section provides another opportunity for students to reinforce number sense.

Use only the [+], [−], [×], [÷], [=] and one of the number keys on your calculator to get the display to read the numbers as shown.

	Number Keys	Display
1.	4	6
2.	5	7
3.	8	4
4.	6	9

1. *[Possible answer: 4 + 4 + 4 + 4 + 4 + 4 + 4 ÷ 4 = 6]*
2. *[Possible answer: 5 + 5 + 5 + 5 + 5 + 5 + 5 ÷ 5 = 7]*
3. *[Possible answer: 8 + 8 + 8 + 8 ÷ 8 = 4]*
4. *[Possible answer: 6 + 6 + 6 + 6 + 6 + 6 + 6 + 6 + 6 ÷ 6 = 9]*

p. 303 Divide mentally.

1. 480 ÷ 60 *[8]*
2. 80 ÷ 40 *[2]*
3. 400 ÷ 80 *[5]*
4. $2,100 ÷ 70 *[30]*
5. 1,200 ÷ 30 *[40]*
6. $4,500 ÷ 50 *[$90]*
7. 8,000 ÷ 20 *[400]*
8. $3,000 ÷ 50 *[$60]*
9. $2,700 ÷ 90 *[$30]*

p. 307 Divide using any method.

1. 20)78 *[3 R18]*
2. 10)35 *[3 R5]*
3. 10)52 *[5 R2]*
4. 128 ÷ 20 *[6 R8]*
5. 239 ÷ 30 *[7 R29]*
6. 187 ÷ 40 *[4 R27]*

p. 309 Solve. Explain your methods. *[Explanations may vary.]*

1. Ms. Tripp made 250 ounces of soup. She wants to put the soup into separate jars to freeze them. Each jar holds 30 ounces. How many jars will she need? *[9 jars]*
2. In Lincoln School 95 students are in 4th grade. There are 13 more boys than girls. How many girls are there? How many boys? *[41 girls, 54 boys]*
3. Buses for field trips hold 40 students. How many buses will be needed for 152 students? *[4 buses]*
4. Max wants to change his 234 pennies to quarters. How many quarters will he get? *[9 quarters]*

Chapter 9 EXTRA PRACTICE

PURPOSE Provide another opportunity for review and practice.

Materials have available: calculators

Using the Extra Practice

The **Extra Practice** can be used to provide further practice during a lesson or as a review later in the chapter.

Using the Additional Practice

The sections below provide additional practice that you can assign. You may wish to write these exercises on the chalkboard or put them on a reproducible master.

extra practice

1. 12 edges, 8 vertices, 6 flat faces

3-Dimensional Figures page 323

Describe each figure. Tell how many edges, vertices, and faces it has.

1 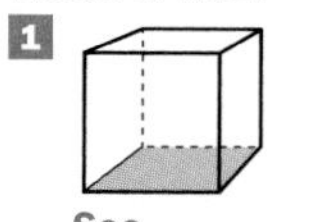 See above.

2  2 curved edges, 0 vertices, 1 curved face, and 2 flat faces

3 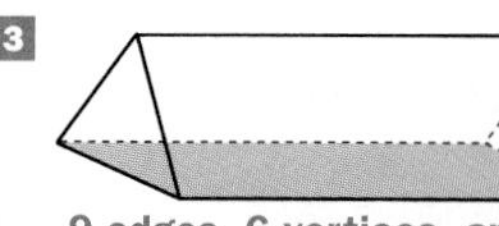 9 edges, 6 vertices, and 5 flat faces

Solve.

4 How many more flat faces does a square pyramid have than a triangular pyramid? 1 more flat face

5 Margarita has 38¢ in a piggy ba[nk]. There are 7 coins in the bank. What are the coins? 3 dimes, 1 nickel, 3 pennies

2-Dimensional Figures and Polygons page 327

Tell if the figure is open or closed.

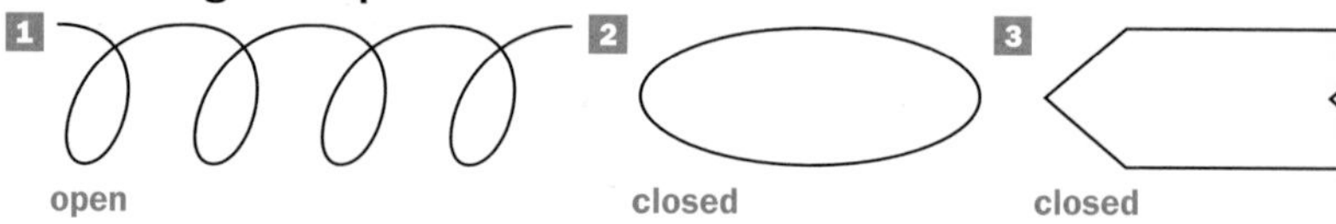

1 open 2 closed 3 closed

Name the polygon.

4 a polygon with 8 sides octagon

5 a quadrilateral with 4 equal corn[ers] square, rectangle

Line Segments, Lines, and Rays page 329

Describe the figure.

1 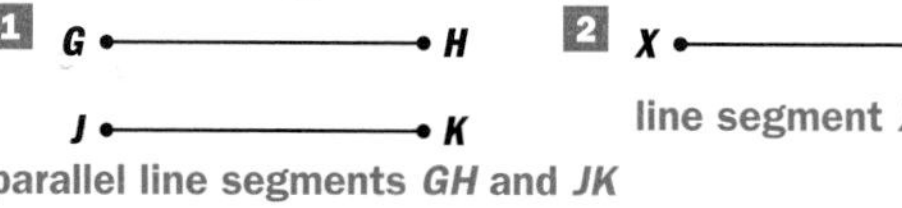

parallel line segments *GH* and *JK*

2 *X* —— *Y* line segment *XY*

3 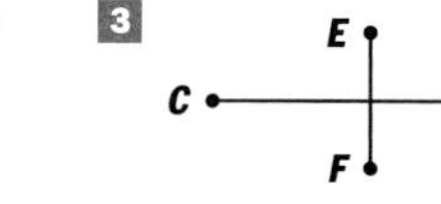

intersecting and/or perpendic[ular] line segments *CD* and *EF*

Solve. Use the figure at the right for problems 4–6.

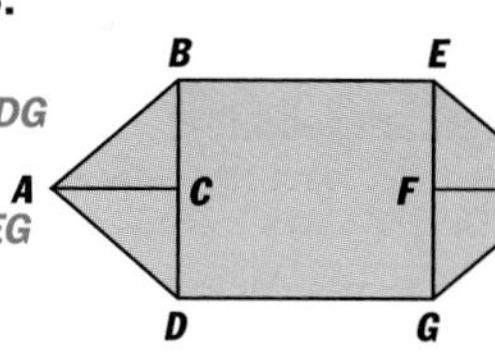

4 List two pairs of parallel line segments. Possible answer: line segments *BD* and *EG*, *BE* and *DG*

5 List two pairs of perpendicular line segments. Possible answer: line segments *AC* and *BD*, *FH* and *EG*

6 List two intersecting line segments that are *not* perpendicular. Possible answer: line segments *EH* and *GH*

516 Extra Practice

Additional Practice

p. 323 Describe each figure. Tell how many edges, vertices, and faces it has.

1.  *[8 edges, 5 vertices, 5 faces]*

2. 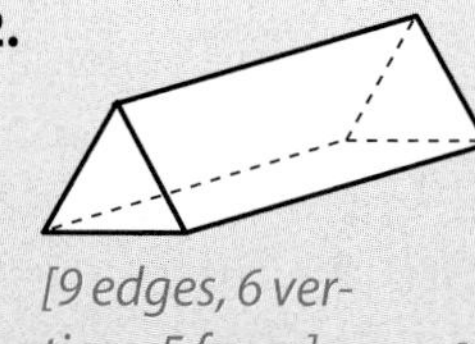 *[9 edges, 6 vertices, 5 faces]*

3. 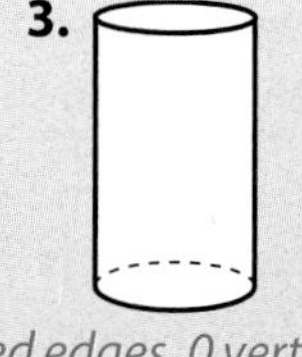 *[2 curved edges, 0 vertices, 1 curved face, 2 flat faces]*

p. 327 Name the polygon that the object looks like.

1. *[octagon]* 2. *[pentagon]* 3. *[triangle]*

p. 329 Describe the figure.

1. 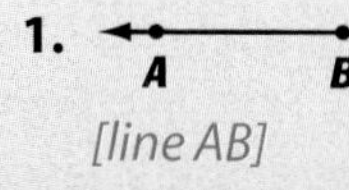

[line AB]

2. 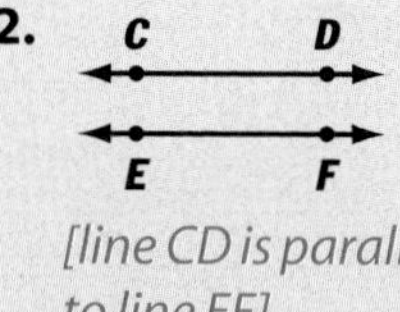

[line CD is parallel to line EF]

3. 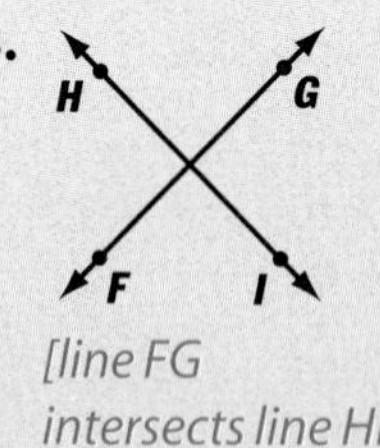

[line FG intersects line HI]

4. 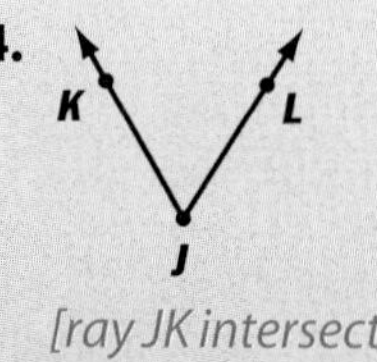

[ray JK intersects ray JL]

5. 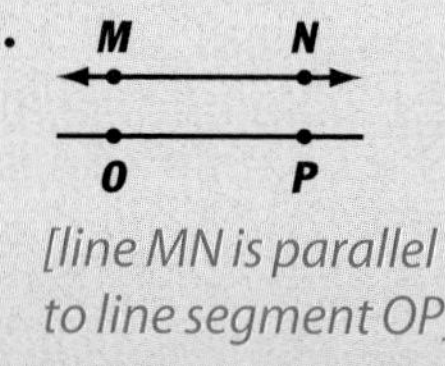

[line MN is parallel to line segment OP]

6. 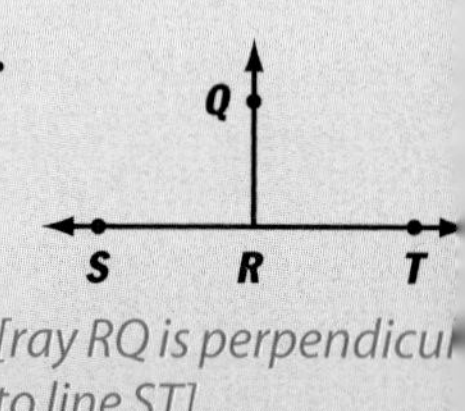

[ray RQ is perpendicu[lar] to line ST]

oblem-Solving Strategy: Make an Organized List page 331
lve. Explain your methods. Explanations may vary.

Spatial reasoning Study the diagram at the right. Then predict how many triangles there will be in the 10-sided figure that extends this pattern. **8 triangles**

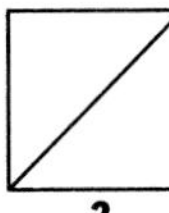

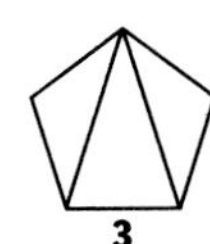

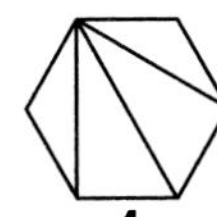

gles page 335
ite *acute, obtuse,* or *right* for the angle.

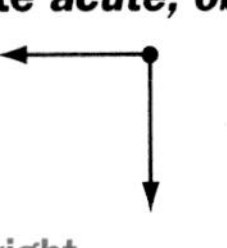
right

2 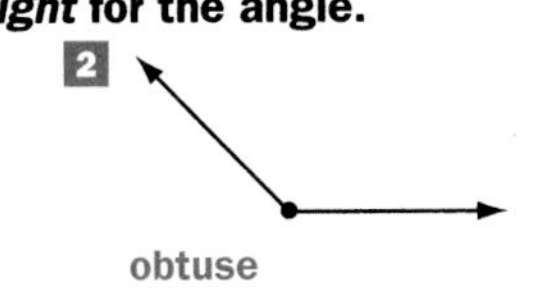
obtuse

3 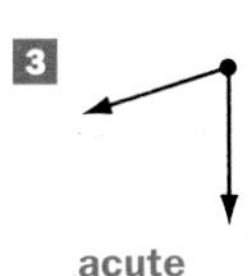
acute

lve.

Dan buys 1 gal of water; Mel buys 3 pints. How many pints do they have in all? **11 pt**

5 How many more right angles are in a square than in a right triangle? **3 more right angles**

ngruent and Similar Figures page 343
rite *congruent* or *similar* for the pair of figures.

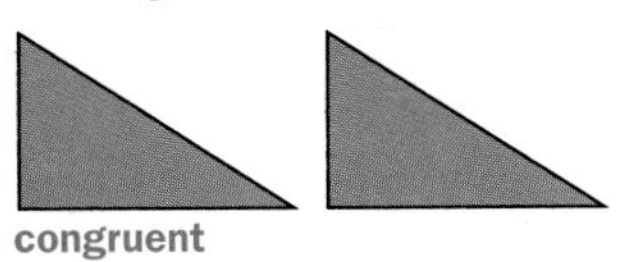
congruent

2 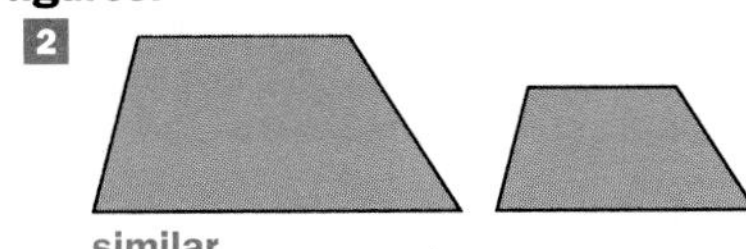
similar

lve.

Matthew hikes 2 kilometers. Jeremy hikes three times as far as Matthew. Zachary hikes half as far as Jeremy. How far does Zachary hike? **3 km**

4 Jill uses 5 tubes of paint to paint 3 pictures. How many tubes will she use to paint 6 pictures? **10 tubes**

Spatial reasoning Put 3 points (not in a straight line) on dot paper. Connect the points to make a polygon and give its name. Write instructions for another student to draw a congruent polygon. **The figure is a triangle; check students' instructions and drawings.**

DEVELOPING ALGEBRA SENSE

This section provides another opportunity for students to reinforce algebraic ideas.

Find the missing length of each figure.

1. 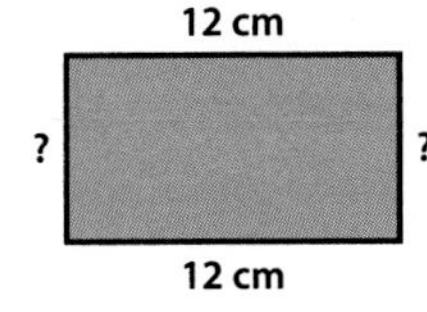

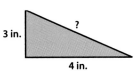

perimeter = 40 cm
[8 cm]

2. 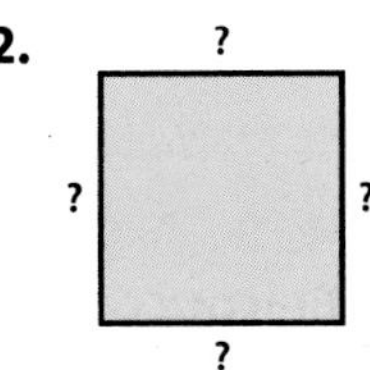

perimeter = 16 cm
[4 cm]

3. 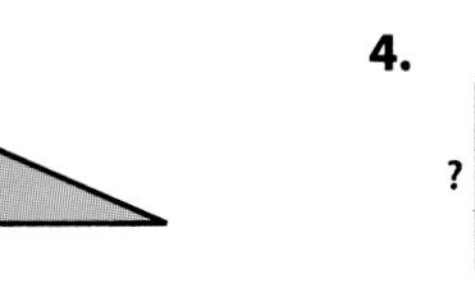

perimeter = 12 in.
[5 in.]

4. 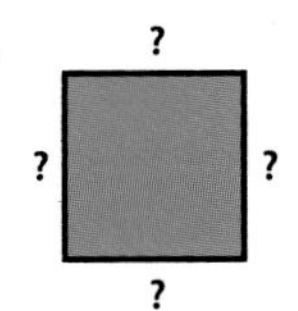

Area = 9 cm^2
[3 cm]

5. 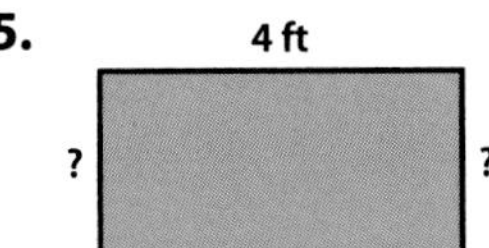

Area = 12 ft^2
[3 ft]

6. 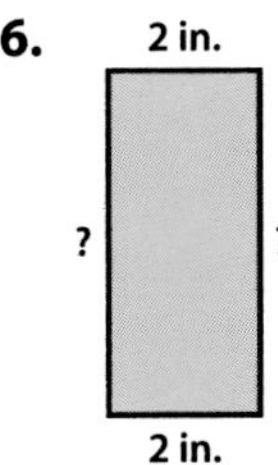

Area = 18 in^2
[9 in.]

p. 331 Solve. Explain your methods. *[Explanations may vary.]*

1. Pedro's soccer league has 6 teams. Each team plays each other team once. How many games will they play? *[15 games]*
2. It costs $87 to buy 3 T-shirts. One T-shirt costs $27. The other two each cost the same. How much does each T-shirt cost? *[$27, $30, $30]*

p. 335 Write acute, obtuse, or right for the angle.

1. 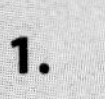 
[obtuse]

2.  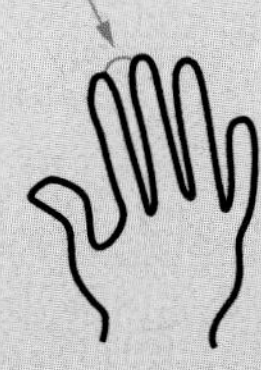
[acute]

3. 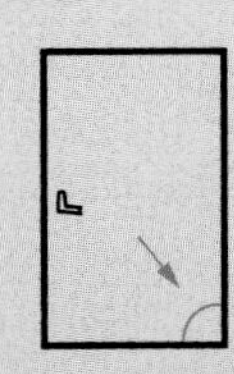
[right]

p. 343 Write *congruent* or *similar* for the pair of figures.

1. 
[congruent]

2. 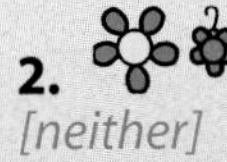
[neither]

3. 
[congruent]

4. 
[similar]

5. 
[congruent]

6. 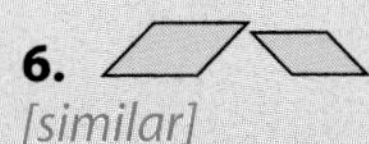
[similar]

Chapter 9 EXTRA PRACTICE

PURPOSE Provide another opportunity for review and practice.

Materials have available: calculators

Using the Extra Practice

The **Extra Practice** can be used to provide further practice during a lesson or as a review later in the chapter.

Using the Additional Practice

The sections below provide additional practice that you can assign. You may wish to write these exercises on the chalkboard or put them on a reproducible master.

Symmetry page 345

Copy and complete the figure to make it symmetrical. Use dot paper. Check students' work.

1 

2 

3 

Solve.

4 How many lines of symmetry can you find in a square? 4 lines

5 **ALGEBRA: PATTERNS** Complete. 1, 3, 6, 10, ■, ■, ■. 15, 21, 28

Slides, Flips, and Turns page 347

Write *flip, slide,* or *turn* to tell how each figure was moved.

1 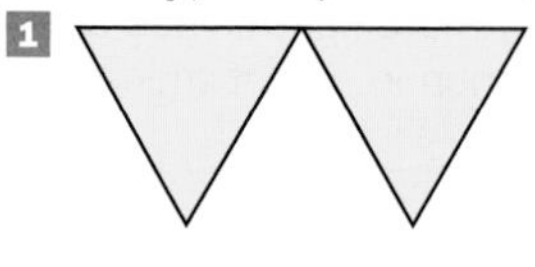
turn

2 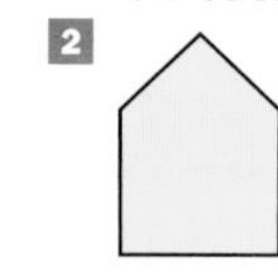 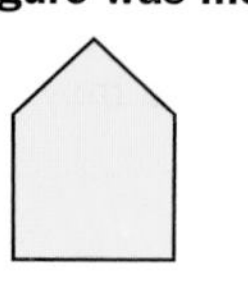
slide

3 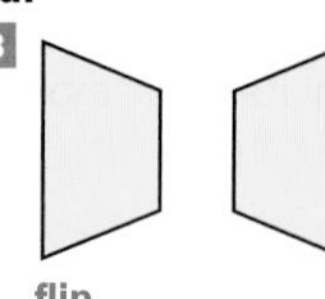
flip

Solve.

4 You can move the left triangle onto the other triangle using a turn. What other two moves would accomplish the same thing? flip, flip

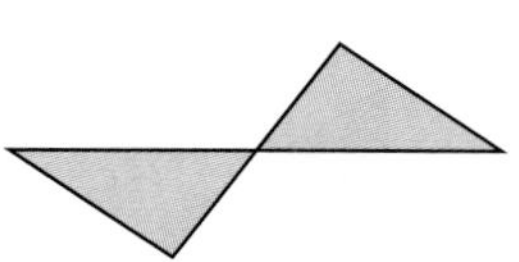

5 Choose any figure. Then draw a pattern using turns and flips. Check students' drawings.

Area page 351

Use graph paper to draw rectangles with the following areas. How many rectangles are possible for each? Check students' drawings.

1 10 square units 2 possible rectangles: 1 × 10 and 2 × 5

2 12 square units 3 possible rectangles: 1 × 12, 2 × 6, and 3 ×

3 16 square units 3 possible rectangles: 1 × 16, 2 × 8, and 4 × 4

4 48 square units 5 possible rectangles: 1 × 48, 2 × 24, 3 × 1 4 × 12, 6 × 8

Additional Practice

p.345 Is the dashed line a line of symmetry?

1. 
[yes]

2. 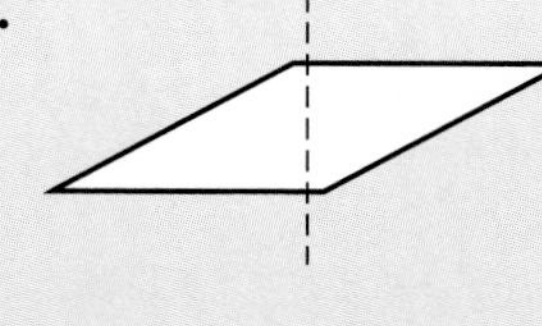
[no]

3. 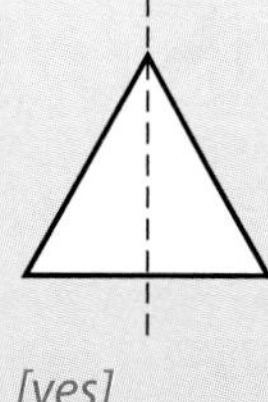
[yes]

p.347 Write *flip, slide,* or *turn* to tell how each figure was moved.

1. 
[flip]

2. 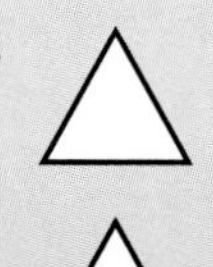
[slide]

3. 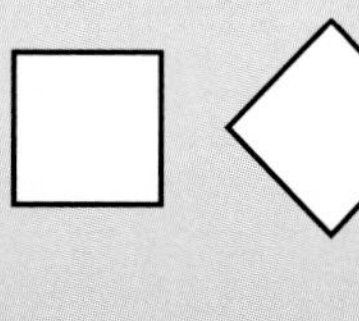
[turn]

p.351 Use graph paper to draw rectangles with the following areas. How many rectangles are possible for each?

1. 12 square units *[3 possible rectangles; 1 × 12, 2 × 6, 3 × 4]*
2. 8 square units *[2 possible rectangles; 1 × 8, 2 × 4]*
3. 15 square units *[2 possible rectangles; 1 × 15, 3 × 5]*
4. 16 square units *[3 possible rectangles; 1 × 16, 2 × 8, 4 × 4]*
5. 24 square units *[4 possible rectangles; 1 × 24, 2 × 12, 3 × 8, 4 × 6]*
6. 9 square units *[2 possible rectangles; 1 × 9, 3 × 3]*

ume page 353
d the volume for each rectangular prism.

length—5 in.
width—4 in.
height—3 in.
60 in.^{3}

2 length—3 in.
width—2 in.
height—4 in.
24 in.^{3}

3 length—9 in.
width—3 in.
height—5 in.
135 in.^{3}

length—7 in.
width—4 in.
height—6 in.
168 in.^{3}

5 length—12 in.
width—8 in.
height—4 in.
384 in.^{3}

6 length—11 in.
width—5 in.
height—4 in.
220 in.^{3}

ve.

List the least and greatest volumes in ex. 1–6. Find the difference.
24 in.^{3}, 384 in.^{3}; 360 in.^{3}

8 Amy's test scores in science were 85, 74, 96, and 89. Find the average. **86**

blem Solvers at Work page 357
ve. Explain your methods. **Explanations may vary.**

Domingo can choose between a Monet art print and a Rubens portrait. He can also choose between a lion statue and an elephant statue. How many choices does he have? Tell what they are. **4 choices; Monet—lion, net—elephant, Rubens—lion, Rubens—elephant**

2 **Logical reasoning** At camp, there are teams only in baseball, volleyball, soccer, and swimming. Eli, Jon, Bob, and Lee each play on a different team. Eli's sport does not use a ball. Jon often kicks the ball. Bob does not play baseball. Who plays baseball? **Lee**

Middleton Grade School is going to take a nature hike. They will use 9-passenger vans to transport 38 students and 3 adults to the trails. How many vans are needed?
5 vans

Brooke buys a sandwich for $3.29, a soda for $1.19, and french fries for $0.89. She hands the clerk $10. How much change will she receive? **$4.63**

Dorita gave 3 cents to each of her 7 friends. Her mother then gave Dorita 6 pennies, so she had 9 pennies in all. How many pennies did she have to begin with? **24 pennies**

There are 32 students in 2 classes studying rocks. There are 6 more students in Ms. Motsinger's class than in Mr. Brown's class. How many are in each class?
Ms. Motsinger—19 students, Mr. Brown—13 students

DEVELOPING SPATIAL SENSE

This section provides another opportunity for students to reinforce spatial sense.

Describe the top, front, and side views of each shape.

1. cylinder
[circle, rectangle, rectangle]

2. 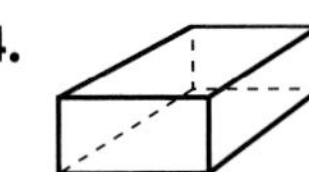
cone
[circle, triangle, triangle]

3. 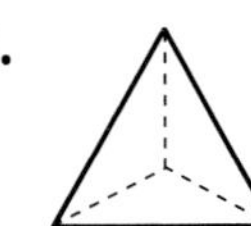
sphere
[circle, circle, circle]

4. 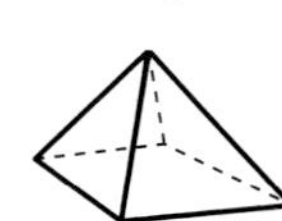
rectangular prism
[rectangle, rectangle, rectangle]

5. triangular pyramid
[triangle, triangle, triangle]

6. square pyramid
[square, triangle, triangle]

p. 353 Find the volume for each rectangular prism.

1. length–3 cm.
width–1 cm
height–4 cm
[12 cm^3]

2. length–5 cm.
width–2 cm.
height–3 cm.
[30 cm^3]

3. length–6 cm.
width–4 cm.
height–5 cm.
[120 cm^3]

4. length–2 in.
width–2 in.
height–2 in.
[8 in.^{3}]

5. length–4 in.
width–3 in.
height–8 in.
[96 in.^{3}]

6. length–5 in.
width–3 in.
height–6 in.
[90 in.^{3}]

p. 357 Solve. Explain your methods. *[Explanations may vary.]*

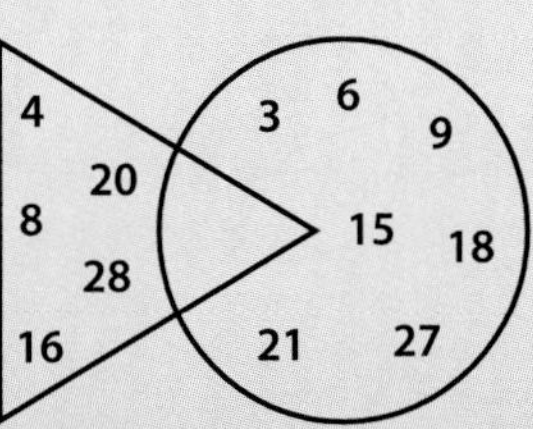

1. The triangle contains numbers that are multiples of 4. The circle contains numbers that are multiples of 3. What numbers should be placed in the overlapping part if all the numbers are less than 30? *[12, 24]*

2. **Logical reasoning** Paul has $0.83. He has 9 coins. What are they?
[2 quarters, 2 dimes, 2 nickels, 3 pennies]

3. Gene measures a box that is 7 in. long, 3 inches wide, and 4 in. high. What is its volume? *[84 in.^{3}]*

Chapter 10 EXTRA PRACTICE

PURPOSE Provide another opportunity for review and practice.

Materials have available: calculators

Using the Extra Practice

The **Extra Practice** can be used to provide further practice during a lesson or as a review later in the chapter.

Using the Additional Practice

The sections below provide additional practice that you can assign. You may wish to write these exercises on the chalkboard or put them on a reproducible master.

Part of a Whole page 371

Write the fraction for the part that is shaded.

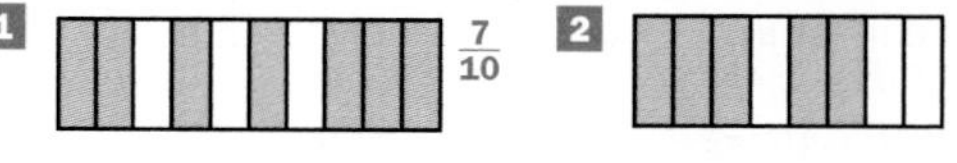

1 $\frac{7}{10}$ 2 $\frac{5}{8}$ 3 $\frac{7}{12}$

Solve.

4 A game board is separated into 12 equal sections. What fraction of the board are 5 sections? $\frac{5}{12}$

5 Grace buys items for \$3.98, \$2.04, \$3.50, and \$0.75. Can s pay for them with a ten-dollar bil Explain. No; the items cost \$10.2 \$10.27 > \$10.

Part of a Group page 373

Choose the fraction that tells which part is blue.

1  a
a. $\frac{7}{12}$ **b.** $\frac{4}{7}$ **c.** $\frac{1}{4}$

2 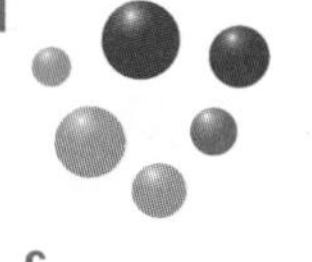 c
a. $\frac{3}{6}$ **b.** $\frac{1}{3}$ **c.** $\frac{1}{6}$

3  b
a. $\frac{3}{4}$ **b.** $\frac{3}{8}$ **c.** $\frac{1}{4}$

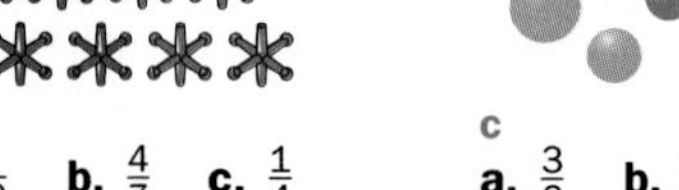

Solve.

4 Three out of four games use number cubes. What fraction of the games use number cubes? What fraction do *not* use number cubes? $\frac{3}{4}$; $\frac{1}{4}$

5 Tiwa wants 20 new hair bows. Th are sold in packages of 6. How many packages must she buy to have at least 20 bows? 4 packag

Find a Fraction of a Number page 375

Find the answer. Use any method.

1 $\frac{1}{2}$ of 22 11
2 $\frac{1}{5}$ of 20 4
3 $\frac{3}{4}$ of 20 15
4 $\frac{2}{3}$ of 15 10
5 $\frac{1}{6}$ of 24 4
6 $\frac{3}{8}$ of 16 6
7 $\frac{1}{3}$ of 18 6
8 $\frac{5}{6}$ of 30 25
9 $\frac{3}{10}$ of 20 6
10 $\frac{1}{4}$ of 24 6
11 $\frac{3}{5}$ of 25 15
12 $\frac{4}{4}$ of 9 9

Solve.

13 Three eighths of the 24 balls at Jay Elementary School are kickballs. How many of the balls are *not* kickballs? 15 balls

Additional Practice

p. 371 Write the fraction for the part that is shaded.

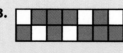

1. 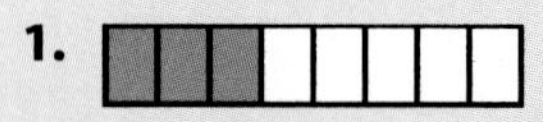 [$\frac{3}{8}$]

2. 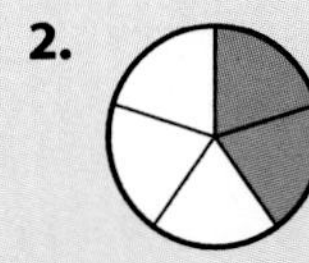 [$\frac{2}{5}$]

3. 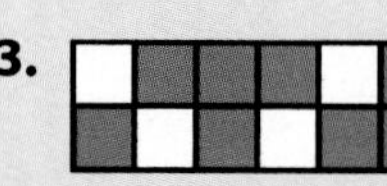 [$\frac{9}{14}$]

p. 373 Write a fraction that tells which parts are circles.

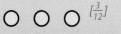

1.  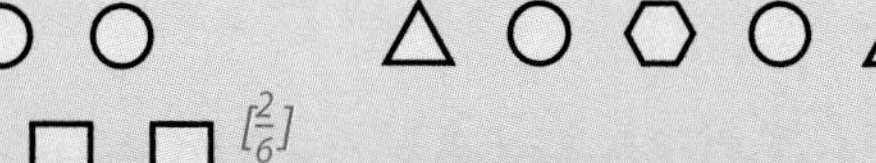 [$\frac{3}{12}$]

2.  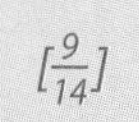 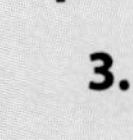 [$\frac{2}{6}$]

3.   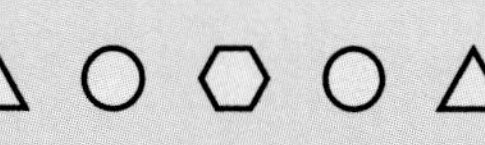 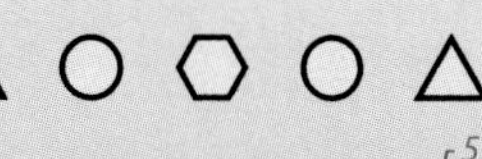 [$\frac{5}{10}$]

p. 375 Find the answer. Use any method.

1. $\frac{1}{4}$ of 28 [7]
2. $\frac{2}{5}$ of 15 [6]
3. $\frac{1}{8}$ of 24 [3]
4. $\frac{1}{6}$ of 36 [6]
5. $\frac{3}{7}$ of 28 [12]
6. $\frac{2}{3}$ of 12 [8]
7. $\frac{5}{9}$ of 18 [10]
8. $\frac{4}{5}$ of 20 [16]
9. $\frac{5}{7}$ of 14 [10]
10. $\frac{3}{4}$ of 24 [18]
11. $\frac{1}{3}$ of 21 [7]
12. $\frac{5}{6}$ of 30 [25]
13. $\frac{1}{9}$ of 18 [2]
14. $\frac{1}{5}$ of 25 [5]
15. $\frac{2}{7}$ of 35 [10]
16. $\frac{4}{9}$ of 36 [16]
17. $\frac{3}{5}$ of 10 [6]
18. $\frac{1}{6}$ of 30 [5]

ivalent Fractions page 379

nplete the equivalent fraction.

$\frac{?}{3} = \frac{8}{■}$ 12 — 6 $\frac{6}{8} = \frac{■}{4}$ 3 — 7 $\frac{4}{5} = \frac{8}{■}$ 10 — 8 $\frac{10}{25} = \frac{2}{■}$ 5

ne three equivalent fractions for the fraction.
any method. Possible answers are given.

	10 $\frac{5}{6}$	11 $\frac{9}{27}$	12 $\frac{6}{14}$	13 $\frac{3}{8}$	14 $\frac{16}{32}$
$\frac{2}{16}, \frac{3}{24}, \frac{4}{32}$	$\frac{10}{12}, \frac{15}{18}, \frac{20}{24}$	$\frac{1}{3}, \frac{3}{9}, \frac{18}{54}$	$\frac{3}{7}, \frac{9}{21}, \frac{12}{28}$	$\frac{6}{16}, \frac{9}{24}, \frac{12}{32}$	$\frac{1}{2}, \frac{2}{4}, \frac{4}{8}$

plify Fractions page 381

ne fraction in simplest form? Write *yes* or *no*.

 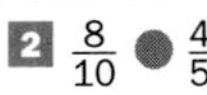  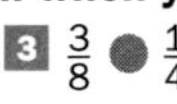  

No. — 2 $\frac{3}{5}$ Yes. — 3 $\frac{35}{42}$ No. — 4 $\frac{3}{12}$ No. — 5 $\frac{25}{26}$ Yes. — 6 $\frac{6}{15}$ No.

te the fraction in simplest form. Show your method. Methods may vary.

$\frac{2}{8}$ $\frac{1}{4}$ — 8 $\frac{6}{21}$ $\frac{2}{7}$ — 9 $\frac{8}{10}$ $\frac{4}{5}$ — 10 $\frac{9}{12}$ $\frac{3}{4}$ — 11 $\frac{6}{16}$ $\frac{3}{8}$ — 12 $\frac{15}{20}$ $\frac{3}{4}$

$\frac{8}{12}$ $\frac{2}{3}$ — 14 $\frac{16}{32}$ $\frac{1}{2}$ — 15 $\frac{24}{30}$ $\frac{4}{5}$ — 16 $\frac{14}{20}$ $\frac{7}{10}$ — 17 $\frac{9}{21}$ $\frac{3}{7}$ — 18 $\frac{12}{48}$ $\frac{1}{4}$

ve.

Lily has 20 marbles. 8 are red. What fraction of the marbles are red? Write in simplest form. $\frac{2}{5}$

20 Write a number that rounds up to 41,200 and down to 41,170. any number from 41,171 through 41,174

npare Fractions page 383

te >, <, or =. Use mental math when you can.

$\frac{6}{12}$ ● $\frac{2}{3}$ < — 2 $\frac{8}{10}$ ● $\frac{4}{5}$ = — 3 $\frac{3}{8}$ ● $\frac{1}{4}$ > — 4 $\frac{12}{16}$ ● $\frac{7}{8}$ < — 5 $\frac{2}{3}$ ● $\frac{9}{15}$ >

te in order from greatest to least.

$\frac{2}{3}, \frac{1}{2}, \frac{5}{6}$ $\frac{5}{6}, \frac{2}{3}, \frac{1}{2}$ — 7 $\frac{3}{8}, \frac{3}{4}, \frac{1}{2}$ $\frac{3}{4}, \frac{1}{2}, \frac{3}{8}$ — 8 $\frac{3}{4}, \frac{5}{6}, \frac{5}{12}$ $\frac{5}{6}, \frac{3}{4}, \frac{5}{12}$

ve.

A player in Wow! wins if she reaches the finish line first. Judy is $\frac{3}{4}$ of the way to the finish line, and Alice is $\frac{5}{8}$ of the way. Who is farther from the finish line? Alice

10 Megan scores 10 points in Socko. Derek scores $\frac{3}{5}$ as many points as Megan, and Kirk scores twice as many as Derek. How many points does each student score? Megan—10 points, Derek—6 points, Kirk—12 points

Extra Practice 521

Developing Algebra Sense

This section provides another opportunity for students to reinforce algebraic ideas.

Find the missing number.

1. $\frac{2}{3} = \frac{◆}{12}$ *[8]*
2. $\frac{8}{10} = \frac{4}{◆}$ *[5]*
3. $\frac{4}{9} = \frac{8}{◆}$ *[18]*
4. $\frac{5}{7} = \frac{◆}{35}$ *[25]*
5. $\frac{12}{16} = \frac{◆}{4}$ *[3]*
6. $\frac{5}{20} = \frac{1}{◆}$ *[4]*

p.379 Name three equivalent fractions for the fraction. Use any method. *[Possible responses given.]*

1. $\frac{2}{3}$ *[$\frac{4}{6}, \frac{6}{9}, \frac{8}{12}$]*
2. $\frac{3}{5}$ *[$\frac{6}{10}, \frac{9}{15}, \frac{12}{20}$]*
3. $\frac{9}{12}$ *[$\frac{3}{4}, \frac{6}{8}, \frac{12}{16}$]*
4. $\frac{16}{20}$ *[$\frac{4}{5}, \frac{8}{10}, \frac{12}{15}$]*
5. $\frac{4}{16}$ *[$\frac{1}{4}, \frac{2}{8}, \frac{3}{12}$]*
6. $\frac{5}{7}$ *[$\frac{10}{14}, \frac{15}{21}, \frac{20}{28}$]*

p.381 Write the fraction in simplest form.

1. $\frac{8}{12}$ *[$\frac{2}{3}$]*
2. $\frac{5}{10}$ *[$\frac{1}{2}$]*
3. $\frac{8}{18}$ *[$\frac{4}{9}$]*
4. $\frac{21}{28}$ *[$\frac{3}{4}$]*
5. $\frac{9}{24}$ *[$\frac{3}{8}$]*
6. $\frac{25}{35}$ *[$\frac{5}{7}$]*

p.383 Write >, <, or =. Use mental math where you can.

1. $\frac{3}{8}$ ◆ $\frac{2}{3}$ *[<]*
2. $\frac{1}{2}$ ◆ $\frac{3}{7}$ *[>]*
3. $\frac{8}{10}$ ◆ $\frac{4}{5}$ *[=]*
4. $\frac{4}{6}$ ◆ $\frac{5}{9}$ *[>]*
5. $\frac{3}{9}$ ◆ $\frac{4}{12}$ *[=]*
6. $\frac{5}{6}$ ◆ $\frac{7}{8}$ *[<]*

Write in order from greatest to least.

7. $\frac{2}{4}, \frac{6}{8}, \frac{4}{5}$ *[$\frac{4}{5}, \frac{6}{8}, \frac{2}{4}$]*
8. $\frac{2}{5}, \frac{7}{9}, \frac{4}{7}$ *[$\frac{7}{9}, \frac{4}{7}, \frac{2}{5}$]*
9. $\frac{5}{8}, \frac{11}{13}, \frac{5}{9}$ *[$\frac{11}{13}, \frac{5}{8}, \frac{5}{9}$]*
10. $\frac{2}{8}, \frac{1}{2}, \frac{4}{5}$ *[$\frac{4}{5}, \frac{1}{2}, \frac{2}{8}$]*
11. $\frac{7}{9}, \frac{3}{6}, \frac{5}{8}$ *[$\frac{7}{9}, \frac{5}{8}, \frac{3}{6}$]*
12. $\frac{1}{12}, \frac{2}{9}, \frac{3}{7}$ *[$\frac{3}{7}, \frac{2}{9}, \frac{1}{12}$]*

PURPOSE Provide another opportunity for review and practice.

Materials have available: calculators

Using the Extra Practice

The **Extra Practice** can be used to provide further practice during a lesson or as a review later in the chapter.

Using the Additional Practice

The sections below provide additional practice that you can assign. You may wish to write these exercises on the chalkboard or put them on a reproducible master.

Mixed Numbers page 385

Rename as a whole number or as a mixed number in simplest form.

1. $\frac{5}{3}$ **$1\frac{2}{3}$**
2. $\frac{7}{4}$ **$1\frac{3}{4}$**
3. $\frac{18}{5}$ **$3\frac{3}{5}$**
4. $\frac{13}{4}$ **$3\frac{1}{4}$**
5. $\frac{25}{6}$ **$4\frac{1}{6}$**
6. $\frac{24}{10}$ **$2\frac{2}{5}$**
7. $\frac{10}{8}$ **$1\frac{1}{4}$**
8. $\frac{40}{6}$ **$6\frac{2}{3}$**
9. $\frac{16}{16}$ **1**
10. $\frac{20}{5}$ **4**
11. $\frac{52}{8}$ **$6\frac{1}{2}$**
12. $\frac{33}{9}$ **$3\frac{2}{3}$**

Solve.

13. Each of two spinners for a game is divided into 8 equal parts. 9 parts are blue. Write a mixed number to describe the blue parts. **$1\frac{1}{8}$**

14. Demi brought 6 pints of water nature hike. Ashley brought 2 quarts. How many more pints Demi bring than Ashley? **2 pt**

Probability page 391

Use the words *more likely, less likely, equally likely, certain,* or *impossible* to describe the probability.

1. picking a red marble **impossible**
2. picking a yellow marble **more likely**
3. picking a blue marble **less likely**

Solve.

4. **Logical reasoning** How can you arrange a marble display to make the probability of picking a red marble certain? **Put only red marbles in the display.**

5. A clerk sold 25 games each mo for 6 months. At this rate, how many will he sell in a year? **300 games**

Fractions and Probability page 393

Find the probability of picking a letter from the cards below.

1. the letter *S* **$\frac{4}{11}$**
2. the letter *I* **$\frac{4}{11}$**
3. the letter *M* **$\frac{1}{11}$**
4. the letter

M S S
S S I
I I P P I

Additional Practice

p.385 Rename as a whole number or as a mixed number in simplest form.

1. $\frac{12}{5}$ *[$2\frac{2}{5}$]*
2. $\frac{9}{9}$ *[1]*
3. $\frac{18}{7}$ *[$2\frac{4}{7}$]*
4. $\frac{35}{4}$ *[$8\frac{3}{4}$]*
5. $\frac{76}{3}$ *[$25\frac{1}{3}$]*
6. $\frac{72}{8}$ *[9]*

p.391 Use the words *more likely, less likely, equally likely, certain,* or *impossible* to describe the probability.

1. picking a square *[less likely]*
2. picking an oval *[impossible]*
3. picking a circle *[equally likely]*
4. picking a circle or square *[more likely]*

p.393 Find the probability of picking a letter from the cards on the right.

1. a vowel *[$\frac{4}{14}$ or $\frac{2}{7}$]*
2. the letter *s* *[$\frac{3}{14}$]*
3. the letter *t* *[$\frac{1}{14}$]*
4. not a vowel *[$\frac{10}{14}$ or $\frac{5}{7}$]*
5. the letter *f* *[$\frac{0}{14}$ or 0]*
6. the letter *a* *[$\frac{2}{14}$ or $\frac{1}{7}$]*

oblem-Solving Strategy: Conduct an Experiment page 395
lve. Explain your methods. **Explanations may vary.**

Toss two pennies 30 times. Record the results as: 2 heads, 2 tails, or 1 head and 1 tail. Based on your experiment, which result is more likely? **1 head and 1 tail, although other results are possible.**

Garth wants to buy several booklets priced at $3 at the art museum. He can buy one booklet and get the next for half price. How many booklets can he buy if he has $25? How much money will he have left? **10 booklets; $2.50**

2 Joy has 13 pairs of shoes in one closet and 8 pairs in another. If she puts them all in one closet with 7 pairs on each shelf, how many shelves will she need? **3 shelves**

4 Four girls ran a 2-kilometer race. Uma was ahead of Mahala and Brianna. Lulu was directly after Uma. Two girls placed between Uma and Mahala. In what order did each girl place? **Uma, Lulu, Brianna, Mahala**

edict and Experiment page 397
e the spinner for problems 1–2. Explain your reasoning.

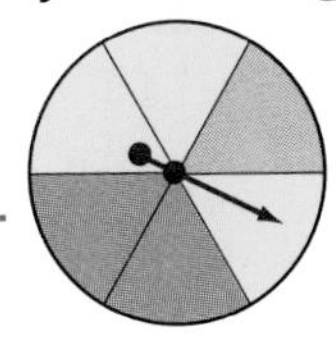

Is it reasonable to predict that the spinner will land on green 10 out of 30 times? **Yes; the probability of landing n green is $\frac{2}{6}$, or $\frac{1}{3}$, and $\frac{1}{3}$ of 30 is 10 times.**

Can you ever expect the spinner to land on blue? **No; the probability of landing on blue is 0.**

Suppose you roll a 1–6 number cube 60 times. Is it reasonable to predict that you will get a number less than 4 about 50 times? **No; the probability of getting a number less than 4 is $\frac{3}{6}$, or $\frac{1}{2}$, and $\frac{1}{2}$ of 60 is 30 times.**

Jay bought $\frac{1}{3}$ of the etchings that were on sale at the art gallery. He bought 6. How many are still on sale? **12 etchings; 6 is $\frac{1}{3}$ of the etchings, so there are $3 \times 6 = 18$, $18 - 6 = 12$.**

roblem Solvers at Work page 401
olve. Explain your methods. **Explanations may vary.**

Delbert works in a video store and earns $18 for 3 hours of work. Irene works in a competing store and earns $42 for 7 hours work. Do Delbert and Irene receive the same amount of money per hour? **Yes, Delbert earns $18 ÷ 3, or $6/hour and Irene earns $42 ÷ 7, or $6/hour.**

2 Alexandra has a $5-off coupon to use at the video store. She rents 3 videotapes at $1.98 each and buys a videotape for $19.98. How much money does she spend at the store? **$20.92**

Developing Spatial Sense

This section provides another opportunity for students to reinforce spatial sense.

Copy each of the shapes on graph paper. Cut them out. Use all four shapes to form a rectangle. What fraction of the rectangle is each shape?

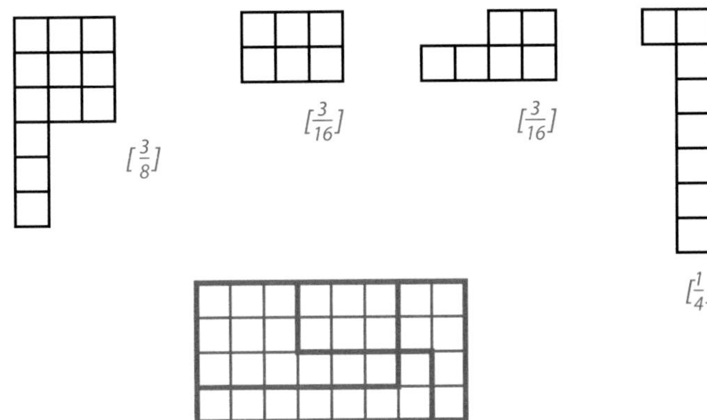

p.395 Solve. Explain your methods. *[Explanations may vary.]*

1. Roll a number cube 30 times. Based on your experiment, did an odd number appear more often than an even number? *[Check students' experiments.]*
2. Mort wants to save $24. He has saved $\frac{3}{4}$ of the amount. How much has he saved? *[$18]*

p.397 Use the spinner for problems 1–2. Explain your reasoning.

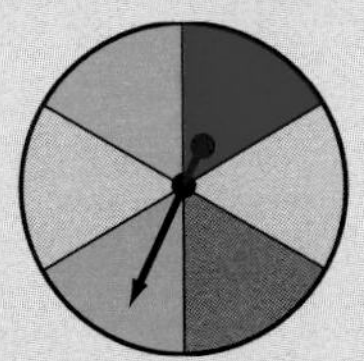

1. How often do you expect the spinner will stop on red in 30 spins? *[$\frac{1}{6} \times 30 = 5$ times]*
2. Is it reasonable to predict that the spinner will land on blue 8 out of 24 times? *[Yes, probability of landing on blue is $\frac{2}{6}$, and $\frac{2}{6} \times 24 = 8$]*

p.401 Solve. Explain your methods. *[Explanations may vary.]*

1. A bag has 8 blocks—4 red, 3 green, and 1 blue—in it. What is the probability of a green block being pulled from the bag? *[$\frac{3}{8}$]*
2. Lisa and Les each earned $5. Lisa saved $\frac{3}{5}$ of her money. Les saved $\frac{6}{10}$ of his. Is this the same amount? *[Yes, $\frac{3}{5} = \frac{6}{10}$]*
3. Dan walks $\frac{3}{4}$ of a mile to school. Don walks $\frac{2}{3}$ of a mile, and Daryl $\frac{3}{8}$ of a mile. Who lives nearest the school? *[Daryl]*
4. Merlo bought 3 CDs that cost $12 each. The tax was $1.80. What was the total bill? *[$37.80]*

PURPOSE Provide another opportunity for review and practice.

Materials have available: calculators, fraction strips

Using the Extra Practice

The **Extra Practice** can be used to provide further practice during a lesson or as a review later in the chapter.

Using the Additional Practice

The sections below provide additional practice that you can assign. You may wish to write these exercises on the chalkboard or put them on a reproducible master.

Add Fractions page 413

Add. You may use models if you wish.

1. $\frac{1}{3} + \frac{1}{3}$ $\frac{2}{3}$
2. $\frac{5}{12} + \frac{7}{12}$ $\frac{12}{12}$, or 1
3. $\frac{4}{5} + \frac{3}{5}$ $\frac{7}{5}$, or $1\frac{2}{5}$
4. $\frac{1}{6} + \frac{1}{6}$ $\frac{2}{6}$, or $\frac{1}{3}$
5. $\frac{5}{8} + \frac{5}{8}$ $\frac{10}{8}$, or $1\frac{2}{8}$, o

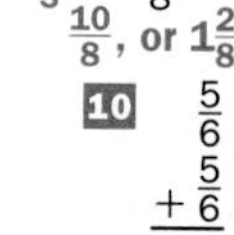

6. $\frac{3}{10} + \frac{4}{10}$ $\frac{7}{10}$
7. $\frac{2}{3} + \frac{2}{3}$ $\frac{4}{3}$, or $1\frac{1}{3}$
8. $\frac{3}{4} + \frac{1}{4}$ $\frac{4}{4}$, or 1
9. $\frac{5}{8} + \frac{7}{8}$ $\frac{12}{8}$, or $1\frac{4}{8}$, or $1\frac{1}{2}$
10. $\frac{5}{6} + \frac{5}{6}$ $\frac{10}{6}$, or $1\frac{4}{6}$, o

Solve.

11. Ben ate $\frac{1}{4}$ of a pizza. Then, he ate another $\frac{1}{4}$. How much pizza did he eat in all? $\frac{2}{4}$ pizza, or $\frac{1}{2}$ pizza
12. **ALGEBRA: PATTERNS** Copy and complete the pattern. Then write the rule.
5, 20, 80, 320, ■ 1,280;
rule: multiply the prior number by 4.

Add Fractions page 415

Add. Write the sum in simplest form.

1. $\frac{1}{5} + \frac{3}{5}$ $\frac{4}{5}$
2. $\frac{5}{8} + \frac{3}{8}$ 1
3. $\frac{1}{4} + \frac{1}{4}$ $\frac{1}{2}$
4. $\frac{7}{10} + \frac{1}{10}$ $\frac{4}{5}$
5. $\frac{3}{8} + \frac{7}{8}$ $1\frac{1}{4}$
6. $\frac{5}{6} + \frac{1}{6}$ 1

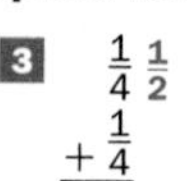
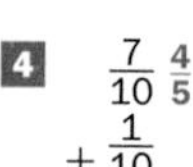
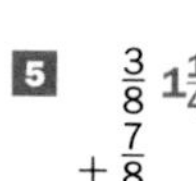

7. $\frac{1}{12} + \frac{7}{12}$ $\frac{2}{3}$
8. $\frac{2}{10} + \frac{9}{10}$ $1\frac{1}{10}$
9. $\frac{3}{6} + \frac{5}{6}$ $1\frac{1}{3}$
10. $\frac{3}{4} + \frac{3}{4}$ $1\frac{1}{2}$

Subtract Fractions page 419

Subtract. Write the difference in simplest form.

1. $\frac{3}{4} - \frac{1}{4}$ $\frac{1}{2}$
2. $\frac{7}{8} - \frac{3}{8}$ $\frac{1}{2}$
3. $\frac{4}{5} - \frac{2}{5}$ $\frac{2}{5}$
4. $\frac{9}{10} - \frac{3}{10}$ $\frac{3}{5}$
5. $\frac{7}{12} - \frac{3}{12}$ $\frac{1}{3}$
6. $\frac{4}{6} - \frac{1}{6}$ $\frac{1}{2}$
7. $\frac{5}{6} - \frac{2}{6}$ $\frac{1}{2}$
8. $\frac{7}{10} - \frac{5}{10}$ $\frac{1}{5}$
9. $\frac{11}{12} - \frac{3}{12}$ $\frac{2}{3}$
10. $\frac{9}{12} - \frac{5}{12}$ $\frac{1}{3}$

Solve.

11. Seven eighths of the students like ice cream. Four eighths prefer chocolate to vanilla. What fraction of the students prefer vanilla ice cream? $\frac{3}{8}$
12. Ramona brought 5 gallons of orangeade to the picnic. Ramona brought 2 more quarts than Jane. How many quarts did they bring altogether? 38 qt

Additional Practice

p.413 Add. You may use models if you wish.

1. $\frac{2}{8}+\frac{3}{8}$ [$\frac{5}{8}$]
2. $\frac{5}{10}+\frac{2}{10}$ [$\frac{7}{10}$]
3. $\frac{3}{5}+\frac{2}{5}$ [$\frac{5}{5}$ or 1]
4. $\frac{3}{4} + \frac{2}{4}$ [$\frac{5}{4}$ or $1\frac{1}{4}$]
5. $\frac{6}{12} + \frac{2}{12}$ [$\frac{8}{12}$ or $\frac{2}{3}$]
6. $\frac{1}{6} + \frac{2}{6}$ [$\frac{3}{6}$ or $\frac{1}{2}$]

p.415 Add. Write the sum in simplest form.

1. $\frac{2}{8} + \frac{3}{8}$ [$\frac{5}{8}$]
2. $\frac{4}{7} + \frac{2}{7}$ [$\frac{6}{7}$]
3. $\frac{4}{10} + \frac{3}{10}$ [$\frac{7}{10}$]
4. $\frac{4}{9}+\frac{2}{9}$ [$\frac{2}{3}$]
5. $\frac{4}{6}+\frac{3}{6}$ [$1\frac{1}{6}$]
6. $\frac{5}{12}+\frac{7}{12}$ [1]

p.419 Subtract. Write the difference in simplest form.

1. $\frac{9}{10}-\frac{2}{10}$ [$\frac{7}{10}$]
2. $\frac{5}{12}-\frac{1}{12}$ [$\frac{1}{3}$]
3. $\frac{3}{4}-\frac{2}{4}$ [$\frac{1}{4}$]
4. $\frac{6}{8}-\frac{3}{8}$ [$\frac{3}{8}$]
5. $\frac{5}{6}-\frac{5}{6}$ [0]
6. $\frac{9}{12}-\frac{7}{12}$ [$\frac{1}{6}$]
7. $\frac{5}{6} - \frac{2}{6}$ [$\frac{1}{2}$]
8. $\frac{7}{10} - \frac{3}{10}$ [$\frac{2}{5}$]
9. $\frac{5}{8} - \frac{3}{8}$ [$\frac{1}{4}$]
10. $\frac{3}{4} - \frac{1}{4}$ [$\frac{1}{2}$]
11. $\frac{11}{12} - \frac{5}{12}$ [$\frac{1}{2}$]
12. $\frac{8}{10} - \frac{6}{10}$ [$\frac{1}{5}$]

tract Fractions page 421
tract. Write the difference in simplest form.

$\frac{5}{8}$ $\frac{1}{8}$ $-\frac{4}{8}$ | 2 $\frac{3}{10}$ $\frac{1}{10}$ $-\frac{2}{10}$ | 3 $\frac{7}{9}$ $\frac{2}{3}$ $-\frac{1}{9}$ | 4 $\frac{3}{4}$ $\frac{1}{2}$ $-\frac{1}{4}$ | 5 $\frac{5}{6}$ $\frac{1}{3}$ $-\frac{3}{6}$ | 6 $\frac{11}{12}$ $\frac{5}{6}$ $-\frac{1}{12}$

$\frac{4}{5}-\frac{1}{5}$ $\frac{3}{5}$ | 8 $\frac{5}{8}-\frac{1}{8}$ $\frac{1}{2}$ | 9 $\frac{10}{10}-\frac{2}{10}$ $\frac{4}{5}$ | 10 $\frac{5}{6}-\frac{1}{6}$ $\frac{2}{3}$

te >, <, or =.

$\frac{5}{8}-\frac{2}{8}$ ● $\frac{7}{8}-\frac{3}{8}$ < | 12 $\frac{3}{6}-\frac{1}{6}$ ● $\frac{5}{6}-\frac{4}{6}$ >

ve.

Eileen cut a loaf of nut bread into eighths. She gave 3 pieces to Fred. What fraction of the loaf did she have left? **$\frac{5}{8}$ loaf**

14 Dee buys 5 cans of corn for $2 at Mott's Grocery. One can of corn at Johnson's Mart costs 39¢. Which grocery charges more for 5 cans of corn? How much more? **Mott's Grocery; 5¢**

d a Common Denominator page 427
ne the common denominator.

$\frac{1}{2}$ and $\frac{3}{4}$ 4 | 2 $\frac{3}{10}$ and $\frac{2}{5}$ 10 | 3 $\frac{1}{2}$ and $\frac{2}{3}$ 6 | 4 $\frac{2}{3}$ and $\frac{3}{4}$ 12 | 5 $\frac{1}{4}$ and $\frac{5}{6}$ 12

te as equivalent fractions with common denominators.

$\frac{3}{4}$ and $\frac{5}{8}$ $\frac{6}{8}, \frac{5}{8}$ | 7 $\frac{5}{6}$ and $\frac{2}{3}$ $\frac{5}{6}, \frac{4}{6}$ | 8 $\frac{3}{4}$ and $\frac{5}{12}$ $\frac{9}{12}, \frac{5}{12}$ | 9 $\frac{2}{3}$ and $\frac{7}{9}$ $\frac{6}{9}, \frac{7}{9}$ | 10 $\frac{1}{2}$ and $\frac{3}{8}$ $\frac{4}{8}, \frac{3}{8}$

$\frac{1}{2}$ and $\frac{2}{3}$ $\frac{3}{6}, \frac{4}{6}$ | 12 $\frac{3}{4}$ and $\frac{1}{3}$ $\frac{9}{12}, \frac{4}{12}$ | 13 $\frac{2}{3}$ and $\frac{3}{5}$ $\frac{10}{15}, \frac{9}{15}$ | 14 $\frac{4}{5}$ and $\frac{1}{2}$ $\frac{8}{10}, \frac{5}{10}$ | 15 $\frac{1}{4}$ and $\frac{1}{6}$ $\frac{3}{12}, \frac{2}{12}$

ve.

Partygoers ate $\frac{1}{4}$ of Nita's birthday cake. Her family ate $\frac{1}{3}$ of the same cake that night. Who ate more cake? Explain how you know. **her family, $\frac{1}{3}$, or $\frac{4}{12} > \frac{1}{4}$, or $\frac{3}{12}$**

17 Jerry places 18 marbles in a sack. 3 are white, 4 are green, 6 are blue, and 5 are red. If he picks one marble without peeking, what is the probability of getting a red marble? **$\frac{5}{18}$**

A ship has 549 gallons of drinking water. The sailors drink 10 gallons each day. How many full days can they stay at sea? **54 full days**

19 Geraldine has $35.34 in her wallet. She cashes a check and then has $82.84. What is the amount of her check? **$47.50**

Developing Algebra Sense

This section provides another opportunity for students to reinforce algebraic ideas.

Find the missing number.

1. $\frac{2}{8}+\frac{◆}{8}=\frac{7}{8}$ *[5]*
2. $\frac{◆}{12}-\frac{5}{12}=\frac{4}{12}$ *[9]*
3. $\frac{◆}{7}+\frac{4}{7}=1$ *[3]*
4. $\frac{5}{9}-\frac{◆}{9}=\frac{2}{9}$ *[3]*
5. $1\frac{2}{5}+2\frac{◆}{5}=3\frac{4}{5}$ *[2]*
6. $4\frac{3}{8}-◆\frac{2}{8}=3\frac{1}{8}$ *[1]*

p.421 Subtract. Write the difference in simplest form.

1. $\frac{6}{7} - \frac{1}{7}$ *[$\frac{5}{7}$]*
2. $\frac{10}{11} - \frac{9}{11}$ *[$\frac{1}{11}$]*
3. $\frac{5}{6} - \frac{2}{6}$ *[$\frac{1}{2}$]*
4. $\frac{5}{8}-\frac{5}{8}$ *[0]*
5. $\frac{5}{9}-\frac{2}{9}$ *[$\frac{1}{3}$]*
6. $\frac{8}{10}-\frac{4}{10}$ *[$\frac{2}{5}$]*

Write >, <, or =.

7. $\frac{8}{9}-\frac{5}{9}$ ◆ $\frac{7}{9}-\frac{6}{9}$ *[>]*
8. $\frac{3}{4}-\frac{1}{2}$ ◆ $\frac{6}{8}-\frac{4}{8}$ *[=]*
9. $\frac{6}{8}-\frac{3}{8}$ ◆ $\frac{7}{8}-\frac{3}{8}$ *[<]*
10. $\frac{11}{12}-\frac{6}{12}$ ◆ $\frac{8}{12}-\frac{6}{12}$ *[>]*

p.427 Name the common denominator.

1. $\frac{2}{3}$ and $\frac{7}{15}$ *[15]*
2. $\frac{3}{5}$ and $\frac{3}{10}$ *[10]*
3. $\frac{1}{2}$ and $\frac{5}{8}$ *[8]*
4. $\frac{1}{3}$ and $\frac{3}{4}$ *[12]*
5. $\frac{1}{2}$ and $\frac{4}{5}$ *[10]*
6. $\frac{1}{6}$ and $\frac{1}{2}$ *[6]*

Write as equivalent fractions with common denominators.

7. $\frac{2}{3}$ and $\frac{7}{9}$ *[$\frac{6}{9}, \frac{7}{9}$]*
8. $\frac{4}{5}$ and $\frac{3}{10}$ *[$\frac{8}{10}, \frac{3}{10}$]*
9. $\frac{7}{8}$ and $\frac{1}{2}$ *[$\frac{7}{8}, \frac{4}{8}$]*
10. $\frac{2}{3}$ and $\frac{5}{12}$ *[$\frac{8}{12}$ and $\frac{5}{12}$]*
11. $\frac{1}{2}$ and $\frac{3}{4}$ *[$\frac{2}{4}, \frac{3}{4}$]*
12. $\frac{1}{3}$ and $\frac{2}{5}$ *[$\frac{5}{15}, \frac{6}{15}$]*

Chapter 11 EXTRA PRACTICE

PURPOSE Provide another opportunity for review and practice.

Materials have available: calculators

Using the Extra Practice

The **Extra Practice** can be used to provide further practice during a lesson or as a review later in the chapter.

Using the Additional Practice

The sections below provide additional practice that you can assign. You may wish to write these exercises on the chalkboard or put them on a reproducible master.

extra practice

Add and Subtract Fractions with Unlike Denominators page 431
Find the equivalent fraction. Then add or subtract.

1 $\frac{1}{4} = \frac{■}{8}$, $+\frac{5}{8} = \frac{■}{8}$, $\frac{■}{8}$ 2; 5; 7

2 $\frac{1}{4} = \frac{■}{4}$, $+\frac{1}{2} = \frac{■}{4}$, $\frac{■}{4}$ 1; 2; 3

3 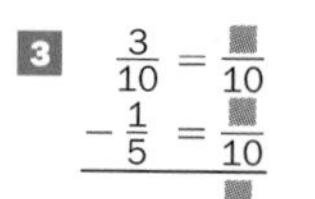 $\frac{3}{10} = \frac{■}{10}$, $-\frac{1}{5} = \frac{■}{10}$, $\frac{■}{10}$ 3; 2; 1

4 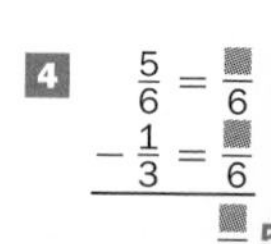 $\frac{5}{6} = \frac{■}{6}$, $-\frac{1}{3} = \frac{■}{6}$, $\frac{■}{6}$ 5

Add or subtract using any method. Write the sum or difference in simplest form.

5 $\frac{1}{6} + \frac{2}{3}$ $\frac{5}{6}$
6 $\frac{1}{4} + \frac{3}{8}$ $\frac{5}{8}$
7 $\frac{3}{5} + \frac{1}{10}$ $\frac{7}{10}$
8 $\frac{1}{12} + \frac{3}{4}$ $\frac{5}{6}$
9 $\frac{1}{4} - \frac{1}{8}$ $\frac{1}{8}$
10 $\frac{2}{3} - \frac{2}{9}$ $\frac{4}{9}$
11 $\frac{7}{8} - \frac{1}{2}$ $\frac{3}{8}$
12 $\frac{3}{5} - \frac{1}{10}$ $\frac{1}{2}$

Solve.

13 Shantelle and Donovan buy $\frac{1}{4}$ pound of pecans. They use $\frac{1}{8}$ pound to bake cookies. Then, they buy another $\frac{1}{4}$ pound. How many pounds of pecans do they then have? $\frac{3}{8}$ lb

14 There are 12 students in the marching band. How many different ways can they line up with the same number of peopl each row? List each way.
6 ways; 1 row of 12, 2 rows of 6, 3 rows o 4 rows of 3, 6 rows of 2, and 12 rows of 1

Problem-Solving Strategy: Draw a Picture page 433
Solve. Explain your methods. Explanations may vary.

1 Use graph paper. Find two shapes with the same area but with different perimeters. Check students' pictures.

2 Jan is 3 times as old as Bob. When they add their ages, the sum is 16. What are their ages? Jan—12, Bob—4

3 **ALGEBRA: PATTERNS** Draw the next three figures.

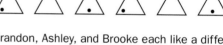

4 Brandon, Ashley, and Brooke each like a different kind of nut—pecans, peanuts, or almonds. Brandon does not like pecans. Ashley likes peanuts. Which is the favorite nut of each student?
Brandon—almonds, Ashley—peanuts, Brooke—pecans

526 Extra Practice

Additional Practice

p. 431 Find the equivalent fraction. Then add or subtract.

1. $\frac{8}{9} \to \frac{◆}{9}$ *[8]*, $-\frac{2}{3} \to \frac{◆}{9}$ *[6]*, $\frac{◆}{9}$ *$[\frac{2}{9}]$*

2. $\frac{3}{4} \to \frac{◆}{12}$ *[9]*, $-\frac{1}{3} \to \frac{◆}{12}$ *[4]*, $\frac{◆}{12}$ *$[\frac{5}{12}]$*

3. $\frac{3}{4} \to \frac{◆}{8}$ *[6]*, $+\frac{3}{8} \to \frac{◆}{8}$ *[3]*, $\frac{◆}{8}$ *$[\frac{9}{8}]$*

Add or subtract using any method.

4. $\frac{7}{10} - \frac{3}{5}$ *$[\frac{1}{10}]$*
5. $\frac{3}{8} + \frac{1}{2}$ *$[\frac{7}{8}]$*
6. $\frac{7}{12} - \frac{1}{4}$ *$[\frac{1}{3}]$*
7. $\frac{5}{6} + \frac{1}{2}$ *$[1\frac{1}{3}]$*
8. $\frac{2}{3} - \frac{1}{2}$ *$[\frac{1}{6}]$*
9. $\frac{5}{9} + \frac{1}{9}$ *$[\frac{2}{3}]$*

p. 433 Solve. Explain your methods. *[Explanations may vary.]*

1. **Logical Reasoning** John, Amy, Kai, and Ezra are sitting beside each other. Kai is between John and Amy. Amy is at the end of the row. In what order are they sitting? *[Ezra, John, Kai, Amy]*
2. One day Brian read $\frac{2}{5}$ of a novel before dinner and $\frac{1}{3}$ of it after dinner. How much of the book did he read that day? *$[\frac{11}{15}]$*
3. On vacation Eva took 7 rolls of film. Each roll had 24 pictures on it. How many pictures did she take? *[168 pictures]*
4. Tony must read a 348 page book in 7 days. About how many pages must he read each day to finish the book on time? *[50 pages]*

dd and Subtract Mixed Numbers page 437

dd or subtract. Use fraction strips if you want. Rename and implify when necessary.

1 $2\frac{1}{4} + 4\frac{1}{4}$ $6\frac{1}{2}$ 2 $1\frac{3}{8} + 2\frac{3}{8}$ $3\frac{3}{4}$ 3 $5\frac{2}{3} + 4\frac{2}{3}$ $10\frac{1}{3}$ 4 $4\frac{1}{2} + 2\frac{1}{2}$ 7

5 $5\frac{5}{8} - 3\frac{3}{8}$ $2\frac{1}{4}$ 6 $7\frac{5}{6} - 3\frac{1}{6}$ $4\frac{2}{3}$ 7 $6\frac{3}{4} - 2\frac{1}{4}$ $4\frac{1}{2}$ 8 $7\frac{9}{12} - 4\frac{1}{12}$ $3\frac{2}{3}$

9 $3\frac{2}{4} + 1\frac{3}{4}$ $5\frac{1}{4}$ 10 $9\frac{3}{8} - 7\frac{3}{8}$ 2 11 $4\frac{5}{6} - 1\frac{3}{6}$ $3\frac{1}{3}$ 12 $4\frac{3}{10} + 2\frac{6}{10}$ $6\frac{9}{10}$

olve. Rename and simplify when necessary.

13 Henry mixed $2\frac{3}{8}$ pounds of hamburger and $1\frac{7}{8}$ pounds of ground veal to make meat loaf. How many pounds of meat did he mix in all? $4\frac{1}{4}$ lb

14 Cynthia is riding to her cooking class. The distance is $3\frac{3}{10}$ miles. She has ridden her bike $1\frac{1}{10}$ miles. How many miles does she have yet to ride? $2\frac{1}{5}$ mi

15 Naomi put decorative tape around the edge of the top of a recipe box. The top of the box measures 9 cm by 15 cm. How many centimeters of tape did she use? 48 cm

16 How many days will be left in the year after September 21? Will your answer be different for a leap year? Explain how you know. 101 d; no, because the extra day is in February and does not occur after September 21.

roblem Solvers at Work page 441

olve. Explain your methods. Explanations may vary.

1 Forty-five students and 5 adults will travel in vans holding 8 passengers on a field trip to Mitzi's Cooking College. How many vans will be needed to take everyone on the field trip? 7 vans

2 Ellie received these scores on some tests in her nutrition class: 85, 98, and 97. She needs an average of 95 points to get an A. What does she need to score on her next test to achieve an A average? 100

3 Jason earned $7 for mowing a lawn. He took the money to the bank and exchanged it for quarters. How many quarters did the bank give Jason? 28 quarters

4 Donna's train departs at 10:45 A.M. A car ride to the train station takes 55 minutes. How long will she have to wait at the train station if she leaves home at 8:55 A.M.? 55 min

Developing Spatial Sense

This section provides another opportunity for students to reinforce spatial sense.

Which patterns could be folded to form a cube? *[a,c]*

a.

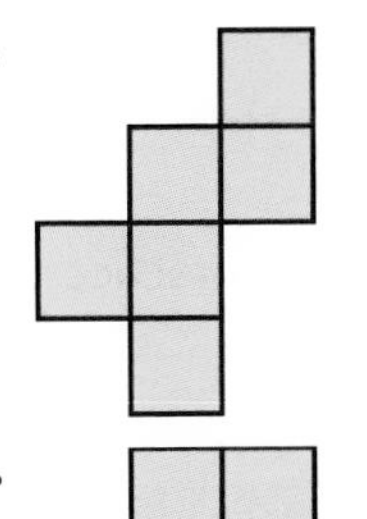

c.

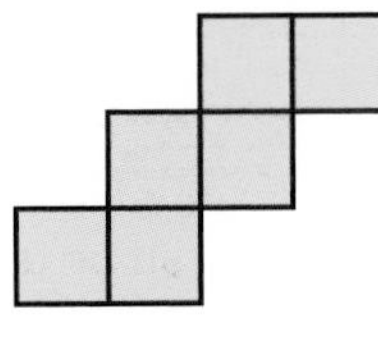

b.

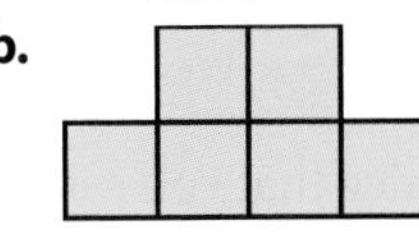

d.

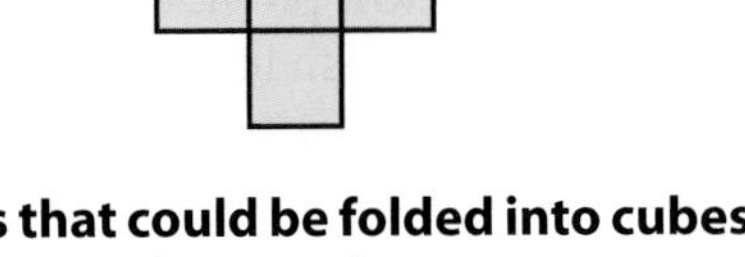

Now design 3 new patterns that could be folded into cubes. Use paper models to help you make sure that your patterns work. *[Answers may vary. Possible answers:]*

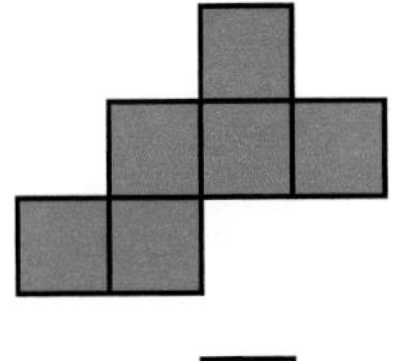

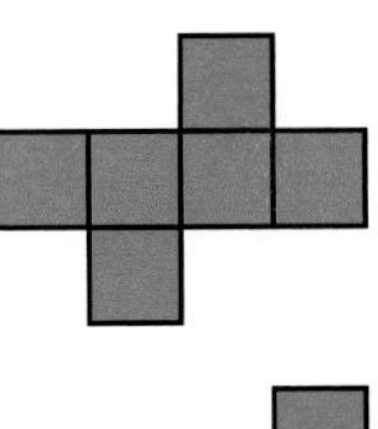

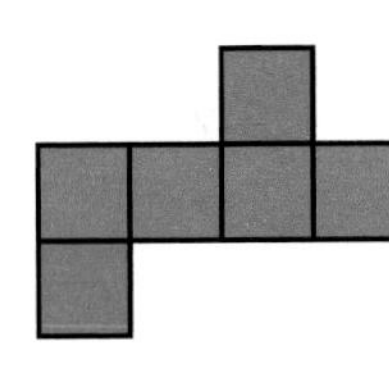

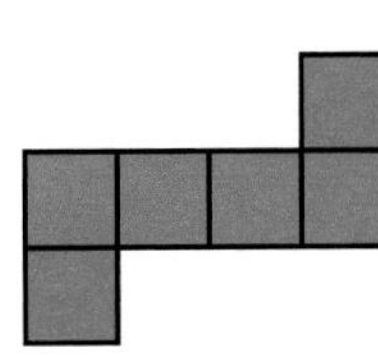

p. 437 Add or subtract. Use fractions strips if you want. Regroup and simplify when necessary.

1. $3\frac{2}{8} + 1\frac{5}{8}$ *[$4\frac{7}{8}$]*
2. $5\frac{9}{10} - 2\frac{3}{10}$ *[$3\frac{3}{5}$]*
3. $3\frac{4}{5} + 2\frac{3}{5}$ *[$6\frac{2}{5}$]*
4. $1\frac{4}{5} + 2\frac{3}{5}$ *[$4\frac{2}{5}$]*
5. $2\frac{3}{7} - 1\frac{3}{7}$ *[1]*
6. $4\frac{7}{8} - 3\frac{5}{8}$ *[$1\frac{1}{4}$]*
7. $5 + 2\frac{3}{7}$ *[$7\frac{3}{7}$]*
8. $6\frac{4}{5} - 2\frac{4}{5}$ *[4]*
9. $7\frac{1}{2} - 3$ *[$4\frac{1}{2}$]*

p. 441 Solve. Explain your methods. *[Explanations may vary.]*

1. Joy bought $1\frac{2}{3}$ lb of cheddar cheese and $1\frac{1}{2}$ lb of brie. How much cheese did she buy? *[$3\frac{1}{6}$ lb]*
2. Mr. Hosado bought 12 rolls at $0.45 each. How much change did he receive from $10? *[$4.60]*
3. Harry made a snack mix. He put together $\frac{1}{2}$ cup of raisins, $\frac{3}{4}$ cup of pretzels, $\frac{3}{4}$ cup of peanuts. How much snack mix did he make? *[2 cups]*
4. Mac, Ned, Rick, and Pete were in a race. Mac and Ned were either first or last. Rick finished before Mac and Pete. In what order did they finish? *[Ned, Rick, Pete, Mac]*

PURPOSE Provide another opportunity for review and practice.

Materials have available: calculators

Using the Extra Practice

The **Extra Practice** can be used to provide further practice during a lesson or as a review later in the chapter.

Using the Additional Practice

The sections below provide additional practice that you can assign. You may wish to write these exercises on the chalkboard or put them on a reproducible master.

Decimals Less Than 1 page 453

Write a decimal.

1 $\frac{4}{10}$ 0.4
2 $\frac{16}{100}$ 0.16
3 $\frac{39}{100}$ 0.39
4 $\frac{97}{100}$ 0.97
5 $\frac{6}{10}$ 0.6
6 $\frac{25}{100}$ 0.25
7 $\frac{54}{100}$ 0.54
8 $\frac{8}{100}$ 0.08
9 $\frac{83}{100}$ 0.83
10 $\frac{72}{100}$ 0.72
11 $\frac{9}{10}$ 0.9
12 $\frac{6}{100}$ 0.06

Solve.

13 Twenty-one out of 100 students have blond hair. Write a decimal for the part of the group that has blond hair. 0.21

14 Gina buys 60 computer disks. She pays $7.38 for each dozen. How much does Gina pay for all the disks? $36.90

Decimals Greater Than 1 page 455

Write a decimal.

1 $3\frac{7}{10}$ 3.7
2 $8\frac{35}{100}$ 8.35
3 $1\frac{12}{100}$ 1.12
4 $4\frac{3}{100}$ 4.03
5 $6\frac{82}{100}$ 6.82
6 $2\frac{8}{10}$ 2.8
7 $5\frac{7}{100}$ 5.07
8 $7\frac{3}{10}$ 7.3
9 $8\frac{91}{100}$ 8.91
10 $1\frac{3}{10}$ 1.3
11 $2\frac{5}{100}$ 2.05
12 $3\frac{4}{10}$ 3.4

Solve.

13 Write a decimal that tells how many sheets of stamps there are. 1.87

14 Renee made 8 calls to students' parents to tell them about the school fair. Jack gives her a list of 20 more names to call. She now has 45 calls to make. How many names did she have when she started calling? 33 names

Compare and Order Decimals page 457

Compare. Write $>$, $<$, or $=$.

1 $0.4 \bullet 0.23$ $>$
2 $0.3 \bullet 0.30$ $=$
3 $4.17 \bullet 4.71$ $<$
4 $4.3 \bullet 4.30$ $=$

Write in order from greatest to least.

5 0.05, 0.4, 0.34 — 0.4, 0.34, 0.05
6 1.5, 1.08, 2.1 — 2.1, 1.5, 1.08
7 3.5, 2.9, 3.08 — 3.5, 3.08, 2.9

Additional Practice

p.453 Write a decimal.

1. $\frac{7}{10}$ *[0.7]*
2. $\frac{38}{100}$ *[0.38]*
3. $\frac{2}{100}$ *[0.02]*
4. four tenths *[0.4]*
5. twelve hundredths *[0.12]*
6. nine tenths *[0.9]*

p.455 Write a decimal.

1. $8\frac{4}{10}$ *[8.4]*
2. $14\frac{37}{100}$ *[14.37]*
3. $35\frac{9}{100}$ *[35.09]*
4. twelve and eight tenths *[12.8]*
5. two and twenty-three hundredths *[2.23]*
6. thirty-nine and five hundredths *[39.05]*

p.457 Compare. Write $>$, $<$, or $=$.

1. $5.3 \blacksquare 5.03$ *[$>$]*
2. $48.6 \blacksquare 48.62$ *[$<$]*
3. $0.7 \blacksquare 0.70$ *[$=$]*
4. $71.5 \blacksquare 71.48$ *[$>$]*
5. $6.2 \blacksquare 6.20$ *[$=$]*
6. $76.35 \blacksquare 67.53$ *[$>$]*

Write in order from greatest to least.

7. 0.20, 0.02, 0.22 *[0.22, 0.20, 0.02]*
8. 3.48, 3.50, 3.05 *[3.50, 3.48, 3.05]*
9. 14.3, 13.4, 14.4 *[14.4, 14.3, 13.4]*
10. 7.72, 7.2, 7.07 *[7.72, 7.2, 7.07]*
11. 0.1, 0.12, 0.08 *[0.12, 0.1, 0.08]*
12. 8.8, 0.88, 8.88 *[8.88, 8.8, 0.88]*

oblem-Solving Strategy: Solve a Simpler Problem page 463
lve. Explain your methods. Explanations may vary.

On Saturday, Dixie's Newsstand sold 328 newspapers at $0.50 each. On Sunday, 435 papers were sold at $1.50 each. How much more money did the stand receive for the Sunday papers than for the Saturday papers? **$488.50**

2 Paula works as a telephone operator from 8:45 P.M. until 5:15 A.M. She has a 30-minute break for a midnight snack and two additional ten-minute breaks. How long does Paula work? **7 h 40 min**

Spatial reasoning How many triangles can you find in the figure below? **12 triangles**

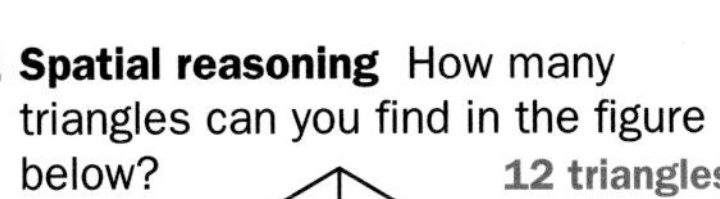

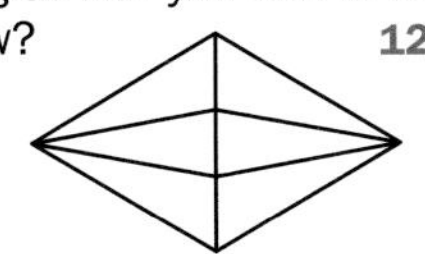

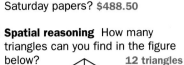

4 Jani saves a penny on Monday. Each day after that, she plans to save twice as much as she saves the day before. How much will Jani save in one week? How much in two weeks? **127 pennies, or $1.27; 16,383 pennies, or $163.83**

Bessie has 24 friends on the Internet. Of these, there are twice as many boys as girls. How many are girls? How many are boys? **8 girls; 16 boys**

6 The area of John's rectangular garden is 80 ft^2. The shorter sides each measure 8 ft. What is the length of each longer side? **10 ft**

stimate Sums and Differences page 465
stimate. Round to the nearest whole number.

3.9 + 4.3 **8**
2 4.7 + 9.2 **14**
3 5.2 − 3.9 **1**
4 21.8 − 4.3 **18**
13.62 − 8.51 **5**
6 7.49 + 8.64 **16**
7 9.75 − 4.38 **6**
8 10.9 − 5.4 **6**
6.2 + 1.9 + 3.5 **12**
10 3.87 + 2.35 + 1.09 **7**
11 8.94 + 6.71 + 9.06 **25**

stimate. Round to the nearest dollar.

$5.48 + $7.65 **$13.00**
13 $10.34 − $4.98 **$5.00**
14 $5.39 − $2.13 **$3.00**
$18.67 + $12.38 **$31.00**
16 $16.75 − $8.98 **$8.00**
17 $13.37 + $5.89 **$19.00**

olve.

Casandra buys an answering machine for $39.98, an extra cord for $10.19, and two tapes for $4.99 each. Can she pay for this purchase with 1 ten-dollar bill and 1 fifty-dollar bill? Explain. **No; even though the estimate is $60, the exact total is $60.15, and $60.15 > $60.**

19 **Logical reasoning** Abraham's CD-ROM sits between the computer and the modem. The printer sits farthest to the left. The computer sits next to the printer. Tell how they are lined up from left to right. **printer, computer, CD-ROM, and modem**

DEVELOPING ALGEBRA SENSE

Complete the function table and choose a graph that reflects the function table.

1. Rule: Multiply by 3 *[a]*

Input	1	2	3	*[4]*	*[5]*	6
Output	3	*[6]*	*[9]*	12	15	*[18]*

a.

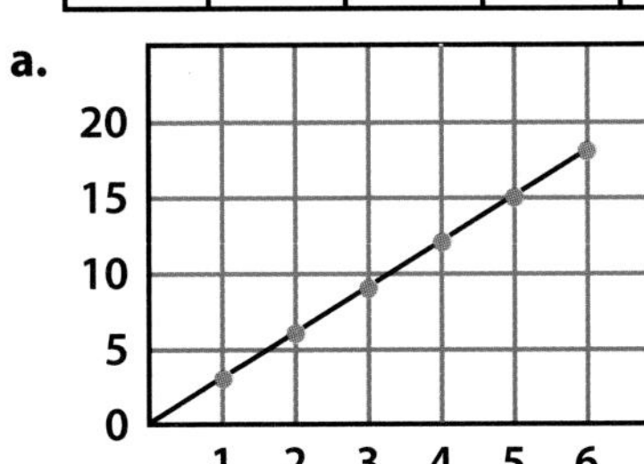

b.

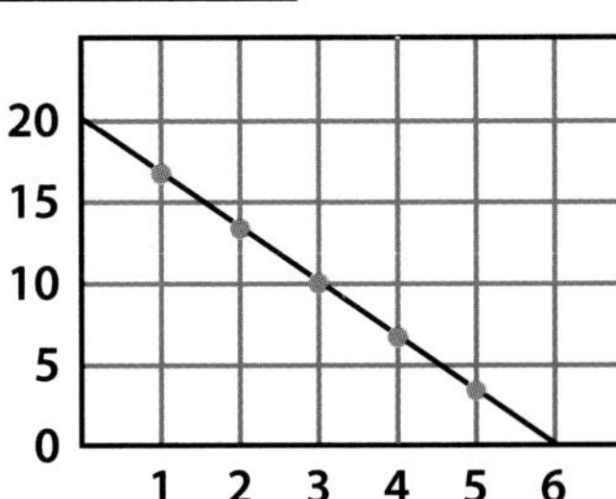

2. Rule: Multiply by 5 *[b]*

Input	*[1]*	2	*[3]*	4	5	6
Output	5	*[10]*	15	*[20]*	25	30

a.

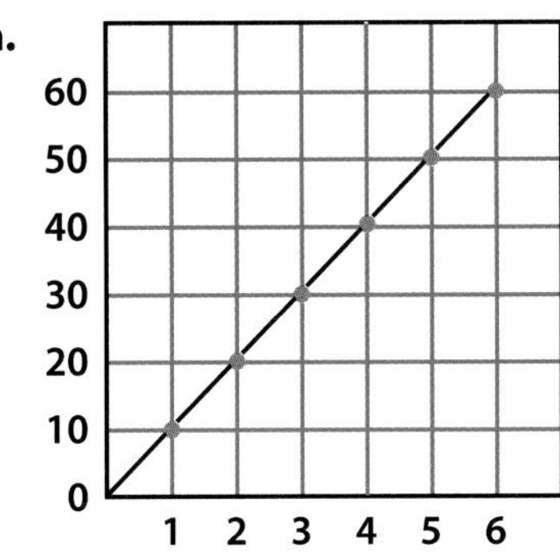

b.

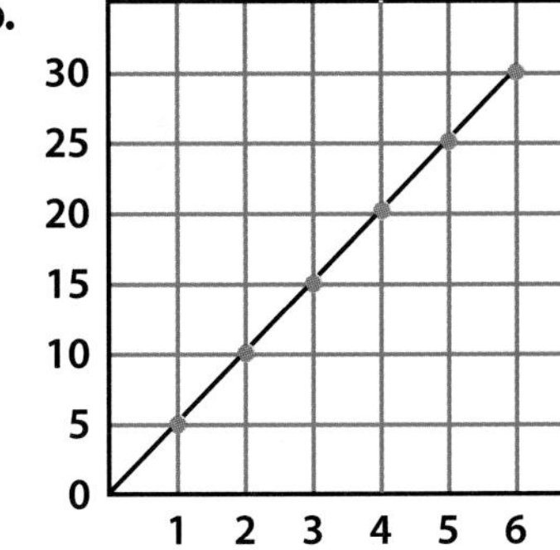

p.463 Solve. Explain your methods. *[Explanations may vary.]*

1. A softball team manager noted that in 54 games her team won twice as many games as they lost. How many had they won and lost? *[36 wins, 18 losses]*
2. Al wants to enclose his backyard. If the width of the yard is 60 ft and the length is 90 ft, how many feet of fencing should he order? *[300 ft]*
3. Peter worked 42 hours last week. He earns $9.25 an hour. What was his pay last week? *[$388.50]*
4. **Spatial reasoning** Draw the top view of the figure below. *[17 and 19]*

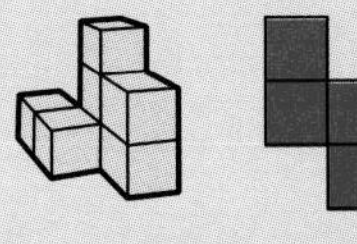

p.465 Estimate. Round to the nearest whole number.

1. 4.2 + 7.1 *[11]* **2.** 6.7 + 2.3 *[9]* **3.** 9.68 + 8.95 *[19]*
4. 8.2 − 3.4 *[5]* **5.** 14.23 − 8.67 *[5]* **6.** 7.81 − 5.96 *[2]*
7. 3.2 + 2.8 + 6.7 *[13]* **8.** 4.23 + 3.94 + 6.58 *[15]*

Estimate. Round to the nearest dollar.

9. $7.28 + $1.84 *[$9]* **10.** $4.79 + $2.38 *[$7]*
11. $9.87 + $2.68 *[$13]* **12.** $8.12 − $3.69 *[$4]*
13. $13.47 − $8.35 *[$5]* **14.** $10.82 − $6.19 *[$5]*

Chapter 12 EXTRA PRACTICE

PURPOSE Provide another opportunity for review and practice.

Materials have available: calculators

Using the Extra Practice

The **Extra Practice** can be used to provide further practice during a lesson or as a review later in the chapter.

Using the Additional Practice

The sections below provide additional practice that you can assign. You may wish to write these exercises on the chalkboard or put them on a reproducible master.

Add and Subtract Decimals page 467

Use decimal squares to add or subtract. **Check students' models.**

1. 0.5 + 0.3 = **0.8**
2. 0.4 + 0.9 = **1.3**
3. 1.45 + 1.78 = **3.23**
4. 2.46 + 1.49 = **3.95**
5. 2.15 + 2.87 = **5.02**
6. 0.9 − 0.4 = **0.5**
7. 3.1 − 0.2 = **2.9**
8. 4.38 − 2.09 = **2.29**
9. 4.09 − 2.28 = **1.81**
10. 3.03 − 2.34 = **0.69**

Solve.

11. Make the problem on the right and its answer reasonable by replacing each ■ with one of these numbers: 4.8, 5.1, or 0.3. Write a number sentence to represent the data. **5.1; 4.8; 0.3; 5.1 − 4.8 = 0.3**

> Al runs the mile in ■ minutes. Jim runs the mile in ■ minutes. Jim runs the mile in ■ fewer minutes than Al.

12. Some glaciers move about 210 inches in 70 years. About how many inches do they move each year? **about 3 in.**

13. Corky the hamster weighs $3\frac{3}{4}$ ounces. Cora weighs $3\frac{5}{8}$ ounces. Who weighs more? **Corky**

Add Decimals page 469

Add using any method. Remember to estimate.

1. 0.5 + 0.7 = **1.2**
2. 3.8 + 0.9 = **4.7**
3. 7.8 + 3.5 = **11.3**
4. 8.3 + 9.8 = **18.1**
5. 2.4 + 3.9 = **6.3**
6. 0.34 + 0.38 = **0.72**
7. $3.49 + 1.98 = **$5.47**
8. 5.36 + 4.25 = **9.61**
9. 4.39 + 8.27 = **12.66**
10. 7.16 + 3.04 = **10.20**
11. 1.23 + 3.45 + 2.89 = **7.57**
12. 34.15 + 14.28 + 9.01 = **57.44**
13. $12.56 + 13.29 + 10.16 = **$36.01**
14. 16.40 + 2.51 + 33.72 = **52.63**
15. 26.4(+ 3.4! + 9.8 = **39.72**

Solve.

16. Brian watches a 2.5-hour sports show, two half-hour sitcoms, and a 2-hour movie. How much time does he spend watching TV? **5.5 h, or $5\frac{1}{2}$ h**

17. **ALGEBRA: PATTERNS** Copy and complete the pattern. Then write the rule.
4.3, 4.7, ■, 5.5, 5.9, ■, 6.7
5.1, 6.3; rule: add 0.4 to the prior number in the sequence.

Additional Practice

p. 467 Use decimal squares to add or subtract. *[Check students' models.]*

1. 0.7 + 0.6 *[1.3]*
2. 1.36 + 0.82 *[2.18]*
3. 3.04 + 2.98 *[6.02]*
4. 2.18 + 1.37 *[3.55]*
5. 0.6 − 0.2 *[0.4]*
6. 1.6 − 0.9 *[0.7]*
7. 2.37 − 0.84 *[1.53]*
8. 5.03 − 2.61 *[2.42]*
9. 4.29 − 1.34 *[2.95]*

p. 469 Add using any method. Remember to estimate.

1. 0.9 + 0.5 *[1.4]*
2. 3.8 + 1.6 *[5.4]*
3. 0.39 + 0.49 *[0.88]*
4. 3.72 + 2.69 *[6.41]*
5. 0.87 + 2.14 *[3.01]*
6. $5.63 + 8.24 *[$13.87]*
7. 14.23 + 7.81 + 5.30 *[27.34]*
8. $32.36 + 4.07 + 2.83 *[$39.26]*
9. 23.60 + 6.28 + 42.30 *[72.18]*

Subtract Decimals page 471

Subtract using any method. Remember to estimate.

1. 0.4 − 0.3 = **0.1**
2. 3.2 − 0.5 = **2.7**
3. 5.4 − 2.7 = **2.7**
4. 6.8 − 3.2 = **3.6**
5. 9.7 − 4.8 = **4.9**
6. 0.58 − 0.35 = **0.23**
7. 7.32 − 4.91 = **2.41**
8. 4.59 − 3.87 = **0.72**
9. 8.54 − 3.07 = **5.47**
10. 10.38 − 6.49 = **3.89**
11. $24.38 − 15.19 = **$9.19**
12. $32.45 − 21.36 = **$11.09**
13. 12.55 − 9.30 = **3.25**
14. 38.90 − 15.92 = **22.98**
15. 23.50 − 14.75 = **8.75**

Solve.

16. A rain barrel holds 35 gallons of water. There are 42.5 quarts already in the barrel. How many more quarts will the barrel hold? **97.5 qt**

17. Suppose you toss a number cube whose sides are labeled 1, 2, 3, 4, 5, and 6. What is the probability you will toss an even number? **$\frac{3}{6}$, or $\frac{1}{2}$**

18. How many characters can a computer print on a page if there are 52 lines per page and 60 characters per line? **3,120 characters**

19. Carly had $38.75. She earned some money and then had $57.35. How much money did she earn? **$18.60**

Problem Solvers at Work page 475

Solve. Write a number sentence to record your work for problems 1–3. Explain your methods. **Explanations may vary.**

1. There are 2,143 jazz CDs, 4,154 country-and-western CDs, and 4,958 rock-and-roll CDs available for loan in the local library. How many music CDs does the library have to loan in all? **11,255 CDs; 2,143 + 4,154 + 4,958 = 11,255**

2. The average teen spends 6.23 hours watching TV each week from 8 P.M. to 11 P.M., while the average adult spends 8.61 hours. Who spends more time watching TV? How much more? **adults; 2.38 h; 8.61 − 6.23 = 2.38**

3. Eugene O'Neill won the Nobel Prize for Literature in 1936. He was born in 1888. How old was he when he won the prize? How many years have elapsed since he won the prize? **He was 48 y old; 1936 − 1888 = 48. Answers vary depending on the current year. Check students' number sentences.**

4. Mark can buy a Macintosh or an IBM computer. He can choose 8, 16, or 32 megabytes of RAM. How many different choices does he have? List the choices. **6 choices; IBM-8 MB, IBM-16 MB, IBM-32 MB, Mac-8 MB, Mac-16 MB, Mac-32 MB**

Developing Number Sense

This section provides another opportunity for students to reinforce number sense.

Write >, <, or = for the ◆.

1. 4.02 + 7.6 ◆ 7.6 + 4.2 *[<]*
2. 3.52 + 8.1 ◆ 3.25 + 8.1 *[>]*
3. 6.3 + 7.23 ◆ 6.30 + 7.23 *[=]*
4. 8.3 + 6.28 ◆ 6.28 + 8.28 *[>]*
5. 9.3 + 2.80 + 7.16 ◆ 9.30 + 7.16 + 2.8 *[=]*
6. 12.37 + 5.72 ◆ 12.4 + 5.72 *[<]*

p. 471 Subtract using any method. Remember to estimate.

1. 0.7 − 0.4 *[0.3]*
2. 8.3 − 3.7 *[4.6]*
3. 5.06 − 2.58 *[2.48]*
4. 0.83 − 0.27 *[0.56]*
5. $14.32 − 6.17 *[$8.15]*
6. 42.40 − 6.39 *[36.01]*
7. 8.2 − 3.8 *[4.4]*
8. 4.70 − 1.04 *[3.66]*
9. $6.03 − $1.35 *[$4.68]*
10. 6.20 − 3.47 *[2.73]*
11. $23.12 − $8.64 *[$14.48]*
12. 8.03 − 2.60 *[5.43]*

p. 475 Solve. Explain your methods. *[Explanations may vary.]*

1. Ms. Bardia bought 2 adult movie tickets at $7.50 each and 3 children's tickets at $4.50 each. How much did she pay? *[$28.50]*
2. Kevin ran the 100-yard dash in 15.3 seconds. Hal ran it 1.17 seconds slower and Jamie 0.85 seconds faster. What were their times? *[Hal—16.47; Jamie—14.45]*
3. **Write a problem** that can be solved using a number sentence that involves multiplication and addition. *[Check students' problem.]*
4. Jerry is 3 ft 8 in. tall. Mark is 48 in. tall. Sam is 50 in. tall, and Harry is 3 ft 10 in. tall. List the boys by height, tallest first. *[Sam, Mark, Harry, Jerry]*

Databank

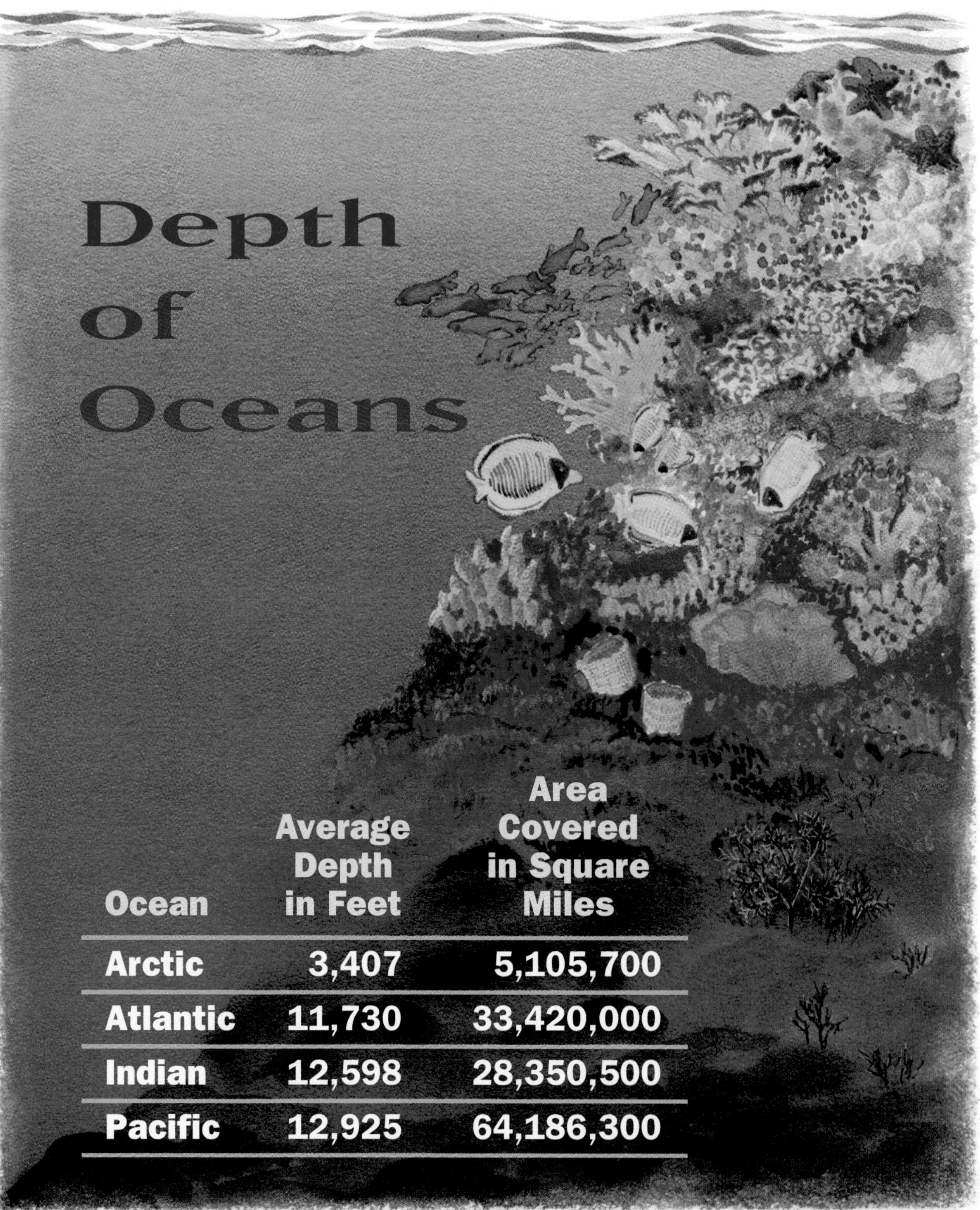

Depth of Oceans

Ocean	Average Depth in Feet	Area Covered in Square Miles
Arctic	3,407	5,105,700
Atlantic	11,730	33,420,000
Indian	12,598	28,350,500
Pacific	12,925	64,186,300

DATABANK

Endangered Animal Populations

Animal Species	Location	Estimated Population in 1970s	Estimated Population in 1990s
Arabian oryx	Asia	35	1,000
African elephant	Africa	1,300,000	600,000
Black rhinoceros	Africa	15,000	4,500
Florida cougar	North America	20	50
Hawaiian monk seal	Hawaiian Islands	2,000	1,000
Indian tiger	Asia	2,500	4,000
Japanese crane	Hokkaido, Japan	220	450
Mauritius parakeet	Africa	50	10
Nene *(similar to a goose)*	Oceania	750	500
Orangutan	Asia	150,000	100,000
Polar bear	Arctic region	5,000	40,000
Red wolf	Texas and Louisiana	100	300
Siberian tiger	Asia	130	400
Woolly spider monkey	South America	3,000	500

Heights of Mountains

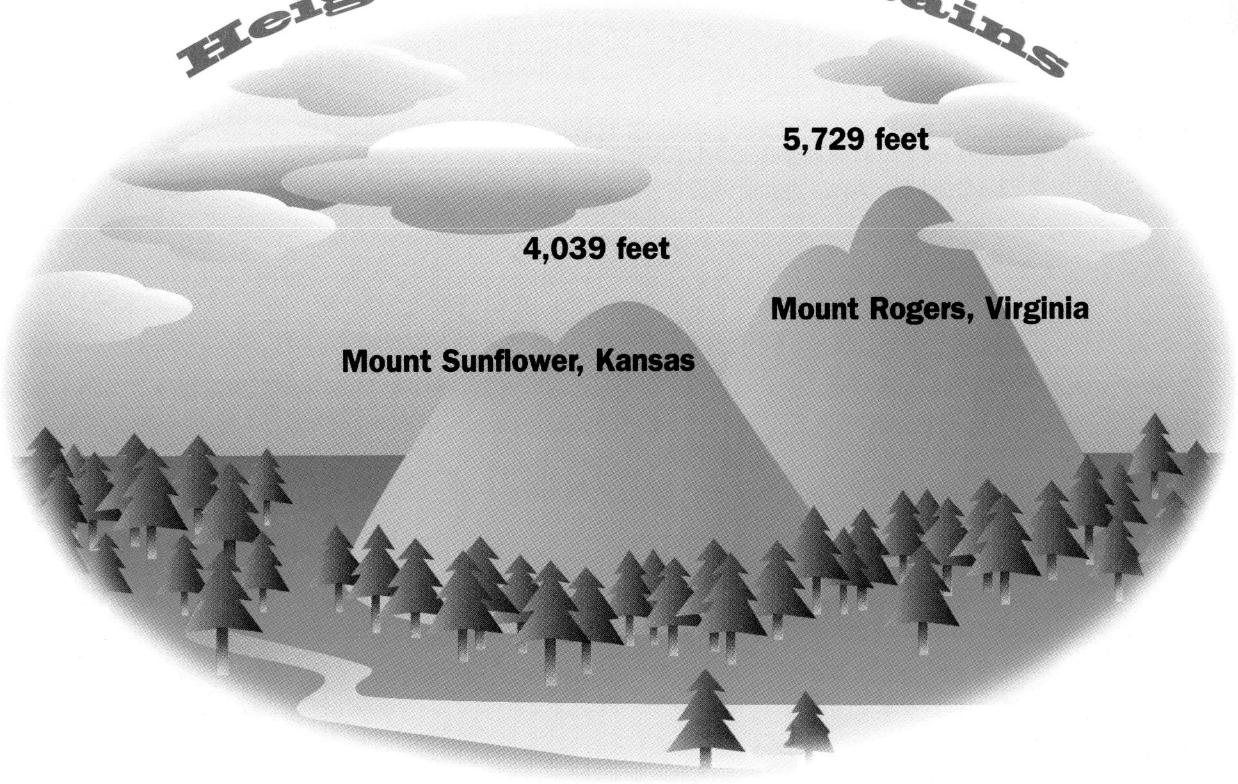

5,729 feet

4,039 feet

Mount Rogers, Virginia

Mount Sunflower, Kansas

DATABANK

Notes and Coins from Different Countries

Country	Note	Coins	Relationship
Botswana	1 pula	50 thebes 25 thebes 10 thebes 5 thebes 2 thebes 1 thebe	100 thebes = 1 pula
China	1 yuan	5 fen 2 fen 1 fen	100 fen = 1 yuan
India	1 rupee	50 paise 25 paise 20 paise	100 paise = 1 rupee
Peru	1 inti	50 centimos 10 centimos 5 centimos	100 centimos = 1 inti
Russia	1 ruble	50 kopeks 20 kopeks 15 kopeks 10 kopeks 5 kopeks 3 kopeks 2 kopeks 1 kopek	100 kopeks = 1 ruble
United States	1 dollar	50 cents 25 cents 10 cents 5 cents 1 cent	100 cents = 1 dollar

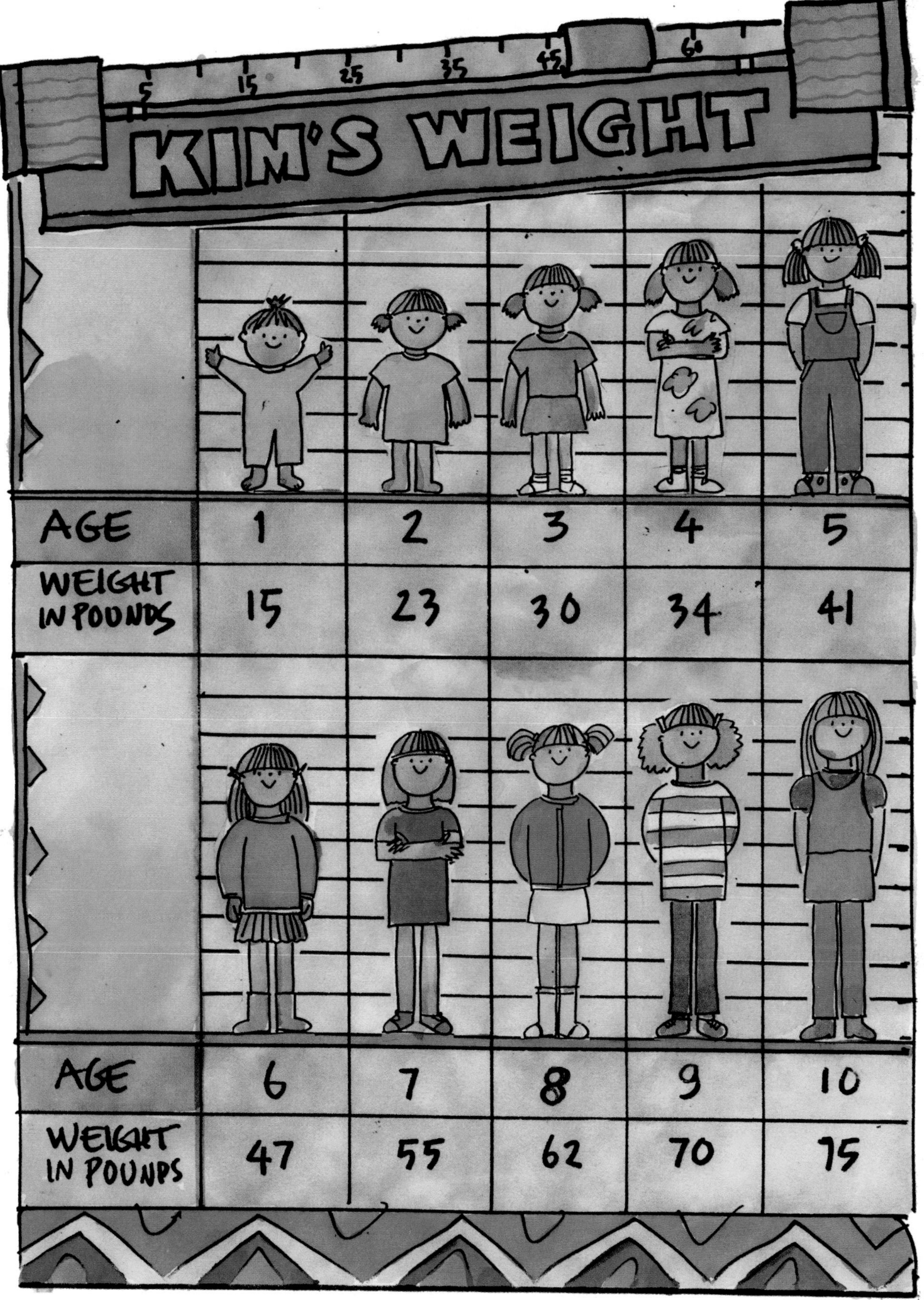
KIM'S WEIGHT
AGE
1
2
3
4
5
WEIGHT IN POUNDS
15
23
30
34
41
AGE
6
7
8
9
10
WEIGHT IN POUNDS
47
55
62
70
75

DATABANK

Giant Trees of the United States

Tree	Height	Location
Palm, Coconut	92 feet	Hilo, Hawaii
Oak, Cherrybark	124 feet	Sussex Co., Virginia
Hickory	125 feet	Monroe Co., Alabama
Beech, American	130 feet	Ashtabula Co., Ohio
Poplar, Balsam	135 feet	Marquette, Michigan
Pecan	143 feet	Cooke Co., Tennessee
Hemlock, Western	227 feet	Olympic National Park, Washington
Fir, Grand	251 feet	Olympic National Park, Washington
Sequoia, Giant	275 feet	Sequoia National Park, California
Douglas Fir, Comet	329 feet	Coos Co., Oregon

Item	Price
X610 laptop computer	$3,899.00
Z14 external modem	$109.00
3.8Y CD-ROM drive	$299.00
76B laser printer	$549.00

CLEANING UP WITH WATER

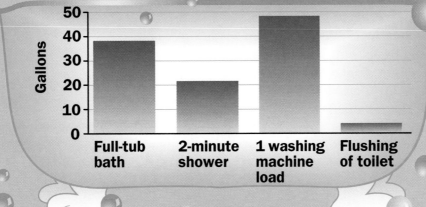

Gallons
50
40
30
20
10
0
Full-tub bath
2-minute shower
1 washing machine load
Flushing of toilet

DATABANK

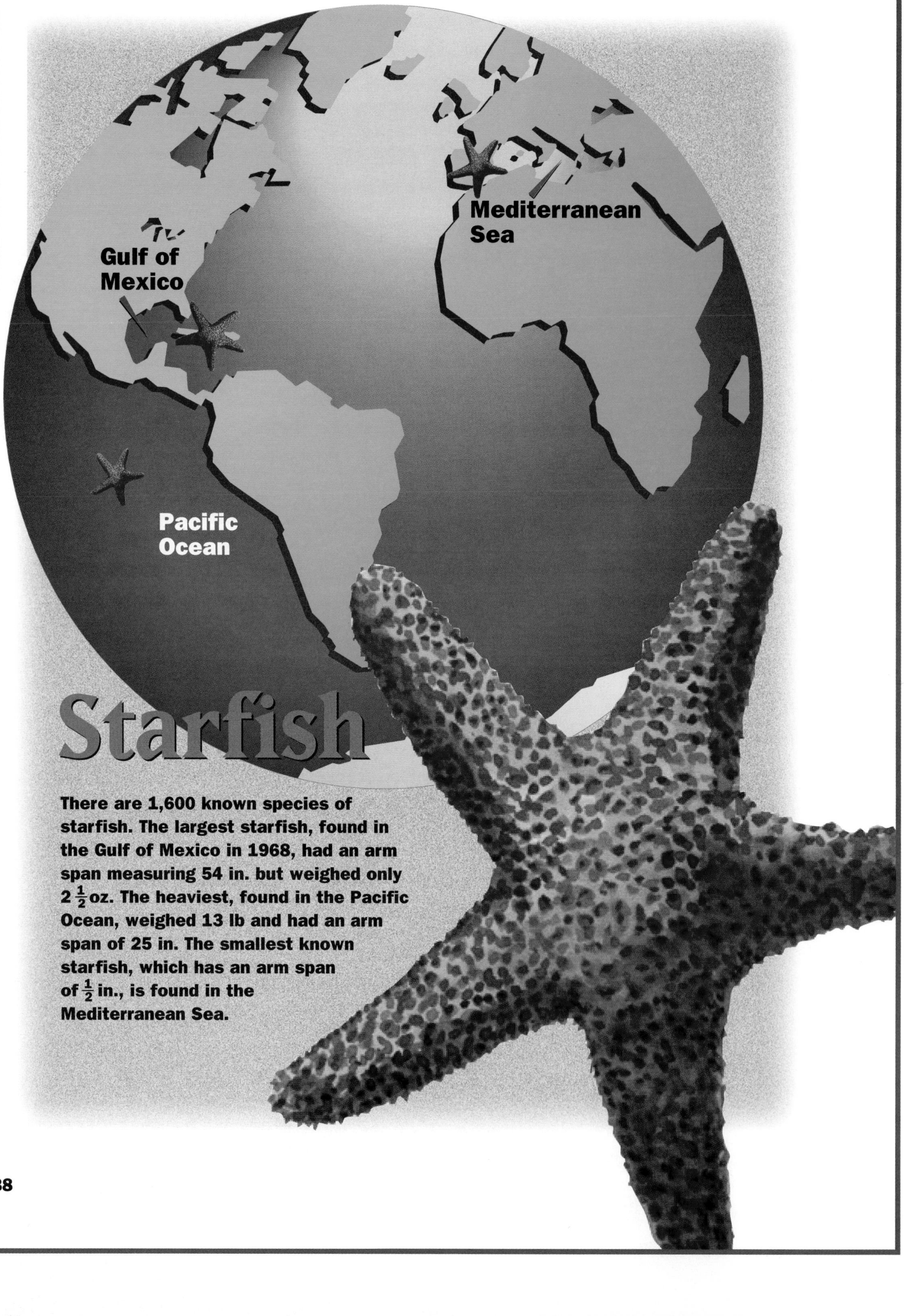

Gulf of Mexico

Mediterranean Sea

Pacific Ocean

Starfish

There are 1,600 known species of starfish. The largest starfish, found in the Gulf of Mexico in 1968, had an arm span measuring 54 in. but weighed only $2\frac{1}{2}$ oz. The heaviest, found in the Pacific Ocean, weighed 13 lb and had an arm span of 25 in. The smallest known starfish, which has an arm span of $\frac{1}{2}$ in., is found in the Mediterranean Sea.

DATABANK

POPULATION OF CAPITAL CITIES

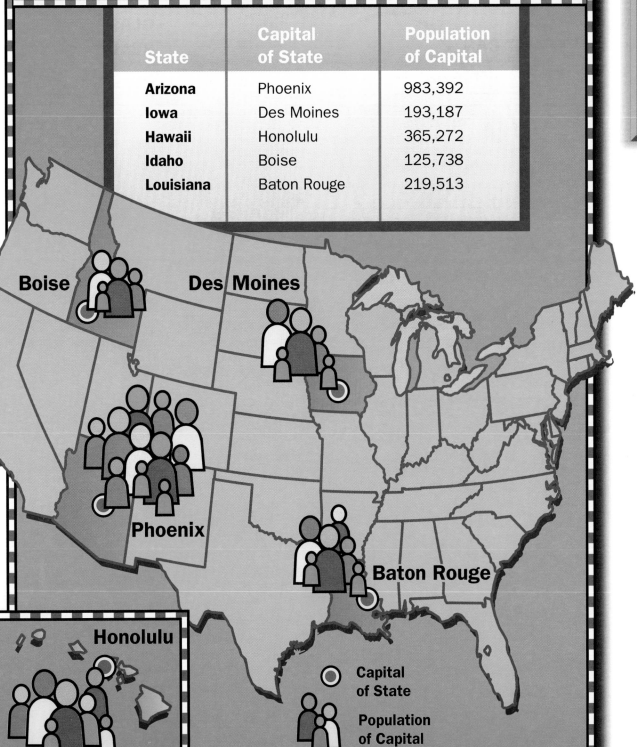

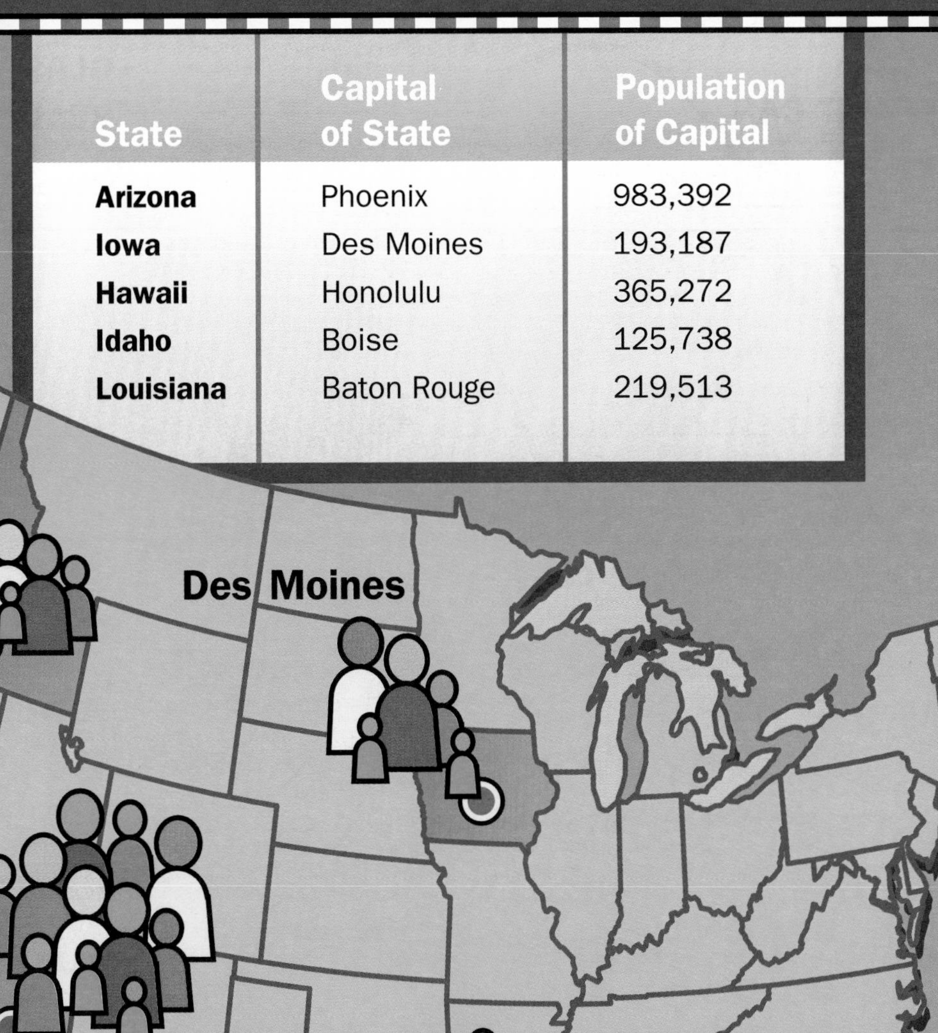

State	Capital of State	Population of Capital
Arizona	Phoenix	983,392
Iowa	Des Moines	193,187
Hawaii	Honolulu	365,272
Idaho	Boise	125,738
Louisiana	Baton Rouge	219,513

DATABANK

SHAPES IN REAL LIFE

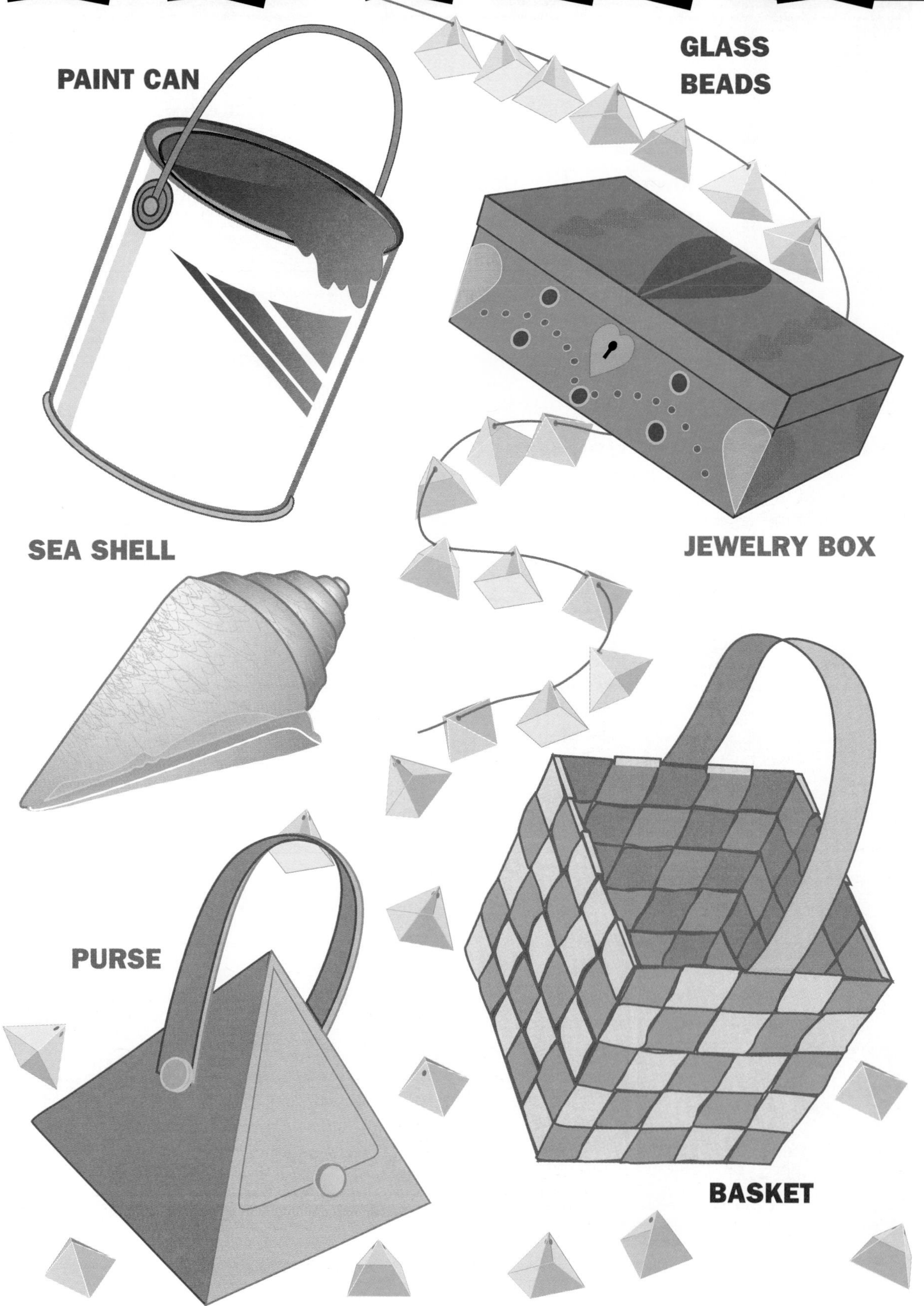

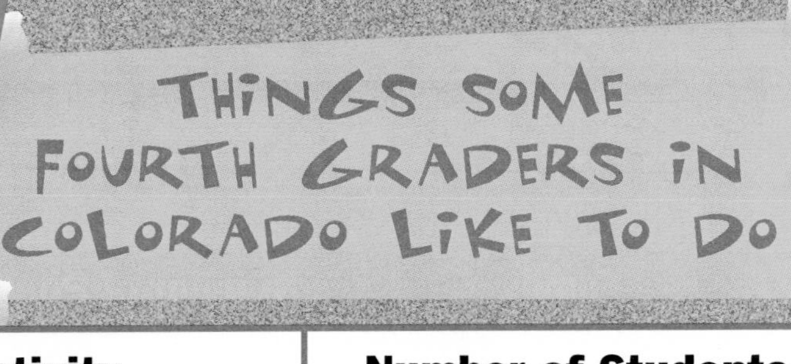

Activity	Number of Students	
Color pictures	卌 卌 |	11
Take photographs	卌 卌 卌	15
Watch it rain	卌 |||	8
Collect foreign coins	||||	4
Collect old jewelry	|||	3
Collect sports posters	卌 |||	8
Swim	卌 卌 卌 |||	18
Play roller hockey	卌 卌 ||||	14
Go fishing	卌 卌 |	11
Garden	卌 ||	7
Make electrical things	卌 卌 卌 ||||	19

Apples Picked by Families

Family	Number of Pounds Picked
The Smiths	38
The Garcias	$25\frac{1}{2}$
The Lohs	$40\frac{3}{4}$
The Crowleys	51

The Story of the Ballpoint Pen

In early times, people wrote with pens made of long reeds. Pens made of goose or swan quills were introduced in Europe around A.D. 600. Workable fountain pens were not invented until 1884. Fountain pens were different from quills in that they had metal points and they could hold their own supply of ink. The first fountain pen was developed by an American named Lewis Waterman.

The idea for a ballpoint pen was patented as early as 1888, but it took a long time to get the pen to work properly. Early ballpoints would only write on rough surfaces. They also tended to leak. The ink in a ballpoint pen is quite thick, but it still must be able to flow smoothly onto the ball so that it can be applied to the paper without skipping and dry almost immediately. It was not until 1944 that two Hungarian inventors named Laszlo and George Biro found the right consistency for the ink and produced a successful ballpoint pen.

Glossary

(*Italicized terms* are defined elsewhere in this glossary.)

A

abacus A counting board used to solve number problems by sliding beads along rods or wires.

acute angle An angle with a measure less than a *right angle.*

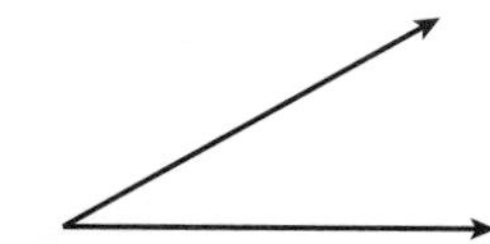

addend A number to be added.

Example: 5 + 4 = 9
The addends are 5 and 4.

addition An operation on two or more numbers that tells *how many in all.*

Example: 9 + 3 = 12 ← sum
↑ ↑
addends

A.M. A name for time between 12:00 midnight and 12:00 noon.

angle A figure formed by two *rays* with the same *endpoint.*

area The number of *square units* needed to cover a surface.

array Objects or symbols displayed in rows and columns.

o o o o
o o o o
o o o o
o o o o

Associative Property When adding or multiplying, the grouping of the numbers does not affect the result.

Examples: 3 + (4 + 5) = (3 + 4) + 5
2 × (3 × 9) = (2 × 3) × 9

average A *statistic* found by adding two or more numbers and dividing their *sum* by the total number of *addends. (See* mean.)

Example: 92 + 84 + 73 = 249
249 ÷ 3 = 83 ← average

B

bar graph A graph that displays *data* using bars of different heights.

C

capacity The amount a container can hold.

centimeter (cm) A *metric unit* of *length.* (*See* Table of Measures.)

circle A closed, curved *2-dimensional figure.* All the points on the circle are the same distance from the center.

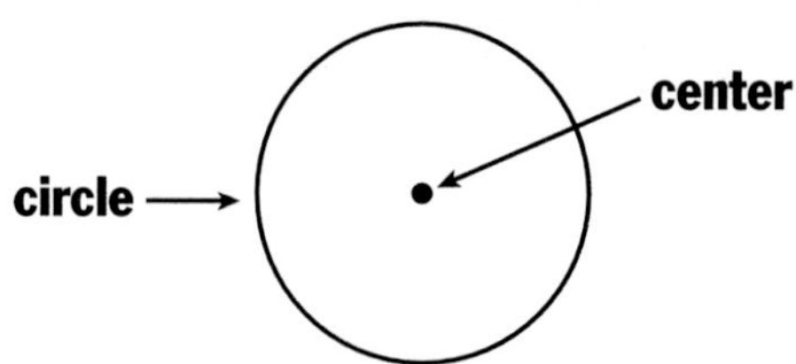

closed figure A figure that starts and ends at the same point.

clustering *Estimating* a *sum* by changing the *addends* that are close in value to one common number and then multiplying that number by the number of *addends.*

Example: 47 + 55 + 59
Estimate: 3 × 50 = 150

common denominator A *denominator* that is a *multiple* of the denominators of two or more fractions.

Example: 48 is a common denominator of $\frac{1}{12}$ and $\frac{1}{8}$.

Commutative Property When adding or multiplying, the order of the numbers does not affect the result.

Examples: 5 + 8 = 8 + 5 = 13
9 × 3 = 3 × 9 = 27

compatible numbers Changing numbers to other numbers that form a basic fact to *estimate* an answer.

Example:
133 ÷ 4 becomes 120 ÷ 4 = 30

composite number A whole number that has *factors* other than itself and 1.

Example: 8 is a composite number. Its factors are 1, 2, 4, and 8.

cone A *3-dimensional figure* whose base is a *circle.*

congruent figures Figures that have the same shape and size.

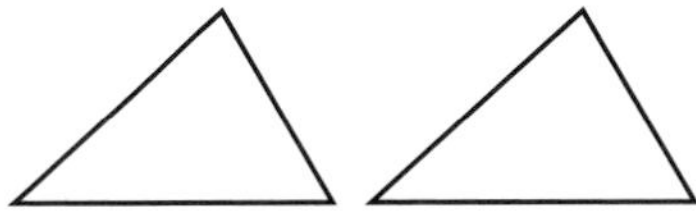

cube A *3-dimensional figure* with six square sides of equal *length.*

cubic unit A unit for measuring *volume.*

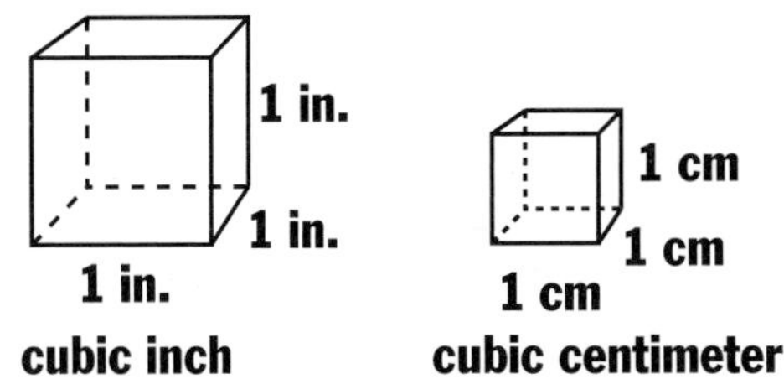

cup (c) A *customary unit* of *capacity.* (*See* Table of Measures.)

customary system A system of measurement whose basic units include *inch, ounce,* and *pound.* (*See* Table of Measures.)

customary unit A unit of measurement in the *customary system.*

cylinder A *3-dimensional figure* with two *faces* that are *circles.*

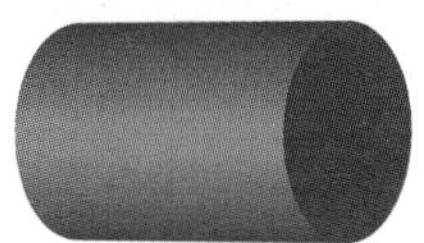

data Information.

decagon A *polygon* with ten sides and ten *angles.*

decimal A number that uses *place value* and a *decimal point* to show tenths, hundredths, and thousandths.

decimal point A period separating the ones and the tenths in a decimal number.

Examples: 0.3, 4.9, 24.752
↑ ↑ ↑
decimal points

decimeter (dm) A *metric unit* of *length.* (*See* Table of Measures.)

degree Celsius (°C) A *metric unit* for measuring *temperature.*

degree Fahrenheit (°F) A *customary unit* for measuring *temperature.*

denominator The number below the bar in a *fraction.*

Example: $\frac{3}{4}$ ← denominator

diagonal A *line segment* that connects two *vertices* but is not a side.

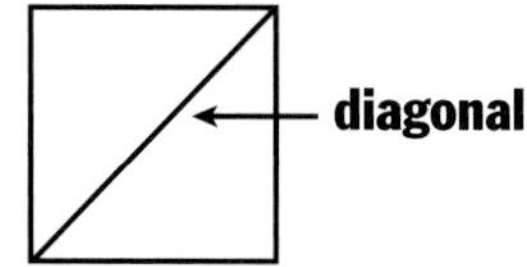

difference The number obtained by subtracting one number from another.

Example: 10 − 6 = 4 ← difference

dividend A number to be divided.

divisible by One number is divisible by another if the *remainder* is 0 after dividing.

division An operation on two numbers that tells *how many groups* or *how many in each group.* Division can also tell *how many are left over.*

Example : quotient
↓
9 R1 ← remainder
divisor → 5)46 ← dividend

divisor The number by which the *dividend* is divided.

edge A *line segment* where two *faces* of a *3-dimensional figure* meet.

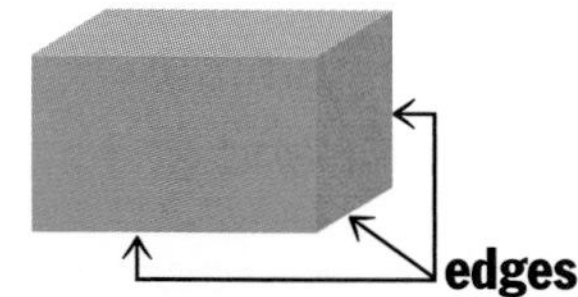

elapsed time The amount of time taken to go from start to finish.

endpoint A point at either end of a *line segment.* The beginning point of a *ray.*

equivalent fractions Two or more fractions that name the same number.

Examples: $\frac{1}{3}$, $\frac{2}{6}$, and $\frac{3}{9}$

estimate To find an answer that is close to the exact answer.

even number A number that ends in 0, 2, 4, 6, or 8.

expanded form A way of writing a number as the *sum* of the values of its digits.

Example: 1,489 can be written as 1,000 + 400 + 80 + 9.

exponent A number that tells how many times a given number is used as a *factor.*

Example: $10^3 = 10 \times 10 \times 10 = 1,000$
↑
exponent

face A side of a *3-dimensional figure.*

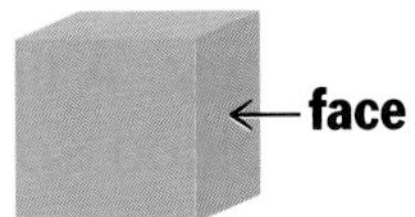

fact family A group of related facts using the same numbers.

Examples: $3 + 2 = 5$ $2 + 3 = 5$
$5 - 2 = 3$ $5 - 3 = 2$

$2 \times 4 = 8$ $4 \times 2 = 8$
$8 \div 2 = 4$ $8 \div 4 = 2$

factors Numbers that are multiplied to give a *product.*

Example: $7 \times 8 = 56$
The factors are 7 and 8.

favorable outcomes Winning results in a *probability* experiment.

flip To move a figure over a *line*; reflection.

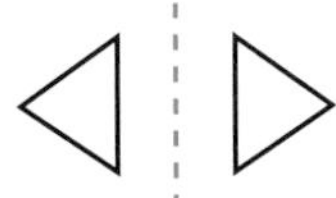

fluid ounce (fl oz) A *customary unit* of *capacity.* (*See* Table of Measures.)

foot (ft) A *customary unit* of *length.* (*See* Table of Measures.)

fraction A number that names part of a whole or part of a group.

Examples: $\frac{2}{3}$, $\frac{7}{10}$, $\frac{1}{100}$

gallon (gal) A *customary unit* of *capacity.* (*See* Table of Measures.)

gram (g) A *metric unit* of *mass.* (*See* Table of Measures.)

Grouping Property When adding or multiplying, the grouping of the numbers does not affect the result.

Examples:
$(3 + 5) + 7 = 15$ $(2 \times 4) \times 5 = 40$
$3 + (5 + 7) = 15$ $2 \times (4 \times 5) = 40$

height The distance from the base to the top of a figure.

heptagon A *polygon* with seven sides and seven *angles.*

hexagon A *polygon* with six sides and six *angles.*

improper fraction A fraction with a *numerator* that is greater than or equal to the *denominator.*

inch (in.) A *customary unit* of *length.* (*See* Table of Measures.)

intersecting lines Lines that meet or cross at a common point.

GLOSSARY

is greater than (>) Symbol to show that the first number is greater than the second.

Example: 439 > 436

is less than (<) Symbol to show that the first number is less than the second.

Example: 852 < 872

key The part of a graph that tells how many items each picture symbol stands for. (*See* pictograph.)

kilogram (kg) A *metric unit* of *mass. (See* Table of Measures.)

kilometer (km) A *metric unit* of *length.* (*See* Table of Measures.)

kite A *quadrilateral* with two pairs of touching *congruent* sides.

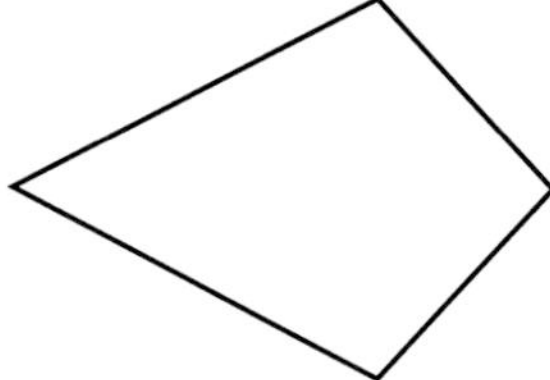

length The measurement of distance between two *endpoints.* (*See also* 2-dimensional figure, 3-dimensional figure.)

line A straight path that goes in two directions without end.

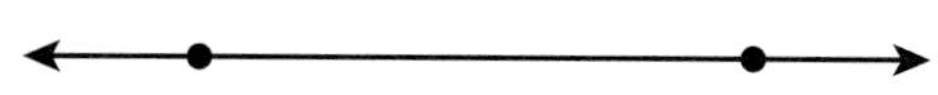

line graph A graph that uses lines to show changes in *data.*

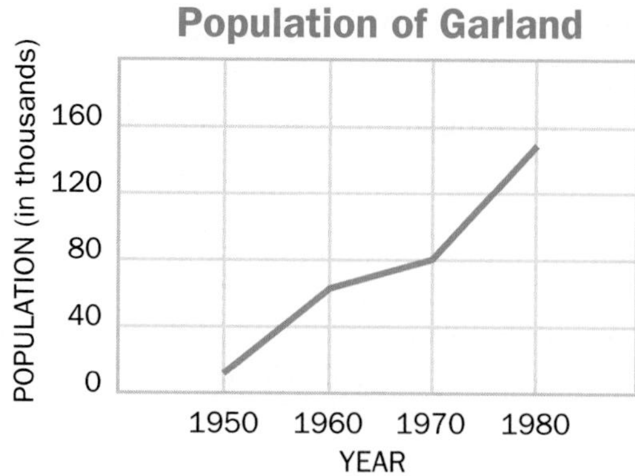

line of symmetry A line on which a figure can be folded so that its two halves match exactly.

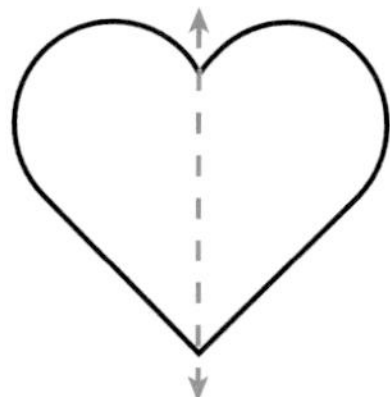

line plot A vertical *graph* that uses Xs above a line to show *data.*

Example:

What is Your Favorite Pet?

	x		
	x		
x	x		
x	x	x	
x	x	x	x
Dog	**Cat**	**Fish**	**Snake**

line segment A straight path that has two *endpoints.*

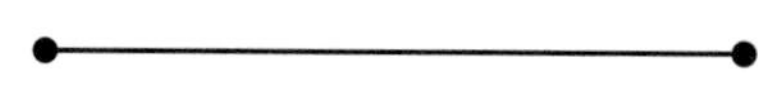

liter (L) A *metric unit* of *capacity.* (*See* Table of Measures.)

mass A measurement that indicates how much of something there is. It is measured by *kilograms* and *grams.*

median The middle number in a group of numbers ordered from the least to the greatest.

Example: The median of 4, 5, and 7 is 5.

meter (m) A *metric unit* of *length.* (*See* Table of Measures.)

metric system A decimal system of measurement whose basic units include *meter, liter,* and *gram.* (*See* Table of Measures.)

metric unit A unit of measurement in the *metric system.*

mile (mi) A *customary unit* of *length.* (*See* Table of Measures.)

milliliter (mL) A *metric unit* of *capacity.* (*See* Table of Measures.)

millimeter (mm) A *metric unit* of *length.* (*See* Table of Measures.)

mixed number A number that has a whole number and a *fraction.*

Example: $8\frac{5}{6}$

mode The number or numbers that occur most often in a collection of *data.*

Example: 2, 6, 1, 6, 4, 8, 6
The mode is 6.

multiple The *product* of a number and any whole number.

Example: 8 is a multiple of 4 because $2 \times 4 = 8$.

multiplication An operation that tells *how many in all* when equal groups are combined.

Example: $5 \times 8 = 40$
↑ ↑ ↑
factors product

numerator The number above the bar in a *fraction.*

Example: $\frac{3}{5}$ ← numerator

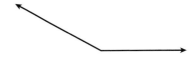

obtuse angle An angle with a measure that is greater than a *right angle.*

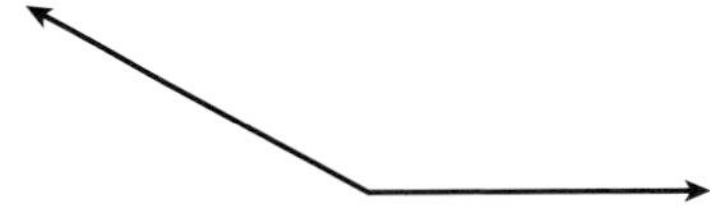

octagon A *polygon* with eight sides and eight *angles.*

odd number A number that ends in 1, 3, 5, 7, or 9.

open figure A figure that does not start and end at the same point.

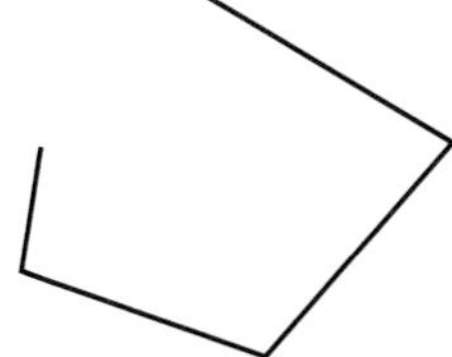

ordered pair A pair of numbers that gives the location of a point on a graph, map, or grid.

GLOSSARY

Order Property When adding or multiplying, the order of the numbers does not affect the result.

Examples: $8 + 9 = 17$ $\quad 4 \times 5 = 20$
$9 + 8 = 17$ $\quad 5 \times 4 = 20$

ordinal number A number used to tell order or position.

Example: second

ounce (oz) A *customary unit* of *weight.* (*See* Table of Measures.)

parallel lines Lines that never intersect.

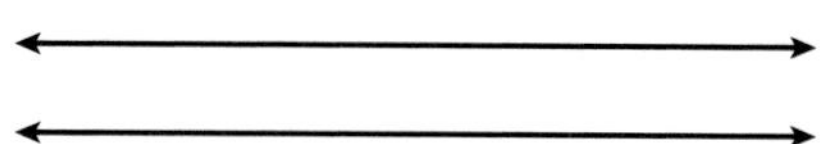

parallelogram A *quadrilateral* with both pairs of opposite sides parallel.

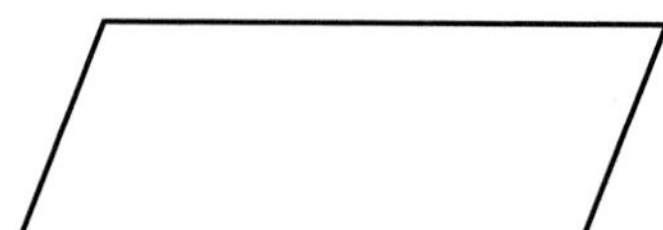

pattern A series of numbers or figures that follows a rule.

Examples: 1, 3, 5, 7, 9, 11, . . .

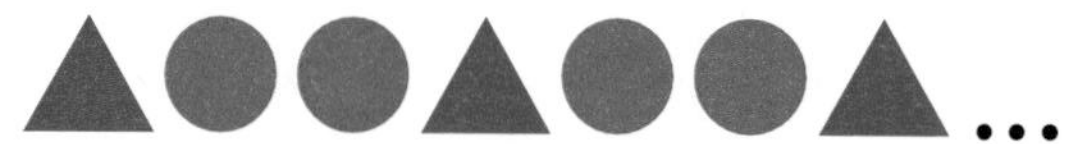

pentagon A *polygon* with five sides and five *angles.*

perimeter The distance around a *closed figure.*

period Each group of three digits in a *place-value* chart.

Example: 527,000

Thousands Period			Ones Period		
Hundred Thousands	Ten Thousands	Thousands	Hundreds	Tens	Ones
5	2	7	0	0	0

perpendicular lines Lines that intersect to form square corners.

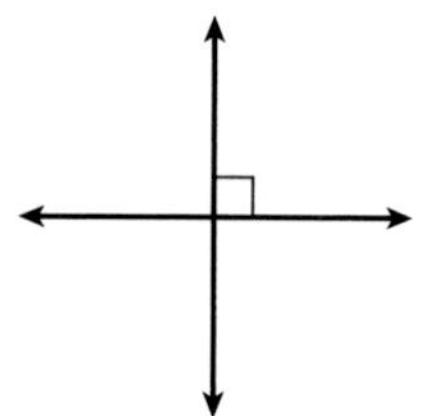

pictograph A graph that shows *data* by using picture symbols. A *key* tells how many items each picture symbol stands for.

pint (pt) A *customary unit* of *capacity.* (*See* Table of Measures.)

place value The value of a digit based on its position in a number.

P.M. A name for time between 12 noon and 12 midnight.

polygon A closed *2-dimensional figure* formed by *line segments.* The sides do not cross each other.

possible outcome Any of the results that could occur in a *probability* experiment.

pound (lb) A *customary unit* of *weight.* (*See* Table of Measures.)

prime number A *whole number* greater than 1 with only itself and 1 as *factors.*

Examples: 7 is a prime number. 2 is the only even number that is prime.

prism A *3-dimensional figure* with two parallel *congruent* bases and *rectangles* or *parallelograms* for *faces.*

probability A number from 0 to 1 that measures the likelihood of an event happening.

product The result of *multiplication.*

Example: 6 × 8 = 48 ← product

pyramid A *3-dimensional figure* that is shaped by *triangles* on a base.

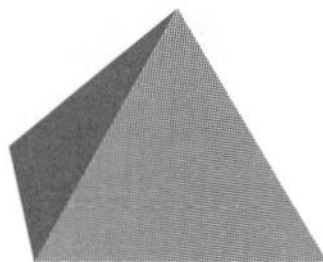

quadrilateral A *polygon* with four sides.

quart (qt) A *customary unit* of *capacity.* (*See* Table of Measures.)

quotient The result of *division.*

Example: 35 ÷ 7 = 5 ← quotient

range The *difference* between the greatest and the least numbers in a group of numbers.

ray A *2-dimensional figure* that has one *endpoint* and goes on forever in one direction.

rectangle A polygon with four sides and four square corners.

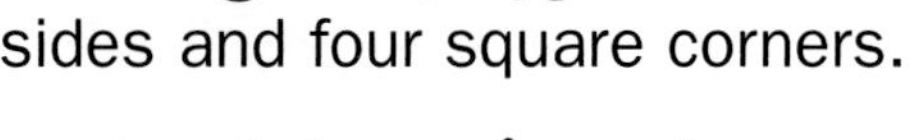

rectangular prism A *3-dimensional figure* with six rectangular *faces.*

regroup To name a number in a different way.

Example: 23 can be regrouped as 2 tens 3 ones or as 1 ten 13 ones.

remainder The number left over after dividing.

Example: 43 ÷ 7 = 6 R1← remainder

rhombus A *parallelogram* with all four sides the same *length.*

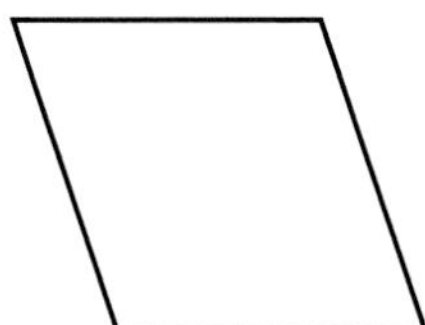

right angle An *angle,* or square corner, formed by *perpendicular lines.*

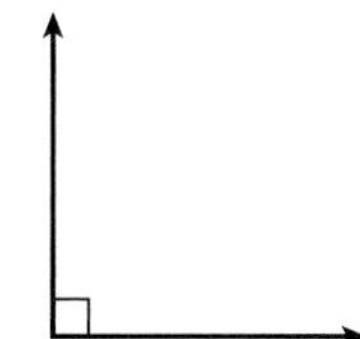

rounding (round) Finding the nearest ten, hundred, thousand, and so on.

Example: 868 rounded to the nearest hundred is 900.

scale Marks that are equally spaced along a line and are used to measure.

GLOSSARY

similar shapes Figures that are the same shape but are different sizes.

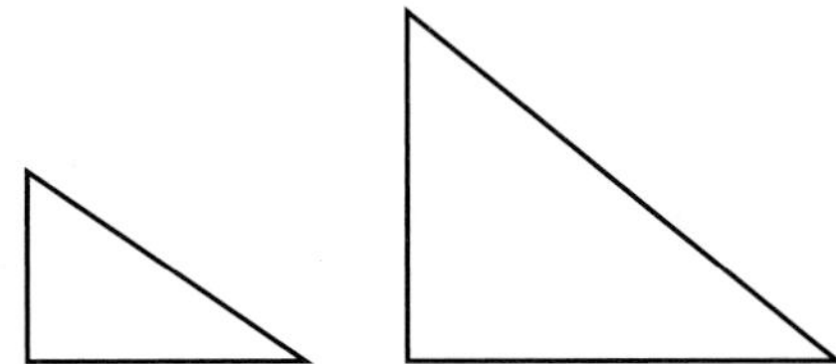

simplest form A *fraction* in which the *numerator* and *denominator* have no common *factor* greater than 1.

skip-count To count by twos, threes, fours, and so on.

Examples:
2, 4, 6, 8, 10, . . . 3, 6, 9, 12, . . .

slide To move a figure along a *line*; translation.

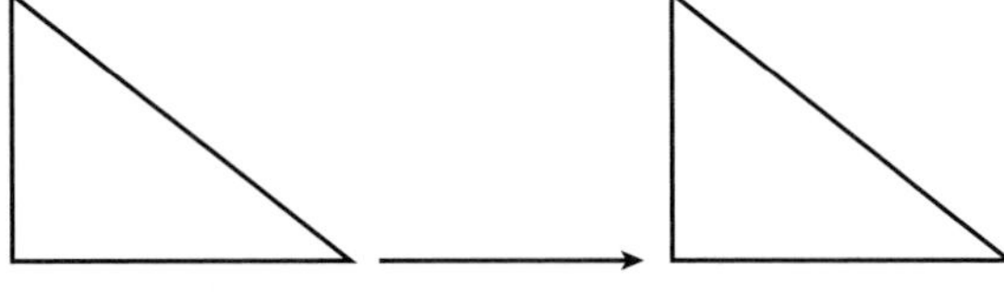

sphere A *3-dimensional figure* that has the shape of a round ball.

spreadsheet A computer program that arranges *data* and formulas in table form.

square A *2-dimensional figure* that has four equal sides and four square corners.

square pyramid A *pyramid* whose base is a *square.*

square unit A unit for measuring *area.*

Examples: square inch (in.^{2}), square foot (ft^2), square centimeter (cm^2), and square meter (m^2)

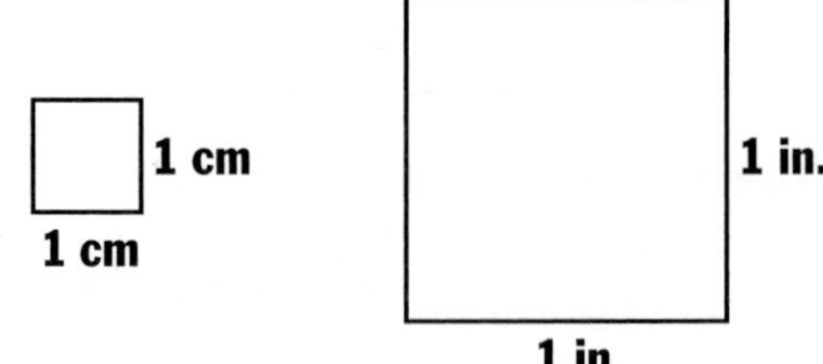

standard form The usual or common way to write a number.

statistics The collecting and arranging of *data* on a particular subject.

subtraction An operation on two numbers that tells *how many are left* when some are taken away. Subtraction is also used to compare two numbers.

Example: $14 - 8 = 6$ ← difference

sum The result of *addition.*

Example: $9 + 6 = 15$ ← sum

temperature A measurement that tells how hot or cold something is.

tessellation Related shapes that cover a flat surface without leaving any gaps; for example, the design on a checkerboard.

3-dimensional figure A figure that has *length, width,* and *height.*

time line A *line* that shows times or dates as points along a *line segment.*

trapezoid A *quadrilateral* with exactly one pair of *parallel* sides.

triangle A *polygon* with three sides and three *angles.*

triangular prism A *prism* whose opposite *faces* are *triangles.*

triangular pyramid A *pyramid* whose base is a *triangle.*

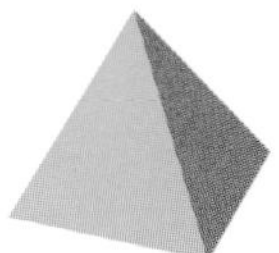

turn To rotate a figure around a point; rotation.

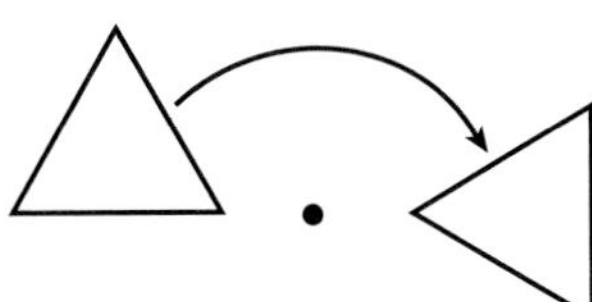

2-dimensional figure A figure that has only *length* and *width.*

variable A symbol used to represent a number or group of numbers.

vertex The common point of the two *rays* of an *angle,* two sides of a *polygon,* or three or more *edges of a 3-dimensional figure.*

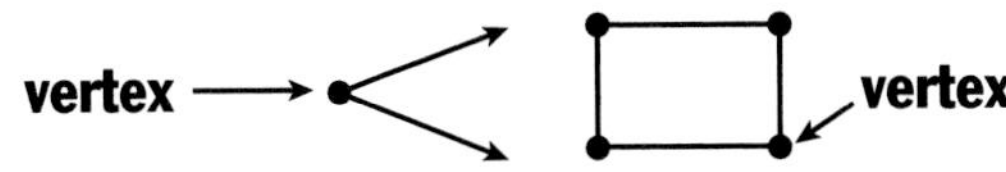

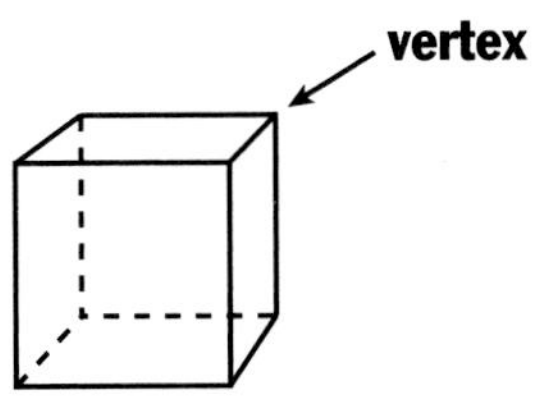

volume The number of *cubic units* that fit inside a *3-dimensional figure.*

weight A measure of how heavy something is.

width The measurement of the shorter of the sides of a *rectangle* that is not a *square.* (*See also* 2-dimensional figure, 3-dimensional figure.)

yard (yd) A *customary unit* of *length.* (*See* Table of Measures.)

Table of Measures

Time

60 seconds (s) = 1 minute (min)
60 minutes (min) = 1 hour (h)
24 hours = 1 day (d)
7 days = 1 week (wk)
12 months (mo) = 1 year (y)
about 52 weeks = 1 year
365 days = 1 year
366 days = 1 leap year

Metric Units

LENGTH	1 centimeter (cm) = 10 millimeters (mm)
	10 centimeters = 1 decimeter (dm)
	10 decimeters = 1 meter (m)
	1,000 meters = 1 kilometer (km)
MASS	1 kilogram (kg) = 1,000 grams (g)
CAPACITY	1 liter (L) = 1,000 milliliters (mL)
TEMPERATURE	0° Celsius (°C) . . . Water freezes
	100° Celsius . . . Water boils

Customary Units

LENGTH	1 foot (ft) = 12 inches (in.)
	1 yard (yd) = 36 inches
	1 yard = 3 feet
	1 mile (mi) = 5,280 feet
	1 mile = 1,760 yards
WEIGHT	1 pound (lb) = 16 ounces (oz)
CAPACITY	1 cup (c) = 8 fluid ounces
	1 pint (pt) = 2 cups
	1 quart (qt) = 2 pints
	1 gallon (gal) = 4 quarts
TEMPERATURE	32° Fahrenheit (°F) . . . Water freezes
	212° Fahrenheit . . . Water boils

Symbols

$<$	is less than	°	degree	$\overrightarrow{AB}$	ray *AB*
$>$	is greater than	$\overleftrightarrow{AB}$	line *AB*	$\angle ABC$	angle *ABC*
$=$	is equal to	$\overline{AB}$	line segment *AB*	(5, 3)	ordered pair 5, 3